Thailand

written and researched by

Paul Gray and Lucy Ridout

with additional contributions by

Ron Emmons, Claire Saunders, Julia Kelly, John Clewley and Tom Vater

ROUGH GUIDES

www.roughguides.com

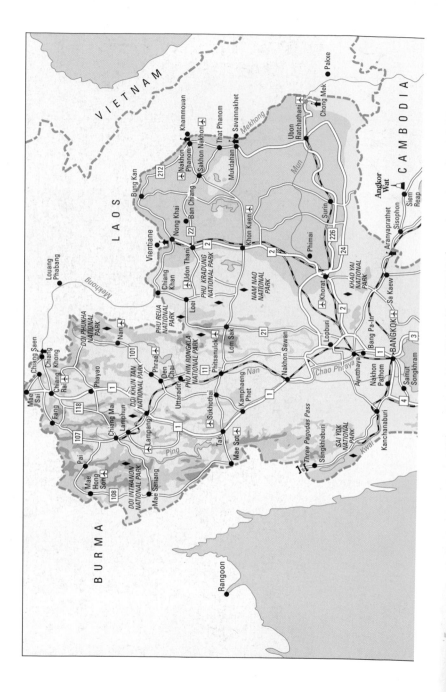

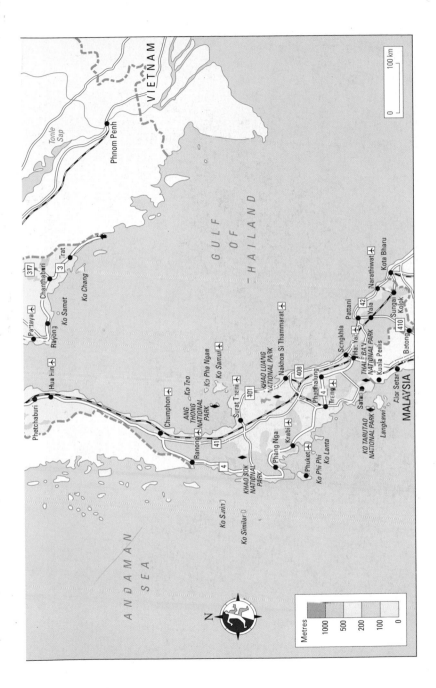

Introduction to

Thailand

With over nine million foreigners flying into the country each year, Thailand has become Asia's primary holiday destination. Yet despite this vast influx of tourists and their cash, Thailand's cultural integrity remains largely undamaged – a country that adroitly avoided colonization has been able to absorb Western influences without wholly succumbing to them. Though the high-rises and neon lights occupy the foreground of the tourist picture, the typical Thai community is still the traditional farming village. Over fifty percent of Thais earn their living from the land, based around the staple, rice, which forms the foundation of the country's unique and famously sophisticated cuisine.

Tourism has been just one factor in the country's development which, once the deep-seated regional uncertainties surrounding the Vietnam War had faded, was free to proceed at an almost death-defying pace. Indeed Thailand enjoyed the fastest-expanding economy in the world, at an average of nine percent growth a year, until it overstretched itself in 1997, sparking a regional financial crisis – but already, with remarkable resilience, the economy's growing again. Politics in Thailand, however, has not been able to keep pace. Coup d'états, which used to be the commonest method of changing government, seem to be a thing of the past, but despite a recently revised constitution and robust criticism from students, grass-roots activists and parts of the press, the malnourished democratic system is characterized by corruption and cronyism.

Through all the changes of the last half-century, the much-revered constitutional monarch, King Bhumibol, who sits at the pinnacle of an elaborate hierarchical system of deference covering the whole of Thai society, has lent a large measure of stability. Furthermore, over ninety percent of the population are still practising Theravada Buddhists, a unifying faith which colours all aspects of daily life – from the tiered temple rooftops that dominate every skyline, to the omnipresent saffron-robed monks and the packed calendar of festivals; it is still the norm for a Thai man to spend three months as a monk at some period during his life.

Where to go

The clash of tradition and modernity is most intense in **Bangkok**, the first stop on almost any itinerary. Within the capital's historic core you'll find resplendent temples, canalside markets and the opulent indulgence of the eighteenth-century **Grand Palace**, while in downtown Bangkok lies the hub of the country's sex industry, the infamous strip known as **Patpong**. After touchdown in Bangkok, much of the package-holiday traffic flows east to **Pattaya**, the country's first and most popular beach resort. Born as a rest-and-recreation base for the US military during the Vietnam War, it has grown into a concrete warren of hotels and strip joints that's just about the least authentic town in Thailand. For unpolluted beaches and clear seas, however, you have to venture just a little further afield, to the islands of **Ko Samet** and **Ko Chang**, with their superb sand and idyllic bamboo beach huts.

Fact file

● Known as Siam until 1939, Thailand lies wholly within the tropics, covering 511,770 square kilometres and divided into 76 provinces or *changwat*. The population of 62 million is made up of ethnic Thais (75 percent) and Chinese (14 percent), with the rest comprising mainly immigrants from neighbouring countries as well as hill-tribespeople; the national language is *phasaa thai*. Buddhism is the national religion, with some 95 percent followers, and Islam the largest of the minority religions at 3.8 percent. Average life expectancy is 69 years.

● Since 1932 the country has been a constitutional monarchy; King Bhumibol, also known as Rama IX (being the ninth ruler of the Chakri dynasty), has been on the throne since 1946. The elected National Assembly (Rathasapha) has five hundred MPs in the House of Representatives (Sapha Phuthaen Ratsadon), led by a prime minister, and two hundred members of the Senate (Wuthisapha). With around a dozen major political parties, governments frequently end up as coalitions.

● Tourism is the country's main industry, and its biggest exports are computers and components, textiles, rice, tapioca and rubber.

Fewer tourists strike north from the east coast into **Isaan**, the poorest and in some ways the most traditionally Thai region. Here, a trip through the gently modulating landscapes of the **Mekhong River** valley, which defines Thailand's northern and eastern extremities, takes in archetypal agricultural villages and a fascinating array of religious sites, while the southern reaches of Isaan hold some of the country's best-kept secrets – the magnificent stone temple complexes of **Phimai**, **Phanom Rung** and **Khao Phra Viharn**, all built by the Khmers of Cambodia almost ten centuries ago. Closer to the capital, in the southwestern corner of Isaan, **Khao Yai National Park** encapsulates the phenomenal diversity of Thailand's flora and fauna, which here range from wild orchids to strangling figs, elephants to hornbills, tigers to macaques.

Attractively sited at the heart of the northern uplands, **Chiang Mai** draws tourists in almost the same quantities as Pattaya, but has

Spirit houses

Although the vast majority of Thais are Buddhist, nearly everyone also believes that the physical world is inhabited by spirits. These spirits can cause trouble if not given enough care and attention, and are apt to wreak particular havoc when made homeless. Therefore, whenever a new building is constructed in Thailand – be it a traditional village house or a multi-storey office block – the owners will also construct a home for the spirits who previously occupied that land. Crucially, these **spirit houses** must be given the best spot on the site – which in Bangkok often means on the roof – and must also reflect the status of the building in question, so their architecture can range from the simplest wooden structure to an elaborate scale model of a particularly ornate temple. Daily offerings of flowers, incense and candles are set inside the spirit house, and sometimes morsels of food are added as well. For an introduction to animist and Buddhist practices in Thailand see p.784.

preserved its looks with far greater care, and appeals to a different kind of visitor. It's a vibrant cultural centre in its own right, with a strong tradition of arts and crafts and a burgeoning line in self-improvement courses – from ascetic meditation to the more earthly pleasures of Thai cookery classes – while the overriding enticement of the surrounding region is the prospect of **trekking** through villages inhabited by a richly mixed population of tribal peoples. With Chiang Mai so firmly planted on the independent tourist trail, the ancient cities of the intervening **central plains** tend to get short shrift. Yet there is rewarding trekking from the Burmese-border towns of **Mae Sot** and **Umphang**, and the elegant ruins of former

The gecko

Whether you're staying on a beach or in a town, chances are you'll be sharing your room with a few **geckos**. These pale green tropical lizards, which are completely harmless to humans and usually measure a cute four to ten centimetres in length, mostly appear at night, high up on walls and ceilings, where they feed on insects. Because the undersides of their flat toes are covered with hundreds of microscopic hairs that catch at even the tiniest of irregularities, geckos are able to scale almost any surface, including glass, which is why you usually see them in strange, gravity-defying positions. The largest and most vociferous gecko is known as the *tokay* in Thai, named after the disconcertingly loud sound it makes. Tokays can grow to an alarming 35cm but are welcomed by most householders, as they devour insects and mice; Thais also consider it auspicious if a baby is born within earshot of a crowing tokay. There's more about Thailand's fauna and flora on p.789.

capitals **Ayutthaya** and **Sukhothai** embody a glorious artistic heritage, displaying Thailand's distinctive ability to absorb influences from quite different cultures. **Kanchanaburi**, stunningly located on the **River Kwai** in the western reaches of the central plains, tells of a much darker episode in Thailand's past, for it was along the course of this river that the Japanese army built the Thailand–Burma Railway during World War II, at the cost of thousands of POW lives.

Sand and sea are what most Thailand holidays are about, though, and the pick of the coasts are in southern Thailand, where the **Samui archipelago** off the **Gulf coast** is one of the highlights: its small resorts, desolate coves and immaculate sweeping beaches draw teenage ravers and solitude-seekers in equal parts.

> **Sand and sea are what most Thailand holidays are about, though, and the pick of the coasts are in southern Thailand.**

Across on the other side of the peninsula, the **Andaman coast** boasts even more exhilarating scenery and the finest coral reefs in the country, in particular around the spectacular **Ko Similan** island chain, which ranks as one of the best dive sites in the world. The largest Andaman coast island, **Phuket**, is one of Thailand's top tourist destinations and is graced with a dozen fine beaches; many of these have been over-developed with expensive high-rises and throbbing nightlife, but quieter corners can still be found. **Ko Phi Phi** has also suffered under unregulated construction, but its coral-rich sea remains an untainted azure, and the sheer limestone

Thai boxing

Such is the national obsession with *muay Thai*, or **Thai boxing**, that when Wijan Ponlid returned home from the Sydney 2000 Olympics with the country's only gold medal (for international flyweight boxing), he was

paraded through town at the head of a procession of 49 elephants, given a new house and over 20 million baht, and offered a promotion at work (he's a policeman). As with soccer and baseball stars in the west, *muay Thai* champions are rarely out of the news even during quieter periods in the sporting calendar, and the national appetite is fed by live TV coverage of major bouts every Sunday afternoon on Channel 7. Though there are boxing venues all around the country, the very best fights are staged at Bangkok's two biggest stadiums, Rajdamnoen and Lumphini, which are well worth attending as a cultural experience even if you have no interest in the sport itself; see p.180 for times and ticket prices and p.69 for more on the rules and rituals of *muay Thai*.

Hill-tribe trekking

Trekking in northern Thailand isn't just about walking through beautiful, rainforested mountain scenery, it also brings you into contact with the **hill** tribes or *chao khao*, fascinating ethnic minorities who are just clinging on to their traditional ways of life. Sometimes termed Fourth World people, in that they are migrants who continue to migrate without regard for national boundaries, the hill tribes have developed sophisticated customs, laws and beliefs to harmonize relationships between individuals and their environment. Despite the disturbance caused by trekking, most *chao khao* are genuinely hospitable to foreigners, but it's important that you go with a knowledgeable guide who has the interests of the local people at heart – and that you act as a sensitive guest in the face of their hospitality. For more on the hill tribes, see p.811; for trekking practicalities, see p.297.

cliffs that characterize the coastline here – and elsewhere around the harbour town and beaches of nearby **Krabi** – are breathtakingly beautiful. The island of **Ko Lanta** has a more understated charm and is a popular destination for families. Inland attractions generally pale in comparison to the coastal splendours, but the rainforests of **Khao Sok National Park** are a notable exception.

Further down the Thai peninsula, in the provinces of the **deep south**, the teeming sea life and unfrequented sands of **Ko Tarutao National Marine Park** are the immediate attractions, though the edgy relationship between Thai sovereignty and Malaysian Islam – the kind of cultural brew that has characterized Thailand throughout its history – makes this region a rewarding one for the more adventurous traveller to explore.

When to go

T he **climate** of most of Thailand is governed by three seasons: rainy (roughly June through October), caused by the southwest monsoon dumping moisture gathered from the Andaman Sea and the Gulf of Thailand; cool (November to February); and hot (March through May). The **rainy season** is the least predictable of the three, varying in length and intensity from year to year, but usually it gathers force between June and August, coming to a peak in September and October, when unpaved roads are reduced to mud troughs and whole districts of Bangkok are flooded. The **cool season** is the pleasantest time to visit, although temperatures can still reach a broiling 30°C in the middle of the day. In the **hot season**, when temperatures often rise to 35°C in Bangkok, the best thing to do is to hit the beach.

Within this scheme, slight variations are found from region to region. The less humid **north** experiences the greatest range of temperatures: at night in the cool season the thermometer occasionally approaches zero on the higher slopes, and this region is often hotter than the central plains between March and May. It's the **northeast** which gets the very worst of the hot season, with clouds of dust gathering above the parched fields, and humid air too. In **southern Thailand**, temperatures are more consistent throughout the year, with less variation the closer you get to the equator.

Rat or raja?

There's no standard system of **transliterating** Thai script into Roman, so you're sure to find that the Thai words

in this book don't always match the versions you'll see elsewhere. Maps and street signs are the biggest sources of confusion, so we've generally gone for the transliteration that's most common on the spot. However, sometimes you'll need to do a bit of lateral thinking, bearing in mind that a classic variant for the town of Ayutthaya is Ayudhia, while among street names, Thanon Rajavithi could come out as Thanon Ratwithi – and it's not unheard of to find one spelling posted at one end of a road, with another at the opposite end. See p.825 for an introduction to the Thai language.

The rainy season hits the **Andaman coast** of the southern peninsula harder than anywhere else in the country – heavy rainfall usually starts in May and persists at the same level until October.

One area of the country, the **Gulf coast** of the southern peninsula, lies outside this general pattern – with the sea immediately to the east, this coast and its offshore islands feel the effects of the northeast monsoon, which brings rain between October and January. This area suffers less than the Andaman coast from the southwest monsoon, getting a comparatively small amount of rain between June and September.

Overall, the **cool season** is generally the **best time** to come to Thailand: as well as having more manageable temperatures and less rain, it offers waterfalls in full spate and the best of the upland flowers in bloom. Bear in mind, however, that it's also the busiest season, so forward planning is essential.

To find out the current weather situation and seven-day forecast in some twenty towns around Thailand, visit the Thai Meteorological Department Web site at Ⓦwww.tmd.motc.go.th/eng/index.html

Thailand's Climate

Average daily temperatures °C and monthly rainfall (mm)

		Jan	Feb	Mar	Apr	May	June	July	Aug	Sept	Oct	Nov	Dec
Bangkok	°C	26	28	29	30	30	29	29	28	28	28	27	26
	mm	11	28	31	72	190	152	158	187	320	231	57	9
Chiang Mai	°C	21	23	26	29	29	28	27	27	27	26	24	22
	mm	8	6	15	45	153	136	167	227	251	132	44	15
Pattaya	°C	26	28	29	30	30	29	29	28	28	28	27	26
	mm	12	23	41	79	165	120	166	166	302	229	66	10
Ko Samui	°C	26	26	28	29	29	28	28	28	28	27	26	25
	mm	38	8	12	63	186	113	143	123	209	260	302	98
Phuket	°C	27	28	28	29	28	28	28	28	27	27	27	27
	mm	35	31	39	163	348	213	263	263	419	305	207	52

41

things not to miss

It's not possible to see everything that Thailand has to offer in one trip — and we don't suggest you try. What follows is a selective and subjective taste of the country's highlights: great places to stay, outstanding national parks, spectacular wildlife, and even good things to eat and drink — arranged in five colour-coded categories to help you find the very best things to see, do and experience. All entries have a page reference to take you straight into the guide, where you can find out more.

01 Phuket Page **635** • It's surprisingly easy to find a tranquil spot on Phuket, especially on the less developed northwest coast.

02 Nan Page **345** • Few travellers make the trip out to Nan, but it's a likeable town set in rich mountain scenery, with a strong handicraft tradition and some intriguing Lao-influenced temples, including the beautiful murals at Wat Phumin.

03 **Sea-canoeing in the Krabi region** Page **677** • Paddling your own canoe is a great way to explore the lagoons, caves and hidden beaches of Krabi's extraordinary coast.

05 **Loy Krathong** Page **267** • At this nationwide festival held in honour of the water spirits, Thais everywhere float miniature baskets filled with flowers and lighted candles on canals, rivers, ponds and seashores.

04 **Silk** Page **504** • The most exquisite weaves and designs are produced by villagers from the northeast, but are sold all over the country.

06 **Khao Yai National Park** Page **458** • Thailand's most popular national park, with decent bird-spotting, plenty of trails and guided night safaris.

07 **Full moon party at Hat Rin, Ko Pha Ngan** Page **588** • *Apocalypse Now* without the war . . .

08 **Khmer ruins** Page **475** • When the ancient Khmers controlled northeast Thailand in the ninth century, they built a chain of magnificent Angkor Wat-style temple complexes, including this one at Phanom Rung.

09 **Diving and snorkelling off Ko Similan** Page **633** • The underwater scenery at this remote chain of national park islands is among the finest in the world.

10 **The National Museum, Bangkok** Page **131** • A colossal hoard of Thailand's artistic treasures.

11 **Ko Chang** Page **439** • Chill out on the long, white sand beaches of Thailand's second-largest, yet still relatively undeveloped, island.

12 **Ko Tao** Page **595** • Take a dive course, or just explore this remote island's contours by boat or on foot.

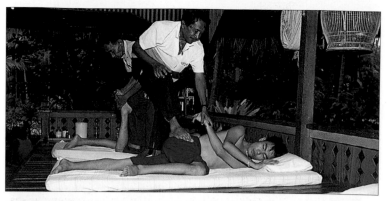

13 **Traditional massage** Page **127** • Combining elements of acupressure and chiropractic, a pleasantly brutal way to help shed jetlag, or simply to end the day.

14 **Trekking from Umphang** Page **286** •
This remote border region of western Thailand offers challenging and relatively untouristed jungle treks to mighty Tee Lor Su Falls.

15 **Krung Ching waterfall, Nakhon Si Thammarat** Page **607**
• On the northern flank of Khao Luang, the south's highest mountain, Krung Ching is probably Thailand's most spectacular drop, reachable only by a nature trail through dense, steamy jungle.

16 **Ko Lanta** Page **695** •
Choose from a dozen different beaches on this long, forested island, inhabited by Muslim fishing families and traditional sea gypsy communities.

17 Jim Thompson's House, Bangkok

Page **152** • The house of the legendary American adventurer, entrepreneur and art collector is a small, personal museum of Thai crafts and architecture.

18 Ko Samet

Page **419** • Petite and pretty, Ko Samet's gorgeous white-sand beaches are justifiably popular.

19 The Grand Palace, Bangkok

Page **121** • No visitor should miss this huge complex, which encompasses the country's holiest and most beautiful temple, Wat Phra Kaeo, and its most important image, the Emerald Buddha.

20 Riding the Death Railway

Page **223** • Thailand's most scenic train journey is also its most historic, using the track constructed by POWs whose story is movingly told in the nearby Hellfire Pass Museum.

22 Wat Phu Thok Page **530** • A uniquely atmospheric meditation temple on a steep, wooded outcrop – clamber around for the spectacular views, if nothing else.

21 Phetchaburi Page **545** • Many of the temples in this charming, historic town date back 300 years and are still in use today.

23 The Mae Hong Son loop Page **351** • Take a bus, car, motorbike or even a bicycle for this 600km trip, winding over implausibly steep forested mountains and through tightly hemmed farming valleys.

24 Vegetarian festival, Phuket Page **643** • During Taoist Lent, fasting Chinese devotees test their spiritual resolve with public acts of gruesome self-mortification.

25 **Amulet market, Bangkok** Page **136** • Nearly everyone wears a sacred talisman – often a miniature Buddha image – to ward off misfortune, and the huge amulet market at Wat Rajnadda is a great place for browsing.

26 **Wat Po, Bangkok** Page **127** • The country's most lavish working temple, a lively complex that encompasses the awesome Reclining Buddha as well as an unmissable massage school.

27 **Khao Sok National Park** Page **625** • Tree-houses, mist-clad outcrops and whooping gibbons make Khao Sok a memorable place to spend the night.

28 **Songkhla** Page **735** • A great all-round base, with miles of sandy beach, some fine restaurants and accommodation, and fascinating sights, including the best museum in the south.

29 **Ko Tarutao National Marine Park** Page **725** • Spectacular and relatively peaceful islands, sheltering a surprising variety of landscapes and fauna.

30 **Folklore Museum, Phitsanulok** Page **257** • One of Thailand's best ethnology museums, complete with a reconstructed village home and a fascinating array of traditional rural crafts.

31 **Thai cookery classes in Chiang Mai** Page **311** • Of the many courses now on offer in the town, these are the most instantly gratifying, including first-class meals and colourful market visits.

32 **Night markets** Page **50** • After-dark gatherings of dramatically lit pushcart kitchens, which are usually the best-value and most entertaining places to eat in any Thai town.

33 Ayutthaya Page **238** • An hour to the north, this former capital provides a sharp contrast to Bangkok, an atmospheric graveyard for temples flanked by good museums and some appealing guest houses.

34 The Mekhong River Page **517** • Forming 750km of the border between Thailand and Laos, the mighty Mekhong provides an endlessly fascinating scenic backdrop to travels in the northeast.

35 Wat Phra That Doi Suthep, Chiang Mai Page **328** • One of the most harmonious ensembles of temple architecture in the country, with mountaintop views over half of northern Thailand thrown in.

36 Chatuchak Weekend Market, Bangkok Page **161** • With over 6000 stalls selling everything from hill-tribe jewellery to cooking pots, Chatuchak Weekend Market is Thailand's top shopping experience.

37 **Rock-climbing on Laem Phra Nang** Page **679** • Even novice climbers can enjoy scaling the limestone cliffs here for unbeatable views of the stunning Andaman coastline.

38 **Tom yam kung** Page **50** • Delicious hot and sour soup with prawns and lemongrass, that typifies the strong, fresh flavours of Thai cuisine.

39 **Sukhothai** Page **259** • Stay in one of the many welcoming guest houses in New Sukhothai and explore the elegant ruins of the nearby old city, Thailand's thirteenth-century capital.

40 **Song-khran** Page **65** • Thai New Year is the excuse for a national waterfight – don't plan on getting much done if you come in mid-April, just join in the fun.

41 **Axe cushions** Page **183** • Much more comfortable than they look, traditional axe cushions make unusual souvenirs and can be bought unstuffed for easy transportation.

contents

using the Rough Guide

We've tried to make this Rough Guide a good read and easy to use. The book is divided into five main sections, and you should be able to find whatever you want in one of them.

colour section

The front colour section offers a quick tour of Thailand. The **introduction** aims to give you a feel for the place, with suggestions on where to go. We also tell you what the weather is like and include a basic country fact file. Next, our authors round up their favourite aspects of Thailand in the **things not to miss** section – whether it's great food, amazing sights or a fabulous beach. Right after this comes the Rough Guide's full **contents** list.

basics

You've decided to go and the Basics section covers all the **pre-departure** nitty-gritty to help you plan your trip. This is where to find out which airlines fly to your destination, what paperwork you'll need, what to do about money and insurance, about internet access, food, security, public transport, car rental – in fact just about every piece of **general practical information** you might need.

guide

This is the heart of the Rough Guide, divided into user-friendly chapters, each of which covers a specific region. Every chapter starts with a list of **highlights** and an **introduction** that helps you to decide where to go, depending on your time and budget. Likewise, introductions to the various towns and smaller regions within each chapter should help you plan your itinerary. We start most town accounts with information on arrival and accommodation, followed by a tour of the sights, and finally reviews of places to eat and drink, and details of nightlife. Longer accounts also have a directory of practical listings. Each chapter concludes with **public transport** details for that region.

contexts

Read Contexts to get a deeper understanding of what makes Thailand tick. We include a brief **history**, articles about **Buddhism**, **the arts**, **hill tribes** and **wildlife**, a detailed further reading section that reviews dozens of **books** relating to the country, and a **language** section which gives useful guidance for speaking Thai and a glossary of words and terms.

index + small print

Apart from a **full index**, which includes maps as well as places, this section covers publishing information, credits and acknowledgements, and also has our contact details in case you want to send in updates and corrections to the book – or suggestions as to how we might improve it.

chapter map of **Thailand**

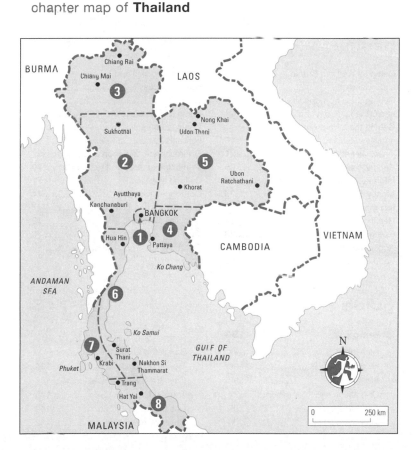

contents

colour section   i–xxiv

basics   9–83

guide   85–748

contexts   749–831

index + small print   833–844

map symbols

symbols

maps are listed in the full index using coloured text

▄▄▄▄▄	International boundary	◖	Cave
▄▄▄▄	Chapter division boundary	◈	Spring
═════	Road	⬚	Waterfall
∷∷∷∷	Unpaved road	⬚	Lighthouse
∙∙∙∙∙	Path	⊠	Gate
▬▬▬	Railway	∩	Arch
─ ─ ─	Ferry route	✕	Airport
─────	Waterway	◆	Museum
◆	Point of interest	ⓘ	Information office
⚐	Border crossing	ℂ	Telephone
▣	Accommodation	⊞	Hospital
◉	Restaurants & bars	⊠	Post office
Ⓧ	Campground	▦	Market
@	Internet access	◐	Swimming pool
⛪	Mosque	▬	Building
⚷	Temple	✚	Church
⛩	Chinese temple	⊹	Christian cemetery
▲	Peak	▦	Park
⋀⋀	Mountains	⬚	Beach
�※	Viewpoint		

basics

basics

Getting there from
Britain and Ireland

The fastest and most comfortable way of reaching Thailand is to fly nonstop from London to Bangkok with either Qantas, British Airways, EVA Airways or Thai International – a journey time of about twelve hours. Many scheduled airlines operate indirect flights to Bangkok (ie flights with one or more connections), which usually take up to four hours longer, but work out significantly cheaper; Lauda Air also flies London–Phuket with a change in Vienna. Prices for these vary throughout the year, but at the time of writing, airlines such as Lufthansa (who fly via Frankfurt) and Royal Jordanian (who stop off in Amman) offer good deals. A small but growing number of charter flights are now available, especially to Phuket, which can get you into the south of the country quickly and cheaply.

There are no nonstop flights from any regional airports in Britain or from any Irish airports, and rather than routing via London, you may find it convenient to fly to another European hub such as Amsterdam, Frankfurt or Vienna, and take a connecting flight from there. From British regional airports, this can sometimes work out as cheap as an indirect flight from London, but if you're looking to save money from Ireland, you're probably best off getting a cheap flight or ferry to England, then catching your flight to Bangkok from London.

If you're continuing **onward** from Thailand, then consider buying a **one-way London–Bangkok ticket** (from £220 plus airport tax) and shopping around for the next leg of your trip once you arrive. If you're planning a long trip with several stops in Asia or elsewhere, buying a **round-the-world (RTW) ticket** makes a lot of sense. A typical one-year ticket, costing from £1250 (plus tax), would depart and return to London, taking in Singapore, Bangkok, Bali, Sydney, Auckland, Tahiti, Los Angeles and New York, leaving you to cover the Singapore–Bangkok and LA–NYC legs overland. Alternatively, you might want to consider **open-jaw** tickets, which can be remarkably good value: flying out London–Bangkok, returning Singapore–London starts from as little as £425 in low season with an airline such as Lufthansa.

Airlines

British Airways ⓦwww.britishairways.com; in the UK ☎0845/773 3377, from the Irish Republic call ☎0141/222 2345 in the UK. Daily nonstop flights from Heathrow to Bangkok.
EVA Airways In the UK ☎020/7380 8300, ⓦwww.evaair.com.tw. Three nonstop Bangkok flights a week from Heathrow.
Lauda Air In the UK ☎020/7630 5924, ⓦwww.laudaair.com. Flies from Gatwick via Vienna twice a week to Bangkok, and once a week to Phuket.
Lufthansa ⓦwww.lufthansa.co.uk; in the UK ☎0845/773 7747, in the Irish Republic ☎01/844 5544. Five flights a week from Heathrow via Frankfurt.
Qantas In the UK ☎0845/774 7767, ⓦwww.qantas.com.au. Daily nonstop flights to Bangkok from Heathrow.
Royal Jordanian Airlines In the UK ☎020 7878 6300, ⓦwww.rja.com.jo. Three flights a week to Bangkok from Heathrow, via Amman.
Thai Airways ⓦwww.thaiair.com; in the UK ☎0870/606 0911 or 0161/831 7861. Daily nonstop Bangkok flights from Heathrow.

Fares

The most expensive times to fly are July, August and December – you may have to book two to three months in advance for cheaper tickets during these **peak periods**. Check the airline's exact seasonal dates through an agent, as you could make major savings by shifting your departure date by as little as one day.

Discounted **nonstop London–Bangkok** return fares start at around £450 low season, rising to £550 during peak periods. For **indirect flights**, Lufthansa works out among the cheapest in high season, at about £440 inclusive of tax; the best low-season rate at the time of writing is £330 with Royal Jordanian. Some agents offer special discounts (around £400 return) with the more reputable airlines for full-time students and/or under-26s. **Fares to Phuket** with Lauda Air via Vienna range from £575 to £685.

Bear in mind that the £20–30 **departure tax** applicable from British airports is not included in prices quoted by many travel agents; we have not included tax in the example fares detailed above, except where noted. Also, you'll always have to pay an airport departure tax (B500) when leaving Thailand on an international flight.

Shopping for tickets

There's little point in buying direct from the airlines unless they happen to be running special offers; any reliable **specialist agent** (see below) will normally be able to undercut airline prices by a hefty percentage (the fares mentioned in this section are agents' prices). These discount deals nearly always carry **restrictions** on your length of stay in Thailand (generally limiting you to seven to ninety days) and usually require a fixed departure date from Thailand – check particulars with your agent.

Before making a final decision on who to book with, it's always worth checking out online agents such as ⓦ www.cheapflights .co.uk and www.ebookers.ie; Teletext, which is especially good for charters; the travel sections in the weekend papers, plus *Time Out* and the *Evening Standard* in London; and free giveaway magazines like *TNT*. Many of the companies advertising in these publications are **bucket shops** who are able to offer extremely cheap deals, but there's a risk attached to companies who don't belong to official travel associations such as ABTA or IATA – if your bucket shop goes bust you get no refund, even on a fully paid-up ticket. With associated agents, such as those listed below, ABTA and IATA will cover any debts in the case of bankruptcy.

You might also like to consider **courier flights**. The deal involves a package being checked through with your luggage, in return for a cheaper flight. Call up armed with the date you'd like to travel and how long you plan to stay, and they can advise whether flights are available; however, return times and luggage are restricted.

Discount flight agents

Britain

Bridge the World, 47 Chalk Farm Rd, London NW1 8AN ☎ 020/7911 0900, ⓦ www.bridgetheworld.com. A wide choice of cut-price flights with good deals aimed at the backpacker market – particularly good for RTW tickets.

Flightbookers, 177–178 Tottenham Court Rd, London W1P 0LX ☎ 020/7757 3000, ⓦ www.ebookers.com. Low fares on an extensive range of scheduled flights.

North South Travel, Moulsham Mill Centre, Parkway, Chelmsford, Essex CM2 7PX ☎ 01245/608 291, ⓦ www.northsouthtravel.co.uk. Friendly, competitive travel agency, offering discounted fares worldwide; profits are used to support projects in the developing world, especially the promotion of sustainable tourism.

STA Travel ⓦ www.statravel.co.uk. 86 Old Brompton Rd, London SW7 3LH ☎ 020/7361 6144; and over forty other branches in British cities. Worldwide specialists in low-cost flights and tours for students and under-26s, though other customers welcome.

Trailfinders ⓦ www.trailfinders.co.uk. 194 Kensington High St, London W8 7RG ☎ 020/7938 3939; plus branches in Birmingham, Bristol, Glasgow and Manchester. One of the best-informed and most efficient agents for independent travellers.

Travelbag, 52 Regent St, London W1R 6DX ☎ 0870/737 7843, ⓦ www.travelbag.co.uk. Discount flights to the Far East; official Qantas agent.

Travel Cuts, 295a Regent St, London W1R 7YA ☎ 020/7255 2082, ⓦ www.travelcuts.co.uk. Specializes in budget, student and youth travel and RTW tickets.

usit CAMPUS, 52 Grosvenor Gardens, London SW1 0AG ☎ 020/7730 8111, ⓦ www.usitcampus.co.uk. Student/youth travel specialists, with over fifty branches, including in YHA shops and on university campuses all over Britain.

Ireland

Joe Walsh Tours ⓦ www.joewalshtours.ie. 69 Upper O'Connell St, Dublin 2 ☎ 01/872 2555; 117

Patrick St, Cork ☎021/277 959. Discount flight agent.

Silk Road Travel, 64 South William St, Dublin 2 ☎01/677 1029 or 677 1147. Specialists in Far Eastern destinations.

Thomas Cook ⓦwww.thomascook.co.uk. 118 Grafton St, Dublin 2 ☎01/677 0469; 11 Donegal Place, Belfast 1 ☎0232/9055 4455. Package holiday and flight agent; also arranges traveller's cheques, insurance and car rental.

Trailfinders, 4–5 Dawson St, Dublin 2 ☎01/677 7888, ⓦwww.trailfinders.ie. Comprehensive and well-informed flight and travel agent, with excellent RTW ticket offers.

usit NOW ⓦwww.usitnow.ie. 19–21 Aston Quay, Dublin 2 ☎01/602 1700; Fountain Centre, College Street, Belfast 1 ☎028/9032 4073; plus branches in Cork, Derry, Galway, Limerick and Waterford. Ireland's main outlet for discounted, youth and student fares.

Courier flight brokers

Ben's Travel, 83 Mortimer St, London W1 ☎020/7462 0022, ⓦwww.benstravel.co.uk.

Bridges Worldwide, Old Mill House, Mill Rd, West Drayton, Middlesex ☎01895/465065, ⓦwww.bridgesworldwide.com.

International Association of Air Travel Couriers, c/o International Features, 1 Kings Rd, Dorchester, Dorset ☎01305/216920, ⓦwww.courier.org or www.aircourier.co.uk. Agents for lots of courier companies; a small membership fee is required to join.

Packages

Package deals come in two varieties: those offering a return flight and a week or more of accommodation, and specialist tours which organize daytime activities and escorted excursions – sometimes in addition to flights, sometimes not. Flight and accommodation deals can work out to be good value if you're planning to base yourself in just one or two places, costing around £700 for eight days in Bangkok and Phuket. **Specialist tour** packages, on the other hand, are pretty expensive compared to what you'd pay if you organized everything independently (from about £1400 including flight for a three-week trip), but they do cut out a lot of hassle, and the most adventurous ones often feature activities and itineraries that wouldn't be easy to set up by yourself. Before booking, make sure you know exactly what's included in the price.

Tour operators

Thailand-wide tour operators based in Bangkok are given on p.188, and local operators in other parts of the country are listed throughout the Guide. Prices below exclude international flights except where noted.

Arc Journeys ☎020/7681 3175, ⓦwww.travelarc.com. Small group and tailor-made tours. Regular departures include a nine-day overland tour from Bangkok to Singapore, taking in visits to the River Kwai, Hua Hin, Ranong, Krabi and Phuket for £900 per person.

Bales Worldwide ☎0870/241 3208, ⓦwww.balesworldwide.co.uk. Traditional high-quality escorted trips, including a fourteen-day "Images of Thailand" tour from £1300 (including flights and some meals) as well as tailor-made itineraries.

British Airways Holidays ☎0870/242 4245, ⓦwww.baholidays.co.uk. Beach- and city-based flight and accommodation packages; for example, five nights in Pattaya from £625. Bookings can be made direct or through most travel agents.

Exodus ☎020/8675 5550, ⓦwww.exodus.co.uk. Small-group adventure tours to Thailand. Flights are included in prices, though land-only options can be arranged. Their "Thailand Adventure" (16 days; from £700) covers Bangkok, cruising on the River Kwai, Erawan National Park, Ayutthaya, Chiang Mai, trekking through hill-tribe villages, and Mae Chan.

Explore Worldwide ☎01252/760000, ⓦwww.explore.co.uk. One of the best adventure-tour operators. Tours, including hill-tribe trekking, from £700 (flights included). Also several Thailand and Laos combinations.

Footprint Adventures ☎01522/804929, ⓦwww.footprint-adventures.com. Tours catering to walkers as well as wildlife and bird enthusiasts, such as their ten-day "Mae Hong Son Jungle Safari", which includes six days' trekking, plus sightseeing in Bangkok and Chiang Mai (£275).

Gecko Travel ☎023/9237 6799, ⓦwww.geckotravel.co.uk. Southeast Asia specialist operating small-group adventure holidays with off-the-beaten-track itineraries; their 21-day tour of Thailand's northern mountains and southern beaches starts at £1400 including flights.

Golden Joy Holidays ☎0870/241 5187, www.goldenjoy.com. Diving-tour organizers; in Thailand the company specializes in the Andaman coast, offering tailor-made packages; five days' day-boat diving in Krabi costs from £225.

Hayes and Jarvis ☎0870/898 9890, www.hayes-jarvis.com. Tours and hotel-based holidays; five nights in Hua Hin cost £580 including flights. Particularly good on diving destinations; exotic weddings also organized.

Imaginative Traveller ☎ 020/8742 8612, ⓦ www.imaginative-traveller.com. Small-group adventure tours off the beaten track with Intrepid Tours, including hill-tribe trekking. From £320 for eight days.

Joe Walsh Tours ☎ 01/676 0991, ⓦ www.joewalshtours.ie. Well-established Irish tour operator offering twelve-day packages to Bangkok and Pattaya from €1250 including flights.

Kuoni Travel ☎ 020/7499 8636, ⓦ www.kuoni.co.uk. Specializes in two-centre holidays, including flights and accommodation, with good family offers. Eight nights in Bangkok and Phuket from £700. Bookings through most travel agents.

Magic Of The Orient ☎ 01293/537700, www.magic-of-the-orient.com. A wide range of upmarket tailor-made packages, including short tours with your own driver, such as three days in Khao Lak and Khao Sok National Park (£300 per person sharing), or a self-drive tour from Chiang Mai to Chiang Dao and Mae Salong (£160).

Peregrine Holidays ☎ 01865/559988, ⓦ www.peregrineadventures.co.uk. Soft adventure holidays with upmarket accommodation; their "Thailand Highlights" tour is an eight-day trip that covers Bangkok, Chiang Mai and the north (£375).

Saga Holidays ☎ 0800/414 383, ⓦ www.saga.co.uk. Long-established company catering exclusively for people aged 50 and over, offering packages such as a sixteen-night stay at a four-star hotel in Chiang Mai from £950 including flights.

Silk Steps ☎ 0117/940 2800, ⓦ www.silksteps.co.uk. Small company specializing in tailor-made itineraries in the Far East, with flights optional. In Thailand, they do both mainstream and off-the-beaten track tours such as a nine-day cycling trip near the Burmese border, through rainforests and along the River Kwai (from £1000).

Skyros ☎ 020/7267 4424, ⓦ www.skyros.com. Large selection of holistic courses from a base in the Ao Prao resort on Ko Samet, ranging from yoga to sailing and art. A two-week session including accommodation and half board starts at £700.

Symbiosis ☎ 020/7924 5906, ⓦ www.symbiosis-travel.co.uk. High-quality tailor-made adventure and special-interest packages, including diving, with a commitment to environmentally sensitive and fair-trade tourism; prices start from around £80 a day, including flights and accommodation.

Thomas Cook Holidays ☎ 01733/563 200, ⓦ www.tcholidays.com. Mainstream tour operator with seven-night packages to Phuket in five-star accommodation from £700, including flights.

Getting there from the **US and Canada**

There are no nonstop flights from North America to Thailand, but plenty of airlines run daily flights to Bangkok from major East- and West-Coast cities with only one stop en route. Bear in mind that the layover time between connecting flights can vary not just from carrier to carrier, but between different flights operated by the same airline. The actual flying time is approximately eighteen hours from LA via Asia, around an hour longer from New York via Europe. From Canada, you can expect to spend something like sixteen hours in the air flying from Vancouver (via Tokyo) or at least twenty hours from Montréal (via Europe).

Some of the major airlines offer **Circle Pacific** deals, often in partnership with other airlines. Generally valid for one year, these tickets allow you to make a certain number of stopovers en route between the West Coast of the US and Canada and Asia. Once you factor in the frequent no-back-tracking proscription, your possible itinerary may be rather limited, and cost more than a more flexible multi-airline choice. A better bet might be a Circle Pacific ticket booked through a discount travel agent (see p.16): this way, for example, an itinerary starting out and ending in Los Angeles, taking in Tokyo, Hong Kong, Bangkok–Singapore, Jakarta, Denpasar (Bali) and Sydney costs around US$2100.

If Thailand is only one stop on a longer journey, you might also want to consider buying a **round-the-world (RTW) ticket**. Some travel agents can sell you an "off-the-shelf" RTW ticket that will have you touching down in about half a dozen cities (Bangkok is on many itineraries); others will have to assemble one for you, which can be more tailored to your needs but is apt to be more expensive. A typical off-the-shelf itinerary, starting and ending in San Francisco with stops in Hong Kong, Bangkok, Delhi, Mumbai (Bombay), London and Boston costs around US$1500.

Airlines

Air Canada ☎1-888/247 2262, ⊛www.aircanada.ca. Daily flights to Bangkok from most major Canadian cities via Osaka, Hong Kong or London.
Air France In the US ☎1-800/237 2747, ⊛www.airfrance.com; in Canada ☎1-800/667 2747, ⊛www.airfrance.ca. Daily flights (though inconveniently scheduled) to Bangkok, via Paris, from over a dozen North American cities.
Cathay Pacific ☎1-800/233-2742, ⊛www.cathaypacific.com. Daily flights via Hong Kong to Bangkok from New York, Los Angeles, San Francisco and Toronto.
China Air Lines ☎1-800/227-5118, ⊛www.china-airlines.com. Flies to Bangkok via Taipei daily from Los Angeles and San Francisco, five times a week from New York and four times a week (summer only) from Anchorage.
Delta Airlines ☎1-800/241 4141, ⊛www.delta.com. Daily flights to Bangkok from most major US cities, via Seoul or Tokyo.
Finnair ⊛www.finnair.fi; in the US ☎1-800/950-5000, in Canada ☎1-800/461-8651. Via Helsinki, three Bangkok flights a week from New York and two summer-only flights a week from Toronto.
Japan Air Lines ☎1-800/525-3663, ⊛www.japanair.com. Flies to Bangkok via Tokyo from Chicago, Dallas, Los Angeles, New York, San Francisco, Los Angeles and Vancouver.
KLM/Northwest ☎www.nwa.com; in the US ☎1-800/374 7747, in Canada ☎1-800/361 5073. Daily flights to Bangkok via Japan from San

Francisco, Los Angeles, Chicago, Detroit, Seattle and New York, or via Amsterdam from New York.
Swissair ⊛www.swissair.com. In the US ☎1-800/221 4750, in Canada ☎1-800/563 5954. Daily flights to Bangkok from Montréal, New York and Toronto via Zürich.
Thai Airways ⊛www.thaiair.com. In the US ☎1-800/426-5204, in Canada ☎1-800/668-8103. Daily flights to Bangkok from Los Angeles via Osaka, and from New York via London.
United Airlines ☎1-800/241-6522, ⊛www.ual.com. Daily flights to Bangkok from most major US cities, via Tokyo.

Fares

Regardless of where you buy your ticket, fares will depend on the **season**, with higher fares applying in December, January and from June to August. The prices quoted below assume midweek travel (where there's a difference in price) and exclude taxes.

There doesn't seem to be much logic behind the pricing of published fares **from the US** to Thailand, although it's probably easier to find a reasonable fare on flights via Asia than via Europe, especially if you're departing from the West Coast. Expect to find regular, high-season published fares at around $1200 minimum from the West Coast and at least $1300 from the East Coast or the Midwest, while low-season fares can go for around $750 from the West Coast and $850 from the East Coast or Midwest. A discount travel agent, however, should be able to dig up, for instance, a high-season fare from LA for around $1050. Be on the lookout also for special limited-offer promotional fares from the major carriers like United Airlines or Thai, which can bring low-season fares down to as little as $600 from the West Coast or $750 from the East Coast.

Air Canada has the most convenient service to Bangkok from the largest number of **Canadian** cities. From Vancouver, expect to pay around CDN$2000 in low season (CDN$300 more in high season), from Toronto, CDN$2300 (CDN$400 more in high season).

Shopping for tickets

Barring special offers, the cheapest of the airlines' published fares is usually an **APEX** ticket, although this will carry certain restrictions:

you will, most likely, have to book and pay up to 21 days before departure and spend at least seven days abroad (maximum stay from one to six months), and you tend to get penalized if you change your schedule.

You can normally cut costs further by going through a specialist flight agent – either a **consolidator**, who buys up blocks of tickets from the airlines and sells them at a discount, or a **discount agent**, who in addition to dealing with discounted flights may also offer special student and youth fares and a range of other travel-related services, such as travel insurance, rail passes, car rentals, tours and the like. Many of these companies sell tickets on the **internet** too, and online-only agents like ⊛travelocity.com are worth a try. If you travel a lot, discount **travel clubs** are another option – the annual membership fee may be worth it for benefits such as cut-price air tickets and car rental.

Don't automatically assume that tickets purchased through a travel specialist will be cheapest – once you get a quote, check with the airlines and you may turn up an even better deal. Be advised also that the pool of travel companies is swimming with sharks – exercise caution and *never* deal with a company that demands cash up front or refuses to accept payment by credit card.

Finally, if you're able to fly at short notice, live in or near one of the major North American airport hubs and don't mind fitting into someone else's schedule, then a **courier flight** would probably be your cheapest option. Bangkok isn't as cheap as some courier destinations, but occasionally good bargains and even free flights come up – check regularly at the websites listed below for details.

Discount agents, consolidators, courier flight brokers and travel clubs

Air Brokers International, 150 Post St, Suite 620, San Francisco, CA 94108 ☏1-800/883-3273 or 415/397-1383, ⊛www.airbrokers.com. Consolidator and specialist in RTW tickets.
Air Courier Association ☏1-800/282-1202, ⊛www.aircourier.org. Courier flight broker; membership costs $50 for one year. A Bangkok flight with them costs $300–$550.
Airtech, 588 Broadway, Suite 204, New York, NY 10017 ☏212/219-7000, ⊛www.airtech.com.

Standby-seat broker; also deals in consolidator fares and courier flights.
Council Travel ☏1-800/226 8624 or 617/528-2091, ⊛www.counciltravel.com. Offices include: 205 E 42nd St, New York, NY 10017 ☏212/822 2700; 530 Bush St, Suite 700, San Francisco, CA 94108 ☏415/421-3473; 931 Westwood Blvd, Los Angeles 90024 ☏310/208-3551; 1153 N Dearborn St, Chicago, IL 60610 ☏312/951 0585. Nationwide US organization specializing in student/budget travel.
Educational Travel Center, 438 N Frances St, Madison, WI 53703 ☏1-800/747-5551 or 608/256 5551, ⊛www.edtrav.com. Student/youth discount agent.
High Adventure Travel, 442 Post St, Suite 400, San Francisco, CA 94102 ☏1-800/350-0612 or 415/912-5600, ⊛www.airtreks.com. RTW and Circle Pacific tickets.
International Association of Air Travel Couriers ☏561/582-8320, ⊛www.courier.org Courier flight broker with membership fee of around $45 a year.
Now Voyager, 74 Varick St, Suite 307, New York, NY 10013 ☏212/431-1616, ⊛www.nowvoyagertravel.com. Consolidator and courier flight broker.
STA Travel ☏1800/777 0112, ⊛www.statravel.com. Branches include: 10 Downing St, New York, NY 10014 ☏212/627-3111; 7202 Melrose Ave, Los Angeles, CA 90046 ☏323/934-8722; 36 Geary St, San Francisco, CA 94108 ☏415/391-8407; 297 Newbury St, Boston, MA 02115 ☏617/266-6014; 429 S Dearborn St, Chicago, IL 60605 ☏312/786-9050; 1905 Walnut St, Philadelphia, PA 19103 ☏215/568-7999. Worldwide specialists in independent travel; also student IDs, travel insurance, car rental, rail passes, etc.
Travac, 989 6th Ave, New York NY 10018 ☏1-800/872-8800, ⊛www.thetravelsite.com. Consolidator and charter broker.
Travel Avenue, 10 S Riverside, Suite 1404, Chicago, IL 60606 ☏1-800/333-3335, ⊛www.travelavenue.com. Full-service travel agent that offers discounts in the form of rebates.
Travel Cuts ☏1-800/667-2887, ⊛www.travelcuts.com. Branches include: 187 College St, Toronto, ON M5T 1P7 ☏416/979-2406; 1613 rue St Denis, Montréal, PQ H2X 3K3 ☏514/843-8511; Student Union Building, University of British Columbia, Vancouver, BC V6T 1Z ☏888/FLY CUTS or 604/822-6890. Canadian student travel organization.
Travelers Advantage ☏1-800/548-1116, ⊛www.travelersadvantage.com. Discount travel club.

Packages

Package tours are often expensive and aimed at those who treasure comfort, but can be excellent value, provided you really want to do all the activities, trips and tours. Those looking for more flexible scheduling would be advised to start with a city package such as those offered by Thai Air (or simply get to Bangkok under their own steam). From the capital, you can then consider a more personal, tailored package to the islands, archipelagos or the wilds. All prices quoted below exclude taxes; unless stated otherwise, round-trip flights are from the West Coast.

Package tour operators

US

Abercrombie & Kent ☎1 800/323-7308 or 630/954-2944, ⓦwww.abercrombiekent.com. Deluxe ten-day "Highlights of Thailand" tour ($2300 not including flight), plus several other packages which include Thailand as part of a more extensive Asian itinerary.
Absolute Asia ☎1-800/736-8187 or 212/627-1950, ⓦwww.absoluteasia.com. Customized tours, covering such specialist interests as archeology and Thai cuisine, as well as a fourteen-day "Discover Thailand" trip taking in Bangkok, Chiang Mai, Chiang Rai and Phuket ($1500 excluding international flights).
Adventure Center ☎1-800/228-8747 or 510/654-1879, ⓦwww.adventure-center.com. Over twenty packages, some covering Thailand exclusively, others including Laos, Malaysia or Singapore. An example is their eleven-day "Golden Triangle" trip in northern Thailand, on which you make journeys by road, longtail boat and on foot, staying in hotels or hill-tribe huts ($500 excluding flight).
Asia Pacific Adventures ☎1-800/825-1680 or 818/886-5190, ⓦwww.asiapacificadventures.com. Customized tours involving an exciting variety of activities – sea canoeing, kayaking, mountain-biking, jungle treks, homestays, Thai cooking etc.
Asia Trans Pacific Journeys ☎1-800/642-2742, ⓦwww.southeastasia.com. Customized tours and packages; their "Explorer's Thailand" tour lasts sixteen days and costs from $2800 excluding flights.
Backroads ☎1-800/462-2848 or 510/527-1555, ⓦwww.backroads.com. They do an eight-day "Golden Triangle" tour involving cycling, trekking and elephant rides, costing $2300 (flight not included) plus $150 for bike rental.
EastQuest ☎1-800/638-3449 or 212/741-1688, ⓔearthquest1@aol.com. Customized tours plus adventure or traditional sightseeing packages.

Elderhostel ☎1-877/426-8056, ⓦwww.elderhostel.org. Specialists in educational and activity programmes, cruises and homestays for senior travellers; they do an eighteen-day "Discovering Thailand" package costing around $3000 including flights.
Geographic Expeditions ☎1-800/777-8183 or 415/922-0448, ⓦwww.geoex.com. Among their offerings is "River of Kings and Northern Caravans", a sixteen-day touring and sailing trip (from $4600; flight not included) and a choice of five four-day Bangkok extensions, including a sea cruise or a trip to Ko Samui (from $1000).
Himalayan Travel ☎1-800/225-2380 or 203/743-2349, ⓦwww.gorp.com/himtravel.htm. Customized tours plus a range of set packages, including the fifteen-day "Northern Thailand Experience", and "The Tropical South", which takes in Phuket and is also fifteen days; each is priced at around $900 excluding flights.
Journeys International ☎1-800/255-8735 or 734/665-4407, ⓦwww.journeys-intl.com. Established ecotourism operator, offering a five-day "Rainforests & Remote Islands" tour to Thailand from $650 excluding flights.
Maupintour ☎1-800/255-4266 or 913/843-1211, ⓦwww.maupintour.com. Twelve-day fully inclusive tours of Thailand, taking in Bangkok, Chiang Mai and Ayutthaya, from $1700 excluding flights.
Mountain Travel-Sobek ☎1-888/687 6235, ⓦwww.mtsobek.com. Their "Treasures of Indochine" is a sixteen-day trip to Thailand, Cambodia and Laos, costing from $3700 excluding flights.
Royal Orchid Holidays ☎1-800/426 5204, ⓦwww.thaiair.com. Subsidiary of Thai Airways; does seven-night Bangkok packages from around $900 in low season, including flights. Also regular promotional offers, when prices for a round-trip flight and four nights in a downtown Bangkok hotel can go for between $550 and $900.
Saga Holidays ☎1-877/265-6862, ⓦwww.sagaholidays.com. Specialists in group travel for senior citizens. Seven nights in Bangkok from $1000 including flights.

Canada

Adventures Abroad ☎1-800/665-3998 or 604/303-1099, ⓦwww.adventures-abroad.com. Small-group tour specialists with several Thailand options; one-week treks start at about CDN$1100 excluding flights.
Goway Travel ☎1-800/387-8850 or 416/322-1034, ⓦwww.goway.com. Wide range of Thailand packages, including three-night tours of Bangkok.

Getting there from **Australia and New Zealand**

There's no shortage of scheduled flights to Bangkok from Australia and New Zealand, with direct services offered by Thai Airways, Qantas and Air New Zealand (flight times from Perth and Sydney are around 9hr, from Auckland around 11hr).

There are a variety of **round-the-world (RTW)** combinations that include Bangkok, with the number of free stopovers ranging from just a few to unlimited. Currently the cheapest is with Qantas/BA, allowing three free stops in each direction for around A$1700/NZ$2100. The most flexible are the mileage-based tickets such as the "Star Alliance 1" offered by the Star Alliance consortium of airlines (ⓦ www.star-alliance.com), and "One World Explorer" by Qantas, Cathay Pacific, British Airways and American Airlines; both tickets allow side trips, backtracking and open-jaw travel (landing in one city and flying out from another). For example, prices for an RTW ticket from Sydney to Bangkok, London, New York, Los Angeles, Auckland and back to Sydney start at around A$2400/NZ$3000. Ultimately your choice will depend on where you want to travel before or after Bangkok. If you don't want to travel outside Asia, a better option is a **Circle Asia** ticket. Put together by an alliance of airlines, these tickets allow you to travel via two or more Asian cities en route, but can be a little complicated to arrange as each sector needs to be costed separately, and backtracking isn't allowed.

Indonesia's proximity to Australia and New Zealand makes it the obvious starting point for **overlanding** to Thailand through Asia. There are regular flights to Denpasar in Bali, where you can connect with boat, rail and bus links through Java and/or Sumatra. Northern Sumatra is just a short boat ride from Malaysia and Singapore, and there are regular ferry connections between Medan and Penang, between Dumai and Melaka, and between the Riau islands and Johor Bahru and Singapore. Once in Malaysia or Singapore, you can proceed into Thailand by train, bus or plane (see p.23). Ansett, Qantas and Garuda fares to Denpasar start at A$800/NZ$1000. Alternatively, you could fly to Singapore or Kuala Lumpur and then continue overland to Thailand by road or rail. If you'd like to travel in a group, then Intrepid's 29-day "Bali to Bangkok Overland" trip (A$2100/NZ$2700 excluding airfare) may be for you.

Airlines

Air New Zealand ⓦ www.airnz.com; in Australia ☎13/2476, in New Zealand ☎09/357 3000 & 0800/737 000. Several flights a week direct to Bangkok from Auckland, Christchurch, Brisbane and Sydney.

Ansett ⓦ www.ansett.com.au; in Australia ☎13 1414 or 02/9352 6707, in New Zealand ☎09/336 2364. Several flights a week from major Australian cities and from Auckland to Denpasar and also to Bangkok, Kuala Lumpur and Singapore.

Egypt Air In Australia ☎02/9267 6979, ⓦ www.egyptair.com.eg. Two flights a week direct to Singapore from Sydney.

Garuda ⓦ www.garuda-indonesia.com; in Australia ☎1300/365330, in New Zealand ☎09/366 1862 & 0800/128510. Several flights a week from major Australian cities and from Auckland to Bangkok, with a stopover in either Denpasar or Jakarta.

Gulf Air ⓦ www.gulfairco.com; in Australia ☎02/9244 2199, in New Zealand ☎09/308 3366. Three flights a week direct to Singapore from Sydney and Melbourne.

Malaysia Airlines ⓦ www.mas.com.my; in Australia ☎13 2476, in New Zealand ☎09/373 2741 or 0800/657472. Several flights a week from Brisbane, Sydney, Melbourne, Perth and Auckland, via Kuala Lumpur, to Bangkok, Phuket, Hat Yai and Chiang Mai.

Olympic Airways In Australia ☎1800/221 663 or 02/9251 2044, ⓦ www.olympic-airways.com. Three direct Sydney–Bangkok flights a week.

Qantas ⓦ www.qantas.com.au; in Australia
☏ 13/1313, in New Zealand ☏ 09/357 8900 or
0800/808 767. Several flights a week direct to
Bangkok from major Australasian cities.
Royal Brunei Airlines In Australia ☏ 07/3221
7757, ⓦ www.bruneiair.com. Three flights a week
to Bangkok via Bandar Seri Begawan from Brisbane,
Darwin and Sydney.
Singapore Airlines ⓦ www.singaporeair.com; in
Australia ☏ 02/9350 0262 or 13/1011, in New
Zealand ☏ 09/303 2129 or 0800/808909. Flights to
Bangkok and Phuket, via Singapore: daily from
Sydney, Melbourne, Perth and Auckland; four flights
a week from Cairns, Brisbane and Christchurch; and
three flights a week from Darwin; also flies three
times a week to Chiang Mai, via Singapore, from
Sydney.
Thai Airways ⓦ www.thaiair.com; in Australia
☏ 1300/651960, in New Zealand ☏ 09/377 3886.
Flies direct to Bangkok three times a week from
Sydney and Auckland, and twice a week from
Brisbane, Melbourne and Perth. Connections
available to Chiang Mai, Hat Yai, Phuket and other
Thai destinations.

Fares

Fares are structured according to **season**;
for most airlines high season is from mid-
November to mid-January and May to the
end of August, when fares rise by about
A/NZ$200–400. Generally airlines have a set
fare from major eastern Australian cities (with
Ansett and Qantas providing a shuttle service to the main point of departure), while
fares from Darwin are around A$200 cheap-
er. From Christchurch and Wellington you'll
pay NZ$150–300 more than from Auckland.
   From Australia, the cheapest direct flights
to **Bangkok** are with Olympic Airlines from
Sydney (around A$850/A$1400 low/high
season), while Thai Airways, Air New
Zealand, BA and Qantas all weigh in around
A$1000/A$1500. The best indirect deals are
with Royal Brunei, via Bandar Seri Begawan
(A$850/A$1100), with other airlines up to
A$400 more expensive. To **Singapore**, the
best deals are with Gulf Air, Egyptair or Royal
Brunei (around A$700/A$1200), with Royal
Brunei flying to **Kuala Lumpur** for the same
prices.
   From New Zealand, Qantas offers the
best direct low-season fares to Bangkok
(around NZ$1100), with Thai Airways only
marginally more expensive; Air New Zealand,
however, charges a pricey NZ$1500. High-

season fares on these airlines are pretty similar, at NZ$1900–2100. In high season, it's
slightly cheaper to get an indirect flight with
Garuda to Bangkok with Garuda, though flying via KL with Malaysia Airlines saves very
little. Singapore Airlines flies to **Singapore**
for NZ$1250/NZ$1900; Malaysia Airlines'
fares to **Kuala Lumpur** are about ten percent cheaper.

Shopping for tickets

Tickets purchased direct from the airlines are
usually expensive; the **discount agents** listed
below offer much better deals on fares and
have the latest information on limited special
offers. Flight Centres and STA Travel generally offer the lowest fares. You might also want
to have a look on the **internet**; ⓦ www.
travel.com.au and ⓦ www.travelforless.co.nz
offer discounted fares, as does ⓦ www.syd-
neytravel.com

Discount travel agents

Anywhere Travel, 345 Anzac Parade, Kingsford,
Sydney ☏ 02/9663 0411,
ⓔ anywhere@ozemail.com.au. Discounted flights as
well as accommodation packages and tours.
Budget Travel ☏ 0800/808 040,
ⓦ www.budgettravel.co.nz. 16 Fort St, Auckland
☏ 09/366 0061, plus branches around the country.
Long-established agent dealing with budget air fares
and accommodation packages.
Destinations Unlimited, 220 Queen St, Auckland
☏ 09/373 4033. Discount fares plus a good
selection of tours and holiday packages.
Flight Centre ⓦ www.flightcentre.com.au. In
Australia: 82 Elizabeth St, Sydney ☏ 02/9235
3522, plus branches nationwide, nearest branch
☏ 13/1600. In New Zealand: 350 Queen St,
Auckland ☏ 09/358 4310, plus branches
nationwide. Competitive discounts on airfares, and a
wide range of package holidays and adventure tours.
Northern Gateway, 22 Cavenagh St, Darwin
☏ 08/8941 1394, ⓔ oztravel@norgate.com.au.
Specializes in low-cost flights to Asia from Darwin.
STA Travel In Australia, nearest branch
☏ 13/1776, fastfare telesales ☏ 1300/360960,
ⓦ www.statravel.com.au; offices at 855 George St,
Sydney; 256 Flinders St, Melbourne; other offices
in state capitals and major universities. In New
Zealand, 10 High St, Auckland ☏ 09/309 0458,
fastfare telesales ☏ 09/366 6673; plus branches in
Wellington, Christchurch, Dunedin, Palmerston
North, Hamilton and at major universities. Fare

discounts for students and under-26s, as well as visas and travel insurance.

Student Uni Travel, 92 Pitt St, Sydney ☏ 02/9232 8444; plus branches in Brisbane, Cairns, Darwin, Melbourne and Perth. Student/youth discounts and travel advice.

Thomas Cook In Australia, 175 Pitt St, Sydney ☏ 02/9231 2877; 257 Collins St, Melbourne ☏ 03/9282 0222; plus branches in other state capitals (local branch ☏ 13/1771, telesales ☏ 1800/801 002). In New Zealand, 191 Queen St, Auckland ☏ 09/379 3920. Low-cost flights, also tours, accommodation and traveller's cheques.

Trailfinders ⓦ www.trailfinders.co.au; offices at 8 Spring St, Sydney ☏ 02/9247 7666; 91 Elizabeth St, Brisbane ☏ 07/3229 0887; Hides Corner, Shield St, Cairns ☏ 07/4041 1199. Independent-travel specialist.

Travel.com.au, 76–80 Clarence St, Sydney ☏ 02/9249 5444 or 1800 000 447, ⓦ www.travel.com.au. Flight discounts.

usit BEYOND ⓦ www.usitbeyond.co.nz. Cnr Shortland St and Jean Batten Place, Auckland ☏ 09/379 4224 or 0800/788 336; plus branches in Christchurch, Dunedin, Palmerston North, Hamilton and Wellington. Student/youth travel specialists.

Package holidays and tours

An **organized tour** is worth considering if you have ambitious sightseeing plans and only a short time to accomplish them, or feel unsure about the language and customs. Most tour companies offer a range of itineraries that take in the major sights and activities. Some of the adventure-oriented tours can help you to get to the more remote areas and include activities such as whitewater rafting, diving, trekking and cycling.

If you can only manage a short visit and are happy to base yourself in one city or resort, **package holidays** can be an economical and hassle-free way of sampling Thailand. Accommodation/flight packages, Bangkok and Chiang Mai city stays, fly-drive options and coach tours are offered by a whole host of operators through your travel agent; most can also arrange add-on trips to resort islands, cruises from Bangkok, air passes and rail travel, and can book accommodation in regional Thailand. Sample city-break prices, including international flights, are around A$1200/NZ$1600 for five nights in Bangkok or eight nights in Phuket (the exact price depends on the type of accom-

modation chosen). Package holidays departing from Darwin, where available, generally cost about A$200 less per person.

Extended journeys through the region cater to all tastes – from those in search of thrills and adventure to those who simply prefer to tour in a group. For example, Gecko's 25-day "Thailand Encompassed" round trip from Bangkok takes in Kanchanaburi and the River Kwai, Ayutthaya, Chiang Mai and the north, and the beach escapes of Ko Samui and Krabi (A$1600/NZ$2000 excluding international flights).

Specialist tour operators and agents

Firms listed below are based in Australia except where noted. Prices below exclude international air fares except where noted.

Abercrombie and Kent In Australia ☏ 03/9699 9766 or 1800/331 429, in New Zealand ☏ 09/579 3369. Their seven-day "Treasures of Thailand" tour (A$4100/NZ$5100 excluding international flights) covers Bangkok and Chiang Mai, and features one night on the Eastern and Oriental Express train (see box on p.24). Also four-day luxury train journeys on the Eastern and Oriental Express from Kuala Lumpur to Bangkok (A$2000/NZ$2500).

Adventure Specialists ☏ 02/9261 2927. Agents for a good selection of overland and adventure tours through Thailand such as Explore's adventure and cultural tours of the country, and Orbitours' customized packages, which include trekking, diving and hill-tribe visits.

Allways Travel ☏ 1800/259 297, ⓦ www.allwaysdive.com.au. All-inclusive dive packages to prime Thai dive sites.

Alma Travel Centre ☏ 03/9670 2288. Thailand trekking specialists.

Asian Explorer Holidays ☏ 07/3832 4266. A selection of tours and accommodation in Bangkok and Chiang Mai.

Asian Travel Centre ☏ 03/9654 8277. A variety of tours and accommodation in Thailand.

Birding Worldwide ☏ 03/9899 9303, ⓦ www.birdingworldwide.com.au. Three-week birdwatching tours in Thailand's national parks and remote regions in the northwest.

Intrepid Travel ☏ 1800/629 186, ⓦ www.intrepidtravel.com.au. A host of one- to four-week low-impact, country-wide adventure tours; also white-water rafting, trekking and cooking holidays. As an example, their fifteen-day "Southern Thailand" trip (A$1200/NZ$1600) explores southern villages, islands and beaches by day, while spending the nights either camping or staying in a variety of local accommodation.

New Horizons Holidays ☎08/9268 3777. Largest Southeast Asian wholesaler in Perth, offering an extensive range of trips to Thailand.

Padi Travel Network ☎02/9417 2800 or 1800/678 100. Dive packages to the prime sites of the Thai coast.

Peregrine Adventures ☎03/9662 2700 or 1300/655 433, ⊛www.peregrine.net.au. Small-group adventure/cultural trips throughout Thailand; their eight-day "Northern Trek and Cycle" from Chiang Mai (A$750/NZ$950) visits the villages and towns around Chiang Dao, the Kok River, the Golden Triangle region and the city of Chiang Rai. Act as agents for Gecko's and Exodus' cycling and adventure holidays.

Pro Dive Travel ☎02/9232 5733 or 1800/820 820. Tailored dive packages to some of Thailand's most popular sights.

San Michele Travel ☎02/9299 1111 or 1800/222 244, ⊛www.asiatravel.com.au. Customized rail tours throughout Southeast Asia; a favourite is their thirteen-day Singapore–Bangkok journey (A$1700/NZ$2100 excluding international flights). They also do city breaks, sightseeing trips, cruises and extended overland tours out of Bangkok.

Thai Binh Travel ☎02/9724 2304. Specialists in accommodation and tours throughout Thailand.

Thailand Travel ☎08/8272 2166. Specialists in all aspects of travel to Thailand.

Travel Indochina ☎02/9321 9133 or 1800/640 823. Four-day city stays in Bangkok, including day tours, as well as extended tours throughout Thailand.

Travel via neighbouring countries

Sharing land borders with Burma, Laos, Cambodia and Malaysia, Thailand works well as part of many overland itineraries, both across Asia and between Europe and Australia. In addition, Bangkok is one of the major regional flight hubs for Southeast Asia.

The most popular multiple-stop Circle Asia and round-the-world air tickets often feature a "surface sector" between Bangkok and either Singapore or Bali; in other words it's up to you to find your own way between these places, either by bus, train, boat or locally purchased flight, or some combination of these. **Travelling overland** in this way is a good means of exploring the country and can save you a significant amount on your air ticket. Other, more unusual overland routes fly you into China and out of Bangkok, leaving you to make your own way across Vietnam and/or Laos and then into Thailand.

The main restrictions on overland routes in and out of Thailand are determined by **visas**, and by where the permitted land crossings lie. Most passport holders should be able to get an on-the-spot thirty-day entry stamp into Thailand at any of the land borders described below, though you may be asked to show proof of onward travel arrangements, which can be tricky for overlanders. Thirty-day stamps are absolutely non-extendable (though it's easy enough to hop across one of the land borders and return on the same day with another thirty-day stamp), so you might want to apply for a sixty-day tourist visa instead, obtainable in advance from Thai embassies; full details on visa requirements are given on p.25.

You may need to buy visas for your next port of call when in Thailand, and details of visa requirements for travel to Thailand's immediate neighbours are outlined below. All **Asian embassies** are located in Bangkok (see p.193 for contact details), but several countries also have visa-issuing consulates outside the capital, where waiting times can be shorter: China and India run consulates in Chiang Mai (see p.326), and Laos and

Vietnam have consulates in Khon Kaen (see p.505).

The right paperwork is also crucial if you're planning to **drive your own car or motorbike into Thailand**. For advice on this, consult The Golden Triangle Rider website (@ www.geocities.com/goldentrianglerider), which has up-to-date first-hand accounts of border crossings with a vehicle between many Southeast Asian countries, including lots about Thailand.

Bangkok has become an important centre for **flights** to many parts of Asia, in particular as a transit point for routes between Europe and Vietnam, Laos and Cambodia; indeed on most flights from Europe to Indochina you have no choice but to be routed via Bangkok. In addition it is now also possible to fly into regional Thai airports from nearby countries, for example from Siem Reap in Cambodia to Phuket, from Phnom Penh to Pattaya, from Louang Phabang and Vientiane in Laos to Chiang Mai, from Kunming in China and from Taipei to Chiang Mai, and from Singapore to Ko Samui. If you're doing a longer trip around Southeast Asia, you may want to consider buying a Circle ASEAN ticket, sold by the national airlines of Thailand, Brunei, Indonesia, Malaysia, the Philippines, Singapore and Vietnam. The pass entitles you to buy two to six flights between and within these countries for around £75/$110 each sector, depending on the distance; these passes must be bought outside the countries concerned.

Burma

At the time of writing, there is no overland access from **Burma** into Thailand and access in the opposite direction is restricted: Western tourists are only allowed to make limited-distance day-trips into Burma at Three Pagodas Pass near Kanchanaburi, at Myawaddy near Mae Sot, at Mae Sai (where three-day tours to Kentung are available), and at Kaw Thaung (Victoria Point) near Ranong. In each of these places you are required officially to exit Thailand, enter Burma on a temporary visa (for a fee of US$5–10), and then re-enter Thailand on a new thirty-day tourist visa; see relevant accounts in the guide for details.

In addition to numerous flights to Bangkok from Burma, there are regular flights to Chiang Mai from Rangoon and Mandalay with Air Mandalay. Tourists who intend to enter Burma by air can buy four-week tourist **visas** at the Burmese embassy in Bangkok (see p.193) for B800; apply to the embassy and you may be able to collect the same day, or definitely the following day.

Cambodia

At the time of writing, there are two legal overland **border crossings** from Cambodia into Thailand, but you should check with other travellers before opting for either as regulations can vary from week to week and border closures are not unheard of.

The most commonly used crossing is at **Poipet**, which lies just across the border from the Thai town of **Aranyaprathet**, at the end of a famously potholed and uncomfortable road. There are reasonable, if time-consuming, public-transport connections to Poipet from Sisophon, Siem Reap and Phnom Penh in Cambodia, and many guest houses in Siem Reap also organize private transport to the border. Bear in mind when arranging transport from your Cambodian departure point that the Thai border closes at 5pm every day, and that the last Aranyaprathet–Bangkok **bus** also leaves at 5pm. Buses from Aranyaprathet take about four and a half hours to reach Bangkok, arriving at the Northern (Mo Chit) Bus Terminal. There are just two **trains** a day from Aranyaprathet to Bangkok, departing at 6.30am and 1.35pm and taking about five and a half hours.

Increasingly popular with travellers is the border crossing in Thailand's Trat province, from Sihanoukville via **Koh Kong** and **Ban Hat Lek** to Trat. The usual route is to get the speedboat from Sihanoukville to Koh Kong, then a taxi-boat from the Koh Kong pier to the Hat Lek border post; however, the Sihanoukville boat doesn't always make it in time before the border closes at 5pm. Minibuses and songthaews run from Ban Hat Lek to Trat, 91km northwest, where you can either pick up a **bus** straight to Bangkok (4–6hr) or stay the night (see p.434) and then proceed to the popular nearby island of Ko Chang, or continue along Thailand's east coast.

The speedier alternative to the above overland routes is to make use of the daily **flights** operated by Bangkok Airways, including services to Phuket and Bangkok from Phnom Penh and from Siem Reap.

Details on exiting Thailand **into Cambodia** via these crossings are given in the box on p.438. At the time of writing, **visas** for Cambodia are issued to travellers on arrival at Phnom Penh and Siem Reap airports, and at both the Aranyaprathet/Poipet and Hat Lek land borders; if you do need to buy an advance thirty-day visa, you can do so from the Cambodian embassy in Bangkok (see p.193; B1000; two working days) or from travel agents in Bangkok's Banglamphu district (for an extra B200).

Laos and Vietnam

There are currently five points along the **Lao border** where it's permissible for tourists to cross into Thailand: Houayxai (for Chiang Khong); Vientiane (for Nong Khai); Thakhek (for Nakhon Phanom); Savannakhet (for Mukdahan); and Pakxe (for Chong Mek). All these are accessible by various combinations of road and river transport; for details, see p.524. As well as the numerous routes to and from Bangkok, Lao Aviation operates handy **flights** between Vientiane and Louang Phabang and Chiang Mai, and Bangkok Airways is planning an outbound flight from Sukhothai to Louang Phabang, with the incoming route probably landing in Bangkok (there are no immigration facilities in Sukhothai). For more on options for travelling to Laos, see p.524.

Visas are required for all non-Thai visitors to Laos. A fifteen-day visa on arrival can bought for US$30 (cash only, plus two photos), but is only available to travellers entering Laos at Vientiane Airport, Louang Phabang Airport or at the Friendship Bridge in Nong Khai. If you want to enter Laos via somewhere other than the above border points, or want a longer visa, you must apply in advance. In Bangkok, thirty-day visas can be obtained directly from the Lao embassy (see p.193) for around B750–1000, depending on nationality; fifteen-day visas cost the same. You need two passport photos, and processing takes three days (or 24hr for an extra B300). It's also possible to get a double-entry visa, that is, two thirty-day visas, costing double the price. An alternative option is to go through one of the travel agents in Banglamphu, who charge B1200–2000 for a fifteen-day visa, and up to

twice as much for a thirty-day visa; allow three working days for processing. The Lao consulate in Khon Kaen in northeast Thailand (see p.505) also issues visas, though fees and processing times are variable. Entering Laos from Chiang Khong in north Thailand, you can get fifteen-day visas in advance through Chiang Khong guest houses and travel agencies: processing takes two to three days and costs about US$30; see p.394.

If you have the right Lao visa and Vietnamese exit stamp, you can travel from **Vietnam** to Thailand via Savannakhet in a matter of hours; you'll need to use Vietnam's Lao Bao border crossing, west of Dong Ha, where you can catch a bus to Savannakhet and then a ferry across the Mekhong to Mukdahan. All travellers into Vietnam need to buy a **visa** in advance. Thirty-day visas take four or five working days to process at the embassy in Bangkok (see p.194) and cost B800–2050 depending on your nationality, or B200 extra through a travel agent. There is also a visa-issuing Vietnamese consulate in Khon Kaen (see p.505).

Malaysia and Singapore

Travelling between Thailand and **Malaysia and Singapore** is straightforward and a very commonly used route. Most Western tourists can spend thirty days in Malaysia and fourteen days in Singapore without having bought a visa beforehand, and transport linking the three countries is excellent. This makes it an ideal route for tourists and expats needing to renew their Thai visas; there are Thai embassies or consulates in Kuala Lumpur, Penang, Kota Bharu and Singapore.

It's possible to take a **train** all the way from Singapore to Bangkok via Malaysia, a journey of just under 2000km. The journey involves several changes, but the overall trip can be done in around thirty hours at an average cost of about £60/US$90; trains leave at least once a day from both ends. Taking the train from Singapore or Johor Bahru in southern Malaysia, you can opt for the west-coast route, via Kuala Lumpur, or the east-coast route, which goes via Kota Bharu but involves a short taxi ride across the border to Sungai Kolok; the two lines rejoin at the southern Thai town of Hat Yai. Travelling from KL to Hat Yai takes about

The Eastern and Oriental Express

It's possible to travel between Singapore and Bangkok in extreme style by taking the **Eastern and Oriental Express** train – a Southeast Asian version of the Orient Express – which transports its passengers in great comfort and luxury. The journey, via Kuala Lumpur, takes around 41 hours in all, departs approximately once a week from either terminus and costs from £800/$1300 per person all-inclusive. For details, go to to ⓦ www.orient-express.com or call ☎ 020/7805 5100 (UK) or ☎ 1-800/524-2420 (US); in Australia, Abercrombie and Kent (see p.20) can organize the journey for you. (Once or twice a month, E&O also runs a Bangkok–Chiang Mai overnight trip, costing from £500/$800 per person.)

thirteen hours and costs about £12/US$18 for a second-class sleeper. For the current timetable and ticket prices, visit the Malaysian Railways website (ⓦ www.ktmb .com.my). Travelling in the reverse direction, you might prefer to change onto a bus or share-taxi at Hat Yai (see p.733), and at Sungai Kolok (p.745) you'll have to get a taxi anyway; details of border formalities are given in the relevant accounts.

Plenty of **buses** also cross the Thai–Malaysian border every day. Hat Yai is the major transport hub for international bus connections, and there are regular buses here from Singapore (around £12/US$18; 18hr) and Kuala Lumpur (£9/US$13; 12hr), and buses and share-taxis from Penang (£9/US$13; 6hr). You'll also find long-distance buses and minibuses to Bangkok, Krabi, Phuket and Surat Thani from Kuala Lumpur, Penang and Singapore, as well as in the reverse direction. If you're coming

from Alor Setar, the nearest big town to the border on Malaysia's west coast, you'll have to get a bus to the border at Bukit Kayu Hitam, then take a share-taxi from the Thai side up to Hat Yai.

It's also possible to travel between Malaysia and Thailand by **ferry**. Frequent boats connect Kuala Perlis and Langkawi with Satun in south Thailand; see p.724 for details.

In addition to the numerous daily **flights** on any number of international airlines from Malaysia and Singapore to Bangkok, Bangkok Airways operates daily flights between Singapore and Ko Samui, while Chiang Mai and Phuket are served by flights from Kuala Lumpur (Malaysia Airlines) and Singapore (Silk Air). There are also regular flights to Hat Yai from Kuala Lumpur and from Johor Bahru (both Malaysia Airlines), and from Singapore (with Singapore Airlines, subsidiary Silk Air).

Red tape and visas

There are three main entry categories for Thailand; for all of them your passport must be valid for at least six months from the date of entry. As visa requirements are often subject to change, you should always check with a Thai embassy or consulate, or a reliable travel agent, before departure.

Most foreign passport holders are allowed to enter the country for **stays of up to thirty days** without having to apply for a visa (New Zealanders are allowed up to ninety days). The period of stay will be stamped into your passport by immigration officials upon entry, but you're supposed to show proof of onward travel arrangements: unless you have a confirmed bus, train or air ticket out of Thailand, you may be put back on the next plane or sent back to get a sixty-day tourist visa from the nearest Thai embassy. Such thirty-day stays cannot be extended under any but the most exceptional circumstances, though it's easy enough to get a new one by hopping across the border into a neighbouring country, especially Malaysia, and back again.

If you're fairly certain you may want to stay longer than thirty days, then from the outset you should apply for a **sixty-day tourist visa** from a Thai embassy or consulate, accompanying your application – which always takes several days to process – with your passport and two photos. The sixty-day visa currently costs £8 per entry in the UK, for example – multiple-entry versions are available, which are handy if you're going to be leaving and re-entering Thailand. Entering on a sixty-day visa, you don't need to show proof of onward travel but, as in all countries, it's up to immigration officials at the port of entry as to what expiry date they stamp on your visa, so it's always advisable to dress respectably (see p.72) when crossing borders.

Thai embassies also consider applications for the slightly more expensive **ninety-day non-immigrant visas** (£15 in the UK) as long as you can offer a good reason for your visit, such as study or business (there are different categories of non-immigrant visa for which different levels of proof are needed). As it's quite a hassle to organize a ninety-day visa from outside the country (and generally not feasible for most tourists), you're better off applying for a thirty-day extension to your sixty-day visa once inside Thai borders.

A note about **day-trips to Burma** at Kaw Thaung, Three Pagodas Pass, Mae Sot and Mae Sai: on re-entering Thailand, you'll generally be given a new thirty-day entry stamp in your passport, regardless of any Thai visa you may already have. This is handy if your permitted time in Thailand is running out, but not so great if you've still got the best part of a sixty- or ninety-day visa left. If you're planning a Burma day-trip, it may well be worth your while to get a multiple-entry visa for Thailand.

If you **overstay** your visa limits, expect to be fined B100 per extra day when you leave Thailand, though an overstay of a month or

Customs regulations

The duty-free allowance on entry to Thailand is 200 cigarettes (or 250g of tobacco) and a litre of spirits or wine. To export **antiques or religious artefacts** – especially Buddha images – from Thailand, you need to have a licence granted by the Fine Arts Department, which can be obtained through Bangkok's National Museum on Thanon Na Phra That (☏02/226 1661 or 281 0433). Applications take at least a week and need to be accompanied by two postcard-sized photos of the object, taken face-on, and photocopies of the applicant's passport. Some antique shops will organize this for you.

more could land you in trouble with immigration officials.

Thai embassies and consulates abroad

For a full listing of Thai diplomatic missions abroad, check out the Thai Ministry of Foreign Affairs' website at ⊛ www.mfa.go.th /embassy/default.htm

Australia Optus Gate, 10 Moore St, Canberra ACT 2600 ☎ 02/6273 1141. Also consulates in Adelaide, Brisbane, Melbourne, Perth and Sydney.

Canada 180 Island Park Drive, Ottawa, Ontario K1Y 0A2 ☎ 613/722 4444, ⊛ www.magma.ca/~thaiott; plus consulates in Vancouver, Montréal, Calgary and Toronto.

Laos Embassy Consular Section, The Regent Centre, Route Luangprabang, Vientiane ☎ 021/217157–8.

Malaysia 206 Jalan Ampang, 50450 Kuala Lumpur ☎ 03/2148 8222; plus consulates at 4426 Jalan Pengkalan Chepa, 15400 Kota Bharu ☎ 09/748 2545; and 1 Jalan Tunku Abdul Rahman, 10350 Penang ☎ 04/226 9484.

New Zealand 2 Cook St, PO Box 17-226, Karori, Wellington ☎ 04/476 8618–19.

UK 29 Queens Gate, London SW7 5JB ☎09003/405456 or 020/7589 2944; plus consulates in Birmingham, Cardiff, Glasgow, Hull and Liverpool.

US 1024 Wisconsin Ave, NW, Suite 401, Washington, DC 20007 ☎ 202/944-3600 or 3608, ⊛ www.thaiembdc.org; plus consulates at 700 North Rush St, Chicago, IL 60611 ☎ 312/644 3129, ⊛ thaichicago@aol.com; 351 East 52nd St, New York, NY 10022 ☎ 212/754 1770, ⊛ thainycg@aol.com; and 611 North Larchmont Blvd, 2nd Floor, Los Angeles, CA 90038 ☎ 323/962-9574, ⊛ www.thai-la.net

Visa extensions and re-entry permits

All sixty-day tourist visas can be **extended** in Thailand for a further thirty days, at the discretion of officials; extensions cost B500 and are issued over the counter at immigration offices (*kaan khao muang*) in nearly every provincial capital – most offices ask for one or two photos as well, plus two photocopies of the first four pages and latest Thai visa page of your passport. Immigration offices also issue **re-entry permits** (B500) if you want to leave the country and come back again within the validity of your visa.

Staying on

Unless you have work or study fixed up before you arrive, **staying on** in Thailand is a precarious affair. Plenty of people do – teaching English, working in resort bars and guest houses, acting as a dive instructor or even unofficially buying into tourist businesses (farangs are generally barred from owning businesses in Thailand) – but it involves frequent and expensive visa runs to neighbouring countries, and often entails hassle from the local police. All non-residents who acquire income while in Thailand should get a tax clearance certificate from the Revenue Department, which has offices in every provincial capital and on Thanon Chakrapong near Democracy Monument in Bangkok (☎ 02/282 9899 or 281 5777). For more on job possibilities in Thailand see p.82.

Information, websites and maps

The efficient Tourism Authority of Thailand (TAT) maintains offices in several cities abroad, where you can pick up a few glossy brochures and get fairly detailed answers to specific pre-trip questions. More comprehensive local information is given at TAT headquarters in Bangkok and its 22 regional branches (all open daily 8.30am–4.30pm), which provide an array of printed information on everything from how to avoid being ripped off to where to learn to dive. In addition, all TAT offices should have up-to-date information on local festival dates and regional transport schedules, but none of them offers accommodation booking and service can be variable. In Bangkok, TAT plays second fiddle to the excellent Bangkok Tourist Bureau, details of which can be found on p.98.

Independent **tour operators** and information docks crop up in tourist spots all over the country and will usually help with questions about the immediate locality, but be on the lookout for self-interested advice, given by staff desperate for commission. As with TAT offices, independent operators won't book accommodation – unless of course they happen to have business links with specific guest houses or hotels. For offbeat, enthusiastic first-hand advice, you can't do better than guest house **noticeboards** and **comment books** – the best of these boast a whole range of travellers' tips, from anecdotal accounts of cross-country bike trips to recommendations as to where to get the perfect suit made.

You'll find plenty of information about Thailand on the **internet** as well, ranging from official government-sponsored sites to travellers' homepages and bulletin boards. The latter can be especially useful if you want to canvass opinions on a particular island or guest house, or if you want to ask other travellers' advice on your proposed itinerary. A selection of the best websites is given in the box on p.28.

TAT offices abroad

TAT's website is at ⊛ www.tat.or.th
Australia 255 George St, Sydney, NSW 2000 ☏ 02/9247 7549; 2 Hardy Rd, South Perth, WA 6151 ☏ 08/9474 3646.

Canada 1393 Royal York Rd, #15, Toronto, Ontario, M9A 4Y9 ☏ 416/ 614-2625 or 1-800-THAILAND, ☏ 416/614-8891.
New Zealand Floor 2, 87 Queen St, Auckland ☏ 09/379 8398.
UK and Ireland 49 Albemarle St, London W1X 3FE ☏ 020/7499 7679; recorded information on 0870/900 2007, ⊛ www.thaismile.co.uk
US ☏ 1-800-THAILAND; 1 World Trade Centre, Suite 3729, New York, NY10048 ☏ 212/432-0433 or 432-0435, ☏ 212/912-0920, ℮ tny@aol.com; 611 North Larchmont Blvd, 1st Floor, Los Angeles, CA90004 ☏ 323/461-9814, ☏ 461-9834.

Maps

One thing neither TAT nor tour operators provide is a decent **map**. For most major destinations, the maps in this book should be all you need, though you may want to supplement them with larger-scale versions of Bangkok and the whole country. Bangkok bookshops are the best source of these maps; where appropriate, detailed local maps and their stockists are recommended in the relevant chapters of the guide. If you want to buy a map before you get there (for outlets at home, see p.28), go for Nelles' 1:1,500,000 map of Thailand, the most consistently accurate of those published abroad, despite leaving many main roads unnumbered. The Bartholomew's 1:1,500,000 is also fairly reliable.

Published by the Roads Association of Thailand in conjunction with Shell, the large-format 1:1,000,000 *Thailand Highway Map* is especially good on **roads**, and is updated annually; it's available at most bookstores in Thailand where English-language material is sold. If you can't get hold of that one, you could go for the set of four 1:1,000,000 regional maps produced by the Highway Department and sold at DK Books all over the country, and in Bangkok at Central department stores. The drawback with this series is that much of the detail is written only in Thai script. **Trekking maps** are hard to come by except in the most popular national parks, where you can usually pick up a free handout showing the main trails on arrival.

Travel bookshops and map outlets

UK

Blackwell's Map and Travel Shop, 53 Broad St, Oxford OX1 3BQ ☎01865/792792, ⓦblackwell.bookshop.co.uk.

Daunt Books, 83 Marylebone High St, London W1M 3DE ☎020/7224 2295; 193 Haverstock Hill, NW3 4QL ☎020/7794 4006.

Heffers Map and Travel, 20 Trinity St, Cambridge, CB2 1TJ ☎01223/586 586, ⓦwww.heffers.co.uk.

John Smith and Sons, 26 Colquhoun Ave, Glasgow, G52 4PJ ☎0141/221 7472, ⓦwww.johnsmith.co.uk.

National Map Centre, 22–24 Caxton St, London SW1H 0QU ☎020/7222 2466, ⓦwww.mapsnmc.co.uk.

Stanfords ⓦwww.stanfords.co.uk; 12–14 Long Acre, London WC2E 9LP ☎020/7836 1321; 29 Corn St, Bristol BS1 1HT ☎0117/929 9966.

The Travel Bookshop, 13–15 Blenheim Crescent, London W11 2EE ☎020/7229 5260, ⓦwww.thetravelbookshop.co.uk.

Ireland

Easons Bookshop, 40 O'Connell St, Dublin 1 ☎01/873 3811, ⓦwww.eason.ie.

Fred Hanna's Bookshop, 27–29 Nassau St, Dublin 2 ☎01/677 1255.

Hodges Figgis Bookshop, 56–58 Dawson St, Dublin 2 ☎01/677 4754, ⓦwww.hodgesfiggis.com.

Waterstones ⓦwww.waterstones.com. Queens Bldg, 8 Royal Ave, Belfast BT1 1DA ☎028/9024 7355; 7 Dawson St, Dublin 2 ☎01/679 1415; 69 Patrick St, Cork ☎021/276 522.

US

The Complete Traveller Bookstore, 199 Madison Ave, New York, NY 10016 ☎212/685-9007.

Elliot Bay Book Company, 101 S Main St, Seattle, WA 98104 ☎206/624-6600 or 1-800/962-5311, ⓦwww.elliotbaybook.com.

Map Link, 30 S La Patera Lane, Unit 5, Santa Barbara, CA 93117 ☎805/692-6777, ⓦwww.maplink.com.

Phileas Fogg's Books & Maps, 87 Stanford Shopping Center, Palo Alto, CA 94304 ☎1-800/533-3644, ⓦwww.foggs.com.

Rand McNally, ⓦwww.randmcnally.com. 444 N Michigan Ave, Chicago, IL 60611 ☎312/321-1751; 150 E 52nd St, New York, NY 10022 ☎212/758-7488; 595 Market St, San Francisco, CA 94105 ☎415/777-3131.

Travel Books & Language Center, 4437 Wisconsin Ave, Washington, DC 20016 ☎1-800/220-2665.

Canada

Open Air Books and Maps, 25 Toronto St, Toronto, ON M5R 2C1 ☎416/363-0719 or 1-800/748-9171.

Travel Bug Bookstore, 2667 West Broadway, Vancouver V6K 2G2 ☎604/737-1122, ⓦwww.swifty.com/tbug.

Ulysses Travel Bookshop, 4176 St-Denis, Montréal H2W 2M5 ☎514/843-9882, ⓦwww.ulysses.ca.

World of Maps, 1235 Wellington St, Ottawa, Ontario K1Y 3A3 ☎613/724-6776, ⓦwww.worldofmaps.com.

World Wide Books and Maps, 1247 Granville St, Vancouver, BC V6Z 1G3 ☎604/687-3320.

Australia and New Zealand

Mapland, 372 Little Bourke St, Melbourne ☎03/9670 4383, ⓦwww.mapland.com.au.

The Map Shop, 6 Peel St, Adelaide ☎08/8231 2033, ⓦwww.mapshop.net.au.

Mapworld, 173 Gloucester St, Christchurch ☎03/374 5399, ⓦwww.mapworld.co.nz.

Perth Map Centre, 1/884 Hay St, Perth ☎08/9322 5733, ⓦwww.perthmap.com.au.

Specialty Maps, 46 Albert St, Auckland ☎09/307 2217, ⓦwww.ubd-online.co.nz/maps.

Travel Bookshop, Shop 3, 175 Liverpool St, Sydney ☎02/9261 8200.

Walkers Bookshop, 96 Lake St, Cairns ☎07/4051 2410.

Worldwide Maps and Guides, 187 George St, Brisbane ☎07/3221 4330.

Online travel bookstores

Adventurous Traveler
ⓦ www.adventuroustraveler.com.
Amazon ⓦ www.amazon.co.uk and
www.amazon.com.
Literate Traveler ⓦ www.literatetraveller.com.

Thailand online

Only general tourist-oriented websites are listed below. For online accommodation-booking services see p.49, for diving websites see p.74, and for websites for gay travellers see p.78.

General Thailand resources

Accommodating Asia: Thailand
ⓦ www.accomasia.com/thailand.htm. Begins with the usual introduction-to-Thailand stuff, but is distinguished by its particularly good "Travellers Notes" section, with links to the diaries, travelogues and homepages of recent travellers to Thailand.
Bangkok Post ⓦ www.bangkokpost.net. The day's main stories from Thailand's leading English-language daily newspaper, plus archive headlines for the last two months, and travel stories. Free access. Recommended.
Geocities ⓦ www.geocities.com. A vast, searchable collection of web pages containing interesting material on travel in Thailand and elsewhere in the region, including travellers' reports, virtual tours and a forum for travel companions.
René Hasekamp's Homepage
ⓦ www.hasekamp.demon.nl/thaiindex.htm. Constructed by a Dutch man who is married to a Thai woman, this site lists practical tips and dos and don'ts for travellers to Thailand, plus info on selected sights and an especially handy list of FAQs.
Siam Net ⓦ www.siam.net/guide. Decent guidebook-style jumping-off point, with general background on Thailand and its main tourist centres, plus hotel bookings services and useful information on visas, prices etc.
Thai Focus ⓦ www.thaifocus.com. Wide-ranging portal site, offering hotel-booking service, domestic and international air tickets, car rental, plus a basic introduction to Thailand's main destinations; the discounts are nothing special though.
Tourism Authority of Thailand (TAT)
ⓦ www.tat.or.th. The official TAT site has general background on the country, plus links to accommodation, weather reports and other standard stuff.

Tourism Authority of Thailand, London
ⓦ www.thaismile.co.uk. The official website for the London TAT office offers special deals on flights to Thailand, has a page for tourist tips and a travellers' bulletin board. It also has an innovative section on Thai culture in the UK, including listings of Thai restaurants across the country, plus recipes for Thai dishes and links to UK shops that specialize in Thai products.

Travellers' resources

About Ecotourism
ⓦ www.ecotourism.about.com. Recommended umbrella site with a wide range of discussions, articles and links concerning the relationship between tourism and the environment, in Thailand and elsewhere. Also some links to eco-aware travel companies.
internet Travel Information Service
ⓦ www.itisnet.com. A really useful resource specifically aimed at budget travellers. Its researchers send weekly reports from the road (Thailand is well covered), so there's heaps of up-to-the-minute information on things like current airfares, border crossings and visa requirements as well as hotel openings and closures.
Journeywoman ⓦ www.journeywoman.com. Highly recommended site aimed at women travellers, with all sorts of imaginative sections, including "What Should I Wear?", which features first-hand tips on acceptable dress in over a hundred different countries. Also includes travel health information, travelogues, advice for solo travellers and links.
Open Directory Project
ⓦ www.dmoz.org/Recreation/Travel/Budget_Travel /Backpacking. Scores of backpacker-oriented links, including plenty of Asia-specific ones, plus travelogues and message boards.
Rec. travel library ⓦ www.travel-library.com. Highly recommended site which has lively pieces on dozens of travel topics about Thailand and elsewhere, from the budget travellers' guide to sleeping in airports, to how to travel light. Excellent links too.
Rough Guides ⓦ www.roughguides.com. Interactive site for independent travellers, with forums, bulletin boards, travel tips and features, plus online travel guides.

Travellers' forums

Lonely Planet Thorn Tree
ⓦ thorntree.lonelyplanet.com. Recommended and popular travellers' forums, divided into regions (eg Mainland Southeast Asia) and topics (Travelling with Kids). A good place to look for travel companions,

exchange information with other travellers or start a debate.

Thailand Tips ⓦ www.thailandtips.com. Thailand-specific forum for travellers' queries and advice about everything from elephant round-ups to the best airport hotel.

Thailand's regions online

Bangkok Metro ⓦ www.bkkmetro.com. The online version of Bangkok's monthly listings magazine includes archives of features, restaurant and club listings, plus readers' letters.

Groovy Map ⓦ www.groovymap.com. Lively site from the company who publish wacky, annotated maps of Bangkok and Phuket, with top-ten lists of things to do by day and night in Bangkok, plus a

what's on calendar for the city. Also has an accommodation booking service for hotels in the main tourist centres in Thailand.

Phuket Gazette ⓦ www.phuketgazette.net. Southern Thailand's resort island of Phuket publishes a weekly independent English-language newspaper, and their online version makes interesting reading, with both local and national news stories, editorials and opinion pieces on a good range of Thailand-related subjects.

Welcome to Chiang Mai and Chiang Rai ⓦ www.infothai.com/wtcmcr. The website of the Chiang Mai listings magazine has some really interesting pages, including background information on hill tribes and north Thai handicrafts, plus regularly updated news of forthcoming events and festivals in the region.

Money, banks and costs

Thailand's unit of currency is the baht (abbreviated to "B"), which is divided into 100 satang. Notes come in B10 (brown), B20 (green), B50 (blue), B100 (red), B500 (purple) and B1000 (beige) denominations, inscribed with Arabic as well as Thai numerals, and increasing in size according to value. The coinage is more confusing, because new shapes and sizes circulate alongside older ones. The tiny brass-coloured 25- and 50-satang pieces are rarely used now, as most prices are rounded off to the nearest baht. There are three different silver one-baht coins, all legal tender; the smallest of these is the newest version, and the one accepted by public call-boxes. Silver five-baht pieces are slightly bigger and have a copper rim; ten-baht coins have a small brass centre encircled by a silver ring.

At the time of writing, **exchange rates** were averaging B42 to US$1 and B62 to £1; note that Thailand has no black market in foreign currency. Daily rates are published in the *Bangkok Post* and the *Nation*, and at all foreign exchange counters and kiosks in Thailand. If you want to check the rates before you leave home, consult one of the online currency converters listed in the box opposite. Because of severe currency fluctuations in the late 1990s, some tourist-oriented businesses now quote their prices in dollars, particularly luxury hotels and dive centres.

Banking hours are Monday to Friday from 8.30am to 3.30pm, but exchange kiosks in the main tourist centres are always open till at least 5pm, sometimes 10pm, and upmarket hotels change money 24 hours a day. The **Don Muang airport exchange counters** also operate 24 hours (and exchange kiosks at overseas airports with flights to Thailand usually keep Thai currency), so there's little point arranging to buy baht before you leave home, especially as it takes seven working days to order from most banks outside Thailand.

Online currency converters

Bangkok Bank
ⓦ bbl.co.th/bankrates/fx_rates_curr.htm.
Tells you the day's rate in Thailand for 23 major currencies against the Thai baht; provided by the Bangkok Bank.
Oanda ⓦ www.oanda.com/cgi-bin/ncc. Gives you the day's baht rate for 164 currencies and compiles "free, wallet-sized conversion tables for travellers", which you simply print out and refer to on the ground.

Costs

In a country where the daily minimum wage is under B165 a day, it's hardly surprising that Western tourists find Thailand an extremely cheap place to travel. At the bottom of the scale, you could manage on a **daily budget** of about B400 (£7/US$10) if you're willing to opt for basic accommodation, stay away from the more expensive resorts like Phuket, Ko Samui and Ko Phi Phi, and eat, drink and travel as the locals do. On this budget, you'll be spending B80–150 for a dorm bed or single room (less if you share the cost of a double room), around B150–200 on three meals (eating mainly at night markets and simple noodle shops, and eschewing beer), and the rest on travel (sticking mainly to non-air-con buses and third-class trains) and incidentals. With extras like air-conditioning in rooms (from B300–800 a double in guest houses and simple hotels) and on long-distance buses, taking tuk-tuks (see p.44) rather than buses for cross-town journeys, and a meal and a couple of beers in a more touristy restaurant (B100–150 per person), a day's outlay would look more like B600–800 (£11–14/US$15–20). Staying in comfortable, upmarket hotels and eating in the more exclusive restaurants, you should be able to live in extreme comfort for around B2000 a day (£35/US$50).

Travellers soon get so used to the low cost of living in Thailand that they start **bargaining** at every available opportunity, much as Thai people do. Although it's expected practice for a lot of commercial transactions, particularly at markets and when hiring tuk-tuks and taxis, bargaining is a delicate art that requires humour, tact and patience. If your price is way out of line, the vendor's vehement refusal should be enough to make you increase your offer: never forget that the few pennies or cents you're making such a fuss over will go a lot further in a Thai person's hands than in your own.

On the other hand, making a tidy sum off foreigners is sometimes official practice: at government-run museums and historical parks, for example, foreigners often pay a B40 admission charge while Thais get in for B10. The most controversial **two-tier pricing** system is the recent innovation at most national parks, where foreigners now have to pay B200 entry while Thais pay just B20 (see p.76 for more on this). A number of privately owned tourist attractions follow a similar two-tier system, posting an inflated price in English for foreigners and a lower price in Thai for locals. This is not illegal, but overcharging tourists on fixed-fare public transport is definitely not acceptable – the best way to avoid getting stung by wily conductors on buses and trains is to watch or ask fellow passengers.

Traveller's cheques, debit and credit cards

The safest way to carry your money is in **traveller's cheques** (a fee of one or two percent is usually levied when you buy them). Sterling and dollar cheques are accepted by banks, exchange booths and upmarket hotels in every sizeable Thai town, and most places also deal in a variety of other currencies; everyone offers better rates for cheques than for straight cash. Generally, a total of B13 in commission and duty is charged per cheque – though kiosks and hotels in isolated places may charge extra. All issuers give you a list of numbers to call in the case of **lost or stolen cheques** and will pay refunds if you can produce the original receipts and a note of your cheque numbers. Instructions in cases of loss or theft vary from issuer to issuer, but you'll usually have to notify the police first and then call the issuing company collect to arrange replacements, usually within 24 hours, either by courier or at a local agent.

American Express, Visa, MasterCard and Diners Club **credit cards**, and Visa and MasterCard/Cirrus **debit cards** are accepted at top hotels as well as in some posh restaurants, department stores, tourist shops and travel agents, but surcharging of up to five percent is rife, and theft and forgery are major industries – always demand the carbon copies, and never leave cards in baggage storage. If you have a personal identification number (PIN) for your debit or credit card, you can also withdraw cash from hundreds of 24-hour **ATMs** ("automatic teller machines" or cash dispensers) around the country. Almost every branch of the Bangkok Bank, Bank of Ayudhya, Siam Commercial and Thai Farmers Bank has ATMs that accept **Visa** cards, **MasterCard** and cards on the **Cirrus** network. For an up-to-the-minute list of ATM locations in Thailand, check the relevant websites (ⓦ www.mastercard .com and ⓦ www.visa.com). If in any doubt call the issuing bank or credit company to find out whether your particular card works in Thailand and, if so, which Thai bank's ATMs accept it. There's usually a handling fee of 1.5 percent on every withdrawal, little different from the total amount of fees and commissions payable on traveller's cheques, but it's wise not to rely on plastic alone, which is more tempting to thieves and less easy to replace than the trusty traveller's cheque.

Wiring money

Wiring money through a specialist agent is a fast but expensive way to send and receive money abroad. The funds should be available for collection, usually in local currency, from the company's local agent within twenty minutes of being sent via Western Union or Moneygram; both charge on a sliding scale, so sending larger amounts of cash is better value.

It's also possible to have money wired directly from a bank in your home country to a bank in Thailand, although this is somewhat less reliable because it involves two separate institutions. Your home bank will need the address of the branch bank where you want to pick up the money and the address and telex number of the Bangkok head office, which will act as the clearing house; money wired this way normally takes two working days to arrive, and costs around £25/US$40 per transaction.

Moneygram and Western Union

Moneygram ⓦ www.moneygram.com; in the UK ☎ 0800/018 0104, in the Irish Republic ☎ 0800/6663 9472, in the US and Canada ☎ 1-800/926-9400, in Australia ☎ 1800/230 100, in New Zealand ☎ 09/379 8243 or 0800/262 263. In Thailand, funds can be collected at many branches of Siam Commercial Bank throughout the country; call the head office in Bangkok on ☎ 02/544 1111 or 544 5000, or drop into your nearest branch. **Western Union** ⓦ www.westernunion.com; in the UK ☎ 0800/833 833, in the Irish Republic ☎ 1800/395 395, in the US and Canada ☎ 1-800/325-6000, in Australia ☎ 1800/649 565, in New Zealand ☎ 09/270 0050. In Thailand, they have agents at many branches of the Bank of Ayudhya; call their Western Union department on ☎ 02/683 1362 to find out which is most conveniently located for you, or check first at ⓦ www.bay.co.th.

Insurance

If you're unlucky enough to require hospital treatment in Thailand, you'll have to foot the bill – this alone is reason enough to make sure you have adequate travel cover before you leave. Besides covering medical expenses and emergency flights home, a good specialist travel policy should include insurance against loss and theft of money and personal belongings, and possibly cover for damage to rented motorbikes and cars as well. Most standard policies exclude so-called dangerous sports – in Thailand these can mean such activities as scuba-diving, white-water rafting and trekking – unless an extra premium is paid

Before shelling out on a new policy, however, it's worth checking whether you are already covered. Many **bank and charge accounts** include some form of travel cover, and insurance is also sometimes included if you pay for your trip with a **credit card** (though usually only medical or accident cover is provided). Some all-risks **home insurance policies** cover your possessions against loss or theft when overseas, and many **private medical schemes** include cover for baggage loss abroad, cancellation or curtailment of your trip and cash replacement as well as sickness or accident. In Canada, provincial health plans usually provide partial cover for medical mishaps overseas, while holders of official student/teacher/youth cards in Canada and the US are entitled to some accident coverage and hospital in-patient benefits. North American students will often find that their student health coverage extends during the vacations and for one term beyond the date of last enrolment.

If **trouble** occurs, make sure you keep all medical bills, and, if possible, contact the insurance company before making any major outlay (for example, on additional convalescence expenses). If you have anything stolen, get a copy of the police report when you notify them of the incident – otherwise you won't be able to claim. Note also that very few insurers will arrange on-the-spot payments in the event of a major expense or loss; you will usually be reimbursed only after going home.

Rough Guides travel insurance

Rough Guides now offers its own **travel insurance**, customized for our readers by a leading UK broker and backed by a Lloyds underwriter. It's available for anyone, of any nationality or age, travelling anywhere in the world.

There are two main Rough Guide insurance plans: **Essential**, for basic, no-frills cover; and **Premier** – with more generous and extensive benefits. Unlike many policies, the Rough Guides schemes are calculated by the day, so if you're travelling for 27 days rather than a month, that's all you pay for. Alternatively, you can take out annual **multi-trip insurance**, which covers you for any number of trips throughout the year (with a maximum of 60 days for any one trip). If you intend to be away for the whole year, the **Adventurer** policy will cover you for 365 days. Each plan can be supplemented with a "**Hazardous Activities Premium**" if you plan to indulge in sports considered dangerous, such as scuba-diving or trekking.

For a **policy quote**, call the Rough Guide Insurance Line on UK freefone ☎0800/015 0906, US tollfree ☎1-866/220 5588, or if you're calling from elsewhere in the world on ☎(+44)1243/621046. Alternatively, get a quote and purchase your policy online at ⊛www.roughguides.com/insurance.

Health

Although Thailand's climate, wildlife and cuisine present Western travellers with fewer health worries than in many Asian destinations, it's as well to know in advance what the risks might be, and what preventive or curative measures you should take.

For a start, there's no need to bring huge supplies of non-prescription medicines with you, as Thai **pharmacies** (*raan khai yaa*; typically open daily 8.30am–8pm) are well stocked with local and international branded medicaments, and of course they are much less expensive than at home. All pharmacies, whatever size the town, are run by highly trained English-speaking pharmacists, who are usually the best people to talk to if your symptoms aren't acute enough to warrant seeing a doctor.

Hospital (*rong phayaabahn*) cleanliness and efficiency vary, but generally hygiene and health-care standards are good and the ratio of medical staff to patients is considerably higher than in most parts of the West. As with head pharmacists, doctors speak English. All provincial capitals have at least one hospital: if you need to get to one, ask at your accommodation for advice on, and possibly transport to, the nearest or most suitable. In the event of a major health crisis, get someone to contact your embassy (see p.193) or insurance company – it may be best to get yourself flown home.

For a comprehensive, and sobering, account of the health problems which travellers encounter worldwide, consult the *Rough Guide to Travel Health* by Dr Nick Jones. In the UK, pick up the Department of Health's free publication *Health Advice for Travellers*, a comprehensive booklet available at the post office (or by calling the Health Literature Line on ☎0800/555777); the content of the booklet, which contains immunization advice, is constantly updated on Ceefax and at ⊛ www.doh.gov.uk/traveladvice/

Inoculations

There are no compulsory **inoculation** requirements for people travelling to Thailand from the West, but it makes sense to ensure your polio and tetanus boosters are up to date (they last ten years); most doctors also strongly advise vaccinations against typhoid (shots last three years or oral capsules are available which need boosting annually) and hepatitis A, and in some cases they might also recommend protecting yourself against Japanese encephalitis, rabies, hepatitis B, tuberculosis and diphtheria. If you do decide to have several injections, plan your course at least four weeks in advance.

In the UK and Ireland, the least costly way of getting immunized is to head first to your local health centre (in the UK some immunizations are free under the NHS while other vaccines must be paid for on prescription,

---

A traveller's first-aid kit

Among items you might want to carry with you – especially if you're planning to go trekking – are:

❑ Antiseptic cream.
❑ Antihistamine cream.
❑ Plasters/band-aids.
❑ Lints and sealed bandages.
❑ Knee supports.
❑ Imodium, Lomotil or Arret for emergency diarrhoea relief.
❑ Paracetamol/aspirin.
❑ Multivitamin and mineral tablets.
❑ Rehydration sachets.
❑ Hypodermic needles and sterilized skin wipes.

but all are administered at no cost by your doctor or health-centre nurse). Though most general practitioners can give advice on inoculation requirements, it's a good idea to come for your appointment armed with a "Health Brief", written information tailored to your journey, provided by return of post by MASTA (see below). However, your local health clinic may not administer some of the less common immunizations and you may have to go to a specialist travel clinic: these work out to be expensive but have the advantage of being staffed by tropical-disease specialists; see below.

North Americans will have to pay full whack for their inoculations, available at an immunization centre – there's one in every city of any size – or most local clinics. In the US, the doctor's consultation fee is generally $75, and the inoculations cost $75–175 each.

Australians and **New Zealanders** can have their jabs administered by their GP for around A$35/NZ$30 per visit plus the cost of the serums. In Australia, sixty percent of the consultation fee is refundable via Medicare, though you still pay for the serums, while Healthcare card-holders are excused the consultation fee and pay only A$2.50 for medicines. In New Zealand, nothing is refundable without medical insurance. In both countries, those who have to pay will find vaccination centres less expensive than doctors' surgeries.

If you forget to have all your inoculations before leaving home, or don't leave yourself sufficient time, you can get them **in Bangkok** at the Australian-run Travmin Bangkok Medical Centre (see p.194 for details), though this is unlikely to work out cheaper than doing it at home. Travmin also advises on and dispenses malaria prophylactics.

Inoculation centres and information

UK and Ireland

British Airways Travel Clinics No appointments necessary at 156 Regent St, London W1 (Mon–Fri 9.30am–5.15pm, Sat 10am–4pm; ☏020/7439 9584). BA also operates other appointment-only clinics in the capital and throughout the country (call ☏01276/685040 or check ⊚www.britishairways.com for locations).
Hospital for Tropical Diseases Travel Clinic, 2nd Floor, Mortimer Market Centre, off Capper St, London WC1E 6AU (Mon–Fri 9am–5pm by

appointment only; ☏020/7388 9600; £15 consultation fee is waived if you have your injections here). Their recorded Health Line (☏09061/337733; 50p per min) gives hints on hygiene and illness prevention as well as listing appropriate immunizations.
MASTA (Medical Advisory Service for Travellers Abroad, ⊚www.masta.org). Call their pre-recorded 24hr Travellers' Health Line (in the UK ☏0906/822 4100, 60p per min; in Ireland ☏1560/147000, €1 per min) to request printed health information tailored to your journey; in the UK they also provide up-to-date information on malaria on ☏0891/600350 (24hr recorded message; 60p per min).
Nomad Pharmacy, 40 Bernard St, London WC1, opposite Russell Square tube station; and 3–4 Turnpike Lane, London N8 (Mon–Fri 9.30am–6pm, ☏020/7833 4114 to book appointment; their telephone helpline is ☏09068/633414, costing 60p a minute).
Trailfinders, 194 Kensington High St, London W8 7RG (Mon–Fri 9am–5pm, Thurs to 6pm, Sat 9.30am–4pm; ☏020/7938 3999). This branch of the travel agency has a no-appointments-necessary immunization clinic.
Travel Health Centre, Dept of International Health and Tropical Medicine, Royal College of Surgeons in Ireland, Mercers Medical Centre, Stephen's St Lower, Dublin ☏01/402 2337. Expert pre-trip advice and inoculations.

US and Canada

International Association for Medical Assistance to Travellers ⊚www.sentex.net/~iamat; 417 Center St, Lewiston, NY 14092 ☏716/754-4883; and 40 Regal Rd, Guelph, Ontario N1K 1B5 ☏519/836-0102. A non-profit organization supported by donations, which can provide leaflets on various diseases and inoculations.
Travelers Medical Center, 31 Washington Square, New York, NY 10011 ☏212/982-1600. Offers a consultation service on immunizations and treatment of diseases for people travelling to developing countries.

Australia and New Zealand

Travellers' Medical and Vaccination Centres ⊚www.tmvc.com.au. In Australia: 2/393 Little Bourke St, Melbourne ☏03/9602 5788; 7/428 George St, Sydney ☏02/9221 7133 and branches in many other cities. In New Zealand: 1/170 Queen St, Auckland ☏09/373 3531; 147 Armagh St, Christchurch ☏03/379 4000; Shop 15, Grand Arcade, 14–16 Willis St, Wellington ☏04/473 0991. Travel medicine and vaccination services.

Mosquito-borne diseases

It isn't only malaria which is spread by **mosquitoes** in Thailand; to a lesser extent, there are risks of contracting both Japanese B encephalitis and dengue fever if you visit during the rainy season. The main message, therefore, is to **avoid being bitten** by mosquitoes. You should smother yourself and your clothes in **mosquito repellent** containing the chemical compound DEET, reapplying regularly (shops, guest houses and department stores all over Thailand stock it, but if you want the highest-strength repellent, or convenient roll-ons or sprays, do your shopping before you leave home). DEET is strong stuff, and if you have sensitive skin a natural alternative is citronella (called Mosiguard in the UK), made from a blend of eucalyptus oils, though still use DEET on clothes and nets. At night you should either sleep under a **mosquito net** sprayed with DEET or in a room with screens across the windows. Accommodation in tourist spots nearly always provides screens or a net (check both for holes), but if you're planning to go way off the beaten track or want the security of having your own mosquito net just in case, wait until you get to Bangkok to buy one, where department stores sell them for about an eighth of what you'd pay in the West. **Mosquito coils** – also widely available in Thailand – help keep the insects at bay; electronic "buzzers" are useless. Prophylaxis advice can change from year to year, so it's worth getting the most up-to-date information from your travel health adviser.

Malaria

Thailand is **malarial**, but the risks involved vary across the country. There is a significant risk of malaria along the **Burmese and Cambodian borders,** including Ko Chang in Trat province; the only anti-malarial drug that is likely to be effective in these areas is **Doxycycline.** In most situations you only need to start taking Doxycycline a couple of days before entering a malarial zone; its use should be discussed with your travel health adviser. Elsewhere in Thailand the risk of malaria is considered to be so low that anti-malarial tablets are not advised.

The first **signs of malaria** are remarkably similar to flu, and may take months to

appear: if you suspect anything go to a hospital or clinic immediately.

Dengue fever

Like malaria, **dengue fever,** a debilitating and occasionally fatal viral disease, is on the increase throughout tropical Asia, and is endemic to many areas of Thailand. Unlike malaria though, dengue fever is spread by a mosquito (the *Aedes*) which bites during daylight hours – usually in early morning or late afternoon, particularly during and just after the rainy season. Symptoms include fever, a rash, headaches and fierce joint pain ("breakbone fever" is another name for dengue) and usually develop between five and eight days after being bitten. There is no vaccine against dengue fever; the only treatment is lots of rest, liquids and paracetamol (or any other acetaminophen painkiller, not aspirin), though more serious cases may require hospitalization.

Japanese encephalitis

If you are travelling for long periods in rural areas between June and September (the rainy season), you may be at risk of contracting **Japanese encephalitis,** a viral inflammation of the brain spread by the *Culex* mosquito which breeds in rice fields. A vaccine is available, and although the risk of travellers catching the disease is low, you should at least consult your health adviser.

Other health problems

Wearing protective clothing is a good idea when **swimming, snorkelling** or **diving:** a T-shirt will stop you from getting sunburnt in the water, while long trousers can guard against coral grazes. Should you scrape your skin on coral, wash the wound thoroughly with boiled water, apply antiseptic and keep protected until healed. Thailand's seas are home to a few dangerous creatures which you should be wary of, principally jellyfish, poisonous sea snakes, sea urchins and a couple of less conspicuous species – stingrays, which often lie buried in the sand, and stonefish, whose potentially lethal venomous spikes are easily stepped on because the fish look like stones and lie motionless on the sea bed.

If **stung or bitten** you should always seek medical advice as soon as possible, but

Carrying essential medications

Make sure that you take sufficient supplies of any essential **medications** and carry the complete supply with you whenever you travel (including on public transport), in case of loss or theft. You should also carry a prescription including the generic name in case of emergency. If travelling for a long time, it may be worth arranging for your doctor or hospital to courier extra supplies to a specific address in Thailand, such as a reputable hotel. It's also a good idea to carry a doctor's letter about your drugs prescriptions with you at all times – particularly when passing through customs at Bangkok airport – as this will ensure you don't get hauled up for narcotics transgressions.

If your medication has to be kept cool, buy a **thermal insulation bag** and a couple of freezer blocks before you leave home. That way you can refreeze one of the two blocks every day, while the other is in use; staff in most hotels, guest houses, restaurants and even some bars should be happy to let you use their freezer compartment for a few hours. If you use **needles and syringes**, you should also take a small sharps bin with you, as garbage disposal in Thailand is haphazard and your used syringes might harm someone.

there are a few ways of alleviating the pain or administering your own first aid in the meantime. If you're stung by a **jellyfish**, the priority treatment is to remove the fragments of tentacles from the skin – without causing further discharge of poison – which is easiest done by applying vinegar to deactivate the stinging capsules. In the case of a poisonous **snake** bite, don't try sucking out the poison or applying a tourniquet: immobilize the limb and stay calm until medical help arrives (all provincial hospitals in Thailand should carry supplies of antivenins. The best way to minimize the risk of stepping on the toxic **spines** of sea urchins, stingrays and stonefish is to wear thick-soled shoes, though these cannot provide total protection; sea urchin spikes should be removed after softening the skin with ointment, though some people recommend applying urine to help dissolve the spines; for stingray and stonefish stings, alleviate the pain by immersing the wound in hot water while awaiting help.

Rabies

Rabies is mainly carried by dogs (between four and seven percent of stray dogs in Bangkok are reported to be rabid), but also cats and monkeys, and is transmitted by bites or scratches. Dogs are everywhere in Thailand and even if kept as pets they're never very well cared for; hopefully their mangy appearance will discourage the urge to pat them as you should steer clear as much as possible. If you are bitten or scratched by an animal, clean and disinfect the wound, preferably with alcohol, and seek medical advice right away.

Worms

Worms can be picked up through the soles of your feet, so avoid going barefoot. Swimming in the southern reaches of the Mekhong River and the lakes of northeastern Thailand can also cause **flukes** to enter through your skin and thence into your bloodstream or liver (they cannot survive in salt water).

Digestive problems

By far the most common travellers' complaint in Thailand, **digestive troubles** are often caused by contaminated food and water, or sometimes just by an overdose of unfamiliar foodstuffs. Break your system in gently by avoiding excessively spicy curries and too much raw fruit in the first few days, and then use your common sense about choosing where and what to eat: if you stick to the most crowded restaurants and noodle stalls you should be perfectly safe. Furthermore, because most Thai dishes can be cooked in under five minutes, you'll rarely have to contend with stuff that's been left to smoulder and stew. You need to be a bit more rigorous about drinking the **water**, though: stick to bottled water, which is sold everywhere, or else opt for boiled water or tea.

Stomach trouble usually manifests itself as simple **diarrhoea**, which should clear up without medical treatment within three to seven days and is best combated by drinking lots of fluids. If this doesn't work, you're in danger of getting **dehydrated** and should take some kind of rehydration solution, either a commercial sachet sold in all Thai pharmacies or a do-it-yourself version which can be made by adding a handful of sugar and a pinch of salt to every litre of boiled or bottled water (soft drinks are *not* a viable alternative). Note that anti-diarrhoeal agents such as Imodium are useful for blocking you up on long bus journeys, but only attack the symptoms and may prolong infections. If diarrhoea persists for more than ten days, or if you have blood or mucus in your stools, you may have contracted bacillary or amoebic dysentery, in which case go to a doctor or hospital.

Heat problems

Aside from the obvious considerations about restricting your exposure to the searing midday sun (using high protection-factor sun creams if you have fair skin, and protecting your eyes with good sunglasses that screen out UV light and your head with a hat), you should avoid **dehydration** by drinking plenty of water and occasionally adding a pinch of salt to fruit shakes. To prevent and alleviate heat rashes, prickly heat and fungal infections, it's a good idea to use a mild antiseptic soap and to dust yourself with prickly heat talcum powder, both of which are sold cheaply in all Thai stores.

AIDS

AIDS is spreading fast in Thailand, primarily because of the widespread sex trade (see p.158), with an alarming 44 percent of prostitutes in Chiang Mai testing HIV positive. Condoms (*meechai*) are sold in pharmacists, department stores, hairdressers, even on street markets. Should you need to have an injection at a hospital, try to check that the needle has been sterilized first; this is not always practicable, however, so you might consider carrying your own syringes. Don't even consider getting yourself tattooed in Thailand.

Due to rigorous screening methods, the country's **medical blood supply** is now considered safe.

Getting around

Travel in Thailand is both inexpensive and efficient, if not always speedy. Unless you travel by plane, long-distance journeys in Thailand can be arduous, especially if a shoestring budget restricts you to hard seats and no air-conditioning. Still, the wide range of efficient transport options makes travelling around this country easier than elsewhere in Southeast Asia. Buses are fast and frequent, and can be quite luxurious; trains are slower but safer and offer more chance of sleeping during overnight trips; moreover, if travelling by day you're likely to follow a more scenic route by rail than by road. Inter-town songthaews, share-taxis and air-conditioned minibuses are handy, and ferries provide easy access to all major islands. Local transport comes in all sorts of permutations, both public and chartered, with relatively little separating them in terms of cost.

For an idea of the frequency and duration of bus, train, air and ferry services between towns, check the **travel details** at the end of each chapter.

Inter-town buses

Buses, overall the most convenient way of getting around the country, come in two categories: **ordinary** (*rot thammadaa*) and air-conditioned (*rot air*), with an additional air-conditioned subcategory known as **tour buses** (*rot tua*). The ordinary and air-conditioned buses are run by Baw Kaw Saw, the government transport company, whereas the misleadingly named tour buses are privately owned and ply the most popular long-distance routes, with no tours involved. Be warned that long-distance overnight buses, particularly the air-conditioned and tour buses, seem to be involved in more than their fair share of accidents; because of this, some travellers prefer to do the overnight journeys by train and then make a shorter bus connection to their destination.

Ordinary buses

The orange-coloured **ordinary buses** are incredibly inexpensive and cover most short-range routes between main towns (up to 150km) very frequently during daylight hours. Each bus is staffed by a team of two or three – the driver, the fare collector and the optional "stop" and "go" yeller – who often personalize the vehicle with stereo systems, stickers, jasmine garlands and the requisite Buddha image or amulet. With an entertaining team and eye-catching scenery, journeys can be fun, but there are drawbacks. For a start, the teams work on a commission basis, so they pack as many people in as possible and might hang around for thirty minutes after they're due to leave in the hope of cramming in a few extra. They also stop so often that their average speed of 60kph can only be achieved by hurtling along at breakneck speeds between pick-ups, often propelled by amphetamine-induced craziness. To flag down an ordinary bus from the roadside you should wait at the nearest **bus shelter**, or *sala*, usually located at intervals along the main long-distance bus route through town or on the fringes of any decent-sized settlement, for example on the main highway that skirts the edge of town. Where there is only a bus shelter on the "wrong" side of the road, you can be sure that buses travelling in both directions will stop there for any waiting passengers. If you're in the middle of nowhere with no *sala* in sight, any ordinary bus should stop for you if you flag it down.

Air-conditioned buses

The blue **air-conditioned buses** stop a lot less often (if at all) and cover the distances faster and more comfortably: passengers are allotted specific seats, and on long journeys get blankets, snacks and nonstop videos. On some routes, you also have the option of taking the VIP air-con bus service, which has fewer seats and more leg room. On the down side, air-con buses usually cost one-and-a-half times as much as the ordinary buses (up to twice as much for VIP buses), depart less frequently and don't cover nearly as many routes; make sure you have some warm clothes, as temperatures can get chilly, even with the blanket. Not all air-con buses have toilets, so it's always worth using bus station facilities before you board.

Tour buses

In a lot of cases **tour buses** are indistinguishable from air-conditioned ones, operating the busiest routes at similar prices and with comparable facilities. However, some tour buses – such as those operated by Nakorn Chai and Win Tour – do offer a distinctly better service, with reclining seats and plenty of leg room, for which they charge more than government-run air-con buses. In general these major tour-bus companies operate out of the government bus terminals and provide a consistently good standard of service. The opposite is unfortunately true of a number of the smaller private tour-bus companies, several of which have a poor reputation for service and comfort, but attract their customers with bargain fares and convenient timetables. The long-distance tour buses that run from Thanon Khao San in Banglamphu to Chiang Mai and Surat Thani are a case in point; travellers on these routes frequently complain about shabby furnishings, ineffective air-conditioning, unhelpful (even aggressive) drivers and a frightening lack of safety awareness – and there are occasional reports of theft from luggage on these routes too. If you're planning to travel either of these routes, you are strongly recommended to go by train instead – the extra comfort and peace of mind are well worth the extra baht.

Tickets and timetables

Tickets for all buses can be bought from the departure terminals, but for ordinary buses it's normal to buy them on board. Air-conditioned buses often operate on a separate station, and tickets for the more popular routes should be booked a day in advance. As a rough indication of **fares**, a trip from Bangkok to Chiang Mai should cost B370–400 for first class, B240 by air-conditioned bus and B130 by ordinary bus.

Long-distance buses often depart in clusters around the same time (early morning or late at night for example), leaving a gap of five or more hours during the day with no services at all. Local TAT offices often keep up-to-date bus **timetables** in English. Or go to the bus terminal the day before you want to leave and check with staff there. That said, if you turn up at a bus terminal in the morning for a medium-length journey (150–300km), you're almost always guaranteed to be on your way within two hours.

Songthaews, share-taxis and air-conditioned minibuses

In rural areas, the bus network is supplemented – or even substantially replaced – by **songthaews** (literally "two rows"), which are open-ended vans (or occasionally cattle-trucks) onto which the drivers squash as many passengers as possible on two facing benches, leaving latecomers to swing off the running board at the back. As well as their essential role within towns (see "Local Transport" on p.43), songthaews ply set routes from larger towns out to their surrounding suburbs and villages, and, where there's no call for a regular bus service, between small towns: some have destinations written on in Thai, but few are numbered. In most towns you'll find the songthaew "terminal" near the market; to pick one up between destinations just flag it down. To indicate to the driver that you want to get out, the normal practice is to rap hard with a coin on the metal railings as you approach the spot (or press the bell if there is one). As a general rule, the cost of inter-town songthaews is comparable to that of air-conditioned buses.

In the deep south they do things with a little more style – **share-taxis**, often clapped-out old limos, connect all the major towns, though they are slowly being replaced by more comfortable **air-conditioned minibuses** (for more details, see p.711). Government-run air-con minibuses are also the norm on certain routes in the central plains, particularly in the Tak and Mae Sot areas. These generally depart frequently and cover the distance faster than the ordinary bus service, but can be uncomfortably cramped when filled to capacity and are not ideal for travellers with huge rucksacks.

In many cases, long-distance songthaews and air-con minibuses will drop you at an exact address (for example a particular guest house) if you warn them far enough in advance – it's generally an expected part of the service.

Trains

Managed by the State Railway of Thailand (SRT), the rail network consists of four main lines and a few branch lines. The **Northern Line** connects Bangkok with Chiang Mai via Ayutthaya and Phitsanulok. The **Northeastern Line** splits into two just beyond Ayutthaya, the lower branch running eastwards to Ubon Ratchathani via Khorat and Surin, the more northerly branch linking the capital with Nong Khai via Khon Kaen and Udon Thani. The **Eastern Line** also has two branches, one of which runs from Bangkok to Aranyaprathet on the Cambodian border, the other of which connects Bangkok with Si Racha and Pattaya. The **Southern Line** extends to Hat Yai, where it branches: one line continues down the west coast of Malaysia, via Butterworth and Kuala Lumpur, to Singapore; the other heads down the eastern side of the peninsula to Sungai Kolok on the Thailand–Malaysia border (20km from Pasir Mas on Malaysia's interior railway). At Nakhon Pathom a branch

Train information

If you want to plan ahead, visit the SRT website (ⓦ www.srt.motc.go.th), which carries timetables for the main routes as well as ticket prices. Alternatively, you could try phoning the 24-hour SRT Hotline on ☏1690, or calling the main Hualamphong office on ☏02/220 4334.

of this line veers off to Nam Tok via Kanchanaburi – this is all that's left of the Death Railway, of *Bridge Over the River Kwai* notoriety.

Fares depend on the class of seat, whether or not you want air-conditioning, and on the speed of the train; those quoted here exclude the "speed" supplements, which are discussed below. Hard wooden third-class seats cost about the same as an ordinary bus (Bangkok–Chiang Mai around B160), and are fine for about three hours, after which numbness sets in. For longer journeys you'd be wise to opt for the padded and often reclining seats in second class (Bangkok–Chiang Mai B320, or B480 with air-con). On long-distance trains, you also usually have the option of second-class berths (for an extra B170–240, or B300–360 with air-con), with day seats that convert into comfortable curtained-off bunks in the evening. Travelling first class (Bangkok–Chiang Mai B1200) means you automatically get a private two-person air-conditioned sleeping compartment, complete with washbasin. Note that you must **buy a ticket before boarding** a train, otherwise you're liable for a fine of B100 on an ordinary train or B200 on a rapid or express train.

There are several different **types of train**: slowest of all is the third-class-only Ordinary service, which is generally (but not always) available only on short and medium-length journeys and has no speed supplement. Next comes the misleadingly named Rapid train (B40 supplement), a trip on which from Bangkok to Chiang Mai, for example, takes nearly fifteen hours; the Special Express (B80 supplement) takes around an hour less to cover the same route; and fastest of all is the Special Express Diesel Railcar (also B80 supplement) which does the journey in eleven to twelve hours. Note that all long-distance trains have **dining cars**, and rail staff will also bring meals to your seat. Tourist menus are written in English but have inflated prices – ask for the similar but less expensive "ordinary" version, the *menu thammadaa*.

Booking at least one day in advance is strongly recommended for second- and first-class seats on all lengthy journeys, and sleepers should be booked as far in advance as possible. It should be possible to make bookings at the station in any major town; for details on how to book trains out of Bangkok, see p.188.

The SRT publishes three clear and fairly accurate free **timetables** in English, for the Northern, Northeastern, and Southern and Kanchanaburi lines respectively (they're sometimes available combined onto a single sheet). The timetables detail types of trains and classes available on each route as well as fares and supplementary charges; the best place to get hold of them is over the counter at Bangkok's Hualamphong station or, if you're lucky, the TAT office in Bangkok. The information desk at Hualamphong also stocks more detailed local timetables covering the Bangkok–Lopburi route via Don Muang airport and Ayutthaya.

Travel agents overseas sell 7-, 14- and 21-day **rail passes**, covering train journeys anywhere in Thailand in non-air-con second-class seats. However, the passes are generally more trouble than they're worth, as the country's network is not extensive enough to make them pay, and many booking offices in Thailand are at a loss as to how to handle them, especially if, as is usually the case, pass-holders want to pay extra for a sleeping berth.

Ferries

Regular **ferries** connect all major islands with the mainland, and for the vast majority of crossings you simply buy your ticket on board. In tourist areas competition ensures that prices are kept low, and fares tend to vary with the speed of the crossing: thus Phuket–Ko Phi Phi costs between B250 (2hr 30min) and B350 (1hr 30 min). Boats generally operate a reduced service during the monsoon season (May–Oct along the east coast and Andaman coast; Nov–Jan on the Gulf coast; the more remote spots become inaccessible in these periods. Details on island connections are given in the relevant chapters.

Flights

The domestic arm of **Thai Airways** (圕www .thaiairways.com) dominates the internal flight network, which extends to all extremities of the country, around two dozen airports. **Bangkok Airways** (圕www.bkkair.co.th) plies some useful additional routes, including Bangkok–Ko Samui, Bangkok–Sukhothai and Bangkok–Ranong, Sukhothai–Chiang Mai, Ko Samui–Phuket, Ko Samui–Krabi and Ko

Samui–Pattaya. There is also a newcomer on the scene, the Phuket-based **Air Andaman** (®www.airandaman.com), which currently only flies Phuket–Krabi, Phuket–Surat Thani and Phuket–Nakhon Si Thammarat, but is intending to extend its service to include Phuket–Chumphon, Phuket–Ranong and Chumphon–Bangkok. In some instances a flight can save you days of travelling: the flight from Chiang Mai to Phuket (around B4000 one way), for example, takes two hours, as against a couple of days by meandering train and/or bus. If you want to plan domestic flights before you leave home, check out the airlines' websites, which list both schedules and fares for all routes.

All towns served by an airport have at least one Thai Airways **booking** office; flights can get booked a long way ahead, so reserve early if possible – but bear in mind it costs much less to book in Thailand than from abroad. The main Bangkok offices for Thai and Bangkok Airways are detailed on p.192, and flight durations and frequencies are listed at the end of each chapter. If you're planning to use the Thai Airways' internal network a lot, you can save money by buying a **Discover Thailand Airpass** (about £140/US$200), available only outside Thailand from Thai Airways' offices and travel agents. The pass covers four one-way flights in a two-month period; you fix the routes when you buy the pass, but dates of travel can be changed in Thailand.

Local transport

Most sizeable towns have some kind of **local transport system**, comprising a network of buses, songthaews or even longtail boats, with set fares and routes but not rigid timetabling; in most cases vehicles leave when they're full – generally at ten- or twenty-minute intervals during the busiest time of day (from about 6am until noon) – and then at least once an hour until 5 or 6pm.

Buses and songthaews

Larger cities like Bangkok, Khorat, Ubon Ratchathani and Phitsanulok have a **local bus** network which usually extends to the suburbs and operates from dawn till dusk (through the night in Bangkok). Most vehicles display route numbers in Arabic numerals, and you pay the conductor B5–10 depending on your destination (on some routes you can choose to take air-con buses, for which you pay a couple of baht extra).

Within medium-sized and large towns, the main transport role is often played by **songthaews**. The size and shape of vehicle used varies from town to town – and in some places they're known as "tuk-tuks" from the noise they make, not to be confused with the smaller tuk-tuks, described below, that operate as private taxis – but all have the tell-tale two facing benches in the back. In some towns, especially in the northeast, songthaews follow fixed routes; in others they act as communal taxis, picking up a number of people who are going in roughly the same direction and taking each of them right to their destination. To hail a songthaew just flag it down, and to indicate that you want to get out, either rap hard with a coin on the metal railings, or ring the bell if there is one. Fares within towns range between B5 and B20, depending on distance.

Longtail boats

Wherever there's a decent public waterway, there'll be a **longtail boat** ready to ferry you along it. Another great Thai trademark, these elegant, streamlined boats are powered by deafening diesel engines – sometimes custom-built, more often adapted from cars or trucks – which drive a propeller mounted on a long shaft that is swivelled for steering. Longtails carry between ten and twenty passengers: in Bangkok and Krabi the majority follow fixed routes, but elsewhere they're for hire at about B100 an hour per boat, more in tourist spots.

Taxi services

Taxis also comes in many guises, and in bigger towns you can often choose between taking a tuk-tuk, a samlor, a motorbike taxi or a car taxi. The one thing common to all modes of chartered transport is that you must establish the **fare** beforehand: although drivers nearly always pitch their first offers too high, they do calculate with traffic and time of day in mind, as well as according to distance – if successive drivers scoff at your price, you know you've got it wrong. See p.104 for advice on how to avoid being ripped off by Bangkok tuk-tuk drivers.

Tuk-tuks

Named after the noise of its excruciatingly unsilenced engine, the three-wheeled open-sided **tuk-tuk** is the classic Thai vehicle. Painted in primary colours, tuk-tuks blast their way round towns and cities on two-stroke engines, zipping around faster than any car and taking corners on two wheels. They aren't as dangerous as they look though, and can be an exhilarating way to get around, as long as you're not too fussy about exhaust fumes. They're also inexpensive: fares start at B10 (B30 in Bangkok) regardless of the number of passengers – three is the safe maximum, though six is not uncommon.

Samlors

Tuk-tuks are also sometimes known as samlors (literally "three wheels"), but the real **samlors** are tricycle rickshaws propelled by pedal power alone. Slower and a great deal more stately than tuk-tuks, samlors operate pretty much everywhere except in Bangkok. Forget any qualms you may have about being pedalled around by another human being: samlor drivers' livelihoods depend on having a constant supply of passengers, so your most ethical option is to hop on and not scrimp on the fare. Drivers usually charge a minimum B10 fee and add B10 per kilometre, possibly more for a heavy load. A further permutation are the motorized samlors, where the driver relies on a motorbike rather than a bicycle to propel passengers to their destination. They look much the same as cycle samlors, often sound as noisy as tuk-tuks and cost something between the two.

Motorbike taxis

Even faster and more precarious than tuk-tuks, **motorbike taxis** feature both in big towns and out-of-the-way places. In towns – where the drivers are identified by coloured, numbered vests – they have the advantage of being able to dodge traffic jams, but are obviously only really suitable for the single traveller, and motorbike taxis aren't the easiest mode of transport if you're carrying luggage. In remote spots on the other hand, they're often the only alternative to hitching or walking, and are especially useful for getting between bus stops on main roads and to national parks or ancient ruins. Within

towns motorbike-taxi fares are comparable to those for tuk-tuks, but for trips to the outskirts the cost rises steeply – about B100–150 for a twenty-kilometre round trip.

Car taxis

Generally available only in the biggest towns, air-conditioned **car taxis** charge fares that begin at around B50. Only major towns and resorts such as Bangkok and Phuket have metered taxis, where you must be sure to establish whether or not the meter is actually working before you set off; if it's not, or if your taxi has no meter, settle on a price at the start.

Vehicle rental

Despite first impressions, and the obvious mayhem that characterizes Bangkok's roads, **driving yourself around Thailand** is fairly straightforward and unstressful. Many roads, particularly in the northeast and the south, are remarkably uncongested. Major routes are clearly signed in English, though this only applies to some minor roads; unfortunately there is no perfect English-language map to compensate, though the Nelles map described on p.27 is adequate.

Outside the capital, its immediate environs and the eastern seaboard, local drivers are considerate and noticeably unaggressive; they very rarely use their horns for example, and will often indicate and even swerve away when it's safe for you to overtake. The most inconsiderate and dangerous road-users in Thailand are bus drivers and lorry drivers, many of whom drive ludicrously fast, hog the road, race round bends on the wrong side of the road and use their horns remorselessly; worse still, many of them are tanked up on amphetamines, which makes them quite literally fearless. Bus and lorry drivers are at their worst after dark (many of them only drive then), so you are strongly advised **never to drive at night** – a further hazard being the inevitable stream of unlit bicycles and mopeds in and around built-up areas, as well as poorly signed roadworks which are often not made safe or blocked off from unsuspecting traffic.

As for local **rules of the road**, Thais drive on the left, and the speed limit is 60km/h within built-up areas and 80km/h outside them. More unusually, a major road doesn't necessarily have right of way over a minor, but the bigger vehicle *always* has right of way. An oncoming vehicle flashing its lights means it's coming through no matter what; a right indicator signal from the car in front usually means it's not safe for you to overtake, while a left indicator signal usually means that it is safe to do so.

Theoretically, foreigners need an international driver's **licence** to hire any kind of vehicle, but most companies accept national licences, and the smaller operations (especially bike rentals) may not ask for any kind of proof at all. **Petrol** (*nam man*, which also means oil) costs around B20 a litre. The big fuel stations are the least costly places to fill up (*hai taem*), and many of these also have toilets and simple restaurants, though some of the more decrepit-looking fuel stations on the main highways only sell diesel. Most small villages have easy-to-spot roadside huts where the fuel is pumped out of a large barrel.

Cars

If you decide to **rent a car**, go to a reputable dealer, preferably an Avis, Budget or SMT branch (see box) or a rental company recommended by TAT, and make sure you got insurance from them. There are international car-rental places at many regional airports, including Bangkok's Don Muang airport, which is not a bad place to kick off, as you're on the edge of the city and within fairly easy (signed) reach of the major regional highways. Car-rental places in provincial capitals and resorts are listed in the relevant accounts. Prices for a small car start at about B1200 per day, depending on the vehicle's condition, which is generally not bad. In most parts of the country, you can count on covering about 70km per hour if travelling long distances on major highways. If appropriate, consider the option of hiring a driver along with the car, which you can often do for no extra charge on day rentals.

Jeeps are a lot more popular with farangs, especially on beach resorts and islands like Pattaya, Phuket and Ko Samui, but they're notoriously dangerous; a huge number of tourists manage to roll their jeeps on steep hillsides and sharp bends. Jeep rental usually works out somewhere between B1000 and B1500.

For all cars and jeeps, renters will often ask for a deposit of at least B2000, and will either want to hold onto your passport or take your credit card details as surety.

Car rental agencies

Avis ⓦ www.avisthailand.com; in the UK ⓣ 0870/606 0100, in the Irish Republic ⓣ 01/605 7555, in the US ⓣ 1-800/331-1084, in Canada 1-800 272 5871, in Australia ⓣ 13 6333, in New Zealand ⓣ 09/526 5231 or 0800/655 111.

Budget ⓦ www.budget.co.th; in the UK ⓣ 0800/181181, in the Irish Republic ⓣ 1850/575757, in North America ⓣ 1-800/527-0700, in Australia ⓣ 1300/362 848, in New Zealand ⓣ 0800/652227 or 09/375 2270.

National Car Rental (SMT in Thailand) esmtcar@samart.co.th; in the UK ⓣ 0870/536 5365, in North America ⓣ 1-800/227-7368.

Motorbikes

One of the best ways of exploring the countryside is to rent a **motorbike**, an especially popular option in the north of the country. Two-seater **80cc** bikes with automatic gears are best if you've never ridden a motorbike before, but aren't really suited for long slogs. If you're going to hit the dirt roads you'll certainly need something more powerful, like a **125cc** trail bike. These have the edge in gear choice and are the best bikes for steep slopes, though an inexperienced rider may find these machines a handful; the less widely available 125cc road bikes are easier to control and much cheaper on petrol.

Rental **prices** for the day usually work out at somewhere between B150 (for a fairly beat-up 80cc) and B350 (for a good trail bike), though you can bargain for a discount on a long rental. As with cars, the renters will often ask for a deposit and your passport or credit-card details, though you're unlikely to have to prove that you've ridden a bike before. Insurance is not often available, so it's a good idea to make sure your travel insurance covers you for possible mishaps.

Before signing anything, **check the bike** thoroughly – test the brakes, look for oil leaks, check the treads and the odometer, and make sure the chain isn't stretched too tight (a tight chain is likelier to break) – and preferably take it for a test run. As you will have to pay an inflated price for any damage when you get back, make a note on the contract of any defects such as broken mirrors, indicators and so on. Make sure you know what kind of petrol the bike takes as well.

As far as **equipment** goes, a helmet is essential – most rental places provide poorly made ones, but they're better than nothing. Helmets are obligatory on all motorbike journeys, and the law is rigidly enforced in major tourist resorts, where on-the-spot fines are the norm. You'll need sunglasses if your helmet doesn't have a visor. As well as being more culturally appropriate, long trousers, a long-sleeved top and decent shoes will provide a second skin if you go over, which most people do at some stage. Pillions should wear long trousers to avoid getting nasty burns from the exhaust. For the sake of stability, leave most of your luggage in baggage storage and pack as small a bag as possible, strapping it tightly to the bike with bungy cords – these are usually provided. Once on the road, oil the chain at least every other day, keep the radiator topped up and fill up with oil every 300km or so.

For expert **advice** on motorbike travel in Thailand, check out David Unkovich's website (⊛www.geocities.com/goldentriangler), which covers everything from how to ship a bike to Thailand to which are the best off-road touring routes in the country. He has also published *A Motorcycle Guide To The Golden Triangle*, which is available in Chiang Mai or via his website.

Bicycles

The safest and most pleasant way of conveying yourself around many towns and rural areas is by **bicycle**, except of course in Bangkok. You won't find bike rentals everywhere, but a lot of guest houses keep a few, and in certain bike-friendly tourist spots, like Kanchanaburi, Chiang Mai and Sukhothai, you'll find larger-scale rental places, who should charge around B20–50 a day. A few rental outlets in the north also offer mountain bikes for around B80.

Hitching

Public transport being so inexpensive, you should only have to resort to **hitching** in the most remote areas, in which case you'll probably get a lift to the nearest bus or songthaew stop quite quickly. On routes served by buses and trains hitching is not standard practice, but in other places locals do rely on regular passers-by (such as national park officials), and as a farang you can make use of this "service" too. As with hitching anywhere in the world, think twice about hitching solo or at night, especially if you're female. Truck drivers are notorious users of amphetamines (as are a lot of bus drivers), so you may want to wait for a better offer.

Accommodation

Cheap accommodation can be found all over Thailand: for the simplest double room prices start at around B100 in the outlying regions and B150 in Bangkok, rising to B250 in some resorts. Tourist centres invariably offer a huge range of more upmarket choices, and you'll have little problem finding luxury hotels in these places. In most resort areas rates fluctuate according to demand, plummeting during the off-season and, in some places, rising at weekends throughout the year.

Whatever the establishment, staff expect you to look at the room before taking it; in the budget ones especially, try out the door-lock, check for cockroaches and mosquitoes and make sure it's equipped with a decent mosquito net or screens. En-suite showers and flush toilets are the norm only in moderately priced and expensive hotels; in the less touristy places you'll be "showering" with a bowl dipped into a large water jar, and using squat toilets.

Guest houses and hostels

Any place calling itself a **guest house** – which could be anything from a bamboo hut to a three-storey concrete block – is almost certain to provide inexpensive, basic accommodation specifically aimed at Western travellers and priced at around B100–250 for a sparse double room with a fan and (often shared) bathroom. You'll find them in all major tourist centres (in their dozens in Bangkok and Chiang Mai), and even in the most unlikely back-country spots: on the beaches, **bungalows** operate in much the same way.

In the main towns guest houses tend to be concentrated in cheek-by-jowl farang ghettos, but even if you baulk at the world travellers' scene that often characterizes these places, guest houses make great places to stay, with attached cafeterias, clued-up English-speaking staff and informative noticeboards. These days, they're providing more and more services and **facilities**, such as internet access, safes for valuables, luggage storage, travel and tour operator desks and their own poste restante. Staying at one out in the sticks, you'll often get involved in local life a lot more than if you were encased in a hotel.

At the vast majority of guest houses **check-out time** is noon, which means that during high season you should arrive to check

Accommodation prices

Throughout this guide, guest houses, hotels and bungalows have been categorized according to the price codes given below. These categories represent the minimum you can expect to pay in the high season (roughly July, Aug & Nov–Feb) for a **double room**. If travelling on your own, expect to pay anything between sixty and one hundred percent of the rates quoted for a double room. Wherever a price range is indicated, this means that the establishment offers rooms with varying facilities – as explained in the write-up. Where an establishment also offers dormitory beds, the prices of these beds are given in the text, instead of being indicated by a price code.

Remember that the top-whack hotels will add seven percent tax and a ten percent service charge to your bill – the price codes below are based on net rates after taxes have been added.

- ❶ under B150
- ❷ B150–250
- ❸ B250–400
- ❹ B400–600
- ❺ B600–900
- ❻ B900–1200
- ❼ B1200–1800
- ❽ B1800–3000
- ❾ B3000+

in at about 11.30am to ensure you get a room: few places draw up a "waiting list" and they rarely take advance bookings unless they know you already and you've paid a deposit.

The **upmarket guest house** is almost a contradiction in terms, but there are a few such places, charging between B250 and B800 for facilities that may include air-conditioning, bathroom, TV and use of a swimming pool. Beware of pricey guest houses or bungalows in mega-resorts like Pattaya, Phuket and Ko Phi Phi, however, which often turn out to be low-quality fan-cooled establishments making a killing out of unsuspecting holidaymakers.

With just twelve officially registered **youth hostels** in the whole country, it's not worth becoming a YHA member just for your trip to Thailand, especially as card-holders get only a small discount anyway. In general, youth-hostel prices work out the same as guest-house rates and rooms are open to all ages, whether or not you're a member. Online reservations can be made via the Thai Youth Hostels Association website (@www.tyha.org).

Budget hotels

Few Thais use guest houses, opting instead for **budget hotels** offering rooms costing up to B600. Beds in these places are large enough for a couple, and it's quite acceptable for two people to ask and pay for a single room (*hong diaw*). Usually run by Chinese-Thais, these three- or four-storey places are found in every sizeable town, often near the bus station. The rooms are generally clean and usually come with attached bathroom and a fan (or air-con), which makes them good value in terms of facilities. Unfortunately they also tend to be grim and unfriendly, staffed by brusque non-English-speakers, and generally lacking in any communal seating or eating area, which makes them lonely places for single travellers. A number of budget hotels also double as brothels, though as a farang you're unlikely to be offered this sideline, and you mayn't even notice the goings-on anyway.

If the hotel's on a busy main road, as many of them are, try asking for a quiet room (*mii hawng ngiap-kwaa mai*?). Advance bookings are accepted over the phone – if you can make yourself understood – but this is rarely necessary, as such hotels rarely fill up.

The only time you may have difficulty finding a budget hotel room is during Chinese New Year (a moveable three-day period in late January or February), when many Chinese-run hotels close and the others get booked up fast.

Moderate hotels

Moderate hotels – priced between B600 and B1200 – can sometimes work out to be good value, offering many of the trimmings of a top-end hotel (TV, fridge, air-con, pool), but none of the prestige. They're often the kind of places that once stood at the top of the range, but were downgraded when the multinational luxury muscled in and hogged the poshest clientele. They still make especially welcome alternatives to the budget hotels in provincial capitals, but, like upmarket guest houses, can turn out to be vastly overpriced in the resorts.

As with the budget hotels, you're unlikely to have trouble finding a room on spec in one of these places, though advance bookings are accepted by phone. Bed size varies a lot more than in the Chinese-run places though, with some making the strict Western distinction between singles and doubles.

Upmarket hotels

Many of Thailand's **upmarket hotels** belong to international chains like Hilton, Holiday Inn, Le Meridien and Sheraton, maintaining top-quality standards in Bangkok and major resorts at prices of B2400 (£40/US$60) and upward for a double – far less than you'd pay for such luxury accommodation in the West. Some of the best home-grown upmarket hotels are up to B1000 cheaper for equally fine service, rooms equipped with TV, mini-bar and balcony, and full use of the hotel sports facilities and swimming pools. Note that, since the collapse of the baht in 1997, a number of luxury hotels now quote rates in US dollars. All upmarket hotels can be booked in advance, an advisable measure in Chiang Mai, Phuket or Pattaya during peak season.

National parks and camping

Unattractive accommodation is one of the big disappointments of Thailand's **national parks**. Generally built to a standard two-

Booking a hotel online

The following online hotel-booking services offer rates discounted by up to sixty percent on the published prices of selected mid-range and upmarket accommodation. Discounted rates for a double room generally start at US$30, but it is occasionally possible to find rooms for US$20.

Hotels across Thailand

Accommodating Asia
ⓦ www.accomasia.com/thailand.htm

Asia Hotels|
ⓦ www.asia-hotels.com

Asia Ways
ⓦ www.asiaways.com

Hotel Thailand
ⓦ hotelthailand.com

Island Net
ⓦ www.islandnet.com

Siam Net
ⓦ www.siam.net

Stay In Thailand
ⓦ www.stayinthailand.com

Thai Focus
ⓦ www.thaifocus.com

Thailand Hotels Association
ⓦ www.thaihotels.org

Thailand Hotels and Resorts
ⓦ www.hotels.siam.net

Regional hotels

Chiang Mai
ⓦ www.infothai.com/wtcmcr

Ko Lanta
ⓦ www.kohlanta.com

Ko Samui
ⓦ www.sawadee.com

Krabi
ⓦ krabihotels.com
ⓦ www.krabi.sawadee.com

Northeast (Isaan)
ⓦ isan.sawadee.com

Phuket
ⓦ www.phuket.com/hotels/index.html

Trang
ⓦ www.trangonline.com

roomed format, these dismal concrete bungalows feature in about half the country's parks, and cost an average B500 for four or more beds plus a probably malfunctioning shower. Because most of their custom comes from Thai family groups, park officials are sometimes loath to discount these huts for lone travellers, though some parks do offer dorm-style accommodation at B100 a bed. In most parks, advance booking is unnecessary except on weekends and national holidays. If you do want to pre-book, then either pay on the spot in Bangkok at the Forestry Department offices (☎02/561 4292–3, ⓕ579 7099), which are near Kasetsart University on Thanon Phaholyothin, about 4km north of the Mo Chit skytrain terminus – this can be quite a palaver, so don't plan on doing anything else that day – or book on the phone (not much English spoken), then send a baht money order and wait for confirmation. If you turn up without booking, check in at the park headquarters – which is usually adjacent to the visitor centre.

In a few parks, private operators have set up low-cost **guest houses** on the outskirts and these make much more attractive and economical places to stay.

Camping

You can usually **camp** in a national park for a minimal fee of B10–30, and some national parks also rent out two-berth tents at anything from B40–200. Unless you're planning an extensive tour of national parks though, there's little point in lugging a tent around Thailand: accommodation everywhere else is too inexpensive to make camping a necessity, and anyway there are no campgrounds inside town perimeters.

Camping is allowed on nearly all **islands and beaches**, many of which are national parks in their own right. Few travellers bother to bring tents for beaches either though, opting for inexpensive bungalow accommodation or simply sleeping out under the stars.

Food and drink

Thai food is now very popular in most Western countries, with a reputation for using fresh ingredients to quickly create dishes that are fiery but fragrant and subtly flavoured. Lemon grass, basil, coriander, galangal, chilli, garlic, lime juice, coconut milk and fermented fish sauce are some of the vital ingredients that give the cuisine its distinctive taste.

Bangkok and Chiang Mai are the country's big culinary centres, boasting the cream of gourmet Thai restaurants and the best international cuisines. The rest of the country is by no means a gastronomic wasteland, however, and you can eat well and cheaply even in the smallest provincial towns, many of which offer the additional attraction of regional specialities. In fact you could eat more than adequately without ever entering a restaurant, as itinerant food vendors hawking hot and cold snacks materialize in even the most remote spots, as well as on trains and buses, and night markets often serve customers from dusk until dawn.

Hygiene is a consideration when eating anywhere in Thailand, but being too cautious means you'll end up spending a lot of money and missing out on some real local treats. Wean your stomach gently by avoiding excessive amounts of chillies and too much fresh fruit in the first few days, and always drink either bottled or boiled water.

You can be pretty sure that any noodle stall or curry shop that's permanently packed with customers is a safe bet, but if you're really concerned about health standards you could stick to restaurants displaying the TAT-approved symbol (also used for shops), which shows a woman seated between two panniers beneath the TAT logo.

Broad **price** categories are appended to restaurant listings throughout this guide: "inexpensive" means you can get a main course for under B60, "moderate" means B60–130, and "expensive" over B130.

Where to eat

Despite their obvious attractions, a lot of tourists eschew the huge range of Thai places to eat and opt instead for the much "safer" restaurants in **guest houses** and **hotels**. Almost all tourist accommodation has a kitchen, and while some are excellent, the vast majority serve up bland imitations of Western fare alongside equally pale versions of common Thai dishes. Having said that, it can be a relief to get your teeth into a processed-cheese sandwich after five days' trekking in the jungle, and guest houses do serve comfortingly familiar Western breakfasts – most farangs quickly tire of eating rice three times a day.

Throughout the country most **inexpensive** Thai restaurants and cafés specialize in one general food type or preparation method – a "noodle shop", for example, will do fried noodles and noodle soups, plus a basic fried rice, but they won't have curries or meat or fish dishes. Similarly, a restaurant displaying whole roast chickens and ducks in its window will offer these sliced, usually with chillies and sauces and served over rice, but their menu probably won't extend to noodles or fish, while in "curry shops" your options are limited to the vats of curries stewing away in the hot cabinet.

To get a wider array of low-cost food, it's sometimes best to head for the local **night market** (*talat yen*), a term for the gatherings of open-air night-time kitchens found in every town. Operating usually from about 6pm to 6am, they are typically to be found on permanent patches close to the fruit and vegetable market or the bus station, and as often as not they're the best and most entertaining places to eat, not to mention the least expensive – after a lip-smacking feast of two savoury dishes, a fruit drink and a sweet you'll come away no more than B70–80 poorer.

A typical night market has some thirty-odd "specialist" pushcart kitchens jumbled together, each fronted by several sets of tables and stools. Noodle and fried-rice vendors always feature prominently, as do sweets stalls, heaped high with sticky rice cakes wrapped in banana leaves or thick with bags of tiny sweetcorn pancakes hot from the griddle – and no night market is complete without its fruit-drink stall, offering banana shakes and freshly squeezed orange, lemon and tomato juices. In the best setups you'll find a lot more besides: curries; barbecued sweetcorn; satay sticks of pork and chicken, fresh pineapple, watermelon and mango; and – if the town's by a river or near the sea – heaps of fresh fish. Having decided what you want, you order from the cook or the cook's dogsbody and sit down at the nearest table; there is no territorialism about night markets, so it's normal to eat several dishes from separate stalls and rely on the nearest cook to sort out the bill.

Some large markets, particularly in Chiang Mai and Bangkok, have separate **food court** areas where you buy coupons first and select food and drink to their value at the stalls of your choice. This is also the modus operandi in the food courts found on the top floor of department stores and shopping centres across the country.

For a more relaxing ambience, Bangkok and the larger towns have a range of **upmarket restaurants**, some specializing in **"royal" Thai cuisine**, which differs from standard fare mainly in the quality of the ingredients and the way the food is presented. As with the nouvelle cuisine of the West, great care is taken over how individual dishes look: they are served in small portions and decorated with carved fruit and vegetables in a way that used to be the prerogative of royal cooks, but has now filtered down to the common folk. The cost of such delights is not prohibitive, either – a meal in one of these places is unlikely to cost more than B500 per person.

How to eat

Thai food is eaten with a fork (left hand) and a spoon (right hand); there is no need for a knife as food is served in bite-sized chunks, which are forked onto the spoon and fed into the mouth. Steamed **rice** (*khao*) is served with most meals, and indeed the most com-

monly heard phrase for "to eat" is *kin khao* (literally, "eat rice"); chopsticks are provided only for noodle dishes, and northeastern sticky-rice dishes are always eaten with the fingers of the right hand. Never eat with the fingers of your left hand, which is used for washing after going to the toilet.

So that complementary taste combinations can be enjoyed, the dishes in a Thai meal are served all at once, even the soup, and shared communally. The more people, the more taste and texture sensations; if there are only two of you, it's normal to order three dishes, plus your own individual plates of steamed rice, while three diners would order four dishes and so on. Only put a serving of one dish on your rice plate each time, and then only one or two spoonfuls.

What to eat

The repertoire of noodles, stir-fries, curries and rice dishes listed below is pretty much standard throughout Thailand. When you get out into the provinces, you'll have the chance to sample a few **specialities** as well, which have evolved either from the cuisines of neighbouring countries or from the crops best suited to that area. Bland food is anathema to Thais, and restaurant tables everywhere come decked out with a **condiment set** featuring the four basic flavours: chopped chillies in watery fish sauce; chopped chillies in vinegar; sugar; and ground red pepper – and often extra bowls of ground peanuts and a bottle of chilli ketchup as well.

Noodle and rice dishes

Thais eat **noodles** (*kway tiaw* or *ba mii*) when Westerners would dig into a sandwich – for lunch, as a late-night snack or just to pass the time – and at B20–30 (around B60 in a posh restaurant) they're the cheapest hot meal you'll find anywhere, whether bought from an itinerant street vendor or ordered in an air-conditioned restaurant. They come in assorted varieties (wide and flat, thin and transparent; made with eggs, soy-bean flour or rice flour) and get boiled up as soups (*kway tiaw nam*), doused in sauces (*kway tiaw rat na*) or stir-fried (*kway tiaw haeng* or *kway tiaw pat*). All three versions include a smattering of vegetables, eggs and meat, but the usual practice is to order the

A food and drink glossary

Note: This glossary includes phonetic guidance to assist you with menu selection; a guide to the Thai language appears in Contexts (p.825).

Basic ingredients

Kài	Chicken
Mŭu	Pork
Néua	Beef, meat
Pèt	Duck
Ahăan thaleh	Seafood
Plaa	Fish
Plaa dùk	Catfish
Plaa mèuk	Squid
Kûng	Prawn, shrimp
Hŏy	Shellfish
Hŏy nang rom	Oyster
Puu	Crab
Khài	Egg
Phàk	Vegetables

Vegetables

Makĕua	Aubergine
Makĕua thêt	Tomato
Nàw mái	Bamboo shoots
Tùa ngâwk	Bean sprouts
Phrík	Chilli
Man faràng	Potato
Man faràng thâwt	Chips
Taeng kwaa	Cucumber
Phrík yùak	Green pepper
Krathiam	Garlic
Hèt	Mushroom
Tùa	Peas, beans or lentils
Tôn hŏrm	Spring onions

Noodles

Ba mìi	Egg noodles
Kwáy tiăw (sên yai/sên lék)	White rice noodles (wide/thin)
Ba mìi kràwp	Crisp fried egg noodles
Kwáy tiăw/ba mìi haêng	Rice noodles/egg noodles fried with egg, small pieces of meat and a few vegetables
Kwáy tiăw/ba mìi nám (mŭu)	Rice noodle/egg noodle soup, made with chicken broth (and pork balls)
Kwáy tiăw/ba mìi rât nâ (mŭu)	Rice noodles/egg noodles fried in gravy-like sauce with vegetables (and pork slices)
Phàt thai	Thin noodles fried with egg, beansprouts and tofu, topped with ground peanuts
Pàt siyú	Wide or thin noodles fried with soy sauce, egg and meat

Rice

Khâo	Rice
Khâo man kài	Slices of chicken served over marinated rice
Khâo mŭu daeng	Red pork with rice
Khâo nâ kài/pèt	Chicken/duck served with sauce over rice
Khâo niăw	Sticky rice
Khâo pàt	Fried rice
Khâo rât kaeng	Curry over rice
Khâo tôm	Rice soup (usually for breakfast)

Curries and soups

Kaeng phèt	Hot, red curry
Kaeng phánaeng	Thick, savoury curry
Kaeng khĭaw wan	Green curry
Kaeng mátsàman	Rich Muslim-style curry, usually with beef and potatoes
Kaeng karìi	Mild, Indian-style curry
Kaeng sôm	Fish and vegetable curry
Tôm khàa kài	Chicken coconut soup
Tôm yam kûng	Hot and sour prawn soup
Kaeng jèut	Mild soup with vegetables and usually pork

dish with extra chicken, beef, pork or shrimps. Most popular of noodle dishes is *kway tiaw phat thai* (usually abbreviated to *phat thai*), a delicious combination of fried noodles, beansprouts, egg and tofu, sprinkled with ground peanuts and the juice of half a lime, and often spiked with tiny dried shrimps.

Fried rice (*khao pat*) is the other faithful standby, much the same price as noodles, and guaranteed to feature on menus right across the country. Curries that come

Other dishes

Hâwy thâwt	Omelette stuffed with mussels
Kài pàt bai kraprao	Chicken fried with basil leaves
Kài pàt nàw mái	Chicken with bamboo shoots
Kài pàt mét mámûang	Chicken with cashew nuts
Kài pàt khīng	Chicken with ginger
Kài yâang	Grilled chicken
Khài yát sài	Omelette with pork and vegetables
Khănom jiin nám yaa	Noodles topped with fish curry
Kûng chúp paêng thâwt	Prawns fried in batter
Lâap	Spicy ground meat
Mūu prîaw wăan	Sweet and sour pork
Néua phàt krathiam phrík thai	Beef fried with garlic and pepper
Néua phàt nám man hŏy	Beef in oyster sauce
Pàt phàk bûng fai daeng	Morning glory fried in garlic and bean sauce
Pàt phàk lăi yàng	Stir-fried vegetables
Pàw pía	Spring rolls
Plaa nêung páe sá	Whole fish steamed with vegetables and ginger
Plaa rât phrík	Whole fish cooked with chillies
Plaa thâwt	Fried whole fish
Sàté	Satay
Sôm tam	Spicy papaya salad
Thâwt man plaa	Fish cake
Yam néua	Grilled beef salad
Yam plaa mèuk	Squid salad
Yam thuù phuu	Wing-bean salad
Yam wun sen	Noodle and pork salad

Thai sweets (khanŏm)

Khanŏm beuang	Small crispy pancake folded over with coconut cream and strands of sweet egg inside
Khâo lăam	Sticky rice, coconut cream and black beans cooked and served in bamboo tubes
Khâo niăw daeng	Sticky red rice mixed with coconut cream
Khâo niăw thúrian/ mámûang	Sticky rice mixed with coconut cream, and durian/mango
Klûay khàek	Fried banana
Lûk taan chêum	Sweet palm kernels served in syrup
Săngkhayaa	Coconut custard
Tàkôh	Squares of transparent jelly (jello) topped with coconut cream

Drinks (khreûang deùm)

Bia	Beer
Chaa ráwn	Hot tea
Chaa yen	Iced tea
Kaafae ráwn	Hot coffee
Kâew	Glass
Khúat	Bottle
Mâekhŏng (or anglicized "Mekhong")	Thai brand-name rice whisky
Nám klûay	Banana shake
Nám mánao/sôm	Fresh, bottled or fizzy lemon/orange juice
Nám plào	Drinking water (boiled or filtered)
Nám sŏdaa	Soda water
Nám tan	Sugar
Nám yen	Cold water
Nom jeùd	Milk
Ohlíang	Iced coffee
Sohdaa	Soda water
Thûay	Cup

Ordering

I am vegetarian/ vegan	*Phŏm* (male)/ *diichăn* (female) *kin ahăan mangsàwirát/jeh*
Can I see the menu?	*Khăw duu menu?*
I would like ...	*Khăw ...*
With/without	*Sài/mâi sài*
Can I have the bill please?	*Khăw check bin?*

served on a bed of steamed rice are more like stews, prepared long in advance and eaten more as a light meal than a main one; they are usually called *khao na* plus the meat of the chosen dish – thus *khao na pet* is duck curry served over rice.

Curries, stir-fries, fish, soups and salads

Thai curries (*kaeng*) are based on coconut milk – which gives them a slightly sweet taste and a soup-like consistency – and get

One of the most refreshing snacks in Thailand is **fruit** (*phŏnlamái*), and you'll find it offered everywhere – neatly sliced in glass boxes on hawker carts, blended into delicious shakes at night market stalls and served as dessert in restaurants. The fruits described below can be found in all parts of Thailand, though some are seasonal. The country's more familiar fruits are not listed here, but include forty varieties of banana (*klûay*), dozens of different mangoes (*mámûang*), three types of pineapple (*sàppàròt*), coconuts (*mapráo*), oranges (*sôm*), lemons (*mánao*) and watermelons (*taeng moh*). To avoid stomach trouble, peel all fruit before eating it, and use common sense when buying it pre-peeled on the street, avoiding anything that looks fly-blown or seems to have been sitting in the sun for hours.

Custard apple (soursop; *nóinà*; July–Sept). Inside the knobbly, muddy green skin you'll find creamy, almond-coloured blancmange-like flesh, having a strong flavour of strawberries and pears with a hint of cinnamon, and many seeds.

Durian (*thúrian*; April–June). Thailand's most prized, and expensive, fruit (see also p.164) has a greeny-yellow, spiky exterior and grows to the size of a football. Inside, it divides into segments of thick, yellow-white flesh which gives off a disgustingly strong stink that's been compared to a mixture of mature cheese and caramel. Not surprisingly, many airlines and hotels ban the eating of this smelly delicacy on their premises. Most Thais consider it the king of fruits, while most foreigners find it utterly foul in both taste and smell.

Guava (*fàràng*; year-round). The apple of the tropics has green textured skin and sweet, crisp flesh that can be pink or white and is studded with tiny edible seeds. Has five times the vitamin C content of an orange and is sometimes eaten cut into strips and sprinkled with sugar and chilli.

Jackfruit (*khanŭn*; year-round). This large, pear-shaped fruit can weigh up to twenty kilograms and has a thick, bobbly, greeny-yellow shell protecting sweet yellow flesh. Green, unripe jackfruit is sometimes cooked as a vegetable in curries.

Lychee (*línjìi*; April–May). Under rough, reddish-brown skin, the lychee has sweet, richly flavoured white flesh, rose-scented and with plenty of vitamin C, round a brown, egg-shaped pit.

Longan (*lamyai*; July–Oct). A close relative of the lychee, with succulent white flesh covered in thin, brittle skin.

Mangosteen (*mangkùt*; April–Sept). The size of a small apple, with smooth, purple skin and a fleshy inside that divides into succulent white segments which are sweet though slightly acidic.

Papaya (paw-paw; *málákaw*; year-round). Looks like an elongated watermelon, with smooth green skin and yellowy-orange flesh that's a rich source of vitamins A and C. It's a favourite in fruit salads and shakes, and sometimes appears in its green, unripe form in salads, notably *som tam*.

Pomelo (*sôm oh*; Oct–Dec). The largest of all the citrus fruits, it looks rather like a grapefruit, though it is slightly drier and has less flavour.

Rambutan (*ngáw*; May–Sept). The bright red rambutan's soft, spiny exterior has given it its name – *rambut* means "hair" in Malay. Usually about the size of a golf ball, it has a white, opaque flesh of delicate flavour, similar to a lychee.

Rose apple (*chomphûu*; year-round). Linked in myth with the golden fruit of immortality, the rose apple is small and egg-shaped, with white, rose-scented flesh.

Sapodilla (sapota; *lámút*; Sept–Dec). These small, brown, rough-skinned ovals look a bit like kiwi fruit and conceal a grainy, yellowish pulp that tastes almost honey-sweet.

Tamarind (*mákhăam*; Dec–Jan). A Thai favourite and a pricey delicacy – carrying the seeds is said to make you safe from wounding by knives or bullets. Comes in rough, brown pods containing up to ten seeds, each surrounded by a sticky, dry pulp which has a sour, lemony taste.

---

their fire from chilli peppers (*phrik*). The best curries are characterized by their **curry pastes**, a subtle blend of freshly ground herbs, spices, garlic, shallots and chilli, the most well known being the red or green curry pastes. It's often possible to request one that's "not too hot" (*mai phet*); if you do bite into a chilli, the way to combat the sear-ing heat is to take a mouthful of plain rice – swigging water just exacerbates the sensation. Alternatively, pick the whole chillies out: contrary to what your eyes might think, the green ones are hotter than the red, and the smaller ones are hotter than the large; thus the tiny green "mouse shit" chillies are small but deadly.

Stir-fries tend to be a lot milder, often flavoured with ginger and whole cloves of garlic and featuring a pleasing combination of soft meat and crunchy vegetables or nuts. Chicken with cashew nuts (*kai pat met mamuang*) is a favourite of a lot of farang-oriented places, as is sweet and sour chicken, pork or fish (*kai/muu/plaa priaw waan*). *Pat phak bung* – slightly bitter morning-glory leaves fried with garlic in a black-bean sauce – makes a good vegetable side dish with any of these.

All seaside and most riverside restaurants rightly make a big deal out of locally caught **fish** and **seafood**. If you order fish it will be served whole, either steamed or grilled with ginger or chillies. Mussels often get stuffed into a batter and shrimps turn up in everything from soups to fried noodles.

You can't make a meal out of a Thai **soup**, but it is an essential component in any shared meal, eaten simultaneously with other dishes, not as a starter. Watery and broth-like, soups are always flavoured with the distinctive tang of lemon grass and kaffir lime leaves, and galangal, and garnished with fresh coriander, and can be extremely hot if the cook adds liberal handfuls of chillies to the pot. Two favourites are *tom kha kai*, a creamy coconut chicken soup; and *tom yam kung*, a prawn soup without coconut milk (the addition of lime juice gives it its distinctive sour flavour).

Another popular part of any proper Thai meal is a spicy, sour **salad** (*yam*), which is often served warm. *Yam* can be made in many permutations – with noodles, meat, seafood or vegetables for example – but at the heart of every variety is a liberal squirt of fresh lime juice and a fiery sprinkling of chopped chillies, a combination which can take some getting used to. The most prevalent variation on this theme is the national dish of the northeast, a spicy green-papaya salad called *som tam*, described under "Regional Dishes".

Sweets

Sweets (*khanom*) don't really figure on most restaurant menus, but a few places offer bowls of *luk taan cheum*, a jellied concoction of lotus or palm seeds floating in a syrup scented with jasmine or other aromatic flowers. Coconut milk is a feature of most other desserts, notably delicious coconut ice cream, and a royal Thai cuisine special of coconut custard (*sangkhayaa*) cooked inside a small pumpkin, whose flesh you can also eat. **Cakes** are sold on the street and tend to be heavy, sticky affairs made from glutinous rice and coconut cream pressed into squares and wrapped in banana leaves.

Regional dishes

Many of the specialities of the **north** originated over the border in Burma; one such is *khao soi*, in which both boiled and crispy egg noodles are served with beef, chicken or pork in a curried coconut soup. Also popular around Chiang Mai are thick spicy sausages (*nam*) made from minced pork, rice and garlic left to cure for a few days and then eaten raw with spicy salad. Somewhat more palatable is the local curry *kaeng hang lay*, made from pork, ginger, garlic and tamarind, and a delicious spicy dipping sauce, *nam phrik ong*, made with minced pork.

The crop most suited to the infertile lands of **Isaan** is **sticky rice** (*khao niaw*), which replaces the standard grain as the staple diet for northeasterners. Served in its own special rattan "sticky rice basket" (the Isaan equivalent of the Tupperware lunchbox), it's usually eaten with the fingers, rolled up into small balls and dipped once (double dipping looks crass to Thai people) into chilli sauces and eaten with side dishes such as the local dish *som tam*, a spicy green-papaya salad with garlic, raw chillies, green beans, tomatoes, peanuts and dried shrimps (or fresh crab).

Although you'll find basted barbecued **chicken** on a stick (*kai yaang*) all over Thailand, it originated in Isaan and is especially tasty in its home region. As with Chiang Mai, Isaan produces its own sausages, called *sai krog isaan*, made from spiced and diced raw pork. Raw minced pork is also the basis of another popular Isaan and northern dish, *larb*, when it is subtly flavoured with mint and served with vegetables.

Aside from putting a greater emphasis on seafood, **southern Thai** cuisine displays a marked Malaysian and Muslim aspect as you near the border. Satays feature more down here, but the two mainstays are the thick, rich and fairly mild Muslim beef curry (*kaeng matsaman*), and the chicken curry served over lightly spiced saffron rice, known as *kaeng karii kai*. You'll find *roti*s in the south, too – pancakes rolled with sickly sweet condensed milk and sugar and sold hot from pushcart griddles.

Vegetarian food

Although very few Thais are **vegetarian** (*mangsawirat*), it's rarely impossible to persuade cooks to rustle up a vegetable-only fried rice or noodle dish, though in more out-of-the-way places that's often your only option unless you eat fish – so you'll need to supplement your diet with the nuts, barbecued sweetcorn, fruit and other non-meaty goodies sold by food stalls. In tourist spots, vegetarians can happily splurge on specially concocted Thai and Western veggie dishes, and some restaurants will come up with a completely separate menu if requested. If you're vegan (*jeh*) you'll need to stress when you order that you don't want egg, as eggs get used a lot; cheese and other dairy produce, however, don't feature at all in Thai cuisine. For an introduction to vegetarianism in Thailand, check out ⓦbangkok.com/healthfood/mangsawirat.shtml.

Drinks

Thais don't drink water straight from the tap, and nor should you; plastic bottles of drinking **water** (*nam plao*) are sold countrywide, even in the smallest villages, for around B10. Cheap restaurants and hotels generally serve free jugs of boiled water which should be fine to drink, though not as foolproof as the bottles.

Night markets, guest houses and restaurants do a good line in freshly squeezed **fruit juices** such as lemon (*nam manao*) and orange (*nam som*), which often come with salt and sugar already added, particularly upcountry. The same places will usually do **fruit shakes** as well, blending bananas (*nam kluay*), papayas (*nam malakaw*), pineapples (*nam sapparot*) and others with liquid sugar or condensed milk (or yoghurt, to make lassi). Fresh **coconut water** (*nam maprao*) is another great thirst-quencher – you buy the whole fruit dehusked, decapitated and chilled; Thais are also very partial to freshly squeezed **sugar-cane juice** (*nam awy*), which is sickeningly sweet.

Bottled brand-name orange and lemon **soft drinks** are sold all over the place for around B10 (particularly in the ubiquitous 7-11 chain stores). Soft-drink bottles are returnable, so some shops and drink stalls have an amazing system of pouring the contents into a small plastic bag (fastened with an elastic band and with a straw inserted) rather than charging you the extra for taking away the bottle. The larger restaurants keep their soft drinks refrigerated, but smaller cafés and shops add ice (*nam khaeng*) to glasses and bags. Most ice is produced commercially under hygienic conditions, but it might become less pure in transit so be wary – and don't take ice if you have diarrhoea. For those travelling with children, or just partial themselves to **dairy products**, UHT-preserved milk and yoghurt drinks are widely available chilled in shops (especially 7-11 stores), as are a variety of soya drinks.

Weak Chinese **tea** (*nam chaa*) makes a refreshing alternative to water and often gets served in Chinese restaurants and roadside cafés. Posher restaurants keep stronger Chinese and Western teas (*chaa*) and **coffee** (*kaafae*), which is nowadays mostly the ubiquitous instant Nescafé. This is usually the coffee offered to farangs even if freshly ground Thai-grown coffee – notably three kinds of hill-tribe coffee from the mountains of the north – is available. If you would like to try Thai coffee, most commonly found at Chinese-style cafés in the south of the country or at outdoor markets, and prepared through filtering the grounds through a cloth, ask for *kaafae thung* (literally, "bag coffee"), normally served very bitter with sugar as well as sweetened condensed milk alongside a glass of black tea to wash it down with. Fresh Western-style coffee, usually brewed, is mostly limited to farang-oriented places, international-style coffee bars and big hotels, in Bangkok, Chiang Mai and beach areas. Tea and coffee are normally served black, perhaps with a sachet of coffee whitener on the side.

Alcoholic drinks

Beer (*bia*) is one of the few consumer items in Thailand that's not a bargain due to the heavy taxes levied on the beverage – at B60 for a 330ml bottle it works out roughly the same as what you'd pay in the West (larger, 660ml bottles, when available, are always slightly better value). The most famous beer is the slightly acrid locally brewed Singha, but Kloster, which is also brewed locally and costs about B5–10 more than Singha, is easier on the tongue. Some places also stock a lighter version of Singha called Singha Gold, and another local beer called Amarit, though it's not widely distributed. Carlsberg and Heineken are now widely found in Thailand, and in the most touristed areas you'll find imported bottles from all over the world, even Corona. Carlsberg, which part-owns a Thai brewery, also produces the ubiquitous Chang (Elephant), usually the cheapest beer available, with a head-banging seven percent alcohol content.

Thai **wine** is now produced in the northeast at a winery called Château de Loei near Phu Reua National Park in Loei province; a red, using shiraz grapes, and a *chenin blanc*, are quite tasty and can be tried at upmarket restaurants or bought at the Maison du Vin wineshop in Thaniya Plaza, Thanon Silom, Bangkok.

At about B60 for a hip-flask-sized 375ml bottle, the local **whisky** is a lot better value,

and Thais think nothing of consuming a bottle a night. The most palatable and widely available of these is Mekhong, which is very pleasant once you've stopped expecting it to taste like Scotch; distilled from rice, Mekhong is 35 percent proof, deep gold in colour and tastes slightly sweet. If that's not to your taste, a pricier Thai **rum** is also available, Sang Thip, made from sugar cane, and even stronger than the whisky at forty percent proof. Check the menu carefully when ordering a bottle of Mekhong from a bar in a tourist area, as they often ask up to five times more than you'd pay in a guest house or shop.

You can **buy** beer and whisky in food stores, guest houses and most restaurants at any time of the day; **bars** aren't really an indigenous feature as Thais rarely drink out without eating, but you'll find a fair number of Western-style drinking holes in Bangkok and tourist centres elsewhere in the country, ranging from ultra-hip haunts in the capital to basic, open-to-the-elements **"bar beers"**.

Telephones, mail and internet access

Thailand boasts a fast and efficient communications network: international mail services are relatively speedy, phoning overseas is possible even from some small islands and internet access is available in every sizeable town.

Mail

Mail takes around seven days to get between Bangkok and Europe or North America, a little longer from the more isolated areas. Almost all **main post offices** across the country operate a **poste restante** service and will hold letters for two to three months. Mail should be addressed: Name (family name underlined or capitalized), Poste Restante, GPO, Town or City,

Thailand. It will be filed by surname, though it's always wise to check under your first initial as well. The smaller post offices pay scant attention to who takes what, but in the busier GPOs you need to show your passport, pay B1 per item received and sign for them. Most GPO poste restantes follow regular post office hours (Mon–Fri 8am–4pm, Sat 8am–noon; some close Mon–Fri noon–1pm and may stay open until 6pm) – exceptions are explained in the guide.

American Express in Bangkok and Phuket also offers a poste restante facility of up to sixty days to holders of Amex credit cards or traveller's cheques: see the relevant accounts in the guide for details.

Post offices are the best places to buy **stamps**, though hotels and guest houses often sell them too, charging an extra B1 per stamp. An airmail letter of under 10g costs around B17 to send to Europe or Australia and B19 to North America; standard-sized postcards cost B12 (anything smaller or larger costs B15), and aerogrammes B15, regardless of where they're going. All **parcels** must be officially boxed and sealed (for a small fee) at special counters within main post offices or in a private outlet just outside – you can't just turn up with a package and buy stamps for it. In tourist centres (especially at Bangkok's GPO) be prepared to queue, first for the packaging, then for the weighing and then again for the buying of stamps. The surface rate for a parcel of up to 5kg is B700 to the UK and the US and B540 for Australia, and the package should reach its destination in three months; the airmail parcel service is almost three times as expensive and takes about a week.

Phones

By and large the Thai phone system works well. Payphones are straightforward enough and generally come in three varieties: red or pale blue for **local calls**, blue or stainless steel for **long-distance calls within Thailand**, and green cardphones for either. Red and pale blue phones take the small one-baht coins and will give you three minutes per B1. Blue and stainless steel ones gobble up B5 coins (inter-provincial rates vary with distance, but on the whole are surprisingly pricey) and are generally unreliable, so you're better off buying a **phonecard**, available in a range of denominations from B25 to B240 from hotels, post offices and a wide variety of shops. In some provincial towns, enterprising mobile-phone owners hang out on the main streets offering cheap long-distance calls.

When dialling any number in Thailand, you must always **preface the number with the area code**, even when dialling from the same area. Anything that's prefaced with a ☏01 is a cell phone or satellite phone number (most guest houses on islands like Ko

Phi Phi and Ko Chang have satellite phones). Where we've given several line numbers – eg ☏02/431 1802–9 – you can substitute the last digit with any number between 3 and 9. For **directory enquiries** within Thailand, call t1133. One final local idiosyncrasy: Thai phone books list people by their first, not their family names.

An increasing number of tourists are taking their **mobile phones** to Thailand. Visitors from the US need to have a tri-band phone though, and not all foreign networks have links with Thai networks, so check with your phone provider before you travel. Whichever your network, you may well have to ask for the "international bar" to be lifted before you set off. It's also worth checking how much coverage there is for your network within Thailand, and asking in advance for a summary of rates for incoming as well as outgoing calls while you're there; some networks offer flat-rate deals on international usage, which can save you a lot of money.

International calls

The least costly way of making an international call is to use the **government telephone centres** (open daily, typically 8am–10pm, 24hr in Bangkok and Chiang Mai), run by the Communications Authority of Thailand, or **CAT**; they're nearly always located within or adjacent to the town's main post office. At government phone centres, you're allotted an individual booth and left to do the dialling.

International dialling codes

If you're dialling from abroad, the international code for Thailand is ☏66. Calling out of Thailand, dial ☏001 and then the relevant country code:

Australia	61
Canada	1
Ireland	353
Netherlands	31
New Zealand	64
UK	44
US	1

Bangkok is seven hours ahead of GMT, twelve hours ahead of Eastern Standard Time and three hours behind Sydney. For **international directory enquiries** call ☏100.

For international IDD phone calls made on private lines and at government telephone offices, there are three time periods with different **rates**. The most expensive, or **standard**, time to call is from 7am to 9pm (a twenty percent discount applies on Sundays); the **economy** period runs from 9pm to midnight and from 5am to 7am; the **reduced** rate applies between midnight and 5am. The per-minute rate for a call to Europe is around B42 standard; B34 economy; and B30 reduced; for North America and Australia it's B24/20/20. An operator-assisted call always costs slightly more. It's possible to call internationally at government rates on the green public **cardphones**, but for international calls these phones only accept phonecards of B500 and above. (You can use any public long-distance phone to call Laos and Malaysia, and can do so on phonecards of less than B500 if you want.)

If you can't get to one of the official government places, try the slightly more expensive **private international call offices** in tourist areas (such as Bangkok's Thanon Khao San), or the even pricier services offered by the posher hotels. Many guest houses on touristy islands like Ko Samet, Ko Chang and Ko Phi Phi have satellite phones which guests can use to call long distance and overseas (phone numbers for these are prefixed by ℗01).

There's also a private international cardphone system called **Lenso**, which operates in Bangkok and the biggest resorts. The phones are bright orange and have been installed all over the place. To use them, you either need a special Lenso phonecard (available from shops near the phones in B200 and B500 denominations), or you can use a credit card. The main drawback with Lenso phones is that the rates are ten percent higher than government IDD rates.

A BT **chargecard** allows British travellers to charge calls from Thailand to their home phone bill; AT&T, MCI and other North American long-distance companies enable their customers to make credit-card calls from Thailand (before you leave, call your company's customer service line to find out the toll-free access code in Thailand). Telephone cards such as Australia's Telstra Telecard or Optus Calling Card and New Zealand Telecom's Calling Card can be used to make calls abroad, which are charged back to a domestic account or credit card.

Collect or **reverse-charge calls** can be made free of charge at government phone centres, or from many guest houses and private phone offices, usually for a fee of B100. You can also make Home Country Direct calls from government phone centres, for which you pay a nominal charge to get through to your home country operator, who arranges for you to make a credit-card or reverse-charge call.

Faxes

Most major post offices offer a domestic and international **fax service** and, as with phone calls, this is where you'll get the cheapest rates – currently around B120 per page to Australia, North America or the UK. Private phone centres will also send faxes for you, as will most guest houses, for which you can expect to pay up to fifty percent more than government rates. Many also offer a "fax restante" service for customers and guests, though as filing systems vary in these places, you might want to check them out before giving fax numbers to your correspondents. Wherever possible, guest-house and hotel fax numbers are given in the guide.

Internet access

Internet access is very widespread and very inexpensive in Thailand. You'll find traveller-oriented **cybercafés** in every touristed town and resort in the country – there are at least twenty in the Banglamphu district of Bangkok, for example – and even islands without land lines, like Ko Samet and Ko Chang, provide (expensive) internet access via satellite phones. In mid-sized towns that don't get much tourist traffic, internet centres are also increasingly popular, making their money from schoolboys who play computer games for hours on end, though travellers are welcome to use these places for emailing as well. Competition keeps prices low: upcountry you could expect to pay as little as B20 per hour, while rates in tourist centres average B1 per minute. Upmarket hotels are the exception, often charging as much as B100 per half-hour or B3–5 per minute. Nearly every mid-sized town in Thailand also offers a public internet service, called **Catnet**, at the government telephone office (usually located inside or adjacent to the main post office). To use the service, you need to buy a B100 card with a Catnet PIN (available at all phone offices), which gives you three hours of internet time at any of these public terminals.

Before leaving home you should check whether your existing **email account** offers a web-based service that enables you to pick up your email from any internet terminal in the world. This is becoming increasingly common and is very useful and straightforward, though it can sometimes be a bit slow. If this does not apply to you, it's well worth setting yourself up with a **free email account** for the duration of the trip, either before you leave home (using someone else's system or through a local cybercafé) or in a cybercafé in Thailand. Several companies offer this free email service, but by far the most popular are those run by Hotmail (ⓦwww.hotmail.com) and Yahoo (ⓦwww.yahoo.com). Both Hotmail and Yahoo are completely free to join, and every cybercafé in Thailand will have them book-marked for speedy access.

If you plan to email from your **laptop** in Thailand, be advised that very few budget guest houses and cheap hotels have telephone sockets in the room, and that many upmarket hotels charge astronomical rates for international calls. One potentially useful way round the cost issue is to become a temporary subscriber to the **Thai ISP** Loxinfo (ⓦwww.loxinfo.co.th), which has local dial-up numbers in every province in Thailand. Their Webnet deal is aimed at international businesspeople and tourists and can be bought online; it allows you 25 hours of internet access for B500 or 45 hours for B700. The usual phone plug in Thailand is the American standard RJ11 phone jack. See the Help for World Travellers website (ⓦwww.kropla.com) for detailed advice on how to set up your modem before you go, and how to hardwire phone plugs where necessary.

The media

To keep you abreast of world affairs there are several English-language newspapers in Thailand, though a mild form of censorship affects the predominantly state-controlled media, even muting the English-language branches on occasion.

Newspapers and magazines

Of the hundreds of **Thai-language newspapers and magazines** published every week, the sensationalist tabloid *Thai Rath* attracts the widest readership, the independent *Siam Rath* the most intellectual. Alongside these, two daily **English-language papers** – the *Bangkok Post* and the *Nation* – both adopt a fairly critical attitude to governmental goings-on and cover major domestic and international stories as well as tourist-related issues. Of the two, the *Bangkok Post* tends to focus more on international stories, while the *Nation* has the most in-depth coverage of Thai and Southeast Asian issues. Both detail English-language cinema programmes, TV schedules and expat social events, and are sold at most newsstands in the capital as well as in major provincial towns and tourist resorts; the more isolated places receive their few copies at least one day late. *Bangkok Metro*, the capital's monthly English-language **listings magazine**, is also a good read; as well as reviews and previews of events in the city, it carries lively articles on cultural and contemporary life in Thailand.

You can also pick up **foreign publications** such as *Newsweek*, *Time* and the *International Herald Tribune* in Bangkok, Chiang Mai, Phuket and Pattaya; expensive hotels sometimes carry air-freighted copies of foreign national newspapers for at least B50 a copy. The weekly current affairs magazine *Asiaweek* is also worth looking out for; available in major bookshops and at newsstands in tourist centres, it generally offers a very readable selection of articles on Thailand and the rest of Asia.

Television

Channel 9 is Thailand's major **TV station**, transmitting news, quiz shows and predominantly imported cartoons and dramas to all parts of the country. Four other networks broadcast to Bangkok – the privately run Channel 3, the military-controlled channels 5 and 7, and the Ministry of Education's Channel 11 – but not all are received in every province. **Cable** networks – available in many mid-range and most upmarket hotel rooms – carry channels from all around the world, including CNN, NBC and MTV from North America, BBC World from the UK, IBC from Australia, the HBO English-language movie channel, and several Star channels from India.

Both the *Bangkok Post* and the *Nation* print the daily TV and cable **schedule**, and they also tell you which English-language programmes are dubbed in Thai. **English soundtracks** for some programmes are transmitted simultaneously on FM radio as follows – Channel 3: 105.5 MHz; Channel 7: 103.5 MHz; Channel 9: 107 MHz; Channel 11: 88 MHz.

Radio

With a shortwave radio, you can pick up the BBC World Service, Radio Australia, Voice of America and various other international stations on a variety of bands right across the country. Times and wavelengths can change every three months, so get hold of a recent schedule just before you travel. The BBC World Service website (✇www.bbc.co.uk/worldservice) carries current frequency details in a useful format that's designed to be printed out and carried with you. For current listings of all major English-language radio station frequencies while you're in Thailand, consult the *Bangkok Post*'s weekly magazine *Real Time*, which comes free with the Friday edition of the paper.

Bangkok is served by a handful of English-language **FM stations**. Radio Thailand broadcasts news, current affairs and sports results in several languages (including English) on 97 MHz from 6am to 11pm. Apart from a few specialist shows, Gold FMX 95.6 pumps out nonstop upbeat chart hits from 5am through to 2am; there are few pauses for chat, except for local and international headlines on the half hour. Proud to dub itself "Bangkok's premier easy-listening station", Smooth 105 FM rarely veers from the middle of the road; international news breaks in on the hour. Bilingual Soft FM (107FM) follows current and classic music trends, with hourly breaks for CNN news reports. At the opposite end of the taste spectrum, Chulalongkorn University Radio (101.5FM) plays a wide selection of Western jazz every day from 4 to 6.30pm, and classical music from 10.30pm to 1am every night.

Crime and personal safety

As long as you keep your wits about you, you shouldn't encounter much trouble in Thailand. Theft and pickpocketing are two of the main problems – not surprising considering that a huge percentage of the local population scrape by on under US$5 per day – but by far the most common cause for concern is the burgeoning number of opportunistic con-artists who manage to dupe ill-informed, over-trusting or foolhardy tourists into unwisely parting with their cash.

To **prevent theft**, most travellers prefer to carry their valuables with them at all times, either in a money belt, neck pouch or inside pocket, but it's sometimes possible to leave your valuables in a hotel or guest-house locker – the safest lockers are those which require your own padlock, as there are occasional reports of valuables being stolen by hotel staff. Padlock your luggage when leaving it in hotel or guest-house rooms, as well as when consigning it to storage or taking it on public transport. Padlocks also come in handy as extra security on your room, particularly on the doors of beachfront bamboo huts.

Avoiding **scams** means that you must be on your guard against anyone who makes an unnatural effort to befriend you – which, as everywhere else in the world, means treading a fine line between paranoia and healthy suspicion. In one of the more well-known scams in Bangkok, pseudo tourist officials hang around the main train station and take unsuspecting travellers to a disreputable private tour company – falling victim to this kind of con is rarely dangerous but always frustrating, so it's worth heeding the specific warnings that you'll find throughout the guide. It's also become increasingly common for Bangkok tuk-tuk drivers to pretend that the Grand Palace or other major sight is closed for the day, so that they get to take you on a round-city tour instead; the easiest way to avoid these rip-offs is to take a metered taxi, but for more advice see p.104. Never buy anything from **touts**: gemstone con-men prey on greedy and gullible tourists, mostly in Bangkok – for information about buying stones and avoiding stings, see p.186.

On a more dangerous note, beware of **drug** scams: either being shopped by a dealer (Chiang Mai samlor drivers are notorious, and there are setups at the Ko Pha Ngan full-moon parties) or having substances slipped into your luggage – simple enough to perpetrate unless all fastenings are secured with padlocks. **Drug smuggling** carries a maximum penalty of death and will almost certainly get you five to twenty years in a Thai prison. Despite occasional royal pardons, don't expect special treatment as a farang: because of its reputation as a major source of drugs, Thailand works hard to keep on the right side of the US and in most cases makes a big show of dishing out heavy sentences. Even more alarming, drug enforcement squads are said to receive 25 percent of the market value of seized drugs, so are liable to exaggerate the amounts involved.

Violent crime against tourists is not common, but it does occur. There have been several serious attacks on women travellers in the last few years, which are good enough reason to be extra-vigilant wherever you are in Thailand, at whatever time of day. However, bearing in mind that over five million foreign tourists visit Thailand every year, the statistical likelihood of becoming a victim is extremely small. Obvious precautions for travellers of either sex include locking accessible windows and doors at night – preferably with your own padlock (doors in many of the simpler guest houses and beach bungalows are designed for this) – and not travelling alone at night in a taxi or tuk-tuk. Nor should you risk jumping into an unlicensed taxi at Don Muang airport at any time of day:

there have been some very violent robberies in these, so take the well-marked authorized vehicles instead or, better still, the airport bus. If you're going hiking on your own for a day, it's a good idea to inform guest-house or hotel staff of where you're planning to go, so they have some idea of where to look for you if necessary.

Be wary of accepting food and drink from strangers, especially on long overnight bus or train journeys, as it may be drugged so as to knock you out while your bags are stolen. This might sound paranoid, but there have been enough drug-muggings for TAT to publish a specific warning about the problem. Unfortunately, it is also necessary for female tourists to think twice about spending time alone with a **monk**, as not all men of the cloth uphold the Buddhist precepts and there have been rapes and murders committed by men wearing the saffron robes of the monkhood (see p.787 for more about the changing Thai attitudes towards the monkhood).

You're more likely to read about armed struggles than experience one, but nevertheless it's advisable to travel with a guide in certain **border areas** or, if you're on a motorbike, to take advice before setting off. As these regions are generally covered in dense unmapped jungle, you shouldn't find yourself alone in the vicinity anyway, but the main stretches to watch are the Burmese border north of Three Pagodas Pass, between Mae Sot and Mae Sariang, around Mae Sai, and between Umphang and Sangkhlaburi – where villages, hideaways and refugee camps occasionally get shelled either by the Burmese military or by rebel Karen or Mon forces – and the border between Cambodia and southern Isaan, which is littered with unexploded mines.

Among hazards to watch out for in the natural world, **riptides** have claimed too many tourist lives to ignore, particularly off Phuket and Ko Samui during stormy periods of the monsoon season, so always pay attention to warning signs and red flags, and always ask locally if unsure. Crazed **elephants** have gored and occasionally killed tourists at elephant shows and theme parks, usually when baited or scared, for example by a flashgun held too close.

Reporting a crime or emergency

TAT has a special department for tourist-related crimes and complaints called the Tourist Assistance Center (**TAC**). Set up specifically to mediate between tourists, police and accused persons (particularly shopkeepers and tour agents), TAC has an office in the TAT headquarters on Thanon Rajdamnoen Nok, Bangkok (daily 8.30am–4.30pm; ☎02/281 5051). In **emergencies**, always contact the English-speaking **tourist police** who maintain a toll-free nationwide line (☎1699) and have offices within or adjacent to many regional TAT offices – getting in touch with the tourist police first is invariably more efficient than directly contacting the local police, ambulance or fire service.

Sexual harassment

Though unpalatable and distressing, Thailand's high-profile sex industry is relatively unthreatening for Western women, with its energy focused exclusively on farang men; it's also quite easily avoided, being contained within certain pockets of the capital and a couple of beach resorts. As for **harassment** from men, it's hard to generalize, but most Western tourists find it less of a problem in Thailand than they do back home. Outside of the main tourist spots, you're more likely to be of interest as a foreigner rather than a woman and, if travelling alone, as an object of concern rather than of sexual aggression.

Opening hours and holidays

Most shops open at least Monday to Saturday from about 8am to 8pm, while department stores operate daily from around 10am to 9pm. Private office hours are generally Monday to Friday 8am–5pm and Saturday 8am–noon, though in tourist areas these hours are longer, with weekends worked like any other day. Government offices work Monday to Friday 8.30am–noon and 1–4.30pm, and national museums tend to stick to these hours too, but some close on Mondays and Tuesdays rather than at weekends.

Most tourists only register **national holidays** because trains and buses suddenly get extraordinarily crowded: although banks and government offices shut down on these days, most shops and tourist-oriented businesses carry on regardless, and TAT branches continue to dispense information. The only time an inconvenient number of shops, restaurants and hotels do close is during Chinese New Year, which, though not marked as an official national holiday, brings many businesses to a standstill for several days in late January or February. You'll notice it particularly in the south, where most service industries are Chinese-managed.

A brief note on **dates**. Thais use both the Western Gregorian calendar and a Buddhist calendar – the Buddha is said to have died (or entered Nirvana) in the year 543 BC, so Thai dates start from that point: thus 2002 AD becomes 2545 BE (Buddhist Era).

National holidays

January 1 Western New Year's Day
February (day of full moon) Maha Puja: Commemorates the Buddha preaching to a spontaneously assembled crowd of 1250.
April 6 Chakri Day: The founding of the Chakri dynasty.
April (usually 13–15) Songkhran: Thai New Year.
May 5 Coronation Day
May (early in the month) Royal Ploughing Ceremony: Marks start of rice-planting season.
May (day of full moon) Visakha Puja: The holiest of all Buddhist holidays, which celebrates the birth, enlightenment and death of the Buddha.
July (day of full moon) Asanha Puja: Commemorates the Buddha's first sermon.
July (the day after Asanha Puja) Khao Pansa: The start of the annual three-month Buddhist rains retreat, when new monks are ordained.
August 12 Queen's birthday
October 23 Chulalongkorn Day: The anniversary of Rama V's death.
December 5 King's birthday
December 10 Constitution Day
December 31 Western New Year's Eve

Festivals

Hardly a week goes by without some kind of local or national festival being celebrated somewhere in Thailand, and most make great entertainment for participants and spectators alike. All the festivals listed below are spectacular or engaging enough to be worth altering your itinerary for, but bear in mind that for some of the more publicized celebrations (notably those in the northeast) you'll need to book transport and accommodation a week or more in advance.

Nearly all Thai festivals have some kind of religious aspect. The most theatrical are generally **Brahmanic** (Hindu) in origin, honouring elemental spirits with ancient rites and ceremonial costumed parades. **Buddhist** celebrations usually revolve round the local temple, and while merit-making is a significant feature, a light-hearted atmosphere prevails, ao the wat grounds are swamped with food- and trinket-vendors and makeshift stages are set up to show *likay* folk theatre, singing competitions and beauty contests.

Many of the secular festivals (like the elephant roundups and the Bridge Over the River Kwai spectacle) are outdoor local culture shows, geared specifically towards Thai and farang tourists and thus slightly artificial, though no less enjoyable for that. Others are thinly veiled trade fairs held in provincial capitals to show off the local speciality, which nevertheless assume all the trappings of a temple fair and so are usually worth a look.

Few of the **dates** for religious festivals are fixed, so check with TAT for specifics. The names of the most touristy celebrations are given here in English; the more low-key festivals are more usually known by their Thai name (*ngan* means "festival").

A festival calendar

January–March

Chaiyaphum Ngan Chao Poh Phraya Lae: The founder of modern Chaiyaphum is feted with parades, music and dance (Jan 12–20).

Chiang Mai Flower Festival: Enormous floral sculptures are paraded through the streets (usually first weekend in Feb).

Nationwide (particularly Wat Benjamabophit in Bangkok and Wat Phra That Doi Suthep in Chiang Mai) Maha Puja: A day of merit-making marks the occasion when 1250 disciples gathered spontaneously to hear the Buddha preach, and culminates with a candlelit procession round the local temple's bot (Feb full-moon day).

Phitsanulok Ngan Phra Buddha Chinnarat: Thailand's second most important Buddha image is honoured with music, dance and *likay* performances (mid-Feb).

Phetchaburi Phra Nakhon Khiri fair: *Son et lumière* at Khao Wang palace (mid-Feb).

That Phanom Ngan Phra That Phanom: Thousands come to pay homage at the holiest shrine in Isaan, which houses relics of the Buddha (Feb).

Pattani Ngan Lim Ko Niaw: Local goddess inspires devotees to walk through fire and perform other endurance tests in public (middle of third lunar month – Feb or March).

Nationwide (particularly Sanam Luang, Bangkok) Kite fights and flying contests (late Feb to mid-April).

Nakhon Si Thammarat Hae Pha Khun That: Southerners gather to pay homage to the Buddha relics at Wat Mahathat, including a procession of long saffron cloth around the chedi (twice a year, coinciding with Maha Puja in Feb and Visakha Puja in May).

Yala ASEAN Barred Ground Dove festival: International dove-cooing contests (first weekend of March).

Phra Phutthabat, near Lopburi Ngan Phra Phutthabat: Pilgrimages to the Holy Footprint attract food- and handicraft-vendors and travelling players (early Feb and early March).

Khorat Ngan Thao Suranari: Nineteenth-century local heroine is honoured with a week of parades and exhibitions (late March).

April and May

Mae Hong Son and Chiang Mai Poy Sang Long: Young Thai Yai boys precede their ordination into monkhood by parading the streets in floral headdresses and festive garb (early April). See p.363 for more.

Nationwide (especially Chiang Mai and Prasat Hin Khao Phanom Rung) Songkhran: The most exuberant of the national festivals welcomes the Thai New Year with massive waterfights, sandcastle building in temple compounds and the inevitable parades and "Miss Songkhran" beauty contests (usually April 13–15).

Prasat Hin Khao Phanom Rung Ngan Phanom Rung: Daytime processions up to the eleventh-century Khmer ruins, followed by *son et lumière* (April full-moon day).

Nationwide (particularly Bangkok's Wat Benjamabophit) Visakha Puja: The holiest day of the Buddhist year, commemorating the birth, enlightenment and death of the Buddha all in one go; the most public and photogenic part is the candlelit evening procession around the wat (May full-moon day).

Sanam Luang, Bangkok Raek Na: The royal ploughing ceremony to mark the beginning of the rice-planting season; ceremonially clad Brahmin leaders parade sacred oxen and the royal plough, and interpret omens to forecast the year's rice yield (early May).

Yasothon Rocket festival (Bun Bang Fai): Beautifully crafted painted wooden rockets are paraded and fired to ensure plentiful rains; celebrated all over Isaan, but especially lively in Yasothon (weekend in mid-May).

June–September

Dan Sai, near Loei Phi Ta Khon: Masked re-enactment of the Buddha's penultimate incarnation (end of June or beginning of July).

Ubon Ratchathani Candle Festival (Asanha Puja): Ubon citizens celebrate the nationwide festival to mark the Buddha's first sermon and the subsequent beginning of the annual Buddhist retreat period (Khao Pansa) with parades of enormous wax sculptures (July, three days around the full moon).

Phra Phutthabat, near Lopburi Tak Bat Dok Mai: Another merit-making festival at the Holy Footprint, this time on the occasion of the start of Khao Pansa, the annual three-month Buddhist retreat period (July around full-moon day).

Nakhon Pathom Food and fruits fair (Ngan Phonlamai): Cooking and fruit-carving demonstrations and folk-theatre performances in the chedi compound (first week of Sept).

Nakhon Si Thammarat Tamboon Deuan Sip: Merit-making ceremonies to honour dead relatives accompanied by a ten-day fair on the town field (Sept or Oct).

October–December

Phuket and Trang Vegetarian Festival (Ngan Kin Jeh): Chinese devotees become vegetarian for a nine-day period and then parade through town performing acts of self-mortification such as pushing skewers through their cheeks. Celebrated in Bangkok's Chinatown with most food vendors and restaurants turning vegetarian for about a fortnight (Oct).

Nationwide (especially Ubon Ratchathani and Nakhon Phanom) Tak Bat Devo and Awk Pansa: Offerings to monks and general merrymaking to celebrate the Buddha's descent to earth from Tavatimsa heaven and the end of the Khao Pansa retreat. Celebrated in Ubon with a procession of illuminated boats along the river and lots of firecrackers, and in Nakhon Phanom with a boat procession and Thai–Lao dragon-boat races along the Mekong (Oct full-moon day).

Surat Thani Chak Phra: The town's chief Buddha images are paraded on floats down the streets and on barges along the river (mid-Oct).

Nan and Phimai Boat races: Longboat races and barge parades along town rivers (mid-Oct to mid-Nov).

Nationwide Thawt Kathin: The annual ceremonial giving of new robes by the laity to the monkhood at the end of the rains retreat (mid-Oct to mid-Nov).

Nationwide (especially Sukhothai and Chiang Mai) Loy Krathong: Baskets (*krathong*) of flowers and lighted candles are floated on any available body of water (such as ponds, rivers, lakes, canals and seashores) to honour water spirits and celebrate the end of the rainy season. Nearly every town puts on a big show, with bazaars, public entertainments, fireworks, and in Chiang Mai, the release of balloons; in Sukhothai it is the climax of a nine-day *son et lumière* festival (late Oct or early Nov).

Wat Saket, Bangkok Ngan Wat Saket: Probably Thailand's biggest temple fair, held around the Golden Mount, with all the usual festival trappings (first week of Nov).

Surin Elephant roundup: Two hundred elephants play team games, perform complex tasks and parade in battle dress (third weekend of Nov).

Nakhon Pathom Ngan Phra Pathom Chedi: Week-long jamboree held in the grounds of the chedi with itinerant musicians, food-vendors and fortune-tellers (Nov).

Kanchanaburi River Kwai Bridge festival: Spectacular *son et lumière* at the infamous bridge (ten nights from the last week of Nov into the first week of Dec).

Khon Kaen Silk Festival: Weavers from around the province come to town to sell their lengths of silk (Nov 29–Dec 10).

Ayutthaya World Heritage Site Festival: Week-long celebration, including a nightly historical *son et lumière* romp, to commemorate the town's UNESCO designation (mid-Dec).

Entertainment and sport

Most travellers confine their experience of Thai traditional culture to a one-off attendance at a big Bangkok tourist show, but these extravaganzas are far less rewarding than authentic folk theatre, music (see p.802) and sports performances. Traditional sport fits neatly into the same category as the more usual theatrical classifications, not only because it can be graceful, even dance-like, to watch, but because, in the case of Thai boxing, Thai classical music plays an important role in the proceedings. Bangkok has one authentic fixed venue for dance and a couple for Thai boxing; otherwise it's a question of keeping your eyes open in upcountry areas for signs that a travelling troupe may soon turn up.

Drama and dance

Drama pretty much equals **dance** in Thai theatre, and many of the traditional dance-dramas are based on the Hindu epic the *Ramayana* (in Thai, *Ramakien*), a classic adventure tale of good versus evil which is taught in all the schools. Not understanding the plots can be a major disadvantage, so try reading an abridged version beforehand (see "Books", p.822) and check out the wonderfully imaginative murals at Wat Phra Kaeo in Bangkok, after which you'll certainly be able to sort the goodies from the baddies, if little else. There are three broad categories of traditional Thai dance-drama –

khon, lakhon and *likay* – described below in descending order of refinement.

Khon

The most spectacular form of traditional Thai theatre is **khon**, a stylized drama performed in masks and elaborate costumes by a troupe of highly trained classical dancers. There's little room for individual interpretation in these dances, as all the movements follow a strict choreography that's been passed down through generations: each graceful, angular gesture depicts a precise event, action or emotion which will be familiar to educated *khon* audiences. The dancers don't speak, and the story is chanted and sung by a chorus who stand at the side of the stage, accompanied by a classical *phipat* orchestra.

A typical *khon* performance features several of the best-known **Ramayana** episodes, in which the main characters are recognized by their masks, headdresses and heavily brocaded costumes. Gods and humans don't wear masks, but it's generally easy enough to distinguish the hero Rama and heroine Sita from the action; they always wear tall gilded headdresses and often appear in a threesome with Rama's brother Lakshaman. Monkey masks are always open-mouthed, almost laughing, and come in several colours: monkey army chief Hanuman always wears white, and his two right-hand men – Nilanol, the god of fire, and Nilapat, the god of death – wear red and black respectively. In contrast, the demons have grim mouths, clamped shut or snarling out of usually green faces; Totsagan, king of the demons, wears a green face in battle and a gold one during peace, but always sports a two-tier headdress carved with two rows of faces.

Khon is performed regularly at Bangkok's National Theatre and nightly at various cultural shows staged by tourist restaurants in Bangkok, Chiang Mai and Pattaya. Even if you don't see a show you're bound to come across copies of the masks worn by the main *khon* characters, which are sold as souvenirs all over the country and constitute an art form in their own right.

Lakhon

Serious and refined, **lakhon** is derived from *khon* but is used to dramatize a greater range of stories, including Buddhist *Jataka* tales, local folk dramas and of course the *Ramayana*. The form you're most likely to come across is *lakhon chatri*, which is performed at shrines like Bangkok's Erawan and *lak muang* as entertainment for the spirits and a token of gratitude from worshippers. Usually female, the *lakhon chatri* dancers perform as a group rather than as individual characters, executing sequences which, like *khon* movements, all have minute and particular symbolism. They wear similarly decorative costumes but no masks, and dance to the music of a *phipat* orchestra. Unfortunately, as resident shrine troupes tend to repeat the same dances a dozen times a day, it's rarely the sublime display it's cracked up to be. Occasionally the National Theatre features the more elegantly executed *lakhon nai*, a dance form that used to be performed at the Thai court and often retells the *Ramayana*.

Likay

Likay is a much more popular derivative of *khon* – more light-hearted with lots of comic interludes, bawdy jokes and over-the-top acting and singing. Some *likay* troupes perform *Ramayana* excerpts, but a lot of them adapt pot-boiler romances or write their own. Depending on the show, costumes are either traditional as in *khon* and *lakhon*, modern and Western as in films, or a mixture of both. *Likay* troupes travel around the country doing shows on makeshift outdoor stages wherever they think they'll get an audience; temples sometimes hire them out for fairs and there's usually a *likay* stage of some kind at a festival – if you happen to be in Thailand on the King's Birthday (December 5th), for example, you'll definitely catch a *likay* show somewhere in town. Performances are often free and generally last for about five hours, with the audience strolling in and out of the show, cheering and joking with the cast throughout. Televised *likay* dramas get huge audiences and always follow romantic plot-lines.

Nang

Nang or shadow plays are said to have been the earliest dramas performed in Thailand, but now are rarely seen except in the far south, where the Malaysian influence ensures an appreciative audience for *nang thalung*. Crafted from buffalo hide, the two-dimensional *nang thalung* puppets play out scenes from popular dramas against a back-lit screen, while the storyline is told through songs, chants and musical interludes. An even rarer *nang* form is the *nang yai*, which uses enormous cut-outs of whole scenes rather than just individual characters, so the play becomes something like an animated film. For more on shadow puppets and puppetry, see p.605.

Film and video

Fast-paced Chinese blockbusters have long dominated the Thai **movie** scene, serving up a low-grade cocktail of sex, spooks, violence and comedy. Not understanding the dialogue is rarely a drawback, as the storylines tend to be simple and the visuals more entertaining than the words. In the cities, Western films are also pretty big, and new releases often get subtitled rather than dubbed.

Thailand's own film industry has been enjoying a bit of a boom recently, with the 2000 **historical epic** *Bang Rajan* proving to be one of the biggest-ever earners at the Thai box-office. Loosely based on real events, it tells the story of a group of plucky Thai villagers who in 1767 fought against the invading Burmese as they made their way to the then-capital Ayutthaya. Capitalizing on the popularity of the genre, *Suriyothai* tells the story of a high-born Thai heroine who also spent her life battling the Burmese; with a budget of 200 million baht, it was the most expensive Thai movie to date when released in 2001, but was set to earn out – in no small part, according to local critics – due to the recent resurgence in real-life tension between Thailand and Burma.

All sizeable towns have a cinema or two and tickets generally start at around B50. Villagers have to make do with the travelling cinema, which sets up a mobile screen in wat compounds or other public spaces, and often entertains the whole village in one sitting. However makeshift the cinema, the king's anthem is always played before every screening, during which the audience is expected to stand up.

Western **videos** come free with your evening meal in guest houses all over Thailand and dissuade many a traveller from venturing anywhere else of an evening. Even if you steer clear of them, you'll get back-to-back Chinese movies on long-distance air-conditioned buses and in some trains too.

Thai boxing

Thai boxing (*muay Thai*) enjoys a following similar to soccer or baseball in the West: every province has a stadium and whenever the sport is shown on TV you can be sure that large noisy crowds will gather round the sets in streetside restaurants and noodle shops. The best place to see Thai boxing is at one of Bangkok's two stadiums, which between them hold bouts every night of the week and on some afternoons as well (see p.180).

There's a strong spiritual and **ritualistic** dimension to *muay Thai*, adding grace to an otherwise brutal sport. Each boxer enters the ring to the wailing music of a three-piece *phipat* orchestra, often flamboyantly attired in a lurid silk robe over the statutory red or blue boxer shorts. The fighter then bows, first in the direction of his birthplace and then to the north, south, east and west, honouring both his teachers and the spirit of the ring. Next he performs a slow dance, claiming the audience's attention and demonstrating his prowess as a performer.

Any part of the body except the head may be used as an **offensive weapon** in *muay Thai*, and all parts except the groin are fair targets. Kicks to the head are the blows which cause most knockouts. As the action hots up, so the orchestra speeds up its tempo and the betting in the audience becomes more frenetic. It can be a gruesome business, but it was far bloodier before modern boxing gloves were made compulsory in the 1930s – combatants used to wrap their fists with hemp impregnated with a face-lacerating dosage of ground glass.

For further **information** about Thai boxing, visit ⊛ www.tat.or.th/do/learn.htm, or contact the Muay Thai Institute at 336/932 Prachathipat, Thanyaburi, Pathum Thani, Bangkok 12130 (☎02/992 0096, ℱ992 0095), which runs forty-hour **training courses** for foreigners at US$160. You can also do one-off training sessions at a gym in central Bangkok; see p.181 for details.

Takraw

You're very unlikely to stumble unexpectedly on an outdoor bout of *muay Thai*, but you're sure to come across some form of **takraw** game at some point, whether in a public park, a wat compound or just in a backstreet alley. Played with a very light rattan ball (or one made of plastic to look like rattan), the basic aim of the game is to keep the ball off the ground. To do this you can use any part of your body except your hands, so a well-played *takraw* game looks extremely balletic, with players leaping and arching to get a good strike.

There are at least five versions of competitive *takraw*, based on the same principles. The one featured in the Southeast Asian Games and most frequently in school tournaments is played over a volleyball net and involves two teams of three; the other most popular competitive version has a team ranged round a basketball net trying to score as many goals as possible within a limited time period before the next team replaces them and tries to outscore them. Other *takraw* games introduce more complex rules (like kicking the ball backwards with your heels through a ring made with your arms behind your back) and many assign points according to the skill displayed by individual players rather than per goal or dropped ball. Outside of school playing fields, proper *takraw* tournaments are rare, though they do sometimes feature as entertainment at Buddhist funerals.

Meditation centres and retreats

Of the hundreds of meditation temples in Thailand, a few cater specifically for foreigners by holding meditation sessions and retreats in English. The meditation taught is mostly Vipassana, or "insight", which emphasizes the minute observation of internal physical sensation, and novices and practised meditators alike are welcome. To join a one-off class in Bangkok, call to check times and then just turn up; for overnight and longer visits to wats in more remote areas, you usually have to contact the monastery in advance, either directly or via the WFB (see opposite).

Longer retreats are for the serious-minded only. All the temples listed opposite welcome both male and female English-speakers, but strict segregation of the sexes is enforced and many places observe a vow of silence. An average day at any one of these monasteries starts with a wake-up call at 4am and includes several hours of group meditation and chanting, as well as time put aside for chores and for personal reflection. However long their stay, all visitors are expected to keep the eight Buddhist precepts, the most restrictive of these being the abstention from food after midday and from alcohol, tobacco, drugs and sex at all times. Most wats ask for a minimal daily donation (around B120) to cover accommodation and food costs. For more information and access details for particular temples, see the relevant sections in the guide.

Meditation centres and retreat temples

House of Dhamma Insight Meditation Centre, 26/9 Soi Chumphon, Soi Lardprao 15, Bangkok ☎02/511 0439, ⊕512 6083, ⓔselena@bkk.loxinfo.co.th. Vipassana meditation

classes in English on the second, third and fourth Sunday of the month (2–5pm) – with weekday classes planned in the future – and weekend and week-long retreats organized. Buddhist library and courses in reiki and other subjects available.
Thailand Vipassana Centre
ⓦ www.dhamma.org. Dhamma Kamala, 200 Thanon Yoopasuk, Prachinburi; and at Dhamma Abha, Ban Huayplu, Phitsanulok. Frequent ten-day residential courses in a Burmese Vipassana tradition. Foreign students must pre-register by email with Pornphen Leenutaphong on
ⓔ pornphen@bkk.a-net.net.th.
Wat Khao Tham, Ban Tai, Ko Pha Ngan, Surat Thani 84280 ⓦ www.watkowtahm.org. Frequent ten-day retreats (Vipassana meditation) led by farang teachers.
Wat Mahathat, Thanon Maharat, Ratanakosin, Bangkok. Situated in Section Five of the wat is its International Buddhist Meditation Centre where Vipassana meditation practice is available in English (daily 7–10am, 1–4pm & 6–9pm; ⓣ02/222 6011 or 01/694 1527 for further information). Participants are welcome to stay in the simple surroundings of the meditation building itself (donation requested) or at a quiet house nearby (B200 per day).
Wat Pa Nanachat Bung Wai, Ban Bung Wai, Amphoe Warinchamrab, Ubon Ratchathani 34310. A group of foreign monks have established this

forest monastery, 17km west of Ubon Ratchathani, specifically for farangs who want to immerse themselves in meditation. Short- and long-term visitors are welcome, but the atmosphere is serious and intense and not for curious sightseers, so you must write to the monastery before visiting.
Wat Ram Poeng (aka Wat Tapotaram), Thanon Canal, Chiang Mai ⓣ053/211620. Month-long, very intensive Vipassana meditation courses (a 20hr day is encouraged) held in English under a resident farang instructor at the Northern Insight Meditation Centre.
Wat Suan Mokkh, Chaiya, Surat Thani
ⓦ www.suanmokkh.org. Popular Anapanasati (mindfulness with breathing) meditation course held on first ten days of every month.
Wat Umong, off Thanon Suthep, Chiang Mai
ⓣ 053/277248. Informal discussions on Buddhism in English and some Anapanasati meditation practice are normally held here on Sunday afternoons at 3pm with one of the farang monks who are often in residence. There is also a Buddhist library with books in English which farangs may borrow. It is possible to arrange to stay.
World Fellowship of Buddhists (WFB), Benjasiri Park, 616 Soi 24, Thanon Sukhumvit, Bangkok
ⓣ02/661 1284, ⓕ661 0555, ⓦwww.wfb-hq.org. The main information centre for advice on English-speaking retreats in Thailand. Holds meditation sessions in English on the first Sunday of every month.

Cultural hints

Tourist literature has so successfully marketed Thailand as the "Land of Smiles" that a lot of farangs arrive in the country expecting to be forgiven any outrageous behaviour. This is just not the case: there are some things so universally sacred in Thailand that even a hint of disrespect will cause deep offence. TAT publishes a special leaflet on the subject, entitled *Do and Don't in Thailand*, which is also reproduced on their website at ⓦ www.tat.or.th – be sure to read it before you travel.

The monarchy

The worst thing you can possibly do is to bad-mouth the **royal family**. The monarchy

might be a constitutional one, but almost every household displays a picture of King Bhumibol and Queen Sirikit in a prominent position, and respectful crowds mass whenever either of them makes a public appearance. When addressing or speaking about royalty, Thais use a special language full of deference, called *rajasap* (literally "royal language").

Aside from keeping any anti-monarchy sentiments to yourself, you should be prepared to stand when the **king's anthem** is played at the beginning of every cinema programme, and to stop in your tracks if the town you're in plays the **national anthem** over its public address system – many small towns do this twice a day at 8am and again at 6pm, as do some train stations. A less obvious point: as the king's head features on all Thai currency, you should never step on a coin or banknote, which is tantamount to kicking the king in the face.

Religion

Almost equally insensitive would be to disregard certain religious precepts. Buddhism plays an essential part in the lives of most Thais, and Buddhist monuments should be treated accordingly – which basically means wearing long trousers or knee-length skirts, covering your arms and removing your shoes whenever you visit one.

All **Buddha images** are sacred, however small, however tacky, however ruined, and should never be used as a backdrop for a portrait photo, clambered over, placed in a position of inferiority or treated in any manner that could be construed as disrespectful. In an attempt to prevent foreigners from committing any kind of transgression the government requires a special licence for all Buddha statues exported from the country.

Monks come only just beneath the monarchy in the social hierarchy, and they too are addressed and discussed in a special language. If there's a monk around, he'll always get a seat on the bus, usually right at the back. Theoretically, monks are forbidden to have any close contact with women, which means, as a female, you mustn't sit or stand next to a monk, or even brush against his robes; if it's essential to pass him something, put the object down so that he can then pick it up – never hand it over directly. Nuns, however, get treated like ordinary women rather than like monks.

The body

The Western liberalism embraced by the Thai sex industry is very unrepresentative of the majority Thai attitude to the body. **Clothing** – or the lack of it – is what bothers Thais most about tourist behaviour. As mentioned above, you need to dress modestly when entering temples, but the same also applies to other important buildings and all public places. Stuffy and sweaty as it sounds, you should keep shorts and vests for the real tourist resorts, and be especially diligent about covering up and, for women, wearing bras in rural areas. Baring your flesh on beaches is very much a Western practice: when Thais go swimming they often do so fully clothed, and they find topless and nude bathing extremely unpalatable. It's not illegal, but it won't win you many friends.

According to ancient Hindu belief the head is the most sacred part of the **body** and the feet are the most unclean. This belief, imported into Thailand, means that it's very rude to touch another person's head or to point your feet either at a human being or at a sacred image – when sitting on a temple floor, for example, you should tuck your legs beneath you rather than stretch them out towards the Buddha. These hierarchies also forbid people from wearing shoes (which are even more unclean than feet) inside temples and most private homes, and – by extension – Thais take offence when they see someone sitting on the "head", or prow, of a boat. On a more practical note, the **left hand** is used for washing after defecating, so Thais never use it to put food in their mouth, pass things or shake hands – as a farang though, you'll be assumed to have different customs, so left-handers shouldn't worry unduly.

Social conventions

In fact, Thais very rarely shake hands anyway, using the **wai** to greet and say goodbye and to acknowledge respect, gratitude or apology. A prayer-like gesture made with raised hands, the *wai* changes according to the relative status of the two people involved: Thais can instantaneously assess which *wai* to use when, but as a farang your safest bet is to go for the "stranger's" *wai*, which requires that your hands be raised close to your chest and your fingertips placed just below your chin. If someone makes a *wai* at you, you should definitely *wai* back, but it's generally wise not to initiate.

Public displays of **physical affection** in Thailand are much more acceptable between friends of the same sex than between lovers, whether hetero- or homosexual. Holding hands and hugging is as common among male friends as with females, so if you're given fairly intimate caresses by a Thai acquaintance of the same sex, don't assume you're being propositioned.

Finally, there are three specifically Thai **concepts** you're bound to come across, which may help you comprehend a sometimes *laissez-faire* attitude to delayed buses and other inconveniences. The first, **jai yen**, translates literally as "cool heart" and is something everyone tries to maintain – most Thais hate raised voices, visible irritation and confrontations of any kind. Related to this is the oft-quoted response to a difficulty, **mai pen rai** – "never mind", "no problem" or "it can't be helped" – the verbal equivalent of an open-handed shoulder shrug which has its basis in the Buddhist notion of karma (see "Religion", p.784). And then there's **sanuk**, the wide-reaching philosophy of "fun", which, crass as it sounds, Thais do their best to inject into any situation, even work. Hence the crowds of inebriated Thais who congregate at waterfalls and other beauty spots on public holidays, and the national waterfight which takes place every April on streets right across Thailand.

Thai names

Although all Thais have a first **name** and a family name, everyone is addressed by their first name – even when meeting strangers – prefixed by the title "Khun" (Mr/Ms); no one is ever addressed as Khun Surname, and even the phone book lists people by their given name. In Thailand you will often be addressed in an Anglicized version of this convention, as Mr Paul or Miss Lucy for example. Bear in mind though, that when a man is introduced to you as Khun Pirom, his wife will definitely not be Khun Pirom as well, as that would be like calling them Mr and Mrs Paul (or whatever).

Many Thai **first names** come from ancient Sanskrit and have an auspicious meaning; for example, Boon means good deeds, Porn means blessings, Siri means glory and Thawee means to increase. However, Thais of all ages are commonly known by the **nickname** given them soon after birth rather than by their official first name. This tradition arises out of a deep-rooted superstition that once a child has been officially named the spirits will begin to take an unhealthy interest in them, so a nickname is used instead to confuse the spirits. Common nicknames – which often bear no resemblance to the adult's personality or physique – include Yai (Big), Oun (Fat) and Muu (Pig); Lek or Noi (Little), Nok (Bird), Noo (Mouse) and Kung (Shrimp); Neung (Number One/Eldest), Sawng (Number Two), Saam (Number Three); and English nicknames like Apple and Joy.

Family names were only introduced in 1913 (by Rama VI, who invented many of the aristocracy's surnames himself), and are used only in very formal situations, always in conjunction with the first name. It's quite usual for good friends never to know each others' surname. Ethnic Thais generally have short surnames like Somboon or Srisai, while the long, convoluted family names – such as Sonthanasumpun – usually indicate Chinese origin, not because they are phonetically Chinese but because many Chinese immigrants have chosen to adopt new Thai surnames and Thai law states that every newly created surname must be unique. Thus anyone who wants to change their surname must submit a shortlist of five unique Thai names – each to a maximum length of ten Thai characters – to be checked against a database of existing names. As more and more names are taken, Chinese family names get increasingly unwieldly, and more easily distinguishable from the pithy old Thai names.

Outdoor activities

The vast majority of travellers' itineraries take in a few days' trekking in the north and a stint snorkelling or diving off the beaches of the south. The big beach resorts of Pattaya, Phuket and Ko Samui also offer dozens of other watersports, and for the well-prepared wildlife enthusiast Thailand offers plenty of national parks to explore. There is also a developing interest in more unusual outdoor activities, such as rock climbing and kayaking. Trekking is concentrated in the north, so we've covered the practicalities of trekking in that chapter (see p.297), but there are smaller, less touristy trekking operations in Kanchanaburi (see p.219), Sangkhlaburi (see p.232) and Umphang (see p.286), all of which are worth considering. Golf has also taken off in Thailand, and there are now dozens of courses across the country, the best of them concentrated near the resort towns of Hua Hin (see p.555) and Pattaya (see p.413). Details of watersports at the major resorts are given in the sections on those towns.

Snorkelling and diving

Thailand has exceptionally rich **marine fauna**, and conditions for coral growth are ideal, with an average sea temperature of about 28°C and very clear waters, so **snorkelling** and **diving** are extremely rewarding. Each coast has at least one resort with a number of equipment-rental shops, diving schools and agencies which organize diving and snorkelling trips to outlying islands, usually at very reasonable prices in worldwide terms. You can dive all year round, too, as the coasts are subject to different monsoon seasons: the diving seasons are from November to April along the Andaman coast, from January to October on the Gulf coast, and all year round on the east coast.

Whether you're snorkelling or diving you should be aware of your effect on the fragile reef structures. Try to minimize your impact by not touching the reefs or asking your boatman to anchor in the middle of one, and don't buy coral souvenirs, as tourist demand only encourages local entrepreneurs to dynamite reefs.

As far as **snorkelling equipment** goes, the most important thing is that you buy or rent a mask that fits. To check the fit, hold the mask against your face, then breathe in and remove your hands – if it falls off, it'll leak water. If you're buying equipment, you should be able to kit yourself out with a mask, snorkel and fins for about B1000; an increasing number of dive centres around the country now sell snorkelling gear as well as dive acessories. Few places rent fins, but a mask and snorkel set usually costs about B50 a day to rent, and if you're going on a snorkelling day-trip they are often included in the price. When renting equipment you'll nearly always be required to pay a deposit of around B200.

The Thai outdoors online

Action Asia ⓦ www.actionasia.com. Digital lifestyle magazine which carries inspirational features on adventure sports in Thailand and the rest of Southeast Asia.
Asian Diver ⓦ www.asian-diver.com. Online version of the divers' magazine, with good coverage of Thailand's diving sites including recommendations, first-hand dive stories and travellers' reports.
Dive Thailand Network ⓦ www.divethailand.net/ontheweb.html. Excellent site with divers' reef reports, masses of links to commercial Thai dive centres and a bulletin board. Especially good on Andaman coast diving.

Diving

All diving centres run programmes of one-day **dive trips**, wreck dives and night dives for B1000–1800 plus equipment, and many of the Andaman coast dive centres (Khao Lak, Phuket, Ko Phi Phi, Ao Nang) also do two- to seven-day liveaboards to the exceptional reefs off the remote Similan and Surin islands (from around B9000) and even further afield to the impressive Burma Banks. Renting a full set of diving **gear**, including wetsuit, from a dive centre costs B600–1000 per day; most dive centres also rent underwater cameras for B1000–1500 per day.

Phuket, Khao Lak, Ao Nang, Ko Phi Phi, Ko Lanta, Ko Tao and Pattaya are the best places to **learn**, and dive centres at all these places offer a range of **courses** from beginner to advanced level, with equipment rental usually included in the cost; Phuket dive centres offer the most competitively priced courses. The most popular courses are the one-day **introductory** or resort dive (a pep talk and escorted shallow dive), which costs anything from B1500 for a very local dive to B4500 for an all-inclusive day-trip to the fabulous Similan Islands; and the four-day **open-water course** which entitles you to

dive without an instructor (B7000–12,000 including at least one dive a day). **Insurance** should be included in the price of courses and introductory dives; for qualified divers, it's available from most reputable diving operators in Thailand for around B60 a day, or B250 a month.

Before you sign up for a diving course or expedition, check that the **diving centre** has proof of membership of either **PADI** (Professional Association of Diving Instructors; ⊕ www.padi.com) or **NAUI** (National Association of Underwater Instructors; ⊕ www.naui.org) and ask other people who've done the course or expedition how they rate it. Both PADI and NAUI post up-to-date lists of their affiliated dive centres in Thailand on their websites. In the guide, we've highlighted those dive centres that are accredited PADI **five-star centres**, which are considered by PADI to offer a very high standard of instruction and equipment, but you should always check with other divers first if possible, no matter how many stars your chosen dive centre has garnered.

Most novice and experienced divers prefer to travel to the dive site in a decent-sized **boat** equipped with a radio and emergency medical equipment rather than in a longtail. If this concerns you, be sure to ask the dive company about their boat before you sign up – any company with a good boat will have photos of it to impress potential customers – though you'll find firms that use longtails will probably charge less.

There are currently three **recompression chambers** in Thailand, one in Sattahip on the east coast near Pattaya (see p.412), one on Ko Samui (see p.569), and the other on Ao Patong in Phuket (see p.638). It's a good idea to check whether your dive centre is a member of one of these outfits, as recompression services are extremely expensive for anyone who's not.

National parks

Over the last forty years almost one hundred areas across Thailand have been singled out for conservation as **national parks**, with the dual aim of protecting the country's natural resources and creating educational and recreational facilities for the public; these parks generally make the best places to observe wildlife. One of the best places for seeing larger animals is **Khao Yai** (see

Thailand's best dives

The East Coast
Pattaya	see p.411

The Andaman Coast
Ao Nang	see p.681
Burma Banks	see p.639
Hin Muang and Hin Daeng	see p.639
Ko Lanta	see p.698
Ko Phi Phi	see p.688
Ko Racha	see p.639
Ko Similan	see p.633
Ko Surin	see p.623
Laem Phra Nang (Railay)	see p.677
Phuket	see p.638

The Gulf Coast
Ko Pha Ngan	see p.586
Ko Samui	see p.569
Ko Tao	see p.598

The Deep South
Ko Losin	see p.744
Ko Phetra	see p.730
Ko Tarutao	see p.727

p.458), the most popular national park, some three hours northeast of Bangkok. If you join a night safari here, you could be rewarded with sightings of elephants, deer, civets, even tigers, while during the day you'll come across gibbons and hornbills at the very least. Bird-watchers consider the national park mountains of **Doi Suthep** (see p.327) and **Doi Inthanon** (see p.352) – both close to Chiang Mai – primary observation spots, and the coastal flats at **Khao Sam Roi Yot** (see p.557) in the south are another good spot. Many of southern Thailand's protected reserves are marine parks, incorporating anything from a single beach, such as the turtle-egg-laying grounds on Phuket (see p.645), to an entire archipelago, such as Ko Similan (see p.633).

All the national parks are administered by the Royal Forestry Department on Thanon Phaholyothin, Chatuchak District, Bangkok 10900 (☎02/561 4292–3, ☏579 7099), about forty minutes' bus ride north of Democracy Monument. To book national park bungalows in advance (advisable for weekends and public holidays) you need to pay up front; see "Accommodation" on p.49 for details.

For all their environmental benefits, national parks are a huge source of **controversy** in Thailand, with vested interests such as fishermen, farmers, loggers, poachers and the tourist industry pitted against environmentalists and certain sections of the government. The Royal Forestry Department has itself come in for voluble criticism over the last few years, particularly over the filming of *The Beach* on the national park island of Ko Phi Phi Leh, and in 2000 when – without warning – it raised the **foreigners' entrance fee** levied at most national parks from B20 to B200 (B100 for children). See "Flora, Fauna and Environmental Issues" on p.789 for a fuller account of these issues and for a more detailed introduction to Thailand's wildlife.

Because of the drastic hike in entrance fees, you may find yourself having to be selective about which parks to visit. At the more popular parks like Khao Yai and Khao Sok you should only have to pay the fee once, however long you stay at the park, even if your accommodation is located outside the entrance gate. And as these parks have plenty of trails and other attractions to keep you occupied, the B200 doesn't seem such bad value. It's the little parks which can only boast of a single waterfall or a lone cave that will probably not seem worth it – at the time of writing not all of these minor attractions were subject to the revised entry fee (those that are have been highlighted in the guide), but the new charges may become more widespread.

Most parks have limited public facilities, very few signposted walking trails and a paucity of usable maps. Nor are many of the parks well served by public transport – some can take a day to reach from the nearest large town, via a route that entails several bus and songthaew changes and a final lengthy walk. This factor, combined with the expense and poor quality of most national park accommodation, means that if you're planning to do a serious tour of the parks you should consider **bringing a tent** (all parks allow this; see p.49 for details) and be prepared to rent your own transport.

Rock climbing

The limestone karsts that pepper south Thailand's Andaman coast make ideal playgrounds for **rock climbers**, and the sport has really taken off here in the last decade. Most climbing is centred round East and West Railay beaches on Laem Phra Nang in Krabi province (see p.679), where there are dozens of routes within easy walking distance of tourist bungalows, restaurants and beaches. Several climbing schools have already established centres here, providing instruction, guides and all the necessary equipment. Ko Phi Phi (see p.688) also offers a few interesting routes and a couple of climbing schools. The best place to **learn** rock climbing is Laem Phra Nang: half-day introductory courses cost B800, a full day's guided climbing B1500 and a three-day course B5000. Equipment rental is charged at about B1000 per day for two people. For further details about climbing courses, visit the rock-climbing schools' websites listed on p.679.

Kayaking and white-water rafting

Kayaking, too, is centred around Thailand's Andaman coast, whose limestone outcrops, sea caves, hongs (hidden lagoons), mangrove swamps and picturesque shorelines all make for rewarding paddling (there are also a handful of operators over on Ko Samui, see p.573). And because you've no roaring engine to disturb the wildlife, you often get to see many more creatures than you would in a more conventional boat.

The longest-established **kayaking operator** in Thailand is SeaCanoe (Ⓦwww.seacanoe.com), who always seems to get good reviews; it is due to this trailblazing company that sea kayaking has taken off in Thailand. They run day-trips out of Phuket (see p.647), Phang Nga (see p.669) and Ao Nang (see p.682), which cost B1700–3000 per person (children aged 4–12 half price), and also do three- to six-day trips. In typical Thai style, SeaCanoe's success has spawned a lot of copycat operations, most of which are based in Krabi (see p.677), Ao Nang, Laem Phra Nang (see p.679) and Phuket, ranging in price from B1200–2700 for a full day or about B900 for half a day. Some of these operators also rent out kayaks for about B300 per hour, as do a couple of places on Ko Phi Phi as well. Phuket-based Paddle Asia (Ⓦwww.paddleasia.com) also offer week-long sea-kayaking trips around the Trang islands and the Tarutao National Marine Park islands at US$100–150 per person per day.

You can go **river kayaking** and **whitewater rafting** on several rivers in north, west and south Thailand, in particular on the River Kwai near Kanchanaburi (see p.219), on the Umphang River near Umphang (see p.286), and on the Pai River near Pai (see p.370).

Some stretches of these rivers can run quite fast, particularly during the rainy season from July to November, but there are plenty of options for novices too. Wild Planet in Bangkok (☎02/629 0977, ☏629 0976, Ⓦwww.wild-planet.co.th) organizes five-day kayaking trips to Umphang (B11,000 per person all-inclusive). In Pai, Thai Adventure Rafting (see p.370) offers two-day rafting trips for B1800 per person; in Chiang Mai, contact Mae Sot Conservation Tour (☎053/814505) for rafting trips in Ob Luang Gorge (B600 per day); and in Trang any tour agent can offer a day's rafting for around B850. Or you can rent your own kayak for about B300 from one of the guest houses in Kanchanaburi.

Gay Thailand

Buddhist tolerance and a national abhorrence of confrontation and victimization combine to make Thai society relatively tolerant of homosexuality, if not exactly positive about same-sex relationships. Most Thais are extremely private and discreet about being gay, generally pursuing a "don't ask, don't tell" understanding with their family. However, most Thais are horrified by the idea of gay-bashing and generally regard it as unthinkable to spurn a child or relative for being gay.

Hardly any public figures are out, yet the predilections of several respected social, political and entertainment figures are widely known and accepted. **Transvestites** (known as *katoey*) and transsexuals are also a lot more visible in Thailand than in the West.

You'll find cross-dressers doing ordinary jobs, even in small upcountry towns, and there are a number of transvestites and transsexuals in the public eye too – including national volleyball stars and champion *muay Thai* boxers. The government tourist office vigorously

77

■

promotes the transvestite cabarets in Pattaya and Phuket, both of which are advertised as family entertainment. *Katoey* also regularly appear as characters in soap operas, TV comedies and films, where they are depicted as harmless figures of fun.

There is no mention of homosexuality at all in Thai **law**, which means that the age of consent for gay sex is sixteen, the same as for heterosexuals. However, this also means that gay rights are not protected under Thai law. This enabled the national Ratchabhat teacher-training institute to implement a bizarre and sudden ban on homosexuals becoming teachers in mid-1997. The ban was greeted with widespread protests and led to a human rights campaign from NGOs at home and abroad, and was eventually dropped. Ironically, there was no gay organization to defend gay men, who were the main target of the ban, their cause being fought by Anjaree, a long-established lesbian activists group.

The scene

Thailand's **gay scene** is mainly focused on mainstream venues like karaoke bars, restaurants, massage parlours, gyms, saunas and escort agencies. For the sake of discretion, gay venues are usually intermingled with equivalent straight venues. As in the straight scene, venues reflect class and status differences. Expensive international-style places are very popular in Bangkok, attracting upper- and middle-class gays, many of whom have travelled or been educated abroad and developed Western tastes. These places also attract a contingent of Thais seeking foreign sugar daddies.

The biggest concentrations of farang-friendly gay **bars and clubs** are found in Bangkok, Chiang Mai, Phuket and Pattaya, and are listed in the guide; recently the gay communities of Bangkok and Phuket have both hosted flamboyant **Gay Pride festivals** in November (check upcoming dates on the websites listed below). Thailand's gay scene is heavily male, and there are hardly any **lesbian**-only venues, though Bangkok has a few mixed gay bars. Where possible, we've listed lesbian meeting-places, but unless otherwise specified, gay means male throughout this guide.

Although excessively physical displays of affection are frowned upon for both hetero-sexuals and homosexuals, Western gay couples should get no hassle about being seen together in public – it's much more acceptable, and common, in fact, for friends of the same sex (gay or not) to walk hand-in-hand, than for heterosexual couples to do so.

The farang-oriented gay **sex industry** is a tiny but highly visible part of Thailand's gay scene. With its tawdry floor shows and host services, it bears a gruesome resemblance to the straight sex trade, and is similarly most active in Bangkok and Pattaya, Patong (on Phuket) and Chiang Mai. Like their female counterparts in the heterosexual fleshpots, many of the boys working in the gay sex bars that dominate these districts are under age. A significant number of gay prostitutes are gay by economic necessity rather than by inclination. As with the straight sex scene, we do not list the commercial gay sex bars in the guide.

Information and contacts for gay travellers

Anjaree, PO Box 322, Rajdamnoen PO, Bangkok 10200 ☎ & ℗ 02/477 1776, ✉ anjaree@loxinfo.com. General information on the lesbian community in Thailand.

Dragon Castle's Gay Asia ✆ dragoncastle.net. Justifiably bills itself as "Gay Thailand's leading website". Carries informed advice on all aspects of the gay scene, good solid tips on potential dangers and pitfalls, plus plenty of listings and links for further information.

Dreaded Ned's ✆ www.dreadedned.com. Information on almost every gay venue in the country, plus some interesting background on gay Thailand and a book list.

Gay Media's Gay Guide to Thailand ✆ www.gay-media.com. Exhaustive listings of gay-friendly hotels in the major tourist centres; also covers gay bars, clubs and saunas in Bangkok.

Metro ✆ www.bkkmetro.com. Bangkok's monthly listings magazine publishes extensive listings of gay venues and events.

Pink Ink ✆ www.khsnet.com/pinkink. Thailand's first gay and lesbian newsletter in English, featuring listings, gossip columns and news clippings, plus personal ads. Available free from major gay venues in Bangkok.

Utopia, 116/1 Soi 23, Thanon Sukhumvit ☎ 02/259 9619, ✆ www.utopia-asia.com. Bangkok's gay and lesbian centre has a café, noticeboards, gallery and shop, and is a good place to find out what's happening on the gay scene. Their website lists clubs, events and accommodation for gays and lesbians and has useful links to other sites in Asia and the rest of the world. Utopia also offers a gay tour-guide service, called Thai Friends, through which English-speaking Thai gay men volunteer to show tourists the sights of Bangkok. It's a strictly non-sexual arrangement and can be organized through the centre or via their website.

Disabled travellers

Thailand makes few provisions for its disabled citizens and this obviously affects the disabled traveller, but these drawbacks are often balanced out by the afford-ability of small luxuries such as taxis, comfortable hotels and personal tour guides, all of which can help smooth the way considerably. Most disabled trav-ellers find Thais only too happy to offer assistance where they can, but hiring a local tour guide to accompany you on a day's sightseeing is particularly recom-mended – with the help of a Thai speaker you will find it much easier to arrange access to temples, museums and other places that may at first not seem wheel-chair-friendly. Government tour guides can be arranged through any TAT office.

Wheelchair users will have a hard time negotiating the uneven pavements, which are high to allow for flooding and invariably lack dropped kerbs, and will find it difficult to board buses and trains. Even crossing the road can be a trial, particularly in Bangkok, where it's usually a question of climbing steps up to a bridge rather than taking a ramped underpass.

One way to cut down the hassle is to go with a **tour**: the extra money is well spent if it guarantees adapted facilities throughout your stay and enables you to explore other-wise inaccessible sights. In the UK, both Kuoni (see p.14) and BA Holidays (see p.13) are used to tailoring package deals to spe-cific needs.

The more expensive international **airlines** tend to be the better equipped: British Airways, Thai Airways and Qantas all carry aisle wheelchairs and have at least one toi-let adapted for disabled passengers. Staff at Bangkok airport are generally helpful to disabled passengers and, if asked, should be able to whisk you past immigration queues; they will also provide wheelchairs if necessary.

Contacts for travellers with disabilities

For general information on disabled travel abroad, get in touch with the organizations listed below, browse the exhaustive links at ⓦwww.independentliving.org or post a query on the forum for travellers with disabil-ities at ⓦthorntree.lonelyplanet.com. For Thailand-specific information, have a look at ⓦwww.infothai.com/disabled, or try the Council of Disabled People of Thailand (ⓣ02/583 3031, ⓕ583 6518), who can pro-vide limited information on the country's resources for the disabled.

UK and Ireland

Access Travel ⓣ01942/888844, ⓕ891811, ⓦwww.access.co.uk. Tour operator who can arrange flights, transfer and accommodation for travellers with disabilities.
Disability Action Group, 2 Annadale Ave, Belfast BT7 3JH ⓣ028/9049 1011.
Holiday Care Service ⓣ01293/774535, minicom 01293/776943 ⓕ784647, ⓦwww.holidaycare.org.uk. Provides free lists of accessible accommodation abroad.

Irish Wheelchair Association In the Irish Republic ☎ 01/833 8241, ℱ 833 3873, ⓔ iwa@iol.ie.
RADAR (Royal Association for Disability and Rehabilitation) ☎ 020/7250 3222, minicom ☎ 020/7250 4119, ⓦ www.radar.org.uk. A good source of advice on holidays and travel abroad. They produce a guide for long-haul holidays.
Tripscope ☎ 08457/585 641, ℱ 020/8580 7022, ⓦ www.justmobility.co.uk/tripscope. This registered charity provides a national telephone information service offering free advice on international transport for those with a mobility problem.

US and Canada

Access-Able ⓦ www.access-able.com. An online resource for travellers with disabilities.
Directions Unlimited ☎ 1-800/533 5343 or 914/241 1700. Tour operator specializing in custom tours for people with disabilities.
Mobility International USA ☎ 541/343 1284, ⓦ www.miusa.org. Information and referral services, access guides, tours and exchange programmes. Annual membership $35 (includes quarterly newsletter).

Society for the Advancement of Travelers with Handicaps (SATH) ☎ 212/447 7284, ⓦ www.sath.org. Non-profit educational organization that has actively represented travellers with disabilities since 1976.
Travel Information Service ☎ 215/456 9600. Telephone-only information and referral service.
Twin Peaks Press ☎ 360/694 2462 or 1-800/637 2256, ⓦ www.twinpeak.virtualave.net. Publisher of a number of resources for the disabled, including the *Directory of Travel Agencies for the Disabled*, listing more than 370 agencies worldwide.
Wheels Up! ☎ 1-888/389-4335, ⓦ www.wheelsup.com. Provides discounted airfares, tour and cruise prices for disabled travelers; also publishes a free monthly newsletter and has a comprehensive website.

Australia and New Zealand

ACROD (Australian Council for Rehabilitation of the Disabled) In Australia ☎ 02/6282 4333, ⓦ www.acrod.org.au.
Disabled Persons Assembly In New Zealand ☎ 04/811 9100.

👫 Travelling with kids

Travelling through Thailand with kids can be both challenging and rewarding. Thais are very tolerant of children so you can take them almost anywhere without restriction, and they always help break the ice with strangers.

Even more than their parents, children need protecting from the sun, unsafe drinking water, heat and unfamiliar **food**. All that chilli in particular may be a problem, even with older kids, so if possible try and make a few visits to Thai restaurants in your home country before launching them into the real thing; consider packing a jar of Marmite or equivalent child's favourite, so that you can always rely on toast if the local food doesn't

go down so well. As diarrhoea could be dangerous for a child, rehydration solutions (see under "Health", p.37) are vital if your child goes down with it. You should also make sure, if possible, that your child is aware of the dangers of rabies; keep children away from animals, and consider a rabies jab.

For a full briefing about the logistics of travelling with kids in Asia, see *Your Child's*

Health Abroad by Dr Jane Wilson-Howarth and Dr Matthew Ellis (Bradt Publications). You might also want to canvass other travellers' opinions, which you can do by posting your queries on the Kids To Go forum at ⓦwww.thorntree.lonelyplanet.com or other travellers' websites (see p.29). For specific advice about kids' health issues, either contact your doctor, or consult one of the travellers' medical services listed on p.35 or, in the UK, call the Nomad Medical Centre (☎020/8889 7014), which publishes a special information sheet on keeping kids healthy when abroad.

Disposable nappies (diapers) are sold in Thailand at convenience stores, chemists and supermarkets in big resorts and sizeable towns; for longer, more out-of-the-way journeys and stays on lonely islands and beaches, consider bringing some washables as back-up. A changing mat is another necessity. If your baby is on powdered **milk**, it might be an idea to bring some of that; you can certainly get it in Thailand but it may not taste the same as at home. Dried baby **food**, too, could be worth taking, though you can get Gerber brand baby food in big towns and resorts and some parents find restaurant-cooked rice and bananas go down just as well.

For touring, child-carrier backpacks such as the Tommy Lightrider are ideal, starting at around £30/US$45, and can weigh less than 2kg. If the child is small enough, a fold up **buggy** is also well worth packing, though you can buy these cheaply in most moderate-sized Thai towns. Don't expect smooth pavements and plentiful ramps however. Children's **clothes** are also very cheap in Thailand, and have the advantage of being designed for the climate. If you haven't already got beach shoes or sports sandals for your child to swim in (to protect against coral, sea urchins and the like), you can buy these in the big cities and in every resort.

Even if you've forgotten a crucial piece of children's equipment, you'll probably find it in Bangkok's well-stocked **children's department store**, Buy Buy Kiddo, (see p.181), which has everything from bottles and dummies to English-language kids' books and games, much of it imported from the West.

Many of the expensive **hotels** listed in this guide offer special deals for families, usually allowing one or two under-12s to share their parents' room for free, so long as no extra bedding is required. It's often possible to cram two adults and two children into the double rooms in inexpensive and mid-range hotels (as opposed to guest houses), as beds in these places are usually big enough for two (see p.48). Few museums or transport companies offer student reductions, but in some cases children get discounts; these vary a lot, one of the more bizarre provisos being the State Railway's regulation that a child aged 3–12 qualifies for half fare only if under 150cm tall; in some stations you'll see a measuring scale painted onto the ticket-hall wall.

A few upmarket hotels arrange special **activities for kids**: the *Laguna Resort* hotels complex on Ao Bang Tao, Phuket (see p.649) is particularly recommended for its family-friendly accommodation and special kids' activities camp, as are the *Novotel Phuket Resort*, and the *Holiday Inn*, both on Patong Beach, Phuket (p.655). In Bangkok, there are several child-friendly theme parks and activity centres, listed on p.179. Several dive centres offer special courses for kids aged 7–11, including Kontiki, which has branches in Phuket (see p.639) and Khao Lak (see p.631). Despite its lack of obvious child-centred activities, many parents find that the moderately developed island of Ko Lanta (see p.695) makes a good destination for kids of all ages, with reasonably priced accommodation, fairly uncrowded sandy beaches and safe seas.

Directory

Addresses Thai addresses can be immensely confusing, mainly because property is often numbered twice, first to show which real estate lot it stands in, and then to distinguish where it is on that lot. Thus 154/7–10 Thanon Rajdamnoen means the building is on lot 154 and occupies numbers 7–10. There's an additional idiosyncrasy in the way Thai roads are sometimes named: in large cities a minor road running off a major road is often numbered as a soi ("lane" or "alley", though it may be a sizeable thoroughfare), rather than given its own street name. Thanon Sukhumvit for example – Bangkok's longest – has minor roads numbered Soi 1 to Soi 103, with odd numbers on one side of the road and even on the other; so a Thanon Sukhumvit address could read something like 27/9–11 Soi 15, Thanon Sukhumvit, which would mean the property occupies numbers 9–11 on lot 27 on minor road number 15 running off Thanon Sukhumvit.

Contact lens solutions Opticians in all reasonable-sized towns sell international brand-name contact lens cleaning and disinfection solutions.

Contraceptives Condoms (*meechai*) are sold in all pharmacies and in many hairdressers and village shops as well. Birth-control pills can be bought in Bangkok (see p.194); supplies of any other contraceptives should be brought from home.

Cookery classes You can take short courses in authentic Thai cookery at schools in Bangkok, Chiang Mai, Hua Hin, Kanchanaburi, Pai, Phuket and Sukhothai; see relevant accounts for details.

Electricity Supplied at 220 volts AC and available at all but the most remote villages and basic beach huts. If you're packing a hair dryer, laptop or other appliance, you'll need to take a set of travel-plug adapters with you as several plug types are commonly in use, most usually with two round pins, but also with two flat-blade pins, and sometimes with both options. Check out the Help for World Travellers website (ⓦ www.kropla.com) which has a very helpful list, complete with pictures, of the different sockets, voltage and phone plugs used in Thailand.

Employment The most common source of employment in Thailand is English teaching, and Bangkok and Chiang Mai are the best places to look. If you have teaching qualifications, you could try the British Council (ⓦ www.britcoun.org/english /teach.htm) and American University Alumni (AUA) schools, as well as the universities. If not, keep an eye on guest-house noticeboards in these two cities, as teachers often advertise for replacements here. The classifieds in the *Bangkok Metro* listings magazine also sometimes carry teachers-wanted ads. If you're a qualified dive master, you might be able to get seasonal work at one of the major resorts – the dive centres on Ko Phi Phi, Ko Lanta and Ko Tao are all good places to ask. Guest-house noticeboards occasionally carry adverts for more unusual jobs such as playing extras in Thai movies.

Film The price of film in Thailand is comparable to that in the West, approximately B100 for 36-exposure Fujicolour print film, or B225 for 36-exposure slide film. Slide film is hard to get outside the main tourist centres but video tape is more widely available. Developing film is a lot less expensive than back home and is done in a couple of hours in the main tourist areas, to about the same quality as in the West.

Laundry services Guest houses and hotels all over the country run low-cost same-day laundry services. In some places you pay per item, in others you're charged by the kilo; ironing is often included in the price.

Left luggage Most major train stations have left-luggage facilities where bags can be stored for up to twenty days; at bus stations you can usually persuade someone official to look after your stuff for a few hours. Many guest houses and hotels also offer an inexpensive and reliable service.

Tampons There's no need to haul boxloads of tampons into Thailand, as you can stock up from department stores in every sizeable town; guest houses often sell them as well.

Tipping Some upmarket hotels and restaurants will add an automatic ten-percent service charge to your bill. It is usual to tip hotel bellboys and porters B10–20, and to round up taxi fares to the nearest B10.

Women's groups An important political focus for Thai women is the Friends of Women Foundation at 218/16 Soi Pradipat 18, Phayathai, Bangkok 10400 (℡02/279 0867), which runs a counselling service and takes up women's rights issues, in particular fighting against the demeaning consequences of sex tourism. The long-established prostitute support group, Empower (PO Box 1065, Silom Post Office, Bangkok 10504; ⓦwww.empowerwomen.org), welcomes committed tourist volunteers who are interested in teaching English to bar girls in Patpong for a minimum period of three months. For more on women's organizations in Thailand see ⓦwww.euronet.nl/~fullmoon/womlist/countries/thailand.html. On a more general note, *Women Travel* (Rough Guides), an informative collection of women's travel essays, includes accounts of experiences in Thailand and other Southeast Asian countries.

guide

guide

Bangkok

CHAPTER 1   # Highlights

* **The Grand Palace** – The country's least missable sight, incorporating its holiest and most dazzling temple, **Wat Phra Kaeo**. **p.121**

* **Wat Po** – Gawp at the Reclining Buddha and the lavish architecture, and leave time for a relaxing massage. **p.127**

* **The National Museum** – The central repository of the country's artistic riches. **p.131**

* **Amulet markets** – Thousands of tiny Buddha images on sale at Wat Rajnadda and Wat Mahathat. **p.136** and **p.131**

* **The canals of Thonburi** – See the Bangkok of yesteryear on a touristy but memorable longtail boat ride. **p.148**

* **Jim Thompson's House** – An elegant Thai design classic. **p.152**

* **Chatuchak Weekend Market** – Six thousand stalls selling everything from triangular cushions to secondhand Levis. **p.161**

* **Thai boxing** – Nightly bouts at the national stadia, complete with live musical accompaniment and frenetic betting. **p.180**

* **Thai Craft Museum** – Shop for the best handicrafts, textiles and souvenirs under one roof. **p.184**

* **Thanon Khao San** – Legendary mecca for Southeast Asian backpackers; the place for cheap sleeps, baggy trousers and tall tales. **p.108**

1

Bangkok

The headlong pace and flawed modernity of **Bangkok** match few people's visions of the capital of exotic Siam. Spiked with scores of high-rise buildings of concrete and glass, it's a vast flatness which holds a population of at least nine million, and feels even bigger. But under the shadow of the skyscrapers you'll find a heady mix of chaos and refinement, of frenetic markets and hushed golden temples, of dispiriting, zombie-like sex shows and early-morning almsgiving ceremonies. One way or another, the place will probably get under your skin – and if you don't enjoy the challenge of slogging through jams of buses and tuk-tuks, which fill the air with a chain-saw drone and clouds of pollution, you can spend a couple of days on the most impressive temples and museums, have a quick shopping spree and then strike out for the provinces.

Most budget travellers head for the **Banglamphu** district, where if you're not careful you could end up watching videos all day long and selling your shoes when you run out of money. The district is far from having a monopoly on Bangkok accommodation, but it does have the advantage of being just a short walk from the major sights in the **Ratanakosin** area: the dazzling ostentation of **Wat Phra Kaeo**, the grandiose decay of **Wat Po** and the **National Museum**'s hoard of exquisite works of art. Once those cultural essentials have been seen, you can choose from a whole bevy of lesser sights, including **Wat Benjamabophit** (the "Marble Temple"), especially at festival time, and **Jim Thompson's House**, a small, personal museum of Thai design.

Accommodation prices

Throughout this guide, guest houses, hotels and bungalows have been categorized according to the **price codes** given below. These categories represent the minimum you can expect to pay in the high season (roughly July, Aug & Nov–Feb) for a **double room**. If travelling on your own, expect to pay anything between sixty and one hundred percent of the rates quoted for a double room. Wherever a **price range** is indicated, this means that the establishment offers rooms with varying facilities – as explained in the write-up. Wherever an establishment also offers **dormitory beds**, the prices of these beds are given in the text, instead of being indicated by price code.

Remember that the top-whack hotels will add seven percent tax and a ten percent service charge to your bill – the price codes below are based on net rates after taxes have been added.

❶ under B150	❹ B400–600	❼ B1200–1800
❷ B150–250	❺ B600–900	❽ B1800–3000
❸ B250–400	❻ B900–1200	❾ B3000+

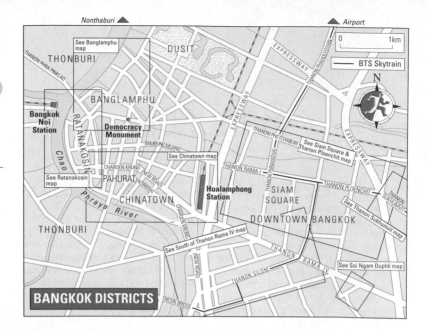

Nonthaburi ▲   ▲ Airport

BANGKOK DISTRICTS

For livelier scenes, explore the dark alleys of **Chinatown**'s bazaars or head for the water: the great **Chao Phraya River**, which breaks up and adds zest to the city's landscape, is the backbone of a network of **canals and floating markets** that remains fundamentally intact in the west-bank Thonburi district. Inevitably the waterways have earned Bangkok the title of "Venice of the East", a tag that seems all too apt when you're wading through flooded streets in the rainy season; indeed, the city is year by year subsiding into the marshy ground, literally sinking under the weight of its burgeoning concrete towers.

Shopping on dry land varies from touristic outlets selling silks, handicrafts and counterfeit watches, through international fashion emporia and home-grown, street-wise boutiques, to completely and sometimes undesirably authentic marketplaces – notably Chatuchak, where caged animals cringe among the pots and pans. Similarly, the city offers the country's most varied **entertainment**, ranging from traditional dancing and the orchestrated bedlam of Thai boxing, through hip bars and clubs playing the latest imported sounds, to the farang-only sex bars of the notorious Patpong district, a tinseltown Babylon that's the tip of a dangerous iceberg. Even if the above doesn't appeal, you'll almost certainly pass through Bangkok once, if not several times – not only is it Thailand's main port of entry, it's also the obvious place to sort out **onward travel**, with some of the world's best deals on international air tickets as well as a convenient menu of embassies for visas to neighbouring countries.

A little history

Bangkok is a relatively young capital, established in 1782 after the Burmese sacked Ayutthaya, the former capital. A temporary base was set up on the western bank of the Chao Phraya, in what is now **Thonburi**, before work started on the more defensible east bank, where the French had built a grand, but short-lived fort in the 1660s. The first king of the new dynasty, Rama I, built

City of angels

When Rama I was crowned in 1782, he gave his new capital a grand 43-syllable name to match his ambitious plans for the building of the city. Since then 21 more syllables have been added. Krungthepmahanakhornbowornrattanakosinmahintarayutthaya-mahadilokpopnopparatratchathaniburiromudomratchaniwetmahasathanamornpim-anavatarnsathitsakkathattiyavisnukarprasit is certified by the *Guinness Book of Records* as the longest place name in the world, roughly translating as "Great city of angels, the supreme repository of divine jewels, the great land unconquerable, the grand and prominent realm, the royal and delightful capital city full of nine noble gems, the highest royal dwelling and grand palace, the divine shelter and living place of the reincarnated spirits". Fortunately, all Thais refer to the city simply as Krung Thep, though plenty can recite the full name at the drop of a hat. Bangkok – "Village of the Plum Olive" – was the name of the original village on the Thonburi side; with remarkable persistence, it has remained in use by foreigners since the time of the French garrison.

his palace at **Ratanakosin**, within a defensive ring of two (later expanded to three) canals, and this remains the city's spiritual heart.

Initially, the city was largely **amphibious**: only the temples and royal palaces were built on dry land, while ordinary residences floated on thick bamboo rafts on the river and canals; even shops and warehouses were moored to the river bank. A major shift in emphasis came in the second half of the nineteenth century, first under Rama IV (1851–68), who as part of his effort to restyle the capital along European lines built Bangkok's first roads, and then under Rama V (1868–1910), who constructed a new residential palace in Dusit, north of Ratanakosin, and laid out that area's grand boulevards.

Since World War II, and especially from the mid-1960s onwards, Bangkok has seen an explosion of **modernization**, which has blown away earlier attempts at orderly planning and left the city without an obvious centre. Most of the canals have been filled in, to be replaced by endless rows of cheap and functional concrete shophouses, sprawling over a built-up area of 330 square kilometres. The benefits of the **economic boom** of the 1980s and early 1990s were concentrated in Bangkok, as well as the calamitous effects of the late-1990s **economic crisis**, both of which attracted migration from all over Thailand and made the capital ever more dominant: the population is now forty times that of the second city, Chiang Mai. Bangkokians now own four-fifths of the nation's automobiles, and there's precious little chance to escape from the pollution in green space: the city has only 0.4 square metres of public parkland per inhabitant, the lowest figure in the world, compared, for example, to London's 30.4 square metres per person.

Arrival and accommodation

Finding a place to stay in Bangkok is usually no problem: the city has a huge range of **accommodation**, from the murkiest backstreet bunk to the plushest five-star riverside suite, and you don't have to spend a lot to get a comfortable place. Getting to your guest house or hotel, however, is unlikely to put you in a good mood, for there can be few cities in the world where **transport** is such a headache. Bumper-to-bumper vehicles create fumes so bad that some days the city's carbon monoxide emissions come close to the international danger level, and it's not unusual for residents to spend three hours getting to work – and these are people who know where they're going. However, the opening in December 1999 of the elevated train network called the Bangkok Transit System, or BTS Skytrain, has radically improved public transport in a few parts of the city, notably the Siam Square, Silom and Sukhumvit areas. Unfortunately for tourists, the Skytrain system does not stretch as far as Ratanakosin or Banglamphu, where boats still provide the fastest means of hopping from one sight to another.

Arriving in Bangkok

Unless you arrive in Bangkok by train, be prepared for a long slog into the centre. Most travellers' first sight of the city is the International Terminal at Don Muang airport, a slow 25km to the north. Even if you arrive by coach, you'll still have a lot of work to do to get into the centre.

By air

Once you're through immigration at either of the two interconnected **international terminals** at **Don Muang airport** (queues are often horrendous, owing to the availability of free short-stay visas on the spot), you'll find 24-hour exchange booths, a couple of helpful TAT information desks (daily 8am–midnight; ☎02/523 8972), a round-the-clock Thai Hotels Association accommodation desk, with prices generally cheaper than rack rates, post offices and international telephone facilities, a pricey left-luggage depot (B70 per item per day), an emergency clinic and, on the fourth floor of the newer Terminal 2 opposite *Pizza Hut*, an expensive cybercafé. Among a wide variety of food and drink outlets (particularly in Terminal 2, which boasts Chinese and Japanese restaurants and a British pub that offers 24hr breakfasts), the cheapest and most interesting options are two food centres serving simple Thai dishes, one on the south side of Terminal 2 on the walkway to the domestic terminal, the other on the fourth floor, accessible from Terminals 1 and 2.

Getting into town

The most economical way of getting into the city is by **public bus**, but this can be excruciatingly slow and the invariably crowded vehicles are totally unsuitable for heavily laden travellers. The bus stop is on the main highway which runs north–south just outside the airport buildings: to find it, head straight out from the northern end of arrivals. Most of the buses run all day and night, with a reduced service after 10pm; see the box on p.100 for a rough sketch of the most useful routes – the TAT office in arrivals has further details. Unless you're already counting your baht, you're better off getting into the city by air-conditioned **airport bus** (daily 4.30am–12.30am; every 30min; B100 payable on bus); the buses depart from outside Terminal 1, Terminal 2 and the domestic terminal (clearly signposted outside each building). Four routes are covered: route AB1 runs along to the west end of Thanon Silom, via Pratunam and Thanon Rajdamri; route AB2 goes to Sanam Luang, via Victory

Monument, Democracy Monument, Thanon Tanao (for Thanon Khao San), Thanon Phra Sumen and Thanon Phra Athit; route AB3 runs down the Dindaeng Expressway and along Thanon Sukhumvit to Soi Thonglor via the Eastern Bus Terminal; and route AB4 runs down the Dindaeng Expressway and west along Thanon Ploenchit to Siam Square, then down to Hualamphong train station. A handy colour leaflet available from the TAT desks details which major hotels each route passes.

The **train** to Hualamphong station (see p.96) is the quickest way into town, and ideal if you want to stay in Chinatown, but services are irregular. To reach the station at Don Muang follow the signs from arrivals in Terminal 1 (if in doubt head towards the big *Amari Airport Hotel*, across the main highway, carry on through the hotel foyer and the station is in front of you). Over thirty trains a day make the fifty-minute trip to Hualamphong, with fares starting from B5 in third class (though express trains command surcharges of up to B80), with services most frequent around the early morning – at other times of the day you might have to wait over an hour.

Taxis to the centre are comfortable, air-conditioned and not too extravagantly priced, although the driving can be hairy. A wide variety is on offer, from pricey limousines, through licensed metered cabs, down to cheap unlicensed and unmetered vehicles – avoid the last-mentioned, as newly arrived travellers are seen as easy prey for robbery, and the cabs are untraceable. Metered taxis, the best option, are operated from clearly signposted counters outside Terminal 1. Even including the B50 airport pick-up fee and B70 tolls for the overhead expressways, a journey to Thanon Ploenchit downtown, for example, should set you back around B250 depending on the traffic.

Airport accommodation

With time to kill and money to spare between flights, you might want to rest and clean up at the *Amari Airport Hotel* (℡02/566 1020, ℗566 1941, ⊛www.amari.com; ➒), just across the road from the international terminal, which rents out very upmarket **bedrooms** for three-hour periods from 8am to 6pm (US$20, no reservations) – far better than the international terminals' day rooms, which are twice the price and designed for transit passengers. To **stay near the airport**, the *Comfort Inn* is a more economical choice (℡02/552 8929, ℗552 8920, ⓔpinap@loxinfo.co.th; ➑) and will pick you up for the five-minute journey from the terminals if you call. Another good option is the huge *Asia Airport Hotel* (℡02/992 6653, ℗992 6828, ⊛www.asiahotel.co.th; ➐), less than ten minutes' drive north of the international terminal, just south of the Rangsit interchange on Thanon Phaholyothin. All rooms are air-conditioned and comfortably furnished, there's a hotel restaurant, a swimming pool and a shopping complex, and free transport to and from the airport; book over the Internet for significant discounts. Cheaper still is the *We-Train* guest house, about 3km west of the airport (℡02/929 2301–10, ℗929 2300, ⊛www.wetrain.linethai.co.th; ➍), run by the Association for the Promotion of the Status of Women, where proceeds go to help distressed women and children; in a peaceful lakeside setting, there are dorms (B140), comfortable fan- or air-conditioned rooms and a swimming pool.

Getting to the rest of the country

To catch a connecting **internal flight**, head to the **domestic terminal** at Don Muang, 500m away from Terminal 2, connected by an air-conditioned covered walkway and by a free shuttle bus (daily 5am–midnight; every 15min); the **domestic departure tax** of B30 is always included in the price of your ticket.

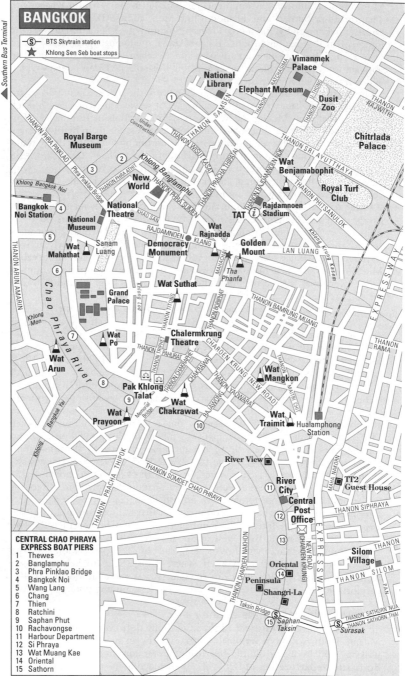

BANGKOK

- Ⓢ BTS Skytrain station
- ★ Khlong Sen Seb boat stops

Nonthaburi ▲

◄ Southern Bus Terminal

National Library
Vimanmek Palace
Elephant Museum
Dusit Zoo
Chitrlada Palace
THANON RATCHASIMA
THANON RAJWITHI
THANON SRI AYUTTHAYA
THANON PHITSANULOK
Royal Barge Museum
Khlong Banglamphu
New World
Wat Benjamabophit
Royal Turf Club
Khlong Bangkok Noi
THANON PHRA PINKLAO
Phra Pinklao Bridge
THANON WISUT KASAT
THANON SANSEN
THANON PRACHA THIPATA
THANON RA-DAMNOEN NOK
Bangkok Noi Station
National Theatre
KHAO SAN
Wat Rajnadda
Rajdamnoen Stadium
TAT ⓘ
THANON RA-DAMNOEN KLANG
National Museum
Wat Mahathat
Sanam Luang
RAJDAMNOEN KLANG
Democracy Monument
Golden Mount
LAN LUANG
Khlong Krung Kasem
Chao Phraya River
THANON ARUN AMARIN
Khlong Mon
Grand Palace
Wat Suthat
Tha Phanfa
THANON BAMRUNG MUANG
E X P R E S S W A Y
THANON RAMA
THANON TRIPHET
THANON TITONG
THANON BOROBAT
Wat Po
Chalermkrung Theatre
CHAROEN KRUNG (NEW ROAD)
Wat Mangkon
THANON MAITRI CHIT
Wat Arun
THANON PAHURAT
THANON CHAKRAPET
THANON CHAKRAWAT
THANON YAOWARAT
Pak Khlong Talat
Wat Chakrawat
Wat Traimit
Hualamphong Station
Bangkok Yai
Wat Prayoon
Memorial Bridge
RAJAWONG
Khlong
THANON PRACHA THIPOK
River View
MAHA NAKORN
TT2 Guest House
THANON SOMDET CHAO PHRAYA
River City
Central Post Office
THANON SIPHRAYA
THANON CHAROEN NAKHON
NEW ROAD (CHAROEN KRUNG)
Silom Village
THANON SILOM
Oriental
Peninsula
Shangri-La
Taksin Bridge Ⓢ
Saphan Taksin
THANON SATHORN NUA
THANON SATHORN THAI
Ⓢ Surasak
PAN

CENTRAL CHAO PHRAYA EXPRESS BOAT PIERS

1. Thewes
2. Banglamphu
3. Phra Pinklao Bridge
4. Bangkok Noi
5. Wang Lang
6. Chang
7. Thien
8. Ratchini
9. Saphan Phut
10. Rachavongse
11. Harbour Department
12. Si Phraya
13. Wat Muang Kae
14. Oriental
15. Sathorn

Marriott Royal Garden Hotel ▼

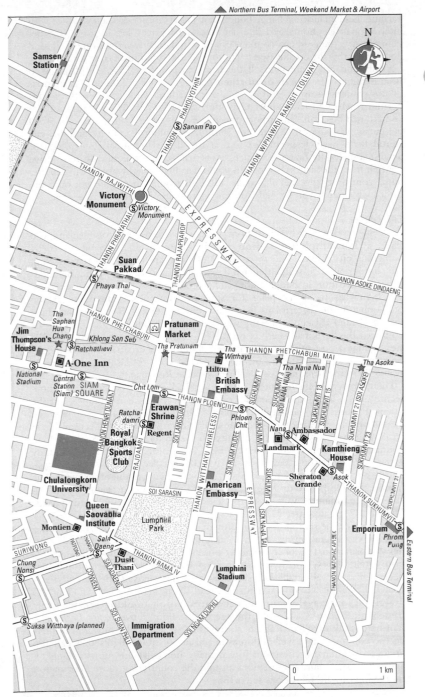

N

Samsen
Station

THANON PHAHOLYOTHIN

Ⓢ Sanam Pao

THANON WIPHAWADI RANGSIT (TOLLWAY)

THANON RAJWITHI

Victory
Monument
Ⓢ Victory
Monument

EXPRESSWAY

THANON PHRAYATHAI

THANON RAJAPRAROP

Suan
Pakkad
Ⓢ
Phaya Thai

THANON ASOKE DINDAENG

THANON PHETCHABURI

Tha
Saphan
Hua
Chang

Pratunam
Market

THANON PHETCHABURI MAI

Jim
Thompson's
House

Khlong Sen Seb
Ⓢ Ratchathevi

Tha Pratunam ★

★ Tha
Witthayu

Tha Asoke ★

A-One Inn

National
Stadium

Central
Station
(Siam)

SIAM
SQUARE

Chit Lom

Hilton

THANON PHETCHABURI MAI

Tha Nana Nua

British
Embassy

SUKHUMVIT 13

SUKHUMVIT 15

SUKHUMVIT 21 (SOI ASOKE)

Ⓢ

THANON PLOENCHIT

Ⓢ

Erawan
Shrine

Phloen
Chit

SOI RUAM RUDEE

SUKHUMVIT 2

SOI NANA NUA

Nana
Ⓢ

Ambassador

Kamthieng
House

SUKHUMVIT 23

THANON HENRI DUNANT

Ratcha-
damri

Ⓢ Regent

SOI LANGSUAN

Landmark

Royal
Bangkok
Sports
Club

SUKHUMVIT 4

SOI NANA TAI

Sheraton
Grande

Asok Ⓢ

THANON SUKHUMVIT

SUKHUMVIT 31

RAJDAMRI

Chulalongkorn
University

SOI SARASIN

American
Embassy

THANON WITTHAYU (WIRELESS)

EXPRESSWAY

THANON RATCHADAPISEK

Queen
Saovablia
Institute

Montien

Sala
Daeng
Ⓢ

Lumphini
Park

Emporium Ⓢ

Phrom
Pong

SURIWONG

SILOM

PATPONG

CONVENT

SALADAENG

Dusit
Thani

THANON RAMA IV

Lumphini
Stadium

Chong
Nonsi
Ⓢ

Ⓢ Suksa Witthaya (planned)

SOI SUAN PHLU

Immigration
Department

SOI NGAM DUPHLI

0   1 km

Ester'n Bus Terminal

Facilities here include exchange booths, hotel reservation desks, a post office with international telephones and internet access, and pricey left luggage (B70 per item per day); metered taxi counters can be found outside arrivals on the ground floor, while the airport bus (see p.92) stops outside the northern end of arrivals.

Finally, you can spare yourself the trip into Bangkok if you're planning to head straight to the **north or northeast** by train or bus: all trains to these parts of the country stop at Don Muang train station, while the Northern Bus Terminal (Mo Chit) is a short taxi ride away. Thai Airways also runs an air-conditioned bus from the airport direct to **Pattaya** three times a day for B200 per person (9am, noon & 7pm; 2hr 30min). Several local and international **car rental** firms have desks and/or reps at the airport terminals (see p.193 for details) and, despite first appearances, it's actually quite straightforward to drive yourself from the airport, so long as you're heading straight out of the city; the rental companies give detailed maps and instructions on how to get onto the right highway, but you'll need a decent route map of your own after that.

By train

Travelling to Bangkok by **train** from Malaysia and most parts of Thailand, you arrive at **Hualamphong station**, which is centrally located and served by numerous **city buses**. The most useful of these are bus #53 (non-air-con), which stops on the east side (left-hand exit) of the station and runs to the budget accommodation in Banglamphu; and the #25 and #40 (both non-air-con), which run east to Siam Square (for Skytrain connections) and along Thanon Sukhumvit to the Eastern Bus Terminal; the westbound #25 runs to Tha Thien (for the Grand Palace), while the westbound #40 heads over the river to the Southern Bus Terminal. See box on p.100 for bus-route details. Station **facilities** include a post office, an exchange booth and a Cirrus/MasterCard cash-point machine (to get to the nearest Visa ATM walk 100m left along Thanon Rama IV to the bank next to *You Sue Vegetarian Restaurant*).

There are two **left-luggage** offices at Hualamphong station. The more secure option is inside the postal service centre at the main entrance, but the opening hours are unhelpfully short (Mon–Fri & Sun 7am–7pm, Sat 8am–4pm) and it's expensive at B30 per day. Alternative storage is available at a cabin halfway down Platform 12, next to the Eastern and Oriental check-in counter; the hours and prices here are more user-friendly (daily 4am–10.30pm; B10 per day for 1–5 days, B15 per day for more than 5 days), but it's not fully enclosed and so doesn't look as secure as the other place. The most economical place to store baggage is at the *TT2 Guest House* (see p.111), about fifteen minutes' walk from the station, which provides the same service for only B7 per item per day.

One service the station does not provide is itinerant tourist assistance staff – anyone who comes up to you in or around the station concourse and offers help/information/transport or ticket-booking services is almost certainly a **con-artist**, however many official-looking ID tags are hanging around their necks. This is a well-established scam to fleece new arrivals; the best advice is to avoid them at all costs and turn instead to the friendly and efficient VC Travel and Tour **travel agent** and **accommodation-booking service** (daily 5am–8pm; ☏02/613 6725) on the mezzanine floor above *Coffee Bucks*. The staff here speak excellent English, so this is the place to buy onward rail tickets (no commission) as well as domestic and international flights; they can also arrange discounted accommodation at many hotels (❹ and up) in Bangkok and other major tourist destinations around the country. For more information on buying onward rail tickets see p.188.

Trains from Kanchanaburi pull in at the small and not very busy **Bangkok Noi Station** in Thonburi, which is on the express-boat line (see p.102), just across the Chao Phraya River from Banglamphu and Ratanakosin.

By bus

Buses come to a halt at a number of far-flung spots. All services from the north and northeast terminate at the **Northern Bus Terminal** (**Mo Chit**) on Thanon Kamphaeng Phet 2; some east-coast buses also use Mo Chit (rather than the Eastern Terminal), including several daily services from Pattaya, and a few daily buses from Rayong (for Ko Samet), Chanthaburi and Trat (for Ko Chang and the Cambodian border). The quickest way to get into the city centre from Mo Chit is to hop onto the **Skytrain** at the Mo Chit BTS station, five minutes' walk from the bus terminal on Thanon Phaholyothin, and then change onto a city bus if necessary – see p.103 for details of Skytrain routes and fares. Otherwise, it's a long bus, tuk-tuk or taxi ride into town: **city buses** from the Mo Chit area include #2 and #77 to Thanon Silom; regular and air-conditioned #3, and air-conditioned #9, #12 and #32 to Banglamphu; and both regular and air-conditioned #29 to Hualamphong Railway station; for details of these routes see the box on p.100.

Most buses from the east coast use the **Eastern Bus Terminal** (**Ekamai**) at Soi 40, Thanon Sukhumvit. This bus station is right beside the Ekamai **Skytrain** stop (see p.103), and is also served by lots of **city buses**, including air-conditioned #11 to Banglamphu and regular #59 to the Northern Bus Terminal (see box on pp.100–1 for details), or you can take a taxi down Soi 63 to Tha Ekamai, a pier on Khlong Sen Seb, to pick up the **canal boat service** to the Golden Mount near Banglamphu (see p.102).

Bus services from Malaysia and the south, as well as from Kanchanaburi, use the **Southern Bus Terminal** (**Sai Tai Mai**) at the junction of Thanon Borom Ratchonni and the Nakhon Chaisri Highway, west of the Chao Phraya River in Thonburi. Drivers on these services nearly always offer to drop passengers on the east side of Thanon Borom Ratchonni before doing a U-turn for the terminus on the west side of the road; if you're heading across the river to Banglamphu or downtown Bangkok you should get off here, along with the majority of the other passengers. Numerous **city buses** run across the river from this bus stop, including air-con #7 to Banglamphu and Hualamphong station, and air-con #11 to Banglamphu and Thanon Sukhumvit (see box on p.100 for routes), and they tend to be pretty empty at this point so quite manageable for luggage-bearing tourists. City buses are especially useful here as the Southern Bus Terminal is renowned for its belligerent **taxi** drivers, nearly all of whom refuse to use the meter and quote anything from B250 to B650 for the trip into central Bangkok. If you are keen to take a taxi to your destination, take any west-bound bus for a few stops to get well away from the bus terminal zone, then hail a metered taxi.

Orientation and information

Bangkok can be a tricky place to get your bearings as it's huge and ridiculously congested, with largely featureless modern buildings and no obvious centre. The boldest line on the map is the **Chao Phraya River**, which divides the city into Bangkok proper on the east bank, and **Thonburi**, part of Greater Bangkok, on the west.

The historical core of Bangkok proper, site of the original royal palace, is **Ratanakosin**, which nestles into a bend in the river. Three concentric canals radiate eastwards around Ratanakosin: the southern part of the area between the canals is the old-style trading enclave of **Chinatown** and Indian **Pahurat**, linked to the old palace by Thanon Charoen Krung (aka New Road); the northern part is characterized by old temples and the **Democracy Monument**, west of which is the backpackers' ghetto of **Banglamphu**. Beyond the canals to the north, **Dusit** is the site of many government buildings and the nineteenth-century palace, which is linked to Ratanakosin by the two stately avenues, Thanon Rajdamnoen Nok and Thanon Rajdamnoen Klang.

"New" Bangkok begins to the east of the canals and beyond the main rail line, and stretches as far as the eye can see to the east and north. The main business district and most of the embassies are south of **Thanon Rama IV**, with the port of Khlong Toey at the southern edge. The diverse area north of Thanon Rama IV includes the sprawling campus of Chulalongkorn University, huge shopping centres around **Siam Square** and a variety of other businesses. A couple of blocks northeast of Siam Square stands the tallest building in Bangkok, the 84-storeyed *Baiyoke Sky Hotel*, whose golden spire makes a good point of reference. To the east lies the swish residential quarter off **Thanon Sukhumvit**.

Information and maps

The newly established **Bangkok Tourist Bureau** (BTB) provides excellent information for tourists on all budgets both from its headquarters, the **Bangkok Information Centre**, located next to Phra Pinklao Bridge at 17/1 Thanon Phra Athit in Banglamphu (daily 9am–7pm; ☎02/225 7612–4), and from its dozen strategically placed information booths around the capital. They all provide reasonable city maps for free, and also run a variety of interesting city tours by boat, bus and bicycle (see p.99). The BTB is the most useful resource for information on the capital, but for destinations further afield you need to visit the **Tourism Authority of Thailand** (**TAT**) which maintains a Tourist Service Centre within walking distance of Banglamphu, at 4 Rajdamnoen Nok (24hr; ☎02/282 9773–4; 24hr freephone tourist assistance ☎1155), a twenty-minute stroll from Thanon Khao San, or a short ride in air-conditioned bus #3. This has plenty of handouts about Bangkok and the provinces, as well as a guide to TAT-approved shops. TAT also has a booth in the airport arrivals concourse. Other useful sources of information, especially about what to avoid, are the travellers' **noticeboards** in many of the Banglamphu guest houses.

If you're staying in Bangkok for more than a couple of days and want to get the most out of the city, it's worth getting hold of *Metro*, a monthly **listings magazine** available in bookstores, hotel shops and 7-11 shops. For B100, you get coverage very similar to London's *Time Out*, including a mixed bag of lively articles and especially useful sections on restaurants, cinemas, nightlife and gay life. If you don't wish to fork out for this, try the two English-language dailies, the *Nation* and the *Bangkok Post*, which give limited information about what's on across the city. Some hotels and tourist offices hand out copies of various free tourist magazines, all of which carry a few articles about local attractions alongside scores of advertisements.

To get around Bangkok without spending much money, you'll need to buy a **bus map**. Of the several available at bookshops, hotels and some guest houses, the most useful is Bangkok Guide's *Bus Routes & Map*, which not only maps all major air-conditioned and non-air-conditioned bus routes but also carries detailed written itineraries of some two hundred bus routes on its flip-side. If you can't find a copy, opt for the long-running bright blue and yellow bus map published by Tour 'n' Guide, which maps bus routes as well as the names of dozens of smaller sois; its street locations are not always reliable however, and it can be hard to decipher exact bus routings. *Litehart's Groovy Map and Guide* pride themselves on marking their bus routes much more clearly – they are nicely colour-coded for ease of use – but only selected routes are given, which is not much good if you find yourself stranded and wanting to know where a particular bus is heading. They also publish a *Bangkok By Night* map, which highlights their recommended bars, restaurants and clubs. The most accurate map for locating small streets and places of interest in the city is *GeoCenter's Bangkok 1:15,000*, best bought before you leave home, though it's also available in some Bangkok bookshops. Serious shoppers might also want to buy a copy of *Nancy Chandler's* idiosyncratic map of Bangkok, which has lots of annotated recommendations on shops and markets across the city; it's available in most tourist areas.

City transport

The main form of transport in the city is **buses**, and once you've mastered the labyrinthine complexity of the route map you'll be able to get to any part of the city, albeit slowly. Catching the various kinds of **taxi** can make a serious dent in your budget, and you'll still get held up by the daytime traffic jams. **Boats** are obviously more limited in their range, but they're regular and as cheap as buses, and you'll save a lot of time by using them whenever possible – a journey between Banglamphu and the GPO, for instance, will take around thirty minutes by water, half what it would take on land. The **Skytrain** has a similarly limited range but is also worth using whenever suitable for all or part of your journey; its network coincides with the Chao Phraya River Express boats at the vital hub of Sathorn Bridge (Saphan Taksin). **Walking** might often be quicker than travelling by road, but the heat can be unbearable, distances are always further than they look on the map, and the engine fumes are stifling.

If you can't face negotiating the public transport network, any taxi or tuk-tuk driver can be hired for the day to take you around the major or minor sights (B500–800), and every travel agent in the city can arrange this for you as well. Alternatively you can join the open-topped, double-decker **Bangkok Sightseeing Bus** which does a ninety-minute guided tour of Ratanakosin, taking in the Grand Palace and Vimanmek (5 daily; B200); contact the Bangkok Tourist Bureau for details. The BTB also runs several quite unusual **tours** of the capital, including a night-time bicycle tour of Ratanakosin (every Sat 7–9.30pm; B290 including bicycle), and a highly recommended 35-kilometre ride along the canal towpaths of Thonburi (see box on p.148).

Buses

Bangkok has three types of bus service, and it's not uncommon for one route to be served by the full trio. **Ordinary** (non-air-con) buses come in a variety of colours and sizes, and fares for most journeys range from B3.5 to B5; most routes maintain a 24-hour service. **Air-conditioned** buses subdivide into three varieties: blue (B6–18 according to distance travelled) and orange (B8–20) public buses, and smaller blue private buses (B8–20); most stop at

Useful bus routes

Except where stated, all buses follow an almost identical route on the return leg of their journey.

#2 (air-con): *Oriental Hotel*–Thanon Silom–Thanon Rama IV–MBK department store (for Siam Square)–Thanon Phayathai–Chatuchak Weekend Market–Lard Phrao–Suwinthawong.

#3 (ordinary): Northern Bus Terminal–Chatuchak Weekend Market–Thanon Phaholyothin–Thanon Samsen–Thanon Phra Athit (for Banglamphu guest houses)–Thanon Sanam Chai–Thanon Triphet–Memorial Bridge (for Pak Khlong Talat)–Taksin Monument–Wat Suwan.

#3 (air-con): Southern Bus Terminal–Thanon Borom Ratchonni–Phra Pinklao Bridge (for Banglamphu guest houses)–Democracy Monument–Rajdamnoen Nok (for TAT and boxing stadium)–Wat Benjamabophit–Thanon Sri Ayutthaya (for Thewes guest houses)–Victory Monument–Chatuchak Weekend Market–Rangsit.

#4 (air-con): Airport–Thanon Rajaprarop–Thanon Silom–Thanon Charoen Krung–Thonburi.

#7 (air-con): Southern Bus Terminal–Thanon Borom Ratchonni–Phra Pinklao (for Banglamphu guest houses)–Sanam Luang–Thanon Charoen Krung (New Road)–Thanon Chakrawat–Thanon Yaowarat (for Chinatown and Wat Traimit)–Hualamphong Station–Thanon Rama IV–Bang Na Intersection–Pak Nam.

#8 (air-con): Wat Po–Grand Palace–Giant Swing (for Wat Suthat)–Thanon Yaowarat–Siam Square–Thanon Ploenchit–Thanon Sukhumvit–Eastern Bus Terminal–Pak Nam (for Ancient City buses).

#9 (air-con): Nonthaburi–Chatuchak Weekend Market–Victory Monument–Thanon Phitsanulok–Democracy Monument–Rajdamnoen Klang (for Banglamphu guest houses)–Phra Pinklao–Thonburi.

#10 (air-con): Airport–Chatuchak Weekend Market–Victory Monument–Dusit Zoo–Thanon Rajwithi–Krung Thon Bridge (for Thewes guest houses)–Thonburi.

#11 (air-con): Southern Bus Terminal–Thanon Borom Ratchonni–Phra Pinklao–Rajdamnoen Klang (for Banglamphu guest houses)–Democracy Monument–Thanon Sukhumvit–Eastern Bus Terminal–Pak Nam (for Ancient City bus).

#12 (air-con): Northern Bus Terminal–Chatuchak Weekend Market–Thanon Phetchaburi–Thanon Larn Luang–Democracy Monument (for Banglamphu guest houses)–Tha Chang–Pak Khlong Talat.

#13 (air-con): Airport–Chatuchak Weekend Market–Victory Monument–Thanon Rajaprarop–Thanon Sukhumvit–Eastern Bus Terminal–Sukhumvit Soi 62.

around 10pm, but some of the more popular services run all night. As buses can only go as fast as the car in front, which at the moment is averaging 4kph, you'll probably be spending a long time on each journey, so you'd be well advised to pay the extra for cool air – and the air-conditioned buses are usually less crowded, too. It's also possible during the day to travel certain routes on flashy, air-conditioned private **microbuses**, which were designed with the

#15 (ordinary): Bamrung Muang–Thanon Phra Athit (for Banglamphu guest houses)–Grand Palace–Sanam Luang–Democracy Monument–Phanfa (for Khlong Sen Seb and Golden Mount)–Siam Square–Thanon Rajdamri–Thanon Silom–Thanon Charoen Krung (New Road)–Krung Thep Bridge–Thanon Rajadapisek.

#16 (ordinary): Thanon Srinarong–Thanon Samsen–Thewes (for guest houses)–Thanon Phitsanulok–Siam Square–Thanon Henri Dunant–GPO–Tha Si Phraya.

#25 (ordinary): Eastern Bus Terminal–Thanon Sukhumvit–Siam Square–Hualamphong Station–Thanon Yaowarat (for Chinatown)–Pahurat–Wat Po and the Grand Palace–Tha Chang.

#29 (air-con and ordinary): Airport–Chatuchak Weekend Market–Victory Monument–Siam Square–Hualamphong Station.

#32 (air-con): Thanon Phra Pinklao–Rajdamnoen Klang (for Thanon Khao San guest houses)– Democracy Monument–Victory Monument–Northern Bus Terminal.

#38 (ordinary): Chatuchak Weekend Market–Victory Monument–Thanon Phetchaburi–Soi Asoke–Eastern Bus Terminal.

#39 (air-con and ordinary): Chatuchak Weekend Market–Victory Monument–Thanon Sri Ayutthaya–Thanon Larn Luang–Democracy Monument–Rajdamnoen Klang (for Thanon Khao San guest houses)–Sanam Luang.

#40 (ordinary): Eastern Bus Terminal–Thanon Sukhumvit–Thanon Rama I (for Siam Square)–Hualamphong Station–Thanon Yaowarat (for Chinatown)–Southern Bus Terminal.

#53 (ordinary): Hualamphong Station–Thanon Krung Kasem–Thanon Samsen and Thanon Phra Athit (for Banglamphu guest houses)–Sanam Luang (for National Museum and Wat Mahathat)–Thanon Mahathat (for Grand Palace and Wat Po)–Pahurat–Thanon Krung Kasem.

#56 (ordinary): Circular route; Phra Sumen–Wat Bowoniwes–Thanon Ratchasima (for Vimanmek Palace)–Thanon Rajwithi–Krung Thon Bridge–Thonburi–Memorial Bridge–Thanon Chakraphet (for Chinatown)–Thanon Mahachai–Democracy Monument–Thanon Tanao (for Khao San guest houses)–Thanon Phra Sumen.

#59 (ordinary): Airport–Chatuchak Weekend Market–Victory Monument–Phanfa (for Khlong Sen Seb and Golden Mount)–Democracy Monument (for Banglamphu guest houses)–Sanam Luang.

#124 and **#127** (ordinary): Southern Bus Terminal–Tha Pinklao (for ferry to Phra Athit and Banglamphu guest houses).

commuter in mind and offer the use of an on-board telephone and newspapers, plus the certainty of a seat (no standing allowed) for a B25 fare (exact money only), which is dropped into a box beside the driver's seat.

Some of the most useful city-bus routes are described in the box above; for a comprehensive roundup of all bus routes in the capital, buy a copy of Bangkok Guide's *Bus Routes & Map* (see p.98), or log onto the Bangkok Mass

Transportation website (W www.bmta.motc.go.th), which also gives details in English of every city-bus route.

Boats

Bangkok was built as an amphibious city around a network of canals – or **khlongs** – and the first streets were constructed only in the second half of the nineteenth century. Although most of the canals have been turned into roads on the Bangkok side, the Chao Phraya River is still a major transport route for residents and non-residents alike, forming more of a link than a barrier between the two halves of the city, and used by several different kinds of boat.

Express boats

The Chao Phraya Express Boat Company operates the vital **express-boat** (*reua duan*) service, using large water buses to plough up and down the river, between clearly signed piers (*tha*) which appear on all Bangkok maps – the important central stops are outlined in the box opposite and marked on our city map (see pp.94–5). Its usual route, ninety minutes in total, runs between Wat Rajsingkorn, just upriver of Krung Thep Bridge, in the south and Nonthaburi in the north. These **"daily standard"** boats set off every ten to fifteen minutes or so between about 6am and 6.30pm, the last boat in each direction flying a blue flag. Boats do not necessarily stop at every landing – they only pull in if people want to get on or off, and when they do stop, it's not for long – when you want to get off, be ready at the back of the boat in good time for your pier. During rush hours (roughly 6–9am & 4–7pm), certain **"special express"** boats operate limited-stop services on set routes, flying either a **yellow** (Nonthaburi to Rajburana, far downriver beyond Krung Thep Bridge) or a **red and orange flag** (Nonthaburi to Wat Rajsingkorn).

   Tickets can be bought on board, and cost B6–12 according to distance travelled, or B15–25 on yellow-flag boats. Don't discard your ticket until you're off the boat, as the staff at some piers impose a B1 fine on anyone disembarking without one.

Cross-river ferries

Smaller than express boats are the slow **cross-river ferries** (*reua kham fak*), which shuttle back and forth between the same two points. Found at every express stop and plenty of other piers in between, they are especially useful for connections to Chao Phraya special express boat stops during rush hours. Fares are B2, which you usually pay at the entrance to the pier.

Longtail boats

Longtail boats (*reua hang yao*) ply the khlongs of Thonburi like buses, stopping at designated shelters (fares are in line with those of express boats), and are available for individual rental here and on the river (see box on p.148). On the Bangkok side, **Khlong Sen Seb** is well served by longtails, which run at least every fifteen minutes during daylight hours from the Phanfa pier at the Golden Mount (handy for Banglamphu, Ratanakosin and Chinatown), and head way out east to Wat Sribunruang, with useful stops at Thanon Phrayathai, aka Saphan Hua Chang (for Jim Thompson's House and Ratchathewi Skytrain stop), Pratunam (for the World Trade Centre and Gaysorn Plaza), Soi Chitlom, Thanon Witthayu (Wireless Road), and Soi Nana Nua (Soi 3), Soi Asoke (Soi 21), Soi Thonglo (Soi 55) and Soi Ekamai (Soi 63), all off Thanon Sukhumvit. This is your quickest and most interesting way of getting between the west and east parts of town, if you can stand the stench of the canal. You may have

Central stops for the Chao Phraya express boat

1. Thewes (all daily standard and special express boats) – for Thewes guest houses.
2. Banglamphu (daily standard) – for Thanon Khao San and Banglamphu guest houses.
3. Phra Pinklao Bridge (all daily standard and special express boats) – for Thonburi shops and city buses to the Southern Bus Terminal.
4. Bangkok Noi (daily standard) – for trains to Kanchanaburi.
5. Wang Lang (or Prannok; all daily standard and special express boats) – for Siriraj Hospital.
6. Chang (daily standard and red and orange flag) – for the Grand Palace.
7. Thien (daily standard) – for Wat Po, and the cross-river ferry to Wat Arun.
8. Ratchini (aka Rajinee; daily standard).
9. Saphan Phut (Memorial Bridge; daily standard and red and orange flag) – for Pahurat, Pak Khlong Talat (and Wat Prayoon in Thonburi).
10. Rachavongse (aka Rajawong; all daily standard and special express boats) – for Chinatown.
11. Harbour Department (daily standard).
12. Si Phraya (all daily standard and special express boats) – walk north past the *Sheraton Royal Orchid Hotel* for River City shopping complex.
13. Wat Muang Kae (daily standard) – for GPO.
14. Oriental (all daily standard and special express boats) – for Thanon Silom.
15. Sathorn (all daily standard and special express boats) – for Thanon Sathorn.

Numbers correspond to those on the **map** on pp.94–5.

trouble actually locating the piers as none are signed in English and they all look very unassuming and rickety; see the map on p.94 for locations and keep your eyes peeled for a plain wooden jetty – most jetties serve boats running in both directions. Once on the boat, state your destination to the conductor when he collects your fare, which will be between B7 and B15. Due to the recent construction of some low bridges, all passengers change onto a different boat at Pratunam and then again at the stop way out east on Sukhumvit Soi 71 – just follow the crowd.

Skytrain

The long-awaited elevated railway known as the **BTS Skytrain**, or *rot fai faa* (ⓦ www.bts.co.th), is now operating in Bangkok, after over thirty years of planning, fudging and building. Although the network is limited, it provides a much faster alternative to the bus, is clean, efficient and vigorously air-conditioned, and – because fares are comparatively high for Bangkokians – is rarely crowded. There are only two Skytrain lines, both running every few minutes from 6am to midnight, with **fares** of around B15–45 per trip depending on distance travelled. Currently, the only **passes** available that are likely to appeal to any visitors cost B250/B300 for ten/fifteen trips (B160/210 for students), but watch out for new deals being introduced.

The **Sukhumvit Line** runs from Mo Chit (stop #N8) in the northern part of the city (near Chatuchak Market and the Northern Bus Terminal), south via Victory Monument (N3) to the interchange, **Central Station** (CS), at Siam Square, and then east along Thanon Ploenchit and Thanon Sukhumvit, via the Eastern Bus Terminal (Ekamai; E7), to On Nut (Soi 77, Thanon Sukhumvit; E9); the whole journey to the eastern end of town from Mo Chit takes around thirty minutes. The **Silom Line** runs from the National Stadium (W1), just west of Siam Square, through Central Station, and then south along Thanon Rajdamri, Thanon Silom and Thanon Sathorn, via Sala Daeng near Patpong (S2), to Saphan Taksin (Sathorn Bridge; S6), to link up with the full gamut of express boats on the Chao Phraya River. Free feeder buses, currently covering seven circular routes mostly along Thanon Sukhumvit, are geared more for commuters than visitors, but pick up a copy of the ubiquitous free BTS **map** if you want more information.   .

The Skytrain network is just the first phase of a planned integrated city transport programme that will be greatly enhanced by the opening of an underground rail system, currently due in 2002. The subway will run from the central Hualamphong Railway station, east along Thanon Rama IV, then north up Soi Asoke/Thanon Ratchadapisek before terminating at Mo Chit in the north of the city.

Taxis

Bangkok **taxis** come in three forms, and are so plentiful that you rarely have to wait more than a couple of minutes before spotting an empty one of any description. Neither tuk-tuks nor motorbike taxis have meters, so you should agree on a price before setting off, and expect to do a fair amount of haggling. Rates for all rise after midnight, and during rush hours when each journey takes far longer.

The most sedate option, Bangkok's metered, air-conditioned **taxi cabs**, is also the most expensive, but well worth the extra in the heat of the day; look out for the "TAXI METER" sign on the roof, which should be illuminated when the cab is available for hire. Fares start at B35, on a clearly visible meter in the front of the vehicle which the driver should reset at the start of each trip, and increase in stages on a combined speed/distance formula. Occasionally, drivers will refuse long, slow, less profitable journeys across town (especially in the middle of the afternoon, when many cabs have to return to the depot for a change of drivers), or, at quieter times of day, will take you on a roundabout, more expensive route to your destination. If a string of metered-cab drivers don't like the sound of your destination, you'll have to try to negotiate a flat fare with one of them, or with one of the now-rare unmetered cabs (denoted by a "TAXI" sign on the roof).

Slightly less stable but typically Thai, **tuk-tuks** can carry three passengers comfortably and are the standard way of making shortish journeys (Banglamphu to Patpong costs at least B80). These noisy, three-wheeled, open-sided buggies fully expose you to the worst of Bangkok's pollution, but are the least frustrating type of city transport – they are a lot nippier than taxi cabs, and the drivers have no qualms about taking semi-legal measures to avoid gridlocks. Be aware, however, that tuk-tuk drivers tend to speak less English than taxi drivers – and there have been cases of robberies and attacks on women passengers late at night. Even during the day it's quite common for tuk-tuk drivers to try and con their passengers into visiting a jewellery or expensive souvenir shop with them, for which they get a hefty commission; the usual tactic involves falsely informing tourists that the Grand Palace is closed (see p.121), and offering instead a ridiculously cheap, even free, city tour – always bear in mind that fuel is around B17/litre and that no honest tuk-tuk driver would make even a short journey for less than B30. Because of the rise in these scams, the Bangkok Tourist Board now advises tourists to take metered taxis instead of tuk-tuks or, failing that, to make sure they take a tuk-tuk with a white "TAXI" sign on the roof, which at least means it's registered to take passengers.

Least costly (a short trip, say from Banglamphu to Wat Po, should cost B20) and quickest of the trio are **motorbike taxis**, though these are rarely used by

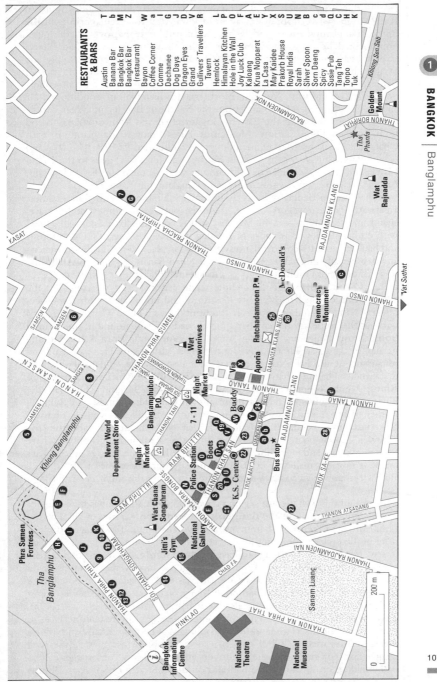

RESTAURANTS & BARS

Austin	T
Banana Bar	b
Bangkok Bar	M
Bangkok Bar (restaurant)	Z
Bayon	W
Coffee Corner	a
Comme	I
Dachanee	G
Dog Days	J
Dragon Eyes	D
Grand	V
Gullivers' Travellers Tavern	R
Hemlock	L
Himalayan Kitchen	P
Hole in the Wall	O
Joy Luck Club	F
Kaloang	A
Krua Nopparat	E
La Casa	Y
May Kaidee	X
Prakorb House	S
Royal India	U
Sarah	N
Silver Spoon	B
Som Daeng	c
Spicy	d
Susie Pub	Q
Tang Teh	C
Tonpo	H
Tuk	K

Phra Sumen Fortress

Tha Banglamphu

Bangkok Information Centre

National Theatre

National Museum

Sanam Luang

National Gallery

Jitti's Gym

Wat Chana Songkhram

Police Station

Boots

7-11

K.S. Center

Night Market

New World Department Store

Banglamphubon P.O.

Wat Bowoniwes

Night Market

Buddy

Via

Aporia

Ratchadamnoen P.

McDonald's

Democracy Monument

Wat Rajnadda

Golden Mount

Wat Suthat

Bus stop

KHLONG BANGLAMPHU

THANON SAMSEN

SAMSEN 1

SAMSEN 4

SAMSEN 6

THANON PHRA ATHIT

SOI CHANA SONGKHRAM

RAM BHUTTRI

THANON CHAKRABONGSE

THANON KHAO SAN

RAM BHUTTRI

CHAO FA

THANON NA PHRA THAT

THANON RAJDAMNOEN NAI

THANON ATSADANG

TROK SAKE

TROK MAYOM

DAMNOEN KLANG NEUA

RAJDAMNOEN KLANG

THANON TANAO

THANON TANAO

THANON TANI

THANON SIBSAM

THANON BOWONIWES

THANON PHRA SUMEN

THANON PRACHA THIPATAI

THANON KRAISI

K.ASAT

PINKLAO

THANON DINSO

THANON DINSO

THANON RAJDAMNOEN KLANG

RAJDAMNOEN NOK

THANON BORIPHAT

Tha Phanfa

Khlong San Saeb

Khlong Banglamphu

200 m

city. Within easy reach of the Grand Palace and other major sights in Ratanakosin (a riverfront walkway from Phra Athit to Ratanakosin is in the offing), Banglamphu is served by plenty of **public transport**. All the guest houses listed lie only a few minutes' walk from one or two Chao Phraya Express boat stops (see the box on p.103), and public longtail boats also ply one of the khlongs in the area (see p.102). Useful **bus routes** in and out of Banglamphu include ordinary bus #3, air-conditioned #12 and air-conditioned #32 to and from Mo Chit Northern Bus Terminal; air-conditioned #7 and air-conditioned #11 to and from the Southern Bus Terminal; air-conditioned #11 to and from the Eastern Bus Terminal; and #53 (ordinary) to and from Hualamphong station. Numerous buses connect Banglamphu with Chatuchak Weekend Market, including air-conditioned #3, #9, #10, #12 and #39; ordinary bus #15 runs to Siam Square; #53 (ordinary) goes to the Grand Palace, and #56 (ordinary) to Chinatown; see box on p.100 for full details. Airport bus AB2 also has several stops in Banglamphu (see p.92).

At the heart of Banglamphu is the legendary **Thanon Khao San** – almost a caricature of a travellers' centre, crammed with guest houses, dodgy travel agents and restaurants serving yoghurt shakes and muesli, the sidewalks lined with ethnic clothes stalls, racks of bootleg music and software CDs, tattooists and hair-braiders. It's colourful, noisy and a good place to meet other travellers, and is especially enjoyable at night when Khao San is closed to cars and the street throngs with milling shoppers and restaurant tables that spill off the pavements. On the down side, the whole scene can get a bit wearing, and the accommodation on Khao San itself is noisy and poor value, with few places offering windows in their rooms. If you want the benefits of Thanon Khao San without the bustle, try the smaller, quieter roads off and around it: **Soi Chana Songkhram**, which encircles the wat of the same name; **Phra Athit**, running parallel to the Chao Phraya River and packed with trendy Thai café-bars and restaurants (it also has a useful express-boat stop); or the residential alleyways that parallel Thanon Khao San to the south, **Trok Mayom** and **Damnoen Klang Neua**. About ten minutes' walk north from Thanon Khao San, the **Thanon Samsen sois** offer a more authentically Thai atmosphere, while a further fifteen minutes' walk in the same direction will take you to **Thanon Sri Ayutthaya**, behind the National Library, a seven-minute walk from the **Thewes** express-boat stop, the most attractive area in Banglamphu, where rooms are larger and guest houses smaller. We've listed only the cream of what's on offer in each small area in Banglamphu: if your first choice is full there'll almost certainly be a vacancy somewhere just along the soi, if not right next door.

Banglamphu is well used to serving travellers' needs, so facilities here are second to none. The excellent **Bangkok Information Centre** is on Thanon Phra Athit, and there's a 24-hour tourist information and assistance booth in front of the police station on the west corner of Thanon Khao San. If you plan to stay in Banglamphu, arrange to have **poste restante** sent to one of the area's two post offices rather than to the GPO, which is inconveniently far away on Charoen Krung; the one closest to Khao San is Ratchadamnoen Post Office on the eastern stretch of Soi Damnoen Klang Neua, but Banglamphubon Post Office near Wat Bowoniwes is also very handy (for full details see p.195). Though there are several private companies offering poste restante services in Banglamphu, their service tends to be haphazard at best; the Khao San business that advertises itself as "GPO" is a private operation. Most guest houses will receive faxes for guests, and their numbers are listed below. Almost every alternate building on Thanon Khao San and on the west arm of Soi Ram Bhuttri offers **internet access**, as do many of the guest houses; intense competition keeps the rates very low. There are also Catnet Internet terminals (see Basics, p.59) at the Ratchadamnoen Post Office. Numerous money **exchange** places can be found on Thanon Khao San, including two branches of national banks (with ATMs), dozens of shops and travel agents, and a couple of self-service laundries.

Thanon Khao San and Soi Damnoen Klang Neua

Chart Guest House, 58–60 Thanon Khao San ☎02/282 0171. Clean, comfortable enough hotel in the heart of backpacker land; the cheapest rooms share bathroom and the priciest have air-con. Rooms in all categories are a little cramped, but they all have windows. ❷–❹

J & Joe House, 1 Trok Mayom ☎02/282 2949. Simple, inexpensive rooms, all with shared bathrooms, in a traditional wooden house located among real Thai homes (very unusual for Banglamphu) in a narrow alley off Khao San. ❷

Khao San Palace Hotel, 139 Thanon Khao San ☎02/282 0578. Clean and well-appointed smallish hotel, where all rooms have attached bathrooms, but only some have windows. The priciest options have air-con and TV. Avoid the rooms overlooking Khao San as they can be noisy at night. ❸–❹

Lek House, 125 Thanon Khao San ☎02/281 8441. Classic Khao San guest house, old-style with small, basic rooms and shared facilities, but less shabby than others in the same price bracket. ❷

Marco Polo Hostel, 108/7–10 Thanon Khao San ☎02/281 1715. Fairly grim windowless boxes in the heart of the ghetto, though all have air-con and private shower. ❸

Nat II, 91–95 Soi Damnoen Klang Neua (aka Soi Post Office) ☎02/282 0211. Large, clean rooms, some with windows, in a fairly quiet location, though you may be woken by the 5am prayer calls at the local mosque. There are only a couple of other guest houses on this road, so it has a friendly, neighbourhood feel to it, even though Khao San is less than 200m away. ❷

Royal Hotel, 2 Thanon Rajdamnoen Klang ☎02/222 9111, ℗224 2083. Used mostly for conferences, this hotel is conveniently located just a 5min stroll from Sanam Luang (it's a further 10min or so to the Grand Palace), but getting to Thanon Khao San entails a life-endangering leap across two very busy main roads. All rooms have air-con, and the facilities are perfectly adequate, though the place lacks atmosphere and isn't exactly plush for the price – the grim facade is enough to put anyone off. ❼

Sawasdee Bangkok Inn, on a tiny soi connecting Thanon Khao San with the parallel Trok Mayom. ☎02/280 1251, ℗281 7818, ⓦwww.sawasdee-hotels.com. Easy to spot because of its mauve-painted facade. Popular and efficiently run mini-hotel, with a good atmosphere and a range of comfortable rooms, though the cheapest are a bit cramped and have no bathroom. Priciest options here include air-con and TV, which makes them good value. You can get Thai massage therapy and lessons on the premises, and there's an attractive garden eating area. ❸–❹

7 Holder Guest House, 216/2–3 Soi Damnoen Klang Neua ☎02/281 3682. Clean and modern, but none of the simply furnished rooms have bathrooms and only some have windows. Fan and air-con available. ❷–❸

Siam Oriental, 190 Thanon Khao San ☎02/629 0312, ℗629 0310. Guest house right in the middle of Thanon Khao San, offering smallish rooms, all with attached bathrooms and some with windows; some have air-con too. ❸

Smile Guest House, 151–161 Trok Sa-ke, off the southern arm of Thanon Tanao ☎02/622 1590, ℗622 0730. Located less than a 5min walk from Khao San, across Rajdamnoen Klang, this is a fairly good-value place that's quiet and out of the tourist ghetto. All rooms have air-con and decent tiled bathrooms, and there's internet access downstairs. ❸

Sweety, Soi Damnoen Klang Neua ☎02/280 2191, ℗280 2192, ⓔsweetygh@hotmail.com. Popular place that's one of the least expensive in Banglamphu; it's nicely located away from the fray but convenient for Khao San. Rooms are very small but all have windows, and beds with thick mattresses; some have private bathrooms. ❶–❷

Vieng Thai Hotel, Soi Ram Bhuttri ☎02/280 5392, ℗281 8153. The best of the options in Banglamphu's upper price bracket: convenient for the shops and restaurants of Thanon Khao San and Banglamphu, and geared towards tourists not business people. All rooms here have air-con, TV, hot water and mini-bar, and there's a big swimming pool. ❼

Soi Chana Songkhram and Phra Athit

Baan Sabai, 12 Soi Rongmai, between Soi Chana Songkhram and Thanon Chao Fa ☎ 02/629 1599. Welcome newcomer to the Banglamphu guest-house scene, located in a quiet soi overlooking the Wat Chana Songkhram compound. Built round a courtyard, this large, hotel-style guest house has a range of clean, comfortable, decent-sized en-suite rooms, some of them air-con, and is host to the pleasant *Bangkok Times* restaurant downstairs. ❸–❹

Chai's House, 49/4–8 Soi Rongmai, between Soi Chana Songkhram and Thanon Chao Fa ☎ 02/281 4901, ℗ 281 8686. Large, clean, simple rooms, all with shared bathrooms. The rate is per person, which makes singles better value than doubles. ❷

Merry V, 35 Soi Chana Songkhram ☎ 02/282 9267. Large, efficiently run and scrupulously clean guest house offering some of the cheapest accommodation in Banglamphu. Rooms are basic and slightly cramped, and they all share bathrooms. Good noticeboard in the downstairs restaurant. ❷

My House, 37 Soi Chana Songkhram ☎ 02/282 9263. Popular place offering a range of simple but exceptionally clean rooms. The cheapest rooms share bathrooms, the most expensive have air-con. ❷–❹

New Siam Guest House, 21 Soi Chana Songkhram ☎ 02/282 4554, ℗ 281 7461. Efficiently run place offering comfortably furnished hotel-style rooms; all with fans and windows, and plenty of clothes hooks. The cheapest rooms share bathrooms, the priciest have air-con. ❸–❺

Peachy Guest House, 10 Thanon Phra Athit ☎ 02/281 6471. Popular, cheap and cheerful place set round a small courtyard, with clean if spartan rooms, most with shared bathrooms but some with air-con. Also has B80 dorm beds, popular with long-stay guests. ❷–❸

Pra Arthit Mansion, 22 Thanon Phra Athit ☎ 02/280 0744, ℗ 280 0742, ℮ praarthit@bkk.a -net.net.th. Recommended mid-range place offering very good, comfortable rooms with air-con, TV, hot water and mini-bar. The fifth-floor rooms have the best views of Banglamphu's rooftops. No restaurant, lobby or other hotel facilities, but staff are friendly and the location is quiet and convenient. ❺

Samsen and Thewes

Backpackers Lodge, Soi 14, 85 Thanon Sri Ayutthaya ☎ 02/282 3231. Quiet, family-run place in the peaceful Thewes quarter of north

Banglamphu. Just a handful of simple rooms, all with shared bathroom, and a communal area downstairs. The cheapest accommodation in this area. ❷

Bangkok International Youth Hostel, 25/2 Thanon Phitsanulok ☎ 02/282 0950, ℗ 628 7416, ⓦ www.tyha.org. Mostly patronized by travelling Thai students: only open to YHA members and nothing special considering the competition. The double rooms have bathrooms, and some have air-con, and there are dorm beds for B70. ❷–❸

New World Lodge Hotel, Samsen Soi 2 ☎ 02/281 5596, ℗ 282 5614, ⓦ www.new-lodge.com. Good-value, large, unadorned rooms, each with a desk, phone, shower and either fan or air-con. All rooms have balconies, and some have khlong views. The cheapest rooms are in the less appealing guest-house wing, are simply furnished and have shared bathrooms. ❷–❺

Shanti Lodge, Soi 16, 37 Thanon Sri Ayutthaya ☎ 02/281 2497. Quiet, attractively furnished and comfortable rooms make this deservedly the most popular place in the Thewes area. Facilities range from rooms with shared bathrooms to en-suite ones with air-con. The vegetarian restaurant downstairs is recommended. ❸–❺

Tavee Guest House, Soi 14, 83 Thanon Sri Ayutthaya ☎ 02/282 5983. Good-sized rooms; quiet and friendly and one of the cheaper places in the Thewes quarter. Offers rooms with shared bathroom plus some en-suite ones with air-con, as well as B80 dorm beds. ❷–❹

Thai Hotel, 78 Thanon Pracha Thipatai ☎ 02/282 2831, ℗ 280 1299. Comfortable enough, but a little overpriced, considering its slightly inconvenient location. All rooms have air-con and there's a decent-sized pool here too. ❼

Villa, 230 Samsen Soi 1 ☎ 02/281 7009. Banglamphu's most therapeutic guest house, a lovely old Thai house and garden with just ten large rooms, each idiosyncratically furnished in simple, semi-traditional style; bathrooms are shared. Fills up quickly, but it's worth going on the waiting list if you're staying a long time. Rooms priced according to their size. ❸–❹

Vimol Guest House, 358 Samsen Soi 4 ☎ 02/281 4615. Old-style, family-run guest house in a quiet but interesting neighbourhood that has just a couple of other tourist places. The simple, cramped rooms have shared bathrooms and a welcoming atmosphere. ❶

Chinatown and Hualamphong station area

Not far from the Ratanakosin sights, **Chinatown (Sampeng)** is one of the most vibrant and quintessentially Asian parts of Bangkok. Staying here, or in one of the sois around the conveniently close **Hualamphong station**, can be noisy, but there's always plenty to look at, and some people choose to base themselves in this area in order to get away from the travellers' scene in Banglamphu. There are a couple of guest houses and a few moderate and expensive hotels here, in among a cluster of seedier places catering mainly to Thais. All listed accommodation is marked on the map on p.140.

Useful **bus** routes for Chinatown include west-bound air-conditioned #7 and ordinary buses #25, #40 and #53, which all go to Ratanakosin (for Wat Po and the Grand Palace); the east-bound #25 and #40 buses both go to Siam Square, where you change onto the Skytrain system. For more details, see box on p.100.

Bangkok Center, 328 Thanon Rama IV ☎ 02/238 4848, ⓕ 236 1862, ⓦ www.bangkokcentrehotel.com. Handily placed upper-mid-range option with efficient service just across the road from the train station. Rooms are smartly furnished, and all have air-con and TV; there's a pool, restaurant and internet access on the premises. ❻

Chinatown Hotel, 526 Thanon Yaowarat ☎ 02/225 0204, ⓕ 226 1295, ⓦ www.chinatown.co.th. Classy Chinese hotel in the heart of the gold-trading district. Comfortably furnished rooms, all with air-con and TV. Kids under 12 can share their parents' rooms for free. ❺–❻

FF Guest House, 338/10 Trok La-0, off Thanon Rama IV ☎ 02/233 4168. The closest budget accommodation to the station, but very basic indeed and a bit of a last resort. To get there from the station, cross Thanon Rama IV and walk left for 200m, and then right down Trok La-0 to the end of the alley. ❷

Krung Kasem Sri Krung Hotel, 1860 Thanon Krung Kasem ☎ 02/225 0132, ⓕ 225 4705. Mid-range but rather shabby Chinese hotel just 50m across the khlong from the station. All rooms have air-con and TV but could do with an overhaul. ❹

New Empire Hotel, 572 Thanon Yaowarat ☎ 02/234 6990, ⓕ 234 6997, ⓔ newempirehotel @hotmail.com. Medium-sized hotel right in the thick of the Chinatown bustle, offering fairly run-of-the-mill rooms, with shower and air-con. ❹

River View Guest House, 768 Soi Panurangsri, Thanon Songvad ☎ 02/235 8501, ⓕ 237 5428. Large but unattractive rooms, with fan and cold water at the lower end of the range, air-con, hot water, TVs and fridges at the top. Great views over the bend in the river, especially from the top-floor restaurant, and handy for Chinatown, Hualamphong station and the GPO. Find it through a maze of crumbling Chinese buildings: head north for 400m from River City shopping centre (on the express-boat line) along Soi Wanit 2, before following signs to the guest house to the left. ❹–❺

TT2 Guest House, 516 Soi Sawang, off Thanon Maha Nakorn ☎ 02/236 2946, ⓕ 236 3054, ⓔ ttguesthouse@hotmail.com. The best budget place in the station area, though significantly more expensive than *FF*. Clean, friendly and well run with good bulletin boards and traveller-oriented facilities, including left luggage at B7 a day and a small library. All rooms share bathrooms, and there are B100 beds in a three-person dorm. Roughly a 15min walk from either the station or the Si Phraya express-boat stop; to get here from the station, cross Thanon Rama IV, then walk left for 250m and right down Thanon Maha Nakorn as far as the *Full Moon* restaurant (opposite Trok Fraser and Neave), where you turn left and then first right. ❸

White Orchid Hotel, 409–421 Thanon Yaowarat ☎ 02/226 0026, ⓕ 225 6403. One of the plushest hotels in Chinatown, right at the hub of the gold-trading quarter. All rooms have air-con and TV, and there's a *dim sum* restaurant on the premises. ❻

Downtown: Siam Square and Thanon Ploenchit

Siam Square – not really a square, but a grid of shops and restaurants between Phrayathai and Henri Dunant roads – and nearby **Thanon Ploenchit** are as central as Bangkok gets, handy for all kinds of shopping, nightlife, the Skytrain and Hualamphong station. There's no budget accommodation here, but a few scaled-up guest houses have sprung up alongside the expensive hotels. Concentrated in their own "ghetto" on **Soi Kasemsan 1**, which runs north off Thanon Rama I just west of Thanon Phrayathai and is the next soi along from Jim Thompson's House (see p.152), these offer an informal guest-house atmosphere, with hotel comforts – air-conditioning and en-suite hot-water bathrooms – at moderate prices. Accommodation here is marked on the map on p.153.

(see p.152)

A-One Inn, 25/13 Soi Kasemsan 1, Thanon Rama I ☎02/215 3029, ⓕ216 4771. The original upscale guest house, owned by a retired police colonel, and still justifiably popular, with helpful staff, satellite TV and a sociable café; no single rooms. ❻

The Bed & Breakfast, 36/42 Soi Kasemsan 1, Thanon Rama I ☎02/215 3004, ⓕ215 2493. Bright, clean, family-run and friendly, though the rooms – carpeted and with en-suite telephones – are a bit cramped. As the name suggests, a simple breakfast is included. ❹

Hilton International, Nai Lert Park, 2 Thanon Witthayu ☎02/253 0123, ⓕ253 6509, ⓦwww.hilton.com. The main distinguishing feature of this member of the international luxury chain is its acres of beautiful gardens, overlooked by many of the spacious, balconied bedrooms; set into the grounds are a verdant landscaped swimming pool, jogging track, tennis courts and popular health club. Good deli-café and French and Chinese restaurants. ❾

Jim's Lodge, 125/7 Soi Ruam Rudee, Thanon Ploenchit ☎02/255 3100–3, ⓕ253 8492, ⓔanant@asiaaccess.net.th. In a relatively peaceful residential area, handy for the British and American embassies; offers luxurious international standards on a smaller scale and at bargain prices; no swimming pool, but there is a roof garden with outdoor jacuzzi. ❼

Le Royal Meridien and **Le Meridien President**, 971 Thanon Ploenchit ☎02/656 0444, ⓕ656

0555, ⓦwww.lemeridien-bangkok.com. Very handily placed for the Erawan Shrine and shopping, the 30-year-old landmark of the *President* has recently been rejuvenated with the building of the towering *Royal Meridien* next door, aimed primarily at business travellers. Room rates compare very favourably with those of other five-star hotels in Bangkok. ❾

Regent, 155 Thanon Rajdamri ☎02/251 6127, ⓕ254 5390, ⓦwww.rih.com. The stately home of Bangkok's top hotels, where afternoon tea is still served in the monumental lobby. ❾

Siam Orchid Inn, 109 Soi Rajdamri, Thanon Rajdamri ☎02/251 4417, ⓕ255 3144, ⓔsiam_orchidinn@hotmail.com. Very handily placed behind the Narayana Phand souvenir centre, this is a friendly, cosy place with an ornately decorated lobby, a tasty restaurant, and air-con, hot water, cable TV, mini-bars and phones in the comfortable bedrooms. The room rate (at the lower end of this price code) includes breakfast. ❼

Wendy House, 36/2 Soi Kasemsan 1, Thanon Rama I ☎02/216 2436–7, ⓕ612 3487. Most spartan of this soi's upmarket guest houses, and no frills in the service either, but clean and comfortable enough. ❹

White Lodge, 36/8 Soi Kasemsan 1, Thanon Rama I ☎02/216 8867 or 215 3041, ⓕ216 8228. Well-maintained, shining white cubicles and a welcoming atmosphere, with very good continental breakfasts at *Sorn's* next door. ❹

Downtown: south of Thanon Rama IV

South of Thanon Rama IV, the left bank of the river contains a full cross-section of places to stay. At the eastern edge of this area is **Soi Ngam Duphli**, a ghetto of budget guest houses which is often choked with traffic escaping the jams on Thanon Rama IV – the neighbourhood is generally on the slide, although the best guest houses, tucked away on quiet **Soi Saphan Khu**, can just about compare with Banglamphu's finest.

Some medium-range places are scattered between Thanon Rama IV and the river, ranging from the notorious (the *Malaysia*) to the sedate (the *Bangkok Christian Guest House*). The area also lays claim to the capital's biggest selection of top hotels, which are among the most opulent in the world. Here you're at least a long

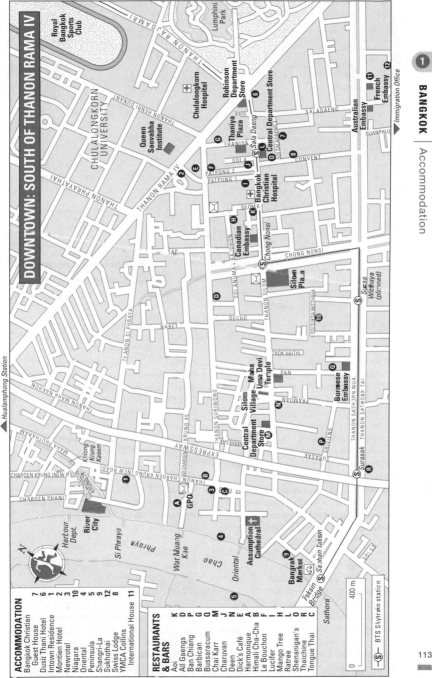

DOWNTOWN: SOUTH OF THANON RAMA IV

ACCOMMODATION

Bangkok Christian Guest House	7
Dusit Thani Hotel	6
Intown Residence	1
Montien Hotel	2
Newrotel	3
Niagara	10
Oriental	4
Peninsula	5
Shangri-La	9
Sukhothai	12
Swiss Lodge	8
YMCA Collins International House	11

RESTAURANTS & BARS

Aoi	K
All Gaengs	D
Ban Chiang	P
Barbican	G
Bussaracum	Q
Chai Karr	M
Charuvan	J
Deen	N
Dick's Café	E
Harmonique	A
Himali Cha-Cha	B
Le Bouchon	F
Lucifer	H
Mango Tree	I
Ratree	L
Shenanigan's	O
Thaichine	R
Tongue Thai	C

Hualamphong Station ▲

▲ Immigration Office

Royal Bangkok Sports Club

Lumphini Park

CHULALONGKORN UNIVERSITY

Queen Saovabha Institute

Chulalongkorn Hospital

Robinson Department Store

Thaniya Plaza

Central Department Store

Bangkok Christian Hospital

Australian Embassy

French Embassy

Canadian Embassy

Silom Plaza

Burmese Embassy

Central Department Store

Silom Village

Maha Uma Devi Temple

Assumption Cathedral

River City

Harbour Dept.

Bangrak Market

GPO

Wat Muang Kae

Chao Phraya

THANON RAMA IV

THANON PHRAYATHAI

THANON HENRI DUNANT

THANON RAJDAMRI

SALADAENG

Sala Daeng (S)

CONVENT

SURIWONG

THANON SILOM

Chong Nonsi (S)

CHONG NONSI

Sala Daeng

SUANPHLU

Surasak (S)

Saphan Taksin (S)

Taksin Bridge

Sathorn

THANON SATHORN TAI

THANON SATHORN NUA

Surasak

Si Phraya

CHAROEN KRUNG (NEW ROAD)

CHAROEN PHANIT

NARET

DECHO

TROK VAITHI

PAN

PRAMUAN

SURIWENG

SURASAK

0	400 m

(S) — BTS Skytrain station

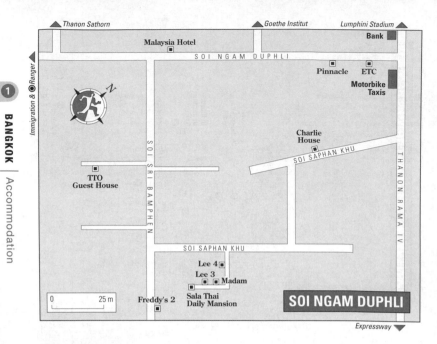

Within the map image: Thanon Sathorn, Goethe Institut, Lumphini Stadium, Malaysia Hotel, Bank, SOI NGAM DUPHLI, Pinnacle, ETC, Motorbike Taxis, Immigration & Ranger, Charlie House, SOI SAPHAN KHU, SOI SRI BAMPHEN, THANON RAMA IV, TTO Guest House, SOI SAPHAN KHU, Lee 4, Lee 3, Madam, 0 25 m, Freddy's 2, Sala Thai Daily Mansion, **SOI NGAM DUPHLI**, Expressway

express-boat ride from the treasures of Ratanakosin, but this area is good for eating and shopping, and has a generous sprinkling of embassies for visa-hunters.

Inexpensive

ETC Guest House, 5/3 Soi Ngam Duphli ☎02/287 1477 or 286 9424, ℻287 1478, ℮ETC@mozart.inet.co.th. Above a branch of the recommended Banglamphu travel agent of the same name, and very handy for Thanon Rama IV, though consequently noisy. Friendly, helpful and very clean, catering mainly to Japanese travellers. Rooms can be dingy, and come with shared or en-suite hot-water bathrooms; breakfast is included. ❷–❸

Freddy's 2, 27/40 Soi Sri Bamphen ☎02/286 7826, ℻213 2097. Popular, clean, well-organized guest house with plenty of comfortable common areas, including a café and beer garden at the rear. Rather noisy. Especially good rates for singles (B100). ❷

Lee 3 Guest House, 13 Soi Saphan Khu ☎02/679 7045, ℻286 3042. The best of the Lee family of guest houses spread around this and adjoining sois. Decent and quiet, though stuffy. ❷

Lee Mansion 4, 9 Soi Saphan Khu ☎02/286 7874 or 679 8116. Simple, airy rooms, most with en-suite cold-water bathrooms, in a dour modern tower; service also dour. ❷

Madam Guest House, 11 Soi Saphan Khu ☎02/286 9289, ℻213 2087. Cleanish, often

cramped, but characterful bedrooms, some with their own bathrooms, in a warren-like, balconied wooden house. Friendly. ❷

Sala Thai Daily Mansion, 15 Soi Saphan Khu ☎02/287 1436. The pick of the area. A clean and efficiently run place at the end of this quiet, shaded alley, with bright, modern rooms (priced according to size) with wall fans; a roof terrace makes it all the more pleasant. ❷–❸

TTO Guest House, 2/35 Soi Sri Bamphen ☎02/286 6783, ℻679 7994. Rough, poorly designed rooms, though all with fridge and phone, some with air-con and hot water, in a friendly establishment. ❸

Moderate

Bangkok Christian Guest House, 123 Soi 2, Saladaeng, off the eastern end of Thanon Silom ☎02/234 1852, ℻237 1742, ℮bcgh@loxinfo .co.th. Well-run, orderly missionary house whose plain air-con rooms with hot-water bathrooms surround a quiet lawn. Breakfast included. ❼

Charlie House, 1034/36–37 Soi Saphan Khu ☎02/679 8330–1, ℻679 7308, ℮charlie_h_th@yahoo.com. Decent mid-range alternative to the crash pads of Soi Ngam Duphli: bright, air-con lobby restaurant, serving good, reasonably priced food, and small, carpeted bedrooms with minimal floral decor, hot-water bathrooms, air-con and TV, close to Thanon Rama IV. Cheap internet access. No smoking. ❹

Intown Residence, 1086/6 Thanon Charoen Krung ⊕02/639 0960–2, ⓕ236 6886, ⓔfann4199@asiaaccess.net.th. Clean, welcoming, rather old-fashioned hotel sandwiched between shops on the noisy main road (ask for a room away from the street). Large, slightly chintzy, comfortable rooms come with air-con, hot-water bathrooms, mini-bars, satellite TVs and phones. ❺

La Residence, 173/8–9 Thanon Suriwong ⊕02/266 5400–1, ⓕ237 9322, ⓔresidenc @loxinfo.co.th. Above *All Gaengs* restaurant, an intimate hotel where the cutesy rooms stretch to TVs and mini-bars. ❼

Malaysia Hotel, 54 Soi Ngam Duphli ⊕02/679 7127–36, ⓕ287 1457, ⓔmalaysia@ksc15.th.com. Once a travellers' legend, famous for its compendious noticeboard, now something of a sleaze pit with a notorious 24hr coffeeshop and massage parlour. The accommodation itself is reasonable value though the rooms are large and have air-con and hot-water bathrooms; some have fridge, TV and video too. There's a swimming pool (B50 per day for non-guests) and reasonably priced internet access. ❺

Newrotel, 1216/1 Thanon Charoen Krung, between the GPO and the *Oriental Hotel* ⊕02/630 6995, ⓕ237 1102, ⓔnewrotel@idn.co.th. Smart, clean, kitschly decorated and good value, with air-con, hot-water bathrooms, fridges and cable TV, the price including American or Chinese breakfast. ❼

Niagara, 26 Soi Suksa Witthaya, off the south side of Thanon Silom ⊕02/233 5783, ⓕ233 6563. No facilities other than a coffeeshop, but the clean bedrooms, with air-con, hot-water bathrooms, satellite TV and telephones are a snip. ❹

Expensive

Dusit Thani Hotel, 946 Thanon Rama IV, on the corner of Thanon Silom ⊕02/236 0450–9, ⓕ236 6400, ⓦwww.dusit.com. Centrally placed top-class hotel, famous for its restaurants, including the *Tiara*, which has spectacular top-floor views. ❾

Montien Hotel, 54 Thanon Surawongse, on the corner of Rama IV ⊕02/233 7060–9, ⓕ236 5219, ⓦwww.montien.com. Grand, airy and solicitous luxury hotel, with a strongly Thai character, very handily placed for business and nightlife. ❾

Oriental Hotel, 48 Oriental Avenue, off Thanon Charoen Krung (New Road) ⊕02/236 0400, ⓕ236 1937, ⓦwww.mandarin-oriental.com. One of the world's best, this effortlessly stylish riverside hotel boasts immaculate standards of service. ❾

Peninsula Bangkok, 333 Thanon Charoennakorn, Klongsan ⊕02/861 2888, ⓕ861 1112, ⓦwww.peninsula.com. Superb top-class hotel with flawless service, which self-consciously aims to rival the *Oriental* across the river, with a stylish modernity that makes its competitor look a little dated. Although it's on the Thonburi side of the Chao Phraya, the hotel operates a shuttle boat across to a pier and reception area by the *Shangri-La Hotel*. ❾

Pinnacle, 17 Soi Ngam Duphli ⊕02/287 0111–31, ⓕ287 3420, ⓦwww.pinnaclehotels.com. Bland but reliable international-standard place, with rooftop jacuzzi and fitness centre; rates, which are towards the lower end of this category, include breakfast. ❼

Shangri-La, 89 Soi Wat Suan Plu, Thanon Charoen Krung ⊕02/236 7777, ⓕ236 8579, ⓦwww.shangri-la.com. Grandiose establishment which, for what it's worth, was voted top hotel in the world by *Condé Nast Traveler* readers in 1996. It boasts the longest river frontage of any hotel in Bangkok, and makes the most of it with gardens, restaurants – including the award-winning *Salathip* for Thai cuisine – and two pools by the Chao Phraya; the two accommodation wings are linked by free tuk-tuk if you can't be bothered to walk. ❾

Sukhothai, 13/3 Thanon Sathorn Thai ⊕02/287 0222, ⓕ287 4980, ⓦwww.hotelsukhothaibangkok .com. The most elegant of Bangkok's top hotels, its decor inspired by the walled city of Sukhothai: low-rise accommodation coolly furnished in silks, teak and granite, around six acres of gardens and lotus ponds. Good Italian and Thai restaurants. ❾

Swiss Lodge, 3 Thanon Convent ⊕02/233 5345, ⓕ236 9425, ⓦwww.swisslodge.com. Swish, friendly, good-value, solar powered boutique hotel, just off Thanon Silom and ideally placed for business and nightlife. The imaginatively named theme restaurant *Café Swiss* serves fondue, raclette and all your other Swiss favourites, while the tiny terrace swimming pool confirms the national stereotypes of neatness and clever design. ❽

YMCA Collins International House, 27 Thanon Sathorn Thai ⊕02/287 1900, 287 1996, ⓦwww.ymcabangkok.com. First-class facilities, including swimming pool and cable TV, with no frills. ❼

Thanon Sukhumvit

Thanon Sukhumvit is Bangkok's longest – it keeps going east all the way to Cambodia. Packed with high-rise hotels and office blocks, mid-priced foreign-food restaurants, souvenir shops, tailors, bookstores and stall after stall selling fake designer gear, it's a lively place that attracts a high proportion of single male tourists to its enclaves of girlie bars on Soi Nana Tai, Soi Cowboy and the Clinton Entertainment Plaza. But for the most part it's not a seedy area, and is home to many expats and middle-class Thais. Although this is not the place to come if you're on a tight budget, it's a reasonable area for mid-range hotels; the four- and five-star hotels on Sukhumvit tend to be more oriented towards business travellers than tourists, but what they lack in glamour they more than make up for in facilities. The best accommodation here is between sois 1 and 21. Advance reservations are accepted at all places listed below and are recommended during high season.

Staying here, you're well served by the **Skytrain**, which has stops all the way along Sukhumvit, making journeys to places such as Siam Square and Chatuchak Weekend Market a fast and hassle-free undertaking. Sukhumvit hotels are also convenient for the Eastern Bus Terminal, with its buses to Pattaya and other east-coast resorts. On the downside, you're a long way from the main Ratanakosin sights, and the sheer volume of traffic on Sukhumvit means that travelling by **bus** across town can take an age – if possible, try to travel to and from Thanon Sukhumvit outside rush hour (7–9am & 3–7pm). Airport bus AB3 has stops all the way along Thanon Sukhumvit (see p.92); useful buses for getting to Ratanakosin include #8 (air-con) and #25 (ordinary); ordinary buses #25 and #40 go to Hualamphong station and Chinatown. Full details of bus routes are given on pp.100-01.

A much faster way of getting across town is to hop on one of the longtail **boats** that ply the canals: Khlong Sen Seb, which begins near Democracy Monument in the west of the city, runs parallel with part of Thanon Sukhumvit and has stops at the northern ends of Soi Nana Nua (Soi 3) and Soi Asoke (Soi 21), from where you can either walk down to Thanon Sukhumvit itself, or take a motorbike taxi. This reduces the journey between Thanon Sukhumvit and the Banglamphu/Ratanakosin area to about thirty minutes; for more details on boat routes, see p.102.

Inexpensive

The Atlanta, at the far southern end of Soi 2 ☎02/252 1650, ℗656 8123, ⊛www. theatlantahotel.bizland.com. Classic old-style hotel with lots of colonial-era character, welcoming staff, and some of the cheapest accommodation on Sukhumvit. Rooms are simple and a bit scruffy, but all have attached bathrooms; some have air-con and hot water. There are two swimming pools, as well as internet access and a left-luggage facility. The hotel restaurant is recommended, serving an extensive Thai menu which includes lots of vegetarian dishes; classic movies set in Asia are shown in the restaurant every night. ❹–❺
Miami Hotel, Soi 13 ☎02/253 5611, ℗253 1266, ℮miamihtl@asiaaccess.net.th. Very popular, long-

established budget hotel built around a swimming pool. Large, spartan and slightly shabby rooms; the cheapest have shared bathrooms, the priciest come with air-con. ❸–❺
Sukhumvit 11, behind the 7-11 store at 1/3 Soi 11 ☎02/253 5927, ℗253 5929, ⊛www.suk11.com. One of the few backpacker-orientated guest houses in this area, with B175 beds in five-person air-con dorms as well as air-con doubles with shared bathroom. Friendly place with informative noticeboards, left luggage and lockers, and a very nice roof terrace/balcony seating area. ❹
SV Guest House, Soi 19 ☎02/253 1747, ℗255 7174. Some of the least expensive beds in the area; the rooms, some of which have air-con, are clean and well maintained, and all share bathrooms. ❸

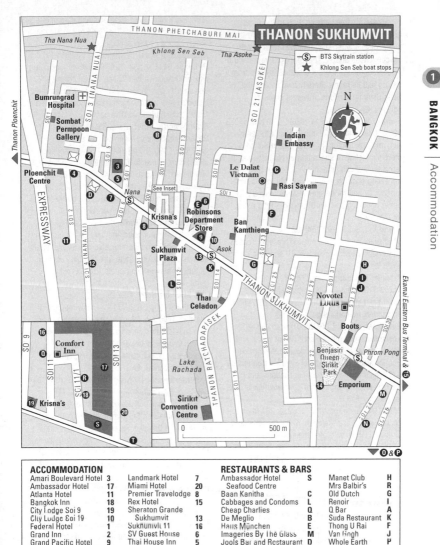

Ekamai Eastern Bus Terminal & ⑮

ACCOMMODATION

Amari Boulevard Hotel	3	Landmark Hotel	7
Ambassador Hotel	17	Miami Hotel	20
Atlanta Hotel	11	Premier Travelodge	8
Bangkok Inn	18	Rex Hotel	15
City Lodge Soi 9	19	Sheraton Grande	
City Lodge Soi 19	10	Sukhumvit	13
Federal Hotel	1	Sukhumvit 11	16
Grand Inn	2	SV Guest House	6
Grand Pacific Hotel	9	Thai House Inn	5
Imperial Queen's Park	14	White Inn	12
J.W. Marriott Hotel	4		

RESTAURANTS & BARS

Ambassador Hotel	S	Manet Club	H
Seafood Centre		Mrs Balbir's	R
Baan Kanitha	C	Old Dutch	G
Cabbages and Condoms	L	Renoir	I
Cheap Charlies	Q	Q Bar	A
De Meglio	B	Suda Restaurant	K
Haus München	E	Thong U Rai	F
Imageries By The Glass	M	Van Gogh	J
Jools Bar and Restaurant	D	Whole Earth	P
La Lunar	O	Yong Lee	T
Lemongrass	N		

Thai House Inn, down a soi beside the *Amari Boulevard* at 1/1 Soi 7 ☏ 02/255 4698, ℱ 253 1780, ✉ thaihouseinn@hotmail.com. Simple, guest-house-style rooms, but reasonably priced for such a central Sukhumvit location. All rooms have air-con, TV and fridge, and there's a Thai-food canteen in the lobby. ❹

Moderate

Bangkok Inn, Soi 11/1 ☏ 02/254 4834, ℱ 254 3545, ⊛ www.bangkokinn.cjb.net. A cosy, friendly, German-run place with clean, smart rooms, all of which have air-con, shower, fridge and TV. Central and good value. ❺

City Lodge, Soi 19 ☏ 02/254 4783, ℱ 255 7340, ⊛ www.amari.com; and Soi 9 ☏ 02/253 7705,

255 4667, same website. Part of the Amari group, these two small, unashamedly mid-range hotels have comfortably equipped rooms with air-con, phone and TV. They are both very centrally located, though the Soi 9 branch suffers from having half its rooms literally overlooking the Nana Skytrain platform. Advance booking advised. ❼

Federal Hotel, 27, Soi 11 ☏02/253 0175, ☏253 5332, ⓔfederalhotel@hotmail.com. Efficiently-run, mid-sized hotel at the far end of Soi 11 so there's a feeling of space and a relatively uncluttered skyline; many rooms look out on the appealing poolside seating area. All rooms have air-con, TV and fridge; the upstairs ones are in better condition and worth paying a little extra for. ❺–❻

Grand Inn, Soi 3 ☏02/254 9021, ☏254 9020. Small, very central hotel offering sizeable, reasonably priced air-con rooms with TV and fridge. Good value. ❺–❻

Premier Travelodge, Soi 8 ☏02/251 3031, ☏253 3195. Well-equipped, centrally located small hotel offering good-value rooms with shower, bathtub, air-con, fridge and TV. ❺

Rex Hotel, Soi 34 ☏02/259 0106, ☏258 6635. Adequate rooms with air-con, TV, hot water, and use of the pool. Its location close to the Eastern Bus Terminal and the Ekamai Skytrain stop makes it convenient for east-coast connections, but it's too isolated from the best of Sukhumvit for a longer stay. ❺

White Inn, Soi 4 ☏02/251 1662, ☏254 8865. Slightly quaint establishment at the far, quiet end of the soi which cultivates the ambience of an Alpine lodge. There are just eighteen fairly good, comfortable air-con rooms, most with a balcony overlooking the small swimming pool. ❻

Expensive

Amari Boulevard Hotel, Soi 5 ☏02/255 2930, ☏255 2950, ⓦwww.amari.com. Medium-sized, unpretentious and friendly upmarket tourist hotel. Rooms are comfortably furnished and all enjoy fine views of the Bangkok skyline; the deluxe ones have private garden patios as well. There's an

attractive rooftop swimming pool and garden terrace which becomes the Thai-food restaurant *Season* in the evenings. ❾

Ambassador Hotel, between sois 11 and 13 ☏02/254 0444, ☏254 7503. Sprawling hotel complex on Sukhumvit that's popular with Asian package tourists and has an excellent range of facilities, including over a dozen restaurants. Rooms are a bit faded, though reasonable value. ❽

Grand Pacific Hotel, above Robinsons Department Store between sois 17 and 19 ☏02/651 1000, ☏255 2441, ⓦwww.grandpacifichotel.com. Conveniently located four-star hotel with smart, well-maintained rooms and good high-rise views. Facilities include three restaurants, a swimming pool, a gym and a business centre. Good value for its class. ❾

Imperial Queen's Park, Soi 22 ☏02/261 9000, ☏261 9530. Enormous and very swish high-rise hotel, whose large, comfortable rooms are nicely decorated with Thai-style furnishings. Facilities include two swimming pools and six restaurants. ❾

J.W. Marriott Hotel, between sois 2 and 4 ☏02/656 7700, ☏656 7711, ⓦwww.marriotthotels.com. Deluxe hotel, offering comfortable rooms with sophisticated phone systems and data ports geared towards business travellers. Facilities include three restaurants, a swimming pool, spa and fitness centre. ❾

Landmark Hotel, between sois 4 and 6 ☏02/254 0404, ☏253 4259, ⓦwww.landmarkbangkok.com. One of the most luxurious hotels on Sukhumvit, oriented towards the business traveller. Several good restaurants, and shops, in the adjacent Landmark Plaza, plus a fitness club and rooftop pool on the premises. ❾

Sheraton Grande Sukhumvit, between sois 12 and 14 ☏02/653 0333, ☏653 0400, ⓦwww.luxurycollection.com. Deluxe accommodation in stylishly understated rooms, all of which offer fine views of the cityscape (the honeymoon suites have their own rooftop plungepools). Facilities include a gorgeous free-form swimming pool and tropical garden on the ninth floor, a spa with a range of treatment plans, and the trendy *Basil* Thai restaurant. Seventeen and unders stay for free if sharing adults' room. ❾

The City

Bangkok is sprawling, chaotic and exhausting: to do it justice and to keep your sanity, you need time, boundless patience and a bus map. The place to start is **Ratanakosin**, the royal island on the east bank of the Chao Phraya, where the city's most important and extravagant sights are to be found. On the edges of this enclave, the area around the landmark **Democracy Monument** includes some interesting and quirky religious architecture, a contrast with the attractions of neighbouring **Chinatown**, whose markets pulsate with the much more aggressive business of making money. Quieter and more European in ambience are the stately buildings of the new royal district of **Dusit**, 2km northeast of Democracy Monument. Very little of old Bangkok remains, but the back canals of **Thonburi**, across the river from Ratanakosin and Chinatown, retain a traditional feel quite at odds with the modern high-rise jungle of **downtown Bangkok**, which has evolved across on the eastern perimeter of the city and can take an hour to reach by bus from Ratanakosin. It's here that you'll find the best shops, bars, restaurants and nightlife, as well as a couple of worthwhile sights. Greater Bangkok now covers an area some 30km in diameter; though unsightly urban development predominates, an expedition to **the outskirts** is made worthwhile by several museums and the city's largest market.

Ratanakosin

When Rama I developed **Ratanakosin** as his new capital in 1782, after the sacking of Ayutthaya and a temporary stay across the river in Thonburi, he paid tribute to its precursor by imitating Ayutthaya's layout and architecture – he even shipped the building materials downstream from the ruins of the old city. Like Ayutthaya, the new capital was sited for protection beside a river and turned into an artificial island by the construction of defensive canals, with a central **Grand Palace** and adjoining royal temple, **Wat Phra Kaeo**, fronted by an open cremation field, **Sanam Luang**; the Wang Na (Palace of the Second King), now doing service as the **National Museum**, was also built at this time. **Wat Po**, which predates the capital's founding, was further embellished by Rama I's successors, who consolidated Ratanakosin's pre-eminence by building several grand European-style palaces (now housing government institutions); Wat Mahathat, the most important centre of Buddhist learning in southeast Asia; the National Theatre and Thammasat University.

Bangkok has expanded eastwards away from the river, leaving the Grand Palace a good 5km from the city's commercial heart, and the royal family have long since moved their residence to Dusit, but Ratanakosin remains the ceremonial centre of the whole kingdom – so much so that it feels as if it might sink into the boggy ground under the weight of its own mighty edifices. The heavy, stately feel is lightened by noisy **markets** along the riverside strip and by **Sanam Luang**, still used for cremations and royal ceremonies, but also functioning as a popular open park and the hub of the modern city's bus system. Despite containing several of the country's main sights, the area is busy

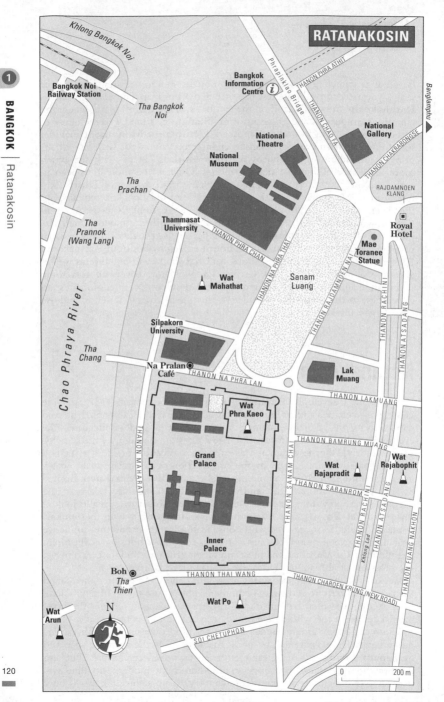

enough in its own right not to have become a swarming tourist zone, and strikes a neat balance between liveliness and grandeur.

Ratanakosin is within easy walking distance of Banglamphu, but is best approached from the river, via the express-boat piers of Tha Chang (for the Grand Palace) or Tha Thien (for Wat Po). A **word of warning**: when you're heading for the Grand Palace or Wat Po, you may well be approached by someone pretending to be a student or an official, who will tell you that the sight is closed when it's not, because they want to lead you on a shopping trip. Although the opening hours of the Grand Palace in particular are sometimes erratic because of state occasions or national holidays, it's far better to put in a bit of extra legwork and check it out for yourself.

Wat Phra Kaeo and the Grand Palace

Hanging together in a precarious harmony of strangely beautiful colours and shapes, **Wat Phra Kaeo** (ⓦ www.palaces.thai.net) is the apogee of Thai religious art and the holiest Buddhist site in the country, housing the most important image, the **Emerald Buddha**. Built as the private royal temple, Wat Phra Kaeo occupies the northeast corner of the huge **Grand Palace**, whose official opening in 1785 marked the founding of the new capital and the rebirth of the Thai nation after the Burmese invasion. Successive kings have all left their mark here, and the palace complex now covers 61 acres, though very little apart from the wat is open to tourists.

The only **entrance** to the complex in 2km of crenellated walls is the Gate of Glorious Victory in the middle of the north side, on Thanon Na Phra Lan. This brings you onto a driveway with a tantalizing view of the temple's glittering spires on the left and the dowdy buildings of the Offices of the Royal Household on the right: this is the powerhouse of the kingdom's ceremonial life, providing everything down to chairs and catering, even lending an urn when someone of rank dies. Turn left at the end of the driveway for the ticket office and entrance turnstiles: **admission** to Wat Phra Kaeo and the palace is B200 (daily 8.30am–3.30pm, palace halls closed Sat & Sun; free tours in English at 10am, 10.30am, 1.30pm & 2pm; personal audioguide B100, with passport or credit card as surety), which includes a free brochure and invaluable map, as well as admission to the Vimanmek Palace in the Dusit area (see p.149). As it's Thailand's most sacred site, you have to show respect by **dressing in smart clothes** – no vests, shorts, see-through clothes, sarongs, miniskirts, fisherman's trousers, slip-on sandals or flip-flops allowed – but if your rucksack won't stretch that far, head for the office to the right just inside the Gate of Glorious Victory, where suitable garments or shoes can be provided (free, socks B15) as long as you leave some identification (passport or credit card) as surety. If you haven't dressed in the right clothes and haven't brought any ID with you, all is not lost: streetsellers opposite the entrance rent out the required attire (sandals with straps, for example, for B50, with a B50 deposit).

Wat Phra Kaeo

Entering the temple is like stepping onto a lavishly detailed stage set, from the immaculate flagstones right up to the gaudy roofs. Although it receives hundreds of foreign sightseers and at least as many Thai pilgrims every day, the temple, which has no monks in residence, maintains an unnervingly sanitized look, as if it were built only yesterday. Its jigsaw of structures can seem complicated at first, but the basic layout is straightforward: the turnstiles in the west wall open onto the back of the bot, which contains the Emerald Buddha; to

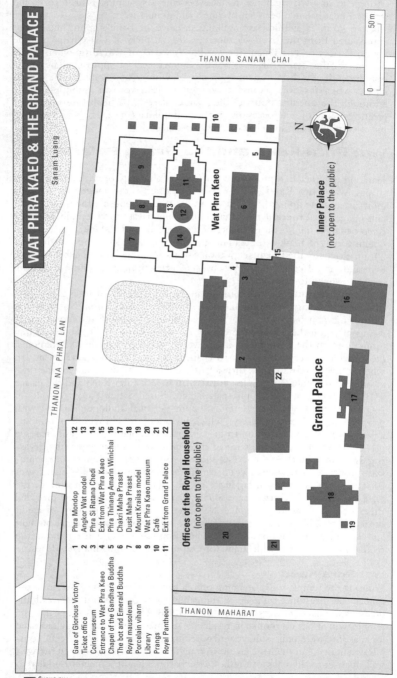

WAT PHRA KAEO & THE GRAND PALACE

THANON SANAM CHAI

Sanam Luang

Wat Phra Kaeo

THANON NA PHRA LAN

Inner Palace
(not open to the public)

Grand Palace

Offices of the Royal Household
(not open to the public)

THANON MAHARAT

Gate of Glorious Victory	**1**
Ticket office	**2**
Coins museum	**3**
Entrance to Wat Phra Kaeo	**4**
Chapel of the Gandhara Buddha	**5**
The bot and Emerald Buddha	**6**
Royal mausoleum	**7**
Porcelain viharn	**8**
Library	**9**
Prangs	**10**
Royal Pantheon	**11**
Phra Mondop	**12**
Angkor Wat model	**13**
Phra Si Ratana Chedi	**14**
Exit from Wat Phra Kaeo	**15**
Phra Thinang Amarin Winichai	**16**
Chakri Maha Prasat	**17**
Dusit Maha Prasat	**18**
Mount Krailas model	**19**
Wat Phra Kaeo museum	**20**
Café	**21**
Exit from Grand Palace	**22**

N

0   50 m

the left, the upper terrace runs parallel to the north side of the bot, while the whole temple compound is surrounded by arcaded walls, decorated with extraordinary murals of scenes from the *Ramayana* (see box on p.125).

The approach to the bot

Immediately inside the turnstiles, you're confronted by six-metre tall *yaksha*, gaudy demons from the *Ramayana*, who watch over the Emerald Buddha from every gate of the temple and ward off evil spirits. Less threatening is the toothless old codger, cast in bronze and sitting on a plinth by the back wall of the bot, who represents a Hindu hermit credited with inventing yoga and herbal medicine. Skirting around the bot, you'll reach its **main entrance** on the eastern side, in front of which stands a cluster of grey **statues** which have a strong Chinese feel: next to Kuan Im, the Chinese goddess of mercy, are a sturdy pillar topped by a lotus flower, which Bangkok's Chinese community presented to Rama IV during his 27 years as a monk; and two handsome cows which commemorate Rama I's birth in the Year of the Cow. Worshippers make their offerings to the Emerald Buddha in among the statues, where they can look at the image through the open doors of the bot without messing up its pristine interior with candle wax and joss-stick ash.

Nearby in the southeastern corner of the temple precinct, look out for the beautiful country scenes painted in gold and blue on the doors of the **Chapel of the Gandhara Buddha**, a building which was crucial to the old royal rainmaking ritual. Adorning the roof are thousands of nagas (serpents), symbolizing water; inside the locked chapel, among the paraphernalia used in the ritual, is kept the Gandhara Buddha, a bronze image in the gesture of calling down the rain with its right hand, while cupping the left to catch it. In times of drought the king would order this week-long ceremony to be conducted, during which he was bathed regularly and kept away from the opposite sex while Buddhist monks and Hindu Brahmins chanted continuously.

The bot and the Emerald Buddha

The **bot**, the largest building of the temple, is one of the few original structures left at Wat Phra Kaeo, though it has been augmented so often it looks like the work of a wildly inspired child. Eight *sema* stones mark the boundary of the consecrated area around the bot, each sheltering in a psychedelic fairy castle, joined by a low wall decorated with Chinese porcelain tiles which depict delicate landscapes. The walls of the bot itself, sparkling with gilt and coloured glass, are supported by 112 golden garudas (birdmen) holding nagas, representing the god Indra saving the world by slaying the serpent-cloud which had swallowed up all the water. The symbolism reflects the king's traditional role as a rainmaker.

Inside the bot, a nine-metre high pedestal supports the tiny **Emerald Buddha**, a figure whose mystique draws pilgrims from all over Thailand – here especially you must act with respect, sitting with your feet pointing away from the Buddha. The spiritual power of the sixty-centimetre jadeite image derives from its legendary past. Reputed to have been created in Sri Lanka, it was discovered when lightning cracked open an ancient chedi in Chiang Rai in the early fifteenth century. The image was then moved around the north, dispensing miracles wherever it went, before being taken to Laos for two hundred years. As it was believed to bring great fortune to its possessor, the future Rama I snatched it back when he captured Vientiane in 1779, installing it at the heart of his new capital as a talisman for king and country.

To this day the king himself ceremonially changes the Buddha's costumes, of which there are three sets, one for each season: the crown and ornaments of an Ayutthayan king for the hot season; a gilt monastic robe dotted with blue enamel for the rainy season, when the monks retreat into the temples; and a full-length gold shawl to wrap up in for the cool season. (The Buddha was granted three new sets of these costumes in 1997, with the old sets put on display in the Wat Phra Kaeo Museum – see p.127.) Among the paraphernalia in front of the pedestal is the tiny, black Victory Buddha, which Rama I always carried with him into war for luck. The two lowest Buddhas were both put there by Rama IX: the one on the left on his sixtieth birthday in 1987, the other when he became the longest-reigning Thai monarch in 1988.

The upper terrace

The eastern end of the **upper terrace** is taken up with the **Prasat Phra Thep Bidorn**, known as the **Royal Pantheon**, a splendid hash of styles. The pantheon has its roots in the Khmer concept of *devaraja*, or the divinity of kings: inside are bronze and gold statues, precisely life-size, of all the kings since Bangkok became the Thai capital. The building is open only on special occasions, such as Chakri Day (April 6), when the dynasty is commemorated.

From here you get the best view of the **royal mausoleum**, the **porcelain viharn** and the **library** to the north (all of which are closed to the public), and, running along the east side of the temple, a row of eight bullet-like **prangs**, each of which has a different nasty ceramic colour. Described as "monstrous vegetables" by Somerset Maugham, they represent, from north to south, the Buddha, Buddhist scripture, the monkhood, the nunhood, the Buddhas who attained enlightenment but did not preach, previous emperors, the Bodhisattva and the future Buddha.

In the middle of the terrace, dressed in deep-green glass mosaics, the **Phra Mondop** was built by Rama I to house the *Tripitaka*, or Buddhist scripture. It's famous for the mother-of-pearl cabinet and solid-silver mats inside, but is never open. Four tiny **memorials** at each corner of the mondop show the symbols of each of the nine Chakri kings, from the ancient crown representing Rama I to the present king's sun symbol, while the bronze statues surrounding the memorials portray each king's lucky white elephants, labelled by name and pedigree. A contribution of Rama IV, on the north side of the mondop, is a **scale model of Angkor Wat**, the prodigious Cambodian temple, which during his reign was under Thai rule. At the western end of the terrace, you can't miss the golden dazzle of the **Phra Si Ratana Chedi**, which Rama IV (1851–68) erected to enshrine a piece of the Buddha's breastbone.

The murals

Extending for over a kilometre in the arcades which run inside the wat walls, the **murals of the Ramayana** depict every blow of this ancient story of the triumph of good over evil, using the vibrant buildings of the temple itself as backdrops, and setting them off against the subdued colours of richly detailed landscapes. Because of the damaging humidity, none of the original work of Rama I's time survives: maintenance is a never-ending process, so you'll always find an artist working on one of the scenes.

The story is told in 178 panels, labelled and numbered in Thai only, starting in the middle of the northern side: in the first episode, a hermit, while out ploughing, finds the baby Sita, the heroine, floating in a gold urn on a lotus leaf and brings her to the city. Panel 109 shows the climax of the story, when Rama, the hero, kills the ten-headed demon Totsagan, and the ladies of the enemy city weep at the demon's death. Panel 110 depicts his elaborate funeral procession, and in 113 you can see the funeral fair, with acrobats, sword jugglers

The Ramayana

The **Ramayana** is generally thought to have originated as an oral epic in India, where it appears in numerous dialects. The most famous version is that of the poet Valmiki, who as a tribute to his king drew together the collection of stories over two thousand years ago. From India, the *Ramayana* spread to all the Hindu-influenced countries of South Asia and was passed down through the Khmers to Thailand, where as the **Ramakien** it has become the national epic, acting as an affirmation of the Thai monarchy and its divine Hindu links. As a source of inspiration for literature, painting, sculpture and dance-drama, it has acquired the authority of holy writ, providing Thais with moral and practical lessons, while its appearance in the form of films and comic strips shows its huge popular appeal. The version current in Thailand was composed by a committee of poets sponsored by Rama I, and runs to three thousand pages.

The central story of the *Ramayana* concerns **Rama** (in Thai, Phra Ram), son of the king of Ayodhya, and his beautiful wife **Sita**, whose hand he wins by lifting and stringing a magic bow. The couple's adventures begin when they are exiled to the forest, along with Rama's good brother, **Lakshaman** (Phra Lak), by the hero's father under the influence of his evil stepmother. Meanwhile, in the city of Lanka (Longka), the demon king **Ravana** (Totsagan) has conceived a passionate desire for Sita and, disguised as a hermit, sets out to kidnap her. By transforming one of his subjects into a beautiful deer, which Rama and Lakshaman go off to hunt, Ravana catches Sita alone and takes her back to Lanka. Rama then wages a long war against the demons of Lanka, into which are woven many battles, spy scenes and diversionary episodes, and eventually kills Ravana and rescues Sita.

The Thai version shows some characteristic differences from the Indian. Hanuman, the loyal monkey king, is given a much more playful role in the *Ramakien*, with the addition of many episodes which display his cunning and talent for mischief, but the major alteration comes at the end of the story, when Phra Ram doubts Sita's faithfulness after rescuing her from Totsagan. In the Indian story, this ends with Sita being swallowed up by the earth so that she doesn't have to suffer Rama's doubts any more; in the *Ramakien* the ending is a happy one, with Phra Ram and Sita living together happily ever after.

and tightrope walkers. In between, Sita – Rama's wife – has to walk on fire to prove that she has been faithful during her fourteen years of imprisonment by Totsagan. If you haven't the stamina for the long walk round, you could sneak a look at the end of the story, to the left of the first panel, where Rama holds a victory parade and distributes thank-you gifts.

The palace buildings

The exit in the southwest corner of Wat Phra Kaeo brings you to the palace proper, a vast area of buildings and gardens, of which only the northern edge is on show to the public. Though the king now lives in the Chitrlada Palace in Dusit, the Grand Palace is still used for state receptions and official ceremonies, during which there is no public access to any part of the palace; in addition the interiors of the Phra Thinang Amarin Winichai and the Dusit Maha Prasat are closed at weekends.

Phra Maha Monthien

Coming out of the temple compound, you'll first be confronted by a beautiful Chinese gate covered in innumerable tiny porcelain tiles. Extending in a straight line behind the gate is the **Phra Maha Monthien**, which was the grand residential complex of earlier kings.

Only the **Phra Thinang Amarin Winichai**, the main audience hall at the front of the complex, is open to the public. The supreme court in the era of the absolute monarchy, it nowadays serves as the venue for the king's birthday speech; dominating the hall is the *busbok*, an open-sided throne with a spired roof, floating on a boat-shaped base. The rear buildings are still used for the most important part of the elaborate coronation ceremony, and each new king is supposed to spend a night there to show solidarity with his forefathers.

Chakri Maha Prasat and the Inner Palace

Next door you can admire the facade – nothing else – of the "farang with a Thai hat", as the **Chakri Maha Prasat** is nicknamed. Rama V, whose portrait you can see over its entrance, employed an English architect to design a purely Neoclassical residence, but other members of the royal family prevailed on the king to add the three Thai spires. This used to be the site of the elephant stables: the large red tethering posts are still there and the bronze elephants were installed as a reminder. The building displays the emblem of the Chakri dynasty on its gable, which has a trident (*ri*) coming out of a *chak*, a discus with a sharpened rim.

The **Inner Palace**, which used to be the king's harem (closed to the public), lies behind the gate on the left-hand side of the Chakri Maha Prasat. The harem was a town in itself, with shops, law courts and a police force for the huge all-female population: as well as the current queens, the minor wives and their servants, this was home to the daughters and consorts of former kings, and the daughters of the aristocracy who attended the harem's finishing school. Today, the Inner Palace houses a school of cooking, fruit-carving and other domestic sciences for well-bred young Thais.

Dusit Maha Prasat

On the western side of the courtyard, the delicately proportioned **Dusit Maha Prasat**, an audience hall built by Rama I, epitomizes traditional Thai architecture. Outside, the soaring tiers of its red, gold and green roof culminate in a gilded *mongkut*, a spire shaped like the king's crown which symbolizes the thirty-three Buddhist levels of perfection. Each tier of the roof bears a typical *chofa*, a slender, stylized bird's head finial, and several *hang hong* (swans' tails), which represent three-headed nagas. Inside, you can still see the original throne, the **Phra Ratcha Banlang Pradap Muk**, a masterpiece of mother-of-pearl inlaid work. When a senior member of the royal family dies, the hall is used for the lying-in-state: the body, embalmed and seated in a huge sealed urn, is placed in the west transept, waiting up to two years for an auspicious day to be cremated.

To the right and behind the Dusit Maha Prasat rises a strange model mountain, decorated with fabulous animals and topped by a castle and prang. It represents **Mount Krailas**, a version of Mount Meru, the centre of the Hindu universe, and was built as the site of the royal tonsure ceremony. In former times, Thai children had shaved heads except for a tuft on the crown which, between the age of five and eight, was cut in a Hindu initiation rite to welcome adolescence. For the royal children, the rite was an elaborate ceremony that sometimes lasted five days, culminating with the king's cutting of the hair knot. The child was then bathed at the model Krailas, in water representing the original river of the universe flowing down the central mountain.

The Wat Phra Kaeo Museum

In front of the Dusit Maha Prasat – next to a small, basic **café** – the air-conditioned **Wat Phra Kaeo Museum** is currently under renovation but you should still be able to get in to see its mildly interesting collection of artefacts associated with the Emerald Buddha and architectural elements rescued from the Grand Palace grounds. Highlights include the Emerald Buddha's original costumes, the bones of various kings' white elephants, and two useful scale models of the Grand Palace, one as it is now, the other as it was when first built.

Wat Po

Where Wat Phra Kaeo may seem too perfect and shrink-wrapped for some, **Wat Po** (daily 8am–5pm; B20), covering twenty acres to the south of the Grand Palace, is lively and shambolic, a complex arrangement of lavish structures which jostle with classrooms, basketball courts and a turtle pond. Busloads of tourists shuffle in and out of the **north entrance** stopping only to gawp at the colossal Reclining Buddha, but you can avoid the worst of the crowds by using the **main entrance** on Soi Chetuphon to explore the huge compound, where you'll more than likely be approached by friendly young monks wanting to practise their English.

Wat Po is the oldest temple in Bangkok and older than the city itself, having been founded in the seventeenth century under the name Wat Potaram. Foreigners have stuck to the contraction of this old name, even though Rama I, after enlarging the temple, changed the name in 1801 to Wat Phra Chetuphon, which is how it is generally known to Thais. The temple had another major overhaul in 1832, when Rama III built the chapel of the Reclining Buddha, and turned the temple into a public centre of learning by decorating the walls and pillars with inscriptions and diagrams on subjects such as history, literature, animal husbandry and astrology. Dubbed Thailand's first university, the wat is still an important centre for traditional medicine, notably **Thai massage**, which is used against all kinds of illnesses, from backaches to viruses. Thirty-hour training courses conducted here in English, usually over a fifteen-day period, cost B6000 (☎02/221 2974 or ✉watpottm@netscape.net for more information). Alternatively you can simply turn up and suffer a massage yourself in the ramshackle buildings (open until 6pm) on the east side of the main compound; allow two hours for the full works (B200 per hr; foot reflexology massage B200 for 45min).

The eastern courtyard

The main entrance on Soi Chetuphon is one of a series of sixteen monumental gates around the main compound, each guarded by stone **giants**, many of them comic Westerners in wide-brimmed hats – ships which exported rice to China would bring these statues back as ballast.

The entrance brings you into the eastern half of the main complex, where a courtyard of structures radiate from the bot – the principal congregation and ordination hall – in a disorientating symmetry. To get to the bot at the centre, turn right and cut through the two surrounding cloisters, which are lined with 394 Buddha images, many of them covered with stucco to hide their bad state of repair – anyone can accrue some merit by taking one away and repairing it. The elegant **bot** has beautiful teak doors decorated with mother-of-pearl, showing stories from the *Ramayana* in minute detail. Look out also for the stone bas-reliefs around the base of the bot, which narrate a longer version of the *Ramayana* in 152 action-packed panels. The plush interior has a well-

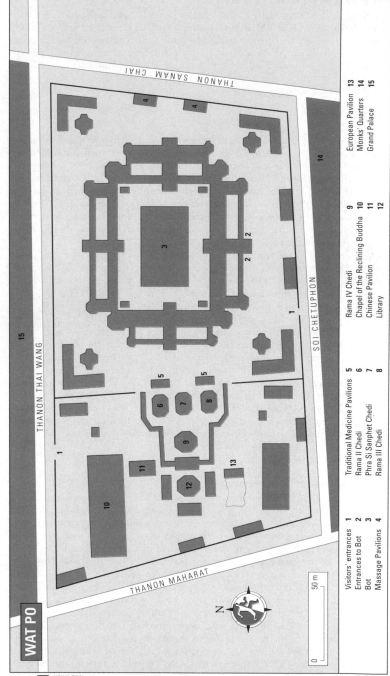

WAT PO

Visitors' entrances	**1**	Traditional Medicine Pavilions	**5**	Rama IV Chedi	**9**
Entrances to Bot	**2**	Rama II Chedi	**6**	Chapel of the Reclining Buddha	**10**
Bot	**3**	Phra Si Sanphet Chedi	**7**	Chinese Pavilion	**11**
Massage Pavilions	**4**	Rama III Chedi	**8**	Library	**12**

European Pavilion	**13**
Monks' Quarters	**14**
Grand Palace	**15**

THANON SANAM CHAI

THANON THAI WANG

SOI CHETUPHON

THANON MAHARAT

Tha Thien

N

0   50 m

proportioned altar on which ten statues of disciples frame a graceful Buddha image containing the remains of Rama I, the founder of Bangkok (Rama IV placed them there so that the public could worship him at the same time as the Buddha).

Back outside the entrance to the double cloister, keep your eyes open for a miniature mountain covered in statues of naked men in tall hats who appear to be gesturing rudely: they are *rishis* (hermits), demonstrating various positions of healing massage. Skirting the southwestern corner of the cloisters, you'll come to a pavilion between the eastern and western courtyards, which displays plaques inscribed with the precepts of traditional medicine, as well as anatomical pictures showing the different pressure points and the illnesses that can be cured by massaging them.

The western courtyard

Among the 95 chedis strewn about the grounds, the four **great chedis** in the western courtyard stand out as much for their covering of garish tiles as for their size. The central chedi is the oldest, erected by Rama I to hold the remains of the most sacred Buddha image of Ayutthaya, the Phra Si Sanphet. Later, Rama III built the chedi to the north for the ashes of Rama II and the chedi to the south to hold his own remains; Rama IV built the fourth, with bright blue tiles, though its purpose is uncertain.

In the northwest corner of the courtyard stands the chapel of the **Reclining Buddha**, a 45-metre-long gilded statue of plaster-covered brick which depicts the Buddha entering Nirvana, a common motif in Buddhist iconography. The chapel is only slightly bigger than the statue – you can't get far enough away to take in anything but a surreal close-up view of the beaming five-metre smile. As for the feet, the vast black soles are beautifully inlaid with delicate mother-of-pearl showing the 108 *lakshanas*, or auspicious signs, which distinguish the true Buddha. Along one side of the statue are 108 bowls which will bring you good luck and a long life if you put 25 satang in each.

Sanam Luang

Sprawling across thirty acres north of the Grand Palace, **Sanam Luang** is one of the last open spaces left in Bangkok, a bare field where residents of the capital gather in the evening to meet, eat and play. The nearby pavements are the marketplace for some exotic spiritual salesmen: on the eastern side sit astrologers and palm readers, and sellers of bizarre virility potions and contraptions; on the western side and spreading around Thammasat University and Wat Mahathat, scores of small-time hawkers sell amulets. In the early part of the year, the sky is filled with kites, which every afternoon are flown in kite-fighting contests (see box on p.130).

As it's in front of the Grand Palace, the field is also the venue for national ceremonies, such as royal funerals and the **Ploughing Ceremony**, held in May at a time selected by astrologers to bring good fortune to the rice harvest. The elaborate Brahmin ceremony is led by an official from the Ministry of Agriculture, who stands in for the king in case the royal power were to be reduced by any failure in the ritual. At the designated time, the official cuts a series of circular furrows with a plough drawn by two oxen, and scatters rice which has been sprinkled with lustral water by the Brahmin priests of the court. When the ritual is over, spectators rush in to grab handfuls of the rice, which they then plant in their own paddies for good luck.

Kite flying

Flying intricate and colourful **kites** is now done mostly for fun in Thailand, but it has its roots in more serious activities. Filled with gunpowder and fitted with long fuses, kites were deployed in the first Thai kingdom at Sukhothai (1240–1438) as machines of war. In the same era, special *ngao* kites, with heads in the shape of bamboo bows, were used in Brahmin rituals: the string of the bow would vibrate in the wind and make a noise to frighten away evil spirits (nowadays noisy kites are still used, though only by farmers, to scare the birds). By the height of the Ayutthayan period (1351–1767) kites had become largely decorative: royal ceremonies were enhanced by fantastically shaped kites, adorned with jingling bells and ornamental lamps.

In the nineteenth century Rama V, by his enthusiastic lead, popularized kite flying as a wholesome and fashionable recreation. **Contests** are now held all over the country between February and April, when winds are strong and farmers have free time after harvesting the rice. These contests fall into two broad categories: those involving manoeuvrable flat kites, often in the shapes of animals; and those in which the beauty of static display kites is judged. The most popular contest of all, which comes under the first category, matches two teams, one flying star-shaped *chula*s, two-metre-high "male" kites, the other flying the smaller, more agile *pakpao*s, diamond-shaped "females". Each team uses its skill and teamwork to ensnare the other's kites and drag them back across a dividing line.

The lak muang

At 6.54am on April 21, 1782 – the astrologically determined time for the auspicious founding of Bangkok – a pillar containing the city's horoscope was ceremonially driven into the ground opposite the northeast corner of the Grand Palace. This pillar, the **lak muang** – all Thai cities have one, to provide a home for their guardian spirits – was made from a twelve-foot tree trunk carved with a lotus-shaped crown, and is now sheltered in an elegant shrine surrounded by immaculate gardens. It shares the shrine with the taller *lak muang* of Thonburi, which was recently incorporated into Greater Bangkok.

Hundreds of worshippers come every day to pray and offer flowers, particularly childless couples seeking the gift of fertility. In one corner of the gardens you can often see short performances of **classical dancing**, paid for by well-off families when they have a piece of good fortune to celebrate.

Mae Toranee

In a tiny park by the hectic bus stops at the northeast corner of Sanam Luang stands the abundant but rather neglected figure of **Mae Toranee**, the earth goddess, wringing the water from her ponytail. Originally part of a fountain built here by Rama V's queen, Saowaba, to provide Bangkokians with fresh drinking water, the statue illustrates a Buddhist legend featured in the murals of many temples. While the Buddha was sitting in meditation at a crucial stage of his enlightenment, Mara, the force of evil, sent a host of earthly temptations and demons to try to divert him from his path. The Buddha remained cross-legged and pointed his right hand towards the ground – the most popular pose of Buddha statues in Thailand – to call the earth goddess to bear witness to his countless meritorious deeds, which had earned him an ocean of water stored in the earth. Mae Toranee obliged by wringing her hair and engulfing Mara's demons in the deluge.

Wat Mahathat

On Sanam Luang's western side, with its main entrance on Thanon Maharat, **Wat Mahathat** (daily 9am–5pm; free), founded in the eighteenth century, provides a welcome respite from the surrounding tourist hype, and a chance to engage with the eager monks studying at **Mahachulalongkorn Buddhist University** here. As the nation's centre for the Mahanikai monastic sect, and housing one of the two Buddhist universities in Bangkok, the wat buzzes with purpose. It's this activity, and the chance of interaction and participation, rather than any special architectural features, which make a visit so rewarding. The many university-attending monks at the wat are friendly and keen to practise their English, and are more than likely to approach you: diverting topics might range from the poetry of Dylan Thomas to English football results gleaned from the BBC World Service.

Every day the twenty-acre grounds host an interesting **herbal medicine market**, and outside, along the pavements of Maharat and surrounding roads, vendors set up stalls to sell some of the city's most reasonably priced **amulets** (though the range and quality are not as good as at the main market at Wat Rajnadda), taking advantage of the spiritually auspicious location.

Situated in Section Five of the wat is its **International Buddhist Meditation Centre** where Vipassana meditation practice is available in English (daily 7–10am, 1–4pm & 6–9pm; ☎02/222 6011 or 01/694 1527 for further information). Participants are welcome to stay in the simple surroundings of the meditation building itself (donation requested) or at a quiet house nearby (B200 per day).

The National Museum

Near the northwest corner of Sanam Luang, the **National Museum** (Wed–Sun 9am–4pm; B40 including free leaflet with map) houses a colossal hoard of Thailand's chief artistic riches, ranging from sculptural treasures in the north and south wings, through bizarre decorative objects in the older buildings, to outlandish funeral chariots and the exquisite Buddhaisawan Chapel, as well as occasionally staging worthwhile temporary exhibitions (details on ☎02/224 1370). It's worth making time for the free **guided tours in English** (Wed & Thurs 9.30am; details on ☎02/215 8173): they're generally entertaining and their explication of the choicest exhibits provides a good introduction to Thai religion and culture. The simple **cafeteria** here serves good, inexpensive Thai food, especially handy if you linger longer than anticipated – and most people do.

History and prehistory

The building which houses the information office and bookshop provides a quick whirl through the **history** of Thailand, a display in which a couple of gems are hidden. The first is a black stone inscription, credited to King Ramkhamhaeng of Sukhothai, which became the first capital of the Thai nation (c.1278–99) under his rule. Discovered in 1833 by the future Rama IV, it's the oldest extant inscription using the Thai alphabet. This, combined with the description it records of prosperity and piety in Sukhothai's Golden Age, has made the stone a symbol of Thai nationhood. Further on is a four-foot-tall carved *kinnari*, a graceful half-human, half-bird creature said to live in one of the Himalayan heavens. This delicate masterpiece is from the best period of Thai woodcarving, the seventeenth and early eighteenth centuries, before the fall of Ayutthaya.

The **prehistory** room is entered through a separate door at the back end of the building. Prominent here are bronze artefacts from Ban Chiang in the northeast of Thailand, one of the earliest Bronze Age cultures ever discovered, including the world's oldest socketed tool, an axe head set in a sandstone mould (3600–2300 BC).

The main collection: southern building

At the back of the compound, two large modern buildings, flanking an old converted palace, house the museum's **main collection**, kicking off on the ground floor of the **southern building**. Look out here for some historic sculptures from the rest of Asia, including one of the earliest representations of the Buddha, from Gandhara in northwest India. Alexander the Great left a garrison at Gandhara, which explains why the image is in the style of Classical Greek sculpture: for example, the *ushnisha*, the supernatural bump on the top of the head, which symbolizes the Buddha's intellectual and spiritual power, is rationalized into a bun of thick, wavy hair.

Upstairs, in the **Dvaravati** rooms (sixth to eleventh centuries), the pick of the stone and terracotta Buddhas is a small head in smooth, pink clay, whose downcast eyes and faintly smiling full lips typify the serene look of this era. You can't miss a voluptuous Javanese statue of elephant-headed Ganesh, Hindu god of wisdom and the arts, which, being the symbol of the Fine Arts Department, is always freshly garlanded. As Ganesh is known as the clearer of obstacles, Hindus always worship him before other gods, so by tradition he has grown fat through getting first choice of the offerings – witness his trunk jammed into a bowl of food in this sculpture.

Room 9 contains the most famous piece of **Srivijaya** art (seventh to thirteenth centuries), a bronze Bodhisattva Avalokitesvara found at Chaiya (according to Mahayana Buddhism, a *bodhisattva* is a saint who has postponed his passage into Nirvana to help ordinary believers gain enlightenment). With its pouting face and sinuous torso, this image has become the ubiquitous emblem of southern Thailand. The rough chronological order of the collection continues back downstairs with an exhibition of **Khmer** and **Lopburi** sculpture (seventh to fourteenth centuries), most notably some dynamic bronze statuettes and stone lintels. Look out for an elaborate lintel which depicts Vishnu reclining on a dragon in the sea of eternity, dreaming up a new universe after the old one has been annihilated in the Hindu cycle of creation and destruction. Out of his navel comes a lotus, and out of this emerges four-headed Brahma, who will put the dream into practice. Nearby, a smooth, muscular stone statue with a sweet smile and downcast eyes shows King Jayavarman VII, last of the great Khmer emperors. Such royal statues are very rare, and the features borrowed from Buddha images suggest that Jayavarman believed that he was close to Buddhahood himself.

The main collection: northern building

The second half of the survey, in the northern building, begins upstairs with the **Sukhothai** collection (thirteenth to fifteenth centuries), which is short on Buddha images but has some chunky bronzes of Hindu gods and a wide range of ceramics. The **Lanna** rooms (thirteenth to sixteenth centuries) include a miniature set of golden regalia, among them tiny umbrellas and a cute pair of filigree flip-flops, which would have been enshrined in a chedi. An ungainly but serene Buddha head, carved from grainy, pink sandstone, represents the **Ayutthaya** style of sculpture (fourteenth to eighteenth centuries): the faintest incision of a moustache above the lips betrays the Khmer influences which came to Ayutthaya after its conquest of Angkor. A sumptuous scripture cabinet, showing a cityscape of old Ayutthaya, is a more unusual piece, one of a surviving handful of such carved and painted items of furniture.

Downstairs in the **Bangkok** rooms (eighteenth century onwards), a stiffly realistic standing bronze brings you full circle. In his zeal for Western naturalism, Rama V had the statue made in the Gandhara style of the earliest Buddha image displayed in the first room of the museum.

The funeral chariots

To the east of the northern building, beyond the café on the left, stands a large garage where the fantastically elaborate **funeral chariots** of the royal family are stored. Pre-eminent among these is the Vejayant Rajarot, built by Rama I in 1785 for carrying the urn at his own funeral. The thirteen-metre-high structure symbolizes heaven on Mount Meru, while the dragons and divinities around the sides – piled in five golden tiers to suggest the flames of the cremation – represent the mythological inhabitants of the mountain's forests. Weighing forty tons and pulled by three hundred men, the teak chariot was used as recently as 1985 for the funeral of Queen Rambhai Bharni, wife of Rama VII.

Wang Na (Palace of the Second King)

The sprawling central building of the compound was originally part of the **Wang Na**, a huge palace stretching across Sanam Luang to Khlong Lod, which housed the "second king", appointed by the reigning monarch as his heir and deputy. When Rama V did away with the office in 1887, he turned the "Palace of the Second King" into a museum, which now contains a fascinating array of Thai *objets d'art*. As you enter (room 5), the display of sumptuous rare gold pieces behind heavy iron bars includes a well-preserved armlet taken from the ruined prang of fifteenth-century Wat Ratburana in Ayutthaya. In adjacent room 6, an intricately carved ivory seat turns out, with gruesome irony, to be a *howdah*, for use on an elephant's back. Among the masks worn by *khon* actors next door (room 7), look out especially for a fierce Hanuman, the white monkey-warrior in the *Ramayana* epic, gleaming with mother-of-pearl.

The huge and varied ceramic collection in room 8 includes some sophisticated pieces from Sukhothai, while the room above (9) holds a riot of mother-of-pearl items, whose flaming rainbow of colours comes from the shell of the turbo snail from the Gulf of Thailand. It's also worth seeking out the display of richly decorated musical instruments in room 15, where you can hear tapes of the unfamiliar sounds they produce.

The Buddhaisawan chapel

The second holiest image in Thailand, after the Emerald Buddha, is housed in the **Buddhaisawan Chapel**, the vast hall in front of the eastern entrance to the Wang Na. Inside, the fine proportions of the hall, with its ornate coffered ceiling and lacquered window shutters, are enhanced by painted rows of divinities and converted demons, all turned to face the chubby, glowing **Phra Sihing Buddha**, which according to legend was magically created in Sri Lanka and sent to Sukhothai in the thirteenth century. Like the Emerald Buddha, the image was believed to bring good luck to its owner and was frequently snatched from one northern town to another, until Rama I brought it down from Chiang Mai in 1795 and installed it here in the second king's private chapel. Two other images (in Nakhon Si Thammarat and Chiang Mai) now claim to be the authentic Phra Sihing Buddha, but all three are in fact derived from a lost original – this one is in a fifteenth-century Sukhothai style. It's still much loved by ordinary people and at Thai New Year is carried out onto Sanam Luang, where worshippers sprinkle it with water as a merit-making gesture.

The careful detail and rich, soothing colours of the surrounding 200-year-old **murals** are surprisingly well preserved; the bottom row between the windows narrates the life of the Buddha, beginning in the far right-hand corner with his parents' wedding.

Tamnak Daeng

On the south side of the Buddhaisawan chapel, the sumptuous **Tamnak Daeng** (Red House) stands out, a large, airy Ayutthaya-style house made of rare golden teak, surmounted by a multi-tiered roof decorated with carved foliage and swan's-tail finials. Originally part of the private quarters of Princess Sri Sudarak, elder sister of Rama I, it was moved from the Grand Palace to the old palace in Thonburi for Queen Sri Suriyen, wife of Rama II; when her son became second king to Rama IV, he dismantled the edifice again and shipped it here to the Wang Na compound. Inside, it's furnished in the style of the early Bangkok period, with some of the beautiful objects that once belonged to Sri Suriyen, a huge, ornately carved box bed, and the uncommon luxury of an indoor toilet and bathroom.

The National Gallery and Silpakorn University Gallery

If the National Museum hasn't finished you off, two other lesser galleries near-by might. The **National Gallery**, across from the National Theatre on the north side of Sanam Luang at 4 Thanon Chao Fa (Wed–Sun 8am–4pm; B30; ℡02/281 2224), houses a permanent collection of largely uninspiring and derivative twentieth-century Thai art, but its temporary exhibitions can be pretty good. The fine old wooden building that houses the gallery is also worth more than a cursory glance – it used to be the Royal Mint, and is constructed in typical early twentieth-century style, around a central courtyard. The **Silpakorn University Gallery** (Mon–Fri 9am–7pm, Sat 9am–4.30pm; free; ℡02/880 7374–6) on Thanon Na Phra Lan, across the road from the entrance to the Grand Palace, also stages regular exhibitions of modern Thai work.

Banglamphu and the Democracy Monument area

Best known as the site of the travellers' mecca, Thanon Khao San, the **Banglamphu** district (see map on p.106) also holds a couple of noteworthy temples. But the most interesting sights in this part of the city are found to the south and east of **Democracy Monument**, within walking distance of Khao San guest houses and equally accessible from the Grand Palace. If coming from downtown Bangkok the fastest way to get to this area is by longtail canal boat along Khlong Sen Seb (see p.102): the Phanfa terminus for this boat service is right next to the Golden Mount compound, just 30m from Wat Rajnadda. For details on bus and boat services to Banglamphu, see p.108.

Wat Chana Songkhram

Sandwiched between Thanon Khao San and the Chao Phraya River at the heart of the Banglamphu backpackers' ghetto stands the lusciously renovated eighteenth-century **Wat Chana Songkhram**. As with temple compounds throughout the country, Wat Chana Songkhram is used for all sorts of neighbourhood activities (including car-parking and football games) and is not at all an ivory tower; in this instance, part of the temple yard has been appropriated by stallholders selling secondhand books and travellers' clothes, making the most of the constant stream of tourists who use the wat as a shortcut between the river and Khao San. It's worth slowing down for a closer look though, as the gables of the bot roof are beautifully ornate, embossed with a golden relief of Vishnu astride Garuda enmeshed in an intricate design of red and blue glass mosaics, and the golden finials are shaped like nagas. Peeking over the compound walls onto the guest houses and internet cafés of Soi Ram Bhuttri are a row of *kuti*, or monks' quarters, elegantly simple wooden cabins on stilts with steeply pitched roofs.

Phra Sumen Fortress and the Chao Phraya Walkway

The crenellated whitewashed tower beside the Chao Phraya River at the junction of Phra Athit and Phra Sumen roads is **Phra Sumen Fortress** (aka Phra Sumeru Fortress), a renovated corner of the original eighteenth-century city walls. It was the northernmost of fourteen octagonal towers built by Rama I in 1783 to protect the royal island of Ratanakosin and originally contained 38 rooms for storing ammunition. (The only other surviving tower, also renovated, is Phra Mahakan Fortress, next to the Golden Mount; see p.138.) Nowadays there's nothing to see inside the Phra Sumen tower, but it makes a striking landmark, and the area around it has been made into a pleasant grassy riverside park, with English-language signs describing the history of the fortifications.

The fort also marks the northernmost limit of a **riverside walkway** which currently only runs as far as the Bangkok Information Centre at Phra Pinklao Bridge, but is due to be extended all the way down to Tha Chang, in front of the Grand Palace. As well as providing a good view of the boats and barges on the Chao Phraya, the Phra Sumen–Phra Pinklao walkway takes you past the front entrances of two very grand old buildings, both of them beautifully restored and currently occupied by international organizations. The United Nations' Food and Agriculture Organization (FAO) now uses the early-twentieth-century mansion known as **Baan Maliwan** as its library (closed to casual visitors), while the nearby UNICEF office is housed in the late nineteenth-century palace of one of the wives of Rama IV, which also served as the headquarters of the clandestine Seri Thai resistance movement during World War II. Both these mansions have their most attractive features facing the river, as in those days most visitors would have arrived by boat. On the eastern side of Thanon Phra Athit, there's another fine early twentieth-century mansion, **Baan Phra Athit**, at #201/1; most of this building is now occupied by a private company, but one wing has been turned into the café-bar *Coffee and More*, with views onto the courtyard.

Wat Indraviharn

Located in the northern reaches of the Banglamphu district on Thanon Wisut Kasat, **Wat Indraviharn** (also known as Wat In) is famous for the enormous standing Buddha that dominates its precincts. Commissioned by Rama IV in the mid-nineteenth century to enshrine a Buddha relic from Sri Lanka, the 32-metre-high image certainly doesn't rate as a work of art: its enormous, overly flattened features give it an ungainly aspect, while the gold mirror-mosaic surface emphasizes its faintly kitsch overtones. But the beautifully pedicured foot-long toenails peep out gracefully from beneath devotees' garlands of fragrant jasmine, and you can get reasonable views of the neighbourhood by climbing the stairways of the tower supporting the statue from behind; when unlocked, the doorways in the upper part of the tower give access to the interior of the hollow image, affording vistas from shoulder level. Elsewhere in the wat's compact grounds you'll find the usual amalgam of architectural and spiritual styles, including a Chinese shrine and statues of Ramas IV and V.

For some reason Wat Indraviharn seems to be a favourite hangout for **con-artists**, and the popular scam here is to offer tourists a tuk-tuk tour of Bangkok for a bargain B20. This is a ridiculous price, especially given that fuel is currently B17/litre, so the driver makes his real fee from taking his passengers to a nearby jewellery shop and making it extremely difficult for them to come away empty-handed. Needless to say, the "rubies and sapphires" are nothing more than prettily coloured glass. Avoid all these hassles by ignoring any tout, persistent tuk-tuk driver or overly helpful "guide" with an ID-card round his neck (there are no official guides), and flag down a passing metered taxi instead.

Democracy Monument

About 300m southeast of Thanon Khao San, and midway along Rajdamnoen Klang, the avenue that connects the Grand Palace and the new royal district of Dusit, looms the imposing **Democracy Monument**. Begun in 1939, it was conceived as a testimony to the ideals that fuelled the 1932 revolution and the changeover to a constitutional monarchy, hence its symbolic positioning between the royal residences. Its dimensions are also significant: the four wings tower to a height of 24m, the same as the radius of the monument – allusions to June 24, the date the system was changed; the 75 cannons around the perimeter refer to the year, 2475 BE (1932 AD). The monument contains a copy of the constitution and is a focal point for public events and demonstrations – it was a rallying-point during the pro-democracy protests of May 1992 and, less traumatically, gets decked out with flowers every year on December 5, in honour of the king's birthday.

The monument was designed by Corrado Feroci, an Italian sculptor who'd been invited to Thailand by Rama VI in 1924 to encourage the pursuit of Western art. He changed his name to Silpa Bhirasi and stayed in Thailand until his death, producing many of Bangkok's statues and monuments – including the Rama I statue at Memorial Bridge and Victory Monument in the Phrayathai district – as well as founding Thailand's first Institute of Fine Arts.

Wat Rajnadda, Loh Prasat and the amulet market

Five minutes' walk southeast of Democracy Monument, at the point where Rajdamnoen Klang meets Thanon Mahachai, stands the assortment of religious buildings known collectively as **Wat Rajnadda**. It's immediately recognizable by the dusky-pink, multi-tiered, castle-like structure called **Loh Prasat**, or "Iron Monastery" – a reference to its 37 metal spires, which represent the 37 virtues that lead to enlightenment. The only structure of its kind in Bangkok, Loh Prasat is the dominant and most bizarre of Wat Rajnadda's components. Each tier is pierced by passageways running north–south and east–west (fifteen in each direction at ground level), with small meditation cells at each point of intersection. The Sri Lankan monastery on which it is modelled contained a thousand cells; this one probably has half that number.

To gain protection from malevolent spirits and physical misfortune, Thais wear or carry at least one **amulet** at all times. The most popular **images** are copies of sacred statues from famous wats, while others show revered holy men, kings (Rama V is a favourite), healers or a many-armed monk depicted closing his eyes, ears and mouth so as to concentrate better on reaching Nirvana – a human version of the hear-no-evil, see-no-evil, speak-no-evil monkeys. On the reverse side a *yantra* is often inscribed, a combination of letters and figures also designed to ward off evil, sometimes of a very specific nature: protecting your durian orchards from gales, for example, or your tuk-tuk from oncoming traffic. Individually hand-crafted or mass-produced, amulets can be made from bronze, clay, plaster or gold, and some even have sacred ingredients added, such as the ashes of burnt holy texts. But what really determines an amulet's efficacy is its history: where and by whom it was made, who or what it represents and who consecrated it. Monks are often involved in the making of the images and are always called upon to consecrate them – the more charismatic the monk, the more powerful the amulet. In return, the proceeds from the sale of amulets contributes to wat funds.

The **belief in amulets** is thought to have originated in India, where tiny images were sold to pilgrims who visited the four holy sites associated with the Buddha's birth, enlightenment, first sermon and death. But not all amulets are Buddhist-related – there's a whole range of other enchanted objects to wear for protection, including tigers' teeth, rose quartz, tamarind seeds, coloured threads and miniature phalluses. Worn around the waist rather than the neck, the phallus amulets provide protection for the genitals as well as being associated with fertility, and are of Hindu origin.

For some people, amulets are not only a vital form of spiritual protection, but valuable **collectors' items** as well. Amulet-collecting mania is something akin to stamp collecting – there are at least six Thai magazines for collectors, which give histories of certain types, tips on distinguishing between genuine items and fakes, and personal accounts of particularly powerful amulet experiences.

In the southeast (Thanon Mahachai) corner of the temple compound, Bangkok's biggest amulet market, the **Wat Rajnadda Buddha Center**, comprises at least a hundred stalls selling tiny Buddha images of all designs, materials and prices. Alongside these miniature charms are statues of Hindu deities, dolls and carved wooden phalluses, also bought to placate or ward off disgruntled spirits, as well as love potions and tapes of sacred music. While the amulet market at Wat Rajnadda is probably the best in Bangkok, you'll find less pricey examples from the streetside vendors who congregate daily along the pavement in front of Wat Mahathat. Prices start as low as B10 and rise into the thousands.

The Golden Mount

The grubby yellow hill crowned with a gleaming gold chedi just across the road from Wat Rajnadda is the grandiosely named Golden Mount, or Phu Khao Tong. It rises within the compound of **Wat Saket**, a dilapidated late eighteenth-century temple built by Rama I just outside his new city walls to serve as the capital's crematorium. During the following hundred years the temple became the dumping ground for some sixty thousand plague victims – the majority of them too poor to afford funeral pyres, and thus left to the vultures.

The **Golden Mount** was a late addition to the compound and dates back to the early nineteenth century, when Rama III built a huge chedi on ground that proved too soft to support it. The whole thing collapsed into a hill of rubble, but Buddhist law states that a religious building can never be destroyed, however tumbledown, so fifty years later Rama V topped the debris with a more sensibly sized chedi in which he placed a few Buddhist relics, believed by some to be the Buddha's teeth.

To reach the base of the mount, follow the renovated crenellations of the eighteenth-century Phra Mahakan Fortress and the old city wall, past the small bird and antiques market that operates from one of the recesses, before veering left when signposted. Climbing to the top, you'll pass remnants of the collapsed chedi and plaques commemorating donors to the temple. The **terrace** surrounding the base of the new chedi is a good place for landmark-spotting: immediately to the west are the gleaming roofs of Wat Rajnadda and the salmon-pink Loh Prasat; behind them the spires of the Grand Palace can be seen and, even further beyond, the beautifully proportioned prangs of Wat Arun on the other side of the river. To the northwest, look for the controversial New World department store, whose multiple storeys contravene the local building laws, which ordain that no structure in the vicinity should compete with the Grand Palace – though the store has yet to be knocked down, its upper floors all lie empty and the ground floor has been colonized by local stallholders.

Wat Saket hosts an enormous annual **temple fair** in the first week of November, when the mount is illuminated with coloured lanterns and the whole compound seethes with funfair rides, food-sellers and travelling performers.

Wat Suthat and Sao Ching Cha

Located about 700m southwest of the Golden Mount, and a similar distance directly south of Democracy Monument along Thanon Dinso, **Wat Suthat** (daily 9am–9pm; B20) is one of Thailand's six most important temples and contains Bangkok's tallest **viharn**, built in the early nineteenth century to house the meditating figure of **Phra Sri Sakyamuni Buddha**. This eight-metre-high statue was brought all the way down from Sukhothai by river, and now sits on a glittering mosaic dais surrounded with surreal **murals** that depict the last twenty-four lives of the Buddha rather than the more usual ten. The galleries that encircle the viharn contain 156 serenely posed Buddha images, making a nice contrast to the **Chinese statues** dotted around the viharn's courtyard and that of the bot in the adjacent compound, most of which were brought over from China during Rama I's reign, as ballast in rice boats: check out the depictions of gormless Western sailors and the pompous Chinese scholars.

The area just in front of Wat Suthat is dominated by the towering, red-painted teak posts of **Sao Ching Cha**, otherwise known as the **Giant Swing**, once the focal point of a Brahmin ceremony to honour Shiva's annual visit to earth. Teams of two or four young men would stand on the outsized seat (now missing) and swing up to a height of 25m, to grab between their teeth a bag of gold suspended on the end of a bamboo pole. The act of swinging probably symbolized the rising and setting of the sun, though legend also has it that Shiva and his consort Uma were banned from swinging in their heavenly abode because doing so caused cataclysmic floods on earth – prompting Shiva to demand that the practice be continued on earth as a rite to ensure moderate rains and bountiful harvests. Accidents were so common with the terrestrial version that it was outlawed in the 1930s.

The streets leading up to Wat Suthat and Sao Ching Cha are renowned as the best place in the city to buy **religious paraphernalia**, and are well worth a browse even for tourists. Thanon Bamrung Muang in particular is lined with shops selling everything a good Buddhist could need, from household offertory tables to temple umbrellas and six-foot Buddha images. They also sell special alms packs for devotees to donate to monks; a typical pack is contained within a (holy saffron-coloured) plastic bucket (which can be used by the monk for washing his robes, or himself), and comprises such daily necessities as soap, toothpaste, soap powder, toilet roll, candles and incense.

Wat Rajabophit

From Wat Suthat, walk south down Thanon Titong for a few hundred metres before turning right (west) on to Thanon Rajabophit, on which stands **Wat Rajabophit** (see map on p.94), one of the city's prettiest temples and another example of Chinese influence. It was built by Rama V and is characteristic of this progressive king in its unusual design, with the rectangular bot and viharn connected by a circular cloister that encloses a chedi. Every external wall in the compound is covered in the pastel shades of Chinese *bencharong* ceramic tiles, creating a stunning overall effect, while the bot interior looks like a tiny banqueting hall, with gilded Gothic vaults and intricate mother-of-pearl doors.

If you now head west towards the Grand Palace from Wat Rajabophit, you'll pass a gold **statue of a pig** as you cross the canal. The cute porcine monument was erected in tribute to one of Rama V's wives, born in the Chinese Year of the Pig. Alternatively, walking in a southerly direction down Thanon Bamruo takes you all the way down to the Chao Phraya River and Memorial Bridge, passing some fine old Chinese shophouses and the exuberant flower and vegetable market, Pak Khlong Talat, en route (see p.144).

Chinatown and Pahurat

When the newly crowned Rama I decided to move his capital across to the east bank of the river in 1782, the Chinese community living on the proposed site of his palace was given no choice but to relocate downriver, to the **Sampeng** area. Two hundred years on, **Chinatown** has grown into the country's largest Chinese district, a sprawl of narrow alleyways, temples and shophouses packed between Charoen Krung (New Road) and the river, separated from Ratanakosin by the Indian area of **Pahurat** – famous for its cloth and dressmakers' trimmings – and bordered to the east by Hualamphong train station. Real estate in this part of the city is said to be the most valuable in the country, with land prices on the Charoen Krung and Thanon Yaowarat arteries reputed to fetch over a million baht per square metre, and there are over a hundred gold/jewellery shops along Thanon Yaowarat alone. For the tourist, Chinatown is chiefly interesting for its markets, shophouses, open-fronted warehouses and remnants of colonial-style architecture, though it also has a few noteworthy temples. The following account covers Chinatown's main attractions and most interesting neighbourhoods, sketching a meandering and quite lengthy route which could easily take a whole day to complete on foot.

Easiest access is to take the **Chao Phraya Express Boat** to Tha Rajavongse (Rajawong) at the southern end of Thanon Rajawong, which runs through the

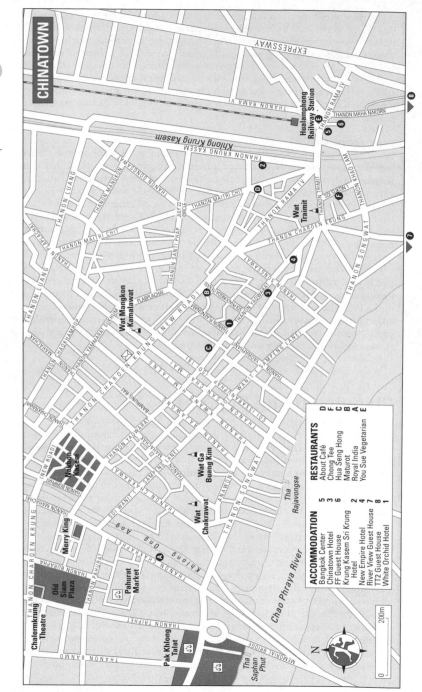

CHINATOWN

ACCOMMODATION
Bangkok Center   5
Chinatown Hotel   3
FF Guest House   6
Krung Kasem Sri Krung
Hotel   2
New Empire Hotel   4
River View Guest House 7
TT2 Guest House   8
White Orchid Hotel   1

RESTAURANTS
About Café   D
Chong Tee   F
Hua Seng Hong   C
Maturot   A
Royal India   B
You Sue Vegetarian   E

The **Chinese** have been a dominant force in the shaping of Thailand, and **commerce** is the foundation of their success. Chinese merchants first gained a toehold here in the mid-fourteenth century, when they contributed so much to the prosperity of the city-state of Ayutthaya that they were the only foreign community allowed to live within the city walls. Soon their compatriots were established all over the country, and when the capital was eventually moved to Bangkok it was to an already flourishing Chinese trading post.

The Bangkok era marked an end to the wars that had dogged Thailand and as the economy began to boom, both Rama I and Rama II encouraged Chinese immigration to boost the indigenous workforce. Thousands of migrants came, most of them young men eager to earn money that could be sent back to families impoverished by civil wars and persistently bad harvests. They saw their overseas stints as temporary measures, intending to return after a few years, though many never did. By the middle of the nineteenth century half the capital's population were of pure or mixed Chinese blood, and they were quickly becoming the masters of the new import-export trade, particularly the burgeoning tin and rubber industries. By the end of the century, the Chinese dominated Thailand's commercial and urban sector, while the Thais remained in firm control of the political domain, an arrangement that apparently satisfied both parties: as the old Chinese proverb goes, "We don't mind who holds the head of the cow, providing we can milk it."

Up until the beginning of the twentieth century, **intermarriage** between the two communities had been common, because so few Chinese women had emigrated – indeed, there is some Chinese blood in almost every Thai citizen, including the king. But in the early 1900s Chinese women started to arrive in Thailand, making Chinese society increasingly self-sufficient and enclosed. **Anti-Chinese feeling** grew and discriminatory laws ensued, including the restricting of Chinese-language education and the closing of some jobs to Chinese citizens, a movement that increased in fervour as Communism began to be perceived as a threat. Since the late 1970s, strict immigration controls have been enforced, limiting the number of new settlers to one hundred per nationality per year, a particularly harsh imposition on the Chinese.

The Chinese still dominate the commercial sector, as can be witnessed over the annual three-day holiday at **Chinese New Year**, when throughout the kingdom nearly all shops, hotels and restaurants shut down. This is the community's most important festival, but is celebrated much more as a family affair than in the Chinatowns of other countries. The nine-day **Vegetarian Festival** in October is a more public celebration, observed with gusto by the Chinese residents of Phuket and Trang provinces (see p.643); in Bangkok, nearly all the city's Chinese restaurants stop serving meat for the duration of the festival, flying special yellow flags to show that they're upholding the community's tradition.

centre of Chinatown. This part of the city is also well served by **buses** from downtown Bangkok, as well as from Banglamphu and Ratanakosin; your best bet is to take any Hualamphong-bound bus (see box on p.100) and then walk from the train station; the non-air-conditioned bus #56 is also a useful link from Banglamphu, as it runs along Thanon Tanao at the end of Thanon Khao San and then goes all the way down Mahachai and Chakraphet roads in Chinatown – get off just after the Merry King department store for Sampeng Lane. Coming from downtown Bangkok and/or the Skytrain network, jump up on a non-air-conditioned #25 or #40, both of which run from Sukhumvit, via Siam Square to Hualamphong, then Thanon Yaowarat and on to Pahurat.

Orientation in Chinatown can be quite tricky: the alleys (known as trok rather than the more usual soi) are extremely narrow, their turn-offs and other road signs often obscured by the mounds of merchandise that clutter the sidewalks and the surrounding hordes of buyers and sellers.

Wat Traimit and the Golden Buddha

Given the confusing layout of the district, it's worth starting your explorations at the eastern edge of Chinatown, just west of Hualamphong station, with the triangle of land occupied by **Wat Traimit** (daily 9am–5pm; B20). Cross the khlong beside the station and walk 200m down (signed) Thanon Tri Mit to enter the temple compound. Outwardly unprepossessing, the temple boasts a quite stunning interior feature: the world's largest solid-gold Buddha is housed here, fitting for a community so closely linked with the gold trade, even if the image has nothing to do with China's spiritual heritage. Over 3m tall and weighing five and a half tons, the **Golden Buddha** gleams as if coated in liquid metal, seated amidst candles and surrounded with offerings of lotus buds and incense. A fine example of the curvaceous grace of Sukhothai art, the beautifully proportioned figure is best appreciated by comparing it with the much cruder Sukhothai Buddha in the next-door bot, to the east.

Cast in the thirteenth century, the image was brought to Bangkok by Rama III, completely encased in stucco – a common ruse to conceal valuable statues from would-be thieves. The disguise was so good that no one guessed what was underneath until 1955 when the image was accidentally knocked in the process of being moved to Wat Traimit, and the stucco cracked to reveal a patch of gold. The discovery launched a country-wide craze for tapping away at plaster Buddhas in search of hidden precious metals, but Wat Traimit's is still the most valuable – it's valued, by weight alone, at $14 million. Sections of the stucco casing are now on display alongside the Golden Buddha.

Sampeng Lane, Soi Issaranuphap and Wat Mangkon Kamalawat

Leaving Wat Traimit by the Charoen Krung/Yaowarat exit (at the back of the temple compound), walk northwest along Thanon Yaowarat, and make a left turn onto Thanon Songsawat, to reach **Sampeng Lane** (also signposted as Soi Wanit 1), an area that used to thrive on opium dens, gambling houses and brothels, but now sticks to a more reputable (if tacky) commercial trade. Stretching southeast–northwest for about 1km, Sampeng Lane is a fun place to browse and shop, unfurling itself like a ramshackle department store selling everything at bargain-basement rates. Among other things, this is the cheapest place in town to buy Chinese silk pyjama pants, electronic pets and other computer games, sarongs, alarm clocks, underwear and hair accessories. And, to complete this perfect shopping experience, there are food stalls every few steps to help keep up your energy.

For a rather more sensual experience, take a right about halfway down Sampeng Lane, into **Soi Issaranuphap** (also signed in places as Soi 16). Packed with people from dawn till dusk, this long, dark alleyway, which also traverses Charoen Krung (New Road), is where you come in search of ginseng roots (essential for good health), quivering fish heads, cubes of cockroach-killer chalk and pungent piles of cinnamon sticks. You'll see Chinese grandfathers discussing business in darkened shops, ancient pharmacists concocting bizarre potions to order, alleys branching off in all directions to gaudy Chinese temples and market squares. Soi Issaranuphap finally ends at the Thanon Plaplachai intersection amid a flurry of shops specializing in paper **funeral art**. Believing that the deceased should be well provided for in their afterlife, Chinese buy miniature paper replicas of necessities to be burned with the body: especially popular are houses, cars, suits of clothing and, of course, money.

If Soi Issaranuphap epitomizes traditional Chinatown commerce, then **Wat Mangkon Kamalawat** (also known as Wat Leng Nee Yee or, in English, "Dragon Flower Temple") stands as a superb example of the community's spiritual practices. Best approached via its dramatic multi-tiered gateway 10m up Charoen Krung (New Road) from the Soi Issaranuphap junction, Wat Mangkon receives a constant stream of devotees, who come to leave offerings at one or more of the small altars inside this important Mahayana Buddhist temple. As with the Theravada Buddhism espoused by the Thais, Mahayana Buddhism (see "Religion: Thai Buddhism" in Contexts) fuses with other ancient religious beliefs, notably Confucianism and Taoism, and the statues and shrines within Wat Mangkon cover the whole spectrum. Passing through the secondary gateway, under the glazed ceramic gables topped with undulating Chinese dragons, you're greeted by a set of four outsize statues of bearded and rather forbidding sages, each clasping a symbolic object: a parasol, a pagoda, a snake's head and a mandolin. Beyond them, a series of Buddha images swathed in saffron netting occupies the next chamber, a lovely open-sided room of gold paintwork, red-lacquered wood, lattice lanterns and pictorial wall panels inlaid with mother-of-pearl. Elsewhere in the compound are little booths selling devotional paraphernalia, a Chinese medicine stall and a fortune-teller.

Wat Ga Buang Kim, Wat Chakrawat and Nakhon Kasem

Less than 100m up Charoen Krung (New Road) from Wat Mangkon, a left turn into Thanon Rajawong, followed by a right turn into Thanon Anawong and a further right turn into the narrow, two-pronged Soi Krai brings you to the typical neighbourhood temple of **Wat Ga Buang Kim**. Here, as at Thai temples upcountry, local residents socialize in the shade of the tiny, enclosed courtyard and the occasional worshipper drops by to pay homage at the altar. This particular wat is remarkable for its exquisitely ornamented "vegetarian hall", a one-room shrine with altar centrepiece framed by intricately carved wooden tableaux – gold-painted miniatures arranged as if in sequence, with recognizable characters reappearing in new positions and in different moods. The hall's outer wall is adorned with small tableaux, too, the area around the doorway at the top of the stairs peopled with finely crafted ceramic figurines drawn from Chinese opera stories. The other building in the wat compound is a stage used for Chinese opera performances.

Back on Anawong, a right turn down Thanon Chakrawat leads to the quite dissimilar **Wat Chakrawat**, home to several long-suffering crocodiles, not to mention monkeys, dogs and chess-playing local residents. **Crocodiles** have lived in the tiny pond behind the bot for about fifty years, ever since one was brought here after being hauled out of the Chao Phraya, where it had been endangering the limbs of bathers. (Unlikely as it sounds, crocodiles still occasionally turn up: the last decade has seen a boy attacked while playing in the Chao Phraya in Nonthaburi.) The original crocodile, stuffed, sits in a glass case overlooking the current generation in the pond.

Across the other side of the wat compound is a grotto two unusual Buddhist relics. The first is a black silhouette on the wall, decorated with squares of gold leaf and believed to be the Buddha's shadow. Nearby, the statue of a fat monk looks on. The story goes that this monk was so good-looking that he was forever being tempted by the attentions of women; the only way he could deter them was to make himself ugly – which he did by gorging himself into obesity.

Further along Thanon Chakrawat, away from the river, is the western limit of Chinatown and an odd assortment of shops in the grid of lanes known as **Nakhon Kasem** (Thieves' Market), bordered by Charoen Krung and Thanon Yaowarat to the north and south and Chakrawat and Boriphat roads to the east and west. In the sois that crisscross Nakhon Kasem, outlets once full of illicitly acquired goods now stock a vast range of metal wares, from antique gongs to modern musical instruments and machine parts.

Pahurat

The ethnic emphasis changes west of Nakhon Kasem. Cross Khlong Ong Ang and you're in **Pahurat** – here, in the small square south of the intersection of Chakraphet and Pahurat roads, is where the capital's sizeable Indian community congregates. Curiosity-shopping is not as rewarding here as in Chinatown, but if you're interested in buying **fabrics** this is definitely the place; Thanon Pahurat is chock-a-block with cloth merchants specializing in everything from curtain and cushion materials, through saree and sarong lengths to wedding outfits and *lakhon* dance costumes complete with accessories. Also here, at the Charoen Krung (New Road)/Thanon Triphet intersection, is the **Old Siam Plaza**: its mint-green and cream exterior, resplendent with shutters and balustraded balconies, is redolent of a colonial summer palace, and its airy, three-storey interior is filled with a strange combination of shops selling either upmarket gifts or hi-tech consumer goods. Most rewarding are the half-dozen shops on the ground floor that carry an excellent range of silk from north and northeast Thailand; many of them offer dressmaking services as well. But most of the ground floor is taken up by a permanent food festival and is packed with stalls selling snacks, sweets and sticky desserts. Pahurat is also renowned for its Indian restaurants, and a short stroll along Thanon Chakraphet takes you past a choice selection of curry houses and street vendors.

Pak Khlong Talat

A browse through the 24-hour **flower and vegetable market**, **Pak Khlong Talat**, is a fine and fitting way to round off a day in Chinatown, though if you're an early riser it's also a great place to come before dawn, when market gardeners from Thonburi boat and truck their freshly picked produce across the Chao Phraya ready for sale to the shopkeepers, restaurateurs and hoteliers. Occupying an ideal position close to the river, the market has been operating from covered halls between the southern ends of Thanon Banmo, Thanon Chakraphet and the river bank since the nineteenth century and is the biggest wholesale market in the capital. The flower stalls, selling twenty different varieties of cut orchids and myriad other tropical blooms, spill onto the streets along the riverfront as well and, though prices are lowest in the early morning, you can still get some good bargains here in the afternoon.

For the most interesting approach to the market from the Old Siam Plaza, turn west across Thanon Triphet to reach Thanon Banmo, and then follow this road south down towards the Chao Phraya River. As you near the river, notice the facing rows of traditional Chinese shophouses, still in use today, which retain their characteristic (peeling) pastel-painted facades, shutters and stucco curlicues; there's an entrance into the market on your right. The Chao Phraya Express Boat service stops just a few metres from the market at Tha Saphan Phut, and numerous city **buses** stop in front of the pier, including the northbound non-air-conditioned #3 and air-conditioned #12, which both run to Banglamphu (see box on p.100).

Thonburi

Bangkok really began across the river from Ratanakosin in the town of **Thonburi**. Devoid of grand ruins and isolated from central Bangkok, it's hard to imagine Thonburi as a former capital of Thailand, but so it was for fifteen years, between the fall of Ayutthaya in 1767 and the establishment of Bangkok in 1782. General Phraya Taksin chose to set up his capital here, strategically near the sea and far from the marauding Burmese, but the story of his brief reign is a chronicle of battles that left little time and few resources to devote to the building of a city worthy of its predecessor. When General Chao Phraya displaced the demented Taksin to become Rama I, his first decision as founder of the Chakri dynasty was to move the capital to the more defensible site across the river. It wasn't until 1932 that Thonburi was linked to its replacement by the **Memorial Bridge** (aka Phra Buddha Yodfa Bridge), built to commemorate the 150th anniversary of the foundation of the Chakri dynasty and of Bangkok, and dedicated to Rama I, whose bronze statue sits at the Bangkok approach. Thonburi retained its separate identity for another forty years until, in 1971, it officially became part of Bangkok.

While Thonburi may lack the fine monuments of Thailand's other ancient capitals, it nevertheless contains some of the most traditional parts of Bangkok and makes a pleasant and evocative place to wander (or even cycle; see box on p.148). As well as the imposing riverside structure of Wat Arun, Thonburi offers a fleet of royal barges and several moderately interesting temples. In addition, life on this side of the river still revolves around the khlongs, on which vendors of food and household goods paddle their boats through the residential areas, and canalside factories transport their wares to the Chao Phraya River artery. The **architecture** along the canals ranges from ramshackle, makeshift homes balanced just above the water – and prone to flooding during the monsoon season – to villa-style residences where the river is kept at bay by lawns, verandas and concrete. Venture on to the Thonburi backroads just three or four kilometres west of the river and you find yourself surrounded by market gardens, nurseries and rural homes, with no hint of the throbbing metropolis across on the other bank. Modern Thonburi, on the other hand, sprawling to each side of Thanon Phra Pinklao, consists of the prosaic line-up of department stores, cinemas, restaurants and markets found all over urbanized Thailand.

Getting to Thonburi is simply a matter of crossing the river – use one of the numerous bridges (Memorial and Phra Pinklao are the most central), take a cross-river ferry, or hop on the express ferry, which makes three stops around the riverside Bangkok Noi station, just south of Phra Pinklao Bridge. You might find yourself taking a train from Bangkok Noi station, as this is the departure point for Kanchanaburi; the Southern Bus Terminal is also in Thonburi, at the junction of Thanon Borom Ratchonni and the Nakhon Chaisri Highway, and all public and air-conditioned buses to southern destinations leave from here.

Wat Arun

Almost directly across the river from Wat Po rises the enormous five-pranged **Wat Arun** (daily 7am–5pm; B20), the Temple of Dawn, probably Bangkok's

most memorable landmark and familiar as the silhouette used in the TAT logo. It looks particularly impressive from the river, as you head downstream from the Grand Palace towards the *Oriental Hotel*, but is ornate enough to be well worth stopping off for a closer look. All boat tours include half an hour here, but Wat Arun is also easily visited by yourself, although tour operators will try to persuade you otherwise: just take a B2 cross-river ferry from the pier adjacent to the Chao Phraya Express Boat pier at Tha Thien.

A wat has occupied this site since the Ayutthaya period, but only in 1768 did it become known as the Temple of Dawn – when General Phraya Taksin reputedly reached his new capital at the break of day. The temple served as his royal chapel and housed the recaptured Emerald Buddha for several years until the image was moved to Wat Phra Kaeo in 1785. Despite losing its special status after the relocation, Wat Arun continued to be revered and was reconstructed and enlarged to its present height of 104m by Rama II and Rama III.

The Wat Arun that you see today is a classic prang structure of Ayutthayan style, built as a representation of Mount Meru, the home of the gods in Khmer mythology. Climbing the two tiers of the square base that supports the **central prang**, you not only enjoy a good view of the river and beyond, but also get a chance to examine the tower's curious decorations. Both this main prang and the four minor ones that encircle it are covered in bits of broken porcelain, arranged to create an amazing array of polychromatic flowers (local people gained much merit by donating their crockery for the purpose). Statues of mythical figures such as *yaksha* demons and half-bird, half-human *kinnari* support the different levels and, on the first terrace, the mondops at each cardinal point contain statues of the Buddha at the most important stages of his life: at birth (north), in meditation (east), preaching his first sermon (south) and entering Nirvana (west). The second platform surrounds the base of the prang proper, whose closed entranceways are guarded by four statues of the Hindu god Indra on his three-headed elephant Erawan. In the niches of the smaller prangs stand statues of Phra Pai, the god of the wind, on horseback.

Wat Prayoon

Downstream of Wat Arun, beside Memorial Bridge, **Wat Prayoon** is worth visiting for its unusual collection of miniature chedis and shrines, set on an artificial hill constructed on a whim of Rama III's, after he'd noticed the pleasing shapes made by dripping candle wax. Wedged in among the grottoes, caverns and ledges of this uneven mass are numerous shrines to departed devotees, forming a phenomenal gallery of different styles, from traditionally Thai chedis, bots or prangs to such obviously foreign designs as the tiny Wild West house complete with cactuses at the front door. Turtles fill the pond surrounding the mound – you can feed them with the banana and papaya sold nearby. At the edge of the pond stands a memorial to the unfortunate few who lost their lives when one of the saluting cannons exploded at the temple's dedication ceremony in 1836.

About ten minutes' walk upstream from Wat Prayoon, the Catholic church of **Santa Cruz** (also known as Wat Kudi Jeen) sits at the heart of what used to be Thonburi's **Portuguese quarter**. The Portuguese came to Thailand both to trade and to proselytize, and by 1856 had established the largest of the European communities in Bangkok: four thousand Portuguese Christians lived in and around Thonburi at this time, about one percent of the total population. The Portuguese ghetto is a thing of the distant past, but this is nonetheless an interesting patch to stroll through, comprising narrow backstreets and tiny shophouses stocked with all manner of goods, from two-baht plastic toys to the essential bottles of chilli sauce.

One of the most popular ways of seeing the sights of Thonburi is by **longtail boat**, taking in Wat Arun and the Royal Barge Museum, then continuing along Thonburi's network of small canals. The easiest place to organize boat tours is at the Bangkok Information Centre, where staff can help hire a boat for you at Tha Wang Nah pier, next to their office on Thanon Phra Athit in Banglamphu (B400 per hour for a boat carrying up to six passengers). Most people however hire boats from Tha Chang, which is conveniently located in front of the Grand Palace, but is renowned for its aggressive and unscrupulous touts and boatmen; if you do go for this option, try to bargain the price down to B400 per hour, but expect to be charged up to B1500 per boat for a two-hour tour.

A less expensive option is to use the **public longtails** that run bus-like services along back canals from central Bangkok-side piers, departing every ten to thirty minutes and charging from B15–30 a round trip. Potentially interesting routes include the Khlong Bangkok Noi service from Tha Chang; the Khlong Mon service from Tha Thien, in front of Wat Po; the Khlong Bang Waek service from Tha Saphan Phut, at Memorial Bridge; and the Khlong Om service from Tha Nonthaburi. There have however been recent reports that taxi-boat drivers are making it impossible for tourists to board the public services from Tha Chang and Tha Thien, so the tourist office suggests starting in Nonthaburi instead.

A fixture of the upper-bracket tourist round is the organized **canal tour** to see Thonburi's **Wat Sai floating market**. This has become so commercialized and land-based that it can't be recommended in preference to the two-hour trip out to the floating markets of Damnoen Saduak (see p.207), but if you're short on time and set on seeing fruit- and flower-laden paddle-boats, then join the longtail Wat Sai market tours from Tha Chang or from Tha Orienten (at the *Oriental Hotel*); these tours leave at around 7am and cost from B400 per person. **Taling Chan floating market**, fairly contrived but picturesque nonetheless, operates every Saturday and Sunday from 9am to 4pm on Khlong Chakphra in front of Taling Chan District Ofice, a couple of kilometres west of Bangkok Noi station. It can be visited as part of a chartered long-tail tour, or you can make your own way there on bus #79 from Democracy Monument/Ratchadamnoen Klang, getting out at Khet Taling Chan, and either watching from the banks or hiring a longtail from the market. Alternatively, every weekend, the Mitchaophya Boat Company (℡02/225 6179) runs a boat **tour** that departs from Tha Chang at 9am and takes in the Royal Barges Museum, floating markets, and the island of Ko Kred, returning at 4pm (Sat & Sun; B200, children B150).

The most peaceful and least touristed way to enjoy the canals of Thonburi is to join the monthly **bicycle tour** organized by the Bangkok Tourist Bureau on Thanon Phra Athit in Banglamphu (℡02/225 7612–4; B650 including bike rental). You need to be reasonably fit to tackle the 35-kilometre route, which is specially designed to follow canal towpaths wherever possible; the tour guides you through exceptionally scenic parts of both Thonburi and Nonthaburi, taking in khlong-side settlements, floating markets, market gardens, orchid nurseries and neighbourhood temples. The tour currently takes place from 7am to 4.30pm on the first Sunday of every month, but there are plans to make it a weekly event, so call ahead to check.

Royal Barge Museum

Until about twenty years ago, the king would process down the Chao Phraya River to Wat Arun in a flotilla of royal barges at least once a year, on the occasion of Kathin, the annual donation of robes by the laity to the temple at the end of the rainy season. Fifty-one barges, filling the width of the river and stretching for almost 1km, drifted slowly to the measured beat of a drum and the hypnotic strains of ancient boating hymns, chanted by over two thousand oarsmen whose red, gold and blue uniforms complemented the black and gold craft.

The 100-year-old boats are becoming quite frail, so such a procession is now a rare event – the last was in 1999, to mark the king's 72nd birthday. The three elegantly narrow vessels at the heart of the ceremony now spend their time moored in the **Royal Barge Museum** on the north bank of Khlong Bangkok Noi (daily 8.30am–4.30pm; B30). Up to 50m long and intricately lacquered and gilded all over, they taper at the prow into magnificent mythical figures after a design first used by the kings of Ayutthaya. Rama I had the boats copied and, when those fell into disrepair, Rama V commissioned the exact reconstructions still in use today. The most important of the trio is *Sri Suphanahongse*, which bears the king and queen and is instantly recognizable by the fifteen-foot-high prow representing a golden swan. In front of it floats *Anantanagaraj*, fronted by a magnificent seven-headed naga and bearing a Buddha image, while the royal children bring up the rear in *Anekchartphuchong*, which has a monkey god from the *Ramayana* at the bow.

The museum is a feature of most canal tours. To get there on your own, cross the Phra Pinklao Bridge (served by air-conditioned buses #3, #7, #9, #11 or #32), and take the first left (Soi Wat Dusitaram), which leads to the museum through a jumble of walkways and houses on stilts. Alternatively, take a ferry to Bangkok Noi station (Tha Rot Fai); from there follow the tracks until you reach the bridge over Khlong Bangkok Noi, cross it and follow the signs. Either way it's about a ten-minute walk.

Dusit

Connected to Ratanakosin via the boulevards of Rajdamnoen Klang and Rajdamnoen Nok, the spacious, leafy area known as **Dusit** has been a royal district since the reign of Rama V (1860–1910). The first Thai monarch to visit Europe, Rama V returned with radical plans for the modernization of his capital, the fruits of which are most visible in Dusit: notably the **Vimanmek Palace** and **Wat Benjamabophit**, the so-called Marble Temple. Today the peaceful Dusit area retains its European feel, and much of the country's decision-making goes on behind the high fences and impressive facades along its tree-lined avenues: Government House is here, and the king lives on the eastern edge of the area, in the Chitrlada Palace.

From Banglamphu, you can get to Dusit by taking the west-bound #56 **bus** from Thanon Tanao or Thanon Phra Sumen and getting off on Thanon Ratchasima. From downtown Bangkok, easiest access is by bus from the Skytrain stop at Victory Monument; there are many services from here, including air-conditioned #10 and #16, both of which run all the way along Thanon Rajwithi. Vimanmek is also served by the open-topped Bangkok Sightseeing Bus (see p.99).

Vimanmek Palace and the Royal Elephant National Museum

Vimanmek Palace (daily 9.30am–4pm; compulsory free guided tours every 30min, last tour 3.15pm; B50, or free with a Grand Palace ticket, which remains valid for one month) was built by Rama V as a summer retreat on Ko Si Chang (see p.404), from where it was transported bit by bit in 1901. Built almost entirely of golden teak without a single nail, the L-shaped "Celestial Residence" is encircled by verandas that look out onto well-kept lawns, flower gardens and lotus ponds. The ticket price also covers entry to half a dozen other small museums in the palace grounds, including the Support Museum and Elephant Museum described below, and all visitors are treated to free performances of traditional Thai dance daily at 10.30am and 2pm. Note that the same **dress rules** apply here as to the Grand Palace (see p.121). The main **entrance** to the extensive Vimanmek Palace compound is on Thanon Rajwithi, but there are also ticket gates on Thanon Ratchasima, and opposite Dusit Zoo on Thanon U-Thong.

Vimanmek Palace

Not surprisingly, Vimanmek soon became Rama V's favourite palace, and he and his enormous retinue of officials, concubines and children stayed here for lengthy periods between 1902 and 1906. All of Vimanmek's 81 rooms were out of bounds to male visitors, except for the king's own apartments, in the octagonal tower, which were entered by a separate staircase.

On display inside is Rama V's collection of artefacts from all over the world, including *bencharong* ceramics, European furniture and bejewelled Thai betel-nut sets. Considered progressive in his day, Rama V introduced many new fangled ideas to Thailand: the country's first indoor bathroom is here, as is the earliest typewriter with Thai characters, and some of the first portrait paintings – portraiture had until then been seen as a way of stealing part of the sitter's soul.

The Support Museum

Elsewhere in the Vimanmek grounds several small throne halls have been converted into tiny museums displaying royal portraits, antique clocks and other collectors' items. The most interesting of these is the **Support Museum Abhisek Dusit Throne Hall**, showcasing the exquisite handicrafts produced under Queen Sirikit's charity project, Support, which works to revitalize traditional Thai arts and crafts. Outstanding exhibits include a collection of handbags, baskets and pots woven from the *lipao* fern that grows wild in southern Thailand; jewellery and figurines inlaid with the iridescent wings of beetles; gold and silver nielloware; and lengths of intricately woven silk from the northeast.

Royal Elephant National Museum

Just inside the eastern, Thanon U-Thong, entrance to the Vimanmek compound stand two whitewashed buildings that once served as the stables for the king's white elephants. Now that the sacred pachyderms have been relocated, the stables have been turned into the **Royal Elephant National Museum**. Inside you'll find some interesting pieces of elephant paraphernalia, including sacred ropes, mahouts' amulets and magic formulae, as well as photos of the all-important ceremony in which a white elephant is granted royal status.

Dusit Zoo (Khao Din)

Just across Thanon U-Thong is **Dusit Zoo**, also known as **Khao Din** (daily 8am–6pm; B30, children B5); once part of the Chitrlada Palace gardens, it is now a public park. All the usual suspects are here, including big cats, elephants, orang-utans, chimpanzees and a reptile house, but the enclosures are pretty basic and not especially heart-warming. However, it's a reasonable place for kids to let off steam, with plenty of shade, a full complement of English-language signs, a lake with pedalos and lots of foodstalls. The main entrance to

The royal white elephants

In Thailand the most revered of all elephants are the so-called **white elephants** – actually tawny brown albinos – which are considered so sacred that they all, whether wild or captive, belong to the king by law. Their special status originates from Buddhist mythology, which tells how the previously barren Queen Maya became pregnant with the future Buddha after dreaming one night that a white elephant had entered her womb. The thirteenth-century King Ramkhamhaeng of Sukhothai adopted the beast as a symbol of the great and the divine, and ever since, a Thai king's greatness is said to be measured by the number of white elephants he owns. The present king, Rama IX, has twelve, the largest royal collection to date.

Before an elephant can be granted official "white elephant" status, it has to pass a stringent assessment of its physical and behavioural **characteristics**. Key qualities include a paleness of seven crucial areas – eyes, nails, palate, hair, outer edges of the ears, tail and testicles – and an all-round genteel demeanour, manifested, for instance, in the way in which it cleans its food before eating, or in a tendency to sleep in a kneeling position. The most recent addition to King Bhumibol's stables was first spotted in Lampang in 1992, but experts from the Royal Household had to spend a year watching its every move before it was finally given the all-clear. Tradition holds that an elaborate ceremony should take place every time a new white elephant is presented to the king: the animal is paraded with great pomp from its place of capture to Dusit, where it's anointed with holy water in front of an audience of the kingdom's most important priests and dignitaries, before being housed in the royal stables. Recently though, the king has decided that as a cost-cutting measure there should be no more ceremonies for new acquisitions, and only one of the royal white elephants is now kept inside the royal palace; the others live in less luxurious rural accommodation.

The expression "white elephant" probably derives from the legend that the kings used to present certain enemies with one of these exotic creatures. The animal required expensive attention but, being royal, could not be put to work in order to pay for its upkeep. The recipient thus went bust trying to keep it.

the zoo is on Thanon Rajvithi, and there's another one across from the Vimanmek elephant museum on Thanon U-Thong.

Wat Benjamabophit

Ten minutes' walk southeast from Vimanmek and the zoo along Thanon Sri Ayutthaya, **Wat Benjamabophit** (daily 7am–5pm; B20) is the last major temple to have been built in Bangkok. It's an interesting fusion of classical Thai and nineteenth-century European design, with its Carrara marble walls – hence the touristic tag "The Marble Temple" – complemented by the bot's unusual stained-glass windows, Victorian in style but depicting figures from Thai mythology. Inside, a fine replica of the highly revered Phra Buddha Chinnarat image of Phitsanulok (see p.256) presides over the small room containing Rama V's ashes. The courtyard behind the bot houses a gallery of Buddha images from all over Asia, set up by Rama V as an overview of different representations of the Buddha.

Wat Benjamabophit is one of the best temples in Bangkok to see religious **festivals** and rituals. Whereas monks elsewhere tend to go out on the streets every morning in search of alms, at the Marble Temple the ritual is reversed, and merit-makers come to them. Between about 6 and 7.30am, the monks line up on Thanon Nakhon Pathom, their bowls ready to receive donations of curry and rice, lotus buds, incense, even toilet paper and Coca-Cola; the demure row of saffron-robed monks is a sight that's well worth getting up early for. The evening candlelight processions around the bot during the Buddhist festivals of Maha Puja (in Feb) and Visakha Puja (in May) are among the most entrancing in the country.

Downtown Bangkok

Extending east from the rail line and south to Thanon Sathorn, **downtown Bangkok** is central to the colossal expanse of Bangkok as a whole, but rather peripheral in a sightseer's perception of the city. This is where you'll find the main financial district, around Thanon Silom, and the chief shopping centres, around Siam Square, in addition to the smart hotels and restaurants, the embassies and airline offices. Scattered widely across the downtown area are just a few attractions for visitors, including the noisy and glittering **Erawan Shrine**, and three attractive museums housed in traditional teak buildings: **Jim Thompson's House**, the **Kamthieng House** and the **Suan Pakkad Palace Museum**. The infamous **Patpong** district hardly shines as a tourist sight, yet, lamentably, its sex bars provide Thailand's single biggest draw for farang men.

If you're heading downtown from Banglamphu, allow at least an hour to get to any of the places mentioned here by **bus**. To get to the southern part of the area, take an **express boat** downriver and then change onto the **Skytrain** or a bus if necessary. For other parts of the downtown area, it might be worth considering the regular **longtails** on Khlong Sen Seb, which runs parallel to Thanon Phetchaburi. They start at the Golden Mount, near Democracy Monument, and have useful stops at Saphan Hua Chang on Thanon Phrayathai (for Jim Thompson's House) and Pratunam (for the Erawan Shrine).

Siam Square to Thanon Sukhumvit

Though Siam Square has just about everything to satisfy the Thai consumer boom – big shopping centres, Western fast-food restaurants, cinemas – don't come looking for an elegant commercial piazza: the "square" is in fact a grid of small streets on the south side of Thanon Rama I, between Phrayathai and Henri Dunant roads, and the name is applied freely to the surrounding area. Further east, you'll find newer, bigger and more expensive shopping malls at Erawan corner, where Rama I becomes Thanon Ploenchit. Life becomes slightly less frenetic along Ploenchit, which is flanked by several grand old embassies, but picks up again once you pass under the expressway flyover and enter the shopping and entertainment quarter of Thanon Sukhumvit.

Jim Thompson's House

Just off Siam Square at 6 Soi Kasemsan 2, Thanon Rama I, **Jim Thompson's House** (daily from 9am, viewing on frequent 45min guided tours in several languages, last tour 4.30pm, café and shop open until 5.30pm; B100, under-25s B50; ⓦ www.jimthompson.com) is a kind of Ideal Home in elegant Thai style, and a peaceful refuge from downtown chaos. The house was the residence of the legendary American adventurer, entrepreneur, art collector and all-round character whose mysterious disappearance in the jungles of Malaysia in 1967 has made him even more of a legend among Thailand's farang community.

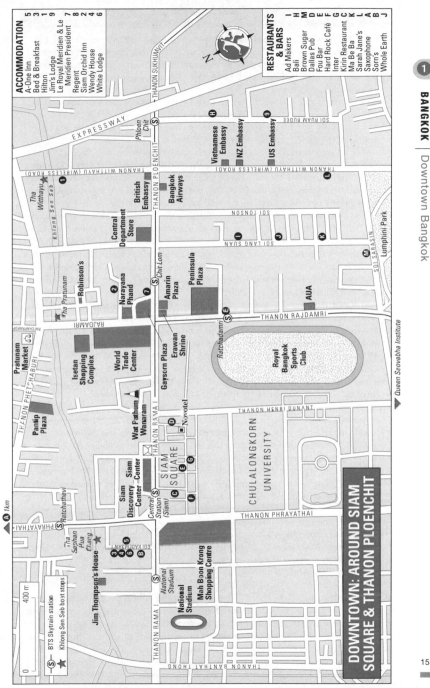

ACCOMMODATION

A-One Inn	5
Bed & Breakfast	3
Hilton	1
Jim's Lodge	9
Le Royal Meridien & Le Meridien President	7
Regent	8
Siam Orchid Inn	2
Wendy House	4
White Lodge	6

RESTAURANTS & BARS

Ad Makers	I
Bali	H
Brown Sugar	M
Dallas Pub	D
Fou Bar	E
Hard Rock Café	F
Inter	G
Kirin Restaurant	C
Ma Be Ba	K
Sarah Jane's	L
Saxophone	A
Som's	B
Whole Earth	J

DOWNTOWN: AROUND SIAM SQUARE & THANON PLOENCHIT

The legend of Jim Thompson

Thai silk-weavers, art-dealers and conspiracy theorists all owe a debt to Jim Thompson, who even now, over thirty years after his disappearance, remains Thailand's most famous farang. An architect by trade, Thompson left his New York practice in 1940 to join the Office of Strategic Services (later to become the CIA), a tour of duty which was to see him involved in clandestine operations in North Africa, Europe and, in 1945, the Far East, where he was detailed to a unit preparing for the invasion of Thailand. When the mission was pre-empted by the Japanese surrender, he served for a year as OSS station chief in Bangkok, forming links that were later to provide grist for endless speculation.

After an unhappy and short-lived stint as part-owner of the *Oriental Hotel*, Thompson found his calling in the struggling silk-weavers of the area near the present Jim Thompson House, whose traditional product was unknown in the West and had been all but abandoned by Thais in favour of less costly imported textiles. Encouragement from society friends and an enthusiastic write-up in *Vogue* convinced him there was a foreign market for Thai silk, and by 1948 he had founded the Thai Silk Company Ltd. Success was assured when, two years later, the company was commissioned to make the costumes for the Broadway run of *The King and I*. Thompson's celebrated eye for colour combinations and his tireless promotion – in the early days, he could often be seen in the lobby of the *Oriental* with bolts of silk slung over his shoulder, waiting to pounce on any remotely curious tourist – quickly made his name synonymous with Thai silk.

Like a character in a Somerset Maugham novel, Thompson played the role of Western exile to the hilt. Though he spoke no Thai, he made it his personal mission to preserve traditional arts and architecture (at a time when most Thais were more keen to emulate the West), assembling his famous Thai house and stuffing it with all manner of Oriental *objets d'art*. At the same time he held firmly to his farang roots and society connections: no foreign gathering in Bangkok was complete without Jim Thompson, and virtually every Western luminary passing through Bangkok – from Truman Capote to Ethel Merman – dined at his table.

If Thompson's life was the stuff of legend, his disappearance and presumed death only added to the mystique. On Easter Sunday, 1967, Thompson, while staying with friends in a cottage in Malaysia's Cameron Highlands, went out for a stroll and never came back. A massive search of the area, employing local guides, tracker dogs and even shamans, turned up no clues, provoking a rash of fascinating but entirely unsubstantiated theories. The grandfather of them all, advanced by a Dutch psychic, held that Thompson had been lured into an ambush by the disgraced former prime minister of Thailand, Pridi Panyonyong, and spirited off to Cambodia for indeterminate purposes; later versions, supposing that Thompson had remained a covert CIA operative all his life, proposed that he was abducted by Vietnamese Communists and brainwashed to be displayed as a high-profile defector to Communism. More recently, an amateur sleuth claims to have found evidence that Thompson met a more mundane fate, having been killed by a careless truck driver and hastily buried.

Apart from putting together this beautiful home, Thompson's most concrete contribution was to turn traditional silk-weaving from a dying art into the highly successful international industry it is today.

The grand, rambling **house** is in fact a combination of six teak houses, some from as far afield as Ayutthaya and most over 200 years old. Like all traditional houses, they were built in wall sections hung together without nails on a frame of wooden pillars, which made it easy to dismantle them, pile them onto a barge and float them to their new home. Although he had trained as an architect, Thompson had more difficulty in putting them back together again; in the end, he had to go back to Ayutthaya to hunt down a group of carpenters who still practised the old house-building methods. Thompson added a few unconventional touches of his own, incorporating the elaborately carved front wall of a Chinese pawnshop between the drawing room and the bedroom, and reversing the other walls in the drawing room so that their carvings faced into the room.

The impeccably tasteful **interior** has been left as it was during Thompson's life, even down to the cutlery on the dining table. Complementing the fine artefacts from throughout Southeast Asia is a stunning array of Thai arts and crafts, including one of the best collections of traditional Thai paintings in the world. Thompson picked up plenty of bargains from the Thieves' Quarter (Nakhon Kasem) in Chinatown, before collecting Thai art became fashionable and expensive. Other pieces were liberated from decay and destruction in upcountry temples, while many of the Buddha images were turned over by ploughs, especially around Ayutthaya. Some of the exhibits are very rare, such as a seventeenth-century Ayutthayan teak Buddha, but Thompson also bought pieces of little value and fakes simply for their looks – a shopping strategy that's all the more sensible in the jungle of today's Thai antiques trade.

The Erawan Shrine

For a break from high culture, drop in on the **Erawan Shrine** (*Saan Phra Pom* in Thai), at the corner of Ploenchit and Rajdamri roads. Remarkable as much for its setting as anything else, this shrine to Brahma, the ancient Hindu creation god, and Erawan, his elephant, squeezes in on one of the busiest and noisiest corners of modern Bangkok, in the shadow of the *Grand Hyatt Erawan Hotel* – whose existence is the reason for the shrine. When a string of calamities held up the building of the original hotel in the 1950s, spirit doctors were called in, who instructed the owners to build a new home for the offended local spirits: the hotel was then finished without further mishap.

Be prepared for sensory overload: the main structure shines with lurid glass of all colours and the overcrowded precinct around it is almost buried under scented garlands and incense candles. You might also catch a lacklustre group of traditional dancers performing here to the strains of a small classical orchestra – worshippers hire them to give thanks for a stroke of good fortune. To increase their future chances of such good fortune, visitors buy a bird or two from the flocks incarcerated in cages here; the bird-seller transfers the requested number of captives to a tiny hand-held cage, from which the customer duly liberates the animals, thereby accruing merit. People set on less abstract rewards will invest in a lottery ticket from one of the physically handicapped sellers: they're thought to be the luckiest you can buy.

Ban Kamthieng

Another reconstructed traditional Thai residence, **Ban Kamthieng** (Tues–Sat 9am–5pm; entry by donation until renovations are completed in 2002) was moved in the 1960s from Chiang Mai to 131 Soi Asoke (Soi 21), off Thanon Sukhumvit, and set up as an ethnological museum by the Siam Society. It differs from both Suan Pakkad and Jim Thompson's House in being the home of a rural family, and the objects on display give a fair representation of country life in northern Thailand.

The house was built on the banks of the Ping River in the mid-nineteenth century, and the ground-level display of farming tools and fish traps evokes the upcountry practice of fishing in flooded rice paddies to supplement the supply from the rivers. Upstairs, the main rooms of the house are much as they would have been 150 years ago – the raised floor is polished and smooth, sparsely furnished with only a couple of low tables and seating mats, and a betel-nut set to hand; notice how surplus furniture and utensils are stored in the rafters. The rectangular lintel above the door to the inner room is a *hum yon*, carved in floral patterns that represent testicles and designed to ward off evil spirits. Walking along the open veranda between the kitchen and the granary, you'll see areca palm (betel-nut) trees to your left (see box on p.503 for more on betel-chewing); the garden, too, is as authentic as possible.

Next door to Kamthieng House, in the same compound, is the more recently acquired **Sangaroon House**, built here to house the folk-craft collection of Thai architect and lecturer Sangaroon Ratagasikorn. Upon his return to Thailand after studying in America under Frank Lloyd Wright, Sangaroon became fascinated by the efficient designs of rural utensils and began to collect them as teaching aids. Those on display include baskets, fishing pots and *takraw* balls, all of which fulfil his criteria of being functional, simple and beautiful, with no extraneous features.

Northern downtown

The area above Thanon Phetchaburi, which becomes increasingly residential as you move north, is cut through by two major roads lined with monolithic company headquarters: Phaholyothin, which runs past the Northern Bus Terminal and the weekend market, and Wiphawadi Rangsit, leading eventually to the airport. The area's chief tourist attraction is Suan Pakkad, a museum of Thai arts and crafts set in a beautiful garden, but it also contains one of Bangkok's most famous landmarks and an important covered market.

Suan Pakkad Palace Museum

The **Suan Pakkad Palace Museum** (daily 9am–4pm; B100), 352–4 Thanon Sri Ayutthaya, stands on what was once a cabbage patch but is now one of the finest gardens in Bangkok. Most of this private collection of beautiful Thai objects from all periods is displayed in six traditional wooden houses, which were transported to Bangkok from various parts of the country. You can either take a mediocre guided tour in English (free) or explore the loosely arranged collection yourself (a free handout is usually available and some of the exhibits are labelled). The attached **Marsi Gallery** has recently opened to display some interesting temporary exhibitions of contemporary art (daily 9am–6pm; ☎02/246 1775–6 for details).

The highlight here is the renovated **Lacquer Pavilion**, across the reedy pond at the back of the grounds. Set on stilts, the pavilion is actually an amalgam of two eighteenth- or late seventeenth-century temple buildings, a *ho trai* (library) and a *ho khien* (writing room), one inside the other, which were found between Ayutthaya and Bang Pa-In. The interior walls are beautifully decorated with gilt on black lacquer: the upper panels depict the life of the Buddha while the lower ones show scenes from the *Ramayana*. Look out especially for the grisly details in the tableau on the back wall, showing the earth goddess drowning the evil forces of Mara. Underneath are depicted some European dandies on horseback, probably merchants, whose presence suggests that the work was executed before the fall of Ayutthaya in 1767.

The carefully observed details of daily life and nature are skilful and lively, especially considering the restraints which the **lacquering technique** places on the artist, who has no opportunity for corrections or touching up: the design has to be punched into a piece of paper, which is then laid on the panel of black lacquer (a kind of plant resin); a small bag of chalk dust is pressed on top so that the dust penetrates the minute holes in the paper, leaving a line of dots on the lacquer to mark the pattern; a gummy substance is then applied to the background areas which are to remain black, before the whole surface is covered in microscopically thin squares of gold leaf; thin sheets of blotting paper, sprinkled with water, are then laid over the panel, which when pulled off bring away the gummy substance and the unwanted pieces of gold leaf that are stuck to it, leaving the rest of the gold decoration in high relief against the black background.

The **Ban Chiang House** has a very good collection of elegant, whorled pottery and bronze jewellery, which the former owner of Suan Pakkad Palace, Princess Chumbot, excavated from tombs at Ban Chiang, the major Bronze Age settlement in the northeast. Scattered around the rest of the museum are some attractive Thai and Khmer religious sculpture among an eclectic jumble of artefacts: fine ceramics as well as some intriguing kiln-wasters, failed pots which have melted together in the kiln to form weird, almost rubbery pieces of sculpture; an extensive collection of colourful papier-mâché *khon* masks; beautiful betel-nut sets (see box on p.503); monks' elegant ceremonial fans; and some rich teak carvings, including a 200-year-old temple door showing episodes from *Sang Thong*, a folk tale about a childless king and queen who discover a handsome son in a conch shell.

Pratunam Market and the Victory Monument

Fifteen minutes' walk southeast of Suan Pakkad and extending northwest from the corner of Rajaprarop and Phetchaburi roads, **Pratunam Market** is famous for its low-cost, low-quality casual clothes. The vast warren of stalls is becoming touristy near the hotels on its north side, though there are still bargains towards the other end, amongst the amphetamine-driven sweatshops.

To the north of Suan Pakkad, the stone obelisk of the **Victory Monument** can be seen from way down the broad Phrayathai and Rajwithi streets, but is viewed most spectacularly from Skytrains as they snake their way round it. It was erected after the Indo-Chinese War of 1940–41, when Thailand pinched back some territory in Laos and Cambodia while the French government was otherwise occupied in World War II, but nowadays it commemorates all of Thailand's past military glories.

Southern downtown

South of Thanon Rama I, commercial development gives way to a dispersed assortment of large institutions, dominated by Thailand's most prestigious centre of higher learning, Chulalongkorn University, and the green expanse of Lumphini Park. Thanon Rama IV marks another change of character: downtown proper, centring around the high-rise American-style boulevard of Thanon Silom, heart of the financial district, extends from here to the river. Alongside the smoked glass banks and offices, the plush hotels and tourist shops, and opposite Bangkok's Carmelite convent, lies the dark heart of Bangkok nightlife, Patpong.

Carrying on to the river, the strip west of Charoen Krung (New Road) reveals some of the history of Bangkok's early dealings with farangs in the fading grandeur of the old trading quarter. Here you'll find the only place in Bangkok where you might be able to eke out an architectural walk, though it's

Bangkok owes its reputation as the carnal capital of the world to a highly efficient sex industry adept at peddling fantasies of cheap sex on tap. More than a thousand sex-related businesses operate in the city, but the gaudy neon fleshpots of Patpong give a misleading impression of an activity that is deeply rooted in Thai culture – the overwhelming majority of Thailand's prostitutes of both sexes (estimated at anywhere between 200,000 and 700,000) work with Thai men, not farangs. It is a phenomenally lucrative industry – according to a Chulalongkorn University study, the 1993 income from the trafficking of women in Thailand amounted to US$20–23 billion, or two-thirds of the national budget.

Prostitution and polygamy have long been intrinsic to the Thai way of life. Until Rama VI broke with the custom in 1910, Thai kings had always kept a retinue of concubines around them, a select few of whom would be elevated to the status of wife and royal mother, the rest forming a harem of ladies-in-waiting and sexual playthings. The practice was aped by the status-hungry nobility and, from the early nineteenth century, by newly rich merchants keen to have lots of sons and heirs. Though the monarch is now monogamous, many men of all classes still keep mistresses, known as *mia noi* (minor wives), a tradition bolstered by the popular philosophy which maintains that an official wife (*mia luang*) should be treated like the temple's main Buddha image – respected and elevated upon the altar – whereas the minor wife is an amulet, to be taken along wherever you go. For those not wealthy enough to take on *mia noi*, prostitution is a far less costly and equally accepted option. Statistics indicate that at least two fifths of sexually active Thai men are thought to use the services of prostitutes twice a month on average, and it's common practice for a night out with the boys to wind up in a brothel or massage parlour.

The farang sex industry is a relatively new development, having had its start during the Vietnam War, when the American military set up seven bases around Thailand. The GIs' appetite for "entertainment" fuelled the creation of instant red-light districts near the bases, attracting women from surrounding rural areas to cash in on the boom; Bangkok joined the fray in 1967, when the US secured the right to ferry soldiers in from Vietnam for R&R breaks. By the mid-1970s, the bases had been evacuated but the sex infrastructure remained and tourists moved in to fill the vacuum, lured by advertising that diverted most of the traffic to Bangkok and Pattaya. Sex tourism has since grown to become an established part of the Thai economy, the two-million-plus foreign males who arrive each year representing foreign-exchange earnings of B50 billion. Even the highly respectable *Bangkok Post* publishes a weekly column on sex-industry news and gossip.

The majority of the women who work in the Patpong bars come from the poorest rural areas of north and northeast Thailand. Economic refugees in search of a better life, they're easily drawn into an industry in which they can make in a single night what it takes a month to earn in the rice fields. In some Isaan villages, money sent home by prostitutes in Bangkok far exceeds financial aid given by the government. Women from rural communities have always been expected to contribute an equal share to the family income, and many opt for a couple of lucrative years

hardly compelling. Incongruous churches and "colonial" buildings (the best of these is the Authors' Wing of the *Oriental Hotel*, where nostalgic afternoon teas are served) are hemmed in by the spice shops and *halal* canteens of the growing Muslim area along Thanon Charoen Krung and the outskirts of Chinatown to the north.

in the sex bars and brothels as the most effective way of helping to pay off family debts and improve the living conditions of parents stuck in the poverty trap. Reinforcing this social obligation is the pervasive Buddhist notion of **karma**, which holds that your lot, however unhappy, is the product of past-life misdeeds and can only be improved by making sufficient merit to ensure a better life next time round.

While most women enter the racket presumably knowing at least something of what lies ahead, younger girls definitely do not. **Child prostitution** is rife: an estimated ten percent of prostitutes are under 14, some are as young as 9. They are valuable property: in the teahouses of Chinatown, a prepubescent virgin can be rented to her first customer for B5000, as sex with someone so young is believed to have rejuvenating properties. Most child prostitutes have been sold by desperate parents as **bonded slaves** to pimps or agents, and are kept locked up until they have fully repaid the money given to their parents, which may take two or more years.

Despite its ubiquity, prostitution has been **illegal** in Thailand since 1960, but sex-industry bosses easily circumvent the law by registering their establishments as bars, restaurants, barbers, nightclubs or massage parlours, and making payoffs to the police. Sex workers, on the other hand, often endure exploitation and violence from employers, pimps and customers rather than face fines and long rehabilitation sentences in prison-like reform centres. Life is made even more difficult by the fact that abortion is illegal in Thailand. In an attempt to redress some of the iniquities, and protect the youngest prostitutes at least, an amendment to the **anti-prostitution law**, passed in April 1996, attempts to treat sex workers as victims rather than criminals. Besides penalizing parents who sell their children to the flesh trade, the amended law is supposed to punish owners, managers and customers of any place of prostitution with a jail sentence or a heavy fine, but this has been met with some cynicism, owing to the number of influential police and politicians allegedly involved in the sex industry. Under this amendment anyone caught having sex with an under-15 is charged with rape, though this has apparently resulted in an increase in trafficking of young children from neighbouring countries as they are less likely to seek help. The extent to which the 1996 law has been misunderstood or just plain ignored by the authorities was underlined in November 2000 when high-ranking police threatened to arrest any Thai sex workers who attended the International Conference of Sex Workers being held in Bangkok.

In recent years, the spectre of **AIDS** has put the problems of the sex industry into sharp focus: according to a joint study by Chulalongkorn University and the European Union, there are currently around one million HIV carriers in Thailand, and there have been over 270,000 AIDS-related deaths in the country since 1985, a disproportionate number of them in the northern provinces. Since 1988, the government has conducted an aggressive, World Health Organization-approved AIDS awareness campaign, a vital component of which has been to send health officials into brothels to administer blood tests and give out condoms. The programme seems to have had some effect, and the number of new HIV infections declined sharply between 1993 and 1996, though there was a rise during the period following the economic crisis of 1997.

The Queen Saovabha Memorial Institute

The **Queen Saovabha Memorial Institute** (*Sathan Saovabha*), often simply known as the **Snake Farm**, at the corner of Thanon Rama IV and Thanon Henri Dunant, is a bit of a circus act, but an entertaining, informative and worthy one at that. Run by the Thai Red Cross, it has a double function: to produce

Snake's blood and other treats

In Thailand's big cities you'll occasionally come across obscure stalls offering restorative glasses of warm **snake's blood**, which appeals mostly to Malaysian, Chinese and Korean visitors. Not just any snake, of course: only poisonous varieties will do, with prices ranging from B100 for a common cobra, through B2000 for a king cobra, up to B30,000 for the rare albino cobra.

Once you've selected your victim from the roadside cages, the proprietor will take the snake behind the stall, hang it up by its head and slit it open with a razor blade. The major artery yields enough blood to fill a wine glass, and when it's been mixed with the bile from the snake's gall bladder, warm whisky and a dash of honey, you down the potion in one. If this doesn't satisfy, delicacies like dried gall bladder and pickled snake genitals might tempt you. But if your health is really in a bad way, all that's left is the shock cure of drinking the **venom**, after it's been mixed with whisky and left standing for quarter of an hour.

There's no evidence to support the claims made for the **medicinal properties** of snakes' innards, but there's no proof to the contrary either. While male impotence remains the main reason for the trade's persistence, the blood is also said to be good for the eyes, for backache, for malodorous urine, and simply to "make happy".

snake-bite serums, and to educate the public on the dangers of Thai snakes. The latter mission involves putting on displays (Mon–Fri 10.30am & 2pm, Sat, Sun & hols 10.30am; B70; ☎02/252 0161) that begin with a slick half-hour slide show illustrating, among other things, how to apply a tourniquet and immobilize a bitten limb. Things warm up with a live demonstration of snake handling and feeding and venom extraction, which is well presented and safe, and gains a perverse fascination from the knowledge that the strongest venoms of the snakes on show can kill in only three minutes. The climax of the display comes when, having watched a python squeezing great chunks of chicken through its body, the audience is invited to handle a docile Burmese constrictor.

Lumphini Park

If you're sick of cars and concrete, head for **Lumphini Park** (Suan Lum; daily 5am–8pm), at the east end of Thanon Silom, where the air is almost fresh and the traffic noise dies down to a low murmur. Named after the town in Nepal where the Buddha was born, the park is arrayed around two lakes, where you can join the locals in feeding the turtles and fish with bread or take out a pedalo or a rowing boat (B40 per hr), and is landscaped with a wide variety of local trees and numerous pagodas and pavilions, usually occupied by Chinese-chess players. In the early morning and at dusk, exercise freaks hit the outdoor gym on the southwest side of the park, or en masse do some jogging along the yellow-marked circuit or some balletic t'ai chi, stopping for the twice-daily broadcast of the national anthem. The wide open spaces here are a popular area for gay cruising, and you might be offered dope, though the police patrol regularly – for all that, it's not at all an intimidating place. To recharge your batteries, make for the inexpensive garden restaurant, *Pop*, in the northwest corner, or the pavement foodstalls at the northern edge of the park.

Patpong

Concentrated into a small area between the eastern ends of Silom and Suriwong roads, the neon-lit go-go bars of the **Patpong** district loom like rides in a tawdry sexual Disneyland. In front of each bar, girls cajole passers-by with a lifeless sensuality while insistent touts proffer printed menus detailing the degradations on show. Inside, bikini-clad or topless women gyrate to Western music and play hostess to the (almost exclusively male) spectators; upstairs, live shows feature women who, to use Spalding Gray's phrase in *Swimming to Cambodia*, "do everything with their vaginas except have babies".

Patpong was no more than a sea of mud when the capital was founded on the marshy river bank to the west, but by the 1960s it had grown into a flash district of nightclubs and dance halls for rich Thais, owned by a Chinese millionaire godfather who gave his name to the area. In 1969, an American entrepreneur turned an existing teahouse into a luxurious nightclub to satisfy the tastes of soldiers on R&R trips from Vietnam, and so Patpong's transformation into a Western sex reservation began. At first, the area was rough and violent, but over the years it has wised up to the desires of the affluent farang, and now markets itself as a packaged concept of Oriental decadence. The centre of the skin trade lies along the interconnected sois of **Patpong 1 and 2**, where lines of go-go bars share their patch with respectable restaurants, a 24-hour supermarket and an over-abundance of chemists. By night, it's a thumping theme park, whose blazing neon promises tend towards self-parody, with names like *French Kiss* and *Love Nest*. Budget travellers, purposeful safari-suited businessmen and noisy lager louts throng the streets, and even the most demure tourists – of both sexes – turn out to do some shopping at the night market down the middle of Patpong 1, where hawkers sell fake watches, bags and designer T-shirts. By day, a relaxed hangover descends on the place. Bar-girls hang out at foodstalls and cafés in respectable dress, often recognizable only by their faces, pinched and strained from the continuous use of antibiotics and heroin in an attempt to ward off venereal disease and boredom. Farang men slump at the bars on Patpong 2, drinking and watching videos, unable to find anything else to do in the whole of Bangkok.

The small dead-end alley to the east of Patpong 2, **Silom 4** (ie Soi 4, Thanon Silom), hosts Bangkok's hippest nightlife, its bars, clubs and pavements heaving at weekends with the capital's brightest and most overprivileged young things. A few gay venues still cling to Silom 4, but the focus of the scene has recently shifted to **Silom 2**. In between, **Thanon Thaniya**'s hostess bars and one of the city's swishest shopping centres, Thaniya Plaza, cater mostly to Japanese tourists, while **Soi 6** (Soi Tantawan) to the west of Patpong attracts a curious mix of Korean and hardcore gay visitors.

Chatuchak and the outskirts

The amorphous clutter of Greater Bangkok doesn't harbour many attractions, but there are a handful of places – principally **Chatuchak Weekend Market**, the cultural theme park of **Muang Boran**, the upstream town of **Nonthaburi** and the tranquil artificial island of **Ko Kred** – which make pleasant half-day escapes. Theoretically, you could also see any one of these sights en route to destinations north, east or west, though lumping luggage around makes negotiating city transport even more trying.

Chatuchak Weekend Market

With six thousand open-air stalls to peruse, and wares as diverse as Laotian silk, Siamese kittens and designer lamps to choose from, the enormous **Chatuchak**

Weekend Market (Sat & Sun 7am–6pm) is Bangkok's most enjoyable shopping experience. It occupies a huge patch of ground between the Northern Bus Terminal and Mo Chit Skytrain station (N8), and is best reached by Skytrain if you're coming from downtown areas. The Mo Chit stop is the most convenient, but some people prefer to get off at Saphan Kwai (N7) and then walk through the amulet stalls that line the road up to the southern (handicraft) part of the market. Coming from Banglamphu, you can either get a bus to the nearest Skytrain stop (probably Ratchathewi or Phya Thai) and then take the train, or take the #3 or #9 bus all the way from Rajdamnoen Klang (1hr).

Though its primary customers are Bangkok residents in search of inexpensive clothes and home accessories, Chatuchak also has plenty of collector- and tourist-oriented **stalls**. Best buys include antique lacquerware, unusual sarongs, cotton clothing and crafts from the north, jeans, traditional musical instruments, silver jewellery and ceramics, particularly the five-coloured *bencharong*. The market is divided into 26 numbered **sections**, plus a dozen unnumbered ones, each of which is more or less dedicated to a certain range of goods, for example household items, plants, used books or handicrafts. If you have several hours to spare, it's fun just to browse at whim, but if you're looking for souvenirs, handicrafts or traditional textiles you should start with sections 22, 24, 25 and 26, which are all in a cluster at the southwest (Saphan Kwai) end of the market; the "Dream" section behind the TAT office is also full of interesting artefacts. *Nancy Chandler's Map of Bangkok* has a fabulously detailed and informatively annotated map of all the sections in the market, but should be bought before you arrive. Alternatively, drop in at the TAT office, located in the Chatuchak market building on the southwest edge of the market, across the car park, as they dish out smaller but useful plans of the market for free.

The market also contains a large, and controversial, **wildlife** section and has long been a popular clearing-house for protected and endangered species such as gibbons, palm cockatoos and Indian pied hornbills, many of them smuggled in from Laos and Cambodia and sold to private animal collectors and foreign zoos, particularly in eastern Europe. The illegal trade goes on beneath the counter, but you're bound to come across fighting cocks around the back (demonstrations are almost continuous), miniature flying squirrels being fed milk through pipettes, and iridescent red and blue Siamese fighting fish, kept in individual jars and shielded from each other's aggressive stares by sheets of cardboard.

There's no shortage of **foodstalls** inside the market compound, particularly at the southern end, where you'll find plenty of places serving inexpensive *pat thai* and Isaan snacks. Close by these stalls is a classy little juice bar called *Viva* where you can rest your feet while listening to the manager's jazz tapes. The biggest restaurant here is *Toh Plue*, behind TAT on the edge of the Dream section, which makes a good rendezvous point. For vegetarian sustenance, head for *Chamlong's* (also known as *Asoke*), an open-air, cafeteria-style restaurant just outside the market on Thanon Kamphaeng Phet (across Thanon Kamphaeng Phet 2), set up by Bangkok's former governor as a service to the citizenry (Sat & Sun 8am–noon). You can **change money** (Sat & Sun 7am–7pm) in the market building at the south end of the market, across the car park from the stalls area, and there's an ATM here too.

The Prasart Museum

Located right out on the eastern edge of the city (and still surrounded by fields), the **Prasart Museum** (Tues–Sun 10am–3pm; B500; call ☎02/379

Joe Louis Puppet Theatre

Still in Nonthaburi but several kilometres east of the express-boat pier, at 96/48 Muu 7, Soi Krungthep–Nonthaburi 12, the **Joe Louis Puppet Theatre** is a unique attraction, which though pricey is well worth the trip for both adults and children. To get there from Nonthaburi pier, take bus #30 or #65 along Thanon Pracharat, the main road back towards the centre of Bangkok, and get off at the entrance to the soi; you then need to hire a motorbike taxi, samlor or songthaew as the theatre is difficult to find deep in the soi. Coming from central Bangkok, you might want to catch the Skytrain to Mo Chit, at the top end of the Sukhumvit line, and take a taxi from there.

The puppets in question are jointed stick puppets (*hun lakorn lek*), an art form which was developed under Rama IV in the mid-nineteenth century but had all but died out before the owner of the theatre, **Sakorn Yangkeowsod** (aka Joe Louis), came to its rescue in the 1980s. Each sixty-centimetre-tall puppet is manipulated by three puppeteers, who are accomplished Thai classical dancers in their own right, complementing their charges' elegant and precise gestures with graceful movements in a harmonious ensemble. Hour-long **shows** (book in advance on ☎02/527 7737–8; B600) are put on daily at the theatre at 10am, with an extra Saturday show at 8pm, but you should turn up an hour in advance for informative demonstrations of how the puppets and *khon* masks are made. The puppets perform mostly stories from the *Ramakien*, accompanied by commentary in English and traditional music of a high standard.

Ko Kred

About 7km north of Nonthaburi, the tiny island of **KO KRED** lies in a particularly sharp bend in the Chao Phraya, cut off from the east bank by a waterway created to make the cargo route from Ayutthaya to the Gulf of Thailand just that little bit faster. Although it's slowly being discovered by day-trippers from Bangkok, this artificial island remains something of a time capsule, a little oasis of village life completely at odds with the metropolitan chaos downriver. Roughly ten square kilometres in all, Ko Kred has no roads, just a concrete path that circles its circumference, with a few arterial walkways branching off towards the interior. Villagers, the majority of whom are Mon (see box on p.234), use a small fleet of motorbike taxis to cross their island, but as a sight-seer you're much better off on foot: a round-island walk takes less than an hour and a half and it's practically impossible to get lost.

There are few sights as such on Ko Kred, but its lushness and comparative emptiness make it a perfect place in which to wander. You'll no doubt come across one of the island's potteries and kilns, which churn out the regionally famous earthenware flower-pots and small water-storage jars and employ a large percentage of the village workforce; several shops dotted around the island sell Ko Kred terracotta, including what's styled as the Ancient Mon Pottery Centre near the island's northeast corner, which also displays delicate and venerable museum pieces and Mon-style Buddha shrines. The island's clay is very rich in nutrients and therefore excellent for fruit-growing, and banana trees, coconut palms, pomelo, papaya and durian trees all grow in abundance on Ko Kred, fed by an intricate network of irrigation channels that crisscrosses the interior. In among the orchards, the Mons have built their wooden houses, mostly in traditional style and raised high above the marshy ground on stilts. A handful of attractive riverside wats complete the picture, most notably **Wat Paramaiyikawat** (aka Wat Poramai), at the main pier at the northeast tip of the island. This engagingly ramshackle eighteenth-century temple was restored by Rama V in honour of his grandmother, with a Buddha relic placed in its Mon-style chedi. Among an open-air scattering of Burmese-style alabaster Buddha images, the tall bot shelters some fascinating nineteenth-century murals, depicting scenes from temple life at ground level and the life of the Buddha above, all set in delicate imaginary landscapes.

Practicalities

On Sundays only, the Chao Phraya Express Boat Company (☎02/623 6001–3) runs **tours** to Ko Kred from central Bangkok (B220), heading upriver from Tha Prachan (Maharat) in Ratanakosin at 9am, taking in Wat Poramai and the Ancient Mon Pottery Centre, before circling the island, dropping in at Wat Chalerm Phra Kiat in Nonthaburi (see p.164) and arriving back at Tha Prachan at about 3pm. At other times, the main drawback of a day-trip to Ko Kred is the difficulty of **getting there**. Your best option is to take a Chao Phraya Express Boat to Nonthaburi, then bus #32 to Pakkred pier – or, if you're feeling flush, a chartered longtail boat direct to Ko Kred (about B150). From Pakkred, the easiest way of getting across to the island is to hire a long-tail boat, although shuttle boats cross at the river's narrowest point to Wat Poramai from Wat Sanam Nua, about a kilometre's walk or a short samlor or motorbike-taxi ride south of the Pakkred pier. The only bright spot about the irksome journey via Pakkred is the chance to eat at the excellent *Hong Seng* **restaurant**, just north of the pier; in a clean, airy wooden building on the river bank, delicious dishes such as *kung plaa* (river shrimp) with hot lemon-grass salad are served up daily from 11am to 3pm.

Muang Boran Ancient City

The brochure for **Muang Boran Ancient City** (daily 8am–5pm; B50, children B25), 33km southeast of the city, sells the place as a sort of cultural fast-food outlet – "a realistic journey into Thailand's past in only a few hours, saving you the many weeks of travel and considerable expense of touring Thailand yourself". The open-air museum is a considerably more authentic experience than its own publicity makes out, showcasing past and present Thai artistry and offering an enjoyable introduction to the country's architecture. To get there from Bangkok, take a bus to **Samut Prakan** on the edge of built-up Greater Bangkok, then a songthaew; air-conditioned **buses** #8 and #11 from Banglamphu/Thanon Rama I/Thanon Sukhumvit, and regular bus #25 from Sanam Luang/Charoen Krung/Thanon Rama I/Thanon Sukhumvit all go to Samut Prakan, where you need to change on to songthaew #36 which passes the entrance to Muang Boran.

Some of Muang Boran's ninety-odd buildings are originals, including the rare scripture library rescued from Samut Songkhram. Others are painstaking reconstructions from contemporary documents (the Ayutthaya-period Sanphet Prasat palace is a particularly fine example) or scaled-down copies of famous monuments such as the Grand Palace. A sizeable team of restorers and skilled craftspeople maintains the buildings and helps keep some of the traditional techniques alive; if you come here during the week you can watch them at work.

A couple of kilometres east of Samut Prakan, the **Crocodile Farm** (daily 7am–6pm; B300, kids B200) figures on tour-group itineraries, but is a depressing place. The thirty thousand reptiles kept here are made to "perform" for their trainers in hourly shows (daily 9, 10 & 11am & 1, 2, 3 & 4pm) and are subsequently turned into handbags, shoes, briefcases and wallets, a selection of which are sold on site. Songthaews run from Samut Prakan. There's also a dinosaur museum at the farm (B60).

Human Imagery Museum and Rose Garden Country Resort

Thirty-one kilometres west of Bangkok on Highway 4, the **Human Imagery Museum** (Mon–Fri 9am–5.30pm, Sat, Sun & holidays 8.30am–6pm; adults B200, children B100) is a Thai version of Madame Tussaud's Wax Museum, but with a less global perspective than its London counterpart. The lifelike **figures**, complete with glistening tongues and dewy eyes, are skilfully cast in fibreglass – wax would melt in the Thai heat apparently – and for the most part represent key characters in Thailand's history. Aside from a group portrait of the first eight kings of the Chakri dynasty, there's a strong emphasis on revered monks, as well as several wry interpretations of everyday life in the kingdom. The upper floor is given over to temporary exhibitions on unusual aspects of Thai history – such as the story of slavery here – with informative English-language captions. On the way to the Human Imagery Museum you'll see signposts for the nearby **Rose Garden Country Resort** (daily 8am–6pm; B10), a rather synthetic experience that caters mainly to tour groups. The lushly landscaped riverside resort makes big bucks from its hotel and golf course, but its main draw is the **Thai Village Cultural Show** (daily at 2.45pm; B300), an all-in-one cultural experience of Thai boxing, cockfighting, a wedding ceremony, elephant training and classical and hill-tribe dancing.

Ordinary **buses** from Bangkok's Southern Bus Terminal to Nakhon Pathom will drop you outside the resort or the museum entrance. To flag a bus down for the return journey from the museum or the Rose Garden, you might have to enlist the help of the museum's car-park attendant.

Food, entertainment, shopping and moving on

As you'd expect, nowhere in Thailand can compete with Bangkok's diversity when it comes to eating and entertainment, and, although prices are generally higher here than in the provinces, it's still easy to have a good time while on a budget. Bangkok boasts an astonishing fifty thousand **places to eat** – that's almost one for every hundred citizens – ranging from grubby streetside noodle shops to the most elegant of restaurants. Below we run through the best of the city's indigenous eateries, with a few representatives of the capital's numerous ethnic minorities.

Bangkok's **bars** and **clubs** have not always been the city's strongest suit, but a vibrant house and techno scene has now emerged around the fringes of

Patpong, and the number of trendy restaurant-bars in the Banglamphu area has recently mushroomed. Getting back to your lodgings is no problem in the small hours: many bus routes run a reduced service throughout the night, and tuk-tuks and taxis are always at hand – though it's probably best for unaccompanied women to avoid using tuk-tuks late at night.

Introductions to more traditional elements of Thai culture are offered by the raucous ambience of the city's **boxing arenas**, its **music and dancing** troupes and its profusion of **shops**, stalls and markets – all of them covered here. This section concludes with an overview of the options for **moving on** from the city – not only to elsewhere in Thailand, but to other countries too, as Bangkok is one of Asia's bargain counters when it comes to buying flights.

Eating

Thai restaurants of all types are found all over the city. The best **gourmet Thai** restaurants operate from the downtown districts around Sukhumvit and Silom roads, proffering wonderful royal, traditional and regional cuisines that definitely merit an occasional splurge. Over in Banglamphu, Thanon Phra Athit has become famous for its dozen or so trendy little restaurant-bars, each with distinctive decor and a contemporary Thai menu that's angled at young Thai diners. At the other end of the scale there are the **night markets** and **street stalls**, so numerous in Bangkok that we can only flag the most promising areas – but wherever you're staying, you'll hardly have to walk a block in any direction before encountering something appealing.

For the non-Thai cuisines, Chinatown naturally rates as the most authentic district for pure **Chinese** food; likewise neighbouring Pahurat, the capital's Indian enclave, is best for unadulterated **Indian** dishes. The place to head for Western, **travellers' food** – from herbal teas and hamburgers to muesli – as

A night on the river

The **Chao Phraya River** looks fabulous at night, when most of the noisy longtails have stopped terrorizing the ferries, and the riverside temples and other grand monuments – including the Grand Palace and Wat Arun – are elegantly illuminated. Joining one of the nightly **dinner cruises** in a converted traditional rice barge along the river is a great way to appreciate it all. Call ahead to reserve a table and check departure details – some places offer free transport from hotels, and some cruises may not run during the rainy season (May through October).

Maeyanang Run by the *Oriental Hotel* ☎02/236 0400. Departs Si Phraya pier at 7pm, returning at 9.30pm. Thai and international buffet. B1600.

Manohra Run by the *Marriott Royal Garden Riverside Hotel*, south of Taksin Bridge in Thonburi ☎02/476 0021. Departs from across the river at 7.30pm, returning 10pm. Eight-course Thai set meal. B1200.

Pearl of Siam ☎02/292 1649. Departs Si Phraya pier at 7.30pm, returning at 9.30pm. Thai and international buffet. B1100.

Shangri-La Horizon ☎02/236 7777. Departs *Shangri-La Hotel* pier at 7.30pm, returning at 10pm. International buffet. B1200.

Thai Wan Fa ☎237 0077. Departs Si Phraya pier at 7pm, returning at 9pm. Thai or seafood set menu. B680 or B730.

well as a hearty range of veggie options is Thanon Khao San, packed with small, inexpensive tourist restaurants; standards vary, but there are some definite gems among the blander establishments.

Fast food comes in two forms: the mainly Thai version, which stews canteen-style in large tin trays on the upper floor **food courts** of department stores all over the city, and the old Western favourites like *McDonald's* and *Kentucky Fried Chicken* that mainly congregate around Thanon Sukhumvit, Siam Square and Thanon Ploenchit – an area that also has its share of decent Thai and foreign restaurants. In addition, downtown Bangkok has a good quota of **coffee shops**, including several branches of Black Canyon and Starbucks, the latter expensive but usually graced with armchairs and free newspapers.

The restaurants listed below are graded by three general price categories based on the cost of a main dish: inexpensive (under B60), moderate (B60–130) and expensive (over B130). In the more expensive places you may have to pay a service charge and ten percent government tax. All the restaurants have English menus unless stated; telephone numbers are given for the more popular or out-of-the-way places, where bookings may be advisable. Most restaurants in Bangkok are open for lunch and dinner; we've noted exceptions in the listings below.

Banglamphu and Democracy area

Banglamphu is a great area for eating. **Khao San** is stacked full of guest-house restaurants serving the whole range of cheap and cheerful travellers' fare; there are also some good veggie places here, as well as Indian, Israeli and Italian joints. For a complete contrast you need only walk a few hundred metres down to riverside **Thanon Phra Athit**, where the pavement positively heaves with arty little café-restaurants; these are patronized mainly by students from Thammasat University up the road, but most offer English-language menus to any interested farangs. The food in these places is generally modern Thai, nearly always very good and reasonably priced. There are also some recommended trendy Thai places on the Banglamphu **fringes**, plus a few traditional options too. For restaurant locations see the map on p.106.

Around Khao San

Coffee Corner, west end of Trok Mayom/Damnoen Klang Neua. Makeshift alleyway café serving ten different blends of freshly brewed coffee, plus espressos and cappuccinos. Inexpensive.

Himalayan Kitchen, 1 Thanon Khao San. First-floor restaurant with good bird's-eye views of Khao San action. Both the food and the decor draw their inspiration from Nepal, with religious *thanka* paintings on the wall and thalis (veg and non-veg) on the menu. Moderate.

La Casa, Thanon Khao San. Stylish Italian place that's the sister operation of the Chiang Mai restaurant. All the standard pizza and pasta formulae are here, plus there are some innovative pasta salads, including a recommended Greek-style one with basil, olives, capers and anchovies. And if you're feeling particularly adventurous you can round off with fettucine doused in chocolate sauce and ice cream. Moderate to expensive.

May Kaidee, 123–125 Thanon Tanao, though actually on the parallel soi to the west; easiest access is to take first left on Soi Damnoen Klang Neua (Soi Post Office). Simple, soi-side foodstall plus tables serving the best vegetarian food in Banglamphu. Try the tasty green curry with coconut, the curry-fried tofu with vegetables or the sticky black-rice pudding. Shuts about 9pm. Inexpensive.

Night markets, In front of 7/11 at the Thanon Tani/Soi Ram Bhuttri intersection, and at the Soi Ram Bhuttri/Thanon Chakrabongse intersection. Small knots of hot-food stalls serving very cheap night-market fare including *pat thai*, *kway tiaw nam*, satay, fresh fruit juices and cold beer. Sets up around 5.30pm and keeps going until the early hours.

Prakorb House, Thanon Khao San. Archetypal travellers' haven, with only a few tables, and an emphasis on wholesome ingredients. Herbal teas, mango shakes, delicious pumpkin curry, and lots more besides. Inexpensive.

Royal India, opposite Boots on Thanon Khao San. Excellent Indian food in copious quantities at this very popular branch of the Pahurat original. Inexpensive to moderate.

Sarah, off Thanon Chakrabongse, between the Shell petrol station and the police station. Inexpensive Israeli restaurant, serving hearty platefuls of workaday falafels, hummus, salads and dips.

Sorn Daeng, southeast corner of Democracy Monument. Standard Thai dishes including unadulterated southern curries like the rich sweet beef *kaeng matsaman*. Inexpensive.

Phra Athit area

Hemlock, 56 Thanon Phra Athit, next door but one from *Pra Arthit Mansion*; the sign is visible from the road but not from the pavement (☎ 02/282 7507). Small, stylish, highly recommended air-con restaurant that's very popular with students and young Thai couples. Offers a long and interesting menu of unusual Thai dishes, including banana flower salad (*yam hua plii*), coconut and mushroom curry, grand lotus rice and various *larb* and fish dishes. The traditional *miang* starters (shiny green wild tea leaves filled with chopped vegetables, fish and meat) are also very tasty, and there's a good vegetarian selection. Mon–Sat 5pm–midnight; worth reserving a table on Friday and Saturday nights. Moderate.

Joy Luck Club, opposite the fort at the point where Thanon Phra Athit turns into Thanon Phra Sumen. Despite its name, the only thing noticeably Chinese about this cute little art-house café-restaurant are the red lanterns hanging outside. Inside are just half a dozen tables (each designed with a glassed-in display of artefacts), modern art on the walls and occasional live music at night. The Thai food is delicious, and there's a big veggie menu too, including various green and *matsaman* curries, plus lots of cocktails. Cheap to moderate.

Krua Nopparat, 130–132 Thanon Phra Athit. The decor in this unassuming air-con restaurant is noticeably plain compared to all the arty joints on this road, but the Thai food is good – try the eggplant wingbean salad and the battered crab – and the prices very inexpensive.

Tonpo, Thanon Phra Athit, next to Tha Banglamphu express-boat pier. Sizeable seafood menu and a relatively scenic riverside location; good place for a beer and a snack at the end of a long day's sightseeing. Moderate.

Tuk, corner of Soi Ram Bhuttri and Soi Chana Songkhram. The perfect breakfast place, with lots of options, ranging from American and European to Israeli and Chinese, plus wholemeal bread and good yoghurt. Cheap.

Samsen, Thewes and the fringes

Bangkok Bar, 591 Thanon Phra Sumen. Housed in an elegant 150-year-old canalside house, complete with high ceilings, wooden floors and fine fretwork, this place is well worth trying both for its setting and for its good-value upmarket Thai cuisine. There's a gallery upstairs to entertain you while you're waiting for food. Recommendations include seafood with young coconut, fish-head curry and deep-fried pillows of tofu. Moderate.

Dachanee, 18/2 Thanon Pracha Thipatai, near *Thai Hotel*. Standard Thai fare such as fiery *tom yam*, plus tasty extras like tofu- and beansprout-stuffed *khanom buang* (crispy Vietnamese-style pancakes), in an air-con restaurant. Inexpensive to moderate.

Dragon Eyes, Thanon Samsen, on the corner of Thanon Wisut Kasat. Small restaurant popular with young Thai couples. Stylish renditions of standard Thai dishes – try the *khao pat* with added fruit and nuts, or the chilli-fried chicken with cashews (*kai pat met mamuang himapaan*). Huge selection of bar drinks as well, and, as you'd expect from a place managed by a *Bangkok Post* music critic, a fine range of music. Daily except Sun 6.30pm–midnight. Moderate.

Isaan restaurants, behind the Rajdamnoen Boxing Stadium on Thanon Rajdamnoen Nok. At least five restaurants in a row serving northeastern fare to hungry boxing fans: take your pick for hearty plates of *kai yaang* and *khao niaw*. Inexpensive.

Kainit, 68 Thanon Titong, next to Wat Suthat. Rather formal Italian restaurant that's mainly patronized by expats, but also works fine as a lunchtime treat after visiting Wat Suthat. The pizza and pastas are tasty but expensive.

Kaloang, beside the river at the far western end of Thanon Sri Ayutthaya. Flamboyant service and excellent seafood attracts an almost exclusively Thai clientele to this open-air riverside restaurant. Try the fried rolled shrimps served with a sweet dip, the roast squid cooked in a piquant sauce or the steamed butter fish. Expensive.

Na Pralan, almost opposite the Gate of Glorious Victory, Thanon Na Phra Lan. Technically in Ratanakosin (it's marked on the map on p.120) but very close to Banglamphu, this small café, only a couple of doors up the street from the Silpakorn University Art College, is ideally placed for refreshment after your tour of the Grand Palace. Popular with students, it occupies a quaint old air-con shophouse with battered, artsy decor. The menu, well thought out with some unusual twists, offers tasty daily specials – mostly one-dish meals with rice – and a range of Thai desserts, coffees, teas and beers. Mon–Sat 10am–10pm. Inexpensive.

Silver Spoon, beside the Tha Thewes express-boat pier at 2/1 Thanon Krung Kasem. Popular place for seafood – and riverine breezes, with decent Chao Phraya views and a huge menu including baked cottonfish in mango sauce, steamed snakehead fish with chillies, and *tom yam kung*. Moderate.

Tang Teh, 269–271 Thanon Wisut Kasat, corner of Thanon Samsen. Quality Thai restaurant, with contemporary art on the walls and high-class food on the menu. Fried catfish with cashews and chilli sauce recommended, as are the superb fishcakes and the steamed sea bass with Chinese plum sauce; also a fairly interesting veggie menu, and home-made ice cream. Moderate.

Chinatown and Pahurat

The places listed below are marked on the map on p.140.

Chong Tee, 84 Soi Sukon 1, Thanon Trimit, between Hualamphong station and Wat Traimit. Delicious pork satay and sweet toast. Inexpensive.

Hua Seng Hong, 371 Thanon Yaowarat. Not too hygienic, but the food is good. Sit outside on the jostling pavement for delicious egg noodle soup with pork, duck or *wonton*, or good-value shark's fin soup, or venture inside to the air con restaurant, where the main thrust is fish and seafood (try the asparagus with scallop), though pricey Chinese spe-cialities like goose feet, smoked whole baby pig and bird's nest are also on offer. If you've still got room for more, head for the stall outside selling delicious *bua loy nga dam nam khing*, soft rice dumplings stuffed with bitter-sweet black sesame in ginger soup (evenings only; inexpensive). Moderate.

Maturot, Soi Phadungdao (aka Soi Texas), Thanon Yaowarat. In a soi famous for its seafood stalls, the fresh, meaty prawns served up here, accompanied by *phak bung fai daeng* (fried morning glory) and *tom yam kung*, stand out. Evenings only, until late. Inexpensive to moderate.

Royal India, just off Thanon Chakraphet. Serves the same excellent curries as its Banglamphu branch, but attracts an almost exclusively Indian clientele. Inexpensive to moderate.

White Orchid Hotel, 409–421 Thanon Yaowarat. Recommended for its *dim sum*, with bamboo bas-kets of prawn dumplings, spicy spare ribs, stuffed beancurd and the like, served in three different portion sizes. *Dim sum* 11am–2pm & 5–10pm. All-you-can-eat lunchtime buffets also worth consid-ering. Moderate to expensive.

You Sue Vegetarian, 75m east of Hualamphong station at 241 Thanon Rama IV; directly across the road from the sign for the *Bangkok Centre Hotel*. Cheap and cheerful Chinese vegetarian café, where standard Thai curries and Chinese one-pot dishes are made with high-protein meal substi-tutes. Daily 6am–10pm.

Yellow-flag heaven for veggies

Every autumn, for nine days during the ninth lunar month (October or November), Thailand's Chinese community goes on a **meat-free** diet in order to mark the onset of the Vegetarian Festival (Ngan Kin Jeh), a sort of Taoist Lent. Though the Chinese citizens of Bangkok don't go in for it as thems-elves like their compatriots in Trang and Phuket (see p.642), many observe the Vegetarian Festival with gusto: nearly every restaurant and food stall turns vegetarian for the period, flying small yellow flags to show they're upholding the tradition. For vegetarian tourists this is a great time to be in town: just look for the yellow flag and you can be sure all dishes will be one hundred per cent vegan. Soya substitutes are a popular feature of Vegetarian Festival food, so don't be surprised to find pink prawn-shaped objects floating in your noodle soup or unappetizingly realistic slices of fake duck. Many veggie restaurants get in on the act during the Vegetarian Festival, running special menus for at least a week or two.

Downtown: Siam Square and Thanon Ploenchit

The map on p.153 shows the places listed below.

Bali, 15/3 Soi Ruam Rudee ☎ 02/250 0711. Top-notch Indonesian food in a cosy nook; closed Mon lunch. Blow out on seven-course *rijstaffel* for B250. Moderate to expensive.

Café Botanica, 1st Floor, Gaysorn Plaza, Thanon Ploenchit ☎ 02/656 1305–6. A haven for footsore shoppers but worth a detour in its own right: excellent Thai and Western food, with an especially good choice of Thai salads and noodles, in a sophisticated, open-plan setting. Moderate.

Inter, 432/1–2 Soi 9, Siam Square ☎ 02/251 4689. Honest, efficient Thai restaurant that's popular with students and shoppers, serving good one-dish meals and more expensive curries in a no-frills, fluorescent-lit canteen atmosphere. Inexpensive.

Kirin Restaurant, 226/1 Soi 2, Siam Square. Swankiest and best of many Chinese restaurants in the area. Expensive.

Kroissant House, Ground Floor, World Trade Center, corner of Thanon Rama I and Thanon Rajdamri. Fine Italian ice creams, cakes and pastries – a good choice for breakfast.

Ma Be Ba, 93 Soi Lang Suan ☎ 02/254 9595. Lively, spacious and extravagantly decorated Italian restaurant dishing up excellent pizzas and daily pasta specials, usually seafood, from a huge open kitchen. Daily 11am–2.30pm & 5.30pm–1am (last food orders 11.30pm). Expensive.

Mah Boon Krong Food Centre, 6th Floor, MBK shopping centre, corner of Thanon Rama I and Thanon Phrayathai. Increase your knowledge of Thai food here: ingredients, names and pictures of dishes (including plenty of vegetarian ones, and a wide range of desserts) from all over the country are displayed at the various stalls. Inexpensive.

Sarah Jane's, Ground Floor, Sindhorn Tower 1, 130–132 Thanon Witthayu ☎ 02/650 9992–3. Long-standing restaurant, popular with Bangkok's Isaan population, serving excellent, simple northeastern food. It's in slick but unfussy modern premises that can be slightly tricky to find at night, towards the rear of a modern office block. Moderate.

Sorn's, 36/8 Soi Kasemsan 1, Thanon Rama I. In this quiet lane of superior guest houses, a laid-back hangout with an atmosphere like a beachside guest-house restaurant. Delicious versions of standard Thai dishes – the *tom kha kai* is especially good – as well as Western meals, varied breakfasts, good coffee and a full-service bar with reasonably priced wine. Moderate.

Talat Samyarn (Samyarn Market), set back on the west side of Thanon Phrayathai, near the corner of Rama IV. Fruitful area for stall-grazing, always busy with Chulalongkorn University students. Inexpensive.

Whole Earth, 93/3 Soi Langsuan ☎ 02/252 5574. The best veggie restaurant in Bangkok, serving interesting and varied Thai and Indian-style food (plus some dishes for carnivores) in a relaxing atmosphere. Moderate.

Zen, 6th Floor, World Trade Center, corner of Thanon Ploenchit and Thanon Rajdamri ☎ 02/255 6462; and 4th Floor, Siam Center, Thanon Rama I ☎ 02/658 1183–4. Good-value Japanese restaurant with wacky modern wooden design and seductive booths. Among a huge range of dishes, the complete meal sets (with pictures to help you choose) are filling and particularly good. Daily 10am–10pm. Moderate to expensive.

Downtown: south of Thanon Rama IV

The places listed below are marked on the map on p.113.

Akane Japanese Noodle, Central department store, Thanon Silom (plus branches around town, including in the World Trade Center, corner of Rajdamri and Rama I). Deliciously authentic *soba*, *udon*, *ramen* and *sushi* dishes in unpretentious style surrounds. Daily 11am–10pm. Moderate.

... ngs, 173/8–9 Thanon Suriwong. Large tasty curries (*kaeng*, sometimes spelt ...ed in cool, modern surrounds. Closed lunchtimes. Moderate.

...ri-La Hotel, 89 Soi Wat Suan Plu, ...ng (New Rd) ☎ 02/236 7777.

One of the capital's best Italians, pricey but not too extravagant. The setting is lively and relaxed, with open-plan kitchen and big picture windows onto the pool and river, though the music can be obtrusive. Whether you're vegetarian or not, it's worth plumping for the pumpkin ravioli with truffle butter sauce; otherwise, there are some unusual main courses as well as old favourites like *ossobucco*, or you can invent your own wood-oven-baked pizza. Daily 11am–late.

Aoi, 132/10–11 Soi 6, Thanon Silom ☎ 02/235 2321–2; branch in Emporium on Thanon Sukhunvit ☎ 02/664 8590. The best place in town for a

Japanese blowout, justifiably popular with the expat community. Excellent authentic food and elegant decor. Lunch sets available and a sushi bar. Daily 11.30am–2pm & 6–11pm. Expensive.

Ban Chiang, 14 Thanon Srivieng, between Thanon Silom and Thanon Sathorn ☎02/236 7045. Fine Thai cuisine in an elegant wooden house. Daily 11.30am–2pm & 5.30–10.30pm. Moderate to expensive.

Bussaracum, 139 Sethiwan Building, Thanon Pan ☎02/266 6312–8. Superb royal Thai cuisine. Expensive, but well worth it. Daily 11am–2pm & 5–10pm.

Chai Karr, 312/3 Thanon Silom ☎02/233 2549. Opposite *Holiday Inn*. Folksy, traditional-style wooden decor is the setting for a wide variety of standard Thai and Chinese dishes, followed by liqueur coffees and coconut ice cream. Daily 11.30am–9pm. Moderate.

Charuvan, 70–2 Thanon Silom, near the entrance to Soi 4. Clean but lackadaisical place, with an air-con room, specializing in inexpensive and tasty duck on rice; the beer's a bargain too.

Deen, 786 Thanon Silom, almost opposite Silom Village (no English sign). Small, basic Muslim café with air-con (no smoking), which offers Thai and Chinese standard dishes with a southern Thai twist, as well as spicy Indian-style curries and specialities such as *grupuk* (crispy fish) and *roti*. Mon–Sat 11am–9.30pm. Inexpensive to moderate.

Harmonique, 22 Soi 34, Thanon Charoen Krung, on the lane between Wat Muang Kae express-boat pier and the GPO ☎02/237 8175. A relaxing, welcoming restaurant that's well worth a trip: tables are scattered throughout several converted houses, decorated with antiques, and a quiet, leafy courtyard, and the Thai food is varied and excellent – among the seafood specialities, try the crab curry. Daily 10am–10pm. Moderate.

Himali Cha-Cha, 1229/11 Thanon Charoen Krung, south of GPO ☎02/235 1569. Fine north Indian restaurant, founded by a character who was chef to numerous Indian ambassadors, and now run by his son; good vegetarian selection. Daily 11am–3.30pm & 6–10.30pm. Moderate.

Laicram, 2nd Floor, Thaniya Plaza, east end of Thanon Silom. Small, proficient restaurant offering some unusual specialities from around Thailand on a huge menu, plus loads of veggie dishes and traditional desserts. Daily 10.30am–3pm & 5–10pm. Moderate.

Le Bouchon, 37/17 Patpong 2, near Thanon Suriwong ☎02/234 9109. Cosy, welcoming French

bistro serving unpretentious food; much frequented by the city's French expats. Daily 11am–11.30pm. Expensive.

Mango Tree, 37 Soi Tantawan, Thanon Suriwong ☎02/236 2820. Excellent authentic Thai food in a surprisingly peaceful haven between Suriwong and Silom, where you can eat indoors or out in the garden to the live strains of a traditional Thai ensemble. Highly rated by Bangkokians, so definitely worth booking. Daily 10am–2pm & 6–10pm. Moderate to expensive.

Mei Jiang, *Peninsula Hotel*, 333 Thanon Charoennakorn, Klongsan. Probably Bangkok's best Chinese restaurant, with beautiful views of the hotel gardens and the river night and day. It's designed like an elegant teak box, without the gaudiness of many Chinese restaurants, and staff are very attentive and graceful. Specialities include duck smoked with tea and excellent lunchtime *dim sum* – a bargain at around B65 a dish. Expensive.

Ranger, Mahamek Driving Range, south end of Soi Ngam Duphli, by the Ministry of Aviation compound ☎02/679 8964. Unusual location in a golf driving range, but the setting for the restaurant itself is cute and pastoral, on tree-shaded platforms above a quiet, lotus-filled pond. Specialities include *yam hua pree*, delicious banana-flower salad with dried shrimp and peanuts; some veggie dishes are available, and the service is friendly and attentive. Daily 6am–10pm. Moderate.

Ratree Seafood, opposite Thaniya Plaza, Soi 1, Thanon Silom. Famous street stall, surrounded by many similar competitors, with twenty or so tables in the adjoining alley. Temptingly displayed, brightly lit on ice, is all manner of fresh seafood (the specialities are *poo chak ka chan* – oily, orange, medium-sized sea crab – and barbecued fish) and there's noodle soup too. Evenings only. Inexpensive to moderate.

Sui Heng, mouth of Soi 65, Thanon Charoen Krung, south of Sathorn Bridge. In a good area for stall-grazing, a legendary Chinese street vendor who has been selling one dish for over seventy years: *khao man kai*, tender boiled chicken breast served with delicious broth and rice. Evenings only, until late. Inexpensive.

Thaichine, 233 Thanon Sathorn ☎02/212 6401. In a grand, century-old building that was formerly the Thai-Chinese Chamber of Commerce, this is an elegant, comfortable restaurant, where the eclectic Asian decor matches the menu's delicious combination of Thai, Vietnamese and Chinese dishes. Daily 10am–11pm. Moderate.

Tongue Thai, 18–20 Soi 38, Thanon Charoen Krung ☎02/630 9918–9. In front of the Oriental Place shopping mall. Very high standards of food and cleanliness, with charming, unpretentious service, in an elegantly decorated 100-year-old shophouse. Veggies are amply catered for with delicious dishes such as tofu in black bean sauce and deep-fried banana-flower and corn cakes, while carnivores should try the fantastic beef curry (*panaeng neua*). Expensive.

Thanon Sukhumvit
See the map on p.117 for locations of the places listed below.

Ambassador Hotel Seafood Centre, inside the *Ambassador Hotel* complex, between sois 11 and 13. Cavernous hall of a restaurant that spills over into a covered courtyard with over a dozen stalls serving all manner of fish and seafood dishes, including soups and barbecued fish. Moderate.

Baan Kanitha, Soi 23. The big attraction at this long-running favourite haunt of Sukhumvit expats is the setting in a traditional Thai house. The food is upmarket Thai and includes lots of fiery salads (*yam*), and a good range of *tom yam* soups, green curries and seafood curries. Expensive.

Basil, *Sheraton Grande Hotel*, between sois 12 and 14. Mouthwateringly fine traditional Thai food with a modern twist is the order of the day at this trendy, relatively informal restaurant in the super-deluxe five-star *Sheraton*. Recommendations include the grilled river prawns with chilli, the *matsaman* curry (both served with red and green rice) and the surprisingly delicious durian cheesecake. Vegetarian menu on request. Expensive.

Cabbages and Condoms, Soi 12. Run by the Population and Community Development Association of Thailand (PDA): diners are treated to authentic Thai food in the Condom Room, and relaxed scoffing of barbecued seafood in the beer garden. Try the *plaa samlii* (fried cottonfish with mango and chilli) or the *kai haw bai toey* (marinated chicken baked in pandanus leaves). All proceeds go to the PDA, and there's an adjacent shop selling all kinds of double-entendre T-shirts, keyrings and of course condoms. Moderate.

De Meglio, Soi 11. Upmarket Italian presided over by a chef who was trained by Anton Mosiman. Antipastos here are unusual Thai-Italian hybrids, and the linguini with clams and the crab cannelloni with fennel salad are recommended. Authentic wood-fired pizzas a speciality. Expensive.

Emporium Food Court, 5th Floor, Emporium Shopping Centre, between sois 22 and 24. Typical food court of twenty stalls selling very cheap but reasonable-quality Thai standards including fish-ball soup, fried chicken and satay. Buy coupons at the entrance booth and find a window table for pleasant views over Queen Sirikit park. For something more upmarket, there are a dozen small restaurant concessions on the same floor as the food court, ranging from Italian to Japanese.

Haus München, Soi 15. Hearty helpings of authentic German classics, from pigs' knuckles to *bratwurst*, served in a restaurant that's modelled on a Bavarian lodge. Moderate.

Jools Bar and Restaurant, Soi 4, a short walk from the Soi Nana go-go strip. Hearty British fare of the meat-and-two-veg variety dished out in the upstairs room of a popular British-run pub. Moderate.

Lemongrass, Soi 24 ☎02/258 8637. Scrumptious Thai nouvelle cuisine in a converted traditional house; vegetarian menu on request. The minced chicken with ginger is a particular winner. Advance reservations recommended. Moderate to expensive.

Mrs Balbir's, Soi 11/1. Deservedly popular veg and non-veg Indian restaurant run by TV cook Mrs Balbir. Specialities include the spicy dry chicken and lamb curries (*masala kerai*) and the daily all-you-can-eat veggie buffet, which is highly recommended at B150 per person. Indian cookery courses held here every week – see Listings on p.193 for details.

Nipa, 3rd Floor, Landmark Plaza, between sois 4 and 6. Tasteful traditional Thai-style place with a classy menu that features an adventurous range of dishes, including spicy fish curry, several *matsaman* and green curries, excellent *som tam* and mouthwatering braised spare ribs. Also offers a sizeable vegetarian selection. Regular cookery classes are held here – see Listings on p.193 for details. Last orders at 10.15pm. Moderate to expensive.

Suda Restaurant, Soi 14. Unpretentious locals' hangout, patronized by office workers at lunchtime, but open till midnight. Standard *kap khao* (dishes served with rice) and noodle dishes, plus some fish: fried tuna with cashews and chilli recommended. Inexpensive to moderate.

Thong U Rai, 22/4–5 Soi 23. Highly recommended bohemian place decked out with paintings and antique curios; serves mid-priced Thai food including especially good minced chicken marinaded in limes.

Whole Earth, a 10min walk down Soi 26 at no.71. Vegetarian restaurant serving meat-free Thai and Indian food plus a few dishes for carnivores (there's another branch off Thanon Ploenchit; see p.172). The mushroom and tofu *larb* served over baked rice is worth the walk, especially if you can get one of the low tables on the first floor where there's more atmosphere than in the ground floor restaurant. Moderate.

Yong Lee, corner of Soi 15. One of the few unpretentious and refreshingly basic rice-and-noodle shops on Sukhumvit. Inexpensive.

Nightlife and entertainment

For many of Bangkok's visitors, nightfall in the city is the signal to hit the **sex bars**, the neon sumps that disfigure three distinct parts of town: along Thanon Sukhumvit's Soi Cowboy (between sois 21 and 23) and Nana Plaza (Soi 4), and, most notoriously, in the two small sois off the east end of Thanon Silom known as Patpong 1 and 2. But within spitting distance of the beer bellies flopped onto Patpong's bars lies **Silom 4**, Bangkok's most happening after-dark haunt, pulling in the cream of Thai youth and tempting an increasing number of travellers to stuff their party gear into their rucksacks: Soi 4, the next alley off Thanon Silom to the east of Patpong 2, started out as a purely **gay** area but now offers a range of styles in gay, mixed and straight pubs, dance bars and clubs. The city's other main gay areas are the more exclusive Silom 2 (towards Thanon Rama IV), and the rougher, mostly Thai bars of Thanon Sutthisarn near the Chatuchak Weekend Market. As with the straight scene, the majority of gay bars feature go-go dancers and live sex shows. Those listed here do not.

On the cultural front, **Thai dancing** is the most accessible of the capital's performing arts, particularly when served up in bite-size portions on tourist restaurant stages. **Thai boxing** is also well worth watching: the live experience at either of Bangkok's two main national stadiums far outshines the TV coverage.

Bars and clubs

For convenient drinking and dancing, we've split the most recommended of the city's bars and clubs into three central areas. In **Banglamphu**, there are two main centres for night-time entertainment. The bars and clubs on and around Thanon Khao San are aimed at young Western travellers, with pool tables, cheap beer and either a programme of back-to-back video showings or a DJ with a good loud set of turntables; some of these places also attract crowds of young Thai drinkers. Khao San itself becomes a traffic-free zone after about 7pm and the kerbside tables make great places to nurse a few beers and watch the parade of other travellers; most of the stalls and shops stay open till 11pm or later, so this is also a good time to browse. A couple of blocks further west, Thanon Phra Athit is more of a Thai scene, though again there are always some farang drinkers in the mix. Here, the style-conscious little restaurant-bars have their tables spill over onto the pavement, and the live music is likely to be a lone piano-player or guitarist.

Downtown bars, which tend to attract both farang and Thai drinkers, are concentrated on adjoining Soi Langsuan and Soi Sarasin (between Thanon Ploenchit and Lumphini Park), and in studenty Siam Square, as well as around the east end of Thanon Silom. Langsuan and Sarasin have their fair share of live-music bars, but the Western covers and bland jazz on offer are often less than inspiring; the better live-music venues are listed below. If, among all the choice of nightlife around Silom, you do end up in one of Patpong's sex bars, be prepared to shell out up to B600 for a small beer. Though many Patpong bars trumpet the fact that they have no cover charge, almost every customer gets ripped off in some way, and stories of menacing bouncers are legion. **Thanon Sukhumvit** watering holes tend to be either British-style pubs, bar-beers (open-sided drinking halls with huge circular bars) packed full of hostesses or full-on girlie bars.

During the cool season (Nov–Feb), an evening out at one of the seasonal **beer gardens** is a pleasant way of soaking up the urban atmosphere (and the traffic fumes). You'll find them in hotel forecourts or sprawled in front of shopping centres – the huge beer garden that sets up in front of the World Trade Centre on Thanon Rajdamri is extremely popular, and recommended; beer is served in pitchers here and bar snacks are available too.

Banglamphu, Ratanakosin and Hualamphong

Except where indicated, all bars listed below are marked on the map on p.106.

About Café, a 5min walk from Hualamphong station at 418 Thanon Maitri Chit (see map on p.140). Arty café-bar that's popular with trendy young Thais. There's a gallery space upstairs and exhibits usually spill over into the ground floor eating and drinking area, where tables and sofas are scattered about in an informal and welcoming fashion. Mon–Sat 10am–midnight.

Austin, just off Thanon Khao San, in the scrum behind *D&D Guest House*. Named in honour of the car (hence the neon silhouette), this homely three-floored bar plays loud music and is hugely popular with students from nearby Thammasat University, though it has yet to attract much of a farang crowd. The favoured drink is a jug of Sang Som rum over ice, mixed with soda and lemon and served with straws to share with your mates. Also on offer are lots of cocktails and fairly pricey beer.

Banana Bar, Trok Mayom/Damnoen Klang Neua. Half a dozen tiny cubbyhole bars open up on this alley every night, each with just a handful of alley-side chairs and tables, loud music on the tape player and a trendy bartender.

Bangkok Bar, west end of Soi Ram Bhuttri. Not to be confused with the restaurant of the same name on Thanon Phra Sumen, this small, narrow dance bar is fronted by a different DJ every night and draws capacity crowds of drinkers and clubbers.

Bayon, Thanon Khao San. Sizeable but not terribly exciting upstairs dance-floor playing disco and rave classics and serving mid-priced drinks to a mixed crowd of Thais and farangs till around 2am.

Boh, Tha Thien, Thanon Maharat. When the Chao Phraya express boats stop running around 7pm, this bar takes over the pier with its great sunset views across the river. Beer and Thai whisky with accompanying spicy snacks and loud Thai pop music – very popular with Silpakorn and Thammasat university students.

Comme, opposite *Tonpo* riverside restaurant at the northern end of Thanon Phra Athit. One of the most sophisticated bar-restaurants on this trendy road, where you can choose between the air-con section and the open-fronted streetside. Serves decent Thai food and well-priced drinks. Daily 6pm–2am.

Dog Days, 100/2–6 Thanon Phra Athit. Quirky little bar-restaurant with a canine theme, a cosy atmosphere and mid-priced food and drink. Tues–Sun 5pm–midnight.

Grand Guest House, middle of Thanon Khao San. Cavernous place lacking in character but popular because it stays open 24hr. Videos are shown non-stop, usually movies in the day and MTV in the early hours.

Gullivers' Travellers Tavern, Thanon Khao San. Backpacker-oriented air-con sports pub with two pool tables, sixteen TV screens, masses of sports memorabilia and reasonably priced beer. Stays open until at least 2am.

Hole in the Wall Bar, Thanon Khao San. Small, low-key drinking-spot at the heart of the back-packers' ghetto. Dim lighting, a more varied than average CD selection and competitively priced beer.

Spicy, Thanon Tanao. Fashionably modern, neon-lit youthful hangout, best for beer, whisky and snacks, but serves main dishes too. Daily 6pm–2am.

Susie Pub, next to *Marco Polo Guest House* off Thanon Khao San. Big, dark, phenomenally popular pub that's usually standing-room-only after 9pm. Has a pool table, decent music, resident DJs and cheapish beer. Packed with farangs and young Thais. Daily 11am–2am.

Siam Square, Thanon Ploenchit and northern downtown

The venues listed below are marked on the map on p.153.

Ad Makers, 51/51 Soi Langsuan ☎02/652 0168. Friendly, spacious bar with Wild West-style wooden decor, featuring nightly "songs for life" bands; cheap drinks.

Brown Sugar, 231/19–20 Soi Sarasin ☎02/250 0103. Chic, pricey, lively bar, acknowledged as the capital's top jazz venue.

Concept CM², *Novotel*, Soi 6, Siam Square ☎02/255 6888. More theme park than nightclub, with live bands and various, barely distinct entertainment zones, including karaoke and an Italian restaurant. Admission price depends on what's on; drinks are pricey.

Dallas Pub, Soi 6, Siam Square ☎02/255 3276. Typical dark, noisy "songs for life" hangout – buffalo skulls, Indian heads, American flags – but a lot of fun: singalongs to decent live bands, dancing round the tables, cheap beer and friendly, casual staff.

Fou Bar, 264/4–6 Soi 3, Siam Square. Smart, modernist but easy-going hangout for students and 20-somethings, with reasonably priced drinks, a good choice of accompanying snacks and some interesting Thai/Italian crossovers for main dishes. Hard to find above a juice bar/internet café by Siam Square's Centerpoint.

Hard Rock Café, Soi 11, Siam Square. Genuine outlet of the famous chain, better for drink than food. Big sounds, brash enthusiasm, bankbreaking prices.

Saxophone, 3/8 Victory Monument (southeast corner), Thanon Phrayathai ☎02/246 5472. Lively, spacious venue that hosts nightly jazz, blues, folk and rock bands and attracts a good mix of Thais and farangs; decent food, relaxed drinking atmosphere and, all things considered, reasonable prices.

Southern downtown: south of Thanon Rama IV

See the map on p.113 for locations of the venues listed below.

The Barbican, 9/4–5 Soi Thaniya, east end of Thanon Silom ☎02/234 3590. Stylishly modern fortress-like decor to match the name: dark woods, metal and undressed stone. With Guinness on tap and the financial pages posted above the urinals, it could almost be a smart City of London pub – until you look out of the windows onto the soi's incongruous Japanese hostess bars. Good food, DJ sessions and happy hours Mon–Fri 5–7pm.

Deeper, Soi 4, Thanon Silom. Long-running hardcore dance club, done out to give an underground feel, all metal and black. Closed after a police raid at the time of writing, but unlikely to remain so.

Hyper, Soi 4, Thanon Silom. Long-standing Soi 4 people-watching haunt, with laid-back music and a fun crowd.

Lucifer, 76/1–3 Patpong 1. Popular rave club in the dark heart of Patpong, largely untouched by the sleaze around it. Done out with mosaics and stalactites like a satanic grotto, with balconies to look down on the dance-floor action. *Radio City*, the interconnected bar downstairs, is only slightly less raucous, with jumping live bands and tables out on the sweaty pavement.

Shenanigans, 1/5 Thanon Convent, off the east end of Thanon Silom ☎02/266 7160. Blarney Bangkok-style: a warm, relaxing Irish pub, tastefully done out in wood, iron and familiar knickknacks and packed with expats, especially on Fri night. Guinness and Kilkenny Bitter on tap (happy hour 4–7.30pm), very expensive Irish food such as Belfast chaps (fried potatoes) and good veggie options (Mon–Thurs set lunches are better value), as well as a fast-moving rota of house bands.

Tapas Bar, Soi 4, Thanon Silom. Cramped, vaguely Spanish-oriented bar (but no tapas), whose outside tables are probably the best spot for checking out the comings and goings on the soi; inside, there's house and garage downstairs, chilled-out ambient and funk upstairs.

Thanon Sukhumvit

The places listed below are marked on the map on p.117.

Cheap Charlies, Soi 11, Thanon Sukhumvit. Hugely popular, long-running pavement bar where it's standing room only, but at a bargain B50 for a bottle of beer it's worth standing.

Imageries By The Glass, 2, Soi 24, Thanon Sukhumvit. Usually packed out with Thai couples who come to hear the nightly live music from the roster of different vocalists including rock-, pop- and folk-singers. Pricey drinks. Mon–Sat 6pm–1.30am.

Jools Bar and Restaurant, Soi 4, Thanon Sukhumvit, a short walk from the Soi Nana go-go strip. Easy-going British-run pub, popular with expat drinkers (photos of regular customers plaster the walls). The cosy downstairs bar is mainly standing room only, and traditional British food is served at tables upstairs.

La Lunar, near *Four Wings Hotel* on Soi 26, Thanon Sukhumvit. Swanky, well-designed place, whose various levels encompass a balconied disco with plenty of room to dance, a sushi bar and a pub with live bands. You need to dress up a bit to get in. B500 including two drinks.

Manet Club, Renoir Club, Van Gogh Club, Soi 33, Thanon Sukhumvit. Three very similar, unexciting, not at all Parisian bars, all almost next door to one another, that are best visited during happy hour (4–9pm).

Old Dutch, Soi 23, Thanon Sukhumvit, at the mouth of the Soi Cowboy strip. Cool, dark, peaceful oasis at the edge of Sukhumvit's frenetic sleaze; a reasonable basic menu and a big stock of current US and European newspapers make this an ideal daytime or early evening watering hole.

Q Bar, far end of Soi 11. Very dark, very trendy, New York-style bar occupying two floors and a terrace. Appeals to a mixed crowd of fashionable people, particularly on Fri and Sat nights when the DJs fill the dance-floor and there's a B300 cover charge that includes two free drinks. Arrive before 11pm if you want a seat; shuts about 2am.

Gay scene

The Balcony, Soi 4, Thanon Silom. Unpretentious, fun place with a large, popular terrace, cheap drinks and decent Thai, Indian and Western food; karaoke and regular talent nights.

Dick's Café, 894/7–8 Soi Pratuchai, Thanon Suriwong. Stylish day-and-night café (daily noon–4am) on a quiet soi opposite the prominent Wall St Tower, ideal for cheap drinking, pastries or just chilling out.

Disco Disco, Soi 2, Thanon Silom. Small, well-designed bar/disco, with reasonably priced drinks and good dance music for a fun young crowd.

DJ Station, Soi 2, Thanon Silom. Highly fashionable but unpretentious disco, packed at weekends, attracting a mix of Thais and farangs; midnight cabaret show. B100 including one drink (B200 including two drinks Fri & Sat).

Freeman Dance Arena, 60/18–21 Thanon Silom (in the soi beside 7-11 store, between Soi Thaniya and Thanon Rama IV). Busy, compact disco playing poppy dance music; regular cabaret shows and chill-out tables out on the soi.

The Icon, 90–96 Soi 4, Thanon Silom. Nightclub with good sounds and sound system, and a large dance floor; singing impersonators at 10.30pm, male dance cabaret at 11.45pm. B200 including two drinks.

JJ Park, 8/3 Soi 2, Thanon Silom. Classy, Thai-oriented bar/restaurant, for relaxed socializing rather than raving, with live Thai music, comedy shows and good food.

Sphinx, 98–104 Soi 4, Thanon Silom. Chic decor, terrace seating and good food attract a sophisticated crowd to this ground-floor bar and restaurant; karaoke and live music upstairs.

Telephone Bar, 114/11–13 Soi 4, Thanon Silom. Cruisey, long-standing eating and drinking venue with good Thai cuisine and a terrace on the alley.

Utopia, 116/1 Soi 23 (Soi Sawadee), Thanon Sukhumvit ☎ 02/259 9619, @ www.utopia-asia.com. Bangkok's first gay and lesbian community venue, comprising a shop for books, magazines, fashion and gifts, gallery, cosy café and bar with weekly women-only nights (currently Fri). "Thai Friends" scheme for visitors to be shown around the city by English-speaking gay Thais. Daily noon–midnight.

Vega, Soi 39, Thanon Sukhumvit. Trendy bar-restaurant run by a group of lesbians. The live music, karaoke and dance floor attract a mixed, fashionable crowd.

Culture shows

Only in Bangkok can you be sure of catching a live display of non-tourist-oriented traditional dance or theatre; few of the outlying regions have resident troupes, so authentic performances elsewhere tend to be sporadic and may not coincide with your visit. The main venue is the National Theatre (☎ 02/224 1342; Mon–Fri 8.30am–4.30pm), next to the National Museum on the northwest corner of Sanam Luang, which puts on special medley shows of **drama and music** from all over the country, performed by students from the

Bangkok for kids

The following theme parks and amusement centres are all designed for kids, the main drawback being that most of them are located a long way from the city centre. Other attractions kids should enjoy include Dusit Zoo (see p.150), the Snake Farm (see p.159), the ice-skating rink inside the World Trade Center on Thanon Rajdamri, and the Joe Louis puppet shows in Nonthaburi (see p.165).

Adventureland, Seacon Square, 904 Thanon Sri Nakarin (Mon–Fri 11am–9pm, Sat & Sun 10am–10pm; free entry). Rollercoasters, go-karts, a "stimulator" cinema and a rollerblade rink. Rides from B15. Skytrain to On Nut, then regular bus #133 from Sukhumvit Soi 77.

Dream World, Thanon Nakhon Nayok, ten minutes' drive north of Don Muang airport (Mon–Fri 10am–5pm, Sat & Sun 10am–7pm; B120, children B95). Theme park with different areas such as Fantasy Land, Dream Garden and Adventure Land. Water rides and other amusements. Regular buses #39 and #59 from Rajdamnoen Klang in Banglamphu to Rangsit, then songthaew or tuk-tuk to Dream World.

MBK Magic Land, 8th Floor, Mah Boon Krong Shopping Centre, at the Rama I/Phrayathai intersection (Mon–Fri 10.30am–6.30pm, Sat & Sun 10.30am–8pm). Centrally located amusements centre in downtown Bangkok, with indoor fairground rides from B15.

Safari World, 99 Thanon Ramindra, Minburi (daily 9am–4.30pm; B600, children B360). Drive-through safari park, complete with monkeys, lions, rhinos, giraffes and zebras, plus a sea-life area with dolphins and sea lions. If you don't have your own car, you can be driven through the park in a Safari World coach. Take regular bus #26 from Victory Monument, then a minibus to Safari World.

Siam Park, 101 Thanon Sukhapiban 2, on the far eastern edge of town (Mon–Fri 10am–6pm, Sat & Sun 9am–7pm; B400, children B300). Waterslides, whirlpools, artificial surf and the like, plus rollercoasters, a small zoo and a beer garden. Air-con bus #14 from Victory Monument.

attached College of the Performing Arts. From November through May, these take place almost every Saturday, and there are also similar shows throughout the year on the last Friday of every month. Spectacular and authentic, the performances serve as a tantalizing introduction to the theatre's full-length shows, which include *lakhon* (classical) and *likay* (folk) theatre and the occasional *nang thalung* (shadow-puppet play). Tickets for these start at around B100; programme details can be checked by calling the theatre or TAT.

The Sala Chalermkrung Theatre (☎02/225 8757) at 66 Thanon Charoen Krung (New Road; on the intersection with Thanon Triphet in Pahurat, next to Old Siam Plaza) shows contemporary Thai drama and comedy most of the week, but occasionally stages traditional, tourist-friendly dance-dramas; call them for details of the current programme. The same is true of the Thailand Cultural Centre, located in the eastern part of the city on Thanon Ratchadapisek (☎02/645 2955).

Many tourist restaurants feature nightly **culture shows** – usually a hotch-potch of Thai dancing and classical music, with a martial-arts demonstration thrown in. Worth checking out are *Baan Thai* (☎02/258 5403), a traditional teak house on Soi 32, Thanon Sukhumvit, where diners are served a set meal during the show (performances at 8.45pm; B550), and the outdoor restaurant in *Silom Village* (☎02/234 4581) on Thanon Silom which also stages a nightly fifty-minute show (7.30pm; B450) to accompany the set menu. In Banglamphu, all tour agents offer a dinner-show package including transport for around B600 per person. The **Joe Louis Puppet Theatre** in Nonthaburi stages entertaining tourist-oriented performances of the *Ramakien* using traditional stick puppets (daily at 10am; B600); see p.165 for details.

Thai dancing is performed for its original ritual purpose, usually several times a day, at the Lak Muang Shrine behind the Grand Palace and the Erawan Shrine on the corner of Thanon Ploenchit. Both shrines have resident troupes of dancers who are hired by worshippers to perform *lakhon chatri*, a sort of *khon* dance-drama, to thank benevolent spirits for answered prayers. The dancers are always dressed up in full gear and accompanied by musicians, but the length and complexity of the dance and the number of dancers depends on the amount of money paid by the supplicant: a price list is posted near the dance area. The musicians at the Erawan Shrine are particularly highly rated, though the almost comic apathy of the dancers there doesn't do them justice.

Cinemas

Central Bangkok has over forty **cinemas**, many of which show recent American and European releases with their original dialogue and Thai subtitles. Most cinemas screen shows four times a day: programmes are detailed every day in the *Nation* and *Bangkok Post*, and full listings and reviews appear in the monthly listings magazine, *Metro*; cinema locations are printed on *Nancy Chandler's Map of Bangkok*. Seats cost from B60 to B120, depending on the plushness of the cinema; whatever cinema you're in, you're expected to stand for the national anthem, which is played before every performance.

The Pata cinema in the department store complex on Thanon Phra Pinklao in Thonburi is convenient for Banglamphu, there are four massive movie theatres in Siam Square, and nearly every major downtown shopping plaza has two or three screens on its top floor. Western films are also occasionally shown at the Japan Cultural Centre, Goethe Institut and Alliance Française: check the English-language press for details. And if it's been a while since you've caught up on the new releases, check out the dozens of video-showing restaurants along Banglamphu's Thanon Khao San, where recent blockbusters are screened back-to-back every day and night of the year, all for the price of a banana smoothie or a cheese sandwich.

Thai boxing

The violence of the average **Thai boxing** match may be offputting to some, but spending a couple of hours at one of Bangkok's two main stadiums can be immensely entertaining, not least for the enthusiasm of the spectators and the ritualistic aspects of the fights. Bouts, advertised in the English-language newspapers, are held in the capital every night of the week at the **Rajdamnoen Stadium**, next to the TAT office on Rajdamnoen Nok (Mon, Wed & Thurs 6pm & 9pm, Sun 5pm), and at **Lumphini Stadium** on Thanon Rama IV (Tues & Fri 6.30pm, Sat 5pm & 8.30pm). Tickets go on sale one hour before and, unless the boxers are big stars, start at B220, rising to B1000 for a ringside seat; tickets for the Sunday bouts at Rajdamnoen cost from B50. You might have to queue for a few minutes, but there's no need to get there early unless there's a really important fight on. Sessions usually feature ten bouts, each consisting of five three-minute rounds (with two-minute rests in between each round), so if you're not a big fan it may be worth turning up an hour late, as the better fights tend to happen later in the billing. It's more fun if you buy one of the less expensive standing tickets, enabling you to witness the wild gesticulations of the betting aficionados at close range. For more on Thai boxing, see p.69.

To engage in a little *muay Thai* yourself, try Jitti's Gym off Thanon Chakrabongse in Banglamphu, which holds open *muay Thai* **classes** every afternoon (3–6pm; B300; ☎02/282 7854). For more in-depth training and further information about Thai boxing, contact the Muay Thai Institute at 336/932 Prachathipat, Thanyaburi, Pathum Thani, Bangkok 12130 (☎02/992 0096, ⓦwww.tat.or.th/do/learn.htm), which runs training courses for foreigners (US$160 for 40hr), including practical instruction, as well as history and theory.

Shopping

Bangkok has a good reputation for **shopping**, particularly for silk, gems and fashions, where the range and quality are streets ahead of other Thai cities, and of many other Asian capitals as well. Antiques and handicrafts are good buys too, and some shops stock curiosities from the most remote regions of the country alongside the more typical items As always, watch out for old, damaged goods being passed off as antiques: if you're concerned about the quality or authenticity of your purchases, stick to TAT-approved shops. Bangkok also has the best English-language bookshops in the country. Department stores and tourist-oriented shops in the city keep late hours, opening at 10 or 11am and closing at about 9pm.

Downtown Bangkok is full of smart, multistoreyed **shopping plazas** with names like Siam Centre, Emporium and the Amarin Plaza, which is where you'll find the majority of the city's fashion stores, as well as designer lifestyle goods and bookshops. The plazas tend to be pleasantly air-conditioned and thronging with trendy young Thais, but don't hold much interest for tourists unless you happen to be looking for a new outfit. You're more likely to find useful items in one of the city's numerous **department stores**, most of which are also scattered about the downtown areas. The Central department stores (on Silom and Ploenchit roads) are probably the city's best, but Robinson's (on Sukhumvit Soi 19, Thanon Rajdamri and at the Silom/Rama IV junction) are also good. Should you need to buy a crucial piece of **children's gear**, you'll find everything from bottles, dummies, slings and mosquito nets to English-language kids' books, clothes and games in the children's department store Buy Buy Kiddo on Sukhumvit Soi 12. The British chain of **pharmacies**, Boots the Chemist, has lots of branches across the city, including on Thanon Khao San, in the Times Square plaza between Sukhumvit sois 12 and 14, and in the Emporium on Sukhumvit.

For travellers, spectating, not shopping, is apt to be the main draw of Bangkok's neighbourhood **markets** – notably the bazaars of Chinatown (see p.142) and the blooms and scents of Pak Khlong Talat, the flower and vegetable market just west of Memorial Bridge (see p.144). The massive Chatuchak Weekend Market is an exception, being both a tourist attraction and a marvellous shopping experience; see p.16 for details. If you're planning on some serious market exploration, get hold of *Nancy Chandler's Map of Bangkok*, an

Counterfeit culture

Faking it is big business in Bangkok, a city whose copyright regulations carry about as much weight as its anti-prostitution laws. Forged **designer clothes** and accessories are the biggest sellers; street vendors along Patpong, Silom, Sukhumvit and Khao San roads will flog you a whole range of inexpensive lookalikes, including Tommy Hilfiger shirts, D&G jeans, Calvin Klein wallets, Prada bags and Hermes scarves.

Along Patpong, after dark, plausible would-be Rolex, Cartier and Tag **watches** from Hong Kong and Taiwan go for about B500 – and are fairly reliable considering the price. If your budget won't stretch to a phoney Rolex Oyster, there's plenty of opportunities for lesser expenditure at the stalls concentrated on Thanon Khao San, where pirated **music CDs** and **software and games CD-ROMs** are sold at a fraction of their normal price. Quality is usually fairly high but the choice is often less than brilliant, with a concentration on mainstream pop and rock albums. Finally, several stallholders along Thanon Khao San even make up passable international **student and press cards** – though travel agencies and other organizations in Bangkok aren't easily fooled.

enthusiastically annotated creation which includes special sections on the main areas of interest. With the chief exception of Chatuchak, most markets operate daily from dawn till early afternoon; early morning is often the best time to go to beat the heat and crowds. The Patpong **night market**, which also spills out on to Thanon Silom, is *the* place to stock up on fake designer goods, from pseudo-Rolex watches to Tommy Hilfiger shirts; the stalls open at about 5pm until late into the evening.

Among the more **esoteric** items you can buy in Bangkok are fossils and Thai wine. The tiny House of Gems (Khun Boonman) at 1218 Thanon Charoen Krung (New Road), near the GPO, deals almost exclusively in **fossils**, minerals and – no kidding – dinosaur droppings. Ranging from sixty million to two hundred million years old, these petrified droppings (properly known as coprolite) were unearthed in the mid-1980s in Thailand's Isaan region; weighing from 150 grams to 8 kilograms, they are sold at B7 per gram. Also on sale here, from B5 to B500 each, are tektites, pieces of glassy rock found in Thai fields and thought to be the 750,000-year-old products of volcanic activity on the moon. As for **wine**, Maison du Vin, 2nd Floor, Thaniya Plaza, Thanon Silom (℡02/231 2185), sell a better-than-passable Chateau de Loei red and white, made by an eccentric Frenchman from grapes grown on the slopes of Phu Reua in Thailand's Isaan region.

Handicrafts and traditional textiles

Samples of nearly all regionally produced **handicrafts** end up in Bangkok, so the selection is phenomenal. Many of the shopping plazas have at least one classy handicraft outlet, and competition keeps prices in the city at upcountry levels, with the main exception of household objects – particularly wickerware and tin bowls and basins – which get palmed off relatively expensively in Bangkok. Handicraft sellers in Banglamphu tend to tout a limited range compared to the shops downtown, but several places on Thanon Khao San sell reasonably priced triangular pillows (*mawn khwaan*) in traditional fabrics, which make fantastic souvenirs but are heavy to post home; some places sell unstuffed versions which are simple to mail home, but a pain to fill when you return! This is also a good place to pick up Thai shoulder bags woven to all specifications and designed with travellers' needs in mind. The cheapest place to buy traditional northern and northeastern textiles – including sarongs, triangular pillows and farmers' shirts – is **Chatuchak Weekend Market** (see p.161), and you might be able to nose out some interesting handicrafts here too.

Come Thai, 2nd Floor, Amarin Plaza (the Sogo building), Thanon Ploenchit. Currently has no English sign, but easily spotted by its carved wooden doorframe. Impressive range of unusual handwoven silk and cotton fabrics, much of it made up into traditional-style clothes such as Chinese mandarin shirts and short fitted jackets.

Kealang, 2nd Floor, Amarin Plaza, Thanon Ploenchit. Huge variety of *bencharong* pots and vases, as well as other multicoloured Thai-Chinese ceramics.

Khomapastr, 1st Floor, River City shopping complex, off Thanon Charoen Krung (New Road). Unusual choice of attractive patterned cotton, in lengths or made up into items such as quirky cushion covers, attractive shirts and *mawn khwaan*.

Krishna's, between sois 9 and 11, Thanon Sukhumvit. The four-storey building is crammed full of artefacts from all over Asia and, though mass-produced metallic statuettes and Balinese masks seem to dominate, there are enough interesting curios (such as Nepalese jewellery and Japanese *netsuke* ornaments) to reward a thorough browse.

The Legend, 2nd Floor, Amarin Plaza, Thanon Ploenchit, and 3rd Floor, Thaniya Plaza, Thanon Silom. Stocks a small selection of well-made Thai handicrafts, from wood and wickerware to fabrics and ceramics, at reasonable prices.

Narayana Phand, 127 Thanon Rajdamri. This government souvenir centre was set up to ensure the preservation of traditional crafts and to maintain standards of quality, and makes a reasonable one-stop shop for last-minute presents. It offers a huge assortment of very reasonably priced goods from all over the country, including *khon* masks and shadow puppets, musical instruments and kites, nielloware and celadon, and hill-tribe crafts. Unfortunately the layout is not very appealing and the place feels like a warehouse – in marked contrast to the much more inspiring Thai Craft Museum in the Gaysorn Plaza next door (see below).

Prayer Textile Gallery, 197 Thanon Phrayathai, on the corner of Thanon Rama I. Traditional fabrics from the north and the northeast, as well as from Laos and Cambodia. The selection is good, but prices for these textiles are getting surprisingly high, particularly for those now classified as antiques.

Rasi Sayam, a 10min hike down Sukhumvit Soi 23, opposite *Le Dalat Vietnamese* restaurant. Very

classy handicraft shop, specializing in eclectic and fairly pricey decorative and folk arts such as tiny betel-nut sets woven from *lipao* fern, sticky rice lunch baskets, coconut wood bowls and *mut mee* textiles. Mon–Sat 9am–5.30pm.

Silom Village, 286/1 Thanon Silom, just west of Soi Decho. A complex of wooden houses that attempts to create a relaxing, upcountry atmosphere as a backdrop for its pricey fabrics and occasionally unusual souvenirs, such as grainy *sa* paper made from mulberry bark.

Sukhumvit Square, between sois 8 and 10, Thanon Sukhumvit. This open-air night-bazaar-style plaza doesn't really get going till nightfall, when it's well worth dropping by to check out the range of quality handicrafts, artefacts, antiques, textiles and clothing sold in the fifty little shops here.

Tamnan Mingmuang, 3rd Floor, Thaniya Plaza, Soi Thaniya, east end of Thanon Silom. Subsidiary of The Legend opposite which aims to foster and popularize crafts from all over the country. Among the unusual items on offer are trays and boxes for tobacco and betel nut made from *yan lipao* (intricately woven fern vines), and bambooware sticky rice containers, baskets and lamp-shades.

Thai Celadon, Sukhumvit Soi 16 (Thanon Ratchadapisek). Classic celadon stoneware made without commercial dyes or clays and glazed with the archetypal blues and greens that were invented by the Chinese to emulate the colour of precious jade. Mainly dinner sets, vases and lamps, plus some figurines.

Thai Craft Museum, 2nd & 3rd Floor of Gaysorn Plaza, entrances on Thanon Ploenchit and on Thanon Rajdamri. Most of the top two floors of Gaysorn Plaza shopping centre are taken over by this collection of three hundred different outlets selling classy, high-quality crafts, textiles, jewellery, art, clothes and souvenirs, much of which is commissioned from villages around the country. You won't find absolute bargains here, but you get what you pay for. The best one-stop souvenir shop in the capital.

Via, 55 Thanon Tanao, Banglamphu. A specialist outlet for miniature reproduction traditional Thai boats. The scale models are all made from teak with fine attention to detail, and cover a dozen different styles of boat including rice barges, royal boats and longtails. Prices from B2000.

Clothes and Thai silk

Noted for its thickness and sheen, **Thai silk** became internationally recognized only about forty years ago after the efforts of American Jim Thompson (see box on p.154). Much of it comes from the northeast, but you'll find the lion's share of outlets and tailoring facilities in the capital. Prices start at about B350 per metre for two-ply silk (suitable for thin shirts and skirts), or B500 for four-ply (for suits).

Bangkok can be a great place to have **tailored clothes** made: materials don't cost much, and work is often completed in only 24 hours. On the other hand, you may find yourself palmed off with artificial silk and a suit that falls apart in a week. Inexpensive silk and tailoring shops crowd Silom, Sukhumvit and Khao San roads, but many people opt for hotel tailors, preferring to pay more for the security of an established business. Be wary of places offering ridiculous deals – when you see a dozen garments advertised for a total price of less than $200, you know something's fishy – and look carefully at the quality of samples before making any decision. If you're staying in Banglamphu, keep an eye on guest-house noticeboards for cautionary tales from other travellers.

Thanon Khao San is lined with stalls selling low-priced **ready-mades**: the tie-dyed shirts, baggy cotton trousers, embroidered blouses and ethnic-style outfits are all aimed at backpackers and New Age hippies; the stalls of Banglamphu Market, around the edges of the abandoned New World department store, have the best range of inexpensive Thai fashions in this area. For the best and latest fashions, however, check out the shops in the Siam Centre and the Siam Discovery Centre, both across from Siam Square, and the high-fashion outlets at the upmarket Emporium on Sukhumvit. **Shoes** and **leather goods** are good buys in Bangkok, being generally hand-made from high-quality leather and quite a bargain: check out the "booteries" along Thanon Sukhumvit.

Ambassador Fashions, 1/10–11 Soi Chaiyot, off Sukhumvit Soi 11 ℡02/253 2993. Long-established and reputable tailor, well versed in making both men's and women's wear. Clothes can be made within 24hr if necessary. Call for free pick-up in Bangkok.

Emporium, between sois 22 and 24 on Thanon Sukhumvit. Enormous and rather glamorous shopping plaza, with a good range of fashion outlets, from exclusive designer wear to trendy high-street gear. Brand name outlets include Versace, Chanel and Louis Vuitton.

Jim Thompson's Thai Silk Company, main shop at 9 Thanon Suriwong, plus branches in the World Trade Center, Central department store on Thanon Ploenchit, at Emporium on Thanon Sukhumvit, and at many hotels around the city. A good place to start looking for traditional Thai fabric, or at least to get an idea of what's out there. Stocks silk and cotton by the yard and ready-made items from dresses to cushion covers, which are well designed and of good quality, but pricey. They also have a home furnishings section and a good tailoring service.

Khanitha, branches at 111/3–5 Thanon Suriwong and the *Oriental* hotel. Specialize in women's suits, evening wear and dressing gowns, tailored from the finest Thai silk.

Mah Boon Krong (MBK), at the Rama I/Phrayathai intersection. Labyrinthine shopping centre which houses hundreds of small, mostly fairly inexpensive outlets, including plenty of high-street fashion shops.

Narry's, 155/22 Sukhumvit Soi 11/1 ℡02/254 9184, ⓦwww.narry.com. Good-value, award-winning tailor of men's and women's clothes. Finished items ready within 24hr if necessary. Call for free pick-up in Bangkok.

Peninsula Plaza, Thanon Rajdamri. Considered the most upmarket shopping plaza in the city, so come here for Louis Vuitton and the like.

Siam Centre, across the road from Siam Square. Particularly good for local labels as well as international high-street chains; Kookaï, Greyhound and Soda Pop are typical outlets.

Siam Discovery Centre, across the road from Siam Square. Flash designer gear, including plenty of name brands like D&G, Morgan, Max Mara and YSL.

Siam Square. Worth poking around the alleys here, especially near what's styled as the area's "Centerpoint" between sois 3 and 4. All manner of inexpensive boutiques, some little more than booths, sell colourful street gear to the capital's fashionable students and teenagers.

Books

English-language **bookstores** in Bangkok are always well stocked with everything to do with Thailand, and most carry fiction classics and popular paperbacks as well. The capital's few **secondhand** bookstores are surprisingly poor value, but you might turn up something worthwhile – or earn a few baht by selling your own cast-offs – in the shops and stalls along Thanon Khao San.

Aporia, Thanon Tanao, Banglamphu. Run by knowledgeable book-loving staff, Banglamphu's main outlet for new books keeps a good stock of titles on Thai and Southeast Asian culture and has a decent selection of travelogues, plus some English-language fiction. Also sells secondhand books.

Asia Books, branches on Thanon Sukhumvit between sois 15 and 19, in Landmark Plaza between sois 4 and 6, in Times Square between sois 12 and 14, and in Emporium between sois 22 and 24; in Peninsula Plaza on Thanon Rajdamri; in Siam Discovery Centre on Thanon Rama I; and in Thaniya Plaza near Patpong off Thanon Silom. English-language bookstore that's especially recommended for its books on Asia – everything from guidebooks to cookery books, novels to art (the Sukhumvit 15–19 branch has the very best Asian selection). Also stocks bestselling novels and coffee-table books.

Books Kinokuniya, 3rd Floor, Emporium Shopping Centre, between sois 22 and 24 on Thanon Sukhumvit. Huge English-language book-store with a broad range of books ranging from bestsellers to travel literature and from classics to sci-fi; not so hot on books about Asia though.

Central Department Store, most convenient branches on Thanon Silom. Paperback fiction, maps and reference books in English.

DK (Duang Kamol) Books, branches on the 3rd Floor of the MBK shopping centre, corner of Rama I and Phrayathai; at 244–6 Soi 2, Siam Square; and at 180/1 Thanon Sukhumvit between sois 8 and 10. One of Thailand's biggest bookseller chains, DK is especially good for maps and books on Thailand.

Shaman Books, two branches on Thanon Khao San, Banglamphu. The best-stocked and most efficient secondhand bookshop in the city, where all books are displayed alphabetically as well as being logged on the computer – which means you can locate your choice in seconds. Lots of books on Asia (travel, fiction, politics and history) as well as a decent range of novels and general interest books. Don't expect bargains though.

Gems and jewellery

Bangkok boasts the country's best **gem and jewellery** shops, and some of the finest lapidaries in the world, making this *the* place to buy cut and uncut stones such as rubies, blue sapphires and diamonds. The most exclusive gem outlets are scattered along Thanon Silom – try Mr Ho's at number 987 – but many tourists prefer to buy from hotel shops, like Kim's inside the *Oriental*, where reliability is assured. Other recommended outlets include Johnny's Gems at 199 Thanon Fuang Nakhon, near Wat Rajabophit in Ratanakosin; Merlin et Delauney at 1 Soi Pradit, off Thanon Suriwong; and Uthai's Gems, at 28/7 Soi Ruam Rudee, off Thanon Ploenchit. For cheap and cheerful silver earrings, bracelets and necklaces, you can't beat the traveller-orientated jewellery shops along Thanon Khao San in Banglamphu.

While it's unusual for established jewellers to fob off tourists with glass and paste, a common **scam** is to charge a lot more than what the gem is worth based on its carat weight. Get the stone tested on the spot, and ask for a written guarantee and receipt. Be extremely wary of touts and the shops they recommend, and note that there are no TAT-endorsed jewellery shops despite any information you may be given to the contrary. Unless you're an experienced gem trader, don't even consider buying gems in bulk to sell at a supposedly vast profit elsewhere: many a gullible traveller has invested thousands of baht on a handful of worthless multi-coloured stones. If you want independent professional advice or precious stones certification, contact the Asian Institute of Gemological Sciences, located inside the Jewelry Trade Center Building, 919/298 Thanon Silom (☏02/267 4315–9). For more on Thailand's ruby and sapphire industry, see p.432.

Antiques and paintings

Bangkok is the entrepôt for the finest Thai, Burmese and Cambodian **antiques**, but the market has long been sewn up, so don't expect to happen upon any undiscovered treasure. Even experts admit that they sometimes find it hard to tell real antiques from fakes, so the best policy is just to buy on the grounds of attractiveness. The River City shopping complex, off Thanon Charoen Krung (New Road), devotes its third and fourth floors to a bewildering array of pricey treasures and holds an auction on the first Saturday of every month (viewing during the preceding week). The other main area for antiques is the stretch of Charoen Krung that runs between the GPO and the bottom of Thanon Silom. Here you'll find a good selection of reputable individual businesses specializing in woodcarvings, bronze statues and stone sculptures culled from all parts of Thailand and neighbouring countries as well. Remember that most antiques require an export permit (see p.25).

Street-corner stalls all over the city sell poor-quality mass-produced traditional Thai **paintings**, but for a huge selection of better-quality Thai art, visit Sombat Permpoon Gallery on Soi 1, Thanon Sukhumvit, which carries thousands of canvases, framed and unframed, spanning the range from classical Ayutthayan-era-style village scenes to twenty-first-century abstracts. The gallery does have works by famous Thai artists like Thawan Duchanee, but prices for the more affordable works by less well-known painters start at B1500.

Moving on from Bangkok

Despite Bangkok's numerous attractions, many travellers feel like getting out of it almost as soon as they arrive – and the city is full of tour operators and travel agents encouraging you to do just that. What's more, on any tour of Thailand you're bound to pass through the capital, as it's the terminus of all major highways and rail lines – there are no through Chiang Mai–Surat Thani links, for example. Fortunately, **public transport** between Bangkok and the provinces is inexpensive and plentiful, if not particularly speedy. This is also an unrivalled place to make arrangements for onward travel from Thailand – the city's travel agents can offer some amazing flight deals and all the major Asian embassies are here, so getting the appropriate **visas** should be no problem.

Travel within Thailand

Having to change trains or buses in Bangkok might sound a tiresome way to travel the country, but it has its advantages – breaking up what would otherwise be an unbearably long trip, and giving the chance to confirm plane tickets and stock up on supplies not so widely available elsewhere. It also means that you can store unwanted clothes in a guest house or hotel – very useful if coming from Chiang Mai (where you might need jumpers and walking boots) and going on to Ko Tao or Krabi (T-shirts and swimwear).

Package tours and tour operators

If your time is short and you want to pack as much as you can into your stay, you might consider booking a **package tour** once you're in Thailand; some recommended tour operators are listed below. A number of tour operators offer inexpensive packages, with deals that range from overnight trips to tailor-made tours of a week or more. All of them include transport and budget accommodation, and most include food as well; prices start at around B1000 for two-day packages. Some of the most popular packages include one or two nights in the **Kanchanaburi** and Sangkhlaburi area (for trekking, river-rafting and elephant riding); three to five nights in **Umphang** (trekking); two or three nights in **Chiang Rai, Chiang Mai** or **Pai** (trekking); and two to four nights in **Khao Sok** national park (trekking, river-rafting and elephant riding). There are also a number of **specialist activity tours**, which are well worth investigating, including rock climbing, kayaking, diving and cycling.

Many of the same tour operators also offer **day-trips** from Bangkok to outlying destinations. These tend to be quite good value as they combine several places which would otherwise take a couple of days to see on your own. The most popular itinerary takes in Damnoen Saduak, Nakhon Pathom and Kanchanaburi.

Bike and Travel, 802/756 River Park, Mu 12, Thanon Phaholyothin ☏02/990 0274, ⓦwww.cyclingthailand.com. Weekend cycling and canoeing trips all over Thailand, tailored for different levels of fitness.

Lost Horizons, Ban Chaophraya Rm 1907, Somded Chaophraya Soi 17 ☏02/863 3180, ⓕ863 1301, ⓦlosthorizonsasia.com. Manages and owns several mid-priced eco-resorts in secluded spots in southern Thailand, and arrange all-inclusive soft-adventure tours to destinations including Khao Sok, the River Kwai, north Thailand and Bangkok canals.

Mama Tour, 144 Thanon Khao San, Banglamphu ☏02/282 3584. Two-day trips from Banglamphu to the River Kwai and Sangkhlaburi, and treks in the north.

Nature Trails, 549 Thantip Soi 2, Thanon Sukhapibaan 3 ☏02/374 6610, ⓕ735 0638, ⓦwww.ntrails.co.th. Regular bird- and butterfly-watching weekends in Thailand's national parks.

Planet Scuba and Wild Planet, across from Thanon Khao San on Thanon Chakrabongse, Banglamphu ☏02/629 0977, ⓕ629 0976, ⓦwww.wildplanet.co.th. PADI Five-Star dive centre and adventure-tour operator which runs a regular programme of activity packages, including dive packages to Ko Tao and Pattaya, trekking from Chiang Mai, kayaking in Umphang and mountain-biking in Chiang Dao.

By train

All trains depart from **Hualamphong Station** except the twice-daily service to Nakhon Pathom and Kanchanaburi, and a couple of the Hua Hin trains, which leave from **Bangkok Noi Station** (also referred to as **Thonburi Station**), across the river from Banglamphu in Thonburi. The "Information" booth at Hualamphong station keeps English-language timetables, or you can try phoning the Train Information Hotline on ☏1690; the State Railway of Thailand website (ⓦwww.srt.motc.go.th) carries an English-language timetable and fare chart for major destinations. For a guide to destinations and journey times from Bangkok, see "Travel Details" on p.196. For details on city transport to and from Hualamphong, left-luggage facilities at the station, and a warning about con-artists operating at the station, see the section on "Arriving in Bangkok" on p.96.

Tickets for overnight trains and other busy routes should be booked at least a day in advance (or at least a week in advance for travel on national holidays), and are best bought from Hualamphong. The clued-up English-speaking staff at VC Travel and Tour on the mezzanine floor of the station concourse (daily 5am–8pm; ☏02/613 6725), above *Coffee Bucks*, sell all types of rail tickets at no commission, and can also book discounted mid-range accommodation at your destination. Alternatively, during normal office hours you can buy rail tickets from the clearly signed State Railway **advance booking office** at the back of the station concourse (daily 8.30am–4pm); at other times you can buy them from ticket counter #2 (daily 5–8.30am & 4–10pm), which is also the place to apply for ticket refunds. Train tickets can also be bought through almost any travel agent and through some hotels and guest houses for a booking fee of about B50. In addition to all types of normal rail ticket, both VC Travel and the Advance Booking Office, sell joint rail and boat or rail and bus tickets, to Ko Samui, Ko Pha Ngan, Ko Tao, Ko Phi Phi and Phuket. Sample prices include B750 to Ko Samui (second-class sleeper and boat ticket) and B800 to Phuket (second-class sleeper and bus transfer).

By bus

Bangkok's three main bus terminals are distributed around the outskirts of town. Leave plenty of time to get to the bus terminals, especially if setting off from Banglamphu, from where you need at least an hour and a half (outside rush hour) to get to the Eastern Bus Terminal, and a good hour to get to the Northern or Southern terminals. Seats on regular long-distance buses don't need to be **booked** in advance, but air-conditioned ones should be reserved ahead of time either at the relevant bus station or through hotels and guest houses. Agencies sometimes provide transport to the bus station for an additional charge.

The **Northern Bus Terminal**, or **Sathaanii Mo Chit** (departure info for both air-con and regular services on ☏02/936 2860), is the departure point for all buses to northern and northeastern towns, including Chiang Mai, Chiang Rai, Nong Khai and Pak Chong (for Khao Yai), and for most destinations in the central plains, including Ayutthaya, Sukhothai and Mae Sot (but excluding Nakhon Pathom and Kanchanaburi, services to which run from the Southern Bus Terminal). Mo Chit also runs a few buses to the east-coast destinations of Pattaya, Chanthaburi and Trat, though there are more regular services to the east coast from the Eastern Bus Terminal. The Northern Bus Terminal is on Thanon Kamphaeng Phet 2, near Chatuchak Weekend Market in the far north of the city; the fastest way to get there is to take the BTS Skytrain to its northernmost terminus, Mo Chit (N8) on Thanon Phaholyothin, which is just a few minutes' walk from the bus terminal. Alternatively, you can take several city buses to Mo Chit, including #2 and #77 from Thanon Silom; both regular and air-con #3, and air-con #9, #12 and #32 from Banglamphu; and both regular and air-con #29 from Hualamphong train station; see box on p.100 for bus route details.

The **Eastern Bus Terminal**, or **Sathaanii Ekamai** (air-con services ☏02/391 2504; regular services ☏02/391 8097), at Sukhumvit Soi 40, serves east-coast destinations such as Pattaya, Ban Phe (for Ko Samet) and Trat (for Ko Chang). The Skytrain stops right by the bus terminal at Ekamai station, as do city buses #11 (from Banglamphu) and #59 (from the Northern Bus Terminal); see box on p.100 for bus route details. Or you can take the Sen Seb canal boat service from the Golden Mount (see p.102) to Tha Ekamai (Sukhumvit Soi 63) and then hop into a taxi down Soi 63 to the bus terminal.

The **Southern Bus Terminal**, or **Sathaanii Sai Tai Mai** (air-con services ☎02/435 1199; regular services ☎02/434 5557), is at the junction of Thanon Borom Ratchonni and the Nakhon Chaisri Highway, west of the Chao Phraya River in Thonburi. It handles departures to all points south of the capital, including Hua Hin, Chumphon (for Ko Tao), Surat Thani (for Ko Samui), Phuket and Krabi (for Ko Phi Phi and Ko Lanta), as well as departures for destinations west of Bangkok, such as Nakhon Pathom and Kanchanaburi. Regular and air-con buses leave from different sections of the Southern Bus Terminal, and anyone there will be able to point you in the right direction for your bus. To get here, take city bus #7 (air-con) from Banglamphu or Hualamphong station, or air-con #11 from Banglamphu or Thanon Sukhumvit (see box on p.100 for bus route details).

Budget transport

Many Bangkok tour operators offer **budget transport** to major tourist destinations such as Chiang Mai, Surat Thani, Krabi, Ko Samet and Ko Chang. In many cases this works out as cheap if not cheaper than the equivalent fare on a public air-con bus and, as most of the budget transport deals leave from the Thanon Khao San area in Banglamphu, they're often more convenient. The main drawbacks, however, are the **lack of comfort** and **poor safety**.

For the shorter trips, for example to **Ko Samet** (around B300 including boat), **Ko Chang** (B480) and **Kanchanaburi** (B100) transport operators always take passengers in minibuses which, if crowded, can be unbearably cramped, and often have insufficient air-conditioning. Drivers usually go as fast as possible, which some travellers find scary. For destinations further afield, such as **Chiang Mai** (11hr) and **Surat Thani** (11hr), travellers are usually taken by larger tour bus; again these tend to be clapped-out old things and drivers on these journeys have an even worse safety record. **Security** on these buses is also a problem, so keep your luggage locked or within view, and passengers often find themselves dumped on the outskirts of their destination city, at the mercy of unscrupulous touts. If you are planning a journey to Chiang Mai or Surat Thani, consider taking the train instead – the extra comfort and peace of mind are well worth the extra baht.

If you're heading for an **island** (such as **Ko Samui**, **Ko Tao** or **Ko Chang**), your bus should get you to the ferry port in time to catch the boat, though there have been complaints from travellers that this does not always happen; always check whether your bus ticket covers the ferry ride. Sample prices for joint bus and boat tickets include B420 for Ko Samui, B520 for Ko Pha Ngan, B570 for Ko Tao and B570 for Ko Phi Phi.

The best overall advice is to consult other travellers before booking with budget transport operators, and to be prepared for the ride not to be particularly comfortable. **Tour operators** open up and go bust all the time, particularly in the Thanon Khao San area, so ask around for recommendations or make your arrangements through a reputable hotel or guest house; never hand over any money until you see the ticket.

By air

Domestic **flights** should be booked as far in advance as possible, though tickets can be bought at the airport if available; the domestic departure tax is included in the price of the ticket. Thai Airways is the main domestic carrier and flies to over twenty major towns and cities; Bangkok Airways currently covers just five routes from the capital: Ko Samui, Sukhothai, Ranong, Hua Hin and Chiang Mai. All domestic flights leave from Don Muang airport (see p.93);

for advice on how to get to the airport see the box below; for details on hotels within ten minutes' drive of the airport see p.93; and for airline phone numbers see "Listings", p.192.

Leaving Thailand

Whether you're moving on within Asia or just trying to get home, Bangkok is one of the best places in the world to buy **low-priced international air tickets**, and there are hundreds of travel agents to buy them from. You'll get the rock-bottom deals from agents who don't belong to the **Association of Thai Travel Agents** (ATTA), but as with their Western counterparts many of these are transient and not altogether trustworthy. Thanon Khao San is a notorious centre of such fly-by-night operations, some of which have been known to flee with travellers' money overnight: if you buy from a non-ATTA outlet it's a good idea to ring the airline and check your reservation yourself – don't hand over any money until you've done that and have been given the ticket. The slightly more expensive ATTA agencies still work out good value by international standards: to check if an agency is affiliated either get hold of the TAT list, ask for proof of membership or call the ATTA office (☎02/237 6046–8). Some tried and tested travel agents are given in "Listings", p.195.

All major **airline offices** are in downtown Bangkok. There's no advantage in buying tickets directly from the airlines – their addresses and phone numbers are given in "Listings", p.192, so you can confirm reservations or change dates.

The **international departure tax** on all foreigners leaving Thailand by air is B500; buy your voucher near the check-in desks at the airport. For advice on getting to the airport see the box below; for a list of accommodation within ten minutes' drive of the airport, see p.93.

Getting to other Asian countries

Bangkok is the regional hub for **flights to Indochina**, and many long-haul flights from Europe to Indochina involve a change of plane in Bangkok. However, if you plan to travel around Thailand before moving on to Laos,

---

Getting to the airport

The fastest, most expensive way of getting to the airport is by metered taxi, which can cost anything from B120 to B350 (plus B40 expressway toll), depending on where you are and how bad the traffic is. If you leave the downtown areas before 7am you can get to the airport in half an hour, but at other times you should set off at least an hour before you have to check in.

Every guest house and travel agent in Banglamphu, and many hotels elsewhere in the city, can book you onto one of the private minibuses to the airport. Those running from Banglamphu depart approximately every hour, day and night, and cost B60–80; though you'll get picked up from your accommodation, you should book yourself onto a minibus that leaves at least an hour and a half before check-in commences as it can take up to 45 minutes to pick up all passengers, after which there's the traffic to contend with.

The airport bus services that are so useful when arriving at Don Muang are less reliable on the outward journey, mainly because the traffic often makes it impossible for them to stick to their half-hourly schedules; at B100 it's not a risk worth taking.

As with in-bound trains, schedules for trains from Hualamphong to Don Muang are not helpfully spread throughout the day, but the service is cheap and fast if the timetable fits yours. A number of city buses run from the city to the airport and are detailed in the box on p.100; they are slow and crowded however.

Cambodia or Singapore, you may not have to return Bangkok as there are an increasing number of interesting inter-Asia flights from Thailand's **regional airports**, including Chiang Mai–Vientiane, Chiang Mai–Louang Phabang, Sukhothai–Siem Reap, Pattaya–Phnom Penh and Ko Samui–Singapore; for more on all these check the relevant accounts in the guide.

Most travellers who choose to make their way **overland from Thailand** to Laos, Cambodia or Malaysia do so slowly, stopping at various places in Thailand en route, but it is possible to make these overland trips in one fell swoop from Bangkok, though in most cases you'll need to spend a night somewhere on the way. To get **from Bangkok to Laos**, you have to take a train or bus to the border at Chiang Khong (see p.393), Nong Khai (see p.522), Nakhon Phanom (see p.531), Mukdahan (see p.536) or Chong Mek (see p.497). For transport **to Cambodia**, either take a bus from Bangkok to the east coast town of Trat and then follow the directions as described in the box on p.438, or take the train or bus from Bangkok to Aranyaprathet and then make the crossing to Poipet, as described on p.439. The easiest way of travelling from Bangkok **to Malaysia** is by train. There is currently one train a day from Bangkok's Hualamphong station to Butterworth (for Penang; 23hr), which costs about B1000 in a second-class sleeper. It's also possible to make onward train connections to Kuala Lumpur (for an extra B420) and Singapore (for an extra B900). A more convoluted option would be to take a bus from Bangkok's Southern Bus Terminal down to Hat Yai (14hr) and then change onto a bus or share-taxi to Penang (6hr); see Basics, p.23, for more.

All the **foreign embassies and consulates** in Bangkok are located in the downtown area; see "Listings", p.193, for details. Before heading off to the embassy, ring ahead to check on the opening hours (usually very limited) and documentation required. Entry formalities for Thailand's near neighbours (other than Malaysia) have undergone radical transformations over the past few years, and may well change again; for an overview of visa requirements for travel to Burma, Cambodia, Laos, Malaysia, Singapore and Vietnam see Basics, p.21–24.

Listings

Airport enquiries General enquiries ℡ 02/535 1111; international departures ℡ 02/535 1254 or 535 1386; international arrivals ℡ 02/535 1310, 535 1301 or 535 1149; domestic departures ℡ 02/535 1192; domestic arrivals ℡ 02/535 1253. **Airlines** Thai Airlines' main offices are at 485 Thanon Silom ℡ 02/234 3100–19, and at 6 Thanon Lan Luang near Democracy Monument ℡ 02/280 0060; the central Bangkok Airways office is at 1111 Thanon Ploenchit ℡ 02/254 2903; and Air Andaman is at 4th Floor, 87 Nailert Building, Unit 402a, Thanon Sukhumvit, ℡ 02/251 4905. International airlines with offices in Bangkok include Aeroflot, 7 Thanon Silom ℡ 02/233 6965; Air France, Unit 2002, 34 Vorwat Building, 849 Thanon Silom ℡ 02/635 1186–7; Air India, 1

Pacific Place, between sois 4 and 6, Thanon Sukhumvit ℡ 02/254 3280; Air Lanka, Charn Issara Tower, 942/34–35 Thanon Rama IV ℡ 02/236 4981; Air New Zealand/Ansett, Sirindhorn Building, Thanon Witthayu (Wireless Road) ℡ 02/254 5440; Biman Bangladesh Airlines, Chongkolnee Building, 56 Thanon Suriwong ℡ 02/235 7643; British Airways, 14th Floor, Abdullrahim Place, opposite Lumphini Park, 990 Thanon Rama IV ℡ 02/636 1747; Canadian Airlines, 6th Floor, Maneeya Centre, 518/5 Thanon Ploenchit ℡ 02/254 0960; Cathay Pacific, Ploenchit Tower, 898 Thanon Ploenchit ℡ 02/263 0616; China Airlines, Peninsula Plaza, 153 Thanon Rajdamri ℡ 02/253 4242–3; Egyptair, CP Tower, 313 Thanon Silom ℡ 02/231 0505–8; Emirates, 356/1 Thanon Vibhavadi

Rangsit ☎02/531 6585; Eva Air, 2nd Floor, Green Tower, Thanon Rama IV ☎02/367 3388; Finnair, Don Muang airport ☎02/535 2104; Garuda, Lumphini Tower, 1168/77 Thanon Rama IV ☎02/285 6470–3; Gulf Air, Maneeya Building, 518/5 Thanon Ploenchit ☎02/254 7931–4; Japan Airlines, 254/1 Thanon Rajadapisek ☎02/274 1401–9; KLM, 19th Floor, Thai Wah Tower 2, 21/133 Thanon Sathorn Thai ☎02/679 1100 extn 11; Korean Air, Kongboonma Building, 699 Thanon Silom ☎02/635 0465; Lao Aviation, Silom Plaza, Thanon Silom ☎02/237 6982; Lauda Air, Wall Street Tower, 33/37 Thanon Suriwong ☎02/233 2544; Lufthansa, Q-House, Soi 21, Thanon Sukhumvit ☎02/264 2400; Malaysia Airlines, 98–102 Thanon Suriwong ☎02/236 4705; Myanmar Airlines, 23rd Floor, Jewelry Trade Center Building, Unit H1, 919/298 Thanon Silom ☎02/630 0338; Northwest, 4th Floor, Peninsula Plaza, 153 Thanon Rajdamri ☎02/254 0790; Olympic Airways, 4th Floor, Charn Issara Tower, 942/133 Thanon Rama IV ☎02/237 6141; Pakistan International (PIA), 52 Thanon Suriwong ☎02/234 2961 6; Philippine Airlines, Chongkolnee Building, 56 Thanon Suriwong ☎02/233 2350–2; Qantas Airways, 14th Floor, Abdullrahim Place, opposite Lumphini Park, 990 Thanon Rama IV ☎02/636 1747; Royal Air Cambodge, 17th Floor, Two Pacific Place Building, Room 1706, 142 Thanon Sukhumvit ☎02/653 2261–6; Royal Nepal, 1/4 Thanon Convent ☎02/233 5957; Singapore Airlines, Silom Centre, 2 Thanon Silom ☎02/236 0440; Swissair, 21st Floor, Abdullrahim Place, opposite Lumphini Park, 990 Thanon Rama IV ☎02/636 2150; United Airlines, 14th Floor, Sirindhorn Building, 130 Thanon Witthayu ☎02/253 0558; Vietnam Airlines, 7th Floor, Ploenchit Center Building, Sukhumvit Soi 2 ☎02/656 9056–8.

American Express c/o Sea Tours, 128/88–92, 8th Floor, Phrayathai Plaza, 128 Thanon Phrayathai, Bangkok 10400 ☎02/216 5934–6. Amex credit-card and traveller's-cheque holders can use the office (Mon–Fri 8.30am–5.30pm, Sat 8.30am–noon) as a poste restante, but mail is only held for sixty days. To report lost cards or cheques call ☎02/273 0044 (cards, office hours), ☎02/273 5296 (traveller's cheques, office hours), or ☎02/273 0022 (after hours for both cards and cheques).

Car rental Avis ⊛www.avis.com; head office, 2/12 Thanon Witthayu (Wireless Road) ☎02/255 5300–4; also at Don Muang international airport ☎02/535 4052; the *Grand Hyatt Erawan Hotel*, 494 Thanon Rajdamri ☎02/254 1234; *Le Meridien Hotel*, 971 Thanon Ploenchit ☎02/253 0444; and the *Amari Airport Hotel* ☎02/566 1020–1. Budget ⊛www.budget.co.th; head office, 19.23 Building A, Royal City Avenue, Thanon Phetchaburi Mai ☎02/203 0250; and at *Comfort Suites Airport Hotel*, 88/107 Thanon Vibhavadi ☎02/973 3752. SMT Rent-A-Car (part of National) ✉smtcar@samart.co.th; head office ☎02/722 8487; and at *Amari Airport Hotel* (☎02/928 1525); plus numerous others on Sukhumvit and Ploenchit roads.

Cookery classes Nearly all the five-star hotels will arrange a Thai cookery class for guests if requested; the most famous is held at the *Oriental* hotel (☎02/437 6211), which mainly focuses on demonstrating culinary techniques and runs for four mornings a week; the Saturday-morning Benjarong Cooking Class at the *Dusit Thani* hotel (☎02/236 6400) takes a more hands-on approach, as does the *Nipa Thai* restaurant (☎02/254 0404 ext 4823), which runs one- to five-day cookery courses on demand, and regular fruit-carving lessons (daily 2–4pm) at the restaurant on the third floor of the Landmark Plaza, between sois 4 and 6 on Thanon Sukhumvit. *Mrs Balbir's* restaurant on Soi 11, Thanon Sukhumvit (☎02/651 0498) holds regular, inexpensive, classes in Thai cookery (Fri 10.30–11.30am) and Indian cookery (Tues 10.30am–noon).

Couriers DHL Worldwide, Grand Amarin Tower, Thanon Phetchaburi Mai ☎02/658 8000.

Embassies and consulates Australia, 37 Thanon Sathorn Thai ☎02/287 2680; Burma (Myanmar), 132 Thanon Sathorn Nua ☎02/233 2237; Cambodia, 185 Thanon Rajdamri (enter via Thanon Sarasin) ☎02/254 6630; Canada, Boonmitr Building, 138 Thanon Silom ☎02/237 4125; China, 57/2 Thanon Rajadapisek ☎02/245 7033; India, 46 Soi 23, Thanon Sukhumvit ☎02/258 0300; Indonesia, 600–602 Thanon Phetchaburi ☎02/252 3135–40; Ireland, either contact the UK embassy, or call the Irish embassy in Malaysia ☎001 60 3/2161 2963; Korea, 51 Soi 26, Thanon Sukhumvit ☎02/278 5118; Laos, 520 Ramkhamhaeng Soi 39 ☎02/539 6667–8, cxtn 103; Malaysia, 35 Thanon Sathorn Thai ☎02/287 3979; Nepal, 189 Soi 71, Thanon Sukhumvit ☎02/391 7240; Netherlands, 106 Thanon Witthayu (Wireless Road) ☎02/254 7701–5; New Zealand, 93 Thanon Witthayu ☎02/254 2530; Pakistan, 31

Soi 3, Thanon Sukhumvit ☎02/253 0288–90; Philippines, 760 Thanon Sukhumvit, opposite Soi 47 ☎02/259 0139–40; Singapore, 129 Thanon Sathorn Thai ☎02/286 2111; Sri Lanka, 75/84 Soi 21, Thanon Sukhumvit ☎02/261 1934–8; Vietnam, 83/1 Thanon Witthayu ☎02/251 5835–8; UK, 1031 Thanon Witthayu ☎02/253 0191–9; US, 20 Thanon Witthayu ☎02/205 4000.

Emergencies For all emergencies, either call the tourist police (free 24hr phoneline ☎1699), visit the Banglamphu Police Station at the west end of Thanon Khao San, or contact the Tourist Police Headquarters, 23rd Floor, 26/56 TPI Tower Building, Thanon Chantadmai, Tungmahamek, Sathorn ☎02/678 6800–9.

Exchange The airport exchange desk and those in the upmarket hotels are open 24hr; many other exchange desks stay open till 8pm, especially along Khao San, Sukhumvit and Silom. If you have a MasterCard/Cirrus or Visa debit or credit card, you can also withdraw cash from hundreds of ATMs around the city, at branches of the Bangkok Bank, the Bank of Ayudhaya, Thai Farmers Bank and Siam Commercial Bank.

Hospitals and clinics If you haven't picked up vaccinations and malaria advice in your home country, or if you need contraceptives or family planning advice, contact the Australian-run Travmin Bangkok Medical Centre, 8th Floor, Alma Link Building, next to the Central department store at 25 Soi Chitlom, Thanon Ploenchit (☎02/655 1024–5; outside clinic hours, call the same number for emergency contacts; B650 per consultation); there's a general clinic here, too. Most expats rate the private Bumrungrad Hospital, 33 Soi 3, Thanon Sukhumvit ☎02/253 0250, as the best and most comfortable in the city. Other recommended hospitals and clinics include Bangkok Adventist Hospital (aka Mission Hospital), 430 Thanon Phitsanulok ☎02/281 1422; Samitivej Sukhumvit Hospital, 133 Soi 49, Thanon Sukhumvit ☎02/392 0011–19; Bangkok Nursing Home Hospital (BNH), 9 Thanon Convent ☎02/632 0550; Bangkok Christian Hospital, 124 Thanon Silom ☎02/233 6981–9; Dental Polyclinic, 211–13 Thanon Phetchaburi Mai ☎02/314 5070; and Pirom Pesuj Eye Hospital, 117/1 Thanon Phrayathai ☎02/252 4141. For rabies advice and treatment, you can also go to the Queen Saovabha Memorial Institute (QSMI) attached to the Snake Farm on Thanon Henri Dunant (Mon–Fri 8.30–10.30am & noon–1pm; ☎02/252 0161).

Immigration office About 1km down Soi Suan Plu, off Thanon Sathorn Thai (Mon–Fri 8am–noon & 1–4pm; ☎02/287 3101–10). Visa extensions take about an hour.

Internet access Banglamphu is packed with internet cafés, in particular along Thanon Khao San and Soi Ram Bhuttri where almost every other business offers internet access; many guest houses offer have internet access too. Competition keeps prices very low, so this is the best area of the city for all cyber activities. The Ratchadamnoen Post Office on Banglamphu's Soi Damnoen Klang Neua (daily 8am–10pm) also has public Catnet internet booths (see p.59). Outside Banglamphu, mid-range and upmarket hotels also offer internet access, but at vastly inflated prices. Thanon Sukhumvit has a number of makeshift phone/internet offices, as well as several more formal and more clued-up internet cafés, including *Cybercafé*, 2nd Floor, Ploenchit Center, Soi 2, Thanon Sukhumvit (daily 10am–9.30pm), and Time Internet Centre on the second floor of Times Square, between sois 12 and 14 (daily 9am–midnight); the Soi Nana Post Office between sois 4 and 6 also has some Catnet internet terminals. Around Siam Square, try Bite Time, 7th Floor, Mah Boon Krong Shopping Centre (daily 11am–10pm); in the Silom area, head for Explorer on Patpong 1 (Mon–Fri & Sun 2pm–1am; Sat 2–10pm). There are also Catnet terminals at the post office counters inside Don Muang airport.

Language courses AUA (American University Alumni), 179 Thanon Rajdamri ☎02/252 8398, and Union Language School, CCT Building, 109 Thanon Suriwong ☎02/233 4482, run regular, recommended Thai language courses.

Laundries Nearly all guest houses and hotels offer same-day laundry services; if yours doesn't, either look for one that does, or use one of the two self-service laundries on Thanon Khao San.

Left luggage At Don Muang airport (international and domestic; B70 per day), Hualamphong train station (B10–30 per day; see p.96), and at most hotels and guest houses (B7–10 per day).

Libraries The National Library at the junction of Samsen and Sri Ayutthaya (Mon–Sat 9am–4.30pm) has a large collection of English-language books, as do AUA at 179 Thanon Rajdamri (Mon–Fri 8.30am–6pm, Sat 9am–1pm) and the British Council in Siam Square (Tues–Fri 10am–7pm, Sat 10am–5pm).

Mail The GPO is at 1160 Thanon Charoen Krung (New Road), a few hundred metres left of the exit for Wat Muang Kae express-boat stop. Poste restante can be collected here Mon–Fri 8am–8pm, Sat, Sun & holidays 8am–1pm; letters are kept for three months. The parcel-packing service at the GPO operates Mon–Fri 8am–4.30pm, Sat 9am–noon. If you're staying on or near Thanon Khao San in Banglamphu, it's more convenient to use the poste restante service at one of the two post offices in Banglamphu itself. The one closest to Khao San is Ratchadamnoen Post Office on the eastern stretch of Soi Damnoen Klang Neua (Mon–Fri 8.30am–5pm, Sat 9am–noon); letters are kept for two months and should be addressed c/o Poste Restante, Ratchadamnoen PO, Bangkok 10002. Banglamphu's other post office is on Soi Sibsam Hang, just west of Wat Bowoniwes (Mon–Fri 8.30am–5pm, Sat 9am–noon); its poste restante address is Banglamphubon PO, Bangkok 10203. You can also send and receive faxes there on ☎02/281 1579. Many of the other non-official post and packing services on Thanon Khao San also offer poste restante, but their systems tend to be chaotic and unreliable; the best option is to use your guest house or hotel fax number. In the Thanon Sukhumvit vicinity, poste restante can be sent to the Thanon Sukhumvit post office between sois 4 and 6, c/o Nana PO, Thanon Sukhumvit, Bangkok 10112.

Massage Traditional Thai massage sessions and courses are held at Wat Po (see p.127), and at dozens of guest houses in Banglamphu.

Meditation centres and retreats The main centres are the House of Dhamma Insight Meditation Centre, Wat Mahathat; and World Fellowship of Buddhists; see Basics, p.70 for details.

Pharmacies There are English-speaking staff at most of the capital's pharmacies, including the numerous branches of Boots the Chemist (they have outlets on Thanon Khao San and Thanon Sukhumvit).

Prison visits A number of farangs are serving long sentences in Nonthaburi Jail, and they appreciate visits from other farangs. When visiting, you need to know the name of the prisoner and which block number they're in; staff at the British embassy keep this information for many nationalities, and guest-house noticeboards often have more details as well as accounts from recent prison visitors. You also need to check the relevant visiting hours for the person you want to visit – many guest-house noticeboards carry this information. Prisoners are only allowed one visitor at a time, and visitors must look respectable, which means no shorts or singlets; all visitors must show their passports at the jail. You can't bring any gifts with you, but you can buy some things at the prison shop – cigarettes and fresh fruit usually go down well. For directions to Nonthaburi, see p.163; at the Nonthaburi pier, take the road straight ahead, and then turn first left for the prison.

Telephones The least expensive places to make international calls are the public telephone offices in or adjacent to post offices. The largest and most convenient of these is in the compound of the GPO on Thanon Charoen Krung (New Road), which is open 24hr and also offers a fax service and a free collect-call service (see above for location details). The post offices at Hualamphong station, on Thanon Sukhumvit (see above) and on Soi Sibsam Hang in Banglamphu (see above) also have international telephone offices attached, but these close at 8pm; the Ratchadamnoen phone office on Soi Damnoen Klang Neua opens daily 8am–10pm. Many private telephone offices claim that they offer the same rates as the public phone offices, but they are almost always at least ten percent more expensive.

Travel agents Diethelm Travel is a huge, recommended agent with branches all over Thailand and Indochina; in Bangkok they're at 12th Floor, Kian Gwan Building II, 140/1 Thanon Witthayu (Wireless Road) ☎02/255 9200, ℗255 9192, ⓦwww.diethelm-travel.com. They sell tickets for domestic and international flights and tours, and are particularly good on travel to Burma, Cambodia, Laos and Vietnam. VC Travel and Tour, Mezzanine Floor, Hualamphong Railway Station ☎02/613 6725, ℗613 6727, are a friendly and efficient travel agent who also provide an accommodation-booking service and sell train tickets at no commission. Also recommended are: Educational Travel Centre (ETC), *Royal Hotel*, Room 318, 2 Thanon Rajdamnoen Klang ☎02/224 0043, ℗622 1420, ⓔFTC@mozart.inet.co.th, also at 180 Thanon Khao San ☎282 2958 and 5/3 Soi Ngam Duphli ☎287 1477 or 286 9424; Exotissimo, 755 Thanon Silom ☎02/223 1510 and 21/17 Soi 4, Thanon Sukhumvit ☎02/253 5240, ⓔexotvlth@linethai.co.th; NS Tours, c/o *Vieng Thai Hotel*, Soi Ram Bhuttri, Banglamphu ☎02/629 0509; and STA Travel, 14th Floor, Wall Street Tower, 33 Thanon Suriwong ☎02/236 0262.

Travel details

Trains

Bangkok Hualamphong Station to: Aranyaprathet (2 daily; 5–6hr); Ayutthaya (20 daily; 1hr 30min); Butterworth (Malaysia; 1 daily; 23hr); Chiang Mai (7 daily; 11hr 10min–14hr 15min); Chumphon (9 daily; 6hr 45min–8hr 20min); Don Muang airport (30 daily; 50min); Hat Yai (5 daily; 14–16hr); Hua Hin (9 daily; 3–4hr); Khon Kaen (5 daily; 7hr 30min–10hr 30min); Khorat (9 daily; 4–5hr); Lampang (7 daily; 11hr); Lamphun (6 daily; 13hr); Lopburi (9 daily; 2hr 15min–3hr); Nakhon Pathom (14 daily; 1hr 20min); Nakhon Si Thammarat (2 daily; 15hr); Nong Khai (3 daily; 11–12hr); Pak Chong (for Khao Yai National Park; 7 daily; 3hr 30min); Pattaya (1 daily; 3hr 45min); Phatthalung (5 daily; 12–15hr); Phitsanulok (9 daily; 5hr 15min–9hr 30min); Si Racha (1 daily; 3hr 15min); Surat Thani (10 daily; 9–12hr); Surin (10 daily; 7–10hr); Trang (2 daily; 16hr); Ubon Ratchathani (6 daily; 10hr 20min–13hr 15min); Udon Thani (5 daily; 10hr); Yala (4 daily; 15–20hr).

Bangkok Noi Station to: Hua Hin (2 daily; 4hr–4hr 30min); Kanchanaburi (2 daily; 2hr 40min); Nakhon Pathom (3 daily; 1hr 10min); Nam Tok (2 daily; 4hr 35min).

Buses

Eastern Bus Terminal to: Ban Phe (for Ko Samet; 12 daily; 3hr); Chanthaburi (18 daily; 5–7hr); Pattaya (every 40min; 2hr 30min); Rayong (every 15min; 2hr 30min); Si Racha (for Ko Si Chang; every 30min; 2–3hr); Trat (for Ko Chang; 21 daily; 6–8hr).

Northern Bus Terminal to: Ayutthaya (every 15min; 2hr); Chaiyaphum (hourly; 6hr); Chiang Mai (19 daily; 10–11hr); Chiang Rai (16 daily; 12hr); Khon Kaen (23 daily; 6–7hr); Khorat (every 15min; 3–4hr); Lampang (10 daily; 8hr); Loei (18 daily; 10hr); Lopburi (every 15min; 3hr); Mae Hong Son (2 daily; 18hr); Mae Sai (8 daily; 13hr); Mae Sot (10 daily; 8hr 30min); Mukdahan (13 daily; 11hr); Nakhon Phanom (17 daily; 12hr); Nan (18 daily; 13hr); Nong Khai (20 daily; 10hr); Pak Chong (for Khao Yai National Park; every 15min; 3hr); Phitsanulok (up to 19 daily; 5–6hr); Sakhon Nakhon (11 daily; 11hr); Sri Chiangmai (4 daily; 12hr); Sukhothai (17 daily; 6–7hr); Surin (up to 20 daily; 8–9hr); Tak (13 daily; 7hr); Ubon Ratchathani (19 daily; 10–12hr); Udon Thani (every 15min; 9hr).

Southern Bus Terminal to: Chumphon (9 daily; 7hr); Damnoen Saduak (every 20min; 2hr); Hat Yai (every 30min; 13hr); Hua Hin (every 25min; 3–3hr 30min); Kanchanaburi (every 15min; 2–3hr); Ko Samui (3 daily; 15hr); Krabi (9 daily; 12–14hr); Nakhon Pathom (every 10min; 40min–1hr 20min); Nakhon Si Thammarat (10 daily; 12hr); Narathiwat (3 daily; 17hr); Pattani (3 daily; 16hr); Phang Nga (4 daily; 11hr–12hr 30min); Phatthalung (4 daily; 13hr); Phuket (at least 10 daily; 14–16hr); Ranong (7 daily; 9–10hr); Satun (2 daily; 16hr); Sungai Kolok (3 daily; 18–20hr); Surat Thani (7 daily; 11hr); Takua Pa (10 daily; 12–13hr); Trang (8 daily; 14hr); Yala (4 daily; 19hr).

Flights

Bangkok to: Buriram (1 daily; 1hr 10min); Chiang Mai (10–13 daily; 1hr); Chiang Rai (5 daily; 1hr 20min); Hat Yai (6 daily; 1hr 25min); Hua Hin (1 daily; 30min); Khon Kaen (4 daily; 55min); Khorat (2 daily; 40min); Ko Samui (9–14 daily; 1hr 20min); Lampang (2 daily; 2hr); Nakhon Phanom (4 weekly; 1hr 10min); Nakhon Si Thammarat (1–2 daily; 1hr 15min); Nan (3 weekly; 2hr); Narathiwat (1 daily; 3hr); Phitsanulok (5 daily; 55min); Phrae (3 weekly; 1hr 20min); Phuket (14 daily; 1hr 20min); Ranong (4 weekly; 1hr 20min); Sakhon Nakhon (4 weekly; 1hr 5min–2hr 10min); Sukhothai (1–2 daily; 1hr); Surat Thani (2 daily; 1hr 10min); Trang (1–2 daily; 1hr 30min); Ubon Ratchathani (2 daily; 1hr 5min); Udon Thani (3–4 daily; 1hr); U-Tapao (for Pattaya; 1–2 daily; 20min).

2

The central plains

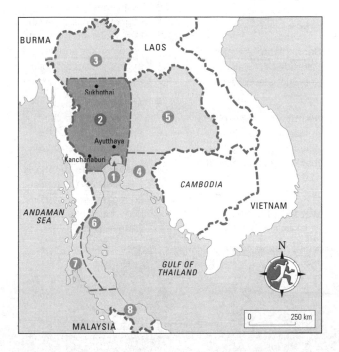

CHAPTER 2

Highlights

✳ **Kanchanaburi** – Stay in a raft house on the River Kwai. **p.208**

✳ **The Death Railway** – Chug through the scenic River Kwai valley and then visit the **Hellfire Pass Museum**, a moving testimony to the World War II POWs who constructed the railway. **p.223** and **p.227**

✳ **Sangkhlaburi** – Peaceful lakeside backwater near the Burmese border. **p.229**

✳ **Ayutthaya** – Atmospheric ruined temples, three fine museums and laid-back guest houses in the broad, grassy spaces of the former capital. **p.238**.

✳ **Wat Phra Phutthabat** – A vibrant introduction to Thai religion at the Temple of the Buddha's Footprint. **p.251**

✳ **Phitsanulok Folklore Museum** – A fascinating look at traditional rural life, complete with reconstructed village homes. **p.257**

✳ **Sukhothai** – A former capital of Thailand, with lots of elegant thirteenth-century ruins and several exceptional guest houses. **p.259**

✳ **Multi-ethnic Mae Sot** – Alluring mix of cultures in this small town on the Burmese border. **p.282**

✳ **Trekking from Umphang** – Remote and untouristed region with waterfalls, river-rafting and Karen villages. **p.285**

2

The central plains

North and west of the capital, the unwieldy urban mass of Greater Bangkok peters out into the vast, well-watered **central plains**, a region that for centuries has grown the bulk of the nation's food and been a tantalizing temptation for neighbouring power-mongers. The most densely populated region of Thailand, with sizeable towns sprinkled among patchworks of paddy and sugar-cane fields, the plains are fundamental to Thailand's agricultural economy. Its rivers are the key to this area's fecundity, especially the Nan and the Ping, whose waters flow from the Chiang Mai hills to irrigate the northern plains before merging to form the Chao Phraya, which meanders slowly south through Bangkok and out into the Gulf of Thailand.

West of Bangkok, beyond the extraordinary religious site of **Nakhon Pathom**, the riverside town of **Kanchanaburi** has long attracted visitors to the notorious Bridge over the River Kwai and is now well established as a budget-travellers' hangout, mainly because of its unique and unpretentious raft-house accommodation. Few tourists venture further west except as passengers on the remaining stretch of the **Death Railway** – the most tangible wartime reminder of all – but the remote and tiny hilltop town of **Sangkhlaburi** holds enough understated allure to make the extra kilometres worthwhile.

Accommodation prices

Throughout this guide, guest houses, hotels and bungalows have been categorized according to the price codes given below. These categories represent the minimum you can expect to pay in the high season (roughly July, Aug & Nov–Feb) for a double room. If travelling on your own, expect to pay anything between sixty and one hundred percent of the rates quoted for a double room. Wherever a price range is indicated, this means that the establishment offers rooms with varying facilities – as explained in the write-up. Wherever an establishment also offers dormitory beds, the prices of these beds are given in the text, instead of being indicated by price code.

Remember that the top-whack hotels will add seven percent tax and a ten percent service charge to your bill – the price codes below are based on net rates after taxes have been added.

❶ under B150
❷ B150–250
❸ B250–400
❹ B400–600
❺ B600–900
❻ B900–1200
❼ B1200–1800
❽ B1800–3000
❾ B3000+

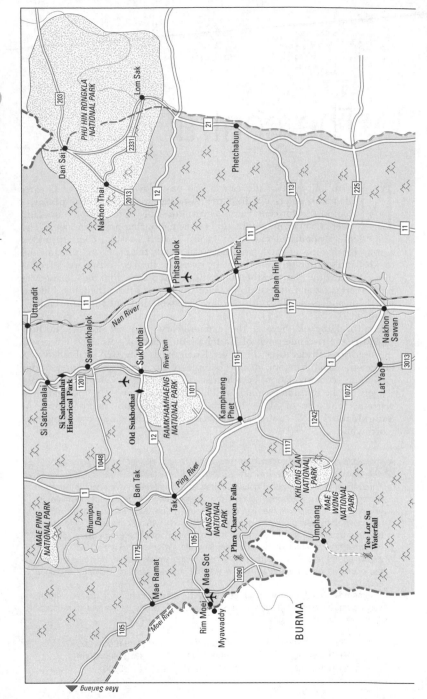

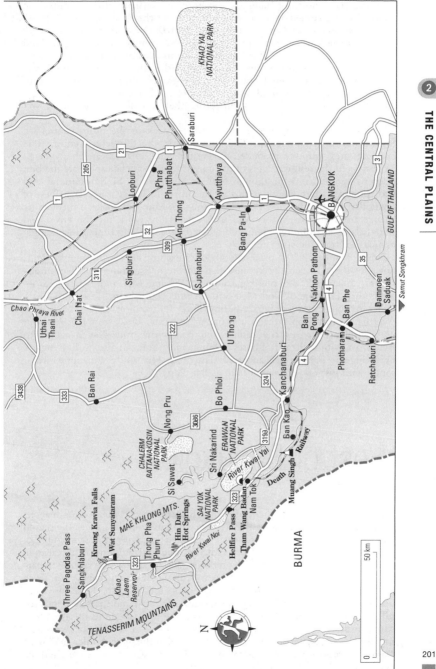

KHAO YAI
NATIONAL PARK

Saraburi

21
205
Lopburi
Phra
Phutthabat
1
1
Ayutthaya
Bang Pa-In
BANGKOK
GULF OF THAILAND
3

Ang Thong
32
309
Singburi
Suphanburi
35

311
Damnoen
Saduak
Samut Songkhram

Chao Phraya River
Chai Nat
Nakhon Pathom
Ban Phe
4

Uthai
Thani
322
U Thong
Ban
Pong
Photharam
Ratchaburi

3438
333
Ban Rai
Nong Pru
Bo Phloi
324
Kanchanaburi
4

3006
ERAWAN
NATIONAL
PARK

CHALERM
RATTANAKOSIN
NATIONAL
PARK
Sri Nakarind
River Kwai Yai
Ban Kao
3199

Kraeng Kravia Falls
Si Sawat
323
Muang Singh
Railway

Wat Sunyataram
SAI YOK
NATIONAL
PARK
Tham Wang Badan
Death

MAE KHLONG MTS.
Hin Dat
Hot Springs
Nam Tok

Three Pagodas Pass
Thong Pha
Phum
Hellfire Pass
BURMA

Sangkhlaburi
323
River Kwai Noi

Khao
Laem
Reservoir

TENASSERIM MOUNTAINS

N

50 km

0

On the plains north of Bangkok, the historic heartland of the country, the major sites are ruined ancient cities which cover the spectrum of Thailand's art and architecture. Closest to Bangkok, **Ayutthaya** served as the country's capital for the four centuries prior to the 1782 foundation of Bangkok, and its ruins evoke an era of courtly sophistication. A short hop north of here, the remnants of **Lopburi** hark back to an earlier time when the predominantly Hindu Khmers held sway over this region, building a constellation of stone temples across central and northeastern Thailand and introducing a complex grammar of sacred architecture that still dictates aspects of wat design today.

A separate nucleus of sites in the northern neck of the plains centres on **Sukhothai**, birthplace of the Thai kingdom in the thirteenth century. The buildings and sculpture produced during the Sukhothai era are the acme of Thai art, and the restored ruins of the country's first official capital are the best place to appreciate them, though two satellite cities – **Si Satchanalai** and **Kamphaeng Phet** – provide further incentives to linger in the area. West of Sukhothai, on the Burmese border, the town of **Mae Sot** makes a therapeutic change from ancient history and is the departure point for the rivers and waterfalls of **Umphang**, a remote border region that's becoming increasingly popular for trekking and rafting.

Chiang Mai (see p.301) makes an obvious next stop after exploring the sights north of Bangkok, chiefly because the Northern Rail Line makes **connections** painless. It's also possible to fly to Chiang Mai and Bangkok from Sukhothai, Phitsanulok and Mae Sot. Or you could branch east into Isaan, either by bus from Lopburi, Sukhothai or Phitsanulok, or by train from Ayutthaya. Most people treat Kanchanaburi as a mini-break from Bangkok, but it's possible to bypass the capital and cut across from Kanchanaburi to Ayutthaya, with a change of buses at Suphanburi. You can also avoid Bangkok by taking the train from Kanchanaburi to Hua Hin and destinations further south, with just one change of train at Ban Pong.

West of Bangkok

Although the enormous chedi of **Nakhon Pathom** and the floating markets of **Damnoen Saduak** are easily seen in a day-trip from the capital, the region west of Bangkok really merits a more extended stay, with at least a couple of nights spent beside the River Kwai in **Kanchanaburi**. All tourist itineraries in this predominantly budget-traveller territory are dictated by the rivers – in particular the Kwai Noi, route of the Death Railway. At Kanchanaburi you reach the outer range of package tours from Bangkok; following the Kwai Noi to its headwaters at **Sangkhlaburi** takes you into a forested and sparsely populated hill region that twenty years ago was considered too dangerous to visit. These days it makes an attractive, unhyped retreat worth a stay of a day or two, offering the possibility of a side trip to the nearby Burmese border at **Three Pagodas Pass**, as well as visits to nearby Mon and Karen settlements and the chance to trek in a relatively uncharted area.

A stupa is born

One of the more colourful explanations of the origin of the Buddhist **stupa** – chedi in Thai – comes from a legend describing the death of the Buddha. Anxious about how to spread the Buddha's teachings after his death, one of his disciples asked for a symbol of the Dharma philosophy. Famously lacking in material possessions, the Buddha assembled his worldly goods – a teaching stick, a begging bowl and a length of cloth – and constructed the stupa shape using the folded cloth as the base, the inverted bowl as the central dome and the stick as the spire.

Upon the Buddha's death, disciples from all over Asia laid claim to his **relics**, burying many of them in specially constructed stupa structures. In Thailand, the temples containing such chedis were given the title **Wat Phra Mahathat** (Temple of the Great Relic) and each royal city had one – today you'll find a Wat Phra Mahathat in Ayutthaya, Lopburi, Phetchaburi, Phitsanulok, Sukhothai, Nakhon Si Thammarat and Bangkok, all enjoying a special status, although the presence of a genuine piece of the Buddha in each is open to question.

Stupa design has undergone many changes since the Buddha's makeshift example, and there are chedis in Thailand reflecting the architectural style of every major historical period. The **Sukhothai** chedi (thirteenth to fifteenth centuries), for example, is generally an elegant reworking of the original Sri Lankan model: early ones are bell-shaped (the bell symbolizing the ringing out of the Buddha's teachings), while the later, slimmer versions evoke the contours of a lotus bud. **Ayutthayan** architects (fourteenth to eighteenth centuries) owed more to the Khmers, elongating their chedis and resting them on a higher square platform, stepped and solid. Meanwhile, the independent **Lanna** kingdom (thirteenth to sixteenth centuries) of northern Thailand built some stupas to a squat pyramidal design that harked back to the seventh century, and other more rotund ones that drew on Burmese influences.

Contemporary chedi-builders have tended to combine historical features at will, but most still pay some heed to the traditional **symbolism** of each stupa component. In theory, the base or platform of the chedi structure should be divided into three layers to represent hell, earth, and heaven. The dome usually supports the cube-shaped reliquary, known as a *harmika* after the Sanskrit term for the Buddha's seat of meditation. Crowning the structure, the "umbrella" spire is graded into 33 rings, one for each of the 33 Buddhist heavens.

Over the centuries, Thailand's chedis have been used to house the ashes of kings and important monks and, in the last two hundred years or so, as reliquaries and memorials for anyone who can afford to have one erected.

up to the **south viharn** are a three-dimensional replica of the original chedi with Khmer prang (east side) and a model of the venerated chedi at Nakhon Si Thammarat (west side). The **west viharn** houses two reclining Buddhas: a sturdy, nine-metre-long figure in the outer chamber and a more delicate por trayal in the inner one.

The museums

There are two museums within the chedi compound and, confusingly, both call themselves **Phra Pathom Museum**. The newer, more formal setup is clearly signposted from the bottom of the chedi's south staircase (Wed–Sun 9am–noon & 1–4pm; B30). It displays a good collection of Dvaravati-era (sixth to eleventh centuries) artefacts excavated nearby, including Wheels of Law – an emblem introduced by Theravada Buddhists before naturalistic images were permitted – and Buddha statuary with the U-shaped robe and thick facial features characteristic of Dvaravati sculpture.

For a broader, more contemporary overview, hunt out the other magpie's nest of a collection, which is halfway up the steps near the east viharn (Wed–Sun 9am–noon & 1–4pm; free). More a curiosity shop than a museum, the small room is an Aladdin's cave of Buddhist amulets, seashells, gold and silver needles, Chinese ceramics, Thai musical instruments, world coins and banknotes, gems and ancient statues.

Sanam Chan Palace

A ten-minute walk west of the chedi along Thanon Rajdamnoen takes you through a large park to the **Sanam Chan Palace** complex. Built as the country retreat of Rama VI in 1907, the palace and pavilions were designed to blend Western and Eastern styles. Several of the elegant wooden structures still stand, complete with graceful raised walkways and breezy verandas. The main palace building has been converted into local government offices, but in one of the new two-storey buildings nearby is a small exhibition displaying photos of Rama Vl and some of his personal effects. In the grounds, Rama VI erected a memorial statue of his favourite dog and a small shrine to the Hindu god Ganesh.

Practicalities

Nakhon Pathom's sights only merit half a day, and at any rate **accommodation** here is no great shakes. If you have to stay the night, probably the quietest of the budget places is *Mitrsampant Hotel* (☎034/242422; ❷), on the corner opposite the west gate of the chedi compound at the Lang Phra/Rajdamnoen intersection, which has fan-cooled rooms and showers. Rooms at the *Mit Thawon* (☎034/243115; ❷), next to the train station, are similarly priced – but don't take the one next to the noisy generator. Thanon Rajvithee, which starts at the southwestern corner of the chedi compound, leads to the unbearably noisy *Muang Thong* and, further along, two much more comfortable hotels: *Nakorn Inn Hotel* (☎034/251152, ℱ254998; ❺) is the town's best, while *Whale Hotel* (☎034/251020, ℱ253864; ❹–❻), down Soi 19 and signposted from the main road (about ten minutes' walk from the chedi), offers good-value mid-range rooms with air-con and TV, plus a disco.

Both the posh hotels have **restaurants** – the *Whale* does hearty American breakfasts as well as Asian and continental versions – but for inexpensive Thai and Chinese dishes head for either *Thai Food* or *Hasang*, both located on Thanon Phraya Gong just south across the khlong from the train station, on the left. Or try one of the garden restaurants along Thanon Rajdamnoen, which runs west from the chedi's west gate. Night-time foodstalls next to the *Muang Thong Hotel* specialize in noodle broth and chilli-hot curries, and during the day the market in front of the station serves up the usual takeaway goodies, including reputedly the tastiest *khao laam* (bamboo cylinders filled with steamed rice and coconut) in Thailand. Alternatively, buy noodles or fried rice from one of the vendors who set up in the chedi compound, and eat out under the trees.

You can **change money** at the exchange booth (open banking hours only) which is one block south of the train station on the road to the chedi, beside the bridge over the khlong. If you're just stopping off for a few hours, leave your **luggage** in the controller's office at the train station (no charge).

Damnoen Saduak floating markets

To get an idea of what shopping in Bangkok used to be like before all the canals were tarmacked over, make an early-morning trip to the **floating markets** (*talat khlong*) of **DAMNOEN SADUAK**, 60km south of Nakhon Pathom. Vineyards and orchards here back onto a labyrinth of narrow canals thick with paddle-boats overflowing with fresh fruit and vegetables: local women ply these waterways every morning between 6 and 11am, selling their produce to each other and to the residents of weatherworn homes built on stilts along the banks. Many of the women wear the deep-blue jacket and high-topped straw hat traditionally favoured by Thai farmers. It's all richly atmospheric, which naturally makes it a big draw for tour groups – but you can avoid the crowds if you leave before they arrive, at about 9am.

The target for most groups is the main **Talat Khlong Ton Kem**, 2km west of the tiny town centre at the intersection of Khlong Damnoen Saduak and Khlong Thong Lang. Many of the wooden houses here have been expanded and converted into warehouse-style souvenir shops and tourist restaurants, diverting trade away from the khlong vendors and into the hands of large commercial enterprises. But, for the moment at least, the traditional water trade continues, and the two bridges between Ton Kem and **Talat Khlong Hia Kui** (a little further south down Khlong Thong Lang) make rewarding and unobtrusive vantage points. Touts invariably congregate at the Ton Kem pier to hassle you into taking a **boat trip** around the khlong network (asking an hourly rate of anything from between B50 per person to B300 for the whole boat) and while this may be worth it to get to the less accessible **Talat Khlong Khun Phitak** to the south, there are distinct disadvantages in being propelled between markets at top speed in a noisy motorized boat. For a less hectic and more sensitive look at the markets, you can explore the walkways beside the canals.

Practicalities

One of the reasons why Damnoen Saduak hasn't yet been totally ruined is that it's a 109-kilometre **bus** journey from Bangkok. To reach the market in good time, you have to catch one of the earliest buses from Bangkok's Southern Bus Terminal: the first air-con buses leave at 6am and 6.30am and take two hours, the first non-air-con bus (#78) leaves at 6.20am and takes half an hour longer. Buses and songthaews from Nakhon Pathom pick up passengers outside the *Nakorn Inn Hotel* on Thanon Rajvithee and take about one hour to get here; the first one leaves at around 6am. From Kanchanaburi, take bus #461 to **Ban Phe** (every 15min from 5.25am; 1hr 15min), then change to the #78. Many tours from Bangkok combine the floating markets with a day-trip to Phetchaburi (p.545), about 40km further south: to get from Damnoen Saduak to Phetchaburi by public bus, you have to change at **Samut Songkhram**. To get to Damnoen Saduak from Phetchaburi or any points further south, catch any Bangkok-bound bus and, depending on which route it takes, change either at Samut Songkhram or at the **Photharam** intersection.

Damnoen Saduak's **bus terminal** is just north of Thanarat Bridge and Khlong Damnoen Saduak on the main Bangkok/Nakhon Pathom–Samut Songkhram road, Highway 325. Songthaews cover the 2km to Ton Kem, but walk if you've got the time: a walkway follows the canal, which you can get down to from Thanarat Bridge, or you can cross the bridge and take the road to the right (west), Thanon Sukhaphiban 1 (unsignposted), through the orchards. Be warned, however, that the drivers on the earliest buses from

Bangkok sometimes do not terminate at the bus station near Thanarat Bridge but instead cross the bridge and then drop unsuspecting tourists a few hundred metres down Thanon Sukhaphiban 1, into the arms of a local boat operator. If you're happy to join a boat tour straight away this is not necessarily a problem, but it can be difficult to extricate yourself from this cunning ruse; to avoid this, get off with the rest of the Thai passengers at the bus station near the bridge.

The best way to see the markets is to **stay overnight** in Damnoen Saduak and get up before the buses and coach tours from Bangkok arrive – and, if possible, explore the khlongside walkways the evening before when you can wander at leisure without the crowds. The only **accommodation** in town is at the Filipino-managed *Little Bird Hotel*, also known as *Noknoi* (T032/254382; ❷–❸), whose sign is clearly visible from the main road and Thanarat Bridge. Rooms here are good value: enormous, clean and all with en-suite bathrooms, and there's air-conditioning if you want it.

Kanchanaburi

Set in a landscape of limestone hills 65km northwest of Nakhon Pathom and 120km from Bangkok, the provincial capital of **KANCHANABURI** unfurls along the northeast bank of the River Kwai Yai to reveal its most attractive feature: a burgeoning number of raft houses and riverside guest houses, any of which makes a wonderful place to unwind for a few days. With most of these catering mainly for modest budgets, Kanchanaburi has blossomed into a popular independent travellers' centre. There's plenty to occupy several days here – the surrounding area offers numerous caves, wats and historical sites to explore, as well as the famous seven-tiered Erawan waterfall (see p.221), some of them easily reached by bicycle; organized treks, rafting trips and elephant rides to destinations further afield are also a major feature.

Kanchanaburi's more official attractions, however, relate to its World War II role as a POW camp and base for construction work on the Thailand–Burma Railway. Day-trippers and tour groups descend in their hundreds on the infamous **Bridge over the River Kwai**, the symbol of Japanese atrocities in the region – though the town's main **war museum** and **cemeteries** are much more moving. Many veterans returning to visit the graves of their wartime comrades are understandably resentful that others have in some cases insensitively exploited the POW experience – the commercial paraphernalia surrounding the Bridge is a case in point. On the other hand, the town's JEATH War Museum provides a shockingly instructive account of a period not publicly documented elsewhere.

Kanchanaburi's history, of course, begins a lot further back – in the Stone Age – when small communities established themselves in the fertile river basin near the present-day town, an era documented in the **Ban Kao Museum** 35km west of town (see p.220). Several millennia later, the people of this area probably paid allegiance to the Mon kings of Nakhon Pathom and subsequently to the Khmers, whose sphere of influence spread north from what is now Cambodia – the temple sanctuary at **Muang Singh**, not far from Ban Kao, stands as a fine example of twelfth-century Khmer architecture. Over the next five hundred years, Kanchanaburi's proximity to Thailand's aggressive Burmese neighbours gained it kudos as a key border stronghold; Rama III built walls around the town in 1743, and a small chunk of these can still be seen towards the western end of Thanon Lak Muang.

Arrival and information

Trains from Bangkok Noi or Nakhon Pathom are the most scenic way to get to Kanchanaburi, if not always the most convenient – there are only two trains daily in each direction. The State Railway also runs special day-trips from Bangkok's Hualamphong station which include short stops at Nakhon Pathom, the Bridge over the River Kwai and Nam Tok, the terminus of the line (Sat, Sun & holidays only; advance booking is essential, see p.189). Coming from Hua Hin, Chumphon and points further south, take the train to Ban Pong and then change onto a Kanchanaburi-bound train (or bus). When moving on to the south, the best option is to take a train or bus to Nakhon Pathom and change onto a night train headed for Chumphon, Surat Thani or beyond, but you must book tickets for these sleepers at least one day in advance, either at Kanchanaburi train station or through a tour operator. The main **Kanchanaburi train station** (☎ 034/511285) is on Thanon Saeng Chuto, about 2km north of the town centre – convenient for riverside lodgings along Soi Rong Heeb Oil and Thanon Maenam Kwai, but a bit of a hike from Thanon Song Kwai accommodation. Thanon Maenam Kwai guest houses usually send a free minibus to pick up passengers who arrive by train. However, if you're staying at *Bamboo House* or the *Felix River Kwai*, or are doing a day-trip and want to see the bridge, get off at the next stop instead, which is **River Kwai Bridge train station**, seven minutes further on and located just in front of the Bridge, on the east bank of the river.

Faster than the train are the various types of air-conditioned **buses** from Bangkok's Southern Bus Terminal; the blue, first-class, #81 bus is the fastest (every 15min; 2hr); the orange second-class air-con bus, also #81, runs every twenty minutes and takes about twenty minutes longer, with some going via Nakhon Pathom. Slower regular bus services (#81; every 15min; 3hr 30min) stop at Nakhon Pathom and several smaller towns en route. From Lopburi, Ayutthaya (for trains from Chiang Mai), or points further north, you'll have to return to Bangkok or change buses at **Suphanburi** (#411; every 20min; 2hr), about 90km north of Kanchanaburi. The Suphanburi route is quite workable in reverse if you're heading north to Ayutthaya and/or Chiang Mai. Arriving at the **bus station** (☎ 034/511182) at the southern edge of the town centre, it's a five-minute walk around the corner to the TAT office, and a ten- to twenty-minute walk, B15 motorbike-taxi ride or B40 samlor ride down Thanon Lak Muang to the raft houses off Thanon Song Kwai or a B40, ten-minute samlor ride to the Soi Rong Heeb Oil and Thanon Maenam Kwai guest houses. If you're coming from Bangkok, the speediest transport of all is to take one of the **tourist minibuses** from Thanon Khao San – they take two hours door to door and should drop passengers at their chosen guest house, but be prepared for a scarily fast ride at times. The same minivans make the return trip to Thanon Khao San every afternoon and can be booked through almost any guest house or tour operator in Kanchanaburi.

The **TAT** office (daily 8.30am–4.30pm; ☎ 034/511200) is a few hundred metres south of the bus station on Thanon Saeng Chuto and keeps up-to-date bus and train timetables.

Town transport

Samlor and **tuk-tuk** drivers armed with sheaves of guest-house cards always meet the trains and buses, so you'll have no problem finding a ride, though getting to the guest house of your choice may take some firm negotiation. As in

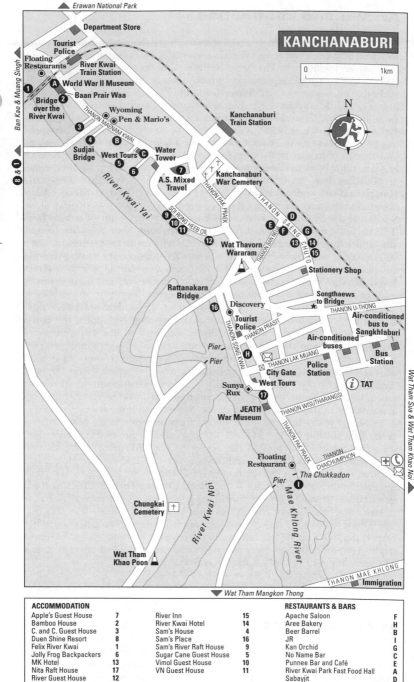

KANCHANABURI

0   1km

Erawan National Park

Department Store

Tourist
Police

Floating
Restaurants

River Kwai
Train Station

A World War II Museum

Baan Prair Waa

2

Bridge
over the
River Kwai

3

Wyoming

B Pen & Mario's

Kanchanaburi
Train Station

4

Sudjai
Bridge

West Tours **C**

5

6

Water
Tower

7

A.S. Mixed
Travel

Kanchanaburi
War Cemetery

THANON MAENAM KWAI

River Kwai Yai

THANON PAK PRAEK

SOI RONG HEEB OIL

9

10

11

12

Wat Thavorn
Wararam

THANON BAN NUA

THANON SAENG CHUTO

D

E

F

G

13

14

15

Stationery Shop

Rattanakarn
Bridge

16

Discovery

Tourist
Police

Songthaews
to Bridge

THANON U-THONG

Air-conditioned
bus to
Sangkhlaburi

THANON SONG KWAI

THANON PRASIT

Air-conditioned
buses

Bus
Station

Pier

Pier

H

THANON LAK MUANG

City Gate

Police
Station

i TAT

West Tours

Sunya
Rux

17

JEATH
War Museum

THANON WISUTHARANGSI

Floating
Restaurant

THANON PAK PRAEK

THANON
CHAICHUMPHON

Tha Chukkadon

Pier

I

Mae Khlong River

Chungkai
Cemetery

River Kwai Noi

Wat Tham
Khao Poon

THANON MAE KHLONG

Immigration

Wat Tham Mangkon Thong

Ban Kao & Muang Singh

1 & 8

Wat Tham Sua & Wat Tham Khao Noi

ACCOMMODATION				RESTAURANTS & BARS	
Apple's Guest House	7	River Inn	15	Apache Saloon	F
Bamboo House	2	River Kwai Hotel	14	Aree Bakery	H
C. and C. Guest House	3	Sam's House	4	Beer Barrel	B
Duen Shine Resort	8	Sam's Place	16	JR	I
Felix River Kwai	1	Sam's River Raft House	9	Kan Orchid	G
Jolly Frog Backpackers	6	Sugar Cane Guest House	5	No Name Bar	C
MK Hotel	13	Vimol Guest House	10	Punnee Bar and Café	E
Nita Raft House	17	VN Guest House	11	River Kwai Park Fast Food Hall	A
River Guest House	12			Sabayjit	D

many tourist towns, samlor drivers extract a hefty commission from guest-house owners and so may charge passengers as little as B5 for a ride that should cost B40. Guest-house owners prefer tourists not to take these ridiculously cheap rides, as the commissions – which range from B50 to B100 per person – are crippling the smaller places and may eventually make only bigger, less homely guest houses financially viable. Many guest houses will pick you up if you phone them from the bus or train station. The Tourist Police have published a list of **acceptable samlor fares** from Kanchanaburi bus station, which states that you should expect to pay B40 for two people to most guest houses or the train station, and B80 to the Bridge.

For transport between the bus station, Maenam Kwai guest houses and the Bridge, your cheapest option is to hop on one of the **songthaews** that run along Thanon Saeng Chuto via the Kanchanaburi War Cemetery (Don Rak) and then up Thanon Maenam Kwai to the Bridge. They start from outside the Bata shoe shop on Thanon Saeng Chuto, one block north of the bus station (every 15min during the day; 15min to the Bridge; B5 per person).

Because Kanchanaburi stretches over 5km from end to end, walking between the main sights can be exhausting. By far the best way to see them, and the surrounding countryside, is by **bicycle**; most guest houses and many tour agencies rent out bikes for about B20 per day, and several also have **motorbikes** (B250 per day) and jeeps for hire. There are dozens of outlets along Thanon Maenam Kwai, as well as one up at the Bridge. Or you can take to the river in a **kayak** (about B300 per 3hr for a two-person craft), available through most guest houses, or directly at River Kwai Canoe on Thanon Taiwan or *C & C Guest House* at 265/2 Thanon Maenam Kwai.

Accommodation

To get the best out of Kanchanaburi, you'll want to stay on or near the river, in either a raft house or a guest house. Most **raft houses** are little more than rattan and cane huts, partitioned into two or three sparsely furnished rooms and balanced on a raft of planks and logs moored close to the river bank. There's nothing romantic about sleeping in them, but the uninterrupted views of the river set against the blue silhouettes of the craggy hills can be magnificent. The one significant drawback is the noise from the karaoke rafts and riverside bars, which can get unbearable at weekends when the singing lasts till dawn. Not all **riverside guest houses** can offer perfect vistas, but the fact these places are built on solid ground provides the option of an attached bathroom and sometimes the bonus of a grassy area on which to loll about.

The river accommodation divides into three distinct areas. The noisier, brasher stretch near **Thanon Song Kwai** is where holidaying groups of Thai students come, so a party atmosphere prevails; it's not the place for peace and quiet. Several hundred metres upriver, the accommodation along **Soi Rong Heeb Oil** and **Thanon Maenam Kwai** offers a greater sense of isolation and a much more peaceful setting, though the best views are bagged by the hotels located on the west bank of the Kwai Yai, to the **north of the Bridge**. The **Thanon Saeng Chuto** hotels are away from the river in the centre of town, so have the least interesting outlooks but the most convenient locations.

Despite Kanchanaburi's increasing popularity, you're unlikely to have a problem finding a room except during the crazy ten days of the annual Bridge Festival (late Nov to early Dec) when every inch of floor space seems to be taken. Details of raft-house accommodation further **upstream** are given under the relevant accounts: Erawan on p.222, Nam Tok and Sai Yok on p.225, and Thong Pha Phum on p.229.

Thanon Song Kwai area

Development in the **Thanon Song Kwai** area has just about reached full capacity: karaoke bars – patronized primarily by Thais although stray farangs are welcome enough – line the road proper, while the river bank is crowded during the daytime with covered one- and two-storey rafts, most of which are for group-hire only and set off upriver in the late afternoon. At night the noise from the disco rafts can be deafening, though they are theoretically only licensed to play until midnight. The construction of a bridge here has been the final nail in the coffin, so even the views are less impressive than they used to be. Not surprisingly, farang tourists are becoming rare in this part of town, and many guest houses on this stretch no longer employ English-speaking staff: the two places listed below are the exception.

Nita Raft House ☎ 034/514521, @ nita-rafthouse @hotmail.com. Kanchanaburi's most inexpensive accommodation option is set away from the main Thanon Song Kwai fray, near the JEATH museum. It's run by a friendly, clued-up family, and offers simple floating rooms, some with shower, and all with some sort of river view. ❶–❷

Sam's Place ☎ 034/513971, ℗ 512023. Attractively designed range of raft houses, the best in this part of town, though the new bridge is right next door so views and noise levels aren't ideal. The cheapest rooms all have en-suite bathrooms, fans, and a view of the river; the more expensive ones have air-con and a small terrace. ❷–❸

Soi Rong Heeb Oil and Thanon Maenam Kwai area

Soi Rong Heeb Oil is little more than a narrow village lane with a handful of pleasant raft-house places, where bicycles and dogs constitute the main traffic and the home-owners sell a few groceries from their front rooms. **Thanon Maenam Kwai** is more of a thoroughfare, stretching 2km from Soi Rong Heeb Oil to the Bridge, and has developed into *the* backpackers' hub, full of small bars, restaurants, tour operators and tourist-oriented minimarts, as well as guest houses, though most of these are situated well off the main road on the river bank.

Apple's Guest House, 293 Thanon Maenam Kwai ☎ 034/512017, ℗ 514958, @ applesguesthouse@hotmail.com. Small, welcoming guest house that runs recommended tours and has the town's best restaurant. The spotless rooms are set round a lawn away from the river and all have fans and attached bathrooms: price depends on the number of beds. Call for free transport from the bus or train station. ❷

Bamboo House, down Soi Vietnam off the Bridge end of Thanon Maenam Kwai ☎ 034/512532. Kanchanaburi's most secluded and peaceful accommodation, if a little inconvenient for shops and restaurants (it's about 4km from the bus station). The nicest bungalows are en-suite and set round a decent-sized lawn that's good for kids; there are also some simple floating huts with a mattress on the floor and shared bathrooms, and a couple of air-con rooms on dry land. ❷–❹

C & C Guest House, Soi England, 265/2 Thanon Maenam Kwai ☎ 034/624547, ℗ 624548. Riverside compound of basic and very inexpensive but idiosyncratically designed huts; those set in the garden have attached bathrooms, and there are also some very cheap floating huts with shared bathrooms. A friendly, family-run place, it organizes unusual treks and rents out kayaks. Call for free transport from the bus or train station. ❶–❷

Jolly Frog Backpackers, 28 Soi China, just off the southern end of Thanon Maenam Kwai ☎ 034/514579, ⓦ www.jollyfrog.fsnet.co.uk. Most backpackers' first choice, this large complex of comfortable bamboo huts (some of them with private bathrooms) is ranged around a riverside garden and also has a few floating rafts. You can swim off the jetty, and the lawn's large enough to sprawl on, though on the down side the place can be noisy at night and is a bit impersonal. Call for free transport from the bus or train station. **①**–**②**

River Guest House, 42 Soi Rong Heeb Oil ⊤034/512491. Beautifully located set of very simple raft houses moored 30m from the river bank. Offers some of the cheapest rooms in Kanchanaburi as well as some with private bathrooms. **①**–**②**

Sam's House, Thanon Maenam Kwai ⊤034/515956, ⊕512023. Attractively located if rather congested set of huts, many of them floating among riverine lotuses; though they look rickety they are all en suite, comfortably furnished and fronted by a small private balcony. There are some less appealing air-con rooms on the river bank. **②**–**③**

Sam's River Raft House, 48/1 Soi Rong Heeb Oil ⊤034/624231, ⊕512023. The nicest of the three *Sam's* places, this has comfortable, thoughtfully designed, air-con raft houses with good beds and

decent river views, plus some cheaper versions with river-bank views, as well as inexpensive en-suite fan rooms on dry land. **②**–**③**

Sugar Cane Guest House, 22 Soi Pakistan, off Thanon Maenam Kwai ⊤034/624520. Peaceful, family-run place with a dozen en-suite huts set round a lawn overlooking the river, plus a block of floating rooms with shared bathroom. Rooms are nicely maintained and comfortably furnished; most have peaceful river views. **②**–**③**

Vimol Guest House, Soi Rong Heeb Oil ⊤ & ⊕034/514831. Unusual, two-storey, A-frame bamboo huts with sleeping quarters in the roof section and bathrooms downstairs. Friendly management and good food. **①**

VN Guest House, Soi Rong Heeb Oil ⊤034/514082. Simple, very cheap, unimaginatively designed concrete riverside huts, some with private bathroom. **①**

Thanon Saeng Chuto

Thanon Saeng Chuto is the town's main thoroughfare, so accommodation here gives you easy access to shops and town centre businesses but offers no prospect of a river view.

MK Hotel, 277/41 Thanon Saeng Chuto ⊤034/621143, ⊕513233. Smartly maintained city-style high-rise hotel that lacks character but compensates with genuinely comfortable rooms and reasonable prices. The most expensive rooms have TV and air-con. Beside the main road, midway between the train and bus stations. **③**–**④**

River Inn, Thanon Saeng Chuto ⊤034/621056. Not near the river at all, but midway between the train and bus stations, this is the cheap wing of

the adjacent *River Kwai Hotel*. Rooms are uninspired, fairly faded, and simply furnished, but all have air-con and TV. **③**

River Kwai Hotel, 284/3–16 Thanon Saeng Chuto ⊤034/513348, ⊕511269, ⓔrkhk@riverkwai .co.th. The town centre's top hotel is nowhere near the river, but all rooms have air-con, and facilities include a swimming pool, nightclub and internet access. Good value for its class but not much atmosphere compared to the competition. **⑤**

North of the Bridge

The hotels on the west bank of the Kwai Yai, to the **north of the Bridge**, are the most luxurious in the area but, though they make the most of their picturesque locations, these places are beyond walking distance from most of the restaurants and sights.

Duen Shine Resort, on the west bank of the Kwai Yai ⊤034/653345, ⊕653346, ⓔ8np9800061.duenshine@sawadee.com.th. Upmarket riverside resort that caters more to Thai tourists than the nearby *Felix*; offers pretty good value rooms, all with air-con and TV, in raft houses, cottages and a small hotel block. There's a swimming pool in the prettily landscaped tropical garden, and a restaurant. **⑦**

Felix River Kwai, on the west bank of the Kwai Yai ⊤034/515061, ⊕515095, ⓦwww.felixriverk-

wai.co.th. Occupying a lovely riverside spot within walking distance of the Bridge (or a 2km drive from Thanon Maenam Kwai – a little inconvenient if you don't have transport), this is the most upmarket resort in the area and offers large deluxe rooms with air-con, TV and mini-bar, plus two swimming pools and several not very interesting restaurants. Rates depend on whether or not you want a river view, and are discounted during the week; reservations are essential for weekends. **⑧**

The Town

Strung out along the east bank of the **River Kwai Yai**, at the point where it divides into the River Kwai Noi and the Maenam Mae Khlong, Kanchanaburi is a long, narrow ribbon of a town. The **war sights** are sandwiched between the river and the busy main drag, Thanon Saeng Chuto, which along with the area around the bus station forms the commercial centre of Kanchanaburi. If you have the time, start with the JEATH War Museum at the far southern end (not to be confused with the inappropriately named World War II Museum near the Bridge), and work your way northwards via the Kanchanaburi cemetery (also known as Don Rak) to the Bridge, preferably on a bicycle, before heading over the river to the town's outlying tourist attractions.

The JEATH War Museum

The **JEATH War Museum** (daily 8.30am–4.30pm; B30) gives the clearest introduction to local wartime history, putting the notorious sights of the Death Railway in context and painting a vivid picture of the gruesome conditions suffered by the POWs who worked on the line (JEATH is an acronym of six of the countries involved in the railway: Japan, England, Australia, America, Thailand and Holland). Notably lacking, though, is any real attempt to document the plight of the conscripted Asian labour force. The museum was set up by the chief abbot of the adjacent Wat Chaichumpon and is housed in a reconstructed Allied POW hut of thatched palm beside the Mae Khlong, about 500m from the TAT office or a fifteen-minute walk southwest of the bus station.

The most interesting **exhibits** are the newspaper articles, paintings and photographs recording conditions in the camps. When things got really bad, photography was forbidden and any sketches had to be done in secret, on stolen scraps of toilet paper; some of those sketches, many by English POW Jack Chalker, were later reproduced as paintings. The simple drawings and paintings of torture methods are the most harrowing of all the evidence.

The Kanchanaburi War Cemetery

Thirty-eight Allied POWs died for each kilometre of track laid on the Thailand–Burma Railway, and many of them are buried in Kanchanaburi's two war cemeteries. Of all the region's war sights, the cemeteries are the only places to have remained completely untouched by the tourist trade. Opposite the train station on Thanon Saeng Chuto, the **Kanchanaburi War Cemetery** (aka Don Rak; daily 8am–4pm; free), is the bigger of the two (the other cemetery, Chungkai, is described on p.217), with 6982 POW graves laid out in straight lines amid immaculately kept lawns and flowering shrubs. Many of the identical stone memorial slabs state simply, "A man who died for his country"; others, inscribed with names, dates and regiments, indicate that the overwhelming majority of the dead were under 25 years old. A commemorative service is held here every year on April 25, Anzac Day.

Asian labourers on the Death Railway – who died in far higher numbers than the Allies – are remembered with rather less ceremony. In November 1990 a **mass grave** of Asians was discovered beneath a sugar-cane field on the edge of town. Digging started after a nearby resident dreamt that the dead couldn't breathe and were asking for his help. The skeletons, many of them mutilated, have since been given a proper burial, but the new graves are not for public viewing – aside from those rather tastelessly displayed in the World War II Museum (see opposite).

The Bridge over the River Kwai

For most people the plain steel arches of the **Bridge over the River Kwai** come as a disappointment: as a war memorial it lacks both the emotive punch of the JEATH museum and the perceptible drama of spots further up the line, and as a bridge it looks nothing out of the ordinary – certainly not as awesomely hard to construct as it appears in David Lean's famous 1957 film, *Bridge on the River Kwai*. But it is the link with the multi-Oscar-winning film, of course, that draws tour buses here by the dozen, and makes the Bridge approach seethe with trinket-sellers and touts. For all the commercialization of the place, however, you can't really come to the Kwai and not see it. To get here either take any songthaew heading north up Thanon Saeng Chuto, hire a samlor, or cycle – it's 5km from the bus station.

The fording of the Kwai Yai at the point just north of Kanchanaburi known as Tha Makkham was one of the first major obstacles in the construction of the Thailand–Burma Railway. Sections of a steel bridge were brought up from Java and reassembled by POWs using only pulleys and derricks. A temporary **wooden bridge** was built alongside it, taking its first train in February 1943; three months later the steel bridge was finished. Both bridges were severely damaged by Allied bombers (rather than commando-saboteurs as in the film) in 1944 and 1945, but the steel bridge was repaired after the war and is still in use today. In fact the best way to see the Bridge is by taking the train over it: the Kanchanaburi–Nam Tok train crosses it three times a day in each direction, stopping briefly at the River Kwai Bridge station on the east bank of the river. Alternatively, check the timetables and stop for a drink at one of the floating restaurants beside the Bridge, which make ideal vantage points for photos, though bear in mind that the trains are nearly always late. You can also walk over the Bridge to the tacky Burmese souvenir stalls on the west bank.

Some of the original World War II **railway engines** used on this stretch have been spruced up and parked beside the Bridge; nearby, a memorial stone commemorates the Japanese soldiers who died while overseeing the construction work.

The Bridge forms the dramatic centrepiece of the annual *son et lumière* **River Kwai Bridge Festival**, held over ten nights from the end of November to commemorate the first Allied bombing of the Bridge on November 28, 1944. The hour-long show uses spectacular effects to sketch the history of the region's wartime role, liberally lacing the commentary with a stodgy anti-war message that doesn't quite square with the climactic go get-'em pyrotechnics. Tourists of all nationalities, including Thais, flock here for the show, and the area around the Bridge turns into an enormous funfair. Book accommodation and air-conditioned buses well in advance if you want to stay during the festival, or join one of the many special tours operating out of Bangkok.

World War II Museum

While at the Bridge, you can't fail to see the signs for the nearby **World War II Museum** (daily 8am–6pm; B30), 30m south along Thanon Maenam Kwai. Not to be confused with the JEATH War Museum (see opposite), this is a more recent, privately owned collection that cynically uses the war to pull in curious coach parties, but it is nevertheless worth visiting for the sheer volume and bizarre eclecticism of its contents. The war section is housed on the lower floors of the building to the left of the entrance, and comprises a very odd mixture of memorabilia (a rusted bombshell, the carpet used by the local Japanese commander), reconstructed tableaux featuring emaciated POWs and sanctimonious quotes from local dignitaries – a marked contrast with the first-hand

Shortly after entering World War II in December 1941, Japan, fearing an Allied blockade of the Bay of Bengal, began looking for an alternative supply route to connect its newly acquired territories that stretched from Singapore to the Burma–India border. In spite of the almost impenetrable terrain, the River Kwai basin was chosen as the route for a new **Thailand–Burma Railway**, the aim being to join the existing terminals of Nong Pladuk in Thailand (51km southeast of Kanchanaburi) and Thanbuyazat in Burma – a total distance of 415km.

About 60,000 Allied POWs were shipped up from captured Southeast Asian territories to work on the link, their numbers later augmented by as many as 200,000 conscripted Asian labourers. Work began at both ends in June 1942. Three million cubic metres of rock were shifted and 14km of bridges built with little else but picks and shovels, dynamite and pulleys. By the time the line was completed, fifteen months later, it had more than earned its nickname, the **Death Railway**: an estimated 16,000 POWs and 100,000 Asian labourers died while working on it.

The appalling conditions and Japanese brutality were the consequences of the **samurai code**: Japanese soldiers abhorred the disgrace of imprisonment – to them, ritual suicide was the only honourable option open to a prisoner – and considered that Allied POWs had forfeited any rights as human beings. Food rations were meagre for men forced into backbreaking eighteen-hour shifts, often followed by night-long marches to the next camp. Many suffered from beri-beri, many more died of dysentery-induced starvation, but the biggest killers were cholera and malaria, particularly during the monsoon. It is said that one man died for every sleeper laid on the track.

The two lines finally met at Konkuita, just south of present-day Sangkhlaburi. But as if to underscore its tragic futility, the Thailand–Burma link saw less than two years of active service: after the Japanese surrender on August 15, 1945, the railway came under the jurisdiction of the British who, thinking it would be used to supply Karen separatists in Burma, tore up 4km of track at Three Pagodas Pass, thereby cutting the Thai–Burma link forever. When the Thais finally gained control of the rest of the railway, they destroyed the track all the way down to Nam Tok, apparently because it was uneconomic. Recently however, an Australian-Thai group of volunteers and former POWs has salvaged sections of track near the fearsome stretch of line known as Hellfire Pass, clearing a memorial walk at the pass and founding an excellent museum at the site, described on p.227.

The history of the Death Railway is recounted in an interesting book by *Bangkok Post* journalist Micool Brooke, which includes first-hand accounts from men who survived the POW camps. It's called *Captive of the River Kwae* (Merman Books, 1995; B350) and can be bought in Kanchanaburi at the World War II Museum and at *Punnee Bar*.

---

accounts at JEATH. Although barely educative, these displays are at least inoffensive, unlike the museum's glass tomb containing the remains of over one hundred of the Asian conscripts found locally in a mass grave.

Elsewhere in the same building are more light-hearted and less unseemly displays, among them stamp and banknote collections, a ceiling painted with illustrations of Thai proverbs and a top-floor gallery of selected "Miss Thailand" portraits from 1934 to 1992. Across the courtyard, a second building seeks to present an overview of Thailand's most venerated institutions with the help of specially commissioned wall-paintings: Buddhism on the ground floor, prime ministers and kings on the middle storeys and family portraits of the museum's founders – the Chansiris – right at the top.

Chungkai Cemetery and Wat Tham Khao Poon

Several of Kanchanaburi's other sights lie some way across the river, and are best reached by bike (or by longtail boat or kayak, organized through your guest house). For Chungkai Cemetery and Wat Tham Khao Poon, both on the west bank of the Kwai Noi, either take the two-minute ferry ride (for pedestrians and bikes) from the pier at the confluence of the two rivers on Thanon Song Kwai, or cycle over Rattanakarn Bridge 1km north of the pier.

Peaceful **Chungkai Cemetery** is built on the banks of the Kwai Noi at the site of a former POW camp. Some 1750 POWs are buried here; most of the gravestone inscriptions include a name and regimental insignia, but a number remain unnamed – at the upcountry camps, bodies were thrown onto mass funeral pyres, making identification impossible.

One kilometre on from Chungkai Cemetery, at the top of the road's only hill, sits the cave temple **Wat Tham Khao Poon** (daily 8am–6pm; donation). This labyrinthine Santa's grotto is presided over by a medley of religious icons – the star being a Buddha reclining under a fanfare of flashing lights. The scenery around here is a good reason for continuing along the road for another few kilometres; once over the hill, the prospect widens to take in endless square kilometres of sugar-cane plantation (for which Kanchanaburi has earned the title "sugar capital of Thailand") fringed by dramatically looming limestone crags. Aside from the odd house, the only sign of human life along here is at the agricultural college in Somdech Phra Srinagarindra Park, 6km south of the temple.

Wat Tham Mangkon Thong (Floating Nun Temple)

The impressive scenery across on the east of the River Kwai Noi makes for an equally worthwhile bike trip, but the cave temple on this side – **Wat Tham Mangkon Thong**, otherwise known as the **"Floating Nun Temple"** – is fairly tacky. The attraction here is a Thai nun who, clad in white robes, will get into the temple pond and float there, meditating – if tourists give her enough money to make it worth her while. It's difficult not to be cynical about such a commercial and unspectacular stunt, though Taiwanese visitors are said to be particularly impressed. The floating takes place on a round pond at the foot of the enormous naga staircase that leads up to the temple embedded in the hillside behind. The temple comprises an unexceptional network of low, bat-infested limestone caves, punctuated at intervals with Buddha statues.

To get to Wat Tham Mangkon Thong by bicycle or motorbike, take the ferry across the Mae Khlong River at Tha Chukkadon and then follow the road on the other side for about 4km. Alternatively, take **bus** #8191 (every 30min; 20 min) from Kanchanaburi bus station.

Eating and drinking

All of Kanchanaburi's guest houses and raft houses have **restaurants**, so similar independent eating places specializing in Western and toned-down Thai dishes have to be pretty outstanding to survive. Local food is, of course, less expensive and more authentic, particularly at the ever-reliable **night market**, which sets up alongside Thanon Saeng Chuto on the edge of the bus station. For seafood, try the two main clusters of **floating restaurants**: around Tha Chukkadon, and north of the Bridge; though dishes are not cheap at these restaurants, they are authentic as they're geared towards Thai tourists, and the river views are great.

Restaurants

Aree Bakery, Thanon Pak Praek. Especially popular for its German-made, home-baked cakes; reasonably priced sandwiches, coffee and ice cream are also served and there's usually a fluctuating pile of secondhand books to peruse or buy. Closes around 4pm.

JR, south of Tha Chukkadon. Floating restaurant that affords especially pretty views across the Mae Khlong and serves good-value, mid-priced set meals of typical Thai-Chinese dishes as well as à la carte standards.

Kan Orchid, next to the *River Kwai Hotel* on Thanon Saeng Chuto. Air-con restaurant with a scrumptious, moderately priced menu of farang-friendly Thai dishes, including recommended steamed river fish with plum sauce. Run by the same family as the highly rated *Krathom Thai*.

Krathom Thai, at *Apple's Guest House*, 293 Thanon Maenam Kwai. Exceptionally delicious food, prepared by guest-house owner Apple to traditional Thai recipes. The extensive, mid-priced menu includes mouthwatering coconut- and

cashew-laced *matsaman* curries – both meat and vegetarian varieties – as well as huge, good-value multi-course set dinners.

Punnee Bar and Café, Thanon Ban Neua. Popular with resident and visiting expats, this English/Thai-run place serves up Thai and Western standards, as well as reasonably priced drinks in the *Ampai Bar Lounge* next door.

River Kwai Park Fast Food Hall, 50m south of the Bridge on Thanon Maenam Kwai. The cheapest place to eat in the vicinity of the Bridge, this is a collection of curry and noodle stalls where you buy coupons for meals that cost just B25 or B30. Only a few of the stalls have English menus, but it's easy enough to point at what you'd like.

Sabayjit, just north of *River Kwai Hotel* on Thanon Saeng Chuto. Unsigned in English, but directly opposite the unmistakable wood-panelled *Apache Saloon*, this place boasts a large and tasty mid-priced menu of sweet-and-sour soups, curries, spicy salads, wontons and noodle dishes.

Bars

Apache Saloon, across from the *River Kwai Hotel* on Thanon Saeng Chuto. Done up inside and out to look like a Wild West sort of bar, this is the place to come for live music (mostly soft rock), mid-priced beer and whisky, and a small menu of snacks.

Beer Barrel, Thanon Maenam Kwai. Rustic-styled outdoor beer garden where the decking is made from actual Death Railway sleepers and you sit at rough-hewn wooden tables amid a jungle of low-lit

trees and vines. The star feature here is the ice-cold draught beer, but there's also a short menu of bar meals including *som tam, kai pat bai kaphrao* (chicken with basil) and *khao pat kung.*

No Name Bar, Thanon Maenam Kwai. Popular farang-run travellers' hangout in among the guest houses and tour operators. Key attractions are the satellite TV showings of the big football matches, the pool table and the well-priced beer. Open till the early hours.

Listings

Books New English-language novels and books about Thailand available at minimarts on Thanon Maenam Kwai and at the stationery shop across from *River Inn* on Thanon Saeng Chuto. Secondhand books bought and sold at *Punnee Bar* on Thanon Ban Neua.

Cookery classes At *Apple's Guest House*, 293 Thanon Maenam Kwai: shop at the morning market and learn how to cook seven different Thai dishes. Minimum three participants; book the day before between 10.30am and 4.30pm (B700).

Emergencies For all emergencies, call the tourist police on the free, 24hr phone line ☎ 1699, or contact them at their booth right beside the Bridge (☎ 034/512795).

Exchange There are several banks with money changing facilities and ATMs on the main Thanon Saeng Chuto. Outside banking hours contact either *Apple's Guest House* on Thanon Maenam Kwai, or *Punnee Bar* on Thanon Ban Neua.

Day-trips, trekking and rafting

All the places listed below advertise treks around the Kanchanaburi and Sangkhlaburi areas, though very few itineraries actually feature any trekking: most concentrate on waterfalls, elephant rides and river rafting instead. Prices listed are per person in a group of four people minimum; smaller groups have to pay proportionally more. If you have plenty of time, you might consider making your own way up to Sangkhlaburi (see p.229) and organizing rafting and elephant riding from one of the two guest houses up there. On the other hand, if you're very short of time it's also possible to organize everything from Bangkok: Mama Tour, NS Tours and Wild Planet all do trips to this region; see p.188 and p.195 for their addresses and phone numbers. All the tour operators listed below also do tailor-made guided tours to the war sights and Damnoen Saduak floating markets.

A.S. Mixed Travel, 293 Thanon Maenam Kwai (☎034/512017, ⊕514958, ⓔapplesguest house@hotmail.com). Small and friendly operation that runs out of *Apple's Guest House* and is led by enthusiastic and well-informed guides. Offers one-day mountain-bike excursions to Than Lot National Park (B600), with the option of a homestay in a remote Karen village (B1450), and more challenging two-day mountain-biking trips around Pha Sawan falls (B1650). Also, standard two-day trips (B1750) up to Three Pagodas Pass, which feature elephant riding, river rafting, plus stops at Hellfire Pass, Pha That waterfall, Hin Dat hot springs and Sangkhlaburi's Mon village; accommodation is at Sangkhlaburi or Thong Pha Phum. Guided one-day trips to Erawan falls, including elephant riding, rafting and a trip on the Death Railway (B750); and car-with-driver (no guide) for a day-trip to Hellfire Pass and Erawan falls (B250 per person plus entrance fees).

C&C Guest House, 265/2 Thanon Maenam Kwai (☎034/624547, ⊕624548). Another low-key, personable outfit, recommended for their two-day trips (B1400) to a Karen village, with elephant rides, rafting and several waterfalls all featured. Their two-nighters (B1800) are one of the few options in Kanchanaburi that include some serious jungle hiking. They also do all sorts of one-day trips (B350–550) featuring various combinations of waterfalls (most popularly Erawan or Pha That), hot springs, river rafting and a ride on the Death Railway. You can rent kayaks through *C&C* as well, at about B300 per three hours.

Punnee Bar and Café, Thanon Ban Neua (☎034/513503). Expat bar-owner Danny will take people pretty much anywhere in the locality for around B600 per person per day, but is especially knowledgeable about Hellfire Pass and the other World War II sights. He can also arrange elephant riding and rafting trips.

River Kwai Canoe, 3/7 Soi Rong Heeb Oil (☎ & ⊕034/620191, ⓔriverkwaicanoe@ yahoo.com). Offers a whole programme of canoeing trips, with all equipment, lunch and connecting transport, from one hour along a short stretch of the Kwai Yai (B250) to a full day on the Kwai Noi in the Sai Yok district, including optional stops at Hellfire Pass and Hin Dat hot springs (B950–1100).

West Tours ⓦwww.westours.net. Branches at 21 Thanon Maenam Kwai (☎034/ 513654, ⊕513655) and on Thanon Song Kwai. Large and efficiently run operation with a dozen different tour plans, including trips to Muang Singh and Hellfire Pass (B600), longtail boat trips up the River Kwai (B600), a twilight elephant safari plus dinner (B800), and a day's rafting and elephant riding including an overnight stay at a Karen village (B1600). Be prepared to be part of a big group if you join the most popular day-trips. They also hire out a car-with-driver for B2000 per day.

Hospitals Kanchanaburi Memorial Hospital, 111 Mu 5 Thanon Saeng Chuto (☎ 034/624191); Thanakan Hospital, 20/20 Thanon Saeng Chuto (☎ 034/622366).

Immigration office At 100/22 Thanon Mae Khlong (☎ 034/513325).

Internet access Available at almost every guest house on Thanon Maenam Kwai as well as at several dedicated internet centres on Thanon Maenam Kwai, and a few more just south of the *River Kwai Hotel* on Thanon Saeng Chuto.

Mail The GPO is 1km south of the TAT office on Thanon Saeng Chuto, but there's a more central post office on Thanon Lak Muang, one block west of Thanon Song Kwai.

Telephones Government telephone office at the GPO, 1km south of the TAT office on Thanon Saeng Chuto (daily 7am–10pm). There are several private telephone offices at guest houses and on Thanon Maenam Kwai.

Around Kanchanaburi

The best way of getting to the main sights in the Kanchanaburi countryside – the temples of **Tham Sua** and **Tham Khao Noi**, the **Ban Kao Museum** and **Erawan National Park** – is to hire a motorbike from one of the guest houses: the roads are good, but the public transport in the immediate vicinity of town is sporadic and wearisome at best. Alternatively, most guest houses in Kanchanaburi organize reasonably priced day-trips to caves, waterfalls and historical sights in the surrounding area, as well as lengthier, more adventurous expeditions (see box on p.219).

Wat Tham Sua and Wat Tham Khao Noi

A twenty-kilometre ride from the town centre gets you to the modern hilltop wats of **Tham Sua** and **Tham Khao Noi**, which both afford expansive views over the river valley and out to the mountains beyond and make a fairly interesting focus for a trip out of town. If you have your own transport, take Highway 323 in the direction of Bangkok and follow signs for Wachiralongkorn Dam; cross the dam – at this point you should be able to see the wats in the distance – and turn right at the T-junction. Otherwise, take any non-air-con Bangkok- or Nakhon Pathom-bound bus as far as Tha Muang, 12km south along Highway 323, then change onto a motorcycle taxi to the temples (about B30).

Designed by a Thai architect, Wat Tham Sua was conceived in typical grandiose style around a massive chedi covered with tiles similar to those used at Nakhon Pathom. Inside, a placid seated Buddha takes centre stage, his huge palms raised to show the Wheels of Law inscribed like stigmata across them; a conveyor belt transports devotees' offerings into the enormous alms bowl set into his lap. The neighbouring Chinese-designed **Wat Tham Khao Noi** is a fabulously gaudy, seven-tiered Chinese pagoda within which a laughing Buddha competes for attention with a host of gesturing and grimacing statues and painted characters.

Ban Kao Museum

Thirty-five kilometres west of Kanchanaburi, the **Ban Kao Museum** (Wed–Sun 8.30am–4.30pm; B30) throws up some stimulating hints about an advanced prehistoric civilization that once settled along the banks of the Kwai Noi. The first evidence that a Stone Age community lived around here was uncovered during World War II, by the Dutch POW and former archeologist H.R. van Heekeren. Recognizing that the polished stone axes he had found might be several millennia old, he returned to the site in 1961 with a Thai–Danish team which subsequently excavated a range of objects covering the period from around 8000 to 1000 BC. Many of these finds are now displayed in the museum.

One of the most interesting discoveries was a group of some fifty **skeletons**, which had been buried with curiously designed pots placed significantly at the head and feet. The graves have been dated to around 1770 BC and the terracotta pot shards reassembled into tripod-shaped vessels of a kind not found elsewhere – they are thought to have been used for cooking over small fires. Polished stone tools from around 8000 BC share the display cabinets with inscribed bronze pots and bangles transferred from a nearby bronze-culture site, which have been placed at around 1000 BC – somewhat later than the bronze artefacts from Ban Chiang in the northeast (see p.507). The hollowed-out tree trunks just in front of the museum are also unusual: they may have been used as boats or as coffins – or possibly as a metaphorical combination of the two.

There's no public **transport** to the museum, so unless you join a tour (see box on p.219) your best option is to hire a motorbike from Kanchanaburi, which also allows you easily to combine Ban Kao with a visit to Prasat Muang Singh, 8km further west (see p.224).

Erawan and Srinakarind national parks

Chances are that when you see a poster of a waterfall in Thailand, you'll be looking at a picture of the falls in **Erawan National Park** (B200), 65km northwest of Kanchanaburi. The seven-tiered waterfall, topped by a triple cascade, is etched into the national imagination not just for its beauty but also for its alleged resemblance to a three-headed elephant – this elephant (*erawan* in Thai) is the former national symbol and the usual mount of the Hindu god Indra. It makes a lovely setting for a picnic, especially just after the rainy season, and on Sundays and holidays Thais flock here to eat, drink and take family photographs against the falls; weekdays are generally a more peaceful time to come.

Access is along the well-maintained Route 3199, which follows the River Kwai Yai upstream, taking in fine views along the way. Buses stop at **Srinakarind** market, from where it's a one-kilometre walk to the Erawan National Park **headquarters** and the trailhead. Although the park covers an area of 550 square kilometres, the only official **trail** is the one that leads you up the course of the rivulet, past each of its seven tiers. Each of these levels comprises a waterfall feeding a pool of invitingly clear water partly shaded by bamboos, rattans, lianas and other clotted vegetation – like seven sets for a Tarzan movie. It's a fairly easy climb up to the fifth stage, but the route on to the sixth and seventh levels gets very steep and slippery and can be a bit scary, especially as you also have to negotiate a few dilapidated bridges and ladders: be sure to wear strong shoes, not flip-flops, and avoid doing levels six and seven alone if you can. The best pools for swimming are levels two (which gets the most crowded), and seven (which is a hard slog but rarely busy). The views over the jungle from the seventh tier are quite stunning.

If you follow the main road along its westerly branch from Srinakarind market for another 10km you'll reach Wat Phrathat, from where it's a five-hundred-metre walk to **Phrathat Cave**. A chartered songthaew from the market to the wat costs about B250: buses don't come this far. The stalactite cave has several large chambers, but is of interest to geologists for the fault lines which run under the Kwai Noi and are clearly visible in the disjointed strata.

The Kwai Yai is dammed a few kilometres north of the turn-off to Erawan and broadens out into the scenic **Srinakarind Reservoir**, a popular recreation spot and site of several resorts, all of which lie within the **Srinakarind National Park** (sometimes spelt Sri Nakarin). From the dam you can hire boats to make the two-hour journey west across the reservoir to **Huay Khamin Falls**, which are said to be the most powerful in the district, and reputedly get the name "Turmeric Streak" from the ochre-coloured limestone rockface. Boats cost about B1500 to charter (though there is a regular Saturday morning service there at 8am, which should cost B150 per person); however, it's quicker and less hassle to join one of the tours from Kanchanaburi, which use four-wheel-drives to cover the very rough track that runs along the western edge of the reservoir to the falls and then on to Hin Dat hot springs and Highway 323 (see p.228).

Practicalities

Buses to Erawan (#8170; 2hr) leave Kanchanaburi every fifty minutes between 8am and 5.20pm; if you miss the 4pm ride back you'll probably be there for the night. Most Kanchanaburi guest houses arrange daily **songthaew** transport to and from Erawan falls for B80 per person, giving you around five hours at the falls and door-to-door service as well. In addition, some tour operators (see p.219) are now offering a very convenient combination transport service to Erawan and Hellfire Pass (see p.226), for about B250 per person. If you have your own transport, simply follow signs from Kanchanaburi for Route 3199 and the falls. You can also combine Erawan with a visit to Hellfire Pass or Sai Yok by taking the minor road to Erawan off Highway 323 near Nam Tok at kilometre-stone 38 (52km north of Kanchanaburi).

Accommodation is plentiful enough along the Kwai Yai valley, if a little select, most so-called "resorts" being peacefully located sets of upmarket raft houses. The *Erawan Resort* (℡01/838 7360 or 034/513568; ❸–❽) is only ten minutes' drive from the park, while the nearby *Kwai Yai Hilton Park* (℡02/421 3179; ❺–❽) and *Pha Daeng Resort* (℡02/579 7145 or 034/513909; ❹–❽) both offer attractive lakeside accommodation. It's also possible to stay in the Erawan National Park bungalows (B250–1000 for two to fifteen people), though these are often full and should ideally be reserved in advance by contacting the Royal Forestry Department in Bangkok (℡02/579 0529 or 579 7223). There are several **foodstalls**, restaurants and shops selling snacks near the trailhead, but they are all closed by 8pm.

Tham Than Lot (Chalerm Rattanakosin) National Park

Ninety-seven kilometres north of Kanchanaburi, off Route 3086, tiny little **Tham Than Lot National Park**, also known as **Chalerm Rattanakosin National Park**, covers just 59 square kilometres but boasts two very nice caves, a decent waterfall and an enjoyable hiking trail that links them; wear comfortable shoes and bring a torch.

It is possible but time-consuming to get to the park without your own transport and would be rather rushed as a day-trip. Take regular **bus** #325 from Kanchanaburi and get off at **BAN NONG PRU** (every 20min; 3hr), then change onto a motorcycle taxi (B100) for the 22-kilometre ride to the park entrance (B200 admission) and visitors' centre. There are five multi-berth **national park bungalows** (B500–1000 for four to twelve people) near the visitors' centre, which should be booked in advance at weekends, or you could stay at the basic *Pasuk Hotel* (**❶–❷**) in Nong Pru if desperate; it's just north of the market. Alternatively, hire your own motorbike from Kanchanaburi, or take a tour (see p.219).

From the visitors' centre, follow the signed trail for about ten minutes to reach the first cave, **Tham Than Lot Noi**, which is 400m deep and illuminated if there are enough people (at weekends for example). A very picturesque 2.5-kilometre, two-hour trail runs on from the other side of Tham Than Lot Noi, along a stream and through a ravine to the first of three **waterfalls**, about an hour and a half's easy walk away, with towering dipterocarps, some fine jungle views and plenty of butterflies to admire en route. The path gets more difficult after the first waterfall, and dangerously slippery in the wet season, passing another couple of waterfalls before coming to the larger of the park's two caves, the impressively deep sink-hole **Tham Than Lot Yai**, site of a small Buddhist shrine. Another ten minutes along the trail brings you to a small forest temple, from where you'll need to retrace your steps to return to the visitors' centre.

The Death Railway: to Nam Tok

The two-hour **rail journey** from Kanchanaburi to **Nam Tok** is one of Thailand's most scenic, and most popular. Leaving Kanchanaburi via the Bridge over the River Kwai, the train chugs through the Kwai Noi valley, stopping frequently at country stations decked with frangipani and jasmine to pick up villagers who tout their wares in the carriages before getting off at the nearest market. There are three trains daily in both directions, which means it's possible to make day-trips from Kanchanaburi to Muang Singh and Nam Tok if you get the timing right. At the time of writing, the train is scheduled to leave Kanchanaburi at 6.11am, 11.01am and 4.37pm and to return from Nam Tok at 5.25am, 1pm and 3.15pm; Kanchanaburi TAT keeps up-to-date **timetables**, so be sure to check with them or station officials before travelling. As it's such a popular trip, the State Railway adds a couple of "**Special Cars**" for tourists on the 11.01 Kanchanaburi–Nam Tok train, for which they charge B150 instead of the usual B17; the seats in the Special Cars are exactly the same as those in the cheap carriages, but you do get a reserved place and several soft drinks and snacks. Tickets for Special Cars are sold from a desk in front of the ticket office from about half an hour prior to travel; standard, cheap tickets are sold from the ticket office fifteen minutes prior to travel – be sure to buy a ticket as non-ticket holders get fined. Whatever ticket you opt for, sit on the left-hand side of the train for the best views, or the right-hand side for shade.

Unfortunately, the trains on this line are often very late, so you may end up having to take the bus on one of the legs: frequent #8203 **buses** connect Kanchanaburi with Nam Tok (every 30min; 1hr 30min) via Highway 323, but don't go anywhere near Muang Singh. Another way of avoiding being trapped by late-running trains is to join one of the **tours** that features a one-way ride on the Railway as well as some of the other local sights, such as Hellfire Pass or Erawan falls (see p.219 for details).

Prasat Muang Singh

Eight hundred years ago, the Khmer empire extended west as far as Muang Singh (City of Lions), an outpost strategically sited on the banks of the River Kwai Noi, 43km west of present-day Kanchanaburi. Thought to have been built at the end of the twelfth century, the temple complex of **Prasat Muang Singh** (daily 9am–5pm; B40) follows Khmer religious and architectural precepts (see p.473), but its origins are obscure – the City of Lions gets no mention in any of the recognized chronicles until the nineteenth century. If you're coming by train, get off at **Tha Kilen** (1hr 15min from Kanchanaburi), walk straight out of the station for 500m, turn right at the crossroads and continue for another 1km to reach the museum. With your own transport, Muang Singh combines well with a trip to the Ban Kao Museum, 8km east of here (see p.220); both sites are on minor road 3445 which forks off from Highway 323 just north of Kanchanaburi, or you can take the signed turn-off from Highway 323 30km north of Kanchanaburi.

Prasat Muang Singh covers one third of a square kilometre, bordered by moats and ramparts which probably had cosmological as well as defensive significance, but unless you fancy a long stroll, you'd be wise to stick to the enclosed **shrine complex** at the heart of it all. Restoration work on this part has been sensitively done to give an idea of the crude grandeur of the original structure, which was constructed entirely from blocks of rough russet laterite.

As with all Khmer prasats, the pivotal feature of Muang Singh is the main prang, as always surrounded by a series of walls and a covered gallery, with gateways marking the cardinal points. The prang faces east, towards Angkor, and is guarded by a fine sandstone statue of **Avalokitesvara**, one of the five great *bodhisattva*s of Mahayana Buddhism, would-be Buddhas who have postponed their entrance into Nirvana to help others attain enlightenment. He's depicted here in characteristic style, his eight arms and torso covered with tiny Buddha reliefs and his hair tied in a top-knot. In Mahayanist mythology, Avalokitesvara represents mercy, while the other statue found in the prasat, the female figure of **Prajnaparamita**, symbolizes wisdom – when wisdom and mercy join forces, enlightenment ensues.

Just visible on the inside of the north wall surrounding the prang is the only intact example of the stucco carving that once ornamented every facade. Other fragments and sculptures found at this and nearby sites are displayed beside the north gate; especially tantalizing is the single segment of what must have been a gigantic face hewn from several massive blocks of stone.

Nam Tok and around

About twenty minutes after Tha Kilen the most hair-raising section of track begins: at **Wang Sing**, also known as Arrow Hill, the train squeezes through thirty-metre-deep solid rock cuttings, dug at the cost of numerous POW lives; 6km further, it slows to a crawl at the approach to the Wang Po viaduct, where a 300-metre-long **trestle bridge** clings to the cliff face as it curves with the Kwai Noi – almost every man who worked on this part of the railway died. The station at the northern end of the trestle bridge is called **Tham Krasae**, after the cave that's hollowed out of the rockface beside the bridge; you can see the cave's resident Buddha image from the train. A couple of raft-house operations here have capitalized on the drama of this stretch of the river. On the viaduct side, *River Kwai Cabin* (☏ 034/591073; ❻–❽) offers upmarket bungalow accommodation; on the other bank, *River Kwai Jungle House*

($\textcircled{T}$034/561052, $\textcircled{F}$636713; $\textbf{❸}$) has well-positioned raft houses. At both places meals are included in the nightly package rates quoted here and accommodation should be booked in advance.

Ten kilometres north of Tham Krasae, the train pulls in at **Wang Po Station** before continuing alongside a particularly lovely stretch of the Kwai Noi, its banks thick with jungle and not a raft house in sight, the whole vista framed by distant tree-clad peaks. Thirty minutes later, the train reaches **NAM TOK**, a small town that thrives chiefly on its position at the end of the line. Few foreign travellers stay here – day-trippers leave when the train begins its return journey, while those on package tours are whisked downriver to pre-booked raft resorts. Nam Tok **train station** is at the top of the town, 3km from the river and 900m north of Highway 323; **buses** usually stop near the T-junction of the highway and the station road.

On rainy-season weekends, Thais flock to the town's roadside **Sai Yok Noi waterfall**, but if you're filling time between trains, you'd be better off stretching your legs on the short trek to the nearby Wang Badan cave or taking a boat trip from Pak Saeng pier to Tham Lawa and Sai Yok Yai falls (see p.228). Impressive stalactites, fathomless chambers and unnerving heat make **Tham Wang Badan** (daily 8.30am–4.30pm) one of the most exciting underground experiences in the region. Located at the western edge of Erawan National Park (see p.221), the cave is reached by a trail that begins from Highway 323 about 1500m northwest of the train station. From the station, walk up the station approach road, cross the tracks, turn left at the roundabout, then first right through the small town, passing a water tower on your left, you'll reach the T-junction with Highway 323 after 900m. The **trail** to the cave is signposted 600m northwest (right) up Highway 323, from the right-hand (east) side of the road. About 1km into the trail, you reach the park warden's office where you can rent feeble torches; it's better to bring your own or to pay the warden at least B50 to accompany you and turn on the cave lights, which is well worth the money. From the office it's 2km of easy walking to the cave, but the descent should be made with care and sturdy shoes.

Longtail boats can be hired from Pak Saeng pier for the upstream **boat ride** to **Tham Lawa**, the largest stalactite cave in the area and home to three species of bat. To get to the pier from the Highway 323 T-junction, cross the road, turn left (southeast) towards Kanchanaburi, then take the first road on your right. It's a two-kilometre walk down this minor road to the river and Pak Saeng pier. There's a small restaurant at the pier, where you can arrange boat-hire. The return journey to the cave takes roughly two hours, including half an hour there, and costs about B700 for the eight-seater boat. Add on at least four more hours and another B800 if you want to continue on to Sai Yok Yai Falls.

Practicalities

The best-value **accommodation** in Nam Tok is at the *Sai Yok Noi Bungalows* ($\textcircled{T}$034/591075; $\textbf{❶–❸}$); to get there from the train station, turn northwest at the T-junction (towards Sangkhlaburi), walk about ten minutes and then turn right at the hotel sign by the fuel station. The roadside *Cola Hotel* ($\textcircled{T}$034/591004; $\textbf{❷–❸}$) is cheap and functional, and conveniently located on the west side of Highway 323 opposite the access road to the train station. Or you can sleep in a floating room, comfortably kitted out with attached bathroom and veranda, beside Pak Saeng pier, at *Kitti Raft* ($\textcircled{T}$034/634168; $\textbf{❸–❹}$). The biggest resort on this section of the river is *River Kwai Jungle Rafts* ($\textcircled{T}$02/246 3079 or 01/215 6402, $\textcircled{F}$02/246 5679, $\textcircled{E}$info@riverkwaifloatel.com; $\textbf{❻}$), about forty minutes upstream from Pak Saeng pier and inaccessible by road. A company called River Kwai Floatel runs the resort, organizing overnight packages starting from Bangkok, which include transport, trips along the river, visits to Kanchanaburi sights, French and Thai meals and raft accommodation. A two-day package costs B2300 per person; packages with only meals and accommodation cost B900 per person per day.

There are lots of small, inexpensive **restaurants** clustered around the train station, and plenty more in the heart of Nam Tok, between the station and Highway 323.

Nam Tok to Three Pagodas Pass

Although the rail line north of Nam Tok was ripped up soon after the end of the war, it casts its dreadful shadow all the way up the Kwai Noi valley into Burma. The remnants of track are most visible at **Hellfire Pass**, while many of the villages in the area are former POW sites – locals frequently stumble across burial sites, now reclaimed by the encroaching jungle. Small towns and vast expanses of impenetrable mountain wilderness characterize this stretch, a landscape typified by the dense monsoon forests of **Sai Yok National Park**, which stretches all the way to the Burmese border. The first significant town beyond Sai Yok is the lakeside **Thong Pha Phum** (147km from Kanchanaburi); from here the road continues a further 73km to the border territory around **Sangkhlaburi**, 18km short of the actual border at **Three Pagodas Pass**, a notorious port of entry for smuggled goods and site of occasional skirmishes between Karen, Mon, Burmese and Thai factions. However, even if you have a visa you won't be allowed to travel any more than 1km into Burma at this point.

The only access to this region is via Highway 323, which runs all the way to the border, past the massive **Khao Laem reservoir**, along a course dominated by the Tenasserim mountains to the west and the less extensive Mae Khlong range to the east. All regular **buses** here originate in Kanchanaburi and run every thirty minutes, via Nam Tok and on to Thong Pha Phum, in both directions, with four a day continuing up to Sangkhlaburi; the last regular bus to Sangkhla leaves Kanchanaburi at midday, passing Hellfire Pass at about 1.15pm and Sai Yok National Park at about 2pm, so it's feasible to stop off for a couple of hours at either Hellfire Pass or Sai Yok National Park before resuming your trip northwards. There are also three daily air-con buses and three daily air-con minibuses from Kanchanaburi to Sangkhlaburi, but these usually pick up passengers only at Thong Pha Phum. As there's nowhere to stay at Hellfire Pass and the budget accommodation at Sai Yok fills up fast, it's advisable to set off from Nam Tok reasonably early and aim to spend the night in Sangkhlaburi; if you get stuck, Thong Pha Phum has a couple of hotels in town, plus several pleasant lakeside hotels for which you need your own transport.

Hellfire Pass

To keep the Death Railway level through the uneven course of the Kwai valley, the POWs had to build a series of embankments and trestle bridges and, at dishearteningly frequent intervals, gouge deep cuttings through solid rock. The most concentrated digging was at **Konyu**, 18km beyond Nam Tok, where seven separate cuttings were made over a 3.5-kilometre stretch. The longest and most brutal of these was **Hellfire Pass**, which got its name from the hellish lights and shadows of the fires the POWs used when working at night – a job which took three months of round-the-clock labour with the most primitive tools.

Hellfire Pass has now been turned into a memorial walk in honour of the POWs who worked and died on it, and their story is documented at the beautifully designed **Hellfire Pass Memorial Museum** (daily 9am–4pm; donation) which stands at the trailhead. This is the best and most informative of all the World War II museums in the Kanchanaburi region, using wartime relics, and POW memorabilia, photos and first-hand accounts to tell the horribly sobering history of the construction of this stretch of the Thailand–Burma Railway. Founded by an Australian-Thai volunteer group, the museum now serves as a sort of pilgrimage site for the families and friends of Australian POWs. A commemorative **booklet** about the construction and maintenance of Hellfire Pass is available at the Museum (B200).

The same Australian-Thai group has also cleared a four-kilometre, ninety-minute circular **memorial walk**, which begins at the Museum and follows the old rail route through the eighteen-metre-deep cutting and on to Hin Tok creek along a course relaid with some of the original narrow-gauge track. The creek was originally forded by a trestle bridge so unstable that it was nicknamed the Pack of Cards Bridge, but this has long since crumbled and disappeared. The trail doubles back on itself, passing through bamboo forest and a viewpoint that gives some idea of the phenomenal depth of rock the POWs had to dig through.

Most Kanchanaburi tour operators (see p.219) offer **day-trips** to Hellfire Pass – to get the most out of the experience, choose an itinerary that combines the pass with a ride on the railway itself. It's also quite easy to get to Hellfire Pass on your own, and to combine it with your own trip on the Railway: from Kanchanaburi or Nam Tok, take any **bus** bound for Thong Pha Phum or Sangkhlaburi and ask to be dropped off at Hellfire Pass, which is signposted on the left-hand side of Highway 323 as you face Sangkhlaburi; it's about a 75-minute journey from Kanchanaburi or 20 minutes from Nam Tok. If you have your own transport, look for the sign shortly after kilometre-stone 64.

Sai Yok National Park

Signed off the highway 104km north of Kanchanaburi, **Sai Yok National Park** also retains some evidence of World War II occupation, but the chief attractions here are caves, waterfalls and teak forests. The park covers five hundred square kilometres of uninhabited land stretching west of Highway 323 as far as the Burmese border, though the public has access only to the narrow strip between the Kwai Noi and the road, an area criss-crossed by short trails and dotted with caves and freshwater springs. It makes a refreshing resting point between Nam Tok and Sangkhlaburi, particularly if you have your own transport; accommodation and restaurant facilities are available, but cater primarily for Thai family groups.

Any of the Kanchanaburi–Thong Pha Phum **buses** will stop at the road entrance to Sai Yok, from where it's a three-kilometre walk to the **visitor centre**, trailheads and river. The last buses in both directions pass the park at about 4.30pm. Motorbike taxis sometimes hang around the road entrance waiting to transport visitors, but a more scenic way of visiting the park would be to join a longtail excursion from Nam Tok (see p.225).

All the trails start from near the visitor centre, and are clearly signposted from there as well as being marked on the map available from the centre. As in most of Thailand's national parks, Thais themselves come here for a waterfall. In this case it's the much-photographed **Sai Yok Yai Falls**, which tumbles right into the Kwai Noi in a powerful cascade – you can shower under it and bathe in the pools nearby, or gaze at it from the suspension bridge. If you come by long-tail from Nam Tok, the boatman will probably also take you another 5km upstream to the stalactite-filled **Daowadung Caves**, a two-kilometre walk west of the river bank.

However, Sai Yok's most unusual feature is its dominant forests of **teak**, an endangered species in Thailand as a consequence of rapacious logging. During the war all the teak in this area was felled for rail sleepers – the present forests were replanted in 1954. The park's other rarity is the smallest known mammal in the world, the hog-nosed or **bumblebee bat**, discovered in 1973 and weighing only 1.75g, with a wingspan of 1.6cm. The bats live in twenty limestone caves in the Kanchanaburi area, of which Sai Yok's **bat cave** is the most accessible. Don't get too excited, though: it's almost impossible to see the bats unless you venture quite far inside with a powerful flashlight, and even then you'll need a fair amount of luck. On the way to the cave along the signposted trail, you might stumble across a few disintegrating rail sleepers which, together with the pile of bricks identified as the "Japanese cooking facility", constitute the park's only visible World War II remains. Although the camp kitchen is not worth making the effort for, follow its signposts from the visitor centre for some secluded bathing spots in the crystal-clear **natural springs** nearby.

Sai Yok has seven national park **bungalows** (B500–1500 for four to twelve people), but more inviting are the *Sai Yok View Raft* (T034/514191; ❹), raft houses near the waterfall; get there early if you want to be sure of a room. The raft house serves **food** and there are plenty of fried rice and noodle stalls near the visitor centre.

Pha That Waterfall and Hin Dat hot springs

Most people come to **Pha That Waterfall** as part of a tour, mainly because it's so laborious to get to without transport. If you do have wheels, look for the big green sign on the left (west) side of the road just after kilometre-stone 104, which directs you onto the very potholed twelve-kilometre track to the falls. There are a couple of foodstalls at the roadside and, if you've arrived on the bus, you may be able to get a ride with a motorcycle taxi from here to Pha That. During and just after the rainy season, Pha That features two long, gently sloping **cascades**; in the dry season there's only one. The setting is pretty, though not as adventurous as Erawan, and the falls are quite peaceful during the week. The rocky steps of the left-hand cascade are quite easy to climb, and you can splash about in the pools en route; there's also a path that follows the falls most of the way up.

Hin Dat hot springs are signed in English off Highway 323 less than 2km north of the Pha That sign, just after kilometre-stone 105 and, as they're only 1km off the highway, they're easy to walk to if you've come by bus – any Thong Pha Phum bus will drop you at the junction. A big pool has been dug at the source of these natural hot springs so you can immerse yourself in soothingly warm water, but there's not much else to detain you here.

Thong Pha Phum and the lakeside hotels

From Sai Yok, Highway 323 continues northwest, following the course of the Kwai Noi. Forty-seven kilometres along the road is **THONG PHA PHUM**, a market town whose prosperity owes much to the tin and silver mines on the nearby Burmese border. There's not much more than a collection of market stalls and missed bus connections to keep you in the town itself, but a couple of inexpensive bungalow-hotels right in the town centre – the medium sized, mid-range *Som Chainuk* (☎034/599067; ❶–❺) and the smaller, cheaper *Sri Thong Pha Phum* (☎034/599058; ❶–❸) – offer decent enough accommodation.

With your own transport, a much better alternative to overnighting in town is to drive 12km west of Thong Pha Phum market to the southeastern fringes of nearby **Khao Laem Reservoir**. Also known as the Kreung Kra Wia reservoir, this vast body of water stretches all the way to Sangkhlaburi 73km to the north and, when created in the early 1980s, flooded every village in the vicinity. The former villagers have been rehoused along the reservoir's banks, and hotels have sprung up here too, making the most of the refreshing, almost Scandinavian, landscape of forested hills and clear, still water that's perfect for swimming in. Here you'll find a string of appealing **raft-house hotels** – most of which also have land-based single and double rooms – that make very pleasant places to stay; to reach these, follow signs from Thong Pha Phum for the Khao Laem Dam, but instead of turning right for the dam continue along the left-hand branch of the road for another 7km. These hotels generally cater for Thai families and groups, so much of the raft-house accommodation is for six to ten people, which means you have to rent the whole raft even if there's only two of you. If your Thai is good enough or if you join a tour from Kanchanaburi – you should be able to arrange for your raft-house to be towed out into the lake and taken for a breakfast-time ride on the water. Recommended hotels include *Phae VIP* (☎034/599001), which has both simple, family-sized raft-houses (B2000 for up to ten people) as well as more comfortable air-conditioned doubles (❻), all with gorgeous views; the adjacent *Wang Pai Resort* (☎01/443 1246; ❺–❽), which has a similar set-up; and 1500m east, the more upmarket *Lake Valley* (☎02/433 6688; ❻), which occupies an equally lovely spot. Even if you've no intention of staying, the moderately priced lakeside **restaurant** at *VIP* makes a soothing place for an hour's break on the way to or from Sangkhlaburi.

Sangkhlaburi and around

Beyond Thong Pha Phum the views get increasingly spectacular as Highway 323 climbs through the remaining swathes of montane rainforest, occasionally hugging Khao Laem's eastern shore, until it comes to an end at the tiny town of **SANGKHLABURI** (often called Sangkhla for short), 73km north of Thong Pha Phum and 220km north of Kanchanaburi. One of those unassuming backwaters where there's nothing much to do except enjoy the scenery and observe everyday life, it has the rough feel of a mountain outpost and is a charming place to hang out for a few days. It's also an increasingly popular destination for overnight "trekking" tours from Kanchanaburi (see p.219) and for Thai tourists at weekends and public holidays.

If you're coming to Sangkhlaburi direct from Kanchanaburi, the most pleasant way to travel is by air-conditioned **minibus** (3 daily at 7.30am, 11.30am & 4.30pm; 3hr), which departs from the office in the far southeastern corner

of Kanchanaburi bus station and should be reserved in advance; there are also three air-con buses (#8203) a day in both directions. The four daily **regular buses** are less expensive but may take twice as long: if you're coming from Nam Tok or Sai Yok, though, these are your only viable option, as the minibuses and air-con buses only pick up passengers at Thong Pha Phum; the last regular bus to Sangkhla leaves Kanchanaburi at midday.

Travelling to Sangkhla under your own steam is scenic if rather tiring, as the **road** is forever twisting and turning after Thong Pha Phum; the last 25km are particularly nerve-wracking for bikers because of the potentially dangerous gravel spots in the many bends. Nonetheless, the views are fabulous, particularly at the signed **viewpoint** just north of kilometre-stone 35 (about 40km south of Sangkhla), where there's a lakeside lay-by that's just perfect for taking photos. You may also be tempted to stop at the roadside **Kraeng Kravia Waterfall**, 1km south of the viewpoint at kilometre-stone 34, beside the army checkpoint. Though not very high, the three-tiered cascade does get quite powerful in and just after the rainy season, and makes a pleasant spot for picnicking on barbecued chicken sold at the nearby stall.

The Town

Located right at the reservoir's northernmost tip, Sangkhlaburi overlooks an eerily beautiful scene of semi-submerged trees. Because of its proximity to the border, Sangkhlaburi's **ethnic mix** is particularly marked: Mon, Karen and Burmese townspeople and traders mingle with indigenous Thais at the central early-morning market. Many wear the checked *longyis* favoured across the border, and the Burmese face powder used as protection against the elements. The older villagers have the hardy, weathered bearing of mountain people: in the cool season, when mist blankets the place until late morning, they make their transactions wrapped in woolly hats and jumpers, sarongs and denim jackets.

Other than people-watching, you could spend a pleasant afternoon **boating** across Khao Laem reservoir in search of the **sunken temple** Wat Sam Phrasop, a former village temple that once stood on a hill but is now almost completely submerged. When water levels are high you can only see the top of its spire, but by the end of the dry season you get to see part of the temple's upper storey as well. The wat is close to the confluence of the three rivers that feed the reservoir and, though the lake is hardly teeming with fish, local villagers do set up their nets here: the strange bamboo contraptions that dot the water are based on an ancient Chinese design and operate on a pulley system. If you paddle close to the cliffside banks of the reservoir you might spot a monkey or two, though sightings apparently get rarer every year. *P Guest House* rents out two-person **canoes** for independent exploring (B25 per hour), or you can join a sunset longtail-boat trip from either *P Guest House* or *Burmese Inn* (B500 per boat with up to ten passengers).

Ban Waeng Ka and Wat Wiwekaram

The Mon village of **BAN WAENG KA**, divided from Sangkhlaburi by the reservoir, grew up in the late 1940s after the outbreak of civil war in Burma when the emergence of an intolerant nationalist regime prompted the country's ethnic minorities to flee across the border (see box on pp.234–5). Illegal immigrants in Thailand, their presence was permitted but not officially recognized, so that thirty years later when the dam was constructed and the valley villages flooded, the Mon refugees weren't entitled to compensation. Despite this, an influential local Mon abbot, Pa U Thama, managed to secure the right to relocate five hundred submerged households to the northwest shore of the reservoir, a settlement which mushroomed into the one-thousand-household village of Waeng Ka, a couple of kilometres west of Sangkhla. Although most now have official Sangkhlaburi residency, the Mon still have limited rights: they must apply for expensive seven-day permits if they wish to travel out of the district, a system which lends itself to corruption.

To explore the village, you can either hail a motorbike taxi (B30), or rent a motorbike from one of Sangkhlaburi's guest houses and cross the spider's web of a **wooden bridge** spanning the lake. Said to be the longest hand-built wooden bridge in the world, it's open to pedestrian and motorbike traffic only; cars use the more solid structure a few hundred metres further north. Once across the bridge, turn left at the cinema to get into the village – a sprawling collection of traditional wooden houses lining a network of steep dirt tracks, with a small but lively dry-goods market at its heart.

Wat Wiwekaram, Ban Waeng Ka's most dramatic sight, stands at the edge of the village, its massive, golden **chedi** clearly visible from Sangkhlaburi. Built in a fusion of Thai, Indian and Burmese styles, the imposing square-sided stupa is modelled on the centrepiece of India's Bodh Gaya, the sacred site of the Buddha's enlightenment, and contains a much-prized Buddha relic (said to be a piece of his skeleton) brought to Ban Waeng Ka from Sri Lanka. The wat is hugely popular with Buddhist pilgrims from all over Thailand, and is also a focal point for the Mon community on both sides of the Thai–Burma border; at Mon New Year in April the wat is packed with men sent by their Mon families to pay their respects. Mon, Karen, Burmese and Thai devotees donate enormous sums of money to temple coffers in honour of the octogenarian **Pa U Thama**, now the wat's abbot, who has been revered as a unifying force ever since he crossed the border into Thailand in 1955. His photograph is displayed in the temple compound, and the opulence of the wat buildings is testimony to his status. There's a good tourist market in the covered cloisters at the chedi compound, with plenty of reasonably priced sarongs, jade and bone jewellery and Burmese woodcarvings. The wat is spread over two compounds, with the gleaming new bot, **viharn** and monks' quarters about 1km away from the chedi, at the end of the right-hand fork in the road. The interior of the viharn is decorated with murals showing tableaux from the five hundred lives of the Buddha, meant to be viewed in anticlockwise order.

Practicalities

Minibuses from Kanchanaburi and Thong Pha Phum terminate in front of the *Pornpailin Hotel* on the eastern edge of Sangkhlaburi; the regular **buses** stop a couple of blocks further west. Sangkhlaburi is small enough to walk round in an hour, and there are plenty of **motorbike taxis** for hire too; rates start at about B15 from the bus terminal to the guest houses and rise to around B50 for a ride from the guest houses to Wat Wiwekaram across the water. There are no bicycles for rent in town, but both guest houses rent **motorbikes** for B200 a day. Armin at *Burmese Inn* can organize the hiring of a pick-up **truck** and driver for around B2000 a day.

The two guest houses organize **day-trips** (around B800 per person) in the area for their guests. A typical full day out includes elephant riding, white-water rafting and a visit to a Mon or Mon-Karen village; other popular itineraries take you to Three Pagodas Pass (see opposite), to the Mon village, temple and market at Ban Waeng Ka, or for a few hours boating on Khao Laem reservoir. Armin at *Burmese Inn* can also arrange four-wheel-drive outings to more remote spots.

Traveller's cheques and dollars can be changed at the **bank**, which is close to the market in the town centre; the post office is near the regular bus stop. If you're heading up to Three Pagodas Pass and want to cross the border into the Burmese side of the market there (see p.235), you currently need to visit the **immigration** office in Sangkhlaburi to get your Thai exit stamp *before* continuing on to Three Pagodas. Sangkhla immigration office (ask for the *kaan khao muang*; Mon–Fri 8.30am–4.30pm) is near the hospital, behind the *Pornpailin* hotel.

Accommodation and eating

Not many independent foreign travellers make it to Sangkhlaburi, but those who do all seem to head for one of the town's two inexpensive **guest houses**: both are run by friendly and informative managers, and offer day-trips and motorbikes for rent. Both guest houses are also used by backpacking tour groups from Kanchanaburi, so it might be worth phoning ahead to reserve a room; you will definitely need to book on weekends and national holidays. *Burmese Inn* (T034/595146; ❷–❸), 800m down the hill from either bus terminal (follow the signs, or take a motorbike taxi), has a range of huts and bungalows, all with attached bathrooms, strung across the hillside, with excellent views of the wooden bridge and Ban Waeng Ka across the lake. The Austrian manager, Armin, is a fount of local knowledge, including current border politics, and will arrange excursions into uncharted national park territory on request. A few hundred metres further down the same road (also well signposted), the efficiently run *P Guest House* (T034/595061, F595139; ❷) is spectacularly sited on the sloping banks of the reservoir, and offers comfortable accommodation in huts with exceptionally smart shared bathrooms. The large but cosy **restaurant** offers good lake views and serves good Thai, Burmese and European food; manager Darunee rents out canoes for exploring the lake and arranges day-trips. If the guest houses are full, try the central *Pornpailin Hotel* (T034/595039; ❸–❹), just behind the market and opposite the army camp; the hotel has large, clean, if slightly overpriced, rooms with attached bathrooms and some air-con, though no views. The Thai-oriented *Forget Me Not* (T034/595015; ❹–❽) occupies a lovely waterside location between *Burmese Inn* and *P Guest House* and has decent rooms with fan or air-con.

Three Pagodas Pass
(Ban Sam Phra Chedi Ong)

Four kilometres before Sangkhlaburi, a road branches off Highway 323 to **Three Pagodas Pass** (signed as **Jadee Sam Ong**), winding its way through cloud-capped, forested hills and passing a few Karen and Mon settlements before reaching the border terminus 18km further on. Songthaews for the pass leave Sangkhlaburi bus station every forty minutes from 6am till about 5pm and take forty minutes; the last songthaew back to Sangkhla leaves at 6pm.

All **border trade** for hundreds of kilometres north and south has to come through Three Pagodas Pass: textiles, sandals, bicycles and medical supplies go out to Burma, in return for cattle and highly profitable teak logs – the felling of which has been illegal in Thailand since 1989. Over the last half-century, the Mon, the Karen and the Burmese government have vied with each other constantly for supremacy at the pass, the rebels relying on the tax on smuggled goods to finance their insurgency campaigns, the government desperate to regain its foothold in rebel territory. Until 1990, an offensive was launched every dry season against the then holder of the pass, but that year the power wrestle ended with the Burmese government gaining command from the Mon, a situation that has so far remained unchallenged.

Dubbed by some "the Palestinians of Asia", the **Mon** people – numbering around four million in Burma and three million in Thailand (chiefly in the western provinces of Kanchanaburi and Ratchaburi, and in the regions of Nonthaburi and Pathum Thani just north of Bangkok) – have endured centuries of persecution, displacement and forced assimilation.

Ethnologists speculate that the Mon originated either in India or Mongolia, travelling south to settle on the western banks of the Chao Phraya valley in the first century BC. Here they founded the **Dvaravati kingdom** (sixth to eleventh centuries AD), building centres at U Thong, Lopburi and Nakhon Pathom and later consolidating a northern kingdom in Haripunchai (modern-day Lamphun). They probably introduced Theravada Buddhism to the region, and produced some of the earliest Buddhist monuments, particularly Wheels of Law and Buddha footprints.

Over on the Burmese side of the border, the Mon kingdom had established itself around the southern city of Pegu well before the Burmese filtered into the area in the ninth century, but over the next nine hundred years consistent **harassment** from the Burmese forced thousands to flee to Thailand. (As Burma was also engaged in an endless series of territorial battles with Thailand, the Mon got their own back by acting as spies and informers for the Thais.) Eventually, in the mid-eighteenth century, the Burmese banned the use of the Mon language in Burma, segregated Mon men and women by force, and decreed that they should be known as Talaings, a pejorative term implying bastardy. Stripped of their homeland, the Mon were once again welcomed into Thailand as a useful source of labour – in 1814, the future Rama IV arrived at the Kanchanaburi border with three royal warboats and a guard of honour to chaperone the exiles. Whole areas of undeveloped jungle were given over to them, many of which are still Mon-dominated today.

The persecution of Burmese Mon continued right through the **twentieth century**. Ever since Burma got independence from the colonial British at the end of World War II, the Mon have fought for the right to administer their own independent Mon State in their historical homelands in lower Burma. In 1982 they joined with Burma's other minority groups such as the Karen (see box on p.280) to form the National Democratic Front and fight together against Burma's repressive

It must be the romantic image of a hilltop smuggling station that attracts the few foreign tourists to the 1400-metre-high pass, because there's nothing substantial to see here. The **pagodas** themselves are diminutive whitewashed structures unceremoniously encircled by a roundabout, though traffic is not exactly heavy up here. They are said to have been erected in the eighteenth century by the kings of Burma and Thailand as a symbolic commitment to peace between the traditionally warring neighbours (during the Ayutthayan period, Burmese troops would regularly thunder through here on elephant-back on their way to attack the capital). Each king supposedly built a chedi on his own side of the border and, at the foot of the central, borderline pagoda, the two kings signed an agreement never to war with each other again. Another interpretation holds that the pagodas represent the three strands of Buddhism – the Buddha, the Dharma (teaching) and the Sangha (monkhood) – and were erected here to boost the morale of Thai soldiers going to and from battle in Burma.

All three pagodas are now on Thai soil, at the edge of **Ban Sam Phra Chedi Ong**, a tiny village comprising not much more than a market, a few

military regime, formerly known as the State Law and Order Restoration Council (SLORC), but now renamed as the State Peace and Development Council (SPDC).

In the early 1990s, SLORC renewed its violence against the Mon in an attempt to round up the labour supply for two **infrastructure projects**: the extension of the Rangoon–Ye rail line as far south as Tavoy, and the construction of a gas pipeline connecting Burmese waters with Kanchanaburi. Though the New Mon State Party entered into a ceasefire agreement with SLORC in June 1995, international human rights organizations continue to report gross violations against civilian Mon living in Burma. Hundreds of thousands of Mon, Karen and Muslim men, women and children have been press-ganged into unpaid labour; furthermore, deaths from malnutrition, malaria and cholera have been reported, as have beatings and gang rapes. Other captive workers are used as human land-mine detectors, and as porters to transport arms for the Burmese attacks on their own rebel army. The junta has also banned the teaching of Mon language and literature in schools, to which the Mon have responded by setting up their own literacy groups during school holidays.

Not surprisingly, Mon have been fleeing these atrocities in droves, the majority ending up in **refugee camps** in the Sangkhlaburi district, the established home to a large community of Mon people. Though the Thai government has always tolerated refugee camps on all its borders, it makes periodic attempts to stem the flow of refugees and send them back across the border (see p.280) – a policy that's been made considerably more urgent by the recent economic crisis in Thailand.

Like Thais, the Mon are a predominantly Buddhist, rice-growing people, but they also have strong animist beliefs. All Mon families have totemic **house spirits**, such as the turtle, snake, chicken or pig, which carry certain taboos: if you're of the chicken-spirit family, for example, the lungs and head of every chicken that you cook have to be offered to the spirits, and although you're allowed to raise and kill chickens, you must never give one away. Guests belonging to a different spirit group from their host are not allowed to stay overnight. Mon **festivals** also differ slightly from Thai ones – at Songkhran (Thai New Year), the Mon spice up the usual water-throwing and parades with a special courtship ritual in which teams of men and women play each other at bowling, throwing flirtatious banter along with their wooden discs.

foodstalls, a songthaew stop, a wat and a tourist restaurant. Burmese land starts 50m away, at the village of Payathonzu, but, at the time of writing, foreign nationals are only allowed to get 1km **across the border** (daily 6am–6pm) here, to the far edge of the border market. Even to make this rather pathetic trip you need to arrive at the border with a Thai exit stamp from the immigration office in Sangkhlaburi (see p.233), whereupon you have to pay US$10 to enter Burma; on re-entry into Thailand you get a new thirty-day Thai tourist visa, regardless of how long you had left on your original one. All of which means it's hardly worth the effort and expense (and some would argue, the $10 to the Burmese government) – especially as the **market** on the Thai side of the border post is actually very enjoyable, inexpensive and full of interesting Burmese goods; items well worth looking out for include the distinctive brightly coloured Karen trousers and jackets, sarongs made of Burmese batik, *longyis,* jade and sapphires, bone jewellery, Burmese face powder, cheroots and all manner of teak-wood artefacts and furniture. Most of the market stalls on the Thai side set up under the roofed area at the back of the car park beside the three chedis.

As somewhere to hang out for a few days, Three Pagodas Pass doesn't compare to the more scenic and essentially more congenial Sangkhlaburi, but it is possible to **stay** on the Thai side of the border, at *Three Pagodas Resort* (T034/595316; ❸–❹) whose rooms and nicer air-con bungalows are set round a very pretty garden, under the lip of a limestone cliff on the edge of Ban Sam Phra Chedi Ong.

Ayutthaya and the Chao Phraya basin

Bisected by the country's main artery, the **Chao Phraya River**, and threaded by a network of tributaries and canals, the fertile plain to the north of the capital retains a spectrum of attractions from just about every period of the country's history. The monumental kitsch of the nineteenth-century palace at **Bang Pa-In** provides a sharp contrast with the atmospheric ruins at the former capital of **Ayutthaya**, where ancient temples, some crumbling and overgrown, others alive and kicking, are arrayed in a leafy, riverine setting. **Lopburi's** disparate remains, testimony to more than a millennium of continuous settlement, are less compelling, but you'll get a frenetic, noisy insight into Thai religion if you visit the nearby **Wat Phra Phutthabat** (Temple of the Buddha's Footprint), still Thailand's most popular pilgrimage site after three and a half centuries.

Each of the attractions of this region can be visited on a day-trip from the capital – or, if you have more time to spare, you can slowly work your way through them before heading north or northeast. **Trains** are the most useful means of getting around, as plenty of local services run to and from Bangkok (note that the State Railway's standard English-language timetable does not list all the local services – phone Hualamphong station on T02/220 4334 for more comprehensive information). The line from the capital takes in Bang Pa-In and Ayutthaya before forking at Ban Phachi: the northern branch heads for Lopburi and goes on to Phitsanulok and Chiang Mai; the northeastern branch serves Isaan. **Buses** between towns are regular but slow, while Bang Pa-In and Ayutthaya can also be reached on scenic but usually expensive **boat** trips up the Chao Phraya.

Bang Pa-In

Little more than a roadside market, the village of **BANG PA-IN**, 60km north of Bangkok, has been put on the tourist map by its extravagant and rather surreal **Royal Palace** (daily 8.30am–5pm, ticket office closes 3.30pm; B50), even though most of the buildings can be seen only from the outside. King Prasat Thong of Ayutthaya first built a palace on this site, 20km downstream from his capital, in the middle of the seventeenth century, and it remained a popular country residence for the kings of Ayutthaya. The palace was abandoned a century later when the capital was moved to Bangkok, only to be revived in the middle of the last century when the advent of steamboats shortened the journey time upriver. Rama IV (1851–68) built a modest residence here, which his son Chulalongkorn (Rama V), in his passion for Westernization, knocked down to make room for the eccentric melange of European, Thai and Chinese architectural styles visible today.

Set in manicured grounds on an island in the Chao Phraya River, and based around an ornamental lake, the palace complex is flat and compact – a free brochure from the ticket office gives a diagram of the layout. On the north side of the lake stand a two-storey, colonial-style residence for the royal relatives and the Italianate **Warophat Phiman** (Excellent and Shining Heavenly Abode), which housed Chulalongkorn's throne hall and still contains private apartments where the present royal family sometimes stays. A covered bridge links this outer part of the palace to the **Pratu Thewarat Khanlai** (The King of the Gods Goes Forth Gate), the main entrance to the inner palace, which was reserved for the king and his immediate family. The high fence which encloses half of the bridge allowed the women of the harem to cross without being seen by male courtiers. You can't miss the photogenic **Aisawan Thiphya-art** (Divine Seat of Personal Freedom) in the middle of the lake: named after King Prasat Thong's original palace, it's the only example of pure Thai architecture at Bang Pa-In. The elegant tiers of the pavilion's roof shelter a bronze statue of Chulalongkorn.

In the inner palace, the **Uthayan Phumisathian** (Garden of the Secured Land) was Chulalongkorn's favourite house, a Swiss-style wooden chalet painted in bright two-tone green. After passing the **Ho Withun Thasana** (Sage's Lookout Tower), built so that the king could survey the surrounding countryside, you'll come to the main attraction of Bang Pa-In, the **Phra Thinang Wehart Chamrun** (Palace of Heavenly Light). A masterpiece of Chinese design, the mansion and its contents were shipped from China and presented as a gift to Chulalongkorn in 1889 by the Chinese Chamber of Commerce in Bangkok. You're allowed to take off your shoes and feast your eyes on the interior, which drips with fine porcelain and embroidery, ebony furniture inlaid with mother-of-pearl and fantastically intricate woodcarving. This residence was the favourite of Rama VI, whose carved and lacquered writing table can be seen on the ground floor.

The simple marble **obelisk** behind the Uthayan Phumisathian was erected by Chulalongkorn to hold the ashes of Queen Sunandakumariratana, his favourite wife. In 1881, Sunanda, who was then 21 and expecting a child, was taking a trip on the river here when her boat capsized. She could have been rescued quite easily, but the laws concerning the sanctity of the royal family left those around her no option. "If a boat founders, the boatmen must swim away; if they remain near the boat [or] if they lay hold of him [the royal person] to rescue him, they are to be executed." Following the tragedy, King Chulalongkorn became a zealous reformer of Thai customs and strove to make the monarchy more accessible.

Turn right out of the main entrance to the palace grounds and cross the river on the small cable car, and you'll come to the greatest oddity of all: **Wat Nivet Dhamapravat**. A grey Buddhist viharn in the style of a Gothic church, it was built by Chulalongkorn in 1878, complete with wooden pews and stained-glass windows.

Bang Pa-In can easily be visited on a day-trip from Bangkok or Ayutthaya. The best way of getting to Bang Pa-In **from Bangkok** is by early-morning **train** from Hualamphong station (7.05am & 8.35am); the journey takes just over an hour. All trains continue to Ayutthaya, with half going on to Lopburi. From Bang Pa-In station (note the separate station hall built by Chulalongkorn for the royal family) it's a two-kilometre hike to the palace, or you can take a samlor for about B30. Slow **buses** leave Bangkok's Northern Terminal every twenty minutes and stop at Bang Pa-In market, a samlor ride from the palace.

Every Sunday, the Chao Phraya Express Boat company (☎02/222 5330) runs a **river tour** to Bang Pa-In, taking in Wat Phailom, a breeding ground for open-billed storks escaping the cold in Siberia, plus a shopping stop at Bang Sai folk arts and handicrafts centre. The boat leaves Prachan (Maharat) pier in Ratanakosin at 8am, and returns at 5.30pm. Tickets, available from the piers, are B330, not including lunch and admission to the palace and the handicrafts centre (B100). Luxury cruises to Ayutthaya also stop at Bang Pa-In.

From Ayutthaya, buses leave Thanon Naresuan every half an hour for the thirty-minute journey to Bang Pa-In market; irregular trains from Ayutthaya's inconveniently located station are less useful for this short hop.

Ayutthaya

In its heyday as the booming capital of the Thai kingdom, **AYUTTHAYA**, 80km north of Bangkok, was so well endowed with temples that sunlight reflecting off their gilt decoration was said to dazzle from three miles away. Wide, grassy spaces today occupy much of the atmospheric site, which now resembles a graveyard for temples: grand, brooding red-brick ruins rise out of the fields, satisfyingly evoking the city's bygone grandeur while providing a soothing contrast to the brashness of modern temple architecture. A few intact buildings help form an image of what the capital must have looked like, while three fine museums flesh out the picture.

The core of the ancient capital was a four-kilometre-wide **island** at the confluence of the Lopburi, Pasak and Chao Phraya rivers, which was once encircled by a twelve-kilometre wall, crumbling parts of which can be seen at the Phom Phet fortress in the southeast corner. A grid of broad roads now crosses the island, with recent buildings jostling uneasily with the ancient remains; the hub of the small, grim and lifeless modern town rests on the northeast bank of the island around the corner of Thanon U Thong and Thanon Chao Phrom, although the newest development is off the island to the east.

Ayutthaya comes alive each year for a week in mid-December, when a **festival** is organized to commemorate the town's status as a UNESCO **World Heritage Site**. The highlight of the celebrations is the nightly *son et lumière* show, usually at Wat Phra Si Sanphet, a grand historical romp featuring fireworks and elephant-back fights.

Some history

Ayutthaya takes its name from the Indian city of Ayodhya (Sanskrit for "invincible"), the legendary birthplace of Rama, hero of the *Ramayana* epic (see p.125). It was founded in 1351 by U Thong – later **King Ramathibodi I** –

after Lopburi was ravaged by smallpox, and it rose rapidly through exploiting the expanding trade routes between India and China. Stepping into the political vacuum left by the decline of the Khmer empire at Angkor and the first Thai kingdom at Sukhothai, by the mid-fifteenth century Ayutthaya controlled an empire covering most of the area of modern-day Thailand. Built entirely on canals, few of which survive today, Ayutthaya grew into an enormous amphibious city, which by 1685 had one million people – roughly double the population of London at the same time – living largely on houseboats in a 140-kilometre network of waterways.

Ayutthaya's great wealth attracted a swarm of **foreign traders**, especially in the seventeenth century. At one stage forty different nationalities, including Chinese, Portuguese, Dutch, English and French, were settled here, many of whom lived in their own ghettos and had their own docks for the export of rice, spices, timber and hides. With deft political skill, the kings of Ayutthaya maintained their independence from outside powers, while embracing the benefits of their cosmopolitan influence: they employed foreign architects and navigators, used Japanese samurai as royal bodyguards, and even took on outsiders as their prime ministers, who could look after their foreign trade without getting embroiled in the usual court intrigues.

In 1767, this 400-year-long **golden age** of stability and prosperity came to an abrupt end. After over two centuries of recurring tensions, the Burmese captured and ravaged Ayutthaya, taking tens of thousands of prisoners back to Burma with them. With even the wats in ruins, the city had to be abandoned to the jungle, but its memory endured: the architects of the new capital on Ratanakosin island in Bangkok perpetuated Ayutthaya's layout in every possible way.

Practicalities

The best way of getting to Ayutthaya **from Bangkok** is by **train** – there are about twenty a day, concentrated in the early morning and evening; trains continue on to the north and the northeast, making connections to Chiang Mai, Nong Khai and Ubon Ratchathani. To get to the centre of town from the station on the east bank of the Pasak, take the two-baht ferry from the jetty 100m west of the station (last ferry 7pm) across to Chao Phrom pier; it's then a five-minute walk to the junction of Thanon U Thong and Thanon Chao Phrom. The station has a useful left-luggage service (daily 5am–10pm; B5 per piece per day). Though frequent, **buses** to Ayutthaya are slower and less convenient, as they depart from Bangkok's remote Northern Terminal. Most buses from Bangkok pull in at the bus station on Thanon Naresuan just west of the centre of Ayutthaya, though some, mainly those on long-distance runs, will only stop at the bus terminal 2km to the east of the centre by the *Ayutthaya Grand Hotel* on Thanon Rojana. Private air-con minibuses from Bangkok's Victory Monument finish their non-stop route opposite the Thanon Naresuan bus station (every 30min during daylight hours). It's also possible to get here by scenic **boat tour** from Bangkok via Bang Pa-In Palace: the *Oriental Hotel* (see p.115), among others, runs swanky day-trips for around B1500 per person, and a couple of plushly converted teak rice barges – the *Mekhala* (☎02/256 7168 or 256 7169) and the *Manohra 2* ☎02/476 0021 – do exorbitantly priced overnight cruises. **From Kanchanaburi**, it's possible to bypass the Bangkok gridlock by taking a bus to Suphanburi (every 30min; 2hr), then changing onto an Ayutthaya bus (every 30min; 1hr 30min), which will drop you off at Chao Phrom market.

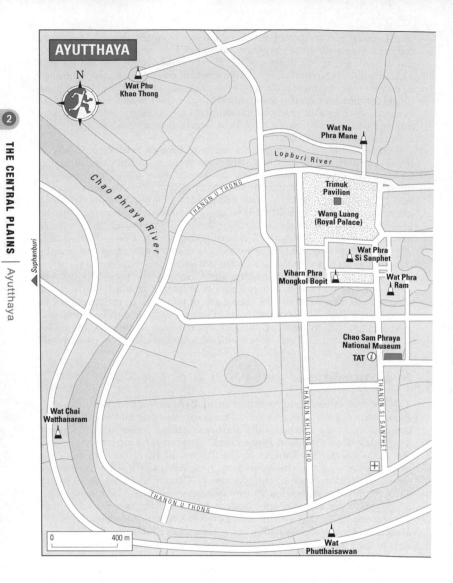

Once in Ayutthaya, the **tourist police** base ℡035/241446 and the helpful **TAT** office (daily 8.30am–4.30pm; ℡035/246076 or 246077, ⓔchedi1@cscoms.com) can be found next to the city hall on the west side of Thanon Si Sanphet, opposite the Chao Sam Phraya National Museum. Under construction just to the south of the TAT office is a grandiose tourist information centre which, it's said, will house multimedia exhibits about Ayutthaya, currency exchange and bike rental facilities, a post office and a café. It's also worth asking TAT about plans to develop the facilities of the sixteenth-century kraal – into which wild elephants were driven for capture and taming – on the northeast side of town, to include a training

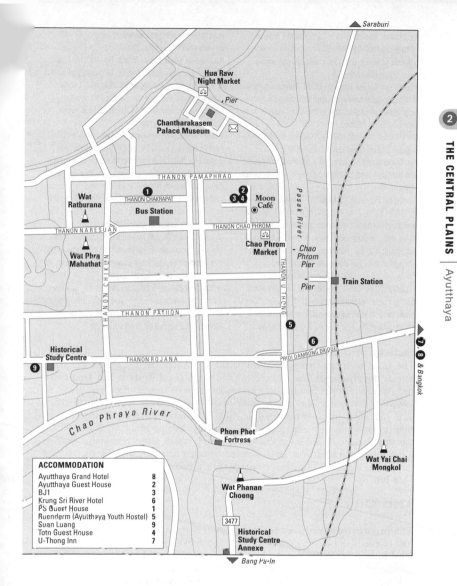

▲ Saraburi

Hua Raw
Night Market

Pier

Chantharakasem
Palace Museum

THANON PAMAPHRAO

Wat
Ratburana

THANON CHAKRAPAT

Bus Station

THANON NARESUAN

Wat Phra
Mahathat

THANON CHIKUN

THANON PATHON

Historical
Study Centre

THANON ROJANA

Chao Phraya River

1
2
3 **4** Moon
Café

THANON CHAO PHROM

Chao Phrom
Market

Chao
Phrom
Pier

Pier

5

6

PRIDI DAMRONG BRIDGE

THANON U THONG

Pasak River

Train Station

▶ **7.8**
& Bangkok

9

Phom Phet
Fortress

Wat Yai Chai
Mongkol

Wat Phanan
Choeng

3477

Historical
Study Centre
Annexe

▼ Bang Pa-In

ACCOMMODATION	
Ayutthaya Grand Hotel	8
Ayutthaya Guest House	2
BJ1	3
Krung Sri River Hotel	6
PS Guest House	1
Ruenderm (Ayutthaya Youth Hostel)	5
Suan Luang	9
Totn Guest House	4
U-Thong Inn	7

school and hospital for elephants and public shows. There are plenty of **internet cafés** around Chao Phrom market and on Thanon Pamaphrao, or try the helpful Net Riverside at Chao Phrom pier (B30 per hr).

Accommodation

Although Ayutthaya is usually visited on a day-trip, there is a good choice of **budget accommodation** for those who want to make a little more of it. A few more upmarket options offer fancier facilities, although two of these, *U-Thong Inn* and *Ayutthaya Grand Hotel*, are a fair distance from town.

Ayutthaya Grand Hotel, 75/5 Thanon Rojana ⌾035/335483–91, ℗335492. Upscale but way out east of town, with hot water, air-con and a large swimming pool. ❻

Ayutthaya Guest House, 12/34 Thanon Naresuan ⌾035/232658. Modern, clean and friendly place on a quiet, unnamed lane in the town centre, with clean, wooden-floored rooms. ❸

BJ 1 Guest House, NG 16/7 Thanon Naresuan ⌾035/251526. Next door to the *Toto* and *Ayutthaya* guest houses, but a bit more cramped and shabby – and justifiably cheaper – than either of them. ❷

Krung Sri River, 27/2 Moo 11, Thanon Rojana ⌾035/244333–7, ℗243777. Ayutthaya's newest and most upmarket accommodation is a grand affair, with swanky lobby, gym and attractive pool, occupying a prime, but noisy, position at the eastern end of the Pridi Damrong Bridge. ❼

PS Guest House, 23/1 Thanon Chakrapat ⌾035/242394. Quiet, homely and sociable spot run by a very helpful retired English teacher. The large, clean and simple rooms (one with air-con) share bathrooms, and there's a balcony to hang

out on overlooking the pleasant garden. ❷–❸, dorm beds B75, singles B100.

Ruenderm (Ayutthaya Youth Hostel), 48 Moo 2 Tambon Horattanachai, Thanon U Thong, just north of Pridi Damrong Bridge ⌾035/241978. Large, simple rooms, with plentiful shared cold-water bathrooms, in a shambolic riverside teak house, scattered with antiques. ❷

Suan Luang, Thanon Rojana ⌾ & ℗035/245537, next to the Historical Study Centre. This training ground for hotel and catering students at Rajabhat College offers functional, bright, spacious and very clean rooms with fridge, TV, air-con and cold-water bathrooms, in a quiet location that's handy for TAT and the museums. ❹

Toto Guesthouse, NG 16/2 Horattanachai ⌾035/251468. Raised two-storey house with clean, plain fan rooms, sharing cold-water bathrooms; same management as *Ayutthaya Guest House* next door. ❷

U-Thong Inn, 210 Thanon Rojana ⌾035/242236–9, ℗242235. Hot water, satellite TV and air-con in all rooms, and a swimming pool. Similar to, and as far out of town as, *Ayutthaya Grand Hotel* but not as good value. ❻

Eating and drinking

The main travellers' hangout is the small, laid-back *Moon Café*, on the same lane as the *Ayutthaya Guest House*, which serves good Western and Thai **food** and occasionally has live music. Otherwise, there's a dearth of decent places to eat; for inexpensive Thai dining your best bet is the Hua Raw night market, near the northernmost point of Thanon U Thong. Riverside restaurants in Ayutthaya are slightly expensive and generally disappointing: your best bet is the atmospheric *Ruenderm* at the youth hostel, which serves reasonable food in some weird combinations, amid gnarled wooden furniture and curios. Around the central ruins are a few pricey restaurants if you need air-conditioning with your lunch.

The City

The majority of Ayutthaya's ancient remains are spread out across the western half of the island in a patchwork of parkland: **Wat Phra Mahathat** and **Wat Ratburana** stand near the modern centre, while a broad band runs down the middle of the parkland, containing the **Royal Palace** and temple, the most revered Buddha image at **Viharn Phra Mongkol Bopit**, and the two main **museums**. To the north of the island you'll find the best-preserved temple, **Wat Na Phra Mane**, and **Wat Phu Khao Thong**, the "Golden Mount", while to the southeast lie the giant chedi of **Wat Yai Chai Mongkol** and **Wat Phanan Choeng**, still a vibrant place of worship.

Busloads of tourists descend on the sights during the day, but the area covered by the old capital is large enough not to feel swamped. Distances are deceptive, so it's best not to walk everywhere if you're doing a full visit: **bicycles** can be hired at the guest houses (B40 per day at *PS*) or if even that sounds too much like hard work, *BJ 1* has a moped for B300 a day. Otherwise it's easy enough to hop on a **tuk-tuk** – B5 for a short, popular journey if you're sharing, B30 if you're on your own. If you're short on time you could hire a tuk-tuk for a whistle-stop tour of the old city for around B150 an hour, either from the train station or from Chao Phrom market.

Big tour **boats** can be chartered from the pier outside the Chantharakasem Palace. A two-hour trip (B600 for the boat, accommodating up to eight passengers) takes in Wat Phanan Choeng (see p.246); **Wat Phutthaisawan**, a fetchingly dilapidated complex founded by Ayutthaya's first king, Ramathibodi; and the recently restored **Wat Chai Watthanaram**, which was built by King Prasat Thong in 1630 to commemorate his victory over Cambodia, taking as its model the imposing symmetry of the Baphuon temple at Angkor. The *Krung Sri River Hotel* (see opposite) organizes occasional Sunday cruises that follow a similar route (B275 per person, including buffet lunch).

Wat Phra Mahathat and Wat Ratburana

Heading west out of the new town centre along Thanon Chao Phrom (which becomes Thanon Naresuan), after about 1km you'll come to the first set of ruins, a pair of temples on opposite sides of the road. The overgrown **Wat Phra Mahathat**, on the left (daily 8.30am–5.30pm; B30), is the epitome of Ayutthaya's nostalgic atmosphere of faded majesty. The name "Mahathat" (Great Relic Chedi) indicates that the temple was built to house remains of the Buddha himself: according to the royal chronicles – never renowned for historical accuracy – King Ramesuan (1388–95) was looking out of his palace one morning when ashes of the Buddha materialized out of thin air here. A gold casket containing the ashes was duly enshrined in a grand 38-metre-high prang. The prang later collapsed, but the reliquary was unearthed in the 1950s, along with a hoard of other treasures including a gorgeous marble fish which opened to reveal gold, amber, crystal and porcelain ornaments – all now on show in the Chao Sam Phraya National Museum (see p.245).

You can climb what remains of the prang to get a good view of the broad, grassy complex, with dozens of brick spires tilting at impossible angles and headless Buddhas scattered around like spare parts in a scrapyard – and look out for the serene head of a stone Buddha which has become nestled in the embrace of a bodhi tree's roots. To the west you'll see the slender fourteenth-century prang of **Wat Phra Ram** and a lake where Ramathibodi I discovered an auspicious conch shell, symbol of victory and righteousness, which confirmed his choice of site for his new city.

Across the road from Wat Phra Mahathat, the towering **Wat Ratburana** (daily 8.30am–5.30pm; B30) was built in 1424 by King Boromraja II to commemorate his elder brothers Ay and Yi, who managed to kill each other in an elephant-back duel over the succession to the throne, thus leaving it vacant for Boromraja. Here four elegant Sri Lankan chedis lean outwards as if in deference to the main prang, on which some of the original stucco work can still be seen, including fine statues of garudas swooping down on nagas. It's possible to go down steep steps inside the prang to the crypt, where on two levels you can make out fragmentary murals of the early Ayutthaya period. Several hundred Buddha images were buried down here, most of which were snatched by grave robbers, although some can be seen in the Chao Sam Phraya Museum. They're in the earliest style that can be said to be distinctly Ayutthayan – an unsmiling Khmer expression, but on an oval face and elongated body that show the strong influence of Sukhothai.

Wat Phra Si Sanphet and the Wang Luang (Royal Palace)

Nearly a kilometre west of Wat Ratburana is **Wat Phra Si Sanphet** (daily 8.30am–5.30pm; B30), built in 1448 by King Boromatrailokanat as his private chapel. Formerly the grandest of Ayutthaya's temples, and still one of the best preserved, it took its name from one of the largest standing metal images of the Buddha ever known, the **Phra Si Sanphet**, erected here in 1503. Towering 16m high and covered in 173kg of gold, it did not survive the ravages of the Burmese, though Rama I rescued the pieces and placed them inside a chedi at Wat Po in Bangkok. The three remaining grey chedis in the characteristic style of the old capital were built to house the ashes of three kings, and have now become the most hackneyed image of Ayutthaya.

The site of this royal wat was originally occupied by Ramathibodi's wooden palace, which Boromatrailokanat replaced with the bigger **Wang Luang** (Royal Palace; same hours and ticket as Wat Phra Si Sanphet), stretching to the Lopburi River on the north side. Successive kings turned the Wang Luang into a vast complex of pavilions and halls with an elaborate system of walls designed to isolate the inner sanctum for the king and his consorts. The palace was destroyed by the Burmese in 1767 and plundered by Rama I for its bricks, which he needed to build the new capital at Bangkok. Now you can only trace the outlines of a few walls in the grass and inspect an unimpressive wooden replica of an open pavilion – better to consult the model of the whole complex in the Historical Study Centre (see opposite).

Viharn Phra Mongkol Bopit and the cremation ground

Viharn Phra Mongkol Bopit (Mon–Fri 8.30am–4.30pm, Sat & Sun 8.30am–5.30pm), on the south side of Wat Phra Si Sanphet, attracts tourists and Thai pilgrims in about equal measure. The pristine hall – a replica of a typical Ayutthayan viharn with its characteristic chunky lotus-capped columns around the outside – was built in 1956, with help from the Burmese to atone for their flattening of the city two centuries earlier, in order to shelter the revered **Phra Mongkol Bopit**, one of the largest bronze Buddhas in Thailand. The powerfully austere image, with its flashing mother-of-pearl eyes, was cast in the fifteenth century, then sat exposed to the elements from the time of the Burmese invasion until its new home was built. During restoration, the hollow image was found to contain hundreds of Buddha statuettes, some of which were later buried around the shrine to protect it.

The car park in front of the viharn used to be the **cremation site** for Ayutthayan kings and high-ranking members of the royal family. Here, on a propitious date decided by astrologers, the embalmed body was placed on a towering *meru* (funeral pyre), representing Mount Meru, the centre of the Hindu-Buddhist universe. These many-gabled and pinnacled wooden structures, which had all the appearance of permanent palaces, were a miracle of architectural technology: the *meru* constructed for King Phetracha in 1704, for example, was 103m tall and took eleven months to raise, requiring thousands of tree trunks and hundreds of thousands of bamboo poles. The task of building at such great heights was given to *yuan-hok*, a particular clan of acrobats who used to perform at the top of long poles during special festivals. Their handiwork was not consigned to the flames: the cremation took place on a pyramid erected underneath the central spire, so as not to damage the main structure, which was later dismantled and its timber used for building temples. The cremation ground is now given over to a picnic area and a clutch of souvenir and refreshment stalls.

The museums

A ten-minute walk south of the viharn brings you to the largest of the town's three museums, the **Chao Sam Phraya National Museum** (Wed–Sun 9am–4pm; B30), where most of the moveable remains of Ayutthaya's glory – those which weren't plundered by treasure-hunters or taken to the National Museum in Bangkok – are exhibited. Apart from numerous Buddhas, it's bursting with **gold treasures** of all shapes and sizes – betel-nut sets and model chedis, a royal wimple in gold filigree, a model elephant dripping with gems and the original relic casket from Wat Mahathat. A second gallery, behind the main hall, explores foreign influences on Thai art and is particularly good on the origins of the various styles of Buddha images. This room also contains skeletons and artefacts from the site of the Portuguese settlement founded in 1540 just south of the town on the banks of the Chao Phraya. The Portuguese were the first Western power to establish ties with Ayutthaya, when in 1511 they were granted commercial privileges in return for supplying arms.

The **Historical Study Centre** (Mon–Fri 9am–4.30pm, Sat & Sun 8.30am–5pm; B100), five minutes' walk away along Thanon Rotchana, is the town's showpiece, with a hefty admission charge to go with it. The visitors' exhibition upstairs puts the ruins in context, dramatically presenting a wealth of background detail through videos, sound effects and reconstructions – temple murals and model ships, a peasant's wooden house and a small-scale model of the Royal Palace – to build up a broad social history of Ayutthaya. The centre's **annexe** (same times and ticket), 500m south of Wat Phanan Choeng on the road to Bang Pa-In, also merits a visit despite its remoteness: built with Japanese money on the site of the old Japanese settlement, it tells the fascinating story of Ayutthaya's relations with foreign powers, using similar multimedia effects and maps, paintings and documents prised from venerable museums around the world.

In the northeast corner of the island, the museum of the **Chantharakasem Palace** (Wed–Sun 9am–4pm; B30) was traditionally the home of the heir to the Ayutthayan throne. The Black Prince, Naresuan, built the first *wang na* (palace of the front) here in about 1577 so that he could guard the area of the city wall which was most vulnerable to enemy attack. Rama IV (1851–68) had the palace rebuilt and it now displays many of his possessions, including a throne platform overhung by a white *chat*, a ceremonial nine-tiered parasol which is a vital part of a king's insignia. The rest of the museum is a jumble of beautiful ceramics, Buddha images and random artefacts.

Wat Na Phra Mane

Wat Na Phra Mane (daily 8.30am–4.30pm; B20 donation), on the north bank of the Lopburi River opposite the Wang Luang, is Ayutthaya's most rewarding temple, as it's the only one from the town's golden age which survived the ravages of the Burmese. The story goes that when the Burmese were on the brink of capturing Ayutthaya in 1760, a siege gun positioned here burst, mortally wounding their king and prompting their retreat; out of superstition, they left the temple standing when they came back to devastate the city in 1767.

The main **bot**, built in 1503, shows the distinctive features of Ayutthayan architecture – outside columns topped with lotus cups, and slits in the walls instead of windows to let the wind pass through. Inside, underneath a rich red and gold coffered ceiling representing the stars around the moon, sits a powerful six-metre-high Buddha in the disdainful, overdecorated royal style characteristic of the later Ayutthaya period.

In sharp contrast is the dark green **Phra Khan Thavaraj** Buddha which dominates the tiny viharn behind to the right. Seated in the "European position", with its robe delicately pleated and its feet up on a large lotus leaf, the gentle figure conveys a reassuring serenity. It's advertised as being from Sri Lanka, the source of Thai Buddhism, but more likely is a Mon image from Wat Phra Mane at Nakhon Pathom dating from the seventh to ninth centuries.

Wat Phu Khao Thong

Head 2km northwest of Wat Na Phra Mane and you're in open country, where the fifty-metre chedi of **Wat Phu Khao Thong** rises steeply out of the fields. In 1569, after a temporary occupation of Ayutthaya, the Burmese erected a Mon-style chedi here to commemorate their victory. Forbidden by Buddhist law from pulling down a sacred monument, the Thais had to put up with this galling reminder of the enemy's success until it collapsed nearly two hundred years later, when King Borommakot promptly built a truly Ayutthayan chedi on the old Burmese base – just in time for the Burmese to return in 1767 and flatten the town. This "Golden Mount" has recently been restored and painted toothpaste-white, with a colossal equestrian statue of King Naresuan, conqueror of the Burmese, to keep it company. You can climb 25m of steps up the side of the chedi to look out over the countryside and the town, with glimpses of Wat Phra Si Sanphet and Viharn Phra Mongkok Bopit in the distance. In 1956, to celebrate 2500 years of Buddhism, the government placed on the tip of the spire a ball of solid gold weighing 2500g, of which there is now no trace.

Wat Yai Chai Mongkol

To the southeast of the island, if you cross the suspension bridge over the Pasak River and the rail line, then turn right at the major roundabout, you'll pass through Ayutthaya's new business zone and some rustic suburbia before reaching the ancient but still functioning **Wat Yai Chai Mongkol**, nearly 2km from the bridge (daily 8.30am–5pm; B20 donation). Surrounded by formal lawns and flower beds, the wat was established by King Ramathibodi in 1357 as a meditation site for monks returning from study in Sri Lanka. King Naresuan put up the celebrated **chedi** to mark the decisive victory over the Burmese at Suphanburi in 1593, when he himself had sent the enemy packing by slaying the Burmese crown prince in a duel. Built on a colossal scale to outshine the Burmese Golden Mount on the opposite side of Ayutthaya, the chedi has come to symbolize the prowess and devotion of Naresuan and, by implication, his descendants down to the present king.

By the entrance, a **reclining Buddha**, now gleamingly restored in toothpaste white, was also constructed by Naresuan; elsewhere in the grounds, the wat maintains its contemplative origins with some highly topical maxims pinned to the trees such as "Cut down the forest of passion not real trees".

Wat Phanan Choeng

In Ayutthaya's most prosperous period the docks and main trading area were located near the confluence of the Chao Phraya and Pasak rivers, to the west of Wat Yai Chai Mongkol. This is where you'll find the oldest and liveliest working temple in town, **Wat Phanan Choeng** (daily 8.30am–4.30pm; B20 donation) – as well as the annexe to the Historical Study Centre (see p.245). The main viharn is often filled with the sights, sounds and smells of an incredible variety of merit-making activities, as devotees burn huge pink Chinese incense candles, offer food and rattle fortune sticks. It's even possible to buy tiny golden statues of the Buddha to be placed in one of the hundreds of niches which line the walls, a form of votive offering peculiar to this temple. If you can get here during a festival, especially Chinese New Year, you're in for an overpowering experience.

The nineteen-metre-high Buddha, which almost fills the hall, has survived since 1324, shortly before the founding of the capital, and tears are said to have flowed from its eyes when Ayutthaya was sacked by the Burmese. However, the reason for the temple's popularity with the Chinese is to be found in the early eighteenth-century shrine by the pier, with its image of a beautiful Chinese princess who drowned herself here because of a king's infidelity: his remorse led him to build the shrine at the place where she had walked into the river.

Lopburi and around

Mention the name **LOPBURI** to a Thai and the chances are that he or she will start telling you about monkeys – the central junction of this tidy provincial capital, 150km due north of Bangkok, swarms with them. So beneficial are the beasts to the town's tourist trade that a local hotelier treats six hundred of them to a sit-down meal at Phra Prang Sam Yod temple every November, complete with menus, waiters and napkins, as a thank-you for the help. In fact, the monkeys can be a real nuisance, but at least they add some life to the town's central **Khmer buildings**, which, though historically important, are rather unimpressive. More illuminating is the **Narai National Museum**, housed in a partly reconstructed palace complex dating from the seventeenth century, and distant **Wat Phra Phutthabat**, a colourful eye-opener for non-Buddhists.

Originally called Lavo, Lopburi is one of the longest-inhabited towns in Thailand, and was a major centre of the Mon (Dvaravati) civilization from around the sixth century. It maintained a tenuous independence in the face of the advancing Khmers until as late as the early eleventh century, when it was incorporated into the empire as the provincial capital for much of central Thailand. Increasing Thai immigration from the north soon tilted the balance against the Khmers and Lopburi was again **independent** from some time early in the thirteenth century until the rise of Ayutthaya in the middle of the fourteenth. Thereafter, Lopburi was twice used as a second capital, first by King Narai of Ayutthaya in the seventeenth century, then by Rama IV of Bangkok in the nineteenth, because its remoteness from the sea made it less vulnerable to European expansionists. Rama V downgraded the town, turning the royal palace into a provincial government office and museum; Lopburi's modern role is as the site of several huge army barracks.

As it's on the main line north to Chiang Mai, Lopburi is best reached by **train**. Nine trains a day, concentrated in the early morning and evening, run here from Bangkok (3hr) via Ayutthaya (1hr 30min): a popular option is to arrive in Lopburi in the morning, leave your bags at the conveniently central station while you look around the town, then catch one of the night trains to the north. **Buses** from Ayutthaya take around two hours to reach Lopburi, having started their journey at Bangkok's Northern Terminal (every 15min; 3hr).

The Town

The centre of Lopburi sits on an egg-shaped island between canals and the Lopburi River, with the rail line running across it from north to south. **Thanon Vichayen**, the main street, crosses the rail tracks at the town's busiest

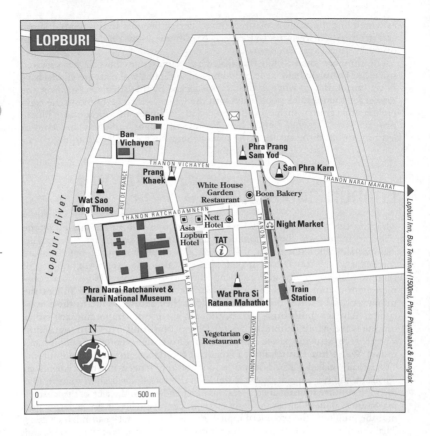

junction before heading eastwards through the newest areas of development to Highway 1. If you're tempted by a gleaming samlor, it'll cost you about B80 per hour to get around the sights.

Wat Phra Si Ratana Mahathat

As you come out of the train station, the first thing you'll see are the sprawled grassy ruins of **Wat Phra Si Ratana Mahathat** (daily 8am–6pm; B30), where the impressive centrepiece is a laterite prang in the Khmer style of the twelfth century, decorated with finely detailed stucco work and surrounded by a ruined cloister. Arrayed in loose formation around this central feature are several more rocket-like Khmer prangs and a number of graceful chedis in the Ayutthayan style, among them one with a bulbous peak and faded bas-reliefs of Buddhist saints. On the eastern side of the main prang, King Narai added to the mishmash of styles by building a "Gothic" viharn, now roofless, which is home to a lonely, headless stone Buddha, draped in photogenic saffron.

Phra Narai Ratchanivet (King Narai's palace)

The imposing gates and high crenellated walls of the **Phra Narai Ratchanivet**, a short walk northwest of the ruins, might promise more than the complex delivers, but the museum in its central courtyard is worth a look, and the grounds are a green and relaxing spot. King Narai built the heavily fortified palace in 1666 as a precaution against any possible confrontation with the Western powers, and for the rest of his reign he was to spend eight months of every year here, entertaining foreign envoys and indulging his love of hunting. After Narai's death, Lopburi was left forgotten until 1856, when Rama IV – worried about British and French colonialism – decided to make this his second capital and lavishly restored the central buildings of Narai's palace.

The outer courtyard

The main **entrance** to the palace complex (daily 7am–5.30pm; free) is through the Phayakkha Gate on Thanon Sorasak. You'll see the unusual lancet shape of this arch again and again in the seventeenth-century doors and windows of Lopburi – just one aspect of the Western influences embraced by Narai. Around the **outer courtyard**, which occupies the eastern half of the complex, stand the walls of various gutted buildings – twelve warehouses for Narai's treasures, stables for the royal hunting elephants, and a moated reception hall for foreign envoys. With their lily ponds and manicured lawns, these well-shaded grounds are ideal for a picnic or a siesta.

The central courtyard and the Narai National Museum

Straight ahead from the Phayakkha Gate another arch leads into the **central courtyard**, where the typically Ayutthayan **Chanthara Phisan Pavilion** contains a fascinating exhibition on Narai's reign – check out the pointed white cap typical of those worn by noblemen of the time, which increased their height by no less than 50cm.

To the left is the colonial-style Phiman Mongkut Hall, now the **Narai National Museum** (Wed–Sun 9am–noon & 1–4pm; B30), whose exhibits concentrate on the period following the Khmer subjugation of Lopburi in the eleventh century. Inevitably there's a surfeit of Buddhas, most of them fine examples of the Khmer style and the distinctive **Lopburi style**, which emerged in the thirteenth and fourteenth centuries, mixing traditional Khmer elements – such as the conical *ushnisha,* or flame on the crown of the Buddha's head – with new features such as a more oval face and slender body. On the top floor is **King Mongkut's bedroom**, filled with his furniture and assorted memorabilia of his reign, including his very short and uncomfortable-looking bed and eerie painted statues of his equally vertically challenged near-contemporaries, Napoleon and Queen Victoria.

On the south side of the museum lies the shell of the **Dusit Sawan Hall**, where foreign dignitaries came to present their credentials to King Narai. Inside you can still see the niche, raised 3.5m above the main floor, where the throne was set; beneath the niche, a modern plaque showing Narai receiving the French envoy, the Chevalier de Chaumont, in 1685 is revered as an icon of the king, with offerings of gold leaf, joss sticks and garlands. The whole building is divided in two around the throne: the front half has "foreign" doors and windows with pointed arches; the rear part, from where the king would have made his grand entrance, has traditional Thai openings. The hall used to be lined with French mirrors in imitation of Versailles, with Persian carpets and a pyramidal roof of golden glazed tiles rounding off the most majestic building in the palace.

The private courtyards

King Narai's private courtyard, through whose sturdy walls only the trusted few were admitted, occupied the southwest corner of the complex. During

Narai's time, hundreds of lamps were placed in niches around the walls of this courtyard by night, shedding a fairy-like light on the palace. Now there's not much more than the foundations left of his residence, the **Sutha Sawan Hall**, and its bathing ponds and artificial grotto.

Rama IV's private courtyard was built to house his harem in the northwest corner of the grounds, behind the present site of the museum. In what used to be the kitchen there's now a small folk museum of central Thai life, containing a loom and various pieces of farming and fishing equipment. In front, you can consult a crude model of the palace as it looked in Narai's time.

Wat Sao Tong Thong and Ban Vichayen

The north gate (now closed) to the palace is called the Vichayen Gate after **Constantine Phaulkon**, a Greek adventurer who had come to Ayutthaya with the English East India Company in 1678. It leads directly to the aptly named Rue de France, the approach to the remains of his grand residence. Halfway along this road, set back on the left, you'll pass a building whose plain terracotta roof tiles and whitewashed exterior give it a strangely Mediterranean look. This is in fact the viharn of **Wat Sao Tong Thong**, and is typical of Narai's time in its combination of Thai-style tiered roof with "Gothic" pointed windows. Erected as either a Christian chapel or a mosque for the Persian ambassador's residence, it was later used as a Buddhist viharn and has now been tastefully restored, complete with brass door-knockers and plush red carpet. Inside there's an austere Buddha image of the Ayutthaya period and, in the lamp niches, some fine Lopburi-style Buddhas.

The complex of **Ban Vichayen** (daily 6am–6pm; B30) was built by Narai as a residence for foreign ambassadors, complete with a Christian chapel incongruously stuccoed with Buddhist flame and lotus-leaf motifs. Though now just a nest of empty shells, it still succeeds in conjuring up the atmosphere of court intrigue and dark deeds which, towards the end of Narai's reign, centred on the colourful figure of Phaulkon. He entered the royal service as interpreter and accountant, rapidly rising to the position of Narai's *ookya vichayen* (prime minister). It was chiefly due to his influence that Narai established close ties with Louis XIV of France, a move which made commercial sense but also formed part of Phaulkon's secret plan to turn Narai and his people to Christianity with the aid of the French. Two missions were sent from Versailles, but both failed in their overt aim of signing a political alliance and their covert attempt at religious conversion. (It was around this time that the word for Westerner, *farang*, entered the Thai language, from the same derivation as *français*, which the Thais render *farangset*.) In 1688, a struggle for succession broke out, and leading officials persuaded the dying Narai to appoint as regent his foster brother, Phetracha, a great rival of Phaulkon's. Phetracha promptly executed Phaulkon on charges of treason, and took the throne himself when Narai died. Under Phetracha, Narai's open-door policy towards foreigners was brought to a screeching halt and the Thai kingdom returned to traditional, smaller-scale dealings with the outside world.

Prang Khaek, Phra Prang Sam Yod and San Phra Karn

Near the northeast corner of the palace, the junction of Thanon Vichayen and Thanon Sorasak is marked by an unusual traffic island, on which perch the three stubby red-brick towers of **Prang Khaek**, a well-preserved Hindu shrine possibly dating from as early as the eighth century. The nearby **Phra Prang Sam Yod** (daily 8am–6pm; B30), at the top of Thanon Na Phra Karn, seems also to have been a Hindu temple, later converted to Buddhism under the Khmers. The three chunky prangs, made of dark laterite with some restored stucco work, are Lopburi's most photographed sight, though they'll only detain you for a minute or two – at least check out some carved figures of seated hermits at the base of the door columns. The shrine's grassy knoll is a good spot for monkey-watching – they run amok all over this area, so keep an eye on your bags and pockets. Across the rail line at the modern red and gold shrine of **San Phra Karn**, there's even a monkey's adventure playground for the benefit of tourists, beside the base of what must have been a huge Khmer prang.

Practicalities

Most of the hotels and just about everything of interest lie to the west of the rail line, within walking distance of the **train station**. The long-distance **bus terminal** is on the south side of the huge Sakeo roundabout, 2km east of the town centre: a city bus or a songthaew will save you the walk. **TAT** has an office in a restored, wooden, colonial-style building on the north side of Wat Phra Si Ratana Mahathat (daily 8.30am–4.30pm; ☎036/422768–9).

Lopburi's choice of **accommodation** is poor. Thanon Na Phra Karn is a minefield of seedy hotels (❶), while the town's most prominent hotel, the *Asia Lopburi* opposite the entrance to Narai's palace, is a ramshackle affair, with a choice of rooms with fan and bathroom, or with air-conditioning and hot water (☎036/411555, ℱ411892, ❷). By far the best option in the heart of town are the en-suite fan or air-con rooms at the clean and friendly *Nett Hotel*, 17/1–2 Soi 2, Thanon Ratchadamnern (☎036/411738 or 421460; ❷–❹). A long trek east of the centre, the air-conditioned rooms at the *Lopburi Inn*, 28/9 Thanon Narai Maharat (☎036/412609, ℱ412457; ❺), are as posh as Lopburi town gets; if money is no object and you have your own transport, head out of town to its sister establishment, the *Lopburi Inn Resort*, off the Saraburi road, an overblown complex of Mediterranean-style buildings with a large swimming pool, gym and sauna (☎036/411265, ℱ412010; ❼).

For **food**, good Western breakfasts and coffee are served at *Boon Bakery* on Thanon Na Phra Karn near the corner of Ratchadamnern, while cheap vegetarian food is served up at an unnamed restaurant on the south side of Wat Phra Si Ratana Mahathat on Thanon Kanchanakhom (look out for the yellow flags outside). In the evening, head for the night market on Thanon Na Phra Karn, or try the classier, open-air *White House Garden Restaurant* on Thanon Praya Kumjud (parallel to and south of Ratchadamnern), which specializes in rich seafood dishes at reasonable prices.

Wat Phra Phutthabat (Temple of the Buddha's Footprint)

Seventeen kilometres southeast of Lopburi along Highway 1 stands the most important pilgrimage site in central Thailand, **Wat Phra Phutthabat**, which is believed to house a footprint made by the Buddha. Any of the frequent **buses** to Saraburi or Bangkok from Lopburi's Sakeo roundabout will get you there in thirty minutes. The souvenir village around the temple, which is on the western side of Highway 1, includes plenty of foodstalls for day-trippers.

The **legend** of Phra Phutthabat dates back to the beginning of the seventeenth century, when King Song Tham of Ayutthaya sent some monks to Sri Lanka to worship the famous Buddha's footprint of Sumankut. To the monks' surprise, the Sri Lankans asked them why they had bothered to travel all that way when, according to the ancient Pali scriptures, the Buddha had passed through Thailand and had left his footprint in their own backyard. As soon as Song Tham heard this he instigated a search for the footprint, which was finally discovered in 1623 by a hunter named Pram Bun, when a wounded deer disappeared into a hollow and then emerged miraculously healed. The hunter pushed aside the bushes to discover a foot-shaped trench filled with water, which immediately cured him of his terrible skin disease. A temple was built on the spot, but was destroyed by the Burmese in 1765 – the present buildings date from the Bangkok era.

A staircase flanked by nagas leads up to a marble platform, where pilgrims make a cacophony by whacking the bells with walking sticks, many of them bought from the stalls below. It's said that if you ring all 93 bells, and count them correctly, you will live that number of years. In the centre of the platform, a gaudy mondop with mighty doors inlaid with mother-of-pearl houses the **footprint**, which in itself is not much to look at. Sheltered by a mirrored canopy, the stone print is nearly 2m long and is obscured by layers of gold leaf presented by pilgrims; people also throw money into the footprint, some of which they take out again as a charm or merit object. The hill behind the shrine, which you can climb for a fine view over the gilded roofs of the complex to the mountains beyond, is covered in a plethora of shrines. The small bot, which elsewhere would be the centrepiece of a temple, is where pilgrims go for a nap.

During the dry season in January, February and March – traditionally, the free time in the rice-farming calendar, between harvesting and sowing – a million pilgrims from all over the country flock to the **Ngan Phrabat** (Phrabat Fair), when other pilgrims are making their way to the other major religious sites at Doi Suthep, Nakhon Si Thammarat and Nakhon Phanom. During the fair, which reaches its peak in two week-long lunar periods, one at the beginning of February, the other at the beginning of March, the stalls selling souvenirs and traditional medicines around the entrance swell to form a small town, and traditional entertainments, magic shows and a Ferris wheel are laid on. The fair is still a major religious event, but before the onset of industrialization it was the highlight of social and cultural life for all ages and classes; it was an important place of courtship, for example, especially for women at a time when their freedom was limited. Another incentive for women to attend the fair was the belief that visiting the footprint three times would ensure a place in heaven – for many women, the Phrabat Fair became the focal point of their lives, as Buddhist doctrine allowed them no other path to salvation. Up to the reign of Rama V (1868–1910) even the king used to come, performing a ritual lance dance on elephant-back to ensure a long reign.

The northern plains

Many tourists bypass the lush northern reaches of the central plains, fast asleep in an overnight train from Bangkok to Chiang Mai, yet it was here, during the thirteenth, fourteenth and fifteenth centuries, that the kingdom of Thailand first began to cohere and assume its present identity. Some of Thailand's finest buildings and sculpture were produced in **Sukhothai**, once the most powerful city in Thailand. Abandoned to the jungle by the sixteenth century, it has now been extensively restored, the resulting historical park making an attractive open-air museum. Less complete renovations have made Sukhothai's satellite cities of **Si Satchanalai** and **Kamphaeng Phet** worth visiting, both for their relative wildness and lack of visitors.

With so many ruins on offer, it's sensible to interweave days of history with days out in the wilds. The nearest hills in which to clear the cobwebs are in **Ramkhamhaeng National Park** near Sukhothai, or further afield at in the rugged Phu Hin Rongkla National Park (see p.515), but to get to either you'll need to hire a motorbike. By public transport from Sukhothai, an easier option is the longer expedition to the Burmese border town of **Mae Sot** and from there down to the **Umphang** region, which offers excellent trekking and white-water rafting.

Phitsanulok stands at the hub of an efficient **transport** network that works well as a transit point between Bangkok, the far north and Isaan. Nearly every Bangkok–Chiang Mai train stops here, and assorted buses head east towards the Isaan towns of Loei, Khon Kaen and Chaiyaphum. It's also possible to fly in and out of the northern plains, through the tiny airstrips at Phitsanulok, Sukhothai and Mae Sot. Within the region, local buses and songthaews ferry tourists between sights, though a less time-consuming way of doing things would be to hire a car or motorbike from Phitsanulok or Sukhothai.

Phitsanulok

Heading north from Lopburi, road and rail plough through Thailand's "rice bowl", a landscape of lurid green paddies interrupted only by the unwelcoming sprawl of **Nakhon Sawan**, sited at the confluence of the Ping and the Nan. A prosperous city of about 100,000 predominantly Chinese inhabitants, Nakhon Sawan plays a vital role as the region's main market and the distribution centre for rice, but is of interest to tourists only as a place to change buses for Kamphaeng Phet, Phitsanulok or Chaiyaphum. The bus station is in the town centre and there are a couple of passable budget hotels close by as a last resort. All Bangkok–Chiang Mai trains stop here, but as the station is 10km out of town, with skeletal local transport and no station hotels, breaking your journey 130km further north at Phitsanulok makes much more sense.

Well equipped with upmarket hotels and pleasantly located on the east bank of the Nan River, **PHITSANULOK** makes a handy base for exploring the historical centres of Sukhothai (see p.259) and Kamphaeng Phet (see p.274). Phitsanulok itself, however, has been basically a one-temple town since fire destroyed most of its old buildings thirty-odd years ago: the country's second most important Buddha image is housed here in Wat Mahathat, drawing pilgrims from all over Thailand. This modest town harks back to a heyday in the late fourteenth and early fifteenth centuries when, with Sukhothai waning in power, it rose to prominence as the favoured home of the crumbling capital's last rulers. After supremacy was finally wrested by the emerging state of Ayutthaya in 1438, Phitsanulok was made a provincial capital, subsequently becoming a strategic army base during Ayutthaya's wars with the Burmese, and adoptive home to Ayutthayan princes.

Arrival, information and transport

There are eleven trains a day from Bangkok and Don Muang airport to Phitsanulok (six of them via Ayutthaya), and six a day from Chiang Mai; the **train station** (T 055/258005) is in the town centre. Buses are more frequent, but to get into town from the regional **bus station** (T 055/242430), 2km east on Highway 12, you'll need to catch local bus #1 (see below). The private **aircon buses** to and from Bangkok, Chiang Mai and Chiang Rai, operated by Win Tour (T 055/243222) and Yan Yon Tour (T 055/2586470), drop off and pick up passengers at their offices near the train station on Thanon Ekathosarot in town. You can also fly to Phitsanulok from Bangkok, Chiang Mai, Lampang, Nan and Phrae; the **airport** is on the southern edge of town, about ten minutes' drive from the train station, and has a tour operators' desk, as well as Avis (T 055/258062, W www.avisthailand.com) and Budget (T 055/258556, W www.budget.co.th) car-rental outlets. Taxis meet all incoming flights, as do free minibuses sent by the upmarket hotels, or you can walk 100m north outside the airport gates and take city bus #4 from the shelter on Thanon Sanambin (see below for details). The helpful and well-informed **TAT** office (daily 8.30am–4.30pm; T & F 055/252742, E tatphs@loxifo.co.th) is on Thanon Sithamtraipidok, east off Thanon Boromtrailokanat.

If you've arrived at Phitsanulok train station and want to make an immediate **bus connection to Sukhothai**, you have two options. The fastest option is to pick up a Sukhothai-bound bus as it passes the *Topland Plaza Hotel* on Thanon Singawat – samlors will take you here for about B30, or you can use local bus #1. If you miss that stop, stay on the #1 until it gets to the regional bus station on the eastern edge of town – quite a lengthy ride in a bus or samlor because of the town's one-way system – where all Sukhothai-bound buses originate (daily 6am to 6pm; every 30min; 1hr).

Local **city buses** all start from the city bus centre on Thanon Ekathosarot, 150m south of the train station; southbound buses leave from outside the *Asia Hotel*, northbound ones from across the road. Most buses cost a standard B5, except air-conditioned ones which cost B7. The most useful bus is route **#1**, which heads north up to the *Topland Plaza Hotel* roundabout, then goes west to the Thanon Singawat bridge (get off between the roundabout and the bridge for Wat Mahathat and long-distance buses to Sukhothai), crosses the bridge and then doubles back along Singawat and heads east to the regional bus station. Bus **#3** also heads west over the river via the Thanon Singawat bridge, but again be sure to get off between the *Topland Plaza* roundabout and the bridge if you want to visit Wat Mahathat or change on to a long-distance bus to Sukhothai. Bus **#4** goes east along Thanon Ramesuan via the junction with Thanon Wisut Kasat (where you should alight for the museum and Buddha foundry) before turning south along Thanon Sanambin, past the *Thani Hotel* and the youth hostel and on to the airport.

Accommodation

Phitsanulok's budget **accommodation** is nowhere near as inviting as Sukhothai's, but the town does have a better selection of upmarket options.

Amarin Lagoon Hotel, 52/299 Thanon Phra Ong Khao T 055/220999, F 220944, W www.amarin-lagoon.com. Probably the poshest place in Phitsanulok, this popular hotel is prettily set in landscaped gardens and has attractively furnished rooms, with air-con and TV, a swimming pool, sauna and fitness centre, and three restaurants. The only drawback is that it's 8km east of the town centre, way beyond the bus terminal. ⑥–⑨

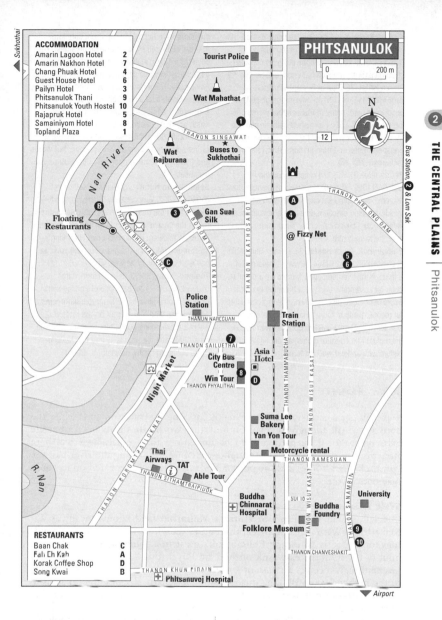

ACCOMMODATION

Amarin Lagoon Hotel	2
Amarin Nakhon Hotel	7
Chang Phuak Hotel	4
Guest House Hotel	6
Pailyn Hotel	3
Phitsanulok Thani	9
Phitsanulok Youth Hostel	10
Rajapruk Hotel	5
Samainiyom Hotel	8
Topland Plaza	1

PHITSANULOK

0   200 m

Tourist Police

Wat Mahathat

THANON SINGAWAT

Wat
Rajburana

Buses to
Sukhothai

Nan River

THANON BOROMTRAILOKNAT

Gan Suai
Silk

Floating
Restaurants

THANON BHUDHABUCHA

@ Fizzy Net

THANON PHRA ONG DAM

Bus Station, 2 & Lom Sak

THANON EKATHOSAROT

Police
Station

THANON NARESUAN

Train
Station

THANON SAILUETHAI

City Bus
Centre

Asia
Hotel

Win Tour

THANON PHYALITHAI

Night Market

THANON BOROMTRAILOKNAT

Suma Lee
Bakery

Yan Yon Tour

Motorcycle rental

THANON RAMESUAN

THANON THAMMABUCHA

THANON WISUT KASAT

Thai
Airways

TAT

Able Tour

THANON SITHAMTRAIPIDOK

R. Nan

Buddha
Chinnarat
Hospital

SOI 10

Buddha
Foundry

University

Folklore Museum

THANON WISUT KASAT

THANON SANAMBIN

THANON CHANVESHAKIT

THANON KHUN PIRAIN

Phitsanuvej Hospital

Airport

RESTAURANTS

Baan Chak	C
Fah Ch Kah	A
Korak Coffee Shop	D
Song Kwai	B

Amarin Nakhon Hotel, 3/1 Thanon Chaophraya ☎ 055/219069, ⓕ 219500, ⓦ www.amarinlagoon.com. Near the train station. Centrally located mid-range business hotel, lacking in character but fine for the price. All rooms have air-con and TV. ❺

Chang Phuak Hotel, next to the rail line on Thanon Thammabucha ☎ 055/252822, ⓕ 252493. Large, slightly shabby rooms with attached bathroom, and fan or air-con. Internet centre next door. ❸
Guest House Hotel, just east of Thanon Wisut Kasat at 99/9 Thanon Phra Ong Dam

℡055/259980, ⑨212737. Misleadingly named, this place is a scaled-down version of the adjoining *Rajapruk Hotel*, offering shabby but passable hotel-style rooms with attached bathroom and air-con. ❸

Pailyn Hotel, 38 Thanon Boromtrailokanat ℡055/252411, ⑨258185. Mid-range place that's good value, with many of the sizeable rooms offering river views, and all furnished with air-con and TV. It's handy for Wat Mahathat, and there's free transport to bus and train stations. Also has two restaurants. ❻–❼

Phitsanulok Thani, 39 Thanon Sanambin ℡055/211065, ⑨211071, ⓦwww.phitsanulokthani.th.com. Fairly upmarket chain hotel, with smart, thickly carpeted air-con rooms plus a restaurant and karaoke bar. Convenient for the airport but 1.5km from the town centre. ❻–❼

Phitsanulok Youth Hostel, 38 Thanon Sanambin ℡055/242060, ⑨210864, ⓦwww.tyha.org. Set in a large, attractive compound fronted by a popular open-air restaurant, this youth hostel is the most traveller-oriented place in town, offering character-ful rooms, plenty of tourist information and bicycles for rent. There's a B120 dorm as well as single and double en-suite rooms, all unusually furnished with antique wooden furniture. Non-IYHA

members have to pay a compulsory surcharge of B50 per night, but all rates include breakfast. The hostel is a 1.5km walk from the centre: take bus #4 from the city bus centre and get off outside the *Phitsanulok Thani Hotel* next door; from the regional bus station take a #1, then a #4. ❸

Rajapruk Hotel, just east of Thanon Wisut Kasat at 99/9 Thanon Phra Ong Dam ℡055/258788, ⑨251395. Well-equipped but rather soulless rooms, all with air-con, hot water and fridge. Swimming pool and nightclub on the premises. ❹

Samainiyom Hotel, 175 Thanon Ekathosarot ℡055/247527. Very centrally located, just a few metres from the train station and city bus centre, this is the best value of the town centre's budget hotels, with clean, comfortable and surprisingly quiet rooms. All rooms have air-con and you can pay a bit extra for TV as well. ❸

Topland Plaza, 68/33 Thanon Ekathosarot ℡055/247800, ⑨247815. One of Phitsanulok's best: all rooms have en-suite marble bathrooms, and you can land a helicopter on the rooftop. There's a swimming pool, Chinese restaurant and beer garden on the premises, and the *Topland Plaza* shopping centre downstairs. ❺–❽

The Town

Typically for a riverside town, "Phi-lok" is long and narrow, and, while the **centre** is small enough to cover on foot, the two **main sights** lie at opposite extremities. You'd be hard pressed to find more than a half-day's worth of attractions to detain you here, though an evening stroll along the river past the ramshackle raft houses and the prospect of a fresh fish dinner eaten on its banks may entice you.

Wat Mahathat

Officially called **Wat Phra Si Ratana Mahathat** (and known locally as Wat Mahathat or Wat Yai), this fourteenth-century temple was one of the few buildings miraculously to escape Phitsanulok's great fire. Standing at the northern limit of town on the east bank of the Nan River (bus #1 or #3 from the city bus centre), it receives a constant stream of worshippers eager to pay homage to the highly revered Buddha image inside the viharn. Because the image is so sacred, a **dress code** is strictly enforced – shorts and skimpy clothing are forbidden – and there's an entrance fee of B10.

Delicately inlaid mother-of-pearl doors mark the entrance to the viharn, opening onto the low-ceilinged interior, painted mostly in dark red and black and dimly lit by narrow slits along the upper walls. In the centre of the far wall sits the much-cherished **Phra Buddha Chinnarat**: late Sukhothai in style and probably cast in the fourteenth century, this gleaming, polished-bronze Buddha is one of the finest of the period and, for Thais, second in importance only to the Emerald Buddha in Bangkok. Tales of the statue's miraculous powers have fuelled the devotion of generations of pilgrims – one legend tells how the Buddha wept tears of blood when Ayutthayan princes arrived in Phitsanulok to oust the last Sukhothai regent. The Phra Buddha Chinnarat stands out among Thai Buddha images because of its *mandorla*, the flame-like halo that frames the upper body and head like a chair-back, tapering off into nagas at the arm rests, which symbolizes extreme radiance and makes any reproductions immediately recognizable. Not surprisingly, the image has spawned several copies, including an almost perfect replica commissioned for Bangkok's Marble Temple by Rama V in 1901. Every February, Phitsanulok honours the Phra Buddha Chinnarat with a week-long **festival**, which features *likay* folk-theatre performances and dancing.

Behind the viharn, the gilded mosaic **prang** houses the holy relic that gives the wat its name (Mahathat means "Great Relic Chedi") – though which particular remnant lies entombed here is unclear – and the cloister surrounding both structures contains a gallery of Buddha images of different styles. As in all such popular pilgrimage spots, the courtyard is crammed with amulet stalls, trinket sellers and lottery-ticket vendors.

Also spared by the fire was the nearby **Wat Rajburana**, just south of Naresuan Bridge and five minutes' walk from Wat Mahathat. Recognizable by the dilapidated brick-based chedi that stands in the compound, the wat is chiefly of interest for the *Ramayana* murals (see p.125) that cover the interior walls of the bot. Quite well preserved, they were probably painted in the mid-nineteenth century.

The Folklore Museum and Buddha foundry

Across town on Thanon Wisut Kasat, southeast of the train station, the **Sergeant Major Thawee Folklore Museum** (Tues–Sun 8.30am–4.30pm; donation) puts a different slant on the region's culture; its fascinating and informatively presented look at traditional rural life makes this one of the best ethnology museums in the country. Local bus #4 will drop you at the Wisut Kasat junction with Thanon Ramesuan, from where it's a five-minute walk to the museum, and a ten-minute walk to the youth hostel. The collection, which is housed in a series of wooden pavilions, belongs to former sergeant-major Dr Thawee, who has pursued a lifelong personal campaign to preserve and document a way of life that's gradually disappearing. Highlights include the reconstructed kitchen, veranda and birthing room of a typical village house, known as a "tied house" because its split bamboo walls are literally tied together with rattan cane, and an exceptionally comprehensive gallery of traps – dozens of specialized contraptions designed to ensnare everything from cockroaches to birds perched on water buffaloes' backs. Among the home accessories, check out the masochistic aid for "improving blood circulation", the range of simple wooden games and the collection of traditional musical instruments. The weaving and natural dyes exhibition is also worth dwelling on, as is the blow-by-blow account – complete with photos – of the routine castration of bullocks and water buffaloes.

Cross the road from the museum and walk south about 50m for a rare chance to see Buddha images being forged at the **Buranathai Buddha Bronze-Casting Foundry**, located behind a big green metal gate at 26/43 Thanon Wisut Kasat. The foundry, which also belongs to Dr Thawi, is open during working hours and anyone can drop in to watch the stages involved in moulding and casting a Buddha image. It's a fairly lengthy procedure, based on the lost-wax method, and best assimilated from the illustrated explanations inside the foundry. Images of all sizes are made here, from thirty-centimetre-high household icons to mega-models destined for wealthy temples. The Buddha business is quite a profitable one: worshippers can earn a great deal of merit by donating a Buddha statue, particularly a precious one, to their local wat, so demand rarely slackens.

Eating

There are half a dozen curry and noodle shops in the town centre on Thanon Ekathosarot, but in the evening, the place to head for is the lively **night market** along the east bank of the river, which gets started at about 6pm: fish and mussels are a speciality – along with cassette tapes, souvenirs and clothes. A smaller night market also sets up on Thanon Sanambin every evening, between the university and the *Thani* hotel. Restaurants serving **"flying vegetables"** are also perennial crowd-pullers: the vegetable in question is the strong-tasting morning-glory (*phak bung*), which is stir-fried before being tossed flamboyantly in the air towards the plate-wielding waiter or customer. Several restaurants around the *Rajapruk Hotel* on Thanon Phra Ong Dam do the honours, and stallholders at the night market put on occasional performances – look out for the specially adapted, stationary two-tiered trucks.

Baan Chak, one block south of the floating restaurants, on the other side of Thanon Buddhabucha. Serves a good range of mid-priced Thai and Chinese dishes plus seafood and curries.

Fah Eh Kah, just east of the railway line on Thanon Phra Ong Dam. A small and friendly family-run Muslim restaurant that specialises in cheap lassi yoghurt drinks and thick *roti* breads served with ladlefuls of the daily curry. Shuts around 2pm.

Korak Coffee Shop, Thanon Ekathosarot. Open-fronted streetside café that serves huge glasses of fresh fruit juice, decent coffee and a small menu of sandwiches and burgers.

Song Kwai, Thanon Bhudhabucha. One of several long-running floating restaurants in a cluster across the road from the post office, this place has a nice atmosphere, eye-catching river views and a decent mid-priced menu of fresh fish and seafood, plus standard Thai-Chinese dishes accompanied by rice.

Listings

Airline The Thai Airways office is near TAT on Thanon Sithamtraipidok ☎055/258020.

Car rental Budget and Avis both have desks at the airport (see p.254), and Avis has another office inside the youth hostel compound on Thanon Sanambin ☎055/242060. For hiring a car with driver, see "Tour Operators", below.

Emergencies For all emergencies, call the tourist police on the free 24hr phone line ☎1699, or contact them at their office north of Wat Mahathat on Thanon Ekathosarot ☎055/245358.

Exchange There are banks with money changing facilities and ATMs on Thanon Naresuan and Thanon Boromtrailokanat.

Hospitals Phitsanuvej Hospital, 211/95 Thanon Khun Pirain ☎055/244911–20; Buddha Chinnarat Hospital, Thanon Sithamtraipidok ☎055/241608.

Internet access At Fizzynet, just south of the *Chang Phuak Hotel* on Thanon Thammabucha.

Mail The GPO is near the river on Thanon Bhudhabucha.

Motorbike rental At Lady Motorcycle for Rent, 17/15–16 Thanon Ramesuan ☎055/242424, at around B200 per day.

Telephones The CAT overseas telephone office is next to the GPO on Thanon Bhudhabucha.

Tour operators Able Tour and Travel (Mon–Sat 8am–5pm; ☎ & ☎055/242206), near the TAT office on Thanon Sithamtraipidok, can arrange minivan tours to Sukhothai or Kamphaeng Phet for B2800 per person if there are only two of you, or half that if you're in a group of five. A cheaper option would be to hire an minivan plus driver for B1200 per day, excluding fuel. Able also sells air tickets, and reconfirms them (for a hefty B300). Next door, Golden Horse ☎055/219510 offers similar services.

Sukhothai

For a brief but brilliant period (1238–1376), the walled city of **SUKHOTHAI** presided as the capital of Thailand, creating the legacy of a unified nation of Thai peoples and a phenomenal artistic heritage. Now an impressive assembly of elegant ruins, **Old Sukhothai**, 58km northwest of Phitsanulok, has been designated a historical park and has grown into one of Thailand's most visited ancient sites.

There are only a few accommodation options near the historical park, not many other facilities, so most travellers stay in so-called **NEW SUKHOTHAI**, a modern market town 12km to the east, which has good travel links with the old city and is also better for restaurants and long-distance bus connections. Straddling the Yom River, it's a small, friendly town, used to seeing tourists but by no means overrun with them. Easy to explore on foot, New Sukhothai offers a couple of outstanding guest houses as well as several other inviting options, which make it a pleasant place to hang out for a few days. The new town also makes a peaceful and convenient base for visiting Ramkhamhaeng National Park, as well as the outlying ruins of Si Satchanalai and Kamphaeng Phet.

Arrival, information and transport

New Sukhothai has direct **bus** connections with several major towns, including Bangkok, Chiang Mai Khon Kaen, Mae Sot and Kamphaeng Phet. At the time of writing, a new integrated bus terminal is being built on the bypass about 2km outside New Sukhothai, but for the moment there are several small bus terminals in town which means you still have to go to the relevant terminal when leaving Sukhothai (see map for locations). When arriving however, most buses drop passengers near the Thanon Singhawat/Thanon Charodvithitong roundabout in the town centre, into the eager hands of waiting **samlor** drivers, some of whom can be pretty intimidating. None of the New Sukhothai guest houses are more than ten minutes' walk from the centre, and if you take a samlor it shouldn't cost more than B20.

A more comfortable, though not necessarily faster, option is to take the **train** from Bangkok, Chiang Mai or anywhere in between as far as Phitsanulok and then change onto one of the half-hourly buses to New Sukhothai, which take about an hour; for details see p.254. This bus service also makes Sukhothai feasible as a day-trip from Phitsanulok, and vice versa.

You can also **fly** to Sukhothai from Bangkok and Chiang Mai with Bangkok Airways; the airport is about 15km north of town, and shuttle buses meet the flights and take passengers to hotels and guest houses for B80 per person. Bangkok Airways also operates three flights a week from Sukhothai to Siem Reap in Cambodia, though not in the reverse direction due to lack of immigration facilities in Sukhothai; see p.438 for more details on travelling from Thailand into Cambodia. A similar flight connection to Louang Phabang in Laos is also on the cards. Passengers departing from Sukhothai airport are subject to a B100 tax for the use of this privately run airport. Bangkok Airways (☏055/613310–5) has a desk at the *Pailyn Hotel* between New and Old Sukhothai, but you can also buy air tickets from the more centrally located Sukhothai Travel Agency (see p.271).

Frequent **songthaews** shuttle between New Sukhothai and the historical park 12km away. During daylight hours they depart about every fifteen minutes

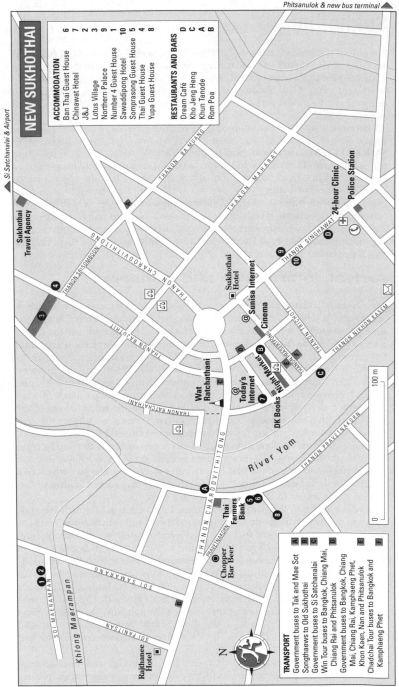

NEW SUKHOTHAI

ACCOMMODATION

Ban Thai Guest House	6
Chinawat Hotel	7
J&J	2
Lotus Village	9
Northern Palace	1
Number 4 Guest House	10
Sawaddipong Hotel	5
Somprasong Guest House	4
Thai Guest House	8
Yupa Guest House	

RESTAURANTS AND BARS

Dream Café	D
Kho Jeng Heng	C
Khun Tanode	A
Rom Poa	B

TRANSPORT

A	Government buses to Tak and Mae Sot
B	Songthaews to Old Sukhothai
C	Government buses to Si Satchanalai
	Win Tour buses to Bangkok, Chiang Mai, Chiang Rai and Phitsanulok
D	Government buses to Bangkok, Chiang Mai, Chiang Rai, Kamphaeng Phet, Khon Kaen, Nan and Phitsanulok
E	Chadchai Tour buses to Bangkok and Kamphaeng Phet
F	

Sukhothai Travel Agency

THANON RAMAUANG

THANON MAHARAT

THANON SRISOMBOON

THANON CHAROOVITHITONG

THANON RAJUTHIT

Sukhothai Hotel

Sunisa Internet

THANON SINGHAWAT

24-hour Clinic

Police Station

Cinema

Wat Ratchathani

Today's Internet

Night Market

DK Books

THANON PRASERTPONG

THANON NIKHON KASEM

THANON PRAVETNAKORN

River Yom

THANON HATCHATHANI

THANON CHAROODVITHITONG

Thai Farmers Bank

PRAVETNAKORN

Chopper Bar Beer

SOI MAERAMPAN

SOI MAERAMPAN

Khlong Maerampan

SOI SAMMANG

SOI PANTISAN

Rajhanee Hotel

N

100 m

0

◄ Old Sukhothai & Paiyn Sukhothai Hotel

from a clearing west of the river on Thanon Charodvithitong, and take around fifteen minutes. **Cycling** is also a good way of getting around, and bikes are available for rent in both New and Old Sukhothai, see "Listings", p.270 for details. There's no TAT office hereabouts, but any guest house can fill you in.

Accommodation

New Sukhothai has a good selection of **budget accommodation** options and several passable mid-range ones, but if you want deluxe rooms you should consider staying either at the *Pailyn Hotel* on the road to Old Sukhothai or in Phitsanulok (see p.254). All accommodation gets packed out during the Loy Krathong festival (see box on p.267), so book in advance if you plan to visit at this time, unless you're willing to sleep sardine-style on a guest-house floor.

New Sukhothai

Ban Thai Guest House, 38 Thanon Pravetnakorn ☎055/610163. On the west bank of the Yom, this comfortable budget option has a few simple rooms with shared bathroom in a small purpose-built house, plus some idiosyncratic wooden bungalows with private bathroom around the back. Home-made yoghurt is the star feature on their breakfast menu. ❶–❷

Chinawat Hotel, 1–3 Thanon Nikhon Kasem ☎055/611385. On the east side of the Yom River, this is a popular place offering adequate if rather faded rooms with fan and shower, plus some with air-con. ❷–❸

J&J, 122/1 Soi Maerampan, off Thanon Charodvithitong ☎055/620095, ✉jjguesthouse@hotmail.com. In a modern family house, this friendly place offers lots of tourist information and a few large but spartan rooms with shared bathrooms. Shares the quiet location of neighbouring *Number 4*, a 10min walk from the town centre; follow the signs from the bus stop for Old Sukhothai. ❷

Lotus Village, 170 Thanon Ratchathani, also accessible from Thanon Rajuthit ☎055/621484, ℱ621463, ✉lotusvil@yahoo.com. Centrally located, stylish accommodation in a traditional Thai compound of teak houses set around a tropical garden with lotus ponds. All rooms are attractively furnished; some have shared bathrooms, others are in en-suite wooden bungalows, and a few have air-con. Run by a well-informed Thai-French couple who organize tours around the region and let guests browse their fine collection of books on Asian and African art and culture. Reception shuts at 10pm. ❷–❺

Northern Palace, 43 Thanon Singhawat ☎055/611193, ℱ612038. This mid-range hotel is not that welcoming; rooms do have air-con and TVs though, and there's a swimming pool. ❹

Number 4 Guest House, 140/4 Soi Maerampan, off Thanon Charodvithitong ☎055/610165. Friendly, traveller-oriented guest house comprising ten charming if simple rattan bungalows, each with a bathroom and veranda, set in a lovely spot surrounded by fields. Run by welcoming and enthusiastic manager Sud who organizes Thai cooking courses and has an excellent book of local DIY motorbike tours. There's a book exchange and a pleasantly breezy upstairs restaurant. A 10min walk from the town centre; follow signs from the bus stop for Old Sukhothai. ❷

Sawaddipong Hotel, 56/2–5 Thanon Singhawat ☎055/611567, ℱ612268. Decent mid-range accommodation offering sizeable, clean rooms with attached bathroom, some with air-con. ❷–❸

Somprasong Guest House, 32 Thanon Pravetnakorn ☎055/611709. Adjacent to the *Ban Thai* and across from *Chinawat*, this large wooden house has sizeable rooms upstairs and affords good views from its riverfront balcony. Also has some newer bungalows with private bathrooms, some of them with air-con. It's a friendly, family-run place and welcomes guests with kids. Offers a B20 discount for those who walk here instead of coming by samlor. ❶–❸

Thai Guest House, 25/4 Thanon Rajuthit ☎055/612853. Makeshift but welcoming home-stay, very much a family enterprise. Simple rooms with fan, plus free tea and coffee throughout the day. ❶–❷

Yupa Guest House, 44/10 Thanon Pravetnakorn ☎055/612578. This converted family home offers some of the cheapest rooms in town and has a nice roof terrace, but lacks the facilities and efficiency of the other guest houses. Rooms are large and share bathrooms, and there's a B50 dorm. ❶

Old Sukhothai and around

Pailyn Sukhothai Hotel, 4km east of the old city at 10/1 Thanon Charodvithitong ☎ 055/613310, ℗ 613317. Top-class hotel where all rooms are air-conditioned and pleasantly furnished, and there's a swimming pool, sauna and disco on site. However, although you're right on the songthaew route, you're still very much between two places, 4km from the historical park and 8km west of the new city. ⑤–⑨

Thai Village Hotel (Mu Ban Thai), just east of the city walls, about 1km from the museum, at 241 Thanon Charodvithitong ☎ 055/611049, 612583. Attractive, air-conditioned wooden bungalows set in a landscaped garden behind the restaurant. ④–⑤

Vitoon Guest House, opposite the entrance to the museum on Thanon Charodvithitong, just outside the central zone ☎ 055/697045. Sprucely kept, very clean rooms with fan and bath in a rather characterless purpose-built little block. Rents bicycles. Very convenient for the historical park, but a songthaew ride away from the best of New Sukhothai's restaurants, markets and shops. ③

Sukhothai Historical Park (Muang Kao Sukhothai)

In its prime, **OLD SUKHOTHAI** boasted some forty separate temple complexes and covered an area of about seventy square kilometres between the Yom River and the low range of hills to the west. At its heart stood the walled royal city, protected by a series of moats and ramparts. **Sukhothai Historical Park**, or **Muang Kao Sukhothai** (daily 6am–6pm), covers all this area and is divided into five zones: all of the most important temples lie within the central zone, as does the Ramkhamhaeng Museum; the ruins outside the city walls are spread out over a sizeable area and divided into north, south, east and west zones. There's an official entrance gate for the central zone, but in the other zones you generally buy your ticket at the first temple you visit. **Entry** to the central zone (excluding the museum, which charges a separate admission fee) is B40, plus B10 for a bicycle, B20 for a motorbike, B30 for a samlor or B50 for a car; all other zones cost B30 each, including your vehicle. Also available are single tickets (B150), valid for one month, covering entry to all five zones plus the museum and the ruins of Si Satchanalai (see p.271).

With the help of UNESCO, the Thai government's Fine Arts Department has restored the most significant ruins and replaced the retreating jungle with lawns, leaving some trees for shade; they have also unclogged a few ponds and moats, and cleared pathways between the wats. The result reveals the original town planners' keen aesthetic sense, especially their astute use of water to offset and reflect the solid monochrome contours of the stone temples. Nevertheless, there is a touch of the too perfectly packaged theme park about the central zone, and while some critics have detected an overly liberal interpretation of the thirteenth-century design, it takes a determined imagination to visualize the ancient capital as it must once have looked. Noticeably absent are the houses and palaces which would have filled the spaces between the wats: like their Khmer predecessors, the people of Sukhothai constructed their secular buildings from wood, believing that only sacred structures merited such a durable and costly material as stone.

Songthaews from New Sukhothai (every 15min; 15min) stop about 300m east of the museum and central zone entrance point. Alternatively you can cycle from New Sukhothai to the Old City along a peaceful canalside track that you can pick up at *Number 4 Guest House*; ask there or at nearby *J&J* for directions. The best way to avoid being overwhelmed (or bored) by so many ruins is to hire a **bicycle** for B20 from one of the numerous outlets near the museum. Paths crisscross the park and circle most of the ruins, particularly in

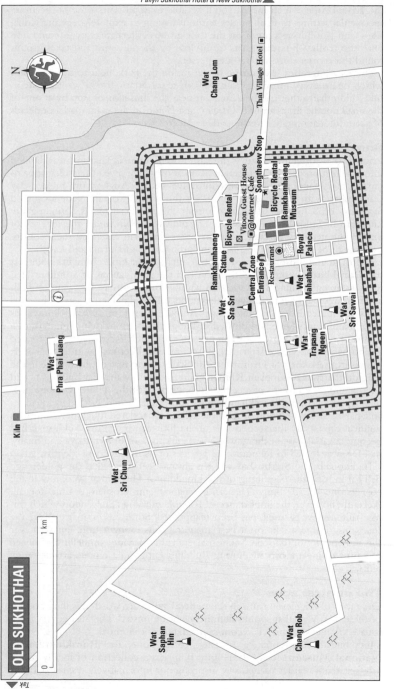

OLD SUKHOTHAI

1 km

0

N

Tak

Wat Chang Lom

Thai Village Hotel

Songthaew Stop

Vitoon Guest House

@Internet Café

Bicycle Rental

Bicycle Rental

Ramkhamhaeng Museum

Ramkhamhaeng Statue

Wat Sra Sri

Central Zone Entrance

Restaurant

Royal Palace

Wat Mahathat

Wat Sri Sawai

Wat Trapang Ngoen

Wat Phra Phai Luang

Kiln

Wat Sri Chum

Wat Saphan Hin

Wat Chang Rob

the central zone, which means you'll be able to appreciate some of the more spectacular settings from all angles without having to explore every individual site – and you'll have a jump on the tour groups. Alternatively, you could hop onto the **trolley bus** that starts from close by the museum and takes groups round the central zone for B20 per person.

There's a **currency exchange** booth inside the park, next to the museum, which opens every morning from 8.30am to 12.30pm. If you want to **eat** in Old Sukhothai, either try the restaurant near the museum, or stop by at one of the small noodle shops around *Vitoon Guest House* on the main road. For details of accommodation close to the park, see p.262.

Some history

Prior to the thirteenth century, the land now known as Thailand was divided into a collection of petty principalities, most of which owed their allegiance to the Khmer empire and its administrative centre Angkor (in present-day Cambodia). With the Khmers' power on the wane, two Thai generals joined forces in 1238 to oust the Khmers from the northern plains, founding the kingdom of **Sukhothai** ("Dawn of Happiness" in Pali) under the regency of one of the generals, Intradit. In short order they had extended their control over much of present-day Thailand, including parts of Burma and Laos.

The third and most important of Sukhothai's eight kings, Intradit's youngest son **Ramkhamhaeng** (c. 1278–1299) laid the foundations of a unique Thai identity by establishing Theravada (Hinayana) Buddhism as the common faith and introducing the forerunner of the modern Thai alphabet; of several inscriptions attributed to him, the most famous, found on what's known as Ramkhamhaeng's Stele and housed in Bangkok's National Museum, tells of a utopian land of plenty ruled by a benevolent monarch. Ramkhamhaeng turned Sukhothai into a vibrant spiritual and commercial centre, inviting Theravada monks from Nakhon Si Thammarat and Sri Lanka to instruct his people in the religion that was to supplant Khmer Hinduism and Mahayana Buddhism, and encouraging the growth of a ceramics industry with the help of Chinese potters. By all accounts, Ramkhamhaeng's successors lacked his kingly qualities and, paying more attention to religious affairs, squandered much of Sukhothai's political capital. By the second half of the fourteenth century, Sukhothai had become a vassal state of the newly emerged kingdom of Ayutthaya and finally, in 1438, was forced to relinquish all vestiges of its independent identity.

Traditionally, the **Sukhothai era** has always been viewed as the golden age of Thai history: the beginning of the kingdom of Thailand as we know it, the cornerstone of all things Thai and a happy and prosperous time for all. Recently, however, the importance of Ramkhamhaeng's Stele, upon which this rose-tinted view is based, has been reappraised. Some historians consider the stele's inscription a fake or at best an outrageous exaggeration, but whatever the authenticity of the stele, Sukhothai-era ruins provide compelling evidence of a time of great prosperity, strong Buddhist faith and a refined artistic sensibility.

The central zone

Only four of the eleven ruins in the **central zone** are worth dwelling on, and of these Wat Mahathat should definitely not be missed. The area covers three square kilometres: a bike is recommended, but not essential.

Just outside the entrance to the central zone, the **Ramkhamhaeng National Museum** (daily 9am–4pm; B30) has a collection of locally found artefacts that's neither particularly inspiring nor informatively displayed, but if

The Sukhothai Buddha

The classic Buddha images of Thailand were produced towards the end of the Sukhothai era. Ethereal, androgynous figures with ovoid faces and feline expressions, they depict not a Buddha meditating to achieve enlightenment – the more usual representation – but an already **enlightened Buddha**: the physical realization of an abstract, "unworldly" state. Though they produced mainly seated Buddhas, Sukhothai artists are renowned for having pioneered the **walking Buddha**, one of four postures described in ancient Pali texts but without precedent in Thailand. These texts also set down a list of the marks of greatness by which future Buddhas could be recognized; of all Thai schools of art, Sukhothai sculptors stuck the most literally to these precepts, as you can see by checking the **features** below against any Sukhothai statue:

Legs like a deer's.
Thighs like the trunk of a banyan tree.
Shoulders as massive as an elephant's head.
Arms tubular like an elephant's trunk, and long enough to touch each knee without bending.
Hands like lotus flowers about to bloom.
Fingertips turned back like petals.
A **head** shaped like an egg.
A **flame** to signify fiery intellect.
Hair like scorpion stings.
A **chin** like a mango stone.
A **nose** like a parrot's beak.
Eyebrows like drawn bows.
Eyelashes like a cow's.
Earlobes elongated by the heavy earrings worn by royalty.
Skin so smooth that dust couldn't stick to it.

you haven't already seen King Ramkhamhaeng's famous stele in Bangkok, you might want to look at the copy kept here. A modern **statue** of the great man sits to the right just inside the zone entrance: cast in bronze, he holds a palm-leaf book in his right hand – a reference to his role as founder of the modern Thai alphabet. Close by stands a large bronze **bell**, a replica of the one referred to on the famous stele (also reproduced here), which told how the king had the bell erected in front of his palace so that any citizen with a grievance could come by and strike it, whereupon the king himself would emerge to investigate the problem.

Wat Mahathat

Turn left inside the gate for Sukhothai's most important site, the enormous **Wat Mahathat** compound, packed with the remains of scores of monuments and surrounded, like a city within a city, by a moat. This was the spiritual focus of the city, the king's temple and symbol of his power; successive regents, eager to add their own stamp, restored and expanded it so that by the time it was abandoned in the sixteenth century it numbered ten viharns, one bot, eight mondops and nearly two hundred small chedis.

Looking at the wat from ground level, it's hard to distinguish the main structures from the minor ruins. Remnants of the viharns and the bot dominate the present scene, their soldierly ranks of pillars which formerly supported wooden roofs) directing the eye to the Buddha images seated at the far western ends.

The one component you can't overlook is the principal chedi complex, which houses the Buddha relic: it stands grandly – if a little cramped – at the heart of the compound, built on an east–west axis in an almost continuous line with two viharns. Its elegant centrepiece follows a design termed **lotus-bud chedi** (after the bulbous finial ornamenting the top of a tower), and is classic late Sukhothai in style. This lotus-bud reference is no mere whimsy but an established religious symbol: though Sukhothai architects were the first to incorporate it into building design – since when it's come to be regarded as a hallmark of the era – the lotus bud had for centuries represented the purity of the Buddha's thoughts battling through the clammy swamp and finally bursting out into flower. The chedi stands surrounded by eight smaller towers on a square platform decorated with a procession of walking Buddha-like monks, another artistic innovation of the Sukhothai school, here depicted in stucco relief. Flanking the chedi are two square mondops, built for the colossal standing Buddhas still inside them today.

The grassy patch across the road from Wat Mahathat marks the site of the former palace, of which nothing now remains.

Around Wat Mahathat

A few hundred metres southwest, the triple corn-cob-shaped prangs of **Wat Sri Sawai** make for an interesting architectural comparison with Wat Mahathat. Just as the lotus-bud chedi epitomizes Sukhothai aspirations, the prang represents Khmer ideals – Wat Sri Sawai was probably conceived as a Hindu shrine several centuries before the Sukhothai kingdom established itself here. The stucco reliefs decorating the prangs feature a few weatherworn figures from both Hindu and Buddhist mythology, which suggests that the shrine was later pressed into Buddhist service; the square base inside the central prang supported the Khmer Shiva lingam (phallus), while the viharn out front is a later, Buddhist addition.

Just west of Wat Mahathat, the particularly fine lotus-bud chedi of **Wat Trapang Ngoen** rises gracefully against the backdrop of distant hills. Aligned with the chedi on the symbolic east–west axis are the dilapidated viharn and, east of that, on an island in the middle of the "silver pond" after which the wat is named, the remains of the bot. It's worth walking the connecting plank to the bot to appreciate the setting from the water. North of the chedi, notice the fluid lines of the walking Buddha mounted onto a brick wall – a classic example of Sukhothai sculpture.

Taking the water feature one step further, **Wat Sra Sri** commands a fine position on two connecting islands north of Wat Trapang Ngoen. The bell-shaped chedi with a tapering spire and square base shows a strong Sri Lankan influence, and the black replica of a freestanding walking Buddha displays many of the "marks of greatness" as prescribed in the Pali texts (see box on p.265).

The outer zones

There's a much less formal feel to the ruins in the four **outer zones**: herds of cows trample nonchalantly through the remains and farming families have built their houses amongst them, growing rice on every available patch of land. You'll need a bicycle or car to get around these zones, but the routes aren't strenuous and all sites are clearly signposted from the city-wall boundaries. The north zone is the closest and most rewarding, followed by the east zone just off the road to New Sukhothai. If you're feeling energetic, head for the west zone,

Loy Krathong: the Festival of Light

Every year on the evening of the full moon of the twelfth lunar month (between late Oct and mid-Nov), Thais celebrate the end of the rainy season with the festival of **Loy Krathong**. One of the country's most beautiful festivals, it's held to honour the spirits of the water at a time when all the fields are flooded and the khlongs and rivers are overflowing their banks. To thank and appease Mae Khong Kha, the goddess of water, Thais decorate **krathong** – miniature basket-boats fashioned from banana leaves – with flowers, load them with burning incense sticks, lighted candles and coins, and set them afloat on the nearest body of water. The bobbing lights of thousands of floating *krathong* make a fantastic spectacle.

Loy Krathong is celebrated all over Thailand, but nowhere more magically than on the ponds of Old Sukhothai. It is here that the festival is said to have originated seven hundred years ago, when the consort of a Sukhothai king adapted the ancient Brahmin custom of paying homage to the water goddess, and began the tradition of placing *krathong* on the lotus ponds. Recently, Sukhothai has developed the original "festival of lights" so that, for the nine nights around the full moon (two weekends and the week in between) both Old and New Sukhothai are *en fête*. Not only are the pond surfaces of the historical park aglow with candles, but the ruins are wreathed in lights and illuminated during a nightly **son et lumière performance** at Wat Mahathat, and there are firework displays at nearby Wat Trapang Ngoen, plus lots of parades, concerts and street-theatre shows.

which requires a much longer bike ride and some hill climbing. The ruins to the south just aren't worth the effort.

The north zone

Continuing north of Wat Sra Si, cross the city walls into the **north zone** and follow the signs for the **information centre** (daily 6am–6pm; free) 500m further on. The centre's breezy pavilions make a pleasant resting place if you're on a bike, and its scale model of Old Sukhothai illustrates the aesthetic awareness of the original planners.

Across the road from the information centre stands **Wat Phra Phai Luang**, one of the ancient city's oldest structures. The three prangs (only one of which remains intact) were built by the Khmers before the Thais founded their own kingdom here and, as at the similar Wat Sri Sawai, you can still see some of the stucco reliefs showing both Hindu and Buddhist figures. It's thought that Phra Phai Luang was at the centre of the old Khmer town and that it was as important then as Wat Mahathat later became to the Thais. When the shrine was converted into a Buddhist temple, the viharn and chedi were built to the east of the prangs: the reliefs of the (now headless and armless) seated Buddhas are still visible around the base of the chedi. Also discernible among the ruins are parts of a large reclining Buddha and a mondop containing four huge standing Buddhas in different postures.

About 500m west from Wat Phra Phai Luang, **Wat Sri Chum** boasts Sukhothai's largest surviving Buddha image. The enormous brick and stucco seated Buddha, measuring over 11m from knee to knee and almost 15m high, peers through the slit in its custom-built mondop. Check out the elegantly tapered fingers, complete with gold-leaf nail varnish and mossy gloves. A passageway – rarely opened up, unfortunately – runs inside the mondop wall, taking you from ground level on the left-hand side to the Buddha's eye level and then up again to the roof, affording a great bird's-eye view of the image.

Legend has it that this Buddha would sometimes speak to favoured worshippers, and this staircase would have enabled tricksters to climb up and hold forth, unseen; one of the kings of Sukhothai is said to have brought his troops here so as to spur them on to victory with encouraging words from the Buddha.

The east zone

About 1km east of the main entrance, the only temple of interest in the **east zone** is **Wat Chang Lom**, just off the road to New Sukhothai, near *Thai Village Hotel*. Chang Lom, which also transliterates as Chang Rob, means "surrounded by elephants": the main feature here is a large, Sri Lankan-style, bell-shaped chedi encircled by a frieze of elephants.

The west zone

Be prepared for a long haul out to the **west zone**, in the forested hills off the main road to Tak. Marking the western edge of Old Sukhothai, almost 5km west of the main entrance, the hilltop temple of **Wat Saphan Hin** should – with sufficiently powerful telescopic lenses – afford a fantastic panorama of the old city's layout, but with the naked eye conjures up only an indistinct vista of trees and stones. If you make it this far, chances are you'll share the view only with the large standing Buddha at the top. The wat is reached via a steep pathway of stone slabs (hence the name, which means "Stone Bridge") that starts from a track running south from the Tak road. This is the easiest approach if you're on a bike as it's completely flat; the shorter route, which follows a lesser, more southerly, road out of the old city, takes you over several hills and past the elephant temple of **Wat Chang Rob**, 1km short of Saphan Hin, where it joins the other track.

Around New Sukhothai

Though Old Sukhothai is the main draw for visitors to New Sukhothai, there are enough other attractions in the area to make it worth staying on for a couple of extra days. Many of these places – such as Si Satchanalai (see p.271) and Kamphaeng Phet (see p.274) – can be fairly easily reached by public transport, but you'll need to **rent your own transport** (see pp.270-1) for trips to Wat Thawet and Ramkhamhaeng National Park.

Some guest houses organize **day-trips** which include several sights, typically a historical park and a waterfall or national park. *Lotus Village* does trips to Si Satchanalai's ruins, textile museum and gold workshop (B1500 for the group excluding fuel or guide); to the waterfalls near Phitsanulok; to the markets of Mae Sot; and to the Kamphaeng Phet ruins and nearby Khlong Lan waterfalls (B2000 per group excluding fuel or guide). *Somprasong* organizes group outings to Si Satchanalai ruins and the waterfalls of Pa-ka National Park for B400 per person (minimum two people). The *Number 4 Guest House* has a resource book full of information on interesting motorbike and bicycle routes through the area, including trips along a canal and to a pottery village.

Sangkhalok Museum

If you have a serious interest in ceramics you'll probably enjoy the Sukhothai-era exhibits at the **Sangkhalok Museum** (Mon–Fri 10am–6pm, Sat & Sun 10am–8pm; B250, children B50), a couple of kilometres east of New Sukhothai on Highway 101, close to the junction with Highway 12, the road to Phitsanulok. If you have your own transport, head southeast and then east along

Thanon Singhawat for about 2km, then turn northwest onto the signed Highway 101 where you'll see the museum almost immediately on your left. A samlor ride here from central New Sukhothai should cost no more than B40.

The ground floor of the museum displays everyday utensils and artefacts from twelfth- to sixteenth-century Sukhothai, including some very fine bowls with scalloped rims and bluish-green patterns and lots of the characteristically expressive figurines; interestingly, many of the works carry the potter's signature. This style of pottery has become known as **Sangkhalok**, after the prosperous city of Sawankhalok near Si Satchanalai that was part of the kingdom of Sukhothai at that time (see p.273 for a description of the Sangkhalok kilns in Si Satchanalai). Also on show are ceramics from twelfth-century Burma, China and Vietnam, all of which were found in the area and so show who the citizens of Sukhothai were trading with at that time – bartering items such as shells and iron balls, bronze pellets and discs are also displayed. The upstairs exhibition presents some of the most exquisite ceramics that were produced in northern Thailand during the **Lanna** era (thirteenth to sixteenth centuries). The Lanna style ceramic figurines are of exceptional quality and there are some gorgeous bowls painted with delicate black and white designs. An upmarket shopping plaza attached to the museum sells reproduction and genuine Thai antiques as well as replicated traditional Sangkhalok pottery.

Wat Thawet

If you're looking for somewhere to **cycle** to, the bizarre modern religious sculptures at Wat Thawet make as reasonable a destination as any, not least because you can do almost the whole sixteen-kilometre round-trip along peaceful canalside tracks. At a leisurely pace it should take you around an hour and a quarter each way, but be sure to wear a hat and take water as there's hardly any shade en route.

Beginning from New Sukhothai, follow riverside Thanon Ratchathani northwards as far as you can beyond *Lotus Village*, then turn right to hit the main road, Thanon Charodvithithong, and continue north up this road for around 300m until you can cross west over the river. At the west edge of the bridge take the concrete path that runs northeast beside the river, and stay on it for the next 8km until you reach Wat Thawet. It's a calm, scenic track that soon runs out of concrete and sees no cars nor even many bikes. On the way you'll pass typical wooden village-style houses, several banana plantations and probably some hopeful fishermen. Some villagers may try to persuade you off the track and onto the main road (Route 1195, to the airport) that mostly runs parallel but out of sight of the river, but the track is much pleasanter and you can get through simply by staying close to the river. The track passes alongside one wooden suspension bridge and, about 1km before the temple, under a major flyover; Wat Thawet is beside the second wooden suspension bridge.

Famous for its one hundred different brightly painted concrete statues depicting morality tales and Buddhist fables, **Wat Thawet** is quite a popular sight for Thai tourists, though some farangs find it a bit tacky. The temple **sculpture park** was conceived by a local monk in the 1970s, with the aim of creating a "learning garden" where visitors could learn about the Buddhist ideas of hell and karmic retribution. For example, people who have spent their lives killing animals are depicted here with the head of a buffalo, pig, cock or elephant, while those who have been greedy and materialistic stand there naked and undernourished, their ribs and backbones sticking out. Then there's the alcoholic who is forced to drink boiling liquids that literally make his concrete guts explode on to the ground.

Ramkhamhaeng National Park

The forested area immediately to the southwest of Sukhothai is protected as **Ramkhamhaeng National Park** (B200) and makes a pleasant day-trip on a motorcycle, with the possibility of a challenging mountain climb at the end of it. Guest houses can also arrange tours to the park, and *Number 4* keeps a detailed route map for motorbikers. To get to the main park entrance from New Sukhothai, follow Highway 101 towards Kamphaeng Phet for 19km, then take the side road signed to Khao Luang for the final 16km to park headquarters. Any Kamphaeng Phet-bound bus will take you as far as the junction with the side road, but unless there happens to be a waiting motorcycle taxi, you'll have trouble hitching into the park from here. You can rent national park **bungalows** (B500 for up to four people) at headquarters.

The park headquarters stands at the foot of the eastern flank of the highest peak, **Khao Luang** (1185m). Several steep paths run from here up to the summit, which can be reached in around four to five hours, though the routes are not very clearly marked; the first couple of kilometres are the worst, after which the incline eases up a little. From the top you should get a fine view over the Sukhothai plains.

Eating and drinking

One of the best places to **eat** in New Sukhothai is the **night market**, which sets up every Wednesday and Thursday in and around the covered marketplace between Thanon Nikhon Kasem and Thanon Ramkhamhaeng; you can often get fresh fish dishes here, and the vendors are used to dealing with farangs. There's another smaller collection of night-time hot-food stalls in front of Wat Ratchathani on Thanon Charodvithitong. A fun place for dawdling over a few beers is the string of pavement tables and chairs between the *Chinawat* and *River View* hotels on Nikhon Kasem; some of these small bar-cafés have karaoke too.

Chinawat Hotel restaurant, Thanon Nikhon Kasem. Sports a large mid-priced menu of good Thai and Western fare that runs the range from *pla rat prik* (fish grilled with chillies) down to cheese sandwiches. Daily 5–10pm.

Dream Café, 88/1 Thanon Singhawat. Has a cosy, cool, dark, coffee-shop atmosphere, with walls and windowsills decked out with curios and Thai antiques, twenty different ice-cream sundaes on the menu and a range of stamina-enhancing herbal drinks. Also does more substantial fare, including mid-priced curries, omelettes and seafood.

Kho Jeng Heng, Thanon Nikhon Kasem. This reasonably priced restaurant specializes in duck dishes, some cooked to Chinese recipes such as the stewed and mildly spiced *pet phalo*, or the roasted

pet yang, and others to Thai specifications as in the thick *kaeng pet* curries.

Khun Tanode, beside the bridge on Thanon Charodvithitong. Recommended little eating place that makes the most of its breezy riverside location and is prettily illuminated at night. The food is cheap and the atmosphere laid back; try the local speciality, crispy-fried chicken drumsticks in Sukhothai sauce, or mussels cooked in a herb sauce.

Rom Poa, signed in English at the edge of the night market. Deservedly popular, fairly inexpensive place that has an interesting English-language menu that includes spicy jelly-thread noodle salads (*yam wun sen*), curries, lots of seafood dishes, fruit shakes and a decent vegetarian selection.

Listings

Banks and exchange There are several banks with money-changing facilities and ATMs on Thanon Singhawat.

Bike rental Most guest houses offer mountain bikes for B50–80 and Chinese bicycles for B30 per day. There are plenty of bicycle-rental places at Old Sukhothai too.

Books There's a tiny selection of new English-language books at DK Books Thanon Nikhon Kasem.

Cookery courses Two-day courses at *Number 4 Guest House* (℡055/610165) cost B1500, including all ingredients and two meals.

Emergencies For all emergencies, call the tourist police on the free, 24hr phoneline ℡1699, or contact the local police station on Thanon Singhawat.

Hospital Sukhothai Hospital (℡055/611782) is west of New Sukhothai on the road to Old Sukhothai; there's a more central 24hr clinic on Thanon Singhawat.

Internet access There are currently around a dozen competitively priced internet centres in New Sukhothai, including Sunisa Internet on Thanon Prasertpong, and Today's Internet on Thanon Charodvithithong. In Old Sukhothai, there's an internet centre across from the museum beside *Vitoon Guest House.*

Mail The GPO is on Thanon Nikhon Kasem.

Motorbike rental Motorbikes can be rented through almost any guest house for B200 per day.

Telephones The CAT overseas telephone office is south off Thanon Singhawat.

Travel agent Domestic and international air tickets are available from Sukhothai Travel Agency, 317/6–7 Thanon Charodvithitong ℡055/613075.

Si Satchanalai and around

In the mid-thirteenth century, Sukhothai cemented its power by establishing several satellite towns, of which the most important was **SI SATCHANALAI**, 57km upriver from Sukhothai on the banks of the Yom. Now a historical park, the restored ruins of Muang Kao Si Satchanalai have a quieter ambience than the grander models at Old Sukhothai, and the additional attractions of the riverside wat in nearby Chalieng, the Sangkhalok pottery kilns in Bang Ko Noi and the Hat Siew textile museum in New Si Satchanalai combine to make the area worth exploring.

Si Satchanalai is for all intents and purposes a day-trip from Sukhothai as local accommodation is thin on the ground. Don't attempt to do the ruins of Si Satchanalai and Sukhothai in a single day: several tour outfits offer this option, but seeing so many dilapidated facades in seven or eight hours is mind-numbing – it's better to opt for one of the Sukhothai-based tour operators that combine ruins with waterfalls or textiles (see p.268).

Half-hourly **buses** bound for Si Satchanalai depart from near Wat Ratchathani on Thanon Charodvithitong in New Sukhothai and take about an hour. The last conveniently timed bus back to New Sukhothai leaves Old Si Satchanalai at 4.30pm; if you miss that one you'll have to wait till about 8pm. Most buses drop passengers on Highway 101 at the signpost for Muang Kao Si Satchanalai, close by a bicycle-rental place and about 2km from the entrance to the historical park. Some buses drop passengers 500m further south, in which case you should follow the track southwest over the Yom River for about 500m to another bicycle-rental place, conveniently planted at the junction for the historical park (1500m northwest) and Chalieng (1km southeast); the kilns are a further 2km north of the park. **Bikes** cost B20 to rent for the day and are much the best way of seeing the ruins – even the walk to the park can be exhausting in the heat; besides the places already mentioned, there's an outlet at the park entrance. If cycling isn't your cup of tea, you could either rent a motorbike in New Sukhothai or join a tour from there.

The historical park stands pretty much on its own with only a couple of hamlets in the vicinity, where you can buy cold drinks but won't get much in the way of food or a place to stay. If you're really determined to see Muang Kao Si Satchanalai on your way elsewhere (like Phrae or Lampang, for example), you could stay at *Wang Yom Resort*, also known as *Suwanthanas*

(℡ 055/611179, ℉ 623448; ❼), which has a range of rather pricey **bungalows** (and a crafts centre) set around an attractive garden 300m south of the park entrance, beside the Yom River and west off Highway 101. Alternatively, if you proceed to the old city's modern counterpart at New Si Satchanalai, 11km north along Highway 101 and the terminus of the Sukhothai buses, you'll find basic but inexpensive accommodation at the *Kruchang Hotel* (❷) near the Bangkok Bank in the town centre.

Muang Kao Si Satchanalai

Muang Kao Si Satchanalai (daily 8am–4pm; B40 plus B10–50 surcharge depending on your vehicle, or free if you have a combined Sukhothai–Si Satchanalai ticket) was built to emulate its capital, but Si Satchanalai is much less hyped than Sukhothai, sees fewer tourists and, most significantly, has escaped the sometimes over-zealous landscaping of the more popular site. It's also a lot more compact, though lacking in the watery splendour of Sukhothai's main temples.

The ruins are numbered and it makes sense to do them in order. Begin with the elephant temple of **Wat Chang Lom**, whose centrepiece is a huge, Sri Lankan-style, bell-shaped chedi set on a square base which is studded with 39 life-sized elephant buttresses. Many of the elephants are in good repair, with most of their stucco flesh still intact; others now have their laterite skeletons exposed. According to a contemporary stone inscription, the chedi was built to house sacred Buddhist relics originally buried in Chalieng. Contrary to the religious etiquette of the time, King Ramkhamhaeng of Sukhothai put the relics on display for a year before moving them – a potentially blasphemous act that should have been met with divine retribution, but Ramkhamhaeng survived unscathed and was apparently even more popular with his subjects afterwards.

Across the road from Wat Chang Lom, **Wat Chedi Jet Taew**'s seven rows of small chedis are thought to enshrine the ashes of Si Satchanalai's royal rulers, which makes this the ancient city's most important temple. One of the chedis is a scaled-down replica of the hallmark lotus-bud chedi at Sukhothai's Wat Mahathat; some of the others are copies of other important wats from the vicinity.

Following the road a short way southeast of Chedi Jet Taew you reach **Wat Nang Phya**, remarkable for the original stucco reliefs on its viharn wall that remain in fine condition; stucco is a hardy material which sets soon after being first applied, and becomes even harder when exposed to rain – hence its ability to survive seven hundred years in the open. The balustraded wall has slit windows and is entirely covered with intricate floral motifs. To the right on the way back to Wat Chang Lom, **Wat Suan Utayan Noi** contains one of the few Buddha images still left in Si Satchanalai.

North of Chang Lom, the hilltop ruins of Wat Khao Phanom Pleung and Wat Khao Suan Khiri afford splendid aerial views of different quarters of the ancient city. The sole remaining intact chedi of **Wat Khao Phanom Pleung** sits atop the lower of the hills and used to be flanked by a set of smaller chedis built to entomb the ashes of Si Satchanalai's important personages – the ones who merited some special memorial, but didn't quite make the grade for Wat Chedi Jet Taew. The temple presumably got its name, which means "mountain of sacred fire", from the cremation rituals held on the summit. **Wat Khao Suan Khiri**'s huge chedi, which graces the summit 200m northwest, has definitely seen better days, but the views from its dilapidated platform – south over the main temple ruins and north towards the city walls and entrance gates – are worth the climb.

Chalieng

Before Sukhothai asserted control of the region and founded Si Satchanalai, the Khmers governed the area from **Chalieng**, just over 2km to the east of Si Satchanalai. Cradled in a bend in the Yom River, all that now remains of Chalieng is a single temple, **Wat Phra Si Ratana Mahathat**, the most atmospheric of all the sites in the Sukhothai area. Left to sink into graceful disrepair, the wat has escaped the perfectionist touch of restorers and now serves both as playground to the kids from the hamlet across the river and as grazing patch for their parents' cows.

Originally a Khmer temple and later adapted by the kings of Sukhothai, Wat Phra Si Ratana Mahathat forms a compact complex of two ruined viharns aligned east–west each side of a central chedi. Of the western viharn only two Buddha images remain, seated one in front of the other on a dais overgrown with weeds, and staring forlornly at the stumps of pillars that originally supported the roof over their heads: the rest has long since been buried under grass, efficiently grazed by the cows. A huge standing Buddha, similar to the two in Sukhothai's Wat Mahathat, gazes out from the nearby mondop. The more important viharn adjoins the central Sri Lankan-style chedi to the east, and is surrounded by a sunken wall of laterite blocks. Entering it through the semi-submerged eastern gateway, you pass beneath a sizeable carved lintel, hewn from a single block of stone. The seated Buddha in the centre of the western end of the viharn is typical Sukhothai style, as is the towering stucco relief of a walking Buddha to the left, which is regarded as one of the finest of its genre.

The Sangkhalok kilns

Endowed with high-quality clay, the area around Si Satchanalai – known as Sawankhalok or Sangkhalok during the Ayutthaya period – commanded an international reputation as a ceramics centre from the mid-fourteenth to the end of the fifteenth century, producing pieces still rated among the finest in the world. More than two hundred **kilns** have been unearthed in and around Si Satchanalai to date, and it's estimated that there could once have been a thousand in all. Two kilometres upstream of Muang Kao Si Satchanalai in **Ban Ko Noi**, the **Sangkhalok Kiln Preservation Centre** (daily 9am–noon & 1–4pm; B30) showcases an excavated production site, with a couple of kilns roofed over as museum pieces.

Unfortunately, there are no English signs to explain how the kilns worked, though a small display of **Sangkhalok ceramics** gives an idea of the pieces that were fired here. Works fall into three broad categories: domestic items such as pots, decorated plates and lidded boxes; decorative items like figurines, temple sculptures and temple roof tiles; and items for export, particularly to Indonesia and the Philippines, where huge Sangkhalok storage jars were used as burial urns. Most Sangkhalok ceramics were glazed – the grey-green celadon, probably introduced by immigrant Chinese potters, was especially popular – and typically decorated with fish or chrysanthemum motifs. Several of Thailand's major museums feature collections of ceramics from both Si Satchanalai and Sukhothai under the umbrella label of Sangkhalok, and there's a dedicated collection of Sangkhalok wares just outside New Sukhothai, described on p.268.

The Sathorn Textile Museum

Eleven kilometres north of the Si Satchanalai ruins, modern Si Satchanalai is worth visiting for the **Sathorn Textile Museum**, located at the northern end of the ribbon-like new town, on the east side of Highway 101. The museum houses the private collection of Khun Sathorn, who also runs the adjacent textile shop, and he or his staff open up the one-room exhibition for anyone who shows an interest. *Lotus Village* guest house in New Sukhothai includes a visit to the museum in its Si Satchanalai day-trip, or you can come here on the bus from New Sukhothai, getting off in modern Si Satchanalai rather than at the ruins.

Most of the **textiles** on show come from the nearby village of Hat Siew, whose weavers have long specialized in the art of *teen jok,* or hem embroidery, whereby the bottom panel of the sarong or *phasin* (woman's sarong) is decorated with a band of supplementary weft, usually done in exquisitely intricate patterns. Some of the textiles here are almost a hundred years old and many of the *teen jok* **motifs** have symbolic meaning which shows what the cloths would have been used for – a sarong or *phasin* used for a marriage ceremony, for example, tends to have a double image, such as two birds facing each other. Elephants also feature quite a lot in Hat Siew weaving, and this is thought to be a reference to the village custom in which young men who are about to become monks parade on elephants to their ordination ceremony at the temple. The tradition continues to this day and elephant parades are held at the mass ordination ceremony every year on April 7 and 8.

Weaving is women's work and, after the rice harvest, the women of Hat Siew settle down at their looms while the men make knives. An experienced weaver takes three weeks to complete a typical band of *teen jok*; the embroidery is done with a porcupine quill. In the garden compound behind the museum you can usually see one of the Hat Siew weavers at work. There's a collection of old agricultural implements in the garden too, including sugar-cane presses, coconut graters and some of the knives made by Hat Siew men.

Once you've seen the Sathorn collection it's tempting to pop into the Sathorn **shop** and look at all the modern Hat Siew textiles for sale. Scarves start at B350, and traditional *teen jok* sarongs range from B600 to B10,000. There are several other Hat Siew textile outlets in modern Si Satchanalai as well, most of them further south down the main road.

Kamphaeng Phet

KAMPHAENG PHET, 77km south of Sukhothai, was probably founded in the fourteenth century by the kings of Sukhothai as a buffer city between their capital and the increasingly powerful city-state of Ayutthaya. Its name, which translates as "Diamond Wall", refers to its role as a garrison town. Strategically sited 100m from the east bank of the Ping, the ruined old city has, like Sukhothai and Si Satchanalai before it, been partly restored and opened to the public as a historical park. The least visited of the three, it should nevertheless rival Si Satchanalai for your attention, mainly because of the eloquently weathered statues of its main temple. A new city has grown up on the southeastern boundaries of the old, the usual commercial blandness offset by a riverside park, plentiful flowers and an unusually high number of traditional wooden houses.

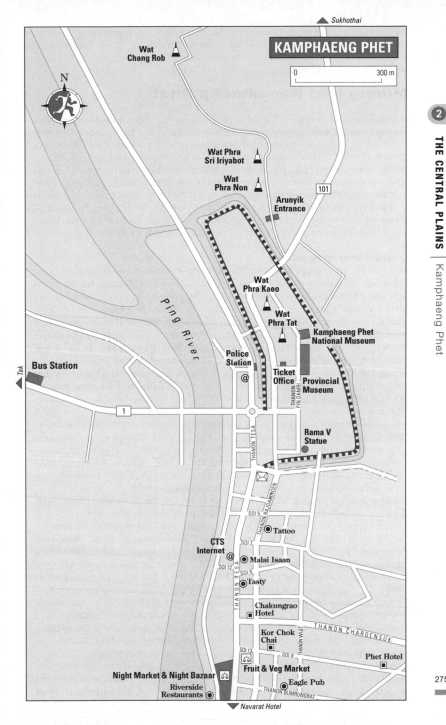

▲ *Sukhothai*

KAMPHAENG PHET

0 ———————— 300 m

Wat Chang Rob

Wat Phra Sri Iriyabot

Wat Phra Non

Arunyik Entrance

101

Ping River

Wat Phra Kaeo

Wat Phra Tat

Kamphaeng Phet National Museum

Police Station

Ticket Office

Provincial Museum

THANON PIN DAMRI

Bus Station

▲ *Tak*

1

Rama V Statue

THANON TESA

THANON RAJDAMNOEN

SOI 5

Tattoo

CTS Internet

SOI 7

SOI 12

Malai Isaan

SOI 9

Tasty

THANON TESA

Chakungrao Hotel

THANON WIJIT

THANON CHAROENSUK

Kor Chok Chai

SOI 12

SOI 8

Phet Hotel

Night Market & Night Bazaar

Fruit & Veg Market

Riverside Restaurants

Eagle Pub

THANON BUMRUNGRAT

▼ *Navarat Hotel*

Highway 1, the region's main north–south route, skirts Kamphaeng Phet on the western side of the river. The town is served by direct **buses** from Bangkok, Chiang Mai and Tak, but most travellers come here as a day-trip from Sukhothai or Phitsanulok.

Muang Kao Kamphaeng Phet

Ruins surround modern Kamphaeng Phet on all sides, but **Muang Kao Kamphaeng Phet** (daily 8am–5pm; B40) takes in the two most interesting areas: the oblong zone inside the old city walls and the forested area just north of that. A tour of both areas involves a five-kilometre round trip; there's no public transport or cycle rental, so if you don't feel like walking you'll have to strike a deal with a samlor driver. If you are coming on a day-trip from Sukhothai or Phitsanulok, consider hiring your own transport there. The ruins that dot the landscape across the Ping River, west of the Thanon Tesa round-about, belong to the even older city of Nakhon Chum, but are now too over-grown, tumbledown and difficult to reach to be worth the effort.

Inside the city walls

Parts of the **city walls** that gave Kamphaeng Phet its name are still in good condition, though Highway 101 to Sukhothai now cuts through the enclosed area and a few shops have sprung up along the roadside, making it hard to visu-alize the fortifications as a whole. Approaching from the Thanon Tesa round-about, you can either walk up Thanon Pin Damri and start your tour at Wat Phra That and the Provincial Museum, or you enter the compound from the western gate and come in at the back end of **Wat Phra Kaeo**. Built almost entirely of laterite and adorned with laterite Buddhas, this was the city's cen-tral and most important structure, and given the name reserved for temples that have housed the kingdom's most sacred image: the Emerald Buddha, now in the wat of the same name in Bangkok, is thought to have been set down here to rest at some point. Seven centuries later, the Buddha images have been worn away into attractive abstract shadows, often aptly compared to the pitted, spi-dery forms of Giacometti sculptures, and the slightly unkempt feel to the place makes a perfect setting. The statues would originally have been faced with stuc-co, and restorers have already patched up the central tableau of one reclining and two seated Buddhas. The empty niches that encircle the principal chedi were once occupied by statues of bejewelled lions.

Adjoining Wat Phra Kaeo to the east are the three chedis of **Wat Phra That**. The central bell-shaped chedi, now picturesquely wreathed in lichen and stray bits of vegetation, is typical of the Sri Lankan style and was built to house a sacred relic. Just east of Wat Phra That, **Kamphaeng Phet National Museum** (Wed–Sun 9am–4pm; B30) displays the artistic and archeological heritage of Kamphaeng Phet. The exhibition on the ground floor looks at the historical development of the city, while upstairs is given over to a display of sculptures found in the locality. The prize exhibit up here is the very fine bronze standing Shiva: cast in the sixteenth century in Khmer–Ayutthayan style, the statue has had a chequered history – including decapitation by a keen nineteenth-century German admirer. Also on this floor is an unusual seventeenth- or eighteenth-century Ayutthayan-style standing Buddha in wood, whose diadem, necklace and even hems are finely carved.

When you're at the National Museum you can't fail to see the alluring col-lection of newly built traditional-style buildings in the adjacent compound which, though unsigned in English, are in fact the **Kamphaeng Phet**

Provincial Museum (Wed–Sun 9am–4pm; free). Inside, exhibits and scale models labelled in English and Thai introduce the history, traditions and contemporary culture of Kamphaeng Phet province, but the real stars of the show are the buildings which houses these displays: glossy tan-coloured teak-wood *sala*s, connected by raised walkways and terraces decorated with flowering shrubs.

The arunyik temples

The dozen or so ruins in the forested area north of the city walls – east 100m along Highway 101 from behind Wat Phra Kaeo, across the moat and up a track to the left – are all that remains of Kamphaeng Phet's **arunyik** (forest) temples, built here by Sukhothai-era monks in a wooded area to encourage meditation.

Once you're through the entrance gate, the first temple on the left is **Wat Phra Non**, otherwise known as the Temple of the Reclining Buddha, though little remains of the enormous Buddha figure save for a few chunks helpfully labelled "neck", "head" and the like. Gigantic laterite pillars support the viharn that houses the statue; far more ambitious than the usual brick-constructed jobs, these pillars were cut from single slabs of stone from a nearby quarry and would have measured up to 8m in height.

A relic's throw to the north, the four Buddha images of **Wat Phra Sri Iriyabot** are in better condition. With cores of laterite and skins of stucco, the restored standing and walking images tower over the viharn, while the seated (south-facing) and reclining (north-facing) Buddhas remain indistinct blobs. The full-grown trees rooted firmly in the raised floor are evidence of just how old the place is.

Follow the path around the bend to reach **Wat Chang Rob**, crouched atop a laterite hill 1km from the entrance gate. Built to the same Sri Lankan model as its sister temples of the same name in Sukhothai and Si Satchanalai, this "temple surrounded by elephants" retains only the square base of its central bell-shaped chedi. Climb one of its four steep staircases for a view out over the mountains in the west, or just for a different perspective of the 68 elephant buttresses that encircle the base. Sculpted from laterite and stucco, they're dressed in the ceremonial garb fit for such revered animals; floral reliefs can just be made out along the surfaces between neighbouring elephants – the lower level was once decorated with a stucco frieze of flying birds.

Practicalities

Arriving by bus from Sukhothai or Phitsanulok, you'll enter Kamphaeng Phet from the east and should ask to be dropped off inside the old city walls rather than wait to be dumped across the river at the **terminal** 2km west of town on Highway 1. If you are coming from the bus terminal, you'll need to hop on a red town **songthaew** (B6), which will take you to the Thanon Tesa roundabout just east of the river (the most convenient disembarkation point for the ruins), or further into the town centre for most of the hotels and restaurants. From the roundabout, songthaews generally do a clockwise circle around the new town, running south down Thanon Rajdamnoen, then west along Bumrungrat, north up Thanon Tesa and west out to the bus station. There's a **bank** with an exchange counter and ATM close to the Thanon Tesa roundabout and several more banks down on Thanon Charoensuk. The main **post office** is on Thanon Tesa, about 200m south of the roundabout, and there are a couple of **internet** centres further south on Thanon Tesa.

Few travellers spend the night in Kamphaeng Phet, not least because **accommodation** here is not exciting and there's currently nothing specifically aimed at the budget traveller. Most foreigners and Thai tourists who do stay over opt for the mid-range *Navarat* (℡055/711211; ❹–❺) on Tesa Soi 21, aka Soi Prapan, 300m south of the night market at the far southern edge of the new town. Staff here speak English, there's a decent restaurant downstairs, and the all air-con rooms are comfortable if a bit shabby at the cheaper end. On the southeastern edge of town at 99 Thanon Wijit, the *Phet Hotel* (℡055/712810, ℻712816; ❺) is a little more upmarket and has a swimming pool and night club as well as decent air-con rooms. For a more economical option, the best bet is *Kor Chok Chai* (℡055/713532; ❷), east of the fruit and veg market on Rajdamnoen Soi 8; the hotel is unsigned but recognizable by its red lanterns. Most of its customers are salespeople, so there's some call-girl activity at night, but it's clean enough and fine for a night.

Food in Kamphaeng Phet rarely rises above the noodles-and-curry level, but *Malai Isaan*, just north of Soi 9 at 77 Thanon Tesa, serves up a reliable range of northeastern food – *khao niaw*, *kai yang* and *som tam* – at very reasonable prices. (There's no English sign, or menu, but you can recognize the place by the enormous sticky-rice baskets hanging out outside.) Just south of Soi 9, the air-conditioned *Tasty* does an English-language menu of ice creams and savouries like fried rice, though for a better view you should walk down to the riverside restaurants behind the night-market plaza. The **night market** itself is a very lively place and sets up in a covered area in the southern part of the new town, between the river and Thanon Tesa; try asking here for the special local noodle dish, *kway tiaw cha kang rao*, made with cow peas and pork. A nice place for a snack or an early evening drink is *Tattoo*, a funky, idiosyncratic little café-bar on Thanon Rajdamnoen, between Tesa sois 5 and 7. In a neighbourhood of majestic old wooden houses, many of which sell typically sticky Thai sweets, this is a tiny shophouse boasting curios on the walls and just four tables, adapted from old sewing-machine trestles; the young couple who run it serve several types of beer and can fry you up some food if you're hungry. The *Eagle Pub*, one block south and east of *Kor Chok Chai* on Thanon Bumrungrat, is a more traditional nightspot, with live music every evening from about 9pm.

West of Sukhothai

Highway 12 heads west from Sukhothai, crossing the westernmost reaches of the northern plains before arriving at the provincial capital of **TAK** (79km), on the east bank of the Ping River. Historically important as the birthplace of King Taksin of Thonburi (who attached the name of his hometown to the one he was born with), Tak is of little interest to tourists except as a place to change **buses** for continuing north to Lampang and Chiang Mai, south to Kamphaeng Phet and Bangkok, or west to Mae Sot and the Burmese border. The Mae Sot service is particularly convenient, with government minivans departing Tak **bus station**, about 3km east of the town centre, every thirty minutes and taking an hour and a half. Tak **airport** is no longer in service, but Thai Airways provides twice-daily complimentary transport between Phitsanulok airport and Tak city centre; contact their Tak office at 485 Thanon Taksin ℡055/512164 for details. **TAT** has a regional office in the town centre at 193 Thanon Taksin (daily 8.30am–4.30pm; ℡055/514341).

The Burmese junta and the Karen

With a population of five million, the **Karen** are Burma's largest ethnic minority, but their numbers have offered no protection against persecution by the Burmese. This mistreatment has been going on for centuries, and entered a new phase after World War II, when the Karen remained loyal to the British. As a reward, they were supposed to have been granted a special settlement when the British left, but were instead left to fend for themselves. Fifteen years after the British withdrawal, the **Burmese army** took control, setting up an isolationist state run under a bizarre ideology compounded of militarist, socialist and Buddhist principles. In 1988, opposition to this junta peaked with a series of pro-democracy demonstrations which were suppressed by the slaughter of thousands.

The army subsequently felt obliged to hold elections, which resulted in an overwhelming majority for the **National League for Democracy** (NLD), led by **Aung San Suu Kyi**, recipient of the 1991 Nobel Peace Prize. In response, the military placed Aung San Suu Kyi under house arrest (where she has remained on and off ever since) and declared all opposition parties illegal. The disenfranchised MPs then joined the thousands who, in the face of the savagery of the Burmese militia against the country's minorities, had fled east to jungle camps along the border north and south of Mae Sot. Armed by the Karen National Union (KNU), all resistance activities of the anti-Rangoon coalition, the Democratic Alliance of Burma, were centred on the jungle camp of Manerplaw, upriver from Mae Sot on the Burmese bank of the Moei River, which was also home to the democratically elected National Coalition Government of the Union of Burma (NCGUB).

In 1995, after seven years of continued armed resistance, several minority groups, including the Mon and the Buddhist Karen, signed temporary **ceasefire agreements** with the Burmese government, which continue to hold at the time of writing. However, a number of factions refused to participate in the ceasefire, the largest of these being the Christian-dominated KNU. The split with their Buddhist compatriots left the Christian Karen vulnerable to the Burmese army and resulted in a mass exodus of around ten thousand Karen across the Thai border in 1995. The KNU have continued to fight the junta, clawing back lost territory every year during the rainy season when their jungle know-how reaps most rewards. Every dry season, however, the Burmese army makes territorial gains, pushing hundreds more civilian **refugees** across the border into Thailand. Common tactics the army employs include the forcible razing and relocation of villages, systematic murder, rape and robbery and the rounding-up of slave labour: according to the International Confederation of Free Trade Unions, nearly one million people are currently subjected to forced labour in Burma, mainly for the building of roads, railways and military projects, and as porters for the Burmese army .

Thailand has been offering temporary asylum to Burmese refugees for almost two decades now, with relief agencies estimating the number living in **camps** on the Thai

If you need a **hotel** in Tak, try the *Mae Ping*, across the road from the fruit and veg market at 231 Thanon Mahattai Bamroong (☎055/511807; ❶–❸), which has faded but inexpensive fan and air-con rooms; the slightly pricier, slightly better *Sa Nguan Thai* (☎055/511153; ❷–❸) is a couple of blocks north of the market at 619 Thanon Taksin and easily identifiable by its red lanterns hanging outside; you can choose between fan and air-con rooms with or without TV. The town's best hotel is the comfortably furnished *Viang Tak 2* (☎055/512507; ❺–❻), one block southwest of the fruit and veg market at 236 Thanon Chumphon; there's a swimming pool here, and some rooms have river

border at over 127,000 in December 2000. Conditions in the camps vary: some of the long-term camps function almost like typical Thai communities with shops, jobs and vegetable plots; other, newer, places are more like holding pens, with refugees living for months if not years under plastic sheeting, forbidden even from cutting wood to make shelters. Unable to cope with the continuing influx from Burma, some of these camps have become inhumanely crowded – as the United Nations High Commissioner for Refugees Sadako Ogata made public, much to Thailand's indignant embarrassment, in October 2000. Worse still, it's not uncommon for Karen refugee camps to be raided by the Burmese military, and even by Karen collaborators. In 2000, repeated devastating attacks on camps along the Moei River near Mae Sot prompted the UNHCR to pressurize Thailand into relocating the refugees to a safer location near Umphang (see p.288). Burma meanwhile is refusing to treat the exiles as refugees, labelling them instead "fugitives, illegal migrants, insurgents and members of unlawful associations opposing the government", who would under no circumstance be allowed to return to Burma without prosecution.

Reactions in the Thai press to the Burmese refugee issue are mixed, with humanitarian concerns tempered by economic hardships in Thailand and by high-profile cases of illegal Burmese workers involved in violent crimes and drug-smuggling (Burma is now one of the world's leading producers and smugglers of methamphetamines, also known as *ya baa*, or Ice, much of which finds its way across Thai borders). Thai public opinion was also swayed when the rebel Burmese splinter-group known as God's Army, led by two teenage twins, laid siege in 1999 to the Burmese Embassy in Bangkok, and the following year to a provincial hospital in Ratchaburi district, taking Thai citizens hostage and demanding asylum for named Burmese dissidents in exchange for their release. The Thai government responded by tightening its entry requirements for all refugees. Meanwhile, the two nations continue to trade, to the obvious benefit of both: every week at Rim Moei alone, Thailand exports some US$6 million worth of goods to Burma, importing produce worth around $400,000 in return.

There may at last be hope on the horizon, for the Karen refugees in Thailand, for the beleaguered Thai authorities and for Burma itself. In early 2001, Aung San Suu Kyi and the military government held **talks** for the first time in five years, with the KNU proclaiming its support for multi-party elections and the creation of a federal structure for Burma.

To offer **support** to the Karen at the refugee camps, you can leave clothes and medicines for the refugees at *Number 4 Guest House* in Mae Sot, or give blood at the Saphan Song Refugees' Clinic, at the far western edge of Mae Sot on Thanon Indharakiri; ask at *Number 4 Guest House* or *The River* restaurant for details. The Human Rights Watch Web site ⓦwww.hrw.org has more information on the current situation at the refugee camps on the Thai–Burma border; for more on the Karen people, see p.813.

views. A more interesting option than staying in town would be to head out to the small village of **BAN TAK**, 20km north of Tak on Highway 1, where an English-Thai couple run the tiny, eight-bed *Ban Tak Youth Hostel* at 9/1 Mu 10, Tambon Taktok (ⓣ & ⓕ055/591286, ⓦwww.tyha.org; ❸, dorm beds B125). The village is right on the Ping River and the hostel rents out bicycles for exploring the area. Songthaews run at least every hour from 7am to 4pm between Tak bus station and Ban Tak and take about forty minutes; coming from Chiang Mai, take any bus bound for Tak and ask to be dropped at Ban Tak.

Most travellers ignore Tak, however, and go straight on to Mae Sot, reached by either of two roads through the stunning western mountain range that divides the northern plains from the Burmese border. Highway 105, the more direct route, is served by cramped government minibuses that leave Tak every thirty minutes between 6.30am and 6pm and take ninety minutes to reach Mae Sot. Rickety but roomy regular buses take twice as long to ply Route 1175, which follows a winding and at times hair-raising course across the thickly forested range, affording great views over the valleys on either side and passing through makeshift roadside settlements built by hill tribes. (Returning along either of these routes to Tak, most public vehicles are stopped at an army checkpoint in an attempt to prevent Burmese entering Thailand illegally, though tourists aren't subject to hassle.) Much of this whole area is conserved as a national park, the most accessible stretch of which falls within **Langsang National Park** and is signposted off Highway 105, 20km west of Tak.

Buses on Route 1175 eventually descend into the valley of the **Moei River** – which forms the Thai–Burmese border here – and join the new northbound section of Highway 105 (formerly Route 1085) at the lovely, traditional village of **Mae Ramat** before continuing south to Mae Sot. Highway 105 carries on northwards, reaching Mae Sariang (see p.356) after a five-hour songthaew ride – a bumpy but extremely scenic journey through rugged border country which is now home to one of the largest Karen refugee camps in the country. Heading south from Mae Sot, the same road becomes Route 1090, nicknamed the Sky Highway because of its panoramic vistas, and eventually winds up in the village of Umphang.

Mae Sot and the border

Located 100km west of Tak and only 6km from the Burmese border, **MAE SOT** boasts a rich ethnic mix of Burmese, Karen, Hmong and Thai residents, a thriving trade in gems and teak, and a laid-back atmosphere. There's little to see in the small town apart from several glittering Burmese-style temples, but it's a relaxed place to hang out with a burgeoning number of good restaurants; the short ride to the border market provides additional, if low-key, entertainment. There are also a couple of pretty waterfalls within day-tripping distance: Nam Tok Mae Kasa is 20km north of town, Nam Tok Phra Charoen 41km south. Don't get excited about crossing into Burma from here as, despite the new bridge at Rim Moei (see p.284), foreign nationals are currently forbidden from going any further into Burma here than the 500m to the town of Myawaddy.

Mae Sot's greatest attraction, however, is as a stopover point on the way to **Umphang** (see p.285), a remote village 164km south of Mae Sot, which is starting to get a name as a centre for interesting rafting and trekking adventures; several tour operators in Mae Sot organize treks out of Umphang and are listed in the box on pp.286–7. The journey to Umphang takes about five hours in a bumpy songthaew so it's usually worth stopping the night in Mae Sot; you can also organize treks to Umphang through Mae Sot tour agencies. If you need to change money for the trip, you should do so in Mae Sot (see "Listings", p.285) as there's nowhere to do so in Umphang. For a list of trekking operators based in Mae Sot and Umphang see the box on pp.286–7.

Arrival and information

Mae Sot has pretty good **bus** connections with towns in the central plains and in the north. There are half-hourly direct government minibuses from Tak

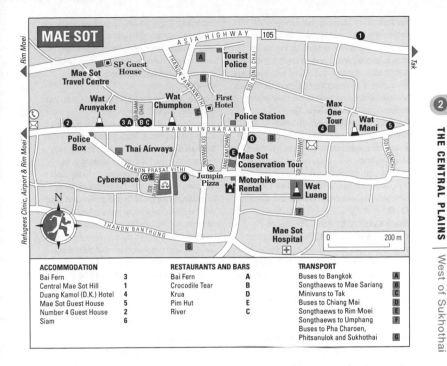

ACCOMMODATION		RESTAURANTS AND BARS		TRANSPORT	
Bai Fern	3	Bai Fern	A	Buses to Bangkok	A
Central Mae Sot Hill	1	Crocodile Tear	B	Songthaews to Mae Sariang	B
Duang Kamol (D.K.) Hotel	4	Krua	D	Minivans to Tak	C
Mae Sot Guest House	5	Pim Hut	E	Buses to Chiang Mai	D
Number 4 Guest House	2	River	C	Songthaews to Rim Moei	E
Siam	6			Songthaews to Umphang	F
				Buses to Pha Charoen,	
				Phitsanulok and Sukhothai	G

(1hr 30min) to Mae Sot and some from Sukhothai as well (2hr 30min), and several daily long-distance buses from Chiang Mai and Bangkok. Songthaews connect Mae Sot with the border towns of Mae Ramat (every 30min; 45min) and Mae Sariang (hourly 6am–midday; 5hr). If you're arriving on a government **minivan**, be sure to tell the driver where you're planning to stay in Mae Sot, and you should be dropped off at your chosen guest house. Otherwise, buses use a variety of different terminals around town: see the map for details. For information on transport between Mae Sot and Umphang, see p.285. Eight **flights** a week connect Mae Sot's tiny airstrip, 3km west of town on the Asia Highway, with Bangkok, four of them via Chiang Mai; to get into town from the airport, either walk out of the airport gates and hop onto a west-bound songthaew to the Thanon Prasat Vithi terminus, or take a motorbike taxi.

There is no TAT office here, but the couple who run *The River* restaurant on Thanon Indharakiri (℡ 055/534593) are an excellent and willing source of local **information**. There is also some tourist information at *Number 4 Guest House*.

Accommodation

Mae Sot's guest houses offer basic **rooms** and some information on the area; the hotels are generally more comfortable but less friendly. If you sign up with a trek at SP Tour, you can stay in one of their guest-house rooms at Mae Sot Travel Centre on the Asia Highway (❶) which are decent enough but too far out of the town centre for anything more than one night.

Bai Fern, 660/2 Thanon Indharakiri ☏055/533343. Very friendly little guest house that's attached to one of the town's best restaurants. Rooms are dark, quite noisy and altogether pretty basic, with mattresses on the floor and shared bathrooms, but the location is good and the staff more welcoming and enthusiastic than those at the other guest houses. Some B50 dorm beds. ❷

Central Mae Sot Hill Hotel, 100 Asia Highway/Highway 105 ☏055/532601, ℱ532600, ⓦwww.centralgroup.com. The most upmarket accommodation in the area, but a 10min drive from the town centre. All rooms are air-con, smartly furnished and have a TV, and there's a swimming pool and tennis courts on the premises. ❻–❼

Duang Kamol (D.K.) Hotel, 298 Thanon Indharakiri ☏055/531699. The nicest and best value of the town hotels is set above the bookshop of the same name, and has huge clean rooms, many of them with little balconies and some with air-con and TV. ❸–❹

Mae Sot Guest House, 10min walk from the town centre at the eastern end of Thanon

Indharakiri ☏055/532745. Sometimes referred to as "Number 2" to distinguish it from *Number 4*, this haphazardly run guest house offers both very basic makeshift rooms as well as more comfortable ones with beds, bathrooms and air-con. ❶–❷

Number 4 Guest House, 736 Thanon Indharakiri ☏ & ℱ055/544976, ⓦwww.geocities.com/no4guesthouse. Located in a nice old teak house about 15min walk west of the town centre, this place is very popular with both travellers and volunteers working at nearby refugee camps. Rooms are clean, and the place has a laid-back feel to it. On the downside, the emphasis is very much on self-service and doing your own thing, which can make it hard to get information or service. All rooms have mattresses on the floor and shared bathrooms; dorm beds cost B50. Also runs recommended treks (see box on p.286) and rents out bicycles. ❶

Siam, 185 Thanon Prasat Vithi ☏055/531176, ℱ531974. Typical Thai-Chinese town hotel, centrally located among the gem and jade shops and with decent enough fan and air-con rooms. ❷–❸

Shopping and Rim Moei border market

Mae Sot is a good place to buy jewellery: the **gem and jade shops** clustered around the *Siam* hotel on Thanon Prasat Vithi offer a larger and less expensive selection than the stalls at the Rim Moei border market, and even if you don't intend to buy, just watching the performance-like haggling is half the fun.

Frequent songthaews ferry Thai traders and a meagre trickle of tourists the 6km from Mae Sot to the border at **RIM MOEI**, where a large and thriving market for Burmese goods has grown up along the high street and beside the banks of the Moei River. It's a bit tacky, and the gems and jade on display are pricier than those in town, but it's not a bad place to pick up Burmese **handicrafts**, particularly wooden artefacts like boxes and picture frames, woven Karen shoulder bags and checked *longyis*. The best buys are the dozens of chunky teak-wood tables and chairs on sale here, most of them polished up to a fine golden brown sheen.

The Asia Highway now zips straight through Rim Moei and into Burma, via the Thai-Burma Friendship Bridge. At the time of writing, access to the Burmese village of **Myawaddy** on the opposite bank of the Moei River is open to any foreign national for a fee of B500, payable at the bridge, though foreign visitors are allowed no further into Burma than this, and must return to Thailand on the same day. When coming back through Thai customs you will automatically be given a new one-month Thai visa on the spot, which is handy if your existing visa is running out, but not so great if you've still got the best part of a sixty-day visa (see Basics p.25 for how to pre-empt this problem).

Eating and drinking

Thanon Prasat Vithi is well stocked with noodle shops and night-market stalls, though the more unusual restaurants are mainly found on the town's other main thoroughfare, Thanon Indharakiri.

Bai Fern, 660/2 Thanon Indharakiri. This small but highly recommended restaurant attached to the guest house of the same name serves some of the best and most imaginative food in the region. The mid-priced menu includes a selection of pepper steaks served with a variety of unusual sauces, authentic Italian *carbonara*, lots of novel stir fries, plus traditional Thai curries and lots of vegetarian options.

Crocodile Tear, Thanon Indharakiri. Dishes out draught beer and stages live soft rock/folk music every night from around 9pm.

Krua, diagonally across from the police station, just off Thanon Indharakiri. Delicious and inexpensive food at this unpretentious, family-run eatery whose menu includes such local specialities as stir-fried frog and bird curry, plus a recommended stir-fried eggplant dish made with beancurd, chilli and basil. Also serves three different blends of local hill-tribe coffee (iced or hot), plus a long menu of veggie dishes.

Pim Hut, Thanon Tang Kim Chang. Popular with locals as well as Thai and farang tourists, and offers a big range of Thai and Western food at reasonable prices – everything from green curries to pizzas.

The River, 626 Thanon Indharakiri. Run by a local-born folk-singer and his wife, this place is becoming known as much for its inviting welcome and useful local information as for its tasty, mid-priced, traveller-oriented menu of pasta, sandwiches, steaks, Thai curries and real coffee.

Listings

Airline Thai Airways is in the town centre at 76/1 Thanon Prasat Vithi ☏ 055/531730.

Banks and exchange There are several banks with money-changing facilities and ATMs on Thanon Prasat Vithi.

Bike rental *Number 4* has rental bicycles for its guests.

Books A small range of new English-language Penguin Classics is available at DK Books on Thanon Indharakiri.

Emergencies For all emergencies, call the tourist police on the free, 24hr phone line ☏1699, or contact them at their booth near the main terminal for buses to Bangkok (☏055/532960). The main police station is in the town centre on Thanon Indharakiri.

Herbal saunas At Wat Mani, near *Mae Sot Guest House*.

Hospitals Mae Sot Hospital is on the southeastern edge of town and Pha Wawa Hospital is on the southwestern edge.

Immigration office At Rim Moei.

Internet access Al Cyber Space, next to the Rim Moei songthaew stop on Thanon Prasat Vithi.

Motorbike rental From a bike-repair shop near the Bangkok Bank on Thanon Prasat Vithi (from B160 per day).

Postal services The GPO is just west of *Number 4* on Thanon Indharakiri, but there's a more central branch near *DK Hotel* on Thanon Indharakiri.

Telephone International calls from the government telephone office just west of *Number 4* on Thanon Indharakiri.

Umphang

Even if you don't fancy doing a trek, consider making the spectacular trip 164km south from Mae Sot to the village of **UMPHANG**, both for the stunning mountain scenery you'll encounter along the way, and for the buzz of being in such an isolated part of Thailand. Umphang-bound songthaews leave Mae Sot from a spot two blocks south of Thanon Prasat Vithi, departing every hour between 7.30am and 3.30pm and costing B120 or B150 if you're lucky enough to get the front seat. The drive generally takes about five hours and for the first hour proceeds in a fairly gentle fashion through the maize, cabbage and banana plantations of the Moei valley. The fun really begins when you start climbing into the mountains and the road – accurately dubbed the **"Sky Highway"** – careers round the edges of endless steep-sided valleys, undulating like a fairground rollercoaster (there are said to be 1219 bends in all). If

A variety of attractions in the area combine to make **Umphang treks** some of the most genuine organized wilderness experiences in Thailand; the vegetation is mainly montane forest, there are numerous varieties of orchid, and you are likely to encounter monkeys and hornbills if not the band of resident wild elephants. There is more emphasis on walking (usually around 3–4hr a day) here than on the more popular treks around Chiang Mai and Chiang Rai, and as yet the number of visitors is reasonably small. The most comfortable **season** for trekking is November through February, though nights can get pretty chilly up here, so you'll need a fleece or equivalent.

The focus of all Umphang treks is the three-tiered **Tee Lor Su Waterfall**, star feature of the Umphang Wildlife Sanctuary, which, unusually for Thailand, flows all year round, even at the end of the dry season. Local people claim that at around 100m high, not only is Tee Lor Su the highest waterfall in Thailand, but it is also the sixth highest in the world. The falls are at their most thunderous just after the rainy season in November, when you can also swim in the beautifully blue lower pool, but trails can still be muddy at this time, which makes walking harder and less enjoyable. During the dry season (Dec–April), you can get close to the falls by road and, mud permitting, it's usually possible to climb up to one of the upper tiers during this period too. At other times the falls are reached by a combination of rafting and walking.

A **typical trek** lasts four days and follows something like the following itinerary. Day one: rafting down the Mae Khlong River via Tee Lor Jor waterfall and some impressively honeycombed cliffs; camp overnight at hot springs or beside the river. Day two: a three- to four-hour jungle trek to Tee Lor Su waterfall; camp near the falls. Day three: a three-hour trek to a Karen village where you stay the night. Day four: a two-hour elephant ride; return to Umphang. Some trekkers find the elephant experience overrated – it's slow and uncomfortable and often covers ground that would be quite manageable on foot; if your group decides to forego this element of the trek you might get a discount. Longer or shorter treks are possible; some of the trek operators listed below can arrange one-day elephant-riding or rafting excursions.

It's possible to **arrange your trek** in Mae Sot, or even in Bangkok (see p.188), but the best place to set up your trip is in Umphang itself. Not only are trips from here usually cheaper and better value (you don't waste half a trek day getting to Umphang), but trek leaders are more flexible and happy to take small groups and to customize itineraries. Being local, they are experts on the area, and your custom helps boost the economy of the village. The main drawback with arranging things from Umphang is that you may have to wait for a couple of days for the trek leader to return from his last trip; the best time to contact them is after 6pm. Guides should provide tents, bedrolls, mosquito nets and sleeping bags, plus food and drinking water; trekkers may be asked to help carry some of the gear.

Mae Sot trekking operators

In addition to the specialist agencies listed below, you can also try asking at *The River* restaurant, and at *Mae Sot Guest House*.

Khun Om, c/o *Number 4 Guest House*, 736 Thanon Indharakiri ☎ & ℱ 055/544976, ⓦ www.geocities.com/no4guesthouse. The treks run by the taciturn Khun Om get rave reviews. He offers the standard three-day Tee Lor Su programme for B3500, does a four-day version for B4500 and – his *pièce de résistance* – a seven-day expedition for US$400 per person. Although it can be hard to elicit information from

you're prone to car-sickness, take some preventative tablets before setting out, as this journey can be very unpleasant, not least because the songthaews get so crammed with people and produce that there's often no possibility of dis-

the staff at *Number 4*, full details of the treks are given on their informative website; book ahead if possible.

Mae Sot Conservation Tour, next to *Pim Hut* at 415/17 Thanon Tang Kim Chang ⓣ055/532818, ⓕ545450, ⓔmaesotco@cscoms.com. This outfit tends to deal more with large groups of Thai trekkers than small groups of farangs. They offer the three-day Tee Lor Su option for around B4000 and also do a one-day "jungle observation" trip to the nearby Mae La Mao River for B3000 per group of six, and a day-trip across the Burmese border for around B2000 per person.

Max One Tour, in the *DK Hotel* plaza at 296/1 Thanon Indharakiri ⓣ055/542942, ⓕ543142, ⓦwww.umphanghill.com. One of two Mae Sot outlets for the Umphang-based Umphang Hill trek operator (see below); the other branch is SP Tour ⓣ055/531409 at the Mae Sot Travel Centre on the northern outskirts of town at 14/21 Asia Highway (Highway 105). Prices start at about B4000 per person for three days and two nights if departing from Mae Sot and include return transport (minimum two people; price may drop for larger groups). See Umphang Hill below for full details.

Umphang trekking operators

The main English-speaking trek leaders operating out of Umphang at the time of writing are listed below, but you can also arrange treks through staff at *Veera Tour* and *Tu Ka Su Guest House*.

Cocoh, c/o BL Tour. Enthusiastic and well informed, Cocoh is a Chinese Burmese and speaks good English. He is keen to arrange tailor-made activities for interested tourists. Three-day treks cost B3000 per person, four-days B3700 (less if there are more than two people). Also arranges one-day trips on rubber rafts, bamboo rafts and elephants.

Mr Boonchuay, reachable at his home ⓣ & ⓕ055/561020, 500m west of the wat. Umphang-born and bred, Mr Boonchuay knows the area well, though his English is not perfect; he does three-day treks for B3000 per person, four day-treks for B3700 (minimum two people). Trekkers can stay at his house for B80 a night.

Mr Tee, c/o *Trekker Hill* ⓣ055/561090, ⓕ561328, 700m northwest of the wat. Mr Tee and his "jungle team" of five guides get good reviews. Besides leading group treks (three days B3500 per person; four days B4000), he is happy to take solo trekkers on three-day trips (B5000). Trekkers can stay in dorms at *Trekker Hill* for B100.

Phu Doi, at *Phu Doi Campsite* ⓣ055/561049, ⓕ561279. Two-day treks for B1500; three-day treks for B2000 (or B3500 with elephant riding and a night in a Karen village); four days for B4000. Minimum two people.

Umphang Hill ⓦwww.umphanghill.com. At *Umphang Hill Resort*, but can also be booked through Max One Tour in Mae Sot. Very efficiently run by a retired local police captain, this place often undercuts rival outfits and has English-speaking staff at the office throughout the day. They do half a dozen basic itineraries in the Umphang area, described in full on their website, and any number of tailor-made permutations; most treks are led by local Karen guides. Three-day treks cost B2500; four days for B3500 (minimum two people; prices drop with larger groups). With a fortnight's advance notice they can also arrange a challenging seven-day trek all the way down to Sangkhlaburi near Kanchanaburi (B12,000 per person, minimum four people).

tracting yourself by staring out of the window. Karen, Akha, Lisu and Hmong people live in the few hamlets along the route, many growing cabbages along the cleared lower slopes with the help of government incentives (part of a

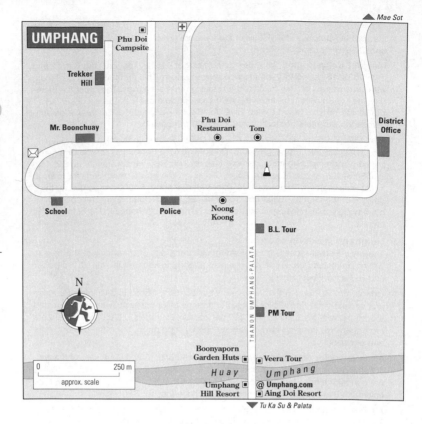

UMPHANG

Phu Doi Campsite

Trekker Hill

Mr. Boonchuay

Phu Doi Restaurant

Tom

District Office

School

Police

Noong Koong

B.L. Tour

THANON UMPHANG-PALATA

N

PM Tour

Boonyaporn Garden Huts

Veera Tour

Huay

Umphang

Umphang Hill Resort

@ Umphang.com

Aing Doi Resort

0   250 m
approx. scale

▼ Tu Ka Su & Palata

national campaign to steer upland farmers away from the opium trade). The Hmong in particular are easily recognized by their distinctive embroidered jackets and skirts edged in bright pink, red and blue bands (see p.813). In 2000, the local population of Karen grew by several thousand when three refugee camps from the Rim Moei area were relocated to a purpose-built village alongside the Sky Highway at the midway point between Mae Sot and Umphang; see box on p.280 for more on Karen refugees. In fact the Umphang region was inhabited by Karen hill tribes before the Thais came to settle in the area in the early twentieth century; later when the Thais began trading in earnest with their neighbours across the Burmese border, the Karen traders from Burma used to carry their identification documents into Thailand in a bamboo container which they called an "umpha" – this is believed to be the origin of the name Umphang.

Surrounded by mountains and sited at the confluence of the Mae Khlong and Umphang rivers, Umphang itself is quiet and sleepy, made up of little more than a thousand or so wooden houses, a few tiny general stores and eating places, a post office, a police station, a primary school and a wat. It won't take long to explore the minute grid of dusty tracks that dissects the village, but independent tourists are still relatively rare here, so you should get quite a warm reception from villagers.

Practicalities

The two main points of **orientation** are the Huay Umphang River at the far southern end of the village, and the wat – about 500m north of the river – that marks the approximate centre of the village. Most of the shops and restaurants are clustered along the two roads that run parallel to the wat, one immediately to the north of the temple, the other along the southern side. There's a knot of guest houses and trekking operators down by the river at the southern end of the village, which is where you'll also find *Umphang.com*, a restaurant with **internet access**.

Mountain bikes can be rented from *Tu Ka Su Guest House* for B200 per day. When it comes to public transport though, Umphang is effectively a dead end, so the only way to travel on from here is to go back to Mae Sot first. **Songthaews** to Mae Sot leave hourly until mid-afternoon; if you tell your guest house when you want to leave they'll arrange for the songthaew to pick you up – be sure to say where in Mae Sot you want to be dropped, then you'll get genuine door-to-door service.

Accommodation and eating

Most of the **accommodation** in Umphang is geared either towards groups of trekkers accompanied by Thai guides, or towards independent travellers who are overnighting just before or after their trek. Because of this, many places charge per person rather than per room; the categories listed below are for two people sharing a room, so expect to pay half if you're on your own. If you've organized a trek here in Bangkok or Mae Sot, accommodation should be included in your package; independent trekkers can usually stay in dorms at their trek leader's house for about B100 (see box on p.287).

Most of the guest houses will at least serve breakfast to their guests. The most popular places for other **meals** are *Phu Doi*, on the road just north of the temple, which has an English-language menu of curries and meat-over-rice dishes; *Umphang Hill*, whose restaurant overlooks the river and has karaoke in the evenings; and the simple and inexpensive noodle shop *Noong Koong*.

Boonyaporn Garden Huts, 106 Thanon Umphang–Palata, on the north bank of the river, ☎ & ℗ 055/561093, ⓦ www.boonyaporn.com. No English sign, but recognizable from its Carlsberg sign. Simple rattan huts in a garden, all with mosquito nets and shared bathrooms; some are better than others so check several if you can. Also some more comfortable wooden huts with bathroom. ❷–❹

Phu Doi Campsite, about 500m northwest of the wat ☎ 055/561049, ℗ 561279. "Campsite" is a complete misnomer as this place has a very nice set of sparklingly clean rooms in a couple of wooden houses with verandas overlooking a pond. All rooms have private bathrooms and mattresses on the floor, and there's free tea and coffee. ❷

Tu Ka Su Guest House, 300m south of the river on Thanon Umphang–Palata ☎ & ℗ 055/561295. Beautifully set in a pretty garden with expansive views over the river, fields and mountains. Rooms cater for different-sized groups of up to eight people, and some have nicely designed garden bathrooms attached. Mountain bikes are available for rent. ❸

Umphang Hill Resort, on the south bank of the river, 500m from the wat, ☎ 055/561063, ℗ 561065, ⓦ www.umphanghill.com. Beautifully set in a flower garden on a slope leading down to the river, with views of the surrounding mountains. Large, basic chalets with verandas, TVs and hot water, plus some trekkers' rooms with B50 mattresses if you come in a group. ❷–❹

Veera Tour, on Thanon Umphang–Palata, on the north bank of the river, ☎ 055/561021, ⓔ veera-tour@hotmail.com. Inexpensive, decent enough rooms with shared bathrooms in a large timber house. ❷

Travel details

Trains

Ayutthaya to: Bangkok Hualamphong (20 daily; 1hr 30min); Chiang Mai (5 daily; 12hr); Lopburi (9 daily; 1hr–1hr 30min); Nong Khai (3 daily; 9hr 30min); Phitsanulok (8 daily; 5hr); Ubon Ratchathani (6 daily; 8hr 30min–10hr).

Kanchanaburi to: Bangkok Noi (2 daily; 2hr 40min); Nam Tok (3 daily; 2hr).

Lopburi to: Ayutthaya (9 daily; 1hr–1hr 30min); Bangkok Hualamphong (9 daily; 2hr 30min–3hr); Chiang Mai (5 daily; 11hr); Phitsanulok (9 daily; 4hr).

Nakhon Pathom to: Bangkok Hualamphong (10 daily; 1hr 20min); Bangkok Noi (3 daily; 1hr 10min); Chumphon (11 daily; 5hr 45 min–8hr 30min); Hat Yai (5 daily; 12hr 15min–16hr); Hua Hin (13 daily; 2hr 15min–3hr 15min); Kanchanaburi (2 daily; 1hr 25min); Nakhon Si Thammarat (2 daily; 15hr); Nam Tok (2 daily; 4hr 20min–4hr 50min); Phetchaburi (12 daily; 1hr 20min–2hr 20min); Sungai Kolok (2 daily; 18hr 30min–20hr); Surat Thani (10 daily; 8hr–11hr 30min); Trang (2 daily; 14–15hr).

Nam Tok to: Bangkok Noi (2 daily; 4hr 35min).

Phitsanulok to: Ayutthaya (6 daily; 4hr 30min–5hr 30min); Bangkok Hualamphong (11 daily; 5hr 40min–8hr), via Don Muang airport (4hr 50min–7hr); Chiang Mai (6 daily; 5hr 50min–7hr 40min); Lamphun (5 daily; 5hr 40min–7hr 20min); Lopburi (8 daily; 3hr–5hr 15min).

Buses

Ayutthaya to: Bangkok (every 15min; 2hr); Bang Pa-In (every 30min; 30min); Chiang Mai (12 daily; 8hr); Lopburi (every 15min; 2hr); Phitsanulok (9 daily; 4–5hr); Suphanburi (every 30min; 1hr 30min).

Bang Pa-In to: Bangkok (every 30min; 2hr).

Damnoen Saduak to: Bangkok (every 20min; 2hr).

Kamphaeng Phet to: Bangkok (7 daily; 6hr 30min); Sukhothai (hourly; 1hr–1hr 30min); Tak (hourly; 1hr).

Kanchanaburi to: Bangkok (every 15min; 2hr–3hr 30min); Erawan (every 50min; 2hr); Nam Tok (every 30min; 1hr 30min); Sai Yok (every 30min; 2hr 30min); Sangkhlaburi (10 daily; 3–6hr); Suphanburi (every 20min; 2hr); Thong Pha Phum (every 30min; 3hr).

Lopburi to: Bangkok (every 15min; 3hr), via Wat Phra Phutthabat (30min); Khorat (every 30min; 3hr).

Mae Sot to: Bangkok (10 daily; 8hr 30min); Chiang Mai (4 daily; 6hr 30min–7hr 30min); Chiang Rai (2 daily; 11hr); Mae Ramat (every 30min; 45min) ; Mae Sai (2 daily; 12hr); Mae Sariang (7 daily; 5hr); Phitsanulok (7 daily; 5hr); Sukhothai (6 daily; 2hr 30min–3hr); Tak (every 30min; 1hr 30min–3hr); Umphang (9 daily; 3hr 30min–5hr).

Nakhon Pathom to: Bangkok (every 10min; 40min–1hr 20min); Damnoen Saduak (every 20min; 1hr); Kanchanaburi (every 10min; 1hr 20min).

Nam Tok to: Sangkhlaburi (4 daily; 3hr 30min).

Phitsanulok to: Bangkok (up to 19 daily; 5–6hr); Chiang Mai (up to 18 daily; 5–6hr); Chiang Rai (9 daily; 6–7hr); Kamphaeng Phet (hourly; 3hr); Khon Kaen (13 daily; 5–6hr); Khorat/Nakhon Ratchasima (10 daily; 6–7hr); Loei (5 daily; 4hr); Mae Sot (7 daily; 5hr); Phrae (hourly; 3hr); Sukhothai (every 30min; 1hr); Tak (hourly; 2–3hr); Udon Thani (5 daily; 7hr).

Sukhothai to: Bangkok (up to 17 daily; 6–7hr); Chiang Mai (up to 16 daily; 5–6hr); Chiang Rai (3 daily; 8–9hr); Kamphaeng Phet (hourly; 1hr–1hr 30min); Khon Kaen (7 daily; 6–7hr); Mae Sot (7 daily; 2hr 30 min–3hr); Nan (2 daily; 6hr); Phitsanulok (every 30min; 1hr); Si Satchanalai (every 30min; 1hr); Tak (every 90min; 2hr).

Tak to: Bangkok (13 daily; 7hr); Ban Tak (hourly; 40min); Chiang Mai (3 daily; 4–6hr); Kamphaeng Phet (hourly; 1hr); Mae Sot (every 30min; 1hr 30min–3hr); Sukhothai (hourly; 1hr 30min).

Flights

Mae Sot to: Bangkok (8 weekly; 1hr 25min–2hr 25min); Chiang Mai (4 weekly; 45min).

Phitsanulok to: Bangkok (4 daily; 45min); Chiang Mai (4 weekly; 2hr 25min); Lampang (1–2 daily; 35min); Nan (4 weekly; 1hr 25min); Phrae (4 weekly; 35min).

Sukhothai to: Bangkok (1–2 daily; 1hr); Chiang Mai (daily; 35min); Siem Reap (Cambodia; 3 weekly; 1hr 40min).

The north

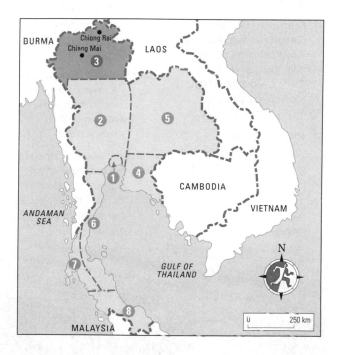

CHAPTER 3

Highlights

✳ **Hill-tribe trekking** – A chance to visit these fascinating peoples and explore the dramatic countryside. **p.297**

✳ **Chiang Mai** – Old-town temples, cookery courses, fine restaurants – still a great place to hang out. **p.301**

✳ **Festivals** – Exuberant Songkhran and glittering Loy Krathong in Chiang Mai, and colourful Poy Sang Long in Mae Hong Son are the pick of many. **p.314** and **p.363**

✳ **Khao soi** – Delicious, spicy, creamy noodle soup, the northern Thai signature dish. **p.322**

✳ **The "Handicraft Highway" to San Kamphaeng** – An extended open-air mall displaying the best of Thai crafts. **p.318**

✳ **Wat Phra That Doi Suthep** – Towering views from this stunning example of temple architecture. **p.327**

✳ **Nan** – An under-rated all-rounder, offering beautiful temple murals, handicrafts and landscapes. **p.345**

✳ **The Mae Hong Son loop** – A rollercoaster journey through the country's wildest mountain scenery. **p.351**

✳ **White-water rafting on the Pai River** – Well-organized excitement taking in rapids, gorges and beautiful waterfalls. **p.370**

3

The north

Travelling up through the central plains, there's no mistaking when you've reached the **north** of Thailand: somewhere between Uttaradit and Den Chai, the train slows almost to a halt, as if approaching a frontier post, to meet the abruptly rising mountains, which continue largely unbroken to the borders of Burma and Laos. Beyond this point the climate becomes more temperate, nurturing the fertile land which gave the old kingdom of the north the name of **Lanna**, "the land of a million rice fields". Although only one-tenth of the land can be used for rice cultivation, the valley rice fields here are three times more productive than those in the dusty northeast, and the higher land yields a great variety of fruits, as well as beans, groundnuts and tobacco.

Until the beginning of the last century, Lanna was a largely independent region. On the back of its agricultural prosperity, it developed its own styles of art and architecture, which can still be seen in its flourishing temples and distinctive handicraft traditions. The north is also set apart from the rest of the country by its exuberant way with festivals, a cuisine which has been heavily influenced by Burma and a dialect quite distinct from central Thai. Northerners proudly call themselves *khon muang*, "people of the principalities", and their gentle sophistication is admired by the people of Bangkok, whose wealthier citizens build their holiday homes in the clean air of the north's forested mountains.

Accommodation prices

Throughout this guide, guest houses, hotels and bungalows have been categorized according to the price codes given below. These categories represent the minimum you can expect to pay in the high season (roughly July, Aug & Nov–Feb) for a double room. If travelling on your own, expect to pay anything between sixty and one hundred percent of the rates quoted for a double room. Wherever a price range is indicated, this means that the establishment offers rooms with varying facilities – as explained in the write-up. Wherever an establishment also offers dormitory beds, the prices of these beds are given in the text, instead of being indicated by price code.

Remember that the top-whack hotels will add seven percent tax and a ten percent service charge to your bill – the price codes below are based on net rates after taxes have been added.

❶ under B150	❹ B400–600	❼ B1200–1800
❷ B150–250	❺ B600–900	❽ B1800–3000
❸ B250–400	❻ B900–1200	❾ B3000+

0 ————— 50 km

BURMA

Salween

Tha Ton

Fang 1089

109

Mae Aw

Mae Lana
Ban Tum

Nai Soi

Mae Suya Soppong

HUAY NAM
DANG
NATIONAL
PARK

Doi Chiang Dao
(2175m)

Chiang
Dao

Phrao

1150

1095

Doi Pai Kit
(1082m)

Soppong

Mae
Hong Son

Pai

Pai

1095

107

1001

108

Mae
Ko Vafe

Doi Mae Ya
(2005m)

Pong Duet
Hot Springs

Mae
Tang

Mae Malai

Ban Mae
Surin

Mae Surin

Mae Rim

Doi
Saket

118

1069

1006

Khun Yuam

1263

Samoeng

Chiang
Mai

Doi
Khun Bong
(1772m)

Doi Inthanon
(2565m)

Doi Suthep
(1668m)

San
Kamphaeng

DOI
INTHANON
NATIONAL
PARK

1269

108

Lamphun

Mae Chaem

Hang
Dong

Doi Khun Tan
(1373m)

Mae La Noi

1266

Ban La Up

1088

Chom
Thong

Pasang

Ping

Mae Tha

11

Hang
Chat

Elephant
Conservation Centre

Thung Kwian

Mae Sariang

108

Hot

106

Kor Kha

Mae Sam Laeb

Salween

Yuam

Wang

105

1

294

Mae Sot

Tak

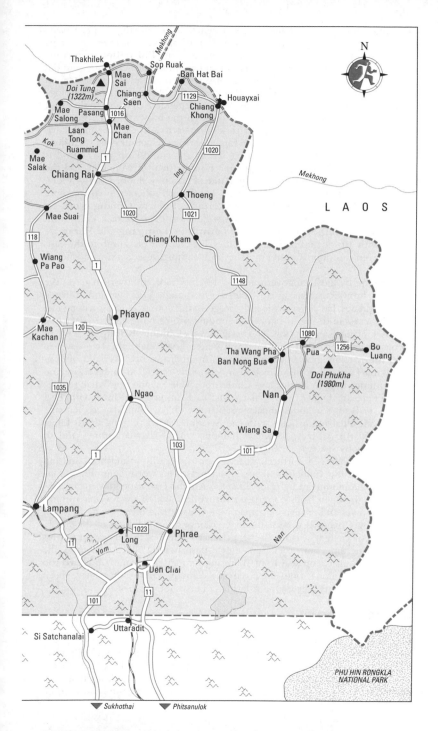

N

Thakhilek
Mekhong
Sop Ruak
Ban Hat Bai
Mae Sai
Doi Tung (1322m)
Chiang Saen
1129
Houayxai
Mae Salong
Pasang
1016
Chiang Khong
Laan Tong
Mae Chan
Ruammid
Kok
1020
Mae Salak
1
Chiang Rai
Ing
Mekhong
Thoeng
L A O S
Mae Suai
1020
1021
118
Chiang Kham
Wiang Pa Pao
1
1148
Phayao
Mae Kachan
120
1080
Tha Wang Pha
Pua
1256
Bo Luang
Ban Nong Bua
Doi Phukha (1980m)
1035
Ngao
Nan
Wiang Sa
103
101
1
Lampang
1023
Phrae
11
Long
Yom
Den Chai
101
11
Nan
Si Satchanalai
Uttaradit
PHU HIN RONGKLA NATIONAL PARK

▼ Sukhothai   ▼ Phitsanulok

Chiang Mai, the capital and transport centre of the north, is a great place just to hang out or to prepare for a journey into the hills. For many travellers, this means joining a trek to visit one or more of the **hill tribes**, who comprise one-tenth of the north's population and are just about clinging onto the ways of life which distinguish them from one another and the Thais around them. For those with qualms about the exploitative element of this ethnological tourism, there are plenty of other, more independent options. To the west, the trip to **Mae Hong Son** takes you through the most stunning mountain scenery in the region into a land with its roots across the border in Burma. Bidding to rival Chiang Mai as a base for exploring the countryside is **Chiang Rai** to the north; above Chiang Rai, the northernmost tip of Thailand is marked by the fascinating, schizophrenic border town of **Mae Sai**, and the junction of Laos and Burma at **Sop Ruak**. Fancifully dubbed the "Golden Triangle", Sop Ruak is a must on every bus party's itinerary – you're more likely to find peace and quiet among the ruins of nearby **Chiang Saen**, set on the leafy banks of the Mekhong River. Few visitors backtrack south from Chiang Mai, even though the towns of **Lamphun**, **Lampang** and **Phrae** are packed with artistic and historical goodies. Further out on a limb to the east, **Nan** is even less popular, but combines rich mountain scenery with eclectic temple art.

An attempt by the Thai government to develop trade and tourism across the northern frontiers, forming a "Golden Quadrangle" of Thailand, Burma, China and Laos, has as yet made little progress, the countries so far having had limited success in trying to cajole one another into relaxing entry restrictions. East of Chiang Saen on the Mekhong River, **Chiang Khong** is now an important crossing point to Laos, from where boats make the two-day trip down the Mekhong to Louang Phabang. Apart from this, overland options for leaving Thailand in this direction are currently restricted to expensive and often arduous trips to Burma and China, from Mae Sai and Sop Ruak respectively. There are flights from Chiang Mai to Kunming in China with Thai Airways, to Rangoon and Mandalay in Burma with Air Mandalay, to Vientiane and Louang Phabang in Laos with Lao Aviation. Other options are to Taipei with Mandarin Airlines, to Kuala Lumpur with Malaysia Airlines and to Singapore with Silk Air.

Transport routes in northern Thailand are necessarily roundabout and bus services often slow, though frequent: in some cases, it's worth considering hopping over the mountains by plane. To appreciate the landscape fully, many people take to the open roads on rented **motorbikes**, which are available in most northern towns and relatively inexpensive – Chiang Mai offers the best choice, followed by Chiang Rai. You should be cautious about biking in the north, however, especially if you are an inexperienced rider; each year several visitors lose precious time from their stay after a mishap on a motorbike. Also, the border police may stop you from venturing into an area that's considered too dangerous, and don't ride alone on any remote trails – there have been occasional incidents where lone riders have been shot.

Some history

The first civilization to leave an indelible mark on the north was **Haripunjaya**, the Mon (Dvaravati) state which was founded at Lamphun in the ninth century. Maintaining strong ties with the Mon kingdoms to the south, it remained the cultural and religious centre of the north for four centuries. The Thais came onto the scene after the Mon, migrating down from

China between the seventh and the eleventh centuries and establishing small principalities around the north. The prime mover for the Thais was **King Mengrai** of Ngon Yang, who, shortly after the establishment of a Thai state at Sukhothai in the middle of the thirteenth century, set to work on a parallel unified state in the north. By 1296, when he began the construction of Chiang Mai, which has remained the capital of the north ever since, he had brought the whole of the north under his control, and at his death in 1317 he had established a dynasty which was to oversee a two-hundred-year period of unmatched prosperity and cultural activity.

However, after the expansionist reign of Tilok (1441–87), a series of weak, squabbling kings came and went, while Ayutthaya increased its unfriendly advances. But it was the **Burmese** who finally snuffed out the Mengrai dynasty by capturing Chiang Mai in 1556, and for most of the next two centuries they controlled Lanna through a succession of puppet rulers. In 1767, the Burmese sacked the Thai capital at Ayutthaya, but the Thais soon regrouped under King Taksin, who with the help of **King Kawila** of Lampang gradually drove the Burmese northwards.

Kawila was succeeded as ruler of the north by a series of incompetent princes for much of the nineteenth century, until colonialism reared its head. After the British took control of Upper Burma, **Rama V** of Bangkok began to take an interest in the north to prevent its annexation. He forcibly moved large numbers of ethnic Thais northwards, in order to counter the British claim of sovereignty over territory occupied by Thai Yai (Shan), who also make up a large part of the population of Upper Burma. In 1877 Rama V appointed a high commissioner in Chiang Mai, and since then the north has built on its agricultural richness to become relatively prosperous. However, the economic boom of the 1980s was concentrated, as elsewhere in Thailand, in the towns, due in no small part to the increase in tourism. The eighty percent of Lanna's population who live in rural areas, of which the vast majority are subsistence farmers, are finding it increasingly difficult to earn a living off the soil, due to rapid population growth and land speculation for tourism and agro-industry.

Hill-tribe treks

Trekking in the mountains of north Thailand differs from trekking in most other parts of the world in that the emphasis is not primarily on the scenery but on the region's inhabitants. Northern Thailand's **hill tribes**, now numbering over 800,000 people living in around 3500 villages, have so far preserved their way of life with little change over thousands of years; see p.811 for more on the tribes themselves. In these days of political correctness, the term **mountain people** is increasingly preferred to describe them; since these groups have no chief, they are technically not tribes. While some of the villages are near enough to a main road to be reached on a day-trip from a major town, to get to the other, more traditional villages usually entails joining a hastily assembled guided party for a few days, roughing it in a different place each night. For most visitors however, these hardships are far outweighed by the experience of encountering peoples of so different a culture, travelling through beautiful tropical countryside and tasting the excitement of elephant riding and river rafting.

On any trek you are necessarily confronted by the **ethics** of your role. Over a hundred thousand travellers now go trekking in Thailand each year, the majority heading to certain well-trodden areas such as the Mae Tang valley,

Trekking etiquette

As the guests, it's up to farangs to adapt to the customs of the hill tribes and not to make a nuisance of themselves. Apart from keeping an open mind and not demanding too much of your hosts, a few simple rules should be observed.

❑ Dress modestly, in long trousers or skirt (or at least knee-length shorts if you must) and a T-shirt or shirt.

❑ Loud voices and boisterous behaviour are out of place. Smiling and nodding establishes good intent. A few hill-tribe phrasebooks and dictionaries are available from bookshops and you'll be a big hit if you learn some words of the relevant language.

❑ If travelling with a loved one, avoid displays of public affection such as kissing, which are extremely distasteful to local people.

❑ Before entering a hill-tribe village, look out for taboo signs (ta-laew), woven bamboo strips on the ground outside the village entrance; these mean a special ceremony is taking place and that you should not enter. Similar signs stuck on the roof above a house entrance or a fresh tree branch mean the same thing. Be careful about what you touch; in Akha villages, keep your hands off cult structures like the entrance gates and the giant swing. Most hill-tribe houses contain a religious shrine: do not touch or photograph this shrine, or sit underneath it. If you are permitted to watch a ceremony, this is not an invitation to participate unless asked. Like the villagers themselves, you'll be expected to pay a fine for any violation of local customs.

❑ Some villagers like to be photographed, most do not. Point at your camera and nod if you want to take a photograph. Never insist if the answer is an obvious "no". Be particularly careful with pregnant women and babies – most tribes believe cameras affect the soul of the foetus or new-born.

❑ Taking gifts is dubious practice – if you must take something, writing materials for children are welcome, as well as sewing tools (like needles) for women, but sweets and cigarettes may encourage begging and create unhealthy tastes.

❑ Do not ask for opium, as this will offend your hosts.

40km northwest of Chiang Mai, and the hills around the Kok River west of Chiang Rai. Beyond the basic level of disturbance caused by any tourism, this steady flow of trekkers creates pressures for the traditionally insular hill tribes. Foreigners unfamiliar with hill-tribe customs can easily cause grave offence, especially those who go looking for drugs. Though tourism acts as a distraction from their traditional way of life, most tribespeople are genuinely welcoming and hospitable to foreigners, appreciating the contact with Westerners and the minimal material benefits which trekking brings them. Nonetheless, to minimize disruption, it's important to take a responsible attitude when trekking. While it's possible to trek independently, the lone trekker will learn very little without a guide as intermediary, and is far more likely to commit an unwitting offence against the local customs, so it's best to go with a sensitive and knowledgeable guide who has the welfare of the local people in mind, and follow the basic guidelines on etiquette outlined in the box above. If you don't fancy an organized trek in a group as described below, it's possible to hire a personal guide from an agent, for which rates begin at about B600 per day.

The hill tribes are big business in northern Thailand: in **Chiang Mai** there are over two hundred agencies which between them cover just about all the trekkable areas in the north. **Chiang Rai** is the second-biggest trekking centre, and agencies can also be found in **Mae Hong Son**, **Pai** and **Nan**, although these usually arrange treks only to the villages in their immediate area. Guided trekking on a much smaller scale than in the north is available in Umphang (see p.286), Kanchanaburi (see p.219) and Sangkhlaburi (see p.232). For the independent traveller, half a dozen **rural guest houses** have been set up either in or near to hill-tribe villages, specifically for those who want to explore the countryside by themselves.

The basics

The right **clothing** is the first essential on any trek. Strong boots with ankle protection are the best footwear, although in the dry season training shoes are adequate. Wear thin, loose clothes – long trousers should be worn to protect against thorns and, in the wet season, leeches – and a hat, and cover your arms if you're prone to sunburn. Antiseptic, antihistamine, anti-diarrhoea **medicine** and insect repellent are essential, and a mosquito net is a good idea. At least two changes of clothing are needed, plus a sarong or towel (women in particular should bring a sarong to wash or change underneath).

If you're going on an organized trek, **water** is usually provided by the guide, as well as a small backpack. **Blankets** or a **sleeping bag** are also supplied, but might not be warm enough in the cool season, when night-time temperatures can dip to freezing; you should bring at least a sweater, and buy a cheap, locally made balaclava to be sure of keeping the chill off.

It's wise not to take anything valuable with you; most guest houses in trekking-orientated places like Chiang Mai have safes and left-luggage rooms, but check that the guest house is long-established and has a good reputation before you consider leaving your things, and then make sure you sign an inventory.

Organized treks

Organized treks can be as short as two days or as long as ten, but are typically of three or four days' duration. The standard size of a group is between six and twelve people, with an average size of eight; being part of a small group is preferable, enabling you to strike a more informative relationship with your guides and with the villagers. Everybody in the group usually sleeps on a bamboo floor or platform in the headman's hut, with a guide cooking communal meals, for which some ingredients are brought from outside and others are found locally.

Each trek usually follows a regular itinerary established by the agency, although they can sometimes be customized, especially for smaller groups and with agencies in the smaller towns. Some itineraries are geared towards serious hikers while others go at a much gentler pace, but on all treks much of the walking will be up and down steep forested hills, often under a burning sun, so a reasonable level of fitness is required. Many treks now include a ride on an elephant and a trip on a bamboo raft – exciting to the point of being dangerous if the river is running fast. The typical trek of three days' duration costs about B1500–2000 in Chiang Mai, often less in other towns, and much less without rafting and elephant riding.

There are several features to look out for when **choosing a trek**. If you want to trek with a small group, get an assurance from your agency that you won't be tagged onto a larger group. Make sure the trek has at least two guides – a leader and a back-marker; some trekkers have been known to get lost for days after becoming separated from the rest of the group. Ask about transport from base at the beginning and end of the trek; most treks begin with a pick-up ride out of town, but on rare occasions the trip can entail a long public bus ride. If at all possible, meet and chat with the guides before leaving. They should speak reasonable English and know about hill-tribe culture, especially the details of etiquette in each village. Finally, ask what food will be eaten, check how much walking is involved per day and get a copy of the route map to gauge the terrain.

While everybody and their grandmother act as **agents**, only a few know their guides personally, so choose a reputable agent. When picking an agent, you should check whether they and their guides have licences and certificates, which they should be able to show you: this ensures at least a minimum level of training, and provides some comeback in case of problems. Word of mouth is often the best recommendation, so if you hear of a good outfit, try it. Each trek should be **registered** with the tourist police, stating the itinerary, the duration and the participants, in case the party encounters any trouble – it's worth checking with the agency that the trek has been registered with the tourist police before departure.

Independent trekking

Unfortunately, the options for **independent trekking** are limited, chiefly by security risks and poor mapping of the area. A series of green Royal Thai Survey Department 1:50,000 maps are available in one or two bookshops in Chiang Mai at B120 each, but each one covers a very limited area. A more useful option is likely to be Hongsombud's *Guide Map of Chiang Rai* (Bangkok Guides) which includes 1:1000 maps of the more popular chunks of Chiang Rai province. The laminated map of *Thailand North* (Berndtson & Berndtson; B190) is a complete road map of the region but is more useful for motorbike trekking than walking; it shows accurately the crisscross of dirt tracks and minor roads on a 1:750,000 map of the north, and also contains a 1:500,000 inset of the Thai section of the Golden Triangle, with relief shading showing the terrain. Another useful map is the one of the *Mae Hong Son Loop* (Golden Triangle Rider; B99), with a scale of 1:375,000, which details many villages and minor roads to the west of Chiang Mai.

For most independent travellers, the only feasible approach is to use as a base one of the half-dozen or so **guest houses** specifically geared for farangs in various parts of the north. They're generally set deep in the countryside, within walking range of several hill-tribe villages, about which the owner can give information in English. Conditions in these guest houses are usually spartan, but the food is generally safe to eat. All these guest houses are covered in the relevant parts of this chapter, and listed in the box below.

If you're confident about finding your way round, it's possible to find **accommodation** in hill-tribe villages themselves. It helps if you speak some Thai, but most villagers, if you hang around for any time, will ask (with the usual "sleep" gesture) if you want to stay. It is usual to stay in the headman's house on a guest platform, but increasingly villages are building small guesthouses. Expect to pay at least B50 per night – for this, you will often be offered dinner and breakfast. It's safe to accept plain rice, boiled drinks and food that's boiled or fried in your presence, but you're taking a risk with anything else, as

---

Guest houses for independent trekking

Between Mae Hong Son and Pai: *Wilderness Lodge* near Mae Suya; *Mae Lana Guest House* at Mae Lana; *Cave Lodge* at Ban Tum.
Between Chiang Mai and Chiang Rai: *Trekker House* near Ban Sop Pong; *Malee's Nature Lovers Bungalows* near Chiang Dao.

it's not unusual for foreigners to suffer food poisoning. Most villages are safe to stay in; to safeguard yourself against the risk of armed bandits who sporadically rob foreigners, try to check with local guides and the district police in the area where you intend to trek.

Chiang Mai

Although rapid economic progress in recent years – due largely to tourism – has brought its share of problems, not least concern about traffic jams and fumes, **CHIANG MAI** manages to preserve some of the atmosphere of an ancient settlement alongside its urban sophistication. A population of about 250,000 makes this the north's largest city, but the contrast with the maelstrom of Bangkok could scarcely be more pronounced: the people here are famously easy-going and even speak more slowly than their cousins in the capital, while the old quarter, set within a two-kilometre-square moat, has retained many of its traditional wooden houses and quiet, leafy gardens. Chiang Mai's elegant temples are the primary tourist sights, but these are no pre-packaged museum pieces – they're living community centres, where you're quite likely to be approached by monks keen to chat and practise their English. Inviting craft shops, rich cuisine and riverside bars further enhance the city's allure, making Chiang Mai a place that detains many travellers longer than they expected. Several colourful festivals attract throngs of visitors here too: Chiang Mai is considered one of the best places in Thailand to see in the Thai New Year – Songkhran – in mid-April, and to celebrate Loy Krathong at the full moon in November, when thousands of candles are floated down the Ping River in lotus-leaf boats.

Chiang Mai – "New City" – loudly celebrated its **700th anniversary** in 1996: founded as the capital of Lanna in 1296, on a site indicated by the miraculous presence of deer and white mice, it has remained the north's most important city ever since. Lanna's golden age under the Mengrai dynasty, when most of the city's notable temples were founded, lasted until the Burmese captured Chiang Mai in 1556. Two hundred years passed before the Thais pushed the Burmese back beyond Chiang Mai to roughly where they are now, and the **Burmese influence** is still strong – not just in art and architecture, but also in the rich curries and soups served here, which are better "Burmese" food than you can find in modern-day Burma. After the recapture of the city, the *chao* (princes) of Chiang Mai remained nominal rulers of the north until 1939, but, with communications rapidly improving from the beginning of the last century, Chiang Mai was brought firmly into Thailand's mainstream as the region's administrative and service centre.

The traditional tourist activities in Chiang Mai are visiting the **temples** and **shopping** for handicrafts, pursuits which many find more appealing here than in the rest of Thailand. These days, increasing numbers of travellers are taking advantage of the city's relaxed feel to indulge in a burst of self-improvement, enrolling for **courses** in **cookery**, **massage** and the like (see box on p.311).

However, a pilgrimage to **Doi Suthep**, the mountain to the west of town, should not be missed, to see the sacred temple and the towering views over the valley of the Ping River, when weather permits. Beyond the city limits, a number of other day-trips can be made, such as to the ancient temples of Lamphun or to the orchid farms and elephant shows of the Mae Sa valley – and, of course, Chiang Mai is the main centre for hill-tribe **trekking**.

Arrival, information and city transport

Bounded by a huge ring road, the Superhighway, Chiang Mai divides roughly into two main parts: the **old town**, surrounded by the well-maintained moat and occasional remains of the city wall, where you'll find most of Chiang Mai's traditional wats, and the **new town centre**, between the moat and the Ping River to the east, for hotels, shops and travel agents. The main concentration of guest houses and restaurants hangs between the two, centred on the landmark of Pratu Tha Pae (**Tha Pae Gate**) in the middle of the east moat.

Many people arrive at the **train station** on Thanon Charoen Muang, just over 2km from Tha Pae Gate on the eastern side of town, or at the Arcade **bus station** on Thanon Kaeo Nawarat, 3km out to the northeast. Getting from either of these to the centre is easy by songthaew or tuk-tuk (see "City transport" opposite). Coming south from Fang or Tha Ton, you'll wind up at the **Chang Phuak bus station** on Thanon Chotana, 500m from the city centre's northern Chang Phuak Gate and 2km northwest of the accommodation concentration around Tha Pae Gate. If you plan to travel with one of the low-cost private bus companies on Bangkok's Thanon Khao San, find out exactly where you'll be dropped in Chiang Mai before making a booking: many of these companies' buses stop on a remote part of the Superhighway, where they "sell" their passengers to various guest-house touts. There's no obligation to go with the touts, but if you try to duck out you'll have a hard job getting downtown and you'll certainly come in for a lot of hassle. The better guest houses – certainly including those we've listed – don't involve themselves in such shenanigans.

Arriving at the **airport**, 3km southwest of the centre, you'll find banks, a post office situated outside with an overseas phone (all open daily 8am–8pm), and an Avis car rental office (☎053/201574). The free courtesy phone for local calls in the arrival hall is helpful to secure accommodation. Though no buses serve the airport, there is a well-organized taxi system which charges B100 for a car to the city centre. If you book accommodation in advance, many hotels and guest houses will pick you up for free from the bus or train station or the airport.

Information

TAT operates out of a swish **information** office (daily 8.30am–4.30pm; ☎053/248604, ℱ248605) at 105/1 Thanon Chiang Mai–Lamphun, on the east bank of the river just south of Nawarat Bridge, where you can pick up various handouts and a simple free **map** of the city. *Nancy Chandler's Map of Chiang Mai*, sold in many outlets all over the city (B120), is very handy for a detailed exploration: like her brightly coloured Bangkok map, it highlights a personal choice of sights, shops, restaurants and various oddities, as well as local transport information.

Trekking around Chiang Mai

The **trekking** industry in Chiang Mai offers an impressive variety of itineraries, with over two hundred agencies covering nearly all trekkable areas of the north. Most treks include a ride on an elephant and a bamboo-raft excursion, though the amount of actual walking included varies enormously. Below we list several reputable trekking operators; if you're particularly concerned about trekking in comfort, contact Lisu Lodge, who will put you up in some style; and if you have a specific interest, such as birdwatching, try the Trekking Collective, who can arrange pricey but high-quality customized treks.

Daret's, 4/5 Thanon Chaiyapoom ☎053/235440, ⓔnootour@hotmail.com.

Eagle House, 16 Thanon Chiang Mai Kao Soi 3 ☎053/235387, ⓦwww.eaglehouse.com.

Lisu Lodge, 172/1–11 Thanon Loy Kroh ☎053/281789, ⓦwww.lisulodge.com.

Trekking Collective, 25/1 Thanon Ratchawithi ☎053/419079, ⓦwww.trekkingcollective.com.

Several free, locally published **magazines**, including *Guidelines* and *Welcome to Chiang Mai and Chiang Rai*, contain information about upcoming events in town and articles about local culture; they're distributed in spots where tourists tend to congregate, including money-exchange booths and the lobby of the *Montri Hotel*. The magazine's website (ⓦ www.infothai.com/wtcmcr), includes extensive listings of the hotels and other businesses in the city and the north. For online information about events in the city, check out ⓦ www.chiangmainews.com; ⓦ northernthailand.com has plenty of suggestions on what to see in the city and elsewhere in northern Thailand. If you expect to stay in Chiang Mai for any length of time, *Exploring Chiang Mai – City, Valley and Mountains* (B350) by local resident Oliver Hargreave is a worthwhile investment, as it is packed with useful information about lesser-known temples and attractions, and suggestions for trips out of town.

City transport

Although you can comfortably walk between the most central temples, **bicycles** are the best way of looking round the old town and, with a bit of legwork, getting to the attractions outside the moat. Trusty sit-up-and-beg models (B30 a day) and mountain bikes (B50) are available at many outlets on the roads along the eastern moat. If you don't fancy pedalling through the heat and pollution, consider a **motorbike** – there are plenty for rent (around B150 a day; see p.326 for addresses of outlets), though these really come into their own for exploring places around Chiang Mai and in the rest of the north.

Unusually for a city the size of Chiang Mai, there are no buses serving the downtown area (for transport to San Kamphaeng, see p.318). The best way of getting around is by red **songthaews** (other colours serve outlying villages) which act as shared taxis within the city, picking up a number of people headed in roughly the same direction and taking each to their specific destination. They charge according to how far you're going – expect to pay B10 for a journey of a couple of kilometres, say from the train station to Tha Pae Gate. With petrol prices rising steadily, however, transport charges are likely to increase.

Chiang Mai is also stuffed with **tuk-tuks**, for which heavy bargaining is expected – allow around B40 for getting from the train station to Tha Pae Gate. They're quick and useful on arrival and departure, and are quite reasonable if you're in a group. You can **hire** a tuk-tuk for about B100 per hour, B300

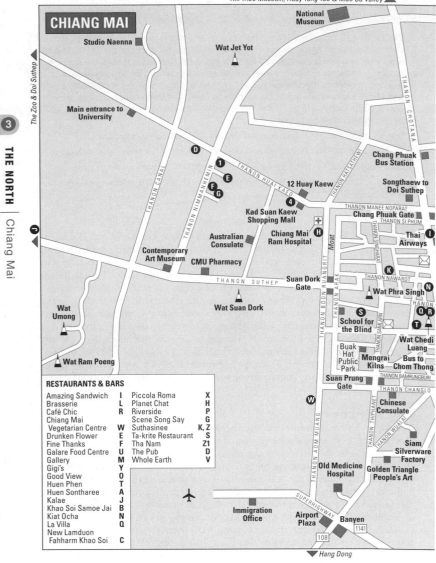

CHIANG MAI

The Zoo & Doi Suthep ◀

Studio Naenna

National Museum

Wat Jet Yot

Main entrance to University

THANON CANAL

THANON NIMMANHEMIN

THANON HUAI KAEO

THANON HATSADHEWI

THANON CHOTANA

D

1

E

F G

12 Huay Kaew

4

Chang Phuak Bus Station

Songthaew to Doi Suthep

THANON MANEE NOPARAT

Chang Phuak Gate

THANON SI PHUM

Kad Suan Kaew Shopping Mall

Chiang Mai Ram Hospital

H

THANON SINGHARAT

Thai Airways

I

Australian Consulate

Contemporary Art Museum

CMU Pharmacy

THANON SUTHEP

Suan Dork Gate

Wat Suan Dork

K

THANON NAWARAT

Wat Phra Singh

N

THANON

O R

Wat Umong

School for the Blind

S

T

Buak Hat Public Park

Mengrai Kilns

Wat Chedi Luang

Bus to Chom Thong

THANON BOON RANGRIT

THANON ARAK

THANON SAMLARN

Moat

Wat Ram Poeng

Suan Prung Gate

THANON BAMRUNGBURI

THANON CHANGLO

W

THANON THIPHANET

Chinese Consulate

RESTAURANTS & BARS

Amazing Sandwich	**I**	Piccola Roma **X**
Brasserie	**L**	Planet Chat **H**
Café Chic	**R**	Riverside **P**
Chiang Mai		Scene Song Say **G**
Vegetarian Centre	**W**	Suthasinee **K, Z**
Drunken Flower	**E**	Ta-krite Restaurant **S**
Fine Thanks	**F**	Tha Nam **Z1**
Galare Food Centre	**U**	The Pub **D**
Gallery	**M**	Whole Earth **V**
Gigi's	**Y**	
Good View	**O**	
Huen Phen	**T**	
Huen Sontharee	**A**	
Kalae	**J**	
Khao Soi Samoe Jai	**B**	
Kiat Ocha	**N**	
La Villa	**Q**	
New Lamduon		
Fahharm Khao Soi	**C**	

THANON AOM MUANG

Old Medicine Hospital

Golden Triangle People's Art

Siam Silverware Factory

Immigration Office

Airport Plaza

Banyen

SUPERHIGHWAY

108

1141

▼ Hang Dong

for half a day or B500 for a full day. Be careful if you use one to go shopping along the San Kamphaeng road, as the drivers usually try to guide you to workshops and showrooms where they can pick up a commission; if you don't mind being led by the nose in this way, you might be able to negotiate a cheaper hire rate with the tuk-tuk driver. The town still has a few **samlors**, which are cheap when used by locals to haul produce home from the market, but not so cheap when chartered by groups of upmarket tourists on sightseeing tours from their hotel.

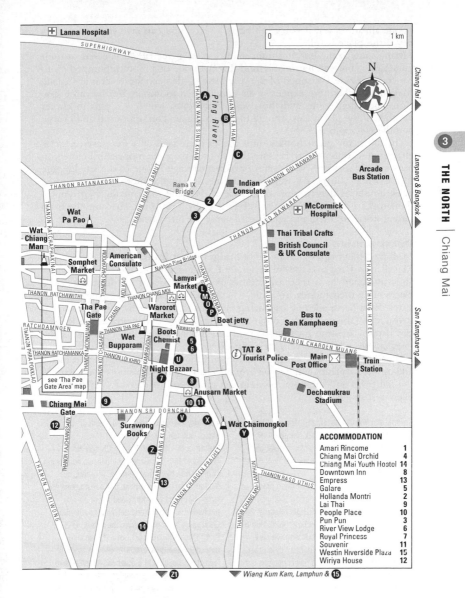

Accommodation

Chiang Mai is well stocked with all kinds of **accommodation**; usually there are plenty of beds to go around, but many places fill up from December to February and at festival time, particularly during Songkhran (April) and Loy Krathong (November). At these times, you need to book to stay at one of the expensive hotels, and for guest houses it's a good idea to phone ahead – even if you can't book a place, you can save yourself a journey if the place is full.

Many touts at the bus and train stations offer a free ride if you stay at their guest house, but you'll probably find that the price of a room is bumped up to pay for your ride. For much of the year there's little need for air-con in Chiang Mai, though the more expensive air-conditioned rooms are usually more spacious and often come with hot-water bathrooms, which is a plus in cooler weather. Some places can arrange to switch the air-con option off and charge you the fan-room rate.

Though many guest houses offer use of their safes as a free service, some charge up to B30 per day. Be sure that you can trust the proprietor before you leave valuables in one of the safes or excess baggage in one of the left-luggage rooms while you go off trekking (choose one of the more well-established guest houses, as they're more conscious of the need to maintain their reputation); make a detailed inventory to be signed by both parties, because the hair-raising stories of theft and credit-card abuse are often true.

Inexpensive

In all ways that matter, the choice of **budget guest houses** is better in Chiang Mai than in Bangkok: they're generally friendlier, quieter and more comfortable, and often have their own outdoor cafés. Many of the least expensive places make their money from hill-tribe trekking, which can be convenient as a trek often needs a lot of organizing beforehand, but equally can be annoying if you're in Chiang Mai for other reasons and come under pressure to trek, as can happen at some guest houses; in the listings below we've indicated the guest houses which are very trekking-orientated.

Most low-cost places are gathered around the eastern side of the old moat, and on the surprisingly quiet sois around Tha Pae Gate. This puts you between the old town and the new town, in the middle of a larder of Thai and travellers' restaurants.

Chiang Mai Youth Hostel, 21/8 Thanon Chang Klan ☎053/276737, ℗204516. About 1500m south of the night bazaar. Very clean, quiet and reliable; rooms have hot showers and fans or air-con. ❷–❸

Eagle House 1, 16 Soi 3, Thanon Chang Moi Kao ☎053/235387, ℗874366, ✆www.eaglehouse.com; and *Eagle House 2*, 26 Soi 2, Thanon Ratchawithi ☎053/210620. Run by an Irishwoman and her Thai husband who are keen to promote ethical eco-tourism, these two friendly, relaxed guest houses have spacious garden terrace areas with good cafés and extensive information boards; well-organized treks also on offer. Rooms in *Eagle House 1*, which all have their own cold-water bathroom, are clean, if basic; the standard of rooms is higher at *Eagle House 2*, a modern compound with clean tiled rooms (the ones on the second floor have air-con), as well as a dorm (B70). ❶–❸

Fang Guest House, 46–48 Soi 1, Thanon Kampangdin ☎053/282940. In a modern building,

with cosy, carpeted rooms, some with air-con, others with fan. ❷–❸

Hollanda Montri, 365 Thanon Charoenrat ☎053/242450, ℮hollandamontri@asia.com. North of the centre by Rama IX Bridge, in a spacious modern building by the river, this guest house has large, clean and well-furnished fan or air-con rooms with balconies and hot-water bathrooms. Good value but a bit far from the action. ❷

Kavil Guest House, 10/1 Soi 5, Thanon Ratchdamnoen ☎ & ℗053/224740. A modern four-storey building in a quiet soi. All the twelve rooms have en-suite hot-water bathrooms; the rooms with fans are small, plain and clean, while those with air-con are pleasantly decorated and more spacious. The downstairs café, at the front (which means there's no noisy courtyard effect), does a small menu of Western food. Trekking orientated, but no pressure. Free safe and luggage storage, inventories signed. ❷–❸

Lek House, 22 Thanon Chaiyapoom ☎053/252686. Near Somphet Market. Central and

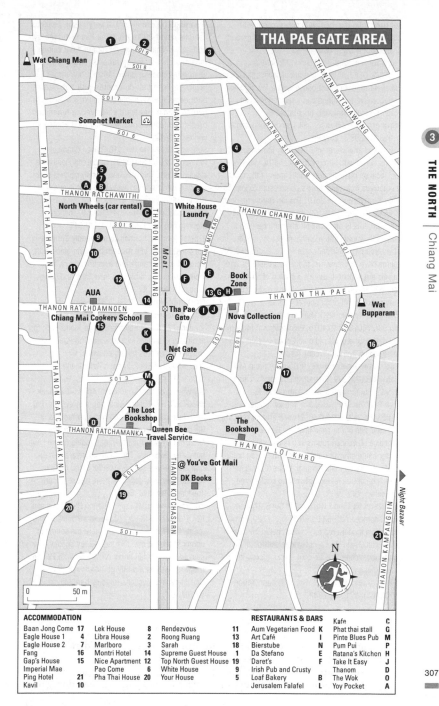

THA PAE GATE AREA

Wat Chiang Man

SOI 9
SOI 8
SOI 7

Somphet Market

SOI 6

THANON CHAIYAPOOM

THANON SITHIWONG

THANON RATCHAWONG

THANON RATCHAWITHI

North Wheels (car rental)

White House Laundry

THANON CHANG MOI

THANON RATCHAPHAKINAI

SOI 5

THANON MOONMUANG

CHANG MOI KAO

Moat

Book Zone

AUA

THANON THA PAE

SOI 2

THANON RATCHDAMNOEN

Chiang Mai Cookery School

Tha Pae Gate

Nova Collection

Wat Bupparam

Net Gate

SOI 6

SOI 5

SOI 4

SOI 3

THANON RATCHAPHAKINAI

The Lost Bookshop

The Bookshop

THANON RATCHAMANKA

Queen Bee Travel Service

THANON LOI KHRO

You've Got Mail

THANON KOTCHASARN

DK Books

SOI 2

SOI 1

THANON KAMPANGOIN

Night Bazaar

N

0   50 m

Baan Jong Come	17	Lek House	8	Rendezvous	11
Eagle House 1	4	Libra House	2	Roong Ruang	13
Eagle House 2	7	Marlboro	3	Sarah	18
Fang	16	Montri Hotel	14	Supreme Guest House	1
Gap's House	15	Nice Apartment	12	Top North Guest House	19
Imperial Mae		Pao Come	6	White House	9
Ping Hotel	21	Pha Thai House	20	Your House	5
Kavil	10				

RESTAURANTS & BARS

Aum Vegetarian Food	K	Kafe	C
Art Café	I	Phat thai stall	G
Bierstube	N	Pinte Blues Pub	M
Da Stefano	E	Pum Pui	P
Daret's	F	Ratana's Kitchen	H
Irish Pub and Crusty		Take It Easy	J
Loaf Bakery	B	Thanom	D
Jerusalem Falafel	L	The Wok	O
		Yoy Pocket	A

THE NORTH | Chiang Mai

3

set back from the road, with clean rooms with cold-water bathrooms set round a shaded garden; shared hot shower available ❶

Libra House, 28 Soi 9, Thanon Moonmuang ☏ & ℗ 053/210687, ℮ libra_guesthouse@hotmail.com. Excellent modern guest house with a few traditional decorative trimmings and keen service. Hot water en suite. Trekking-orientated. ❶

Marlboro Guest House, 138 Thanon Sithiwongse ☏ 053/232598 or 232599, ℬ www.infothai.com/mgh. Tastefully furnished rooms, some with air-con, fridge and TV, in convenient location near the northeast corner of the moat. It organizes treks, but there's no pressure to join. ❸

Nice Apartment, 15 Soi 1, Thanon Ratchdamnoen ☏ 053/210552, ℗ 419150. In a quiet lane in the old town, this is an excellent choice for a longer stay, with weekly and monthly rates; for longer stays, you pay their daily rate minus about B50. All rooms have hot showers, fridge and cable TV, and towels are supplied; there's a choice of air-con or fan. Very friendly. No trekking-tour hassle, but it's very popular and often booked out. ❸

Pha Thai House, 48/1 Thanon Ratchaphakinai ☏ 053/278013, ℗ 274075. Efficiently run modern building with a quiet patio and solar-heated water in all rooms (fan or air-con). ❷–❸

Pao Come Guest House, 9 Thanon Chang Moi Kao ☏ 053/252377. Friendly place; basic, clean rooms with fan and shared bathrooms. ❶

Pun Pun Guest House, 321 Thanon Charoenrat ☏ 053/243362, ℗ 246140, ℬ www.armms.com. On the east side of the river, near the Rama IX Bridge. A choice of wooden rooms in a house with hot-water bathrooms, or bungalows with shared bath. Under American management, it has a small garden and popular restaurant serving back-home favourites. ❷

Rendezvous Guest House, 3/1 Soi 5, Thanon Ratchdamnoen ☏ 053/213763, ℗ 217229. Large, attractive modern rooms – which could be cleaner, but include satellite TV, hot-water bathroom, fan and fridge (some are air-con). Lacks a cosy lounge area, though. ❸

Sarah Guest House, 20 Soi 4, Thanon Tapae ☏ 053/208271, ℗ 279423,

ℬ sarahgh.hypermart.net. A very clean, peaceful establishment 200m from Tha Pae Gate, run by an English-Thai couple. All rooms have ceiling fans and cold-water bathrooms, and there's a shared hot shower downstairs; a few large, nicely furnished air-con rooms with hot-water bathrooms are available too. There's a pleasant garden with a courtyard café serving American breakfasts, continental and Thai food and sandwiches. ❷–❸

Souvenir Guest House, 118 Thanon Charoen Prathet ☏ & ℗ 053/818786, ℮ souvenirguesthouse @hotmail.com. This spacious, friendly place is clean and well run, boasting rooms with air-con or fan (some with bathrooms). ❷–❸

Supreme Guest House, 44/1 Soi 9, Thanon Moonmuang ☏ 053/222480, ℗ 218545, ℮ peter_kim80@hotmail.com. Friendly German-run guest house in a modern concrete block with a pleasant roof veranda and a useful library. The rooms are comfortable and have fans and solar-heated showers. ❷

The White House, 12 Soi 5, Thanon Ratchdamnoen ☏ 053/357130, ℗ 357129, ℮ neung7711@hotmail.com. Large rooms with fan or air-con in a quiet location near Tha Pae Gate. Trekking orientated but no pressure. ❸

Your House, 8 Soi 2, Thanon Ratchawithi ☏ 053/217492, ℗ 419093, ℬ www.siprog.com/yourhouse. An old-town teak house with a suitably welcoming atmosphere. Big, airy, clean rooms share hot-water bathrooms; in the modern annexe across the road there are small rooms with their own bathrooms (some have hot water) and fans. The small courtyard restaurant area serves good French food and buffalo steaks. Free pick-ups from train, bus or airport. Trekking orientated. ❷

Wiriya House, 10/4 Soi 1, Thanon Rajchiangsaen Kor ☏ 053/272948, ℗ 272346, ℮ wiriyah@loxinfo .co.th. Located in a quiet lane near the southeast corner of the old city, this four-storey building has cosy rooms with fan or air-con, some with TV and fridge, as well as a pretty garden to relax in. Considerable reductions for long-term stays. ❷–❸

Moderate

For a little over B400 for a double, you can buy yourself considerably more comfort than the bottom-bracket accommodation provides. By far the best of these **moderate** places are the upmarket guest houses and lodges, which as well as good facilities (hot water, often air-con too) offer decent decor and atmosphere. Chiang Mai also has dozens of bland, no-frills hotels in the same price range.

Baan Jong Come Guest House, 47 Soi 4, Thanon Tha Pae ☎053/274823. This family-run place combines modern motel/hotel-style rooms – fan or air-con – with a guest-house atmosphere. The rooms, which are upstairs, are very clean and spacious, with cool tiled floors and big comfortable beds made up with sheets and blankets; bathrooms with hot shower are attached. Below there's a pleasant courtyard with a café. Popular with Americans. ❸–❹

Downtown Inn, 172/1–11 Thanon Loi Khro ☎053/270662, ⓕ272406. Western-style comforts without the extras of the big luxury hotels; quiet considering its central location near the night bazaar. ❻

Galare Guest House, 7 Soi 2, Thanon Charoen Prathet ☎053/818887 or 821011, ⓕ279088, ⓦwww.galare.com. Near Narawat Bridge, a smart, popular place with fan or air-con rooms, as well as a terrace and shady lawn overlooking the river. ❺

Gap's House, 3 Soi 4, Thanon Ratchdamnoen ☎053/278140, ⓕ270143, ⓦthai-culinary-art.infothai.com. Set around a relaxing, leafy compound strewn with antiques are plush air-con rooms with hot showers, as well as simpler rooms with fan and shared bathrooms. The price of a double includes American breakfast, and a vegetarian buffet is served in the evening; one- or two-day cookery courses available. ❸–❹

Lai Thai Guesthouse, 111/4–5 Thanon Kotchasarn ☎053/271725, 271414 or 271534, ⓕ272724, ⓦwww.laithai.com. On the southeast

corner of the moat. Frenetic place, very popular with families, who are no doubt attracted by the (small) courtyard swimming pool around which the three floors of this attractive 120-room modern Thai-style building are arranged. Besides hot-water en suite bathrooms, the rooms boast traditional wooden floors, bamboo walls and air-con or fan. Free pick-ups from bus and train station. ❹

Montri Hotel, 2–6 Thanon Ratchdamnoen ☎053/211069 or 211070, ⓕ217416, ⓔm.intl@cm.ksc.co.th. Smart, clean and good-value multistorey modern hotel. Beside noisy Tha Pae Gate, so ask for a room at the back; there's an excellent attached coffee shop, (see p.324). ❹

People Place, 9 Soi 8, Thanon Charoen Prathet ☎053/282487, ⓕ270060, ⓦwww.infothai.com/people. A compact building just a few steps from the night bazaar, with spacious, comfy en-suite rooms. ❺

Roong Ruang Hotel, 398 Thanon Tha Pae ☎053/234746, ⓕ252409. Tucked away off the main road near Tha Pae Gate, this great-value place has attractive rooms. some air-con, snuggled around a pretty courtyard, some rooms also come with TV and fridge. ❸–❹

Top North Guest House, 15 Soi 2, Thanon Moonmuang ☎053/278900 or 278684, ⓕ278485, ⓔtopnorth@hotmail.com. Modern, unpretentious place with a small swimming pool, in a quiet enclave of guest houses. Fan-cooled and air-con rooms available. ❹.

Expensive

Clustered around the night bazaar, and along Thanon Huai Kaeo, Chiang Mai's **expensive hotels** aren't quite up to Bangkok's very high standards, though room rates are generally more reasonable here; the best hotels lay on all the expected luxuries plus traditional Lanna architectural touches, and breakfast is included at most places. Worth considering in this price range is the *Regent Resort*, out in the Mae Sa valley (see p.333); they'll collect you from the airport if you've made a booking and lay on a shuttle bus service into Chiang Mai for guests.

Amari Rincome Hotel, 1 Thanon Nimmanheimin ☎053/894884–93, ⓕ221915, ⓦwww.amari.com. Popular with tour groups, this hotel has an elegant lobby, tastefully furnished rooms and an excellent swimming pool; its *La Gritta* restaurant does a blow-out buffet lunch. Though it's a bit far from the centre, there are lots of restaurants and shops nearby. ❾

Chiang Mai Orchid, 100 Thanon Huai Kaeo ☎053/222091, ⓕ221625, ⓔcmorchid@loxinfo.co.th. Grand, tasteful hotel with efficient service and a health club, inconveniently located on the northwest side of town. ❽

Imperial Mae Ping Hotel, 153 Thanon Sri Dornchai ☎053/270160–8, ⓕ270181, www.imperialhotels.com. Massive and characterless luxury hotel in an ugly high-rise building; popular with Asian tourists, it's convenient for the night bazaar. 6

Empress, 199 Thanon Chang Klan ☎ 053/270240, ⓕ 272467, ⓦ www.empresshotels.com. Grand international-class hotel conveniently placed on the south side of town: within walking distance of the night bazaar, yet far enough removed to get some peace and quiet. 6

River View Lodge, 25 Soi 2, Thanon Charoen Prathet ☎ 053/271109–10, ⓕ 279019. Tasteful alternative to international-class hotels, with a beautiful riverside garden, a swimming pool and neat decorative touches in the rooms. Quiet and

very well run; the most expensive rooms have balconies overlooking the river balconies. 7

Royal Princess, 112 Thanon Chang Klan ☎ 053/281033–43, ⓕ 281044, ⓦ www.royalprincess.com. Tidy, centrally located hotel close to the night bazaar, with elegant rooms, a swimming pool, fine restaurants and impeccable service. 8

Westin Riverside Plaza, 318/1 Thanon Chiang Mai–Lamphun ☎ 053/275300, ⓕ 272292, ⓦ www.westin.com. The city's most luxurious hotel is located in one of its tallest buildings, a few kilometres south of town by the river. Facilities include a pool, business centre and health club as well as several top-class restaurants. 9

The City

Chiang Mai feels less claustrophobic than most cities in Thailand, being scattered over a wide plain and broken up by waterways. In addition to the moat encircling the temple-strewn old town, the gentle Ping River brings a breath of fresh air to the eastern side of the pungent food markets above Nawarat Bridge, and the modern, hectic shopping area around Thanon Chang Klan. To make the most of the river, take a **boat trip** (2hr; B100) in a converted rice barge from the jetty beside the *Riverside Restaurant*, on the east bank just north of Nawarat Bridge. Slow but sturdy, the boats offer a clear view of the surroundings as they take visitors through lush countryside north of town; boats leave on the hour every hour between 10am and 3pm. Alternatively, contact Mae Ping River Cruises (☎ 053/274822), based at Wat Chaimongkol on Thanon Charoen Prathet, who offer pick-up from your hotel and charge B300 per person for a two-hour cruise, usually in a longtail boat; they take you 8km upstream from the centre for a look round a farmer's fruit and flower gardens, plus refreshments and fruit tasting, before returning to the city.

Wat Phra Singh

If you see only one temple in Chiang Mai it should be **Wat Phra Singh**, perhaps the single most impressive array of buildings in the city, at the far western end of Thanon Ratchdamnoen in the old town. Just inside the gate to the right, the wooden scripture repository is the best example of its kind in the north, inlaid with glass mosaic and set high on a base decorated with stucco angels. The largest building in the compound, a colourful modern viharn fronted by naga balustrades, hides from view a rustic wooden bot, a chedi constructed in 1345 to house the ashes of King Kam Fu, and – the highlight of the whole complex – the beautiful **Viharn Lai Kam**. This wooden gem from the early nineteenth century is a textbook example of Lanna architecture, with its squat, multi-tiered roof and exquisitely carved and gilded pediment: if you feel you're being watched as you approach, it's the sinuous double arch between the porch's central columns, which represents the Buddha's eyebrows.

Inside sits one of Thailand's three **Phra Singh** (or Sihing) Buddha images (see p.604), a portly, radiant and much-revered bronze in a fifteenth-century

THE NORTH | Chiang Mai

310

In recent years there's been a steady increase in the number of visitors who come to Chiang Mai looking to return home with a new skill by taking a self-improvement course. An obvious thing to learn was how to cook Thai food, but a variety of other courses blossomed, and it's now possible to tackle just about any local subject or skill, including Thai massage, meditation and – perhaps most challenging of all – the Thai language.

Cookery
There has been an explosion of interest in preparing Thai food, and many Chiang Mai guest houses and cookery schools now offer lessons. The original – and still the best – is the Chiang Mai Thai Cookery School, 1–3 Thanon Moonmuang ☏ 053/206388, ⓕ 206387, ⓔ nabnian@loxinfo.co.th run by Somphon and Elizabeth Nabnian. They offer courses of one to five days (B900–B4200), in groups of eight to eighteen people, covering traditional Lanna and common Thai dishes, including vegetarian options and the use of substitute ingredients available in the West. While the fees might seem expensive, the courses are well worth it, including a first-class meal and fruit tasting, a recipe book and transport from their office to Somphon's house, a 15min drive. It's good to book a day or two in advance as the classes are very popular, but you can just turn up and attempt to secure a place.

Massage courses
While the best place to study Thai massage in Thailand is considered to be at Bangkok's Wat Po (see p.127), some well-regarded schools make Chiang Mai a popular alternative as a more relaxing base for courses which can run several weeks (they also offer massages to customers). The longest-established centre is the Old Medicine Hospital, 78/1 Soi Moh Shivagakomarpaj, off Thanon Wualai opposite the Old Chiang Mai Cultural Center (daily 9am–4pm; ☏ 053/275085). Highly respected ten-day courses in English (B3500) are held twice a month, though the group size can get a bit too big at popular times; a massage costs B250 for two hours. The college of Thai Massage Therapy at 49/2 Thanon Kampangdin ☏ 01/6811698 offers smaller classes and three levels of study, each taking a week and costing B2000. Traditional massages by extremely competent, blind masseurs can be had (B150 per hour) at the School for the Blind, 41 Thanon Arak ☏ 053/278009.

Meditation
Northern Insight Meditation Centre, at Wat Ram Poeng (aka Wat Tapotaram) on Thanon Canal near Wat Umong ☏ 053/211620, offers month-long Vipassana courses and has a resident farang instructor. At the Raja Yoga Meditation Centre, 181/52 Soi 2, Superhighway Muu 3 ☏ 053/218604, you can drop in for their evening meditation session at 7pm. Sunshine House, 24 Soi 4, Thanon Kaeo Nawarat (no phone), is a centre for alternative courses: meditation, yoga and t'ai chi.

Thai language
AUA, 24 Thanon Ratchadamnoen ☏ 053/211377 or 278407 is the most central and longest-established school, with each course normally lasting sixty hours and costing B3300, though shorter thirty-hour courses are available. Australia Centre, 75/1 Moo 14, Tambon Suthep, ☏ 053/810552–3, ⓕ 810554, at the back of the university, offers two-week (30hr; 3hr daily) introductory Thai-language courses costing B2900, or four-week language and culture programmes.

Lanna style. Its setting is enhanced by the colourful **murals** of action-packed tableaux, which give a window on life in the north a hundred years ago: courting scenes and piggyback fights, merchants, fishermen and children playing. The murals illustrate two different stories: on the right-hand wall is an old folk tale, the *Sang Thong*, about a childless king and queen who are miraculously

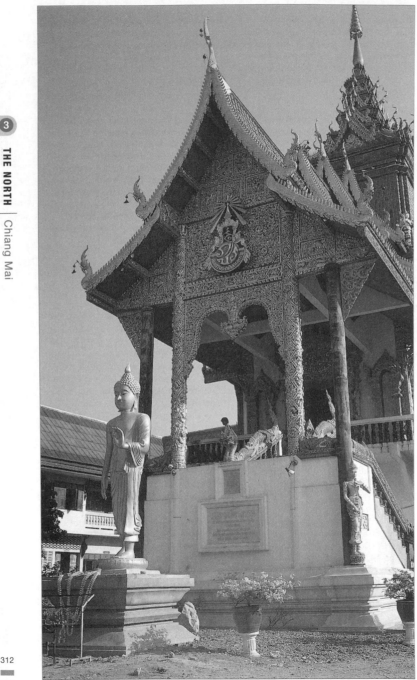

given a beautiful son, the "Golden Prince", in a conch shell. The murals on the left, which have been badly damaged by water, show the story of the mythical swan Suwannahong, who forms the magnificent prow of the principal royal barge in Bangkok. Incidentally, what look like Bermuda shorts on the men are in fact Buddhist **tattoos**: in the nineteenth century, all boys in the north were tattooed from navel to kneecap, an agonizing ordeal undertaken to show their courage and to enhance their appeal to women. On one side of the wat is a high school for young yellow-sashed novices and schoolboys in blue shorts, who all noisily throng the temple compound during the day. Dally long enough and you'll be sure to have to help them with their English homework.

Wat Chedi Luang

From Wat Phra Singh a ten-minute walk east along Thanon Ratchadamnoen brings you to **Wat Chedi Luang** on Thanon Phra Pokklao, where an enormous chedi, toppled from 90m to its present 60m by an earthquake in 1545, presents an intriguing spectacle – especially in the early evening when the resident bats flit around. You'll need a titanic leap of the imagination, however, to picture the beautifully faded pink-brick chedi, in all its crumbling grandeur, as it was in the fifteenth century, when it was covered in bronze plates and gold leaf, and housed the Emerald Buddha (see p.123). Recent attempts to rebuild the entire chedi to its former glory, now abandoned, have nevertheless led to modern replacements of the elephants at the base, the nagas which line the lengthy staircases, and the Buddha images in its four niches. In an unprepossessing modern building (which women are not allowed to enter) by the main entrance stands the city's navel pillar, the *lak muang*, sheltered by a stately gum tree which, the story has it, will stand for as long as the city's fortunes prosper.

Wat Chiang Man

From Wat Chedi Luang, the old town's main commercial street, Thanon Phra Pokklao, heads north past a monument to King Mengrai, the founder of Chiang Mai, set in its own small piazza. Behind the monument, the attractive old provincial office is scheduled to open as an Arts and Culture Museum in the near future. Turn right along Thanon Wiang Kaeo to reach the oldest temple in Chiang Mai, **Wat Chiang Man**, fifteen minutes' walk from Chedi Luang.

Erected by Mengrai on the site where he first pitched camp, the wat is most notable for two dainty and very holy Buddha images housed in the viharn to the right of the entrance: the **Phra Sila**, a graceful stone work carved in northern India in the sixth century BC, stands in the typical *tribunga*, or hipshot stance; its partner, the **Phra Setangamani** (or Crystal Buddha), made four centuries later probably in Lavo (modern Lopburi), is much revered by the inhabitants of Chiang Mai for its rain-making powers and is carried through the streets during the Songkhran festival to help the rainy season on its way. Neither image is especially beautiful, but a powerful aura is created by making them difficult to see, high up behind three sets of iron bars. Check out the chedi at the back of the compound for the herd of stone elephants on whose backs it sits.

Wat Bupparam

On the east side of town at the mid-point of the main shopping drag, Thanon Tha Pae, **Wat Bupparam** makes for a mildly interesting stroll from the main guest-house area around Tha Pae Gate. Housed in the new wedding-cake

Chiang Mai festivals

Chiang Mai is the best and busiest place in the country to see in the Thai New Year, **Songkhran**, which takes over the city between April 13 and 16. The most obvious role of the festival is as an extended "rain dance" in the driest part of the year, when huge volumes of canal water are thrown about in a communal water-fight that spares no one a drenching. The other elements of this complex festival are not as well known but no less important. In the temple compounds, communities get together to build sandcastles in the shape of chedis, which they cover with coloured flags – this bestows merit on any ancestors who happen to find themselves in hell and may eventually release them from their torments, and also shows an intent to help renovate the wat in the year to come. Houses are given a thorough spring-clean to see out the old year, while Buddha images from the city's main temples are cleaned, polished and sprinkled with lustral water, before being ceremonially carried through the middle of the water-fight, to give everyone the chance to throw water on them and receive the blessing of renewal. Finally, younger family members formally visit their elders during the festival to ask for their blessings, while pouring scented water over their hands.

Loy Krathong, on the night of the full moon in November, has its most showy celebration at Sukhothai, but Chiang Mai is not far behind. While a spectacular but unnerving firework fiesta rages on the banks, thousands of candles are gently floated down the Ping River in beautiful lotus-leaf boats. People hope in this way to float away any sins or ill luck they have incurred, and give thanks for the rainy season to Mae Kong Kha, the ancient water goddess. As well as floating *krathong*s, people release **khom loy**, paper hot-air balloons that create a magical spectacle as they float heavenward with firecrackers trailing behind. As with *krathong*s, they are released to carry away problems and bad luck, as well as to honour the Buddha's top-knot, which he cut off when he became an ascetic (according to legend, the top-knot is looked after by the Buddha's mother in heaven).

Chiang Mai's brilliantly colourful **flower festival**, usually on the first weekend of February, also attracts huge crowds. The highlight is a procession of floats, modelled into animals, chedis and even scenes from the *Ramayana* (see p.125), and covered in flowers. In early April, the **Poy Sang Long** festival (which has its most elaborate manifestation in Thailand in Mae Hong Son; see box on p.363), centred around Wat Pa Pao near the northeast corner of the old city, is an ordination ritual for young Shan men, who are paraded round town on the shoulders of relatives. The boys are dressed in extravagant, colourful clothing with huge floral headdresses, which they symbolically cast off at the end of the festival to don a saffron robe. In late May or early June, the **Inthakin** festival, a life-prolonging ceremony for the city of Chiang Mai, is focused around the *lak muang* at Wat Chedi Luang, which throngs with locals making offerings.

---

structure at the centre of the temple is a magnificent black Buddha, which was apparently made for King Naresuan of Ayutthaya nearly four hundred years ago from a single piece of teak. The **temple well** (off-limits for women) was used for watering the Buddha relics enshrined in the chedi and is also Chiang Mai's representative in the *murathaphisek* ceremony, when holy waters are gathered from Thailand's most auspicious localities for the ritual bathing of a new king.

Chiang Mai National Museum

For a fuller picture of Lanna art and culture, head for the **National Museum**, on the northwestern outskirts of Chiang Mai (Wed–Sun 9am–4pm; B30). To get to the museum with your own transport, leave the old to[...] Chang Phuak Gate on the northern moat, then go 2km up Thano[...] a crowded shopping street, before turning left along the Superhigh[...] you must go past the museum, then make a U-turn along the road[...] divider and head back towards your target along the eastboun[...] Alternatively, charter a tuk-tuk or songthaew from the centre of [...] (B30–40). The building is easy to identify by its soaring *kalae* motifs – e[...] rately carved extensions to the bargeboards that create a "V" shape over [...] apex of each roof and are a hallmark of Lanna architecture.

Inside, the airy rooms are cool enough for a long browse, and the collectic[...] is engrossing and liberally labelled in Thai and English. As you enter, you ar[...] greeted on the left by the head of a smiling bronze Buddha that is as tall as a man, but you need to go right to follow the displays which are grouped into six sections. The first of these displays artefacts and skeletons unearthed by local archaeological digs, as well as photographs of cave paintings found in the area. This leads into the the second section, which chronicles the golden age of the Lanna kingdom, from the fourteenth to the sixteenth centuries, and includes some lovely ceramics. The third part recounts relations between Chiang Mai and the Siamese Court of Bangkok from the late eighteenth to the mid-twentieth century, while the fourth section (upstairs) focuses on the expansion of trade in the late nineteenth century, particularly due to the activities of logging companies. The fifth section shows how the process of modernization continued throughout the twentieth century with advances in educational opportunities, health facilities and the development of handicraft industries such as silverware.

The biggest section is given over to **Thai religious art**, with a particular focus on Lanna art. Hundreds of Buddha images are on display, ranging from a humble, warmly smiling sandstone head of the Haripunjaya (Lamphun) era, representing the earliest northern style, to gleaming images in the Ratanakosin (Bangkok) style. In the golden age of Lanna images were produced in two contrasting styles. One group, which resembles images from northern India, has been called the "**lion-type**", after the Shakyamuni (Lion of the Shakyas) archetype at the great Buddhist temple at Bodh Gaya, the site of the Buddha's enlightenment. It's been conjectured that a delegation sent by King Tilok to Bodh Gaya in the 1450s brought back not only a plan of the temple to be used in the building of nearby Wat Jet Yot, but also a copy of the statue, which became the model for hundreds of Lanna images. These broad-shouldered, plump-bellied Buddhas are always seated with the right hand in the touching-the-earth gesture, while the face is well rounded with pursed lips and a serious, majestic demeanour. The second type is the "**Thera Sumana**" style named after the monk Mahathera Sumana, who came from Sukhothai in 1369 to establish his Sri Lankan sect in Lanna. The museum is well stocked with this type of image, which shows strong Sukhothai influence, with an oval face and a flame-like *ushnisha* on top of the head.

Wat Jet Yot

Set back from the Superhighway two minutes' walk west of the museum, the peaceful garden temple of **Wat Jet Yot** is named after the "seven spires" of its unusual chedi. The temple was built in 1455 by King Tilok, to represent[...] seven places around Bodh Gaya in India which the Buddha visited in the [...] weeks following his enlightenment. Around the base of the chedi, deli[...] cos portray cross-legged deities serenely floating in the sky, a role m[...] yogic fliers; their faces are said to be those of King Tilok's relativ[...]

...etre north of the Superhighway off Thanon Chotana, the **Tribal** (daily 9am–4pm; free) enjoys a superb location behind the artfully ...d **Ratchamangkla Park**. Originally established in 1965 as part of ...al Research Institute at Chiang Mai University, the museum was ... in 1997 to the present edifice, in the style of a Chinese pagoda. ...ooking a tree-lined lake, the very pretty and peaceful setting makes a visit ...hwhile, as does the opportunity to learn something about the various hill ...es before heading off on a trek. It's about a ten-minute walk from the park ...te on Thanon Chotana to the museum entrance, but, if you are getting here ...y songthaew, drivers can take their vehicles round the park directly to the museum. However, when it's time to leave you have to take the ten-minute walk to the gate to find transport back into town.

Set out on three floors, the museum has its main exhibition area on the ground floor, where displays about each of the main hill tribes are accompanied by concise information printed in both Thai and English. A useful wall chart shows the calendar of traditional village life, giving a month-by-month picture of the agricultural activities, ceremonies and festivals of the tribes featured; there are also photos and models of village dwellings, giving a good idea of the different styles of architecture, and a display of hill-tribe instruments accompanied by taped music. If you are especially interested, ask to see the slide show (15min) and video (55min), for which the combined cost is B50 per person. Despite the saccharine American narrator, the video is interesting, describing the six main tribes and showing a festival for each; by the end of it you should be able confidently to distinguish between the modes of dress of the various tribes.

As you trawl through the exhibition, glimpses of the lake through the windows are very appealing, and it's worth taking a look at the reconstructions of hill-tribe houses erected along the lake's south side. The road around the lake is popular with joggers in the morning and evening, and snack stalls clustered around the southeast corner of the lake attract groups of local people late in the day. Since the park is right next door to Chiang Mai's horse-racing track, you might even be lucky enough to see the stirring sight of horses swimming in the lake with their trainers. Walking around to the east side of the lake takes you into the park and more formal gardens, with pretty flower beds, and a smaller lake around which a sculpture garden is set, the hills making an attractive backdrop. Another cluster of snack stalls near the park entrance does a brisk trade at sundown.

The zoo and arboretum

About 1km beyond Wat Jet Yot, the Superhighway crosses Thanon Huai Kaeo, a broad avenue of posh residences and hotels which starts out from the northwest corner of the moat and ends at the foot of Doi Suthep. Heading out up Thanon Huai Kaeo, past the sprawling campus of Chiang Mai University, brings you to **Chiang Mai Zoo** (daily 8am–7pm; last entry 5pm; B30 adults, B30 per vehicle), in an attractive 36-acre park, run by the municipality, at the base of the mountain. It's easy to get there and back from the centre by tuk-tuk or songthaew (B30–40 one way).

Originally a menagerie of a missionary family's pets, the zoo now houses a ...re collection of colourful Asian birds, monkeys and larger mammals – ...co...ing the most popular attraction, Thai elephants – in modern, relatively vis...ble conditions. Despite a disorientating layout, it makes a diverting ...ly for kids. Feeding times for animals are posted clearly, and refreshment stalls for humans are never far away. The grounds are too big to walk round, but as bicycles and motorbikes are not allowed, you may need to hire a songthaew at the entrance to take you around. The zoo is better visited in the morning to avoid the afternoon heat. In an idyllic location in the upper reaches of the grounds there's a small campsite, mostly used for picnics by day-trippers.

Next door to the zoo entrance, an unprepossessing park, where you'll often see joggers toiling and itinerant monks sleeping or meditating under their parasols, is in fact a small **arboretum**, with name tags stuck to the plants and trees, so you can mug up on them before going upcountry.

Wat Umong

More of a park than a temple, **Wat Umong** makes an unusual, charming place for a stroll in the western suburbs. If you're heading here from the zoo, it's best to take a tuk-tuk or songthaew around the university campus; from the centre of town, take a songthaew or cycle east along Thanon Suthep for about 2km and turn left after Wang Nam Gan (a royal agricultural produce project), then continue for another kilometre following the signs to the wat along a winding lane.

According to legend the wat was built in the 1380s by King Ku Na for a brilliant but deranged monk called Jan, who was prone to wandering off into the forest to meditate. Because Ku Na wanted to be able to get Jan's advice at any time, he founded this wat and decorated the **tunnels** (*umong*) beneath the chedi with paintings of trees, flowers and birds to simulate the monk's favoured habitat. Some of the old tunnels can still be explored, where obscure fragments of paintings and one or two small modern shrines can be seen. Above the tunnels, frighteningly lavish nagas guard the staircase up to the overgrown **chedi** and a grassy platform supporting a grotesque black statue of the fasting Buddha, all ribs and veins: he is depicted as he was during his six years of self-mortification, before he realized that he should avoid extremes along the Middle Path to enlightenment. Behind the chedi, the ground slopes away to a **lake** inhabited by hungry carp, where locals come to relax and feed the fish. On a tiny island here, reached by a concrete bridge, stands a statue of Buddhadasa Bhikkhu, whose eclectic philosophy is followed at Wat Umong. Informal discussions in English on Buddhism, and some meditation practice, are normally held in the Chinese pavilion on the lake's edge here on Sunday afternoons at 3pm, with one of the farang monks who are often in residence.

Throughout the tranquil wooded grounds, the temple's diverse education-focused philosophy comes vividly alive: as you enter the compound you pass through a shady grove where signs pinned to nearly every tree, displaying simple Buddhist maxims in Thai and English and the botanical name of the species. At certain times of the day, your stroll is accompanied by a soothing Thai voice emanating from loudspeakers, expounding on Buddhism; the subject can be explored in more depth in the library, in the centre of the temple grounds, with some books in English, and at the adjacent bookshop – and outside at tables and covered seating areas local people read, study and conduct discussions. Up some nearby steps, the path leading to the chedi is lined with outrageous cartoons of sinning anthropomorphized dogs, moral maxims underneath each one, while colourful and surreal didactic paintings also cover the modern hall near the tunnel entrances. At the entrance gate, handicrafts are sold by the community of disabled people who have a house and workshop in the wat.

The Contemporary Art Museum

From the turn-off to Wat Umong, Thanon Suthep heads back towards town, eventually meeting the western moat at Suan Dork Gate. A short way along on the left, at the junction with Thanon Nimmanheimin, the new **Chiang Mai Contemporary Art Museum** (Tues–Sun 9.30am–5pm; ℡053/944833; free) is not only confirmation of the city's growing importance, but also a boon to the large local artistic community. The large exhibition areas are well lit and the exhibitions generally change each month, giving visitors insights into the minds of modern Thai artists.

Wat Suan Dork

A little further along Thanon Suthep, the Hill Tribe Products Foundation (see p.320) sits on the right in front of **Wat Suan Dork**, the "Flower Garden Temple", which was later surrounded by walls as part of Chiang Mai's fortifications. Legend says that Mahathera Sumana, when he was invited to establish his Sri Lankan sect here in 1369, brought with him a miraculous glowing relic. The king of Chiang Mai ordered a huge chedi – the one you see today – to be built in his flower garden, but as the pea-sized relic was being placed inside the chedi, it split into two parts: one half was buried here, the other found its way to Doi Suthep, after more miracles.

The brilliantly whitewashed chedi now sits next to a garden of smaller, equally dazzling chedis containing the ashes of the Chiang Mai royal family; framed by Doi Suthep to the west, this makes an impressive and photogenic sight, especially at sunset. Standing in the way of a panoramic shot of all the chedis, the huge, open-sided viharn on the east side has been crudely restored, but the bot at the back of the dusty compound is more interesting – decorated with lively *Jataka* murals, it enshrines a beautifully illuminated, 500-year-old Buddha.

Shopping

Shopping is an almost irresistible pastime in Chiang Mai, a hotbed of traditional cottage industries offering generally high standards of workmanship at low prices. Two main tourist shopping areas, conveniently operating at different times of the day, sell the full range of local handicrafts.

The **road to San Kamphaeng**, which extends due east from the end of Thanon Charoen Muang for 13km, is the main daytime strip; also known as the "Handicraft Highway", it's lined with every sort of shop and factory, where you can usually watch the craftsmen at work. The biggest concentrations are at Bo Sang, the "umbrella village", 9km from town, and at San Kamphaeng itself, once important for its kilns but now dedicated chiefly to silk-weaving. While it's a worthwhile trip to watch age-old crafts in process, the main problem is getting there. Frequent white **songthaews** to San Kamphaeng leave Chiang Mai from the central Lamyai market, but it's difficult to decide when to get off if you don't know the area. You could sign up for a tour or hire a **tuk-tuk** for a few hundred baht, but the catch here is that the drivers will want to take you to the shops where they'll pick up a commission. The best way to go is by **bicycle** or **motorbike**, which allows you to stop where and when you please, though you need nerves of steel to brave the fast-moving traffic and narrow road.

The other shopper's playground is the **night bazaar**, sprawling around the junction of Thanon Chang Klan and Thanon Loi Khro, where bumper-to-bumper street stalls and several indoor market areas and shopping centres sell just about anything produced in Chiang Mai, plus crafts from other parts of Thailand and counterfeit designer goods; the action starts up at around 5pm. Lots of the items are junk or fakes, but there are bargains tucked away here and there. Even if you're not into shopping, there's lots to see here, including rock climbers in action at The Peak, a fifteen-metre-high climbing wall surrounded by shops and cafes, and traditional dancing at the Galare Food Centre (see p.322).

During the day, bustling **Warorot market**, along the river immediately north of Thanon Tha Pae, has lots of cheap and cheerful cotton, linen and ceramics for sale on the upper floors. In the heart of the market, you can watch locals buying chilli paste, sausage and sticky rice from their favourite stalls, and maybe even join the queue. There's also a flower market here which is open late at night until the early hours of the morning.

Since the 1997 economic crash **secondhand markets** have become a phenomenon in Chiang Mai, selling both new and used clothes, books and trinkets in the evenings; they are hugely popular among the young and make fascinating places just to wander. No particular location can be recommended as they tend to occupy a patch of empty land for six months, then move on, but if you happen to pass such a cluster of temporary stalls and a mass of motorbikes, check it out.

Fabrics and clothes

The **silk** produced out towards **San Kamphaeng** is richly coloured and hardwearing, with various attractive textures. Bought off a roll, the material is generally less costly than in Bangkok, though more expensive than in the northeast – prices start from around B450 a metre for two-ply (for thin shirts and skirts) and B750 a metre for four-ply (suitable for suits). Ready-made silk clothes and made-to-measure tailoring, though inexpensive, are generally staid and more suited to formal wear. With branches 5km out of Chiang Mai and in San Kamphaeng itself, Piankusol is the best place to follow the **silk-making** process right from the cocoon. If you've got slightly more money to spend on better quality silk, head for Shinawatra (branches 7km out and in San Kamphaeng), which was once graced by no less a personage than the late Princess Diana.

Shops in San Kamphaeng and Chiang Mai sell traditional, locally made pastel-coloured **cotton** starting at B150 per metre, which is nice for furnishings. Outlets in the basement of the main night bazaar building on Thanon Chang Klan have good, cheap selections of this sort of cloth, plus hand-painted and batik-printed lengths. On the third floor of the Chiang Inn Plaza, just north on the same street, the upmarket Loom by Nandakwang shop has an excellent range of attractive cotton goods, including quality bedspreads and shirts. Chiang Mai is also awash with geometric *mut mee* cloth and the Technicolor weaves of the Thai Lue (see p.350), but both are far better and much less expensive in their place of origin: the former in the northeast, the latter around Chiang Khong and Nan. Another shop worth a root around is Pa Ker Yaw, 180 Thanon Loi Khro, a weather-beaten wooden shophouse stuffed with a selection of rich fabrics, as well as folksy jewellery and other crafts.

For the all-over ethnic look, Classic Lanna Thai, on the first floor of the night bazaar and on Thanon Moonmuang, sells classy ready-to-wear clothes, made from local fabrics by traditional northern methods. If you just need to replenish your rucksack, try Ga-Boutique at 1/1 Thanon Kotchasarn (opposite Tha

Pae Gate), which sells ordinary casual clothes of reasonable quality at low prices.

If you're interested in the whole process of traditional fabric production, particularly the use of **natural dyes**, Studio Naenna, 138/8 Soi Changkhian, Thanon Huay Keow at the base of Doi Suthep (phone ℡053/226042 for an appointment and possibly a free pick-up), is an excellent place to begin. It's run by a lecturer at Chiang Mai University, who will show you her dyeshop, the dyes and the plants from which they are extracted; you can then watch the weavers in action and buy the finished products, which consist of top-quality ready-made garments and accessories, in their showroom.

To make sure more of your money goes to those who make the goods, take your custom to one of the non-profit-making shops whose proceeds go to the hill tribes. These include the Hill Tribe Products Foundation, on Thanon Suthep in front of Wat Suan Dork, which sells beautiful lengths of cotton and silk and a variety of hill-tribe gear; Thai Tribal Crafts, 204 Thanon Bamrungrat off Thanon Kaeo Nawarat – *yaam*, the embroidered shoulder bags popular with Thai students, are particularly good here (around B250); and Golden Triangle People's Art and Handicrafts, 137/1 Thanon Nantharam ℡053/276194, which works mainly with Akha women. The last of these has an excellent library/research centre, the Mountain People Culture and Development Highland Research Institute; specializing in oral history, and with useful information in English, it's located in another building in the same compound and can be used by appointment.

Woodcarving

Chiang Mai has a long tradition of **woodcarving**, which expresses itself in everything from salad bowls to half-size elephants. In the past the industry has relied on the cutting of Thailand's precious teak, but manufacturers are now beginning to use other imported hardwoods, while bemoaning their inferior quality. Carl Bock, who travelled through the region in 1882, observed a habit which is still common today, particularly in Ban Tawai (see below): "The woodcarvers have a quaint taste for inlaying their work with odd bits of coloured glass, tinsel or other bright material: such work will not bear close inspection, but it has a remarkably striking effect when the sun shines on these glittering objects."

The best place for carving is **Chiangmai Banyen Company**, 201 Thanon Wualai, at the junction with the Superhighway: their workmanship is top-notch and the wood is treated to last. Prices are quite high though – a statue of a chubby, reclining boy of the kind found all over Chiang Mai will set you back B350 here. With refreshing honesty, the proprietors explain that a lot of their stuff is left outside for a few rainy seasons to give it a weathered look – elsewhere, pieces that have been weathered in this way are often passed off as antiques. Banyen also has an absorbing **folk museum** of wooden objects collected from around the north.

If you're a real aficionado and have your own transport, head for **Ban Tawai**, a large village of shops and factories where prices are low and you can watch the woodworkers in action. One of Thailand's most important woodcarving centres, Ban Tawai relied on rice farming until thirty years ago, but today virtually every home here has carvings for sale outside and each backyard hosts its own cottage industry. To get there, follow Highway 108 south from Chiang Mai 13km to Hang Dong, then head east for 2km.

Lacquerware

Lacquerware can be seen in nearly every museum in Thailand, most commonly in the form of betel-nut sets, which used to be carried ceremonially by the slaves of grandees as an insignia of rank and wealth (see box on p.503). Betel-nut sets are still produced in Chiang Mai according to the traditional technique, whereby a woven bamboo frame is covered with layers of rich red lacquer and decorated with black details. A variety of other objects, such as trays and jewellery boxes, are also produced, some decorated with gold leaf on black gloss. Lacquerware makes an ideal choice for gifts, as it is both light to carry, and at the same time typically Thai. Just about every other shop in town sells lacquerware: Laitong, 6km out towards San Kamphaeng, is a good place to see the intricate process of manufacture, though prices are lower elsewhere.

Celadon

Celadon, sometimes known as greenware, is a delicate variety of stoneware which was first made in China over two thousand years ago and later produced in Thailand, most famously at Sukhothai and Sawankhalok. Several kilns in Chiang Mai have revived the art, the best of them being Mengrai Kilns at 79/2 Soi 6, Thanon Samlarn. Sticking to the traditional methods, Mengrai produces beautiful handcrafted items, thrown in elegant shapes and covered with transparent green and blue glazes, from as little as B160 for a small vase, B180 for a medium-sized decorated bowl, B95 for a large cup and B80 for a plate.

Umbrellas and paper

The village of **Bo Sang** bases its fame on souvenir **umbrellas** – made of silk, cotton or mulberry paper and decorated with bold, painted colours (from about B120 for a kid's parasol) – and celebrates its craft with a colourful **umbrella fair** every January. The artists who work here can paint a small motif on your bag or camera in two minutes flat. The grainy mulberry (*sa*) **paper**, which makes beautiful writing or sketching pads, is sold almost as an afterthought in many of Bo Sang's shops; it can also be bought from stalls at the night market (typically ten envelopes and ten pieces of paper for B70), while Tonpao, in the basement of the Chiang Mai Night Bazaar Building, sells a very wide range of *sa* paper in the form of albums, notepaper and so on.

Jade, silver and jewellery

Chinese soft **jade** and nine colours of hard jade from Burma are worked into a great variety of objects, from chopsticks (B3000) to large Buddha images (B30,000); the finest, translucent, hard jade is reserved for jewellery, usually deep green in colour, which is supposed to bring the wearer good health. Several outlets along Thanon Tha Pae and Thanon Chang Klan display a wide selection.

Of the traditional craft quarters, only the **silversmiths'** area on Thanon Wualai remains in its original location. The Siam Silverware Factory on Soi 3, a ramshackle and sulphurous compound loud with the hammering of hot metal, gives you a whiff of what this zone must have been like in its heyday. The end results are repoussé plates, bowls and cups, and attractive, chunky jewellery. Silver is often priced by the gram, with current rates at about B10–15 per gram, so a thin, engraved sterling-silver bracelet costs around B250–350 and a chunky bangle around B500–700.

A good general **jewellery** store is Nova Collection at 210 Thanon Tha Pae, which has some lovely rings and necklaces blending gold, silver and precious stones in striking and original designs – but for the very best workmanship and prices you need to visit Mae Sai on the Burmese border (see p.387).

Eating

The main difficulty with **eating** in Chiang Mai is knowing when to stop. All over town there are inexpensive and enticing restaurants serving typically northern food, which has been strongly influenced by Burmese cuisine, especially in curries such as the spicy *kaeng hang lay* (usually translated on menus as "Northern Thai curry"), made with pork, ginger, garlic and tamarind. Another favourite local dish is Chiang Mai *nem*, spicy pork sausage – although the uncooked, fermented varieties are usually too sour for Western palates. At lunchtime the thing to do is to join the local workers in one of the simple, inexpensive cafés that put all their efforts into producing just one or two special dishes – the traditional meal at this time of day is *khao soi*, a thick broth of curry and coconut cream, with egg noodles and a choice of meat. At the opposite extreme, the city's major hotels mostly provide a Thai/Western lunchtime buffet for something over B200, which is good value if you're hungry.

None of the Western food in Chiang Mai is brilliant, and it's generally more expensive than Thai, but there's plenty of it, particularly Italian-slanted, and sometimes it's very hard to resist. Easier to refuse are the restaurants which lay on touristy **cultural shows** with *khan toke* dinners, a selection of northern dishes eaten on the floor off short-legged lacquer trays. There are better places to sample the region's food, and the hammy dancing displays, often with embarrassing audience participation, are a dubious diversion.

Thai

Anusarn Market, off Thanon Chang Klan. Happy night-time hunting ground of open-air stalls and restaurants. One-dish operators (serving up *hawy thawt* fried up with great panache, or *khao soi*, or very good *phat thai*) square up to each other across a shared courtyard of tables; beyond lie *halal* restaurants specializing in barbecued chicken with honey, and several good seafood places including the old favourite *Fatty's*. Inexpensive to moderate.

Aum Vegetarian Food, on the corner of Ratchdamnoen and Moonmuang roads. Small and dingy, but it does interesting veggie dishes. Inexpensive.

Chiang Mai Vegetarian Centre, Thanon Aom Muang. Run by the Santi Asoke group, like the café at Bangkok's Chatuchak Market: a cavernous traditional *sala* serving good veggie dishes on rice, and desserts. Mon–Thurs & Sun 6am–2pm. Inexpensive.

Galare Food Centre, Thanon Chang Klan, night bazaar. A coupon system operates at this open-air collection of foodstalls and bars. It's a good lively place for a break from shopping, a budget meal and a beer, with free shows of traditional dancing on a stage between 9pm and 10.30pm, making a nice background accompaniment without being too loud or intrusive. Inexpensive.

The Gallery, 25 Thanon Charoenrat. Refined restaurant on soothing riverside terraces, behind a gallery for local artists. Interesting selection, big portions, slow service. Moderate to expensive.

Huen Phen, 112 Thanon Ratchamanka. Probably Chiang Mai's most authentic northern restaurant, with bags of ambience. The selection of hors d'oeuvres at B80 gives a great taste of all the local specials. It's not yet on the tourist trail, so no English sign. Moderate.

Huen Sontharee, 46 Thanon Wang Sing Kham. A convivial riverfront restaurant (not signed in English) owned by the famous northern Thai folk-singer Sontharee Wechanon, who entertains diners from her balcony-level stage and serves up northern specialities. Food highlights include fried Chiang Mai sausage with whole baby garlic – the garlic is quite delicious, crunchy and almost sweet. Split levels allow a choice of seating – on a riverside terrace, near the stage or at round low tables on a balcony overlooking the action. Evenings only until 1am. Moderate.

Kalae, 65 Thanon Suthep. Follow this road to the western end, then climb 200m up the hill to find this relaxing spot on the bank of a small reservoir, where tables are set beneath trees and between bright flower beds. With a good, though limited, menu of Thai favourites, it's a useful place to head for after a visit to Wat Umong or the zoo. Moderate.

Khao Soi Samoe Jai, Thanon Faham (no English sign). Thick and tasty *khao soi*, delicious satay and other noodle dishes pack the locals in each lunchtime. Daily 9am–3pm. Inexpensive.

Kiat Ocha, 41–43 Thanon Nawarot, off Thanon Phra Pokklao (no English sign). Delicious and very popular satay and *khao man kai* – boiled chicken breast served with a special sauce, broth and rice. This and the surrounding cafés are especially handy if you're looking round the old town. Daily 5am–2pm. Inexpensive.

New Lamduon Fahharm Khao Soi, 352/22 Thanon Charoenrat. Excellent *khao soi* prepared to a secret recipe. Also satay, waffles and *som tam*. Daily 9am–3pm. Inexpensive.

Phat thai stall, opposite Soi 5, Thanon Tha Pae. Great *phat thai*, served on a banana leaf with a generous side dish of raw vegetables. Open after dark. Inexpensive.

Ratana's Kitchen, 320–322 Thanon Tha Pae. A favourite among locals both for Northern specialities like *kaeng hang lay* and *khao soi* and for tasty Western breakfasts, sandwiches and steaks. Inexpensive to moderate.

Suthasinee, 164/10 Thanon Chang Klan. Great, creamy *khao soi*, and good *som tam* ordered from the stall outside. Another branch in the Old Town at 1/5 Thanon Khang Ruanjum. Daily 11am–3pm. Inexpensive.

Ta-krite Restaurant, 7 Soi 1, Thanon Samlarn. On the south side of Wat Phra Singh. Delicious and varied cuisine, in a simple wooden house surrounded by plants. Inexpensive to moderate.

Tha Nam, 43/3 Moo 2, Thanon Chang Klan. Restaurant on the southern edge of town serving traditional northern Thai food in a ramshackle teak house, where the musicians can sometimes be a bit noisy playing their traditional music. It's better to eat on the huge terrace overlooking a quiet green stretch of the river (you can even hear the frogs croaking) – a much nicer view than the bare concrete banks that face the more popular *Riverside* (see "Nightlife", p.325). Moderate to expensive.

Thanom Restaurant, 8 Thanon Chaiyapoom, near Tha Pae Gate (no English sign). Great introduction to northern Thai and Burmese-style cooking, in startlingly clean surroundings. The fastidious management aren't over-fond of tourists and expect you to be dressed modestly (so no sleeveless tops or shorts) before they'll let you in, and to eat early: lunch is 11am–1pm, dinner 5–7.30pm. Moderate.

Whole Earth, 88 Thanon Sri Dornchai. Mostly veggie dishes from Thailand and India, plus a big fish and seafood selection; soothing atmosphere with occasional live mood music in a traditional Lanna house. Moderate to expensive.

The Wok, 44 Thanon Ratchamanka. Centrally located, with a relaxing ambience, and quality guaranteed as it's run by the Chiang Mai Cookery School. Moderate.

European and all-rounders

Amazing Sandwich, 252/3 Thanon Phra Pokklao. Situated in the old city near Chang Phuak Gate, this is the place to go if you hanker for a sandwich or baguette made up to order, or fancy munching on a pie or pasty. Mon–Sat 9am–8.30pm. Moderate.

Art Café, 291 Thanon Tha Pae. This brightly decorated Italian-run place exhibits local art, and is a popular *farang* hangout with a good ambience. All the café favourites (yoghurt and muesli as well as the usual American and continental breakfasts, sandwiches, soups, salads and ice cream) and full meals (mainly pasta, but Thai fare too, including a big selection of vegetarian options) are served, so it's useful for a snack or coffee any time. There are mags, newspapers and books to read: you'll need them as service can be very slow. A big selection of wines from B400. Daily 10am–10pm. Moderate to expensive.

Bierstube, 33/6 Thanon Moonmuang. Friendly and efficient service combined with generous portions of German or Thai food at reasonable prices make this place a favourite among locals. The tables outside provide a good people-watching spot, too. Inexpensive to moderate.

Cafe Chic, 105/5 Thanon Phra Pokklao. A perfect place to cool down after sweating round temple compounds in the old city. Its limited menu of Thai food and Western sandwiches is supplemented with home-made cookies and a wide choice of teas and coffees. Decorative items and household accessories are also on sale. Daily except Sun 10am–8pm. Moderate.

Daret's, 4 Thanon Chaiyapoom ☏ 053/235440. The definitive budget travellers' hangout with outdoor trestles and a friendly buzz. Famous fruit shakes, good breakfasts and back-home staples, though the Thai food is rather bland. Inexpensive to moderate.

Da Stefano, 2/1–2 Thanon Chiang Moi Kao. Just round the corner from Tha Pae Gate, this has quickly become one of Chiang Mai's most popular Italian restaurants. It's easy to see why: it has a winning combination of tasteful ambience, efficient service and delicious food. Mon–Sat 11.30am–11pm, Sun 5–11pm. Moderate to expensive.

Irish Pub and Crusty Loaf Bakery, 24/1 Thanon Ratchawithi. With a spacious garden, this place, painted green and white, is more of a casual café-restaurant than a pub. A window display of freshly baked breads – including soda bread – makes for satisfying sandwiches and there are jacket potatoes of course, plus pizzas and a good vegetarian selection with Guinness (bottled only), Carlsberg (on tap) and reasonably priced wine to wash it down. Moderate.

Jerusalem Falafel, 35/3 Thanon Moonmuang. Small and simple café serving up pitta bread and Israeli food right near Tha Pae Gate. Daily except Fri 9am–11pm. Inexpensive to moderate.

JJ Coffee Shop and Bakery, *Montri Hotel*, corner of Ratchadamnoen and Moonmuang roads. Phenomenally popular with tourists (and local folk too), boasting a bustling, sanitized atmosphere, air-con and indoor garden. All kinds of food, but best for breakfast, with bread and croissants baked in front of your eyes, great muesli and yoghurt, and brewed coffee. Smaller branch at Chiang Inn

Plaza, Thanon Chang Klan. Daily 6.30am–10.30pm. Moderate to expensive.

Kafe, 127–129 Soi 5, Thanon Moonmuang. Long-time favourite among locals, with tasty burgers, good Thai food and a wide range of drinks in a warm and welcoming ambience. Inexpensive to moderate.

La Villa, 145 Thanon Ratchdamnoen. Relaxing conservatory-style Italian-run restaurant with big windows looking out onto a garden where there are more tables. Good salads, pasta and risotto, the best pizzas in town – baked in a wood-fired oven – and probably the best coffee too. Expensive.

Piccola Roma, 3/2–3 Thanon Charoen Prathet ☎053/271256. The genuine article, with especially good pasta, which would stand the test back in Italy, and an extensive wine list. Phone for free pick-up. Reservations recommended. Very expensive.

Pum Pui, 24 Soi 2, Thanon Moonmuang ☎053/278209. Trattoria-style Italian-run place where you're guaranteed huge servings; the food is mostly pasta (including an excellent lasagne), but there's pizza too, and the menu has a long vegetarian section. Seating is outside in a tree-filled courtyard off a quiet fume-free lane. Moderate to expensive.

Drinking and nightlife

Although there's a clutch of hostess bars bordering the east moat and along Loi Khro, and several gay bars offering sex shows, Chiang Mai's **nightlife** generally avoids Bangkok's sexual excesses. In other respects, however, the city throbs after dark. If your heart's set on **dancing**, try the big hotels, some of which have predictable, westernized nightclubs (like Space Bubble at the *Porn Ping* on Thanon Charoen Prathet) which charge about B100 admission, including one drink; for something more adventurous, head for one of the more Thai-style nightclubs such as *Channel X* or *Gigi's* (see opposite). Some of the places listed here are geared to a relaxing night out, while others get rocking as the night wears on.

Though there are **bars** scattered throughout the city, the main concentrations are on the east bank of the Ping River, around Tha Pae Gate, along Thanon Thanon Ratchawithi and to the west of town along Thanon Nimmanheimin, which swarms with students from nearby Chiang Mai University. For a gentle introduction to the city's **gay scene**, check out the bars in the basement of the night bazaar on Thanon Chang Klang – places like *Happy Happy Bar* and *Dragon Boys Bar* boast a welcoming atmosphere – and see ⓦwww.chiang-maigossip.com for more information.

There are often free or inexpensive classical **concerts** at Chiang Mai University, Payap University and the AUA language school (see box on p.311) – check in the local free magazines.

Brasserie, 37 Thanon Charoenrat. Good restaurant with pretty riverside terraces, more famous as the venue for some of the city's best live blues and rock. Warms up around 11pm.

Channel X, 12 Thanon Huai Kaeo. This is just one of several nightclubs in the 12 Huai Kaeo complex that are geared towards the city's youth, with bands performing covers of current hits at top volume. Gets going around midnight.

Drunken Flower, 295/1 Soi 1, Thanon Nimmanheimin. Tucked away in a lane beside the *Amari Rincome Hotel*, this quirky venue is a favourite among university students. Reasonable prices for food and drinks and an eclectic range of background music.

Fine Thanks, 119 Thanon Nimmanheimin. Another spot that's popular among Thais, yet welcoming to farangs, and features Thai bands playing a mix of Thai and Western songs.

Gigi's, 68/2 Thanon Chiang Mai–Lamphun, 500m south of TAT and Narawat Bridge. Fun, full-on massive videotheque club, packed with young Thais dancing around their bar stools, though there is a small dance-floor in front of the performance stage; a balcony level provides an excellent vantage point for the action below. Live music (strictly Thai pop covers) and video music. No admission but pricey drinks.

Good View, 13 Thanon Charoenrat. An upmarket clone of the neighbouring *Riverside*, this large venue appeals to fashionable Thais with its smart staff, extensive menu and slick, competent musicians, who play anything from country to jazz.

Pinte Blues Pub, 33/6 Thanon Moonmuang. The frontage of this simple bar is so small that you could miss it if you blink, but it is one of the city's longest-standing venues, and an ideal spot for a chat over cheap drinks with blues in the background.

Planet Chat, 8/4 Thanon Boonruangrit. Located just outside the northwest corner of the old city, this stylish nightspot gets packed out at weekends, when Thai bands play a mix of Thai and Western tunes.

Take It Easy, 283–287 Thanon Tha Pae. A bar occupying a double shophouse right near Tha Pae Gate; popular among backpackers, it features live bands playing loud rock.

The Pub, 189 Thanon Huai Kaeo. Homely, relaxing expat hangout, once rated by *Newsweek* as one of the world's best bars. As the name suggests: draught beer, darts, separate sports bar. Mon–Sat from 5pm, Sun from 11am.

Riverside, 9 Thanon Charoenrat ☎ 053/243239. Archetypal farang bolthole: candlelit terraces by the water, reliable Western and Thai food (moderate to pricey), extensive drinks list and inexpensive draught beer. Various bands perform nightly and the tempo increases as the night wears on. They do dinner cruises for an extra B50 per person on top of the cost of the meal; call for times.

Scene Song Say, 120/2 Soi 7, Thanon Nimmanheimin. One of Chiang Mai's more intriguing live-music venues, where the bands play anything from acid jazz to blues and reggae. Inexpensive cocktails are an added attraction.

Yoy Pocket, 30 Thanon Ratchawithi. The walls here are full of Americana, but the jukebox is just about purely Asian so it's a good spot to listen to some Thai pop music, an essential experience. Packed at night with twenty-something Thais. Daily noon–midnight.

Listings

Airlines Air Mandalay, Room 107, Doi Ping Mansion, 148 Thanon Charoen Prathet ☎ 053/818049; Bangkok Airways, Chiang Mai airport ☎ 053/281519; Lao Aviation, 240 Thanon Phra Pokklao, behind Thai Airways ☎ 053/418258–9; Malaysia Airlines, *Mae Ping Hotel*, 153 Thanon Sri Dornchai ☎ 053/276523 or 276538; Mandarin Airlines, 4th Floor, 414/21 Thanon Chang Klan ☎ 053/205157–8; Silk Air, *Mae Ping Hotel*, 153 Thanon Sri Dornchai ☎ 053/276459 for info, ☎ 053/276495 or 276459 reservations; Thai Airways, 240 Thanon Phra Pokklao ☎ 053/210210.

Banks and exchange Dozens of banks are dotted around Thanon Tha Pae and Thanon Chang Klan, and many exchange booths here stay open for evening shoppers.

Books Book Zone at 318 Thanon Tha Pae stocks a wide range of English-language publications, including novels, books about Thailand and maps. Two other large book stores, Suriwong at 54/1 Thanon Sri Dornchai (Mon–Sat 8am–7.30pm, Sun 8am–12.30pm) and DK Books at 79/1 Thanon Kotchasarn also have a wide selection; the former's display is the better organized. There is an excellent selection of secondhand books at the Lost Bookshop, 34/3 Thanon Ratchamanka, though the advertised opening hours (daily 9am–2pm & 5–8pm) are unreliable. Another place with a good selection of new and used books is The Bookshop at 59/7 Thanon Loi Khro (daily except Thurs 11am–9pm).

Buses The main terminus is Arcade Bus Station, Thanon Kaeo Nawarat ☏053/242664.

Car rental Many outlets in the Tha Pae Gate area rent out cars and four-wheel drives, from around B800 a day: reliable companies offering insurance include Queen Bee, 5 Thanon Moonmuang ☏053/275525; Journey, 283 Thanon Tha Pae ☏053/208787; and North Wheels, 127/2 Thanon Moonmuang ☏053/216189. For comprehensive insurance and back-up it might be worth paying the full whack (from B1400 a day) at Avis, Royal Princess Hotel, 112 Thanon Chang Klan ☏053/281033; or at Budget, 201/2 Thanon Mahidol ☏053/202871, opposite Airport Plaza.

Cinemas Call Movieline ☏053/262661, operated by the Raintree Community Centre ☏www.raintreecenter.org, for details of which English soundtrack or English-subtitled films are showing around town. The Vista chain screens some English-language films at its Kad Suan Kaew shopping plaza cinemas on Thanon Huai Kaeo: at Vista 1–4 actually in the plaza and at 12 Thanon Huai Kaeo, opposite. French-language films with English subtitles are screened at the Alliance Française, 138 Thanon Charoen Prathet (usually Fri 8pm; ☏053/275277).

Consulates Australia, 165 Thanon Sirimangklachan (Mon–Fri 8am–5pm, Sat 8am–noon; ☏053/221083); Canada, 151 Chiang Mai–Lampang Superhighway (Mon–Fri 9am–noon; ☏053/850147); China, 111 Thanon Chang Lo (Mon–Fri 9–11am; ☏053/276125); India, 344 Thanon Charoenrat (Mon–Fri 9am–noon; ☏053/243066); UK, 198 Thanon Bamrungrat ☏053/263015; US, 387 Thanon Witchayanon (Mon & Wed 8–10.30am; ☏053/252629). The Australian, Canadian and UK consulates are honorary.

Hospitals Lanna, at 103 Superhighway ☏053/211037–41 or 215020–2, east of Thanon Chotana, has a 24hr emergency service and dentistry department; McCormick ☏053/240823–5 is used to farangs and is nearer, on Thanon Kaeo Nawarat; Chiang Mai Ram at 8 Thanon Boonruangrit ☏053/224851–69 also has a good reputation.

Immigration office On the southern leg of the Superhighway, 300m before the airport, on the left (Mon–Fri 8.30am–4.30pm; ☏053/277510).

Internet access Most guest houses and hotels offer access to the internet, and every second shop in town appears to be an internet café, so you should have no problem getting online. Rates vary from as little as B15 per hour in locations near Chiang Mai University to as much as B120 in downtown areas; B60 an hour is the most typical rate, charged at You've Got Mail, with branches at 10 and 69/1 Thanon Kotchasarn; and Net Gate, 22 Thanon Kotchasarn.

Laundry Most guest houses and hotels have an efficient laundry service; if you're stuck, try White House, 31–35 Chang Moi Kao (behind Thanon Chaiyapoom), which charges by the kilo and is affordable and reliable.

Mail The GPO is on Thanon Charoen Muang near the train station. Poste restante and other postal services are available at the usual times (private packing services operate outside on Thanon Charoen Muang); poste restante should be addressed to: Chiang Mai Post and Telegraph Office, Thanon Charoen Muang, Chiang Mai 50000. There are also poste restante facilities at the Phra Singh post office (43 Thanon Samlarn) and the Mae Ping post office on Thanon Wichayanon near Nawarat Bridge. Other post offices can be found on Thanon Phra Pokklao at the junction with Thanon Ratchawithi, at 195/8–9 Thanon Chotana, and at the airport.

Motorbike rental Motorbikes of all shapes and sizes are available for rent around Tha Pae Gate, starting from about B150 per day for a 100cc step-through. Check brakes, lights etc before agreeing to rent. Among rental outlets, the reliable Queen Bee Travel Service, 5 Thanon Moonmuang ☏053/275525 can also offer limited insurance. An expert in motorbike trekking in northern Thailand, David Unkovitch ☏www.geocities.com/goldentriangleerider, lives in Chiang Mai and often leads trekking groups.

Pharmacy Boots, Thanon Chang Klan, in front of the Chiang Inn Plaza; CMU Pharmacy, north side of Thanon Suthep, just east of the junction with Thanon Nimmanheimen.

Swimming Non-guests can use the pool at the *Amari Rincome Hotel*, 301 Thanon Huai Kaeo (daily 10am–7pm; B90); Pong Pot Swimming Pool, 73/22 Soi 4 Thanon Chotana, (daily 8.30am–7.30pm; B20) has one big and one small pool.

Telephones The main office for calling abroad is the Chiang Mai Telecommunication Center (open 24hr) on the Superhighway, just south of the east end of Thanon Charoen Muang, but a more convenient, though pricier, location from which to call abroad is in the basement of the night bazaar. Many Internet cafes offer cheap international calls, but the line is often not clear. The GPO has an overseas phone and fax service until 4.30pm every day.

Tourist police 105/1 Thanon Chiang Mai–Lamphun ☎053/248130 or nationwide helpline ☎1699.
Trains Tickets cannot be booked by phone, but you can call ☎053/247462 (daily 6am–9pm) to check on availability and departure times.
Travel agents TransWorld Travel, 259–261 Thanon Tha Pae ☎053/272415, is reliable for plane and train tickets, while Travel Shoppe, 2/2 Thanon Chaiyapoom ☎053/874091, is good for plane tickets and VIP bus tickets; neither firm charges commission.

Around Chiang Mai

You'll never feel cooped up in Chiang Mai, as the surrounding countryside is dotted with day-trip options in all directions. Dominating the skyline to the west, **Doi Suthep** and its eagle's-nest temple are hard to ignore, and a wander around the pastoral ruins of **Wiang Kum Kam** on the southern periphery has the feel of fresh exploration. Further south, the quiet town of **Lamphun** offers classic sightseeing in the form of historically and religiously significant temples and a museum. To the north, the **Mae Sa valley** may be full of tour buses, but its highlights, the elephant camp and the botanic gardens, as well as the nearby lake of **Huay Tung Tao**, merit an independent jaunt. For honest, unabashed commerce, head for the shopping strip which stretches east towards San Kamphaeng (see p.318); about 23km beyond the weaving village, you can relax at some **hot springs**. All the trips described here can be done in half a day; longer excursions are dealt with later in the chapter.

Doi Suthep

A jaunt up **DOI SUTHEP**, the mountain which rises steeply at the city's western edge is the most satisfying brief trip you can make from Chiang Mai, chiefly on account of beautiful **Wat Phra That Doi Suthep**, which dominates the hillside and gives a towering view over the goings-on in town. This is the north's holiest shrine, its pre-eminence deriving from a magic relic enshrined in its chedi and the miraculous legend of its founding. The original chedi here was built by King Ku Na at the end of the fourteenth century, after the glowing relic of Wat Suan Dork had self-multiplied just before being enshrined. A place had to be found for the clone, so Ku Na put it in a travelling shrine on the back of a white elephant and waited to see where the sacred animal would lead: it eventually climbed Doi Suthep, trumpeted three times, turned round three times, knelt down and died, thereby indicating that this was the spot. Ever since, it's been northern Thailand's most important place of pilgrimage, especially for the candlelit processions on **Maha Puja**, the anniversary of the sermon to the disciples, and **Visakha Puja**, the anniversary of the Buddha's birth, enlightenment and death.

Frequent **songthaews** leave the corner of Manee Noparat and Chotana roads for the sixteen-kilometre trip up to Wat Phra That (B30 to the wat, B60 return, B150 return to include Phuping Palace and Doi Pui village). The road, although steep in places, is paved and well suited for **motorbikes**. At the end

Khruba Srivijaya

Khruba Srivijaya, the most revered monk in northern Thailand, was born in 1877 in a small village 100km south of Chiang Mai. His birth coincided with a supernatural thunderstorm and earthquake, after which he was named In Fuan, "Great Jolt", until he joined the monkhood. A generous and tireless campaigner, he breathed life into Buddhist worship in the north by renovating over a hundred religious sites, including Wat Phra That Haripunjaya in Lamphun and Wat Phra That Doi Tung near Mae Sai. His greatest work, however, was the construction in 1935 of the paved road up to Wat Phra That Doi Suthep, which beforehand could only be reached after a climb of at least five hours. The road was constructed entirely by the voluntary labour of people from all over the north, using the most primitive tools. The project gained such fame that it attracted donations of B20 million, and on any one day as many as four thousand people were working on it. So that people didn't get in each other's way, Khruba Srivijaya declared that each village should contribute 15m of road, but as more volunteers flocked to Chiang Mai, this figure had to be reduced to 3m. The road was completed after just six months, and Khruba Srivijaya took the first ride to the temple in a donated car.

When Khruba Srivijaya died in 1938, Rama VIII was so moved that he sponsored a royal cremation ceremony, held in 1946. The monk's relics were divided up and are now enshrined at Wat Suan Dork in Chiang Mai, Wat Phra Kaeo Don Tao in Lampang and at many other holy places throughout the north.

of Thanon Huai Kaeo, a statue of Khruba Srivijaya, the monk who organized the gargantuan effort to build the road from here to the wat, points the way to the temple.

A signpost halfway up is about the only indication that Doi Suthep is a **national park** (B200), though an entry fee is not levied if you are only visiting the wat, Phuping Palace and Doi Pui village. Despite the nearness of the city, its rich mixed forests support 330 species of birds, and the area is a favoured site for nature study, second in the north only to the larger and less disturbed Doi Inthanon National Park. On the higher slopes near park headquarters (℡ 053/295117) there's a **campsite**, which can only be reached if you have your own transport, and national park **bungalows** (B2000 for ten persons).

About 5km from the statue of Khruba Srivijaya, an unpaved road – rather rutted, so be careful – on the right leads 3km to **Mon Tha Than Falls**, a beautiful spot, believed by some to be home to evil spirits. Camping is possible beside the pretty lower cascade, where refreshment stalls are open during the day. The higher fall is an idyllic five-metre drop into a small bathing pool, completely overhung by thick, humming jungle.

Wat Phra That Doi Suthep

Opposite a car park and souvenir village, a flight of three hundred naga-flanked steps is the last leg on the way to **Wat Phra That Doi Suthep** – a nearby funicular (B20 return) provides a welcome alternative. From the temple's **lower terrace**, the magnificent views of Chiang Mai and the surrounding plain, 1000m below, are best in the early morning or late afternoon, though peaceful contemplation of the view is frequently shattered by people sounding the heavy, dissonant bells around the terrace – it's supposed to bring good luck. At the northwestern corner is a two-metre-high statue of the elephant who, so the story goes, expired on this spot.

Before going to the **upper terrace** you have to remove your shoes – and if you're showing a bit of knee or shoulder, the temple provides wraps to cover your impoliteness. This terrace is possibly the most harmonious piece of temple architecture in Thailand, a dazzling combination of red, green and gold in the textures of carved wood, filigree and gleaming metal – even the tinkling of the miniature bells and the rattling of fortune sticks seem to keep the rhythm. A cloister, decorated with gaudy murals, tightly encloses the terrace, leaving room only for a couple of small minor viharns and the altars and ceremonial gold umbrellas which surround the central focus of attention, the **chedi**. This dazzling gold-plated beacon, a sixteenth-century extension of Ku Na's original, was modelled on the chedi at Wat Phra That Haripunjaya in Lamphun – which previously had been the region's most significant shrine – and has now become a venerated emblem of northern Thailand.

A small *hong*, or swan, on a wire stretching to the pinnacle is used to bless the chedi during major Buddhist festivals: a cup in the swan's beak is filled with water, and a pulley draws the swan to the spire where the water is tipped out over the sides of the chedi. Look out also for an old photograph opposite the northwestern corner of the chedi, showing a cockerel which used to peck the feet of visitors who entered with their shoes on.

Beyond the wat

Songthaews continue another 4km up the paved road to **Phuping Palace** (Fri–Sun & public holidays 8.30–11.30am & 1–4pm; B50), the residence for the royals when they come to visit their village development projects in the north (usually Dec–Feb, when it is closed to the public). There is a viewpoint over the hills to the south, a rose garden and some pleasant trails through the forest, but the buildings themselves are off-limits. About 3km from the palace along a dirt side road and accessible by songthaew, **Ban Doi Pui** is a highly commercialized Hmong village, only worth visiting if you don't have time to get out into the countryside – seeing the Hmong is about all you get out of it.

Wiang Kum Kam

The well-preserved and rarely visited ruins of the ancient city of **WIANG KUM KAM** – traditionally regarded as the prototype for Chiang Mai – are hidden away in the picturesque, rural fringe of town, 5km south of the centre. According to folklore, Wiang Kum Kam was built by King Mengrai as his new capital of the north, but was soon abandoned because of inundation by the Ping River. Recent excavations, however, have put paid to that theory: Wiang Kum Kam was in fact established much earlier, as one of a cluster of fortified satellite towns that surrounded the Mon capital at Lamphun. After Mengrai had conquered Lamphun in 1281, he resided at Kum Kam for a while, raising a chedi, a viharn and several Buddha statues before moving on to build Chiang Mai. Wiang Kum Kam was abandoned sometime before 1750, probably as a result of a Burmese invasion.

About 3km square, the ancient city is best explored on a bicycle or a motorbike, though it's possible to see it by hiring a tuk-tuk for half a day (about B300). The best way to approach Wiang Kum Kam without getting lost is from Route 1141, the southern leg of the Superhighway, which links the airport to Highway 11; immediately to the east of the Ping River bridge, take the signposted turning to the south.

About half of Wiang Kum Kam's 22 known temple sites have now been uncovered, along with a stone slab (now housed in the Chiang Mai National

Museum) inscribed in a unique forerunner of the Thai script, and a hoard of terracotta Buddha images. It's easiest to head first for **Chedi Si Liam**, reached 1km after the Ping River bridge, which provides a useful landmark: this much-restored Mon chedi, in the shape of a tall, squared-off pyramid with niched Buddha images, was built by Mengrai on the model of Wat Kukut in Lamphun, and is still part of a working temple.

Backtracking along the road you've travelled down from Chiang Mai, take the first right turn, turn right again and keep left through a scattered farming settlement to reach, after about 2km, **Wat Kan Thom** (aka Chang Kham), the centre of the old city and still an important place of worship. Archeologists were only able to get at the site after much of it had been levelled by bulldozers building a playground for the adjacent school, but they have managed to uncover the brick foundations of Mengrai's viharn. The modern spirit house next to it is where Mengrai's soul is said to reside. Also in the grounds are a white chedi and a small viharn, both much restored, and a large new viharn displaying fine craftsmanship.

The real joy now is to head off along the trails through the thick foliage of the longan plantations to the northwest of Wat Kan Thom, back towards Chedi Si Liam. On this route, you come across surprisingly well-preserved chedis and the red-brick walls of Wiang Kum Kam's temples in a handful of shady clearings, with only a few stray cows and sprouting weeds for company.

Lamphun

Though capital of its own province, **LAMPHUN** lives in the shadow of the tourist attention (and baht) showered on Chiang Mai, 26km to the north. Yet for anyone interested in history, a visit to this former royal city is a must. The town's largely plain architecture is given some character by the surrounding waterways, beyond which stretch lush rice fields and plantations of *lam yai* (longan); the sweetness of the local variety is celebrated every year in early August at the **Ngan Lam Yai** (Longan Festival), when the town comes alive with processions of fruity floats, a drum-beating competition and a Miss Lam Yai beauty contest. Lamphun also offers a less frantic alternative to Chiang Mai during the Songkhran and Loy Krathong festivals (see box on p.314), the Khuang River being a far less congested place to float your *krathong* than Chiang Mai's Ping River. Though the streets of the town are usually sleepy, the ancient working **temples** of Wat Phra That Haripunjaya and Wat Kukut are lively and worth aiming for on a half-day trip from Chiang Mai. A full-day visit could include Wat Mahawan and the Chama Thevi monument, as well as a stroll round the town's market.

Lamphun claims to be the oldest continuously inhabited town in Thailand, and has a history dating back to the early ninth century when the ruler of the major Dvaravati centre at Lopburi sent his daughter, Chama Thevi, to found the Buddhist state of **Haripunjaya** here. Under the dynasty she established, Haripunjaya flourished as a link in the trade route to Yunnan in southwest China, although it eventually came under the suzerainty of the Khmers at Angkor, probably in the early eleventh century. In 1281, after a decade of scheming, King Mengrai of Chiang Mai conquered Lamphun and integrated it once and for all into the Thai state of Lanna, which by then covered all of the north country.

The Town

Chama Thevi's planners are said to have based their design for the town on the shape of an auspicious conch shell. The rough outcome is a rectangle, narrower at the north end than the south, with the Khuang River running down its kilometre-long east side, and moats around the north, west and south sides. The main street, Thanon Inthayongyot, bisects the conch from north to south, while the road to Wat Kukut (Thanon Chama Thevi) heads out from the middle of the west moat.

One of the north's grandest and most important temples, **Wat Phra That Haripunjaya** (B20) has its rear entrance on Thanon Inthayongyot and its bot and ornamental front entrance facing the river. The earliest guess at the date of its founding is 897, when the king of Haripunjaya is said to have built a chedi to enshrine a hair of the Buddha. More certain is the date of the main rebuilding of the temple, under King Tilokaraja of Chiang Mai in 1443, when the present ringed chedi was erected in the then-fashionable Sri Lankan style (later copied at Doi Suthep and Lampang). Clad in brilliant copper plates, it has since been raised to a height of about 50m, crowned by a gold umbrella.

The plain open courtyards around the chedi contain a compendium of religious structures in a wild mix of styles and colours. On the north side, the tiered Haripunjaya-style pyramid of **Chedi Suwanna** was built in 1418 as a replica of the chedi at nearby Wat Kukut. You get a whiff of southern Thailand in the open space beyond the Suwanna chedi, where the **Chedi Chiang Yan** owes its resemblance to a pile of flattened pumpkins to the Srivijayan style. On either side of the viharn (to the east of the main chedi) stand a dark red **belltower**, containing what's claimed to be the world's largest bronze gong, and a weather-beaten **library** on a raised base. Just to add to the temple's mystique, an open pavilion at the southwestern corner of the chedi shelters a stone indented with four overlapping **footprints**, believed by fervent worshippers to confirm an ancient legend that the Buddha once passed this way. Next to the pavilion can be seen a small **museum** which houses bequests to the temple, including some beautiful Buddha images in the Lanna style. Finally, beside the back entrance, is the **Phra Chao Tan Jai**, a graceful standing Buddha, surrounded by graphic murals that depict a horrific version of Buddhist hell.

Across the main road from the wat's back entrance, the **National Museum** (Wed–Sun 9am–noon & 1–4pm; B30) contains a well-organized but not quite compelling collection of religious finds, and occasionally stages some interesting temporary exhibitions. The terracotta and bronze Buddha images here give the best overview of the distinctive features of the Haripunjaya style: large curls above a wide, flat forehead, bulging eyes, incised moustache and enigmatic smile.

Art-history buffs will get a thrill out of **Wat Chama Thevi** (aka Wat Kukut), where two brick chedis, dated to 1218, are the only complete examples not just of Haripunjaya architecture, but of the whole Dvaravati style. Queen Chama Thevi is supposed to have chosen the site by ordering an archer to fire an arrow from the city's western gate – to retrace his epic shot, follow the road along the National Museum's southern wall to the west gate at the city moat, and keep going for nearly 1km along Thanon Chama Thevi. The main chedi – Suwan Chang Kot – is tiered and rectangular, the smaller Ratana Chedi octagonal, and both are inset with niches sheltering beautiful, wide-browed Buddha images in stucco, typical of the Haripunjaya style. Suwan Chang Kot, believed to enshrine Chama Thevi's ashes, lost its pinnacle at some stage, giving rise to the name Wat Kukut, the temple with the "topless" chedi.

On your way back to the town centre from Wat Chama Thevi, you might like to pop in at **Wat Mahawan**, located just outside the west gate. The temple has been recently renovated and features some huge and fearsome nagas standing guard at the entrance to the viharn. Following the moat to the south from here brings you in about five minutes to the **Queen Chama Thevi monument**, situated in a large square by the moat in the southwest corner of the city; the monument receives a steady stream of locals making offerings to their heroine. Beside it is the town's main market, which mostly sells fresh produce and buzzes with activity in the morning.

Practicalities

The direct (and scenic) route from Chiang Mai to Lamphun is Highway 106, for much of the way a stately avenue lined by thirty-metre-tall *yang* trees. The best way to cover this route is to rent a motorbike, or catch a blue **songthaew** from the Chiang Mai–Lamphun road, just south of Narawat bridge and opposite the TAT office, which will put you off outside the back entrance of Wat Haripunjaya. If you turn up at Lamphun by **train**, it's a thirty-minute walk or a samlor ride southwest to the town centre.

Among the few **restaurants** in Lamphun with an English-language menu is *Lamphun Ice*, which serves tasty Thai food at reasonable prices; it's conveniently situated just south of Wat Haripunjaya at 6 Thanon Chaimongkol. Basic inexpensive Thai food is available at cafés on Thanon Inthayongyot to the south of Wat Haripunjaya. It's unlikely you'll want to stay overnight in Lamphun, as it makes a perfect day-trip from Chiang Mai and there's not a wide range of **accommodation**. The only decent choice in town is the *Supamit Holiday Inn* (☎053/534865–6; ❹), a large modern building with en-suite rooms on Thanon Chama Thevi opposite Wat Kukut.

The hot springs

Thirty-five kilometres east of Chiang Mai, the **San Kamphaeng hot springs**, with their geysers, baths and gardens, as well as a resort, make for a wonderfully indulgent day-trip, easily accomplished by motorbike. The quickest way there, about 45 minutes at a good speed, is to take Highway 11 southeast of Chiang Mai, then turn left onto Route 1317, which heads eastwards as dual carriageway for much of the way before veering north towards Highway 118, the main Chiang Mai–Chiang Rai road (look for the turning on the left after about 35km, signposted "Hot Springs" in English). The slow route, heading east out of the city on Route 1008 through San Kamphaeng (see p.318) before turning north onto Route 1317, allows you to combine mineral bathing with some handicrafts shopping.

The government-run hot springs (B20) have pleasantly landscaped gardens, geysers that spout scalding water about 10m high, and mineral baths. Right next door, set in its own expansive gardens, is the *Rong Aroon Hot Springs Resort* (☎053/248475, ⓕ248491). It's perfect for a visit of a few hours, providing a soothing tonic to the general stresses of travel, though options do include staying in **bungalows** (❼), which have hot spring water piped into them. If you're not a guest, the main gate charges B20 admission to the property, and for another B60 you can take advantage of the utilitarian bath house which offers hot baths in a private room (towels provided). Massages, mud baths and facials are available at reasonable prices in a separate building to the left of the main bath house, and there are even jacuzzi baths (B120) and a swimming pool. The water at the source is over 90°C (Thai visitors can be seen here boiling eggs in tiny bamboo baskets). You can have a restaurant lunch on the bougainvillea-draped terrace overlooking the hot spring geyser, or take a picnic to eat in the grounds.

Huay Tung Tao and the Mae Sa valley

On the north side of Chiang Mai, Thanon Chotana turns into Highway 107, which heads off through a flat, featureless valley, past a golf course and an army camp, towards the small market town of **Mae Rim** 16km away. With your own transport, you can head off down side roads to the west of Highway 107, either to Huay Tung Tao for a swim and chillout, or to the Mae Sa valley, which despite its theme-park atmosphere has sufficient attractions for an interesting half- or full day out, and some pretty resorts that might even tempt you to spend a night out of Chiang Mai. Without your own vehicle, it's best to visit as part of a tour group as public transport here is at best sporadic — try Gem Travel, 209/2 Sridornchai Soi 6, Chiang Mai (℡053/272855; around B550 for a half-day trip).

About 10km out of Chiang Mai, look for the signpost to the left to **Huay Tung Tao**, a large lake at the base of Doi Suthep, 2km to the west of the turn-off along a dirt road which is easily driven. A great place to cool off during the hot season, the lake is safe to swim in and is also used by anglers and windsurfers. Simple shelters along the water's edge provide shade from the sun, and food vendors sell sticky rice, grilled chicken and *som tam* (green papaya salad).

Turn left about 1km after Mae Rim to enter the **Mae Sa valley**, where a good sealed road, Route 1069, leads up into the hills. The main road through the valley passes a snake farm, a monkey circus, orchid and butterfly farms and the unspectacular **Mae Sa Waterfall** (B200 national park fee payable), where you can walk up a peaceful trail passing lots of little cascades along the way. Several elephant camps also lie along the route, of which the best is the **Mae Sa Elephant Camp**, 10km along the valley road (though you'd be better off going to the more ecologically sound Elephant Conservation Centre near Lampang; see p.341). Mae Sa offers logging shows at 8am and 9.40am daily (B80, children B40) and you can take a short ride on an elephant (B80) or a more expensive ride into the countryside (about B400 an hour).

Two kilometres beyond the Mae Sa Elephant Camp, the magnificent **Queen Sirikit Botanic Gardens** (B20, children B10, vehicles B50) are well worth a look, and if you are at all botanically inclined, you could easily spend the whole day here as it covers such a large area. A vehicle is certainly necessary to get to the upper area where glasshouses display a fantastic array of plants.

Among several **resorts** in the Mae Sa valley, the pick is the *Regent* (℡053/298181–9, ℻298190, ⓦwww.regenthotels.com; ❾), down a side road on the left just 1km after the turning into the valley from Mae Rim. The last word in Lanna luxury, this award-winning resort has superbly appointed pavilions, plush apartments, a swimming pool, a gym and spa, set among beautifully landscaped grounds. Even if you're not staying there, it's a good spot to stop, especially in the late afternoon or early evening, to enjoy a meal or drink on a terrace with a lovely view across hills to the west. Other resorts in the valley are far simpler than the *Regent*, but attractive nonetheless; among these the *Pong Yang Garden Resort* (℡053/879151–2, ℻879153; ❼) stands out, located a couple of kilometres beyond the botanic gardens on the south side of the road. It boasts well-equipped bungalows as well as a restaurant with a view of an attractive waterfall.

Once you've seen all you want to in the valley, you have the option of retracing your route to Chiang Mai, or continuing west for a scenic drive in the country. For the latter, turn left on to Route 1269 before Samoeng, and follow this road as it swoops up and down over hills, skirting Doi Suthep to join Highway 108 8km south of Chiang Mai, a two-hour drive in all.

East of Chiang Mai

From Chiang Mai, visitors usually head west to Mae Hong Son or north to Chiang Rai, but a trip eastwards to the ancient city-states of Lampang, Phrae and Nan can be just as rewarding, not only for the dividends of going against the usual flow, but also for the natural beauty of the region's upland ranges – seen to best effect from the well-marked trails of **Doi Khun Tan National Park** – and its eccentric variety of Thai, Burmese and Laotian art and architecture. Congenial **Lampang** contains Thai wats to rival those of Chiang Mai for beauty – in Wat Phra That Lampang Luang the town has the finest surviving example of traditional northern architecture anywhere – and is further endowed with pure Burmese temples and some fine old city architecture, while little-visited **Phrae**, to the southeast, is a step back in time to a simpler Thailand. Harder to reach but a more intriguing target is **Nan**, with its heady artistic mix of Thai and Laotian styles and steep ring of scenic mountains.

A few major **roads**, served by regular through buses from Chiang Mai, cross the region: Highway 11 heads southeast through Lampang and the junction town of Den Chai before plummeting south to Phitsanulok; from Lampang Highway 1 heads north to Chiang Rai; and from Den Chai Highway 101 carries on northeast through Phrae to Nan, almost on the border with Laos. With the completion of Route 1148 between Tha Wang Pha and Chiang Kham, it is now much easier to continue north from Nan to Chiang Rai, through some spectacular scenery. The northern **rail line** follows a course roughly parallel with Highway 11 through the region, including a stop at Doi Khun Tan National Park, and although trains here are generally slower than buses, the Lampang and Den Chai stations are useful if you're coming up from Bangkok.

Doi Khun Tan National Park

One of three national parks close to Chiang Mai, along with Suthep and Inthanon, **DOI KHUN TAN NATIONAL PARK** (B200) is easily accessible by train from Chiang Mai: the 1362-metre-long rail tunnel, thought to be the longest in Thailand, and completed by German engineers in 1918, actually cuts through the mountain slope. Even so, the park is actually the least spoilt of the three; a former hill station, it was not declared a national park until 1975 and a lack of tourist infrastructure until recently has meant that it has had few visitors. With food and accommodation now more easily available, it is cautiously opening up to tourists: two café-restaurants have been opened, the campsite has been improved and the bungalow accommodation is very good. One of the other appeals of Doi Khun Tan National Park is that no road runs through the park itself – it can most easily be reached by **train** from Chiang Mai.

The park

Covering 255 square kilometres, the park's vegetation varies from bamboo forests at an altitude of 350m to tropical evergreen forests between 600 and 1000m; the 1363-metre summit of Doi Khun Tan is known for its wild flowers, including orchids. Most of the small mammal species in the park are squirrels, but you're more likely to see some birds, with over 182 species found here. A leaflet on the park's ecology can be obtained at the park **headquarters**. The **trails** have all been improved and are clearly marked. There are short nature trails around the park headquarters (where self-guided maps are available), while three major trails all eventually lead to the summit of **Doi Khun Tan**, the highest summit reachable on self-guided trails in the Chiang Mai area; with impressive views of the surrounding countryside, it's clear how it fulfilled its role as a World War II military lookout. The main 8.3-kilometre trail from the train station to the Doi Khun Tan summit, though steep, is very easy, divided into four quarters of approximately 2km each with each quarter ending at a resting place. While you shouldn't have a problem reaching the summit and returning to the station in a day, a more rewarding option is to do the walk in two days, staying overnight in the bungalows or the campsite – both situated on picturesque peaks – approximately halfway along the trail. Alternatively, you can take a circular route to the summit and back, forsaking a large chunk of the main trail for the two subsidiary trails which curve around either side, taking in two **waterfalls**.

Practicalities

Though there are five daily **trains** from Chiang Mai (1hr 30min) which stop at the park, at least three of these arrive after dark, so day-trippers should make a very early start (leaving Chiang Mai at 6.35am and taking the last train back at 6.32pm; check current timetables). Get off at Khun Tan station, from where the park headquarters are 1300m up the summit trail. A **car** or motorbike can also take you to the park headquarters, though no further: follow Highway 11 to the turn-off to Mae Tha and head northeast along a partly paved road, following signs for the park, a further 18km away.

The park is most popular on weekends, when the majority of Thai people visit, and during the cool season. Park **bungalows** (B1200 for six people), are located 2.5km along the main trail from the headquarters, while tents can be hired (B100) for the **campsite**, which is a little further along the trail (pitching your own costs B30). There is a small **restaurant** just up from the train ticket office, and food is also available at a shop and café near the headquarters. Campground stalls sell meals at weekends except in the rainy season.

Lampang and around

Slow passes and long tunnels breach the narrow, steep belt of mountains between Chiang Mai and **LAMPANG**, the north's second-largest town, 100km to the southeast. Lampang is an important transport hub – Highway 11, Highway 1 and the northern rail line all converge here – and given its undeniably low-key attractions, nearly all travellers sail through it on their way to the more trumpeted sights further north. But unlike most other provincial capitals, Lampang has the look of a place where history has not been completely wiped out: houses, shops and temples survive in the traditional style, and the town makes few concessions to tourism. Out of town, the beautiful complex of Wat Phra That Lampang Luang is the main attraction in these parts, but while you're in the neighbourhood you could also stop by to watch a show at the Elephant Conservation Centre, on the road from Chiang Mai.

Founded as Kelang Nakhon by the ninth-century Haripunjaya queen Chama Thevi, Lampang became important enough for one of her two sons to rule here after her death. After King Mengrai's conquest of Haripunjaya in 1281, Lampang suffered much the same ups and downs as the rest of Lanna, enjoying a burst of prosperity as a **timber** town at the end of the nineteenth century, when it supported a population of twenty thousand people and four thousand working elephants. Many of its temples are financially endowed by the waves of outsiders who have settled in Lampang: refugees from Chiang Saen (who were forcibly resettled here by Rama I at the beginning of the nineteenth century), Burmese teak-loggers and workers, and, more recently, rich Thai pensioners attracted by the town's sedate charm.

The Town

The modern centre of Lampang sprawls along the south side of the Wang River, with its most frenetic commercial activity taking place along Thanon Boonyawat and Robwiang near Ratchada Bridge. Here, you'll find stalls and shops selling the famous local pottery, a kitsch combination of whites, blues and browns, made from the area's rich kaolin clay.

Lampang's few sights are well scattered; the best place to start is on the north side of the river (the site of the original Haripunjaya settlement), whose leafy suburbs today contain the town's most important and interesting temple, **Wat Phra Kaeo Don Tao** (B20). An imposing, rather forbidding complex on Thanon Phra Kaeo, 1km northeast of the Ratchada Bridge, the temple was founded in the fifteenth century to enshrine the Phra Kaeo Don Tao image, now residing at Wat Phra That Lampang Luang (see p.339). For 32 years it also housed the Emerald Buddha (local stories aver this to be a copy of Phra Kaeo Don Tao), a situation which came about when an elephant carrying the holy image from Chiang Rai to Chiang Mai made an unscheduled and therefore auspicious halt here in 1436. The clean, simple lines of the white, gold-capped **chedi**, which is reputed to contain a hair of the Buddha, form a shining backdrop to the wat's most interesting building, a Burmese **mondop** stacked up in

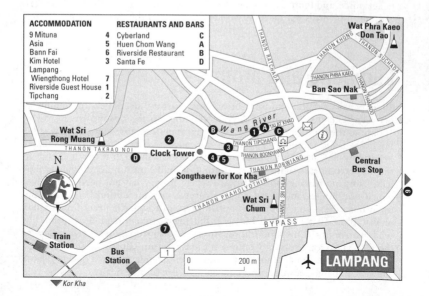

extravagantly carved tiers; it was built in 1909 by craftsmen from the local Burmese community, employed for the task by a Thai prince (whose British-style coat of arms can be seen on the ceiling inside). All gilt and gaudy coloured glass, the interior decoration is a real fright, mixing Oriental and European influences, with some incongruously cute little cherubs on the ceiling. The mondop's boyish bronze centrepiece has the typical features of a Mandalay Buddha, with its jewelled headband, inset black and white eyes, and exaggerated, dangling ears, which denote the Buddha's supernatural ability to hear everything in the universe. In front of the Buddha is an image of Khruba Srivijaya, the north's most venerated monk (see box on p.328).

The small, gloomy **museum** diagonally opposite the mondop displays some dainty china among its exhibits, but its main focus is woodcarving, a craft at which Burmese artisans excel. To see a better, though still small, display of ceramics, lacquerware and teak furnishings, make your way to **Ban Sao Nak** ("many pillar house") at 6 Thanon Ratwattana, not far from Wat Phra Kaeo Don Tao (daily 10am–5pm, B30 with free soft drink). This sprawling wooden mansion is supported by a maze of teak pillars and contains some interesting fading photographs of its former occupants, who were local notables.

The Burmese who worked on Wat Phra Kaeo Don Tao were brought to Lampang in the late nineteenth century when, after the British conquest of Upper Burma, timber companies expanded their operations as far as northern Thailand. Fearing that the homeless spirits of fallen trees would seek vengeance, the Burmese logging workers often sponsored the building of temples, most of which still stand, to try to appease the tree spirits and gain merit. Though the spirits had to wait nearly a century, they seem to have got their revenge: due to a short circuit in some dodgy wiring, the viharn of **Wat Sri Chum**, the most important and beautiful Burmese temple in town, burnt to the ground in 1992. Now restored to its former glory, with fresh carvings and murals by Burmese craftsmen, it's sited in a small grove of bodhi trees five minutes' walk south of Thanon Robwiang. None of the remaining wats is of outstanding architectural merit, but to get more of a flavour of Burma, try **Wat Sri Rong Muang**, towards the west end of Thanon Takrao Noi, which presents a dazzling ensemble: the crazy angles of its red and yellow roof shelter more Mandalay Buddhas and several extravagantly carved gilt sermon thrones, swimming in a glittering sea of coloured-glass wall tiles.

When you've had your fill of temples, the streets of the **Talat Kao**, the "Old Market" (also known as Talat Jiin, "Chinese Market") around Thanon Tipchang, are good for a stroll, especially in the early morning. Now a quiet area of shophouses and mansions, it shows a mixture of Burmese, Chinese and European influence, with intricate balconies, carved gables and unusual sunburst designs carved over some of the doors. Small lanes on the north side of the Talat Kao lead down to the Wang River, whose waters are as green as some of its overgrown banks – what used to be the main thoroughfare for trading boats and huge rafts of felled timber has been reduced almost to stagnation by an upriver dam. Unfortunately a large section of the river bank through the main part of town is now stripped of its greenery, and the sandy soil and concrete tiers make for an ugly view.

Practicalities

Buses from Nawarat Bridge in Chiang Mai run to Lampang every thirty minutes from Thanon Chiang Mai–Lamphun, just south of Narawat bridge, for most of the day, some of which then trundle on up Highway 1 to Phayao and Chiang

Rai. Ten buses a day from Chiang Mai's Arcade station also stop at Lampang on their way to Nan. Only six **trains** a day stop here in each direction; the **train and bus stations** lie less than 1km to the southwest of town, and many buses also stop on Thanon Phaholyothin in the centre. The **airport** is located just south of town, and songthaews are on hand for the short ride to the centre. The small, primitive **tourist information** centre (Mon–Fri 9am–noon & 1–4pm), at the Provincial Office on the corner of Thanon Boonyawat and Pakham, can help with advice on excursions to the elephant training centre and the like.

The whole town can be covered on foot without trouble, though to get out to Wat Phra Kaeo Don Tao you might want to hop on one of the many **songthaews** which cruise the streets. **Horse-drawn carriages**, which have become an incongruous symbol of Lampang (in fact, Thais call it "horse-cart city"), can be hired in the centre (B150 for 10min, B200 for 30min or B300 for 1hr), complete with Stetson-wearing driver.

Accommodation

Among its accommodation prospects, Lampang has two delightful **guest houses** which themselves provide reason enough to stay here. Run by the owners of the restaurant of the same name (see below), the *Riverside Guest House*, 286 Thanon Talat Kao (T054/227005, F322342; ❸–❹), is a peaceful traditional compound of elegantly decorated rooms, all with hot- or cold-water bathrooms; some rooms boast balconies overlooking the river. The helpful Belgian owner is a good source of local information and she can rent out motorbikes. About 4km from the centre on the east side of Highway 1 towards Chiang Rai, *Bann Fai* (T & F054/224602; ❸) is most useful for those with their own transport. Named "Cotton House" for the spinning and weaving which you can watch in a small workshop, the complex also comprises a good handicrafts shop and an attractive outdoor restaurant, as well as rooms in a wooden house at the back, sparsely but tastefully decorated with low antique dressing tables and triangular "axe" pillows, and sharing bathrooms.

The town's lowest-priced **hotels** queue up to the west of the centre along Thanon Boonyawat. Among them are some dismal, dirty affairs, but the best of the bunch has long been *9 (Kao) Mituna Hotel*, set back from the road at no. 285 (T054/217438, 222261; ❶–❷) with basic fan and air-con rooms. For a little more cash, standards improve markedly: the *Kim Hotel* at no. 168 (T054/217721; ❹) has rooms with air-con, TV and hot water, while those almost opposite at the *Asia Lampang Hotel*, 229 Thanon Boonyawat (T054/227844–7, F224436, Easiahotel@lampang1.a-net.th; ❹), are clean, comfortable and good value. At the top end are two luxury hotels, the sprawling 235-room *Lampang Wiengthong Hotel*, 138/109 Thanon Phaholyothin (T054/225801–2, F225803; ❼), popular with businessmen; and the smaller, more tourist-orientated *Tipchang Hotel*, to the west at 54/22 Thanon Takrao Noi (T054/226501–6, F225362; ❺), both with their own swimming pools.

Eating and drinking

A popular place to **eat and drink** is the *Riverside* at 328 Thanon Tipchang, a cosy, relaxing spot on terraces overlooking the water. A wide variety of excellent Thai and Western food (moderate–expensive), including pizza, is served here to the sounds of live music. A quieter ambience prevails at *Huen Chom Wang*, 276 Thanon Talat Kao, where guests are greeted by beautifully arranged blossoms floating in water bowls on the stairway. The sprawling wooden building has fine views of the river and its menu features many northern specialities (moderate–expensive). *Cyberland*, at 258/13–14 Thanon Tipchang, provides a clever combination of cheap eats and drinks along with cable TV and inexpensive web surfing. The stretch of Thanon Takrao Noi between the clocktower and Thanon Wienglakon is lively at night with many simple restaurants and a night market running off its side streets. Also along Thanon Takrao Noi are a few Wild West **bars** – Lampang obviously takes its Stetson-wearing image seriously – including *Santa Fe*, near the corner of Thanon Wienglakon. In this area, there are also pubs, discos and karaoke bars that attract the town's youth after dark.

Wat Phra That Lampang Luang

If you've made it as far as Lampang, a visit to **Wat Phra That Lampang Luang**, a grand and well-preserved capsule of beautiful Lanna art and architecture, is a must, one of the architectural highlights of northern Thailand. However, although the wat is a busy pilgrimage site, **getting there** without your own transport isn't always straightforward: some songthaews will take you to the temple direct from outside the Thai Farmers Bank on Thanon Robwiang (B30); otherwise, take one to **Kor Kha**, 10km southwest on Highway 1 (B15), then take another towards **Hang Chat** and get off at the temple entrance. If you're getting there yourself on a motorbike (which can be rented in Lampang from the *Riverside Guest House*) or other transport, cross the bridge over the Mae Nam Wang at Kor Kha and turn right, heading north on a paved road.

The wat was built early in the Haripunjaya era as a *wiang* (fortress), one of a satellite group around Lampang – you can still see remains of the threefold ramparts in the farming village around the temple. A naga staircase leads you up to a wedding cake of a gatehouse, richly decorated with stucco, which is set in the original brick boundary walls. Just inside, the oversized **viharn** is open on all sides in classic Lanna fashion, and shelters a spectacular centrepiece: known as a *ku*, a feature found only in the viharns of northern Thailand, this gilded brick tower looks like a bonfire for the main Buddha image sitting inside, the Phra Chao Lan Thong. If you're over 1.8m tall, mind your head on the panels hanging from the low eaves, which are decorated with attractive, though fading, early nineteenth-century paintings of battles, palaces and nobles in traditional Burmese gear.

This central viharn is snugly flanked by three others. In front of the murky, beautifully decorated viharn to the left, look out for a wooden *tung chai* carved with flaming, coiled nagas, used as a heraldic banner for northern princes. The battered, cosy **Viharn Nam Tame**, second back on the right, dates back to the early sixteenth century. Its drooping roof configuration is archetypal: divided into three tiers, each of which is divided again into two layers, it ends up almost scraping the ground. Under the eaves you can just make out fragments of panel paintings, as old as the viharn, illustrating a story of one of the exploits of the Hindu god Indra.

Hundreds of rainy seasons have turned the copper plates on the wat's huge central **chedi** into an arresting patchwork of greens, blues and purples: safe inside are supposed to be a hair of the Buddha and ashes from the right side of his forehead and neck. By the chedi's northwest corner, a sign points to a drainage hole in the wat's boundary wall, once the scene of an unlikely act of derring-do: in 1736, local hero Thip Chang managed to wriggle through the tiny hole and free the *wiang* from the occupying Burmese, before going on to liberate the whole of Lampang.

A gate in the south side of the boundary wall leads to a spreading **bodhi tree** on crutches: merit-makers have donated hundreds of supports to prop up its drooping branches. The tree, with its own small shrine standing underneath, is believed to be inhabited by spirits, and the sick are sometimes brought here in search of a cure.

Don't miss the small, unimpressive viharn to the west of the main complex – it's the home of **Phra Kaeo Don Tao**, the much-revered companion image to Bangkok's Emerald Buddha, and the wat's main focus of pilgrimage. Legend has it that the statuette first appeared in the form of an emerald found in a watermelon presented by a local woman to a venerated monk. The two of them tried to carve a Buddha out of the emerald, without much success, until the god Indra appeared and fashioned the marvellous image, at which point the ungrateful townsfolk accused the monk of having an affair with the woman and put her to death, thus bringing down upon the town a series of disasters which confirmed the image's awesome power. In all probability, the image was carved at the beginning of the fifteenth century, when its namesake wat in Lampang was founded. Peering through the dim light and the rows of protective bars inside the viharn, you can just make out the tiny meditating Buddha – it's actually made of jasper, not emerald – which on special occasions is publicly displayed wearing a headdress and necklace.

Cashing in on Phra Kaeo Don Tao's supernatural reputation, a shop in the viharn sells amulets and Buddha images. Outside the wat, simple snacks, handicrafts and antiques can be bought from market stalls; also available are the small china cows with which devotees make merit, inscribing the models first with

---

The elephant in Thailand

To Thais the Asian elephant has profound spiritual significance, derived from both Hindu and Buddhist mythologies. Carvings and statues of Ganesh, the Hindu god with an elephant's head, feature on ancient temples all over the country and, as the god of knowledge and remover of obstacles, Ganesh has been adopted as the symbol of the Fine Arts Department – and is thus depicted on all entrance tickets to historical sights. The Hindu deity Indra rarely appears without his three-headed elephant mount Erawan, and miniature devotional elephant effigies are sold at major Brahmin shrines, such as Bangkok's Erawan shrine. In Buddhist legend, the future Buddha's mother was able to conceive only after she dreamt that a white elephant had entered her womb: that is why elephant balustrades encircle many of the Buddhist temples of Sukhothai, and why the rare white elephant is accorded royal status (see p.151) and regarded as a highly auspicious animal.

The practical role of the elephant in Thailand was once almost as great as its symbolic importance. The kings of Ayutthaya relied on elephants to take them into battle against the Burmese – one king assembled a trained elephant army of three hundred – and during the nineteenth century King Rama IV offered Abraham Lincoln a male and a female to "multiply in the forests of America" and to use in the Civil War. In times of peace, the phenomenal strength of the elephant has made it invaluable as a beast of burden: elephants hauled the stone from which the gargantuan Khmer temple complexes of the north and northeast were built, and for centuries they have been used to clear forests and carry timber.

The traditional cycle for domestic elephants is to be born in captivity, spending the first three years of their lives with their mothers (who get five years' maternity leave), before being forcibly separated and raised with other calves in training schools. From the age of three each elephant is assigned its own mahout – a trainer, keeper and driver rolled into one – who will stay with it for the rest of its working life. Training begins gently, with mahouts taking months to earn the trust of their charge; over the

their name and the date in black ink and then offering them to the shrine in front of the chedi, making a curious display.

The Elephant Conservation Centre

The **Elephant Conservation Centre** (℡054/229042 or 228034), 37km northwest of Lampang on Highway 11, is the most authentic place in Thailand to see elephants displaying their skills and, being more out of the way, is less touristy than the elephant showgrounds to the north of Chiang Mai.

Run by the veterinary section of the Thai forestry organization, the conservation centre was originally set up in 1969 in another nearby location as a young elephant training centre, the earliest of its kind in Thailand. However, with the high levels of elephant unemployment since the ban on logging (see box below), the new centre, opened in 1992, emphasizes the preservation of the elephant in Thailand. By promoting eco-tourism the centre is providing employment for the elephants and enabling Thai people to continue their historically fond relationship with these animals. Money raised from entrance fees helps to finance the **elephant hospital** here, which cares for sick, abused, ageing and abandoned elephants. Its yearly expenses are 12–14 million baht, with huge expenses incurred from nursing about sixty elephants; the enormous amounts of money the centre needs to feed and care for its elephants mean it is in a permanent funding crisis.

next thirteen years the elephant is taught about forty different commands, from simple "stop" and "go" orders to complex instructions for hooking and passing manoeuvres with the trunk. By the age of sixteen an elephant is ready to be put to work and is expected to carry on working until it reaches 50 or so; the law requires it must be retired at 60, though it can live for another 20 years.

Ironically, the **timber industry** has been the animal's undoing. Mechanized logging has destroyed the wild elephant's preferred river-valley grassland and forest habitats, forcing them into isolated upland pockets. As a result, Thailand's population of wild elephants is now only about two thousand. With the 1989 **ban on commercial logging** within Thai borders – after the 1988 catastrophe when the effects of deforestation killed a hundred people and wiped out villages in Surat Thani province, as mudslides swept down deforested slopes carrying cut timber with them – the domesticated population, numbering about three thousand, is becoming less useful. The biggest problem facing these elephants and their mahouts nowadays is **unemployment**. The estimated 250 elephants working on the illegal teak-logging trade are often abused and overworked, while mahouts who can no longer find work for their animals are forced to abandon them since they cannot afford the vast amount of food needed to sustain the creature – about 125kg a day. The discarded animals destroy forests and crops and are often hunted down and killed. In town streets and on beaches, you'll often see those mahouts who keep their elephants charging both tourists for the experience of handfeeding them bananas, and Thais for the chance to stoop under their trunks for good luck. Training schools now concentrate as much on perfecting shows for tourists as on honing the elephants' practical skills, and another lucrative alternative tourist industry is elephant trekking. The Elephant Conservation Centre near Lampang estimates that if drastic measures are not taken, in twenty years' time the elephant could be extinct in Thailand, where the population has dropped by about fifteen thousand since 1984.

An interpretive centre has exhibits on the history of the elephant in Thailand and elephant rides (B100 for 10min, B200 for 30min or B400 for 1hr) are available, while **shows** (daily 10am & 11am plus Sat & Sun 1.30pm; B50) put the elephants through their paces, with plenty of amusing showmanship and loud trumpeting for their audience. After some photogenic bathing, they walk together in formation and go through a routine of pushing and dragging logs, then proceed to paint pictures, play instruments and walk through scattered eggs without breaking them. You can buy bananas and sugar cane to feed them after the show.

Practicalities

The Elephant Conservation Centre is best visited en route between Chiang Mai and Lampang: ask the bus conductor for Suan Pa (Forest Park) Thung Kwian, 70km from Chiang Mai. On a day-trip from Lampang, a bus towards Lamphun or Chiang Mai should get you to the entrance gates in around thirty minutes, but you'll still have a couple of kilometres to walk from there. If you have your own vehicle, the Thung Kwian **market**, 21km from Lampang on Highway 11, offers not only a useful stop for refreshments near the Elephant Centre, but also a chance to view the panoply of forest products on sale – from wild pigs, squirrels and birds to honeycombs, bugs and creepy crawlies of every description. This is a favourite spot for city Thais to pick up some exotic taste to take back home with them.

Phrae and around

From Lampang, buses follow Highway 11 to the junction town of Den Chai (Bangkok–Chiang Mai trains also stop here), 83km to the southeast, then veer northeastwards on Highway 101 through the tobacco-rich Yom valley, dotted with distinctive brick curing-houses. Frequent songthaews from Den Chai head for the small city of **PHRAE**, 20km further on, the capital of the province of the same name which is famous for woodcarving and the quality of its *seua maw hawm*, the deep-blue, baggy working shirt seen all over Thailand (produced in the village of Ban Thung Hong, 4km north of Phrae on Highway 101). If you're driving here from Lampang, turn left from Highway 11 at **Mae Khaem** onto Route 1023 and approach the town via Long and some lovely scenery.

The main reason to stop in Phrae is to explore the old city, delineated by an earthen moat, with its lanes filled with traditional teak houses – as in Lampang, the former logging industry attracted Burmese workers and the influence is evident – and to enjoy the old-fashioned and friendly nature of a place still virtually untouched by tourism. More teak is on show at Ban Prathup Jai, a colossal house west of the centre, while several wats showing Lanna and Burmese influences are of architectural merit. Out of town, 18km to the northeast, are the so-called ghost pillars at **Phae Muang Phi**, a geological quirk of soil and wind erosion, which are probably only worth visiting if you are going on through to Nan with your own transport.

The Town

Sited on the southeast bank of the Yom River, Phrae is clearly divided into old and new town; an earthen wall surrounds the roughly oval-shaped old town, with a moat along its eastern edge. At the centre of the **old town**, a large roundabout is the main orientation point; a tidy park beside it where the locals like to play *petanque* (a French version of bowls) makes a central oasis. Running northwest–southeast through the roundabout and into the new town is Thanon Charoen Muang, where several shops sell the trademark deep indigo shirts. The main street in the new town, Thanon Yantarakitkoson, intersects Thanon Charoen Muang at a right angle about 300m southeast of the old town, and leads northeast to the bus station.

Dotted around the old town, several wats are worth visiting and are easily reached on foot; in fact, a stroll through the area's quiet lanes is recommended, with traditional **teak houses** to gaze at and a glimpse of local life as extended families congregate sociably outside. You will really find the Thai smile here: people are friendly and will probably try to talk to you with any English they have.

Wat Luang and Wat Phra Non

In the northwest corner of the old town, Phrae's oldest temple complex, **Wat Luang**, dates from the town's foundation around the twelfth century; it contains the only intact original brick entrance gate to the city, though unfortunately it has been closed up and turned into an ugly shrine. From the new town you can reach the wat by continuing up Thanon Charoen Muang past the roundabout until just before you hit the ramparts, then turning left. Apart from the gate, the oldest component of the wat is the crumbling early Lanna-style **chedi** called Chang Kham after the four elephants – now mostly trunkless – which sit at its octagonal base; these alternate with four niches containing Buddha images and some haphazardly leaning gilded bronze parasols. Architectural experts have been called in from Bangkok to plan the restoration of the chedi and the overall complex: unfortunately, over the years, Wat Luang has been added to and parts of it have been quite spoilt in a gaudy modernization process. Until recently, a dishonest monk was even taking down parts of the temple to sell for a profit. Apart from the ruined entrance gate, this meddling is most evident in the **viharn**, where an ugly and very out-of-place brick facade has been placed in front of the original Lanna-style sixteenth-century entrance. Opposite the chedi, a **museum** on two floors houses some real treasures, the most important being a collection of sixteenth-century bronze Buddhas and several glass cases containing old manuscripts with beautifully gilded covers, which are located upstairs.

Still within the old city, about a block west of Wat Luang along the boundary road is **Wat Phra Non**, established three centuries ago, whose name comes from the reclining Buddha in a small viharn; look out for the bot's finely carved wooden pediment showing scenes from the *Ramayana*.

Ban Prathup Jai

Turn right out of Wat Phra Non, then right again at the first crossroads, to leave the old town; follow this road to a junction, then first right and first left to reach the massive two-storey teak house of **Ban Prathup Jai** (daily 8am–5pm; B20), constructed out of nine old houses in the mid-1980s. A visit here allows you to appreciate the beauty and strength of the wood, even if the overall effect is just too ornate: the lower floor has an impressive interior of 130 pillars of solid teak carved with jungle scenes; huge wooden elephants wander among the columns set against solid teak walls and ornately carved furniture (plus a souvenir shop where you can buy all things wooden). Upstairs has the feel of a traditional house, and the furniture and objects are those that you might find in a well-to-do Thai home: ornately carved cabinets crammed with bowls and other ordinary household objects, tables displaying framed family portraits, wall carvings and even a teak bar.

Wat Sra Bo Kaeo

Just to the east of the old city, near the northern end of Thanon Nam Khue (which runs parallel to the moat), **Wat Sra Bo Kaeo** is set in a peaceful, shady grove of trees. Its Burmese-style viharn is of no great age, but has an intriguing marble Buddha image and beautiful teak floorboards. The most striking aspect of the temple is the brightly-painted Shan chedi with two unusually attractive guardian figures in flowing robes. Also note the intricate, decorative stucco work on the spire of the bot to the left of the viharn.

Practicalities

Phrae's **bus station**, off Thanon Yantarakitkoson, is 1km northeast of the modern centre. There are usually some **samlors**, the form of transport around town, congregating here, while **songthaews** head for out-of-town routes, including the train station at Den Chai. The **airport** is 9km southeast, from where Thai Airways (office at 42–44 Thanon Ratsadamnoen; ☎054/511123) runs a shuttle bus into town.

Accommodation in Phrae comprises several **hotels** in the new town clustered around Thanon Charoen Muang, Thanon Yantarakitkoson and Thanon Ratsadamnoen (which runs parallel to and just south of Thanon Charoen Muang). In the budget range, the best of these is the *Toongsriphaibool Hotel* at 84 Thanon Yantarakitkoson (☎054/511011; ❶), near the junction with Thanon Charoen Muang. A large three-storey hotel, it's arranged around a courtyard and so is off the noisy road; the clean, simply furnished rooms have fans and attached (cold-water) bathrooms. Even cheaper and nearer the centre, though a little dingy, is the *Thepwiman Hotel,* 226–228 Thanon Charoen Muang (☎054/511003; ❶); try to avoid the rooms that face the street. A popular midrange hotel, close to the old city, is the *Nakhon Phrae Hotel*, with two sections either side of Thanon Ratsadamnoen (☎054/511122, ℱ521937; ❸–❹); most of its rooms have air-conditioning, hot water en-suite rooms and cable television. The city's best hotel is the *Mae Yom Palace* near the bus station at 181/6 Thanon Yantarakitkoson (☎054/521028–36, ℱ522904;˙❻); a swimming pool features among its amenities.

For **eating**, you could start with the foodstalls at the lively **night market** by Pratuchai Gate on the southern edge of the old city, at the junction of Thanon Rob Muang and Thanon Charoen Muang. Nearby on Thanon Ratsadamnoen around the *Nakhon Phrae Hotel*, there are a few places to choose from including some simple Chinese cafés: the *Ah Hui*, right next to the *Nakhon Phrae Hotel*, serves several tasty rice dishes, though like most eateries in Phrae, it has no English menu. For this luxury, you have to pay higher prices at the coffee shop of the *Nakhon Phrae Hotel*, or head a couple of kilometres south to 57/6 Thanon Yantarakitkoson, where *Ban Fai*, serving Thai, Chinese and Western dishes, is popular among tour groups. As you might expect, Phrae's nightlife is pretty much nonexistent, but the *Beer Corner*, on Thanon Rob Muang just southwest of the Pratuchai Gate, provides live folk music, and the night market, selling clothes and trinkets, attracts locals along the section of Thanon Rob Muang going northeast from Pratuchai Gate.

Wat Phra That Cho Hae

Wat Phra That Cho Hae, 9km east of town (1km on from the village of Padang), is an important pilgrimage centre sited on a low hill, led up to by two naga stairways through a grove of teak trees. One staircase leads to a shrine where a revered Buddha image, Phra Chao Tan Chai, is said to increase women's fertility. The small grounds also house a gilded 33-metre-high **chedi**, traditionally wrapped in the yellow satin-like cloth, *cho hae* (which gives the wat its name) in March or April, and a brightly decorated viharn with an unusual cruciform layout. To the north of the main compound, a new viharn houses a shiny Buddha and some well-crafted murals and window carvings. To get to the wat, take a songthaew (around B150 there and back, with a wait) from Thanon Charoen Muang near the Thanon Yantarakitkoson intersection.

Nan

After leaving the Yom, Highway 101 gently climbs through rolling hills of cotton fields and teak plantations to its highest point, framed by limestone cliffs, before descending into the high, isolated valley of the Nan River, one of the two great tributaries of the Chao Phraya. Ringed by high mountains, the sleepy but prosperous provincial capital of **NAN**, 225km east of Lampang, rests on the grassy west bank of the river. This stretch of water really comes alive during the **Lanna boat races**, usually held in late October or early November, when villages from around the province send teams of up to fifty oarsmen here to race in long, colourfully decorated canoes with dragon prows. The lush surrounding valley is noted for its cotton-weaving, sweet oranges and the attractive grainy paper made from the bark of local *sa* (mulberry) trees.

Although it has been kicked around by Burma, Laos and Thailand, Nan province has a history of being on the fringes, distanced by the encircling barrier of mountains. Rama V brought Nan into his centralization programme at the start of the twentieth century, but left the traditional ruling house in place, making it the last province in Thailand to be administered by a local ruler (it remained so until 1931). During the troubled 1970s, communist insurgents holed up in this twilight region and proclaimed Nan the future capital of the liberated zone, which only succeeding in bringing the full might of the Thai Army down on them. The insurgency faded after the government's 1982 offer of amnesty, though there is still a noticeable military presence. Today, energies are focused on development, and the province has become less isolated with the building of several new roads. Nan still has a slight reputation for lawlessness, but most of the bandits nowadays are illegal loggers.

The Town

Nan's unhurried centre comprises a disorientating grid of crooked streets, around a small core of shops and businesses where Thanon Mahawong and Thanon Anantaworarichides meet Thanon Sumondhevaraj. The best place to start an exploration is to the southwest at the **National Museum** (Wed–Sun 9am–noon & 1–4pm; B30), located in a tidy palace with superb teak floors, which used to be home to the rulers of Nan. Its informative, user-friendly displays give you a bite-sized introduction to Nan, its history and its peoples, the prize exhibit being a talismanic elephant tusk with a bad case of brown tooth decay, which is claimed to be magic black ivory. The tusk was discovered over

NAN

ACCOMMODATION
Amazing Guest House	2
City Park	7
Dhevaraj	5
Doi Phukha Guest House	1
Fahthanin	3
Nan Guest House	6
Sukkasem	4

RESTAURANTS
Da Dario	A
PoAom Sam	B
Suan Issan	D
Tanaya Kitchen	C

Airport & Tha Wang Pha

THANON SUAN TAN

Station for Bangkok & Phitsanulok Buses

THANON KHA LUANG

Pra Nan

Night Market   Songthaew to Tha Wang Pa and Pua

Main Bus Station

THANON ANANTAWORARICHIDES

THANON NOR KHAM

THANON MAHAYOT

Thai-Payap Development Association

THANON JETABOOT

THANON SUMONTHEWARAJ

Oversea

THANON MAHAWONG

Fhu Travel

THANON PHAKWANG

Wat Chang Kham

THANON MAHAPHOM

Thai Airways   National Museum

THANON SURIYA PONG

Wat Phumin

THANON CHAO FA

THANON ARIYAWONG

THANON THALI

Nan River

Sa Paper Factory

Wat Phra That Chae Haeng

Phayao

0   200 m

Phrae, Wat Phra That Khao Din (2 km) & Sao Din

three hundred years ago and now sits on a colourful wooden *khut*, a mythological eagle. The museum also houses elegant pottery and woodcarving, gorgeously wrought silverware and some rare Laotian Buddhas.

Nearby on Thanon Phakwang, **Wat Phumin** will grab even the most overtempled traveller. Its 500-year-old centrepiece is an unusual cruciform building, combining both the bot and the viharn, which balances some quirky features in a perfect symmetry. Two giant nagas pass through the base of the building, with their tails along the balustrades at the south entrance and their heads at the north, representing the sacred oceans at the base of the central mountain of the universe. The doors at the four entrances, which have been beautifully carved with a complex pattern of animals and flowers, lead straight to the four Buddha images arranged around a tall altar in the centre of the building – note the Buddhas' piercing onyx eyes and pointed ears, showing the influence of Laos, 50km away. What really sets the bot apart are the recently restored **murals**, whose bright, simple colours seem to jump off the walls. Executed in 1857, the paintings take you on a whirlwind tour of heaven, hell, the Buddha's previous incarnations, local legends and incidents from Nan's history, and include stacks of vivacious, sometimes bawdy, detail, which provides a valuable pictorial record of that era. Diagonally opposite Wat Phumin, **Wat Chang Kham** is also over 500 years old, though the two viharns that stand side by side are unexceptional in design. The main feature here is a gorgeous, gold-capped chedi, supported by elephants on all sides; those on the corners are adorned with gold helmets. The temple is attached to a school, a reminder that temples were once the only source of education in the country.

Wat Phra That Chae Haeng, on the opposite side of the river 2km southeast of town, is another must, as much for its setting on a hill overlooking the Nan valley as anything else. The wat was founded in 1300, at a spot determined by the Buddha himself when he passed through this way – or so local legend would have it. The nagas here outdo even Wat Phumin's: the first you see of the wat across the fields is a wide driveway flanked by monumental serpents gliding down the slope from the temple. A magnificent gnarled bodhi tree with hundreds of spreading branches and roots guards the main gate, set in high boundary walls. Inside the walls, the highlight is a slender, 55-metre-high golden chedi, surrounded by four smaller chedis and four carved and gilded umbrellas, as well as small belfries and stucco lions. Close competition comes from the viharn roof, which has no fewer than fifteen Laotian-style tiers, stacked up like a house of cards and supported on finely carved *kan tuei* (wood supports) under the eaves.

You can get another great overview of the Nan valley by turning right just after the bridge on Highway 101 to the south of town. Follow the lane a couple of kilometres, and go up the hill to **Wat Phra That Khao Noi**, where you can join a huge image of a standing Buddha in contemplating the lush panorama below.

Crafts and shops

Loyalty to local traditions ensures the survival of several good **handicrafts shops** in Nan, most of which are found on Thanon Sumondhevaraj north of the junction with Anantaworarichides. Traditional lengths of superb **cotton** (much of it *pha sin*, used as wraparound skirts) woven in local villages are sold at Pha Nan, 21/2 Thanon Sumondhevaraj; as the owner is a teacher, the shop has unusual hours (Mon–Fri 5–10pm, Sat & Sun 8am–10pm). The staff are friendly and you can happily browse the huge selection of cloths for hours without hard sell. Jantragun, at nos. 304–306 (see also Ban Nong Bua, p.350), also has a good selection of *seua maw hawm*, Phrae's famous blue working shirts, and a few notebooks made from **sa paper**. You can watch the smelly, sticky, fascinating process of making this paper on the south bank of the Nan River just west of the town bridge. Look out for what appears to be a field of solar panels as you cross the bridge: the *sa* bark is softened and milled in water to form a gluey soup, into which these finely meshed frames are gently dunked before drying on the river bank. The resulting coarsely grained white sheets can be bought here at the factory for B5 each.

The Thai-Payap Development Association, a **non-profit-making organization** set up to bring extra income to local hill tribes, has its shop beside its head office at 24 Thanon Jetaboot. On sale here are bags, basketware, woodcarving, honey and all manner of fabrics, even Hmong baby-carriers.

A large **silverware** showroom and workshop named Chom Phu Phukha is situated about 2km west of town along the road to Phayao (Route 1091), on the right opposite a petrol station. They stock a wide range of bracelets, necklaces, bowls and trays, priced according to design and weight (about B10–15 per gram), and are happy for visitors to look round the workshop, where young hill-tribe people fashion the items. A good variety of local cloth, hand-woven by the hill tribes, is also on sale here.

Practicalities

If you're coming here direct from Chiang Mai, you might want to weigh up the seven-hour bus journey to Nan (around B85 non-air-con, B120–150 air-con) against the one-hour flight (B500). The **airport** is on the north side of town, from where songthaews head into the centre, and a minibus operated by Thai Airways runs to the hotels. The main **bus station** is on Thanon Anantaworarichides on the west side of town, but Bangkok and Phitsanulok services use a smaller station to the east of the centre on Thanon Kha Luang; arriving at either leaves a manageable walk or a samlor ride to the central accommodation area. For exploring Nan, Oversea, at 488 Thanon Sumondhevaraj, rents out decent **bicycles** (B30–50 a day) and **mopeds** (B150).

Accommodation

Despite being a small town with few visitors, Nan has some attractive accommodation options, ranging from family-run guest houses to clean, reasonably priced hotels. The only time of year when finding somewhere to stay might be a problem is when the Lanna boat races take place in town (late Oct or early Nov).

Amazing Guest House, 25/7 Thanon Rat Amnuay ☎054/710893. About 1km north of the centre. Offers clean, simple rooms in a family-style, wooden house with shared bathroom. ❶

City Park Hotel, 99 Thanon Yantarakitkoson ☎054/741343–52, ℗773135. About 2km from the centre on Highway 10.1 to Phrae. The best place in town, its tasteful rooms (all with cable TV), all in low-rise buildings, giving onto balconies overlooking a large swimming pool. ❻

Dhevaraj Hotel, 466 Thanon Sumondhevaraj ☎054/710078 or 710212, ℗771365. Rooms at this centrally positioned place are quite plush, with fan or air-con, and cable TV; all are en suite. ❸

Doi Phukha Guest House, 94/5 Soi 1, Thanon Sumondhevaraj ☎054/751517. On the north side of town, this fine guest house occupies a beautiful wooden house in a quiet compound; the simple rooms share hot and cold showers, and there's an informative noticeboard and excellent maps of the province available. ❶

Fahthanin Hotel, 303 Thanon Anantaworarichides ☎054/757321–4. Carpeted, air-con rooms here come with TV and minibar. ❺

Nan Guest House, 57/16 Thanon Mahaphom ☎054/771849. Adequate, if rather basic rooms in a wooden house, separated by rather flimsy partitions. ❶

Sukkasem Hotel, 119–121 Thanon Anantaworarichides ☎054/710141. A bargain hotel in the centre, with simple clean rooms just across from the night market. ❷

Eating

Plenty of simple Thai **restaurants** line Thanon Anantaworarichides, among them *Poom Sam*, just next to the *Sukkasem Hotel*. It may look like any other street food outlet, but they prepare excellent Thai and Chinese food with great service at rock-bottom prices. Next to *Poom Sam* is *Tanaya Kitchen*, a tiny, homely café that serves good vegetarian food. Nan's big culinary surprise, however, is *Da Dario* at 37/4 Thanon Rat Amnuay (☎054/750258), which runs west off Thanon Sumondhevaraj. Right next door to *Amazing Guest House*, *Da Dario* serves both authentic Italian and Thai food rated by the locals, with moderate to expensive prices. The **night market** includes an excellent *phat thai* stall (B20 per generous serve), and for a taste of Isaan food, check out *Suan Issan* at 2/1 Thanon Anantaworarichides, which despite its address is actually in the narrow alley off Thanon Sumondhevaraj, just south of the junction with this road. Cheap and clean, with lots of plants out front, this restaurant has good service, and the fiery Isaan food will have your tongue flapping.

Around Nan

The remote, mountainous countryside around Nan runs a close second to the headlong scenery of Mae Hong Son province, but its remoteness means that Nan has even worse transport and is even more poorly mapped. This does, of course, make it an exciting region to explore, when you may encounter the ethnic minorities of the area – the Thai Lue, the Htin and the little-known Phi Tong Luang.

Without your own vehicle or motorbike, your easiest option for exploring this region is to head for the reliable Fhu Travel, the only fixer in Nan at 453/4 Thanon Sumondhevaraj (℡054/710636, ℻775345). Besides organizing popular and enjoyable, if slightly pricey, guided **tours** and trekking trips, Fhu and Ung his wife can advise you where to go according to your interests or even arrange customized tours. One-day tours to Wat Nong Bua, including a visit to the local weavers and views of Doi Phukha from nearby Pua, cost B2000 for two to three people or B600 per person for four to six people, including transport, driver/guide and lunch. Treks (two days B1200 per person, three days B1500 per person; minimum four people) head west, through tough terrain of thick jungle and high mountains, visiting at least one Phi Tong Luang village (see box, below) and nearby Hmong and Mien villages where they work, as well as settlements of **Htin**, an upland Mon–Khmer people most of whom migrated into Nan province after the Communist takeover of Laos in 1975. For those who want to go it alone, the bus service is sketchy, but Oversea (see opposite) rents out motorbikes.

Sao Din

One of several brief excursions from Nan possible with your own transport, **Sao Din** ("earth pillars"), 60km to the south, provides a more

---

Spirits of the yellow leaves

Inhabiting the remote hill country west of Nan, the **Phi Tong Luang** – "Spirits of the Yellow Leaves" – represent the last remnant of nomadic hunter-gatherers in Thailand, and their way of life, like that of so many other indigenous peoples, is rapidly passing. Believing that spirits will be angered if the tribe settles in one place, grows crops or keeps animals, the Phi Tong Luang build only temporary shelters of branches and wild banana leaves, moving on to another spot in the jungle as soon as the leaves turn yellow; thus they earned their poetic Thai name, though they call themselves Mrabri – "Forest People". Traditionally they eke out a hard livelihood from the forest, hunting with spears, trapping birds and small mammals, digging roots and collecting nuts, seeds and honey.

Recent deforestation by logging and slash-and-burn farming has eaten into the tribe's territory, however, and many of the Phi Tong Luang have been forced to sell their labour to Hmong and Mien farmers (the spirits apparently do not get angry if the tribe settles down and works the land for other people). They are paid only in food – because of their docility and their inability to understand and use money, they often get a raw deal for their hard work. They are also particularly ill equipped to cope with curious and often insensitive tourists, although one of the American missionaries working with the tribe believes that occasional visits help the Phi Tong Luang to develop by teaching them about people in the outside world. The future doesn't look bright: they number only about 100–200 members; their susceptibility to disease (especially malaria) is high and life expectancy low.

intriguing example of soil erosion than the heavily-promoted Phae Muang Phi near Phrae. Here the earth pillars cover a huge area and appear in fantastic shapes, the result of centuries of erosion by wind and rain. The site is almost impossible to reach by public transport, but if you have a motorbike or car, head south on Highway 101 to Wiang Sa, then turn left and follow Route 1026 to Na Noi; a turning on the right just after Na Noi leads into the site. If you visit, take care to wear long trousers and boots, especially in the cool season, as a thorny plant which grows in the region can cause discomfort.

Ban Nong Bua

The easiest and most varied day-trip out of Nan is to the north, heading first for **BAN NONG BUA**, site of a famous muralled temple of the same name. If you're on a bike, ride 40km up Route 1080 to the southern outskirts of the town of **Tha Wang Pha**, where signs in English point you left across the Nan River to Wat Nong Bua, 3km away. Buses from Nan's main bus station on Thanon Anantaworarichides make the hour-long journey to Tha Wang Pha roughly hourly, or you can take a songthaew there from in front of the petrol station by the night market on the same road – then either hire a motorbike taxi in the centre of Tha Wang Pha, or walk the last 3km.

Wat Nong Bua stands behind the village green on the west side of the unpaved through road. Its beautifully gnarled viharn was built in 1862 in typical Lanna style, with low, drooping roof tiers surmounted by stucco finials – here you'll find horned nagas and tusked *makaras* (elephantine monsters), instead of the garuda finial which invariably crops up in central Thai temples. The viharn enshrines a pointy-eared Laotian Buddha, but its most outstanding features are the remarkably intact **murals** which cover all four walls. Executed between 1867 and 1888, probably by the Wat Phumin painters, they depict with much humour and vivid detail scenes from the *Chanthakhat Jataka* (the story of one of the Buddha's previous incarnations, as a hero called Chanthakhat). This is a particularly long and complex *Jataka* (although a leaflet, available from the monks in return for a small donation to temple funds, outlines the story in English), wherein our hero gets into all kinds of scrapes, involving several wives, other sundry liaisons, some formidably nasty enemies and the god Indra transforming himself into a snake. The crux of the tale comes on the east wall (opposite the Buddha image): in the bottom left-hand corner, Chanthakhat and the love of his life, Thewathisangka, are shipwrecked and separated; distraught, Thewathisangka wanders through the jungle, diagonally up the wall, to the hermitage of an old woman, where she shaves her head and becomes a nun; Chanthakhat travels through the wilderness along the bottom of the wall, curing a wounded naga-king on the way, who out of gratitude gives him a magic crystal ball, which enables our hero to face another series of perils along the south wall, before finally rediscovering and embracing Thewathisangka in front of the old woman's hut, at the top right-hand corner of the east wall.

Ban Nong Bua and the surrounding area are largely inhabited by **Thai Lue** people, distant cousins of the Thais, who've migrated from China in the past 150 years. They produce beautiful cotton garments in richly coloured geometric patterns; walk 200m behind the wat and you'll find weavers at work under the stilted sky-blue house of Khun Chunsom Prompanya, who sells the opulent fabrics in the shop behind. The quality of design and workmanship is very high here, and prices, though not cheap, are reasonable for the quality.

Doi Phukha National Park

East of Tha Wang Pha, Route 1080 curves towards the town of **Pua**, on whose southern outskirts Route 1256, the spectacular access road for **Doi Phukha National Park**, begins its journey eastwards and upwards. It's difficult to get into the park on public transport, and you'll have to stay the night: songthaews from Thanon Anantaworarichides or hourly buses from Nan's main station both run to Pua, from where infrequent songthaews (usually only one a day between 8am and 9am) serve the handful of villages along Route 1256. The trip is most exciting if tackled on a bike (though watch out for loose chippings on the bends): the road climbs up a sharp ridge, through occasional stands of elephant grass and bamboo, towards Doi Dong Ya Wai (1939m), providing one of the most jaw-droppingly scenic drives in Thailand: across the valleys to north and south stand rows of improbably steep mountains (including the 1980-metre Doi Phukha itself, far to the south), covered in lush vegetation with scarcely a sign of human habitation.

At park headquarters, 24km up the road, **accommodation** ranges from a campsite (B100 to rent a tent) to two bungalows (one sleeps six for B1200, the other seven for B1600); as they're often full, it's best to book through the Forestry Department in Bangkok (see p.48). There are several trails within the park but they're not well marked, so it's best to hire a **guide** at headquarters (B300 per day). The guides lead visitors to Hmong and Htin villages and up the arduous slope to the nearest summit, Dong Khao (1305m). You can arrange to have **meals** cooked for you in the staff cafeteria.

The Mae Hong Son loop

Two roads from Chiang Mai head over the western mountains into Mae Hong Son, Thailand's most remote province, offering the irresistible prospect of tying the highways together into a six-hundred-kilometre loop. The towns en route give an appetizing taste of Burma to the west, but the journey itself, winding over implausibly steep forested mountains and through tightly hemmed farming valleys, is what will stick in the mind.

The southern leg of the route, Highway 108, first passes **Doi Inthanon National Park**, with its lofty views over half of northern Thailand and enough waterfalls to last a lifetime, then **Mae Sariang**, an important town for trade across the Burmese border. The provincial capital, **Mae Hong Son**, at the midpoint of the loop, still has the relaxing atmosphere of a large village and makes the best base for exploring the area's mountains, rivers and waterfalls. The northern leg, Route 1095, heads northeast out of Mae Hong Son into an area of beautiful caves and stunning scenery around **Mae Lana** and **Soppong**: staying at one of the out-of-the-way guest houses here will enable you to trek independently around the countryside and the local hill-tribe villages. Halfway back towards Chiang Mai from Mae Hong Son is **Pai**, a cosy travellers' hangout with some gentle walking trails in the surrounding valley.

We've taken the loop in a clockwise direction here, in part because Doi Inthanon is best reached direct from Chiang Mai and in part because this dispenses with the straight, fast and boring section of the journey (Chiang Mai–Hot) at the beginning. These considerations apart, you could just as easily go the other way round. Travelling the loop is straightforward, although the mountainous roads go through plenty of bends and jolts. Either way, Mae Hong Son is about eight hours' travelling time from Chiang Mai by **bus**, although services along the northern route are slightly less frequent. The 35-minute Chiang Mai–Mae Hong Son **flight** is surprisingly inexpensive (B420), and is worth considering for one leg of the journey, especially if you're short on time. Above all, though, the loop is made for **motorbikes** and **jeeps**: the roads are quiet (but watch out for huge, speeding trucks) and you can satisfy the inevitable craving to stop every five minutes and admire the mountain scenery. A useful piece of equipment for this journey is the **map** of the Mae Hong Son Loop published by Golden Triangle Rider, available in local bookshops at B99.

Highway 108: Chiang Mai to Mae Hong Son

Bus drivers on **Highway 108** are expected to have highly sharpened powers of concentration and the landlubber's version of sea legs – the road negotiates almost two thousand curves in the 349km to Mae Hong Son, so if you're at all prone to travel sickness plan to take a breather in Mae Sariang. Buses to Mae Sariang and Mae Hong Son depart from Chiang Mai's Arcade bus station; services to Chom Thong (for Doi Inthanon National Park) leave from the southern end of Thanon Phra Pokklao (Chiang Mai Gate).

Doi Inthanon National Park

Covering a huge area to the southwest of Chiang Mai, **DOI INTHANON NATIONAL PARK**, with its hill-tribe villages, dramatic waterfalls and panoramas over rows of wild, green peaks to the west, gives a pleasant, if sanitized, whiff of northern countryside, its attractions and concrete access roads kept in good order by the Thai Forestry Department. The park, named after the highest mountain in the country and so dubbed the "Roof of Thailand", is geared mainly to wildlife conservation but also contains a hill-tribe agricultural project producing strawberries, apples and flowers for sale. Often shrouded in mist, Doi Inthanon's temperate forests shelter a huge variety of flora and fauna, which make this one of the major destinations for naturalists in Southeast Asia. The park supports about 380 bird species, the largest number of any site in Thailand – among them the ashy-throated warbler and a species of the green-tailed sunbird, both unique to Doi Inthanon – as well as, near the summit, the only red rhododendrons in Thailand (in bloom Dec–Feb) and a wide variety of ground and epiphytic orchids. The waterfalls, birds and flowers are at their best in the cool season, but night-

time temperatures sometimes drop below freezing, making warm clothing a must.

The gateway to the park is **CHOM THONG**, 58km southwest of Chiang Mai on Highway 108, a market town with little to offer apart from the attractive **Wat Phra That Si Chom Thong**, whose impressive brass-plated chedi dates from the fifteenth century. The nearby bo tree has become an equally noteworthy architectural feature: dozens of Dalí-esque supports for its sagging branches have been sponsored by the devoted in the hope of earning merit. Inside the gnarled sixteenth-century viharn, a towering, gilded *ku* housing a Buddha relic just squeezes in beneath the ceiling, from which hangs a huge, sumptuous red and green umbrella. Weaponry, gongs, umbrellas, thrones and an elephant-tusk arch carved with delicate Buddha images all add to the welcoming clutter. Two doors up from the wat, *Watjanee* is a simple but clean and well-run vegetarian **restaurant**.

The main road through the park turns west off Highway 108 1km north of Chom Thong, winding generally northwestwards for 48km to the top of Doi Inthanon, passing the park headquarters about 30km in. A second paved road forks left 10km before the summit, reaching the riverside market of **Mae Chaem**, southwest of the park, after 20km. Sticking to public transport, you can reach the park headquarters using one of the **songthaews** that shuttle between Chom Thong and Mae Chaem, along the mountain's lower slopes; to get to the summit however, you'll have to hitch from the Mae Chaem turn-off (generally manageable), unless you want to charter a whole songthaew from Chom Thong's temple for around B1000 to the peak and back. By **motorbike** or **jeep**, you could do the park justice in a day-trip with an early start from Chiang Mai, or treat it as the first stage of a longer trip to Mae Hong Son, following Route 1088 south from Mae Chaem to pick up Highway 108 again 20km west of Hot.

The park

Three sets of waterfalls provide the main roadside attractions on the way to the park headquarters: overrated **Mae Klang Falls**, 8km in, which with its picnic areas and food vendors gets overbearingly crowded, especially at weekends; **Vachiratharn Falls**, the park's most dramatic, with a long, misty drop down a granite escarpment 11km beyond; and the twin cascades of **Siriphum Falls**, backing the park headquarters a further 11km on. With your own wheels you could reach a fourth and much more beautiful cataract, **Mae Ya**, which is believed to be the highest in Thailand – the winding, fourteen-kilometre paved track to it heads west off the main park road 2km north of Highway 108. A rough unpaved side road offers a roundabout but culturally more enlightening route to the headquarters, leaving the main road 3km beyond Vachiratharn Falls, taking in three traditional and unspoilt Karen villages before rejoining the main road at the more developed Hmong village of **Ban Khun Klang**, 500m before the headquarters.

For the most spectacular views in the park, continue 11km beyond the headquarters along the summit road to the sleek, twin chedis looming incongruously over the misty green hillside: on a clear day you can see the mountains of Burma to the west from here. Built by the Royal Thai Air Force, the chedis commemorate the sixtieth birthdays of the Thai king and queen; the king's monument, **Napamaytanidol Chedi** (1987), is brown to the more feminine lilac of the queen's **Napapolphumsiri Chedi** (1992). Starting a short distance up the road from the chedis, the rewarding **Kew Mae Pan Trail**, a two-hour circular walk, wanders through sun-dappled forest and open savanna as it skirts the steep western edge of Doi Inthanon, where violent-red rhododendrons (Dec–Feb) are framed against open views over the canyoned headwaters of the Pan River, when the weather allows. A signpost on the summit road opposite the helipad marks the trailhead, and the well-cut path from there is easy to follow, but you need to get a permit from headquarters to show at the beginning of the trail.

Doi Inthanon's **summit** (2565m), 6km beyond the chedi, is a big disappointment – from the car park you can see little beyond the radar installation. For many people, after a quick shiver and a snapshot in front of a board proclaiming this the highest point in Thailand, it's time to hop in the car and get back to warmer climes. A small, still-revered stupa behind this board contains the ashes of King Inthanon of Chiang Mai (after whom the mountain was renamed): at the end of the nineteenth century he was the first to recognize the importance of this watershed area in supplying the Ping River and ultimately the Chao Phraya, the queen of Thailand's rivers. One hundred metres back down the road, it's an easy walk to the bog which is the highest source of these great waterways, and one of the park's best bird-watching sites. The cream and brown sphagnum mosses which spread underfoot, the dense ferns that hang off the trees and the contorted branches of rhododendrons give the place a creepy, primeval atmosphere.

The paved **Mae Chaem road** skirts yet another set of waterfalls, 7km after the turn-off: look for a steep, unpaved road to the right, leading down to a ranger station and, just to the east, the dramatic long drop of **Huai Sai Luaeng Falls**. A circular two-hour trail from the ranger station takes in creeks and small waterfalls as well as **Mae Pan Falls**, a series of short cascades in a peaceful, shady setting. Continuing southwest, the paved road affords breathtaking views as it helter-skelters down to the sleepy valley of **Mae Chaem**. Bikers can take on a tough, though mostly paved, route towards Mae Hong Son from here, heading north up Route 1088 then west along Route 1263 (past the Buatong Fields and Mae Surin Waterfall – see p.359), joining Highway 108 just north of Khun Yuam. For saner souls, the southern 45-kilometre stretch of Route 1088 joins Highway 108 25km west of Hot.

Practicalities

A checkpoint by Mae Klang Falls collects **entrance fees** of B200 for foreigners, plus B20 per motorbike, and B30 per car. For detailed information on the park, stop at the **visitor centre** (daily 8.30am–4.30pm), 1km beyond the checkpoint, which puts on a fairly interesting slide show with English commentary about the park (just ask to see it). Information is also available at the **park headquarters**, a further 22km on, where you need to stop if you plan to stay overnight or to request a permit to walk the Kew Mae Pan trail. Two hundred metres beyond the headquarters on the left, the **Birding Visitor Centre** has a useful logbook and information in English for birders to consult, and sells a primitive map of birding sites (B5).

Accommodation and eating

Accommodation in the park is of the log-cabin variety, a bit dilapidated and without the blessing of hot water. Three- to ten-berth national park bungalows (B300–3000; bookings in Bangkok on ☏02/579 7223 or 579 5734, or at the park on 01/881 7346), set among dense stands of pine near the headquarters, come with cold-water bathrooms, electricity, mattresses and bedding. They are often fully booked at weekends and national holidays, but at other times you should be all right turning up on the day. Elsewhere, the *Little Home Guest*

House and Restaurant, 7km along the main park road from Chom Thong (℡01/224 3446; ❸–❺), has clean, breeze-block huts, either fan-cooled or air-conditioned, and with inside bathrooms, some with hot water. The *Navaroung Resort*, just before reaching Mae Chaem from Doi Inthanon (℡ & 🖷053/828477; ❺) offers small, cosy chalets with hot water and fan, set in a colourful garden with pleasant views across the valley that are shared by its restaurant.

Camping, an often chilly alternative, is permitted on a site about 500m from the park headquarters and another site at Huai Sai Luaeng Falls (B30 per person per night). Two-person tents can be rented at the shop beside headquarters for B70 per night, as can blankets at B20 each per night.

Food stalls operate in the daytime at Mae Klang Falls and also through the evening beside park headquarters. The Birding Visitor Centre serves up cheap but tasty dishes, and there's a popular canteen with a reasonable variety of food by the twin chedis. All these places will prepare food to take away if you need a packed lunch.

West to Mae Sariang and Mae Sam Laeb

South from Chom Thong, there are several **weaving** villages bordering Highway 108, and a **textile museum** at **Ban Rai Pai Ngam** (on the east side of the road at kilometre-stone 68) is well worth a look. The museum is dedicated to the work of Saeng-da Bansiddhi, a local woman who started a co-operative practising traditional dyeing and weaving techniques using only natural products. Saeng-da died in the late 1980s, and the museum, which displays looms, fabrics and plants used in dyeing, was established to honour her efforts to revive these disappearing skills. It is situated on the upper floor of a large wooden building, while on the ground floor weavers can be seen busy at work. Bolts of cloth and a small range of clothes are on sale at reasonable prices.

Highway 108 parallels the Ping River downstream as far as **Hot**, a dusty, forgettable place 27km from Chom Thong, before bending west and weaving through pretty wooded hills up the valley of the Chaem River. Four kilometres west of town, the twee *Hot Resort* (℡053/461070; ❹) has well-appointed chalets with hot water, and a riverside restaurant which serves tasty food at moderate prices.

Another 13km brings you to **Ob Luang Gorge National Park** (B200), billed with wild hyperbole as "Thailand's Grand Canyon". A wooden bridge over the short, narrow channel lets you look down on the Chaem River bubbling along 50m below. Mae Sot Conservation Tour (℡053/814505 or 814424), based in Chiang Mai, organizes combination hiking and white-water rafting trips here on weekends (B1300–2700, depending on number in group). Upstream from the bridge, you can relax at the roadside foodstalls and swim in the river when it's not too fast, and the shady park contains a **campsite** (B30 to pitch your own tent; B150 to hire a tent and blankets). Two hundred metres west of the park entrance, *Khao Krairaj Resort* (℡053/384542–3, 🖷865181; ❻) offers a variety of tastefully rustic rooms and bungalows with fan and hot water in shady grounds. West of Ob Luang, the highway gradually climbs through pine forests, the road surface bad in patches and the countryside becoming steeper and wilder.

Mae Sariang

After its descent into the broad, smoky valley of the Yuam River, Highway 108's westward progress ends at **MAE SARIANG**, 183km from Chiang Mai,

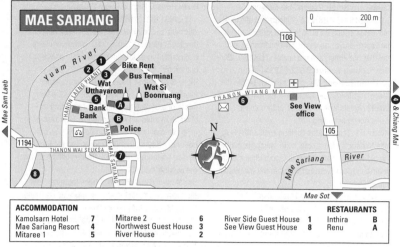

ACCOMMODATION						RESTAURANTS	
Kamolsarn Hotel	7	Mitaree 2	6	River Side Guest House	1	Inthira	B
Mae Sariang Resort	4	Northwest Guest House	3	See View Guest House	8	Renu	A
Mitaree 1	5	River House	2				

a quietly industrous market town showing a marked Burmese influence in its temples and its rows of low wooden shophouses. Halfway along the southern route between Chiang Mai and Mae Hong Son, this is an obvious place for a stopover. From here you can make an intriguing day-trip to the trading post of Mae Sam Laeb on the river border with Burma, and it's also possible to strike off south on a bone-rattling journey to Mae Sot.

Apart from soaking up the atmosphere, there's nothing pressing to do in this border outpost, which is regularly visited by local hill tribes and dodgy traders from Burma. If you want something more concrete to do, stroll around a couple of temples off the north side of the main street, whose Burmese features provide a glaring contrast to most Thai temples. The first, **Wat Si Boonruang**, sports a fairy-tale bot with an intricate, tiered roof piled high above. Topped with lotus buds, the unusual *sema* stones, which delineate the bot's consecrated area, look like old-fashioned street bollards. The open viharns here and next door at **Wat Uthayarom** (aka Wat Jong Sung) are mounted on stilts, with broad teak floors that are a pleasure to get your feet onto. Both wats enshrine Burmese-style Buddhas, white and hard-faced.

Practicalities

Buses enter Mae Sariang from the east along the town's main street, Thanon Wiang Mai, and pull in at the **terminal** on Thanon Mae Sariang, one of two north–south streets; the other, Thanon Laeng Phanit, parallels the Yuam River to the west. **Motorbikes** (Honda Dreams B200 per day; big bikes B380 per day) for exploring local temples and Karen villages can be hired from Pratin Kolakan, a small outlet opposite the bus terminal, or from the *See View Guest House* (see p.358); the latter also rents mountain bikes (B50).

When it's time for **food**, don't be put off by the basic appearance of the *Inthira Restaurant* on Thanon Wiang Mai – it's the locals' favourite, and dishes up excellent Thai dishes at moderate prices. *Renu Restaurant*, opposite, is less highly favoured but specializes in "wild food" such as nuthatch curry and wild boar. For such a tiny town, Mae Sariang has a good range of **accommodation**, listed below.

Kamolsarn Hotel, Thanon Mae Sariang ☎053/681524, ℻681204. A clean and efficient mid-range option on a fairly quiet street south of the centre; most rooms are air-conditioned and have TV, hot water, and unusually, a bathtub. ❹ **Mae Sariang Resort** ☎053/682344–5. Go 2km out towards Chiang Mai, then turn left before the bridge and follow the track for a further 1km. Simple chalets with hot-water bathrooms in an idyllic riverside setting. ❸ **Mitaree 1**, Thanon Mae Sariang ☎053/681110. Mae Sariang's oldest hotel, with cheap rooms in the old wooden part out back, and a choice of fan or air-con rooms with hot water in the main building. ❶–❸ **Mitaree 2**, Thanon Wiang Mai ☎053/681109. Around 50m east of the post office (15min from Thanon Laeng Phanit on foot). Part guest house, part hotel and part resort, with diverse facilities to match. ❸–❻ **Northwest Guest House**, Thanon Laeng Phanit ☎053/681188, ℻681353. The same deal as the *River Side* opposite – ie a mattress on the floor in a wooden room, but with smart, new shared bathrooms. ❶

River House, Thanon Laeng Phanit ☎053/681188, ℻681353. Sharing the same management as the *Northwest Guest House* opposite, this is set up more like a hotel, with river views and comfy fan or air-con rooms with hot-water bathrooms. ❹ **River Side Guest House**, 85 Thanon Laeng Phanit ☎053/681188. Along with the *See View*, this is one of Mae Sariang's long-standing travellers' hangouts, with basic rooms (mattress only) in an old-fashioned wooden house with shared hot-water bathrooms. The rooms and the pretty terrace restaurant occupy a choice position above the curving river. ❶ **See View** ☎053/681556. Across the river from the town centre; call in at their office at 70 Thanon Wiang Mai and they'll take you from there (they also meet buses from Chiang Mai and Mae Hong Son and songthaews from Mae Sot). The best budget place to stay in town, with a choice of big, comfortable, concrete rooms, each with a hot-water bathroom, or well-designed wooden A-frames in the garden, where there's also a cosy restaurant. Their enthusiastic and helpful owner, Aekkasan, is a mine of local information. ❷

Mae Sam Laeb

Some 46km southwest of Mae Sariang is **MAE SAM LAEB**, lying on the Salween River, which forms the border with Burma at this point. Songthaews for the 75-minute journey (B50) are sporadic, and only leave when they have a full complement of passengers – you can usually catch one at around 8am from the market, but it's best to get current information from one of the town's guest houses first.

Mae Sam Laeb is no more than a row of bamboo stores and restaurants, yet has a classic frontier feel about it. As the Burmese army has in the past mounted attacks against the Karen insurgents downstream from Mae Sam Laeb, you should check with staff at your accommodation that all is quiet before heading there. In the dry season, depending on the security situation, it may be possible to hire a longtail boat on the rocky river to view the steep, wooded banks on both sides of the frontier.

South from Mae Sariang: Highway 105 to Mae Sot

Highway 105, which drops south for 230km to Mae Sot (see p.282), makes a scenic and quiet link between the north and the central plains, though it has some major drawbacks. Setting off through the Yuam valley, the road winds over a range of hills to the Burmese border, formed here by the Moei River, which it then hugs all the way down to Mae Sot. Along the way, you'll pass through traditional Karen villages which still keep some working elephants, and dense forests with occasional forlorn stands of teak.

The major deterrent against travelling this way is the standard of public transport: though the route is paved, it's covered only by **songthaews** (7 daily), with a journey time of about six hours – really too much on a rattling bench seat – at a cost of B150 per person. In addition to the discomfort, this border area is rather remote and lawless, and is the scene of occasional **skirmishes** between the Burmese army and the opposition freedom fighters – most of the fighting is conducted on the Burmese side, but check that the coast is clear before leaving Mae Sariang.

North to Mae Hong Son

North of Mae Sariang, wide, lush valleys alternate with tiny, steep-sided glens – some too narrow for more than a single rice paddy – turning Highway 108 into a winding roller coaster. With your own transport, an attractive side trip can be made by turning right on the south side of **Ban Mae La Noi**, 32km from Mae Sariang, onto Route 1266. This all-weather unpaved road climbs sharply eastwards against a stunning backdrop of sawtoothed, forested mountains, speckled here and there with incongruous grids of bright-green cabbage patches. After 25km, the friendly Lawa settlement of **Ban La Up** appears, strung along a razor-blade ridge, where the village elephant, if not on agricultural duty, can be hired for a two-hour round trip to the pretty Pang Tai waterfall.

The market town of **KHUN YUAM**, 95km north of Mae Sariang, is a popular resting spot, especially for bikers who've taken the direct route here (Route 1263) over the mountains from Mae Chaem. There's not much here in the way of attractions, though the **Khun Yuam Cultural Centre**, on the left of Thanon Rajaburana opposite Wat Muai Tor at the north end of town, has a curious collection of rusting relics from the Japanese World War II occupation – old trucks, rifles, water canisters and uniforms. Hundreds of black and white photos lining the walls are a grim reminder that this area has not always been as peaceful as it is today.

The *Ban Farang* **guest house** (☎053/622086; ❷–❸), well signposted at the north end of town just off the main thoroughfare, Thanon Rajaburana, can put you up in fine style. Each of its smart, very clean twin rooms has duvets and a hot- or cold-water bathroom, with access to a shared hot shower; the restaurant serves up good Thai and French food, at reasonable prices. Less pricey rooms can be had at the friendly but dingy *Mitkhunyuam Hotel*, 115 Thanon Rajaburana (☎053/691057; ❶–❹), with the cheaper rooms in the original old wooden building at the front, and more expensive rooms, some with air-con and hot-water bathrooms, in the comfy new building behind.

Just north of Khun Yuam, Route 1263 branches off to the east over the hills towards Mae Chaem; after about 12km, a side road leads north up to the **Buatong fields**, where Mexican sunflowers make the hillsides glow butteryellow in November and early December. Much of the roadside elsewhere is bordered by these same flowers at this time of year, but the sheer concentration of blooms at Buatong, combined with sweeping views over endless ridges to the west, make it worth sharing the experience with the inevitable tour groups. Just 10km further down the same road from Buatong, **Mae Surin Waterfall** in Mae Surin National Park (B200) is arguably the most spectacular waterfall in the whole country, the waters hurtling over a cliff and plunging almost 100m before crashing on huge boulders and foaming down a steep gorge. The kind topography of the region allows a great view of the falls from directly in front, but the best view, from below, requires a steep and at times precarious three-hour hike down and back from the well-appointed **camping** area (free; tent rental B30). Basic food is available from a stall at the campsite (Nov–Feb). To reach the park without your own transport, join a tour from Mae Hong Son (see p.364).

Back on the main road, 10km north of Khun Yuam, the landscape broadens for the river crossing at **Ban Mae Surin**, gracefully complemented by a typical Burmese temple and chedi. A right turn about 23km beyond Mae Surin leads up to **Mae Ko Vafe** – a Thai rendition of "microwave", referring to the transmitters that grace the mountain's peak; the road climbs for 10km to a Hmong village, where the view west stretches far into Burma. Around 15km beyond this turn-off Highway 108 climbs to a roadside **viewing area**, with fine vistas, this time to the east, of the sheer, wooded slopes and the Pha Bong Dam in the valley far below. Subsequently the road makes a dramatic, headlong descent towards Mae Hong Son, passing the **Ban Pha Bong** hot springs, 7km north of the viewing area (11km before Mae Hong Son). These have been turned into a small spa complex, with showers, toilets and a restaurant – swimming is discouraged, so you're expected to haul out buckets full of the healing waters with which to douse yourself.

Mae Hong Son and around

MAE HONG SON, capital of Thailand's northwesternmost province, sports more nicknames than a town of just under ten thousand people seems to deserve. In Thai, it's Muang Sam Mok, the "City of Three Mists": set deep in a mountain valley, Mae Hong Son is often swathed in mist, the quality of which differs according to the three seasons (in the hot season it's mostly composed of unpleasant smoke from slash-and-burn agriculture). In former times, the town, which wasn't connected to the outside world by a paved road until 1968, was known as "Siberia" to the troublesome politicians and government officials who were exiled here from Bangkok. Nowadays, thanks to its mountainous surroundings, it's increasingly billed as the "Switzerland of Thailand": eighty percent of Mae Hong Son province is on a slope of more than 45 degrees.

To match the hype, Mae Hong Son has become one of the fastest-developing tourist centres in the country, sporting dozens of backpacker guest houses and more latterly, for Thais and farangs who like their city comforts, luxury hotels. Most travellers come here for **trekking** and day-hiking in the beautiful countryside, others just for the cool climate and lazy upcountry atmosphere. The town is still small enough and sleepy enough to hole up in for a quiet week, though in the high season (Nov–Feb) swarms of minibuses disgorge tour groups who hunt in packs through the souvenir stalls and fill up the restaurants. It is also a popular location for film-makers, and sometimes the peaceful hillsides reverberate with the lucrative sounds of explosions and machine-gun fire, as they did during the 1995 filming of *The Quest* starring Roger Moore and Jean-Claude van Damme.

Mae Hong Son was founded in 1831 as a training camp for elephants captured from the surrounding jungle for the princes of Chiang Mai (Jong Kham Lake, in the southeastern part of the modern town, served as the elephants' bathing spot). The hard work of hunting and rearing the royal elephants was done by the **Thai Yai**, who account for half the population of the province and bring a strong Burmese flavour to Mae Hong Son's temples and festivals. The other half of the province's population is made up of various hill tribes (a large number of Karen, as well as Lisu, Hmong and Lawa), with a tiny minority of Thais concentrated in the provincial capital.

The latest immigrants to the province are **Burmese refugees**: as well as rural Karen, driven across the border when the Burmese army razed their villages (see box on p.280), many urban students and monks, who formed the hard core of the brutally repressed 1988 uprising, have fled to this area to join the resistance forces. The latter are susceptible to malaria and generally suffer most from the harsh jungle conditions here; many refugees live in camps between Mae Hong Son and the border, but these do not encourage visitors as they've got quite enough on their plates without having to entertain onlookers.

Arrival, information and accommodation

Running north to south, Mae Hong Son's main drag, Thanon Khunlumprapas, is intersected by Thanon Singhanat Bamrung at the traffic lights in the centre of town, and lined by laid-back shops and businesses. Arriving at Mae Hong Son's **bus station**, towards the north end of Thanon Khunlumprapas, puts you

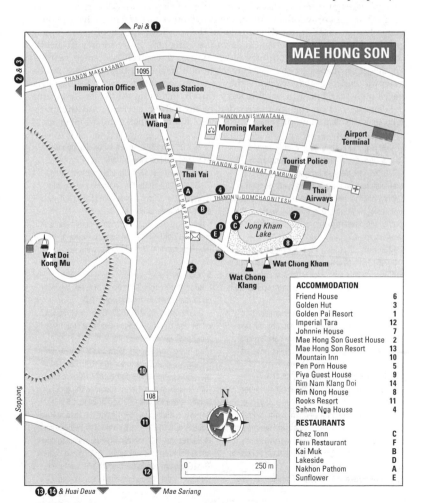

MAE HONG SON

Pai & ❶

2 & 3

THANON MAKKASANDI 1095

Immigration Office   Bus Station

Wat Hua Wiang

THANON PANISHWATANA
Morning Market

THANON KHUNLUMPRAPAS

Airport Terminal

Thai Yai

THANON SINGHANAT BAMRUNG

Tourist Police

Ⓐ   ❹

Ⓑ

THANON U-DOMCHAONITESH

Thai Airways

❺

Ⓓ Ⓒ ❻   ❼

Ⓔ   Jong Kham Lake

❽

❾

Wat Doi Kong Mu

Ⓕ   Wat Chong Kham

Wat Chong Klang

ACCOMMODATION	
Friend House	6
Golden Hut	3
Golden Pai Resort	1
Imperial Tara	12
Johnnie House	7
Mae Hong Son Guest House	2
Mae Hong Son Resort	13
Mountain Inn	10
Pen Porn House	5
Piya Guest House	9
Rim Nam Klang Doi	14
Rim Nong House	8
Rooks Resort	11
Sahan Nga House	4

RESTAURANTS	
Chez Tonn	C
Fern Restaurant	F
Kai Muk	B
Lakeside	D
Nakhon Pathom	A
Sunflower	E

❿

108

⓫

N

Sopong

0   250 m

⓬

⓭, ⓮ & Huai Deua   Mae Sariang

within walking distance of the guest houses. If you arrive at the **airport** and are not sure where to stay, go to the Mae Hong Son Business Association desk, and they will help fix you up. Tuk-tuks (B40) run from the airport to the centre, though if you're already booked into a resort or hotel, a car or minibus should pick you up. Motorbike taxis also operate in and around the town: the local transport hub is the north side of the morning market.

The Burmese army has been known to attack villages and camps along the border, so if you're planning any trips other than those described on p.364, you should check first with the **tourist police**, who have sketchy free maps of the area and the town, on Thanon Singhanat Bamrung (℡053/611812). Check out ⓦ www.maehongsontravel.com for information about tour options in the area, as well as maps and transport details.

Accommodation

At the lower end of the accommodation spectrum, Mae Hong Son has a healthy roster of **guest houses**, most of them being good-value, rustic affairs built of bamboo or wood and set in their own quiet gardens; many have ranged themselves around Chong Kham Lake in the southeast corner of town, which greatly adds to their scenic appeal. If you've got a little more money to spend, you can get out into the countryside to one of several self-contained **resorts** on the grassy banks of the Pai River, though staying at one of these is not exactly a wilderness experience – they're really designed for weekending Thais travelling by car. Finally, several **luxury hotels**, including the *Rooks Resort* and the *Imperial Tara* on the southern edge of town, have latched onto the area's meteoric development, offering all the usual international-standard facilities.

Guest houses

Friend House, 21 Thanon Pradit Jongkham ℡053/620119. Very smart and clean modern teak, concrete and rattan house with upstairs balcony giving views of the lake. They have large rooms sleeping up to four, with hot-water bathrooms, and smaller rooms which share hot showers. ②–③

Golden Hut, 253/1 Moo 11, Thanon Makkasandi ℡053/611544. Situated in a sloping garden on the northwest side of town facing open country, with good-value brightly designed concrete rooms with hot water. ③

Johnnie House, Thanon U-domchaonitesh ℡053/611667. In a small compound by the lake, this clean, friendly place has some basic rooms which share hot showers, while others have en-suite hot-water bathrooms. ②–③

Mae Hong Son Guest House, 295 Thanon Makkasandi ℡053/612510. Relaxing old-timer that's moved out to the suburbs for a view over the town. Choice of bare wooden rooms, some with cold-water bathrooms; clean and simple leaf-roofed huts; or large attractive bungalows with their own hot-water bathrooms; all have access to shared hot showers. ②–③

Pen Porn House, 16/1 Thanon Padunomuaytaw ℡ & ⓕ 053/611577. Smart, motel-like doubles with fans and hot showers. ③

Rim Nong House, 4/1 Thanon Chamnansathit ℡053/611052–3. On the south side of the lake. Cramped but decent rooms with shared hot showers, plus towels, sheets and fans. ①

Saban Nga House, 14 Thanon U-domchaonitesh ℡053/612280. Clean and central; rooms have mattress, fan and shared hot showers. ①

Resorts

Golden Pai Resort, 6km north of town, signposted to the left of the road towards Pai ℡053/612265–6, ⓕ 611523. Clean, well-appointed air-con chalets arranged around a smart swimming pool. ⑦

Mae Hong Son Resort, 6km south of town, on the road to Huai Deua ℡053/613138. Poshest of the resorts – a friendly and quietly efficient place, with chalets by the river or rooms in the grounds behind. Price includes cooked breakfast. ⑤

Rim Nam Klang Doi, 5km along the road to Huai Deua ℡053/612142, ⓕ 612086. The best-situated of the resorts, with rambling gardens sloping down to the Pai River and swimming, fishing and boating. The rooms are comfortable and well-maintained, with hot-water bathrooms and fan or air-con. ⑤

Hotels

Imperial Tara Hotel, 149 Moo 8, Tambon Pang Moo ☏ 053/611473, ℻ 611252, ⊛ www.imperial-hotels.com. On the south side of the town by the turn-off for Huai Deua, this grand building is set in pretty landscaped gardens, overlooked by spacious rooms featuring TV and mini-bar; there's a swimming pool too. ❾

Piya Guest House, 1/1 Thanon Khunlumprapas ☏ 053/611260. Despite its name, this is more like a hotel, boasting spacious rooms with hot-water bathrooms, TV and air-con in a lush garden, with a restaurant overlooking the lake. ❺

Mountain Inn, 112 Thanon Khunlumprapas ☏ 053/611309, ℻ 612284. Large, neat and tasteful rooms with air-con, hot-water bathrooms, carpeting and TV, set round a flower-strewn garden. ❺

Rooks Resort, 14/5 Thanon Khunlumprapas ☏ 053/611390, ℻ 611524. Comfy rooms, swimming pool, tennis courts and nightclub. ❽

The Town

Beyond the typical concrete boxes in the centre, Mae Hong Son sprawls lazily across the valley floor and up the lower slopes of Doi Kong Mu to the west, trees and untidy vegetation poking through at every possible opportunity to remind you that open country is only a stone's throw away. Plenty of traditional Thai Yai buildings remain – wooden shophouses with balconies, shutters and corrugated-iron roof decorations, homes thatched with *tong teung* leaves and fitted with herringbone-patterned window panels – though they take a severe beating from the weather and may eventually be replaced by inexpensive, all-engulfing concrete.

Mae Hong Son's classic picture-postcard view is its twin nineteenth-century Burmese-style temples from the opposite, north shore of Jong Kham Lake, their gleaming white and gold chedis and the multi-tiered spires of their viharns reflected in the water. In the viharn of **Wat Chong Kham** is a huge, intricately carved sermon throne, decorated with the *dharmachakra* (Wheel of Law) in coloured glass on gold; the building on the left has been built around the temple's most revered Buddha image, the benign, inscrutable Luang Pho To. Next door, **Wat Chong Klang** is famous for its paintings on glass, which are over 100 years old; they're displayed over three walls on the left-hand side of the viharn. The first two walls behind the monks' dais (on which women are not allowed to

---

Poy Sang Long

Mae Hong Son's most famous and colourful festival is **Poy Sang Long**, held at the beginning of April, which celebrates the ordination into the monkhood, for the duration of the schools' long vacation, of Thai Yai boys between the ages of seven and fourteen. Similar rituals take place in other northern Thai towns at this time, but the Mae Hong Son version is given a unique flavour by its Thai Yai elements. On the first day of the festival, the boys have their heads shaved and are anointed with turmeric and dressed up in the gay colours of a Thai Yai prince, with traditional accessories: long white socks, plenty of jewellery, a headcloth decorated with fresh flowers, a golden umbrella and heavy face make-up. They are then announced to the guardian spirit of the town and taken around the temples. The second day brings general merry-making and a spectacular parade, headed by a drummer and a richly decorated riderless horse, which is believed to carry the town's guardian spirit. The boys, still in their finery, are each carried on the shoulders of a chaperone, accompanied by musicians and bearers of traditional offerings. In the evening, the novices tuck into a sumptuous meal, waited on by their parents and relatives, before the ordination ceremony in the temple on the third day.

stand) depict *Jataka* stories from the Buddha's previous incarnations in their lower sections, and the life of the Buddha himself in their upper, while the third wall is devoted entirely to the Buddha's life. A small room beyond houses an unforgettable collection of **teak statues**, brought over from Burma in the middle of the nineteenth century. The dynamically expressive, often humorous figures are characters from the *Vessantara Jataka*, but the woodcarvers have taken as their models people from all levels of traditional Burmese society, including toothless emaciated peasants, butch tattooed warriors and elegant upper-class ladies.

The town's vibrant, smelly **morning market**, just south of the bus station, is worth dragging your bones up at dawn to see. People from the local hill tribes often come down to buy and sell, and the range of produce is particularly weird and wonderful, including, in season, porcupine meat, displayed with quills to prove its authenticity. Next door, the many-gabled viharn of **Wat Hua Wiang** shelters, under a lace canopy, one of the most beautiful Buddha images in northern Thailand, the **Chao Palakeng**. Copied from a famous statue in Mandalay, the strong, serene bronze has the regal clothing and dangling ears typical of Burmese Buddhas. Though the town is generally quiet during the day while visitors are out exploring the hills, the main streets come alive in the evening as **handicraft stalls** display colourful bolts of cloth, lacquerware, Burmese puppets, ceramics and jewellery.

For a godlike overview of the area, drive or climb up to **Wat Doi Kong Mu** on the steep hill to the west. From the temple's two chedis, which enshrine the ashes of respected nineteenth-century monks, you can look down on the town and out across the sleepy farming valley north and south. Behind the chedis, the viharn contains an unusual and highly venerated white marble image of the Buddha, surrounded in gold flames. If you've got the energy, trek up to the lemon-coloured bot on the summit, where the view extends over the Burmese mountains to the west.

Around Mae Hong Son

Once you've exhausted the few obvious sights in town, the first decision you'll have to grapple with is whether to visit the **"long-neck" women**. Our advice is don't, though many travellers do. Less controversial, **boat and raft trips** on the babbling Pai River are fun, and the roaring **Pha Sua Falls** and the Kuomintang village of **Mae Aw** make a satisfying day out. If all that sounds too easy, Mae Hong Son is now Thailand's third-largest centre for **trekking**. Other feasible targets include the hot springs at Ban Pha Bong (see p.360) and, at a push, Tham Lot (see p.369).

Local transport, in the form of songthaews from the morning market, is thinly spread and unreliable, so for all of these excursions it's best to rent your own vehicle or join an organized tour. The best fixer in town is the helpful and reliable Sunflower (see box on p.366), though there are many other **tour agents** clustered around the junction of Thanon Khunlumprapas and Thanon Singhanat Bamrung. *Thai Yai*, which doubles as an office for the *Mae Hong Son Guest House*, at 20 Thanon Singhanat Bamrung (℡053/620105) rents out **bicycles** at B100 a day and Honda Dream **motorbikes** for B180. Several places on the main street rent out **four-wheel drives**, though the most reliable place is Avis at the airport (℡053/611367; B1200 per day).

Nai Soi

The original village of long-neck Padaung women in the Mae Hong Son area, **NAI SOI**, 35km northwest of town, has effectively been turned into a human

Long-neck women

The most famous – and notorious – of the Mae Hong Son area's spectacles is its contingent of **"long-neck" women**, members of the tiny Padaung tribe of Burma who have come across to Thailand to escape Burmese repression. Though the women's necks appear to be stretched to 30cm and more by a column of brass rings, the "long-neck" tag is a technical misnomer: a *National Geographic* team once X-rayed one of the women and found that instead of stretching out her neck, the pressure of eleven pounds of brass had simply squashed her collarbones and ribs. Girls of the tribe start wearing the rings from about the age of six, adding one or two each year up to the age of sixteen or so. Once fastened, the rings are for life, for to remove a full stack would cause the collapse of the neck and suffocation – in the past, removal was a punishment for adultery. Despite the obvious discomfort, and the laborious daily task of cleaning and drying the rings, the tribeswomen, when interviewed, say that they're used to their plight and are happy to be continuing the tradition of their people.

The **origin** of the ring-wearing ritual remains unclear, despite an embarrassment of plausible explanations. Padaung legend says that the mother of their tribe was a dragon with a long, beautiful neck, and that their unique custom is an imitation of her. Tour guides will tell you the practice is intended to enhance the women's beauty. In Burma, where it is now outlawed as barbaric, it's variously claimed that ring-wearing arose out of a need to protect women from tiger attacks or to deform the wearers so that the Burmese court would not kidnap them for concubines.

In spite of their handicap (they have to use straws to drink, for example), the women are able to carry out some kind of an ordinary life: they can marry and have children, and they're able to weave and sew, although these days they spend most of their time posing like circus freaks for photographs. Only half of the Padaung women now lengthen their necks; left to its own course, the custom would probably die out, but the influence of tourism may well keep it alive for some time yet.

zoo for snap-happy tourists, with an entrance fee of B250 per person. The "long necks" pose in front of their huts and looms, every now and then getting it together to stage a good-luck song – all a visitor can do is stand and stare in embarrassed silence or click away with a camera. All in all it's a disturbing spectacle, offering no opportunity to discover anything about Padaung culture. At least, contrary to many reports, the "long necks" are not held as slaves in the village: the entrance fee is handled by the Karenni National People's Party, to whom the Padaung, in their precarious plight as refugees, have offered their services (the KNPP is fighting for the independence of Burma's Kayah state, where the Padaung come from). Much of the fee is used to support the KNPP, and some goes to help improve conditions in the village, while the "long necks" themselves are each paid a living wage of about B1500 per month.

Without your own transport, you have to hitch up with an expensive tour (about B750 per person, including entrance fee) from a travel agent in town. By motorbike, head north along Route 1095 for 2km and turn left after the police box; cross the suspension bridge over the Pai River, turn left at the next village and continue for another 10km.

Trips on the Pai River

Scenic **boat trips** on the Pai River start from Huai Deua, 7km southwest of town near the *Mae Hong Son Resort*. There's no need to go on an organized tour: take a motorbike taxi, tuk-tuk or one of the infrequent songthaews from

There's no getting away from the fact that **trekking** up and down Mae Hong Son's steep inclines is tough, but the hill-tribe villages are generally unspoilt and the scenery is magnificent. To the west, trekking routes tend to snake along the Burmese border, occasionally nipping over the line for a quick thrill, and can sometimes get a little crowded as this is the more popular side of Mae Hong Son. Nearly all the hill-tribe villages here are Karen, interspersed with indigenous Thai Yai settlements. To the east of Mae Hong Son the Karens again predominate, but by travelling a little further you'll also be able to visit Hmong, Lisu and Lahu; many villages here are very traditional, having little contact with the outside world. If you're very hardy, you might want to consider the five- to six-day route to Pai, which by all accounts has the best scenery of the lot.

About a dozen guest houses and travel agencies run treks out of Mae Hong Son. Among the reliable operators, *Mae Hong Son Guest House* charges from B600–700 per person per day, depending on how far into the more remote, interesting areas the trek ventures. Sunflower, 2/1 Soi 3, Thanon Khunlumprapas (T & F 053/620549) offers something a little different: a wide range of treks with the emphasis on eco-tourism and appreciating nature, especially bird-watching. On some treks you can enjoy a herbal sauna prepared by villagers. Staying rough in the jungle is possible – rates for this range from B850 per person per day (with two people in the group) to B500 per person (with six or more).

Mae Hong Son market to Huai Deua and approach the owners at the boat station. Twenty minutes downriver from Huai Deua (B500, plus B250 admission charge to the village) will get you to **Huai Phu Kaeng**, where a dozen or so "long-neck" women display themselves in a set-up similar to that at Nai Soi. You're better off enjoying the river for its own sake, as it scythes its way between cliffs and forests to the Burmese border, another ten minutes beyond (B500), or travelling upriver to **Soppong** (B400), a pretty, quiet Thai Yai village 5km due west of Mae Hong Son (not to be confused with the Soppong on Route 1095, northeast of Mae Hong Son). **Elephant rides** into the surrounding jungle, for B400 per hour for two people, can be arranged at the *Mae Hong Son Resort*.

A small stretch of the Pai River between **Sop Soi**, 10km northwest of Mae Hong Son, and Soppong is clear enough of rocks to allow safe clearance for bamboo **rafts**. The journey takes two hours at the most, as the rafts glide down the gentle river, partly hemmed in by steep wooded hills. Most of Mae Hong Son's travel agents can fix this trip up for you, including travel to Sop Soi and from Soppong, charging around B500 per raft (two or three passengers).

Pha Sua Falls and Mae Aw

North of Mae Hong Son, a trip to Pha Sua Falls and the border village of Mae Aw takes in some spectacular and varied countryside. Your best options are to rent a motorbike or join a tour – most agents charge around B400 per person, which includes a visit to the highly overrated Fish Cave – as there are only occasional (B50 to Mae Aw) songthaews from the market in the morning, and no guarantees for the return journey to Mae Hong Son. Under your own steam, the best route is to head north for 17km on Route 1095 (ignore the first signpost for Pha Sua, after 10km) and then, after a long, steep descent, turn left onto a side road, paved at first, which passes through an idyllic rice valley and the Thai Yai village of **Ban Bok Shampae**. About 9km from the turn-off you'll reach **Pha Sua Falls**, a wild, untidy affair, which crashes down in several cataracts through a dark, overhung cut in the limestone. The waterfall is in full roar in October after the rainy season, but has plenty of water all year round. Take care when swimming, as several people have been swept to their deaths here.

Above the falls the paved road climbs precipitously, giving glorious, broad vistas of both Thai and Burmese mountains, before reaching the unspectacular half-Hmong, half-Thai Yai village of **Naphapak** after 11km. A decent, largely flat stretch covers the last 7km to **MAE AW** (aka Ban Ruk Thai), a settlement of Kuomintang anti-Communist Chinese refugees (see p.384), right on the Burmese border. In the past, this area saw fighting between the Kuomintang and the army of Khun Sa, the opium warlord who, having been kicked out of the Mae Salong area by the Thai army in 1983, set up base somewhere in the uncharted mountains across the border northeast of Mae Aw. The road up here was built by the Thai military to help the fight against the opium trade and all has been quiet for several years. Mae Aw is the highest point on the border which visitors can reach, and provides a fascinating window on Kuomintang life. The tight ring of hills around the village heightens the feeling of being in another country: delicate, bright-green tea bushes line the slopes, while Chinese ponies wander the streets of long, unstilted bamboo houses. In the central marketplace on the north side of the village reservoir, shops sell great bags of oolong and Chian Chian teas, as well as dried mushrooms, and rustle up simple noodle dishes for visitors.

Eating and drinking

Nobody comes to Mae Hong Son for the **food** – the available options are limited, although a few good restaurants have sprung up in order to cater specifically to foreigners. If you fancy a change from guest-house breakfasts, head for the morning **market**, where a stall on the south side rustles up good, cheap, *roti* (pancakes with condensed milk and sugar). At night, several **foodstalls** open up on Thanon Khunlumprapas, offering a cheap alternative to restaurant fare.

Chez Tonn, next to *Friend House* near the lake. Serves tasty Thai and Western food. Inexpensive.

Fern, 87 Thanon Khunlumprapas. A showy, tourist-oriented eating place specializing in Thai food, with a nice candlelit terrace. Moderate to expensive.

Kai Muk, Thanon U-Domchaonitesh. Attractive, efficient and popular, with a huge variety of excellent Thai dishes on its menu. Moderate.

Lakeside Bar and Restaurant, 2/3 Thanon Khunlumprapas. A good place for a drink and some tasty Thai dishes. Here you can relax to the sounds of a live band playing Western and Thai pop and folk music, on a terrace overlooking Jong Kham Lake and the fairy lights on the temples behind. Moderate.

Nakhon Pathom, Thanon Khunlumprapas. Specializes in tasty pork on rice and noodle soup. Inexpensive.

Sunflower, 116/115 Soi 3, Thanon Khunlumprapas. A small quiet café with a few outdoor tables, serving very good Western food including excellent breakfasts with home-made bread and filter coffee. Moderate.

Listings

Airline The Thai Airways office is at 71 Thanon Singhanat Bamrung ☎053/611297.
Airport For flight information, call ☎053/612221.
Exchange The airport has a bank currency exchange (daily 10am–4pm). There are also several banks and exchange booths along Thanon Khunlumprapas.

Immigration office On Thanon Khunlumprapas (daily 9am–4pm; ☎053/612106).
Internet access Several cybercafés cluster around the junction of Thanon Khunlumprapas and Thanon Singhanat Bamrung.
Mail and telephones The post office is on Thanon Khunlumprapas; you can make phone calls here.

Route 1095:
Mae Hong Son to Chiang Mai

Route 1095, the 243-kilometre northern route between Mae Hong Son and Chiang Mai, is every bit as wild and scenic as the southern route through Mae Sariang – if anything it has more mountains to negotiate, with a greater contrast between the sometimes straggly vegetation of the slopes and the thickly cultivated valleys. Much of the route was established by the Japanese army to move troops and supplies into Burma after its invasion of Thailand during World War II. The labour-intensive job of paving every hairpin bend was completed in the 1990s, but ongoing repair work can still give you a nasty surprise if you're riding a motorbike. If you're setting off along this route from Chiang Mai by public transport, go to the Arcade station and catch either a bus to Pai where you change, or one direct to Mae Hong Son; routes are signed in English.

Mae Suya and Mae Lana

The first stretch north out of Mae Hong Son weaves up and down the west face of Doi Pai Kit (1082m), giving great views over the lush valley to the north of town. Beyond the turn-off for Mae Aw (see p.366) and the much-touted but unspectacular Fish Cave, the highway climbs eastward through many hairpin bends before levelling out to give tantalizing glimpses through the trees of the Burmese mountains to the north, then passes through a hushed valley of paddy fields, surrounded by echoing crags, to reach the Thai Yai/Kuomintang village of **MAE SUYA**, 40km from Mae Hong Son. Take the left turning by the police box, 3km east of the village to reach *Wilderness Lodge* after a further 1km of dirt road. Set in wild countryside, the friendly guest house offers primitive bungalows (**❶**) and dorm beds (B60) in the barn-like main house, and does a wide range of vegetarian and meat-based Thai food.

The owner of the lodge can give you directions and maps for cave exploration and beautiful wilderness day walks through the mountains to hill-tribe villages. Two hours' walk to the north, **Tham Nam Pha Daeng** is a pretty, 1600-metre-long cave (open Nov–May) with, like Tham Lot (see opposite), ancient coffins; apart from a few low crawls, the journey through the cave is relatively easy. To the south beyond Route 1095, **Tham Nam Lang**, one of the most capacious caves in the world, has a towering entrance chamber which anyone can appreciate, although the spectacular 9km beyond it demands full-on caving, again in the dry season only, and the proper equipment. Ask about trekking from *Wilderness Lodge* to **Wat Tham Wua Sunyata**, a peaceful forest monastery with a highly respected abbot, which looks more like a country club than a spiritual centre; you can stay here, join in meditation and share in the sole meal of the day.

One further remote guest house lies in the sleepy valley of **MAE LANA**, a Thai Yai village 6km north of the highway, reached by a dirt road which branches off to the left 56km from Mae Hong Son and leads uphill through dramatic countryside. By a stream on the edge of the village, the clean and cosy *Mae Lana Guest House* (**❶–❷**), with rooms and bungalows all sharing hot showers, serves good Thai food. The village is within easy walking distance of Lahu villages, plus several caves including **Tham Mae Lana**, with its white-water flows and phallic formations – hopefully this sensitive cave, which is difficult to access and explore at any rate, will soon be protected by the government. A five-hour walk along easy-to-follow tracks through beautiful mountain scenery will also save you the fare to Ban Tum (see below).

Soppong and Tham Lot

The small market town of **SOPPONG**, 68km from Mae Hong Son, gives access to the area's most famous cave, **Tham Lot**, 9km north in **BAN TUM** (or Ban Tham). There's no public transport along the gentle paved forest road to the village, so if you haven't got your own wheels, you'll have to hitch, walk or rent a motorbike taxi (B60).

Turn right in the village to find the entrance to the **Tham Lot Nature Education Station** set up to look after the cave, where you can hire a guide with lantern for B100. A short walk through the forest brings you to the entrance of Tham Lot, where the Lang River begins a 600-metre subterranean journey through the cave, requiring you to hire a bamboo raft (at B100 per group of one to four) for the journey through to the other side. Two hours should allow you enough time for travelling through the broad, airy tunnel, and for the main attraction, climbing up into the sweaty caverns in the roof.

The first of these, **Column Cavern**, 100m from the entrance on the right, is dominated by a twenty-metre-high cave stalagmite snaking up towards the ceiling. Another 50m on the left, bamboo ladders lead up into **Doll Cave**, which has a glistening, pure white wall and a weird red and white formation shaped like a Wurlitzer organ; deep inside, stalagmites look like dolls. Just before the vast exit from the cave, wooden ladders on the left lead up into **Coffin Cave**, named after the remains of a dozen crude log coffins discovered here, one of them preserved to its full length of 5m. Hollowed out from tree trunks, they are similar to those found in many of the region's caves: some are raised 2m off the ground by wooden supporting poles, and some still contained bones, pottery and personal effects when they were discovered. These are now on display in a small museum at the cave's entrance. The coffins are between 1200 and 2200 years old, and local people attribute them to *phi man*, the cave spirits. It's worth hanging round the cave's main exit at sunset, when hundreds of thousands of tiny black chirruping swifts pour into the cave in an almost solid column, to find their beds for the night.

Practicalities

Cave Lodge (❶–❸), on the other side of Ban Tum from the cave, makes an excellent and friendly base for exploring the area. The owners, a local Shan woman and her Australian husband, have plenty of useful information about Tham Lot and some of the two hundred other caves in the region, and organize occasional **guided trips** through the more interesting ones. They also offer **kayaking** trips through Tham Lot at B400 for a couple of hours. Walking to local Karen, Lahu and Lisu villages from the lodge is possible, as well as elephant riding at a nearby Karen village (B200 per person per hour). There is a swimming hole right in front of the lodge, a funky communal area for eating and hanging out, and the kitchen bakes its own bread and cakes. Dorm beds here are B60, and the wooden bungalows, some with shared hot showers and others with their own bathrooms, are scattered over the overgrown hillside.

On the main road at the western end of Soppong, *Jungle Guest House* (☎053/617099; ❶–❸) is the most popular of several places in town, and can give advice on local walks to Lisu villages or organize inexpensive trekking trips to Lisu, Lahu and Karen settlements further to the south. Accommodation here is in simple bamboo huts with shared hot showers, a dorm or some sturdier teak bungalows with hot-water bathrooms attached; the food, both Thai and Western, is great. A short walk east of Soppong's bus stop and a little upmarket, *Lemonhill Guest House* (℡053/617039; ❷) has chalets with their own hot-water bathrooms, in a pretty garden sloping down to the Lang River.

Pai

Beyond Soppong, the road climbs through the last of Mae Hong Son province's wild landscape before descending into the broad, gentle valley of **PAI**, 43km from Soppong. Once treated as a stopover on the tiring journey to Mae Hong Son, Pai is now a destination in its own right, and travellers settle into the town's laid-back feel for weeks or even months. There's nothing special to do in Pai, but the atmosphere is relaxing and the guest houses and restaurants have tailored themselves to the steady flow of travellers who make the four-hour bus journey out from Chiang Mai. The small town's traditional buildings spread themselves liberally over the west bank of the Pai River, but everything is within walking range of the bus station at the north end. On the town's main drag, Thanon Rungsiyanon, an odd mix of hill-tribe people, shrouded Thai Muslims and Westerners mingle together.

Several undemanding **walks** can be made around Pai's broad, gently sloping valley. The easiest – one hour there and back – takes you across the river bridge on the east side of town and up the hill to Wat Mae Yen, which commands a great view over the whole district (the much-touted hot springs, 7km south of the wat, are a big disappointment). On the way to the wat, you'll pass the town's open-air **swimming pool** (usually daily 10am–7pm; B30). To the west of town, an unpaved road (accessible by motorbike) heads out from Pai hospital, passing, after 3km, Wat Nam Hu, whose Buddha image has an unusual hinged top-knot containing holy water, before gradually climbing through comparatively developed Kuomintang, Lisu and Lahu villages to **Mo Pang Falls**, with a pool for swimming, about 10km west of Pai.

Pai makes a good base for **trekking**, which can be arranged for around B500 per day through the guest houses or trekking agents, of which *Back Trax* at 67/1 Thanon Rungsiyanon is reliable. Karen, Lisu and Lahu villages are within range, and the terrain has plenty of variety: jungles and bamboo forests, hills and flat valleys. The area north of town, where trekking can be combined with **elephant riding**, can get rather touristy, but the countryside to the south is very quiet and unspoilt, with a wider range of hill tribes; hardened walkers could arrange a trek to Mae Hong Son, five days away to the southwest. If you just fancy the elephant riding without the trekking, head for the elephant camp office at no. 5/3 Thanon Rungsiyanon (B300 for 90min, B400 for 2hr 30min).

With a little more cash to spare, you could strike up with the French-run Thai Adventure Rafting (℡053/699111), in an office next to *Chez Swan* on Thanon Rungsiyanon, for a **rubber-raft trip** south down the Khong River from Mae Suya, then west along the Pai River, before finishing up just north of Mae Hong Son where Route 1095 crosses the river. Sturdier than bamboo rafts, these craft can negotiate the exciting Hin Mong rapids, and will also take you through the Pai Kit gorges and past Suza Waterfalls, a series of twenty travertine falls cascading from a jungle delta, which make a good place for swimming. The journey takes two days, including a night under canvas by the river, and costs B1800 per person (four people minimum); the season runs from July to the end of January, with the highest water from August to early September, and participants must be able to swim.

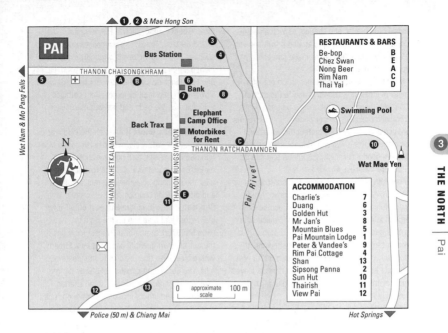

Practicalities

Pai's **bus station** is near the junction of Thanon Rungsiyanon and Thanon Chaisongkhram. The most reliable place to rent **motorbikes** is MS Motors at 6 Thanon Rungsiyanon, which has Honda Dreams (B150) and trail bikes (B250); *Duang Guest House* has plenty of **mountain bikes** (B50 old, B80 new). You can **change money** at the bank at the north end of Thanon Rungsiyanon. The **post office** is at the southern end of Thanon Khet Kalang; you can make international calls here. Several shops near the intersection of Thanon Rungsiyanon and Thanon Ratchadamnoen offer **internet access**. The police are just south of town, on the road to Chiang Mai.

Accommodation

Coinciding with the town's soaring popularity, **guest houses** are springing up all the time. There are now forty or so within town, as well as several options in the countryside around Pai, useful for escaping the growing bustle downtown; we've listed the pick of the bunch below. Several upmarket **resorts** have also sprung up in the countryside, catering largely for Thai weekenders with their own transport. The best of these is *Pai Mountain Lodge*, 6km west of Pai on the road to Mo Pang Falls (℡053/699995; ❹), which has large chalets with proper fireplaces (a great boon in the cool season) in a flower-strewn upland bowl.

Charlie's Guest House, 9 Thanon Rungsiyanon ℡053/699039. Offers a variety of rooms, including kitsch "romantic houses", set around a lush garden, all of them clean (Charlie is the district health officer) with access to hot showers; it also has B50 dorm beds. ❶–❷

Duang Guest House, 5 Thanon Rungsiyanon ℡053/699101, ℻699581. Opposite the bus station, this is a reasonable place to stay, though in a rather cramped compound; some rooms have hot-water bathrooms. ❶–❸

Golden Hut, on the river bank, northeast of the bus station ℡053/699949. Has simple rooms and huts, both en-suite and sharing, as well as a B40 dorm in a quiet, shady spot around a fruit and vegetable plot, and offers home-made jam and yoghurt for breakfast. ❶–❸

Mr Jan's, Thanon Sukhaphibun 3. On one of a mess of small streets behind and to the east of *Charlie's*, this offers quiet, simple bamboo bungalows with mosquito nets or pricier concrete rooms with cold-water en-suite bathrooms, all set in a delightfully overgrown and fragrant medicinal herb garden; good massages (B150/hour) and saunas (B50) are available. ❶–❷

Mountain Blues, 174 Thanon Chaisongkhram ☎053/699282. On the outskirts of town; head west from the bus station past the hospital. Set around a lily pond, this rather chaotic place offers a choice of a dormprice, or A-frame bamboo huts with mosquito nets and shared hot showers, or bungalows (some of which sleep four; B200) with en-suite hot-water bathrooms. Live blues is played most evenings in the bar out front, and a jam session is held every Friday. ❶

Peter & Vandee's, on the road heading east out of town, just after the bridge. Has basic bamboo huts set on a low hill beside the town's swimming pool. Despite their names, both owners are Thai and have earned a reputation for their well-organized one- to five-day cookery classes (B400–1200). ❶

Rim Pai Cottage, 17 Moo 3, Viang Tai ☎053/699133, ☎699234. In a beautiful setting by the river to the east of the bus station, this is as posh as Pai gets; first choice among its rustic but comfortable log cabins, all with hot showers, are the riverside treehouses. ❹–❺

Shan Guest House, Thanon Rungsiyanon ☎053/699162. Almost in open countryside at the southern end of town, this is a friendly establishment in large unruly grounds around a pond; old bamboo bungalows with cold-water bathrooms are slowly being replaced by large, smart cottages with quilts on the beds and hot-water en-suites. ❶–❸

Sipsong Panna Guest House, on the Pai River north of town. Follow signs 1km north on the Mae Hong Son road, then turn right for another kilometre. Besides just four en-suite rooms, named after the elements, they have a small art studio and offer cooking courses. ❸

Sun Hut, on the road heading east out of town just before Wat Mae Yen on the right ☎053/699730. In one of the nicest locations of the out-of-town guest houses, set by a stream with a view over rice paddies to the western hills. The compound consists of sturdy bungalows named after the planets, some sharing bathrooms and others en-suite, arranged around a pond and a communal, open-sided lounging area. ❶–❸

Thairish, Thanon Rungsiyanon ☎053/699149. In a solid wooden building; upstairs there are rooms with shared bathroom, while downstairs is a congenial bar and restaurant. ❶–❷

View Pai Hotel, on the main road at the south end of town ☎053/699174. Somewhat shabby, this place has en-suite rooms with fan or aircon; it's only worth resorting to if you happen to arrive at a busy time and the guest houses are full. ❸–❹

Eating

As with the guest–house scene, new **restaurants** are opening practically every week, but those mentioned here have been established for some time and are generally reliable. Best of the travellers' haunts is *Thai Yai* at 12 Thanon Rungsiyanon (Mon–Sat 7.30am–9.30pm, Sun 7.30am–noon), which rustles up generous portions of back-home favourites at surprisingly low prices. The menu includes lots of veggie options, good coffee and delicious bread baked daily – and they even do a packed lunch for day-trips. Bringing a cosmopolitan touch to this rural town, *Chez Swan*, also on Thanon Rungsiyanon, lays on good French food at moderate prices. At the junction of Thanon Chaisongkhram and Khetkalang, *Nong Beer Restaurant* turns out a mean *khao soi* at lunch time. Reasonably priced versions of standard Thai dishes are served at *Rim Nam Restaurant*, which occupies a pleasant spot by the bridge on the east side of town, with a covered terrace raised over the river. At night, a popular spot for travellers to congregate is at *Be-Bop*, on Thanon Chaisongkhram, a small but busy **bar** which hosts live music.

From Pai to Chiang Mai

Once out of the Pai valley, Route 1095 climbs for 35km of hairpin bends, with beautiful views north to 2175-metre Doi Chiang Dao near the top. In the cool season, with your own transport, you can witness – if you get started from Pai an hour before dawn – one of the country's most famous views of the sun rising over a sea of mist at **Huay Nam Dang National Park** (B200). The viewpoint is signposted on the left 30km out of Pai, after a long climb up the valley; take this turning and go on 6km to the park headquarters. Similar views can be glimpsed from the road over the next few kilometres, though finding a spot to stop off isn't easy. Once over the 1300-metre pass, the road steeply descends the south-facing slopes in the shadow of Doi Mae Ya (2065m), before working its way along the narrow, more populous lower valleys. After 55km (at kilometre-stone 42), a left turn leads 6.5km over some roller-coaster hills to **Pong Duet hot springs**, where scalding water leaps into the air, generating copious quantities of steam in the cool season. A few hundred metres downstream of the springs, a series of pools allow you to soak in the temperature of your choice. The last appealing detour of the route is to **Mokfa Falls** (part of Doi Suthep National Park; B200), where a cascade tumbles about 30m into a sand-fringed pool that is ideal for swimming, making an attractive setting for a break – it's 2km south of the main road, 76km from Pai. Finally, at **Mae Malai**, turn right onto the busy Highway 107 and join the mad, speeding traffic for the last 34km across the wide plain of rice paddy to Chiang Mai.

Chiang Rai and the borders

The northernmost tip of Thailand, stretching from the Kok River and **Chiang Rai** to the border, is a schizophrenic place, split in two by Highway 1, Thailand's main north–south road. In the western half, rows of wild, shark's-tooth mountains jut into Burma, while to the east, low-lying rivers flow through Thailand's richest rice-farming land to the Mekhong River, which forms the border with Laos here. In anticipation of Burma and Laos throwing open their frontiers to tourism, the region is well connected and has been thoroughly kitted out for visitors. Chiang Rai now has well over two thousand hotel rooms, catering mostly to upmarket fortnighters, who plough through the countryside in air-conditioned Scenicruisers in search of quaint, photogenic primitive life. What they get – fairground rides on boats and elephants, a sanitized presentation of the Golden Triangle's opium fields and colourfully dressed hill people performing artificial folkloric rituals – generally satisfies expectations, but has little to do with the harsh realities of life in the north.

Chiang Rai itself pays ever less attention to independent travellers, so although you will probably have to pass through the provincial capital, you should figure on spending most of your time in the border areas to the north, exploring the dizzy mountain heights, frenetic border towns and ancient ruins.

Trekking, the prime domain of the backpacker, has also taken the easy route upmarket, and is better embarked on elsewhere in the north.

Chiang Mai to Chiang Rai

From Chiang Mai you can choose from three main approaches to Chiang Rai. The quickest and most obvious is Highway 118, a fast, 185-kilometre road that swoops through rolling hill country. Buses make the run in three hours, and most travellers end up passing this way once – it's best saved for the return journey, when you may well want to speed back to the comforts of Chiang Mai. For do-it-yourself **trekking**, this route has the benefit of running close to the primitive *Trekker House*, set in a beautiful landscape among a plethora of hill-tribe settlements: to get there from Chiang Mai, take any Chiang Rai bus and get off at the signpost 64km from Chiang Mai, just before Ban Sob Pong, from where it's a seven-kilometre walk up a dirt road. But unless you're in a desperate hurry getting to and from Chiang Rai, you'll probably opt for one of the scenic routes to Chiang Rai described below. The westerly of the two follows Highway 107 to **Tha Ton** and then completes the journey by longtail boat or bamboo raft down the **Kok River**. The other follows Highway 118 as far as Mae Kachan, then branches right on Highway 120 to the tranquil lakeside town of **Phayao**, and approaches Chiang Rai via Highway 1.

Tha Ton and the Kok River

Set aside two days for this road and river journey along the **Kok River**, allowing for the almost inevitable overnight stay in Tha Ton. Buses between Chiang Mai's northern Chang Phuak bus station and Tha Ton take about four hours; the standard boat trip takes the better part of the following afternoon. If you're on a motorbike, once at Tha Ton you have the choice of stowing your bike on the longtail for Chiang Rai, or pushing on northeastwards to Mae Salong or Mae Chan.

Chiang Mai to Fang

From Chiang Mai the route heads north along Highway 107, retracing the Mae Hong Son loop in the early going and, after 56km, passing an **elephant training centre** on the right, which puts on logging shows daily at 9am and 10am (B60). It's a more attractive setting than the Mae Sa valley camps, especially good for elephant rides and bamboo rafting, but if you're planning to visit Lampang, there is a less hyped equivalent with a better show en route (see p.341). Around kilometre-stone 72 **Chiang Dao**, an oversized market village, stretches on and on along the road as the crags and forests of Thailand's third-highest peak, Doi Chiang Dao (2175m) loom up on the left. With almost sheer sides rising from the rice paddies to neck-stretching heights, it is probably the most dramatic mountain in the country. The Chiang Mai–Fang **bus** stops at both the elephant camp and Chiang Dao.

A road heads northwest of the village after 5km to an extensive complex of interconnected caverns, **Tham Chiang Dao**, with an attached monastery (the caves have been given religious significance by the local legend of a hermit sage who is said to have dwelt in them for a millennium). Several of the caverns can be visited; a couple have electric light but others need the services of a guide with a lantern. Admission to the caves is B10 and guides ask around B80–100 for a tour of about half an hour, during which they point out unusual rock formations. About 1500m further north along the road from the caves, the secluded *Malee's Nature Lovers Bungalows* (℡01/9618387, ⓔmaleenature @hotmail.com; ❶–❹) is a cosy compound delightfully set in the shadow of the mountain; call them to be picked up from the main road. Half a dozen comfy bungalows of varying size, some with hot water, as well as dorm accommodation and camping facilities are available here. They can arrange treks to the top of the mountain or to surrounding hill-tribe villages, and also point birders in the right direction.

Back on Highway 107, the road shimmies over a rocky ridge marking the watershed separating the catchment areas of the Chao Phraya River to the south and the Mekhong River ahead, before descending into the flat plain around Fang and the Kok River. Branching off to the left some 60km from Chiang Dao, a steep and winding 25-kilometre road, Route 1249, leads up to **Doi Angkhang** (1928m). Besides an agricultural station here that produces peaches, raspberries and kiwis in the cool climate, the mountain is home to the **Angkhang Nature Resort** (℡053/450110, ⓕ450120, ⓦwww.amari.com /angkhang; ❽), where the luxurious teak pavilions have balconies with great views, and mule riding, mountain biking and bird-watching are the main activities. There are several hill-tribe villages in the region and the roads around here are fun for bikers.

En route to Tha Ton on public transport, you may have to change buses in the ugly frontier outpost of **Fang**, 153km from Chiang Mai, but you're far better off pushing on to Tha Ton for somewhere to stay, as Fang's few hotels are cheap and nasty. With your own transport, you can give Fang a miss altogether by branching west on a bypass signposted to Chiang Rai. Another option is cut east 5km before Fang on Highway 109 for Chiang Rai (125km), but this route is not as interesting as going down the beautiful Kok valley.

Tha Ton

The tidy, leafy settlement of **THA TON**, nearly 180km north of Chiang Mai, huddles each side of a bridge over the Kok River, which flows out of Burma 4km to the west upstream. Life in Tha Ton revolves around the bridge – buses and boats pull up here, and most of the accommodation is clustered nearby. The main attractions here are longtail-boat and bamboo-raft rides downstream to Chiang Rai, but on the south side of the bridge the over-the-top ornamental gardens of **Wat Tha Ton**, endowed with colossal golden and white Buddha images and an equally huge statue of Chao Mae Kuan Im, the Chinese goddess of mercy, are well worth the short climb. From any of the statues, the views up the narrow green valley towards Burma and downstream across the sun-glazed plain are heady stuff.

Thip's Traveller House (℡ & ⓕ053/459312; ❶), on the south side of the bridge, is a convenient and cheap **place to stay**, with decent en-suite rooms in a crowded compound, and good food. The formidable Mrs Thip is a great source of information and organizes rafting packages to Chiang Rai (see p.377) as well as scenic longtail-boat trips to the Burmese border (20min). Mrs Thip has opened a second guest house (❷) 4km east along Route 1089 on a rise above the Kok valley, with a variety of comfortable rooms – ask at *Thip's* for a lift out there. Another place to try if *Thip's* is full is the nearby *Apple Guesthouse* (℡053/4593158; ❶), whose quiet, shady flower-filled compound is backed by a field. It offers a choice of A-frame bamboo bungalows or clean pleasant rooms in a modern building; all have their own bathrooms, screens and fans. To reach the guest house, head 200m south from the bridge, then walk 150m up the first lane on the left after Mrs Thip's. *Apple* also operates a smarter, newer place – also called *Apple* – right in front of the boat landing, with attractive rooms, all with hot water and TV (☎053/373144–5; ❸). On the north side of the river, *Garden Home* (☎053/373015; ❷–❻), 300m west from the bridge, is another appealing option, with attractive en-suite bungalows (some with hot water and air-con) sheltering under an orchard of lychees and mangoes, and bikes available for rent.

With its own gardens and choice of restaurants (moderate to expensive) about half a kilometre east of the bridge, on the south bank of the river, *Mae Kok River Village Resort* (☎053/459355–6, Ⓕ459329, Ⓔ tiger@loxinfo.co.th; ❼) is Tha Ton's best **upmarket** choice. Well-designed, air-conditioned suites and family villas are set around a pool, while its three restaurants and two bars enjoy riverside locations. The owner, Shane Beary, also runs Track of the Tiger, which offers a wide variety of **soft adventure tours**, taking visitors off the well-trodden trekking trails in a measure of luxury (around B1500 per day, depending on itinerary). Tours are pitched at families, and options include a motorized river barge which takes people to their riverfront jungle camp (with simple bamboo bungalows), group barbecue dinners, mountain-biking trips (day and half-day) and rafting (see p.377). At the resort, visitors can sign up for courses in Thai cooking or massage, rock climbing or canoeing.

The biggest building in Tha Ton is the *Tha Ton Chalet* (☎053/373155–7; ❻), right next to the bridge on the north side of the river, which has top-class rooms with great views downriver, but lacks character. About half a kilometre upstream on this side, beyond *Garden Home*, the *Tha Ton River View Resort and Restaurant* (☎053/373173–5; ❼) is yet another smart riverside complex where all rooms have air-con and hot water.

Beyond Tha Ton, the drab Route 1089 heads to Mae Chan and Highway 1; 20km out of town, an exciting roller coaster of a side road leads north to Mae Salong (see p.384). There's no direct public transport from Tha Ton to Mae Salong, though you can get there on one of the yellow songthaews which leave a few hundred metres north of the bridge in Tha Ton (B50); change onto a green songthaew at the turn-off for the side road to Mae Salong (also change here for songthaews to Mae Chan).

Along the Kok River

Travelling down the hundred-kilometre stretch of the **Kok River** to Chiang Rai gives you a chance to soak up a rich diversity of typical northern land-scapes, which you never get on a speeding bus. Heading out of Tha Ton, the river traverses a flat valley of rice fields and orchards, where it's flanked by high reeds inhabited by flitting swallows – be sure to take a look back for the best view of Wat Tha Ton's beacon-like Buddhas, which remain in sight for at least the first thirty minutes of the trip. About the same time as the statue disappears, you pass the 900-year-old **Wat Phra That Sop Fang**, with its small hilltop chedi and a slithering naga staircase leading up from the river bank. After a five-minute break in **Mae Salak**, 20km from Tha Ton, where dozens of Akha women and children beg and hawk necklaces, you find the river starts to meander between thickly forested slopes. From among the banana trees and giant wispy ferns, kids come out to play, adults to bathe and wash clothes, and water buffalo emerge simply to enjoy the river.

About two hours out of Tha Ton the hills get steeper and the banks rockier, leading up to a half-hour stretch of small but feisty rapids, where you might well get a soaking. Here and there, denuded slopes studded with burnt tree stumps attest to recent deforestation. Beyond the rapids, crowds of boats suddenly appear, ferrying camcorder-toting tour groups from Chiang Rai to the Karen village of **Ruammid**, 20km upstream, for elephant riding. From here on, the landscape deteriorates as the bare valley around Chiang Rai opens up. The best time of year to make this trip is in the cool season (roughly Nov–Feb), when the vegetation is lushest and the rapids most exciting. Canopied **longtail boats** (B200, motorbikes B300) leave from the south side of the bridge in Tha Ton every day at 12.30pm for the trip to Chiang Rai, which takes around four rather noisy hours. The slower, less crowded journey upriver gives an even better chance of appreciating the scenery – the longtails leave Chiang Rai at 10.30am.

If you have more time, the peaceful **bamboo rafts** which glide downriver to Chiang Rai in two days almost make you part of the scenery. Rafts, which leave at about 8am, can fit up to six paying passengers – there are usually plenty of travellers to hitch up with during the high season, when you shouldn't have to wait more than a day for a full complement (minimum of four people); the price includes mats, sleeping bags and food. Each party is accompanied by two steersmen who dismantle the rafts in Chiang Rai and bring the bamboo back to be recycled in Tha Ton. *Mrs Thip's* Guest house (see p.375) is the best place organizing the standard two-day, one-night raft trips (B1500) with a night spent in a Lahu village, a visit to the hot springs in Doi Fang National Park and a one-hour elephant ride at Ruammid. Their popular three-day, two-night trips combine the raft trip with trekking to a variety of hill-tribe villages and an elephant ride (B2200).

Mae Kok River Village Resort offers an upmarket version of the two-day rafting trip in a sturdier and more manoeuvrable adapted bamboo raft, using inner tubes and a steel frame with bamboo on top; the price (from B1700 per person with a full complement of eight passengers) includes an elephant safari and hill-tribe visit and, in line with their soft adventure focus, an overnight stay in their jungle lodge base camp. Their two- to three-day river barge trips down the Kok River to Chiang Rai combine 4WD visits to hill-tribe villages, some trekking, canoeing, an elephant safari and overnighting in the base camp (from B2500 per person with a full complement of eight passengers).

River boats used to be easy pickings for bandits, but the police have successfully clamped down on them by setting up riverside checkpoints. The most important of these is at Mae Salak, where you'll be asked to show your **passport**.

To Chiang Rai via Phayao

Another alternative to racing straight up Highway 118 to Chiang Rai is to turn right onto Highway 120 at Mae Kachan, and follow the route between rolling hills to **PHAYAO**, an ancient, sleepy town facing the 1800-metre peak of Doi Bussaracum. Buses pull in at the station on the north side of town off Thanon Phaholyothin.

Phayao is worth a stop to visit its bizarre wat or to have lunch on the east shore of its large hyacinth-strewn lake. According to legend, the lakeside position of **Wat Sri Khom Kham** – a twenty-minute walk or a songthaew ride north along Thanon Phaholyothin from the bus station – was chosen by the Buddha himself, when, wilting in the notorious Phayao heat, he received shelter from a tree which miraculously sprouted from a seed planted by a passing bird. The main object of worship here is the Phra Chao Ton Luang, a huge pointy-nosed Buddha in the crude, angular local style of the fifteenth century. The limelight has been stolen, however, by a gruesome, modern **statue garden** at the north end of the temple: the supposedly educational statues, which look like special-effects models from a particularly nasty fright movie, are inspired by the Buddhist scriptures and represent the torments of hell. In contrast to these horrors, a modern **viharn**, which has been built on stilts over the lake at the south end of the wat, is all elegance and good taste. The interior has been vibrantly decorated with murals by Angkarn Kalyanapongsa, a famous artist and poet who has followed traditional Lanna styles, incorporating typically homely comic detail with the addition of a sharp, modern edge. The wat apart, Phayao is blessed with many lovely old **teak houses**, which can be seen dotted around the centre.

The town's best budget **hotel** is the central *Tharn Thong*, 55 Thanon Donsanam (T 054/431302, F 481256; ❷–❸), which has clean, reasonably quiet rooms with hot water and fan or air-conditioning. Several **restaurants**, many of which specialize in fish dishes, cluster along the lakeside promenade, catching what breeze they can.

Chiang Rai

Having lived in the shadow of Chiang Mai for all but thirty years of its existence, **CHIANG RAI** – sprawled untidily over the south bank of the Kok River – is now coming up on the rails to make a challenge as an upmarket tourist centre, with all the hype and hustle that goes with it. The long arm of the package-tour industry has reached this northern outpost, bringing snap-happy bus-bound tourists and well-heeled honeymooners, who alight for a couple of days of excursions and then shoot off again. Paradoxically, this leaves the town to get on with its own business during the day, when the trippers are out on manoeuvres, but at night the neon lights flash on and souvenir shops and ersatz Western restaurants are thronged. Meanwhile, the town keeps up its reputation as a dirty-weekend destination for Thais, a game given away by just a few motels and car-ports – where you drive into the garage and pay for a discreet screen to be pulled across behind you. Budget travellers have been sidelined, but they still turn up for the trekking and for the excellent **handicraft shopping**.

Chiang Rai is most famous for the things it had and lost. It was founded in 1263 by King Mengrai of Ngon Yang who, having recaptured a prize elephant he'd been chasing around the foot of Doi Tong, took this as an auspicious omen for a new city. Tradition has it that Chiang Rai prevailed as the capital of the north for thirty years, but historians now believe Mengrai moved his court directly from Ngon Yang to the Chiang Mai area in the 1290s. Thailand's two holiest images, the Emerald Buddha (now in Bangkok) and the Phra Singh Buddha (now perhaps in Bangkok, Chiang Mai or Nakhon Si Thammarat, depending on which story you believe), also once resided here before moving on – at least replicas of these can be seen at Wat Phra Kaeo and Wat Phra Singh.

Arrival, information and transport

Arriving at the **bus station** on Thanon Phaholyothin on Chiang Rai's south side leaves a long walk to most of the guest houses, so you might want to bundle into a samlor (around B20–30) or a songthaew, the two main forms of transport around town (there are also some tuk-tuks around). Longtails from Tha Ton dock at the **boat station,** which occasionally moves if the water level is too low: it's currently situated northwest of the centre on the north side of the Mae Fah Luang bridge. Taxis run into town from the **airport**, 8km northeast, for B150, or Avis and Budget have a car service for B200 per passenger.

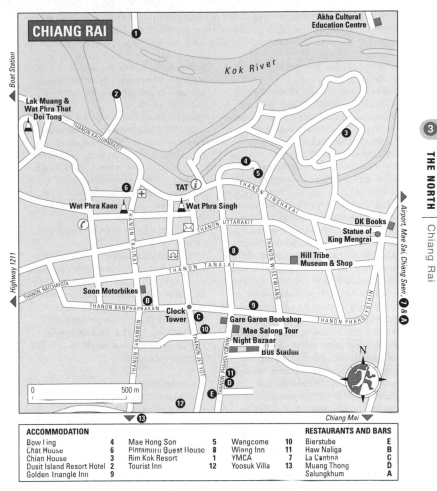

CHIANG RAI

Akha Cultural
Education Centre

Boat Station

K o k   R i v e r

Lak Muang &
Wat Phra That
Doi Tong

THANON KAISORNRASIT

Highway 1211

THANON RATCHAYOTA

THANON SANAMBIN

THANON RATRAT

TAT

Wat Phra Kaeo

Wat Phra Singh

THANON SINGHAKAI

THANON UTTARAKIT

THANON TANALAI

THANON BANPHAPRAKAN

THANON WISETWIANG

THANON JETYOT

THANON PHAHONYOTHIN

DK Books
Statue of
King Mengrai

Hill Tribe
Museum & Shop

Soon Motorbikes

Clock
Tower

Gare Garon Bookshop

Mae Salong Tour

Night Bazaar

Bus Station

THANON PHAHONYOTHIN

Airport, Mae Sai, Chiang Saen,

N

0   500 m

Chiang Mai

ACCOMMODATION					RESTAURANTS AND BARS	
Bow I ing	4	Mae Hong Son	5	Wangcome	10	Bierstube	E
Chat House	6	Pintamin Guest House	8	Wiang Inn	11	Haw Naliga	B
Chian House	3	Rim Kok Resort	1	YMCA	7	La Cantina	C
Dusit Island Resort Hotel	2	Tourist Inn	12	Yoosuk Villa	13	Muang Thong	D
Golden Triangle Inn	9					Salungkhum	A

TAT has a helpful office at 448/16 Thanon Singhakai near Wat Phra Singh (daily 8.30am–4.30pm; ℡053/717433) with some useful free maps and well-written information brochures; it's also shared by the **tourist police** (℡053/717779) who offer a 24–hour service.

Songthaews, which have no set routes, cost locals B5 for short hops; you can flag them down and arrange a price for other trips. Most guest houses rent out **motorbikes** but **bicycles** can be more difficult to find; both are for hire at Soon Motorbikes, 197/2 Thanon Trairat (℡053/714068) – mountain bikes at B100 per day, small motorbikes at B150.

Accommodation

Chiang Rai is overstuffed with **accommodation** in all categories, but much of it offers poor quality for the price; that said, one or two guest houses compare with Chiang Mai's best, and in the *Dusit* it boasts one of the north's finest hotels. Much of the more expensive accommodation is clustered around the commercial centre on Thanon Phaholyothin, while the guest houses can be found along the south bank of the river and on the fringes.

Inexpensive and moderate

Bow Ling Guest House, off Thanon Singhakai ☎053/712704; near the *Mae Hong Son Guest House*. A cute, peaceful place in a very local residential soi with tiny, concrete rooms off a fragrant courtyard filled with pot plants. Run by a young family, this place is very friendly and homely. The five rooms all have their own cold-water bathrooms, and a shared hot shower is available. ❶

Chat House, 3/2 Soi Sangkaew, Thanon Trairat ☎053/711481. Located behind its own garden café on a quiet soi, this is Chiang Rai's longest-running travellers' hangout, with a very laid-back atmosphere. The rooms are modern, colourfully decorated and have en-suite bathrooms with hot water, though they could be a little cleaner; satellite TV is on nightly in the café. Treks, motorbike hire (B150–400) and free pick-ups from the airport are offered by the casual, friendly management. ❶

Chian House, 172 Thanon Sri Boonruang ☎053/713388. In a lively, ramshackle compound around a small swimming pool; accommodation here includes pleasant en-suite rooms (all hot water) and spacious, clean and nicely furnished wooden bungalows with cool tiled floors. Motorcycles (B150–200) and jeeps (B800) for hire; boat trips, elephant rides and one- to five-day treks offered. ❶–❸

Golden Triangle Inn, 590 Thanon Phaholyothin ☎053/711339, ℻713963. Large, tastefully decorated rooms in a garden compound in the heart of town. Tours and treks offered. ❹

Mae Hong Son Guest House, 126 Thanon Singhakai ☎053/715367. This friendly establishment, in a quiet local street, comprises wooden buildings arranged around a very green, pleasant courtyard with neat bar and café. Very pleasant rooms – some en suite (hot water), others sharing hot showers. Tours and treks offered, motorbikes for hire. ❶–❷

Pintamorn Guest House, 509/1 Thanon Rattanaket ☎053/714161, ℻713317. Centrally located, this is one of the best deals in town, its big, well-lit rooms boasting hot-water bathrooms and fan or air-con, with a rambling restaurant downstairs. ❷–❸

Tourist Inn Guesthouse, 1004/4–6 Thanon Jet Yot ☎053/714682. Immaculately clean hotel-style guest house in a modern four-storey building run by a Japanese-Thai team. The reception area downstairs has a European-style bakery, a seating area with big comfy armchairs, TV area and library, while bright, light rooms all come with hot-water bathrooms and air-con or fan. There are cheaper rooms in an attached building, which are not as modern but have hot showers. ❷–❸

YMCA, 70 Thanon Phaholyothin ☎053/713785 or 713786, ℻714336. Ever reliable, with comfortable rooms, some with air-con, in a modern building on the northern edge of town, and dorm beds (B90) available. There's a swimming pool, too. ❹

Yoosuk Villa, 952/13 Thanon Ruamjitthawai ☎053/711946, ℻712376. A good deal in the moderate price range: neat rooms with air-con, TV, fridge and hot water. ❸

Expensive

Dusit Island Resort Hotel, 1129 Thanon Kraisorasit ☎053/715777–9, ℻715801, ⊛ www.dusit.com. Set on a ten-acre island in the Kok River, with unbeatable views of the valley, this is the top of the top end. Facilities include a health club, tennis courts, swimming pool and children's playground, with high standards of service. ❾

Rim Kok Resort, 6 Moo 4, Thanon Chiang Rai–Tha Ton ☎053/716445–60, ℻715859. Palatial luxury hotel in sprawling grounds on the quiet north side of the river. ❽

Wangcome, 869/90 Thanon Pemavipat ☎053/711800, ℻712973. Chintzy hotel, not quite up to international five-star standards. ❼

Wiang Inn, 893 Thanon Phaholyothin ☎053/711533, ℻711877. A bit smarter than the *Wangcome*, and with a swimming pool. ❼

The Town

A walk up to **Doi Tong**, the hummock to the northwest of the centre, is the best way to get your bearings and, especially at sunset, offers a fine view up the

Kok River as it emerges from the mountains to the west. On the highest part of the hill stands the most interesting of Chiang Rai's few sights, a kind of phallic Stonehenge centred on the town's new **lak muang**, representing the Buddhist layout of the universe. Historically, the erection of a *lak muang* marks the official founding of a Thai city, precisely dated to January 26, 1263 in the case of Chiang Rai; the new *lak muang* and the elaborate stone model around it were erected 725 years later to the day, as part of the celebrations of King Bhumibol's sixtieth birthday. The *lak muang* itself represents Mount Sineru (or Meru), the axis of the universe, while the series of concentric terraces, moats and pillars represent the heavens and the earth, the great oceans and rivers, and the major features of the universe. Sprinkling water onto the garlanded *lak muang* and then dabbing your head with the water after it has flowed into the basin below brings good luck.

The old wooden *lak muang* can be seen in the viharn of **Wat Phra That Doi Tong**, the city's first temple, which sprawls shambolically over the eastern side of the hill. Look out for the small golden prang, the old-fashioned wooden spirit house and the Chinese shrine, with which the wat shares the hillside in a typically ecumenical spirit.

The Emerald Buddha, Thailand's most important image, was discovered when lightning cracked open the chedi (since restored) at **Wat Phra Kaeo** on Thanon Trairat. A beautiful replica, which was carved in China from 300kg of milky green jade and presented by a Chinese millionaire in 1991, can now be seen here in the Hor Phra Yok, a tiny, Lanna-style pavilion situated to the right behind the viharn. At 47.9cm wide and 65.9cm high, the replica is millimetres smaller; the Buddha image is not an exact copy as religious protocol dictated that the replica could not have exactly the same name, materials or appearance as the original. The whole complex has recently been renovated and the decorative trimmings show a high level of craftsmanship, including those on the large wooden building to the left of the viharn, which houses ancient religious objects and texts. Though no other temples in Chiang Rai are of such historic importance, admirers of temple art and architecture will find many interesting curiosities in the other temple compounds scattered around the town.

The **statue of King Mengrai** in the northeast corner of town is also an interesting place to wander to, if only to observe the regularity with which locals arrive to pay homage and make offerings to their local hero, who founded the kingdom of Lanna. The small island on which the statue stands is often surrounded by roaring traffic, yet the statue itself stands serenely amid the scent of incense and flowers.

As Chiang Rai is surrounded by such a variety of hill tribes and visited by such a weight of tourists, there are plenty of **handicraft shops**, though most of those lined up along Thanon Phaholyothin are merely trinket stalls. For a more authentic selection, head for the **Hill Tribe Museum and Handicrafts Shop** at 620/25 Thanon Tanalai, which stocks tasteful and well-made hill-tribe handicrafts. The shop, on the second floor, was started by the country's leading development campaigner, Meechai Viravaidya, under the auspices of the PDA (Population and Community Development Association) and all proceeds go to village projects. The museum (Mon–Fri 8.30am–8pm; Sat & Sun 10am–8pm; B40) is a good place to learn about the hill tribes before going on a trek, and includes a slick, informative slide show (25min); they also organize treks themselves which you can ask about while you're here. All sorts of handicrafts, some of good quality and competitively priced, are on sale at the **night bazaar** which is set up off Thanon Phaholyothin next to the bus station, and it might at least give you something to do in the evening.

Eating and drinking

Chiang Rai's **restaurants** congregate along Thanon Banphaprakan, Jet Yot and Phaholyothin, with a growing number of unimpressive Western places scattered around. However, there are some good Thai options in the moderate to expensive range. There's a **food centre** in the night bazaar with lots of delicious snacks and a beer garden too, where you can catch a free performance of transvestite cabaret, local folk-singers or traditional dancers. On Thanon Jed Yod, just south of the junction with Thanon Banphaprakan, a clutch of go-go **bars** down a side alley add a touch of sleaze, while several western-style bars further down the road offer a more relaxed atmosphere, with satellite TV, music or just drinks and a chat.

Bierstube, south of the *Wiang Inn* at 897/1 Thanon Phaholyothin. A well-run and easy-going watering hole, with inexpensive draught beer and good German food, including its own smoked sausages and pickles. Expensive.

Cabbages and Condoms, Ground Floor, Hill Tribe Museum, 620/25 Thanon Tanalai. Proudly proclaiming "our food is guaranteed not to cause pregnancy", this restaurant covers its walls with paraphernalia devoted to birth control, including condom campaign posters and pictures of Meechai Viravaidya, who began this organization to promote family planning and HIV/AIDS prevention. The yummy menu of Thai food, including some traditional northern dishes, is well described in English, with a few dishes suitable for vegetarians. Daily 11am–midnight. Moderate.

Chiang Rai Island Restaurant, in the grounds of the *Dusit Island Resort*, 1129 Thanon Kraisorasit. An elegant, open-sided pavilion well worth a splurge for its wide range of delicious Thai cuisine. Expensive.

Haw Naliga, 402/1–2 Thanon Banphaprakan. To the west of the clocktower after which it's named, this eating place has seen better days, but is centrally located and boasts a varied Thai menu. Moderate.

La Cantina, 1025/40 Thanon Jet Yot. The Italian owner rustles up a long menu of good pastas, pizzas and veggie options, accompanied by home-baked bread. Moderate to expensive.

Muang Thong, on the corner of Thanon Phaholyothin, just south of the *Wiang Inn Hotel*. Does a wide range of Thai and Chinese dishes, and displays a huge selection of ingredients outside its open-sided eating area. Popular among Thais, Chinese and foreigners alike. Moderate.

Salungkhum, 843 Thanon Phaholyothin. Between King Mengrai's statue and the river. Rated by locals as serving the best food for the price in town, with a garden at the back for evening dining; there's no sign in English, but look out for the Cosmo petrol station on the opposite side of the road. Moderate.

Listings

Airlines The Thai Airways office is at 870 Thanon Phaholyothin ☎ 053/711179.

Boat trips Mae Salong Tour, 882–4 Thanon Phaholyothin ☎ 053/712515, ⨍ 711011, run boat trips (albeit infrequent and extremely expensive ones) up the Mekhong to China, departing from and returning to Sop Ruak. The tour operator takes care of visa arrangements, but since these trips are geared towards Thais, you aren't guaranteed an English-speaking guide.

Bookshop Gare Garon, 869/18 Thanon Phaholyothin, has a small range of new and used books in English, or you could try DK Books on the same street near the Mengrai statue.

Car and motorbike rental For renting a motorbike, Soon at 197/2 Thanon Trairat ☎ 053/714068 is the most reliable place in Chiang Rai and has the best choice with small bikes, starting from B150. Four-wheel drives are available for B1500–2400 a day at Avis in the *Dusit Island Resort* ☎ 053/715777 and SMT (Inter-rent) at the airport ☎ 053/793048, while local agencies like the reliable P.D. Tour, 869/108 Thanon Pemavipat, near the Wiang Come department store ☎ 053/712829, can rent cheaper jeeps for around B800 per day; they also organize expensive car tours in the area.

Tours and trekking from Chiang Rai

Communities from all the hill tribes have settled around **Chiang Rai**, and the region offers the full range of terrain for **trekking**, from gentle walking trails near the Kok River to tough mountain slopes further north towards the Burmese border. The river is deep enough for rafts both to the west and the east of the town, and elephant riding is included in most treks. However, this natural suitability has attracted too many agencies and trekkers, and many of the hill-tribe villages, especially between Chiang Rai and Mae Salong, have become weary of the constant to-ing and fro-ing. Some of the agencies in Chiang Rai have recently widened their net to include the rest of the province, such as Chiang Khong, where there's a large population of Hmong and Mien, and provinces like Nan, 270km to the southeast. Sizes of group treks from Chiang Rai tend to be smaller than those from Chiang Mai, often with just two or three people, with a maximum of about seven in a group; an average three-day, two-night trek with an elephant trek costs B2200 each for two people and B1800–2000 each for up to five. All guest houses in Chiang Rai can fit you up with a trek – *Chat*, *Chian* and *Mae Hong Son* are responsible and reliable, and the tourist office publishes a trekking leaflet with a list of trekking outfits they've vetted.

The PDA (℡053/740088; see p.381) offers two- to five-day jungle treks, and you can chat about them and look at itineraries at the Hill Tribe Museum; a three-day, two-night trek with two to five people costs B2500–3000 and includes overnights in Lahu and Akha villages, elephant trekking and a longtail-boat ride. They also offer one-day versions from B1000–3000 (depending on the size of the group), and tours to Mae Salong and other places of interest. As well as its treks, *Mae Hong Son Guest House* offers a day-trip to Doi Tung (B1000 per person), while *Chian Guest House* offers a half-day combined boat trip along the Kok River to a Karen village followed by an elephant ride (B700).

For comprehensive and accurate coverage of trails and hill-tribe villages in Chiang Rai province, the *Guide Map of Chiang Rai* by V. Hongsombud (Bangkok Guides) is essential; it's available at the Chiang Rai bookshops listed opposite.

Exchange There are banks and currency exchange counters on Thanon Tanalai, Thanon Uttarakit and Thanon Rhanon Phaholyothin, near the bus station.

Internet access Many hotels and guest houses in Chiang Rai offer internet access, and there are many cybercafés on the small streets between Thanon Jet Yot and Phaholyothin.

Mail The post office is on Thanon Uttarakit, just south of Wat Phra Singh.

Pharmacy A few well-stocked pharmacies can be found on Thanon Tanalai.

Telephones A convenient place for making international calls is at the Telecom Centre on Thanon Ngam Muang, near Wat Phra Kaeo.

North of Chiang Rai

At a push, any one of the places described in this section could be visited on a day-trip from Chiang Rai, but if you can devote three or four days, you'd be better off moving camp to make a circuit of **Mae Salong** with its mountain-top Chinese enclave, **Mae Sai**, an intriguing border town, and **Chiang Saen**, whose atmospheric ruins by the banks of the Mekhong contrast sharply with the commercialism of nearby **Sop Ruak**. Given more time and patience, you could also stop over on the way to Mae Sai at **Doi Tung** to look down over Thailand, Laos, Burma and China, and continue beyond Chiang Saen to **Chiang Khong** on the banks of the Mekhong, which is now a popular crossing point to Laos.

Chiang Rai province is well enough mapped for independent exploration: the *Guide Map of Chiang Rai* (see box above) is indispensable for getting the most out of a rented vehicle (see p.382 for rental outlets), and might well give you some ideas for day walks away from the major attractions. If you just want to hop around the main towns by **public transport**, the set-up is straightforward enough: frequent buses to Mae Sai run due north up Highway 1; to Chiang Saen, they start off on the same road before forking right onto Highway 1016; for most other places, you have to make one change off these routes onto a songthaew.

Mae Salong (Santikhiri)

Perched 1300m up on a ridge with commanding views of sawtoothed hills, the Chinese Nationalist outpost of **MAE SALONG** lies 36km along a roller coaster of a road that ploughs into the harsh border country west of Highway 1. Songthaews make the dizzying ninety-minute journey frequently, starting from **Ban Pasang**, 32km north of Chiang Rai on Highway 1. A few marginally interesting attractions might tempt you to hop off en route, notably the **Hill Tribe Culture Centre**, 12km from Ban Pasang, where local minorities are taught how to farm cash crops other than opium, and a couple of Mien and Akha souvenir villages. You should have no trouble flagging down another pick-up when you're done, though you may have to wait.

Mae Salong is the focal point for the area's fourteen thousand **Kuomintang**, who for two generations now have held fast to their cultural identity, if not their political cause. The ruling party of China for 21 years, the Kuomintang (Nationalists) were swept from power by the Communist revolution of 1949 and fled in two directions: one group, under party leader Chiang Kai-shek, made for Taiwan, where it founded the Republic of China; the other, led by General Li Zongren, settled in northern Thailand and Burma. The Nationalists' original plan to retake China from Mao Zedong in a two-pronged attack never came to fruition, and the remnants of the army in Thailand became major players in the heroin trade. Over the last twenty years, the Thai government has worked hard to "pacify" the Kuomintang by a mixture of force and more peaceful methods, such as crop programmes to replace opium. Around Mae Salong at least, its work seems to have been successful, as evidenced by the slopes to the south of the settlement, which are covered with a carpet of rich green tea bushes. Since its rehabilitation, Mae Salong is now officially known as **Santikhiri** (Hill of Peace).

The Town and beyond

Though it has temples, a church and a mosque, it's the details of Chinese life in the back streets – the low-slung bamboo houses, the pictures of Chiang Kai-shek, ping-pong tables, the sounds of Yunnanese conversation punctuated with throaty hawking – that make the village absorbing. Mae Salong gets plenty of Thai visitors, especially at weekends, who throng the main street's souvenir stalls to buy such delicacies as sorghum whisky (pickled with ginseng, deer antler and centipedes) and locally grown Chinese tea and herbs. If you want to sample the wares for yourself in a less commercialized environment, look out for the **traditional medicine shop**, on the right of the main street 50m before *Shin Sane Guest House*. Here they sell medicinal teas, pellets and biscuits which are good for the various parts of the body. It's also worth braving the dawn chill to get to the **morning market**, held in the middle of town from 5am to 7am, which pulls them in from the surrounding Akha, Lisu and Mien villages.

The minor road which branches off the main street in the centre of town leads after an hour to a clutch of very traditional and conservative **Akha**

A variety of circumstances have led to North Thailand being notorious for the production of **illegal drugs**, especially **opium**, which comes from the resin that oozes from the seed heads of the opium poppy when slit. Though opium is associated with the Far East in the popular imagination, the opium poppy actually originated in the Mediterranean. It arrived in the East, however, over twelve centuries ago, and was later brought to Thailand from China with the hill tribes who migrated from Yunnan province.

Opium growing has been illegal in Thailand since 1959, but during the 1960s and 1970s rampant production and refining of the crop in the lawless region on the borders of Thailand, Burma and Laos earned the area the nickname "**the Golden Triangle**". Two "armies" have traditionally operated most of the trade within this area. The **Shan United Army**, which was fighting the Burmese government for an independent state for the Shan people, funded its weapons and manpower from the production of **heroin** (a more refined form of opium). Led by the notorious warlord Khun Sa, the Shan United Army attempted to extend their influence inside Thailand during the 1960s, where they came up against the troops of the **Kuomintang** (KMT). These refugees from China, who fled after the Communist takeover there, were at first befriended by the Thai and Western governments, who were pleased to have a fiercely anti-Communist force patrolling this border area. The Kuomintang were thus able to develop the heroin trade, while the authorities turned a blind eye.

At first the Kuomintang and Shan armies were powerful enough to operate unhindered within Thai borders. Since the 1980s, however, the danger of Communist incursion into Thailand has largely disappeared, and the government has been able to concentrate on the elimination of the crop. The Kuomintang in the area around Mae Salong have been put on a determined "pacification" programme, though it appears they still play an important role as middlemen in the traffic in heroin. In 1983 the Shan United Army was pushed out of its stronghold at nearby Ban Hin Taek, over the border into Burma, and in 1996, Khun Sa cut a deal with the corrupt Burmese military dictatorship. The man once dubbed the "Prince of Death" now lives under Burmese army protection in a comfortable villa in Rangoon and has turned his attention to supposedly legitimate business ventures.

The Thai government's concerted attempt to eliminate opium growing within its borders has succeeded in reducing the size of the crop to an insignificant amount. However, Thailand still has a vital role to play as a conduit for heroin; most of the production and refinement of opium has simply moved over the borders into Burma and Laos, where opium yields stand at well over 2500 tonnes per year and are still rising.

The destruction of huge areas of poppy fields has had far-reaching repercussions on the hill tribes. In many cases, with the raw product not available, opium addicts have turned to injecting heroin from shared needles, leading to a devastating outbreak of AIDS. It has been necessary for the Thai government to give the hill tribes an alternative livelihood through the introduction of more legitimate cash crops, yet these often demand the heavy use of pesticides, which later get washed down into the lowland valleys, incurring the wrath of Thai farmers.

Though the trafficking of heroin from across the borders with Burma and Laos still presents a serious problem for the Thai authorities, its importance has been eclipsed by a flood tide of *ya baa*, or **methamphetamines**, that is infiltrating the traditional fabric of Thai society, particularly the schools. Produced in vast quantities in factories just across the Burmese border, these pills are the main objective of vehicle searches in border areas, yet despite frequent arrests of traffickers, consumption appears to be on the increase.

villages – notably Ban Mae Do – whose inhabitants moved here from Burma only in the last few years. The Kuomintang live up to their Thai nickname – *jiin haw*, meaning "galloping Chinese" – by offering treks on horses, a rare sight in Thailand. Trips to Akha villages can be arranged at the *Shin Sane Guest House* (see below) from B400 for four to five hours.

Towering above the town on top of the hill, the **Princess Mother Pagoda**, a huge, gilt-topped chedi, stands beside a small cruciform viharn and is so distinctive that it has quickly become the town's proud symbol. It is a long and steep climb to get there, but with a rented vehicle you can follow the road to the edge of town, and branch right opposite a school and market on a road that carries you heavenward, revealing some breathtaking views on the way.

Beyond Mae Salong, newly paved roads let you nip the back way to Tha Ton; half-hourly songthaews cover the distance in ninety minutes. North of Mae Salong lies **Ban Therd Thai**, although to get to it by road you'd have to backtrack down the main road 12km to Sam Yaek and then make your own way up a paved side road a further 13km into the hills. In its former incarnation as Ban Hin Taek, this mixed village was the opium capital of the notorious Khun Sa (see p.385): the Thai army drove Khun Sa out after a pitched battle in 1983, and the village has now been renamed and "pacified" with the establishment of a market, school and hospital.

Practicalities

The best of Mae Salong's budget **accommodation** is *Shin Sane Guest House* (☎053/765026; ❶), a friendly place on the west side of the main road, which has small rooms in the funky wooden main building and smart bungalows (with hot showers) in the yard behind. Right next door are the tidy spacious rooms of the *Akha Guest House* (☎053/765103; ❶), the polished-wood two-storey home of a Christianized Akha family. Downstairs they have a small shop selling Akha stuff where the family mostly hang out. Of the upmarket places, *Mae Salong Villa* (☎053/765114–9, ℻765039; ❺) on the main road at the eastern end of the village offers most value, with a choice of functional rooms or comfy wooden bungalows with balconies facing the Princess Mother Pagoda and Burmese mountains, all with hot-water bathrooms. The terrace **restaurant** shares the same view and cooks up the best food in town, including delicious but expensive Chinese specialities like *het hawm* (wild mushrooms) and *kai dam* (black chicken). A slightly cheaper alternative is the *Mae Salong Central Hills Hotel* (☎053/765113, ℻765349; ❹), on the right in the middle of town. Also with expansive views, the small rooms are clean and carpeted, and all have hot water and TV.

Doi Tung

Steep, wooded hills rise abruptly from the plains west of Highway 1 as it approaches the Burmese border. Crowned by a thousand-year-old wat, the central peak here, 1300-metre **DOI TUNG**, makes a worthwhile outing just for the journey. A broad paved road runs up the mountainside, beginning 43km north of Chiang Rai on Highway 1, just before **Ban Huai Khrai**. It's best to have your own vehicle or go on a tour from Chiang Rai, though you will also find songthaews in Ban Huai Khrai ferrying villagers up the mountain in the morning and at weekends (about B50 return). The only other options are to hitch (easy at weekends) or charter a whole songthaew for B500.

The summit road ascends past Thai Yai, Chinese, Akha and Lahu villages, shimmies over a precarious saddle with some minor temple buildings 2km before the top, and finally climbs through a tuft of thick woods to **Wat Phra That Doi Tung** – look out for the strange collection of small Indian, Chinese and Thai statues, brought as offerings by pilgrims, in a rocky glade just before you reach the main temple buildings. Pilgrims to the wat earn themselves good fortune by clanging the rows of dissonant bells around the temple compound and by throwing coins into a well, which are collected for temple funds. For non-Buddhist travellers, the reward for getting this far is the stunning view out over the cultivated slopes and half of northern Thailand. The wat's most important structures are its twin **chedis**, erected to enshrine relics of the Buddha in 911. When the building of the chedis was complete, King Achutaraj of Ngon Yang ordered a giant flag (*tung*), reputedly 2km long, to be flown from the peak, which gave the mountain its name.

Doi Tung became the country seat of the Princess Mother until her death in 1995 (the mother of the present king, she was never queen herself, but was affectionately known as *Mae Fa Luang*, "great mother of mankind"). The **Royal Villa** and **Mae Fa Luang Garden**, 12km up the summit road then left up a side road, are open to visitors (daily 7.30am–6pm; garden B50, villa B70, both B100) and well worth a visit. Regular guided tours take visitors round some parts of the Swiss-style building that was the country home of the Princess Mother in her later years, passing the Grand Reception Hall, where astral constellations have been embedded in the ceiling, then her living room, bedroom and study, all left as when she lived there. Below, the immaculate ornamental gardens throng with snap-happy day-trippers at weekends. The Princess Mother's hill-tribe project has helped to develop local villages by introducing new agricultural methods: the slopes which were formerly blackened by the fires of slash-and-burn farming are now used to grow teak and pine, and crops such as strawberries and coffee, which are sold in the shop by the entrance to the gardens.

A steep **back road** north to Mae Sai (22km) begins at the saddle beneath the peak. This area has been the scene of conflict among the Kuomintang, the hill tribes and others involved in the opium trade, but is now safe to travel in with the development of Doi Tung under the Princess Mother's project, though it remains a little intimidating, with two checkpoints en route to Mae Sai. After 4km of asphalt, you reach the chedi and arboretum at the pinnacle of **Doi Chang Moob**, an even higher and better viewpoint than Doi Tung – on a clear day, you can make out the Mekhong River and the triangular outline of 2600-metre Loi Pangnao, on the border between Burma and China. A difficult, dangerously steep road then follows the sharp ridge north before snaking down to **Ban Pha Mee**, an Akha village where you can get refreshments, and thence to Mae Sai 7km further on.

Mae Sai and around

MAE SAI, with its hustling tourist trade and bustling border crossing, is not to everyone's taste, but it can be an intriguing place to watch the world go by, and with some good-value guest houses it can also be used as a base for exploring Doi Tung or Sop Ruak. Thailand's most northerly town lies 61km from Chiang Rai at the dead end of Highway 1, which forms the town's single north–south street and is the site of the bus stop. Wide enough for an armoured battalion, this ugly boulevard still has the same name – **Thanon Phaholyothin** – as at the start of its journey north in the suburbs of Bangkok.

Thanon Phaholyothin ends at a short but commercially important **bridge** over the Mae Sai River, which forms the border with Burma. During daylight hours (6am–6pm), Thais have long been allowed to travel up to 5km into Burmese territory (though the frontier is sporadically closed during international disputes between the two countries), but this dubious pleasure is now also open to farangs.You'll need first to get stamped out ofThailand at the Mae Sai immigration office (see opposite); on the other side of the bridge, you simply pay B250 (or US$5) for a one-day stay; and on your return to Thailand, you'll automatically be given a new thirty-day entry stamp. Prospering on the back of growing cross-border trade, **Thakhilek**, the Burmese town opposite, looks remarkably similar to the concrete boxes of Mae Sai, one of the few obvious differences being that traffic in Burma is rather perversely made to drive on the right (a snook cocked at the British after the overthrow of colonial rule, though most vehicles in the country are still right-hand drive). Thakhilek's handful of temples have next to nothing of architectural interest, the town's big draw being – for farangs and for the hundreds of Thai day-trippers who crowd the narrow streets – a frenzy of **shopping**.The huge market on the right after the bridge is an entrepôt for a bizarre diversity of goods from around the world – from Jacob's Cream Crackers to bears' paws and tigers' intestines – but its main thrust is to cater to the everyday demands of Thai customers, with a selection of ordinary, cheap clothes and bedding.The array of Burmese handicrafts – tatty Pagan lacquerware and crude woodcarving – is disappointing.

Shopping is the main activity in Mae Sai, too: from the central morning market crowded with purposeful Burmese, to the stores around the bridge which hawk "Burmese" handicrafts – mostly made in the factories of Chiang Mai, though slightly better quality than in Thakhilek – and coloured glass posing as gems. Village Product, 51/24 Moo 10, Thanon Muang Daeng (about 500m south of the border, turn left then 200m on your right) offers more interesting stuff, such as hill-tribe fabric and clothes from both Thailand and Burma. Thong Tavee, further south at 17 Thanon Phaholyothin, is the place to buy good-quality jade and to watch the delicate process of cutting, decorating and polishing the stone in the workshop behind.

For a better perspective on the town, climb up to the chedi of **Wat Phra That Doi Wao**, five minutes' walk from the bridge (behind the *Top North Hotel*). As well as Doi Tung to the south and the hills of Laos in the east, you get a good view up the steep-sided valley and across the river to Thakhilek. There is a market in the grounds with Burmese and Chinese stuff sold, running from about 5am to 6pm, or later if it's busy.

Most travellers staying in Mae Sai end up making **day-trips** out to Doi Tung (from Mae Sai take a songthaew to Ban Huai Khrai, then see p.386) and Sop Ruak (see opposite). A third, less compelling choice would be **Tham Luang**: this "Royal Cave" has an impressive entrance cavern, flooded with natural light, and 7km of low, sweaty passageways beyond.Tourists have become lost in here before, so try to find a local guide to show you around if you're curious. Without a bike you have to hop on a bus south on Highway 1 for 5km, to where a row of roadside stalls sell strawberries in the cool season; the cave is a signposted 3km from there. On the way, look out for the elaborate mausoleums of Mae Sai's Chinese cemetery, 2km south of town.

Pricey and uncomfortable package tours into Burma are available, arranged through the very dour Ananda Tours, 22 Moo 7, Thanon Phaholyothin (☎053/731038, ☏731749), with a three-day, two-night trip to Kentung costing US$300 per person for a minimum of four people; the sorting out of visas is included in the price but it's best to arrive a few days in advance of the date you want to travel. *King Kobra Maesai Guest House* also organizes trips to Kentung.

Practicalities

A handful of **inexpensive guest houses** are strung out along the river bank west of the bridge. The best of these is the furthest away: *Mae Sai* (T053/732021; ❷–❸) is a beautiful, relaxing place to stay with a wide variety of bungalows, wedged between a steep hill and the river, fifteen minutes from the main road. Much closer to the bridge, *King Kobra Maesai Guest House* (T & F053/733055, ✉kkmaesai@loxinfo.co.th; ❶–❹) has very cheap cell-like rooms downstairs sharing hot-water bathrooms and better en-suite (hot-water) rooms upstairs, some with air-con and cable TV; in addition, they offer tours and treks. *Chad Guest House* on Soi Wiangpan – look out for the signpost on the left, 1km before the bridge – scores low for location but is the classic travellers' rest (T053/732054; ❶): the family is welcoming and well informed about the area (B20 for maps and information for non-guests), the food is good and it's an easy place to meet people. The *Wang Tong*, on the east side of the bridge at 299 Thanon Phaholyothin (T053/733388–95, F733399; ❻), is Mae Sai's best **hotel**, with a huge, ornate lobby and a swimming pool but sloppy service. Much less pretentious and better value is the *Mae Sai Hotel* at 125/5 Thanon Phaholyothin (T053/731462; ❶–❹), which has simple, clean rooms with attached bathrooms, some with air-conditioning.

A popular **eating** place is *Rabieng Kaew*, a wooden house with an open-air terrace, opposite the Krung Thai Bank on Thanon Phaholyothin – the menu lists a wide choice of excellent Thai cuisine, though it's not inexpensive by local standards. The terrace of the *Rim Nam* (*Riverside*), under the western side of the bridge, is crowded during the day with tourists watching the border action, but the Thai dishes are surprisingly good and generous, and not too pricey. The night market, across the main road from the *Sri Wattana Hotel*, is inexpensive and very popular. *JoJo*, 233 Thanon Phaholyothin (daytime only), serves up decent Western breakfasts, Thai fast food and fancy ice creams at a price.

For getting around the local area, **motorbikes** can be rented from Tong Service on Thanon Sairomjoy just west of the bridge, or Pon Chai, opposite the Bangkok Bank on Thanon Phaholyothin, for B150 a day. If you're travelling on to Mae Salong, take a songthaew to **Pasang** (about B20) and then another to Mae Salong (B50). Mae Sai has an **immigration office**, inconveniently located 2km south of the bridge on Thanon Phaholyothin (Mon–Fri 8.30am–4.30pm; T053/731008).

Sop Ruak

The Golden Triangle, which actually denotes a huge opium-producing area spreading across Burma, Laos and Thailand (see p.385), has, for the benefit of tourists, been artificially concentrated into the precise spot where the borders meet, 70km northeast of Chiang Rai. Don't come to the village of **SOP RUAK**, at the confluence of the Ruak and Mekhong rivers, expecting to run into sinister drug-runners, addicts or even poppy fields – instead you'll find souvenir stalls, pay-toilets, an opium museum and lots of signs saying "Golden Triangle" which pop up in a million photo albums around the world.

While it may look terribly touristy and commercial, the small **Opium Museum** in the centre of town, identifiable by a green tin-roofed pagoda above the entrance gate (daily 7am–6pm; B20), is actually worth a visit. All the paraphernalia of opium growing and smoking, accompanied by a well-written English commentary, is housed in several display cases. A display of agricultural tools and photographs shows how the poppy is scored to extract opium once it has lost its petals. Other cases display beautifully carved teakwood opium

storing boxes; weights cast from bronze and brass in animal shapes – from elephants, swans, and rabbits to sleeping ducks; a collection of opium pipes including one of silver, one of jade and one of ivory; and, perhaps most fascinating, a
ceramic opium pillow in the shape of a crouching man on which an addict
would rest his head while smoking.

The meeting of the waters is undeniably monumental, but to get an unobstructed view of it you need to climb up to **Wat Phra That Phu Khao**, a
1200-year-old temple perched on a small hill above the village: to the north,
beyond the puny Ruak (Mae Sai), the mountains of Burma march off into
infinity, while eastwards across the mighty Mekhong spread the hills and villages of Laos. This pastoral scene has now been transformed, however, by the
appearance of a Thai luxury hotel (part-owned by drugs warlord Khun Sa)
over on the uninhabited strip of Burmese land immediately upstream of the
confluence. The attached casino bypasses Thai laws against gambling, and the
usually strict border formalities are waived for visitors coming from Thailand.

For B300, you can have the thrill of stepping on Laotian soil. A longtail boat
from the pier in the centre of the village will give you a kiss-me-quick tour of
the "Golden Triangle", including five minutes on a sand bar in the Mekhong
which belongs to Laos.

To get to Sop Ruak you'll have to go via Chiang Saen or Mae Sai. **From
Chiang Saen** you can go by regular songthaew (departing from in front of the
school on the west side of the T-junction), rented bicycle (an easy 10-km ride
on a paved road, though not much of it runs along the river bank) or longtail
boat up the Mekhong (B500 round trip). **From Mae Sai**, songthaews make
the 45-minute trip from the side of the *Sri Wattana Hotel* on Thanon
Phaholyothin (they leave when they're full).

Practicalities

There's nowhere decent to **stay** in Sop Ruak for budget travellers, but for
those willing to splurge, one of the north's finest hotels, the *Le Meridien Baan
Boran* (℡ 053/784086, ℻ 784090, ⓦ www.lemeridien.com; ➒), tastefully
designed in impeccable traditional style and set in extensive grounds, is located 1km north out of the village. The balconies of all its rooms and its swimming pool offer great views over the countryside to the Mekhong, Burma and
Laos. Among many amenities available to guests, **mountain bikes** (B200) can
be hired to explore the local area.

Chiang Saen

Combining tumbledown ruins with sweeping Mekhong River scenery,
CHIANG SAEN, 60km northeast of Chiang Rai, makes a rustic haven and a
good base camp for the border region east of Mae Sai. The town's focal point,
where the Chiang Rai road meets the main road along the banks of the
Mekhong, is a lively junction thronged by buses, songthaews, longtails and
cargo boats from Laos and China. Turning left at this junction soon brings you
to Sop Ruak, and you may well share the road with the tour buses that sporadically thunder through. Very few tourists turn right in Chiang Saen along
the road to Chiang Khong, even though this is the best way to appreciate the
slow charms of the Mekhong valley.

Originally known as Yonok, the region around Chiang Saen seems to have
been an important Thai trading crossroads from some time after the seventh
century. The city of Chiang Saen itself was founded around 1328 by the successor to the renowned King Mengrai of Chiang Mai, Saen Phu, who gave up

his throne to retire here. Coveted for its strategic location guarding the Mekhong, Chiang Saen passed back and forth between the kings of Burma and Thailand for nearly three hundred years until Rama I razed the place to the ground in 1804. The present village was established only in 1881, when Rama V ordered a northern prince to resettle the site with descendants of the old townspeople mustered from Lamphun, Chiang Mai and Lampang.

The Town

The layout of the old, ruined city is defined by the Mekhong River running along its east flank; a tall rectangle, 2.5km from north to south, is formed by the addition of the ancient ramparts, now fetchingly overgrown, on the other three sides. The grid of leafy streets inside the ramparts is now too big for the modern town, which is generously scattered along the river road and across the middle on Thanon Phaholyothin. For serious temple explorers, the Fine Arts Department has an **information centre** (daily 8.30am–4pm), opposite the National Museum, devoted to the architecture and conservation of the city, which is an ongoing, well-funded project. The information, written in Thai and English, is accompanied by photographs.

The **National Museum** (Wed–Sun 8.30am–4.30pm; B30) makes an informative starting point, housing some impressive Buddha images and architectural features rescued from the surrounding ruins, with good labelling in English. The art of northern Thailand was once dubbed "Chiang Saen style" because the town had an important school of bronze-casting. The more appropriate name "Lanna style" is now preferred, though you'll still come across the traditional term. As in many of Thailand's museums, the back end is given over to exhibits on folk culture, one of many highlights being the beautiful wooden lintel carved with *hum yon* (floral swirls representing testicles), which would have been placed above the front door of a house to ward off evil. **Wat Phra That Chedi Luang**, originally the city's main temple, is worth looking in on next door for its imposing octagonal chedi, now decorated with weeds and a huge yellow ribbon, while handicraft stalls in the grounds sell Thai Lue cloths among their wares.

Beyond the ramparts to the west, **Wat Pa Sak**'s brick buildings and laterite columns have been excavated and restored by the Fine Arts Department, making it the most accessible and impressive of Chiang Saen's many temples (there's an entrance fee of B30 whenever the custodian is about). The wat's name is an allusion to the hundreds of teak trees which Saen Phu planted in the grounds when he built the chedi in 1340 to house some Indian Buddha relics. The central chedi owes its eclectic shape largely to the grand temples of Pagan in Burma: the square base is inset with niches housing alternating Buddhas and *deva* (angels) with flowing skirts, and above rises the tower for the Buddha relic, topped by a circular spire. Beautiful carved stucco covers much of the structure, showing intricate floral scrolls and stylized lotus patterns as well as a whole zoo of mythical beasts.

The open space around modern Chiang Saen, which is dotted with trees and another 140 overgrown ruins (both inside and outside the ramparts), is great for a carefree wander. A spot worth aiming for is the gold-topped, crooked chedi of **Wat Phra That Chom Kitti**, which gives a good view of the town and the river from a small hill outside the northwest corner of the ramparts.

Practicalities

Buses from Chiang Rai and **songthaews** from Sop Ruak stop just west of the T-junction of Thanon Phaholyothin and the river road, a short walk or a samlor ride from Chiang Saen's main guest houses, while songthaews and the one daily bus from Chiang Khong stop on the river road about 250m south of the T-junction near Wat Pong Sanuk. **Longtail boats** for Sop Ruak (B500 return) congregate just south of the T-junction. If you're travelling from Chiang Rai by **bike or car**, follow Highway 1 north as far as **Mae Chan** (30km), then bear northeastwards along a secondary route (Route 1016) for the last 30km to Chiang Saen. To get around the ruins and the surrounding countryside, **bicycles** (B60 per day) and **motorbikes** (B180 per day) can be rented at *Gin's Guest House* (see below).

Accommodation

Chiang Saen has one **hotel** and just a few **guest houses**, the best of which are listed below. The most convenient are along the riverfront, but though they have great views across the massive Mekhong, they can also be very noisy with roaring trucks, whining speedboats and wailing nightclub singers trying to outdo each other.

Ban Suan, near Wat Phrathat Chom Kitti on the town's western bypass ☎ 053/650907. Perhaps the best deal in town is out; this has large, well-designed rooms with solar-heated water ranged around a sloping garden. Some have air-con, TV and fridge, others just fans. ❶–❹

Chiang Saen Guesthouse, just a block north of the main junction ☎ 053/650196. Basic rooms with shared bathrooms, and a riverfront café selling Western fare such as banana pancakes. ❶

Gin's Guest House, outside the ramparts, 2km north of the T-junction ☎ 053/650847. At this attractive guest house, also facing the river, there's a choice between large A-frame bungalows in a lychee orchard, or pricier spacious, well-furnished rooms in the main house, with polished wood floors, all with access to hot water; the owner, a

knowledgeable teacher, can organize visas to Laos. ❷–❸

JS Guest House, in a lane leading north from the post office ☎ 053/777060. A cheap but clean option near the museum and main temples; here you get a mattress on the floor with a fan, and shared use of a bathroom. ❶

River Hill, south of the T-junction and a block back from the river road ☎ 053/650826–9, ℻ 650828. This hotel sets a high standard in a modern four-storey brick building with some traditional touches. Pleasant, friendly and well run, it's sited in a quiet rustic street with bamboo houses and trees to look out at; the rooms, all of which have air-con, TV, fridge, telephone and hot-water bathrooms, are very nicely done out right down to the Thai cushion seats on the floor. ❺

Eating

Food in Chiang Saen is nothing special; you can eat standard travellers' fare at the *Chiang Saen Guesthouse*, or try the street stalls, which set up low pavement tables in the evening, along the riverfront by the cargo pier and Wat Pha Kao Pan. In the same lane as *JS Guesthouse* is *Chat Cha*, a small shophouse that serves American breakfast and tasty, cheap Thai food. Five kilometres north of the centre on an undeveloped part of the river is the best of a mediocre bunch of riverfront **restaurants**, the *Rim Khong*, a *sala*-style open-sided place where the views are great, the standard Thai food is decent but the service slow. For pleasant service and crisply clean and colourful surrounds, but no river view, the moderate-to-expensive *Wieng Saen Phu Restaurant* at the *River Hill Hotel* is worth a try.

East to Chiang Khong

Several routes lead from Chiang Saen to **Chiang Khong**, 70km downriver, the only other town on the Mekhong before it enters Laos; once a peaceful backwater, it is now frequently visited as a crossing point to Laos (indeed it is the only international crossing point in the north). The most scenic way to get to Chiang Khong is by **motorbike**, following the northward kink in the river for two hours along winding, scenic roads. An exciting but expensive alternative is to run the rapids on a hired **longtail boat**, which takes about three hours and costs around B1500. There is one **bus** a day between the two towns as well as several **songthaews**, which head off along the river before cutting across country on Route 1129, to reach Chiang Khong after two hours. If you're going straight to Chiang Khong from Chiang Rai, direct **buses** leaving every hour cover the ground in just over two hours.

Heading out of Chiang Saen by the river road, you pass through tobacco fields and, after 4km, can see the tall, brick gate of **Wat Phra That Pha Ngao** on the right. The tenth-century temple contains a supposedly miraculous chedi perched on top of a large boulder, but the real attraction is the view from the new chedi on the hillside above: take the one-kilometre paved track which starts at the back of the temple and you can't miss the lumbering **Chedi Ched Yod**, designed by an American in the style of a concrete bunker and built over and around a ruined brick chedi. From here the panorama takes in Chiang Saen's ruins, the wide plain and the slow curve of the river. To the east, the Kok River, which looks so impressive at Chiang Rai, seems like a stream as it pours into the mighty Mekhong.

Twenty-three kilometres from Chiang Saen, turn left off Route 1129 to follow the course of the Mekhong, reaching the Thai Lue settlement of **Ban Hat Bai** after 9km. Signposts will lead you to Sukhawadee in the heart of the village, a small unkempt shop selling a wide selection of the beautifully coloured cotton for which the Thai Lue are famous – if you ask you'll be taken to see the old women of the village weaving (*tor pha*) at their looms in the space beneath their stilted houses. Beyond Hat Bai, the hills close in and the river enters a stretch of rocky rapids, forcing the road to climb up the valley side and making for some dramatic vantage points.

Chiang Khong

CHIANG KHONG first achieved fame among travellers as the starting point for the old Laotian loop, lost after the Pathet Lao government closed Laos in 1975, but coming back to prominence with the recent loosening of attitudes towards tourism. Chiang Khong is currently one of five places in Thailand where it's possible for farangs to **cross to Laos** (the others are Nong Khai, Nakhon Phanom, Mukdahan and Chang Mek in the northeast), and word has clearly got around about the pleasures of the Mekhong boat journey to Louang Phabang, as the small town these days is constantly bustling with foreigners. At the north end of town is Chiang Khong's main pier, **Hua Wiang**. The departure-point for frequent passenger ferries (B20) to **Houayxai** across the border (from where the Louang Phabang boats leave), it is being showered with money to develop it into a major port for trade with Laos and China. For fishing boats, the port is **Ban Hat Khrai**, just south of town, which springs to life during the annual giant catfish hunt: at this time the good but pricey restaurant above the port is the place to sample catfish. In between the two ports, Chiang Khong is strung out along a single north–south street, Thanon Sai Klang, on a high, steep bank above the river. Once you've admired the elevated view of the traffic on the Mekhong and the turrets of the French-built Fort Carnot across in Houayxai, there's little to do (if you're not crossing to Laos) but relax and enjoy the fact that none of the hustle is directed at you.

The **giant catfish** (*pla buk*), found only in the Mekhong, is said to be the largest freshwater fish in the world, measuring up to 3m in length and weighing in at 300kg. Chiang Khong is the catfish capital of the north, attracting fish merchants and restaurateurs from Chiang Rai and Chiang Mai – the tasty meat of the *pla buk* is prized for its fine, soft texture and can fetch up to B400 a kilo. The catfish season is officially opened at the port of Ban Hat Khrai on April 18 with much pomp, including an elaborate ceremony to appease Chao Por Pla Buk, the giant catfish god. Around a hundred fishing boats then set out from both the Thai and Laotian banks, as they do every morning before dawn for the rest of the season, vying with one another to see who can make the first catch. Gone is the old challenge and excitement of harpooning the fish, however: the fishermen now trawl the river over several kilometres of its course with 250-metre nylon nets. The season's haul is usually between thirty and sixty fish all told, but recent years have been so disappointing (the grand total for the year 2000 was two) that Thailand's Fishery Department has begun an artificial spawning programme. At the time of writing, a museum devoted to the giant catfish was being built at Ban Hat Khrai, which should open soon.

If you do decide to cross over into Laos, there are several possibilities for onward travel once over the border. From Houayxai, cargo boats that have been converted to accommodate passengers leave at 11am each day, gliding down the scenic Mekhong and taking two days – overnighting in a village en route – to reach Louang Phabang (B430). Cramped and noisy speedboats cover the same stretch in six to seven hours for B1000 per person, but these are not recommended as fatalities occur regularly despite the requirements for passengers to wear helmets and life jackets. As an alternative to buses on Laos's appalling road system, flights leave Houayxai for Louang Phabang daily, twice daily for Vientiane.

If you have time to spare and want to explore the area around Chiang Khong, try a trip to **Thung Na Noi**, a Hmong village 8km west. You can get there by renting a bike from a guest house (get directions from the proprietor), or taking a songthaew (daily from 9am; B15) from Soi 8, near the new post office. First go to the village school, where you will be given a student guide and taken around the village; contribute at least a B20 donation to the school. Ask the teacher to find a guide from the village to take you on the 3km walk to the attractive Huai Tong waterfall.

Practicalities

Most buses stop on the main road at the east end of town, though a few pull into the town centre itself. If you need to get from the bus to the ferry, or anywhere else about town, the local version of a **tuk-tuk**, a converted motorbike, should take you there for B20. For exploring the local area with your own transport, *Ban Tam-Mi-La* and other guest houses hire **bicycles** (B100–150) or **motorcycles** (B200 per day). Several **banks** on Thanon Sai Klang have a foreign exchange service; the post office in the centre of town is along the same road.

Most of Chiang Khong's guest houses now organize **visas for Laos**, or you can get one through one of the many travel agents that line the town's only street; allow two or three working days for your application to be processed (this may come down if the immigration office in Houayxai reopens). Fifteen-day tourist visas cost B1300 (see p.524 for information about other means of getting a Lao visa).

Even if you have to wait around in Chiang Khong for a Lao visa to come through, a few days here is no hardship given the high standard of its **guest houses**. The best is *Ban Tam-Mi-La*, at 113 Thanon Sai Klang (⊤ & Ⓕ 053/791234; ❷–❸), signposted down a lane in the middle of town among a cluster of small restaurants. The staff are helpful and the atmosphere is easy-going and restful; the place has half a dozen tasteful, well-designed wooden bungalows (from shared cold-water bathrooms to en-suites with hot shower). They also offer a **homestay** option 20km out of town, where you can learn about life on a Thai farm and how to cook Thai food. Among the twenty or so other guest houses in town, *Ban Fai* at 27 Thanon Sai Klang (⊤ 053/791394; ❶) or *Border*, just across the road (⊤ 053/791448; ❶), offer clean rooms with shared bath in family-style wooden houses. The *Chiang Khong Hotel* at 68/1 Thanon Sai Klang (⊤ 053/791182, Ⓕ 655640; ❷–❸) has large rooms set back off the street with fan or air-con. The swankiest place in town is the *Huan-Thai Sopaphan Resort* (⊤ 053/791023, Ⓕ 791446; ❷–❹), right next to *Ban Tam-Mi-La*; there are a few basic rooms within this large teak house, but most are en-suite with cable TV and breakfast included in the price. *Ban Tam-Mi-La* has an excellent **restaurant** with a sweeping view of the river and lots of vegetarian options – come early as the food finishes at 8.30pm.

Travel details

Trains

Chiang Mai to: Bangkok (7 daily; 13hr).
Den Chai to: Bangkok (8 daily, 9hr), Chiang Mai (7 daily; 4hr).
Doi Khun Tan to: Bangkok (5 daily; 12hr); Chiang Mai (3 daily; 1hr).
Lampang to: Bangkok (6 daily; 11hr); Chiang Mai (6 daily; 2hr).
Lamphun to: Bangkok (7 daily; 13hr); Chiang Mai (8 daily; 20min).

Buses

Chiang Khong to: Bangkok (10 daily; 13–14hr); Chiang Mai (3 daily; 6hr); Chiang Rai (hourly; 3hr); Chiang Saen (1 daily; 2hr).
Chiang Mai to: Bangkok (19 daily; 10–11hr); Chiang Khong (3 daily; 6hr); Chiang Rai (48 daily; 3–6hr); Chiang Saen (4 daily; 5hr); Chom Thong (every 30min; 1hr); Fang (every 30min; 3hr 30min); Khon Kaen (7 daily; 12hr); Khorat (9 daily; 12hr); Lampang (every 20min; 2hr); Lamphun (every 10min; 1hr); Loei (4 daily; 9hr); Mae Hong Son (9 daily via Mae Sariang; 8hr); Mae Sai (10 daily; 4hr); Mae Sot (4 daily; 6hr); Nan (10 daily; 6–7hr); Pai (5 daily; 4hr); Phayao (11 daily; 3hr); Phitsanulok (10 daily; 5–6hr); Phrae (15 daily; 4hr); Rayong (8 daily; 15hr); San Kamphaeng (every 30min; 30min); Sukhothai (12 daily; 5hr); Tak (4 daily; 4hr); Tha Ton (7 daily; 4hr); Ubon

Ratchathani (6 daily; 17hr); Udon Thani (4 daily; 12hr).
Chiang Rai to: Bangkok (16 daily; 12hr); Chiang Khong (hourly; 2hr); Chiang Mai (37 daily; 3–6hr); Chiang Saen (every 15min; 1hr 30min); Khon Kaen (5 daily; 12hr); Khorat (4 daily; 13hr); Lampang (every 20min; 5hr); Mae Sai (every 15min; 1hr 30min), Mae Sot (2 daily; 11hr); Nakhon Phanom (4 daily; 16hr); Nan (1 daily; 6–7hr); Pattaya (4 daily; 16hr); Phayao (every 20min; 2hr); Phitsanulok (6 daily; 6hr); Sukhothai (3 daily; 6hr); Tha Ton (3 daily; 2hr), Udon Thani (3 daily; 13hr).
Lampang to: Bangkok (10 daily; 8hr); Chiang Mai (every 20min; 2hr); Chiang Rai (every 20min; 5hr); Nan (10 daily; 5hr); Phayao (21 daily; 3hr).
Mae Hong Son to: Bangkok (2 daily; 18hr); Chiang Mai via Mae Sariang (6 daily; 8hr); Chiang Mai via Pai (4 daily; 7hr).
Mae Sai to: Bangkok (8 daily; 13hr); Chiang Mai (11 daily; 5hr); Chiang Rai (every 15min; 1hr 30min).
Nan to: Bangkok (13 daily; 13hr); Chiang Mai (10 daily; 6–7hr); Chiang Rai (1 daily; 6–7hr); Den Chai (5 daily; 3hr); Phrae (13 daily; 2hr–2hr 30min).
Pai to: Chiang Mai (4 daily; 4hr); Mae Hong Son (4 daily; 4hr).
Phayao to: Chiang Mai (11 daily; 3hr); Chiang Rai (every 20min; 2hr); Nan (2 daily; 5hr).

Phrae to: Chiang Mai (15 daily; 4hr); Nan (13 daily; 2hr–2hr 30min).

Flights

Chiang Mai to: Bangkok (10–13 daily; 1hr); Chiang Rai (2 daily; 40min); Kuala Lumpur (Malaysia; 2 weekly; 1hr 40min); Kunming (China; 2 weekly; 2hr 30min); Louang Phabang (Laos; 2 weekly; 1hr); Mae Hong Son (3 daily; 40min); Mae Sot (4 weekly; 1hr); Mandalay (Burma; 1 weekly; 50min); Nan (4 weekly; 1hr); Phitsanulok (4 weekly; 2hr); Phrae (4 weekly; 1hr 30min); Phuket (7 weekly; 2hr); Rangoon (Yangon in Burma; 3 weekly; 40min); Singapore (4 weekly; 3hr); Sukhothai (1 daily; 35min); Taipei (Taiwan; 2 weekly; 4hrs); Vientiane (Laos; 2 weekly; 2hr 10 min).

Chiang Rai to: Bangkok (5 daily; 1hr 20min); Chiang Mai (2 daily; 40min).

Lampang to: Bangkok (2 daily; 2hr); Phitsanulok (1 or 2 daily; 35min); Petchabun (3 weekly; 45min).

Mae Hong Son to: Chiang Mai (3 daily; 40min).

Nan to: Bangkok (3 weekly; 2hr); Chiang Mai (4 weekly; 40min); Phitsanulok (4 weekly; 1hr 25min); Phrae (1 daily; 30min).

Phrae to: Bangkok (3 weekly; 1hr 20min); Chiang Mai (4 weekly; 1hr 30min); Nan (1 daily; 30min); Phitsanulok (4 weekly; 35min).

The east coast

CHAPTER 4   Highlights

* **Ko Si Chang** – Tiny,
  barely touristed island
  with craggy coastlines
  and an appealingly laid-
  back ambience. **p.402**

* **Diving from Pattaya** –
  Away from the girlie bars
  and high-rise hotels,
  there's rewarding year-
  round wreck and reef
  diving nearby. **p.411**

* **Ko Samet** – Pretty (and
  popular) little island
  fringed with dazzlingly
  white beaches. **p.419**

* **Chanthaburi** – Watch
  gem dealers polishing
  piles of uncut sapphires,
  and explore the
  Vietnamese quarter.
  p.430

* **Ko Chang** – Large,
  sparsely populated
  island, with several good
  beaches and lots of
  accommodation. **p.439**

* **Ko Mak** – Stay in a
  teepee-hut on this
  diminutive island with
  fine white-sand beaches.
  p.450

4

The east coast

Located within easy reach of the capital, the **east coast** resorts and islands attract a mixed crowd of weekending Bangkokians, pleasure-seeking expats and budget-conscious backpackers. Transport connections are good, prices are generally more reasonable than at the biggest southern resorts and, if you're heading overland to Cambodia, the east coast beaches make the perfect chance to indulge yourself en route before adventuring into more challenging territory across the border. You'll find the whitest beaches on the offshore islands – the five-hundred-kilometre string of mainland strands are disappointingly grey and the resorts here cater more for Thai groups than solitary horizon-gazing farangs. In addition, the discovery of oil and natural gas fields in these coastal waters has turned pockets of the first hundred-kilometre stretch into an unsightly industrial landscape of refineries and depots, sometimes referred to as the Eastern Seaboard. Offshore, however, it's an entirely different story, with island beaches as peaceful and unsullied as many of the more celebrated southern retreats.

The first worthwhile stop comes 100km east of Bangkok at the less than scintillating town of **Si Racha**, which is the point of access for tiny **Ko Si Chang**, whose dramatically rugged coastlines and low-key atmosphere make it a restful haven. In complete contrast, **Pattaya**, just half an hour south, is Thailand's number-one package-tour destination, its customers predominantly middle-

Accommodation prices

Throughout this guide, guest houses, hotels and bungalows have been categorized according to the price codes given below. These categories represent the minimum you can expect to pay in the high season (roughly July, Aug & Nov–Feb) for a double room. If travelling on your own, expect to pay anything between sixty and one hundred percent of the rates quoted for a double room. Wherever a price range is indicated, this means that the establishment offers rooms with varying facilities – as explained in the write-up. Wherever an establishment also offers dormitory beds, the prices of these beds are given in the text, instead of being indicated by price code.

Remember that the top-whack hotels will add seven percent tax and a ten percent service charge to your bill – the price codes below are based on net rates after taxes have been added.

❶ under B150	❹ B400–600	❼ B1200–1800
❷ B150–250	❺ B600–900	❽ B1800–3000
❸ B250–400	❻ B900–1200	❾ B3000+

aged Western and Chinese males enticed by the resort's sex-market reputation and undeterred by its notoriety as the country's most polluted beach. Things soon look up, though, as the coast veers sharply eastwards towards Ban Phe, revealing the island of **Ko Samet**, the prettiest of all the beach resorts within comfortable bus-ride range of Bangkok.

East of Ban Phe, the landscape starts to get more lush and hilly as the coastal highway nears **Chanthaburi**, the dynamo of Thailand's gem trade and one of only two provincial capitals in the region worth visiting. The other appealing inland city is **Trat**, 68km further along the highway and an important departure point for **Ko Chang**, a huge forested island with long, fine beaches, plentiful accommodation and a host of smaller, less developed islets off its coasts. East of Ko Chang lies the Cambodian border post of Ban Hat Lek, one of two points – the other being Aranyaprathet, a little way north – where it is currently legal to **cross overland into Cambodia**; details of these border crossings are given on p.438.

Highway 3 extends almost the entire length of the east coast – beginning in Bangkok as Thanon Sukhumvit, and known as such when it cuts through towns – and hundreds of **buses** ply the route, connecting all major mainland destinations. Buses from Bangkok's Eastern (Ekamai) Bus Terminal serve all the provincial capitals and tourist spots; there are a few services here from Bangkok's Northern (Mo Chit) Bus Terminal as well, and tourist minibuses run direct from Banglamphu in Bangkok to the ferry piers for Ko Samet and Ko Chang. It's also possible to travel between the east coast and the northeast without doubling back through the capital: the most direct routes into **Isaan** start from Pattaya, Rayong and Chanthaburi, and all pass through fairly spectacular upland scenery, crossing the two ranges of invariably cloud-capped mountains which mark the climatic and geological divide between the fertile, fruit-growing east coast and the almost barren scrublands of the Khorat plateau. One Eastern Line **train** a day runs in each direction between Bangkok, Si Racha and Pattaya, and there are two trains a day from Bangkok to Aranyaprathet and back. There's an **airport** at U-Tapao naval base, midway between Pattaya and Rayong, served by Bangkok Airways **flights** to and from Ko Samui and Phnom Penh in Cambodia; an airport is also scheduled to open in Trat in 2003.

Si Racha and Ko Si Chang

Almost 30km southeast of Bangkok, Highway 3 finally emerges from the urban sprawl at the fishing town of Samut Prakan. It then follows the edge of the plain for a further 50km before reaching the provincial capital of **Chonburi**, whose only real attraction is its annual October bout of buffalo racing. Thai holidaymakers are very keen on the expensive beach resort of Bang Saen, 10km south of Chonburi, particularly as a day-trip break from Bangkok. As an off-the-beaten-track experience, however, the nearby island of **Ko Si Chang** is more rewarding, with the possibility of a night in an atmospheric waterside hotel on the mainland at **Si Racha** on the way there or back.

Si Racha and around

Access to Ko Si Chang is from the fishing port and refinery town of **SI RACHA**, famous throughout Thailand as the home of *nam phrik Si Racha*, the orange-coloured, chilli-laced ketchup found on every restaurant and kitchen table in the country. You'll probably only find yourself staying here if you miss the last boat to the island, though the idiosyncratic seafront hotels make this an unexpectedly enjoyable experience, and the town is not without charm, especially at twilight, when the rickety, brightly painted fishing boats load up with ice and nets before setting off into the night. Si Racha's other claim to fame is its Tiger Zoo, an increasingly popular tourist attraction.

Practicalities

Buses to Si Racha leave Bangkok's Eastern (Ekamai) Bus Terminal every thirty minutes and take about two hours. Air-conditioned buses stop near Laemtong department store on Thanon Sukhumvit (Highway 3), from where you can take a samlor or tuk-tuk to the pier for **ferries to Ko Si Chang** (for details of these see p.402); most regular buses stop nearer the waterfront, on Thanon Chermchompon (also spelt Thanon Jermjompol), within walking distance of the pier. There are also direct buses between Si Racha and Rayong (for Ban Phe and Ko Samet), Pattaya, and Trat (for Ko Chang). White songthaews from Naklua (the northern suburb of Pattaya, see p.407) run around twice an hour to Si Racha, dropping passengers near the clocktower on the southern edge of town. One **train** a day in each direction connects Si Racha with Bangkok; the **train station** is on the eastern edge of the town and is most easily reached by tuk-tuk.

Strung out along the wooden jetties are the simple, cabin-like rooms of three pleasant waterfront **hotels**, all of which are on Thanon Chermchompon, within five minutes' walk of the Ko Si Chang pier. The English-speaking managers give a slight advantage to *Sri Wattana* on the (unmarked) Soi 8 at 35 Thanon Chermchompon (☎038/311037; ❷), but the adjacent *Siwichai* at 38 Thanon Chermchompon (☎038/311212; ❷–❹) is just as pleasant, as is the *Samchai* – which also has some air-con rooms – at the end of the signposted Soi 10, officially 3 Thanon Chermchompon (☎038/311234; ❷–❸). For **eating**, try any of the seafood restaurants along Thanon Chermchompon, especially the Chinese-style *Chua Lee* between sois 8 and 10, or the night-market stalls by the clocktower further south down the road.

Sriracha Tiger Zoo

Nine kilometres southeast of Si Racha, the **Sriracha Tiger Zoo** (daily 9am–6pm; B250, children B150) is usually visited by day-trippers from Pattaya, but is also easily accessible from Si Racha. Said to be the most successful tiger breeding centre in the world, the zoo currently has some two hundred Bengal tigers in its care, as well as thousands of crocodiles and a host of other typical zoo creatures, including elephants, camels, wallabies and Peruvian guinea pigs. One of the zoo's philosophies is that different animals should interact with each other as if they were members of the same family, so you're quite likely to see tiger cubs being suckled by pigs, and ducks hanging out with the crocodiles. Visitors are usually allowed to cuddle the zoo-bred baby tigers, and elephant shows, pig racing and an animal circus are staged several times a day.

All tour companies in Pattaya (see p.405) offer day-trips to the Tiger Zoo. Alternatively, there is **public transport** there from the southern edge of Si Racha town centre: walk south a few hundred metres down Thanon Sukhumvit from the town centre as far as Robinson's department store (get off here if coming by bus **from Pattaya**), then cross the road onto minor road 3241 and wait outside the Assumption College for a songthaew (at least hourly; 20min) to the zoo.

Ko Si Chang

The unhurried pace and the absence of consumer pressures make tiny, rocky **Ko Si Chang** a satisfying place to hang out for a few days. Unlike most other east-coast destinations, it offers no real beach life – fishing is the major source of income, and there's little to do here but explore the craggy coastline and gaze at the horizon, though there are several appealing hotels and guest houses.

Practicalities

Ferries to Ko Si Chang leave from Si Racha and run approximately hourly from 6am to 8pm. Nearly all the ferries depart from the pier at the end of Si Racha's Soi 14, off Thanon Chermchompon, though occasionally they set off instead from Wat Ko Loi, the "island temple" at the end of the very long causeway 400m further along. The hop across to Ko Si Chang should take about forty minutes, but this varies according to how many passengers need to be transferred to and from the cargo ships between which the ferries weave.

On **arrival**, you'll probably dock at Ko Si Chang's Tha Bon, the more northern of the two piers on the east coast, though some boats pull in at Tha Lang.

The first boat back to the mainland leaves at 6am and the last at 6pm; all but the 6.40am departing boats stop off at Tha Lang on their way back.

Both piers connect with Thanon Asadang, a small ring road on which you'll find the market, shops and most of the island's houses. The rest of the island is accessible only by paths and tracks. It's easy enough to walk from place to place, the simplest point of reference for **orientation** being *Tiew Pai Guest House*, which stands at the southwest "corner" of Thanon Asadang, about 750m from Tha Lang. Alternatively, you can jump in one of the bizarrely elongated 1200cc motorbike **samlors** which, as there are probably fewer than a dozen private cars on Ko Si Chang, virtually monopolize the roads. A ride from the pier to any of the guest houses in one of these contraptions costs about B30, and a tour of the island will set you back around B250; some of the drivers speak good English. You can rent **motor-bikes** (B250 per day) and **mountain bikes** (B50) from *Sripitsanu Bungalows*, whose managers can also arrange boat trips to nearby islands for B1000–1600 per boat with up to twenty passengers.

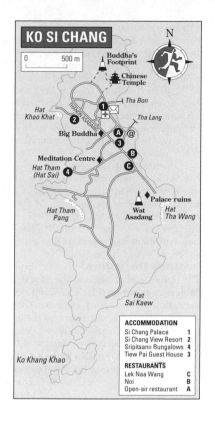

There are **exchange facilities** (but no ATM) at the Thai Farmers Bank near the market between the two piers. The post office and hospital are near Tha Bon, and **internet access** is available inside the video rental store near Tha Lang. For a fee of B50, non-guests can use the **swimming pool** at *Sichang Palace Hotel*.

Accommodation and eating

There's a surprising range of **accommodation** on Ko Si Chang, including some places with superb sea views. Most backpackers stay in the centrally located *Tiew Pai Guest House* (℡038/216084; ❸–❺), where rooms range from simple doubles with shared bathrooms to air-conditioned ones with private facilities. The restaurant serves a good range of food and the friendly managers speak English. If you prefer a coastal spot, and are willing to pay a bit more, your first choice should be *Sripitsanu Bungalows* (℡038/216336, ⓔsripit-sanu@hotmail.com; ❹), which has just half a dozen comfortably furnished bungalows almost right at the edge of the Hat Tham cliff – some of the lower rooms are actually built into the rockface. It's a really relaxing place, run by a well-informed couple. Further along the coast, at Hat Khao Khat, *Si Chang View Resort* (☎038/216210, ℉216211; ❹–❺) occupies another prime spot, though sadly you can't see the rugged coastline clearly from the otherwise very attractive fan and air-con rooms. Finally, the most upmarket place on the island is *Si Chang Palace* (☎038/216276, ℉216030; ❼–❽), set across from Tha Bon on Thanon Asadang; facilities here include a swimming pool, and all rooms have air-con and TV. For the very best and personally selected sea views, nothing can beat **camping** on your chosen spot: the cliffs at Hat Khao Khat are a particularly popular site, though quite exposed.

The two best **restaurants** on the island are southeast of *Tiew Pai*, on the road to the old palace. Both *Lek Naa Wang* and *Noi* serve up recommended Thai food, including an excellent choice of fish and seafood dishes, at moderate prices. Otherwise, *Tiew Pai* does decent travellers' food (with nightly karaoke-style entertainment from teenage Thai girls at night) and there are several small noodle shops between the piers. As the island caters for the crews of the cargo ships which choke the deep channel between Ko Si Chang and the mainland, a couple of open-air restaurants near the piers employ singing hostesses to entertain them in the evenings.

Around the island

The most famous site on the island is the overgrown ruins of **Rama V's palace**, near pebbly Hat Tha Wang beach on the southeast coast (just follow the road from *Tiew Pai Guest House*). Built here in the 1890s as a sort of health resort where sickly members of the royal family could recuperate in peace, King Chulalongkorn's teakwood palace formed the heart of a grand and extensive complex comprising homes for royal advisers, quarters for royal concubines and administrative buildings. By the turn of the century, however, the king had lost interest in his island project and so in 1901 his golden teak palace was moved piece by piece to Bangkok, and reconstructed there as Vimanmek Palace (see p.149). The other buildings were left to disintegrate in their own good time: aside from the stone steps and balustrades which still cling to the shallow hillside, the only structure on the site to survive intact was the circular **Wat Asadang**, right at the top and surmounted by a chedi. Nonetheless it's an evocative site and a pleasant focus for a not particularly strenuous outing; you can walk to the ruins in less than half an hour from *Tiew Pai*.

The main beach on the west coast, and the most popular one on the island, is **Hat Tham Pang**, a kilometre-long stretch of sand complete with deckchairs and beach umbrellas for rent. A samlor to this beach costs around B70 from *Tiew Pai*. North of Hat Tham Pang, and also accessible via a fork off Thanon Asadang opposite *Tiew Pai*, you'll find the Tham Yai Prik meditation centre and the dramatically situated *Sripitsanu Bungalows*, both located above a tiny, rocky cove known as **Hat Tham** or Hat Sai.

Back down on the ring road, continuing in a northwesterly direction, you'll pass beneath the gaze of a large yellow Buddha before reaching the rocky northwest headland of **Khao Khat**, a few hundred metres further along Thanon Asadang. The uninterrupted panorama of open sea makes this a classic sunset spot, and it's safe enough for cliffside scrambling.

From here the road heads east to reach the gaudy, multi-tiered Chinese temple, **Saan Chao Paw Khao Yai** (Shrine of the Father Spirit of the Great Hill), stationed at the top of a steep flight of steps and commanding a good view of the harbour and the mainland coast. Established here long before Rama V arrived on the island, the shrine was dedicated by Chinese seamen who saw a strange light coming out of one of the **caves** behind the modern-day temple.

The caves, now full of religious statues and offertory paraphernalia, are visited by boatloads of Chinese pilgrims, particularly over Chinese New Year.

Continue on up the cliffside to reach the small pagoda built for Rama V and enshrining a **Buddha's Footprint**. Two very long, very steep flights of stairs give access to the footprint: the easternmost one starts at the main waterfront entrance to the Chinese temple and takes you past a cluster of monks' meditation cells, while the westerly one rises further west along the ring road and offers the finest lookouts. It's well worth the vertiginous ascent, not least for the views out over Thailand's east coast; looking down over a gulf congested with cargo boats from Ayutthaya and Bangkok, you'll see the tiny island of Ko Khram and, clearly visible on the horizon, the Si Racha coast.

4

THE EAST COAST | Pattaya

Pattaya

With its murky sea, streets packed with high-rise hotels and touts on every corner, **PATTAYA** is the epitome of exploitative tourism gone mad. But most of Pattaya's visitors don't mind that the place looks like Torremolinos or that the new water treatment plant has only recently stopped businesses from dumping their sewage straight into the bay – what they are here for is sex. The town swarms with male and female **prostitutes**, spiced up by a sizeable population of transvestites (*katoey*), and plane-loads of Western men flock here to enjoy their services in the rash of go-go bars and massage parlours for which "Patpong-on-Sea" is notorious. The ubiquitous signs trumpeting "Viagra for Sale" say it all. Pattaya also has the largest **gay scene** in Thailand, with several exclusively gay hotels and a whole area given over to gay sex bars.

Pattaya's evolution into sin city began with the Vietnam War, when it got fat on selling sex to American servicemen. Tempted by the dollars, outside investors moved in, local landowners got squeezed out, and soon the place was unrecognizable as the fishing village it once was. When the soldiers and sailors left in the mid-1970s, Western tourists were enticed to fill their places, and as the seaside Sodom and Gomorrah boomed, ex-servicemen returned to run the sort of joints they had once blown their dollars in. Almost half the bars, cafés and restaurants in Pattaya are Western-run, specializing in home-from-home menus of English breakfasts, sauerkraut and bratwurst, hamburgers and chips. More recently, there is said to have been an influx of criminal gangs from Germany, Russia and Japan, who reportedly find Pattaya a convenient centre for running their rackets in passport and credit-card fraud as well as child pornography and prostitution.

Yet Pattaya does have its good points even if you don't fit the lecherous profile of the average punter, as attested by the number of **families** and older couples who choose to spend their package fortnights here. Although very few people swim off Pattaya's shore, the beach itself is kept clean so lots of tourists make use of the deckchairs and parasols that line its length, stirring only to beckon one of the iced-drink vendors. Pattaya's watersports facilities are among the best in the country, and there are masses of tourist-oriented theme parks, cultural attractions and golf courses within day-tripping distance. Holidaying here is not cheap (with no makeshift, low-budget bamboo huts for backpackers, and few bargain foodstalls), but travellers on a modest budget can find good accommodation at relatively low cost.

405

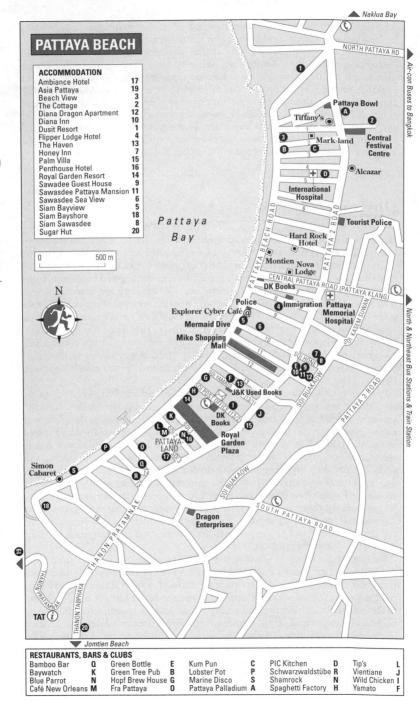

PATTAYA BEACH

ACCOMMODATION

Ambiance Hotel	17
Asia Pattaya	19
Beach View	3
The Cottage	2
Diana Dragon Apartment	12
Diana Inn	10
Dusit Resort	1
Flipper Lodge Hotel	4
The Haven	13
Honey Inn	7
Palm Villa	15
Penthouse Hotel	16
Royal Garden Resort	14
Sawadee Guest House	9
Sawasdee Pattaya Mansion	11
Sawasdee Sea View	6
Siam Bayview	5
Siam Bayshore	18
Siam Sawasdee	8
Sugar Hut	20

0 — 500 m

N

Naklua Bay

NORTH PATTAYA RD

Air-con Buses to Bangkok

Pattaya Bowl **A**

Tiffany's

Mark-land

Central Festival Centre

Alcazar

International Hospital

Tourist Police

North & Northeast Bus Stations & Train Station

Hard Rock Hotel

Pattaya Bay

Montien

Nova Lodge

CENTRAL PATTAYA ROAD (PATTAYA KLANG)

DK Books

Police

Explorer Cyber Café

Mermaid Dive

Mike Shopping Mall

Immigration

Pattaya Memorial Hospital

J&K Used Books

POST OFFICE

DK Books

Royal Garden Plaza

PATTAYA-LAND

Simon Cabaret

Dragon Enterprises

SOUTH PATTAYA ROAD

TAT

Jomtien Beach

RESTAURANTS, BARS & CLUBS

Bamboo Bar	**Q**	Green Bottle	**E**	Kum Pun	**C**	PIC Kitchen	**D**	Tip's	**L**
Baywatch	**K**	Green Tree Pub	**B**	Lobster Pot	**P**	Schwarzwaldstübe	**R**	Vientiane	**J**
Blue Parrot	**N**	Hopf Brew House	**G**	Marine Disco	**S**	Shamrock	**N**	Wild Chicken	**I**
Café New Orleans	**M**	Fra Pattaya	**O**	Pattaya Palladium	**A**	Spaghetti Factory	**H**	Yamato	**F**

Orientation

Pattaya comprises three separate bays. At the centre is the four-kilometre **Pattaya Beach**, the noisiest, most unsightly zone of the resort, crowded with yachts and tour boats and fringed by a sliver of sand and a paved beachfront walkway. Known by its English name, and signed as such, **Pattaya Beach Road** (Thanon Hat Pattaya) runs the length of the beach and is connected to the parallel Pattaya 2 Road (Thanon Pattaya Sawng) by a string of sois numbered from 1 in the north to 17 in the south. The core of this block, between sois 6 and 13, is referred to as **Central Pattaya** and is packed with hotels, restaurants, bars, fast-food joints, souvenir shops and tour operators. During the day this is the busiest part of the resort, but after dark the neon zone south of Soi 13/2 – **South Pattaya** – takes over. Known locally as "the strip", this is what Pattaya's really about, with sex for sale in go-go bars, discos, massage parlours and open-sided "bar-beers". The town's enclave of gay sex bars is here too, focused mainly on the interlinked network of small lanes known as **Pattayaland** sois 1, 2 and 3, but actually signed as Sois 13/3, 13/4 and 13/5, between the Royal Garden Plaza and Soi 14. Pattaya Beach Road continues south from its junction with South Pattaya Road (Thanon Pattaya Tai) all the way down to the *Siam Bayshore Hotel*; this stretch of road is also known as **Walking Street** because it's pedestrianized every evening from 7pm, though proposed development may put a stop to that. **North Pattaya**, between Central Pattaya Road (Thanon Pattaya Klang) and North Pattaya Road (Thanon Hat Pattaya Neua), also has its "bar-beers", but is a more sedate, upmarket district.

The southerly bay, **Jomtien Beach**, is also fronted by enormous high-rises, many of which are condominiums, though there are some low-rise mid-priced hotels along the beachfront road, Jomtien Beach Road (Thanon Hat Jomtien), as well. Fourteen kilometres long, it is safer and a little cleaner than Pattaya Beach, and is considered Thailand's number-one windsurfing spot. Trees provide shade in some stretches and in other parts there are sun loungers with parasols for rent. The far northern tip of Jomtien, beyond the end of the road, is mainly a gay cruising beach. The atmosphere in Jomtien is almost sleepy in comparison to Pattaya, with just a handful of restaurant-shacks, the occasional minimarket, and half-a-dozen bar-beers between the hotels and condos.

Naklua Bay, around the northerly headland from Pattaya Beach, is the quietest of the three enclaves, and has managed to retain its fishing harbour and indigenous population despite the onslaught of condominiums, holiday apartments and expat homes. Most of the accommodation here is in time-shared condos, and there's no decent beach.

Arrival and information

Most people **arrive** in Pattaya direct **from Bangkok**, either by public **bus** from the Eastern (Ekamai) Bus Terminal (every 30min until 10.30pm; 2–3hr), the Northern (Mo Chit) Bus Terminal (every 30min until 5pm; 2–3hr), or by air-conditioned tour bus from a Bangkok hotel or Don Muang airport (3 daily; 2hr 30min). Air-con buses to and from Bangkok and the airport use the bus station on North Pattaya Road, from where share-taxis deliver travellers to the hotel of their choice for B40 per person. Non-air-con buses use the Baw Kaw Saw government bus station on Thanon Chaiyapruk in Jomtien. **From Si Racha** it's a thirty-minute ride to Pattaya in one of the frequent buses or songthaews, and you'll probably get dropped just east of the resort on Thanon

Sukhumvit, from where songthaews will ferry you into town; a few Si Racha songthaews will take you all the way. Buses **from Rayong** and **Trat** generally drop passengers on Thanon Sukhumvit as well. To travel to Rayong (for Ban Phe and Ko Samet) or Trat (for Ko Chang), you need to wait at one of the bus *sala* on Thanon Sukhumvit and flag down any of the frequent government buses that pass. Malibu Travel offers a faster and more direct B150 minibus service between Pattaya and the Ban Phe pier; the ticket includes pick-up from your hotel and can be booked through most hotels and tour agents in Pattaya. It's also possible to get to Pattaya direct **from Isaan** – buses to and from Khorat, Ubon Ratchathani and Nong Khai use the Northeastern Bus Station on Central Pattaya Road, just east of the Pattaya 3 Road intersection. Buses to and **from Chiang Mai** drop passengers at the terminus on Thanon Sukhumvit, across from the Central Pattaya Road intersection.

Pattaya is on a branch line of the eastern rail line, and there is one **train** a day in each direction between the resort and Bangkok, which takes almost four hours. Though this seems a lot longer than the bus, it can work out faster if you factor in the time it takes to cross Bangkok to the Eastern Bus Terminal. Pattaya's **train station** is on Thanon Sukhumvit, about 500m north of the Central Pattaya Road interesction.

Pattaya's U-Tapao **airport** (☎038/245595) is located at the naval base near Sattahip, about 25km south of the resort; it's served by Bangkok Airways flights to and from Ko Samui and Phnom Penh in Cambodia (through flights to Siem Reap are planned). If you're travelling to Cambodia from U-Tapao you'll have to pay a B400 departure tax at the airport; the domestic departure tax of B30 is included in the price of the ticket.

Information

The **TAT** office is inconveniently located at 609 Thanon Pratamnak (sometimes referred to as Cliff Road) between South Pattaya and Jomtien (daily 8.30am–4.30pm; ☎038/428750, 🖷429113, ✉tatpty@chonburi.ksc.co.th). The *Pattaya Mail* prints local news stories, entertainment listings and details of community events; it comes out every Friday and is available at most newsstands and bookstores. There are several free what's-on magazines published in Pattaya, which are dished out at tour agencies and pricier hotels.

Transport

The easiest way to get around Pattaya is by **songthaew** – though on all routes beware of being overcharged. Most follow a standard anticlockwise route up Pattaya 2 Road as far as North Pattaya Road and back down Pattaya Beach Road, for a fixed fee of B10 per person. Never jump in a parked songthaew, as you'll be charged for chartering the whole vehicle; instead just flag down a passing one and press the bell when you want to get off. Songthaews **to Jomtien** leave from the junction of Pattaya 2 Road and South Pattaya Road (but can be flagged down anywhere along their route) and cost B10 to Thanon Boonkanjana. Songthaews **to Naklua** start from the junction of Pattaya 2 Road and Central Pattaya Road and cost B10 to Naklua Soi 12.

The alternative is to rent your own transport: Pattaya Beach Road is full of touts offering motorbikes and jeeps for rent. **Motorbike rental** costs from B150 to B700 per day depending on the bike's size; beware of faulty vehicles, and of scams – some people have reported that rented bikes get stolen from tourists by touts so they can keep the customer's deposit. Avis **car rental** (☎038/361627, 🌐www.avisthailand.com) have an office inside the *Dusit*

Resort Hotel in North Pattaya, Budget ($\textcircled{\tiny T}$038/720613, ⓦwww.budget.co.th) has an office off Soi Diana Inn, and many of the motorbike touts also rent out jeeps for about B1000 per day.

Accommodation

Really cheap **hotels** are almost impossible to find in Pattaya, and a depressing number of the lowest-priced options suffer from poor maintenance, musty rooms and unfriendly staff. Only one of the "inexpensive" hotels listed below has rooms for B150, but there are a number of places offering fan rooms for B250 and air-con rooms for B300. Rooms that cost B400 and up usually offer reasonable facilities, including air-conditioning, TV and use of a swimming pool as well. Advance reservations are advisable to stay in the best-value hotels. Prices in all categories plummet by up to fifty percent when demand is slack, so it's often worth asking around two or three places before checking in. If your budget can't stretch to B250, you may have to resort to one of the less pricey "rooms for rent" advertised in the shops along Pattaya 2 Road between Soi 11 and Soi 13/2 (Soi Post Office), along Soi 13/2 itself, on Soi 13/1 (Yamato) and on Soi Buakaow. These tend to be dingy back rooms, and usually operate only until the owner finds something more lucrative to do with the premises.

Bear in mind that the sex industry ensures that all rooms have beds large enough for at least two people; rates quoted here are for "single" rooms with one big double bed (a "double" room will have two big double beds and cost more). Another effect of the sex industry is that hotel guests are often assumed to be untrustworthy, so when checking in you're likely to be asked for a deposit against the loss of your room key and against the use of your mini-bar and phone. Though all hotels are easy-going about gay couples, we've listed a couple of exclusively gay hotels as well.

Some people prefer to stay on **Jomtien Beach**, which is quieter and has a bit more of a beach scene, but lacks the shops and restaurants of Pattaya – as well as the go-go bars. Prices here are about the same as on Pattaya Beach.

Pattaya

Inexpensive and moderate

Ambiance Hotel, 325/91 Pattayaland Soi 3 (Soi 13/5), South Pattaya $\textcircled{\tiny T}$038/424099, ⓕ424626. Well-appointed hotel aimed at gay customers and located right in the heart of the gay district. Has just thirty rooms, all of them furnished with air-con, TV and mini-bar. ⑤–⑦

Beach View, Soi 2, Pattaya Beach Rd, North Pattaya $\textcircled{\tiny T}$038/422660, ⓕ422664. Medium-sized mid-range high-rise with swimming pool just across the road from the beach. Many rooms have sea view and some have air-con. Extremely reasonable for its class. ④–⑤

The Cottage, off Pattaya 2 Rd, North Pattaya $\textcircled{\tiny T}$038/425660, ⓕ425650. Excellent-value, well-appointed fan and air-con bungalows, attractively designed and pleasantly located in a quiet garden compound a good distance off the main road. Convenient for the shops and restaurants in the Central Festival Centre complex. Facilities include two small swimming pools, a bar and a restaurant. ④–⑤

Diana Dragon Apartment, 198/16 Soi Diana Inn, opposite Soi 11, Central Pattaya $\textcircled{\tiny T}$038/423928, ⓕ411658. Enormous fan and air-con rooms with fridge, and use of the pool at *Diana Inn*, 100m away; favoured by long-stay tourists. Very good value. ③

Diana Inn, 216/3–9 Pattaya 2 Rd, opposite Soi 11, Central Pattaya $\textcircled{\tiny T}$038/429675, ⓕ424566, ⓦwww.golfasia.com. Popular, centrally located mid-range hotel with rather dark, faded rooms, most with air-con and TV. Swimming pool and buffet breakfast included in the price. ③–⑤

Flipper Lodge Hotel, 520/1 Soi 8, Pattaya Beach Rd, Central Pattaya $\textcircled{\tiny T}$038/426401, ⓕ426403, ⓔflippers@ptty.loxinfo.co.th. Very good-value mid-range hotel at the lower end of this price category. Smart air-con rooms, all with TV, some with sea view, and two swimming pools, one of them on the rooftop. Advance reservations advisable. **⑤**–**⑥**

The Haven, 185 Soi 13, Pattaya Beach Rd, Central Pattaya ☎038/710988, ℱ426200, ℮fobe@loxinfo.co.th. Small, friendly establishment offering fifteen clean, comfortable and remarkably good value air-con rooms set around a small courtyard with a swimming pool and seafood restaurant. All rooms have TV, video player and phone. Fairly peaceful despite being in a soi that's lined with bar-beers. **⑤**

Honey Inn, 529/2 Soi Honey Inn, opposite Soi 10, Pattaya 2 Rd, Central Pattaya ☎038/428117. Mid-sized hotel with swimming pool offering large, air-con rooms in fairly good condition, all with a decent balcony and TV. **④**

Palm Villa, 485 Pattaya 2 Rd, opposite Soi 13/2, Central Pattaya ☎ & ℱ038/429099. Peaceful haven close to the nightlife, with small garden, a swimming pool, and sizeable fan and air-con rooms. **③**–**④**

Penthouse Hotel, Pattayaland Soi 2 (Soi 13/4), South Pattaya ☎038/429639, ℱ421747. Small hotel for gay tourists offering inexpensive, good-value air-con rooms, all with TV. Located in the gay district. **④**

Sawasdee Guest House, 502/1 Soi Honey Inn, opposite Soi 10, Pattaya 2 Rd, Central Pattaya ☎038/425360, ℱ720261, ℠www.sawasdee-hotels.com. The cheapest branch of the excellent Sawasdee chain of budget hotels has the most inexpensive rooms in Pattaya, decently if spartanly outfitted and available with fan or air-con. **②**–**③**

Sawasdee Pattaya Mansion, 367 Soi Diana Inn, Central Pattaya ☎038/720563, ℱ720261, ℠www.sawasdee-hotels.com. Perhaps the nicest of all the Sawasdee hotels, this one has appealingly cosy rooms with TV and air-con, a small pool and a friendly atmosphere. **③**–**④**

Sawasdee Sea View, 302/1 Soi 10, Central Pattaya ☎038/710566, ℱ720261, ℠www.sawasdee-hotels.com. Recommended place occupying a great location in a still quiet soi just a few dozen metres off the beachfront road. Rooms are smallish but clean, air-conditioned and fairly well kept; the pricier ones have TV, and some rooms on the upper floors do indeed have a faint sea view. **③**–**④**

Siam Sawsadee, corner of Soi Honey Inn and Soi Buakaow, Central Pattaya ☎038/720330, ℱ720261, ℠www.sawasdee-hotels.com. Breezy, good-value hotel with a swimming pool and 206 big, comfortable rooms, all with air-con, TV and fridge. **④**

Expensive

Asia Pattaya, 325 Thanon Pratamnak (Cliff Rd), South Pattaya ☎038/250602–6, ℱ250496, ℠www.asiahotel.co.th. Attractively placed on a private bay between the *Royal Cliff* and Jomtien Beach. Extensive facilities including nine-hole golf course, tennis courts, swimming pool and snooker tables. **⑧**–**⑨**

Dusit Resort, 240/2 Pattaya Beach Rd, North Pattaya ☎038/425611–4, ℱ428239, ℠www.dusit.com. In the thick of the high-rises, it has an excellent reputation for high-quality service and facilities, which include two pools, a gym, tennis and squash courts. **⑨**

Royal Garden Resort, 218 Pattaya Beach Rd, Central Pattaya ☎038/412120, ℱ429926, ℠www.royal-garden.com. Set right in the heart of the resort, across the road from the beach, and enclosed by a tropical garden, this well-equipped hotel has standard-issue top-notch rooms, floodlit tennis courts, a huge pool and a spa. **⑧**–**⑨**

Siam Bayshore, 559 Pattaya Beach Rd ☎038/428678, ℱ428730, ℠www.siamhotels.com. At the far southern end of the South Pattaya strip, set in a secluded wooded spot overlooking the beach, this popular hotel comprises 270 rooms spread over twelve wings and is set in exceptionally lush tropical gardens. Many rooms have balconies offering uninterrupted sea views, and there are two pools as well as tennis courts and snooker, table-tennis and badminton facilities. **⑧**–**⑨**

Siam Bayview, Pattaya Beach Rd, on the corner of Soi 11, Central Pattaya ☎038/423871, ℱ423879, ℠www.siamhotels.com. Very centrally located upscale hotel that has smart, good-sized rooms, many of them with ocean views. Good value considering its location and facilities, which include two swimming pools, tennis courts, snooker and several restaurants. **⑧**–**⑨**

Sugar Hut, 391/18 Thanon Tabphaya, midway between South Pattaya and Jomtien ☎038/251686, ℱ251689, ℠www.sugarhut.co.th. The most unusual, least corporate accommodation in Pattaya comprises a charming collection of just 33 Ayutthaya-style traditional wooden bungalows set in a fabulously lush garden with three swimming pools. The bungalows are in tropical-chic style, with low beds, open-roofed shower rooms, mosquito nets and private verandas; the more expensive ones have a sitting room as well. It's an appealingly laid-back place but best with your own transport as it's nowhere near the restaurants, shops or sea. **⑨**

Jomtien Beach

DD Inn, just back from the beach, on a tiny soi opposite *KFC* at the far north end of Beach Rd ☏038/232995, ✉ddinnguesthouse@hotmail.com. Friendly, good-value guest-house-style little hotel in an ideal spot just a few metres from the beach. Rooms with balconies are slightly pricier, but all rooms come with air-con, TV, hot water – and duvets! Recommended. ❹

Grand Jomtien Palace, 365 Beach Rd, at the corner of Thanon Wat Boonkanjana (aka Wat Bun) ☏038/231405, ℱ231404, ✉grandjt@ptty2.loxinfo.co.th. Upmarket high-rise hotel where many of the comfortable, air-con rooms have a decent sea view. Facilities include a swimming pool, a beer garden and restaurant, and a small shopping arcade. ❽

JB Guest House, 75/14 Soi 5 (Soi Post Office), off Beach Rd ☏038/231581. Exceptionally good-value rooms in this small, friendly, Bangkok-style guesthouse. All rooms have TV and hot water; you pay slightly more for air-con. ❸

Mermaid's Beach Resort, 75/102 Soi 7, off Beach Rd ☏038/232210, ℱ231908. Nicely appointed, mid-range, low-rise hotel that's smartly furnished and well maintained. There's a swimming pool, dive centre, restaurant and baby-sitting service, and all 120 rooms have air-con and TV. Price depends on whether you want a view of the pool or the street. ❺–❼.

Sea Breeze Hotel, next to Soi 10 on Beach Rd ☏038/231056, ℱ231059. Decent sized air-con rooms, all with TV and most overlooking a garden. Swimming pool and pool table on the premises. ❺

Silver Sand Villa, next to Soi White House at the northern end of Beach Rd ☏038/231288, ℱ232491, ✉sweetsea@cbi.cscom.com The huge, nicely furnished air-con rooms in the old wing are good value, but you need to book ahead for a view of the pool (rather than a wall); most of the rooms are wheelchair-accessible. Rooms in the new wing are more expensive; though plainly furnished, they all have balconies and pool views. Two swimming pools and restaurant. ❺–❼

Surf House, between Sois 5 and 7 at the north end of Beach Rd ☏038/231025, ℱ231029. Popular mid-range place across from the beach. Rooms are a bit faded, but all have air-con and TV, and some have a sea view. ❺

Daytime activities

Most tourists in Pattaya spend the days recovering from the night before: not much happens before midday, breakfasts are served until early afternoon, and the hotel pool generally seems more inviting than a tussle with water-skis. But the energetic are well catered for, with a decent range of dive centres, watersports facilities, golf courses and theme parks to enjoy.

Snorkelling and scuba diving

Snorkelling and scuba diving are popular in Pattaya, though if you've got the choice between diving here or off the Andaman coast (see pp.638–9), go for the latter – the reefs there are a lot more spectacular. The big advantage of Pattaya is that it can be dived year-round. The main destinations for local **dive trips** are the group of "outer islands" about 25km from shore, which include Ko Rin, Ko Man Wichai and Ko Klung Badaan, where you have a good chance of seeing big schools of barracuda, jacks and tuna, as well as moray eels and blue-spotted stingrays. There are also two rewarding wreck dives in the Samae San/Sattahip area: the 21-metre-deep freighter *Phetchaburi Bremen*, which went down in the 1930s; and the 64-metre-long cargo ship *Hardeep*, which was sunk during World War II and can be navigated along the entire length of its interior. A one-day dive trip including two dives, equipment and lunch generally costs around B3000, with accompanying snorkellers paying B800. Several companies along Pattaya Beach Road run **snorkelling** trips to nearby Ko Larn and Bamboo Island, though mass tourism has taken its toll on these two islands and their coral.

Pattaya is also an easy place to learn to dive: one-day introductory dives start at about B3000, and four-day open-water **courses** average out at B12,000. Be

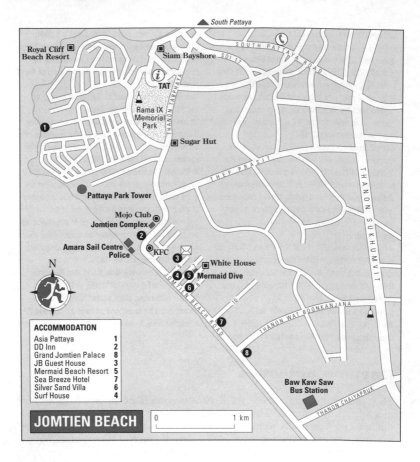

South Pattaya

Royal Cliff
Beach Resort

Siam Bayshore — SOI 17

SOUTH PATTAYA ROAD

TAT

Rama IX
Memorial
Park

THANON TAPPRAYA

Sugar Hut

① THEP PRASIT

Pattaya Park Tower

Mojo Club
Jomtien Complex

②

Amara Sail Centre
Police

KFC

③

White House

④ ⑤ Mermaid Dive

⑥

N

⑦

THANON WAT BOONKANJANA

THANON SUKHUMVIT

JOMTIEN BEACH ROAD

ACCOMMODATION
Asia Pattaya	1
DD Inn	2
Grand Jomtien Palace	8
JB Guest House	3
Mermaid Beach Resort	5
Sea Breeze Hotel	7
Silver Sand Villa	6
Surf House	4

⑧

Baw Kaw Saw
Bus Station

THANON CHAIYAPRUK

JOMTIEN BEACH   0 ———————— 1 km

careful when signing up for a dive course or expedition: unqualified instructors and dodgy equipment are a fact of life in Pattaya, and it's as well to question other divers about all operators, TAT-approved or not (see p.75 of Basics for more guidelines). The local **recompression chamber** is at the Apakorn Kiatiwong Naval Hospital (☎038/601185) in Sattahip, 26km south of Pattaya; it's open 24 hours. TAT-approved dive shops that run diving expeditions and internationally certificated courses include:

Aquarelax Diving Center, 183/31 Soi 13/2 (Soi Post Office), Central Pattaya ☎038/710900, ⓕ7109-01, ⓦwww.dive-pattaya.com. PADI Five-Star Instructor Development Centre; German management.
Dave's Divers Den, 190/11 Central Pattaya Rd, Central Pattaya ☎038/420411, ⓕ360095, ⓔdrd @loxinfo.co.th. Pattaya's longest-running dive centre.
Mermaid's Dive Centre, Soi White House, Jomtien ☎038/232219, ⓕ232221, ⓦwww .mermaiddive.com; and between sois 10 and 11

on Beach Rd, Central Pattaya. PADI Five-Star Instructor Development Centre.
Paradise Scuba Divers, *Siam Bay View Hotel*, corner Soi 10, Pattaya Beach Rd, Pattaya ☎038/710567, ⓔlscuba@loxinfo.co.th. PADI Five-Star dive centre.
Seafari Sports Center, 359/2 Soi 5, Pattaya Beach Rd, North Pattaya ☎038/429060, ⓕ361356, ⓦwww.seafari.net. PADI Five-Star Instructor Development Centre; American management.

Water sports

Jomtien Beach is the place for **windsurfing, water-skiing, jet-skiing** and **parasailing** (the latter is also popular in North Pattaya): you can either book up in the outlets along Pattaya's Beach Road or head down to Jomtien itself and sign up there. One of Jomtien's biggest watersports outlets is the Amara Sail Centre, located on the beach just north of the police station and the Thanon Tabphaya/Beach Road junction. *Surf House Kitchen* restaurant between sois 5 and 7 at the north end of Jomtien's Beach Road also rents out water-sports equipment, as do several nearby shops, and there are heaps of jetskis for rent on the beach north of Soi 5. Average prices start at about B1000 per hour for water-skiing, B500 for windsurfing, and B500 for one round of parasailing. Or you might want to try **cable skiing** at the Lakeland lagoon (daily 10am–9pm; B300 for 2hr) on Thanon Sukhumvit, about 5km north of Pattaya. *Deutsches House* restaurant on Soi 4, North Pattaya (☎038/428725) runs day-long **deep-sea fishing** expeditions for about B2000 per person; you could also try asking about fishing trips at the *Shamrock* bar on Pattayaland Soi 2 (Soi 13/4) in Central Pattaya.

Land sports

All top-end hotels have **tennis courts** and some offer badminton and gym facilities too, though these are generally open only to guests. The Pattaya Bowl, just north of Soi 1, Pattaya 2 Road in North Pattaya (daily 10am–midnight), has twenty **bowling** lanes (B60–80 per game); there's a **shooting range** at *Tiffany's* on Pattaya 2 Road, North Pattaya (daily 9am–10pm; B120), and a **go-kart circuit** in Jomtien that's suitable for 7-year-olds as well as adults (daily 9.30am–6.30pm; B100–200 for 10min). And at weekends there's always the prospect of watching a **speedway race** at the Bira International Circuit, 14km northeast of Pattaya on Highway 36 (B80–150). Six bouts of **Thai boxing** are staged at 8pm every Thursday night at the Sityodtong stadium, near the Siam Country Club on the far eastern fringes of Pattaya; tickets cost B400, plus B100 for return transport and can be bought through Dragon Enterprises (☎038/427585), on Soi Day-Night Hotel in South Pattaya.

There are currently seventeen international-standard **golf courses** within easy reach of Pattaya, some of them designed by famous golfers. Visitors' green fees average B750 on a weekday, B1500 on a weekend, plus B200 for a caddy, and a set of clubs can usually be rented for B200–300. One popular option is to join the golf **package** run by Golf Bus (☎038/720370), which includes transport to and from the Phoenix Golf and Country Club and all fees except club rental (B1500 on weekdays, or B2100 weekends). The *Diana Inn* at 216/3–9 Pattaya 2, opposite Soi 11, Central Pattaya (☎038/429675, ⓦwww.golfasia.com), also organizes all-inclusive golfing packages to local courses. The following courses are all less than an hour's drive from Pattaya, with the closest listed first and the furthest last; for directions, either call the course or ask at your hotel. Phoenix Golf and Country Club (27 holes; ☎038/239391), Siam Country Club (18 holes; ☎038/249381); Laem Chabang International Country Club (27 holes; ☎038/338351); and Eastern Star Golf Course (18 holes; ☎038/630410).

Theme parks and other attractions

One of the most enjoyable attractions in the resort is **Ripley's Believe It Or Not** (daily 11am–11pm; B280), located on the third floor of the Royal Garden Plaza shopping and entertainments centre on Pattaya Beach Road. It's part of a worldwide chain of similar curiosity museums inspired by the bizarre collections of the early twentieth-century American cartoonist and adventurer Robert Leroy Ripley, and displays lots of outlandish objects (including fetishes, torture contraptions and tribal masks), and real-life novelties from Thailand and further afield (such as models of the world's tallest, smallest and fattest men), as well as an exhibition on sharks. Amazing facts are presented in a lively way which makes it fun for all the family, so long as the kids have a penchant for the gruesome. When the kids tire of Ripley's they can always play on the arcade games, dodgems and ride-simulators found nearby on the same floor of the plaza.

Advertised as the only one of its kind in the world, the **Museum of Bottle Art** (daily 11am–8pm; B100), 100m south of the bus station on Thanon Sukhumvit, contains three hundred pieces of art in bottles, all of them painstakingly assembled by Dutch expat Pieter Bij de Leij. The artist has spent the best part of his 60-plus years pursuing this hobby and the result is a huge collection of miniature replicas – including Dutch windmills, Thai temples, a Saudi mosque and a British coach and horses – encased in glass bottles. He is usually on hand to demonstrate his technique, and there's also a video showing him at work. To get to the museum, take an eastbound songthaew along Central Pattaya Road, get off as soon as you reach Thanon Sukhumvit, and walk 200m south.

The hugely ambitious **Sanctuary of Truth**, also known as **Wang Boran** and **Prasat Mai** (daily 8am–6pm; B500; ☎038/225407), is also a kind of replica, but on a 1:1 scale. Conceived by the man behind the Muang Boran Ancient City complex near Bangkok (see p.166), it's a huge temple-palace designed to evoke the great ancient Khmer sanctuaries of Angkor and built entirely of wood. Begun in 1981, the sanctuary is still a work-in-progress (and still a hard-hat zone), with construction workers and woodcarvers swarming over the site and as yet no English-language tourist information available, but if you have an interest in ancient Khmer architecture or modern Thai woodcraft then it's probably worth the steep entry fee. The sanctuary is located behind imposing crenellated walls off the west end of Naklua Soi 12, close to the *Garden Sea View* hotel; to get there from Central Pattaya, take a Naklua-bound songthaew as far as Soi 12, then a B10 motorbike taxi. Built in a fabulously dramatic spot beside the sea, the temple rises to 105m at its highest point (each of the central pillars is made from a single tree) and fans out into four gopura, or entrance pavilions, each of which is covered in symbolic religious and mythological woodcarvings. The **carvings** on the north (seaside) gopura are inspired by Cambodian mythology, and include a tower above the gopura that's crowned with an image of the four-headed Hindu god Brahma, plus a lotus flower and two three-headed elephants; those on the east gopura refer to China, so the Mahayana Buddhist *bodhisattva*s have Chinese faces; the carvings on the west gopura evoke India and include scenes from the Hindu epic the *Mahabarata*; and the southern entrance has images from Thailand, such as scenes from the Hindu tale the *Ramayana*. For more on the symbolism of Hindu and Buddhist sculptures, see the piece on Art and Architecture in "Contexts", p.772.

There are several theme parks, "culture villages" and wildlife parks on the outskirts of Pattaya, all well signed off the main roads. **Mini Siam**, just north of the North Pattaya Road/Thanon Sukhumvit intersection, is just what it sounds like: two hundred of Thailand's most precious monuments reconstructed to 1:25 scale; Mini Europe is supposedly coming soon. **Nong Nooch Village**, 18km south of Pattaya off Thanon Sukhumvit, serves life-sized Thai culture in the form of traditional dancing and elephant rides against the backdrop of an attractively landscaped park. It's a popular feature of many tour-operators' programmes (B350 half-day), but it's worth coming here if you're into flowers: the **orchid garden** is said to be the world's largest. The **Elephant Village**, 6km northeast of Pattaya, offers ninety-minute elephant "treks" round its park for B700, plus the option of doing some rafting as well; there's also an elephant training show every afternoon (B400). For details and transport, call ⊕038/361868, or contact *Novotel Tropicana Hotel*, off Soi 6, Pattaya Beach Road. **Sriracha Tiger Zoo**, about 30km north of Pattaya, also offers the chance to interact with creatures of the wild, and is described on p.402.

Plenty of agents fix up **day-trips** to tourist spots further afield, like Ko Samet (B800), the River Kwai (B1500) and Bangkok (B1500), though the journey times for all these are so long as to make them hardly worth the effort.

Shopping

Pattaya is not a bad place for **shopping**, though unless you're keen to snap up dozens of fake designer boxer shorts and mass-produced woodcarvings you're probably best keeping away from the ubiquitous street stalls that clog the pavements of Pattaya Beach Road day and night. Better to retreat inside one of the resort's glossy shopping plazas – like the Central Festival Centre on Pattaya 2 Road in North Pattaya, which has a tempting array of fairly classy shops, ranging from designer clothes outlets such as D&G to smart gift and handicraft shops; there's also a cineplex (see p.418), several restaurants and a food court. Pattaya's other main shopping centre is Royal Garden Plaza in South Pattaya, where you'll find international fashion outlets like Timberland, as well some handicraft stalls, Boots the Chemist, *Pizza Hut* and *McDonald's*, lots of coffee shops, Ripley's Believe it or Not (see p.413) and a cinema screen.

Pattaya boasts Thailand's best English-language **bookshops** outside Bangkok. DK Books (daily 8am–11pm) on Soi 13/2 (Soi Post Office) stocks a phenomenal range of books on Asia, from guidebooks to novels to coffee-table glossies, and has a pile of anecdotal "farang in Thailand" and "confessions of a bar girl" literature too; there's a much smaller branch of DK north up Beach Road, on the corner of Central Pattaya Road. Bookazine on the corner of Pattayaland 1 (Soi 13/3) and Beach Road in South Pattaya also has an impressive range of books on Asia, as well as several shelves of novels and general-interest titles; their magazine section is unrivalled, and you should be able to find almost any major international newspaper or magazine here. J&K Used Books, which occupies an upstairs room above a grocery shop on Soi 13/1 (Soi Yamato), keeps a small stock of inexpensive secondhand novels and non-fiction titles, arranged alphabetically and catalogued on computer.

Eating

Overall, **food** in Pattaya is expensive compared to the rest of the country and not nearly as interesting. The scores of expat restaurateurs in Pattaya have made Western food the resort's primary dining option, a generally dismal situation worsened by the host of fast-food joints along Pattaya Beach Road – *McDonald's*, *KFC*, *Mr Donut* and so on. For inexpensive Thai food, hunt out the curry and noodle vendors on Soi Kasem Suwan – they are concentrated between Central Pattaya Road and Soi Honey, but might pitch up anywhere. Top-quality Thai restaurants are a bit thin on the ground – not surprisingly, given the setting, there's more of an emphasis on seafood than on classical cuisine. Most hotels offer fairly good value all-you-can eat breakfast buffets for around B75 per head, the majority of which are open to non-guests as well.

Baywatch, Pattaya Beach Rd, between Pattayaland sois 1 and 2 (sois 13/3 and 13/4), Central Pattaya. Open 24hr, this is a good, if pricey, place to get your all-day breakfast, complete with sea view and sidewalk vantage point. Cappuccinos, filter coffees, burgers, sandwiches and pancakes.

Blue Parrot, Pattayaland Soi 2 (Soi 13/4), Central Pattaya. Mexican café and bar, good for moderately priced lunchtime tacos, enchiladas and chilli.

Café New Orleans, Pattayaland Soi 2 (Soi 13/4), Central Pattaya. Specializing in mid-priced Cajun and Creole dishes, this place is especially recommended for its tasty baby back ribs and its all-you-can-eat lunchtime deals on weekends.

Fra Pattaya, South Pattaya Rd, South Pattaya. Big menu of moderately priced staple Thai and Chinese dishes; authentic taste and workaday atmosphere.

Lobster Pot, opposite Soi 14, Pattaya Beach Rd, South Pattaya. Enormous, moderately priced seafront restaurant specializing in fresh seafood, in particular tiger prawns and giant lobsters.

PIC Kitchen, Soi 5, North Pattaya. One of Pattaya's finest traditional Thai restaurants, set in a stylish series of teak buildings. Mouth-watering, mid-priced menu of elegantly presented curry, seafood, rice, noodle and vegetarian dishes. Nightly live jazz from 7pm.

Royal Garden Plaza Food Court, top floor of the Royal Garden Plaza, Pattaya Beach Rd, Central Pattaya. Lots of hot-food stalls serving specialities from different parts of Thailand, plus Japanese and Italian options too. Not exactly haute cuisine, but fast, hassle-free and fairly inexpensive for Pattaya.

Decide what you want and then buy coupons to the right value.

Schwarzwaldstube, Soi 15, Central Pattaya. Hearty Swiss and German dishes with lots of reasonably priced steak and an unusually good cheese selection.

Spaghetti Factory, corner of Soi 13/2 (Soi Post Office) and Pattaya Beach Rd, Central Pattaya. Pleasant and popular streetside branch of this chain restaurant. Hearty portions of pasta and pizza at moderate prices.

Sugar Hut, 391/18 Thanon Tabphaya, mid-way between South Pattaya and Jomtien. Attached to the delightful tropical hotel described on p.410, this restaurant gives you the chance to soak up the ambience and enjoy the tropical gardens without shelling out for a bungalow. Food is served in an open-sided *sala* and is mainly classy (and expensive) traditional Thai; recommendations include fried catfish in coconut milk and chilli, and chicken baked with pineapple. Worth the splurge.

Tip's, 22/10 Pattaya Beach Rd, between Pattayaland sois 2 and 3 (sois 13/4 and 13/5), South Pattaya. Long-running Pattaya institution offering over a dozen different set breakfasts at cheap prices.

Vientiane, between sois 13/1 and 13/2 on Pattaya 2 Rd. Specializes in moderately priced Southeast Asian food, including Lao-inspired curries and some Indonesian dishes.

Yamato, Soi 13/1 (Soi Yamato), Central Pattaya. Good-value, relatively inexpensive Japanese fare including sushi, *soba* and *udon* dishes, *tempura* and *sashimi*. Open evenings only during the week, and for lunch and dinner at weekends.

Drinking and nightlife

Entertainment is Pattaya's *raison d'être* and the **nightlife** is what most tourists come for, as do oilfield workers from the Arabian Gulf and US marines on R&R. Of the four hundred-odd **bars** in Pattaya, the majority are the so-called "bar-beers", relatively innocent open-air drinking spots staffed by hostesses whose primary job is to make you buy beer not bodies. However, sex makes more money than booze in Pattaya – depending on who you believe, there are between six thousand and twenty thousand Thais working in Pattaya's sex industry, a workforce that includes children as young as 10. It's an all-pervasive trade: the handful of uninspiring discos depend more on prostitutes than on ravers, while the transvestite cabarets attract audiences of thousands.

Bars

Pattaya's often nameless outdoor **"bar-beers"** group themselves in clusters all over North, Central and South Pattaya. The set-up is the same in all of them:

the punters – usually lone males – sit on stools around a brashly lit circular bar, behind which the hostesses keep the drinks, bawdy chat and well-worn jokes flowing. Beer is generally quite inexpensive at these places, the atmosphere low-key and good-humoured, and couples as well as single women drinkers are almost always made welcome.

Drinks are a lot more expensive in the bouncer-guarded **go-go bars** on the South Pattaya "strip" where near-naked hostesses serve the beer and live sex shows keep the boozers hooked through the night. The scene follows much the same pattern as in Patpong, with the women dancing on a small stage in the hope they might be bought for the night – or the week. Go-go dancers, shower shows and striptease are also the mainstays of the **gay scene**, centred on Pattayaland Soi 3 (Soi 13/5), South Pattaya.

There's not a great deal of demand for bars where the emphasis is on simple companionable drinking, but those listed below are comparatively low-key and welcoming. Most are open-sided streetside joints, with a few bar stools and a number of chairs set out around low tables in the front. Even here, bartenders are nearly always young and female, and many of them earn extra money by occasionally sleeping with customers.

Bamboo Bar, seafront end of South Pattaya Rd. An exuberant in-house band pulls in a sizeable crowd to this large streetside lounge-style bar.

Green Bottle, adjacent to *Diana Inn*, Pattaya 2 Rd, Central Pattaya. A cosy, air-con, pub-style bar which has forged a studiously unsleazy atmosphere. Serves food.

Hopf Brew House, between sois 13/1 (Yamato) and 13/2 (Post Office), Pattaya Beach Rd, Central Pattaya. Cavernous air-con pub, designed like a German beer hall around an internal courtyard with a stage for the nightly live music. Attracts a youngish crowd, including vacationing couples, and serves bar snacks as well as beer.

Kum Pun, Soi 2, North Pattaya. Bar and restaurant known for its live bands who play nightly sets of authentic Thai folk music as well as soft rock.

Mojo Club, near Jomtien Complex, off Thanon Thep Prasit, North Jomtien. Laid-back bar run by a couple of jazz musicians, with live jazz and blues nightly.

Shamrock, Pattayaland 2 (Soi 13/4), South Pattaya. This British-run bar is a good place to catch local expat gossip. The manager sometimes entertains customers on his banjo, and his collection of folk-music tapes is also worth listening out for. On the edge of the gay district, but attracts a very mixed crowd.

Shenanigans, *Royal Garden Resort* hotel complex, Pattaya Beach/Pattaya 2 Rd, Central Pattaya. Irish pub that's a sister operation to the hugely popular outfit in Bangkok. Serves Guinness and Kilkenny Bitter every day of the week, enlivened by a timetable of different theme nights with appropriate food. The big screen shows major sports events, and there are nightly sets from a roster of live bands who start playing around 11pm.

Wild Chicken, the Pattaya 2 end of Soi 13/2 (Soi Post Office), South Pattaya. Attracts a friendly expat crowd, including the local Hash House Harriers. Discreet hostesses and amiable managers.

Discos

Pattaya's **discos** tend to be pick-up joints with few frills, no admission charges, relatively inexpensive beer and a large number of unattached women hanging round the edges. The huge and sleazy *Marine Disco*, in the heart of "the strip", is the ultimate meat market, with its cramped upstairs dance-floor encircled by ringside seats, and a more official boxing ring downstairs, starring prepubescent boys. The more hi tech *Pattaya Palladium*, at the intersection of Soi 1 and Pattaya 2 Road in North Pattaya, boasts a more salubrious ambience, but is not exactly intimate – it's the biggest of its kind in Asia and is supposed to have a capacity of six thousand, with a troupe of 35 dancers to entertain them.

Cabarets

Tour groups – and families – constitute the main audience at Pattaya's **transvestite cabarets**. Glamorous and highly professional, these shows are performed three times a night at three theatres in the resort: at Alcazar, opposite Soi 4 on Pattaya 2 Road in North Pattaya; at Tiffany's, north of Soi 1 on Pattaya 2 Road in North Pattaya; and also at Simon Cabaret on Beach Road in South Pattaya. Each theatre has a troupe of sixty or more transvestites who run through twenty musical-style numbers in fishnets and crinolines, ball gowns and leathers, against ever more lavish stage sets. All glitz and no raunch, the shows cost from B400.

Listings

Airlines Bangkok Airways, 2nd Floor, *Royal Garden Plaza*, South Pattaya ☎ 038/411965; Thai Airways, inside the *Dusit Resort*, North Pattaya ☎ 038/429347.

Cinemas Central Cineplex, on the top floor of the Central Festival Centre on Pattaya 2 Rd in North Pattaya, has four English-language shows a day at each of its four screens. There's also a three-screen cinema on the top floor of *Royal Garden Plaza* in South Pattaya. Tickets from B70.

Cookery classes At the *Royal Cliff Beach Resort*, Royal Cliff Bay, 353 Thanon Pratamnak ☎ 038/250421, between South Pattaya and Jomtien. Held every Mon, Wed and Fri at 10am; B990.

Emergencies For all emergencies, call the tourist police on the free, 24hr phoneline ☎ 1699. Alternatively, contact the tourist police on Pattaya 2 Rd, just south of Soi 6, Central Pattaya ☎ 038/429371, or call in at the more central police station on Beach Rd, just south of Soi 9.

Exchange Numerous exchange counters and ATMs, particularly on Pattaya Beach Rd and Pattaya 2 Rd.

Hospitals The two most central private hospitals are the Pattaya International Hospital on Soi 4 ☎ 038/428374–5, and Pattaya Memorial Hospital

on Central Pattaya Rd ☎ 038/429422–4. The Bangkok-Pattaya Hospital ☎ 038/427751–5 is on Thanon Sukhumvit, about 400m north of the intersection with North Pattaya Rd. The nearest divers' recompression chamber is at the Apakorn Kiatiwong Naval Hospital ☎ 038/601185 in Sattahip, 26km south of Pattaya; it's open 24hr a day.

Immigration office Opposite *Flipper Lodge* on Soi 8 (Mon–Fri 8.30am–4.30pm; ☎ 038/429409). Many travel agents offer cheap visa-renewal day-trips to Cambodia: check advertisements and local press for details.

Internet access At dozens of internet centres throughout the resort, including the very efficient, 24hr *Explorer Internet Café* , between sois 9 and 10 on Pattaya Beach Rd; Catnet at the small public CAT phone office on Soi 13/2.

Mail The post office is, not surprisingly, on Soi Post Office in Central Pattaya, though the road has now officially been re-signed as Soi 13/2.

Telephones The main CAT international telephone office is on South Pattaya Rd, just east of the junction with Pattaya 2 Rd, and there's a smaller, more central branch on Soi 13/2 in Central Pattaya. There are lots of private international call centres in the resort.

Pattaya to Ko Samet

South of Pattaya, buses race along Highway 3 past the turn-off to the deep-sea fishing port of **Bang Saray**, before stopping to offload returning sailors at **Sattahip**, site of the Thai Navy headquarters. The few swimmable beaches along this stretch of shoreline are reserved for the exclusive use of holidaying sailors and their families. Though the nearby **U-Tapao** air base also belongs to the military, it is also used by Bangkok Airways – for details of their routes, see p.42.

Few farang travellers choose to stop for longer than they have to in the busy provincial capital of **RAYONG**, but it's a useful place for **bus connections**, particularly if you're travelling between the east coast and the northeast, or if you're trying to get to Ko Samet; Ban Phe, the ferry pier for Ko Samet, is served by frequent songthaews from Rayong bus station (see p.421 for details). Rayong is famous for producing the national condiment *nam plaa* – a sauce made from decomposed fish – and for the pineapples and durian grown in the provincial orchards, but there's nothing much for tourists here. The **TAT office** (T 038/655420, F 655422, E tatry@infonews.co.th) for the Rayong region and Ko Samet is inconveniently located 7km east of Rayong town centre at 153/4 Thanon Sukhumvit (Highway 3), on the way to Ban Phe; any Ban Phe-bound bus or songthaew will drop you at its door.

In the unlikely event that you get stuck here overnight, there are three passable moderately priced **hotels** within walking distance of the bus terminal, a few hundred metres east along Thanon Sukhumvit, past the hospital. All three offer fan-cooled and air-conditioned rooms with attached bathroom; the least costly but dingiest rooms belong to the *Asia Hotel*, just north off Thanon Sukhumvit at no. 84 (T 038/611022; ❶–❸), otherwise try the *Rayong Otani* at no. 69 (T 038/611112; ❷–❺) or the nearby *Rayong Hotel* at no. 65/3 (T 038/611073; ❷–❹), both of them on the south side of the road. If you prefer a sea view, you could stay at one of the high-rise hotels or family bungalows along the **Rayong coast** that are finding increasing favour with Thai weekenders, despite the superiority of beaches elsewhere in the vicinity. Sandwiched between the seafront and the Rayong River estuary, a couple of kilometres southwest of Thanon Sukhumvit and the bus terminal, *Rayong Seaview* at 46 Beach Road (T 038/611364; ❻–❼) is the most moderately priced, while the *PMY Beach Hotel*, west along the shorefront at no. 147 (T 038/613002, F 614887; ❽–❾) has a swimming pool, fitness centre and snooker club. The exclusive *Rayong Resort* (T 038/651000, F 651007, W www.rayongresort.com; ❾) is much further east along the coast and occupies a nice spot on a headland just west of Ban Phe with sea views out to Ko Samet; facilities here include three shorefront swimming pools, tennis courts, table tennis and boat trips to Ko Samet.

Ko Samet

Attracted by its proximity to Bangkok and its powdery white sand, backpackers, package tourists and Thai students flock to the island of **Ko Samet**, 80km southeast of Pattaya, whose former name, Ko Kaew Phitsadan, means "the island with sand of crushed crystal". Only 6km long, Ko Samet was declared a **national park** in 1981, but typically the ban on building has been ignored and there are now over thirty bungalow operations here. Inevitably, this has had a huge impact on the island's resources: the sea is no longer pristine, and you occasionally stumble across unsightly piles of rubbish. Though the authorities did try closing the island to overnight visitors in 1990, they have since come to a (controversial) agreement with the island's bungalow operators who now pay rent to the Royal Forestry Department.

Samet's beaches tend to be characterized by the type of **accommodation** you find there, though as the island gets increasingly upmarket, it is becoming more difficult to find a bungalow for under B300 a double in high season on any of the beaches. Ao Phrao, Ao Wong Duan and Hat Sai Kaew have the most upmarket places to stay, but all the other beaches still have at least a few budg-

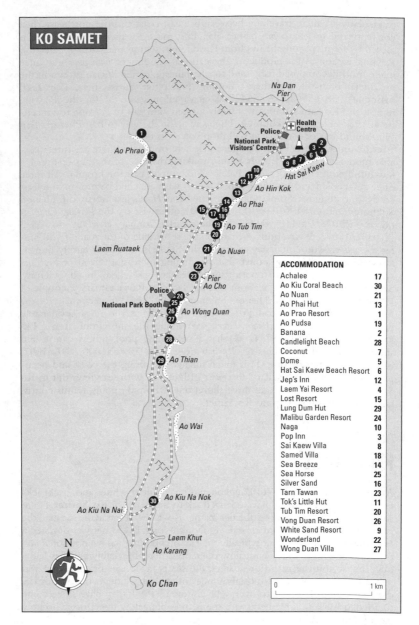

KO SAMET

Na Dan
Pier

Health
Centre

Police

National Park
Visitors' Centre

Ao Phrao

Hat Sai Kaew

Ao Hin Kok

Ao Phai

Ao Tub Tim

Laem Ruataek

Ao Nuan

Pier
Ao Cho

Police

National Park Booth

Ao Wong Duan

Ao Thian

Ao Wai

Ao Kiu Na Nok

Ao Kiu Na Nai

Laem Khut

Ao Karang

N

Ko Chan

ACCOMMODATION	
Achalee	17
Ao Kiu Coral Beach	30
Ao Nuan	21
Ao Phai Hut	13
Ao Prao Resort	1
Ao Pudsa	19
Banana	2
Candlelight Beach	28
Coconut	7
Dome	5
Hat Sai Kaew Beach Resort	6
Jep's Inn	12
Laem Yai Resort	4
Lost Resort	15
Lung Dum Hut	29
Malibu Garden Resort	24
Naga	10
Pop Inn	3
Sai Kaew Villa	8
Samed Villa	18
Sea Breeze	14
Sea Horse	25
Silver Sand	16
Tarn Tawan	23
Tok's Little Hut	11
Tub Tim Resort	20
Vong Duan Resort	26
White Sand Resort	9
Wonderland	22
Wong Duan Villa	27

0   1 km

et-orientated bungalows, with the most accessible beaches – Ao Hin Kok, Ao Phai and Ao Tub Tim – being the most popular in this category. Typically you can expect to pay B150 for the simplest bamboo hut equipped only with a large, well-worn mattress, a blanket and a mosquito net; the same kind of huts with private bathrooms and electric fans cost B200–400. More upmarket bungalows are usually made of concrete and have good, tiled bathrooms; the most expensive have air-con, but prices also depend on whether or not you have an uninterrupted view of the sea. Samet has no fresh water, so water is trucked in from the mainland and should be used sparingly; most sets of bungalows offer at least a few huts with attached bathroom. Electricity in a few places is rationed for evening consumption only, but even these outfits have video shows after dark to help keep the beer flowing.

All beaches get packed on **weekends** and national holidays, so at these times you'd be sensible to take the first available room and if necessary change early the following day. You could also try phoning ahead to reserve a room, though not all bungalows accept bookings and it can be hard getting through in the first place as most places on Ko Samet still rely on satellite phones (code ℡01). At Songkhran (the Thai New Year, in April) it's said to be impossible to find a bungalow even on the most remote beaches, so it's probably worth altering your itinerary accordingly. Many bungalow managers raise their rates by sixty percent during peak periods and sometimes for weekenders as well: the rates quoted here are typical high-season rates. If all affordable accommodation is booked up, you can always **camp** – in accordance with national park rules, camping is permissible on any of the beaches, despite what you might be told.

Until a few years ago, Samet was considered to be malarial, but has now been pronounced safe. You'll still encounter plenty of **mosquitoes** at dusk though, so take lots of repellent; nets or screens are supplied by all bungalow operations and repellent is available from stalls and shops on the island.

En route to the island: Ban Phe

The mainland departure-point for Ko Samet is the tiny fishing port of **BAN PHE**, about 200km from Bangkok. There are hourly direct **buses** from Bangkok's Eastern (Ekamai) Bus Terminal to the Ban Phe pier, departing between 5.30am and 5.30pm (some air-con services; 3hr), but if you miss those you can easily take one of the more frequent buses to **Rayong** (every 15min; 2hr 30min) and then change onto songthaews, which leave Rayong bus station about every thirty minutes and take half an hour to reach Ban Phe pier. Alternatively, you could take one of the **tourist minibuses** from Thanon Khao San to Ban Phe; prices for these do not include the boat fare and you should be prepared for some fairly crazed driving. From **Pattaya**, there are hardly any direct Ban Phe buses so you're probably best off taking a bus to Rayong (every 30min; 1hr 30min) and then one of the half-hourly songthaews. There are tourist minibuses from Pattaya as well, which can be booked through most hotels and cost B150 – be warned that the B50 boat ticket available as an add-on to the minibus ticket from Pattaya is for Ao Wong Duan, so if you want to go to one of the other beaches, wait and buy your boat ticket at Ban Phe. Coming by bus from points further east, such as **Chanthaburi** or **Trat** for example, you'll most likely be dropped at the Ban Phe junction on Highway 3, from where a songthaew or motorbike taxi will take you the remaining 5km to the pier.

If you get stuck with nothing to do between ferries, several places to check your **email** – a good idea here as internet access is very expensive on Ko Samet – can be found on and around Ban Phe's main pier-head, including a couple on the pier itself. There are a couple of **hotels** on the two-hundred-metre stretch of road between the main Saphaan Nuan Tip pier and the Ao Phrao (Saphaan Sri Ban Phe) pier. *TN Place* (❷–❹) has simple guest-house rooms with or without private bathroom; it's the cheaper and more traveller-oriented of the two.

It also has internet access and there's a restaurant next door. The nearby mid-range *Diamond Hotel* (☎038/651757; ❸–❹) has simple rooms with fan and more comfortable air-con ones with TV; you can check-in 24 hours a day, which could be useful.

Boats to Ko Samet

Once in Ban Phe, you need to decide which beach you want and then choose your **boat** accordingly. Some boats are owned by individual resorts and ferry both pre-paid package tourists and fare-paying independent travellers; others make the crossing as soon as they have enough passengers (minimum eighteen people) or sufficient cargo to make it worth their while. In theory, boats to the two main piers on Ko Samet run hourly from 8am to 5pm during high season (Nov–Feb) and on national holidays, and every two hours at other times. In practice, many of the boats leave at the same time, so you may well end up waiting a couple of hours. Probably the best strategy is to get on the boat with the most people and buy your ticket on board rather than from one of the boat-specific booths on the pier-head. All boats charge the same fares.

The easiest place to get to on Ko Samet is **Na Dan pier** on the northeastern tip of the island, which is the most convenient arrival point for the beaches of Hat Sai Kaew, Ao Hin Kok, Ao Phai, Ao Tub Tim and Ao Nuan, and quite feasible for all the other beaches as well; songthaews meet the boats at Na Dan (see opposite) and will take you as far as Wong Duan, or you can walk to your chosen beach. Boats to Na Dan leave from Ban Phe's Saphaan Nuan Tip pier, opposite the 7-11 shop; they take thirty minutes to get to Samet and charge B40 one way.

Leaving Ko Samet

Four **scheduled boats** leave Ko Samet's Na Dan pier every day, the first one at about 7am, the last at 5pm, and there are usually a few extra ones in between; times are posted at the pier, but if you have a plane to catch you should allow for boat delays. There are also regular departures from Ao Wong Duan, every two hours between 8.30am and 4.30pm and, in high season, you'll find at least one Ban Phe boat a day from Ao Cho and Ao Phrao.

Arriving at Ban Phe, you can pick up **buses** to Bangkok, Chanthaburi or Trat, or a songthaew to Rayong, from where buses to all these destinations, plus Pattaya and Si Racha, are far more frequent. The Ban Phe bus and songthaew stop is 400m east of the 7-11, though most buses and songthaews pass the pier-head and will pick up passengers there. If you're heading straight back to Bangkok's Thanon Khao San, to Don Muang airport or to Pattaya, your easiest (and most expensive) option is to buy a direct **minibus** ticket from one of Ko Samet's tour operators (there's at least one on every beach); these tickets don't include the boat fare, but departure times from Ban Phe are arranged to coincide with boat arrivals. You can also book tourist minibuses at the tour operators' offices in Ban Phe on the little soi beside the 7-11 shop, across from the main pier, though they may not always have room for last-minute bookings. Travelling **to Ko Chang**, it takes just two and a half hours by tourist minibus from Ban Phe to the Laem Ngop pier, though it's expensive at B250 (bookable at the *White Sand Resort* on Hat Sai Kaew); the alternative route by ordinary bus can take all day and often entails changing buses at Chanthaburi and then getting onto a Laem Ngop-bound songthaew in Trat, though it works out at half the price. Note that if you're going overland **to Cambodia** via Koh Kong near Trat and need to buy an advance visa (check with the embassy first to find out whether this is necessary), the *White Sand Resort* travel agent on Ko Samet can do this, avoiding the need for you to go back to Bangkok yourself; the service takes five days.

There are equally frequent boats to **Ao Wong Duan** (40min; B50), which is also convenient for the nearby beaches of Ao Cho and Ao Thian. Some boats go to Wong Duan direct from Ban Phe's Saphaan Nuan Tip pier, others stop at Na Dan first – it's often a question of how many passengers there are. Some of the bungalow resorts on the smaller beaches also run boats from Ban Phe direct to their beach – see the individual beach accounts below for details. Boats to **Ao Phrao** leave from a different pier, called Saphaan Sri Ban Phe pier, which is 200m west of the 7-11. The boat service is free to guests of the *Ao Phrao Resort*, or B90 return for non-guests; there are usually four boats a day, but call the resort on ☏038/616883 to check times.

Island practicalities

Foreign visitors are charged the B200 national-park **entrance fee** on arrival (B100 for children under 14 or free for the under-3s), payable either at the checkpoint between the Na Dan pier and Hat Sai Kaew (where there is a national park visitor centre, with displays on Ko Samet's marine life) or at the booth near the Ao Wong Duan pier. There is a sporadic **songthaew** service on Ko Samet, but you may have to wait quite a while for your ride to fill up, and you shouldn't rely on the songthaews as a way to travel between beaches. Songthaews start at Na Dan pier and drive as far as Wong Duan, down the pot-holed track that runs along the centre of the island; fares are posted at Na Dan pier and range from B10 to Hat Sai Kaew (or B100 if you charter the songthaew) to B50 to Ao Kiu (B500 to charter). There are **motorbikes** for rent on every beach at a prohibitive B150 per hour, and a place next to *Sai Kaew Villa* on Hat Si Kaew rents out mountain bikes for B150 per day.

Ko Samet's **health centre** and **police station** are in Na Dan, and the island's **post office** is run by *Naga Bungalows* on Ao Hin Kok, they offer a poste restante service as well as basic postal facilities (see p.425 for details). You can make **international phone calls** at *Naga*, and at the bigger bungalow operations on every main beach; nearly all Ko Samet's phones are satellite phones so the charges are high, at around B100 per minute. Both *Naga* and *Sai Kaew Villa* on Hat Sai Kaew offer **internet access** by satellite phone, which is not surprisingly very expensive at around B7–10 per minute. The biggest bungalows also **change money**, though obviously rates are less favourable than on the mainland. In Na Dan and on Hat Sai Kaew, Ao Phai and Ao Wong Duan, small shops sell basic travellers' necessities, again at higher prices than in Ban Phe and Rayong.

The beaches

Most of the islanders not associated with the tourist trade live in the **north-east** of the island, near Na Dan, where there are a few shops and foodstalls, as well as the island's only school, health centre and wat. Samet's best **beaches** are along the **east coast**, and this is where you'll find nearly all the bungalow resorts. A rough track connects some of them; otherwise it's a question of walking along the beach at low tide or over the low, rocky points at high water. Long stretches of the **west coast** are well-nigh inaccessible, though at intervals the coastal scrub has been cleared to make way for a track. The views from these clifftop clearings can be magnificent, particularly around sunset, but you can only safely descend to sea level at the bay up near the northwest headland. A few narrow tracks cross the island's forested central ridge to link the east and west coasts, but much of the **interior** is dense jungle, home of hornbills, gibbons and spectacular butterflies.

Samet has no decent coral reefs of its own, so you'll have to take a boat trip to the islands of Ko Kudi, Ko Thalu and Ko Mun, off the northeast coast, to get good **snorkelling** and **fishing**. Trips cost from B450 to B650 including equipment, and can be booked through at least one bungalow resort on every main beach. Some places also offer boat trips around Samet itself for about B400 for a full day. Despite the lack of great reefs, there are a couple of **dive operators** on Samet: Ploy Scuba (℡01/218 7636), next to *Sai Kaew Villa* on Hat Sai Kaew, offers introductory dives lasting one hour for B1200, or one day for B1600, and teaches the four-day open water course for B9500. Ao Prao Divers (℡038/616883, Ⓔaopraodivers@hotmail.com), based at *Ao Prao Resort* and with a branch at *Sea Breeze* on Ao Phai, is slightly more expensive, but has a big programme of dive trips and cruises and is PADI-certified.

Hat Sai Kaew

Arriving at **Na Dan** pier, a ten-minute walk south along the track, past the health centre and school, brings you to **HAT SAI KAEW**, or Diamond Beach, named for its beautiful long stretch of luxuriant sand, so soft and clean it squeaks underfoot – a result, apparently, of its unusually high silicon content, which also makes it an excellent raw material for glass-making. Songthaews from Na Dan to Hat Sai Kaew cost B10 per person, or B100 when chartered.

The most popular – and congested – beach on Samet, this is the only part of the island where the beachfront is lined with bungalows, restaurants, beachwear stalls, deck chairs and parasols; the northern end is usually a lot more peaceful than the southern. Holidaying Thais and farangs flock here in pretty much equal numbers, especially at weekends and on public holidays, but big groups of day-tripping package tourists make stretches of the beach almost unbearable from around 11am to 4pm. At night, you have the option of enjoying a leisurely dinner at one of the big seafront seafood **restaurants**, watching videos at one of the bungalow cafés, hanging out at the beachside *Reggae Bar* or heading up the track that connects Hat Sai Kaew with the pier at Na Dan, where you'll find congenial little drinking dens such as *Roger's Vodka Bar* and the *Banana Bar*. *White Sand Resort* has a good **travel agent** which sells minibus tickets to Ko Chang and offers a Cambodian visa service, as well as doing all the usual day-trips and bus tickets. There is **internet access** at *Sai Kaew Villa* and a **dive shop** next door.

Much of the **accommodation** on Hat Sai Kaew is crammed uncomfortably close together. The best-value place on the beach is *Laem Yai Resort* (℡01/293 0208; ❹), whose decent, comfortable wooden bungalows occupy a pretty position under the Laem Yai headland at the nicest, far northern end of Hat Sai Kaew. Nearby the few simple huts at *Pop Inn* (❸) and *Banana* (℡01/218 5841; ❸) are set further back but also have access to the calmer stretch of the beach; they are the cheapest places on Hat Sai Kaew. The distinctive blue and white bungalows of *Hat Sai Kaew Beach Resort* are stylish and thoughtfully designed, which makes them the best in their price bracket (❽), with phones, TV and air-con in every room. The terraced bungalows at *Coconut* (℡01/294 6822; ❹–❼) are overpriced, though the detached air-conditioned bungalows are a lot more comfortable and may be worth splashing out for. A short walk south along the beach, the large and efficiently run *Sai Kaew Villa* (℡ & Ⓕ038/615852, Ⓦwww.saikaew.com; ❺–❽) comprises a dozen smart, clean rooms with fan or air-con in a hotel-like block, plus some prettier, more expensive bungalows; it also has internet access. The southern end of the beach is occupied by *White Sand Resort* (℡038/617195; ❹–❺), a huge complex of standard-issue bungalows set in a garden back from the shorefront; rooms here are unexciting but relatively well priced for this beach, and there's a choice between fan or air-con.

Ao Hin Kok

Separated from Hat Sai Kaew by a low promontory on which sits a mermaid statue – a reference to Sunthorn Phu's early nineteenth-century poem, *Phra Abhai Mani* (see box on p.426) – **AO HIN KOK** is smaller and less cluttered than its neighbour. There are three bungalow outfits here, looking over the beach from the grassy slope on the far side of the track. **Songthaews** from Na Dan will drop you at Ao Hin Kok for B20 per person (or B150 when chartered), or you can walk here in about fifteen minutes.

Ao Hin Kok is a particularly good beach for food, with all three bungalows offering exceptional fare at their attached **restaurants**. *Naga* is especially recommended for its vegetarian dishes, its cocktails and its home-made bread and cakes; it also stages regular pool competitions and puts on fire-juggling shows. *Tok's Little Hut* is known for its seafood, and *Jep's Inn* serves up a fine menu of curries, seafood and travellers' fare at its tables on the beach, prettily decorated with fairy lights and given extra atmosphere by mellow music.

The English-run *Naga Bungalows* (☎01/353 2575; ❶–❸) has the cheapest **accommodation** on Ko Samet, offering a range of simple huts with mattresses on the floor, mosquito nets and shared facilities, with the price depending on whether you want a fan or air-con. It's extremely popular, and there's a pool table and a table-tennis table on the premises as well. Next door, *Tok's Little Hut* (☎01/218 1264; ❷–❸) offers slightly more comfortable bungalows, all with attached bathrooms. At the welcoming *Jep's Inn* (☎01/853 3121; ❸–❹) you have the option of staying in quite pleasant small bungalow blocks or in larger, more expensive detached wooden huts, all of them en-suite, but none with a sea view.

Ko Samet **post office** is run out of *Naga Bungalows* and offers a parcel packing, phone, fax and **internet** service as well as poste restante; letters are kept for three months and should be addressed c/o Poste Restante, Ko Samet Post Office, Naga Bungalows, Ko Samet.

Ao Phai

Beach accommodation gets a little more upmarket around the next collection of rocks on the narrow but pleasant enough **AO PHAI**, where the bungalows tend to be well built and comfortable, and most have attractive tiled bathrooms. Facilities on Ao Phai include an outdoor bar and a minimarket, and *Sea Breeze* has a small library, sells boat trips and minibus tickets, rents out windsurfing equipment and offers overseas telephone and money-exchange facilities. **Songthaews** from Na Dan cost B20 per person to Ao Phai (or B150 when chartered), or you can walk it in twenty minutes.

The recommended *Ao Phai Hut* (☎01/353 2644; ❹–❺) occupies a lovely position on the rocky divide between Ao Phai and Hin Kok, and offers attractive, simply furnished **huts** which are nicely spaced in among the trees. All huts have attached bathrooms and some have air-con, though electricity is only available in the evenings. *Sea Breeze* (☎01/218 6397, Ⓕ239 4780; ❸–❺) is the largest set of bungalows on the beach, offering inexpensive wooden huts, more solid concrete ones and bigger versions with air-con; they all have private bathrooms, but, as they're built up a sparsely wooded slope, none has a sea view. The adjacent *Silver Sand* (☎01/218 5195; ❸–❺) is good value for Ko Samet, offering decent, well-maintained bungalows with nice bathrooms, the price depending on distance from the sea (the cheapest ones are quite far back, with

Over thirty thousand lines long and written entirely in verse, the nineteenth-century romantic epic **Phra Abhai Mani** tells the story of a young prince and his adventures in a fantastical land peopled not only by giants and mermaids, but also by gorgeous women with whom he invariably falls in love. Seduced by an ogress who lives beneath the sea, and kept captive by her for several months, Phra Abhai Mani pines for dry land and eventually persuades a mermaid to help him escape. Naturally, the two fall in love, and decide to spend some time together on the near-by island of Ko Samet (hence the mermaid statue on Ao Hin Kok). But the prince soon tires of the mermaid's charms, and leaps aboard a passing ship in pursuit of another ill-fated affair, this time with a princess already engaged to someone else. And so it goes on.

Widely considered to be one of Thailand's greatest-ever poets, **Sunthorn Phu** (1786–1856) is said to have based much of his work on his own life, and the romantic escapades of *Phra Abhai Mani* are no exception. By all accounts, the man was a colourful character – a commoner alternately in and out of favour at Bangkok's Grand Palace, where he lived and worked for much of his life. The child of a broken marriage, he was taken to the palace as a baby when his mother got a job as wet nurse to a young princess (his father had returned to his home town of Klaeng in Rayong province). His first brush with court officialdom came sometime before his twentieth birthday, when he was temporarily imprisoned for having an affair with a court lady. Soon pardoned, the couple married, and Sunthorn Phu was employed as the court poet. By the time Rama II ascended the throne in 1809, he was an established royal favourite, acting as literary aide to the king. However, he took to the bottle, was left by his wife and participated in a drunken fight that landed him in jail again. It was during this stint inside (estimated to be around 1821) that he started work on *Phra Abhai Mani*. The poem took twenty years to complete and was rented out in instalments to provide the poet with a modest income – necessary as royal patronage had ceased with the ascent to the throne of Rama III (1824–51), whose literary efforts Sunthorn Phu had once rashly criticized. Eventually, poverty forced the poet to become a monk, and he was only reinstated at court a few years before his death when Rama IV (1851–68) was crowned.

Aside from authoring several timeless romances, Sunthorn Phu is remembered as a significant **poetic innovator**. Up until the end of the eighteenth century, Thai poetry had been the almost exclusive domain of high-born courtiers and kings, written in an elevated Thai incomprehensible to most of the population, and concerned mainly with the moral Hindu epics the *Mahabarata* and the *Ramayana* (see p.125). Sunthorn Phu changed all that by injecting huge doses of realism into his verses. He wrote of love triangles, thwarted romances and heartbreaking departures, and he also composed travel poems, or *nirat*, about his own journeys to well-known places in Thailand. Most crucially, he wrote them all in the common, easy-to-understand language of vernacular Thai. Not surprisingly, he's still much admired. In Bangkok, the centenary of his death was celebrated by the publication of several new anthologies and translations of his work. And in the province of Rayong, he's the focus of a special memorial park, constructed, complete with statues of his most famous fictional characters, on the site of his father's home in Klaeng.

no view and some unsightly rubbish nearby), and whether or not you want air-con. The sturdy chalet-style bungalows at the well-appointed *Samed Villa* (T 01/494 8090, F 945 5481; ❹–❺) are scenically sited along the rocks and up the slope behind the restaurant, so most have a sea view; they are all comfortably designed inside and the price depends on whether or not you want air-con. The cheapest huts on this part of the island are at *Achalee* (❷–❸), set behind *Samed Villa*, away from the beach; they're pretty scruffy but the pricier ones have private bathrooms.

Ao Tub Tim

Also known as Ao Pudsa, **AO TUB TIM** is a small white-sand bay sandwiched between rocky points, partly shaded with palms and backed by a wooded slope. It feels secluded, but is only a short stroll from Ao Phai and the other beaches further north, so you get the best of both worlds. **Songthaews** will bring you here from Na Dan pier for B20 per person (or B150 when chartered), or you can walk it in about thirty minutes.

Of the two **bungalow** operations on the beach, *Tub Tim Resort* (T & F 038/615041, W tubtimresort.hypermart.net; ❹–❼) offers the greatest choice of accommodation, from simple wooden huts through to big air-conditioned bungalows; prices also depend on proximity to the sea, though no hut is more than 200m away. Huts at the adjacent *Ao Pudsa* (T 01/239 5680; ❸–❹) are decent enough, with price depending on distance from the shore; the restaurant here occupies a nice site on the sand, with several tables fixed under the palm trees. *Ao Pudsa* also organizes boat trips, sells ferry tickets and has money-exchange facilities.

Ao Nuan

Clamber up over the next headland (which gives you a panoramic take on the expanse of Hat Sai Kaew) to reach Samet's smallest beach, the secluded **AO NUAN**. The best way to get here from the pier is to take a **songthaew** from Na Dan for B20 per person (B150 when chartered).

The atmosphere here is relaxed and much less commercial than the other beaches, and the mellow restaurant of the friendly *Ao Nuan* has some of the best veggie food on the island. Because it's some way off the main track, the beach gets hardly any through traffic and so feels quiet and private. The huts are idiosyncratic (❷–❹), each built to a slightly different design (some circular, some A-frame, some thatched), and dotted across the slope that drops down to the bay; a few are built right on the beach. None of the huts has an attached bathroom, electricity is only available at night, and they all have mattresses on the floor and a mosquito net. Although not brilliant for swimming, the rocky shore reveals a good patch of sand when the tide withdraws, and the good beach at Ao Tub Tim is only five minutes' walk away.

Ao Cho

A five-minute walk south along the track from Ao Nuan brings you to **AO CHO**, a fairly wide stretch of beach with just a couple of bungalow operations plus a pier, a minimarket and motorbikes for rent. Despite being long and partially shaded, this beach seems is less popular than the others, so it may be a good place to try if you want a low-key atmosphere, or if the bungalows on other beaches are packed out. There's some coral off the end of the pier, and you can rent snorkelling gear on the beach. It's also possible to arrange night-time trips on a squid boat, available through *Wonderland* for B5000 per boat (up to about twenty passengers). The easiest way to get to Ao Cho is to take a **boat** to Ao Wong Duan and then walk here, or you could take the normal boat to Na Dan and then hang around for a songthaew (B30). Alternatively call *Wonderland* the day before you arrive and they should send a boat to pick you up from Ban Phe (B50 per person).

Wonderland (☎01/943 9338; ❷–❺) has some of the cheapest **bungalows** on Ko Samet which, though small and basic and away from the shore, do have fans and private bathrooms; they also have lots of better bungalows with sea views and can organize snorkelling and fishing trips. Most of the bungalows at the Italian-managed *Tarn Tawan* (☎01/429 3298, ⓦwww.kosamet.com; ❹–❺) also have a sea view; here the price depends on whether you go for a semi-detached unit with fan and private bathroom, or a larger, free-standing bungalow.

Ao Wong Duan

The horseshoe bay of **AO WONG DUAN**, round the next headland, is dominated by mid-range and upmarket bungalow resorts with rather inflated prices. Few backpackers come here, but it is popular with older couples and with package tourists. Although the beach is fairly long and broad, it suffers revving jet-skis and an almost continual stream of day-trippers, and the shorefront is consequently fringed with a rash of beach bars and tourist shops. Both *Malibu* and *Sea Horse* have minimarts, motorbike rental, money exchange and overseas telephone services, and both places sell boat tickets and snorkelling trips. There's a national-park booth on the beach, where you must pay your B200 entry fee if alighting from a Ban Phe boat, and a police box. At least four direct **boats** a day should run from Na Dan to Wong Duan (B50); look for the *Malibu*, the *Sea Horse* and the *Wong Duan Resort* boats. Alternatively, take a boat to Na Dan, then a B30 ride in a songthaew (or a B200 taxi ride). Return boats depart every two hours between 8.30am and 4.30pm; if you're in a hurry you can charter a seven-person speedboat from the Wong Duan pier to Ban Phe for B1000.

The whitewashed concrete **bungalows** at *Malibu Garden Resort* (☎01/218 5345, Ⓔsamet@loxinfo.co.th; ❺–❼) are set round a shady tropical garden with a small swimming pool; the rooms are uninspiring but decent enough and come with fan or air-con and TV. Accommodation at the adjacent *Seahorse* (☎01/451 5184; ❻–❼) is currently the least good value on the beach in high season, though there are discounts of up to fifty percent from April through October. Rooms here are very plain and pricey considering there's no pool (though the beach is perfectly swimmable); the most expensive ones have air-con. *Vong Duan Resort* (☎038/651777, Ⓕ651819; ❺–❻) is the best-value place to stay on the beach; its bungalows have character, are attractively designed inside and out (with or without air-con) and stand around a pretty tropical garden. Neighbouring *Wong Duan Villa* (☎ 038/652300, Ⓕ651741; ❻–❼) also has nicely appointed bungalows, spacious, comfortably furnished and with big balconies, though the less expensive fan rooms seem overpriced.

Ao Thian (Candlelight Beach)

Off nearly all beaten tracks, **AO THIAN** (also known as Candlelight Beach) is the best place to come if you want seclusion: though facilities are simple, prices are reasonable and the setting is quite lovely. Should you need provisions or distractions, Wong Duan is only a ten-minute walk away. Ao Thian's narrow white-sand bay is dotted with wave-smoothed rocks and partitioned by larger outcrops that create several distinct beaches; as it curves outwards to the south you get a great view of the east coast. Though occasional supply **boats** do travel from Ban Phe to Ao Thian, the most reliable route here is to get a boat to Wong Duan and then walk.

At the northern end, *Candlelight Beach* (☎01/218 6934; ❹–❺) has a dozen or so basic **huts** ranged along the shorefront slope and a few more along the coast itself; all have attached bathrooms, though they seem a little dilapidated. Right down at the other end of the beach is the much more interesting *Lung Dum*

Hut (☎ 01/458 8430; ❸–❹), where the thirty simple but idiosyncratic bunga-lows are all slightly different in design; the best are built right on the rocks with the sea just metres from the door. All huts have a private bathroom, fan and mosquito net, with electricity only available in the evenings; the price depends on the location. If you're looking for a romantic spot then this is a good choice; the staff are friendly and there are two little restaurants.

Ao Kiu

You have to really like the solitary life to plump for Samet's most isolated beach, **AO KIU**, over an hour's walk south of Ao Thian through unadulterat-ed wilderness – the track begins behind *Wong Duan Resort* and can be joined at the back of *Lung Dum Hut* at Ao Thian. It's actually two beaches: Ao Kiu Na Nok on the east coast and Ao Kiu Na Nai on the west, separated by a few hun-dred metres of scrub and coconut grove. The bungalows here belong to *Ao Kiu Coral Beach* (☎ 038/652561; ❸–❻), and most are set in among the palms on the east shore, although a couple look down on the tiny west-coast coral beach; you can also rent tents here for B100.

The most convenient way of **getting here** is by direct boat from the main-land; during high season at least one *Coral Beach* boat makes the run daily – call to check departure times. Songthaews here from Na Dan cost B50 per person or B500 to charter.

Ao Phrao (Paradise Bay)

Across on the west coast, the rugged, rocky coastline only softens into beach once – at **AO PHRAO**, also known as Paradise Bay, on the northwestern stretch, some 4km north of Ao Kiu Na Nai. Ao Phrao gets nowhere near as many overnight visitors, but the beach is shady and not at all bad and, outside the weekends, you have lots of space to yourself. The most direct route from the east-coast beaches is via the inland **track** from behind *Sea Breeze* on Ao Phai, which takes about twenty minutes on foot, though the track from the back of *Tub Tim* on Ao Tub Tim will also get you there. Direct **boats** to Ao Phrao leave four times a day from Ban Phe's private Sri Ban Phe pier, and are free for guests of *Ao Phrao Resort*, or B90 return for non-guests. You can also get here by songthaew from Na Dan for B30 per person, or B200 on charter.

The best reason for coming to Ao Phrao is to stay at *Ao Prao Resort* (☎ 038/616883, ⓕ 02/439 0352, ⓦ www.aopraoresort.com; ❽–❾), which offers the most stylish **accommodation** on the island, with comfortable wooden chalets set in a tropical flower garden that slopes down to the beach. All chalets have air-conditioning, TVs and balconies overlooking the sea; rooms are discounted on weekdays, but advance booking is advisable for any time of the week. There's a dive centre here (see p.424), internet access and an overseas phone service. The nicest of the handful of other options on Ao Phrao, none of which are budget-oriented, is *Dome* (☎ 01/218 7693, ⓕ 038/652600; ❺–❼), whose bungalows are built up the side of a small slope and have sea views; some also have air-con.

Chanthaburi

For over five hundred years, precious stones have drawn prospectors and traders to the provincial capital of **CHANTHABURI**, 80km east of Ban Phe, and it's this pivotal role within Thailand's most lucrative **gem-mining** area that makes it one of the most appealing of all the east-coast towns. Seventy percent of the country's gemstones are mined in the hills of Chanthaburi and Trat provinces, a fruitful source of sapphires and Thailand's only known vein of rubies. Since the fifteenth century, hopefuls of all nationalities have flocked here, particularly the Shans from Burma, the Chinese and the Cambodians, many of them establishing permanent homes in the town. The largest ethnic group, though, are Catholic refugees from Vietnam, vast numbers of whom arrived here in the wake of the recurrent waves of religious persecution between the eighteenth century and the late 1970s. The French, too, have left their mark: during their occupation of Chanthaburi from 1893 to 1905, when they held the town hostage against the fulfilment of a territorial treaty on the Lao border, they undertook the restoration and enlargement of the town's Christian cathedral.

This cultural diversity makes Chanthaburi an engaging place, even if there's less than a day's worth of sights here. Built on the wiggly west bank of the Maenam Chanthaburi, the town fans out westwards for a couple of kilometres, though the most interesting parts are close to the river, in the district where the Vietnamese families are concentrated. Here, along the soi running parallel

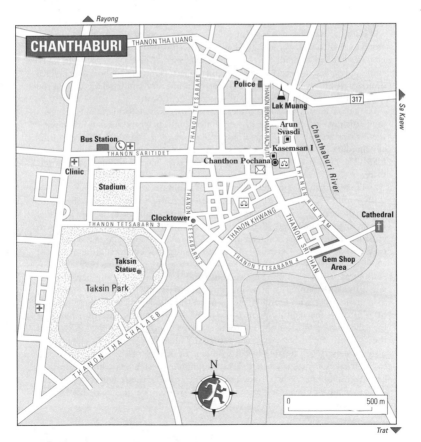

Rubies and sapphires

As long ago as the fifteenth century, European travellers noted the abundance of precious stones in Chanthaburi and Trat, but the first **gem-mining rush** happened in 1857, when stories of farmers ploughing up cartloads of rubies and fishermen trawling precious stones from the sea bed brought in hundreds of prospectors from ruby-rich Burma. Before long they had been joined by Cambodians and Vietnamese, and then the British mine companies from Burma came over to organize the industry. By 1900, Sapphires and Rubies of Siam Ltd had bought up nearly all the mining fields in eastern Thailand, but it proved an unwise move, as most immigrant miners refused to work for the colonials and moved on elsewhere. When Thailand lost many of its best sapphire mines in a border dispute with Cambodia, the company decided to pull out, leaving the Chanthaburi fields once more to independent self-employed miners.

The next great transformation came half a century later, as a consequence of the upheavals in Burma, which until then had been the world's main supplier of **corundum** – the term for all crystalline forms of aluminium oxide, such as ruby and sapphire. In 1962 the Burmese effectively sealed their country against the outside world, ousting all foreign companies and ceasing all external trade. The Thai dealers promptly muscled in to fill the gap in the world corundum market, and rapidly achieved their current dominant status by forcing the government to ease import and export duties.

Locally produced stones account for a small fraction of the total trade in and around Chanthaburi, whose mines have now been exploited for so long that high-cost mechanical methods are the only viable way of getting at the rocks. Self-employed panhandlers have rushed to work on new veins in Cambodia, while Thai dealers pull the strings in Vietnam's embryonic industry and regularly buy up the entire annual production of some of Australia's gem fields.

Though artificially produced stones are now used where formerly only the genuine article would do – in the glasses of most high-quality watches for example – the demand for top-notch natural stones from jewellers and watchmakers is virtually limitless. In view of the profits to be made – an uncut 150-carat ruby sold for US$1.2 million in 1985 – it's inevitable that sharp practice should be commonplace.

Doctoring the classification of a stone is a common act of skulduggery. A low-quality rough stone from Africa might emerge from the cutter's workshop with a label identifying it as Burmese or Kashmiri, the top rank in the gem league. But perhaps the most prevalent form of fraud involves **heating the stones** to enhance their colour, a cosmetic operation recorded as long ago as the first century, when Pliny the Elder described the technique of enhancing the quality of agate by "cooking" it. Trace elements are what give corundums their colour – in the case of blue sapphires it's titanium and iron that create the hue. To convert a weakly coloured sapphire into an expensive stone, factories now pack the low-grade rocks with titanium and iron oxide, heat the lot to within a whisker of 2050°C – the melting point of sapphire – and thereby fuse the chemicals into the surface of the stone to produce an apparently flawless gem. As long as the cutter and polisher leave the new "skin" intact when they do their work, only an expert will be able to tell whether the highly priced end product is a sham. It takes a lot less effort to fool the gullible Westerners who reckon they can make a killing on the Chanthaburi market: tumble the red glass of a car taillight in a tub of gravel, and after an hour or two you've got a passable facsimile of a ruby.

to the river, the town presents a mixture of pastel-painted, colonial-style housefronts and traditional wooden shophouses, some with finely carved latticework.

Continuing south along this soi, you'll reach a footbridge on the other side of which stands Thailand's largest **cathedral**: the Church of the Immaculate Conception. There's thought to have been a church on this site ever since the first Christians arrived in town, though the present structure was revamped in French style in the late nineteenth century. West of the bridge, the **gem dealers' quarter** begins, where shopkeepers sit sifting through great mounds of tiny coloured stones, peering at them through microscopes and classifying them for resale. Some of these shops also cut, polish and set the stones: Chanthaburi is as respected a cutting centre as Bangkok, and Thai lapidaries are considered among the most skilled – not to mention most affordable – in the world. Most of Chanthaburi's market-trading is done on weekend mornings, when buyers from Bangkok descend in their hundreds to sit behind rented tables and haggle with local dealers.

Chanthaburi has a reputation for high-grade fruit too, notably durian, rambutan and mangosteen, all grown in the orchards around the town and sold in the daily **market**, a couple of blocks northwest of the gem quarter. Basketware products are also good buys here, mostly made by the Vietnamese.

West of the market and gem quarter, the landscaped **Taksin Park** is the town's recreation area and memorial to King Taksin of Thonburi, the general who reunited Thailand between 1767 and 1782 after the sacking of Ayutthaya by the Burmese. Chanthaburi was the last Burmese bastion on the east coast – when Taksin took the town he effectively regained control of the whole country. The park's heroic bronze statue of Taksin is featured on the back of the B20 note.

Practicalities

Even if you're not planning a visit to Chanthaburi, you may find yourself stranded here for a couple of hours between **buses**, as this is a major interchange for east-coast services (some Rayong–Trat journeys require you to change here for example) and a handy terminus for buses to and from the northeast: eight daily buses make the scenic six-hour Chanthaburi–Sa Kaew–Khorat journey in both directions, with Sa Kaew being a useful interchange for buses to Aranyaprathet and the Cambodian border. Buses to and from all these places, as well as Bangkok's Eastern (Ekamai) and Northern (Mo Chit) stations, use the Chanthaburi **bus station** (☎039/311299) on Thanon Saritidet, about 750m northwest of the town centre and market. There are several **banks** with ATMs on Thanon Khwang.

The two best-located **accommodation** options are both near the river. The small and basic *Arun Svasdi* at 239 Thanon Sukha Phiban (☎039/311082; ❶–❷), down a soi off the eastern end of Thanon Saritidet, has quiet rooms with fan and bathroom and is in the heart of the Vietnamese part of town. Around the corner at 98/1 Thanon Benchama-Rachutit, the much larger *Kasemsan 1* (☎039/312340; ❷–❹) offers a choice between the sizeable, clean rooms with fan and bathroom on the noisy street side, and the similar but more expensive air-conditioned ones in the quieter section. The **restaurant** next door to *Kasemsan 1*, called *Chanthon Pochana* (no English sign), serves a range of standard rice and seafood dishes. Otherwise, check out the foodstalls in the market and along the riverside soi for Vietnamese spring rolls (*cha gio*) served with sweet sauce, and for the locally made Chanthaburi rice noodles (*kway tiaw Chanthaburi*).

Trat and around

Most travellers who find themselves in and around the minor provincial capital of **Trat** are heading either for the island of **Ko Chang**, via the tiny fishing port of Laem Ngop, or for **Cambodia**, via the border at Ban Hat Lek. Trat itself has a certain charm, with its compact business district dominated by a traditional covered market, and its residential streets still lined with wooden houses. As the overland crossing into Cambodia gets increasingly popular, Trat will no doubt develop into more of a travellers' centre – new little inexpensive guest houses are already popping up all over the town. If you head out of the town, east along the coast road towards the Cambodian border, you'll travel through some exhilarating countryside before getting to the port of **Khlong Yai** and the border post at **Ban Hat Lek**; this route also passes the Khao Lan refugee camp museum, a testimony to one of the bleakest episodes of recent local history.

Trat

The small and pleasantly unhurried market town of **TRAT**, 68km east of Chanthaburi, is the perfect place to stock up on essentials, change money, make long-distance telephone calls or extend your visa before striking out for the idylls of Ko Chang or the challenges of Cambodia.

Trat is served by lots of buses from Bangkok, including seven daily air-con government **buses** and at least half a dozen private tour buses from the Eastern (Ekamai) Bus Terminal (5–6hr), and three daily buses from the Northern (Mo Chit) Bus Terminal, which take about four hours. Trat also has useful bus connections with Ban Phe (for Ko Samet), Chanthaburi, Pattaya and Si Racha. All air-con buses, whether government or privately operated, drop passengers somewhere on the central four-hundred-metre stretch of Thanon Sukhumvit, at the relevant **bus office** as shown on the map opposite. Buses also depart from these different spots, where timetables for all Bangkok-bound services are clearly posted so you can easily see which company is running the next service. Non-air-con buses from Bangkok and other east-coast towns use the **regular bus station** near the *Thai Roong Roj Hotel*. If you're planning on travelling straight on **to Ko Chang** in the same day you should aim to get the 6am or 8.30am air-con bus here from Bangkok's Eastern Bus Terminal, though the 9am service might make it as well, so long as you're willing to charter a songthaew from Trat to the port at Laem Ngop. For details on transport to Ko Chang see p.441. An airport is due to open in Trat in 2003, and will be served by Bangkok Airways flights.

Trat's official **TAT** office is in Laem Ngop (see p.437), but any guest house will help you out with local information; alternatively, visit *Jean's Café* (see p.43) for a browse through the legendary travellers' comment books.

Accommodation

Guest houses in Trat are small, friendly and inexpensive places, most of them very much traveller-oriented and run by well-informed local people who are used to providing up-to-date information on boats to Ko Chang and Cambodian border crossings. All the guest houses listed here are within ten minutes' walk of the bus and songthaew stops on Thanon Sukhumvit.

Coco, on the corner of Soi Yai Onn and Thanon Thoncharoen ☎039/530462. Run by an exceptionally friendly family who run a great restaurant downstairs, this place has very cheap and basic rooms with shared bathrooms. ❶

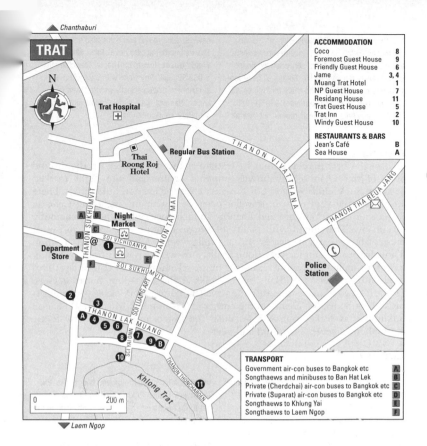

TRAT

N

Trat Hospital ✚

Thai Roong Roj Hotel

Regular Bus Station

THANON VIVATTHANA

THANON THA REUA JANG

Night Market

Department Store

SOI VICHIDANYA

THANON TAT MAI

THANON SUKHUMVIT

SOI SUKHUMVIT

SOI LUANG APT

Police Station

THANON LAK MUANG

SOI YAI ONN

THANON THONCHAROEN

Khlong Trat

0   200 m

ACCOMMODATION	
Coco	8
Foremost Guest House	9
Friendly Guest House	6
Jame	3, 4
Muang Trat Hotel	1
NP Guest House	7
Residang House	11
Trat Guest House	5
Trat Inn	2
Windy Guest House	10

RESTAURANTS & BARS	
Jean's Café	B
Sea House	A

TRANSPORT	
Government air-con buses to Bangkok etc	A
Songthaews and minibuses to Ban Hat Lek	B
Private (Cherdchai) air-con buses to Bangkok etc	C
Private (Suparat) air-con buses to Bangkok etc	D
Songthaews to Khlong Yai	E
Songthaews to Laem Ngop	F

4

THE EAST COAST | Trat and around

Foremost Guest House, 49 Thanon Thoncharoen ☏039/511923. One of the longest-running guest houses in town; rooms here are basic and share a common bathroom, but there's a communal seating area downstairs and the very pleasant *Jean's Cafe* next door. The guest house is run by very well-informed people and offers lots of local information as well as a set of exceptionally useful travellers' comment books containing up-to-the-minute recommendations on Ko Chang and Cambodia (the books are available either at the guest house or at *Jean's Café*). Has B50 dorm beds. ❶

Friendly Guest House, 106–110 Thanon Lak Muang ☏039/524053. Rooms in the extended modern home of an exuberant family; all have windows and share bathrooms. ❶

Jame, 45/1 Thanon Lak Muang ☏039/530458. Very clean rooms of varying sizes, depending on how much you want to pay, all with shared bath.

Split between two houses on opposite sides of the road. ❶–❷

Muang Trat Hotel, 24 Soi Vichidanya ☏039/511091. On the edge of the night market, a typically basic and rather grubby town hotel, where the rather overpriced rooms are all en-suite and you can opt for air-con and TV if you want. ❸

NP Guest House, 10 Soi Yai Onn ☏039/512270. Friendly option, with simple but fair enough rooms with shared bathrooms; not all of them have windows. Plenty of information available from the manager. ❶

Residang House, 87/1–2 Thanon Thoncharoen ☏039/530103. The most comfortably appointed of all the guest houses in Trat, this place feels like a small hotel. Rooms are large and very clean and all have thick mattresses; bathrooms are shared. There are lockers downstairs and lots of local information. ❷

435

Trat Guest House, 4 Soi Khunpoka, off Thanon Lak Muang ☎039/511152. Decent, very inexpensive rooms in a characterful converted old house, located down a quiet little soi. Rooms all have windows and bamboo walls and share bathrooms. ❶
Trat Inn, 1–5 Thanon Sukhumvit ☎039/511028. Slightly seedy hotel with basic rooms, but they all have en-suite rooms and some also have air-con. There's internet access downstairs. ❶–❷
Windy Guest House, 63 Thanon Thoncharoen ☎039/523664. Tiny place with a very laid-back atmosphere that's perfectly situated right on the khlong. Has just three simple rooms and a B50 dormitory, so it's often full. ❶

Eating

Two of the best **places to eat** in Trat are at the day market, on the ground floor of the Thanon Sukhumvit shopping centre, and the night market, between Soi Vichidanya and Soi Kasemsan, east of Thanon Sukhumvit. There are also several very pleasant traveller-oriented restaurants, including *Coco*, on the corner of Soi Yai Onn and Thanon Thoncharoen, which has a deliciously imaginative Thai menu with plenty of veggie options, real coffee and great music, all at bargain prices. In a similar vein, *Jean's Café* on Thanon Thoncharoen is another very popular place to while away an hour or two; it has a nice mellow atmosphere, a good music selection and of course tasty Thai food and travellers' fare. Run by the folks at the next-door *Foremost Guest House*, it's a good place to peruse the travellers' comment books if you're heading to Cambodia. *Sea House*, on the corner of Thanon Lak Muang and Thanon Sukhumvit, is decked out with sea shells and fosters an invitingly artsy-folksy atmosphere; it serves Thai food and beer.

Listings

Banks and exchange There are several banks on the central stretch of Thanon Sukhumvit.
Emergencies For all emergencies, call the tourist police on the free 24hr phoneline ☎1699. Alternatively, contact the local police station off Thanon Vivatthana ☎039/511035.
Hospital Trat hospital ☎039/511986 is off Thanon Sukhumvit on the north edge of town.
Immigration office Located on the Trat–Laem Ngop road, 3km northeast of Laem Ngop pier (Mon–Fri 8.30am–4.30pm; ☎ 039/597215).

Internet access On the ground floor of the *Trat Inn* at 1–5 Thanon Sukhumvit, near the day market further north up Thanon Sukhumvit, and at the CAT overseas telephone office on Thanon Vivatthana.
Mail At the GPO on Thanon Tha Reua Jang.
Telephones The CAT overseas telephone office is on Thanon Vivatthana on the eastern edge of town (daily 7am–10pm).

The road to the border

From Trat, the obvious land-based excursion is a trip as far as the Cambodian border. **Songthaews** to the small, thriving fishing port of Khlong Yai, 74km east, leave Trat about every thirty minutes from behind the shopping centre; they all travel via Khao Lan and take about an hour and a quarter. From Khlong Yai it's just a short journey on to Ban Hat Lek and the border.

The journey into this narrow tail of Thailand passes through some of the most enthralling countryside in the region, with sea views to the south and a continuous range of forested mountains to the north, pierced by a couple of waterfalls so mighty you can see them from the road. Midway to Khlong Yai, you might consider stopping off for an hour at the **Khao Lan refugee camp museum** (daily 8.30am–4pm; donation); ask the songthaew driver for "phipitapan Khao Lan" – though it's easy to spot because of the enormous Red Cross symbol outside. During the last few months of 1978, Cambodians started pouring across the Ban That mountains into eastern Thailand, desperate to escape the brutalities of Pol Pot's "Year Zero" mania and the violence that erupted with the Vietnamese invasion. Trat province received the heaviest influx of refugees, and Khao Lan became the largest of the six camps in Thailand, eventually comprising a hospital, an orphanage and an arts and crafts workshop as well as thousands of makeshift dwellings. In its nine years of operation, this Red Cross camp served as a temporary home to some 200,000 people. By the time it ceased operation in 1987, most of its refugees had been resettled, and Thailand's last Cambodian refugee camp was closed in April 1993.

Nothing now remains of the original Khao Lan camp: the museum is housed in a modern building close to the road, and the few other new structures on the site were purpose-built for the Thai soldiers stationed here. The contents of the museum are disappointingly sparse, offering only a sketchy historical and political context, spiced up with a few photos and a couple of waxwork tableaux of life in the camp. The overall tone of the place seems inappropriately ingratiating, with each exhibit presented more as a memorial to Queen Sirikit's gracious patronage of the camp (the queen is president of the Thai Red Cross and made several visits to the Khao Lan site) than as a testimony to the resilience of its displaced residents.

Forty kilometres to the south, **Khlong Yai** boasts a great setting, the town's long pier jutting way out to sea, partly flanked by rows of stilt houses that form a shelter for the fishing boats. It's a dramatic place to visit during rough weather, when the turbulent seas lash against the housefronts and the end of the pier disappears beneath low-lying storm clouds. There's little point venturing all the way on to **Ban Hat Lek** unless you're planning to cross into Cambodia (see box on p.438 for details).

Laem Ngop

The departure point for Ko Chang and the outer islands is **LAEM NGOP**, 17km southwest of Trat and served by share-taxis (songthaews) every half-hour or so; rides can take anything from twenty to forty minutes, so leave plenty of time to catch the boat. The usual songthaew fare is B20 per person with a full load or about B30 with a minimum of eight people; if there aren't many passengers but everyone's in a hurry to catch the boat, there's sometimes a whip round to make up the difference. For details of **boat services** from here to Ko Chang, see p.441, and for boat services to the outer islands, see p.450.

If you do miss the boat or the seas are too rough to negotiate, it's no great hardship to be stuck in this tiny port, which consists of little more than a wooden pier, one main road and a small collection of traditional houses inhabited mainly by fisherfolk, many of whom are Muslim. If you happen to be in the area between January 17 and 21, it may be worth staying here for the festival commemorating the repulsing of French forces from Laem Ngop in 1941 and the loss of three Thai warships in the process.

Although it still retains its small-town atmosphere, Laem Ngop caters well to the Ko Chang tourist trade: there's a cluster of partisan **tourist information** booths around the main pier-head at which you can buy ferry tickets and reserve accommodation on the island – definitely worthwhile in peak season. There's also an official TAT office (daily 8.30am–4.30pm; ☎ & ℱ 039/597255) close by, which offers independent advice on the island and may be able to give

There are currently two legal **border crossings** for tourists travelling to **Cambodia**: one at Ban Hat Lek, near the east-coast town of Trat, and the other at Aranyaprathet, midway between the east coast and Isaan. Recent reports claim that it is possible to buy a thirty-day Cambodian **visa on arrival** at both these points (it's worth checking the latest information with the Cambodian Embassy in Bangkok; see p.193), as well as at the airports in Phnom Penh and Siem Reap: you need US$20 and a photo for this. You may also want to bring a (real or fake) International Quarantine Booklet showing dates of your vaccinations, as border guards at both overland crossings have been known to (illegally) charge foreigners without vaccination cards a US$5 penalty fee.

If you're travelling nonstop from Bangkok to Cambodia, the fastest route is via Ban Hat Lek. If you don't fancy the overland route, you can **fly** with Bangkok Airways from Sukhothai to Siem Reap, from Pattaya to Phnom Penh and from Bangkok to both Siem Reap and Phnom Penh; details are given in the relevant city accounts. Full details on **entering Thailand from Cambodia** are given in Basics on p.22, where you'll also find information on Thai visa requirements.

Trat–Ban Hat Lek–Koh Kong–Sihanoukville

As Ban Hat Lek (on the Thai side) and Koh Kong (in Cambodia) are on opposite sides of the Dong Tong River estuary, crossing the border here involves taking at least one taxi-boat before you can board the scheduled public boat on to Sihanoukville. The first leg of the trip from Trat takes you to the Thai border post at **Ban Hat Lek**, 91km southeast of Trat (border open daily 7am–5pm). Share-taxis (songthaews) and air-con minibuses to Ban Hat Lek leave from Thanon Sukhumvit in central Trat and cost B100 per person. If you want to reach Sihanoukville in one day, you'll need to be at the minibus stop for about 4.30am, when drivers meet passengers off the overnight bus from Bangkok (departing the Eastern Bus Terminal at 11.30pm) and whisk them straight to Ban Hat Lek in time for the opening of the border at 7am. This gives you just enough time to catch the daily scheduled **boat** to **Sihanoukville** from the nearby town of **Koh Kong** across on the eastern bank of the estuary (sometimes referred to as Krong Koh Kong), which at the time of writing sets off at around 8am. To get to the Koh Kong pier, take a motorcycle or car taxi from the Ban Hat Lek immigration post to the west bank of the estuary (a 10min drive) and then a taxi-boat across to Koh Kong on the east bank.

you current boat times. You can **change money** at the Thai Farmers' Bank (usual banking hours), five minutes' walk back down the main road from the pier, or at the currency exchange booth on the pier, which has longer opening hours. There are several small **internet centres** on the road up to the pier and around the pier-head itself.

Your best bet for **accommodation** in Laem Ngop is the friendly and efficiently run *Chut Kaew* guest house (☎039/597088; ❷), close to the bank on the main road, and about seven minutes' walk from the pier. Besides simple rooms with shared bathrooms, it has plenty of information on Ko Chang (you can store luggage here while you're on the island) and rents bicycles to explore Laem Ngop. *Chut Kaew* also serves good travellers' **food**, and even if you're not staying in Laem Ngop it's worth getting an early songthaew from Trat and eating breakfast here before catching the first boat of the day to Ko Chang. There are a couple of large, scenically located restaurants on the pier-head too, where you can order anything from banana pancakes to seafood dinners; they're probably nicest at sunset though, after the crowds of ferry passengers have gone.

Shortly after leaving Koh Kong, the Sihanoukville boat makes a brief stop at **Pak Khlong** (aka Bak Kleng) at the western side of the river mouth, which can be reached directly from Ban Hat Lek. Doing so involves taking a taxi-boat across open sea all the way down to the mouth of the estuary, and is reportedly not very safe as the boats are old; if you want to take the risk, you can hire a taxi-boat from the pier near the Ban Hat Lek immigration post.

If you leave Trat later in the day and can't find transport all the way to Ban Hat Lek, take a songthaew to Khlong Yai, then change on to another songthaew or a motor-cycle taxi for the sixteen-kilometre ride to Ban Hat Lek. Once through immigration, follow the route described above to Koh Kong, where you can stay the night before catching the Sihanoukville boat the next morning.

For up-to-the minute details on routes, times and prices, check the travellers' comment books at Trat's *Foremost Guest House*, and for a thorough guide to Koh Kong and how to reach it from both sides of the border, visit ⊛kohkong .com/kohkong.

Aranyaprathet–Poipet–Siem Reap

The other overland crossing into Cambodia is at **Poipet**, 4km east of the Thai town of **Aranyaprathet**. The border here is open daily from 7am to 5pm; once through the border, you have to face a gruelling eight- to twelve-hour journey in the back of a pick-up to cover the notoriously hellish 150km of potholed road between Poipet and Siem Reap. If you need a **hotel** in Aranyaprathet, try either the comfortable *Inter Hotel* on Thanon Chatasingh (☎037/231291, ⓟ232352; ❹–❺), or the cheaper *Aran Garden II* at 110 Thanon Rat Uthit (❷–❸).

From **Bangkok**, the easiest way to get to Aranyaprathet is by **train**: there are two services a day, which take about six hours; you'll need to catch the one at 5.50am to ensure reaching the border before 5pm. Tuk-tuks will take you the 4km from the train station to the border post. Alternatively, take a **bus** from Bangkok's Northern (Mo Chit) Bus Terminal to Aranyaprathet (4 daily until 5.30pm; 4hr 30min), then a tuk-tuk from the bus station to the border. It's also possible to buy a **through ticket to Siem Reap** from Bangkok from almost any travel agent in Banglamphu for about B1600; transport is by minibus to the border and then by pick-up to Siem Reap. Travelling to Cambodia **from east-coast towns**, the easiest route is to take a bus from Chanthaburi to the town of **Sa Kaew**, 130km to the northeast, and then change onto a bus for the 55-kilometre ride east to Aranyaprathet.

Ko Chang

The focal point of a national marine park archipelago of 52 islands, **Ko Chang** is Thailand's second-largest island (after Phuket) and is mainly characterized by a broad central spine of jungle-clad hills, the highest of which, **Khao Salak Pet**, tops 740m. Though it measures 30km north to south and 8km across, Ko Chang supports fewer than five thousand inhabitants, many of whom make their living from fishing and reside in the hamlets scattered around the fringes of the island. But it is the island's long, white-sand beaches that are now the main income-earner here, for Ko Chang is an increasingly mainstream destination for foreign and domestic tourists alike.

Ko Chang's west coast has the prettiest **beaches** and is the most developed, with Hat Sai Khao (White Sand Beach) drawing the biggest crowds. The east coast is closer to the mainland and less exposed to storms, but has hardly any-where to stay. During **peak season**, accommodation on the west coast tends to fill up very quickly – and you'd be wise to avoid the island altogether on

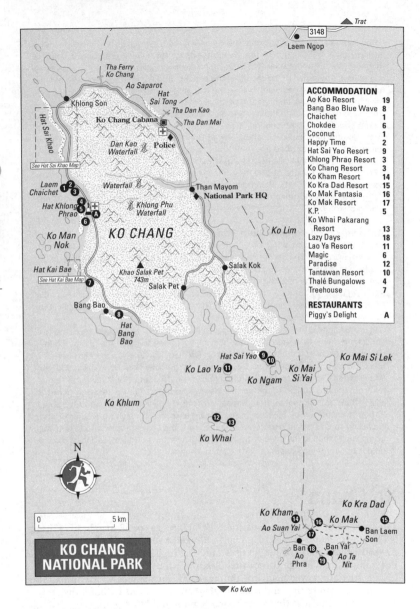

ACCOMMODATION

Ao Kao Resort	19
Bang Bao Blue Wave	8
Chaichet	1
Chokdee	6
Coconut	1
Happy Time	2
Hat Sai Yao Resort	9
Khlong Phrao Resort	3
Ko Chang Resort	3
Ko Kham Resort	14
Ko Kra Dad Resort	15
Ko Mak Fantasia	16
Ko Mak Resort	17
K.P.	5
Ko Whai Pakarang Resort	13
Lazy Days	18
Lao Ya Resort	11
Magic	6
Paradise	12
Tantawan Resort	10
Thalé Bungalows	4
Treehouse	7

RESTAURANTS

Piggy's Delight	A

KO CHANG
NATIONAL PARK

national holidays, when most places are booked out by groups of Thai students – but it gets a lot quieter (and cheaper) from May to October, when fierce storms batter the huts and can make the sea too rough to swim in.

A wide road runs almost all the way round the island, served by fairly frequent public **songthaews**; you can also rent motorbikes and mountain bikes on most beaches, and should be able to arrange a motorbike taxi from the same places if necessary. Only the southeastern and southwestern coasts remain

Diving and snorkelling off Ko Chang

The **reefs** off Ko Chang are nowhere near as spectacular as Andaman coast dive sites, but they're decent enough and – a major advantage – not at all crowded. Local **dive sites** range from the beginners' reefs at the Southern Pinnacle, with lots of soft corals, anemones, myriad reef fish and the occasional moray eel at depths of 4–6m, to the more challenging 31-metre dive off Ko Rang, where you're likely to see snapper and possibly even a whale shark.

Just three **dive schools** currently operate out of Ko Chang. The longest running of the these is Sea Horse Diving at *Kai Bae Hut* on Hat Kai Bae (℡01/996 7147, ℮adidive@hotmail.com); PADI-certificated Eco Divers operates from the upmarket *Ban Pu Resort* on Hat Sai Khao (℡01/865 6408, ℗01/983 7127, ℮crispine75@hotmail.com); while a less formal dive centre runs out of one of the huts at *Bamboo Bungalow* (℡01/829 6721, ℮schmidti@tr.ksc.co.th), also on Hat Sai Khao. Waves permitting, the dive centres run trips to reefs off Ko Chang's more sheltered east coast during the **monsoon season** from June through September, though visibility is unlikely to be very rewarding during that period. Prices for dive trips should include two dives, transport and lunch, and be in the range B1800–2400 depending on the operator and the destination; accompanying **snorkellers** generally pay B600–800 including lunch and equipment. All three dive centres also offer PADI **dive courses**: the two-day Scuba Diver averages B6500, the four-day Open Water B8500–10,000, and the two-day Advanced B7000–8000. The nearest **recompression chamber** is at the Apakorn Kiatiwong Naval Hospital in Sattahip (℡038/601185), 26km south of Pattaya. See p.75 in Basics for a general introduction to diving in Thailand and for advice as to what to look for in a dive centre.

inaccessible to vehicles. The island is now fully wired up for **electricity**, though a few bungalows ration their supply for evening consumption only. Many accommodation places are on the phone system, but as they use satellite **phones** (their numbers prefaced by the ℡01 code wherever you call from), it's not always possible to get through; some places can also be contacted via a land line on the mainland. **Internet access** on Hat Sai Khao and Hat Kai Bae is very expensive (B8 per minute) because it too relies on satellite phones, so you might want to get your emailing done in Trat or Laem Ngop before you hit the island. There are **money-exchange** facilities and small **shops** on Hat Sai Khao and Hat Kai Bae, including a couple of secondhand bookshops.

Though mosquitoes don't seem to be much in evidence, Ko Chang is one of the few areas of Thailand that's still considered to be **malarial**, so you may want to start taking your prophylactics before you get here, and bring repellent with you – refer to p.36 of Basics for more advice on this. Sand flies can be more of a problem on the southern beaches, but there's not a lot you can do about them except soothe your bites with calamine; apart from that, watch out for **jellyfish**, which plague the west coast in April and May, and for **snakes** sunbathing on the overgrown paths into the interior. Although there are a couple of **clinics** on Ko Chang, for anything serious you'll need to be taken to the hospital in Trat (see p.436).

Travel practicalities

All **passenger boats** to Ko Chang depart from Laem Ngop (see p.437) and take 45 minutes to one hour to reach the island; **tickets** (B50) can be bought in Trat, at the Laem Ngop pier or on the boats themselves. During high season (Nov–April), boats should depart Laem Ngop every hour from 7am–5pm, though it's always worth checking in Trat first. Outside high season, weather permitting, boats leave every two hours from 9am–5pm. The boats arrive at

Tha Dan Kao on Ko Chang's northeast coast, from where **songthaews** (B30–50 per person) ferry passengers on to the main beaches. They should drop you outside your chosen bungalows; the more remote bungalows to the south of Hat Kai Bae sometimes send their own songthaew to meet the 3pm boats, but you'll still have to pay. From late October through to late May there's also one daily boat from Laem Ngop (at 3pm; B80) direct to *White Sand Beach Resort* on Hat Sai Khao.

If schedules run according to plan, it's possible to do the whole **Bangkok–Ko Chang** trip in a day by public transport, catching the 6am or 8.30am air-con bus from the Eastern (Ekamai) Bus Terminal, arriving in Trat by 2.30pm, and making the short connection to Laem Ngop in plenty of time for the 4pm boat; if you catch the 9am from Bangkok and arrive in Trat for 3.30pm, you should charter a songthaew right away and head speedily on to Laem Ngop. Budget tour operators in Bangkok run **tourist minibuses** from Thanon Khao San through to Laem Ngop (6hr) for B270; the big advantage of these is that you don't have to add on an extra couple of hours to get yourself through the early morning traffic jams between Thanon Khao San and the Eastern Bus Terminal, though the drivers of these minibuses are notoriously reckless.

If you have your own vehicle, you need to use one of the **car ferries** that operate between the Laem Ngop coast and Ao Saparot, on Ko Chang's northeast coast. There are two companies offering this service, from two different piers west of Laem Ngop, both clearly signposted off the Trat–Laem Ngop road; Ko Chang Ferry is at kilometre-stone 4 on Route 3156, while Ferry Ko Chang is at kilometre-stone 10. Both companies run five ferries a day in each direction between 7am and 5pm, charging B400 per car with driver, plus B30 per extra passenger; motorbikes cost B120 with driver. The journey takes 25 minutes. The vehicle ferries mean there may soon be a door-to-door service between Bangkok guest houses and Ko Chang bungalows, without the need to change on to the public ferry at Laem Ngop.

Leaving Ko Chang, boats run from Tha Dan Kao to an hourly timetable between 7am and 5pm in high season and to a two-hourly one between 9am and 5pm in low season. To get to Tha Dan Kao from Hat Sai Khao, simply stand on the main road and flag down a north-bound songthaew; from the other beaches, ask at your bungalows as there may be organized transport to your boat. Tickets for the daily **tourist minibuses** from Laem Ngop to Bangkok's Thanon Khao San (B270), Ban Phe (for Ko Samet; B220) and Pattaya (B300) are best bought from bungalows and tour agents on Ko Chang, but you should also be able to buy them once you've landed in Laem Ngop. Alternatively, hop on one of the public songthaews that meet the boat and make your onward travel arrangements in Trat.

Hat Sai Khao (White Sand Beach)

Framed by a broad band of fine white sand at low tide, a fringe of casuarinas and palm trees and a backdrop of forested hills, **Hat Sai Khao** (White Sand Beach) is the island's longest beach and, some would argue, its prettiest too. It is also the busiest and most commercial, with over twenty different bungalow operations squashed in between the road and the shore, plus an increasing number of upmarket hotel-style developments – which inevitably detract from its loveliness. However, it's a lively and friendly place to be, with a regular Saturday-night disco on the central stretch of beach next to *Mac Bungalows* and several volleyball nets where players gather every evening at sunset. Should you prefer to be on the edge of the fray, there are several more isolated places to stay at the northern end of the beach, beyond *Yakah*, where each bungalow has its own sea view, there's hardly any passing pedestrian traffic and the road is out of earshot. Be warned, though, that there have been rumours of a dope-busting scam on Hat Sai Khao, whereby sellers inform the police straight away and then buyers are obliged to pay big fines. You should also be careful when swimming off Hat Sai Khao: currents are very strong here, so it's best to stay within your depth, particularly during low season when there may not be other swimmers around to help you out.

Practicalities

Songthaews take about 25 minutes to drive from Tha Dan Kao to Hat Sai Khao. If you want the bungalows at *KC, Rock Sand* or *White Sand Beach Resort*, get off as soon as you see the sign for *Yakah*, and then walk along the beach. For bungalows further south, the songthaew should drop you right outside your chosen one. In high season there's also a daily **boat** from Laem Ngop direct to *White Sand Beach Resort*; see opposite for details.

You can rent **motorbikes** at several roadside stalls on Hat Sai Khao for B50 an hour or B350 a day – these prices are justified, apparently, because the road is poor and the demand high. The same places will act as a **taxi**

HAT SAI KHAO

ACCOMMODATION

Apple	11
Arunee	4
Bamboo Bungalow	10
Ban Pu Ko Chang Hotel	12
Cookie	7
Grand View	13
KC Beach Resort	3
Ko Chang Lagoon	9
Mac Bungalows	8
Moonlight	14
Plaloma Cliff Resort	15
Rock Sand	2
Sangtawan	6
White Sand Beach Resort	1
Yakah	5

0   500 m

Ao Saparot & Tha Dan Kao

THE EAST COAST | Ko Chang

Police box

Clinic

N

Internet Centre & Bookshop

Hillside Minimart

RESTAURANTS AND BARS

Ban Nuna	C
15 Palms	A
Sabay Bar	B

Laem Chaichet & Hat Khlong Phrao ▼

service if you ask, charging about B60 for a ride to Khlong Phrao or B100 to Kai Bae, but you're better off waiting for a songthaew to drive past: so long as the songthaew is heading that far anyway, you should be able to get to Hat Khlong Phrao for B20 and to Hat Kai Bae for B30.

Several bungalows run **snorkelling** and **fishing trips** to nearby islands, typically charging B250 per person for a three-hour outing, including equipment. Other places sell snorkelling trips to the islands of Ko Whai, Ko Mak and Ko

Rang organized by the Trat-based boat company Island Hopper (☎039/597060). *Sangtawan* bungalows runs day-long **jungle treks** through Ko Chang's forests for B250, while the folk at *Rock Sand* bungalows do overnight expeditions, which include a swim in a waterfall, forest walks and accommodation in tents or hammocks (B400 per person plus a share of the B1000 fee for the National Park guide). There are currently two **dive centres** on Hat Sai Khao (see the box on p.441 for details).

Several **shops** can be found on Hat Sai Khao, both on the beach and across the road from it: as well as all obvious necessities, including mosquito repellent, suntan lotion and toilet rolls, the *Ban Pu* minimarket complex also sells new and secondhand books and has **internet access** upstairs. There's a **clinic** on the main road, opposite the *Sabay Bar*.

Accommodation

All the bungalow operations listed here are on the beach, and some of them offer rooms for B200 and under, but if they're full you may want to check out the small, inexpensive guest houses set among the shops and restaurants across the road from the beach: *Arunee*, *Ban Nuna*, *Tiger Hut* and *Jida* all offer simple rooms in small single-storey blocks in the ❷ category.

Northern Hat Sai Khao

KC Beach Resort ☎01/833 1010. The most popular place on Hat Sai Khao, and deservedly so, *KC* has almost fifty huts strung out under the palm trees over a long stretch of beach so that each hut feels a little bit private and has a view of the sea. It's under friendly management and has an extremely laid-back atmosphere. The original huts are simple bamboo constructions with mosquito nets, electric lights and shared bathrooms; the newer wooden ones are en suite and are staggered to give each a sea view. Electricity is available in the evenings only. ❸–❹

Rock Sand ☎01/863 7611. Just seventeen simple, idiosyncratic huts perched up on a rocky promontory; price depends on size and amenities, with the cheapest offering just a mattress and a mosquito net, and the better ones having en-suite bathrooms, a good view, and the option of air-con. ❷–❺

White Sand Beach Resort ☎01/863 7737. Located in a quiet, attractive spot at the far north end of the beach (about 10min walk along the sand from the next set of bungalows at *Rock Sand*), *White Sand* offers a big range of nicely spaced huts, many of which are still only lit by paraffin lamps. Lots of huts have uninterrupted sea views, some have private bathrooms and a few have electricity as well; price depends on amenities and which of the three rows you're in. There's a restaurant here, but you have to walk a fair way to get a change of menu. The *White Sand* boat comes here once a day from late October through May, departing Laem Ngop at 3pm and costing B80. ❷–❹

Central Hat Sai Khao

Apple ☎01/863 3398. Just a handful of good wooden bungalows, all with mosquito nets and electricity; a few have sea views, others have en-suite bathrooms. ❸–❹

Bamboo Bungalow ☎01/829 6721, ✉schmidti@tr.ksc.co.th. Many of the huts here are, not surprisingly, made of bamboo, and they all have mosquito nets and electricity. There's a small dive centre here too. The cheapest huts share bathrooms, though there are more solid huts with en-suite facilities. ❷–❸

Ban Pu Ko Chang Hotel ☎01/863 7314, ☎983 7127, ✉banpu_kohchang@hotmail.com. The nicest upmarket accommodation on Hat Sai Khao, comprising a low-rise hotel block and spacious wooden bungalows with unusual, open-roofed bathrooms built around a pretty tropical garden and a small swimming pool. All rooms have sea view, air-con, TV and a veranda. There's internet access across the road and a dive centre in the hotel. ❽

Cookie ☎01/861 4327. Deservedly the most popular of the mid-range places on this beach, *Cookie* is the best in its price bracket on the central stretch of Hat Sai Khao. The smart bungalows all have small verandas, attached tiled bathrooms and electric fans, and are thoughtfully kitted out with clothes-hangers, pegs and towels. Huts are set very close together, but only those in the third row have no sea view; price depends on which row you're in. ❸–❹

Ko Chang Lagoon ☎01/863 1530. Large, resort-style two-storey hotel complex where all rooms are comfortably furnished with air-con, fridge and veranda. ❼

Mac Bungalows ☎01/864 6463. Sturdy wooden huts, all with veranda seating, good beds, fans and nice clean bathrooms; some have air-con. The pricier bungalows have sea views, but the huts are packed a little too close together to be worth the money. ❹–❼

Yakah ☎01/862 2795. This collection of basic, old-style bamboo huts is crowded together under the trees and furnished with mattresses and mosquito nets; some have beach views, others back onto the road. The pricier ones have attached bathrooms. ❷–❹

Southern Hat Sai Khao

Grand View (formerly *SunSai*) ☎01/863 7802. Efficiently run, child-friendly place with a big range of unusually well-spaced rooms set in a garden; there's a table-tennis table and dart board in the restaurant. Although the hotel garden drops down to a rocky part of the beach, the sandy bit is just a few steps away. The cheapest rooms share facilities but are close to the beach; mid-range places are en suite and located across the road from the beach; the most expensive ones are by the sea and have air-con and TV. ❷–❼

Moonlight ☎01/861 7672. Large, simple, en-suite bungalows widely spaced above a rocky part of the beach (though just a few metres from sand), most of them with sea view. It's a peaceful, unhurried place; the restaurant serves recommended barbecued seafood. ❸

Plaloma Cliff Resort ☎01/863 1305, ℱ219 3867. Offers a big range of accommodation, from simple bamboo huts and sturdy bungalows on the lawn to plush air-con rooms in a hotel block with panoramic coastal views. As it's built on a rocky point there's no direct access to the sea from here, and the management can be a little off-hand. ❸–❼

Eating and drinking

All the bungalow operations on Hat Sai Khao have **restaurants**, most of which offer very passable European food and standard Thai fare. Many of them do fish barbecues at night as well: the freshly caught barracuda, shark, tuna, king prawns, crab and squid are usually laid out on ice shavings for you to select yourself, and many places set out tables on the beach. Across the road from the beach, *Ban Nuna* makes a pleasant place for an evening meal: seating is Thai-style on cushions in a breezy open-sided *sala*, and the menu includes Thai curries, heaps of seafood dishes and pizzas. It's also well worth checking out *15 Palms*, where you can sit at tables right on the sand, enjoying real coffee and home-made bread as well as mid-priced English pies, pizzas and a good range of Thai food. After sundown, one of the most popular places on the beach is *Sabay Bar*, where you can either sit beside low tables on mats laid over the sand and work your way through the huge menu of cocktails, or take to the small dance-floor which pumps out European rave music till the early hours.

Laem Chaichet and northern Hat Khlong Phrao

Four kilometres south along the tarmac road from southern Hat Sai Khao, **LAEM CHAICHET** is a small cape whose rocky headland curves round into a secluded casuarina-fringed bay to make an attractive and peaceful setting. There are currently just four bungalow operations on this little stretch of coast, and no shops as yet, but you can rent **motorbikes** (B60 per hour or B400 per day) and arrange boat trips here. **Songthaews** take about ten minutes to reach Laem Chaichet from Hat Sai Khao (B20), fifteen minutes from Hat Kai Bae, or 35 minutes from Tha Dan Kao. The access track from the main road leads straight to *Coconut Beach Bungalows* (☎01/949 3838; ❸–❽), which offers row upon row of **accommodation**, from simple wooden huts on the seafront with shared facilities, to mid-range huts and upmarket concrete versions with air-con and TV, a few of which have sea views. The six wooden bungalows on the edge of the *Coconut Beach* enclave belong to another branch of the same family and are rented out under the name *Coconut Restaurant* (℡01/932 0519; ❹); all are en suite and have sea views. *Coconut Restaurant* itself caters to guests at both sets of bungalows, serving travellers' fare, Thai standards plus regular seafood barbecues. If you follow the path 100m to the right of *Coconut Restaurant*, across a small khlong (with a bridge) and past the tiny boat harbour, you'll come to *Chaichet* (℡01/862 3430; ❷–❼), prettily located on the headland and with a range of accommodation, from simple A-frame huts to bigger bungalows with bathrooms, fans and fine sea views, or rooms with air-con. If you don't mind staying away from the beach, the cheapest accommodation at Laem Chaichet is offered by *Happy Time* (❷), which has a handful of ultra-basic bamboo huts right beside the main island road.

Ten minutes' walk south along the beach from *Coconut*, or a five-minute drive along the main road, brings you to the northern stretch of **HAT KHLONG PHRAO**. The beach here gets a fair bit of flotsam washed up, but is long and never gets crowded. The southern end is defined by quite a wide khlong (Khlong Phrao itself), which is only wadeable (up to your thighs) at low tide; if you want to get to the southern stretch of Hat Khlong Phrao on the other side of the khlong (see below), you're better off going via the road. There are two **accommodation** options on this northern stretch, both upmarket and neither that interesting. *Ko Chang Resort*, also known as *Rooks Ko Chang Resort* (℡ & ℻01/912 0738, ⓦwww.thaitrader.com/rooks; ❽) has sixty rooms, most of them in bungalows and a few in a central block; all have air-con, TV and mini-bar, though they're not exactly in mint condition. During high season, guests at *Ko Chang Resort* can take a direct boat from the private Centrepoint pier in Laem Ngop, a few kilometres west of the regular pier; call to confirm times and availability. Five minutes' walk further south down the beach, the mid-range *Khlong Phrao Resort* (℡01/830 0126, ℻039/597106; ❺–❽) is built round a seawater lagoon and offers slightly more reasonably priced rooms. The cheaper ones all have verandas from where you can cast fishing lines directly into the lagoon; the more expensive rooms have air-con, TVs and hot water. *Khlong Phrao Resort* can arrange snorkelling and fishing trips for guests.

Khlong Phu waterfall and southern Hat Khlong Phrao

The road gets more potholed and bumpy south of the turn-off for the *Khlong Phrao Resort*. A couple of kilometres on, you'll see a sign for **Khlong Phu waterfall** (Nam Tok Khlong Phu), which is about 1500m east off the main road. The track to the falls is accessible on foot, mountain bike or motorbike; occasionally there's a guy on a motorbike waiting by the main road to ferry people up there, but most people come with their own wheels. The route fords the shallow khlong and cuts through pineapple fields and shady tropical forest before emerging at the falls. Some 20m high, Nam Tok Khlong Phu plunges into an invitingly clear pool defined by a ring of smooth rocks which are ideal for sunbathing.

Beyond the turn-off for the falls, the main road passes signs for *Thalé Bungalows* and then for *KP*; take either one of these signed tracks to get down to the southern stretch of **Hat Khlong Phrao** (a **songthaew** ride here from Hat Sai Khao costs B20–30). The beach here is very long, partially shaded by casuarinas and backed by a huge coconut grove. It has an appealingly mellow atmosphere and the beach invariably feels almost empty, which makes it one of the best places on Ko Chang to escape the crowds; as yet there are no shops or commercial outlets of any kind here other than the two bungalow operations, though there is a **clinic** and a fuel station on the main road, about 500m south of the *KP* access road, across from Wat Khlong Phrao. Like northern Hat Khlong Phrao, the beach here gets a fair bit of natural debris washed up along its sand, and the southern end is also cut off by a khlong, wider and deeper than the one at the northern end and only crossable by swimming.

Seven hundred metres off the main road, *KP* (℡01/863 5448; ❷–❹) is efficiently run by a former national-park ranger and his wife and is the more popular of the two **bungalow** outfits on this beach. The forty huts here are pretty simple, and come either with or without a fan and bathroom, but they are all attractively scattered through a coconut grove just a few steps from the beach. There's a nice restaurant here, as well as a bar shack further up the beach. The management rents out mountain bikes (B40 per hour or B200 per day), kayaks and windsurfers, and organizes snorkelling and fishing day-trips as well as a three-day sea-safari to Ko Kud (see p.451). *KP* is guaranteed to be open year-round and should be reserved well ahead for the Christmas–New Year period. Ten minutes' walk up the beach, and separated from *KP* by an extensive coconut grove, *Thalé Bungalows* (℡01/926 3843; ❷) occupies the southern bank of the northern khlong and a fair length of the shorefront too. It offers some of the most basic bamboo huts on the island, with mattresses on the floors, shared bathrooms and no mosquito nets (it's probably worth buying your own from Trat if you plan to stay here). On the plus side, it does have electricity and has a certain romance, especially as it gets relatively few guests; the managers are friendly and serve meals.

South across the next khlong (again, impassable except by swimming) and round a headland, the main road runs past Wat Khlong Phrao and skirts the back of a couple more **bungalows** which, though officially also on Hat Khlong Phrao, are actually on a completely different little white-sand bay, which is palm-fringed and secluded. There are lots of options to choose from at *Magic* (℡01/861 4829; ❶–❼), which stands right on the beach, from very cheap no-frills bamboo huts at the bottom of the scale through to larger, more comfortable wood and stone bungalows with private facilities, sea views and the option of air-con. *Magic* rent out motorbikes (B80 per hour) and can arrange boat trips. The adjacent *Chokdee* (℡01/910 9052; ❷–❹) sits on a rocky promontory but of course has access to the sand in front of *Magic*; you can choose between huts with shared bathrooms or better en-suite ones with sea views. Five minutes' walk north from *Magic*, along the main road, the vegetarian **restaurant** and massage centre *Piggy's Delight* (Mon–Sat 4–10pm) gets rave reviews and makes a nice change from bungalow food.

Hat Kai Bae

South of *Chokdee*, the road runs through a scenic swath of palm trees and past a few roadside restaurants and an internet centre (see p.448) before veering down to **HAT KAI BAE**, a couple of kilometres south along the coast. Though narrow, the beach here is overhung with trees and blessed with soft white sand and pale blue water – which would make a pretty scene if it were not for the unsightly piles of abandoned building rubble. Though almost all of the shorefront has been built on, the bungalows are mostly discreet bamboo and wood huts, nicely set among the palms and casuarinas. North of the access track, the shore becomes very rocky, loses the beach completely as it's dissected by a lagoon-like khlong and a shrimp farm, and then re-emerges as a sandy mangrove-fringed strand a bit further on. There are a couple of bungalows – *Coral* and *Nang Nual* – next to the khlong, which makes a surprisingly charming setting and feels not unlike staying in a small fishing village. But on the main part of Hat Kai Bae, the atmosphere lies somewhere between the good-time buzz on Hat Sai Khao and the solitary romance of southern Hat Khlong Phrao. Aside from a little pocket of commercialism around *Kai Bae Hut*, most of Kai Bae is peaceful and, above all, mellow. When the tide is in, people seem to spend their time swinging in hammocks that have been strung up on their verandas or making shell mobiles, and at night there are a handful of beach bar shacks for lounging in.

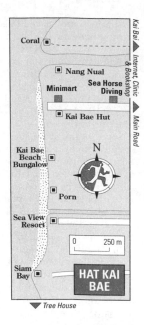

Big chunks of Kai Bae's beach completely disappear at high tide, so you might prefer to seek out the wider and more swimmable bay about twenty minutes' walk further south – just follow the road south from *Siam Bay* restaurant at the southernmost end of Kai Bae. If you carry on even further, the path takes you to so-called Lonely Beach, site of *Tree House*, thirty minutes' walk south of *Siam Bay*.

Practicalities

Arriving by **songthaew** from Tha Dan Kao (50min; B50), you should ask to be dropped at your chosen bungalow. If not, you'll need to walk along the beach to your destination – it's less than fifteen minutes on foot from *Kai Bae Hut* to *Siam Bay* at the far southern end. Coming by songthaew from Hat Sai Khao, expect to pay B30 to *Kai Bae Hut*; the journey takes around 25 minutes. If you're on a motorbike, be prepared for the road to be in very poor condition – even washed away – in places.

All bungalows on Hat Kai Bae offer **snorkelling** outings to local reefs and islands from about B200 per person. Sea Horse Diving at *Kai Bae Hut* organizes **diving** trips in the area: see the box on p.441 for details. You can rent **motorbikes** at *Kai Bae Beach* (B60 per hour or B400 per day), and *Nang Nual* has **canoes** and boats for rent.

Kai Bae Hut has a well-stocked **minimart** that sells fishing tackle and snorkels as well as all the usual travellers' essentials. You can buy stamps and postcards at *Kai Bae Beach*, which also **changes money**, as does *Sea View*. There's a cluster of useful little businesses just east of the beach, on the stretch of main road opposite the access road to *Coral* and *Nang Nual*; here you'll find **internet access** at Kai Bae internet, a secondhand **bookshop** and a **clinic**.

Accommodation and eating

All the Kai Bae bungalows have restaurants, but the best **food** on the beach is served up by *Coral* restaurant, which occupies a gorgeous breezy spot on the coral rocks north of the access road. The menu includes specialities from Isaan like *som tam* and minced pork *larb*, as well as Thai curries and consistently good barbecued seafood. For a few relaxed **beers**, you could do worse than drop in at the ultra-laid-back *Comfortable Bar*, a few metres further north.

Coral ⓣ01/292 2562. Large concrete and wood bungalows built near the khlong on the coral rocks north of the access road, but only a 5min walk from a quiet stretch of sand. The bungalows are fairly simple but have bathrooms and fans. ❹
Kai Bae Beach Bungalow ⓣ01/862 8103. Popular, well-run outfit with lots of bungalows stretching over quite a big patch of the seafront and a restaurant at either end. Simple bamboo huts with shared facilities and comfortable wooden ones with fan and bathroom. ❸–❹
Kai Bae Hut ⓣ01/862 8426. Expensive place on the busiest part of Hat Kai Bae, next to the main access road. Wooden chalets with fan and bathroom, and concrete bungalows with air-con and TV. ❹–❽
Nang Nual ⓣ01/295 1348. Set beside the lagoon-like khlong just north of the access road, this place has no beach of its own. Offers simple huts of slit bamboo, all with en-suite bathrooms. ❸
Porn ⓣ01/864 1608. Laid-back, long-running travellers' hangout with a big range of simple bamboo bungalows (with and without bathrooms) set on the beach. There's an attractive shoreside eating area full of cushions and low tables, plus table-tennis and volleyball. ❶–❸

Sea View Resort ⓣ01/830 7529, ⓕ218 5055. The most upmarket place on the beach, *Sea View* is set in a tropical flower garden and has a table-tennis table under the palm trees, and a currency exchange desk. The wooden chalets here are hardly deluxe, but they all have private bathrooms and TVs, and some have air-con; rooms in the hotel block are slightly cheaper. Big discounts offered July–Sept. ❻–❼
Siam Bay ⓣ01/859 5529. Set right at the southern end of the beach, *Siam Bay* has a beautifully sited restaurant overlooking the rocks. The cheapest huts are simple bamboo ones set right on the beach, some with fan, bathroom and mosquito screens, others with shared facilities and mozzie nets. The sturdier concrete bungalows on the slope and by the beach are more expensive. ❷–❺
Treehouse A 30min walk south of Hat Kai Bae, or 10min by bike or songthaew, this German-Thai-managed place is set in its own little rocky bay known as Lonely Beach, and is an increasingly popular spot for getting away from the crowds. Huts are simple affairs mostly set on the rocks, and there's a fairly pricey restaurant. A regular taxi service runs here throughout the day from near *Kai Bae Hut*. Closed May–Sept. ❸

Hat Bang Bao

From Kai Bae, the road gets rougher as it worms its way south through inland forest until it reaches Bang Bao fishing village and the isolated, sandy beach, **HAT BANG BAO**. During high season there's one daily boat here leaving from Laem Ngop at 3pm (2hr 30min; B120). Otherwise you can either try and persuade a songthaew to take you all the way, or walk from Hat Kai Bae in about three hours. From November through April you can stay on the beach at *Bang Bao Blue Wave* (ⓣ01/439 0349; ❷–❹), which offers simple huts with or without attached bathrooms, and electricity in the evenings.

The east coast

The east coast is not nearly as inviting as the west, and the few bungalows that used to operate on some of the beaches here seem to have been abandoned. The road runs south of the piers at Ao Saparot and Tha Dan Kao to **Than Mayom**, site of the national park office and national park bungalows, and then continues for another 4km before terminating at **Hat Salak Pet** on the south coast.

The southeast headland holds the best beach on this coast, **Hat Sai Yao** (also known as Long Beach), which is best reached by taking the 3pm Ko Whai boat from Laem Ngop during high season and asking to be dropped at Long Beach. Hat Sai Yao is excellent for swimming and has some coral close to shore. Depending on the sea conditions, some boats will take you directly into Hat Sai Yao, while others will drop you just around a small promontory close to *Tantawan Resort* (❷), an appealingly local, family-run place with just a dozen basic huts in a rocky spot that's good for fishing and just ten minutes' walk from the sands of Long Beach. For slightly better accommodation, follow the path westwards for ten minutes to the beachfront *Hat Sai Yao Resort* (☎039/511145 extn 218; ❶–❹), located on Long Beach itself, where large, simple huts are equipped with fans and electric lights. Both bungalows serve food.

The outer islands

South of Ko Chang lies a whole cluster of **islands** of all different sizes, many of them now home to at least one set of tourist accommodation. All the islands are pretty much inaccessible during the rainy season, but from November to April the main islands – such as Ko Mak, Ko Kham and Ko Whai – are served by daily boats from Laem Ngop. For the latest information on boat times and weather conditions, ask at any guest house in Trat, or at the ticket offices near the pier in Laem Ngop.

Ko Mak and Ko Kham

The island of **Ko Mak** (sometimes spelt "Maak") is the most visited and accessible of the outer islands. It lies off the south coast of Ko Chang, and boasts fine white-sand beaches along the south and west coasts; the rest of the sixteen-square-kilometre island is dominated by coconut and rubber plantations. The most recent population count, taken in 1995, put the number of residents at four hundred, most of whom either fish or work in the plantations. During the dry season, from November to April, there's one **boat** a day between the mainland and Ko Mak, leaving Laem Ngop at 3pm (3hr 30min; B170); the return boat leaves Ko Mak every morning at 8am. There are just a few **places to stay** on Ko Mak. One of the most popular is the British-run *Lazy Days* (ⓔkohmak@hotmail.com; ❶–❸), which has nicely positioned teepees and bungalows (with and without private bathrooms) on a rather rocky stretch of beach on the southwest coast. The managers here organize dive trips to local reefs. Further down the coast, *Ao Kao Resort* (☎038/225263 or 01/457 6280, ⓕ039/597239; ❶–❺) is also recommended and has a range of nice huts amongst the palms with and without bathrooms. Near the pier on the northwest coast, *Ko Mak Resort* (☎02/3196714 or 01/219 1220, ⓕ02/3196715; ❺–❻) offers some of the largest and most comfortable bungalows on the island, while *Ko Mak Fantasia* (☎01/219 1220; ❶–❸), further up on the north coast, has simpler A-frame huts among the palm trees beside a narrow beach.

Miniature **Ko Kham** lies off the northern tip of Ko Mak, and has room for just one set of bungalows, *Ko Kham Resort* (☎039/538055 or 01/212 1814, ⓕ538054). Accommodation here is in twenty simple bamboo structures and meals at the resort restaurant are included in the price of B500 per person per day. There's little to do here except swim, sunbathe and enjoy being surrounded by sea. A daily **boat** sails from Laem Ngop to Ko Kham at 3pm (3hr; B170); the return boat leaves Ko Kham at around 8am daily.

Ko Whai and Ko Lao Ya

The beaches on **Ko Whai**, which lies midway between Ko Chang and Ko Mak, tend to be rocky, which means that sunbathing here is not always so pleasurable, but the snorkelling is pretty good and the fishing is said to be rewarding here too. People who come here for the quiet are rarely disappointed.

There are currently two **places to stay** on the island: *Paradise* (℡039/597031; ❶–❷), which offers inexpensive bamboo huts on the western end of the island, and the more comfortable *Ko Whai Pakarang Resort*, sometimes known as *Coral Resort* (℡039/512581 or 01/945 4383; ❷–❹) which has forty bungalows across towards the eastern headland. **Boats** to Ko Whai depart Laem Ngop once a day at 3pm (Nov–April; 2hr 30min; B130).

Petite **Ko Lao Ya**, which sits just off Ko Chang's southeastern headland, is a package-tour island. Graced with pretty waters and white-sand beaches, it takes about two and a half hours to reach by tour boat from Laem Ngop. **Accommodation** at the *Lao Ya Resort* (℡039/531838) is in upmarket, air-conditioned bungalows and the all-inclusive price, for boat transfers, bungalow and three meals, is B1800 per person. Contact the resort for details and times of boats, which vary according to the number of tourists.

Ko Kud

The second-largest island in the archipelago after Ko Chang, **Ko Kud** (also spelt Ko Kut and Ko Kood), south of Ko Mak, is known for its sparkling white sand and its exceptionally clear turquoise water. Accommodation here is in upmarket resorts and needs to be booked in advance: *Ko Kud Sai Kaeo* (℡ & ℻039/511429; ❼) is located on Ao Ta Tin on the northwest coast, while across on the northeast coast at Ao Kluay you'll find the super-deluxe *Ko Kood Island Resort* (℡ & ℻02/233 7276; ❾), and nearby *Kood Island Resort* (℡039/511145, ℻02/398 2444; ❼–❾). The resorts only operate November to April, when the boat can make the five- or six-hour journey from Dan Kao pier, which is about 4km west of Trat town centre; you'll need to check schedules when you book your accommodation.

Travel details

Trains

Aranyaprathet to: Bangkok (2 daily; 5hr 20min–5hr 40min).

Pattaya to: Bangkok (1 daily; 3hr 45min); Si Racha (1 daily; 30min).

Si Racha to: Bangkok (1 daily; 3hr 15min); Pattaya (1 daily; 30min).

Buses

Aranyaprathet to: Bangkok (4 daily; 4hr 30min).

Ban Phe to: Bangkok (12 daily; 3hr); Chanthaburi (6 daily; 1hr 30min); Rayong (every 30min; 30min); Trat (6 daily; 3hr).

Chanthaburi to: Bangkok (Eastern Bus Terminal; 18 daily; 4–5hr); Bangkok (Northern Bus Terminal; 3 daily; 3hr); Khorat (8 daily; 6hr); Rayong (8 daily; 2hr); Sa Kaew (for Aranyaprathet; 8 daily; 3hr); Trat (every 1hr 30min; 1hr 30min).

Pattaya to: Bangkok (Don Muang airport; 3 daily; 2hr 30min); Bangkok (Eastern Bus Terminal; every 30min; 2–3hr 30min); Bangkok (Northern Bus Terminal; every 30min; 2–3hr); Chanthaburi (6 daily; 3hr); Chiang Mai (6 daily; 12hr); Khorat (4 daily; 5–6hr); Nong Khai (7 daily; 12hr); Rayong (every 30min; 1hr 30min); Trat (6 daily; 4hr 30min); Ubon Ratchathani (7 daily; 10hour).

Rayong to: Bangkok (Eastern Bus Terminal; every 15min; 2hr 30min); Bangkok (Northern Bus Terminal; 2 daily; 2hr 30min); Ban Phe (for Ko Samet; every 30min; 30 min); Chanthaburi (8 daily; 2hr); Khorat (18 daily; 4hr).

Si Racha to: Bangkok (every 30min; 2hr); Chanthaburi (6 daily; 3hr 30min); Pattaya (every 20min; 30min); Rayong (for Ban Phe and Ko Samet; 2hr); Trat (6 daily; 5hr).

Trat to: Bangkok (Eastern Bus Terminal; 13 daily; 5–6hr); Bangkok (Northern Bus Terminal; 3 daily;

4hr); Chanthaburi (every 1hr 30min; 1hr 30min); Pattaya (6 daily; 4hr 30min); Rayong (for Ko Samet; 6 daily; 3hr 30min); Si Racha (6 daily; 5hr).

Ferries
Ban Phe to: Ko Samet (4–18 daily; 30min).
Laem Ngop to: Ko Chang (5–10 daily; 45min–3hr); Ko Kham (Nov–April 1 daily; 3hr); Ko Mak (Nov–April 1 daily; 3hr 30min); Ko Whai (Nov–April 1 daily; 2hr 30min).
Si Racha to: Ko Si Chang (hourly; 40min).

Flights
U-Tapao (Pattaya) to: Ko Samui (1 daily; 1hr); Phnom Penh (Cambodia; 1 daily; 1hr 10min).

The northeast: Isaan

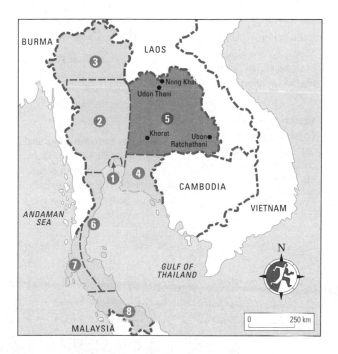

CHAPTER 5 # Highlights

✴ **Khao Yai National Park** – A dozen trails, lots of birds, several waterfalls and organized night safaris. **p.458**

✴ **Khmer ruins** – Exquisite Angkor Wat-style temples at Phimai, Phanom Rung and Khao Phra Viharn. **p.471**, **p.475** and **p.484**

✴ **Silk** – A northeastern speciality, available all over the region but particularly in Khon Kaen. **p.504**

✴ **Yasothon Rocket Festival** – Bawdy rain-making ritual involving ornate home-made rockets. **p.498**

✴ **Phu Kradung** – Teeming table mountain, the most dramatic of the region's national parks. **p.512**

✴ **Mekhong "backpackers' resorts"** – Lie back and get to know the mighty river between Chiang Khan and Nong Khai. **p.517**

✴ **Wat Phu Tok** – Extraordinary meditation temple on a steep sandstone outcrop. **p.530**

✴ **Wat Phra That Phanom** – Isaan's most fascinating holy site, especially during the February pilgrimage. **p.534**

✴ **Som tam, kai yang and sticky rice** – The Isaan classic, a perfect combination of simple ingredients, found all over the northeast.

5

The northeast: Isaan

Bordered by Laos and Cambodia on three sides, the tableland of **north-east Thailand** – known as **Isaan**, after the Hindu god of death and the northeast – comprises a third of the country's land area and is home to nearly a third of its population. This is the least-visited region of the kingdom, and the poorest: over seventy percent of Isaan villagers earn less than the regional minimum wage of B130 a day. Farming is the livelihood of virtually all northeasterners, despite appallingly infertile soil (the friable sandstone contains few nutrients and retains little water) and long periods of drought punctuated by downpours and intermittent bouts of flooding. In the 1960s, government schemes to introduce hardier crops set in motion a debt cycle that has forced farmers into monocultural cash-cropping to repay their loans for fertilizers, seeds and machinery. For many families, there's only one way off the treadmill: each January and February, Bangkok-bound trains and buses are crammed with northeasterners leaving in search of seasonal or short-term work; of the twenty million who live in Isaan, an average of two million seasonal economic refugees leave the area every year, and northeasterners now make up the majority of the capital's lowest-paid workforce.

Most northeasterners speak a dialect that's more comprehensible to residents of Vientiane than Bangkok, and Isaan's historic allegiances have tied it more closely to Laos and Cambodia than to Thailand. Between the eleventh and

---

Accommodation prices

Throughout this guide, guest houses, hotels and bungalows have been categorized according to the **price codes** given below. These categories represent the minimum you can expect to pay in the high season (roughly July, Aug & Nov–Feb) for a **double room**. If travelling on your own, expect to pay anything between sixty and one hundred percent of the rates quoted for a double room. Wherever a **price range** is indicated, this means that the establishment offers rooms with varying facilities – as explained in the write-up. Wherever an establishment also offers **dormitory beds**, the prices of these beds are given in the text, instead of being indicated by price code.

Remember that the top-whack hotels will add seven percent tax and a ten percent service charge to your bill – the price codes below are based on net rates after taxes have been added.

❶ under B150	❹ B400–600	❼ B1200–1800
❷ B150–250	❺ B600–900	❽ B1800–3000
❸ B250–400	❻ B900–1200	❾ B3000+

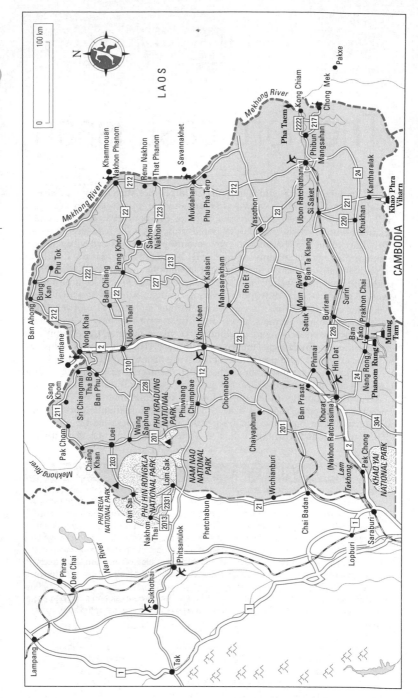

thirteenth centuries, the all-powerful **Khmers** covered the northeast in magnificent stone temple complexes, the remains of which constitute the region's most satisfying tourist attractions. During subsequent centuries the territories along the Mekhong River changed hands numerous times, until the present border with Laos was set at the end of World War II. In the 1950s and 1960s, **Communist insurgents** played on the northeast's traditional ties with Laos; a movement to align Isaan with the Marxists of Laos gathered some force, and the Communist Party of Thailand, gaining sympathy among poverty-stricken northeastern farmers, established bases in the region. At about the same time, major US air bases for the **Vietnam War** were set up in Khorat, Ubon Ratchathani and Udon Thani, fuelling a sex industry that has plagued the region ever since. When the American military moved out, northeastern women turned to the tourist-orientated Bangkok flesh trade instead, and nowadays the majority of prostitutes in the capital come from Isaan.

These cities, like Isaan's other major population centres, are chaotic, exhausting places, with precious little going for them apart from accommodation and onward transport. For tourists, Isaan's prime sights are its **Khmer ruins**, and the trails through **Khao Yai National Park**. Three huge northeastern **festivals** also draw massive crowds: in May, Yasothon is the focus for the bawdy rocket festival; in July, Ubon Ratchathani hosts the extravagant candle festival; while the flamboyant, though inevitably touristy, "elephant round-up" is staged in Surin in November.

Isaan's only mountain range of any significance divides the uninspiring town of **Loei** from the central plains and offers some stiff walking, awesome scenery and the possibility of spotting unusual birds and flowers in the national parks which spread across its heights. Due north of Loei, the **Mekhong River** begins its leisurely course around Isaan with a lush stretch where a sprinkling of guest houses has opened up the river countryside to travellers. Marking the eastern end of this upper stretch, the fast-developing border town of **Nong Khai** is surrounded by possibly the most outlandish temples in Thailand. The grandest and most important religious site in the northeast, however, is **Wat Phra That Phanom**, way downstream beyond **Nakhon Phanom**, a town which affords some of the finest Isaan vistas.

The other big draw for travellers are Isaan's four **border crossings into Laos**. The most popular of these is at Nong Khai, a route which provides easy road access to the Lao capital, Vientiane, and gives foreigners a Lao visa on arrival. But if you already have a visa you can also enter Laos via the Isaan towns of Nakhon Phanom, Mukdahan and Chong Mek, as well as via Chiang Kong in north Thailand; see p.524 for a full run-down on overland travel into Laos. You can get your advance **Lao visa** from the consulate in the central Isaan town of Khon Kaen, where there's also a Vietnamese consulate issuing visas for Vietnam.

The most comfortable **time of year** in Isaan is the cool season (Nov–Feb), which is also when the waters of the Mekhong are highest and the scenery greenest – but if you want to catch the region's most exciting festivals you'll have to brave the hotter months, when temperatures can soar to 40°C. Many travellers **approach Isaan** from the north, either travelling directly from Chiang Mai to Loei, a nine-hour bus ride, or stopping off at Phitsanulok, in the northern reaches of the central plains, and crossing into Isaan via the Phetchabun hills, arriving at Khon Kaen or Chaiyaphum. But there are a number of other equally viable routes into Isaan: a regular and efficient **bus** service connects the east-coast towns of Pattaya, Rayong and Chanthaburi with Khorat, and direct bus services run from Bangkok to all major northeastern centres. It's also possible to arrive by **train** from Bangkok: two rail lines cut through Isaan, one extending eastwards across the south of the region, the other pursuing the northern route up as far as the Lao border. Thai Airways operates regular **flights** between Bangkok and the major northeastern cities.

All major towns and cities in Isaan are connected by **public transport**, as are many of the larger villages. Compared to many other regions of the country, northeastern roads are fairly traffic-free, so **renting your own vehicle** is also a good option: there are car-rental places in every city, and motorbike rental is available in some of the smaller, more touristed towns. Alternatively, you could rent a car from Bangkok's Don Muang airport (see p.96), as it's quite a straightforward two- to three-hour run to Khao Yai National Park and Khorat from Don Muang, with no need to face the capital's traffic jams.

Southern Isaan

Southern Isaan more or less follows one of two branches of the northeastern rail line as it makes a beeline towards the eastern border, skirting the edge of **Khao Yai National Park** before entering Isaan proper to link the major provincial capitals of **Khorat**, **Surin** and **Ubon Ratchathani**. The rail line is handy enough for entering the region, but once here it's as well to follow a route that takes in smaller towns and villages wherever possible, which means switching to buses and songthaews. It is in these smaller places that you'll learn most about Isaan life, particularly if you head for the exceptionally welcoming **guest houses** in Surin, Phimai and Kong Chiam, all of which are run by highly informed English-speaking locals who sometimes arrange tours to nearby villages. For even more of an immersion into a rural community, consider booking yourself on to the **homestay** programme in the village of **Ban Prasat**.

Even if your time is limited, you shouldn't leave this part of Isaan without visiting at least one set of Khmer ruins: **Prasat Hin Phimai** is the most accessible of the region's top three sites, but it's well worth making the effort to visit either **Prasat Hin Khao Phanom Rung** or **Khao Phra Viharn** as well, both of which occupy spectacular hilltop locations. Relics of an even earlier age, prehistoric cliff paintings also draw a few tourists eastwards to the town of **Kong Chiam**, which is prettily set between the Mekhong and Mun rivers and is well worth a visit in its own right. Nearby **Chong Mek** is best known as a legal entry point into Laos, but is also the site of a very enjoyable Thai-Lao border market.

Khao Yai National Park

About 120km northeast of Bangkok, the unrelieved cultivated lushness of the central plains gives way to the thickly forested Phanom Dongrek mountains. A

2168-square-kilometre chunk of this sculpted limestone range has been conserved as **KHAO YAI NATIONAL PARK**, one of Thailand's most rewarding reserves, and certainly its most popular. Spanning five distinct forest types, Khao Yai (Big Mountain) sustains three hundred bird and twenty large landmammal species, and offers a plethora of waterfalls and several undemanding walking trails.

Although Khao Yai can be done as a long day-trip from Bangkok, it really deserves an overnight stop: there's camping and basic accommodation in the park itself, and plenty of more comfortable options just beyond the perimeter and in the nearby town of **Pak Chong**. It's quite easy to trek around the park by yourself, as long as you stick to the official trails, but as some of Khao Yai's best features – its waterfalls, caves and viewpoints – are as much as 20km apart, you might get more satisfaction from joining a tour (see box on p.460). Try to avoid visiting at weekends and holidays, when the trails and waterfalls get ridiculously crowded and the animals make themselves scarce. Even at quiet times, don't expect it to be like a safari park – patience, a soft tread and a keen-eyed guide are generally needed, and it's well worth bringing your own binoculars if you have them. Finally, be prepared for patches of fairly rough terrain, and pack some warm clothes, as the air can get quite cool at the higher altitudes in the park, especially at night.

Practicalities

Whether you decide to see Khao Yai on your own or as part of a tour, your first port of call has to be the small market town of **PAK CHONG**, 37km north of Khao Yai's visitor centre and major trailheads, and served by trains and buses from lots of major towns (see below). One of the two recommended Khao Yai tour leaders operates from Pak Chong, and there are a couple of places to stay in town too, should you decide to base yourself outside the park. If, on the other hand, you want to head straight up to Khao Yai, you need to get a songthaew from Pak Chong's town centre.

Thanon Tesaban cuts right through the middle of Pak Chong and is essentially the town centre. Small side roads (sois) shoot off Thanon Tesaban in parallel lines to the north and south; the sois to the north are odd-numbered in ascending order from west to east (Soi 13 to Soi 21) and the sois on the south side of the road have even numbers, from west to east (from Soi 8 to Soi 18). There's a **currency-exchange** counter (bank hours) on the south side of the main road between the footbridge and Soi 18, a supermarket about 200m further west, plenty of minimarkets and several **internet** centres, including Prints @ Paper, 100m up Soi 17 on the right.

Getting to Khao Yai and back

Trains from Bangkok, Ayutthaya, Khorat, Surin and Ubon Ratchathani all stop at Pak Chong **train station** on the northern edge of Pak Chong, one block north of the main road, Thanon Tesaban. **Buses** to Pak Chong tend to be faster and more frequent: the most useful direct services include those from Bangkok and Khorat. Long-distance buses all stop in the town centre, on the main road: buses from Bangkok generally pull in beside the footbridge on the north (railline) side of the road, while buses from the north and the northeast drop passengers on the other, south, side of the footbridge.

The cheapest way to get **from Pak Chong to Khao Yai** is to take a **songthaew**: these leave from outside the 7-11 shop, 200m west of the footbridge on the north side of the main road, or sometimes from the corner of

Khao Yao tours and guides

Tours of Khao Yai are reasonably priced and cater primarily for independent tourists rather than big groups. The two best reasons for joining one of these tours are that you get to be accompanied by at least one expert wildlife spotter (all tour operators have to take a park ranger with them), and that you have transport around the park, so you don't have to backtrack along trails and can see the waterfalls without having to hitch a ride. On the downside, you probably won't be able to choose which trails you cover, and may find the amount of walking unsatisfactorily slight; in addition it's usual, though not compulsory, to stay in the tour operator's own accommodation. Perhaps the best option would be to hire a park ranger to be your own personal **guide** on the more remote trails; you can arrange this at the park headquarters, but don't expect to get transport as well as a guide. There's no set fee, but a fair rate would be B300 for a few hours, or around B500 for the whole day; organize your guide the night before and be sure to specify a start time.

In recent years, Khao Yai has unfortunately been plagued with unscrupulous **tour operators**, and readers have reported a number of horror stories, including drunk and unpleasant guides and the theft of travellers' cash and credit cards. As it's not possible to keep track of all fly-by-night operators in Pak Chong and Khao Yai, we are recommending only two tour outfits, both of them highly reputable and long-established. In Pak Chong, the recommended tour operator is Wildlife Safari (T & F044/312922, Emarkread@ksc.th.com), which was set up by an English biologist (now a park ranger), and emphasizes plant-spotting and animal observation rather than hearty hikes. The standard one-and-a-half day programme features walks along one or two trails, depending on the season and on recent sightings, as well as a night safari; it costs B850 per person, plus the B200 park entry fee. Tailor-made programmes can also be arranged if you phone in advance. Wildlife Safari is based about 2km north of Pak Chong train station at 39 Thanon Pak Chong Subsanun, Nong Kaja (call ahead to arrange free transport from Pak Chong); their accommodation here features a range of spacious and comfortably furnished rooms in the garden of the family home, some with private bathrooms and air-con (❷–❹).

The other recommended operator is *Khao Yai Garden Lodge* (T044/365178, F365179, Wwww.khaoyai-garden-lodge.de), based out of Pak Chong at kilometre-stone 7 on the road into the park. *Garden Lodge* offers a one-and-a-half day programme (B950 per person plus B200 park entry fee) which includes a trip to the bat cave at dusk, plus a full day of trail hikes, a swim at one of the waterfalls and a night safari; they also do more taxing three- and four-night expeditions into the park at B1500 per person per day, including food, guides, porters, tents and hammocks.

nearby Soi 21; they depart about every thirty minutes between 6.30am and 5pm, take around half an hour and cost B15. Songthaews, however, are not allowed to enter the park itself, so you will be dropped at the **park checkpoint**, about 14km short of the Khao Yai visitor centre, park headquarters and most popular trailheads. At the checkpoint (where you pay the B200 national park entrance fee), park rangers will flag down passing cars and get them to give you a ride up to the visitor centre; this is normal practice and quite safe. The whole journey from Pak Chong to Khao Yai visitor centre takes about an hour; if you want to stay in the park overnight (see opposite) you should try to arrive at the visitor centre well before 5pm when the office shuts, as after that it may be impossible to organize your accommodation and blankets.

It's also possible to **charter a songthaew** from Pak Chong to the park: chartered songthaews count as private vehicles, so they're allowed to go past the checkpoint and will take you wherever you like. The current asking price is about B600 for the ride from Pak Chong to Haew Suwat waterfall, or about

B1000 for a return trip, including several hours in the park. Songthaews can be chartered from the stop outside the 7-11 shop.

Coming back from the park is often easier, as day-trippers will usually give lifts all the way back down to Pak Chong. If you don't fancy that, either get a lift as far as the checkpoint, or walk to the checkpoint from the visitor centre – it's a pleasant three- to four-hour, fourteen-kilometre walk along the fairly shaded park road, and you'll probably spot lots of birds and some monkeys and deer as well. At the checkpoint you can pick up a songthaew to Pak Chong: the last one usually leaves here at about 5.30pm.

Accommodation and eating

You have several options when it comes to **accommodation** in and around Khao Yai, but note that if you decide to do a tour, it's usual to stay in the lodgings run by your tour guide.

Staying in the park

If you're intending to do several days' independent exploring in the park, the most obvious place to stay is the **national park dormitories** next to the park headquarters and visitor centre in the heart of Khao Yai. Accommodation here is extremely basic and can get very cold, but at B30 per person plus B15 per blanket it's cheap and very convenient. Showers and toilets are provided and you should be able to beg a sleeping mat if you don't have your own. On week nights you may well have one of the big wooden huts to yourself, but on weekends they can get packed out with groups of Thai students and you may even not be able to get a space. You can also hire a **tent** (from B150, depending on the size) at the Pha Kluai **campground**, which is about 4km east of the park headquarters, on the road to Haew Suwat falls; there are showers and toilets on site, and you can pitch your own tent here for B20. If you want to be sure of getting a dorm bed or tent you'll need to book ahead through the Royal Forestry Department in Bangkok (☎02/561 4292–3), as described in Basics on p.48, but most travellers simply turn up at the park on the day.

There's no need to bring food and water supplies with you as there are half a dozen **foodstalls** and snack sellers in a building near the park headquarters. They serve hot noodles, curries and rice dishes and sell fresh fruit, drinking water, beer, hot coffee and crisps. The stalls open from about 6am to 8pm; bring plenty of small denomination notes with you as change can be a problem.

The park road

The 23-kilometre road that runs from Pak Chong up to the park checkpoint (Thanon Thanarat) is dotted with luxurious **"lodges"**, aimed squarely at Thai weekenders but by no means unfriendly to vacationing farangs. Thai guests nearly always arrive by car, but most lodges can arrange transport from Pak Chong; the Pak Chong songthaew will also bring you here. Addresses are determined by the nearest kilometre marker on Thanon Thanarat. If you don't have your own transport you'll be restricted to your lodge's restaurant for most of your meals.

Set in a lush and beautifully landscaped garden, complete with a swimming pool, ponds and an aviary, *Khao Yai Garden Lodge* (☎044/365178, ℗365179, ⓦwww.khaoyai-garden-lodge.de; ❷–❼) is a nicely designed bungalow resort 12km out of Pak Chong, at kilometre-stone 7. Run by the congenial and well-informed Klaus, it offers a few simple rooms with shared facilities as well as a range of better-appointed en-suite ones, some of which have air-con and extra beds for kids. Klaus organizes day and overnight tours of the park (see box on p.460), as well as day-trips to the Khmer temples and other major sights of Isaan. *Juldis Khao Yai Resort* (℡044/297297, ℻297291, ⓦwww.khaoyai.com; ❼), at kilometre-stone 17, offers good-value upmarket accommodation in its large, comfortably furnished air-conditioned rooms, each of which has a balcony with garden or pool view. There are three swimming pools, several tennis courts, a not very interesting restaurant and a pub on the premises, and the hotel rents mountain bikes and can arrange tours into the park.

Pak Chong

The obvious drawback to basing yourself in Pak Chong itself is that it's about an hour's journey from the Khao Yai trailheads. On the plus side, there's a passable, inexpensive hotel here and an exceptionally good night market, so if you only want to do one day's walking in the park, it's not such a hardship to make an early start and take the songthaew there and back.

Pak Chong's most acceptable budget **hotel** is the *Phubade Hotel* (℡044/314964; ❷–❸), located just 50m south of the train station on Tesaban Soi 15; from the station, go straight down the steps and look for the "Hotel" sign on your right, opposite the ice-cream shop. Coming from the bus stop, cross to the north side of the main road if necessary, walk 400m west and then turn right up Tesaban Soi 15. The hotel is spartan and shabby but fairly clean, and has both fan and air-conditioned rooms, all with bathrooms. Alternatively, you could try the *Happy Trail Tour Guest House* (℡044/311861; ❶), located just a few metres from the train station on the same soi. Rooms here are cheap and simple, with a mattress on the floor and a shared bathroom, though the management seems at best distracted. Smarter and more appealing, but not as central, *Rim Tarn Inn* (℡044/313364, ℻312933; ❹–❺) is located on the south side of the main road, about 800m west of the bus stops; it has huge, luxurious rooms, all with air-con, hot water and TV, and there's a swimming pool, restaurant and beer garden on the premises. You should be able to get a good discount on a week night.

The night market sets up along the edge of the main road, with most of the stalls on the north side of the road, between Tesaban sois 17 and 19. It's an enjoyable **place to eat**, with plenty of inexpensive savouries to choose from. There's a decent bakery on Tesaban Soi 16, off the south side of the main road, and, while you're there, you should check out the Mei Ort sweet shop across the road, whose window displays a rainbow selection of home-made candies. If you're looking for somewhere to have a beer, try the *Riverside* **bar** and restaurant, signed off the southern end of Tesaban Soi 8, which stages live music most nights.

The park

During the daytime you're bound to hear some of the local wildlife even if you don't catch sight of it. Noisiest of all are the white-handed (or lar) **gibbons** and the pig-tailed **macaques**, which hoot and whoop from the tops of the tallest trees. **Hornbills** also create quite a racket, calling attention to themselves by flapping their enormous wings; Khao Yai harbours large flocks of four different hornbill species, which makes it one of the best places in Southeast Asia to observe these creatures. The great hornbill in particular is an incredibly beautiful bird, with brilliant yellow and black undersides; the magnificent oriental pied hornbill boasts less striking black and white colouring, but is more commonly seen at close range because it swoops down to catch fish, rats and reptiles. You might also see silver pheasants, woodpeckers and Asian fairy-bluebirds, and – from November to

March – several species of **migrant birds,** including the yellow-browed warbler from North Asia and the red-breasted flycatcher from Europe.

A herd of about two hundred Asian **elephants** lives in the park, and its members are often seen at night – it's the only place in Thailand where you have much likelihood of spotting wild elephants. Khao Yai is also thought to harbour Thailand's largest population of **tigers,** currently estimated at fifty; sightings are rare though not mythical, and occasionally the park rangers use dead deer to try and attract them close to the observation towers. You're almost certain to spot **civets,** and you might come across a **slow loris,** while barking **deer** and sambar deer are less nervous after dark. **Wrinkle-lipped bats** assemble en masse at sunset, especially at the cave entrance on Khao Luuk Chang (Baby Elephant Mountain), 6km north of the north (main) gate into the park, which every evening disgorges millions of them on their nightly forage.

Exploring the park

Twelve well-worn **trails** – originally made by elephants and other park species, and still used by these animals – radiate from the area around the visitor centre and park headquarters at kilometre-stone 37, and a few more branch off from the roads that traverse the park. The main trails are numbered and should be easy to follow, and sketch maps and brief trail descriptions are available at the visitor centre; a few paths are signposted en route or marked with coloured flashes. Rangers sometimes alter the course of a trail, or decommission it altogether, if the path is becoming eroded or overgrown, or (more likely) if they are trying to protect animals or birds in the locality. It's probably worth checking the state of each trail with the rangers at their headquarters before you set off. Wear good boots, be prepared for some wading through rivers, and take a hat and plenty of water.

Snacks, bottled water, hot meals and mosquito repellent can be bought at the **foodstalls** next to the park headquarters and visitor centre (see "Staying in the Park" on p.461 for details). You will probably be glad of a strong repellent to deter not just the usual insects but also **leeches,** which can be quite a problem on some of the trails, particularly during and just after the rainy season; though not harmful, they are pretty disgusting. Apply the repellent liberally, particularly round the neck of your boots (it's best to sprinkle the boots as well, just to be sure), wear long sleeves and long trousers, and cover your neck too. If you've only got shorts or thin trousers, consider buying a pair of leech socks (canvas gaiters) from the foodstalls by the visitor centre. Because these bloodsuckers stick fast to your skin, you can't just pick them off or even squash them. Instead you should burn them with a lighted cigarette, or douse them in salt; oily suntan lotion or insect repellent sometimes makes them lose their grip and fall off.

The trails

The shortest and least taxing of the park's trails is the **Nature Trail,** which starts just behind the visitor centre. It's paved all the way and takes just thirty minutes in each direction; if it's not too crowded, you could see gibbons, woodpeckers and kingfishers en route.

Of the more adventurous hikes that begin from the park headquarters, the most popular is **trail 6,** which runs to **Nong Pak Chee observation tower** in the west of the park. This is a fairly easy walk through forest and grassland which culminates at an observation tower built next to a lake. En route you'll hear (if not see) white-handed gibbons in the tallest trees, and might spot barking deer in the savanna. If you stay at the tower long enough you could see needletails dive-bombing the lake; elephants and gaurs sometimes come to drink here, too, and you may even glimpse a tiger. The walk takes about two and a half hours to the observation tower (4km), from where it's another kilo-metre down a dirt track which meets the main road between kilometre-stones 35 and 36. From the road, you can walk or hitch back either to the headquar-ters (2km) or down to the checkpoint (12km) and then travel on to Pak Chong. If you just want to spend a few hours at the observation tower and for-get the main part of the walk, stop beside the main road between kilometre stones 35 and 36 (before reaching the park headquarters) and walk the kilo-metre down the access track to the tower.

Trails 7 and 9 both branch off trail 6 into slightly shorter alternatives. **Trail 7**, from park headquarters to **Wong Cham Pi** (sometimes spelt "Wong Jumpee"), is a two- to three-hour loop which ends on the main road just 1km north of the headquarters at kilometre-stone 36. **Trail 9**, from the headquar-ters to **Mo Sing To,** is about a two-hour loop and passes through a different stretch of grassland and goes past a small lake.

Another good focus for walks is the area around **Haew Suwat Falls**, east of the visitor centre. These 25-metre-high falls are a great place for an invigorat-ing shower and featured in the recent film *The Beach*. To get to the falls from the park headquarters, either follow trail 1 (see below), or walk, drive or hitch the six-kilometre road beyond the headquarters to Haew Suwat – it's a popu-lar spot, so there should be plenty of cars.

Trail 1 runs from the visitor centre (8.3km one way; 3–4hr), beginning on the Nature Trail behind the visitor centre, then veering off it, along a path marked with red flashes, to **Haew Suwat**. En route to Haew Suwat you'll pass a turn-off to **trail 3** (which goes to Pha Kluai campsite and waterfall, see below); about forty minutes before reaching Haew Suwat is a signed trail off to the left that leads to nearby Haew Pratun falls; twenty minutes further down trail 1 you may hear Haew Sai falls in the distance, though these are easier to reach from Haew Suwat itself.

Day-trippers often do the shorter walk from Haew Suwat waterfall to **Pha Kluai campsite (trail 4)**, which is paved most of the way and takes two hours at most. You've a good chance of spotting gibbons and macaques along this route, as well as kingfishers and hornbills. The area around nearby Pha Kluai falls is famous for its impressive variety of orchids. **Trail 5**, from Haew Suwat waterfall to the **Khao Laem ranger post**, is a more strenuous undertaking, whose main attractions are the waterfall, the wide expanse of grassland near Khao Laem and the impressive view of Khao Laem hill itself. You should ask permission from HQ before setting out on this trail, and don't attempt it in the rainy season, as the river gets too high to cross. The trail 5 walk starts just upstream of the falls, from where it's about two hours to Khao Laem and then two hours back (along the same route): approximately 6km altogether.

Night safaris

A much-touted park attraction are the hour-long **night safaris** – officially known as "night lightings" – which take truckloads of tourists round Khao Yai's main roads in the hope of catching some interesting wildlife in the glare of the specially fitted searchlights. Regular night-time sightings include deer and civets, and elephants and tigers are sometimes spotted as well. However, opin-ions differ on the quality of the night-lighting experience: some people find it thrilling just to be out on the edges of the jungle after dark, others see it as rather a crass method of wildlife observation. Whatever your conclusion, you will enjoy the outing a lot more if you take warm clothes with you – Khao Yai is quite high up and gets very chilly after sunset.

The night-lighting trucks leave the park headquarters every night at 7pm and 8pm (they can pick you up from the campsite if requested). During weekends the park can feel like a town centre at night, with four or five trucks following each other round and round the main roads, raking the forests as they go. All night lightings are run by the park rangers, so tour operators sometimes join forces to hire a truck with ranger and searchlights. If you're on your own, you'll probably need to accompany one of these groups, as the trucks cost B300 to rent and can take up to eight people: book your place at the national park headquarters.

Khorat (Nakhon Ratchasima) and around

Beyond Pak Chong, Highway 2 and the rail line diverge to run either side of picturesque Lam Takhong Reservoir, offering a last taste of undulating, forested terrain before gaining the largely barren Khorat plateau. They rejoin at **KHORAT** (officially renamed **Nakhon Ratchasima**) – literally, "Frontier Country" – which is still considered the gateway to the northeast.

If this is your first stop in Isaan, it's not a particularly pleasant introduction: Khorat's streets are far too narrow for the traffic they're expected to cope with, and there's nothing here you could call a genuine "tourist attraction". It can also be a confusing place to get to grips with: the **commercial centre** used to be contained within the old city moat, at the eastern end of town, but it has spilt over westwards and there are shops and markets as well as hotels and restaurants in both areas. But Khorat is at the centre of a good **transport network** and makes an obvious base for exploring the potteries of Ban Dan Kwian. Also within striking distance are the **Khmer ruins** of Phimai, Phanom Rung and Muang Tham, as are the archaeological remains of **Ban Prasat**. Aside from serving Bangkok and all the main centres within Isaan, Khorat's bus network extends south along Highway 304 to the east coast, enabling you to travel directly to Pattaya, Rayong and Chanthaburi without going through the capital.

Arrival, information and transport

There are two bus terminals in town, of which **Bus Terminal 2** (T044/256006–9), situated on the far northern edge of the city on Highway 2, is by far the busier and more useful. Terminal 2 is the arrival and departure point for regular and air-con buses serving all destinations, including regional towns such as Phimai, Pak Chong (for Khao Yai) and Pak Tong Chai, as well as long-distance destinations such as Bangkok, Chiang Mai, Surin, Khon Kaen, Nong Khai, Rayong (for Ko Samet) and Pattaya. The easiest way to get to and from Bus Terminal 2 is by tuk-tuk. **Bus Terminal 1** (T044/242889), which is located just off Thanon Suranari, close to the town centre and most hotels, also runs both fan and air-con buses to Bangkok, but you're better off using the more frequent service from Terminal 2. Arriving at the **train station** on Thanon Mukkhamontri (T044/242044), you're midway between the commercial centre to the east and the TAT office to the west; the train station is on city bus routes #1, #2, and #3, described on p.467. It's possible to fly to Khorat from Bangkok; the **airport** is 20km east of town on Highway 226

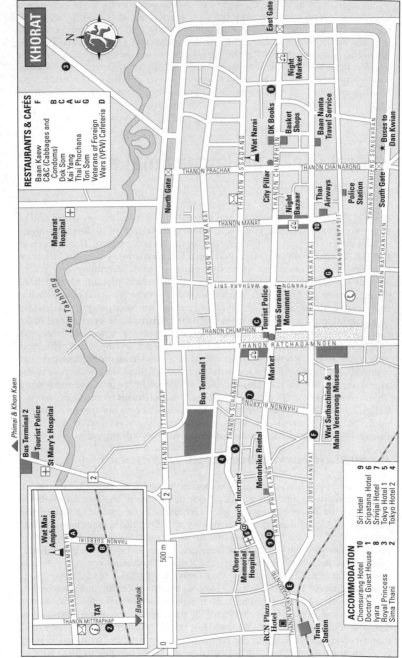

KHORAT

RESTAURANTS & CAFÉS
Baan Kaew   F
C&C (Cabbages and
Condoms)   B
Dok Som   C
Kai Yang   A
Thai Phochana   E
Ton Som   G
Veterans of Foreign
Wars (VFW) Cafeteria   D

ACCOMMODATION
Chomsurang Hotel   10   Sri Hotel   9
Doctor's Guest House   1   Sripatana Hotel   6
Iyara   8   Srivijai Hotel   5
Royal Princess   3   Tokyo Hotel 1   1
Sima Thani   2   Tokyo Hotel 2   4

(✆044/254834), and all planes are met by taxis and hotel minibuses which charge B80 for the trip into town.

If you're basing yourself in Khorat for more than a night you'd do well to trek out to the main **TAT office** (daily 8.30am–4.30pm; ✆044/213666, ☏213667, ✉tatsima@tat.or.th), on the western edge of town, to pick up a free map of the convoluted city bus network; access from the city centre is by city bus #2 or #3, as described below.

Flat-fare **songthaews** (B4) and air-conditioned **city buses** (B7) travel most of the main roads within town. The most useful routes are the yellow **#1** (served by both buses and songthaews), which heads west along Thanon Chumphon, past the train station and out to *Doctor's Guest House*, and returns east via Thanon Yommarat; **#2** (buses only), which runs between the main TAT office in the west, via the train station, and Suranari and Assadang roads, to beyond the *lak muang* (city pillar) in the east; and **#3** (buses only), which also runs right across the city, via Mahathai and Jomsurangyat roads, past the train station, to the TAT office in the west.

Accommodation

Khorat isn't short of **accommodation**, but many of the city's budget places rate as pretty poor value. Noise is the main problem in the more economical central hotels – it's best to request a room away from the main road. If you're planning a visit to Phimai, consider staying in the lovely old guest house there rather than commuting from Khorat.

Chomsurang Hotel, 2701/2 Thanon Mahathai ✆044/257088, ☏252897; near the night bazaar. One of Khorat's affordable best, and the usual choice of business people and better-off tourists. All rooms have air-con; the pricier ones have TV and mini bar, and there's a swimming pool. ❺–❼

Doctor's Guest House, 78 Soi 4, Thanon Suebsiri, 500m east of TAT ✆044/255846. The most peaceful place in town, with a quaint B&B atmosphere, just five rooms with shared bathrooms, and a garden seating area, though it's currently managed by a couple who don't speak much English. A ten-minute ride from the city centre: local yellow bus/songthaew #1 stops opposite the soi entrance (ask for "*thanon Suebsiri soi sii*"), while #2 passes the Thanon Suebsiri junction, so get off at the huge "American Standard" billboard across from the ornate Wat Mai Amphawan. Buses from Bangkok or Khao Yai can drop you outside the *Sima Thani* hotel, a 10min walk away. ❷

Royal Princess, 1137 Thanon Suranari ✆044/256629, ☏213121, ⓦwww.royalprincess.com. Part of the *Royal Princess* hotel chain, Khorat's newest top-notch accommodation is out on the northeastern fringes of town and has 186 comfortable air-con rooms and two restaurants, plus a large swimming pool, a jogging track and a business centre. ❼–❾

Sima Thani, Thanon Mittraphap ✆044/213100, ☏213121, ⓦwww.simathani.co.th; next to the TAT office. One of the city's most upmarket hotels, with smart air-con rooms, a swimming pool and three restaurants. There's a relaxed feel to the place despite its popularity with business-people, and the rooms are good value. Its location beside Highway 2 (the Bangkok–Nong Khai road) makes it very convenient for drivers, and buses from Bangkok or Khao Yai can drop you at the door en route to Bus Terminal 2, but it's too far to walk from the hotel to the town centre. ❻–❾

Sri Hotel, 688–690 Thanon Pho Klang ✆044/242831. More central than *Doctor's* and a recommended alternative for budget travellers. The en-suite rooms, which come with either fan or air-con, are surprisingly quiet and spacious, and there are some cheaper ones near the road. The management can arrange minibuses to Phimai (B900 for up to 3 people). ❷–❸

Sripatana Hotel, 346 Thanon Suranari ✆044/255349, ☏251655. Reasonably priced for the facilities, which include air-con in all rooms, TV and mini-bar in some, and a swimming pool on site. Significant discounts often available. ❹–❺

Srivijai Hotel, 9–11 Thanon Buarong ✆044/242194, ☏267254. Very noisy streetside location near the regular bus station. All rooms are en-suite and some have air-con. ❸–❹

Tokyo Hotel I, 329–333 Thanon Suranari ☏044/242873, ℗252335. Conveniently located budget option that's both clean and friendly. Also check out the adjacent *Tokyo Guest House*, and the nearby *Tokyo Hotel 2*, all under the same congenial management. Rooms in all three places have attached bathrooms, though the degree of comfort varies according to price; the most expensive have air-con. ❶–❸

The City

Sights are thin on the ground in Khorat, but if you spend more than a couple of hours in the city you're bound to come across the landmark statue at the western gate of the old city walls. This is the much-revered **Thao Suranari Monument**, erected to commemorate the heroic actions of the wife of the deputy governor of Khorat, during an attack by the kingdom of Vientiane – capital of modern-day Laos – in 1826. Local chronicles proffer several versions of her feat: some say she organized a feast for the Lao army and enticed them into bed, where they were then slaughtered by the Thais; another tells how she and the other women of Khorat were carted off as prisoners to Vientiane, whereupon they attacked and killed their guards with such ferocity that the Lao retreated out of fear that the whole Thai army had arrived. At any rate, Thao Suranari saved the day and is still feted by the citizens of Khorat, who lay flowers at her feet, light incense at her shrine and even dance around it. At the end of March, the town holds a week-long **festival** in her honour, with parades through the streets and the usual colourful trappings of Thai merry-making.

The closest thing Khorat has to a public **park** is the strip of grass that runs north and south of the monument, between Chumphon and Ratchadamnoen roads; all sorts of things happen here, from haircuts and massages to chess tournaments and picnics. Otherwise, check out the city's **Maha Veeravong Museum** (daily 9am–4pm; B10), which houses a small and unexceptional collection of predominantly Dvaravati- and Lopburi-style Buddha statues found at nearby sites; it's in the grounds of Wat Suthachinda, on Thanon Ratchadamnoen.

Tourist shops and crafts outlets don't really feature in Khorat, but if you're not going further east to Surin, or north to Chaiyaphum, this is a good place to buy **silk**, much of which is produced in Pak Tong Chai, an uninteresting and over-exploited town 32km south of Khorat on Highway 304; the specialist shops along Thanon Chumphon sell the fabric at reasonable prices and stock a bigger range than places in the town of origin. The reverse is true of **ceramics**: there's far more choice at the local pottery village of **Dan Kwian** (see opposite) than at Khorat's night bazaar. Across the road from DK Books on Thanon Chumphon is a cluster of shops selling traditional **basketware** goods – though the sticky-rice baskets, fish traps and rice winnowers are sold as functional items, many are so deftly made that they make attractive souvenirs. If you're looking for cheap **clothes**, take a stroll through the **night bazaar** that sets up at dusk every evening along the *Chomsurang Hotel* end of Thanon Mahathai.

Eating

The night bazaar on Thanon Mahathai includes a few hot-food stalls, but there's a bigger selection of **night-market**-style foodstalls, with some streetside tables, way out east near the *Iyara* hotel on Thanon Chumphon.

Baan Kaew, 105/17–19 Thanon Jomsurangyat. Huge Thai-Chinese restaurant that's famous for its seafood dishes and its roast-duck curry. Moderate.
C&C (Cabbages and Condoms), next to the Soi 4 intersection on Thanon Suebsiri, close to the *Doctor's Guest House* and TAT. Typical Thai fare at this restaurant managed along the same lines as its sister operation in Bangkok, with all proceeds going to the Population and Community Development Association of Thailand (PDA). Moderate.
Dok Som, 142 Thanon Chumpon. Centrally located place with an attractive garden seating area as well as an air-conditioned dining room. Serves Thai, Chinese and European food. Moderate.
The Emperor, inside the *Sima Thani* hotel on Thanon Mittraphap, next to TAT. Khorat's best Chinese restaurant, with a long menu of high quality Chinese standards. Expensive.
Kai Yang, Thanon Suebsiri. Popular place for lunchtime fried chicken with sticky rice. Inexpensive.
Thai Phochana, 142 Thanon Jomsurangyat. Centrally located air-con restaurant known for its duck curries (*kaeng pet*) and Khorat-style noodles cooked with coconut cream (*mii khorat*). Moderate.
Ton Som, 125–129 Thanon Washara Srit. Long-running fairly upmarket restaurant serving classical Thai cuisine that includes seasonal dishes such as *khao chae*, jasmine rice served with seven different condiments, plus Chinese and Western standards. Moderate to expensive.
Veterans of Foreign Wars (VFW) Cafeteria, next to the *Sri Hotel* on Thanon Pho Klang. A combination of greasy spoon and local pub, this dishevelled place was set up by and for the GIs who've settled in the city. More popular with Khorat residents than tourists, it dishes up hearty helpings of steak and fries, pork chops, pizzas and sandwiches (drinks only after 7pm). Inexpensive.

Listings

Airlines The Thai Airways office is at 14 Thanon Manas (☎044/257211), close to the night bazaar.
Bookshops A branch of DK Books east of the *lak muang* on Thanon Chumphon stocks a good selection of cheap Penguin Classics, and upstairs has a few English-language books about Thailand and some Thai novels in translation.
Hospitals The private St Mary's Hospital (☎044/242385) is at 307 Thanon Mittraphap (Highway 2), near Bus Terminal 2; the government Maharat Hospital is on the northeast edge of town (☎044/254990–1).
Internet access At Touch Internet, next to *Sripatana Hotel* on Thanon Suranari, and at Zap, a few hundred metres west of the train station at 81 Thanon Mukhamontri, as well as (expensively) at the *Sima Thani* and *Royal Princess* hotels.
Mail There are post offices next to TAT on Thanon Mittraphap, inside the city walls on Thanon Assadang, and just west of the city walls on Thanon Jomsurangyat.
Motorbike rental You can hire a motorbike from Virojyarnyon, 554 Thanon Pho Klang, for B200 a day.
Telephones The CAT overseas telephone office is inside the city walls on Thanon Sanpasit.
Tourist police Their main office is opposite Bus Terminal 2 on Highway 2 (☎044/341777–9), and there's a more central booth beside the Thao Suranari Monument on Thanon Chumphon.
Tours Baan Nanta Travel Service, located at 168 Thanon Mahathai (☎044/257359, ⓦwww.nanta-travel.com), east of *Chomsurang Hotel*, can arrange private day-trips to local sights such as Phanom Rung, Muang Tam and Dan Kwian for around B2000 per car. *Siri Hotel* organizes inexpensive B900 minibus trips to Phimai for up to three people.

Dan Kwian

Some of the most sought-after modern pottery in Thailand is produced by the potters of **DAN KWIAN**, a tiny village 15km south of Khorat on Route 224. To get there, take local bus #1307 (destination Chok Chai; every 30min; 30min) from Bus Terminal 2, or pick it up at Khorat's southern city gate; get off as soon as you see the roadside pottery stalls. Inevitably, the popularity of the highly distinctive Dan Kwian ceramics has made the village something of a tourist trap, but the place remains remarkably untacky (and the wares under-priced). The roadside stalls display the whole range of products, from inexpensive sunbaked clay necklaces to traditional urn-shaped water jars; in the background the potters work the clay without much regard for curious onlookers.

Characteristic of **Dan Kwian pottery** is its unglazed metallic finish. The local clay, dug from the banks of the Mun, has a high iron content, which when fired in wood-burning kilns combines with ash to create the shimmering end result. Different shades are achieved by cramming the pots into the kiln to achieve uneven firing: the greater their exposure to heat, the darker the finish. The usual technique consists of building the pots through the continuous addition of small pieces of clay. From this method comes the most typical Dan Kwian motif, the geometrical latticework pattern, which is incorporated into all sorts of designs, from incense burners and ashtrays to vases and storage jars. The potters also mould clay into sets of ceramic tiles and large-scale religious and secular murals – increasingly popular decorations in modern wats and wealthy city homes.

First settled by Mon in the mid-eighteenth century, Dan Kwian has always been a convenient rest spot for travellers journeying between the Khorat plateau and Cambodia – hence its name, which means "Cart Place" or "Wagon Station". The tag still applies, as the village is now home to a **cart museum** (always open; free), a ramshackle outdoor collection of traditional vehicles and farming implements assembled at the back of the pottery stalls. Look out for the monster machine with two-metre wheels, designed to carry two tons of rice, and the covered passenger wagons with their intricately carved shafts. The exhibits aren't all as archaic as they look – Isaan farmers still use some of the sugar-cane presses on display, and the fish traps and lobster pots are a common sight in this part of the country.

Ban Prasat

The quintessentially northeastern village of **BAN PRASAT** has become a source of great interest to archeologists following the discovery in the 1990s of a series of **burial grounds** within its boundaries, some of which date back 3000 years. The skeletons and attendant artefacts have been well preserved in the mud, and many of the finds are now on public display in Ban Prasat; the village has made extra efforts to entice tourists with low-key craft demonstrations and a homestay programme. It's also a pleasant village in its own right, a traditional community of stilt houses and flowering shrubs set beside the Tarn Prasat river, which rises in Khao Yai National Park; water from Tarn Prasat, one of the nine most sacred rivers in Thailand, was used in the religious ceremonies for the king's 72nd birthday celebrations in 1999. All this makes Ban Prasat well worth a couple of hours of your time on the way between Khorat and Phimai – or even an overnight stay if you organize it in advance.

There are currently three **excavation pits** open to the public, each clearly signed from the centre of the village and informatively labelled in English and Thai. From these pits archaeologists have surmised that Ban Prasat was first inhabited about 1000 BC. Its residents, rice farmers who built dykes and moats to channel water to and from Tarn Prasat, traded their wares with coastal people, from whom they received shell jewellery among other goods. Each pit contains bones and objects from different eras, buried at different depths but also with the head pointing in different directions, suggesting a change in religious or superstitious precepts; for example skeletons at the deepest (oldest) level in Pit 1 point southeast, whereas those on the next level in the same pit point east and those nearest the surface point either north or south. **Artefacts** found and displayed alongside them include stone discs, or *chakra,* believed to date back to 1000 BC, lots of wide-lipped or "trumpet-rim" earthenware vessels decorated with patterns applied in red slip, glazed Khmer-style pottery, and glass and bronze bangles. There are additional exhibits at the **Ban Prasat Museum** beside the car park, though its opening hours seem rather erratic.

Signs in the village direct you to local projects such as the family who do **silk weaving**, where you should be able to see several stages of the sericulture process (see box on p.481 for more on the local silk industry), beginning with the silkworms and the mulberry trees they feed on, the raw silk cocoons they produce and then the loom at which the cloth is woven; the family has a small selection of pieces to sell. Other interesting village crafts include the weaving of floor mats from locally grown bulrushes, and the making of household brooms.

Ban Prasat is located a couple of kilometres off Highway 2, 46km north of Khorat and 17km southwest of Phimai. Any Khorat–Phimai bus (#1305 from Khorat's Bus Terminal 2; every 30min; about 50min from Khorat or 20min from Phimai) will drop you at the Highway 2 junction, from where you have to walk the 2km to the village if you can't flag down a passing car. There are no hotels or restaurants in the village, but there is a **home-stay** programme, which is a great opportunity to savour typical village life. Home-stays cost B400 per person per night including two meals and should be arranged at least a week in advance by contacting Khun Teim Laongkarn of the Eco-tourism Society, 282 Mu 7, Tambon Tarn Prasat, Amphoe Non Sung, Nakhon Ratchasima 30420 (℡044/367075). Alternatively, staff at the Khorat TAT office may be able to help (℡044/213666, ℻213667, ℮tatsima@tat.or.th).

Phimai

Hemmed in by its rectangular old city walls and encircled by tributaries of the Mun River, the small modern town of **PHIMAI**, 60km northeast of Khorat, is completely dominated by one of the most impressive Khmer sites in Thailand – the charmingly restored temple complex of **Prasat Hin Phimai**. No one knows for sure when the prasat was built or for whom, but as a religious site it probably dates back to the reign of the Khmer king Suriyavarman I (1002–49); the complex was connected by a direct road to Angkor and orientated southeast, towards the Khmer capital. Over the next couple of centuries Khmer rulers made substantial modifications, and by the end of Jayavarman VII's reign (1181–1220), Phimai had been officially dedicated to Mahayana Buddhism. Phimai's other claim to fame is **Sai Ngam** (Beautiful Banyan), reputedly the largest banyan tree in Thailand, still growing a couple of kilometres beyond the temple walls.

The ruins are the focus of a **sound and light show**, which is held here on the second Saturday evening of every month and costs B500 including dinner; contact the organizers for details on ℡044/260331, or check with the Khorat TAT office (℡044/213666, ℻213667, ℮tatsima@tat.or.th). The biggest event of the year, however, is the annual festival of **boat races**, held on the Mun's tributaries over a weekend in late October or early November. In common with many other riverside towns throughout Thailand, Phimai marks the end of the rainy season by holding fiercely competitive longboat races on the well-filled waterways, and putting on lavish parades of ornate barges done up to emulate the Royal Barges of Bangkok.

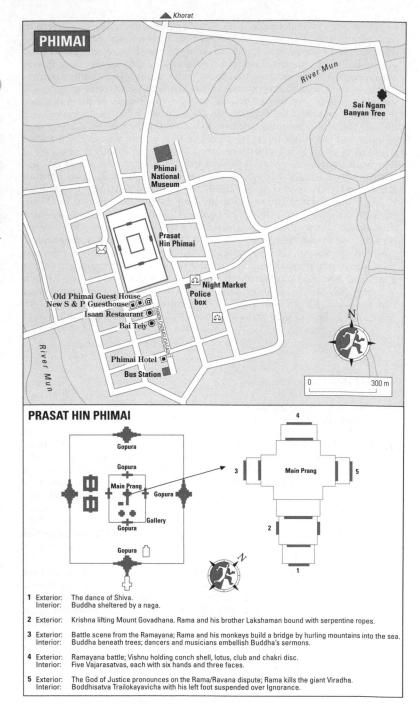

PHIMAI

Khorat

River Mun

Sai Ngam
Banyan Tree

Phimai
National
Museum

Prasat
Hin Phimai

Night Market

Old Phimai Guest House
New S & P Guesthouse
Isaan Restaurant
Bai Teiy

Police
box

THANON CHOMSUDASADET

River Mun

Phimai Hotel

Bus Station

N

0   300 m

PRASAT HIN PHIMAI

Gopura

Gopura

Main Prang

Gopura

Gallery

Gopura

Gopura

4

3   Main Prang   5

2

1

N

1 Exterior: The dance of Shiva.
   Interior: Buddha sheltered by a naga.

2 Exterior: Krishna lifting Mount Govadhana. Rama and his brother Lakshaman bound with serpentine ropes.

3 Exterior: Battle scene from the Ramayana; Rama and his monkeys build a bridge by hurling mountains into the sea.
   Interior: Buddha beneath trees; dancers and musicians embellish Buddha's sermons.

4 Exterior: Ramayana battle; Vishnu holding conch shell, lotus, club and chakri disc.
   Interior: Five Vajarasatvas, each with six hands and three faces.

5 Exterior: The God of Justice pronounces on the Rama/Ravana dispute; Rama kills the giant Viradha.
   Interior: Boddhisatva Trailokayavicha with his left foot suspended over Ignorance.

Khmer temples

To make sense of the **Khmer ruins** of Thailand, it's essential to identify their common architectural features. At the centre of the rectangular temple compound is always the **main prang**, a pyramidal or corn-cob-shaped tower built to house the temple's most sacred image. Each prang has four entrance chambers or **gopura**, the most important of which (usually the eastern one, facing the dawn) is often extended into a large antechamber. The **lintels** and **pediments** above the gopura are carved with subjects from relevant mythology: typical Hindu reliefs show incidents from the *Ramayana* epic (see box on p.125) and lively portraits of the Hindu deities Shiva and Vishnu, while Buddhist scenes come from the lives of the Buddha and other *bodhisattva*s. **Antefixes** on the roof of the prang are often carved with the Hindu gods of direction, some of the most common being Indra on the three-headed elephant (east); Yama on a buffalo (south); Varuna on a naga or a *hamsa*, a sacred goose (west); Brahma on a *hamsa* (north); and Isaana on a bull (northeast).

Originally, the prang would have sheltered a **shiva lingam**, continuously bathed by lustral water dripping from a pot suspended over it; the water then flowed out of the inner chamber by means of a stone channel, a process which symbolized the water of the Ganges flowing from the Himalayan home of Shiva. In most prasats, however, the lingam has disappeared or been replaced with Hindu or Buddhist statues.

One or two **minor prangs** usually flank the main prang: often these were added at a later date to house images of less important gods, though in some cases they predate the main structure. Concentric sets of walls shield these shrines within an inner courtyard. In many temples, the innermost wall – the **gallery** – was roofed, either with wood (none of these roofs has survived) or stone. At their cardinal points some galleries have gopuras with carved lintels and pediments, which are usually approached by staircases flanked with **naga balustrades**; in Khmer temples, nagas generally appear as symbolic bridges between the human world and that of the gods. Most prangs enclose ponds between their outer and inner walls, and many are surrounded by a network of moats and **reservoirs**: historians attribute the Khmers' political success in part to their skill in designing highly efficient irrigation systems (see p.752 for the history of the Khmers in Thailand).

The ruins

Built mainly of dusky pink and greyish white sandstone, **Prasat Hin Phimai** (daily 7.30am–6pm; B40) is a seductive sight for so solemn a set of buildings. Even from a distance, the muted colours give off a far from austere glow; closer inspection reveals a mass of intricate carvings.

From the main southeastern gate, a staircase ornamented with classic naga balustrades leads to a gopura in the **outer walls**, which are punctuated on either side by false balustraded windows – a bit of sculptural sleight-of-hand to jazz up the solid stonework without piercing the defences. A raised pathway bridges the space between these walls and the inner gallery that protects the prangs of the **inner sanctuary**. The minor prang to the right, made of laterite, is attributed to the megalomaniac twelfth century King Jayavarman VII. Enshrined within is a statue of him; it's a copy of the original which was found in the same location, but is now kept in the National Museum in Bangkok. The pink sandstone prang to the left, which is connected to a Brahmin shrine where seven stone linga were found, was probably built around the same time.

After more than twenty years of archeological detective work and painstaking reassembly, the magnificent **main prang** has now been restored to its original cruciform groundplan and conical shape, complete with an almost full set of carved lintels, pediments and antefixes, and capped with a stone lotus bud. The **carvings** around the outside of the prang depict predominantly Hindu themes. Shiva – the Destroyer – dances above the main entrance to the southeast antechamber: his destruction dance heralds the end of the world and the creation of a new order, a supremely potent image that warranted this position over the most important doorway. For more on these legends, see "Art and Architecture" in Contexts, (p.774). Most of the other external carvings pick out momentous episodes from the *Ramayana* (see box on p.125), starring heroic Rama, his brother Lakshaman and their band of faithful monkeys in endless battles of strength, wits and magical powers against Ravana, the embodiment of evil. Inside, more sedate Buddhist scenes give evidence of the conversion from Hindu to Buddhist faith, and the prasat's most important image, the Buddha sheltered by a seven-headed naga, sits atop a base that once supported a Hindu Shiva lingam.

Much of the ancient carved stonework discovered at Phimai but not fitted back into the renovated structure can be seen at the **Phimai National Museum** (daily 9am–4pm; B30) northeast of the ruins, just inside the old city walls. They're easier to appreciate here, being at eye-level, well labelled and backed up by a photographic lesson on the evolution of the different styles.

Sai Ngam

Two kilometres northeast of the museum – get there by bicycle (see below) or samlor – **Sai Ngam** is a banyan tree so enormous that it's reputed to cover an area about half the size of a soccer pitch (approximately 2300 square metres). It might look like a grove of small banyans, but Sai Ngam is in fact a single *ficus bengalensis* whose branches have dropped vertically into the ground, taken root and spawned other branches, thereby growing further and further outwards from its central trunk. Banyan trees are believed to harbour animist spirits, and you can make merit here by releasing fish into the artificial lake which surrounds Sai Ngam. The tree has become a popular recreation spot, and several restaurants have sprung up alongside. En route to the tree, you'll pass a large-scale model of the Thungsunrit Irrigation Project, an indication of the northeast's dependence on a well-regulated water supply.

Practicalities

Regular **bus** #1305 runs direct to Phimai from Khorat's Bus Terminal 2 (every 30min; 1hr 30min) and stops within sight of the ruins; the last return bus departs at 6pm. The bus passes the turn-off to Ban Prasat (see p.470), so if you get up early you can combine the two places on a day-trip from Khorat. It's also feasible, if a bit of an effort, to visit Phimai en route to points east or west without having to pass through Khorat. You can do this by taking an ordinary, or "rapid" (read "slow"), **train** to the tiny station of **Hin Dat**, which is about an hour and forty minutes' train ride west of Surin, or about 55 minutes' ride east of Khorat. Hin Dat is 25km south of Phimai, so from here you should either wait for one of the infrequent songthaews to Phimai, splash out on an expensive motorbike taxi or try hitching. Songthaews back to Hin Dat from Phimai are generally timed to link up with east-bound trains; check with the *Old Phimai Guest House*, (see opposite), for current timetables.

Once in Phimai, the best way to get about is by **bicycle**, although this isn't permitted inside the ruins. *Bai Teiy* restaurant has bicycles for rent and issues free maps of cycling routes around town, while *Old Phimai Guest House* has bicycles for guests only. Aside from the ride out to Sai Ngam, the area just west of the ruins, beyond the post office, is especially atmospheric – many of the traditional wooden houses here double as workshops, and you'll often see householders weaving cane chairs in the shade beneath the buildings. There are several **internet** centres in Phimai, the most convenient of which is on Thanon Chomsudasadet, near the *Old Phimai*.

Accommodation

Though most people visit the ruins as a day-trip, Phimai has two inexpensive **places to stay** as well as an unpretentious hotel, and makes a much more attractive and peaceful overnight stop than Khorat. Your first choice should be the *Old Phimai Guest House* (T044/471918; ❷–❸), a lovely old wooden house with a roof garden and sun rooms, just off Thanon Chomsudasadet and only a couple of minutes from the ruins; YHA members get a ten-percent discount on room rates, and there are also B90 dorm beds available. The rooms here all have shared bathrooms, and you can choose to have a fan or air-conditioning. The *Old Phimai* is an excellent source of information, with a big noticeboard and full details of local travel connections; they also run day-trips to Phanom Rung at B450 per person. Even if you're just passing through and need somewhere to leave your luggage for a few hours, this is the place to ask. The other option in this category is the *New S&P Guest House* (T044/471797; ❷) just across the narrow soi from the *Old Phimai*, with large clean rooms and dorms beds at B80. More upmarket but nowhere near as atmospheric as the budget places, the friendly *Phimai Hotel*, next to the bus station, (T044/471306, F471940, Wwww.korat.in.th/phimaihotel/eindex.htm; ❷–❸) is a typical small hotel where rooms are reasonably comfortable and all have private bathrooms; the air-conditioned rooms also have TVs.

Eating

Bai Teiy on Thanon Chomsudasadet, the town's most popular **restaurant**, serves tasty Thai dishes, including fresh fish from the river; it also acts as an informal tourist information service and can help with bus and train timetables. For typical northeastern fare try around the corner at *Isaan Excellent Taste*, but if you prefer a meal with a view, go to the string of interchangeable restaurants alongside Sai Ngam – they serve up decent enough food, though prices are pitched high because of the location. The night market sets up at dusk on the road just southeast of the ruins and is a good place to sample genuine local fare at genuine local prices.

Phanom Rung and Muang Tham

East of Khorat the bleached plains roll blandly on, broken only by the occasional small town and, if you're travelling along Highway 24, the odd tantalizing glimpse of the smoky Phanom Dongkrek mountain range above the southern horizon. That said, it's well worth jumping off the Surin-bound bus for a detour to the fine Khmer ruins of **Prasat Hin Khao Phanom Rung** and **Prasat Muang Tham**. Built during the same period as Phimai, and for the same purpose, the temple complexes form two more links in the chain that once connected the Khmer capital with the limits of its empire. Sited dramatically atop an extinct volcano, Phanom Rung has been beautifully restored, and the newly renovated Muang Tham lies on the plains below.

To get to the ruins, you first need to take a **bus** to the small town of **Ban Tako**, located on Highway 24 about 115km southeast of Khorat or 83km southwest of Surin. Bus #274 travels between the two provincial capitals, leaving approximately every thirty minutes from dawn till dusk and taking just over two hours from Khorat or just under two hours from Surin. From Ban Tako it's 12km south to Phanom Rung and another 8km southeast along a side road to Muang Tham; as there's no public transport direct to the ruins, you either have to hitch or rent a **motorbike taxi** – they usually charge B200 per person for the round-trip to Phanom Rung, Muang Tham and back to Ban Tako. If you don't want to splash out on a taxi, you can try **hitching** – a time-consuming option during the week (so you should take a very early bus from Khorat or Surin), but a lot easier at weekends. The best place to hitch from is a small village south of Ban Tako called **Ban Don Nong Nae**, which you can reach from Ban Tako by taking a ten-minute songthaew ride. Alternatively, join one of the inexpensive day-tours organized from Phimai by the *Old Phimai Guest House* (B450 per person; see p.475). There are two car parks and two **entrances** to the Phanom Rung complex; if you have your own transport, ignore the first (west) entrance, signed off the access road, and carry on to the main (east) entrance and car park – the drama of the site is lost if you explore it back-to-front. Motorbike taxis should take you to the main entrance. There is a prettily located resort behind the car park at the western entrance, built on platforms down the hillside, but at the time of writing it was closed and is unlikely to reopen in the foreseeable future. Most people do the ruins as a day-trip from Khorat or Surin, but you could **stay** in the town of **NANG RONG**, 14km west of Ban Tako on Highway 24, where there's a guest house called *Honey Inn* (℡044/622825; ❷); call them first though as the handful of rooms fills up fast, and you need to ask for specific directions as it's difficult to find. Alternatively, stay in the provincial capital of **BURIRAM**, 50km northeast of Nang Rong and served by frequent buses between the two that take just over an hour, as well as by daily Thai Airways flights from Bangkok. In Buriram, you could try the cheap but decent enough hotel *Chai Jaroen* (℡044/601505; ❶–❷) at 114–16 Thanon Niwat; it's not signed in English but is in front of the train station and right (west) a few metres, very near the night market. A more comfortable, recommended option is the *Vongthong Hotel* (℡044/612540, ℻620859, Ⓔvongthong@isan.sawadee.com; ❻), in the southern part of town at 512/1 Thanon Jira, where rooms have air-con, mini-bar and satellite TV.

Prasat Hin Khao Phanom Rung

Prasat Hin Khao Phanom Rung (daily 6am–6pm; B40) stands as the finest example of Khmer architecture in Thailand, its every surface ornamented with exquisite carvings and its buildings so perfectly aligned that on the morning of April's full-moon day you can stand at the westernmost gopura and see the rising sun through all fifteen doors. This day marks Songkhran, the Thai New Year, which is celebrated with a day-long **festival** of huge parades all the way up the hill to the prasat – a tradition believed to go back eight hundred years. As at most Khmer prasats, building at Phanom Rung was a continuous process that spanned several reigns: the earliest structures are thought to date to the beginning of the tenth century and final additions were probably made three hundred years later, not long before it was abandoned. Restoration work was begun in 1971 and lasted seventeen years: the results are impressive and give the most complete picture of Khmer architecture in Thailand.

The **approach** to the temple compound is one of the most dramatic of its kind. Symbolic of the journey from earth to the heavenly palace of the gods,

the ascent to the inner compound is imbued with metaphorical import: by following the 200-metre-long avenue, paved in laterite and sandstone and flanked with lotus-bud pillars, you are walking to the ends of the earth. Ahead, the main prang, representing Mount Meru, home of the gods, looms large above the gallery walls, and is accessible only via the first of three **naga bridges**, a raised cruciform structure with sixteen naga balustrades, each naga having five heads. Once across the bridge you have traversed the abyss between earth and heaven. A series of stairways ascends to the eastern entrance of the celestial home, first passing four small ponds, thought to have been used for ritual purification. A second naga bridge crosses to the **east gopura**, entrance to the inner sanctuary, which is topped by a lintel carved with Indra (god of the east) sitting on a lion throne. The gopura is the main gateway through the **gallery** which runs right round the inner compound and has one main and two minor entranceways on each side. Part of the gallery has been restored to its original covered design, with arched roofs, small chambers inside and false windows. The chambers may have been used for exhibiting as well as storing artefacts.

Phanom Rung is surprisingly compact, so the east gopura leads almost directly into the **main prang**, separated from it only by a final naga bridge. A dancing Shiva, nine of his ten arms intact, and a lintel carved with a relief of a **reclining Vishnu** preside over the eastern entrance to the prang. The Vishnu image has a somewhat controversial history: stolen from the site in the early 1960s, it mysteriously reappeared as a donated exhibit in the Art Institute of Chicago; for over ten years the curators refused to return it to Thailand, but as restoration work on Phanom Rung neared completion in 1988, the Thai public took up the cause and the Institute finally relented. The relief depicts a common Hindu creation myth, known as "Reclining Vishnu Asleep on the Milky Sea of Eternity", in which Vishnu dreams up a new universe, and Brahma (the four-faced god perched on the lotus blossom that springs from Vishnu's navel) puts the dream into practice. On the pediment above this famous relief is a lively carving of Shiva's Dance of Destruction (see p.774 for more on the Hindu legends). Of the other recurring figures decorating the prang, one of the most important is the lion head of Kala, also known as Kirtimukha, symbolic of both the lunar and the solar eclipse and – because he's able to "swallow" the sun – considered far superior to other planetary gods. Inside the prang you can see the all-powerful Shiva lingam, for which the prang was originally built; the stone channel that runs off the lingam and out of the north side of the prang was designed to catch the lustral water with which the sacred stone was bathed.

Two rough-hewn laterite libraries stand alongside the main prang, in the northeast and southeast corners, and there are also remains of two early tenth-century brick prangs just northeast of the main prang. The unfinished **prang noi** (little prang) in the southwest corner now contains a stone Buddha footprint, which has become the focus of the merit-making that underlies the annual April festivities, thus neatly linking ancient and modern religious practices.

Prasat Muang Tham
The dishevelled ruins of **Prasat Muang Tham** (daily 6am–6pm; B40) used to make a wonderful counterpoint to the renovated Phanom Rung, but now that Muang Tham has been almost completely restored as well, you may find it lacks something in comparison to its more dramatic neighbour. Like Phanom Rung, Muang Tham was probably built in stages between the tenth and thirteenth centuries, and is based on the classic Khmer design of a central prang flanked by minor prangs and encircled by a gallery punctuated with gopura. The four stone-rimmed L-shaped ponds, located between the gallery and the outer wall,

may have been used to purify worshippers as they entered the complex, or they may have served as straightforward reservoirs.

Surin and around

Best known for its much-hyped elephant round-up, the provincial capital of **Surin**, 197km east of Khorat, is an otherwise typical northeastern town, a good place to absorb the easy-going pace of Isaan life, with the bonus of some atmospheric Khmer ruins nearby. The elephant tie-in comes from the local Suay people, whose prowess with the pachyderms is well known and can be seen first-hand in the nearby village of **Ban Ta Klang**. Thais, Lao and Khmers make up the remainder of the population of Surin province – the Khmers have lived and worked in the region for over a thousand years, and their architectural legacy is still in evidence at the ruined temples of **Ta Muen Toj**, **Prasat Ta Muen Tam** and **Bay Kream**. The local Khmer population was boosted more recently, during the Khmer Rouge takeover of Cambodia in the 1970s, when many upper-class Cambodians fled here.

The Town

Surin's only official sight is its **museum** (Mon–Fri 8.30am–4.30pm; free), a tiny one-room exhibition on Thanon Chitramboong featuring stacks of carved antefixes and, more interestingly, several sacred elephant ropes formerly used by the Suay in their hunts to capture wild elephants for taming. Made of buffalo hide and measuring up to 100m, these ropes were considered so special by the men who handled them that women weren't allowed to touch them and, as the essential tools of the hunt, they were blessed by ancestral spirits before every expedition. As added protection the hunters wore the specially inscribed protective clothing on display here: the *yantra* designs are produced by combinations of letters and numbers arranged in such a way as to invoke magic and ward off evil.

You won't find "magic" clothing on sale in Surin, but the local **silk** weave is famous for its variety: seven hundred designs are produced in Surin province alone, many of them of Cambodian origin, including the locally popular rhomboid pattern. Not surprisingly, Surin is one of the best places in the country to buy silk: there are usually four or five women selling their cloth around the Tannasarn–Krungsrinai intersection, or you can try the **shop** opposite the *Ubon Hotel* on Thanon Tannasarn, the Ruen Mai Silk Shop on Thanon Chitramboong, or Netcraft next to the *Phetkasem Hotel*, which also sells locally made silver earrings and buttons. Though it is possible to visit the nearby **villages** where women weave most of Surin's silk and cotton, you'll need to go with a guide, not only to understand the weavers' explanations of what they do, but also to get a more behind-the-scenes look at the less obvious aspects of the process, like the breeding of the silkworms and the extracting of the thread; *Pirom's House*, listed on p.482, should be able to arrange a guide for you. Timing is also important if you want to see the weavers in action: the best months to see them are between November and June, when the women aren't required to work day and night in the fields.

Surin's **elephant round-up**, held every year on the third weekend of November, draws some forty thousand spectators to watch elephants play soccer,

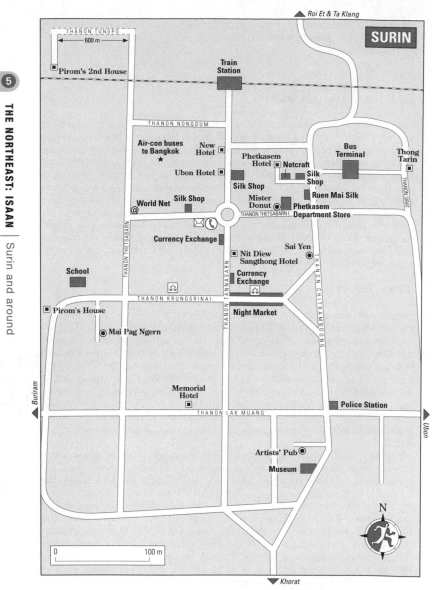

Roi Et & Ta Klang

SURIN

THANON TUNGPO
← 600 m →

■ Pirom's 2nd House

Train
Station

THANON NONGDUM

Air-con buses
to Bangkok
★

New
Hotel ■

Bus
Terminal

Thong
Tarin
■

Phetkasem
Hotel ■ Netcraft

Ubon Hotel ■

Silk
Shop

Silk Shop

Ruen Mai Silk

World Net
@

Silk Shop

Mister
Donut ◉

Phetkasem
Department Store

THANON THETSABARN I.

Currency Exchange

Sai Yen
◉

■ Nit Diew
Sangthong Hotel

School
■

Currency
Exchange
⟨⟩

THANON KRUNGSRINAI

■ Pirom's House

Night Market

◉ Mai Pag Ngern

Memorial
Hotel
■

THANON LAK MUANG

Police Station ■

Burriam ◄

Ubon ►

Artists' Pub ◉

Museum

N

0   100 m

Khorat ▼

THANON THETSABARN

THANON TANNASARN

THANON CHITRAMBOONG

THANON SIRAI

engage in tugs of war and parade in full battle garb. These shows last about three
hours and give both trainers and animals the chance to practise their skills, but
however well controlled the elephants appear, you should always approach them
with caution – when frightened or taunted, the elephants have caused tourist
fatalities. Tickets cost B200 (for a seat with no shade) or B500 (a seat in the shade
plus English commentary); local people offer car-parking facilities in their own
backyards, for which you can expect to pay anything up to B100. If you miss

Silk production

Most hand-woven **Thai silk** is produced by Isaan village women, some of whom oversee every aspect of sericulture, from the breeding of the silkworm through to the dyeing of the fabric. A principal reason for Isaan's pre-eminence in the silk industry is that its soils are particularly suitable for the growth of mulberry trees, the leaves of which are the **silkworms'** favoured diet. The cycle of production begins with the female silk-moth, which lives just a few days but lays around 300–500 microscopic eggs in that time. The eggs take about nine days to hatch into tiny silkworms which are then kept in covered rattan trays and fed on mulberry leaves three or four times a day. The silkworms are such enthusiastic eaters that after three or four weeks they will have grown to about 6cm in length (around ten thousand times their original size), ready for the cocoon-building **pupal** stage.

The silkworm constructs its **cocoon** from a single white or yellow fibre that it secretes from its mouth at a rate of 12cm a minute, sealing the filaments with a gummy substance called sericin. The metamorphosis of the pupa into a moth may take as few as two days or as many as seven, but the sericulturist must anticipate the moment at which the new moth is about to break out of the cocoon, in order to prevent the destruction of the precious fibre – which at this stage is often 900m long. At the crucial point the cocoon is dropped into boiling water, killing the moth (which is often eaten as a snack) and softening the sericin, so that the unbroken filament can be unravelled. The fibres from several cocoons are "reeled" into a single thread, and two or three threads are subsequently twisted or "thrown" into the yarn known as **raw silk** (broken threads from damaged cocoons are worked into a second-rate yarn called "spun silk"). In most cases, the next stage is the "degumming process", in which the raw silk is soaked in soapy water to dissolve the sericin entirely, reducing the weight of the thread by as much as thirty percent and leaving it soft and lustrously semi-transparent.

Extremely absorbent and finely textured, reeled silk is the perfect material for dyeing; most silk producers now use chemical dyes, though traditional vegetable dyes are making a bit of a comeback. Once dyed, the silk is ready for **weaving**. This is generally done during slack agricultural periods, for example just after the rice is planted and again just after it's harvested. Looms are usually set up in the space under the house, in the sheltered area between the piles, and most are designed to produce a sarong length of around 1m x 2m. Isaan weavers have many different weaving techniques and can create countless patterns, ranging from the simplest single-coloured plain weave for work shirts to exquisitely complex wedding sarongs that may take up to six weeks to complete.

the Surin show, you might catch the lesser round-up in Ayutthaya (see p.238) – or better still, take a trip out to Ban Ta Klang.

Practicalities

Ten **trains** a day make the Bangkok–Surin connection, stopping at the **station** on the northern edge of town, less than ten minutes' walk from the central market area on Thanon Krungsrinai. The **bus** terminal is one block east of the train station. Extra trains and buses are laid on to cope with the crowds that flock here for the elephant round-up, and these can be booked through the Bangkok TAT office (see p.98); alternatively you could join one of the overnight packages organized by Bangkok travel agencies (see p.195). The **post and telephone offices** are next to each other at the Thetsabarn 1 roundabout; **internet** access is available at World Net, on the corner of Thanon Thetsabarn and Thanon Thetsabarn 1; and you can change money and withdraw cash from ATMs at several **banks** along Thanon Tannasarn.

One of the best reasons for coming to Surin is to take one of the excellent **local tours** organized from *Pirom's House* (see below). Pirom is a highly informed former social worker who genuinely enjoys conversing with foreigners, and his day-trips give tourists an unusual chance to see glimpses of rural northeastern life as it's really lived. Tours cost from B500 per person; groups should be a minimum of four people and a maximum of eight. Pirom's **village tours** feature visits to local silk weavers and basket-makers, as well as to Ban Ta Klang elephant trainers' village (see opposite), and at time of writing he was planning to introduce three-day trips which will include staying in local villages and will emphasize traditional music, cookery and crafts. His tours to ancient **Khmer ruins** take in prasats Ban Pluang, Bay Kream, Ta Muen Toj, and Ta Muen Tam (see p.484), all of which are close to the Cambodian border and inaccessible to anyone without transport, and he will also take visitors to Phanom Rung and Khao Phra Viharn if requested.

Accommodation

During the elephant round-up, room rates in Surin double, and **accommodation** fills up weeks in advance, so book well ahead and make use of the accommodation-booking websites listed in Basics on p.49. During the rest of the year you'll have no trouble finding a place to stay.

Memorial Hotel, 186 Thanon Lak Muang ☏044/511288. Average mid-range place; some rooms have air-con and TV. ❹–❺

New Hotel, 22 Thanon Tannasarn ☏044/511341, ℗538410, just a few metres from the train station. Clean rooms with fan and shower, plus some with air-con. ❷–❸

Nit Diew Sangthong Hotel, near the post office at 155–161 Thanon Tannasarn ☏044/512099, ℗514329. Friendly, well-run hotel, where the best rooms have air-con and TV. ❷–❸

Phetkasem Hotel, 104 Thanon Chitramboong ☏044/511274, ℗514041, ℮pkhotel@cscoms.com. One of Surin's best hotels, offering sizeable air-con rooms with TV, and a swimming pool. ❹–❻

Pirom's House, 242 Thanon Krungsrinai ☏044/515140, one block west of the market. Pirom and Aree's teak-wood home is one of the friendliest guest houses in Isaan, and almost a reason in itself to stop off in Surin. Rooms have shared facilities, and there's a B70 dorm. As the tenancy on their current home was under threat at

time of writing, Pirom has constructed a new guest house in a peaceful spot surrounded by rice fields off Thanon Tungpo, northwest of the railway tracks. The set-up here is the same as at the original guest house and for the foreseeable future the two guest houses will be running in tandem, though it's probably wise to phone first to check. To get to the new guest house, follow Thanon Tesaban north over the railway tracks, take the first left and then turn left again after about 600m down a track close to the radio mast. ❷

Thong Tarin Hotel, 60 Thanon Sirirat ☏044/514281, ℗511580, ℮thongtarin@isan.sawadee.com. The poshest hotel in town, with upmarket rooms equipped with air-con and TV, plus a swimming pool on the premises. Discounts available outside the festival weekend. ❻–❾

Ubon Hotel, 156 Thanon Tannasarn ☏044/511133. Bottom of the range, and a last resort if all else is booked out, this place has spartan and very basic en-suite rooms with fan or air-con. At least it's close to the train station. ❷–❸

Eating and drinking

For the best in Isaan **food**, head for *Sai Yen* on Thanon Chitramboong, where a constant stream of local office workers and families dine in traditional style, rolling the sticky rice into little balls and dipping them into assorted chilli sauces, *larb* curries and spicy *som tam* salads. Try the (unsigned) *Mai Pag Ngern* restaurant, off the western end of Thanon Krungsrinai, for good food from central Thailand – curries, noodle soups and the like – and inexpensive beer in a garden setting. Surin's lively **night market** on the eastern end of Thanon Krungsrinai is one of Isaan's best, boasting a remarkably large and tasty selection of local food (including roasted crickets and barbecued locusts), as well as a good range of stalls selling clothes and toys. More prosaically, the restaurant and bowling alley in the forecourt of the *Phetkasem Hotel* specializes in ice creams and Western food.

Aspiring local rock **musicians** and their friends hang out in the *Artist's Pub* down a small soi just north of the museum, where the atmosphere is laid-back and welcoming, if not always exactly bustling, and the beer is a bargain. For traditional music, it's worth checking out the *Phetkasem Hotel* bar on a Friday or Saturday evening, as Cambodian ensembles play a regular slot here, performing their particular brand of Khmer folk music known as *kantrum* (see "Music" in Contexts, p.810, for more on this). Not surprisingly, given the ethnic make-up of Surin, there are quite a few *kantrum* bands in the town, and although they don't have fixed venues you could well stumble across a group if you try out two or three local bars of an evening.

Ban Ta Klang

Fifty-eight kilometres north of Surin, the "elephant village" of **BAN TA KLANG** is the main settlement of the Suay people and training centre for their elephants. One out of every two Ta Klang families owns its own elephant, using it as a Western farmer would a tractor, but otherwise treating it as a much-loved pet (see box on p.340 for an introduction to the role of the elephant in Thailand). There are around eighty elephants living in the village, and you can see them honing their skills at the weekly **elephant shows** staged in the village (Sat 9.30am; B100) – miniature, ninety-minute-long versions of the world-famous elephant round-up, held in Surin every year on the third weekend of November (see p.479). Even if you're not in the area on a Saturday, you might want to come to Ban Ta Klang anyway, for a visit to the **Centre for Elephant Studies** (daily 8.30am–4.30pm), which looks at many aspects of elephant life, including the lifestyle of a wild elephant, its anatomy, its historical relationship with humans and the traditional dress and rituals used in sacred elephant ceremonies; you can also sometimes see elephants taking their daily bath in the nearby Mun River. (Every year, on the first weekend of November, the elephants compete in **swimming races**, held further up the Mun in the town of **Satuk**, 30km west of Ta Klang.) The most authentic of the elephant spectacles staged in Ta Klang is the annual **ordination ceremony** held in the village as part of the preparations for the beginning of Khao Pansa (Buddhist Lent). Usually held in May (contact TAT for exact dates), the ceremony involves the young men of the village riding to the temple on ceremonially clad elephants.

Traditionally regarded as the most expert hunters and trainers of elephants in Thailand, the **Suay** tribe migrated to the region from Central Asia before the rise of the Khmers in the ninth century. It was the Suay who masterminded the use of elephants in the construction of the great Khmer temples, and a Suay chief who in 1760 helped recapture a runaway white elephant belonging to the king of Ayutthaya, earning the hereditary title "Lord of Surin". Surin was governed by members of the Suay tribe until Rama V's administrative reforms of 1907.

The role of elephants has diminished with the advent of modern machinery and the 1989 ban on teak logging, but other Asian governments occasionally ask for their help as hauliers, and one of the stranger Thai superstitions provides the Suay with a handy money-spinner. Many Thais believe that it's good luck to walk under an elephant's belly (pregnant women who do so are guaranteed an easy birth), so it's not unheard of for a Suay mahout to walk his elephant the 450km from Surin to Bangkok, charging around B20 per limbo en route. As a mahout and his elephant can earn up to B20,000 a month in this way, there has been a significant exodus from the village to the metropolis in recent years. Local authorities have responded by making a big effort to counter this enticement with more lucrative village-based activities – hence the weekly shows and other events at Ban Ta Klang.

Local **buses** to Ta Klang depart approximately hourly from the Surin terminal and take about two hours. If driving yourself, head north along Highway 214 for 36km, turn left at the village of Ban Nong Tad and continue for 22km until you reach Ban Ta Klang.

Ta Muen Toj, Prasat Ta Muen Tam and Bay Kream

The cluster of Khmer ruins called **Ta Muen Toj**, **Prasat Ta Muen Tam** and **Bay Kream**, close to the Cambodian border east of Surin, are best visited on a tour from *Pirom's House* in Surin (see p.482), for this is not a zone to explore unguided. The two-hour drive to the frontier area passes through several checkpoints along the way, and as the road nears Phanom Dongrek – the mountains that divide Thailand from Cambodia – it runs through villages whose inhabitants live under the daily threat of unexploded landmines whenever they go fishing in remote parts of the river or wood-cutting off the main forest paths. These legacies from the war in Cambodia continue to claim lives and limbs, and there's not a village in this area without its disabled victims, though the pathways to the ruins have of course been cleared.

It's thought that the tiny **Ta Muen Toj** was a resting place for worshippers at the nearby **Prasat Ta Muen Tam**, a walled temple compound in the clutches of enormous trees – a testament to the age of the place and to the durability of the materials with which the temple was built. A kilometre or so further, **Bay Kream** stands on a mound, like an island in the suffocating jungle. This is the largest and the most recognizable of the three sites, with carved lintels and large stone blocks strewn between the dilapidated walls; piled-up earth now fills many of the rooms to ceiling height and the window frames have subsided beneath ground level, giving the whole complex a wonderful air of decomposition. Beyond Bay Kream, the unconquered Cambodian jungle stretches to the horizon.

Khao Phra Viharn, Si Saket and Kantharalak

Perched atop a 547-metre-high spur of the Dongkrek mountains on the Thai–Cambodian border, about 140km southwest of Ubon and 220km southeast of Surin, the ninth- to twelfth-century Khmer ruins of **KHAO PHRA VIHARN** (also known as Preah Vihear) surpass even the spectacularly set Phanom Rung. A magnificent avenue over 500m long rises to the clifftop sanctuary, from where you get breathtaking views over the jungle-clad hills of Cambodia. The temple buildings themselves, built of grey and yellow sandstone, retain some fine original carvings and have been sufficiently restored to give a good idea of their original structure. Constructed over a three-hundred-year period, Khao Phra Viharn was dedicated to the Hindu god Shiva and is thought to have served both as a retreat for Hindu priests – hence the isolated site – and an object of pilgrimage, with the difficulty of getting there an extra challenge for devotees. The large complex would have also been inhabited by a big cast of supporting villagers who took care of the priests and the pilgrims – hence the presence of several large reservoirs on the site.

An added attraction for modern-day tourists is that the whole complex was only reopened to visitors in 1998, following almost a century of **territorial dispute** between Thailand and Cambodia over who owned the site. The situation was further complicated by Cambodia's civil war, with the Khmer Rouge taking control of the temple in 1975 and laying mines around it, making the temple far too dangerous to visit. Although the ruins have now been de-mined, there are skull-and-cross-bones signs in the vicinity which should be heeded. It's now accepted that the central sanctuary of the Khao Phra Viharn complex stands on Cambodian land, but the temple is only accessible by the cliffside-staircase, which starts just inside Thailand's southern border. For the tourist, this dual ownership means having to pay twice to get into the ruins: there's a B200 National Park **entry fee** payable to the Thai authorities about 12km north of the temple car park, at the barrier near the Ban Phum Saron junction (where you have to relinquish your passport); and another B200 entry fee at the base of the temple steps, which goes to the Cambodians. In addition to the expense involved, Khao Phra Viharn is very difficult to get to without your own **transport** (see Practicalities, p.486) – and when you do get there you have to contend with large crowds of tourists and a big gaggle of very persistent hawkers. But, if you can ignore the hassle, the ruins are worth the effort.

The temple car park is lined with souvenir stalls and a score of cheap restaurant shacks. From here it's about 1km to the base of the temple steps – if you can't face the walk, wait for the **shuttle-bus** which ferries people to and fro continuously throughout the day for B5. En route you'll pass the beginning of the path up to the **Pha Mo I Daeng viewpoint**, from where you get a good view of the temple cliff and can just about make out the Khao Phra Viharn complex on its summit. There's not much information on the temple available at the site, so if you have a serious interest in the ruins, buy a copy of the excellent *Preah Vihear* **guidebook** before you come; published by River Books, it's available from most Bangkok bookshops. For a brief guide to the main architectural features and symbolism of Khmer ruins in Thailand see box on p.473.

The ruins

The approach to the **temple complex** (daily from 8.30am; last entry 3.30pm; total entry fee B400) begins with a steep stairway and continues up the cliff-face via a series of pillared causeways, small terraces with naga balustrades and four cruciform-shaped **gopura** (pavilions), each built with doorways at the cardinal points, and decorated with carved reliefs of tales from Hindu mythology. Beyond the first gopura, as you walk along the first of the pillared causeways, you'll see to the left (east) one of the temple's biggest **reservoirs**, a large stone-lined tank sunk into the cliff and guarded by statues of lions.

As you pass through the last, southernmost, doorway of the second gopura, look back at the door to admire the pediment carving which depicts the

Hindu creation myth, the **Churning of the Sea of Milk**, in which Vishnu appears in his tortoise incarnation and, along with a naga and a sacred mountain (here symbolized by the churning stick), helps churn the cosmic ocean and thereby create the universes, as well as the sacred nectar of immortality; see p.775 for the full story. The third gopura is much larger than the others and is extended by east and west wings. Its central doorways are all decorated with clearly discernible carvings; a particularly eye-catching one above the outside of the northern doorway shows an episode from the Hindu epic the *Mahabarata*, in which the god **Shiva fights with the heroic Arjuna** over who gets the credit for the killing of a wild boar – in fact the carving here looks as if they are enjoying an affectionate embrace. A causeway flanked with two naga balustrades links the third gopura to the fourth; the buildings on either side of the fourth gopura are thought to have been libraries.

The ascent up the cliff-face finally reaches its climax at the **central sanctuary**, built on the summit and enclosed within a courtyard whose impressive colonnaded galleries are punctuated by windows to the east and west. Cambodian monks tend the modern Buddha image inside the sanctuary, keeping a fire burning and selling offertory garlands and incense to tourists. The pediment above the northern entrance to this shrine is carved with an image of the multi-armed **dancing Shiva**, whose ecstatic dance brings about the destruction of the existing world and the beginning of a new epoch (see p.775). Climb through one of the gallery windows to walk across to the cliff edge, from where you get far-reaching views of Cambodia, and can appreciate just how isolated the temple must have been. A look back at the temple complex shows that though the sanctuary's southernmost wall is punctuated by a couple of beautifully carved false doors, there are no genuine south-facing doors or windows – experts assume that this was a deliberate design feature to stop priests being distracted by the cliff-top panorama.

Practicalities: Kantharalak and Si Saket

Khao Phra Viharn is not served by public **transport**, so by far the easiest way of getting to the ruins is to hire a car (with or without driver) or motorbike from Ubon Ratchathani (see p.491), Surin (see p.479) or Si Saket, all of which towns have a decent range of hotels and good long-distance transport connections. Alternatively, you could take a motorcycle taxi to the temple from the nearest sizeable town to Khao Phra Viharn, Kantharalak, or from the road junction and national park barriers at Ban Phum Saron.

Kantharalak

KANTHARALAK is located just off the Khao Phra Viharn–Si Saket road (Highway 221), 36km north of the temple. There is an hourly **bus** service here from Ubon Ratchathani (1hr 30min), which departs from a terminus just across the Mun River in the Warinchamrab suburb of Ubon, and a half-hourly service here from Si Saket; buses arrive at Kantharalak bus station, 50m from the market on the main street.

There is no **songthaew** service from Kantharalak to the temple, but occasional songthaews do connect Kantharalak with **Ban Phum Saron**, the junction near the national-park barrier 12km north of Khao Phra Viharn, from where you can get a **motorcycle taxi** to the temple; you can also get a motorcycle taxi all the way from Kantharalak to Khao Phra Viharn (about B100 each way).

Kantharalak is a two-street town, with the best of the budget **hotels**, the *Kantharalak Hotel* (☏045/661085; ❸), situated on the main street at no.131/35–36, about 1km off Highway 221; its rooms, scruffy but serviceable, are set back off the road, all with en-suite bathrooms and TV, some with air-conditioning.

Si Saket

The quiet provincial capital of **SI SAKET** is a more enjoyable place to base yourself than Kantharalak, with a better choice of hotels, a good night market, a tourist office, train connections from Bangkok, Surin and Ubon, and bus links with Ubon, Phibun Mangsahan, Chong Mek, Surin and Bangkok; however, it is 98km from Khao Phra Viharn. Si Saket **train station** is in the centre of the town, at the southern end of Thanon Si Saket; Thanon Ratchakan Rot Fai 3 runs parallel to and to the south of the railway tracks and the station building. The **bus station** is in the southern part of town, two blocks south of the *Kessiri Hotel* and one block west, just off Thanon Chotiphan; there are no buses from here to Khao Phra Viharn, so you have to get the #523 to Kantharalak (hourly; 2hr) and make onward arrangements from there.

Si Saket sees very few tourists, but there is a **Tourism Co-ordination Centre** (Mon–Fri 8.30am–4.30pm; ☏045/611574), in front of the Provincial Hall at the junction of Thanon Lak Muang and Thanon Thay Pha. Staff here can arrange a **car and driver** to take you to Khao Phra Viharn and other nearby ruins (approximately B1200/day). About 50m east of the Tourism Centre, on Thanon Thay Pha is a **post office** and, just east of that, an **internet** centre.

There are three reasonable **hotels** within easy walking distance of the train station. The *Si Saket Hotel* (☏045/611846; ❷), one block directly north of the station at 384/5 Thanon Si Saket, offers basic en-suite rooms; at the slightly better *Phrompinan* (☏045/612677, ☏612696; ❸–❹), located at 849/1 Thanon

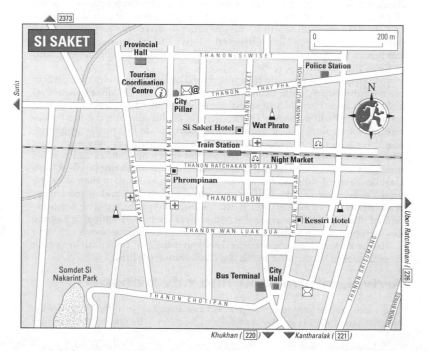

Lak Muang, the ground-floor fan rooms are grotty and to be avoided, though the upstairs air-con ones are much more comfortable and reasonable value – to get there, exit the station via the southern exit and walk right (west) along Thanon Ratchakan Rot Fai 3 as far as the junction with Thanon Lak Muang. If instead you turn left (east) outside the station's southern exit, along Thanon Ratchakan Rot Fai 3, and then right (south) down Thanon Kukhan, after a couple of blocks you'll come to the *Kessiri Hotel*, 1102–5 Thanon Kukhan (T045/614007, F614008; ❺); it's the most comfortable place in town, with good rooms, all furnished with TV and air-con, and there's a restaurant downstairs. The best place to **eat** in town is the unusually diverse night market, which sets up around a small plaza along the southern edge of the rail line on Thanon Ratchakan Rot Fai 3, just west of Thanon Kukhan. Otherwise there are half-a-dozen small Thai-Chinese restaurants on Thanon Kukhan, between the *Kessiri Hotel* and the rail line; along this road you'll also find several handicraft shops selling locally produced lengths of silk and triangular "axe"-cushions.

Ubon Ratchathani

East of Surin, Highway 226 and the rail line run in tandem through desiccated, impoverished plains before coming to a halt at **UBON RATCHATHANI** (Royal City of the Lotus), a provincial capital which, despite its name, is of neither regal nor botanical distinction. Almost always referred to simply as Ubon – not to be confused with Udon (Udon Thani) to the north – Thailand's fifth-largest city holds little in the way of atmosphere or attraction beyond a couple of wats, a decent museum and a lingering hangover from its days as a US airbase site. It's only really worth visiting in order to make trips out: eastwards to the small town of Kong Chiam beside the River Mekhong (see p.494) and the Lao border market at Chong Mek (see p.497), or southwest to the Khmer ruins of Khao Phra Viharn (see p.484).

If you're near Ubon in early July, you should definitely consider coming into town for the local **Asanha Puja** festivities, an auspicious Buddhist holiday celebrated all over Thailand to mark the beginning of Khao Pansa, the annual three-month Buddhist retreat. Ubon's version of this festival is the most spectacular in the country: local people make huge wooden or plaster sculptures, coat them in orange beeswax and then carve intricate decorations in the wax. The sculptures are mounted on floats around enormous candles and paraded through the town – hence the tourist name for the celebrations, the **Ubon Candle Festival** – before being presented to various wats; in most wats the candle is kept burning throughout the retreat period. The end of the retreat, **Awk Pansa** (early to mid-Oct), is also exuberantly celebrated with a procession of illuminated boats along the Mun River, each representing one of the city's temples, as well as parades, market stalls and *likay* theatre shows in Thung Si Muang Park, and lots of fireworks throughout the city. Traditional long-boat races are staged on the river in the days following Awk Pansa.

Arrival, information and city transport

The most painless way to get to Ubon from Bangkok is to fly: Thai Airways operates two **flights** a day between Ubon and Bangkok; the **airport**

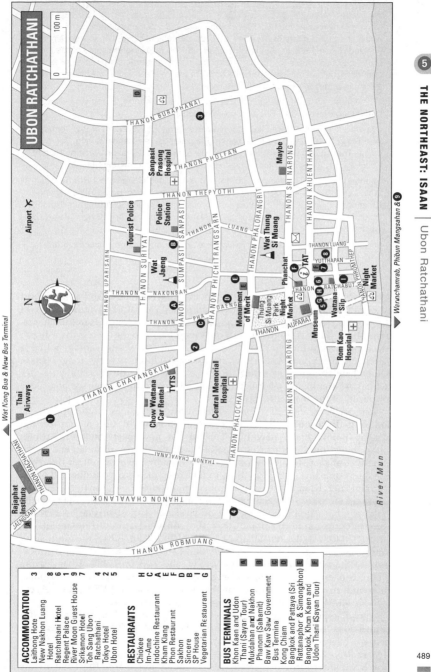

UBON RATCHATHANI

Airport ✈

Thai Airways ❶

◀ Wat Nong Bua & New Bus Terminal

Rajaphat Institute Ⓐ

THANON CHAYANGKUN

Chow Wattana Car Rental
TYTS

THANON CHAYANGKUN

THANON CHAVALOK

Central Memorial Hospital ✚

THANON PHALOCHAI

❹

THANON ROBMUANG

THANON UPARISARN

Tourist Police

Wat Jaeng

THANON SURIYAT

THANON NAKONBAN

THANON
Ⓐ

❷ Ⓒ

THANON PHA

THANON DAENG Ⓓ

THANON PHICHITRANGSARN

Monument of Merit Ⓔ

THANON AUPARAT

Museum

Rom Kao Hospital ✚

THANON SRI NARONG

THANON SRI NARONG

Sanpasit Prasong Hospital ✚

THANON PHOLFAN

Police Station Ⓑ

SANPASIT

THANON SUMPASIT

THANON LUANG

THANON THEPYOTHI

Wat Thung Si Muang ⛩

Thung Si Muang Park

Phanchat

Night Market

Ⓕ TAT ℹ

Wattana Silp

❺ Ⓖ Ⓗ

RATCHABUT

THANON PHROMTHEP

❼ ❽

YUTTHAPAN

THANON LUANG

Night Market

THANON SRI NARONG

THANON BURAPHANAI

Ⓓ

Maybe

THANON SRI NARONG

THANON PHALORANGRIT

THANON KHUENTHANI

❾

❻

Ⓘ

River Mun

▶ Warinchamrab, Phibun Mangsahan & ❾

N

0   100 m

ACCOMMODATION

Laithong Hote	3
New Nakhon Luang Hotel	8
Ratchathani Hotel	6
Regent Palace	1
River Moon Guest House	9
Srikamon Hotel	7
Toh Sang Ubon Ratchathani	4
Tokyo Hotel	2
Ubon Hotel	5

RESTAURANTS

Chiokee	H
Im-Ame	C
Indochine Restaurant	A
Kham Kiang	E
Phon Restaurant	F
Sakhon	D
Sincere	B
SP House	I
Vegetarian Restaurant	G

BUS TERMINALS

Khon Kaen and Udon Thani (Sayar Tour)	Ⓐ
Mukdahan and Nakhon Phanom (Sahamit)	Ⓑ
Baw Kaw Saw Government Bus Termina	Ⓒ
Kong Chiam	Ⓓ
Bangkok and Pattaya (Sri Rattanaphor & Simongkhon)	Ⓔ
Bangkok, Khon Kaen and Udon Thani (Sayan Tour)	Ⓕ

⑤

City bus routes

Ubon is fairly well served by a fleet of numbered and differently coloured city buses, which charge a flat fare of B5. They are especially useful for getting to the train station and regional bus depots in Warinchamrab. The following are some of the most useful city bus routes for hotels, sights and transport terminals – not all pass the front door, but should leave you with no more than a five-minute walk; buses cover the same routes in reverse on the return leg.

#1 (white): Thanon Jaengsanit–Thanon Sumpasit–Thanon Buraphanai–Thanon Phromthep–Nakorn Chai Bus Terminal–Warinchamrab.

#2 (white): Thanon Chayangkun (for New Bus Terminal, Government Bus Terminal, Wat Nong Bua, *Tokyo Hotel*)–Thanon Phichitrangsarn–Thanon Luang (for post office)–Thanon Khuenthani (for TAT, hotels & museum)–Thanon Auparat–Nakorn Chai Bus Terminal–*River Moon Guest House* –Warinchamrab Train Station.

#3 (pink): Thanon Chayangkun (for New Bus Terminal, Government Bus Terminal, Wat Nong Bua)–Thanon Sumpasit–Thanon Luang (for post office)–Thanon Khuenthani (for TAT, hotels & museum)–Thanon Yutthapun–Thanon Phromthep–Nakorn Chai Bus Terminal–Talat Warinchamrab (for Kong Chiam and Chong Mek buses).

#6 (pink): Thanon Auparat (for *Tokyo Hotel*, museum, Thanon Khuenthani hotels, TAT)–Nakorn Chai Bus Terminal–Warinchamrab.

(☎045/244073) is just north of the town centre. A cheaper and arguably just as enjoyable way of travelling here from the capital (and most places in between) is to come by **train** – the line terminates at Ubon Ratchathani station (☎045/321004) in the suburb of **Warinchamrab**, just across the sluggish Maenam Mun. White city bus #2 meets all trains at Warinchamrab and takes passengers north across the river into central Ubon, passing along Thanon Khuenthani, location of several hotels and the TAT office. City buses #1 (white), #3 (pink) and #6 (pink) also cross the river into Ubon; see box above for details of the main city bus routes.

There are currently half a dozen different **bus** companies running provincial and **long-distance services** in and out of Ubon, with as many drop-off and pick-up points, but a new **bus station** has now been built on Thanon Chayangkun, on the northwest edge of town, which may mean an end to the current confusion. In the meantime, services run by the government Baw Kaw Saw bus company (☎045/241831; to and from Bangkok, Yasothon, Roi-Et, Buriram and Khorat) use the terminal in the north of town off Thanon Chayangkun (served by city buses #2 and #3), while those operated by Nakorn Chai (☎045/269385), one of Thailand's largest private air-con bus companies (to and from Khorat, Surin, Buriram, Chaiyaphum, Phitsanulok and Chiang Mai), use the terminal just south of the Mun River, on the road to Warinchamrab, which is served by city buses #1, #2, #3 and #6. For the locations of the other bus company depots, see the map on p.489. When leaving Ubon, you can only buy air-con bus **tickets** from the appropriate terminal; train and air tickets, however, can be bought through TYTS Travel Agent (☎045/246043) on Thanon Chayangkun in the city centre.

Regular **local buses** and songthaews to and from Phibun Mangsahan (for connections to Kong Chiam and Chong Mek) and Si Saket use the terminal near the Talat Kao marketplace in Warinchamrab, southeast of the river; city bus #3 can drop you within five minutes' walk of Talat Kao. Buses to Kantharalak (for Khao Phra Viharn) leave from a terminus just across the Mun in the

Warinchamrab suburb of Ubon, served by city buses, #1, #2, #3 and #6. If you're thinking of going out to Kong Chiam and the cliff paintings (see p.494), then consider renting a **motorbike** (B200–500 per day) or **car** (B1200 per day with or without a driver) from Chow Wattana (☎045/242202) at 39/8 Thanon Suriyat, opposite Nikko Massage.

Staff at the **TAT office** on Thanon Khuenthani (daily 8.30am–4.30pm; ☎045/243770) can help you out with specific queries on all bus and train departures.

Accommodation

Ubon's choice of **hotels** is fair enough, but as there's not much of a travellers' scene in the city there's just one guest house, south of the river in Warinchamrab; instead, the emphasis is on mid-range accommodation.

Laithong Hotel, 50 Thanon Pichitrangsarn ☎045/264271, ℗264270. Fairly central top-notch hotel with well-furnished air-con rooms, a sizeable pool, and Thai and Chinese restaurants. ❻–❼

New Nakhon Luang Hotel, 84–88 Thanon Yutthapan ☎045/254768, ℗246075. Central budget hotel with clean, slightly scruffy rooms, either fan-cooled or air-con. ❷–❸

Ratchathani Hotel, 229 Thanon Khuenthani ☎045/254599, ℗243561. Very central and popular city hotel, offering reasonable value fan and air-con rooms, all with hot water and TV, if rather spartan furnishings. ❸–❹

Regent Palace, 256 Thanon Chayangkun ☎045/245046, ℗245597. Fairly smart rooms on the northern edge of town, all with air-con and hot water. ❻–❾

River Moon Guest House, 43–45 Thanon Si Saket 2, Warinchamrab ☎045/322592. Just a few hundred metres from the train station, and clearly signed, this is a good budget option, a friendly, traveller-oriented place with clean, simple rooms in a traditional wooden house. ❷

Srikamon Hotel, 22 Thanon Ubonsak ☎045/241136, ℗243792. Comfortable air-con rooms right in the heart of downtown Ubon; a good mid-range option. ❹–❺

Toh Sang Ubon Ratchathani, 251 Thanon Phalochai ☎045/241925, ℗244814, ⓦwww.tohsang.com. Smart, comfortable and well-maintained rooms make this the best value in the top bracket, especially as significant discounts are usually available. Located a little way from the centre, on the west edge of town. ❼–❽

Tokyo Hotel, 178 Thanon Auparat ☎045/241739, ℗263140. About a 5min walk north of the museum, this is the best and friendliest of central Ubon's budget hotels. Fan and air-con rooms in the old block are adequate if a little shabby, while those in the new wing are nicer and come with TV at the top of the range. ❸–❺

Ubon Hotel, 333 Thanon Khuenthani ☎045/241045, ℗262017. Centrally located place offering unremarkable but decent enough rooms with fan or air-con. ❹

The City

Aside from its confusing number of arrival points, central Ubon is easy enough to negotiate. The main accommodation and eating area is confined to a fairly compact area between Thanon Sumpasit in the north and the Maenam Mun in the south. Of the city's eight main wats, **Wat Thung Si Muang**, in the middle of this zone near the post office, is the most noteworthy, mainly for its unusually well-preserved teak library – raised on stilts over an artificial pond to keep book-devouring insects at bay. The murals in the bot, to the left of the library, have also survived remarkably well: the lively scenes of everyday life in the nineteenth century include musicians playing *khaen* pipes and devotees performing characteristic Isaan merit-making dances, as well as conventional portraits of city life in Bangkok.

Off Thanon Chayangkun at the northern edge of town, the much more modern **Wat Nong Bua** (city bus #2 or #3) is modelled on the stupa at Bodh Gaya in India, scene of the Buddha's enlightenment; the whitewashed replica is carved with scenes from the *Jataka* and contains a scaled-down version of the stupa covered in gold leaf. Of more interest, especially if you don't happen to be here during the candle festival, is the wax float kept in a small building behind the chedi.

For an overview of all things to do with southern Isaan, pay a visit to the **museum** (Wed–Sun 8.30am–4.30pm; B10), housed in the blue and grey building opposite the *Ubon Hotel* on Thanon Khuenthani. This is a real something-for-everyone offering, with thematic displays on the region's geology, ancient history, folk crafts, musical instruments and more, most with informative descriptions in English. Particularly worth looking out for are a ninth-century Khmer statue of Ganesh, examples of the star-embroidered fabric that is a speciality of Ubon and a pre-fourth-century bronze bell and ceremonial drum found in the vicinity. Also on show is a serviceable reproduction of the Pha Taem cliff-paintings – much easier to get to than the originals, though hardly as atmospheric.

Silk, cotton and silverware are all good buys in Ubon. Several shops along Thanon Khuenthani specialize in reasonably priced clothes made from the stripey rough **cotton** weaves peculiar to the Ubon area, but by far the biggest selection is at Maybe, on the eastern end of Thanon Sri Narong. The **silver handicrafts** shop Wattana Silp on Thanon Ratchabut (just north of the *SP House* restaurant near the riverside night market) has a good selection of Lao-style silver filigree belts and accessories, as well as lots of other jewellery. The best place for **northeastern crafts** is Phanchat, which has two branches along Thanon Ratchabut (50m east of the museum, off Thanon Khuenthani). The larger branch, unsigned in English, stands next to a motorbike showroom at no. 158, between the park and Thanon Khuenthani; the smaller branch is off the south side of Thanon Khuenthani. Both shops specialize in fine-quality regional goods, like triangular "axe" pillows (*mawn khwaan*) as well as lengths of **silk** and clothes made to local designs, and also stock antique farm and household implements.

Eating

Ubon is a good place for sampling local Isaan specialities, which you can enjoy either in air-conditioned comfort at one of the restaurants listed below, or at one of the city's **night markets**. The largest and liveliest of these markets sets up on the north bank of the Mun River and serves especially good *hawy thawt*. There are smaller night markets on Thanon Ratchabut (north off Thanon Khuenthani), and on the sidewalk next to the *Tokyo Hotel*.

Chiokee, between the *Ubon* and *Ratchathani* hotels on Thanon Khuenthani. Friendly, café-style place serving a large menu of Thai and Western staples. Especially popular at breakfast time, when farangs come for the ham and eggs, local office workers for rice gruel. Inexpensive.

Im-Ame, Thanon Pha Daeng (no English sign). Smart air-con place that's renowned for its Isaan specialities, and also serves dishes from other parts of Thailand. Moderate.

Indochine Restaurant, 12/10 Thanon Sumpasit, just west of Wat Jaeng (no English sign, but easily recognizable by the photos of speciality dishes on the walls). One of Ubon's more interesting eating experiences, with a good menu of mainly Vietnamese food, much of it based around stuffed rice-noodle pancakes with spicy sauces and lashings of fresh mint. Closes at 6pm. Moderate.

Kham Klang, Thanon Nakonban. Atmospheric garden restaurant whose predominantly northeastern menu is popular with Ubon residents. Moderate.

Phon Restaurant, round the corner from TAT (no English sign). Air-con Thai and Chinese restaurant whose ribs in black-bean sauce are well worth sampling. Moderate.

Sakhon, Thanon Pha Daeng. Another of Ubon's top northeastern restaurants, particularly recommended for its more unusual dishes, like *tom yam* with fish eggs and red ant eggs. Moderate.

Sincere, Thanon Sumpasit, between the police station and Wat Jaeng. Highly regarded, predominantly French menu, with an emphasis on steaks and classic sauces. Closed Sun. Expensive.

SP House, southern leg of Thanon Ratchabut, near the night market and the river. The place to come for coffee, cakes and ice-cream sundaes. Moderate.

Vegetarian Restaurant, in front of the *Ubon Hotel* on Thanon Khuenthani. Tiny workaday meat-free café serving mainly *kap khao* ("with rice") dishes made with soya chunks. Shuts about 6pm. Inexpensive.

Listings

Airline The Thai Airways office is at 364 Thanon Chayangkun ☎045/313340, in the north part of town.

Airport Call ☎045/244073 for arrivals and departures information.

Exchange At several banks and ATMs, including next to TAT on Thanon Khuenthani and on Thanon Ratchabut.

Hospitals Phyathai Ubon Hospital, north of the city at 512/3 Thanon Chayangkun ☎045/879030; more central is Rom Kao Hospital, near the bridge on Thanon Auparat.

Immigration office In the town of Phibun Mangsahan (see below), 45km to the east; if you're travelling to Laos via Chong Mek (see

p.497) it's a wise precaution to come to this immigration office (Mon–Fri 8.30am–4.30pm; ☎045/441108) for a Thai exit stamp, as travellers without exit stamps have been known to get turned back at the border.

Internet access At the CAT telephone office, next to the GPO on the Thanon Srinarong/Thanon Luang intersection.

Mail The GPO is centrally located at the Thanon Srinarong/Thanon Luang intersection.

Telephones The CAT telephone office is next to the GPO on the Thanon Srinarong Thanon Luang intersection.

Tourist police On Thanon Suriyat ☎045/245505.

Around Ubon

On the whole, the area **around Ubon** is a good deal more interesting than the metropolitan hub, particularly if you venture eastwards towards **Kaeng Tana National Park**, the appealing Mekhong riverside town of **Kong Chiam**, the prehistoric paintings at **Pha Taem** and the Lao border market at **Chong Mek.** Nearly all the routes detailed on the following pages can be done as a day-trip from Ubon – most comfortably with your own transport, but manageable on buses and songthaews if you set off very early in the morning – though there's a lot to be said for taking things more slowly and spending a night or two in the rural reaches of Ubon Ratchathani province. Another interesting outing from Ubon would be to head southwestwards to the hilltop Khmer temple of Khao Phra Viharn that straddles the Cambodian border (see p.484).

Phibun Mangsahan

There are several routes east out of Ubon, but they nearly all begin with Highway 217, which starts in Ubon's southern suburb of Warinchamrab and then follows the Mun River eastwards for 45km before splitting into two at the town of **PHIBUN MANGSAHAN**. From here, Highway 217 continues in a southeasterly direction to the border at Chong Mek, passing through Kaeng Tana National Park, while the northeasterly fork out of Phibun, called Route 2222, follows the course of the Mun to its confluence with the Mekhong at Kong Chiam.

Sited at a turbulent point of the Mun called Kaeng Saphue (*kaeng* means rapids), there's little more to Phibun Mangsahan (known locally as Phibun) than a chaotic central bus station and a sprawling market that caters for the riverine catchment area, but for travellers it's an inevitable interchange on any eastbound journey. In April, Ubon celebrates the Thai New Year festival of Songkhran by staging performances of Isaan folk music and dance beside the Kaeng Saphue rapids; these **Maha Songkhran** festivities run from April 12 to 15. Phibun's one exceptional sight, **Wat Phokakaew**, stands on the western outskirts of town, 1km from the town limit, and is signposted off Highway 217. An unusually attractive modern temple, it's worth a look for its exceptionally elegant proportions, eye-catchingly tiled exterior and fine naga–encircled platform from which you can see the hills of Laos on the horizon. The wat's interior walls are decorated with reliefs of twelve of Thailand's most revered temples, including the Golden Mount in Bangkok and Nakhon Pathom's monumental chedi. The space under the temple has been converted into a serene meditation hall.

To get to Phibun from Ubon, first take **city bus** #1, #3 or #6 across the river to the Warinchamrab bus station near Talat Kao, and then change onto a **local bus** bound for Phibun (every 10min until 4.30pm). These terminate in Phibun's town centre, from where it's a ten-minute walk or short tuk-tuk ride through town to the songthaew stop beside the Kaeng Saphue bridge, the departure point for transport to Kong Chiam and Chong Mek.

Kong Chiam and the Pha Taem paintings

Thirty kilometres northeast of Phibun, along Route 2222 (or 75km from Ubon), the riverside village of **KONG CHIAM** is a popular destination for day-tripping Thais, who drive out here to see the somewhat fancifully named "two-coloured river" for which the village is nationally renowned. Created by the merging of the muddy brown Mun with the muddy brown Mekhong at "the easternmost point of Thailand", the water is hardly an irresistible attraction, but the village has a certain appeal and makes a very pleasant stopover point. Comprising little more than a collection of wooden houses, the requisite post office, school and police station, a few guest houses, several restaurants and two wats, Kong Chiam feels like an island, with the Mun defining its southern limit and the Mekhong its northern edge. A paved walkway runs several hundred metres along the banks of the Mekhong, beginning in front of the District Office and running down to the large *sala* which is built right over the confluence and affords uninterrupted views. Behind the *sala*, **Wat Kong Chiam** is the more charming of the village's two temples and has an old wooden bell tower in its compound; the cliffside **Wat Tham Khu Ha Sawan**, located near the point where Route 2222 turns into Kong Chiam, is unprepossessing, with a huge modern Buddha image staring down on the villagers below.

Kong Chiam's sights are thin on the ground, but you can rent motorbikes from *Apple Guest House* (see opposite) and explore the area, or charter a **longtail boat** for a trip up the Mekhong River, taking in the Pha Taem cliff-paintings on the way. Even though Laos is just a few hundred metres away from Kong Chiam, on the other bank of the Mekhong, foreigners are not allowed to cross the border here – for this you must go downstream to Chong Mek (see p.497).

Pha Taem cliff-paintings

The most popular outing from Kong Chiam is a visit to the **Pha Taem paintings** (daily 6am–6pm; B200), which cover a 170-metre stretch of cliff-face 18km up the Mekhong. Clear proof of the antiquity of the fertile Mekhong valley, these bold, childlike paintings are believed to be between 3000 and 4000 years old, the work of rice-cultivating settlers who lived in huts rather than caves. Protected from the elements by an overhang, the red paint – a mixture of soil, tree gum and fat – has kept its colour so well that the shapes and figures are still clearly discernible; human forms, handprints and geometric designs appear in groups alongside massive depictions of animals and enormous fish – possibly the prized catfish still caught in the Mekhong.

Pha Taem (Taem Cliff) is clearly signposted from Kong Chiam, but try to avoid coming here on a weekend when the place gets swamped with scores of tour buses. If you're lucky, you might get a ride on one of the infrequent Ubon-bound buses as far as the Pha Taem turn-off, from where you can try and hitch the rest of the way (about 8km), but otherwise, unless you rent a motorbike, you'll have to hitch all the way or charter a tuk-tuk or taxi from the village – ask at *Apple Guest House* for advice. The road passes a group of weird, mushroom-shaped sandstone rock formations known as **Sao Chaliang** before reaching the Pha Taem car park on top of the cliff. There are foodstalls and a visitor centre here, where you have to pay the B200 national park entry fee. From the car park, follow the path that's signed "Pha Taem Loop 3km", which runs down the cliff-face and along the shelf in the rock to the paintings. If you continue along the path past the paintings, you'll eventually climb back up to the top of the cliff again, via the **viewpoint** at Pha Mon, taking in fine views of the fertile Mekhong valley floor and glimpses of hilly western Laos. It's about 1700m from Pha Mon back to the car park, along a signed trail across the rocky scrub.

Practicalities

Kong Chiam-bound **songthaews** leave Phibun Mangsahan's Kaeng Saphue bridge every half-hour throughout the morning and then hourly until 4.30pm, and take sixty to ninety minutes. A few **buses** go directly from Ubon to Kong Chiam, leaving in the morning from a spot on the eastern end of Ubon's Thanon Suriyat, but these are painfully slow, taking a convoluted back-road route and stopping for long breaks along the way. Songthaews and buses terminate at the Kong Chiam **bus station** at the west end of Thanon Kaewpradit, a few hundred metres' walk from *Apple Guest House*. If you have your own transport, Kong Chiam combines well with visits to Chong Mek and Kaeng Tana National Park; *Apple* rents motorbikes for B150 per day.

Accommodation

Kong Chiam has a nice range of reasonably priced guest houses and "resorts", which is a good incentive to stay over in this pleasant, slow-paced village.

Apple Guest House, opposite the post office on Thanon Kaewpradit ☎045/351160. About 5min walk from the bus station and the Mekhong. The most traveller-oriented place to stay in Kong Chiam, this is a convivial set-up with good, clean, en-suite rooms set around a garden, as well as a restaurant, motorbike rental and a useful notice-board. The pricier rooms have air-con. ❷–❸

Araya Resort, towards the eastern end of Thanon Phukamchai ☏045/351191, 10min walk from the bus station. Good-value set of steeply roofed, whitewashed, chalet-style bungalows, built around a garden with several ponds; the rooms are comfortable and have air-con, hot water and TV. **④**

Ban Rim Khong Resort, 37 Thanon Kaewpradit ☏045/351101. Also has another entrance one block north on the road in front of the Mekhong River, between the district office and the wat. Great-looking little resort with half a dozen timbered chalets wreathed in bougainvillea and ranged round a lawn, plus a couple with uninterrupted views of the Mekhong. The actual rooms are disappointingly scruffy, but have air-con, TV and fridge. Discounts for stays of more than one night. **⑥**

Kong Chiam Guest House, Thanon Phukamchai ☏045/351074. One block southeast of the bus station. Priced the same as *Apple* and of a similar standard, though not quite so appealing or traveller-oriented; fine as a second choice. All rooms are en-suite and some have air-con. **②–③**

Toh Sang Kong Chiam, on the south bank of the Mun ☏045/351174, ℗351162, ⓦwww.tohsang.com. A 5min taxi-boat ride across from Kong Chiam or a 25km drive via the Pak Mun Dam (see box opposite). Romantically located upmarket resort where all rooms have balconies overlooking the river and are very comfortably, if a little kitschly furnished. There's a swimming pool, table-tennis room and mini-gym, plus a couple of restaurants and boat trips to Pha Taem and other riverine sights. Well-priced, but you're a bit stuck without your own transport, though boats to Kong Chiam can be arranged through the hotel: to get here by road, take the Pak Mun (dam) road 2173 from either Phibun, Chong Mek or Kong Chiam and turn off it at kilometre-stone 7, following signs for Ban Woen Buk. **⑦–⑧**

Eating

The most popular places to eat are, not surprisingly, the two **floating restaurants** moored on the Mekhong in front of the district office. Both serve fairly pricey menus of Thai-Chinese dishes and of course plenty of fish. Be sure to ask if they have any *pla buk*, the giant catfish which is very much a local speciality (see box on p.394). There are a string of cheaper, less flashy little restaurants on the bank behind the floating restaurants, along with a few food vendors offering sweet potatoes, grilled bananas and fried chicken.

Kaeng Tana National Park and the Pak Mun dam

Nine kilometres east out of Phibun, Route 2172 forks off the main Highway 217 and heads straight to the so-called **Emerald Triangle**, the spot where Thailand, Laos and Cambodia meet (the name echoes the more famous border area in north Thailand, the Golden Triangle, where Thailand, Laos and Burma meet). A further 10km along Highway 217, the road begins to run alongside one of the largest reservoirs in Isaan (measuring some 43km north to south), held back by the **Sirindhorn dam**, and dotted with permanent fishing-net platforms. Thirty-two kilometres from Phibun, Route 2296 veers north off Highway 217 to take traffic across the Mun River via the controversial **Pak Mun dam** (see box opposite) and on to Kong Chiam, while Highway 217 continues east to Chong Mek and the Lao border (see below).

Kaeng Tana National Park (☏045/243120) is signed off Route 2296 (the dam road), and you pay the B200 national park entry fee at the barrier close to the junction. Although the park offers only a couple of short trails (starting from the headquarters), through predominantly scrubby vegetation to waterfalls and caves, it's a reasonably pleasant excursion. The best picnic spot is beside **Kaeng Tana**, less than 1km beyond the headquarters; formerly a much wilder set of rapids than those at Kaeng Saphue, these are reported to have lost most of their force since the construction of the Pak Mun dam. If desperate, you could consider staying in the park: six-berth national-park bungalows here go

The Pak Mun dam

The landscape between Phibun and Kong Chiam has changed drastically over the last few years, thanks to the construction of the hydroelectric **Pak Mun dam** across the Mun River, a few kilometres west of Kong Chiam. Completed in 1994, its creation was bitterly contested, not only by the three-thousand-plus families whose homes and livelihoods were to be severely affected, but also by environmental pressure groups and NGOs across the world. The former residents and fishermen lost out, and 117 square kilometres of previously farmed and inhabited land were flooded.

As a partial sop to local fishermen and environmentalists, EGAT, the Thai electricity board, responded by commissioning a ground-breaking **fish ladder** on the downstream wall of the dam to address concerns about the movement of fish between the Mekhong and the Mun rivers. During June and July when the fish spawn, the river water is funnelled down two maze-like channels that are supposed to slow the current sufficiently to enable the spawning fish to swim up the Mun from the Mekhong, as they did before the dam was built. However, a study by the independent World Commission on Dams, released in November 2000, shows that both the dam and its fish ladder have been a financial and environmental disaster. According to their report, out of the 265 fish species originally found in the Mun river, only 96 remained after the dam's completion, and the catch upstream of the dam has declined by between sixty and eighty percent. The whole project is made even more of a mockery by the fact that the dam has apparently only been producing around one sixth of its potential power output. Loss of livelihood and the government's reneging in 1998 on promised compensation to the families affected by the dam has prompted increasingly vociferous **protests** by Pak Mun villagers, including the establishment of a temporary "protest village" in front of the dam and frequent mass demonstrations in Bangkok – where they have joined with other grassroots activists affected by similar large-scale projects to create the Assembly of the Poor (see Contexts, p.799, for more).

for B500–800, though accommodation in Kong Chiam, 30km away via the dam road, is more comfortable and better value. To see this area by public transport, take a Kong Chiam-bound **songthaew** from Phibun and get off when you see the dam road (Route 2296) signed off Route 2222; you'll have to hitch the 6km from this junction to the park.

Chong Mek and the Lao border

Highway 217 finally peters out 44km east of Phibun Mangsahan at the Lao border village of **CHONG MEK**, site of a busy Thai-Lao market, and one of the legal border crossings for foreigners. **Songthaews** leave approximately hourly between 7am and 4pm from beside Kaeng Saphue bridge in Phibun Mangsahan, taking about ninety minutes to reach Chong Mek. There is also a long-distance **bus** service between Chong Mek and Bangkok: two air-con buses a day depart from Chong Mek market at 4pm and 5pm, arriving at Mo Chit Northern Bus terminal about twelve hours later.

To **cross into Laos** via Chong Mek, farangs must be possession of a Lao visa which specifies Chong Mek as the entry point (see the box on p.524 for information on how to arrange this; the nearest Lao consulate to Chong Mek is in Khon Kaen, listed on p.505). It's also a wise precaution to stop at the immigration office in Phibun Mangsahan near Ubon (see p.493) before continuing to

Chong Mek, in order to get your Thai exit stamp – sometimes it's possible to get stamped out at Chong Mek itself, but some travellers have reported being sent back to Phibun to get their stamp. If you have the right paperwork you can simply walk across the border (it's open daily 8.30am–4pm) to the Lao town of Ban Muang Kao, from where songthaews run fairly frequently to the city of Pakxe 40km away. There are currently no hotels in Chong Mek, and little else beside the market and a few small shops and restaurants on its fringes, but a tourist information centre was under construction at the time of writing.

Even if you're not planning to cross into Laos, the **border market** at Chong Mek is well worth a couple of hours, especially at weekends when it's at its liveliest. Among the stalls are traditional herbalists, whose stock includes pieces of bark, weirdly shaped roots and all sorts of bizarre-looking dried vegetable and animal matter; lots of basketware sellers displaying very inexpensive fish traps, winnowing trays, sticky rice baskets and small tables; vendors of cheap clothes, including jeans, combat gear and very good-value sarongs; plus a mouthwatering number of restaurant shacks serving both Thai and Lao goodies. Few farangs visit the market, and there's plenty of good-humoured bargaining here without the hassle of more touristed places.

Yasothon and Roi Et

By the beginning of May, Isaan is desperate for rain; there may not have been significant rainfall for six months and the rice crops need to be planted. In northeastern folklore, rain is the fruit of sexual encounters between the gods, so at this time villagers all over Isaan hold the bawdy **Bun Bang Fai** – a merit-making **rocket festival** – to encourage the gods to get on with it. The largest and most public of these festivals takes place in **YASOTHON**, 98km northwest of Ubon, on a weekend in mid-May. Not only is the fireworks display a spectacular affair, but the rockets built to launch them are superbly crafted machines in themselves, beautifully decorated and carried proudly through the streets before blast-off. Up to 25 kilograms of gunpowder may be packed into the nine-metre-long rockets and, in keeping with the fertility theme of the festivities, performance is everything. Sexual innuendo, general flirtation and dirty jokes are essential components of Bun Bang Fai; rocket builders compete to shoot their rockets the highest, and anyone whose missile fails to leave the ground gets coated in mud as a punishment. At other times of the year, Yasothon has nothing to tempt tourists – just a faceless high street full of motorbike-part shops and a handful of unremarkable wats.

All Khon Kaen-bound **buses** from Ubon stop in Yasothon, at the bus station on Thanon Rattanakhet, as do some heading for Chaiyaphum. If you want to stay here during festival time, book your **hotel** well in advance and be prepared to pay double what the room's worth. *Yot Nakhon*, one block northwest of the market and two blocks northwest of the bus station at 141–143 Thanon Uthai-Ramrit (℡045/711481, ℻711476; ❷–❺) has plenty of decent fan and air-conditioned rooms, while the newest and best hotel in town is the comfortable, mid-range *JP Emerald* (℡045/724847, ℮jpemerald@isan.sawadee.com; ❼), close to the city hall at 36 Thanon Pha Pa.

If Yasothon's booked out, you might want to commute there from either Ubon (see p.488) or **ROI ET**, a pleasant if unarresting town 71km further northwest and also on the Ubon–Khon Kaen bus route. Roi Et's **bus station** (℡043/511939) is way out beyond the western fringes of town on Thanon Thawa Phiban, so you need to take a samlor or tuk-tuk to the town-centre hotels. Just off the eastern shore of Roi-Et's artificial lake, Beung Phlan Chai, the centrally located *Banchong* **hotel**, at 99–101 Thanon Suriyadet Bamrung (☎043/511235; ②), has reasonable enough fan rooms for the price, while the nearby *Sai Thip* at 133 Thanon Suriyadet Bamrung (☎043/511365; ②–③) is also convenient and has both fan and air-con rooms, but at slightly inflated prices. The air-conditioned rooms with TV at the *Mai Thai*, 99 Thanon Haisok (☎043/511038, ⑤512277; ④), used to be the best in town, but are now rather faded though still decent value; more luxurious accommodation is available at the *Roi Et Thani* (☎043/520387, ⑤520401, ⓔroietthani@isan.sawadee.com, ⑥–⑦) at 78 Thanon Ploenchit on the eastern edge of town, which offers a swimming pool, business centre and gym as well as large comfortable rooms. The night market sets up two blocks east of the *Banchong* hotel and is an enjoyable **place to eat**; there's more upmarket dining at the restaurants around the edge of the lake.

Central Isaan

The more northerly branch of the northeastern rail line bypasses Khorat, heading straight up through **central Isaan** to the Lao border town of Nong Khai via Khon Kaen and Udon Thani, paralleling Highway 2 most of the way. West of these arteries, the smaller Highway 201 is shadowed by the thickly wooded Phetchabun hills and Dong Phaya Yen mountain range, the westernmost limits of Isaan, chunks of which have been turned into the **national parks** of Phu Kradung, Phu Reua and Phu Hin Rongkla. But hills play only a minor part in central Isaan's landscape, most of which suffers from poor-quality soil that sustains little in the way of profitable crops and, quite apart from what it does to the farmers who work it, makes for drab views from the bus or train window.

Nevertheless, there are a handful of towns worth stopping off at: **Chaiyaphum** provides the opportunity to visit silk weavers in a nearby village; **Khon Kaen**, for its museum of local history, its textiles and its excellent handicraft shops; **Udon Thani**, a departure point for the Bronze Age settlement of **Ban Chiang**; and **Loei**, for its access to the mountainous national parks. Trains connect only the larger towns, but **buses** link all the above centres, also conveniently serving the town of Phitsanulok (see p.254) – the springboard for a tour of the ruins of Sukhothai and a junction for onward travel to Chiang Mai – via a spectacularly hilly route through the rounded contours of Phetchabun province.

Chaiyaphum

Travellers used to come to **CHAIYAPHUM** for the provincial capital's annual elephant round-up, but since this has now been downgraded into a simple elephant procession during the annual town festival, there's little to draw you here. Nonetheless, it's a fairly calm place and compact enough for you to walk easily from end to end in half an hour, and if you do happen to be in the area between January 12 and 20 it's probably worth stopping by to see the elephants and all the other festivities that make up the week-long celebration in honour of Chao Poh Phraya Lae, the nineteenth-century founder of the modern town, whose statue graces the main roundabout at its southern end.

The only notable sight in Chaiyapum is **Prang Ku**, a ruined Khmer temple probably built in the late twelfth century at the site of a resting place along the route between Phimai and northern outposts of the Khmer empire. All that's left here is the central prang, now housing a sandstone Dvaravati-era Buddha, and the remnants of a surrounding wall. Prang Ku is on Thanon Bannakarn, about 2km east of the main roundabout. If you have your own transport, you can make a pleasant round-trip by continuing past the prang, through rice fields interspersed with villages, eventually ending up on Thanon Niwet Rat, 1km east of the bus station at the northern edge of the town centre.

Chaiyaphum's other attraction is its proximity to the **silk-weaving** villages of **Ban Khwao** and **Ban Tawn**, 15km west of town and accessible by songthaew from Thanon Nonmuang (on the west side of town). If you're lucky and can communicate a little in Thai, you may be able to get a look at the whole silk-weaving process, from breeding through spinning, dyeing and weaving (see box on p.481), but in general you'll learn more if you join a tour led by an English-speaking guide, such as those run from the town of Surin (see p.479). Nonetheless, buying silk direct from the weavers makes economic sense for both parties as it cuts out the middle merchants – 6m of good-quality plain-coloured silk can cost as little as B2000 – though there are a wider range of patterns and colours in Khon Kaen and Surin. Tailors in Chaiyaphum can make up the cloth for you, but for complicated designs you should wait until you reach the savvy stitchers of Chiang Mai or Bangkok.

For a therapeutic shower and peaceful jungle picnic, you could head out to one of two **waterfalls** in the area. The most impressive is the multi-tiered, fifty-metre-wide **Nam Tok Thad Tone**, 21km north of Chaiyaphum in the small Thad Tone National Park off the end of Route 2051. To get there from Chaiyaphum, take a songthaew from the bus station on Thanon Niwet Rat (3 daily at 10am, 11am & noon) to **Ban Nam Tok Thad Tone**, the falls village at the end of the road, and then walk the 2km to the waterfall. Coming back, you'll have to rely on hitching a lift, which shouldn't be too difficult. Alternatively, make the trip to **Nam Tok Pa Eung**, 26km to the northwest; from the bus station take a songthaew bound for **Nong Bua Daeng** and ask to get out at the waterfall, 45 minutes on. Follow the dirt track on the right to a car park (1500m), cross the river and continue for 1km to the next pair of bridges – the falls are just beyond.

Practicalities

From Bangkok, **buses** to Chaiyaphum leave at least once an hour and take about six hours. There are also connections from Phitsanulok in the central plains, Chiang Mai and Chiang Rai in the north, and Khorat, Surin, Ubon, Khon Kaen, Loei and Chiang Khan in Isaan. All ordinary buses stop at the **station** on Thanon Niwet Rat at the eastern edge of town; air-conditioned tour buses stop at the southern end of Thanon Nonmuang.

If you need a **hotel**, try the typically basic Thai-Chinese *Sirichai Hotel* (☎044/811461, ℱ812299; ❷–❸), which has spartan fan and air-con rooms and a restaurant, halfway down Thanon Nonmuang at no.565; to get there from the ordinary bus station, walk a short distance down Thanon Niwet Rat to the roundabout, cross over onto Thanon Chaiprasit and continue for about 200m before turning left down Thanon Nonmuang. The *Lert Nimit* (℡044/811522, ℻822335; ❸–❺) opposite the ordinary bus station at 447 Thanon Niwet Rat, has better rooms for the price, some with air-conditioning.

For value and variety the best place to **eat** is, as usual, the **night market**, which starts from about 6pm just off Thanon Ratchathani, a couple of blocks east of Thanon Nonmuang. Alternatively, the **curry stalls** in front of the department store on Thanon Ratchathani serve through the evening and during most of the day as well. If you prefer to eat inside, there are **noodle shops** on Thanon Ratchathani and Thanon Nonmuang, as well as a "boat noodle" place near the *Lert Nimit* at 447/22 Thanon Niwet Rat, where *kway tiaw reua* (noodles cooked in a dark, strong-tasting broth) are served from a traditional wooden sampan stationed in the dining area.

Khon Kaen and around

Geographically at the virtual centre of Isaan, **KHON KAEN** has been the focus of government plans to regenerate the northeast, and is now the seat of a highly respected university as well as the Channel 5 television studios. Considering its size and importance, the city is surprisingly uncongested and spacious, and there's a noticeably upbeat feel, underlined by its apparently harmonious combination of traditional Isaan culture – huge markets and hordes of street vendors – and flashy shopping plazas and world-class hotels. Its location, 188km northeast of Khorat on the Bangkok–Nong Khai rail line and Highway 2, makes it a convenient resting point, even though the provincial museum is just about the only sight here. The farangs staying in the city tend to be business people or university teachers rather than tourists, though an increasing number of travellers are stopping here for **Indochinese visas** now that Khon Kaen has both a Lao and a Vietnamese consulate.

Arrival, transport and information

Khon Kaen is easily reached by road or rail from Bangkok and most other major towns in the northeast. **Trains** from Bangkok leave five times daily, with one service going via Khorat and continuing as far as Udon Thani; the others bypass Khorat en route to the end of the line at Nong Khai. The **train station** (℡043/221112) is just off Highway 2 on the southwestern edge of town, about fifteen minutes' walk from the main hotel area. Over twenty air-conditioned **buses** arrive from Bangkok daily; regular bus connections also serve Chaiyaphum, Nong Khai via Udon Thani, Khorat, Ubon and Phitsanulok. The main, non-air-conditioned **bus station** (℡043/237300) is on Thanon Prachasamoson, a five-minute walk northwest of the Thanon Klang Muang hotels; the air-conditioned-bus terminal (℡043/239910) is right in the town centre, at the junction of Thanon Ammat and Thanon Klang Muang. Five daily **flights** make the Bangkok–Khon Kaen trip in both directions. The **airport** (℡043/246305) is 6km west of the city centre, and has Avis and Budget car-rental desks (see p.505 for details); taxis meet all flights.

Local buses and songthaews ply Khon Kaen's streets from 5am to 8pm, charging a standard fare of B4, or B6 for air-con journeys. The most useful of these are: **#1** (yellow and red or orange), which runs up Thanon Na Muang from the Si Chan junction, via the regular bus terminal to the museum; **#3** (yel-

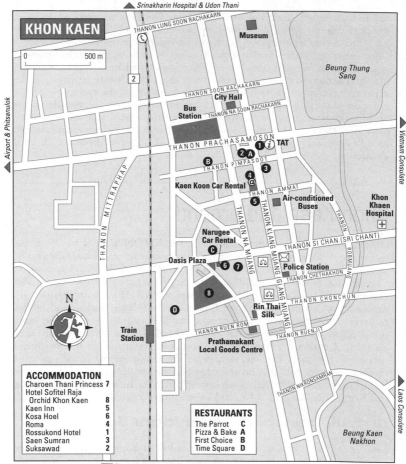

Srinakharin Hospital & Udon Thani

KHON KAEN

0   500 m

THANON LUNG SOON RACHAKARN

Museum

Beung Thung Sang

THANON SOON RACHAKARN

City Hall

Bus Station

THANON NA SOON RACHAKARN

THANON PRACHASAMOSON   **TAT**

THANON PIMPASOOT

Kaen Koon Car Rental

THANON AMMAT

Air-conditioned Buses

Khon Khaen Hospital

Narugee Car Rental

THANON SI CHAN (SRI CHANT)

Oasis Plaza

Police Station

THANON CHETHAKHON

THANON CHONCHUN

Rin Thai Silk

Train Station

THANON RUEN ROM

Prathamakant Local Goods Centre

THANON RUENJIT

THANON NIKRONSAMRAN

Beung Kaen Nakhon

N

THANON MITTRAPHAP

THANON PRACHASAMRAN

THANON KLANG MUANG

THANON NA MUANG

THANON GLANG MUANG

THANON ROBMUANG

Airport & Phitsanulok

Vietnam Consulate

Laos Consulate

ACCOMMODATION
Charoen Thani Princess **7**
Hotel Sofitel Raja
  Orchid Khon Kaen   **8**
Kaen Inn   **5**
Kosa Hoel   **6**
Roma   **4**
Rossukond Hotel   **1**
Saen Sumran   **3**
Suksawad   **2**

RESTAURANTS
The Parrot   **C**
Pizza & Bake   **A**
First Choice   **B**
Time Square   **D**

Chonnabot, Khorat & Bangkok

low and blue) which connects the train station and the regular bus terminal; **#6** (green) which travels up Thanon Na Muang from the junction with Thanon Ruen Rom, as far as the regular bus terminal; **#8** (light blue), **#9** (light blue) and **#13** (orange) which all connect the regular bus terminal with the air-con terminal, via Thanon Klang Muang; and **#11** (white) which connects the air-con bus terminal with the railway station, via Thanon Si Chan. A short **tuk-tuk** ride should cost you B30, while the minimum fare in a **samlor** is B15.

The **TAT** office (daily 8.30am–4.30pm; ☏043/244498) is on Thanon Prachasamoson, about five minutes' walk east of the bus station.

Accommodation

Accommodation in Khon Kaen is plentiful and reasonably priced, particularly in the middle price range. Most of the hotels are centrally located along Thanon Klang Muang.

Charoen Thani Princess, 260 Thanon Si Chan ⊺043/220400, ⓕ220438, ⓦwww.royalprincess.com. Chain hotel with a pool, several bars and restaurants, a nightclub and a range of moderately luxurious rooms. ❺–❼

Hotel Sofitel Raja Orchid Khon Kaen, 9/9 Thanon Prachasumran ⊺043/322155, ⓕ322150, ⓔsofitel@kkaen.loxinfo.co.th. Gorgeously appointed luxury hotel, with extremely comfortable rooms, a swimming pool and plenty of bars and restaurants. Significant discounts are often available, which makes it worth splashing out for. One of the nicest hotels in the northeast. ❼–❽

Kaen Inn, 56 Thanon Klang Muang ⊺043/245420, ⓕ239457. Good-value upper mid-range place, where all rooms have air-con and come with shower, TV and fridge. ❹–❺

Kosa Hotel, 250 Thanon Si Chan ⊺043/225014, ⓕ225013. Huge, high-rise hotel offering reasonably priced rooms, all with air-con and TV, plus a beer garden and snooker hall. ❻–❽

Roma, 50/2 Thanon Klang Muang ⊺043/236276, ⓕ242458. The fan-cooled rooms here aren't very interesting, but the better maintained air-con ones are fairly good value and have TV. ❸

Saen Sumran, 55 Thanon Klang Muang ⊺ & ⓕ043/239611. One of the oldest hotels in town, this is also the most traveller-orientated place in Khon Kaen, with a useful noticeboard and friendly, helpful staff. The large, wood-floored rooms upstairs are quite comfortable and the cheapest in the city. ❷

Suksawad, 2/2 Thanon Klang Muang ⊺043/236472. Family-run budget hotel in a quiet location set back from the road; all rooms have fan and shower but the standard is a little lower than the Saen Sumran across the road. ❷.

The Town

In keeping with its status as a university town, Khon Kaen has several fine collections in its **museum**, two blocks north of the bus station on Thanon Lung Soon Rachakarn (daily 9am–4pm; B30). To get there by local bus, catch the yellow and red or orange #1 from anywhere on Thanon Na Muang that's

---

Betel

Betel-chewing is a habit indulged in all over Asia, and in Thailand nowhere more enthusiastically than in the northeast, where the three essential ingredients for a good chew – betel leaf, limestone ash and areca palm fruit – are found in abundance. You chew the coarse red flesh of the narcotic fruit (best picked when small and green-skinned) first, before adding a large heart-shaped betel leaf, spread with limestone ash paste and folded into manageable size; for a stronger kick, you can include tobacco and/or marijuana at this point. An acquired and bitter taste, betel numbs the mouth and generates a warm feeling around the ears. Less pleasantly, constant spitting is necessary: in traditional houses you spit through any hole in the floorboards, while in more elegant households a spittoon is provided. It doesn't do much for your looks either: betel-chewers are easily spotted by their rotten teeth and lips stained scarlet from the habit.

When travelling long distances, chewers carry basketloads of the ingredients with them; at home, guests are served from a betel set, comprising at least three small covered receptacles, and sometimes a tray to hold these boxes and the knife or nutcracker used to split the fruit. Betel-chewing today is popular mainly with elderly Thais, particularly northeastern women, but it used to be a much more widespread social custom, and a person's betel tray set was once a Thai's most prized possession and an indication of rank: royalty would have sets made in gold, the nobility's would be in silver or nielloware, and poorer folk wove theirs from rattan or carved them from wood. Betel sets still feature as important dowry items in Isaan, with tray-giving processions forming part of northeastern engagement ceremonies.

north of the Thanon Sri Chan junction, and you'll be dropped outside the museum. The star attraction on the ground floor of the museum is a *sema* carved with a sensuous depiction of Princess Bhimba wiping the Buddha's feet with her hair on his return to Kabilabasad after years of absence in search of enlightenment. In the same room, the scope of the **Ban Chiang** collection of reassembled pots, bronze tools and jewellery rivals those held in Bangkok's National Museum and at Ban Chiang itself (see p.507), and is put into context by a map showing the distribution of contemporaneous settlements in the region. The display of **folk craft** in one of the smaller ground-floor galleries includes traditional fish traps and animal snares, and a selection of **betel trays** that run the gamut of styles from crude wooden vessels carved by Isaan farmers to more intricate silver sets given by the better-off as a dowry. Upstairs, the displays of Buddha sculptures feature the most perfect small bronze Lanna-style images outside of northern Thailand.

If you have an evening to fill, you could take a samlor tour of **Beung Kaen Nakhon**, the artificial lake 1500m south of the bus station on the southern outskirts of town, and then eat at one of the lakeside restaurants. It takes an hour and a half to walk the perimeter of the lake; aside from a couple of wats and some upmarket residences on its shores, there's nothing else much here, but it's the nearest Khon Kaen has to a public park and as such attracts families and kids on weekends and holidays.

Shopping

Khon Kaen is great for **shopping**, its stores boasting a huge range of regional **arts and crafts**, including high-quality Isaan **silk** of all designs and weaves. One of the best outlets is the cavernous Prathamakant Local Goods Centre (daily 8am–8.30pm) at the southern end of town at 81 Thanon Ruen Rom. Although aimed squarely at tourists, the selection here is quite phenomenal: hundreds of gorgeous *mut mee* (see p.523) cotton and silk weaves, as well as clothes, furnishings, triangular "axe" pillows of all sizes, *khaen* pipes and silver jewellery. To get to Prathamakant from the north part of town, take green local bus #6 from anywhere on Thanon Na Muang. Rin Thai Silk on Thanon Na Muang stocks a smaller range of Isaan silk, but will tailor clothes from their fabrics too. Itinerant vendors, who wander the main streets with panniers stuffed full of silk and cotton lengths, also offer competitive prices, and though the choice is restricted you can be sure most of the money will go to the weavers; they often gather on the steps of the *Kaen Inn* and along the stretch of Thanon Klang Muang just north of the hotel. Weavers from across the province gather in the city to display and sell their fabrics at the annual **Silk Festival** (Nov 29–Dec 10), which takes place at the City Hall on Thanon Na Soon Rachakan. Lined with small but often specialized shops and a huge covered fresh- and dry-goods market, Thanon Klang Muang is another good area for local products. Neam Lap La, at the top end of Thanon Klang Muang, just north of *Roma Hotel*, is the place to buy spicy sausages, sugar-coated beans and other Khon Kaen delicacies.

Eating and drinking

Khon Kaen has a reputation for very **spicy food**, particularly sausages, *sai krog isaan*, which are served with cubes of raw ginger, onion, lime and plenty of chilli sauce, at stalls along Thanon Klang Muang between the *Suksawad* and *Kaen Inn*. These and other local favourites – such as pigs' trotters, roast duck and shellfish – can be sampled at the stalls along the northern edge of Bueng Kaen Nakhon. There's quite a choice of restaurants around the lake as well, including one that actually juts out over it, which makes a pleasant spot to spend the evening. Steaks, pizzas and Thai curries are the most popular dishes at the cosy *Parrot*, opposite the entrance road to the *Kosa Hotel* on Thanon Si Chan, but its real forte is the huge **breakfasts**, served from 7.30am, which include real coffee, eggs, sausages, bacon and hash browns. You can also get real coffee at *Pizza and Bake* on Thanon Klang Muang. For inexpensive *phat thai* and *khao pat*, with air-conditioning, go to *Coffee Break*, west of Thanon Klang Muang off Thanon Sri Chan. *First Choice* on Thanon Pimpasoot is another farang-friendly restaurant, offering air-conditioned premises and an English-language menu detailing a large range of moderately priced Thai, Western and Japanese options, plus a sizeable vegetarian selection. The *Underground* food and drink complex in the basement of the *Hotel Sofitel* has half a dozen small restaurant concessions, including a surprisingly authentic pizzeria as well as German and Chinese eateries.

Khon Kaen is the only place in Thailand where you can drink the exclusive brand of Johnnie Walker whisky known as the Royal Lochnager, and the place that sells it – along with dozens of other Johnnie Walker whiskies, as well as Venezuelan rum and unusual imported beers – is the *Johnnie Walker* **bar** inside the *Charoen Thani Princess* hotel on Thanon Si Chan. The nearby *Hotel Sofitel* has its own microbrewery, the *Krönen Brauhaus*, in the basement *Underground* complex, where German-style beer flows strong and dark. The bizarre outdoor eating and drinking plaza called *Time Square* just west of the *Hotel Sofitel* does not seem to attract much custom to its half-dozen small bar-restaurants and live music acts – despite the Las Vegas style over-the-top neon that advertises the place.

Listings

Airline The Thai Airways office is inside the *Hotel Sofitel* on Thanon Prachasumran ☏ 043/227710.

Banks and exchange There's a currency-exchange booth in front of the Bangkok Bank on Thanon Si Chan, between the *Charoen Thani* and the *Kosa* hotels (daily 9am–5pm).

Car rental Avis ☏ 043/344313, ⊛ www.avis.com and Budget ☏ 043/345460, ⊛ www.budget.co.th both have desks at the airport, but there are also several local firms based in the city centre, which offer cars with or without driver: Narugee Car Rent, next to Oasis Plaza department store and the *Kosa Hotel* off Thanon Si Chan ☏ 043/224220; and Kaen Koon Car Rent at 54/1–2 Thanon Klang Muang ☏ 043/239458.

Consulates The Lao consulate is located at the far southern end of town, about 1500m east of Beung Kaen Nakhon lake, at 19/3 Thanon Ban Nonthun Photican (Mon–Fri 8.30–11.30am & 1.30–4.30pm; ☏ 043/223698). Visas take three working days to process. For more details on applying for a Lao visa, and travel into Laos, see the box on p.524. There's also a Vietnamese consulate in Khon Kaen (Mon–Fri 8.30am–4pm; ☏ 043/242190), about 1500m east of the TAT office, off Thanon Prachasamoson at 65/6 Thanon Chaiaphadung.

Hospitals Srinakarin Hospital, attached to Khon Kaen University, north of town on Highway 2 ☏ 043/242331–44; Khon Kaen Hospital, off Thanon Si Chan ☏ 043/236005–6.

Internet access Available at the shop next to the *Roma Hotel* on Thanon Klang Muang.

Mail The most centrally located post office is at on Thanon Si Chan, and there's another branch next to the phone centre on Thanon Lung Soon Rachakarn.

Telephones The CAT international telephone centre is in the north of town on Thanon Lung Soon Rachakarn.

Tourist police At the TAT office on Thanon Prachasamoson ☏ 043/236937.

Travel agent Domestic and international air tickets can be bought and changed at Kaen Koon Car Rent at 54/1–2 Thanon Klang Muang ☏ 043/239458.

Around Khon Kaen

The outer reaches of Khon Kaen province hold a few places that are worth exploring on **day-trips**. Two of these are easily accessible on public transport, the third is best visited by hired car or motorbike, or you might want to combine them all into a tailor-made tour and hire a car with driver for the day. If you're looking for other things to occupy yourself, don't be duped by the TAT brochure on the "tortoise village" in the village of Ban Kok, about 5km west of Chonnabot. Though the tourist literature makes the place look interesting, the reality is both depressing and dull and is definitely not worth the effort.

Phra That Kham Kaen

One moderately interesting way of killing a few hours in Khon Kaen is to make a trip out into the countryside north of town, to visit the revered **that** (reliquary tower) which gave the town and province its name, and to take in some typical northeastern hamlets. The monument, called **Phra That Kham Kaen**, is located within the compound of Wat Chediyaphum in the hamlet of **Nan Pong**, 30km north of Khon Kaen; large yellow songthaews make the ninety-minute journey from Khon Kaen bus station about every half-hour. On the way you'll pass through a string of settlements consisting of little more than a few wooden houses raised on stilts to provide shelter for livestock and storage space for looms and ox-carts, and surrounded by small groves of banana and areca palm trees. Outside every house you'll see at least one enormous *ohng*, the all-important water storage jars that are left to collect rainwater for use during the debilitating annual drought. The journey to Nan Pong is more rewarding than the arriving: the whitewashed *that* looks too inconsequential to merit such a significant place in local mythology. The story goes that two monks once rested here beneath a dead tamarind tree (*kham*); when they returned to the spot a couple of months later it had sprung back into life, so they had the miraculous tree enshrined – and the name Khon Kaen followed from the Kham Kaen shrine.

Chonnabot

Khon Kaen also makes a reasonable base from which to explore the local silk-weaving centre of **Chonnabot**, about 54km southwest of the city. Traditionally a cottage industry, this small town's **silk production** has become centralized over the last few years, and weavers now gather in small workshops in town, each specializing in just one aspect of the process. You can walk in and watch the women (it's still exclusively women's work) at their wheels, looms or dye vats, and then buy from the vendors in the street out front. For more details on silk-weaving processes, see box on p.481. To get to Chonnabot from Khon Kaen, take any ordinary Khorat-bound bus to **Ban Phae** (every 30min), then a songthaew for the final 10km to Chonnabot.

Dinosaurland

Khon Kaen hit the international headlines in 1996 when the oldest-ever fossil of a tyrannosaur **dinosaur** was unearthed in Phuwiang National Park, about 90km northwest of Khon Kaen city. Estimated to be 120 million years old, it measures just 6m from nose to tail and has been named *Siamotyrannus isanensis* – Siam for Thailand, and Isaan after the northeastern region of Thailand. Before this find at Phuwiang, the oldest tyrannosaur fossils were the 65-million- to 80-million-year-old specimens from China, Mongolia and North America. These younger fossils are twice the size of the *Siamotyrannus*; the latter's age and size have therefore established the *Siamotyrannus* as the ancestor of the *Tyrannosaurus rex*, and confirmed Asia as the place of origin of the tyrannosaur genus, which later evolved into various different species.

The fossil of this extraordinary dinosaur – together with eight moderately interesting paleontological finds – is on show to the public at **Dinosaurland** in Phu Wiang National Park, and can be visited free of charge at any time. The Dinosaurland tag is a little misleading as there are no theme-park attractions here, just nine quarries and a small visitor centre which holds some factual displays on dinosaur evolution and the fossilization of dinosaur bones. Nearly all the information is in Thai, however, so it's worth picking up the informative English-language brochure on Dinosaurland from Khon Kaen's TAT office before you come.

The *Siamotyrannus isanensis* is displayed in **Quarry #9**, which is accessible via the 1500-metre track that starts across the road from the visitor centre; from the car park at the end of the track, it's a five-hundred-metre walk to the quarry. The fossil is an impressive sight, with large sections of the rib cage almost completely intact. **Quarry #1** contains the other displays, as well as two previously undiscovered species. The theropod *Siamosaurus sutheethorni* (named after the paleontologist Warawut Suteehorn) is set apart from the other, carnivorous, theropods by its teeth, which seem as if they are unable to tear flesh; the fifteen- to twenty-metre-long *Phuwiangosaurus sirindhornae* (named in honour of Thailand's Princess Royal) is thought to be a new species of sauropod.

Though it's just about feasible to get to Dinosaurland by public transport, it's a time-consuming, convoluted and quite expensive trip, so you're much better off hiring your own wheels in Khon Kaen. To **get to the park**, head west out of Khon Kaen on Highway 12, following the signs for Chumpae as far as kilometre-stone 48, where you'll see an unmissable dinosaur statue beside the road. Turn right off the main road here, and continue for another 38km, passing through the small town of Phuwiang and following signs all the way for Dinosaurland. Make your way first to the visitor centre, from where you can follow the relevant tracks. There's a **food** and drink stall at the car park in front of Quarry #3, which is about one kilometre's drive north of the visitor centre.

Udon Thani and Ban Chiang

Economically important but charmless, **UDON THANI** looms for most travellers as a misty, early-morning sprawl of grey cement seen from the window of the overnight train to Nong Khai. The capital of an arid sugar-cane and rice-growing province, 137km north of Khon Kaen, Udon was given an economic shot in the arm during the Vietnam War with the siting of a huge American military base nearby, and despite the American withdrawal in 1976, the town has maintained its rapid industrial and commercial development. The only conceivable reason to alight here would be to satisfy a lust for archeology at the excavated Bronze Age settlement of **BAN CHIANG**, 50km to the east in sleepy farming country, though plenty of travellers avoid spending time in Udon by visiting Ban Chiang on a day-trip from the much preferable base of Nong Khai (see p.522) or by staying in the village itself.

Listed as a UNESCO World Heritage site in 1992, the village of Ban Chiang is unremarkable nowadays, although its fertile setting is attractive and the

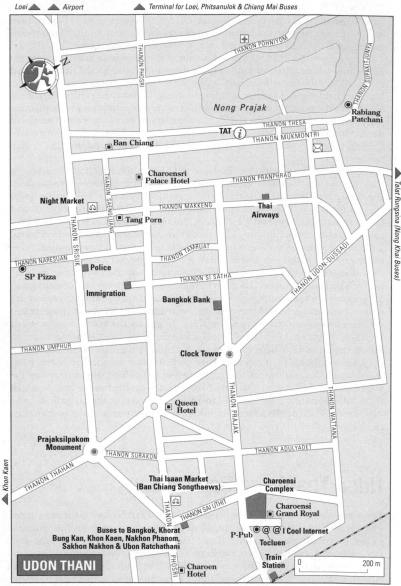

Top labels:

Loei ▲▲   ▲ Airport   ▲ Terminal for Loei, Phitsanulok & Chiang Mai Buses

Side labels:

5

THE NORTHEAST: ISAAN | Udon Thani and Ban Chiang

◀ Khon Kaen

▶ Talat Rungsina (Nong Khai Buses)

▼ Talat Nong Bua

Map labels:

THANON POHNIYOM

THANON PHOSRI

THANON SUPAKITJUNYA

Nong Prajak

Rabiang Patchani

THANON THESA

TAT ⓘ

THANON MUKMONTRI

Ban Chiang

Charoensri Palace Hotel

THANON PRANPHRAO

THANON SAENGUANG

Night Market

THANON MAKKENG

Thai Airways

Tang Porn

THANON SRISUK

THANON TAMRUAT

THANON NARESUAN

Police

SP Pizza

THANON SI SATHA

THANON UDON-DUSSADI

Immigration

Bangkok Bank

THANON UMPHUR

Clock Tower ◉

THANON PRAJAK

THANON WATANA

Queen Hotel

Prajaksilpakom Monument

THANON ADULYADET

THANON SURAKON

THANON THAHAN

Thai Isaan Market (Ban Chiang Songthaews)

Charoensi Complex

Charoensi Grand Royal

THANON SAI UTHIT

Buses to Bangkok, Khorat Bung Kan, Khon Kaen, Nakhon Phanom, Sakhon Nakhon & Ubon Ratchathani

P-Pub @ @ I Cool Internet

Tocluen

Train Station

UDON THANI

THANON PHOSRI

Charoen Hotel

0   200 m

villagers are noticeably friendly to visitors. It achieved worldwide fame in 1966, when a rich seam of archeological remains was accidentally discovered: clay pots, uncovered in human graves alongside sophisticated **bronze** objects, were dated to around 3000 BC, implying the same date for the bronze pieces. Ban Chiang was immediately hailed as the vanguard of the Bronze Age, seven hundred years before Mesopotamia's discovery of the metal – a revelation which shattered the accepted view of mainland Southeast Asia as a cultural backwater during that era. Despite continuing controversy over the dating of some of the finds, Ban Chiang stands as one of the world's earliest bronze producers; its methods of smelting show no signs of influence from northern China and other neighbouring bronze cultures, which suggests the area was the birthplace of Southeast Asian civilization.

The present village's fine **National Museum** (daily 9am–4pm; B30) displays some of the choicest finds from Ban Chiang and provides a richly informative commentary. It also contains the country's best collection of characteristic late-period Ban Chiang clay pots, with their red whorled patterns on a buff background, and takes you through their stages of manufacture; although not of prime historical significance, these pots have become an attractive emblem of Ban Chiang, and freely adapted by local souvenir producers. A single room in the museum is dedicated to the modern village; the tale it tells, of the rapid disappearance of traditional ways, is an all-too-familiar lament in Thailand. The story, however, doesn't quite end there: the influx of tourists has encouraged local farmers to turn to their looms again, producing especially rich and intricate lengths of silk and cotton *mut mee*, for sale as they are in the souvenir shops around the museum, or transformed into garments and other articles by the inhabitants of Ban Chiang itself, many of whom can be glimpsed through doorways hard at work on their sewing machines.

In the grounds of **Wat Pho Si Nai**, on the south side of the village, part of an early dig has been canopied over and opened to the public (same times and ticket as the museum). Two burial pits have been left exposed to show how and where artefacts were found.

Practicalities

Buses pull into Udon Thani at a variety of locations, depending on where they've come from: Loei, Phitsanulok and Chiang Mai services use the terminal on the town's western bypass; Nong Khai buses leave from Talat Rungsina (Rungsina market, also used by Ban Phu buses) on the north side of town; Bangkok, Khorat, Bung Kan, Khon Kaen, Nakhon Phanom, Sakhon Nakhon and Ubon Ratchathani services leave from the other main terminal on Thanon Sai Uthit; east of the centre, Ban Chiang-bound songthaews (big, multi-coloured truck versions) base themselves at the morning market, Talat Thai Isaan. Arriving by **train** is no more convenient, as the station lies a good 2km east of the town centre. The best way of connecting these points is in a **skylab**, Udon's version of a tuk-tuk (B20 and upwards per journey). From the **airport**, 3km south of the centre, Thai Airways' air-conditioned minibuses run passengers downtown (B50 per person) and direct to Nong Khai (B100 per person). Alternatively, both Avis (☎042/244770, ⓔuth@avisthailand.com) and Budget (☎042/246805, ⓔbracuth@budget.co.th) have **car-rental** desks at the airport, with daily rates starting from around B1400 for a jeep.

To **get to Ban Chiang** from Udon, either take a direct songthaew (every 30min until 3.45pm) or catch a Sakhon Nakhon-bound bus (every 20min) to Ban Palu and then a motorized samlor (B30 per person) for the last 5km or so from the main road to the village. Heading back to Udon the same day by songthaew is problematic as the service runs only until about 10.30am (every 30min) so any later in the day you'll have to make do with a samlor and bus combination.

Udon has a friendly **TAT office** (daily 8.30am–4.30pm; ☎042/325406–7, ⓕ325408, ⓔtatudon@tat.or.th), which also covers Nong Khai, Nong Bua

Lamphu and Loei provinces; it's housed at 16/5 Thanon Mukmontri on the south side of Nong Prajak, a newly landscaped lake and park to the northwest of the centre. There's **internet access** at I Kool Internet on Thanon Prajak (daily 10am–midnight, Thurs until 9pm; B20 per hour), opposite the Charoensi Complex shopping centre, and at the slightly smaller Tocluen, a few doors down (same hours and rate).

Accommodation and eating

It's possible to stay overnight in Ban Chiang at the excellent *Lakeside Sunrise Guesthouse* (T042/208167; ❷), and in fact many guests linger for a few days. Run by Australian Alex Ovenden and his wife Tong, the guest house is just a few minutes' walk from the museum (where Tong works): facing the museum, head left then turn right at the first intersection and look for a large Western-style wooden two-storey house. Guests here sleep in clean top-floor rooms with fans and mosquito screens and can relax on a huge balcony – equipped with a helpful noticeboard and small library – overlooking an artificial lake; there are shared cold-water showers downstairs, though hot water can be brought to you for a small fee. Alex can rustle up food and even real coffee; otherwise food possibilities are limited to the simple village cafés – the place directly opposite the museum does an excellent *raht nah* (noodles in a thick gravy). Bicycles are available for exploring the surrounding countryside, or Alex can arrange motorcycle rental; there's a bird sanctuary 6km away, and a couple of interesting forest wats closer to the village, all marked on Alex's useful hand-drawn map of the area.

In Udon, the centrally located *Queen Hotel* at 6–8 Thanon Udon–Dussadi (T042/221451; ❶–❷) is the best budget bet, with decent fan-cooled and air-con rooms and a friendly owner who speaks some English; the *Tang Porn*, 289/1 Thanon Makkeng (T042/221032; ❶), also has a reasonable location and clean rooms. In the middle of the range, the excellent-value *Charoensi Palace Hotel*, 60 Thanon Phosri (T042/242611–3; ❸), is a popular businessmen's haunt which offers large, clean bedrooms with air-con and hot water. Further up the scale, the *Charoen Hotel* at 549 Thanon Phosri (T042/248155, F241093, @charoen@edtech.co.th; ❻) has air-con rooms with hot showers and TVs, and a swimming pool outside, but better still are the luxury *Charoensri Grand Royal*, next to the Charoensi Complex at 277/1 Thanon Prajak (T042/343555, F343550; ❽), and the *Ban Chiang* at 5 Thanon Mukmontri (T042/327911–29, F223200, @bchiang@udon.ksc.co.th; ❻) – both with health club, pool and karaoke bar among their offerings. All three of Udon's upmarket hotels regularly offer discounts of as much as sixty percent on their official rates, making them well worth a splurge if you can afford it.

Delicious *kai yaang* (barbecued chicken) and *khao niaw* (sticky rice) are served at several inexpensive **restaurants** around the junction of Thanon Prajak and Thanon Pranphrao. For a greater variety of low-priced comestibles – Thai, Chinese and Vietnamese – head for the night market on Thanon Makkeng between Thanon Saengluang and Thanon Srisuk. One of Udon's most popular restaurants is the *Rabiang Phatchani*, northeast of the centre in Nong Prajak park, with a large menu of Thai and Chinese dishes and outdoor seating on a leafy terrace overlooking the lake. Among the town's hangovers from Nam days is *SP Pizza* at 63/2 Thanon Naresuan, which rustles up good steaks, pizzas, burgers and french fries, while more fast food of the *Pizza Hut* and *KFC* ilk is eagerly consumed by the locals at the Charoensri Complex. Opposite the complex, there's a cluster of decent eating and drinking options, including the air-con *P-Pub*, with beer on tap and a cosy, wood-beamed interior.

Loei and around

Most people carry on from Udon Thani straight north to Nong Khai (see p.522), but making a detour via **LOEI**, 147km to the west, takes you within range of four towering national parks and sets you up for a lazy tour along the Mekhong River. The capital of a province renowned for the unusual shapes of its stark, craggy mountains, Loei is, more significantly, the crossroads of one of Thailand's least tamed border regions; from Laos come all manner of illegal goods and refugees, especially Hmong tribespeople, still punished by the Communist Pathet Lao for siding with the Americans during the Vietnam War, who seized control of Laos at the end of the war in 1975.

Despite its frontier feel, the town, lying along the west bank of the small Loei River, is friendly and offers legitimate products of its own: tamarind paste and pork sausages are sold in industrial quantities along Oua Thanon Aree (off Thanon Charoenrat, Loei's main street, which runs roughly parallel to the river), while local quilts and lengths of silk and cotton in strong, simple designs are available at Dork Fai, 138/2 Thanon Charoenrat.

One reason to make a special trip to this region is to attend the unique rain-making **festival of Phi Ta Kon**, held over three days either at the end of June or the beginning of July in the small town of **Dan Sai**, 80km southwest of Loei. In order to encourage the heavens to open, townsfolk dress up as spirits in patchwork rags and fierce, brightly painted masks (made from coconut palm fronds and the baskets used for steaming sticky rice), then parade the town's most sacred Buddha image round the streets while making fun of as many onlookers as they can, waving wooden phalluses about and generally having themselves a whale of a time. The afternoon of the second day of the festival sees the firing off of dozens of bamboo rockets. The carnival can be visited in a day from Loei, though rooms are hard to come by at this time; a tamer version of the procession is tacked onto the otherwise uninspiring Cotton Blossom Festival, held in Loei town in February.

Practicalities

Beyond its meagre attractions, Loei is really only useful as a transport hub and as a base for the nearby national parks; the Tourism Authority of Thailand has plans to open a new office here in the next few years to help promote the parks – check with the Udon Thani office (see p.509) for the latest. **Buses** run here from Udon Thani and Khon Kaen every thirty minutes, from Phitsanulok in the central plains five times a day and from Bangkok (via Chaiyaphum) eighteen times a day. Songthaews (every 30min) and small green buses (every 15min) link the town to Chiang Khan, an hour to the north at the start of the Mekhong River route, while minibuses run hourly in the mornings to Sang Khom (3hr, bypassing Chiang Khan) and all the way to Nong Khai (6–7hr) – though it's quicker to catch a bus to Udon and change if you're going straight from Loei to Nong Khai. All of these arrive and depart at the **bus terminal** on Highway 201, the main through north–south road, about 2.5km south of the centre.

For **internet access**, PA Computer is at Thanon Charoenrat 139 (daily 9am–midnight; B20 per hour), and there are a couple more places on Thanon Chumsai, which runs east–west between Thanon Charoenrat and Highway 201: KR Computer is at no. 22/38 (daily 9am–midnight; same rate), and PP Net is next door (daily 10am–11pm; same rate).

Accommodation and eating

Unless it's festival time, finding a decent **place to stay** in Loei shouldn't be a problem. The more traveller-friendly of its two guest houses is the *Muang Loei*, in a modern terrace at 103/128 Thanon Raat Uthit off the western end of Thanon Ruamjai, which runs parallel to and north of Thanon Chumsai (⊕042/832839; ❶); the rooms and dorm (B60 per person) are basic and share cold-water bathrooms, but the downstairs seating area compensates with its comfy sofas and information boards. The helpful English-speaking owner, Khun Charoen, can organize day-trips to Phu Reua (B1200 including lunch), as well as motorcycle and car rental (B250/B1000 per day respectively) for those who prefer to go it alone; he also has several bicycles available free of charge to guests. Loei's other guest house, *Friendship House*, close to the bus station at 219 Thanon Charoenrat (⊕042/832230; ❶), is a notch up in comfort and price; large, clean rooms come with fan and en-suite cold-water bathroom, and there's a homely restaurant attached; the owners are very friendly, but speak no English. Comfortable and centrally placed, *Thai Udom Hotel*, at 122/1 Thanon Charoenrat (⊕042/811763, ⓕ830187; ❷–❸), has rooms with fan or air-conditioning, all with hot-water bathrooms. The quieter *Muang Fai* (*Cotton Inn*), south of the centre at 191/1–9 Thanon Charoenrat (⊕042/811302, ⓕ832680; ❸), offers the same choice of facilities but is not as good value, though some of its rooms on the higher floors offer good mountain views.

The **food** at the *Nawng Neung Restaurant*, 8/22 Thanon Ruamjai, is delicious and very economical – *khao man kai* and noodle soup are specialities – but it's only open until 2pm. During the evening the central night market, on the east side of Thanon Charoenrat, serves up the usual budget eats, as well as the distinctly uncommon local delicacy, *khai ping* – barbecued eggs on skewers, which taste like coarse, salty soufflés. The clean and airy *Saw Ahaan*, 100m west of the clocktower on Thanon Nok Kaew, has a large range of moderately priced Thai dishes on its English-language menu, while the *Kungsee*, slightly south of the centre at 167/1 Thanon Charoenrat, is a simple open-air noodle restaurant, with a terrace offering pretty views over the river and the thickly forested hills beyond.

Phu Kradung National Park

The most accessible and popular of the parks in Loei province, **PHU KRADUNG NATIONAL PARK**, about 80km south of Loei, protects a grassy 1300-metre plateau whose temperate climate supports a number of tree, flower and bird species not normally found in tropical Thailand. Walking trails crisscross much of sixty-square-kilometre Phu Kradung (Bell Mountain), and you ought to reckon on spending three days here if you want to explore them fully – at a minimum you have to spend one night, as the trip from Loei to the top of the plateau and back can't be done comfortably in a day. The park is closed during the rainy season (June–Sept), owing to the increased risk of mud-slides and land-slips, and is at its busiest during weekends in December and January, when the summit headquarters is surrounded by a sea of tents.

Access and accommodation

To get to the park, take any bus between Loei and Khon Kaen and get off at the village of **Phu Kradung** (1hr 30min), then hop on a B20 songthaew for the remaining 7km to the well-organized **visitor centre** (Oct–May daily 7am–2pm), where you can pick up a trail map and pay the B200 admission fee. You can also leave your gear at the visitor centre, or hire a porter to tote it to the top for B10 per kilo. At park headquarters, up on the plateau 8km from the visitor centre, there are ten national park **bungalows** sleeping from eight people upwards (B100 per person); at busy times it is best to reserve in advance through the Forestry Department in Bangkok (see p.49). There are also kitsch wooden wigwams available for B100 per night, as well as conventional tents (B50; or you can pitch your own for B10); blankets (needed on cool-season nights) and pillows both go for B10 each, and mats for B5–10. Simple **restaurants** at park headquarters compete with several at the rim of the plateau, all of which can rustle up inexpensive, tasty food from limited ingredients, so there's no need to bring your own provisions. On the plain beneath the plateau a private concern with its own restaurant, *Phu Kradung Resort*, operates 2–3km from the visitor centre towards Phu Kradung village (☎042/871076; ❸); its bungalows, with attached cold-water bathrooms, electricity and blankets, sleep five or six people.

The park

The gruelling main **trail** leads from the visitor centre 5.5km up the eastern side of Phu Kradung, passing occasional refreshment stalls, and becoming steeper and rockier on the last 1km, with wooden steps over the most difficult parts; most people take at least three hours, including rest stops. The trail is occasionally closed for maintenance, when a parallel 4.5-kilometre trail, running just a few hundred metres to the north of the main trail, is opened up in its place. At the end of the climb, the unbelievable view as your head peeps over the rim more than rewards the effort: flat as a playing field, the broad plateau is dotted with odd clumps of pine trees thinned by periodic lightning fires, which give it the appearance of a country park. Several feeder trails fan out from here, including a 9.5-kilometre path along the precipitous southern edge that offers sweeping views of Dong Phaya Yen, the untidy range of mountains to the southeast that forms the unofficial border between the northeast and the central plains. Another trail heads along the eastern rim for 2.5km to Pha Nok An – also reached by a two-kilometre path due east from the headquarters – which looks down on neat rice fields and matchbox-like houses in the valley below, an outlook that's especially breathtaking at sunrise.

The attractions of the mountain come and go with the **seasons**. October is muddy after the rains, but the waterfalls which tumble off the northwestern edge of the plateau are in full cascade and the main trail is green and shady. December brings out the maple leaves; by February the waterfalls have disappeared and the vegetation on the lower slopes has been burnt away. April is good for the rhododendrons and wild roses, which in Thailand are only found at such high altitudes as this.

Among the park's **wildlife**, mammals such as elephants, sambar deer and gibbons can be seen very occasionally, but they generally confine themselves to the evergreen forest on the northern part of the plateau, which is out of bounds to visitors. In the temperate pines, oaks and beeches that dot the rest of the plateau you're more likely to spot resident **birds** such as jays, sultan tits and snowy-browed flycatchers if you're out walking in the early morning and evening.

Nam Nao National Park

Amongst the undulating sandstone hills of the Phetchabun range, the flat-topped summit of Phu Phajit (1271m), **Nam Nao National Park**'s highest peak, can be seen to the southwest from nearby Phu Kradung National Park.

At just under a thousand square kilometres, Nam Nao is larger and more ecologically valuable than its neighbour, with a healthy population of possibly over a hundred mammal species, including large animals such as forest elephant, banteng and a handful of tigers, and more often-seen barking deer, gibbons and leaf monkeys, as well as over two hundred bird species. These creatures thrive in habitats ranging from tropical bamboo and banana stands to the dominant features of dry evergreen forest, grasslands, open forest and pine stands that look almost European. Though the park was established in 1972, it was regarded as unsafe for visitors, remaining a stronghold for guerillas of the Communist Party of Thailand until the early 1980s; still much less visited than Phu Kradung, it can provide a sense of real solitude. The range of wildlife here also benefited from a physical isolation which stopped abruptly in 1975, when Highway 12 was cut through the park and poachers could gain access more easily. However, as the park adjoins the **Phu Khieo Wildlife Sanctuary**, there is beneficial movement by some species between the two areas.

The turn-off to the park is on Highway 12; look out for the sign at kilometre-stone 50, 147km west of Khon Kaen and 160km by road from Loei. Several **buses** a day run through the park from Khon Kaen and Loei – both about two-to-three-hour journeys. Once you've paid the B200 admission fee, walk or hitch the 2km down the potholed road past the park headquarters to the **visitor centre** (daily 8am–4pm), where you can pick up an English-language brochure which contains a rough sketch map of the park. **Accommodation** here consists of ten bungalows (B500 for an eight-person bungalow), and a campsite where two-man tents can be hired (B40 per day) or you can pitch your own (B10 per person); blankets (B10) and gas lamps (B100) are also available for rent. Stalls near headquarters sell simple **meals**.

A good network of clearly-marked circular forest **trails** begin near the park headquarters, ranging from a one-kilometre nature trail teeming with butterflies, to a six-kilometre track known for occasional elephant sightings; another 3.5-kilometre trail climbs through mixed deciduous forest to the Phu Kor outlook, with its sweeping views across to Phu Phajit. Other trails can be accessed directly from Highway 12, most of them clearly signposted from the road: at kilometre-stone 39, a steep climb up 260 roughly hewn steps leads to the Tam Par Hong viewpoint, a rocky outcrop offering stunning panoramas of the park; and at kilometre-stone 67, a seven-hundred-metre trail leads to the beautiful Haew Sai waterfall, best seen during or immediately after the rainy season. Experienced walkers can reach the top of Phu Phajit along a rugged trail which begins from kilometre-stone 69; you need to hire a guide from the visitor centre (book in advance through the Forestry Department in Bangkok – see p.75) for the steep six-hour climb. Most people camp on top, bringing their own gear and supplies, before making the descent the next day.

Phu Reua National Park

About 50km west of Loei, the 120-square-kilometre **Phu Reua National Park** gets the name "Boat Mountain" from its resemblance to an upturned sampan, with the sharp ridge of its hull running southeast to northwest. The highest point of the ridge, Phu Reua Peak (1365m), offers one of the most spectacular panoramas in Thailand: the land drops away sharply on the Laos side, allowing views over toy-town villages to countless green-ridged mountains spreading towards Louang Phabang. To the northwest rises Phu Soai Dao (2102m) on Laos's western border; to the south are the Phetchabun mountains.

Access and accommodation

The nine-kilometre paved road north from Highway 203 to the summit, means the park can get crowded at weekends, though during the week you'll probably have the place to yourself. The snag is that there's no organized **public transport** up the steep summit road – regular Lom Sak and Phitsanulok buses from Loei can drop you at the turn-off to the park on Highway 203, but then you'll have to walk/hitch or wait for a songthaew to fill up (B40 one way). The easiest option would be to **rent a motorbike** at the *Muang Loei* guest house in Loei (see p.512). Once on the summit road, you have to pay B200 admission at a checkpoint, before reaching the **visitor centre** after 4km (daily 5am–8pm), which has a trail map, several simple restaurants with erratic opening hours, and, in the pretty, pine-shaded grounds, four standard-issue, five-berth national park **bungalows** (B250 per bungalow). **Tents** are available to rent at the visitor centre for B50 (or there's a B30 charge if you bring your own) and can be pitched at the campsite (4km further up the mountain and 1500m along a dirt road from the summit road), where foodstalls set up shop at weekends. Warm clothes are essential on cool-season nights – the lowest temperature in Thailand (-4°C) was recorded here in 1981 – and even by day the mountain is usually cool and breezy.

The park

A day's worth of well-marked trails fan out over the meadows and pine and broad-leaved evergreen forests of Phu Reua, taking in gardens of strange rock formations, the best westerly viewpoint, Phu Kut, and, during and just after the rainy season, several waterfalls. The most spectacular viewpoint, Phu Reua Peak, is an easy one-kilometre stroll from the top of the summit road where the songthaews drop you. The park's population of barking deer, wild pigs and pheasants has declined over recent years – rangers' attempts to stop poaching by local villagers have been largely unsuccessful and have resulted in occasional armed clashes – but you may be lucky enough to spot one of 26 bird species, which include the crested serpent-eagle, green-billed malkoha, greater coucal, Asian fairy-bluebird, rufescent prinia and white-rumped munia, as well as several species of babbler, barbet, bulbul and drongo.

Phu Hin Rongkla National Park

Thailand's densely forested hills and mountains have always harboured bandits and insurgents, and the rugged 300-square-kilometre tract of highland known as **PHU HIN RONGKLA NATIONAL PARK** is no exception: for over a decade these mountains, straddling Phitsanulok, Phetchabun and Loei provinces, were the stronghold of the **Communist Party of Thailand**. Founded in 1942 and banned ten years later, the CPT went underground and by 1967 had established a self-contained command centre in Phu Hin Rongkla, complete with a hospital, library and a printing press that even issued birth and death certificates. Despite assaults on the Phu Hin Rongkla base from government forces, numbers swelled in the wake of the murderous suppression of Bangkok pro-democracy demonstrations in 1973 and 1976. Then, in 1978, a policy of amnesty in return for the surrender of weapons was extended to the students and others who had fled to the hills; over the next few years, as CPT members returned to the cities, the party began to crumble. As the threat of insurgence diminished, the government built roads through Phu Hin Rongkla and other inaccessible parts of Isaan; finally, in 1982, Phu Hin Rongkla was declared a national park.

The park's history is a significant part of its appeal, but for most visitors Phu Hin Rongkla is principally a refreshing change of scenery – and temperature – from the plains to the east and west. At an elevation that rises to about 1800m, much of the park's vegetation is typical of a tropical mountain forest, with trees growing much further apart than they do in the valleys, leaving occasional expanses of exposed rock, peppered by low-lying scrub and mon-tane flowers. Walking through these open forests is relatively easy, and the park's few short trails take you across some of the most attractive parts of the stony terrain.

Access and accommodation

Getting to Phu Hin Rongkla by public transport is a hassle, involving uncertain connections and lengthy journeys. **From Loei**, take a Phitsanulok-bound bus to either **Nakhon Thai** (130km southwest on the junction of routes 2013 and 2331), or **Lom Sak** (140km down Highway 203); **from Phitsanulok**, take an hourly bus direct to Nakhon Thai. Route 2331 is the main access road through the park, and about three songthaews make the daily 20km run from Nakhon Thai to the park visitor centre and back. From Lom Sak you have to hire a motorbike taxi to take you the 30km to the visitor centre (about B150).

All in all, considering you have to trek fair distances along Route 2331 to get between trailheads once you're in the park, you're much better off renting your own transport from either Phitsanulok or Loei. If travelling by **car** or **motorbike** from Loei, your quickest route is west via Highway 203, then south on Route 2013 to Nakhon Thai, and southeast on Route 2331. From Phitsanulok, follow Highway 12 eastwards towards Lom Sak for 68km, then north along Route 2013 to Nakhon Thai.

About 10km after entering the park gates via Nakhon Thai on Highway 2331, you'll reach the **visitor centre**, alongside the park headquarters and a rudimentary restaurant. The centre doubles as a small CPT **museum** and provides free maps giving trail distances and routes. There's not really enough in the park to merit an **overnight stay**, though there are bungalows here (❹–❺) and tents (from B150). It's also possible to stay in Lom Sak: *Pen Sin 1* at 33/8 Thanon Wachi (☎056/701545; ❷) and *Sawang Hotel* at 147/6 Thanon Samakkichai (☎056/701642; ❶–❷) are both within a few minutes' walk of the bus station.

The park

The best of the park's trails is the 3.5-kilometre **Lan Hin Pum** (One Million Knotty Rocks), which starts about 5km east of the visitor centre. It runs through a superb natural rock garden that's particularly pretty in the rainy season when wild orchids and all kinds of hardy flowers bloom amongst the mosses, ferns and lichen. Halfway through the circuit you come to a precipice overlooking dense jungle, usually with plenty of mist to heighten the atmosphere; the route also passes the office of the Communist Party's headquarters, as well as Pha Chu Thong, the so-called "flag-raising cliff" where the red flag was unfurled after every CPT victory.

A less dramatic 1500-metre walk across **Lan Hin Daeg** (One Million Broken Rocks) begins 3km west of the visitor centre; the rocks here are so deeply fissured that at times it feels like picking your way across a stegosaurus's back. Clogged with ferns and mosses, the well-camouflaged crevices made ideal natural hideouts and air-raid shelters for the CPT – with full command of terrain like this, it's hardly surprising that they withstood some fifteen years of persistent battery from the government forces.

Along the Mekhong

The **Mekhong** is the one of the great rivers of the world, the third longest in Asia, after the Yangtse and the Yellow River. From its source 4920m up on the east Tibetan plateau it roars down through China's Yunnan province – where it's known as Lancang Jiang, the "Turbulent River" – before snaking its way a little more peaceably between Burma and Laos, then, by way of the so-called Golden Triangle, as the border between Thailand and Laos. After a brief shimmy into rural Laos via Louang Phabang, the river reappears on the scene in Isaan to form 750km of the border between Thailand and Laos. From Laos it crosses Cambodia and continues south to Vietnam, where it splinters into the many arms of the Mekhong delta before flowing into the South China Sea, 4184km from where its journey began.

This dramatic stretch around Isaan is one of the more accessible places to observe the mighty river, and as Laos opens further border crossings to visitors, the Mekhong is slowly becoming more of a transport link and less of a forbidding barrier. The guest houses along the upper part of this stretch, east from **Chiang Khan**, are geared towards relaxation and gentle exploration of the rural way of life along the river bank. **Nong Khai**, the terminus of the rail line from Bangkok and the principal jumping-off point for trips to the Lao capital of Vientiane, is the pivotal town on the river, but has lost some of its restful charm since the building of the massive Thai-Australian Friendship Bridge and the ensuing increase in cross-border trade. East of Nong Khai you're into wild country; here the unique natural beauty of **Wat Phu Tok** is well worth the hefty detour, and your Mekhong journey wouldn't be complete without seeing **Wat Phra That Phanom**, a place of pilgrimage for 2500 years. Sights get sparse beyond that, although by continuing south through **Mukdahan** you can join up with the southern Isaan route at Ubon Ratchathani (see p.488).

A road, served by very slow **buses** and **songthaews**, runs beside or at least parallel to the river as far as Mukdahan. If you've got the time (allow at least a week to do it any sort of justice) you could make the entire marathon journey described in this section, although realistically you'll probably start in Nong Khai and work your way either upstream or downstream from there. **Motorbike** rental may provide another incentive to base yourself in Nong Khai: having your own transport will give you more freedom of movement in this region, and the roads are quiet and easy to negotiate, though often in a state of disrepair. There's no official long-distance **boat** transport along this stretch of the river, at least from the Thai side, though if you're willing to spend the money it's possible to arrange private charters downstream from Chiang Khan all the way to Nong Khai.

Chiang Khan to Tha Bo

Rustic "backpackers' resorts" – and the travelling between them – are the chief draw along the reach of the Mekhong between **Chiang Khan** and **Tha Bo**. Highway 211 covers this whole course: songthaews take you from Chiang Khan to Pak Chom, from where buses complete the journey, stopping at all towns en route.

Chiang Khan

The Mekhong route starts promisingly at **CHIANG KHAN**, a friendly town that happily hasn't been converted to concrete yet. Rows of shuttered wooden shophouses stretch out in a two-kilometre-long ribbon parallel to the river, which for much of the year runs red with what locals call "the blood of the trees": rampant deforestation on the Lao side causes the rust-coloured topsoil to erode into the river. The town has only two streets – the main through route (Highway 211, also known as Thanon Sri Chiang Khan) and the quieter Thanon Chai Khong on the waterfront – with a line of sois connecting them numbered from west to east.

Arguably the most enjoyable thing you can do here is to hitch up with other travellers for a **boat trip** on the river, organized through one of the guest houses. If you opt to go **upstream**, you'll head west towards the lofty mountains of Khao Laem and Khao Ngu on the Thai side and Phu Lane and Phu Hat Song in Laos, gliding round a long, slow bend to the mouth of the Heuang River tributary, 20km from Chiang Khan, which forms the border to the west of this point; stops can be arranged at the Ban Khok Mat Queen's Project to see silk- and cotton-weaving and an agricultural experiment area, and at Hat Sai Kaew, a sandy beach for swimming. Upstream trips cost between B200 and B400 per person depending on how far you venture and the number of people in the boat, and take two to three hours. A ride **downstream to Pak Chom** will take you through some of the most beautiful scenery on the Thai Mekhong: hills and cliffs of all shapes and sizes advance and recede around the winding flow, and outside the rainy season, the rapids are dramatic without being dangerous (best between December and April), and the shores and islands are enlivened by neat grids of market gardens. This jaunt costs around B1300 for the boat (maximum of three people), and takes around six hours, including an hour in Pak Chom, if you go both ways. Private charters all the way **downstream to Nong Khai** will set you back around B8500 for the boat (maximum of eight people); the journey takes around eight hours. Most guest houses also offer a **sunset on the Mekhong** cruise for about B150 per person.

It's also worth taking a walk towards the eastern end of the river road to **Wat Tha Khok**, by Soi 20, for its unobstructed view across the majestic Mekhong. The Lao viharn shows some odd French influences in its balustrades, rounded arches and elegantly coloured ceiling. Continuing another 2km east along the main highway, a left turn back towards the river will bring you to **Wat Tha Khaek**, a formerly ramshackle forest temple which, on the back of millions of bahts' worth of donations from Thai tourists, has embarked on an ambitious building programme in a bizarre mix of traditional and modern styles. One kilometre further along this side road lies the reason for the influx of visitors: at this point, the river runs over rocks at a wide bend to form the modest rapids of **Kaeng Kut Khu**. Set against the forested hillside of imaginatively named

Phu Yai (Big Mountain), it's a pretty enough spot, with small restaurants and souvenir shops shaded by trees on the river bank. If you're feeling brave, try the local speciality *kung tun*, or "dancing shrimp" – fresh shrimp served live with a lime juice and chilli sauce.

Practicalities

Songthaews from Loei and Pak Chom (every 30min) and **buses** from Loei (every 15min) stop at the west end of town near the junction of Highway 201 (the road from Loei) and Highway 211. There's **internet access** at the northern end of Soi 10, near the junction with Highway 211 (daily 8am–10pm; B50 per hour), and a Thai Farmers' Bank on the highway between sois 8 and 9. You can extend your visa at the **immigration office** (Mon–Fri 8.30am–4.30pm; ☎042/821911 or 821175), a ten-minute walk east along Thanon Chai Khong from the *Rabieng* restaurant.

When it comes to **accommodation**, there are three excellent options strung out along the riverside Thanon Chai Khong, all of which can arrange boat trips and tours of the area. The *Ton Kong Guest House* at no. 299/3, between sois 9 and 10 (☎042/821547; ❶–❸), is run by a welcoming Thai couple and has eight clean rooms – some en suite, one with air-conditioning – and a first-floor terrace overlooking the river, perfect for lounging; the popular restaurant downstairs serves a good range of Thai dishes, as well as Western breakfasts and a mean margarita. Extras on offer include traditional massage (B120 per hour), herbal steam baths (B150 per hour), bicycle rental (B60 per day), motorbike rental (B200 per day), boat trips and tailor-made tours to just about anywhere – from home-stays in local villages to a karaoke night out that finishes up with a 3am tipple at the morning market. Opposite at no. 300, the *Friendship Guest House* (☎042/822052; ❷) has eight cosy wood-panelled rooms with spotlessly clean shared bathrooms in a lovely 50-year-old teak house; the hot showers are free of charge, and alongside the usual boat trips, massages and bike rental, the Thai-Swedish owners can also arrange car rental for B1000 per day. A little further west along Thanon Chai Khong opposite Soi 8, the riverside *Rimkong Pub and Restaurant* at no. 294 (☎042/821125; ❶) is run by a helpful Thai-French couple who have lived in Chiang Khan for over nine years and are a great source of information on the area; basic wooden rooms share clean cold-water bathrooms, and there's a small terrace on the top floor. Boat trips and a huge range of tours are available here, as well as transport to nearby towns. A more traditional hotel is the *Souksomboon* (☎042/821064; ❷), built around a courtyard on Thanon Khong, between sois 8 and 9; its best rooms overlook the river with attached cold-water bathrooms, or there are cheaper share-bathroom options available. For more in the way of luxury, the *Chiang Khan Hill Resort* (☎042/821285, ℱ821415, ⓦwww.geocities.com/chkhill; ❺–❼) offers fan-cooled and air-conditioned bungalows, all with hot-water bathrooms, in a pretty garden overlooking the river at Kaeng Kut Khu.

The most fruitful hunting grounds for **food** are the day market (which opens at 3am and is at its best before 9am), on the south side of Thanon Sri Chiang Khan between sois 9 and 10; and the night market (6–8pm), between sois 18 and 19 on the same road. For a hearty *phat thai*, head for *Lom Look* on the east side of Soi 9. The best restaurant in town, with peaceful water views and inexpensive Chinese and Thai dishes, is *Rabieng*, nearby at the T-junction with Soi 9 and the river road.

Pak Chom, Sang Khom and Wat Hin Ma Beng

Half-hourly songthaews from Chiang Khan cover the beautiful, winding route to **PAK CHOM**, 41km downriver, where you can pick up a bus from Loei (7 daily) to continue your journey towards Nong Khai via Sang Khom and Sri Chiangmai. Pak Chom used to be the site of a refugee camp for fifteen thousand Lao Hmong, who were moved in 1992 to Chiang Rai province; its array of largely redundant administrative buildings has something of the air of a ghost town, offering little incentive to stay. If you get stuck, the *Pak Chom Guest House* (❶), at the west end of town, is at least set in leafy grounds, with primitive bungalows on stilts overlooking the river, and extras are laid on such as boat trips (B60 per hour), massages (B100 per hour) and a communal Thai-Lao dinner (B70). The riverside *Jumpee Guest House* (❶), signposted down the same road, has three slightly nicer huts and a tiny restaurant.

Beyond Pak Chom, the road through the Mekhong valley becomes flatter and straighter. After 50km, a sign in English points down a side road to **Than Tip Falls**, 3km south, which is well worth seeking out. The ten-metre-high waterfall splashes down into a rock pool overhung by jungle on three sides; higher up, a bigger waterfall has a good pool for swimming, and if you can face the climb you can explore three higher levels.

Staying in one of the **"backpackers' resorts"** in idyllic, tree-shaded **SANG KHOM**, 63km east of Pak Chom, puts you in the heart of an especially lush stretch of the river within easy **biking** distance of several backroad villages and temples. You can rent bicycles (B70 per day) and motorbikes (B200–300 per day) at *River Huts* (☎042/441012, ✉riverhuts@hotmail.com; ❶), which occupies a patch of shady river bank, with bungalows that run to tables, chairs and verandas, and a casual pally atmosphere provided by the American-Thai owners. The establishment offers really delicious Thai food prepared by Noopit, a professional cook (she can also do Western dishes on request), a large library, **internet access** and an inflatable boat. Fifty metres further upstream, *Buoy Guest House* (☎042/441065; ❶) enjoys the best location: decent bamboo huts, with beautiful views out over the river, are set in a spacious compound, half of it on a spit of land reached by a wooden bridge over a small tributary. The obliging owners also have inner tubes, dugout canoes and fishing boats to get you onto the Mekhong, or if that sounds too strenuous, you can settle for a massage instead (B100 per hour) or just relax in the hammocks strung from the veranda of every hut. Food is available on a deck overlooking the stream (most of it also in vegetarian versions), and motorbikes can be rented here for B200 per day. Next door, just upstream of Buoy, the *New TXK (Mama's) Guest House* is the oldest guest house in Sang Khom, but isn't a patch on its neighbours. Two kilometres east of Sang Khom on the Nong Khai road, the French-run *Siam Bungalows* (☎042/441399; ❸) offers a little more luxury; the pristine bungalows, some with hot-water showers attached are set in a beautiful shady garden – book ahead for the nicest bungalow, set directly on the river. Amenities include a pleasant open-air bar/restaurant, complete with pool table and small library, and there are plans to build a swimming pool. Bikes are available (B50 per day) for exploring the local area, or the owners can arrange boating/camping trips along the Mekhong.

Another 19km east on Route 211, midway between Sang Khom and Sri Chiangmai, **Wat Hin Ma Beng** is a famous meditation temple, popular with Thai pilgrims and rich donors. The long white boundary wall and huge modern buildings are evidence of the temple's prosperity, but its reputation is in fact based on the asceticism of the monks of the Thammayut sect, who keep themselves in strict poverty and allow only one meal a day to interrupt their meditation. The flood of merit-makers, however, proved too distracting for the founder of the wat, Luang Phu Thet, who before his death in 1994 decamped to the peace and quiet of Wat Tham Kham near Sakhon Nakhon. Visitors have the opportunity to revere an unnervingly lifelike waxwork of the great monk that has been set up next to the river, near a large statue of a tiger, the symbol of hermits. Across the narrow stretch of water here, you can get a good look at a much less prosperous Lao forest wat.

Sri Chiangmai and Wat Nam Mong

Unprepossessing it may be, but **SRI CHIANGMAI**, 38km east of Sang Khom, is known in Chinese catering circles as one of the world's leading manufacturing centres of spring-roll wrappers: if the weather's fine, production of these rice-flour discs, which you can see drying on bamboo racks around the town and taste in local restaurants, hits 200,000 pieces per day. Outside of the rainy season, the resourceful burghers of Sri Chiangmai also reclaim vast tracts of land from the Mekhong to grow tomatoes, which has led to the establishment of Thailand's largest ketchup factory and a jolly tomato festival, featuring messy tomato-eating contests and the election of a Miss Tomato, in February. Many of these tomato growers and spring-roll-wrapper makers are Vietnamese, victims of the upheavals caused by World War II and two Indochina wars since, who have fled across Laos to safe haven in Thailand; today you'll still hear older Vietnamese people speaking French in the streets. The town also offers the unique opportunity of gazing at the backstreets of Vientiane, directly across the Mekhong, without having to go through all the expensive red tape to get there. It looks quite unappealing and lifeless, replicating the concrete architecture of the Thai side.

Here again, one outstanding **guest house** makes the town accessible to farangs who want to experience its daily life. *Tim Guest House* (T & F 042/451072, W www.nk.ksc.co.th/timgh; 1) has clean, quiet rooms – shared bathrooms have solar-heated water – at 553 Moo 2, Thanon Rimkhong (the riverfront road), as well as a well-stocked library and lots of helpful information boards. The hospitable Swiss owner spoils homesick guests with ham, pâté, French bread (also available fresh from the town bakery's oven at 3.30pm every day), pizzas and good coffee, as well as some tasty Thai food. In addition to herbal saunas and massages, he can arrange bicycle and motorbike rental (respectively B30 and B150–200 per day) and provide some simple hand-drawn maps – the guest house is a handy jumping-off point for **Ban Phu** (see p.528), 35km south, just one hour away by motorbike along a new paved road. Also on offer are **boat trips** to Wat Hin Ma Beng (B800 per boat), past the suburbs of Vientiane, river islands and swimming beaches; on the way you might be lucky enough to see gold-panners and fishermen at work, as well as wild ducks, herons and kingfishers, or you could opt for the shorter version, a one-hour sunset trip (B40 per person). It's also possible to charter a boat down to Nong Khai (B180–800 per person depending on the number of passengers). The easiest way to get on the water, however, is to take advantage of the large, permanently moored raft down on the river, which the owner has set up as a place where guests can sit, read and drink; it's a lovely spot at the end of the day, bobbing about on the water and watching the sun set.

Thanks to ketchup and spring-roll traffic, the condition of Highway 211 and the frequency of buses improve noticeably east of Sri Chiangmai. **Wat Nam Mong** can be seen across the fields on the west side of the road, 12km out of

Sri Chiangmai and 3km before **Tha Bo**. A slender Lao-style viharn makes the perfect setting for the gaunt Phra Ong Thu image inside. Stern but handsome, the 300-year-old bronze image is the brother of a more famous Buddha in Laos – it's much revered, especially by Lao emigrants, some of whom even send their sons from the US to serve as monks here.

Nong Khai and around

The major border town in these parts is **NONG KHAI**, still a backwater but developing fast since the construction of the huge Thai-Australian Friendship Bridge over the Mekong on the west side of town in 1994. Occupying a strategic position at the end of Highway 2 and the northeastern rail line, and just 24km from Vientiane, Nong Khai acts as a conduit for goods bought and sold by Thais and Lao, who are allowed to pass between the two cities freely for stays of up to three days. For the souvenir markets that have sprung up around the main pier, **Tha Sadet**, and the slipway to the bridge, the Lao bring across silver, wood and cane items, and sundry goods from the old Soviet bloc; they return with noodles, soap powder, ketchup, warm clothes and toilet rolls.

As with most of the towns along this part of the Mekong, the thing to do in Nong Khai is just to take it easy, enjoying the riverside atmosphere and the peaceful settings of its guest houses, which offer good value. Before you lapse into a relaxation-induced coma, though, try joining an evening river tour, or make a day-trip out to see the sculptures and rock formations in the surrounding countryside.

The Town

Nong Khai lays itself out along the south bank of the Mekong in a four-kilometre band which is never more than 500m deep. Running from east to

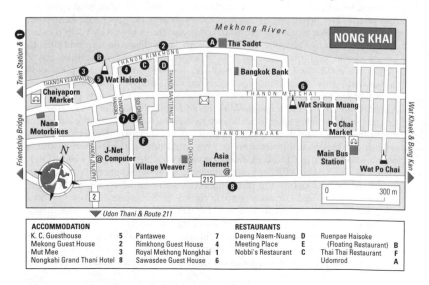

ACCOMMODATION				RESTAURANTS			
K. C. Guesthouse	5	Pantawee	7	Daeng Naem-Nuang	D	Ruenpae Haisoke	
Mekong Guest House	2	Rimkhong Guest House	4	Meeting Place	E	(Floating Restaurant)	B
Mut Mee	3	Royal Mekong Nongkhai	1	Nobbi's Restaurant	C	Thai Thai Restaurant	F
Nongkahi Grand Thani Hotel	8	Sawasdee Guest House	6			Udomrod	A

west, Thanon Meechai dominates activity: the main shops and businesses are plumb in the middle around the post office, with more frenetic commerce to the east at the Po Chai day market by the bus station, and to the west at the Chaiyaporn night market. Although most of the buildings have been replaced by concrete boxes, a few weather-beaten wooden houses remain, their attractive balconies, porticoes and slatted shutters showing the influence of colonial architecture, which was imported from across the river before the French were forced out of Laos in 1954.

The most pleasant place for a stroll, however, is the riverside area. Although built up in the centre around Tha Sadet, it becomes rustic and leafy around the fringes, which are often busy with people bathing, washing their clothes and fishing, especially in the early morning and evening. The largest freshwater fish in the world, the *pla buk*, or **giant catfish**, which can weigh in at 300kg, lives in the Mekhong (see box on p.394): instead of the old method of harpooning, fishermen now trawl the river with nets during the catfish season (April–June), when you can occasionally see them struggling with these leviathans on the river bank. If you're lucky, you might also catch sight of a sunken chedi, **Phra That Nong Khai**, which slipped into the river in 1847 and has since subsided so far that it's only visible in the dry season.

To catch the best of life on the river, take the **boat trip** which sets out from the *Ruenpae Haisoke* floating restaurant behind the temple at the top of Thanon Haisoke every evening at 5.30pm. At B30 it's the least expensive way of getting onto the Mekhong in Thailand, and runs up and down the length of Nong Khai for an hour and a half to two hours, sticking to the Thai side. Reasonably priced drinks can be ordered from the bar; food – expensive and best avoided – has to be ordered twenty minutes before the boat leaves. There's no stunning scenery, but plenty of activity on both river banks as the sun sets behind the Friendship Bridge.

The main temple of the region is **Wat Po Chai** at the east end of Thanon Prajak. The cruciform viharn with its complex and elegant array of Lao tiers shelters a venerated gold image, the Phra Sai Buddha. Prince Chakri, the future Rama I, is said to have looted the image from Vientiane along with the Emerald Buddha, but the boat which was bringing back the Phra Sai overturned and sank in the Mekhong. Later, the statue miraculously rose to the surface and the grateful people of Nong Khai built this great hangar of a viharn to house it, where the present king, Chakri's descendant, comes every year to pay his respects. It's worth a visit for the Buddha's stagy setting, in front of a steep, flame-covered altar, dazzlingly lit from above and below in green. The solid gold is so highly polished that you have to peer carefully to make out the Sukhothai influence in its haughty expression and beaked nose.

Fifteen minutes' walk west of Wat Po Chai at 1151 Soi Chitapanya, just off Thanon Prajak, **Village Weaver Handicrafts** (daily 8am–6pm; ☏042/411236, ⓔvillage@udon.ksc.co.th) specializes in **mut mee** (literally "tied strings"), the northeastern method of tie-dyeing bundles of cotton thread before hand-weaving, which produces geometrical patterns on a coloured base. Through a self-help project initiated in 1982 to help local rural women earn cash, the work is produced in nearby villages and in the yard behind the shop, where you can watch the weaving process (daily except Sun). White on indigo is the simplest, most traditional form, but the shop also carries a wide range of more richly patterned lengths of silk and cotton, as well as ready-made clothes, bags and "axe" pillows; they offer a very reasonable and professional posting and packing service back to your home country, and it's also possible to order by email. Five kilometres south of Nong Khai on the road to Udon

Thani, the **Village Vocational Training Centre** is another self-help initiative by the Good Shepherd Sisters, producing **pottery** and handicrafts sold at the Isan Shop, 1km back towards Nong Khai on the same road; you're welcome to visit the centre to see the artisans at work (centre and shop both open Mon–Sat 9am–5pm).

Practicalities

From Bangkok, you'll most likely be coming to Nong Khai by night **train**, arriving just after dawn at the station 2km west of the centre. Day **buses** from all points in Isaan and night buses from further afield pull in at the terminal on the east side of town off Thanon Prajak. As everything in Nong Khai is so spread out, you might want to consider hopping on a **tuk-tuk** (B20 for a medium-length journey such as Chaiyaporn Market to Tha Sadet) for getting around. To get to some of the area's remoter spots, **motorbikes** can be rented (from B200 a day) at the *K.C. Guesthouse* and at the travel agency within the *Pantawee Hotel* (see opposite), while Village Weaver Handicrafts (see p.523) offers **four-wheel drives** for around B1000 per day including insurance; alternatively, you can hire a car and driver from the *Nongkhai Grand Thani Hotel* (see

---

Trips to Laos

As Laos has loosened its attitudes towards tourism in recent years, the means of getting a tourist visa for independent travel have changed rapidly, and can be expected to continue changing over the next few years. What follows is an outline of the options at the time of going to press, and some pointers as to how things might develop. In Nong Khai, the *Mut Mee Guest House* is a good source of information on visas and travel to Laos.

You can now get a fifteen-day tourist visa on arrival at Vientiane airport, at Louang Phabang airport and at the Friendship Bridge, Nong Khai, for US$30 (it's possible to pay in baht at the bridge). Fifteen-day visas can also be obtained at the Lao embassy in Bangkok or the consulate in Khon Kaen for up to B1000 in three working days or so, and can be extended for a further fifteen days at any Vientiane travel agent or at the immigration department in Vientiane for US$2 per day. Thirty-day, non-extendable visas are available from the Bangkok embassy (see p.193) and the Khon Kaen consulate (see p.505). Travel agents in Bangkok, Chiang Mai, Chiang Khong and other major tourist centres are another source of visas.

You need to specify your chosen point of entry into Laos if you apply for your visa in advance. There are currently five permissible overland crossing points: Chiang Khong in northern Thailand, and Nong Khai, Nakhon Phanom, Mukdahan and Chong Mek in Isaan. (Plans are afoot for a new bridge across the Mekhong at Mukdahan, with construction due to begin in late 2002.)

The transport options for crossing to Laos are much simpler. From Bangkok and Chiang Mai there are regular flights to Vientiane (daily and twice-weekly respectively), and frequent public ferries traverse the Mekhong from Chiang Khong, Nakhon Phanom and Mukdahan, while at Chong Mek it's just a question of walking between the two border posts. The ferry service from Nong Khai is now reserved for Thais and Lao, so farangs have to use the Thai-Australian Friendship Bridge (daily 8am–8pm; at lunchtime between 2pm and 4pm and at weekends there is a B10 "overtime" charge to get across). From downtown Nong Khai, take a tuk-tuk to the foot of the bridge (about B20–30), then a minibus (B10) across the span itself, before catching a taxi (about B400 for up to four people), tuk-tuk (B25) or bus (B5) to Vientiane, 24km away. An air-conditioned minibus meets incoming passengers at Udon Thani airport to carry them to the Lao side of the bridge (40min; B100).

below) for around B1500 per day. For local exploration, **bicycles** are available at *Mut Mee*, *K.C.* and *Mekong* guest houses (all listed below).

There's a small **TAT information booth** (daily 8.30am–4.30pm; ⓣ & ⓕ042/467844) at the Tha Udom market on the road leading up to the Friendship Bridge, although its opening hours (and days) can be erratic as it's only staffed by one person. If time's running out on your Thai tourist visa, you should be able to get an extension at the **immigration office** (Mon–Fri 8.30am–4.30pm; ⓣ042/420242) further south on the same road. See the box opposite for details of how to get to Laos from Nong Khai, with fifteen-day visas available on arrival across the Friendship Bridge; longer thirty-day ones are only available from Khon Kaen and Bangkok.

There are several places offering **internet access**, including J-Net Computer, 1205 Thanon Jenjophit (daily 8.30–9pm; B20 per hour), and Asia Internet, on Highway 212 opposite the *Nongkhai Grand Thani Hotel* (daily 9am–9pm; B15 per hour). More central, but slightly pricier, are the terminals at the Wasambe Bookshop, on the funky little lane leading to *Mut Mee Guest House*; you can also send faxes and make international calls from here. The bookshop, run by American Michael Wilson, stocks an excellent selection of new **books** in English specially imported from the US, as well as a smaller selection of secondhand cast-offs. Bangkok Bank on Thanon Sisaket, off Thanon Meechai, has a daily **currency exchange** service until 5pm.

Accommodation

Nong Khai has a good choice of inexpensive **places to stay**, the best among which are *Mut Mee* and *Sawasdee*. In the wake of the Friendship Bridge has come a rash of luxury developments, of which more are to be expected.

K.C. Guesthouse, 1018 Thanon Keawworut ⓔnongsaa@hotmail.com; next to Wasambe Bookshop. This two-storey all-wooden guest house is a cheaper, more intimate alternative to *Mut Mee*, and just nearby so you can still hang out/eat there, as *K.C.* itself offers no food. Sharing two cold-water bathrooms, the simple, clean rooms have mosquito screens, shutters and fans, and there are bikes (B50 per day) and motorbikes (B200 per day) for rent; friendly management. ❷

Mekong Guest House, Thanon Rimkhong by Tha Sadet ⓣ042/460689. Good for watching the bustle at the pier from the pleasant riverside restaurant/bar with beer on tap, but noisy when it comes to sleeping. Recently refurbished, with clean tiled-floor rooms and hot-water bathrooms (both en-suite and shared), and a few dorm beds (B80). The nicest rooms overlook the river. ❷–❸

Mut Mee Guest House, 1111 Thanon Keawworut ⓕ042/460717, ⓦbkk.loxinfo.co.th/~wasambe /mutmee.html. The attractive riverside terrace is a magnet for travellers; well-kept rooms and bamboo huts, all fitted with fans and screens, sprawl around it. Bathrooms (hot water) are either shared or en-suite, and three-bed dorms are available (dorm bed B80). With helpful, well-informed staff and a good

riverside restaurant, it's also the home of the Nong Khai Alternative Center for irregular yoga and meditation and t'ai chi workshops. Mountain bikes are available for rent at a rate of B40 a day (ask for the hand-drawn map of local sights). ❷–❸

Nongkhai Grand Thani Hotel, 589 Moo 5, Nongkhai–Phonpisai road ⓣ042/420033, ⓕ412026, ⓦwww.nongkhaigrand.com. On the southern bypass, a luxury hotel with the *Dusit Thani* group's usual high standards of service. ❻

Pantawee Hotel, 1049 Thanon Haisoke ⓣ042/411568–9. A good mid-range choice that's surprisingly comfortable for the price: immaculately clean rooms come with hot-water bathrooms – some with fan, others with air-con. ❸

Rimkhong Guesthouse, 815/1–3 Thanon Rimkhong ⓣ042/460625. Looking across to the river, these two concrete buildings, each with six rooms, are set in a spacious park-like garden with trees and flowers, though the basic rooms, with overhead fans, mosquito nets and shared cold-water bathrooms, are pretty disappointing, and the management is off-hand. Okay if other guest houses are full. ❷

Royal Mekong Nongkhai, 222 Jommanee Beach ⓣ042/420024, ⓕ421280, ⓔMekong_Royal@

hotmail.com; in the riverside grounds west of town, 200m past the Friendship Bridge. Two-hundred-bed international-standard hotel; no beach, but there's a large swimming pool. ❻ **Sawasdee Guest House**, 402 Thanon Meechai ☏042/412502. A well-equipped, grand old wooden house round a pleasant courtyard, with helpful management: luggage storage and showers available for those catching a night train or bus. Fan-cooled rooms sharing cold-water bathrooms (try to avoid those overlooking the noisy main road), and air-con rooms with en-suite hot showers. ❶–❸

Eating

Among local people and tourists alike, the most popular **restaurants** in Nong Khai are the handful of moderately priced riverside terraces clustered around the pier on Thanon Rimkhong, though these compete with travellers' fare at guest houses and some excellent Vietnamese places.

Daeng Naem-Nuang, 1062/1–2 Thanon Banterngjit. Absolutely delicious Vietnamese food at this immaculately clean, popular and airy place: the speciality here is *nam nueng* – make-it-yourself fresh spring rolls with barbecue pork. The obliging owner will demonstrate how to build the rolls using fresh soft rice wrappers, the pork, vermicelli noodles, lettuce, mint, lemony *chat mooung* leaves, chopped starfruit, green banana, cucumber, garlic, chilli and a rich peanut sauce. Takeaways also available. Closes at 7pm. Inexpensive.
Meeting Place, 1117 Soi Chuenjitt. The speciality at this Australian-run bar/restaurant is fish and chips – the fish fresh from the Mekhong and fried in beer batter – but there are also burgers and pizza on offer, as well as beer on tap. The decor is somewhat spartan, but the place is friendly enough, and there's a pool table to help while away the evenings.
Mut Mee Guesthouse, Thanon Keawworut. This relaxed riverfront eating place under bamboo shelters is deservedly popular: good Thai dishes, particularly vegetarian versions, vie with tasty Western efforts including marinated pork steaks with french fries, French bread and home-made yoghurt, plus there's French red wine at a reasonable B55 a glass and beer on tap. Inexpensive.

Nobbi's Restaurant, 997 Thanon Rimkhong. Run by a German-Thai couple, this bright and busy restaurant is popular with expats for its all-day Western breakfasts, tasty pizzas and beer on tap. Books, newspapers and board-games are welcome extras. Happy hour 4–6pm.
Ruenpae Haisoke, behind Wat Haisoke. Justifiably popular: as well as running the boat trip mentioned on p.523, it has a floating restaurant that is permanently moored to the bank, where you can enjoy large portions of standard Thai dishes. Moderate.
Thai Thai Restaurant, 1155/8 Thanon Prajak. The place to come for honest, inexpensive Thai food; the menu in English is limited, but you can point out anything else you fancy on the impressive display counter. The similar *Dee Dee Pochana Restaurant* next door is also very popular. Daily noon–3am. Inexpensive.
Udomrod, Thanon Rimkhong. Particularly good food and atmosphere at this riverside terrace restaurant, specializing in *paw pia yuan* (Vietnamese spring rolls) and *plaa raat phrik* (whole fish cooked in chillies and garlic), and occasionally serving up fresh giant catfish in season.

Around Nong Khai

By far the easiest and most popular day-trip out of Nong Khai takes in **Sala Kaeo Kou**, with its surreal sculptures, a short songthaew hop to the east. To the southwest of town and also fairly easy to get to, **Wat Phra That Bang Phuan** offers classic temple sightseeing, while the natural rock formations at **Ban Phu** require much more effort and a full day out. Some of the sights upstream along the Mekhong described on the previous pages are also within day-tripping distance, and it's quite possible to get to Ban Chiang and back in a day, changing buses at Udon Thani.

Sala Kaeo Kou

Just off the main highway 5km east of Nong Khai, **Sala Kaeo Kou** (aka Wat Khaek; daily 7am–5pm; B10) is best known for its bizarre sculpture garden, which looks like the work of a giant artist on acid. The temple was founded by the late **Luang Phu Boonlua Surirat**, an unconventional Thai holy man who studied under a Hindu guru in Vietnam and preached in Laos until he was thrown out by the Communists in the late 1970s. His charisma – those who drank water offered by him would, it was rumoured, give up all they owned to the temple – and heavy emphasis on morality attracted many followers among the farmers of Nong Khai. Luang Phu's popularity suffered, however, after his eleven-month spell in prison for insulting King Bhumibol, a crime alleged by jealous neighbours and probably without foundation; he died a year after his release in August 1996.

Arrayed with pretty flowers and plants, the **sculpture garden** bristles with Buddhist, Hindu and secular figures, all executed in concrete with imaginative abandon by unskilled followers under Luang Phu's direction. The religious statues, in particular, are radically modern. Characteristics that marked the Buddha out as a supernatural being – tight curls and a bump on the crown of the head called the *ushnisha* – are here transformed into beehives, and the *rashmis* on top (flames depicting the Buddha's fiery intellect) are depicted as long, sharp spikes. The largest statue in the garden shows the familiar story of the kindly naga king, Muchalinda, sheltering the Buddha, who is lost in meditation, from the heavy rain and floods: here the Buddha has shrunk in significance and the seven-headed snake has grown to 25m, with fierce, gaping fangs and long tongues.

Many of the statues illustrate **Thai proverbs**. Near the entrance, an elephant surrounded by a pack of dogs symbolizes integrity, "as the elephant is indifferent to the barking dogs". The nearby serpent-tailed monster with the moon in his mouth – Rahoo, the cause of eclipses – serves as an injunction to oppose all obstacles, just as the people of Isaan and Laos used to ward off eclipses by banging drums and firing guns. In the corner furthest from the entrance, you enter the complex Circle of Life through a huge mouth representing the womb, inside which a hermit, a policeman, a monk, a rich man and a beggar, among others, represent different paths in life. A man with two wives is shown beating the older one because he is ensnared by the wishes of the younger one, and an old couple who have made the mistake of not having children now find they have only each other for comfort.

The disturbingly vacant, smiling faces of the garden Buddhas bear more than a passing resemblance to Luang Phu himself, whose picture you can see in the **temple building**, a huge white edifice with mosque-like domes – he's the one with the bouffant hairdo, dressed in white. Don't leave Sala Kaeo Kou without **feeding the fish**, an activity that's immensely popular with Thais and farangs alike; you can buy bags of food from the stalls near the garden's small lake. If you're heading over to **Laos**, the **Xiang Khouan** sculpture garden – Sala Kaeo Kou's precursor – shouldn't be missed; Luang Phu spent twenty years working on the sculptures there before his expulsion from the country in the late 1970s. The park is 25km from downtown Vientiane on the Mekhong River.

Wat Phra That Bang Phuan

More famous as the site of a now concealed 2000-year-old Indian chedi than for its modern replacement, rural **Wat Phra That Bang Phuan** remains a highly revered place of pilgrimage. The wat is in the hamlet of **Ban Bang**

Phuan, southwest of Nong Khai on Highway 211; buses west from Nong Khai no longer pass this way (they use the paved road along the river bank to Tha Bo), so to get here by public transport, take an Udon-bound service 12km down Highway 2 to Ban Nong Song Hong, then change onto an Udon–Sri Chiangmai bus for the remaining 12km. If you fancy breaking the journey in Nong Song Hong, look out for Nisachon, which sells a wide selection of attractive cotton next to its posh restaurant; it's on the east side of Highway 2 south of the police checkpoint.

The original **chedi** is supposed to have been built by disciples of the Buddha to hold 29 relics – pieces of breastbone – brought from India. A sixteenth-century king of Vientiane piously earned himself merit by building a tall Lao-style chedi over the top of the previous stupa; rain damage toppled this in 1970, but it was restored in 1977 to the fine, gleaming white edifice seen today. The unkempt compound also contains a small museum, crumbling brick chedis and some large open-air Buddhas.

Ban Phu

Deep in the countryside 61km southwest of Nong Khai, the wooded slopes around **BAN PHU** are dotted with strangely eroded sandstone formations which have long exerted a mystical hold over people in the surrounding area. Local wisdom has it that the outcrops, many of which were converted into small temples from the seventh century onwards, are either meteorites – believed to account for their burnt appearance – or, more likely, were caused by under-sea erosion some fifteen million years ago. Together with a stupa enshrining a Buddha footprint that is now an important pilgrimage site (especially during its annual festival, held between March 11 and 15), the rock formations have been linked up under the auspices of fifty-square-kilometre **Phu Phra Bat Historical Park** (daily 8am–4.30pm; B30). A well-signposted network of **paths** has been cleared from the thin forest to connect 25 of the outcrops, each of which has a helpful English-language information board attached. It would take a good five hours to explore the whole park, but the most popular route – a two-kilometre circuit covering the sights listed below – can be completed in an ambling hour or two.

On **public transport**, the easiest way of getting there from Nong Khai is to take the 7.15am bus to Ban Phu; if you leave any later you won't have time to see the park properly, as the whole journey takes a couple of hours and the last bus back to Nong Khai leaves at 3pm. From Ban Phu, it's another 13km west to the historical park; take a songthaew for the first 10km until you come to a right fork in the road; from here a motorbike taxi will bring you the final 3km up to the main park entrance, which the Fine Arts Department has helpfully sprinkled with site maps.

Among the most interesting of the outcrops are **Tham Wua** and **Tham Khon**, two natural shelters whose paintings of oxen and human stick figures suggest that the area was first settled at least six thousand years ago. A local legend accounts for the name of nearby **Kok Ma Thao Barot** (Prince Barot's Stable), a broad platform overhung by a huge slab of sandstone. A certain Princess Ussa, banished by her father to these slopes to be educated by a hermit, sent out an SOS which was answered by a dashing prince, Barot. The two fell in love and were married against the wishes of Ussa's father, prompting the king to challenge Barot to a distinctly oriental sort of duel: each would build a temple, and the last to finish would be beheaded. The king lost. Kok Ma Thao Barot is celebrated as the place where Barot kept his horse when he visited Ussa.

The furthest point of the circuit is the viewpoint at **Pha Sadej**, where the cliff drops away to give a lovely view across green fields and forest to the distant mountains. More spectacular is **Hor Nang Ussa** (Ussa's Tower), a mushroom formed by a flat slab capping a five-metre-high rock pillar. Under the cap of the mushroom, a shelter has been carved out and walled in on two sides. The *sema* found scattered around the site, and the square holes in which others would have been embedded, indicate that this was a shrine, probably in the Dvaravati period (seventh to tenth centuries). Nearby, a huge rock on a flimsy pivot miraculously balances itself against a tree at **Wat Por Ta** (The Father's Temple); the walls and floor have been evenly carved out to form a vaguely rectangular shrine, with Dvaravati Buddha images dotted around.

The left fork on the way to the park entrance leads to **Wat Phra Bat Bua Bok**: a crude chedi built in imitation of Wat Phra That Phanom (see p.534), it's decorated with naive bas-reliefs of divinities and boggle-eyed monsters, which add to the atmosphere of simple, rustic piety. In a gloomy chamber in the tower's base, the only visible markings on the sandstone **Buddha footprint** show the Wheel of Law. Legend has it that the Buddha made the footprint here for a serpent which had asked to be ordained as a monk, but had been refused because it was not human. Higher up the slope, a smaller *that* perches on a hanging rock that seems to defy gravity.

Downstream to Mukdahan

East of Nong Khai, the land on the Thai side of the Mekhong becomes gradually more arid, while jagged forest-covered mountains loom on the Laos side. Few visitors make it this far, to the northeast's northeast, though the attractions are surprisingly varied, ranging from painterly riverscapes to Isaan's major religious site, **Wat Phra That Phanom**. **Transport** along Highway 212 out of Nong Khai is fairly straightforward: sixteen buses a day from Nong Khai run to Bung Kan, six of which continue to Nakhon Phanom, where you have to change onto one of the hourly buses to get to That Phanom and Mukdahan.

Ban Ahong and Wat Phu Tok

Just over 100km east of Nong Khai, at Isaan's northernmost point, **BAN AHONG** is a traditional farming village of eight hundred inhabitants which would go unnoticed but for an unusual forest wat sited at the eastern end of the village, on a beautiful winding stretch of the river opposed by lofty hills on the Laos side. **Wat Paa Ahong**, set among huge boulders, is inhabited by a single "monk-herbalist", Luang Phor Phraeng, who maintains a beautiful garden here; he's sometimes joined by novice monks, and lay visitors may stay here for a day or two.

Ban Ahong's nearest town, **Bung Kan**, 137km from Nong Khai, is a reasonably prosperous riverside settlement, but dusty and ugly, and its handful of cheap and nasty hotels are only recommended if you get stuck here. Any bus between Nong Khai and Bung Kan will drop you at Ban Ahong, and it's then a fifteen-minute walk to Wat Paa Ahong. If you're passing through the village, it's well worth asking around to see if the *Hideaway Guesthouse* has reopened; this was closed at the time of writing, after a change in ownership, but was previously a popular stop-off point along this stretch of the river, where tourist-friendly accommodation is otherwise scarce.

Wat Phu Tok

You'll almost certainly have to change buses in Bung Kan to get to the area's most compelling destination, the extraordinary hilltop retreat of **Wat Phu Tok**. One of two sandstone outcrops which jut steeply out of the plain 35km southeast of Bung Kan, Phu Tok has been transformed in the past few years into a meditation wat, its fifty or so monks building their scattered huts on perches high above breathtaking cliffs. The outcrop comes into sight long before you get there, its sheer red face sandwiched between green vegetation on the lower slopes and tufts of trees on the narrow plateau above. As you get closer, the horizontal white lines across the cliffs reveal themselves to be painted wooden walkways, built to give the temple seven levels to represent the seven stages of enlightenment.

In an ornamental garden at the base, reflected in a small lake, an elegant, incongruously modern marble chedi commemorates **Phra Ajaan Juen**, the famous meditation master who founded the wat in 1968 and died in a plane crash ten years later. Within the chedi, the monk's books and other belongings, and diamond-like fragments of his bones, are preserved in a small shrine.

The first part of the ascent of the outcrop takes you to the third level up a series of long, sometimes slippery, wooden staircases, the first of many for which you'll need something more sturdy than flip-flops on your feet. A choice of two routes – the left fork is more interesting – leads to the fifth and most important level, where the **Sala Yai** houses the temple's main Buddha image in an airy, dimly lit cavern. The artificial ledges which cut across the northeast face are not for the fainthearted, but they are one way of getting to the dramatic northwest tip here on level five: on the other side of a deep crevice spanned by a wooden bridge, the monks have built an open-sided Buddha viharn under a huge anvil rock (though the gate to the viharn is usually locked). This spot affords stunning **views** over a broad sweep of countryside and across to the second, uninhabited outcrop. The flat top of the hill forms the seventh level, where you can wander along overgrown paths through thick forest.

Practicalities

Getting to Wat Phu Tok isn't easy – the location was chosen for its isolation, after all – but the trip out gives you a slice of life in remote countryside. Coming from Nong Khai, change at Bung Kan and catch one of the half-hourly buses south along Route 222 towards Pang Khon; get off after 25km at **Ban Siwilai** – which has a couple of very basic hotels – from where songthaews make the hour-long, twenty-kilometre trip east to Phu Tok when they have a full complement of passengers (services are more frequent in the morning).

Since some foreign tourists misbehaved while staying overnight at Phu Tok (a couple allegedly sleeping together in one of the *salas*), the hospitality of the temple unfortunately no longer extends to farangs, a fact stressed by prominent signs. Unless you want to stay in Bung Kan, Ban Ahong or Ban Siwilai, it's best to come on a day-trip from Nong Khai as there is no accommodation in the attached village either, though **food** is available: just outside the grounds, a collection of foodstalls and a simple restaurant dish up the usual noodles and grilled chicken. One stall sells parcels of dried bark, wood, leaf and herbs as infusions for medicinal teas which you'll be pressed to try.

Nakhon Phanom

Beyond Bung Kan, the river road rounds the hilly northeastern tip of Thailand before heading south through remote country where you're apt to find yourself stopping for buffalo as often as for vehicles. The Mekhong can only be glimpsed occasionally until you reach **NAKHON PHANOM** (meaning "city of mountains"), 313km from Nong Khai, a clean and prosperous town which affords the finest view of the river in northern Isaan, framed against the giant ant hills of the Lao mountains opposite.

The town makes a pleasant place to hang out, its quiet broad streets lined with some grand old public buildings, colonial-style houses and creaking wooden shophouses. During the Indochina wars, Nakhon Phanom was an important gateway for thousands of Vietnamese refugees, whose influence can be seen in the dilapidated and atmospheric hybrid, **Wat Or Jak**, opposite the pier for Laos. The ferry from this pier to Khammouan (Tha Khaek) in Laos can be used by farangs, as long as they have a visa, of course – and at the time of writing, visas were not available anywhere in Nakhon Phanom, so you would have to equip yourself with one before you left Bangkok or Khon Kaen. If that all sounds like too much hassle, the closest you can get to Laos is to hire a **boat** from the pier for an hour (B500 for up to fifteen people), providing the best perspective on the beautiful riverscape. Walking around town, you'll see several lit-up boat shapes around the place, a reminder of Nakhon Phanom's best-known festival, the **illuminated boat procession**, which is held on the river every year, usually in October at the end of the rainy season. The week-long celebrations – marking the end of the annual three-month Buddhist Rains Retreat – also feature colourful dragon-boat races along the Mekhong, pitting Thai and Lao teams against each other.

The biggest Buddha in Isaan is at **Wat Phra Yai**, but the image is an unattractive 25-metre-high architectural feature covered in rust-coloured tiles, which forms the roof of a small viharn, squeezed in underneath its crossed legs. To reach the temple, take a tuk-tuk or walk west of town on the road to Udon Thani (Highway 22) for 2km, then turn left down the western bypass for another 2km.

Practicalities

The main **bus station** is about half a kilometre west of the centre. You can fly to Nakhon Phanom from Bangkok (B1820 one way) with Thai Airways; the airline's limousine from the **airport** costs B50 per person. The **ferry to Laos** (daily 8.30am–noon & 1–4pm; every 20–30min; B50) goes from opposite the riverfront market; after 4pm you can charter the whole boat (B500 for up to ten people) to take you across.

TAT has an impressive office at 184/1 Thanon Suntorn Vichit, corner of Thanon Salaklang (daily 8.30am–4.30pm; ☎042/513490–1, ℉513492, ⓔtatphnom@tat.or.th), 500m north of the pier for Laos; they also cover Sakhon Nakhon and Mukdahan provinces. Ask here if you're interested in village homestays around Nakhon Phanom; the enthusiastic director, Khun Pongsan, has plans to set up a scheme in the area. The efficient North by Northeast Tours (☎042/513572, ℉513573, ⓦwww.thaitourism.com), situated underneath the *Mae Namkhong Grand View Hotel* on Highway 212, is a US-Thai-run outfit which offers a range of tours around the Mekhong region, including a three-day eco-tour of rural Laos (B2000); it can also organize visas for Laos and tailor-made itineraries. There's **internet access** at the J-Net Cybercafe, 203–207 Thanon Suntorn Vichit (daily 10am–midnight; B20 per hour), just north of the pier.

The run-down *River Inn* at 137 Thanon Suntorn Vichit (☎042/511305, ℱ520450; ❸–❹) may have the best location of Nakhon Phanom's budget **hotels**, but that's about all it has to recommend it: the dilapidated fan and air-con rooms are pricey for what you get; its riverside restaurant is good for a beer-with-a-view, but avoid the food. A much better option is the friendly four-storey *Grand Hotel*, at 210 Thanon Sri Thep (☎042/511526, ℱ511283; ❷–❸), a block back from the river just south of the passenger ferry and market, with bright modern rooms, all en-suite, ranging from fan and cold-water rooms (with access to a shared hot shower) to hot-water and air-con. Less central, but excellent value and well worth a splurge is the *Mae Namkhong Grand View*, on Highway 212 at the southern edge of town (☎042/513564, ℱ511037; ❹); the international-standard rooms here come with en-suite hot-water bathrooms and the nicest boast balconies and river views. At the luxury end, the best option is the eight-storey *Nakhonphanom River View* (☎042/522333–40, ℱ522780, ⓔriverview@cscoms.com; ❼), a few hundred metres south of the *Mae Namkhong Grand View*, with tasteful rooms boasting facilities ranging from cable TV to bathtubs, as well as an outdoor swimming pool overlooking the river. Discounts of up to forty percent are common here, so it's worth calling ahead to check.

A few small, reasonable **restaurants** with riverside terraces, specializing in Mekhong giant catfish dishes, are clustered around the passenger pier and the old clocktower, at the corner of Suntorn Vichit and Sri Thep roads: the *New Suan Mai* and the *Giant Catfish* are both reliable. North along Thanon Suntorn Vichit at no. 165, 500m past the TAT office, the popular *Rabieng Chomkom* serves up excellent Thai food and fresh fish in a lovely outdoor setting. There are a couple of good Vietnamese eateries along Thanon Sri Thep: *Dararat*, 50m north of the *Grand Hotel* at no. 91, has tasty *nam nueng* (unfried spring rolls) on offer, while the *Phorn Thep* at no. 344 is a popular spot for breakfast – *khai krata* (eggs, Vietnamese sausages and French bread) is available until around 9am. Thanon Fueng Nakhon, running west from the old clocktower, has a choice of several simple eateries and is a lively spot at night.

Sakhon Nakhon

On Highway 22, 90km west of Nakhon Phanom, unappealing **SAKHON NAKHON** only justifies a detour off the Mekhong River route if you're interested in temples – though if you're travelling by bus from Udon Thani or Khon Kaen to Nakhon Phanom or That Phanom you'll have to pass through here in any case. Though Sakhon Nakhon is separated from the heart of Isaan by the forested Pan mountains, Thai Airways fly here from Bangkok four times a week, so it's not as cut off as it seems.

Top of the wats is **Wat Phra That Choeng Choom**, near Nong Harn Lake just west of the centre, where an angular, white Lao chedi has been built around and on top of a Khmer laterite prang dating from the eleventh century. The chedi affords glimpses of the prang through its three outer doors and can be entered through a door at the back of the adjacent viharn. Legend has it that the chedi was built to enshrine four pairs of footprints made by the Buddha in his different manifestations. Elsewhere in the spacious grounds is a tower with a huge wooden bell, hollowed from a single tree trunk.

A small, well-restored Khmer prang, **Wat Phra That Narai Cheng Weng**, lies 6km northwest of town, 100m to the left off Highway 22 opposite the turning for Nakhon Phanom. The laterite prang, set among coconut palms on a grassy knoll, is said to contain ashes of the Buddha. The lintel above the eastern doorway displays a well-preserved bas-relief of twelve-armed Shiva, dancing a jig to destroy the universe. On the northern pediment is shown the next stage in the never-ending cycle of destruction and rebirth, with Vishnu reclining on a dragon dreaming up the new creation. An umbilical cord topped by a lotus extends from his navel, but the figure of Brahma on top of the lotus, whose job it is to put Vishnu's dream into practice, has been eroded. Beneath is a lively carving of Krishna, one of the incarnations of Vishnu, locked in combat with a toothy lion.

For **accommodation**, the large, shabby rooms with en-suite bathrooms at the *Krong Thong Hotel*, 645/2 Thanon Charoen Muang (℡042/711235; ❶–❷), are your best bet in the budget range, but if you're stuck in Sakhon you might well feel like upgrading to the much cleaner and more comfortable *Dusit Hotel*, 1784 Thanon Yuvapatana (℡ & ℻042/711198–9; ❸–❹), where all rooms have air-conditioning and hot water, and there is free use of a nearby swimming pool.

That Phanom and around

Fifty kilometres south of Nakhon Phanom, **THAT PHANOM**, a small, green and friendly town of weather-beaten wooden buildings, sprawls around Isaan's most important shrine. Popularly held to be one of the four sacred pillars of Thai religion (the other three are Chiang Mai's Wat Phra That Doi Suthep, Wat Mahathat in Nakhon Si Thammarat, and Wat Phra Phuttabat near Lopburi), **Wat Phra That Phanom** is a fascinating place of pilgrimage, especially at the time of the ten-day Ngan Phra That Phanom festival, usually in February, when thousands of people come to pay homage and enjoy themselves in the holiday between harvesting and sowing; pilgrims believe that they must make the trip seven times during a full moon before they die.

This far-northeastern corner of Thailand may seem like a strange location for one of the country's holiest sites, but the wat used to serve both Thais and Lao, as evidenced by the ample boat landing in the village, now largely disused; since the Pathet Lao took over in 1975, Lao have only been allowed to cross the river for the Ngan Phra That Phanom and the fascinating Monday and Thursday morning waterfront **market** where Lao people offer for sale such items as wild animal skins, black pigs and herbal medicines, alongside the usual fruit and veg. The temple reputedly dates back to the eighth year after the death of the Buddha (535 BC), when five local princes built a simple brick chedi to house bits of his breastbone. It's been restored or rebuilt seven times, most recently after it collapsed during a rainstorm in 1975; the latest incarnation is in the form of a Lao *that*, 57m high, modelled on the That Luang in Vientiane.

The best approach to the temple is from the river: a short ceremonial way leads directly from the pier, under a Disneyesque victory arch erected by the Lao, through the temple gates to the **chedi** itself, which, as is the custom, faces water and the rising sun. A brick and plaster structure covered with white paint and gold floral decorations, the chedi looks like nothing so much as a giant, ornate table leg turned upside down. From each of the four sides, an eye forming part of the traditional flame pattern stares down, and the whole thing is surmounted by an umbrella made of 16kg of gold, with precious gems and gold rings embedded in each tier. The chedi sits on a gleaming white marble platform, on which pilgrims say their prayers and leave every imaginable kind of offering to the relics. Look out for the brick reliefs in the shape of four-leaf clovers above three of the doorways in the base: on the northern side, Vishnu mounted on a garuda; on the western side, the four guardians of the earth putting offerings in the Buddha's alms bowl; and above the south door, a carving of the Buddha entering Nirvana. At the corners of the chedi, brick plaques, carved in the tenth century but now heavily restored, tell the stories of the wat's princely founders.

That Phanom is only an hour away from Nakhon Phanom, Sakhon Nakhon and Mukdahan, and served by frequent **buses** from each, which stop on Thanon Chayangkun, immediately outside the wat. The centre of the village is 200m due east of here, clustered around the pier on the Mekhong.

Practicalities

That Phanom's outstanding **accommodation** choice is the welcoming *Niyana Guest House*, 288 Moo 2, Thanon Rimkhong (☎042/540588, ✉niyanaguesthouse@hotmail.com; ❶), four blocks north of the pier, set in a garden with café area facing the river. The effusive owner, Niyana, is a fund of local information, and rustles up excellent Thai and Western food (breakfast and dinner only), as well as renting out bicycles (B60 per day) and organizing boat trips and occasional tours of Mukdahan National Park (see p.537). The pleasant rooms (and one dorm; B60 per person) in her quiet modern two-storey house are decorated with her own paintings and share cold-water bathrooms; a huge upstairs balcony serves as an open-air common area with an impressive library and noticeboard. Niyana has a sideline selling unstuffed axe floor cushions, rarely available unfilled elsewhere in Thailand, and much cheaper to post home. If Niyana can't put you up, try the *Sang Thong Hotel* (❷), south of the victory arch at 34 Phanom Thanon Phanarak. In a wooden house around a family courtyard, they offer basic rooms with their own cold- or hot-water bathrooms, as well as some reasonable bungalows (❸) down on the riverfront Thanon Rimkhong. Alternatively, *Rim Khong Bungalows*, three sois north of the arch, just back from the river (☎042/541634; ❷–❸), can offer hot-water bathrooms and air-conditioning, or cheaper fan and cold-water combinations; the utilitarian concrete rooms, reasonably clean though drab, are arranged around a courtyard.

For somewhere to **eat**, there are a few simple restaurants around the victory arch, the best of these being *That Phanom Pochana*, on the north side of the arch, a big airy place which is good for a *phat thai* or a choice of Chinese dishes. Further south along the same road at no. 39, the friendly *Bom* restaurant serves similar fare and is slightly cheaper.

There are a few **internet** places scattered around town; TK internet is 100m west of Thanon Chayangkun on Highway 212 (daily 9am–11pm; B20 per hour). Siam Commercial Bank has a branch, with an ATM and exchange facilities, at 359 Thanon Chayangkun.

Around That Phanom

From That Phanom the weaving village of **Renu Nakhon**, 15km northwest, can be reached by regular songthaews to the Renu junction, then 8km north by tuk-tuk. The wat at the centre of the village has a smaller, stubbier imitation of the Phra That Phanom, crudely decorated with stucco carvings and brown paint, and an attached cultural centre where local dance performances are sometimes held. Around the wat, stalls and shops sell a huge variety of reasonable cotton and silk, much of it in simple, colourful *mut mee* styles.

An interesting cycle ride from That Phanom (bikes can be hired from *Niyana Guest House*; see above) takes the road following the river – a mixture of deteriorating paved road and red dirt – through green countryside and a couple of villages 18km south to the **Kaeng Kabao rapids**. Here Thai tourists gather to watch the white water; their numbers are catered for with bamboo *salas* overlooking the river where they can picnic, and many stalls selling simple food such as barbecued chicken or pork. There are several restaurants too, further back from the river; the best (and cleanest) place to eat is the *Kaeng Kaboo Restaurant*, which does a particularly good fried rice with squid.

Continuing 3km south of the rapids along the river road is the incongruous sight of a very lavish Catholic church, the **Our Lady of the Martyrs of Thailand Shrine** (called Wat Songkhon in Thai), which was blessed and dedicated in December 1995. It's situated on an idyllic stretch of the Mekhong, with manicured lawns looking across a few river islands and some longtail-boat activity to Laos. Many of the people who live along the stretch of the river between That Phanom and Mukdahan are Catholic, and in the 1950s some were accused of being Communist sympathisers and killed by the Thai authorities; at the rear of the church, seven glass coffins hold models of the bodies of the Thais who have been declared martyrs by the Catholic Church. The minimalist modern complex is surrounded by a terracotta-coloured laterite circular wall with Stations of the Cross, and the square glass-walled church comes complete with a gold-coloured floating Jesus; note that, just as with temples, it's customary to take off your shoes before going inside. To get there from Mukdahan, head north up Highway 212, then 9km east, then look out for a sign of the cross at a turning and head the final 5km north.

Mukdahan and beyond

Fifty kilometres downriver of That Phanom, **MUKDAHAN** is the last stop on the Mekhong trail before Highway 212 heads off inland to Ubon Ratchathani, 170km to the south. You may feel as if you're in the Wild East out here, but this is one of the fastest-developing Thai provinces, owing to increasing friendship between Laos and Thailand and the proximity of **Savannakhet**, the second-biggest Lao city, just across the water. A bridge across the Mekhong here is planned for completion by 2005; further into the future, a new train line linking Mukdahan with the existing Thai rail network at Ubon Ratchathani has also been discussed. Very few farang visitors make it this far, though the B50 ferry trip is an officially sanctioned crossing to Laos (see box on p.524 for more crossings into Laos).

In the heart of town, the main river **pier** serves the cross-border trade, which accounts for a large part of the local economy. By the pier, a pleasant tree-lined promenade overlooks Sawannakhet, and a daily **market** (especially busy at weekends), spills over into the compound of Wat Sri Mongkon. On sale here are household goods and inexpensive ornaments, such as Vietnamese mother-of-pearl and Chinese ceramics, brought over from Laos; the market is also good for local fabrics like large lengths of coarsely woven cotton in lovely muted colours for a bargain B200, and expensive but very classy silks. At the southern edge of town rises the 65-metre-high **Mukdahan Tower** (daily 8am–6pm; B20), a modern white edifice that looks somewhat out of place in the low-rise outskirts. Opened in 1996, the tower houses an interesting array of historic artefacts from the Mukdahan area, including traditional Isaan costumes, coins, parchments and vicious-looking weaponry; look out for the delicate fifteen-centimetre-high gold and silver trees on display on the first floor – each year Mukdahan has to pay tribute to the king with a tree weighing 180 grams in gold and another of the same weight in silver. The highlight of the tower, however, is the expansive view from the sixth floor over Mukdahan and the Mekhong into Laos.

Practicalities

Half-hourly buses from That Phanom and Ubon Ratchathani stop at the **bus terminal** about a kilometre northwest of the centre on Highway 212. **Ferry** services for Savannakhet leave Mukdahan daily (Mon–Fri at 9.15am, 10.15am, 11.15am, 2.30pm & 3.30pm, Sat 10.30am, 11.30am, 2.30pm & 4pm; Sun 10.30am). There's **internet access** at 11/1 Thanon Kaew Kinnaree (daily 8am–midnight; B20 per hour), one block west of *Saensuk Bungalows*.

The best budget **accommodation** option is the *Ban Thom Kasem* (no English sign) at 25–25/2 Thanon Samut Sakdarak (℡042/611235 or 612223; ❶–❷). Centrally located, this four-storey hotel has wood-floored and -panelled rooms (fan or air-con) with hot-water bathrooms and welcome extras like towels and toilet paper; there's an attached clean and pleasant Chinese-style café too. If you want a little more comfort, turn south off the main east–west street, Thanon Pitakpanomkhet, at the town's largest traffic circle, onto Thanon Phitak Santirat, where you'll find the friendly *Saensuk Bungalows* (℡042/611214, ℗632985; ❸) at no. 2, 100m down on your right: clean air-conditioned rooms, all with hot water, are ranged around a tidy courtyard. Further west at 40 Thanon Pitakpanomkhet, *Ploy Palace Hotel* (℡042/663111, ℗611223, ✉ploypalace@muk.a-net.net.th; ❼), a grand pink edifice with an overblown marbled lobby and tasteful bedrooms, is the best of Mukdahan's three luxury options, with excellent service and a rooftop swimming pool and gym among its attractions.

Of the **restaurants** which dot the riverside promenade, Thanon Somranchaikhong, the best – and priciest – is the popular *Riverview*, 1km south of the pier, which serves excellent food on a pretty bougainvillea-covered terrace built out over the Mekong. En route you'll pass by a couple of cheaper places on the same street, including the friendly *Wine, Wild, Why*, a tiny restaurant-bar with a wooden terrace overlooking the river and a good range of simple one-dish Thai meals. Alternatively, you can eat on the river itself: standard Thai food is served on board the *Morris* (moderate–expensive; open until 11pm), a slightly ramshackle three-storey boat permanently moored about 200m south of the main pier and lit up with coloured bulbs, so you can't miss it. The emphasis here is more on drinking, which is no bad thing, sitting on the top deck and watching the moon rise. For breakfast, the *Pith Bakery*, one block north of *Saensuk Bungalows* on the same road, is a good bet, with Western-style breakfasts, fresh juices and thirteen different varieties of coffee beans.

Mukdahan National Park

If you're tired of concrete Isaan towns, stretch your legs exploring the strange rock formations and beautiful waterfalls of **Mukdahan National Park** (aka Phu Pha Terp; daily 8am–6pm; B200), down a minor road along the Mekong southeast of Mukdahan. Regular songthaews pass the turning for the park 14km out of town, and from there it's a two-kilometre walk uphill to the park headquarters. Just above the headquarters is a hillside of bizarre rocks, eroded into the shapes of toadstools and crocodiles, which is great for scrambling around. The hillside also bears two remnants of the area's prehistory: the red finger-painting under one of the sandstone slabs is reckoned to be 4000 years old, while a small cage on the ground protects a 75-million-year-old fossil. Further up, the bare sandstone ridge seems to have been cut out of the surrounding forest by a giant lawnmower, but in October it's brought to life with a covering of grasses and wildflowers. A series of ladders leads up a cliff to the highest point, on a ridge at the western end of the park (a two-kilometre walk from the park headquarters), which affords a sweeping view over the rocks to the forests and paddies of Laos. Halfway up the cliff is a cave in which villagers have enshrined scores of Buddha images, and nearby, at least from July to November, is the park's most spectacular waterfall, a thirty-metre drop through thick vegetation.

The park, which can be readily visited on a day-trip from Mukdahan or That Phanom, has no official accommodation, but you can camp with your own gear free of charge. The simple **foodstalls** near headquarters will keep you going with fried rice and noodles.

Travel details

Trains

Buriram to: Ayutthaya (9 daily; 4hr 30min–7hr 45min); Bangkok (10 daily; 6hr–9hr 30min), via Don Muang airport (5hr 30min–8hr 30 min); Khorat (10 daily; 1hr 30min–2hr 40min); Pak Chong (10 daily; 2hr 30min–5hr); Si Saket (7 daily; 1hr 45min–3hr 20min); Surin (10 daily; 35–65min); Ubon Ratchathani (7 daily; 2hr 30min–4hr 15min).

Khon Kaen to: Ayutthaya (5 daily; 6hr–8hr 20min); Bangkok (5 daily; 7hr 30min–10hr 20min), via Don Muang Airport (6hr 45min–9 hr 20min); Khorat (1 daily; 3hr 20min); Nong Khai (3 daily; 2hr 45min); Udon Thani (5 daily; 1hr 40min).

Khorat to: Ayutthaya (7 daily; 3hr 30min); Bangkok (9 daily; 4–5hr); Khon Kaen (1 daily; 2hr 45min); Si Saket (7 daily; 4hr–5hr 30min); Surin (7 daily; 2hr 30min–3hr 40min); Ubon Ratchathani (7 daily; 5hr–6hr 40min); Udon Thani (1daily; 4hr 45min).

Nong Khai to: Ayutthaya (3 daily; 10hr); Bangkok (3 daily; 11hr 30min–12hr 30min); Khon Kaen (3 daily; 3hr); Khorat (1 daily; 6hr 40min); Udon Thani (3 daily; 1hr).

Pak Chong (for Khao Yai) to: Ayutthaya (9 daily; 2hr–2hr 45min); Bangkok (10 daily; 3hr 30min–4hr 45min) via Don Muang airport (2hr 50min–4hr); Khorat (10 daily; 1hr 30min–2hr); Si Saket (7 daily; 4hr 20min–7hr 30min); Surin (10 daily; 3hr 10min–5hr 15min); Ubon Ratchathani (7 daily; 6hr 50min–8hr 40min).

Prachinburi to: Aranyaprathet (2 daily; 2hr 20min); Bangkok (2 daily; 2hr 30min).

Surin to: Ayutthaya (9 daily; 5hr 10min–9hr); Bangkok (10 daily; 7–10hr), via Don Muang airport (6hr 30min–9hr); Buriram (10 daily; 35–65min); Khorat (10 daily; 2–4hr); Pak Chong (10 daily; 3–6hr); Sikhoraphum (6 daily; 30–55min); Si Saket (7 daily; 1hr 35min–2hr 10min); Ubon Ratchathani (7 daily; 2hr 30min–3hr 30min).

Ubon Ratchathani to: Ayutthaya (7 daily; 7–12hr); Bangkok (7 daily; 8hr 30min–14hr), via Don

Muang airport (8–13hr); Buriram (7 daily; 2hr 30min–4hr 15min); Khorat (7 daily; 5hr–6hr 40min); Si Saket (7 daily; 1hr 10min); Surin (7 daily; 2hr 30min–3hr 30min).

Udon Thani to: Ayutthaya (5 daily; 7hr 30min–10hr 30min); Bangkok (5 daily; 9–12hr 30min); Khon Kaen (7 daily; 1hr 30min–3hr); Khorat (3 daily; 4hr 30min–6hr 30min); Nong Khai (4 daily; 1hr).

Buses

Bung Kan to: Bangkok (4 daily; 8hr); Nakhon Phanom (6 daily; 4hr); Nong Khai (17 daily; 2hr); Sakhon Nakhon (hourly; 3hr); Udon Thani (every 70min; 4hr).

Chaiyaphum to: Bangkok (hourly; 6hr); Khon Kaen (10 daily; 2–3hr); Khorat (about every 30min; 2hr); Phitsanulok (6 daily; 3hr); Surin (5 daily; 4hr); Ubon Ratchathani (5 daily; 6–7hr).

Chiang Khan to: Bangkok (6 daily; 9–11hr); Chiang Mai (8 daily; 6hr); Loei (every 30min by songthaew; 1hr); Pak Chom (every 30min by songthaew; 1hr).

Chong Mek to: Bangkok (2 daily; 12 hr); Phibun Mangsahan (every 30min; 90min).

Khon Kaen to: Bangkok (23 daily; 6–7hr); Chaiyaphum (hourly; 2–3hr); Khorat (hourly; 2hr 30min–3hr); Loei (every 30min; 4hr); Nong Khai (10 daily; 2–3hr); Phitsanulok (hourly; 5–6hr); Sri Chiangmai (6 daily; 3hr); Ubon Ratchathani (15 daily; 6hr); Udon Thani (10 daily; 1hr 30min–2hr).

Khorat to: Bangkok (every 20min; 4–5hr); Ban Tako (for Phanom Rung; every 30min; 2hr); Buriram (every 30min; 3hr); Chaiyaphum (every 30min; 2hr); Chanthaburi (every 30min; 6–8hr); Chiang Mai (7 daily; 12–14hr); Chiang Rai (5 daily; 14–16hr); Dan Kwian (every 30min; 30min); Khon Kaen (hourly; 2hr 30min–3hr); Lopburi (11 daily; 3hr 30min); Nakhon Phanom (3 daily; 8hr); Nong Khai (7 daily; 6–8hr); Pak Tong Chai (every 30min; 45min); Pattaya (7 daily; 6–8hr); Phimai (every 30min; 1hr–1hr 30min); Phitsanulok (7 daily;

7–9hr); Rayong (for Ko Samet; every 30min; 6–8hr); Sri Chiangmai (6 daily; 6hr 30min); Surin (every 30min; 4–5hr); Ubon Ratchathani (7 daily; 5–7hr); Udon Thani (hourly; 3hr 30min–5hr).

Loei to: Bangkok (18 daily; 10hr); Chiang Khan (every 30min by songthaew, every 15min by minibus; 1hr); Chiang Mai (4 daily; 9–12hr); Chiang Rai (4 daily; 9–11hr); Khon Kaen (every 25min; 4hr); Nong Khai (hourly minibus; 6–7hr); Pak Chom (7 daily, or every 30min by minibus; 2hr 30min); Phitsanulok (5 daily; 4hr); Sang Khom (hourly minibus; 3hr); Udon Thani (every 30min; 3hr).

Mukdahan to: Bangkok (13 daily; 11hr); Nakhon Phanom (hourly; 2hr); Sakhon Nakhon (hourly; 2hr); That Phanom (every 30min; 1hr 20min); Ubon Ratchathani (every 30min; 2–3hr); Udon Thani (5 daily; 4hr–4hr 30min).

Nakhon Phanom to: Bangkok (17 daily; 12hr); Chiang Rai (4 daily; 16hr); Khon Kaen (6 daily; 4–5hr); Khorat (20 daily; 8hr); Mukdahan (hourly; 2hr); Nong Khai (7 daily; 6hr); Phitsanulok (4 daily; 10hr); That Phanom (hourly; 1hr); Ubon Ratchathani (7 daily, 4hr); Udon Thani (12 daily; 5–6hr).

Nong Khai to: Bangkok (20 daily; 10hr); Bung Kan (16 daily; 2hr); Loei (13 daily; 6–7hr); Nakhon Phanom (6 daily; 6hr); Rayong (7 daily; 12hr); Sang Khom (5 daily; 3hr); Sri Chiangmai (3 daily; 2hr); Udon Thani (every 30min; 1hr).

Pak Chom to: Chiang Khan (every 30min by songthaew; 1hr); Loei (7 daily, or every 30min by minibus; 2hr 30min); Nong Khai (7 daily; 5hr).

Pak Chong to: Bangkok (every 15min; 3hr); Khorat (every 20min; 1hr 30min).

Sakhon Nakhon to: Bangkok (11 daily; 11hr); Chiang Rai (1 daily; 12hr); Khon Kaen (6 daily; 4hr); Khorat (6 daily; 7hr); Mukdahan (hourly; 3hr); Nakhon Phanom (hourly; 1hr 30min); That Phanom (7 daily; 2hr); Ubon Ratchathani (9 daily; 5hr); Udon Thani (every 30min; 3hr).

Sang Khom to: Loei (7 daily; 3hr); Nong Khai (7 daily; 3–4hr).

Si Saket to: Bangkok (6 daily; 11hr); Surin (12 daily; 1hr 30min); Ubon Ratchathani (at least 12 daily; 45min–1hr).

Sri Chiangmai to: Bangkok (4 daily; 12hr); Khon Kaen (5 daily; 4hr); Khorat (7 daily; 6hr); Loei (7 daily; 4hr 30min); Nong Khai (17 daily; 1hr 30min), Udon Thani (every 30min; 1hr 30min).

Surin to: Bangkok (up to 20 daily; 8–9hr); Ban Tako (every 30min; 2hr); Chaiyaphum (5 daily; 4–5hr); Khorat (every 30min; 4hr); Si Saket (at least 12 daily; 1hr 30min); Ta Klang (hourly; 2hr); Ubon Ratchathani (at least 12 daily; 2hr 30min–3hr); Yasothon (hourly; 2–3hr).

That Phanom to: Bangkok (4 daily; 12hr); Mukdahan (hourly; 1hr 20min); Nakhon Phanom (by bus: 9 daily, 1hr 20min; by songthaew: every 10min 6am–5pm, 1hr 20min); Sakhon Nakhon (7 daily; 2hr); Ubon Ratchathani (10 daily; 3–4hr); Udon Thani (4 daily; 4–5 hr).

Ubon Ratchathani to: Bangkok (19 daily; 10–12hr); Chaiyaphum (5 daily; 6–7hr); Chiang Mai (5 daily; 9hr); Kantharalak (8 daily; 1hr 30min); Khon Kaen (16 daily; 6hr); Khorat (17 daily; 5hr); Phibun Mangsahan (every 25min; 1hr); Rayong (7 daily; 9hr); Roi Et (16 daily; 3hr); Si Saket (at least 12 daily; 45min–1hr); Surin (12 daily; 2hr 30min); 2hr 30min–3hr); Udon Thani (11 daily; 5–7hr); Yasothon (18 daily; 1hr 30min–2hr).

Udon Thani to: Ban Chiang (every 20min; 1hr 30min); Bangkok (every 15min; 9hr); Ban Phu (every 45min; 1hr); Bung Kan (every 70min; 4hr); Chiang Mai (6 daily; 11–13hr); Chiang Rai (5 daily; 12–14hr); Khon Kaen (every 15min; 1hr 30min–2hr); Khorat (every 45min; 3hr 30min–5hr); Loei (every 25min; 3hr); Nakhon Phanom (9 daily; 5–7hr); Nong Khai (every 30min; 1hr); Phitsanulok (5 daily; 8hr); Rayong (9 daily; 12hr); Sakhon Nakhon (every 20min; 3hr); Sri Chiangmai (every 30min; 1hr 30min); That Phanom (4 daily; 4–5hr); Ubon Ratchathani (11 daily; 5–7hr).

Yasothon to: Khon Kaen (hourly; 3hr–3hr 30min); Roi Et (hourly; 1hr).

Flights

Buriram to: Bangkok (daily; 1hr 10min).

Khon Kaen to: Bangkok (5 daily; 55min); Chiang Mai (1 daily; 50min–1hr 30min).

Khorat to: Bangkok (2 daily; 50min).

Nakhon Phanom to: Bangkok (1–2 weekly; 1hr 10min).

Sakhon Nakhon to: Bangkok (1–2 weekly; 1hr 5min–2hr 10min); Nakhon Phanom (2–3 weekly; 25min).

Ubon Ratchathani to: Bangkok (2 daily; 1hr 5min); Chiang Mai (3 weekly; 1hr 50min); Khon Kaen (3 weekly; 40min).

Udon Thani to: Bangkok (3–4 daily; 1hr).

Southern Thailand:
the Gulf coast

CHAPTER 6

Highlights

✻ **Phetchaburi** – Charming historic town, boasting several fine old working temples. **p.545**

✻ **Squid-pier hotels in Hua Hin** – Breezy, characterful rooms built on converted jetties. **p.553**

✻ **Bird-watching in Khao Sam Roi Yot National Park** – Especially rewarding Sept–Nov. **p.557**

✻ **Ang Thong National Marine Park** – A dramatic boat-trip from Samui or Pha Ngan. **p.572**

✻ **Samui resorts** – A great choice of beachside pads, from simple bungalows to luxurious cottages. **pp.568–585**

✻ **Ao Thong Nai Pan on Ko Pha Ngan** – Beautiful, secluded bay with good accommodation. **p.593**

✻ **Full moon at Hat Rin** – DIY beach parties draw ravers in their thousands. **p.588**

✻ **A boat trip round Ko Tao** – Satisfying exploration and great snorkelling. **p.597**

✻ **Nakhon Si Thammarat** – Historic holy sites, shadow puppets and excellent cuisine. **p.601**

✻ **Krung Ching waterfall** – Walk past giant ferns and screeching monkeys to reach this spectacular drop. **p.607**

Southern Thailand: the Gulf coast

The major part of southern Thailand's **Gulf coast**, gently undulating from Bangkok to Nakhon Si Thammarat, 750km away, is famed above all for the **Samui archipelago**, three small idyllic islands lying off the most prominent hump of the coastline. This is the country's most popular seaside venue for independent travellers, and a lazy stay in a Samui beachfront bungalow is so seductive a prospect that most people overlook the attractions of the mainland, where the sheltered sandy beaches and warm clear water rival the top sun spots in most countries. Added to that you'll find scenery dominated by forested mountains that rise abruptly behind the coastal strip, and a sprinkling of historic sights – notably the crumbling temples of ancient **Phetchaburi**, which offer an atmospheric if less grandiose alternative to the much-visited attractions at Ayutthaya and Lopburi, on the other side of Bangkok. Though not a patch on the islands further south, the stretch of coast south of Phetchaburi, down to the traditional Thai resorts of **Cha-am** and **Hua Hin**, is handy for weekenders escaping the oppressive capital. In the early 1900s, the royal family "discovered" this stretch of the coast, making regular expeditions here to take the sea air and to go deer- and tiger-hunting in the

Accommodation prices

Throughout this guide, guest houses, hotels and bungalows have been categorized according to the **price codes** given below. These categories represent the minimum you can expect to pay in the high season (roughly July, Aug & Nov–Feb) for a double room. If travelling on your own, expect to pay anything between sixty and one hundred percent of the rates quoted for a double room. Wherever a **price range** is indicated, this means that the establishment offers rooms with varying facilities – as explained in the write-up. Wherever an establishment also offers **dormitory beds**, the prices of these beds are given in the text, instead of being indicated by price code.

Remember that the top-whack hotels will add seven percent tax and a ten percent service charge to your bill – the price codes below are based on net rates after taxes have been added.

❶ under B150	❹ B400–600	❼ B1200–1800
❷ B150–250	❺ B600–900	❽ B1800–3000
❸ B250–400	❻ B900–1200	❾ B3000+

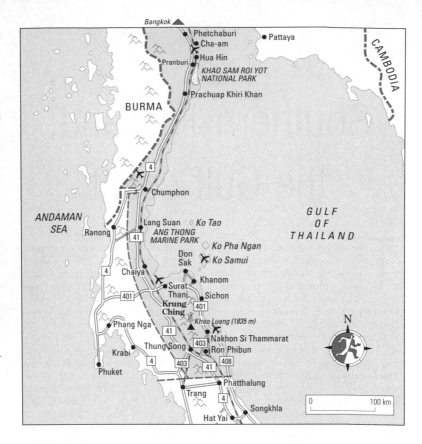

inland jungle. It soon became a fashionable resort area for the lower echelons of Thai society, and Cha-am and Hua Hin are now crammed with condos, high-rise hotels, bars and restaurants. There are no more tigers in the area, but nearby **Khao Sam Roi Yot National Park** is one of Thailand's most rewarding bird-watching spots. **Chumphon**, 150km further down the coast, has little to offer in its own right, but is the most convenient departure point for direct boats to Ko Tao.

Southeast of Chumphon lies **Ko Samui**, by far the most naturally beautiful of the islands, with its long white sand beaches and arching fringes of palm trees. The island's beauty has not gone unnoticed by tourist developers of course, but this at least means you can buy a little extra comfort if you've got the cash. In recent years the next island out, **Ko Pha Ngan**, has drawn increasing numbers of backpackers away from its neighbour: its bungalows are generally simpler and cost less than Ko Samui's, and it offers a few stunning beaches with a more laid-back atmosphere. **Hat Rin** is the distillation of all these features, with back-to-back white sands, relaxed resident hippies and t'ai chi classes – though after dusk it swings into action as Thailand's rave capital, a reputation cemented by its farang-thronged full moon parties. The furthest inhabited island of the archipelago, the small, rugged outcrop of **Ko Tao**, has taken off as a **scuba-diving** centre, but remains on the whole quieter and less sophisticated than Samui and Pha Ngan.

Tucked away beneath the islands, **Nakhon Si Thammarat**, the cultural capital of the south, is well worth a short detour from the main routes down the centre of the peninsula – it's a sophisticated city of grand old temples, delicious cuisine and distinctive handicrafts. With its small but significant Muslim population, and machine-gun dialect, Nakhon begins the transition into Thailand's deep south.

The **train** from Bangkok connects all the mainland towns, and **bus** services, along highways 4 (also known as the Phetkasem Highway, or, usually, Thanon Phetkasem when passing through towns) and 41, are frequent. Daily boats run to the islands from two jumping-off points: **Surat Thani**, 650km from Bangkok, has the best choice of routes, but the alternatives from **Chumphon** get you straight to the tranquillity of Ko Tao.

Phetchaburi

Straddling the River Phet about 120km south of Bangkok, the provincial capital of **PHETCHABURI** (aka Phetburi) has been settled ever since the eleventh century, when the Khmers ruled the region, but only really got going six hundred years later, when it began to flourish as a trading post between the Andaman Sea ports and Burma and Ayutthaya. Despite periodic incursions from the Burmese, the town gained a reputation as a cultural centre – as the ornamentation of its older temples testifies – and after the new capital was established in Bangkok it became a favourite country retreat of Rama IV, who had a hilltop palace built here in the 1850s. Today the town's main claim to fame is as one of Thailand's finest sweet-making centres, the essential ingredient for its assortment of *khanom* being the sugar extracted from the sweet-sapped palms that cover Phetchaburi province. This being very much a cottage industry, modern Phetchaburi has lost relatively little of the ambience that so attracted Rama IV: the central riverside area is hemmed in by historic wats in varying states of disrepair, and wooden rather than concrete shophouses still line the river bank.

Despite the obvious attractions of its old quarter, Phetchaburi gets few overnight visitors as most people do it on a day-trip from Bangkok, Hua Hin or Cha-am – a reason in itself for bucking the trend. It's also possible to combine a day in Phetchaburi with an early morning expedition from Bangkok to the floating markets of Damnoen Saduak, 40km north (see p.207); budget tour operators in the Thanon Khao San area offer this option as a day-trip package for about B500 per person.

Arrival, information and transport

Arriving by **bus**, you are likely to be dropped in one of three places. The main station for **non-air-con buses** is on the southwest edge of Khao Wang, about thirty minutes' walk or a ten-minute songthaew ride from the town centre. However, non-air-con buses to and from **Cha-am and Hua Hin** use the small terminal in the town centre, just east of the market and one block south of Thanon Phongsuriya – less than ten minutes' walk from the Chomrut Bridge accommodation. The **air-con bus terminal** is also about ten minutes' walk from Chomrut Bridge, located near the post office just off Thanon

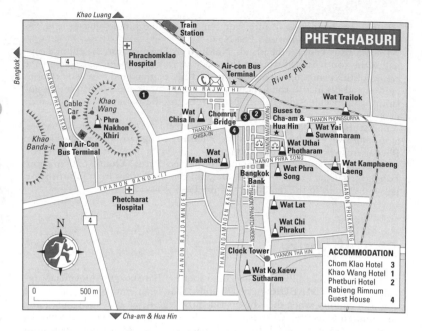

Rajwithi. Phetchaburi **train station** is on the northern outskirts of town, not far from Khao Wang, about 1500m from the main area of sights.

There is no TAT office in town, but *Rabieng Rimnum Guest House* is a good source of local **information**; they also offer **internet access** in the evenings, or you can check your email at the CAT **phone office** (daily 8am–8pm), which is next to the **GPO** on Thanon Rajwithi. The branch of Bangkok Bank 150m east of Wat Mahathat on Thanon Phra Song does **currency exchange** and has an ATM.

Phetchaburi's town centre might look compact, but to see the major temples in a day and have sufficient energy left for climbing Khao Wang and exploring the lesser sights, you might want to hire a **samlor** for a couple of hours (about B100 per hour) – also, samlor drivers have no qualms about riding through wat compounds, so you can get close-up views of the crumbling facades without getting out. Alternatively make use of the public **songthaews** which circulate round the town and charge B6, or **rent a motorbike** from *Rabieng Rimnum Guest House*.

Accommodation

Most travellers **stay** at the *Rabieng Rimnum (Rim Nam) Guest House*, centrally located at 1 Thanon Chisa-in, on the southwest corner of Chomrut Bridge (☎032/425707, ☎410695; ❷). Occupying a century-old house next to the Phetburi River and, less appealingly, a noisy main road, the guest house offers half a dozen simple rooms with shared bathrooms, lots of local info, internet access and the best restaurant in town; they also rent motorbikes and organize overnight trips to a nearby national park for bird-watching and hiking. Less traveller-oriented, but quieter and cheaper, is the friendly *Chom Klao* hotel across on the northeast corner of Chomrut Bridge at 1–3 Thanon Phongsuriya (☎032/425398; ❶–❷); it's not signed in English, but is easily recognized by its pale blue doors and riverside location. Some of the rooms give out onto the riverside walkway and you can choose whether or not you want an en-suite bathroom. The other central option is the shabby *Phetburi Hotel*, at 39 Thanon Phongsuriya (☎032/425315; ❶). Across on the other side of town, near the base of Khao Wang, the slightly seedy *Khao Wang Hotel*, 174/1–3 Thanon Rajwithi (☎032/425167; ❷–❸), has both fan and air-con rooms, all with TV, but don't expect immaculate decor or furnishing.

The Town

The pinnacles and rooftops of the town's thirty-odd wats are visible in every direction, but only a few are worth stopping off to investigate; the following description takes in the three most interesting, and can be done as a leisurely two-hour circular walk beginning from Chomrut Bridge.

Of all Phetchaburi's temples, the most attractive is the still-functioning seventeenth-century **Wat Yai Suwannaram** on Thanon Phongsuriya, about 700m east of Chomrut Bridge. The temple's fine old teak *sala* has elaborately carved doors, bearing a gash said to have been made by the Burmese in 1760 as they plundered their way towards Ayutthaya. Across from the *sala* and hidden behind high whitewashed walls stands the windowless Ayutthaya-style bot. The bot compound overlooks a pond, in the middle of which stands a small but well-preserved scripture library, or *ho trai*: such structures were built on stilts over water to prevent ants and other insects destroying the precious documents. Enter the walled compound from the south and make a clockwise tour of the cloisters filled with Buddha statues before entering the bot itself via the eastern doorway (if the door is locked, one of the monks will get the key for you). The bot is supported by intricately patterned red and gold pillars and contains a remarkable, if rather faded, set of murals, depicting Indra, Brahma and other lower-ranking divinities ranged in five rows of ascending importance. Once you've admired the interior, walk to the back of the bot, passing behind the central cluster of Buddha images, to find another Buddha image seated against the back wall: climb the steps in front of this image to get a close-up of the left foot, which for some reason was cast with six toes.

Fifteen minutes' walk east and then south of Wat Yai, the five tumbledown prangs of **Wat Kamphaeng Laeng** on Thanon Phra Song mark out Phetchaburi as the probable southernmost outpost of the Khmer empire. Built to enshrine Hindu deities and set out in a cruciform arrangement facing east, the laterite corncob-style prangs were later adapted for Buddhist use, as can be seen from the two which now house Buddha images. There has been some attempt to restore a few of the carvings and false balustraded windows, but these days worshippers congregate in the modern whitewashed wat behind these shrines, leaving the atmospheric and appealingly quaint collection of decaying prangs and casuarina topiary to chickens, stray dogs and the occasional tourist.

Continuing west along Thanon Phra Song from Wat Kamphaeng Laeng, across the river, you can see the prangs of Phetchaburi's most fully restored and important temple, **Wat Mahathat**, long before you reach them. Boasting the "Mahathat" title only since 1954, when the requisite Buddha relics were donated by the king, it was probably founded in the fourteenth century, but suffered badly at the hands of the Burmese. The five landmark prangs at its heart are adorned with stucco figures of mythical creatures, though these are nothing compared with those on the roofs of the main viharn and the bot. Instead of tapering off into the usual serpentine *chofa*, the gables are studded with miniature *thep* and *deva* figures (angels and gods), which add an almost mischievous vitality to the place. In a similar vein, a couple of gold-embossed crocodiles snarl above the entrance to the bot, and a caricature carving of a bespectacled man rubs shoulders with mythical giants in a relief around the base of the gold Buddha, housed in a separate mondop nearby.

Leaving Wat Mahathat, it's a five-minute walk north up Thanon Damnoen Kasem to Thanon Phongsuriya and another few minutes back to Chomrut Bridge, but if you have the time, backtrack a little and return via the **market**, which lines Thanon Matayawong and spills over into the alleyways on either side – there are enough stalls selling the locally famous *khanom* to make it worth your while.

Khao Wang and Khao Banda-It

Dominating the western outskirts, about thirty minutes' walk from Wat Mahathat, stands Rama IV's palace, a stew of mid-nineteenth-century Thai and European styles scattered over the crest of the hill known as **Khao Wang**. During his day, the royal entourage would struggle its way up the steep brick path to the summit, but now there's a **cable car** (daily 8am–4pm; B50) which starts from the western flank of the hill off Highway 4, quite near the non-air-con bus terminal. To get to the base of the hill from the town centre, take a white local **songthaew** from Thanon Phongsuriya and ask for Khao Wang. If you want to walk to the summit, get off as soon as you see the pathway on the eastern flank of the hill, just across from the junction with Thanon Rajwithi; for the cable car, stay put until you've passed the last of the souvenir stalls on Highway 4, then walk south about 700m. If you do walk, you'll have to contend with the hundreds of opportunistic monkeys who hang out at the base of the hill and on the path up to the top.

Up top, the wooded hill is littered with wats, prangs, chedis, whitewashed gazebos and lots more, in an ill-assorted combination of architectural idioms – the prang-topped viharn, washed all over in burnt sienna, is possibly the ugliest religious building in the country. Whenever the king came on an excursion here, he stayed in the airy summer house, **Phra Nakhon Khiri** (daily 9am–4pm; B40), with its Mediterranean-style shutters and verandas. Now a museum, it houses a moderately interesting collection of ceramics, furniture and other artefacts given to the royal family by foreign friends. Besides being cool and breezy, Khao Wang also proved to be a good star-gazing spot, so Rama IV had an open-sided, glass-domed observatory built close to his sleeping quarters. The king's amateur astronomy was not an inconsequential recreation: in August 1868 he predicted a solar eclipse almost to the second, thereby quashing the centuries-old Thai fear that the sun was periodically swallowed by an omnipotent lion god.

If you've got energy to spare, the two cave wats out on the western edges of town make good time-fillers. **Khao Banda-it**, a couple of kilometres west of Khao Wang, comprises a series of stalactite caves filled with Buddha statues and a 200-year-old Ayutthaya-style meditation temple. A bizarre story goes with this wat, attempting to explain its design faults as an intentional whim. The money for the three wat buildings was given by a rich man and his two wealthy wives: the first wife donated the bot, the second wife gave the viharn and the husband stuck the chedi in the middle. The chedi, however, leans distinctly southwards towards the viharn, prompting local commentators to point this out as subtle public acknowledgement of the man's preferences. Five kilometres north of Khao Wang, the caves of **Khao Luang** have the distinction of being a favourite royal picnic spot, and have also been decorated with various Buddha images.

Eating

Phetchaburi's best **restaurant** is the *Rabieng Rimnum (Rim Nam)*, which occupies a traditional wooden house beside the Chomrut Bridge, overlooking the Phetburi River; it's attached to the guest house of the same name but is open to non-guests as well. The restaurant boasts a long and interesting menu of inexpensive Thai dishes, from banana blossom salad to spicy crab soup, and is deservedly popular with local people. If you fancy sampling one of the local **sweet snacks**, such as *khanom maw kaeng* (sweet egg custard), you won't have to look far: almost half the shops in the town centre stock the stuff, as do many of the souvenir stalls crowding the base of Khao Wang, not to mention the day market on Thanon Matayawong.

Cha-am and around

Forever in the shadow of its more famous neighbour Hua Hin, the beach resort of **CHA-AM**, 41km south of Phetchaburi, is burgeoning now as it picks up the overspill from Hua Hin and positions itself as a more sedate alternative. It used to be a typically Thai resort, with accommodation catering mainly to families and student groups from Bangkok and an emphasis on shorefront picnics rather than swimming and sunbathing, but that's beginning to change as the Europeans and expats move in, bringing with them jet-skis and minimarkets, travellers' accommodation and package-holiday high-rises. The most developed bit of Cha-am's coastal strip stretches about 3km along Thanon Rumachit (sometimes spelt Ruamjit), from the *Mark Land Hotel* in the north to the *Santisuk* bungalows in the south. The beach here is pleasantly shaded, though rather gritty and very narrow at high tide, and the water is perfectly swimmable if not pristine. During the week the pace of life in Cha-am is slow and peaceful, and it's easy to find a solitary spot under the casuarinas, particularly up at the northerly end of the beach – something that's rarely possible at weekends, when prices shoot up and traffic thickens considerably. Away from the seafront there's not all that much to do here, but there are several **golf-courses** within striking distance (see p.555) and buses shuttle between Cha-am and Hua Hin (25km south) every half-hour, taking just 35 minutes.

Practicalities

Nearly all regular and air-con **buses** to and from Bangkok, Phetchaburi, Hua Hin, Chumphon and destinations further south stop in the town centre on Thanon Phetkasem (Highway 4), close to the junction with Thanon Narathip, 1km west of this beach. The **train station** (☏032/471159) is a few short blocks west of this junction. Thanon Narathip is the most useful of the side roads linking Thanon Phetkasem and the beachfront, and ends at a small seaside promenade and **tourist police** booth on Thanon Ruamchit, roughly halfway down the three-kilometre strip of beachfront development. To get down to the beach from Thanon Phetkasem, either walk or take a B20 motorbike taxi. Some private air-con buses to and from Bangkok use the depot at the little plaza on the beachfront Thanon Ruamchit, just south of the Ruamchit/Narathip junction.

Thanon Ruamchit is where you'll find most of the hotels and restaurants, as well as a few tourist-oriented businesses, including a small **post office** just south of *Scandy Resort*, a couple of places offering **internet access**, and several stalls where you can rent **motorbikes** as well as three-person pushbikes (B20). Cha-am's main business district occupies the small grid of streets west of Thanon Phetkasem, between the bus drop and the train station. Here you'll find the market, most of the shops, the **police station** (☎032/471323), the **GPO** and banks with **exchange** facilities and ATMs. The local **TAT** office (daily 8.30am–4.30pm; ☎032/471005, ⓔtourism@np.a-net.net.th) is about 1km south of the centre on Highway 4.

Accommodation

Most of the cheaper accommodation is concentrated in **central Cha-am**, set along the west side of beachfront Thanon Ruamchit; there are no hotels on the beach itself. All the Thanon Ruamchit hotels are described as being either north or south of the Narathip junction. The more expensive accommodation occupies the 25km of coastline **between Cha-am and Hua Hin**, where resorts are able to make the most of their extensive plots of land and enjoy what are in effect private beaches, though guests without transport have to rely on hotel shuttles or public buses to get to the shops and restaurants of Cha-am or Hua Hin. Many of the mid-market resorts in the Cha-am/Hua Hin strip are package-tour-oriented, but independent travellers can get reasonable **discounts** by booking online through almost any of the hotel finders listed in Basics on p.49; in addition, many hotels here give a fifteen to thirty percent discount from Sunday to Thursday.

Central Cha-am

Arunthip, south of the Narathip junction at 263/40 Thanon Ruamchit ☎032/471503. In a shophouse block; reasonable enough fan and air-con rooms, some with sea-view balconies, above a street-level reception desk and restaurant. ❸–❹

Happy Home, north of the Narathip junction on Thanon Ruamchit ☎032/471393. Ten rather scruffy semi-detached bungalows in two facing rows, though they all have air-con and TV and are just a hop and a skip from the shore. ❹

Kaen Chan Hotel, north of the Narathip junction at 241/3 Thanon Ruamchit ☎032/471314, ⓕ471531. Mid-sized hotel with a sixth-floor swimming pool and rooms that are fairly good value, if unexciting, all featuring air-con, TV and distant sea view. ❺

Mark Land Hotel, north of the Narathip junction at 208/14 Thanon Ruamchit ☎032/433821, ⓕ433834. Recommended, good-value high-rise where the nicely appointed deluxe rooms all have a balcony, most of which afford a partial long-distance view of the sea. All rooms are equipped with air-con, TV and mini-bar, and there's a swimming pool and fitness room. ❼–❽

Nirandorn Resort, just north of the Narathip junction on Thanon Ruamchit ☎032/471893. Uninspired but adequate fan and air-con bungalows and hotel rooms. ❸–❹

Santisuk, south of the Narathip junction at 263 Thanon Ruamchit, beside the intersection with Thanon Racha Phli 2 ☎032/471212. The charming exterior of this collection of traditional-style cottages on stilts unfortunately belies very plain and shabby interiors. Accommodation is geared towards Thai family groups, with bungalows comprising two double bedrooms for a total price of B2000, though there are also a few double en-suite rooms in a larger stilt-house, with either fan or air-con. ❸–❹

Scandy Resort, north of the Narathip junction at 274/32–33 Thanon Ruamchit ☎ & ⓕ032/471926, ⓦwww.scandyresort.thethai.com. Small, mid-market guest house above a restaurant where the best rooms are huge, good value and have air-con, TV, balconies and good sea views. Also has a few cheaper fan rooms. Recommended. ❸–❹

Between Cha-am and Hua Hin

Beach Garden Hotel, about 7km south of Cha-am at 949/21 Soi Suan Loi, off Thanon Phetkasem ☎032/471350, ⓕ471291. Set in a lush tropical garden that runs down to the sea, accommodation in this good-value resort is in either attractive, comfortably furnished cottages or a less characterful but smart hotel block. Has a swimming pool, games room, tennis courts, windsurfing and other watersports facilities. ❼–❽

Dusit Resort and Polo Club, 14km south of Cha-am and 9km north of Hua Hin at 1349 Thanon Phetkasem ☎032/520009, ℱ520296, ℬwww.dusit.com. One of the most luxurious and elegant spots on this stretch of coast, boasting five restaurants, a huge pool as well as a children's pool, all manner of sporting facilities – including a polo field, riding and sailing lessons and tennis courts – and cultural entertainments; there's an Avis car-rental desk here too. ⑨
Golden Sands, about 9km south of Cha-am at 854/2 Thanon Burirom, off Thanon Phetkasem ☎032/471617, ℱ471984. Standard upmarket rooms with private balconies and sea views in a 22-storey seaside block set in pleasantly landscaped gardens. There's a good pool and plenty of water-sports facilities. ⑧–⑨
Regent Cha-am, about 8km south of Cha-am at 849/21 Thanon Phetkasem ☎032/451240, ℱ471491, ℬwww.regent-chaam.com. Well-regarded upmarket resort set in appealing gardens that run down to a nice stretch of beach. Rooms are comfortably furnished; facilities include three swimming pools, squash and tennis courts and a fitness centre. ⑧–⑨

Eating and drinking

The choice of **restaurants** in Cha-am is not a patch on the range you get in Hua Hin, but for a change from hotel food you might want to try the Mexican specials at *Chicken Coop*, signed off Thanon Narathip; or drop by the *Tipdharee*, next to *Scandy Resort*, which boasts a huge menu of mid-priced Thai dishes, including lots of seafood, curries and one-plate dishes. *Baan Plang Pub and Restaurant* on Thanon Narathip opens nightly from 7pm to 2am and stages **live music**, as does the *Jeep Pub*, located in the little enclave of bars and other businesses between *Scandy Resort* and *Kaen Chan Hotel*.

Phra Ratchaniwet Marukhathaiyawan

Midway between Cha-am and Hua Hin lies the lustrous seaside palace of Rama VI, **Phra Ratchaniwet Marukhathaiyawan** (daily 8am–4pm; by donation), a rarely visited place despite the easy access; the half-hourly Cha-am–Hua Hin buses stop within a couple of kilometres' walk of the palace at the sign for Rama VI Camp – just follow the track through the army compound.

Designed by an Italian architect and completed in just sixteen days in 1923, the golden teak building was abandoned to the corrosive sea air after Rama VI's death in 1925. Restoration work began in the 1970s and today, most of the structure looks as it once did, a stylish composition of verandas and latticework painted in pastel shades of beige and blue, with an emphasis on cool simplicity. The spacious open hall in the north wing, hung with chandeliers and encircled by a first-floor balcony, was once used as a theatre, and the upstairs rooms, now furnished only with a few black-and-white portraits from the royal family photo album, were given over to royal attendants. The king stayed in the centre room, with the best sea view and access to the promenade, while the south wing (still not fully restored) contained the queen's apartments.

Hua Hin

Thailand's oldest beach resort, **HUA HIN** used to be little more than an overgrown fishing village with one exceptionally grand hotel, but the arrival of mass tourism, high-rise hotels and farang-managed hostess bars have begun to make a serious dent in its once idiosyncratic charm. With the far superior beaches of Ko

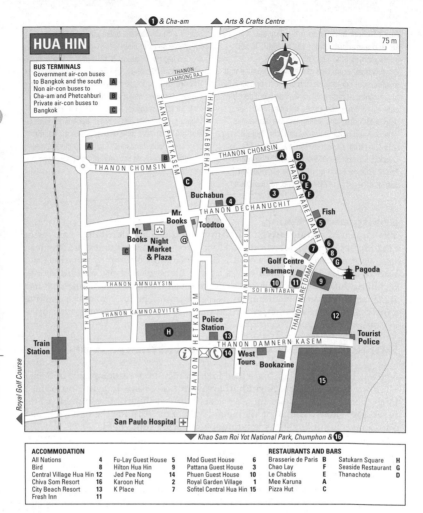

HUA HIN

& Cha-am • Arts & Crafts Centre

N

0   75 m

BUS TERMINALS
Government air-con buses
to Bangkok and the south   **A**
Non air-con buses to
Cha-am and Phetchaburi   **B**
Private air-con buses to
Bangkok   **C**

THANON DAMRONG RAJ

THANON PHETKASEM

THANON NAEBKEHAT

THANON CHOMSIN

THANON CHOMSIN

THANON NARED DAMRI

Buchabun

Mr. Books

THANON DECHANUCHIT   Fish

Mr. Books   Toodtoo

Night Market & Plaza

@

THANON SA SONG

THANON AMNUAYSIN

THANON KAMNOADVITEE

THANON POON SUK

Golf Centre Pharmacy

SOI BINTABAN

Pagoda

THANON NARED DAMRI

Police Station

THANON DAMNERN KASEM

Tourist Police

West Tours   Bookazine

Train Station

THANON PHETKASEM

San Paulo Hospital ✚

Royal Golf Course

Khao Sam Roi Yot National Park, Chumphon & 16

ACCOMMODATION						RESTAURANTS AND BARS			
All Nations	4	Fu-Lay Guest House	5	Mod Guest House	6	Brasserie de Paris	B	Satukarn Square	H
Bird	8	Hilton Hua Hin	9	Pattana Guest House	3	Chao Lay	F	Seaside Restaurant	G
Central Village Hua Hin	12	Jed Pee Nong	14	Phuen Guest House	10	Le Chablis	E	Thanachote	D
Chiva Som Resort	16	Karoon Hut	2	Royal Garden Village	1	Mee Karuna	A		
City Beach Resort	13	K Place	7	Sofitel Central Hua Hin	15	Pizza Hut	C		
Fresh Inn	11								

Samui, Krabi and Ko Samet so close at hand, there's little here to draw the sun-seeker, but it's nonetheless a convivial place in which to drink and enjoy fine seafood and, if you can afford it, stay in the atmospheric former *Railway Hotel*. In addition, the town makes a convenient base for day-trips to Khao Sam Roi Yot National Park, 63km south, and there are half a dozen golf courses in the area.

At the start of the twentieth century, **royalty** were Hua Hin's main visitors, but the place became more widely popular in the 1920s, when the opening of the Bangkok–Malaysia rail line made short excursions to the beach much more viable. The Victorian-style *Railway Hotel* was built soon after to cater for the leisured classes, and in 1926 Rama VII had his own summer palace, Klai Klangwon (Far from Worries), erected at the northern end of the beach. It was here, ironically, that Rama VII was staying in 1932 when the coup was launched in Bangkok against the system of absolute monarchy. The current king spends a lot of time here now, apparently preferring the sea breezes to the traffic fumes of the capital.

Arrival, information and transport

Hua Hin is conveniently located on the Bangkok–Surat Thani rail line, but journeys tend to be slow (3hr 30min–4hr from Bangkok), and most of the trains arrive late in the afternoon or very early in the morning. The most conveniently timed train from Bangkok leaves Thonburi station at 7.20am; if you're coming from Kanchanaburi, you can pick up this train from Ban Pho (not listed on English-language timetables) at about 9.30am. Hua Hin **train station** (☏032/511073) is at the west end of Thanon Damnern Kasem, about ten minutes' walk from the seafront.

Hua Hin's **bus** service is more useful. Non-air-con **Cha-am** and **Phetchaburi** buses arrive and depart every half-hour, using the terminal at the junction of Thanon Phetkasem and Thanon Chomsin, while government air-con buses to and from the Southern Bus Terminal in **Bangkok, Chumphon** and the south use the depot further west along Thanon Chomsin. The private air-con buses to southern destinations beyond Chumphon, such as **Phuket** (B680), **Krabi** (B700) and **Ko Samui** (B680 including ferry), all leave from town in the late evening; tickets should be booked through tour agents (see p.557). Bangkok Airways runs daily Bangkok–Hua Hin and Ko Samui–Hua Hin flights; the **airport** is about 5km north of town, beside the Phetkasem Highway, so you can flag down any south-bound bus into town or make use of the taxis that meet the flights.

The **tourist information** desk at the local government office (daily 8.30am–4.30pm; ☏032/532433), on the corner of Thanon Damnern Kasem and Thanon Phetkasem, offers advice on getting to Khao Sam Roi Yot National Park and sells bus tickets for southern destinations.

Hua Hin has plenty of samlors and motorbike taxis, but many tourists rent cars and motorbikes to explore the area by themselves. Avis (☏032/512021, ⓦwww.avis.com) have desks inside the *Hotel Sofitel*, and at the *Dusit Resort*, 9km north of Hua Hin (see p.551); several Hua Hin tour agencies also act as agents for Budget (ⓦwww.budget.co.th). The transport touts outside the *Hotel Sofitel* rent out 150cc bikes for around B200 a day.

Accommodation

A night or two at the former *Railway Hotel* (now the *Sofitel*) is reason in itself to visit Hua Hin, but there are plenty of other **places to stay**, both in the luxury and the more budget-orientated categories. The most unusual guest houses are built on converted squid piers, with rooms strung out along wooden jetties so you can hear and feel the waves beneath you, even if you can't afford a room overlooking them. Rooms at jetty guest houses are fairly inexpensive, the only drawback being the rather strong aroma of seashore debris at low tide. Rates can drop significantly from Mondays to Thursdays, so don't be afraid to ask for a discount. Resorts beyond the northern fringes of Hua Hin, on the stretch of coast between Hua Hin and Cha-am, are described on pp.550–1.

Inexpensive and moderate

All Nations, 10 Thanon Dechanuchit ☏032/512747, ✉cybercafehuahin@hotmail.com. Large, comfortable and exceptionally spruce rooms, many of them with balconies and some

with air-con. Bathrooms are shared between two rooms. Also has a nice roof terrace. ❸–❹

Bird, 31/2 Thanon Naretdamri ☏032/511630. A classic jetty guest house, with smallish but very clean, smart rooms set over the water, plus a nice breezy sea-view terrace at the end. All rooms have attached bathrooms, and some have air-con. Book ahead as it's very popular. ❸–❹

Fresh Inn, 132 Thanon Naretdamri ⊤032/511389, Ⓕ532166. Small Italian-run hotel, with a friendly, cosy atmosphere; all rooms are spacious and comfortable, and have air-con, TV and hot water. ❺

Fu-Lay Guest House, 110/1 Thanon Naretdamri ⊤032/513670, Ⓕ530320, Ⓦwww.huahinguide.com/guesthouse/fulay. A beautifully appointed jetty guest house with a high standard of rooms, nice en-suite bathrooms, friendly staff, plus the characteristic breezy seating area set right over the water. The priciest ones have air-con and TV. Recommended. ❹–❺

Jed Pee Nong, 17 Thanon Damnern Kasem ⊤032/512381, Ⓕ532063. This welcoming, though slightly shabby, low-rise hotel has a pool, which makes it decent value. The more expensive rooms have air-con and TV. ❺

Karoon Hut, 80 Thanon Naretdamri ⊤032/530737. Friendly jetty guest house, with an open-air seating area at the end of the pier. The rooms, some with air-con, are simple but fine. ❹–❺

K Place, 116 Thanon Naretdamri ⊤032/513908. Large, comfortable and well-appointed rooms, all with air-con and TV, make this small place a good-value mid-range option. ❺

Mod Guest House, 116 Thanon Naretdamri ⊤032/512296. Jetty guest house with some good rooms (a few with air-con), others fairly basic but very cheap (for Hua Hin), plus an attractive seafront terrace-restaurant and seating area. Call ahead to secure a room. ❷–❹

Pattana Guest House, 52 Thanon Naretdamri ⊤032/513393, Ⓕ530081, Ⓦhuahinpattana@hot-mail.com. Simple, inexpensive rooms in an appealingly traditional teak-wood house, quietly located at the end of a small soi. Some rooms have private bathrooms. ❸–❹

Phuen Guest House, Soi Bintaban (also spelt Binthabat) ⊤032/512344. Traditional wooden house in a busy street of bars, crammed with lots of small, basic rooms, most en suite and a few with air-con. ❷–❸

Expensive

Central Village Hua Hin, Thanon Damnern Kasem ⊤032/512036, Ⓕ511014, Ⓦwww.central-group.com. Like its sister operation the *Sofitel*, the *Central Village*, comprised of 41 cream-painted wooden villas set in a seafront garden, has a distinctive old-fashioned charm,. All the villas have large verandas, and some have two rooms and an uninterrupted sea view, though they're not exactly the last word in contemporary luxury. There's a pool and a restaurant on the premises, and guests can also use the facilities at the *Sofitel* over the road. ❾

Chiva Som International Health Resort, south of Hua Hin at 73/4 Thanon Phetkasem ⊤032/536536, Ⓕ511154, Ⓦwww.chivasom.net. Internationally renowned super-deluxe spa and health resort with just 57 exclusive bungalows and hotel rooms set in tropical beachfront gardens. A whole range of health treatments on offer, from aqua-aerobics and traditional massage to cardiac rehabilitation and skin consultations. Recently voted the best spa resort in the world by readers of Condé Nast's *Traveller* magazine. All-inclusive room-and-treatment packages start at about $250 per person per day. ❾

City Beach Resort, 16 Thanon Damnern Kasem ⊤032/512870, Ⓕ512448, Ⓦwww.citybeach.co.th. Reasonably priced, centrally located high-rise hotel with comfortable, well-equipped rooms, all with air-con and TV and most enjoying a sea view from the balcony. Has a swimming pool and a couple of restaurants. ❽

Hilton Hua Hin, 33 Thanon Naretdamri ⊤032/512879, Ⓕ511135, Ⓦwww.hilton.com. Set bang in the centre of Hua Hin's beachfront, the *Hilton's* high-rise profile disfigures the local skyline, but the facilities are extensive and the views excellent. Has an impressive stepped swimming pool right on the seafront, and a pretty water garden. Rooms are comfortable though not exciting; rates start at B7000. ❾

Hotel Sofitel Central Hua Hin, 1 Thanon Damnern Kasem ⊤032/512021, Ⓕ511014, Ⓦwww.sofitel.com. The former *Railway Hotel* remains a classic of colonial-style architecture, with cool, high ceilings, heavy-bladed ceiling fans, polished wood panelling and wide sea-view balconies. All is much as it was in 1923, except for the swimming pools and tennis courts which were built especially for the filming of *The Killing Fields* – the *Railway Hotel* stood in as Phnom Penh's plushest hotel. Rates start at B5600; weekends get booked out several weeks in advance. ❾

Royal Garden Village, just north of Hua Hin at 43/1 Thanon Phetkasem ⊤032/520250, Ⓕ520259, Ⓦwww.royal-garden.com. Award-winning, atmospheric top-notch hotel comprising attractive traditional Thai-style pavilions set in fourteen acres of beachfront land. Has three restaurants, a free-form pool and its own stretch of beach. ❾

The resort

The prettiest part of Hua Hin's five-kilometre-long **beach** is the patch in front of the *Sofitel*, where the sand is at its softest and whitest. North of here the shore is crowded with tables and chairs belonging to a string of small restaurant shacks, which is great if you're hungry but not ideal for solitary sunbathing; the beach then ends at a Chinese-style pagoda atop a flight of steps running down to Thanon Naretdamri. The coast to the north of the pagoda is dominated by the jetties and terraces of guest houses and seafood restaurants right up to the fishing pier, where the daily catch is still unloaded every morning. South of the *Sofitel*, upmarket hotels and condos overshadow nearly the whole run of beach down to Khao Takiab (Chopstick Hill), 8km further south.

Among the resort's myriad souvenir **shops**, Buchabun, at 22 Thanon Dechanuchit (Mon–Fri 5–10pm), stands out for its fine eclectic range of unusual antique arts and crafts collected from different parts of Thailand, and for its modern ceramics and other contemporary handicrafts. The Hua Hin Arts and Crafts Centre (daily 11am–10pm) at 18 Thanon Naeb Kehat, about 500m north of the junction with Thanon Chomsin, also sells antique and modern Thai paintings, woodcarvings and sculptures, and there are usually artists working on site too. Back in town at 27 Thanon Naretdamri, Fish is a small but alluring outlet selling gorgeous hand-made clothes in local cotton and silk fabrics. Plenty of other shops on and around Thanon Naretdamri sell beachwear and there are dozens of tailors here too. Other fun places to shop for clothes and souvenirs (after 6pm only) are the stalls at the night market on the west end of Thanon Dechanuchit, the more upmarket little shops in the Night Plaza that runs off it, and the collection of small shops selling good-quality handicrafts, textiles and clothes among the restaurants in Satukarn Square at the Thanon Phetkasem/Thanon Damnern Kasem crossroads.

When you tire of eating, drinking and shopping, you can always make an **excursion** to Khao Sam Roi Yot National Park (described on p.557), either by renting a car or as part of a tour (see p.557 for details of tour operators). Most tour operators also sell day-trips to Pala-u Falls near the Burmese border, as well as to Phetchaburi (see p.545), Damnoen Saduak floating markets (see p.207), Kanchanaburi and the River Kwai (see p.208) and Bangkok. It's quite feasible to do Phetchaburi as a day-trip by public bus from Hua Hin, and even easier to visit the old summer palace of Phra Ratchaniwet Marukhathaiyawan, described on p.551.

Golf courses

The Thai enthusiasm for **golf** began in Hua Hin in 1924, with the opening of the Royal Hua Hin Golf Club behind the train station, and now there are another five courses of international standard in the Hua Hin/Cha-am area. Visitors' green fees average B1200 on a weekday, B1800 on a weekend (though a couple are significantly cheaper), plus about B180 for a caddy. Some club houses also rent sets of clubs for B600, or you can ask at the Hua Hin Golf Centre (☎032/530119, ℻512085, ⓦwww.huahingolf.com), on Thanon Naretdamri across from the *Hilton*, which sells and repairs clubs, stocks golfing accessories and organizes trips and packages to local golf courses.

The eighteen-hole Royal Hua Hin Golf Course (☎032/512475) is the most centrally located of the **courses**, easily reached on foot by simply crossing the railway tracks to the west side of Hua Hin Railway Station. To get to the other courses (all eighteen holes except where noted), you'll need to drive: the Palm Hills Golf Resort (☎032/520800) is just fifteen minutes' drive north of Hua

Hin, on the way to Cha-am; the Jack-Nicklaus designed Springfield Royal Country Club (☏032/471303) is a few kilometres further north, just to the south of Cha-am itself; and the 27-hole Imperial Lake View (☏032/520091) is on the northern side of Cha-am. Half an hour's drive west of Hua Hin is the Majestic Creek Country Club (☏032/520102); and 25 minutes' south of Hua Hin is the Bangkok Golf Milford (☏032/572437).

Eating and drinking

Hua Hin is renowned for its **seafood**, and some of the best places to enjoy the local catch are the seafront restaurants along Thanon Naretdamri. Fish also features heavily at the **night market**, which sets up at sunset along the western end of Thanon Dechanuchit. For authentic European food, try any one of the farang-run bars and restaurants along Soi Bintaban or Thanon Damnern Kasem, where managers offer menus of pizzas and pasta, fish and chips, baked beans and German sausage. The biggest concentration of **bars** is along Soi Bintaban and around the back of the *Hilton* hotel; many of these places are so-called "bar-beers", with lots of seating round a large oval bar, and several hostesses dispensing beer and flirtation through the night.

Brasserie de Paris, 3 Thanon Naretdamri. Refined French restaurant that's known for its seafood and has an appealing terrace over the water. Specialities include crab Hua Hin, coquilles St Jacques and filet à la Provençal. Expensive.

Chao Lay, Thanon Naretdamri. Large and popular seafront restaurant specializing in quality seafood. Moderate.

Le Chablis, Thanon Naretdamri. Tasty and authentic French cuisine, plus some Thai dishes too. Moderate to expensive.

Mee Karuna, 26/1 Thanon Naretdamri. Upmarket restaurant, popular with Thai holidaymakers, which serves authentic, good-quality Thai classics such as *tom yang kung*. Moderate to expensive.

Satukarn Square, at the Thanon Phetkasem/Damern Kasem junction. Every evening

from around 6pm this tourist version of the more traditional night market becomes one of the most enjoyable places to be in Hua Hin. There are about twenty small restaurants in the partially open-air plaza (plus about the same number of handicraft shops) including specialist Italian, Indian, German and seafood outlets, all serving very reasonably priced food.

Seaside Restaurant, Thanon Naretdamri. Sample locally caught fish and seafood right on the seafront; worth the fairly steep rates. Moderate to expensive.

Thanachote, 11 Thanon Naretdamri. Atmospheric seafood restaurant, set on its own pier over the sea and serving exceptionally good fish dishes. Moderate.

Listings

Banks and exchange There are currency-exchange counters all over the resort, especially on Thanon Damnern Kasem and Thanon Naretdamri; most of the main bank branches with ATMs are on Thanon Phetkasem.

Books Hua Hin is well stocked with English-language bookstores: there are two branches of Mr Books, one on Thanon Phetkasem and the other at the west end of Thanon Dechanuchit, plus a Bookazine opposite the *Hotel Sofitel*.

Cookery classes One-day courses (B990) can be arranged through the Buchabun handicrafts shop

at 22 Thanon Dechanuchit (Mon–Fri 5–10pm; ☏032/547053); call to check when the next class is scheduled, or drop by the shop.

Diving No local reefs, but the bigger tour operators (see below) offer diving day-trips to Chumphon (see p.559) for B3000.

Emergencies For all emergencies, call the tourist police on the free, 24hr phoneline ☏ 1699, or contact them at their office opposite the *Sofitel* at the beachfront end of Thanon Damern Kasem ☏032/515995. The Hua Hin police station is further west on Damern Kasem ☏032/511027.

Hospitals The best private hospital in Hua Hin is the San Paulo, 222 Thanon Phetkasem ☎032/532576, south of the tourist information office. The government Thonburi Hua Hin Hospital is on the north edge of town at 17/155 Thanon Phetkasem ☎032/520900.

Internet access Available at several outlets in the resort, including on Thanon Phetkasem and at the CAT international phone office on Thanon Damnern Kasem.

Mail The GPO is on Thanon Damnern Kasem.

Pharmacy Several in the resort, including the exceptionally well-stocked Medihouse (daily 9am–10pm) opposite the *Hilton* on Thanon Naretdamri.

Telephones The CAT overseas telephone office (daily 8am–midnight) is on Thanon Damnern Kasem, next to the GPO.

Tour operators Both Toodtoo Tours, inside the Apilat Plaza on Thanon Phetkasem (☎032/530553, ℗512209, ✉www.toodtoo.com), and Western Tours at 11 Thanon Damnern Kasem (☎ & ℗032/512560) sell bus and air tickets and do day-trips to the Sam Roi Yot National Park (B900 per person), Pala-u falls and diving excursions to Chumphon. Toodtoo rents out jeeps and 750cc bikes, and Western offers a car-plus-driver service.

South to Chumphon

The 270-kilometre-long coastal strip between Hua Hin and Chumphon sees very few foreign tourists, though the beaches and birdlife of **Khao Sam Roi Yot National Park**, 63km south of Hua Hin, make a refreshing day-trip or even overnight stay. Less than 30km further south, the provincial capital of **Prachuap Khiri Khan** is famed for its seafood if not for its sand, but though it's a nice enough town there's nothing much to see there.

Khao Sam Roi Yot National Park

With a name that translates as "The Mountain with Three Hundred Peaks", the magnificent **KHAO SAM ROI YOT NATIONAL PARK**, 63km south of Hua Hin, boasts a remarkable variety of terrain, vegetation and wildlife within its 98 square kilometres. The dramatic **limestone crags** after which it is named are indeed its dominant feature, looming up to 650m above the gulf waters and the forested interior, but perhaps more significant are the mud flats and freshwater marsh which attract and provide a breeding ground for thousands of migratory birds. **Bird-watching** is the major draw, but great caves, excellent trails through forest and along the coast and a couple of secluded beaches provide strong competition. Pick up a **park map** from Hua Hin's tourist information desk before you go – it's sketchy but better than nothing.

Access and accommodation

Like most of Thailand's national parks, Khao Sam Roi Yot's chief drawback is also the secret of its appeal – it's very hard to visit by public transport. From Hua Hin, you need to take a local **bus** (every 20min; 40min) to **Pranburi** (23km) and then charter either a songthaew or a motorbike taxi (B150–250) to the park headquarters. But even once you're there, it's difficult to get about without wheels, as the sights, all accessible by park road, are spread all over the place – Hat Laem Sala and Tham Phraya Nakhon are 16km from HQ, Tham Sai is 8km, and the marsh at Rong Jai is 32km away. You can bypass the headquarters altogether and go directly to the beach at Laem Sala and the cave of Phraya Nakhon; from 6am to noon, hourly songthaews go from Pranburi market to the fishing village of **Bang Phu**, then it's a thirty-minute boat ride or a steep twenty- to thirty-minute trek from Bang Phu's temple – note that the last songthaew back leaves Bang Phu at 1pm.

Your best bet is to rent your own transport from Hua Hin, then follow Highway 4 south to Pranburi, turn left at Pranburi's main intersection and drive another 23km to the park checkpoint; carry on past the turn-off to Laem Sala, and continue 13km to the **park headquarters** and **visitor centre**, near the village of Khao Daeng. Alternatively, you could join a one-day **tour** from Hua Hin for about B900 (see p.557), though these tend to focus on the caves and beaches rather than the birds and animals.

The park's **accommodation** sites are around the headquarters and at Laem Sala; at both places it's a choice between camping, at B40 per person, or staying in one of the national park bungalows (B500–1000), which sleep up to twenty people. A more appealing option would be to stay a few kilometres outside the park entrance on the white-sand beach of Hat Phu Noi, where *Dolphin Bay Resort* (℡032/559333, ℻559334, ⓦwww.explorethailand.com; ⑥) offers air-con bungalows with sea views and a swimming pool, plus lots of excursions into the park, as well as dolphin-watching, sailing, snorkelling and fishing trips plus motorbike and car rental. To reach the resort, call to arrange transport from Hua Hin, or follow the above directions for the national park until you see the *Dolphin Bay* signs.

The park

Wildlife-spotting is best begun from the **visitor centre**, which has easy access to the mud flats along the shore, and is the starting point for the park's two official **nature trails** – the "Horseshoe Trail", which takes in the forest habitats of monkeys, squirrels and songbirds, and the "Mangrove Trail", which leads through the swampy domiciles of crabs, mudskippers, monitor lizards and egrets (for more on mangrove habitats, see p.791). When hungry, the **long-tailed (crab-eating) macaque** hangs around the mangrove swamps, but is also quite often spotted near the park headquarters, along with the **dusky langur**, or leaf monkey (also known as the spectacled langur because of the distinctive white skin around its eyes); the nocturnal **slow loris** (very furry and brown, with a dark ring around each eye and a dark stripe along its back) is a lot shyer and rarely seen. The park's forested crags are home to the increasingly rare **serow** (a black ungulate that looks like a cross between a goat and an antelope), as well as hordes of monkeys. Eminently spottable are the small, tawny-brown **barking deer** and **palm civets**; **dolphins** are also sometimes seen off the coast.

The park hosts up to three hundred species of **bird**. Between September and November, the mud flats are thick with migratory shore birds from Siberia, China and northern Europe – some en route to destinations further south, others here for the duration. The freshwater marsh near the village of **Rong Jai** is a good place for observing **waders** and **songbirds**, and is one of only two places in the whole country where the **purple heron** breeds. It's worth picking up a photocopied "bird-watchers' guide" – and a pair of binoculars – from the visitor centre.

The park also has a number of trails leading to **caves**, **beaches** and **villages**, the most popular heading to the area around **Hat Laem Sala**, a sandy, casuarina-fringed bay shadowed by limestone cliffs (see p.557 for access). Nearby, the huge, roofless **Tham Phraya Nakhon** is also quite a draw: it houses an elegant wooden pavilion constructed here by Rama V in 1890, and subsequent kings have left their signatures on the limestone walls. A three-hour trek from Phraya Nakhon, **Tham Sai** is a genuine dark and dank limestone cave, complete with stalactites, stalagmites and petrified waterfalls. The trek offers some fine coastal views, but a shorter alternative is the twenty-minute trail from **Khung Tanot** village (accessible by road), where you can rent a (very necessary) flashlight.

Prachuap Khiri Khan

Between Hua Hin and Chumphon there's only one place that makes a decent way-station on the route south, and that's the provincial capital of **PRA-CHUAP KHIRI KHAN**, 90km beyond Hua Hin. Prachuap has attractive streets of brightly painted wooden houses and vibrant bougainvillea and hibiscus blossoms set out in a neat grid to the west of the not very interesting beach. The town is only 12km east of the Burmese border, and you can see the Burmese mountains clearly if you climb up the 417 steps the monkey-infested **Khao Chong Krajok** at the northern end of town.

Prachuap is on the main Southern Railway Line, with connections to Chumphon and Surat Thani in the south, and Hua Hin, Phetchaburi and Bangkok to the north. The **train station** is on the west edge of town at the western end of Thanon Kong Kiat, which runs eastwards down to the sea and the main pier. The **bus station**, which also runs services to Chumphon, Surat Thani, Hua Hin, Phetchaburi and Bangkok, is one block east of the train station and two blocks north, on Thanon Phitak Chat. For overnight stops, try the *Yutichai Hotel*, about 50m east of the train station at 115 Thanon Kong Kiat (☎032/611055; ❶–❷), which has fan **rooms** with or without private bathroom, or the fairly similar *Inthira Hotel* (☎032/611418; ❷), about 20m north around the corner and across from the inland night market (south of the bus station) at 118 Thanon Phitak Chat. At the better-appointed *Tesaban (Thaed Saban) Bungalows* (☎032/611204; ❸–❹), on Thanon Prachuap Khiri Khan just south of Khao Chong Krajok at the north end of the beach, you can choose between fan and air-con bungalows, most of which have good sea views. Prachuap has two exceptionally good **night markets**, one in the town centre on Thanon Phitak Chat and the other north of the pier on the seafront – both of them serve delicious fresh fish.

Chumphon and around

South Thailand officially starts at **CHUMPHON**, where the main road splits into west- and east-coast branches, and inevitably the provincial capital saddles itself with the title "gateway to the south". Yet Chumphon has only recently begun to sell itself to tourists, an area of economic potential that assumed vital significance after November 1989, when Typhoon Gay – the worst typhoon to hit Thailand in recent decades – crashed into Chumphon province, killing hundreds of people and uprooting acres of banana, rubber and coconut plantations. With the mainstays of the region's economy in ruins, TAT and other government agencies began billing the beaches 12km east of town as a **diving** centre for the February to October season, when west-coast seas get too choppy. But although the nearby dive centre offers competitive prices and trips to unpolluted offshore reefs (see p.562), the town is simply not in the same league as neighbouring Ko Samui (see p.569). It's relaxed and friendly for sure, and not yet overrun with farangs, but the beaches are twenty minutes' drive out of

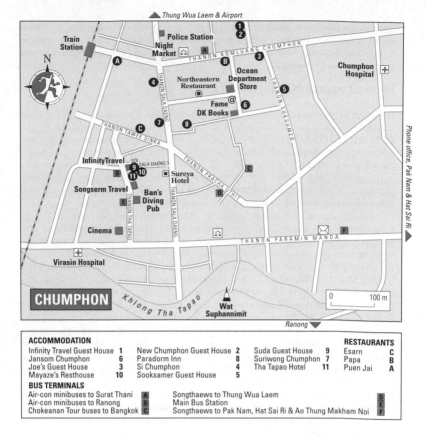

Thung Wua Laem & Airport

Ranong

CHUMPHON

Khlong Tha Tapao

Wat Suphannimit

ACCOMMODATION				RESTAURANTS	
Infinity Travel Guest House	1	New Chumphon Guest House	2	Suda Guest House	9	Esarn	C
Jansom Chumphon	6	Paradorm Inn	8	Suriwong Chumphon	7	Papa	B
Joe's Guest House	3	Si Chumphon	4	Tha Tapao Hotel	11	Puen Jai	A
Mayaze's Resthouse	10	Sooksamer Guest House	5				

BUS TERMINALS

Air-con minibuses to Surat Thani A · Songthaews to Thung Wua Laem
Air-con minibuses to Ranong B · Main Bus Station
Chokeanan Tour buses to Bangkok C · Songthaews to Pak Nam, Hat Sai Ri & Ao Thung Makham Noi D E F

town and the resorts there are seemingly unwilling to accommodate the budget visitor. For most travellers it is Chumphon's proximity to the island of **Ko Tao** that is the biggest draw, with three different boat services running out to the island every day, weather permitting. So it is that most backpackers stop by Chumphon for a night, take the boat to Ko Tao and spend another night here on their way back north; the town is well equipped to serve passers-through, offering clued-up travel agents, efficient transport links and plenty of internet cafés.

Arrival and information

Chumphon is conveniently located on the Southern Railway Line and has several **trains** a day to and from Surat Thani and Hat Yai in the south and Hua Hin, Phetchaburi and Bangkok to the north. The train station (☏077/511103) is on the northwest edge of town, at the western end of Thanon Komluang Chumphon, less than ten minutes' walk from most guest houses and hotels. The main **bus terminal** (☏077/570294) is on Thanon Tha Tapao, within a few minutes' walk of many guest houses and travel agents; all non-air-con buses use this terminal, as do most air-con services including those to and from Bangkok, Phetchaburi, Hua Hin, Ranong, Phuket, Surat Thani and Hat Yai. There are also several private **air-con bus and minibus** services that leave from other parts of town: air-con minibuses to Surat Thani leave from Thanon Komluang Chumphon every half-hour; hourly air-con minibuses to Ranong leave from Thanon Tha Tapao; and Chokeanan Tour air-con buses to Bangkok (4 daily) leave from just off Thanon Pracha Uthit. There is an **airport** (T077/591068) 35km north of town, which should be running Air Andaman **flights** to and from Bangkok and Phuket in the near future; check with any travel agent in town or contact the airline (T02/2514905, Wwww.airandaman.com).

There are three different **boat services from Chumphon to Ko Tao**, all of which leave from the port area at Pak Nam, 14km southeast of Chumphon; tickets for all boats can be bought from travel agents and guest houses. The fastest but most stomach-churning option is the Numhasin (aka Nama Hamsin) **speed boat** (T077/521755), which leaves at 7.30am (1hr 45min; B400); Numhasin provides free transfers from Chumphon guest houses, but the boat cannot run in windy weather. The **Songserm express boat** (T077/503735) leaves at 7.30am every day from January through October (the seas are too rough in November and December) from Tha Yang pier (2hr 30min; B400 one-way, B750 return). A Songserm bus meets the morning trains arriving from Bangkok and takes passengers to their office in town, from where there's onward transport to the ferry at 7am; they will also pick up from guest houses in town. The **slow boat** (T077/521615) departs at midnight from the Tha Reua Ko Tao pier (aka the Tha Thai and Seafood pier); services (6hr; B200) run in all but the very worst weather. To get to Tha Reua Ko Tao you'll need to take the taxi vans offered by guest houses, which leave town at about 10pm and cost B50 per person.

Travel agents in Chumphon are very accommodating to travellers' needs, and as well as Ko Tao boat tickets, they all sell bus, train and air tickets, and store luggage free of charge; some also offer free showers and video shows to travellers awaiting onward connections. The three best travel agents are all on Thanon Tha Tapao, within a few minutes' walk of the main bus station: Songserm Travel (T077/506205) lets travellers kip down on the office floor while waiting for the boat and are open 24 hours; and both Infinity Travel (T077/501937) and *Ban's Diving Pub* (T077/570751) have internet access and a restaurant, and offer free showers and video shows to waiting travellers.

Accommodation

As with most other Thai towns, Chumphon's **guest houses** are the friendliest places to stay, if not exactly the last word in comfort, and they're all geared up for travellers, with farang-friendly menus, bikes for hire and plenty of local information. The **hotels** in town are less pricey than those on the beaches, but nothing special.

Chumphon's guest houses are used to accommodating Ko Tao-bound travellers, so it's generally no problem to check into a room for half a day before catching the night boat. Most places will also store luggage for you until your return to the mainland.

Infinity Travel, check in through their office on Thanon Tha Tapao T077/501937. One of Chumphon's most clued-up travel agencies, *Infinity* has three rooms above its office on Thanon Tha Tapao, and another eight rooms in a characterful old wooden house on Soi 1, Thanon Komluang Chumphon. All rooms share bathrooms, and the old house has a nice seating area downstairs plus motorbike rental. ❷

Jansom Chumphon, off Thanon Sala Daeng T077/502502, F502503. Chumphon's top hotel offers air-con, TV and all the usual trimmings, but is starting to look a little faded. ❹–❺

Mayaze's Resthouse, off Thanon Sala Daeng at 111/35 Soi 3 (aka Soi Bangkok Bank) T077/504452, F502217, Emayazes@hotmail.com. Small, friendly guest house with comfortable fan and air-con rooms, all

of which share bathrooms. Plenty of local information and free tea and coffee. ❸
New Chumphon Guest House (aka *Miao*), Soi 1, Thanon Komluang Chumphon ☎077/502900. Smallish rooms with shared facilities in a house on a quiet, residential soi. Nice outdoor seating area, and friendly clued-up staff. Price depends on the size of the room. ❷
Paradorm Inn, 180/12 Thanon Paradorm, east off Thanon Sala Daeng ☎077/511598, ℱ501112. The best value of the town's mid-range hotels: all rooms have air-con and TV, and there's a pool and restaurant. ❹
Si Chumphon, 127/22–24 Thanon Sala Daeng ☎077/511379. Very similar to neighbouring *Suriwong Chumphon*, with no ambience but reasonable rooms. Fan and air-con rooms available. ❷–❸
Sooksamer Guest House, 118/4 Thanon Suksumer ☎077/502430. Located on a peaceful

street, this place is friendly and exceptionally cheap if a little ragged round the edges. Rooms in the traditional house are a bit box-like and share facilities, though the communal seating area is pleasant. ❶
Suda Guest House, off Thanon Sala Daeng on Soi 3 (aka Soi Bangkok Bank) ☎077/504366. Clean and well-maintained, with just three rooms with shared bathroom in the owner's own modern house, and the option of fan or air-con. Motorbikes for rent and breakfast on request. ❸
Suriwong Chumphon, 125/27–29 Thanon Sala Daeng ☎077/511397, ℱ502699. Large and characterless, but the rooms are clean and en suite and some have air-con. ❷–❸
Tha Tapao Hotel, 66/1 Thanon Tha Tapao ☎077/511479, ℱ502479. Unexciting mid-range hotel that's used to dealing with farang tourists, is convenient for the bus station, and has both fan and air-con rooms. ❸

Beaches and islands

Chumphon's best beach is **THUNG WUA LAEM**, 12km north of town and served by frequent yellow songthaews from halfway down Thanon Pracha Uthit (B25). The long sandy stretch has a few bungalow resorts and a handful of seafood restaurants. *Chumphon Cabana* (☎077/560245, ℱ504442, Ⓦwww.cabana.co.th; ❺–❽) offers a selection of well-appointed fan and air-con bungalows at the southern end of the beach, and also runs a **dive centre** (Jan–Sept only), featuring trips to nearby islands for B900 per diver and B500 per snorkeller, and offering NAUI-certificated five-day courses for B11,500. They provide free transport (3 daily) to the resort from their Chumphon office, which is next to Infinity Travel on Thanon Tha Tapao. Further up the beach, there's cheaper fan and air-con accommodation at *Seabeach Bungalow* (☎077/560115; ❸–❹).

If you're keen to go diving or snorkelling independently, then you should make for **HAT SAI RI**, 20km south of town and reached by frequent songthaews from Thanon Paramin Manda (B20). Though dirtier and busier than Thung Wua Laem, this is the best place to hire boats to the tiny offshore **islands**, some of the best of which are visible from the beach: it's well worth exploring the reefs around **Ko Mattra** and **Ko Rat** (the one with a profile like a half-submerged rhino), and although nearby **Ko Lang Ka Chiu** is out of bounds because of its birds'-nest collecting business (see box on p.695), it's permissible to dive in the surrounding waters. Further afield, about 18km offshore, the reefs and underwater caves around **Ko Ngam Yai** and **Ko Ngam Noi** are the usual destination of the *Chumphon Cabana* diving and snorkelling expeditions. To get to any of the above islands on your own, either negotiate directly with the fishermen on Hat Sai Ri or enlist the help of the amenable manager of *Sai Ri Lodge* (☎077/521212; ❻) at the southern end of the beach; a day's boat ride around all or some of these islands should cost about B2000 per ten-person boat (excluding any diving or snorkelling equipment). If you want to stay at the *Lodge*, you can choose between fan and air-con bungalows.

About 5km south of Hat Sai Ri, **Ao Thung Makham Noi** has become a popular spot with German tourists because of *MT Resort*, also known as *Mother Hut* (☎077/558153, ℱ558152; ❸), which offers appealing bungalows set among the palm trees beside the beach. There's a restaurant on the beach and you can organize snorkelling trips to Ko Thong Lang, just a few minutes off shore, as well as longer expeditions in squid boats. To get to Ao Thung Makham Noi, either take one of the songthaews from Thanon Paramin Manda or arrange transport through *Mayaze's Resthouse*.

Eating

There are a couple of very good northeastern **restaurants** in town – the one next to the Ocean department store off Thanon Sala Daeng serves *kai yang, som tam* and sticky rice all day; the other, *Esarn* on Thanon Tawee Sinka, has basic Thai dishes in the daytime and northeastern fare in the evening. For freshly caught seafood, try the large, open-air *Papa* on Thanon Komluang Chumphon, or the similar *Puen Jai*, an upmarket garden restaurant across from the train station. After dark, the **night market** sets up along both sides of Thanon Komluang Chumphon and is a popular and enjoyable place to eat. For Western food, check out the breakfasts at *Paradorm Inn*; or the coffee bar on the third floor of the Ocean department store, which stocks ten different coffee blends; or the pizzas in the food centre on the same floor.

Listings

Banks and exchange The main banks, with exchange counters and ATMs, are on Thanon Sala Daeng and Thanon Pracha Uthit.

Books A few English-language books and the *Bangkok Post* at DK Books opposite the *Jansom Chumphon* hotel.

Emergencies For all emergencies, call the tourist police on the free, 24hr phoneline ☎1699, or contact the Chumphon police station on the north end of Thanon Sala Daeng ☎077/511505.

Hospitals The government Chumphon Hospital (☎077/503672) is on the northeast edge of town; the private Virasin Hospital (☎077/503238) is in the southwest, on Thanon Paramin Manda.

Internet access Available at lots of places on Thanon Tha Tapao, including *Ban's Diving Pub* and Infinity Travel, as well as at Fame, opposite the *Jansom Thara* hotel.

Mail The GPO is on the southeastern edge of town, on Thanon Paramin Manda.

Motorbike rental For B150 per day from *Suda Guest House, New Chumphon Guest House* and Infinity Travel.

Pharmacy Several in the resort, including the exceptionally well-stocked Medihouse (daily 9am–10pm) opposite the *Hilton* on Thanon Naretdamri.

Telephones The main CAT overseas phone centre is on the far southeastern edge of town, several hundred metres east of the GPO on Thanon Paramin Manda: any Paramin Manda songthaew will drop you outside. The more central Fame, opposite the *Jansom Thara* hotel, also offers overseas phone and fax services.

Chaiya and around

About 140km south of Chumphon, **CHAIYA** was the capital of southern Thailand under the Srivijayan empire, which fanned out from Sumatra between the eighth and thirteenth centuries. Today there's little to mark the passing of the Srivijayan civilization, but this small, sleepy town has gained new fame as the site of **Wat Suan Mokkh**, a progressively minded temple whose meditation retreats account for the bulk of Chaiya's farang visitors. Unless you're interested in one of the retreats, the town is best visited on a day-trip, either as a break in the journey south, or as an excursion from Surat Thani.

Chaiya is 3km from Highway 41, the main road down this section of the Gulf coast: **buses** from Chumphon to Surat Thani will drop you off on the highway, from where you can catch a motorbike taxi or walk into town; from Surat Thani's local bus station, hourly buses take an hour to reach Chaiya. Although the town lies on the main Southern Rail Line, most **trains** arrive in the middle of the night; only the evening trains from Bangkok are useful, getting you to Chaiya first thing in the morning.

The Town

The main sight in Chaiya is **Wat Phra Boromathat** on the western side of town, where the ninth-century chedi – one of very few surviving examples of Srivijayan architecture – is said to contain relics of the Buddha himself. Hidden away behind the viharn in a pretty, red-tiled cloister, the chedi looks like an oversized wedding cake surrounded by an ornamental moat. Its unusual square tiers are spiked with smaller chedis and decorated with gilt, in a style similar to the temples of central Java.

The **National Museum** (Wed–Sun 9am–4pm; B10) on the eastern side of the temple is a disappointment. Although the Srivijaya period produced some of Thailand's finest sculpture, much of it discovered at Chaiya, the best pieces have been carted off to the National Museum in Bangkok. Replicas have been left in their stead, which are shown alongside fragments of some original statues and an exhibition of local handicrafts. The best remaining piece is a serene stone image of the Buddha from **Wat Kaeo**, an imposing chedi on the south side of town. Heading towards the centre from Wat Phra Boromathat, you can reach this chedi by taking the first paved road on the right, which brings you first to the brick remains of Wat Long, and then after 1km to Wat Kaeo, enclosed by a thick ring of trees. Here you can poke around the murky antechambers of the chedi, taking care not to trip over the various dismembered stone Buddhas that are lying around.

Ban Phum Riang

If you've got some time on your hands, you could take one of the regular songthaews to **BAN PHUM RIANG**, 5km east of Chaiya, a Muslim crab-fishing village of wooden stilt houses clustered around a rickety mosque. The weavers here are famous for their original designs of silk and cotton; although the cottage industry is on the decline, you might still be able to pick up a bargain in the village's handful of shops.

Wat Suan Mokkh

The forest temple of **Wat Suan Mokkh** (Garden of Liberation), 6km south of Chaiya on Highway 41, was founded by **Buddhadasa Bhikkhu**, southern Thailand's most revered monk until his death in 1993 at the age of 87. His back-to-basics philosophy, encompassing Christian, Zen and Taoist influences, lives on and continues to draw Thais from all over the country to the temple, as well as hundreds of farangs. It's not necessary to sign up for one of the wat's retreats to enjoy the temple, however – all buses from Chumphon and Chaiya to Surat Thani pass the wat, so it's easy to drop by for a quiet stroll through the wooded grounds.

The layout of the wat is centred on the Golden Hill: scrambling up between trees and monks' huts, you'll reach a hushed clearing on top of the hill which is the temple's holiest meeting-place, a simple open-air platform decorated with nothing more than a stone Buddha with the Wheel of Law. At the base of the hill, the outer walls of the Spiritual Theatre are lined with bas-reliefs, replicas of originals in India, which depict scenes from the life of the Buddha. Inside, every centimetre is covered with colourful didactic painting, executed by resident monks and visitors in a jumble of realistic and surrealistic styles.

Meditation retreats

Meditation retreats are held by farang and Thai teachers over the first ten days of every month at the International Dharma Heritage, a purpose-built compound 1km from the main temple at Wat Suan Mokkh. Large numbers of farang travellers, both novices and experienced meditators, turn up for the retreats, which are intended as a challenging exercise in mental development – it's not an opportunity to relax and live at low cost for a few days. Conditions imitate the rigorous lifestyle of a *bhikkhu* (monk) as far as possible, each day beginning before dawn with meditation according to the Anapanasati method, which aims to achieve mindfulness by focusing on the breathing process. Although talks are given on Dharma (the doctrines of the Buddha – as interpreted by Buddhadasa Bhikkhu) and meditation technique, most of each day is spent practising Anapanasati in solitude. To aid concentration, participants maintain a rule of silence, broken only by daily chanting sessions, although supervisors are available for individual interviews if there are any questions or problems. Men and women are segregated into separate dormitory blocks and, like monks, are expected to help out with chores.

Each course has space for about one hundred people – turn up at the information desk in Wat Suan Mokkh by early afternoon on the last day of the month to enrol. The fee is B1200 per person, which includes two vegetarian meals a day and accommodation in simple cells. Bring a flashlight (or buy one outside the temple gates) and any other supplies you'll need for the ten days – participants are encouraged not to leave the premises during the retreat. For further information, go to ⓦwww.suanmokkh.org or contact TAT in Surat Thani.

Surat Thani

Uninspiring **SURAT THANI**, 60km south of Chaiya, is generally worth visiting only as the jumping-off point for the Samui archipelago (see p.566, p.586 and p.597), though it might be worth a stay when the Chak Phra Festival (see box on p.567) is on, or as a base for seeing the nearby historic town of Chaiya.

Strung along the south bank of the Tapi River, with a busy port for rubber and coconuts near the river mouth, the town is experiencing rapid economic growth and paralysing traffic jams. Its only worthwhile attraction is the **Monkey Training College** (daylight hours; from B300 per show; ☎077/227351), a thirty-minute trip out of town, where young monkeys are trained to pick coconuts from trees which are too tall for humans to reach. To get there, charter a songthaew, or take a local bus 6km east towards Kanchanadit and Don Sak and then walk the last 2km, following the signpost south from the main road. The serious business of the college is undoubtedly worthy – coconuts are the province's most important crop, providing a much-needed cash livelihood for small farmers – but the hour-long coconut-picking display that the owner, Somphon Saekhow, and his champion pig-tailed

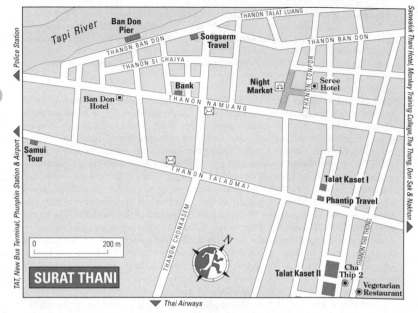

TAT, New Bus Terminal, Phunphin Station & Airport

Thai Airways

SURAT THANI

macaque put on for visitors may feel a little exploitative. At the end of the display, Khun Somphon will show you the stable at the back where the most laborious parts of the training take place. The three-month course costs the monkeys' owners B3000 per student, and graduates can farm up to one thousand coconuts a day.

Practicalities

Buses to Surat Thani arrive at three different locations, two of which are on Thanon Taladmai in the centre of town, at Talat Kaset I on the north side of the road (local buses) and opposite at Talat Kaset II (many long-distance buses, including those from Phuket and Hat Yai). The new bus terminal, 2km southwest of the centre on the road towards Phunphin, handles services from Bangkok and a few other provinces. Arriving by **train** means arriving at **Phunphin**, 13km to the west, from where buses run into Surat Thani every ten minutes between 6am and 7pm, and share-taxis leave when full (B15 per person or about B90 to charter the whole car into town). It's also possible to buy express-boat and vehicle-ferry tickets to Ko Samui and Ko Pha Ngan from the train station, including a connecting bus to the relevant pier (Tha Thong, Don Sak or Khanom). If you're planning to leave by train, booking tickets at the reliable Phantip Travel, in front of Talat Kaset I at 293/6–8 Thanon Taladmai (℡077/272230 or 272906), will save an extra trip to Phunphin.

Phunphin and the bus stations are teeming with touts offering to escort you onto their employer's service to **Ko Samui** or **Ko Pha Ngan** – they're generally reliable but make sure you don't get talked onto the wrong boat. If you manage to avoid getting hustled, you can buy tickets direct from the boat operators: Songserm Travel, on Thanon Ban Don opposite the night-boat pier (℡077/285124–6), handles the express boats to Samui and Pha Ngan; Samui

At the start of the eleventh lunar month (September or October) the people of Surat Thani celebrate the end of Buddhist Lent with the **Chak Phra Festival** (Pulling the Buddha), which symbolizes the Buddha's return to earth after a monsoon season spent preaching to his mother in heaven. On the Tapi River, tugboats pull the town's principal Buddha image on a raft decorated with huge nagas, while on land sleigh-like floats bearing Buddha images and colourful flags and parasols are hauled across the countryside and through the streets. As the monks have been confined to their monasteries for three months, the end of Lent is also the time to give them generous offerings in the *kathin* ceremony, of which Surat Thani has its own version, called Thot Pha Pa, when the offerings are hung on tree branches planted in front of the houses before dawn. Longboat races, between teams from all over the south, are also held during the festival.

Tour, 326/12 Thanon Taladmai (⊕077/282352), handles connecting buses for the vehicle ferries.

Arriving by **air**, you can take a B80 Songserm/Phantip minibus for the 27-kilometre journey south into Surat Thani, or a B280 combination ticket to Ko Samui; if you're flying out of Surat, you can catch the minibus from town to the airport at the Thai Airways office, south of the centre at 3/27–28 Thanon Karoonrat, off Thanon Chonkasem (⊕077/272610 or 273710), or at the *Wangtai Hotel* (see below).

If you're coming from points south by **air-conditioned minibus** or **share-taxi**, you should be deposited at the door of your destination; when leaving Surat, minibus tickets can be booked at Phantip or the offices around Talat Kaset II; share-taxis also congregate at Talat Kaset II.

TAT has an office at the western end of town at 5 Thanon Taladmai (daily 8am–4pm; ⊕077/288817–9, ℰtatsurat@samart.co.th), which stocks free, sketchy maps. Small **share-songthaews** buzz around town, charging around B10 per person.

Accommodation and eating

Most budget **accommodation** in Surat Thani is noisy, grotty and overpriced – you'd probably be better off on a night boat to Ko Samui or Ko Pha Ngan. If you do get stuck here, head for the *Ban Don Hotel*, above a restaurant at 268/1 Thanon Namuang (⊕077/272167; ❷), where clean rooms with fans and en-suite bathrooms are set back from the noise of the main road. A little upmarket but not as good value, *Seree Hotel*, 2/2–5 Thanon Tonpor (⊕077/272279; ❸–❹), is also clean and quiet, with fan-cooled and air-con rooms. At the western end of town, *Wangtai Hotel*, 1 Thanon Taladmai (⊕077/283020–39, ℰ281007; ❺), was for a long time Surat Thani's only luxury option, and is still very good value with large, smart rooms around a swimming pool; its main challenger at the opposite end of town, the *Saowaluk Thani*, 99/99 Thanon Surat–Kanchanadit (⊕077/213700–30, ℰ213735; ❽), is more spacious and swankier, but over twice the price.

For tasty, inexpensive Thai and Chinese **food** in large portions, head for the restaurant on the ground floor of the *Ban Don Hotel*. The night market between Thanon Si Chaiya and Thanon Ban Don displays an eye-catching range of dishes; a smaller offshoot by Ban Don pier offers less choice but is handy if you're taking a night boat. During the day, *Cha Thip 2* on the east side of Talat Kaset II bus station serves good dim sum and coffee, while one block east on

Thanon Tha Thong, an unnamed restaurant offers a wide selection of cheap and delicious tray food or fried dishes, mostly vegetarian though with some fish (look out for the yellow flags outside and a sign saying "vegetarian food"; closes 7pm). For more upmarket food, you could do a lot worse than the *Wangtai Hotel*, which at various restaurants and times of the day can offer buffet breakfasts, dim sum and tasty Thai and Western food, with friendly service and fierce air-conditioning.

Ko Samui

An ever-widening cross-section of visitors, from globetrotting backpackers to suitcase-toting fortnighters, come to southern Thailand just for the beautiful beaches of **KO SAMUI**, 80km from Surat – and at 15km across and down, Samui is large enough to cope, except during the rush at Christmas and New Year. The paradisal sands and clear blue seas have kept their good looks, which are enhanced by a thick fringe of palm trees that gives a harvest of three million coconuts each month. However, development behind the beaches – which has brought the islanders far greater prosperity than the crop could ever provide – speeds along in a messy, haphazard fashion with little concern for the environment. A local bye-law limits new construction to the height of a coconut palm (usually about three storeys), but the island's latest hotel complexes bask in the shade of some suspiciously lofty trees, rumoured to have been brought in from northern Thailand.

For most visitors, the days are spent indulging in a few watersports or just lying on the beach waiting for the next drinks seller, hair braider or masseur to come along. For a day off the sand, you should not miss the almost supernatural beauty of the **Ang Thong National Marine Park**, which comprises many of the eighty islands in the Samui archipelago. A motorbike day-trip on the fifty-kilometre round-island road throws up plenty more gorgeous beaches, and nighttime entertainment is provided by a huge number of beach bars, tawdry barbeers and clubs. Buffalo fighting, once a common sport on the island, is now generally restricted to special festivals such as Thai New Year; the practices and rituals are much the same as those of bullfighting in Hat Yai (see p.731).

The island's most appealing beaches, **Chaweng** and **Lamai**, have seen the heaviest development and are now the most expensive places to stay, while quieter beaches such as **Maenam** are generally less attractive. **Choeng Mon** in Samui's northeast corner makes a good compromise: the beaches are nothing to write home about but the views of the bay are, the seafront between the handful of upmarket hotels is comparatively undeveloped, and Chaweng's nightlife is within easy striking distance. **Accommodation** on the island is generally in bungalow resorts, from the basic to the very swish: at the lower end of the scale, there are very few places left for under B150, but nearly all bottom-end bungalows now have en-suite bathrooms and constant electricity; for the most upmarket places you can pay well over B3000 for the highest international standards. The price codes on the following pages are based on high-season rates, but out of season (roughly April–June, Oct & Nov) dramatic reductions are possible.

No particular **season** is best for coming to Ko Samui. The northeast monsoon blows heaviest in November, but can bring rain at any time between October and January, and sometimes makes the sea on the east coast too chop-

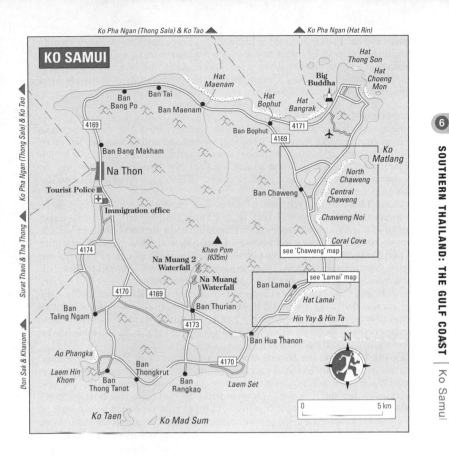

KO SAMUI

Hat Thong Son

Big Buddha

Hat Choeng Mon

Hat Maenam

Ban Tai

Ban Bang Po

Ban Maenam

Ban Bophut

Hat Bophut

Hat Bangrak

Ban Bang Makham

Na Thon

Tourist Police

Immigration office

Ko Matlang

North Chaweng

Ban Chaweng

Central Chaweng

Chaweng Noi

Coral Cove

see 'Chaweng' map

Khao Pom (635m)

Na Muang 2 Waterfall

Na Muang Waterfall

Ban Lamai

see 'Lamai' map

Hat Lamai

Ban Thurian

Hin Yay & Hin Ta

Ban Taling Ngam

Ban Hua Thanon

Ao Phangka

Laem Hin Khom

Ban Thongkrut

Ban Thong Tanot

Ban Rangkao

Laem Set

N

0   5 km

Ko Taen

Ko Mad Sum

4169

4171

4169

4174

4170

4169

4173

4170

py for swimming. (The north coast is generally calm enough for swimming all year round.) January is often breezy, March and April are very hot, and between May and October the southwest monsoon blows mildly onto Samui's west coast and causes some rain.

TAT runs a small but helpful office (daily 8.30am–noon & 1–4.30pm; ☏077/420504, ℮tatsamui@samart.com), tucked away on an unnamed side road in Na Thon (north of the pier and inland from the post office). Another useful source of **information** is Ⓦwww.sawadee.com, a website set up by a German based at Lamai, which allows, among other things, direct bookings at a range of hotels on the island.

Ko Samui has around a dozen **scuba-diving** companies, offering trips for qualified divers and a wide variety of courses throughout the year, and the only **recompression chamber** in this part of Thailand, at Bangrak. Although the coral gardens at the north end of Ang Thong National Marine Park offer good diving between October and April, most trips for experienced divers head for the waters around Ko Tao (see p.595), which contain the best sites in the region; a day's outing costs around B3000, though if you can make your own way to Ko Tao, you'll save money and have more time in the water. The range of courses is comparable to what's on offer at Ko Tao, though prices are generally higher. Established and reliable PADI Five-Star Dive Centres include Samui International Diving School (ⓦwww.planet-scuba.net), which has its head office at the *Malibu Resort* towards the north end of Central Chaweng (ⓣ077/422386); and Easy Divers (ⓦwww.thaidive.com), which has its head office opposite *Full Circle* on Chaweng (ⓣ077/413372–3).

Getting to the island

The most obvious way of getting to Ko Samui is on a boat from the Surat Thani area. Services fluctuate according to demand and extra boats are often laid on in high season, but the longest-established ferry is the night boat which leaves Ban Don pier in **Surat Thani** itself for **Na Thon** – the main port on Samui – at 9pm every night (7–8hr); tickets (B150) are sold at the pier on the day of departure.

From **Tha Thong**, 5km east of Surat, one express boat a day, handled by Songserm Travel (see p.566) runs to Na Thon (2hr 30min); the B150 ticket includes bus transport from Surat or Phunphin train station to the pier. Vehicle ferries run seven times a day between **Don Sak** pier, 68km east of Surat, and Thong Yang, 8km south of Na Thon (1hr 30min; B55); to coincide with these boats, Samui Tour (see p.566) runs buses from Surat or Phunphin to Don Sak and from Thong Yang to Na Thon, costing B40 for ordinary buses, B50 for air-conditioned buses; similarly vehicle ferries operate from **Khanom**, 100km east of Surat (4 daily; 1hr 30min; B55), with coinciding air-con buses from Surat or Phunphin run by Songserm (B50). The total journey time using the vehicle ferries is much the same as on an express boat, and if the sea is turbulent, the shorter voyage can be a blessing.

From **Bangkok**, the State Railway, in association with Surat travel agency Phanthip, does train/bus/boat packages through to Ko Samui which cost almost exactly the same as organizing the parts independently – around B550 if you travel in a second-class bunk. Government-run overnight bus–boat packages from the Northern Terminal cost from B300, and are far preferable to some of the cheap deals offered by private companies on Thanon Khao San (from around B250), as the vehicles used on these latter services are often substandard and several thefts have been reported. At the top of the range, you can get to Ko Samui direct **by air** on Bangkok Airways (in Bangkok ⓣ02/229 3456; at Samui airport ⓣ077/422513); between twelve and fourteen flights a day leave Bangkok, and there are even daily flights from Phuket, Krabi, U-Tapao (near Pattaya) and Singapore. Air-con minibuses meet incoming flights (and connect with departures) at the **airport** in the northeastern tip of the island, charging B100 to Chaweng for example; the rustic terminal has a reservations desk for some of the island's moderate and expensive hotels, currency-exchange facilities, a post office with international telephones (daily 8am–8pm), restaurants, and a Budget car-rental branch (ⓣ077/427188, ⓦwww.budget.co.th).

Finally, it's possible to hop to Ko Samui from **Ko Pha Ngan**: three express boats a day do the 45-minute trip from Thong Sala to Na Thon (B95), while two vehicle ferries cover the same route for the same price in 1hr 10min; from Hat Rin three passenger boats a day take an hour to reach Bangrak (B100). Between January and September, if there are enough takers and the weather's good enough, one boat a day starts at Thong Nai Pan, on Ko Pha Ngan's east coast, and calls at Hat Rin before crossing to Maenam.

Island transport

Songthaews, which congregate at the car park between the two piers in Na Thon, cover a variety of set routes during the daytime, either heading off clockwise or anti-clockwise on Route 4169, to serve all the beaches; destinations are marked in English and fares for most journeys range from B20 to B45. In the evening, they tend to operate more like taxis and you'll have to negotiate a fare to get them to take you exactly where you want to go. Ko Samui now also sports a handful of **air-con taxis**, whose drivers hang out at the same car park and will ferry you to Chaweng for about B300. You can **rent a motorbike** from B150 in Na Thon, but it's hard to find a decent new bike in the capital, so it's probably safer, and more convenient, to rent at one of the main beaches – dozens are killed on Samui's roads each year, so proceed with caution.

Na Thon

The island capital, **NA THON**, at the top of the long western coast, is a frenetic half-built town which most travellers use only as a service station before hitting the sand: although most of the main beaches now have post offices, currency-exchange facilities, supermarkets, travel agents and clinics, the biggest and best concentration of amenities is to be found here. The town's layout is simple: the two piers come to land at the promenade, Thanon Chonvithi, which is paralleled first by narrow Thanon Ang Thong, then by Thanon Taweeratpakdee, aka Route 4169, the round-island road; the main cross-street is Thanon Na Amphoe, just north of the piers.

Practicalities

Ferry agent Songserm has its office on Thanon Chonvithi opposite the piers (℡077/421316–9), while tickets for the bus–ferry combination to Surat via Thong Yang and Don Sak can be bought from Samui Tour at The Bamboo House, south of the piers on Thanon Chonvithi. Bangkok Airways (℡077/422513) have an office next to Songserm's. Some of the **banks** have automatic teller machines, late-night opening and safe-deposit boxes; all the supermarkets and department stores are geared up for beachside needs. At the northern end of the promenade, there's a **post office** (Mon–Fri 8.30am–4.30pm, Sat & Sun 8.30am–noon) with poste restante and packing services and an IDD (international direct dialling) telephone service upstairs that's open daily from 8.30am to 9pm. Nathon Book Store, on Thanon Na Amphoe, is the best secondhand English-language **bookshop** in this part of Thailand.

For emergencies, the main police station is on Thanon Taweeratpakdee just north of Thanon Na Amphoe, or better still contact the **tourist police** (℡1699 or 077/421281 or 421441), who are based 1km south of town on Route 4169; private **clinics** operate on Thanon Ang Thong and Thanon Taweeratpakdee, while the less costly state **hospital** (℡077/421230–2 or 421399), 3km south of town off Route 4169, has recently been upgraded and is now preferable to the private hospitals on Chaweng. Tourist visas may be extended at the **immigration office**, also south of town, 2km down Route 4169 (Mon–Fri 8.30am–4.30pm; ℡077/421069). Finally, on a more soothing note, the Garden Home Health Center, 2km north along Route 4169 in Ban Bang Makham, dispenses some of the best **massages** (B150 per hr) and herbal **saunas** (B250) on the island, though note that it closes at sunset.

Accommodation and eating

If you really need a **place to stay** in Na Thon, the best budget option is the *Seaview Guesthouse* which, though it fails to provide views of the sea, has quiet rooms at the rear; it's housed in a modern building at 67/15 Thanon Taweeratpakdee (☎077/236236; ❷). If you're on a slightly higher budget, head for *Jinta Residence* towards the south end of Thanon Chonvithi (☎077/420630-1, ℻420632, ⓦwww.tapee.com; ❸–❺), with smart, bright bungalows (some with en-suite hot-water bathrooms, air-con and TV) and its own **internet café** (B2 per min).

Several stalls and small cafés purvey inexpensive Thai **food** around the market on Thanon Taweeratpakdee and on Thanon Chonvithi (including a lively night market by the piers), and there are plenty of Western-orientated places clustered around the piers. Justifiably popular, especially for breakfast, is cheerful and inexpensive *RT (Roung Thong) Bakery*, with one branch opposite the piers and another on Thanon Taweeratpakdee, which supplies bread to bungalows and restaurants around the island and also serves Thai food. For lunch, head for the modern block of shops behind the large Samui Mart department store on Thanon Taweeratpakdee: here you can choose between *Zheng Teck*, a neat and simple Chinese-run veggie restaurant (daily 7am–3pm) which also sells vegetarian supplies, and *Yemeng*, a popular, well-run café serving duck or pork on rice.

Ang Thong National Marine Park

Even if you don't get your buns off the beach for the rest of your stay, it's worth taking at least a day out to visit the beautiful **ANG THONG NATIONAL MARINE PARK**, a lush, dense group of 41 small islands strewn like dragon's teeth over the deep blue Gulf of Thailand, 31km west of Samui. Once a haven for pirate junks, then a Royal Thai Navy training base, the islands and their coral reefs, white-sand beaches and virgin rainforest are now preserved under the aegis of the National Parks Department. Erosion of the soft limestone has dug caves and chiselled out fantastic shapes which are variously said to resemble seals, a rhinoceros, a Buddha image and even the temple complex at Angkor.

The surrounding waters are home to dolphins, wary of humans because local fishermen catch them for their meat, and *pla thu* (short-bodied mackerel), part of the national staple diet, which gather in huge numbers between February and April to spawn around the islands. On land, long-tailed macaques, leopard cats, common wild pig, sea otters, squirrels, monitor lizards and pythons are found, as well as dusky langurs which, because they have no natural enemies here, are unusually friendly and easy to spot. Around forty bird species have had confirmed sightings, including the white-rumped shama noted for its singing, the brahminy kite, black baza, little heron, Eurasian woodcock, several species of pigeon, kingfisher and wagtail, as well as common and hill mynah; island caves shelter swiftlets, whose homes are stolen for bird's nest soup (see box on p.695).

The largest land mass in the group is **Ko Wua Talab** (Sleeping Cow Island) where the park headquarters shelter in a hollow behind the small beach. From there it's a steep 430-metre climb (about 1hr return; bring walking sandals or shoes) to the island's peak to gawp at the panorama, which is especially fine at sunrise and sunset: in the distance, Ko Samui, Ko Pha Ngan and the mainland; nearer at hand, the jagged edges of the surrounding archipelago; and below the peak, a secret cove on the western side and an almost sheer drop to the clear blue sea to the east. Another climb from the beach at headquarters, only 200m but even harder going (allow 40min return), leads to Tham Buabok, a cave set high in the cliff-face. Some of the stalactites and stalagmites are said to resemble lotuses, hence the cave's appellation, "Waving Lotus". If you're visiting in

September, look out for the white, violet-dotted petals of **lady's slipper orchids**, which grow on the rocks and cliffs.

The feature which gives the park the name Ang Thong, meaning "Golden Bowl", and which was the inspiration for the setting of recent cult bestseller, *The Beach*, is a landlocked lake, 250m in diameter, on **Ko Mae Ko** to the north of Ko Wua Talab. A well-made path (allow 30min return) leads from the beach through natural rock tunnels to the rim of the cliff wall which encircles the lake, affording another stunning view of the archipelago and the shallow, blue-green water far below, which is connected to the sea by a natural underground tunnel.

Practicalities

Apart from chartering your own boat at huge expense, the only way of **getting to Ang Thong** is on an organized day-trip; boats leave Na Thon every day at 8.30am, returning at 5.30pm. In between, there's a two-hour stop to explore Ko Wua Talab (just enough time to visit the viewpoint, the cave and have a quick swim, so don't dally), lunch on board the moored boat, some cruising through the archipelago, a visit to the viewpoint over the lake on Ko Mae Ko and a snorkelling stop (snorkel hire is an extra B50). Tickets cost B550 per person (including entry to the national park), available from Highway Travel (☎077/421285 or 421290) by Na Thon pier and through agencies on Samui's main beaches. Similar trips run from Ban Bophut on Ko Samui (contact Air Sea Travel on ☎077/422262–3, who also run speedboat trips to Ang Thong for B850) and from Thong Sala pier on Ko Pha Ngan, but less frequently; *Seaflower*, at Ao Chaophao on Ko Pha Ngan's west coast, does three-day "treks" (see p.594). It's also possible to combine a boat trip to Ang Thong with **kayaking** among the islands in the northern part of the park. The best operator of this kind of day-trip is Blue Stars, based near the *Green Mango* nightclub on Chaweng (☎077/413231), which has English guides and charges B1800, including a light breakfast, lunch, kayaking and snorkelling.

If you want to **stay at Ko Wua Talab**, the National Parks Department maintains simple four- to fifteen-berth bungalows (B600–1500) at the headquarters. To book accommodation, contact the Ang Thong National Marine Park Headquarters (☎077/420225), or the Forestry Department in Bangkok (see p.48). Camping is also possible in certain specified areas: if you bring your own tent, the charge is B50 per night, or two-person tents can be hired for B100 a night. If you do want to stay, you can go over on a boat-trip ticket – it's valid for a return on a later day. For getting around the archipelago from Ko Wua Talab, it's possible to charter a motor boat from the fishermen who live in the park; the best snorkelling, with the highest density and diversity of living coral, is off the west side of Ko Sam Sao or "Tripod Island", so named after its towering rocky arch. The limited canteen at park headquarters is open daily from 7am to 10pm.

Maenam

The most westerly of the beaches on the north coast is **MAENAM**, 13km from Na Thon and now Samui's most popular destination for shoestring travellers. The exposed four kilometre bay is not the island's prettiest, being more of a broad dent in the coastline, and the sloping beach is relatively narrow and coarse. But Maenam has the lowest rates for bed and board on the island, unspoilt views of fishing boats and Ko Pha Ngan, good swimming and – despite the recent opening of a luxury hotel – is the quietest of the major beaches. Jet-skis give way to windsurfing here (available from *Santiburi Dusit Resort* and on the beach just east of *Cleopatra's Palace*), and there's very little in the way of nightlife – though if you want to go on the razzle, there are late-night songthaews to and from Chaweng and Lamai. The main road is set back far from the beach among the trees, and runs through the sizeable fishing village of **Ban Maenam**, in the centre of the bay, one of the few places on Samui where there's more to life than tourism.

Practicalities

Most visitors to Maenam **eat** in their hotel or resort restaurant, though a couple of unaffiliated places in Ban Maenam stand out. *Gallery Pizza* on the pier road (closes 8.30pm; ☎077/247420) dishes up delicious, authentic pizza to take away from a wood-fired oven. *Angela's Bakery* (closes 5.30pm), opposite the **police station** on the main through-road to the east of the pier, is a popular expat hangout, offering a wide choice of sandwiches, cakes and pies, plus a few other Western dishes and deli goods such as meats and cheeses to stock up on. Further east, beyond the access road to *Cleopatra's Palace*, is a **post office** with poste restante, while SK Travel, near *Gallery Pizza* on the pier road, provides **internet access** (B2 per min).

Accommodation

As well as one or two upmarket resorts, Maenam has over twenty inexpensive bungalow complexes, most offering a spread of accommodation. There's little to choose between these places, although the best of the bunch are at the far eastern end of the bay.

Axolotl Village, not on Maenam itself, but 2km west at Ban Tai ☎ & ☎077/420017, ⊛www.axolotlvillage.com. A peaceful, friendly place with Italian-German management, offering meditation and a variety of other courses. Clean, attractive bungalows, the more expensive with hot water and air-con, and an excellent Thai and Italian beachside restaurant. ❹–❼

Cleopatra's Palace, at the eastern end of the bay, 1km from the village ☎077/425486. A variety of clean wooden and concrete bungalows, all with fans and bathrooms, stand in a rather higgledy-piggledy, cramped compound; the Thai and Western food is recommended. ❷–❹

Friendly ☎ & ☎077/425484. About 500m east of *Cleopatra's Palace*. Easy-going place with helpful staff. All the bungalows are very clean and have their own bathrooms, though the place feels exposed, with no trees to provide shade. ❷–❹.

Home Bay, at the far western end of Maenam ☎077/247214 or 247241, ☎247215. Has a grandiose-looking restaurant overlooking its own large stretch of untidy beach, tucked in beside a small cliff; sleeping options range from smart wooden bungalows with mosquito screens to big, concrete family cottages. ❸–❹

Maenam Resort, 500m west of the village ☎077/247286, ☎ & ☎425116. Just beyond *Santiburi Dusit Resort*. A moderately priced beach-front resort in tidy grounds, with a clean restaurant. The rooms and large bungalows, with verandas and air-con, offer good-value comfort. ❺–❻

Naplarn Villa, at the far western end, off the access road to *Home Bay* ☎077/247047. Good value if you don't mind a 5min walk to the beach: excellent food and clean, well-furnished, en-suite wooden bungalows with ceiling fans, mosquito screens and verandas, arrayed around a pleasant garden. ❷

Rose, next door to *Friendly* at the eastern end of the bay. Laid-back old-timer that has resisted the urge to upgrade: basic thatched-roofed wooden huts in a shady compound have mosquito nets and bathrooms but no fans, and the electricity still comes from a generator (lights out 11pm). ❷

Santiburi Dusit Resort, 500m west of the village ☎077/425031–8, ☎425040, ⊛www.dusit.com. Luxury hotel in beautifully landscaped grounds spread around a huge freshwater swimming pool and stream. Accommodation is mostly in Thai-style villas, inspired by Rama IV's summer palace at Phetchaburi, each with a large bathroom and separate sitting area, furnished in luxurious traditional design. Facilities include watersports on the private stretch of beach, a health centre, an Avis car-rental desk, and an excellent "royal" cuisine restaurant, the *Sala Thai*. ❾

Shangrilah, west of *Maenam Resort*, served by the same access road ☏ 077/425189. A friendly place in a flower-strewn compound which sprawls onto the nicest, widest stretch of sand along

Maenam. Accommodation is in a variety of smart, well-maintained en-suite bungalows with verandas, decent furniture, mosquito screens and ceiling fans. The restaurant serves good Thai food. ❷–❹

SR, the far eastern end of the bay ☏ 01/891 8874. A quiet, welcoming place with a very good restaurant. Accommodation is in basic beachfront bamboo huts with bathrooms, verandas and chairs. ❷

Bophut

The next bay east along from Maenam is **BOPHUT**, which has a similar look to Maenam but shows a marked difference in atmosphere and facilities. The quiet two-kilometre beach attracts a mix of young and old travellers, as well as families, and **Ban Bophut**, at the east end of the bay, is well geared to meet their needs with a bank currency-exchange booth, several scuba-diving outlets, a small bookstore, travel agents and supermarkets crammed into its two narrow streets. However, it mostly maintains a sleepy village feel, momentarily jostled when the speed boats to Ko Tao (see p.597) offload and pick up passengers. Many of the visitors here are French, whose culinary preferences are satisfied by a clutch of good Gallic-run restaurants on the beach road in Ban Bophut, most with fine views of the bay and Ko Pha Ngan from their terraces. The part of the beach which stretches from *Peace* to *World* bungalows, at the west end of the bay, is the nicest, but again the sand is slightly coarse by Samui's high standards.

Active pursuits are amply catered for, with jet-skis available just to the west of the village, kayaks at *Peace*, and sailboards, water-skiing and all sorts of other watersports near *Samui Palm Beach Resort*; Samui Go-kart, a **go-karting** track (daily 9am–9pm; ☏ 077/425097; from B300 for 10min) on the main road 1km west of the village, offers everyone the chance to let off steam without becoming another accident statistic on the roads of Samui.

Accommodation

There's very little ultra-cheap accommodation left among Bophut's twenty or so resorts. Most establishments are well spaced out along the length of the beach, though a handful of places cluster together on the west side of Ban Bophut.

Eddy's, beyond *World*, at the far west end of Bophut back towards Maenam ☏ 077/245221, ☏ 245127, ✉ Eddy_samui10@hotmail.com. Poor location on the main road, but only a 2min walk to the beach and good value for the facilities: large, stylish rooms with verandas, TVs, mini-bars and hot water (some rooms with air-con), helpful staff and a popular restaurant for Thai and Western food ❺

The Lodge, towards the western end of the village ☏ 077/425337, ☏ 425336. Apartment-style block with immaculately clean and tastefully decorated modern rooms, all with balconies looking over the water, and boasting air-con, ceiling fan, fridge,

satellite TV, plus spacious bathrooms with tubs to soak in. There's a waterfront bar downstairs where you can get breakfast. ❼

Peace, at the mid-point of the beach ☏ 077/425357, ☏ 425343, ✉ www.kohsamui.net/peace. This large, well-run concern has shady and attractive lawned grounds, and being well away from the main road – and free of televisions – lives up to its name. Spotless bungalows, all with mosquito screens and their own bathroom, are brightly decorated and thoughtfully equipped; the larger ones, with hot water and air-con, are well suited to families. There's a small children's playground, a beautiful new pool with

fountains and jacuzzi, and a beachside restaurant serving good Thai and European food. ❹–❼
Samui Euphoria ☎077/425100–6, ℱ425107, ⓦwww.samuieuphoria.com. Just to the east of *Peace*. A well-run, upmarket resort with several restaurants, watersports facilities and a large pool. In low-rise buildings, the rooms are spacious and smart, with plenty of traditional Thai decorative touches, and all come with TV, air-con, mini-bar and their own balconies, overlooking the mani-cured lawns or the beach. ❾
Samui Palm Beach Resort, west of *Peace*, from which it's next door-but-two ☎077/425494 or 425495, ℱ425358, ⓔspbhotel@samart.co.th.

Expensive but reasonable value, with frequent large discounts and American breakfast included in the price. Cottages are elegant – though a little frayed at the edges – with air-con, satellite TV, fridges and hints of southern Thai architecture, and there's an attractive swimming pool. ❾
Smile House, across the road from *The Lodge*, at the western end of the village ☎077/425361, ℱ425239. Firmly in the moderate range, *Smile* has a reliable set of chalets grouped around a small, clean swimming pool. At the bottom end of the range you get a clean bathroom, mosquito screens and a fan; at the top, plenty of space, hot water and air-con. ❹–❼

Bangrak

Beyond the sharp headland with its sweep of coral reefs lies **BANGRAK**, some-times called Big Buddha Beach after the colossus which gazes sternly down on the sun worshippers from its island in the bay. The beach is no great shakes, espe-cially during the northeast monsoon, when the sea retreats and leaves a slippery mud flat, but Bangrak still manages to attract the watersports crowd.

The **Big Buddha** is certainly big and works hard at being a tourist attrac-tion, but is no beauty despite a recent face-lift. A short causeway at the eastern end of the bay leads across to a clump of souvenir shops and foodstalls in front of the temple, catering to day-tripping Thais as well as farangs. Ceremonial dragon-steps then bring you up to the covered terrace around the Big Buddha, from where there's a fine view of the sweeping north coast.

Bangrak's **bungalows** are squeezed together in a narrow, noisy strip between the road and the shore, underneath the airport flight path. The best of a disap-pointing bunch is *LA Resort* (☎077/425330; ❸), a welcoming family-run place in a colourful garden, with clean and sturdy en-suite bungalows.

The northeastern cape

After Bangrak comes the high-kicking boot of the **northeastern cape**, where quiet, rocky coves, overlooking Ko Pha Ngan and connected by sandy lanes, are fun to explore on a motorbike. Songthaews run along the paved road to the largest and most beautiful bay, **Choeng Mon**, whose white sandy beach is lined with casuarina trees which provide shade for the bungalows and upmarket resorts.

Accommodation

Most of the accommodation on the northeastern cape is found around Choeng Mon. The tranquillity and prettiness of this bay have attracted two of Samui's most expensive hotels and a handful of bungalows and beach restau-rants, but on the whole the shoreline is comparatively underdeveloped and laid-back.

Boat House Hotel, south side of Choeng Mon ☎077/425041–52, ℱ425460, ⓦwww.imperial-hotels.com. Run by the reliable Imperial group, *Boat House* is named after the two-storey rice

barges which have been converted into suites in the grounds. It also offers luxury rooms in more prosaic modern buildings, often filled by package tours. Beyond the boat-shaped pool, the full gamut of watersports is drawn up on the sands.

9

Choeng Mon Bungalows, north of *Boat House* on Choeng Mon ☎077/425372, ℱ425219, ℮siriyong@samart.co.th. A shady compound with a good beachside restaurant, notable mostly for having the cheapest rooms on Choeng Mon – spartan wooden affairs with fans and en-suite showers – as well as top-of-the-range bungalows with air-con, mini-bars and hot-water bathrooms. **2–6**

Ô Soleil ☎ & ℱ077/425232. Next door to *PS Villas*. A lovely, orderly place, with sturdy, pristine wooden bungalows. The most basic have fans and en-suite bathrooms, while the best have TV, mini-bar and air-con. **3–7**

PS Villas ☎077/425160, ℱ425403. Next door to *White House*. Friendly place in large, beachfront grounds, offering a range of spacious, attractive fan-cooled or air-con bungalows with verandas and mosquito screens. **3–7**

The Tongsai Bay Cottages and Hotel, north side of Choeng Mon ☎077/425015–28, ℱ425462,

℗www.tongsaibay.co.th. Easy-going establishment with the unhurried air of a country club and excellent service. The luxurious hotel rooms and red-tiled cottages command beautiful views over the spacious, picturesque grounds, the private beach (with plenty of watersports), a vast salt-water swimming pool and the whole bay; most of them also sport second bathtubs on their secluded open-air terraces, so you don't miss out on the scenery while splashing about. The hotel's very fine restaurants include *Chef Chom's*, which specializes in improvising Thai dishes from the day's freshest ingredients, and there's a delightful health spa. **9**

White House, next door to *Choeng Mon Bungalows* ☎077/245315–7, ℱ245318, ℗www.whitehouse.kohsamui.net. Swiss-managed luxury hotel with narrow beach frontage and correspondingly cramped grounds around a small swimming pool and pretty courtyard garden. What it lacks in space it makes up for in style, with plants and beautiful traditional decor in the common areas and rooms. **8**

Chaweng

For sheer natural beauty, none of the other beaches can match **CHAWENG**, with its broad, gently sloping strip of white sand sandwiched between the limpid blue sea and a line of palm trees. Such beauty has not escaped attention, which means, on the plus side, that Chaweng can provide just about anything the active beach bum demands, from thumping nightlife to ubiquitous and surprisingly diverse watersports. The negative angle is that the new developments are ever more expensive, building work behind the palm trees and repairs to the over-commercialized main drag are always in progress – and there's no certainty that it will look lovely when the bulldozers retreat.

The six-kilometre bay is framed between the small island of Ko Matlang at the north end and the 300-metre-high headland above Coral Cove in the south. From **Ko Matlang**, where the waters provide some colourful snorkelling, an often exposed coral reef slices southwest across to the mainland, marking out a shallow lagoon and **North Chaweng**. This S-shaped part of the beach has some ugly pockets of development, but at low tide it becomes a wide, inviting playground, and from October to January the reef shelters it from the worst of the northeast winds. South of the reef, the idyllic shoreline of **Central Chaweng** stretches for 2km in a dead-straight line, the ugly village of amenities on the parallel main drag largely concealed behind the treeline and the resorts. Around a low promontory is **Chaweng Noi**, a little curving beach in a rocky bay, which is comparatively quiet in its northern part, away from the road.

South of Chaweng, the road climbs and dips into **Coral Cove**, a tiny isolated beach of coarse sand hemmed in by high rocks, with some good coral for snorkelling. It's well worth making the trip to the *Beverly Hills Café*, towards the tip of the headland dividing Chaweng from Lamai, for a jaw-dropping view over Chaweng and Choeng Mon to the peaks of Ko Pha Ngan (and for some good, moderately priced food).

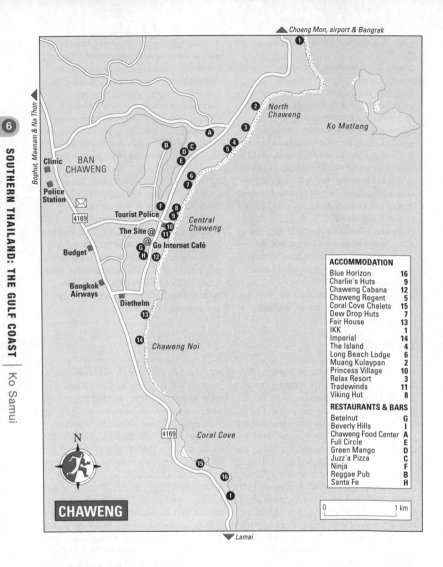

ACCOMMODATION

Blue Horizon	16
Charlie's Huts	9
Chaweng Cabana	12
Chaweng Regent	5
Coral Cove Chalets	15
Dew Drop Huts	7
Fair House	13
IKK	1
Imperial	14
The Island	4
Long Beach Lodge	6
Muang Kulaypan	2
Princess Village	10
Relax Resort	3
Tradewinds	11
Viking Hut	8

RESTAURANTS & BARS

Betelnut	G
Beverly Hills	I
Chaweng Food Center	A
Full Circle	E
Green Mango	D
Juzz'a Pizza	C
Ninja	F
Reggae Pub	B
Santa Fe	H

CHAWENG

Practicalities

Small **banks** and **supermarkets** can be found at many locations along the main drag, as can **rental motorbikes** (from B150 a day) and **four-wheel drives** (from B800 a day); if reliability is your main priority, contact Budget in Ban Chaweng (☎077/427188, ⓦwww.budget.co.th; 4WD from around B1400 per day). Among dozens of places offering **internet access** are Go Internet Café, at the south end of Central Chaweng opposite the *Central Samui Beach Resort*; and The Site, a little to the north opposite *Tradewinds* (both B2 per min); while Diethelm (☎077/422320, ⓔditssum@samart.co.th), at the far south end of the beach road just before it joins Route 4169, is a reliable and knowledgeable – though expensive – **travel agent**. There's a **tourist police** booth in front of *Princess Village* in the heart of Central Chaweng. The original village of **Ban Chaweng**, 1km inland of Central Chaweng beach on the round-island road, has a **police station**, a **post office** with poste restante, a small **clinic** and a branch of Bangkok Airways (☎077/422512–8 or 420133).

Accommodation

Over fifty **bungalow resorts** and **hotels** at Chaweng are squeezed into thin strips running back from the beachfront at right angles. In the inexpensive and moderate range, prices are generally over the odds, although a few places, all of them listed below, offer reasonable value. More and more expensive places are sprouting up all the time, offering sumptuous accommodation at top-whack prices.

Inexpensive to moderate

Blue Horizon, above Coral Cove ☎077/422426, ℱ230293, ℮bluehorizon@samuitourism.com. One of several resorts clinging to the steep hillside, this is a friendly, well-ordered place, where some of the sturdy, balconied bungalows have air-con and hot water. ❹–❼

Charlie's Huts, in the heart of Central Chaweng ☎077/422343 or 230285. Some of the cheapest accommodation options left on Chaweng are the wooden huts with shared bathrooms, mosquito nets and fans in the grassy compound here; en-suite and air-con bungalows also available, but no hot water in any of them. ❷–❺

Chaweng Cabana, south end of Central Chaweng ☎077/422184, ℱ422377. Reliable, well-run option, for those who don't feel the need of a swimming pool with their luxuries; bungalows in a lush garden with bland but tasteful decor, some with air-con, cable TV and fridge. ❻–❾

Dew Drop Huts, at the top end of Central Chaweng ☎077/422238, ℮jah_dub@hotmail.com. Secluded among dense trees, *Dew Drop* ignores the surrounding flash development to offer a friendly, laid-way-back ambience, old-fashioned primitive huts – now joined by some upgraded pads with air-con on the beach – plus herbal saunas and massages. ❶–❻

IKK, around the point at the far north end of North Chaweng ☎077/422482–3. Comfortable en-suite bungalows on an unusually spacious and peaceful stretch of sand. ❸

The Island, in the middle of North Chaweng ☎077/230751–3, ℱ230942. A spread of well-designed accommodation with air-con and hot-water bathrooms encompassing concrete rooms at the back of the shady, orderly compound, as well as grand beachside cottages; there's also a good restaurant on the beach. ❺–❽

Long Beach Lodge, towards the north end of Central Chaweng ☎ & ℱ077/422372. An unusually spacious and shady sandy compound, which may attract the beady eyes of developers. All the orderly, clean bungalows are a decent size and have fans and en-suite bathrooms; the larger, more expensive ones have hot water and air-con. ❹–❼

Relax Resort, in the middle of North Chaweng ☎077/422280, ℱ422113. Friendly spot that lives up to its name, with a range of very clean and well-maintained fan-cooled and air-con rooms and chalets, all with en-suite hot-water bathrooms. ❹–❺

Viking Hut, Central Chaweng ☎077/413304, ℮living99@loxinfo.co.th. A cheap, friendly place next door and similar to *Charlie's Huts*, with a little more shade. Good basic huts, some en suite. ❷–❹

Expensive

Chaweng Regent, at the bottom end of North Chaweng ☎077/422389–90, ℱ422222, ℗www.chawengregent.com. Elegant bungalows with all mod cons around lotus ponds and a pool, though conditions are a little cramped. ❾

Coral Cove Chalets, above Coral Cove ☎077/422260–1, ℱ422496, ℗www.kohsamui.net/ccc. Especially good-value and stylish place with bright, tasteful bungalows, each with balcony, TV and mini-bar, grouped around an attractive pool and jacuzzi. ❽

Fair House, north end of Chaweng Noi ☎077/422255–6, ℱ422373, ℮fairhouse@sawadee.com. A great location on a lovely stretch of beach, with extensive, lush gardens and two pools. The colourfully decorated bungalows are preferable to the large hotel rooms, which have good facilities but lack style. ❾

Imperial, on a small rise above Chaweng Noi ☎077/422020–36, ℱ422396–7, ℮www. imperialhotels.com. The longest-established luxury hotel on Samui is a grand but lively establishment with a Mediterranean feel, set in leafy grounds around two pools. ❾

Muang Kulaypan, North Chaweng ☎077/422305, ℱ230031, ℮kulaypan@sawadee.com. Original, stylish boutique hotel arrayed around a large, immaculate garden with a black-tiled swimming pool. Rooms – each with their own private balcony or garden – combine contemporary design with traditional Thai-style comforts. ❾

Princess Village, Central Chaweng ☎077/422216, ℱ422382,

℮www.princess.kohsamui.net. Traditional Ayutthaya-style houses on stilts set in plenty of space around beautiful lotus ponds. Decorated with carved wooden panels, "axe" pillows and traditional cotton fabrics, which sit a little uneasily with the Western-style bathrooms, minibars and air-con. ❾

Tradewinds, next door to *Princess Village*, Central Chaweng ☎077/230602–4, ℱ231247, ℮tradewinds@sawadee.com. A cheerful, well-run place of characterful bungalows (all with air-con, hot water and mini-bar) with plenty of room to breathe in colourful tropical gardens. The resort specializes in sailing, with its own catamarans and yacht (instruction available). ❽

Eating

It's hard to find good, reasonably priced **Thai food** here, but one place that's worth making a beeline for is the friendly and efficient beachside restaurant of *Relax Resort*. Avoid the curries in favour of the house speciality – seafood. Prawn cakes make a delicious starter, then choose your own ultra-fresh fish and have it weighed and cooked as you wish (red snapper in plum sauce is recommended). To go with it, there's a good selection of wine and draft Carlsberg at decent prices. Decent backstops are the *Chaweng Food Center*, 200m along the road to Ban Chaweng from North Chaweng, a day-and-night market of cheap and cheerful foodstalls that's popular with local workers; and *Ninja*, a very basic Thai restaurant near *Charlie's Huts* on Central Chaweng, that's unexceptional bar the fact that it stays open 24 hours. Moving upmarket, the *Budsaba Restaurant* at *Muang Kulaypan* fully justifies the journey: here you get to recline in your own open-sided beachfront hut, while tucking into unusual and excellent Thai dishes such as banana flower and shrimp salad.

For well-prepared **Western food**, especially if you're tired of the breakfast at your accommodation, head for the beachside restaurant at *The Island. Juzz'a Pizza* (daily 5pm–1am) does a lot more than its name (almost) suggests, with very good pizza, pasta and other Western fare, in surprisingly homely surroundings on the noisy lane leading to the *Green Mango*, at the north end of Central Chaweng. At the top end of the price range, *Betelnut* (☎077/413370, ℮www.thaisite.com/betelnut), down a small lane at the south end of Central Chaweng opposite the landmark *Central Samui Beach Resort*, is by far Samui's best restaurant, serving exceptional Californian-Thai **fusion food**. On the other side of the same lane, you can take a highly recommended **Thai cookery course**, or just buy some choice ingredients to take home with you, at the Samui Institute of Thai Culinary Arts (SITCA; ☎077/413172, ℮www.sitca.net).

Drinking and nightlife

Avoiding the raucous bar-beers and English theme pubs on the main through road, the best place to **drink** is on the beach: at night dozens of resorts and dedicated bars lay out small tables and candles on the sand, especially towards the north end of Central Chaweng and on North Chaweng. Also on the beach, *Jah Dub* at *Dew Drop Huts* specializes in reggae, and holds parties in high season, usually on Tuesday and Friday nights.

Bang in the heart of Central Chaweng but set well back from the beach, *The Reggae Pub* is not just an unpretentious, good-time **nightclub**, but a venerable Samui institution, with a memorabilia shop, foodstalls, internet access and upstairs snooker tables. Chaweng's other long-standing dance venue, *Green Mango* at the north end of Central Chaweng, occupies a similarly huge shed which combines an industrial look with that of a tropical greenhouse, complete with fountain, fairy lights and ornamental garden. The title of Samui's best club, however, goes to *Full Circle*, a hip and stylish place with British DJs playing house music, done out in minimalist metal with splashes of primary colours; it's set amid a forest of bar-beers on North Chaweng (look out for flyers or ask about regular beach parties the club hosts at Hat Thong Son on the island's northeastern cape). Its sister club, *Santa Fe*, at the south end of Central Chaweng, has a Native American theme, with totem-like statues and a mosaic-decorated dance floor; it now caters mostly for Thais, with poppy "love" music (as they call it) and live bands, but is great fun nonetheless, and there are good pool tables if you need a break.

Lamai

Samui's nightlife is most tawdry at **LAMAI** (though Chaweng is fast catching up these days): planeloads of European package tourists are kept happy here at go-go shows and dozens of open-air hostess bars, sinking buckets of booze while slumped in front of boxing videos. Running roughly north to south for 4km, the white palm-fringed beach is, fortunately, still a picture – though it doesn't quite match Chaweng – and it's possible to avoid the boozy mayhem by staying at the quiet extremities of the bay, where the backpackers' resorts have a definite edge over Chaweng's. At the northern end, the spur of land which hooks eastward into the sea is perhaps the prettiest spot: it has more rocks than sand, but the shallow sea behind the coral reef is protected from the high seas of November, December and January.

The action is concentrated into a farang toytown of bars and Western restaurants that has grown up behind the centre of the beach, packed cheek-by-jowl along the noisy, dusty rutted backroads. Crowded among them are supermarkets, clinics, banks and travel agents; jet-skis and water-skiing are available on the beach just south of *Lamai Inn 99*, level with the central crossroads.

The original village of **Ban Lamai**, set well back at the northern end, remains aloof from these goings-on, and its wat contains a small museum of ceramics, agricultural tools and other everyday objects. Most visitors get more of a buzz from **Hin Yay** (Grandmother Rock) and **Hin Ta** (Grandfather Rock), small rock formations on the bay's southern promontory, which never fail to raise a giggle with their resemblance to the male and female sexual organs. If the excitement gets too much for you, head for *The Spa Resort* (see p.583) at the far north end of the beach: its "Rejuvenation Menu" covers everything from colonic irrigation to healing clay facials, along with more traditional treatments such as Thai massage (B250 per hour) and herbal saunas (B250 per hour). In similar vein, but much more upmarket, is Tamarind Springs (☎077/230571 or 424436, ⓦwww.tamarindretreat.com), set in a beautiful, secluded coconut grove just north of *Spa Resort* off the main road; here a herbal sauna and two-hour Thai massage, for example, costs B1200.

Practicalities
Internet access is provided at several places around the central crossroads and at Sawadee, next to the petrol station, on the road between *The Spa Resort* and Ban Lamai (B2/min; see also p.569).

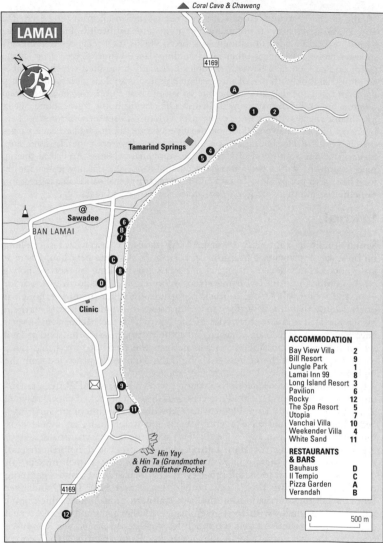

▲ *Coral Cave & Chaweng*

LAMAI

4169

Tamarind Springs

Ⓐ
❶ ❷
❸
❹
❺

@
Sawadee
BAN LAMAI

❻
Ⓑ
❼

Ⓒ
❽

Ⓓ

Clinic

❾

❿ ⓫

Hin Yay
& Hin Ta (Grandmother
& Grandfather Rocks)

4169

⓬

ACCOMMODATION	
Bay View Villa	2
Bill Resort	9
Jungle Park	1
Lamai Inn 99	8
Long Island Resort	3
Pavilion	6
Rocky	12
The Spa Resort	5
Utopia	7
Vanchai Villa	10
Weekender Villa	4
White Sand	11

RESTAURANTS & BARS	
Bauhaus	D
Il Tempio	C
Pizza Garden	A
Verandah	B

0 ——————— 500 m

▼ *Ban Hua Thanon & Na Thon*

To tempt you away from your guest-house kitchen, there are several good Italian **restaurants**, such as *Il Tempio*, a short way north of the tourist village's main crossroads, and, a couple of hundred metres on, the German-run *Verandah* at *Mui Bungalows*, which serves excellent, well-presented international and Thai food. To work up an appetite, walk to the northern end of the bay where the Austrian-run *Pizza Garden*, on the headland above *Jungle Park*, bakes great pizzas and baguettes, and serves good pastas and coffee.

Lamai's **nightlife** is all within spitting distance of the central crossroads. Apart from the hostess bars, *Bauhaus* is the main draw, a barn-like entertainment complex with pool, darts, a big screen showing satellite sport and a dance floor.

Accommodation

Lamai's **accommodation** is generally less cramped and slightly better value than Chaweng's, though it presents far fewer choices at the top end of the market. The far southern end of the bay towards the Grandparent Rocks has the tightest concentration of budget bungalows.

Bay View Villa, on the bay's northern headland ☎ & ⓕ077/418429. Neat, stylish bungalows with verandas and en-suite bathrooms in an extensive, flower-bedecked compound. Offers a friendly welcome and great sunset views of the beach from the attractive restaurant. ❹

Bill Resort, at the far southern end of the bay ☎077/424403, ⓕ424286. An efficient and orderly setup, crammed into a fragrant, overgrown garden on a rocky stretch of beach and up the hill behind; clean bungalows with en-suite hot-water bathrooms, some with air-con. ❹–❼

Jungle Park, on the bay's northern headland ☎077/418034, ☎ & ⓕ077/424110. Next door to *Bay View Villa*. The shady compound with large swimming pool feels a little like a holiday camp but is reliable and well maintained; choose between rooms with fan and cold showers or spacious, sturdy bungalows with air-con and hot water. ❹–❻

Lamai Inn 99, on the beach by the tourist village's main crossroads ☎077/424212 or ☎ & ⓕ077/424427. A surprisingly spacious establishment, which offers a variety of bungalow styles and sizes, some with hot water and air-con. If you want to be near the throbbing heart of Lamai's nightlife, this is your place. ❹–❻

Long Island Resort, at the far north end of the beach ☎077/424202 or 418456, ⓕ424023, ⓦwww.sawadee.com/samui/longisland. A self-styled "boutique resort" with stylish but cosy bungalows (the cheapest with cold-water bathrooms, the priciest with air-con, cable TV and mini-bars), a decent-sized pool, a "mini spa" offering massages, steam and various other treatments, and a good Thai and Western restaurant serving up some interesting southern Thai dishes. ❹–❽

Pavilion, on the central stretch of Lamai, north of the crossroads ☎077/232083–6, ⓕ424029, ⓦwww.sawadee.com/samui/pavilion. Lamai's best upmarket choice, just far enough from the pubs and clubs to get some peace; the atmosphere is friendly and lively, and there's a good beachside

pool and restaurant. Most of the accommodation is in comfortable hotel rooms, but if your purse will stretch that far, go for one of the beachside cottages. ❽–❾

Rocky, beyond the headland, at the far southern end of the bay ☎ & ⓕ077/424326. Squeezes as much as it can into its beachside strip: a small swimming pool, a restaurant and a wide choice of rooms and bungalows, all with bathrooms, some with hot water and air-con. ❸–❺

The Spa Resort, at the far north end of the beach ☎077/230855, ⓕ424126, ⓦwww.spasamui.com Next to *Weekender Villa*. A wide variety of cosy, well-constructed rooms, decorated with shells and other bric-a-brac, though they're often full with people being rejuvenated (see p.581); delicious veggie and non-veggie food. ❸–❹

Utopia, on the central stretch of Lamai, north of the crossroads ☎077/233113, ⓕ233115, ⓔjim_utopia@hotmail.com. Good-value, welcoming place on a narrow strip of land stuffed with flowers. The cheapest bungalows have mosquito screens, fans and en-suite bathrooms, while those at the top of the price range boast air-con and hot water. Good coffee and breakfasts, and plenty of free beach equipment. ❸–❺

Vanchai Villa, on the access road to *White Sand*, at the far southern end of the bay ☎077/424296. Quiet, family-run operation set back from the beach, offering a range of very clean, spacious bungalows with verandas among the palm trees, and excellent, cheap food. ❷–❹

Weekender Villa, between the main road and the beach to the east of Ban Lamai ☎077/424116. Despite its location this is a quiet spot; the staff are friendly and the large, en-suite wooden bungalows shelter in an airy coconut grove. ❷

White Sand, at the far southern end of the bay ☎077/424298. Long-established and laid-back budget place with around fifty simple beachside huts which attract plenty of long-term travellers. ❷

The south and west coasts

Lacking the long beaches of the more famous resorts, the **south and west coasts** rely on a few charming, isolated spots with peaceful accommodation, which can usually only be reached by renting a motorbike or four-wheel drive. Heading south from Lamai, you come first to the Muslim fishing village at **Ban Hua Thanon** and then, about 3km south and well signposted off Route 4170, one of the island's most secluded hotels: originally founded as a private club on a quiet south-facing promontory, the *Laem Set Inn* (℡077/424393, ℻424394, ⓦwww.laemset.com; ➑–➒) offers a wide range of elegant rooms and suites – some of them reassembled village houses – as well as an excellent restaurant, plenty of free watersports equipment and a scenically positioned swimming pool (open to non-guests who come for lunch).

The gentle but unspectacular coast beyond is lined with a good reef for snorkelling, which can be explored most easily from the fishing village of **Ban Bangkao**. Snorkellers rave about the coral around **Ko Mad Sum**, 4km offshore: an all-day tour from Ban Bangkao or the next village to the west, **Ban Thongkrut**, including mask, snorkel and lunch, will set you back around B350 per person. About 5km inland, near **Ban Thurian**, the **Na Muang falls** make a popular outing as they're not far off the round-island road (each of the two main falls has its own signposted kilometre-long paved access road off Route 4169). The lower fall splashes and sprays down a twenty-metre wall of rock into a large pool, while Na Muang 2 upstream is a more spectacular, shaded cascade but requires a bit of foot-slogging from the car park (about 15min uphill); alternatively you can walk up there from Na Muang 1, by taking the 1500-metre trail which begins 300m back along the access road from the lower fall. The self-styled "safari camp" at the Na Muang 2 car park offers thirty-minute **elephant rides**, taking in the falls, for B600 per person. The best budget place to stay hereabouts is the welcoming *Diamond Villa* (℡077/424442; ➊–➍), in a secluded beachside coconut grove 1km west of Ban Bangkao, where you can choose either a wooden shack, with or without bathroom, or a smart concrete hut.

At the base of the west coast, **AO PHANGKA** (Emerald Cove) is a pretty horseshoe bay, sheltered by Laem Hin Khom, the high headland which forms Samui's southwestern tip, and by a coral reef which turns it into a placid paddling pool. The beach is poor and often littered with flotsam but, like the whole of the west coast, gives fine views of the tiny offshore islands of Ko Si Ko Ha – where birds' nests are harvested for the health-giving Chinese soup (see box on p.695) – with the sun setting over the larger Ang Thong archipelago behind. The best budget place to stay here is the laid-back *Seagull* on the north shore of the bay (℡077/423091; ➋–➍), where a wide variety of clean bungalows, all with showers, is spread out on a flowery slope, and there's a good, if slow, restaurant. Across the headland on the south-facing shore of Laem Hin Khom and further upmarket, the quiet and welcoming *Coconut Villa* (℡ & ℻077/423151; ➌–➏) commands stunning views of Ko Mad Sum and its neighbouring islands; the fan-cooled or air-con bungalows all have en-suite bathrooms, the food is recommended, and there's an excellent swimming pool set in attractive gardens by the sea.

Further up the coast, the flat beaches are unexceptional but make a calm alternative when the northeast winds hit the other side of the island. In a gorgeous hillside setting near the village of the same name, *Baan Taling Ngam* (℡077/423019–22, ℻423220, ⓦwww.meridien-samui.com; ➒), part of the international Meridien group, boasts a rather excessive total of seven swimming pools. The accommodation is in villas or balconied rooms on the resort's steep slopes, luxuriously decorated in traditional style. There's a spa and a Thai cooking school, and the hotel lays on the largest array of sports and watersports facilities on the island.

Ko Pha Ngan

In recent years backpackers have tended to move over to Ko Samui's little sibling, **KO PHA NGAN**, 20km to the north, but the island still has a simple atmosphere, mostly because the lousy road system is an impediment to the developers. With a dense jungle covering its inland mountains and rugged granite outcrops along the coast, Pha Ngan lacks the huge, gently sweeping beaches for which Samui is famous, but it does have plenty of coral to explore and some beautiful, sheltered bays: **Hat Khuat** and **Hat Khom** on the north coast; **Thong Nai Pan** and half a dozen remote, virgin beaches on the east coast; and, on an isolated neck of land at the southeast corner, **Hat Rin**, a

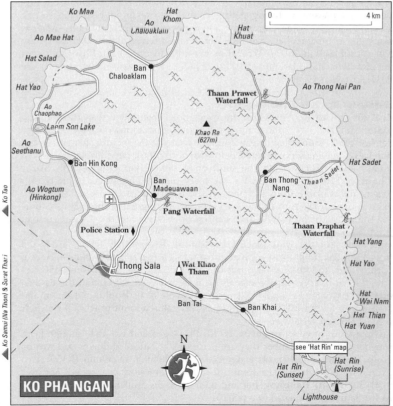

pilgrimage site for ravers. Most of Pha Ngan's development, however, has plonked itself along the less attractive south and west sides, linked by the only coastal roads on the island, which fan out from **Thong Sala**, the capital.

Pha Ngan's **bungalows** all now have running water and electricity (on the remoter beaches, only in the evenings and from individual generators), and most offer the choice of shared or en-suite bathrooms. There are no luxury hotels, and only a handful of places offer air-con. The two hundred or so resorts generally have more space to spread out than on Ko Samui, and the cost of living is lower; the prices given on the following pages are standard for most of the year, but in slack periods you'll be offered discounts, and at the very busiest times (especially in December and January) Pha Ngan's bungalow owners are canny enough to raise the stakes. As on Ko Samui, nearly all the bungalow resorts have inexpensive, traveller-orientated **restaurants**; at one or two of the cheapest resorts, however, where they make their money from food more than accommodation, owners have been known to kick out guests who don't eat at the in-house restaurant.

There's no TAT office on Ko Pha Ngan, but you might want to take a look at ⓦ www.kohphangan.com, a website with a miscellany of **information** about the island, set up by the owner of Phangan Batik in Thong Sala (see opposite). If you're going to be exploring, well worth picking up from supermarkets on the island is Visid Hongsombud's excellent, regularly updated **map** of Ko Pha Ngan and Ko Tao (B70; ⓦ www.thaiguidemap.com). The island isn't a great base for **scuba diving**: getting to the best sites around Ko Tao (see box on p.599) involves time-consuming and expensive voyages, and there aren't as many dive companies here as on Ko Samui or Ko Tao – of those that exist, Easy Divers on Hat Rin (☏ 077/375258, ⓦ www.thaidive.com) and Phangan Divers on Hat Rin and Hat Yao (☏ 077/375117, ⓦ www.phangandivers.com) are PADI Five-Star Centres.

Getting to Ko Pha Ngan

Boat services to Ko Pha Ngan are even more changeable than those to Ko Samui and Ko Tao. Politicking for landing concessions, variable passenger demand and seasonal fluctuation combine to make the picture changeable and unreliable, but the services listed below seem the most dependable.

The slowest **ferry** from the Gulf coast leaves Ban Don pier in **Surat Thani** at 11pm every night for the ferry pier at Thong Sala (7hr; B200); tickets are available from the pier on the day of departure. One Songserm express boat a day runs from Tha Thong to Thong Sala (4hr; B200 including transport to the pier). Three express boats a day do the 45-minute trip from Na Thon on **Ko Samui** (B100), while two vehicle ferries cover the same route for the same price (1hr 10min). Two vehicle ferries a day sail from Don Sak, 68km east of Surat Thani, to Thong Sala (2hr 30min; B120), with connecting buses from Surat to Don Sak, run by Samui Tour (B50 aircon, B40 ordinary). Small boats also shuttle between Samui and the eastern side of Pha Ngan (see p.570), and speed boats from Bophut, Maenam and Nathon on Samui call in at Thong Sala after thirty minutes (B250) on their way to Ko Tao.

Three kinds of vessel run between Ko Pha Ngan and **Ko Tao**, though from roughly June to November they are occasionally cancelled due to bad weather. At least two speed boats a day cover the distance in 50min (B350), two express boats a day take 1hr 30min (B225), and one slow boat spends 3hr over it (B150). **From Bangkok**, bus and train packages similar to those for getting to Ko Samui are available (see p.570).

Thong Sala and the south coast

Like the capital of Samui, **THONG SALA** is a port of entrance and little more, where the incoming ferries are met by touts sent to escort travellers to bungalows elsewhere on the island. In front of the pier, transport to the rest of the island (songthaews, jeeps and motorbike taxis) congregates by a dusty row of banks, travellers' restaurants, supermarkets, scuba-diving outfits and motorbike (from B150 a day) and jeep (B1000) rental places. If you go straight ahead from the pier, you can turn right onto the town's high street, a leafy mix of shops and houses that's ghostly and windswept at night. A short way down here you'll find laundries and, set back on the west side of the street, the multi-talented Phangan Batik (daily 10am–10pm; ℡077/377254, ℗www.kohphangan.com), which, besides selling batiks, rents out good-quality mountain bikes (B100 a day) and offers internet access (B100 per hr). Further on are a couple of clinics and, about 500m from the pier, the post office (Mon–Fri 8.30am–noon & 1–4.30pm, Sat 9am–noon). Thong Sala's sprinkling of travel agents can organize train and plane tickets, and visa extensions, and they sometimes put together trips to Ang Thong National Marine Park for B550 a head (see p.573). The island's hospital (℡077/377034) lies 3km north of town, on the inland road towards Mae Hat, while the police station (℡077/377114) is nearly 2km up the Ban Chaloaklam road.

In the vicinity of Thong Sala, an easy excursion can be made to the grandiosely termed Than Sadet–Ko Pha Ngan National Park, which contains **Pang waterfall**, Pha Ngan's biggest drop, and a stunning viewpoint overlooking the south and west of the island. The park lies 4km northeast of Thong Sala off the road to Chaloaklam – if you don't have a bike, take a Chaloaklam-bound songthaew as far as Ban Madeuawaan, and then it's a one-kilometre signposted walk east. A roughly circular trail has been laid out through the park, as mapped out by the signboard in the car park. The main fall bouncing down in stages over the hard, grey stone – is a steep 250-metre walk up a forest path. The trail then continues for over 1km upriver beyond the falls, before skirting through thick rainforest to the viewpoint and back to the car park in a couple of hours.

The long, straight **south coast** is well served by songthaews and motorbike taxis from Thong Sala, and is lined with bungalows, especially around **Ban Khai**, to take the overspill from nearby Hat Rin. It's hard to recommend staying here, however: the beaches are mediocre by Thai standards, and the coral reef which hugs the length of the shoreline gets in the way of swimming.

On a quiet hillside above **Ban Tai**, 4km from Thong Sala, **Wat Khao Tham** holds ten-day meditation retreats most months of the year (B2900 per person to cover food; minimum age 20); the American and Australian teachers emphasize compassion and loving kindness as the basis of mental development. Only forty people can attend each retreat (they're especially heavily subscribed Dec–March), so it's best to pre-register; for further information, write to Wat Khao Tham, PO Box 18, Ko Pha Ngan, Surat Thani 84280, or go to ℗www.watkowtahm.org, where the schedule of retreats is posted.

If you need to **stay** around Thong Sala, walk 800m north out of town to *Siriphun* (℡077/377140, ℗377242; ❸–❺). The owner is helpful, the food very good and the bungalows are clean and well positioned along the beach; all have showers and mosquito screens on the windows, and an extra wad of baht buys air-con and one of the island's few bathtubs. Alternatively, *Charm Beach Resort*, a friendly, sprawling place only 1500m southeast of Thong Sala (℡077/377165 or 377412; ❶–❺), has a wide variety of decent bungalows and good Thai food.

The incongruous white high-rise overshadowing Thong Sala's pier is the *Pha Ngan Chai Hotel* (☎ & ℱ077/377068; ❻), makes a fair stab at international-standard features, with air-conditioning, warm water, TVs, mini-bars and, in some rooms, sea-view balconies.

Hat Rin

HAT RIN is now firmly established as the major **rave** venue in Southeast Asia, especially in the high season of December and January, but every month of the year people flock in for the full moon party (ⓦwww.thaisite.com/fullmoonparty) – something like *Apocalypse Now* without the war. There's a more sedate side to Hat Rin's alternative scene, too, with old- and new-age hippies packing out the t'ai chi, yoga and meditation classes, and helping consume the drugs that are readily available. Drug-related horror stories are common currency round here, and many of them are true: dodgy Ecstasy, MDMA omelettes, speed punch, diet pills, and special teas containing the local fungus, *hed khi kwai* (buffalo-shit mushrooms), put an average of two farangs a month into hospital for psychiatric treatment. The local authorities have started clamping down on the trade in earnest, setting up a permanent police box at Hat Rin, instigating regular roadblocks and bungalow searches, and drafting in scores of police (both uniformed and plain-clothes) on full-moon nights. It doesn't seem to have dampened the fun, only made travellers a lot more circumspect (the police's going rate for escaping a minor possession charge is a B50,000 "fine").

Hat Rin occupies the flat neck of Pha Ngan's southeast headland, which is so narrow that the resort comprises two back-to-back beaches, joined by transverse roads at the north and south ends. The eastern beach, usually referred to as **Sunrise**, or Hat Rin Nok (Outer Hat Rin), is what originally drew visitors here, a classic curve of fine white sand between two rocky slopes, where the swimming's good and there's even some coral at the southern end to explore. This is the centre of the action, with a solid line of beachside bars, restaurants and bungalows tucked under the palm trees. **Sunset** beach, or Hat Rin Noi (Inner Hat Rin), which for much of the year is littered with flotsam, looks ordinary by comparison but has plenty of quieter accommodation.

Practicalities

The awkwardness of **getting to Hat Rin** in the past helped to maintain its individuality, but this is changing now that the road in from Ban Khai has been paved. Songthaews and motorbike taxis from Thong Sala now cover the steep roller-coaster route – take care if you're driving your own motorbike. The easiest approach of all, however, if you're coming from Ko Samui, or even Surat Thani, is by direct boat from Samui's north coast: three boats a day (currently 10.30am, 1pm & 4pm; B100) cross to Sunset beach from Bangrak in under an hour, and occasional longtails cover the Maenam–Hat Rin–Thong Nai Pan route.

The area behind and between the beaches – especially around what's known as Chicken Corner, where the southern transverse road meets the road along the back of Sunrise – is crammed with small shops and businesses: there are clinics, a post office (by Chicken Corner), secondhand bookstores, travel agents, motorbike rental places (from B150 a day), offices with expensive overseas phone facilities, bank currency-exchange booths, even a gym, tattooists and video-game arcades. Dozens of places offer **internet access**, but your best bet is probably *Bulan Cyber Café* (☎077/375201, ⓔbulancybercafe@hotmail.com) off the southern transverse road towards the pier on Sunset.

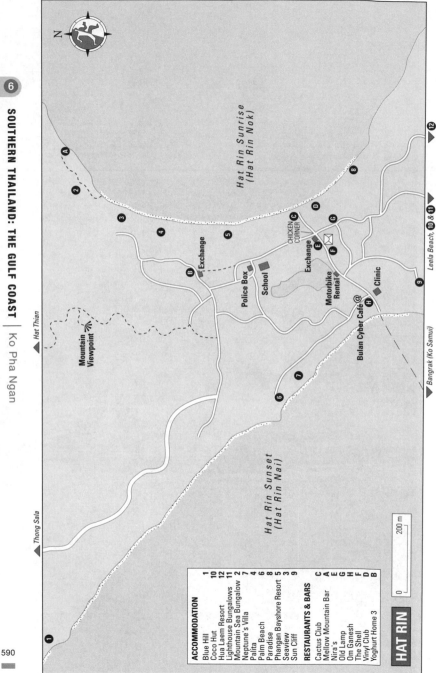

N

▲ *Thong Sala*

▲ *Hat Thian*

Mountain Viewpoint

Hat Rin Sunset (Hat Rin Nai)

Hat Rin Sunrise (Hat Rin Nok)

Exchange

Police Box

School

Exchange

CHICKEN CORNER

Motorbike Rental

Clinic

Bulan Cyber Café @

▲ *Leela Beach,* 10 & 11

▲ *Bangrak (Ko Samui)*

12

0   200 m

HAT RIN

ACCOMMODATION

Blue Hill	1
Coco Hut	10
Hua Laem Resort	12
Lighthouse Bungalows	11
Mountain Sea Bungalow	2
Neptune's Villa	7
Palita	4
Palm Beach	6
Paradise	8
Phangan Bayshore Resort	5
Seaview	3
Sun Cliff	9

RESTAURANTS & BARS

Cactus Club	C
Mellow Mountain Bar	A
Nira's	E
Old Lamp	G
Om Ganesh	H
The Shell	F
Vinyl Club	D
Yoghurt Home 3	B

Accommodation

For most of the year, Hat Rin has enough bungalows to cope, but on **full-moon nights** as many as eight thousand revellers turn up. There's a little over three thousand rooms on the whole island, so your options are either to arrive early, to forget about sleep altogether or to hitch up with one of the many party boats (about B300 per person) organized by guest houses and restaurants on Ko Samui, especially on Bangrak and Bophut, which usually leave at 9pm and return around dawn. Even at other times, staying on **Sunrise** is often expensive and noisy, though a few places can be recommended. On **Sunset**, the twenty or more resorts are laid out in orderly rows, and are especially quiet and inexpensive between June and September.

Blue Hill, at the far northern end of Sunset, a 20min walk from Chicken Corner. Quiet spot run by a friendly, laid-back couple, with slighly ramshackle en-suite bungalows, good, cheap food in generous portions, and great views of the sunset and across to Samui. Catch a songthaew or motorbike taxi to *Bird Bungalows*, then walk northwest for 5min along the beach. ❷

Coco Hut, Leela Beach, out towards the lighthouse on the west side of the headland ☎077/375369, ⊛www.cocohut.com. On a clean, quiet stretch of beach, about a 20min walk from Chicken Corner along a well-signposted route, these newly built bungalows are roomy and bright; internet access is available. The owners were building a 24-room guest-house extension next door at the time of writing. ❻

Hua Laem Resort, about 1km south along the coast from Sunrise ☎077/375222. Reached by following signs from Chicken Corner which take you along a well-maintained cliffside walk, offering stunning views across the whole of Hat Rin Sunrise below. Set in a charming, secluded spot, rooms are basic but in good order and clean (some have private balconies); the owners are friendly and obliging and the panoramic restaurant offers good, cheap food. ❷

Lighthouse Bungalows, on the far southwestern tip of the headland ⊛Lighthouse_bg@hotmail.com. A 30min walk from Chicken Corner, the last section along a rickety wooden walkway over the rocky shoreline, which can be a bit disconcerting at night. At this friendly haven, wooden bungalows, sturdily built to withstand the wind and backed by trail-filled jungle, either share bathrooms or have their own. The restaurant food is varied and tasty. ❶–❸

Mountain Sea Bungalow, at the quieter northern end of Sunrise. A great spot, bungalows rising up on the rocks at the end of the beach, with verandas to take in the views. Set in the very

peaceful, shady garden, all have bathrooms and fans. ❸

Neptune's Villa, near the small promontory at the centre of Sunset ☎01/956 3575. A popular, laid-back place in grassy, shady grounds giving onto the beach. Rooms are basic but cheap – pay extra if you want a Western-style toilet. ❷–❸

Palita, at the northern end of Sunrise ☎077/375170, ⊛palitas9@hotmail.com. Clean, well-run place with en-suite bungalows (some aircon) giving on to the beach, and large, simple, better-value huts (some with their own bathrooms) among the coconut palms behind. The food gets rave reviews. ❶–❻

Palm Beach, on and around the tiny head at the centre of Sunset ☎077/375240. This place is typical of the establishments here, but offers a little more room as it spreads over the headland. In a peaceful setting, the clean, sturdy wooden bungalows, most of them fronting the sand, either share bathrooms or have their own. ❷–❸

Paradise, spread over the far southern end of Sunrise and up the slope behind ☎077/375244. Well-established place, with a good restaurant – the original full moon party began here, and it's still a party focus once a month. All bungalows are en suite and some of the cheaper hillside options offer fine views over the bay from their verandas. ❸–❺

Phangan Bayshore Resort, on the middle of Sunrise ☎077/ 375227, ⊛375226. An upmarket, well-ordered place, though staff seem somewhat jaded and service is brusque. Big bungalows with spacious verandas, some with air-con, are set on a green lawn, shaded with palms. ❺–❻

Seaview, at the quieter northern end of Sunrise ☎077/375160. On a big plot of shady land, this clean, orderly place is a similar setup to *Palita* next door. Simple, en-suite huts at the back, posher bungalows (some air-con) beachside. ❸–❻

Sun Cliff, high up on the tree-lined slope above the south end of Sunset ☎077/375134. Friendly place with great views of the south coast and Ko Samui, and a wide range of bright, well-maintained bungalows, some with large balconies, fridges, hot water and air-con. ②–⑥

Eating and nightlife

As well as good simple Thai fare at some of the bungalows, Hat Rin sports an unnerving choice of world **foods** for somewhere so remote, and vegetarians are unusually well provided for. All-day breakfasts of croissants, cakes and good coffee at *Nira's* bakery café near Chicken Corner are especially popular (the bakery shop stays open 24hr), as well as at *Yoghurt Home 3* behind the north end of Sunrise, which offers home-made yoghurt in many combinations, as well as newspapers and generous servings of veggie food. Also worth seeking out are comparative old-timer *The Shell* on the southern transverse, for reasonably priced pasta; *Om Ganesh*, an excellent Indian restaurant on the same street with cheerful service, whether eat-in or delivered to your bungalow (☎077/375123); and *The Old Lamp*, just south of Chicken Corner, where simple but delicious Western and Thai food is served at relaxing low tables.

Nightlife normally centres around the bars and clubs at the south end of Sunrise – notably the *Cactus Club* for pop/handbag rave and the *Vinyl Club* for heavy trance – which pump out music onto their indoor dance-floors and low-slung beach tables. Up the hill behind the southern end of Sunrise, the *Back Yard* nightclub makes a good alternative venue, with a large balcony area overlooking the beach; this is where the full moon party continues into the next day and beyond. For somewhere to chill, head for *Mellow Mountain Bar*, which occupies a great position up in the rocks on the north side of Sunrise beyond *Seaview Bungalows*, and has an eclectic play-list, from drum 'n' bass to ambient. On full moon night itself, *Paradise* styles itself as the party host, but the mayhem spreads along most of Sunrise, fuelled by hastily erected drinks stalls and sound systems.

The east coast

North of Hat Rin, the rocky, exposed **east coast** stretches as far as Ao Thong Nai Pan, the only centre of development. No roads run along this coast, only a rough, steep, fifteen-kilometre trail, which starts from Hat Rin's northern transverse road (signposted) and runs reasonably close to the shore, occasionally dipping down into pristine sandy coves with a smattering of bungalows. In season (roughly Jan–Sept), if the weather's good enough, boats run to the east coast beaches (occasionally as far as Hat Khuat) from Hat Rin, some of them starting from Thong Sala or Maenam on Ko Samui, or you can arrange a boat on Sunrise if you're staying at one of the bungalows up the coast (B50 per head to *The Sanctuary*, for example). A few of the resorts on Sunrise, such as *Paradise*, organize occasional boat trips with snorkelling and fishing up this coast (typically B300 a head including dinner); otherwise you can splash out on chartering your own longtail (around B1500 to Thong Nai Pan and back).

About ninety minutes up the trail, **HAT THIAN**, a shady bay that's good for snorkelling, has established a reputation as a quiet alternative to Hat Rin. Accommodation is available at the friendly *Haad Tien Resort* (contact *Yoghurt Home 3* in Hat Rin, ☎01/229 3919, for further details, or go to ⓦwww.haadtien-resort.com; ②), with well-built en-suite wooden bungalows on the slope above the beach; and at the even mellower *Sanctuary* (in Bangkok ☎02/551 9082, ⓦwww.kohphangan.com/sanctuary; ③–⑤), which offers a wider range of en-suite bungalows, as well as dorm accommodation (B60), and good vegetarian fare and seafood, and hosts courses in yoga, meditation, massage and the like.

Steep, desolate **HAT SADET**, 12km up the trail from Hat Rin, has a handful of basic bungalow operations, sited here because of their proximity to **Thaan Sadet**, a boulder-strewn brook which runs out into the sea. The spot was popularized by various kings of Thailand who came here to walk, swim and vandalize the huge boulders by carving their initials on them. A rough road has been bulldozed through the woods above and parallel to Thaan Sadet to connect with the equally rough track from Thong Sala to Ao Thong Nai Pan.

AO THONG NAI PAN is a beautiful, semicircular bay backed by steep, green hills, which looks as if it's been bitten out of the island's northeast corner, leaving a tall hump of land dividing the bay into two parts. The southern half has the better sand and a hamlet which now sports a few farang bars and shops; the northern half is quieter, disturbed only by the little bit of surf which squeezes in. Both halves are sheltered and deep enough for swimming, and there's good snorkelling around the central headland and along the outer rim of the bay's southern half. A bumpy nightmare of a dirt road winds its way for 12km over the steep mountains from Ban Tai on the south coast to Thong Nai Pan. Jeeps connect with incoming and outgoing boats at Thong Sala every day, but if there's heavy rain they don't chance it.

Half a dozen resorts line the southern half of the bay, where the friendly *Pingjun* (☎077/299004; ❶–❸) has a range of large, en-suite bungalows with verandas and hammocks on a broad stretch of beach. But with most of the northern beach to themselves, *Star Huts I* and *II* (☎077/299005 or 01/219 1136; ❶–❸) get the nod as Thong Nai Pan's best budget choice. Very clean, well-maintained bungalows, with en-suite or shared bathrooms, line the sand, and the friendly owners dish up good food, have canoes for rent and can provide information about local walks. The steep slopes of the central outcrop make a beautiful setting for *Panviman* (☎077/238544, ☎238543, ⓦwww. koliphangan.com/panviman; ❼–❽), Ko Pha Ngan's only attempt at a luxury resort, with pricey fan-cooled or air-conditioned cottages and hotel style rooms. For non-guests it's worth making the climb up here for the view from the restaurant perched over the cliff edge.

The north coast

The village of **BAN CHALOAKLAM**, on the largest bay on the **north coast**, has long been a famous R&R spot for fishermen from all over the Gulf of Thailand, with sometimes as many as a hundred trawlers littering the broad and sheltered bay. Nowadays it is also a low-key tourist destination, as it can easily be reached from Thong Sala, 10km away, by songthaew or motorbike taxi along the island's best road. Facilities include travel agencies, motorbike rental, clinics, international phone and internet services and scuba outfits The best bit of beach is at **Hat Khom**, a tiny cove dramatically tucked in under the headland to the east, with a secluded strip of white sand and good coral for snorkelling. For **accommodation**, try *Fanta* (☎077/374065; ❷–❸) at the eastern end of Ban Chaloaklam, on a wide spread of beach backed by casuarinas with clean, en-suite bungalows and good food. Or walk out to friendly *Coral Bay* (☎01/677 7241; ❶–❹), which has plenty of space and great views on the grassy promontory dividing Hat Khom from the rest of Ao Chaloaklam. The sturdy bungalows range from simple affairs with mosquito nets and shared bathrooms to large pads with funky bathrooms built into the rock; snorkelling equipment is available to make the most of Hat Khom's reef.

If the sea is not too rough, longtail boats run three times a day for most of the year from Ban Chaloaklam to secluded **HAT KHUAT** (Bottle Beach), the best of the beaches on the north coast, sitting between steep hills in a perfect cup of a bay; you could also walk there along a testing trail from Hat Khom in around ninety minutes. The four friendly resorts here are all owned by the same extended family, so there's little to choose between them. The original is *Bottle Beach* (℡01/229 4762; ❶–❸), which has smart beachfront bungalows, tightly packed huts behind and highly recommended food.

The west coast

Pha Ngan's **west coast** has attracted about the same amount of development as the forgettable south coast, but the landscape here is more attractive and varied, broken up into a series of long sandy inlets with good sunset views over the islands to the west; most of the bays, however, are sheltered by reefs which can keep the sea too shallow for a decent swim, especially between April and October. The roads from Thong Sala as far up as Hat Yao are in decent condition, but routes beyond that as far as Ao Mae Hat (which is best reached from Ban Chaloaklam on the north coast), especially the side roads down to Hat Salad, have not as yet been similarly upgraded, and are testing if you're on a bike. Motorbike taxis run as far as Hat Yao; songthaews, jeeps or even boats cover the rest.

The first bay north of Thong Sala, Ao Wogtum (aka Hinkong), yawns wide across a featureless expanse which turns into a mud flat when the sea retreats behind the reef barrier at low tide. The nondescript bay of **AO SEETHANU** beyond is home to the excellent *Loy Fah* (℡077/377319 or 01/979 2050; ❶–❹), a well-run place which commands good views from its perch on top of Seethanu's steep southern cape, and offers decent snorkelling and swimming from the rocks; lodgings range from simple huts with mosquito nets and showers, to concrete cottages with verandas and chairs.

Continuing north, there's a surprise in store in the shape of **Laem Son Lake**, a beautiful, tranquil stretch of clear water cordoned by pines which spread down to the nearby beach. Under the shade of the pines, the rudimentary en-suite huts of *Bovy Resort* (❶) can only be recommended for their beachfront peace and quiet. *Seethanu Bungalows* (℡077/274106 for the phone booth outside the restaurant, ℮seetanubungalow@hotmail.com; ❷–❻), actually round the next headland on the small bay of **AO CHAOPHAO**, is a lively spot with a popular restaurant; sturdy, characterful wooden bungalows (all en-suite) are arrayed around a slightly messy garden, with the more expensive options by the beach. Next door, *Seaflower* (❶–❸) is quieter and more congenial, set in a well-tended garden: bungalows with their own bathrooms vary in price according to their size and how far you have to roll out of bed to land on the beach, and the veggie and meaty food is excellent. If you're feeling adventurous, ask the owner about the occasional three-day longtail-boat treks to Ang Thong National Marine Park (see p.572), which involve snorkelling, caving, catching your own seafood, and sleeping in hammocks or rough shelters (B1800 per person). Two doors away, friendly *Haad Chao Phao* (❷) is also recommended: in a shady garden, the ten clean and well-kept en-suite bungalows (all with mosquito nets and verandas) lead down to an attractive patch of beach.

Beyond Chaophao, livelier **HAT YAO** offers a long, gently curved beach, a diving outfit and a nonstop line of bungalows, with a swankier resort under construction towards its north end. Good bets here are *Ibiza* (℡01/229 4721; ❷), with smart, airy en-suite bungalows in a spacious garden, and the friendly

Bay View (☎01/229 4780; ❶–❹), which offers good food and views from a wide range of bungalows on the quiet northern headland. The only bay to the north of that, **HAT SALAD**, is probably the best of the bunch: it's pretty and quiet, with good snorkelling off the northern tip. *My Way* and *Salad Hut* (both ❶–❷) are relaxing places for chilling out here, featuring primitive bungalows with shared or en-suite bathrooms, and recommended, though moderately expensive, food.

On the island's northwest corner, **AO MAE HAT** is good for swimming and snorkelling among the coral which lines the sand causeway to the tiny islet of Ko Maa. The bay, which is most easily reached by the road west from Ban Chaloaklam, also supports several decent bungalow resorts, including *Island View Cabana* (☎077/377144; ❶–❸), a popular place with a well-positioned, thatch-roofed restaurant, snooker tables and a variety of well-designed bungalows shaded by casuarina trees.

Ko Tao

KO TAO (Turtle Island) is so named because its outline resembles a turtle nose-diving towards Ko Pha Ngan, 40km to the south. The rugged shell of the turtle, to the east, is crenellated with secluded coves where one or two bungalows hide among the rocks. On the western side, the turtle's underbelly is a long curve of classic beach, facing Ko Nang Yuan, a beautiful Y-shaped group of islands offshore, also known as Ko Hang Tao (Turtle's Tail Island). The 21 square kilometres of granite in between is topped by dense forest on the higher slopes and dotted with huge boulders that look as if they await some Easter Island sculptor. It's fun to spend a couple of days exploring the network of rough trails, after which you'll probably know all 750 of the island's inhabitants. Ko Tao is now best known as a venue for **scuba diving**, with most companies at Mae Hat, the main village and arrival point; see the box on p.598 for further details.

The island is the last and most remote of the archipelago which continues the line of Surat Thani's mountains into the sea. There were over ninety sets of **bungalows** at the latest count (still not enough at times during the peak season from December to March, when travellers occasionally have to sleep on the beach until a hut becomes free) concentrated along the west and south sides. Some still provide the bare minimum, with plain mattresses for beds, mosquito nets and shared bathrooms, but most places can now offer en-suite bathrooms and a few comforts, and there are even a few air-con chalets knocking around. Electricity still comes from private generators, usually evenings only, with few kept running 24 hours a day. If you're just **arriving**, it might be a good idea to go with one of the touts who meet the ferries at Mae Hat, with pickup or boat on hand, since at least you'll know their bungalows aren't full or closed – the former is possible from December to March, the latter from June to August; failing that, call ahead as even the remotest bungalows now have mobile phones. Some resorts with attached scuba-diving operations have been known to refuse guests who don't sign up for diving trips or courses; on the other hand, some of the bigger dive companies now have their own functional lodgings, staying at which is often included in the price of a dive course.

Food can be a little pricey and limited in range because most of it is brought across on the ferry boats. As is the case on Ko Pha Ngan, at some of

◀ Chumphon

◀ Ko Pha Ngan, Ko Samui & Surat Thani

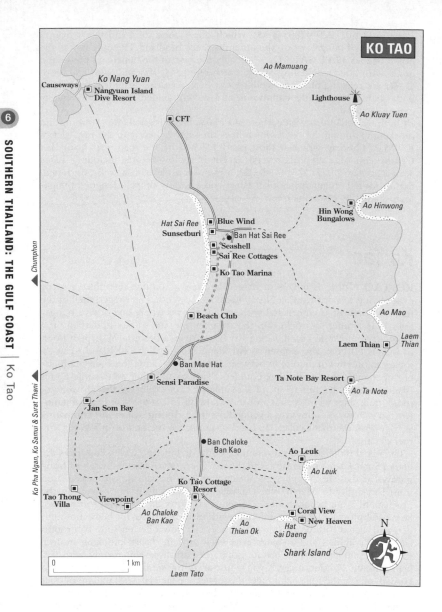

KO TAO

Ko Nang Yuan

Causeways
■ Nangyuan Island
Dive Resort

■ CFT

Ao Mamuang

Lighthouse ▲

Ao Kluay Tuen

Hat Sai Ree
Sunsetburi
■ Blue Wind
● Ban Hat Sai Ree
■ Seashell
■ Sai Ree Cottages
■ Ko Tao Marina

■ Ao Hinwong
Hin Wong
Bungalows

■ Beach Club

Ao Mao

Laem Thian ■
Laem
Thian

● Ban Mae Hat

■ Sensi Paradise

Ta Note Bay Resort ■
Ao Ta Note

■ Jan Som Bay

● Ban Chaloke
Ban Kao

Ao Leuk ■
Ao Leuk

Tao Thong
Villa ■
Viewpoint ■

Ko Tao Cottage
Resort ■
Ao Chaloke
Ban Kao

Ao
Thian Ok

■ Coral View
■ New Heaven
Hat
Sai Daeng

Shark Island

N

0   1 km

Laem Tato

the cheapest resorts, where they make their money from food more than accommodation, owners have been known to kick out guests who don't eat at the in-house restaurant.

The **weather** is much the same as on Pha Ngan and Samui, but being that bit further off the mainland, Ko Tao feels the effect of the southwest monsoon more: June to October can have strong winds and rain, with a lot of debris blown onto the windward coasts.

Getting to Ko Tao

There are three different boat services **from Chumphon** to Ko Tao: the Numhasin **speed boat** (departs daily in fine weather only at 7.30am; 1hr 45min; B400); the **Songserm express boat** (departs daily from January through October at 7.30am; 2hr 30min; B400); and the **slow boat** (departs daily in all but the very worst weather at midnight; 6hr; B200). **Tickets** for all boats can be bought in Chumphon at any guest house or travel agent, all of whom provide transport to the port and some of whom also offer free showering facilities and video shows between connections; see the Chumphon account on p.561 for full details.

Three kinds of vessel run between Thong Sala on **Ko Pha Ngan** and Ko Tao: at least two speed boats a day (50min; B350), two express boats a day (1hr 30min; B225) and one slow boat (3hr; B150). The speed boats originate at Bophut, Maenam and Na Thon on **Ko Samui** (total journey time to Ko Tao 1hr 30min; B450–550). There's also a night boat from **Surat Thani**, departing at 11pm (9hr; B400).

These services fluctuate according to demand and so on, and in high season extra boats may appear. All voyages to and from Ko Tao are also at the mercy of the weather, especially between June and November; plenty of travellers have missed onward connections through being stranded on the island, so it's best not to plan to visit at the end of your holiday.

Island transport

You can **get around** easily enough on foot, but there are roads of sorts now to most of the resorts, though some are still four-wheel drive only, motorbike taxis and pickups (B20–50 per person, more for 4WD), and even rental mopeds (B150–200 a day), are available in Mae Hat. Mountain **bikes** can be rented for around B100 per day from the island's all-purpose fixer, Mr J, with outlets just north of Mae Hat by the school and at Ao Chaloke Ban Kao behind *Buddha View Dive Resort*. **Longtail-boat taxis** are available at Mae Hat or through your bungalow, or you could splash out on your own **round-island boat tour**, allowing you to explore the coastline fully with stops for snorkelling and swimming, including a visit to Ko Nang Yuan (about B1500 for the boat for the day); alternatively you could hook up with a group tour, again through your resort or at Mae Hat (usually about 5hr; B250–300 a head).

The west coast and Ko Nang Yuan

All boats to the island dock at **MAE HAT**, a small, lively village with a few seafront restaurants, clinics, a Krung Thai Bank currency-exchange booth (daily 9am–3pm; cash advances on credit cards available) and a post office in one of the larger supermarkets (daily 8.30am–10pm), with phone, currency-exchange and poste restante facilities. Worth singling out among the **eating and drinking** options here are the *Swiss Bakery*, 100m straight ahead from the pier up the hill, serving good coffee and a wide range of pastries and savouries, including delicious croissants; and *Whitening*, a cool restaurant, bar and nightclub, 200m south of the pier overlooking the bay, which dishes up interesting and tasty Thai and Western food.

South of Mae Hat

For somewhere good to stay on the southern edge of Mae Hat, try *Sensi Paradise Resort* (☎077/456244, ℗456245), which has taken over the former *Coral Beach Resort* and now sprawls over the lower slopes of the headland to

Some of the best dive sites in Thailand are found around Ko Tao. The island is blessed with outstandingly clear (visibility up to 35m) and deep water relatively close to shore, and provides near-perfect conditions for a wide range of coral species. On top of that, there's a kaleidoscopic array of marine life, and you may be lucky enough to encounter whale sharks, barracudas, leatherback turtles and pilot whales. Diving is possible at any time of the year, with sheltered sites on one or other side of the island in any season – the changeover from southwest to northeast monsoon in November is the worst time, while visibility is best from April to July, in September (usually best of all) and October.

To meet demand, Ko Tao has about thirty dive companies, nearly all of them based at Mae Hat, Hat Sai Ree or Ao Chaloke Ban Kao. The companies have by agreement set fixed prices across the island: by far the most popular course, PADI's four-day "Openwater" for beginners, costs B7800 at the time of writing; one-day introductions to diving are also available for B1500, as is the full menu of PADI courses, up to "Dive Master"; for qualified divers, one dive costs B800, a ten-dive package B5500, with fifteen percent discounts if you bring your own gear. Some of the companies, including Easy Divers, will take snorkellers along on their dive trips, providing good-quality snorkel, mask and fin sets for B300 a day.

With no distinction in price, other factors come into play when choosing a company in such a competitive market. Make sure that the gear and the boat are well maintained and check out the kind of instruction and whether you get on with the instructors. Companies often throw in your accommodation for the duration of an Openwater course, but ask exactly how long it's for (3 or 4 nights), where it is and what it's like; some will also throw in a free fun dive at the end of the course; free snacks and drinking water should be provided on the boat. PADI Five-Star Dive Centres, all of which are committed to looking after the environment, involving maintaining their own dive sites as well as taking part in regular, organized clean-ups around the island, include Scuba Junction on Hat Sai Ree ⓦwww.scuba-junction.com, Big Blue at Mae Hat ☏077/456050, ⓦwww.bigbluediving.com, Easy Divers at Mae Hat ☏077/456010, ⓦwww.thaidive.com and on Ko Nang Yuan (see

the south of the village. It offers some of the best upmarket accommodation on the island, with well-designed, air-con wooden cottages, including some large family units, in pretty, flower-covered sloping grounds (❾), as well as cheaper bungalows with shared bathrooms (❸); five minutes beyond the edge of the property, there's a sandy, palm-sheltered cove for secluded sunbathing and swimming.

In this direction, also handy for the village (15min walk) is *Jan Som Bay* (☏077/502502–10; ❹), a characterful place overlooking a beautiful rocky beach, with snorkels and fins to rent. In traditional Thai style, the large wooden chalets have only shutters on the windows and slits under the roof to catch the breeze (bed nets rather than screens keep the mosquitoes off), as well as large verandas with deckchairs and tables.

A good way further down the coast (40min walk from Mae Hat or B50 in a taxi-boat), *Tao Thong Villa* (☏077/456078; ❶) offers plenty of shady seclusion and good snorkelling and swimming. Sturdy bungalows with decent mosquito nets are dotted around a rocky outcrop and the slope behind, with a breezy restaurant on the small, sandy isthmus in between.

North of Mae Hat

Five minutes' walk north of Mae Hat, sheltering on the south side of a small promontory, the quiet and friendly *Beach Club* caters to a wide range of budg-

p.600), and Planet Scuba at Mae Hat and next to *Sai Ree Cottages* on Hat Sai Ree
⊕01/229 4336, ⓦwww.planet-scuba.net.

Main dive sites

Ko Nang Yuan. Perfect for beginners and good for snorkelling; hard coral, sponges
and granite boulders.

White Rock (Hin Khao). Sarcophyton leather coral turns the granite boulders here
white when seen from the surface; also wire, antipatharian and colourful soft corals,
and gorgonian sea fans. Plenty of fish, including titan triggerfish.

Shark Island. Large granite boulders with acropora, wire and bushy antipatharian
corals, sea whips, gorgonian sea fans and barrel sponges. Reef fish include
angelfish, parrotfish and groupers; occasional whale sharks.

Hinwong Pinnacle. Generally for experienced divers, often with strong currents.
Similar scenery to White Rock, over a larger area, with beautiful soft coral at 30m depth.
A wide range of fish, including blue-spotted fantail stingrays and large groupers.

Chumphon or **Northwest Pinnacle.** A granite pinnacle, over 30m in depth, its top
covered in anemones, with the possibility of exceptional visibility. Barrel sponges,
tree and antipatharian corals at deeper levels; a wide variety of fish, in large numbers, attract local fishermen; occasional whale sharks and huge groupers.

Southwest Pinnacle. Probably the top site in terms of visibility, scenery and marine
life. A huge pyramid-like pinnacle rising to 6m below the surface, its upper part covered in anemones, with smaller pinnacles around; at lower levels, granite boulders,
barrel sponges, sea whips, bushy antipatharian and tree corals. Big groupers and
snappers; occasionally, large stingrays, leopard and sand sharks, swordfish, finback
whales and whale sharks.

Sail Rock (Hin Bai). Visibility of up to 25m, and a ten-metre-deep underwater chimney. Antipatharian corals, both bushes and whips, and carpets of anemones. Large
groupers, snappers and fusiliers, bright blue-ringed angelfish, curious batfish and
juvenile clown sweetlips; occasional whale sharks.

ets (⊕ and ⓕ077/456222, ⓔbeachclub@kohtao.com; ❸–❼): choose between
clean, en-suite thatched huts, some with verandas on the beach, and smart concrete chalets with cold-water bathrooms, fridges and fans or air-conditioning;
windsurfers can be rented here for B300–400 per hour.

Beyond the promontory, you'll find **Hat Sai Ree**, Ko Tao's only long beach.
The strip of white sand stretches for 2km in a gentle curve, backed by a smattering of coconut palms. Over twenty bungalow resorts have set up shop here,
and a small village, **BAN HAT SAI REE**, with bars, supermarkets, a clinic and
a bakery, has evolved at its northern end. Towards the midpoint of the beach,
twenty minutes' walk from Mae Hat, *Ko Tao Marina* (⊕077/456173, ⓕ456213,
ⓔkohtaomarina@hotmail.com; ❸–❻) is a well-maintained, family-run operation that offers small bungalows with mosquito nets, fans and their own bathrooms, or larger, swankier affairs with mosquito screens, and a good beachside
restaurant. In another shady, flower-strewn garden a couple of doors up, *Sai Ree
Cottages* (⊕077/456126; ❶–❷) has primitive huts and sturdy en-suite bungalows by the beach, and serves excellent grub; a branch of Planet Scuba behind
the cottages rents out two-person **sea kayaks** at B400 per half-day or B700
per day. The spacious, tidy compound next door belongs to *Seashell Resort*
(⊕077/456271 or 01/229 4621), a friendly, well-run place under the tall palm
trees; it offers internet access as well as very smart, sturdy bungalows, with en-

suite showers and mosquito screens, either with fans (**❸**) or with air-con and baths (**❻**). A hundred metres or so further up the beach by the village is the new *Sunsetburi Resort* (☎077/456266, ℱ377801; **❼**), Ko Tao's most upmarket lodgings, with its own large swimming pool and air-con, hot water and mini-bars in smart, modern concrete cottages.

Blue Wind (☎077/456116, ✉Bluewind_wa@yahoo.com), next door but one, is another good choice here: the smart, well-kept bungalows are scattered about a shady compound, and the very good beachside restaurant serves up home-made breads, croissants and cakes, as well as Western and Thai meals. The track north of the village ends beyond the beach at secluded *CFT* (**❶–❹**) on the rocky northwest flank of the island, which offers cheap shacks or en-suite bun-galows, and excellent food; there's no beach here, but the views over to Ko Nang Yuan are something else.

Ko Nang Yuan

One kilometre off the northwest of Ko Tao, **KO NANG YUAN**, a close-knit group of three tiny islands encircled by a ring of easily accessible coral, provides the most spectacular beach scenery in these parts, thanks to the causeway of fine white sand which joins up the islands. Longtail boats scheduled for day-trippers leave Mae Hat and Hat Sai Ree in the morning, returning in the late afternoon (B60 return). A boat also meets incoming and outgoing ferries at Mae Hat, for people staying at the *Nangyuan Island Dive Resort* (☎077/456088–91 or 01/229 5212, ℱ077/456093, ⓦwww.nangyuan.com; **❼–❾**), which makes the most of its beautiful location, its swanky fan and air-con bungalows spreading over all three islands. Rules to protect the environment here include banning visitors from bringing cans and plastic bottles with them; one of Thailand's foremost diving operations, Easy Divers, works out of the resort.

The east and south coasts

The sheltered inlets of the **east coast**, most of them containing one or two sets of bungalows, can be reached by boat or four-wheel drive. The most northerly inhabitation here is at **Ao Hinwong**, a deeply recessed bay strewn with large boulders, which has a particularly remote, almost desolate air. Nevertheless, *Hin Wong Bungalows* (☎01/229 4810; **❸**) is welcoming and pro-vides good, basic accommodation on a steep, grassy slope above the rocks. In the middle of the coast, the dramatic tiered promontory of **Laem Thian** shel-ters a tiny beach and a colourful reef on its south side. With the headland to itself, *Laem Thian* (☎01/229 4478; **❶–❸**) offers simple rooms or comfy bunga-lows, decent food and a secluded, castaway feel. Laem Thian's coral reef stretch-es down towards **Ao Ta Note**, a horseshoe inlet sprinkled with boulders and plenty of coarse sand, with the best snorkelling just north of the bay's mouth. The pick of the handful of resorts here is *Ta Note Bay Dive Resort* (☎01/970 4703; **❷–❺**), whose well-designed wooden bungalows, set among thick bougainvillea, range from simple affairs with mosquito nets, shared bathrooms and no fans, to en-suite chalets with large verandas and views out towards Ko Pha Ngan and Ko Samui; snorkelling equipment and kayaks are available to rent. The last bay carved out of the turtle's shell, **Ao Leuk**, has a well-recessed rocky beach and deep water for swimming and snorkelling. The simple en-suite huts at *Ao Leuk Resort* (**❷**) are a bit ramshackle, but they're cheap and enjoy plenty of space and shade in a palm grove.

The **southeast corner** of the island sticks out in a long, thin mole of land, which shelters the sandy beach (Hat Sai Daeng) on one side if the wind's coming from the northeast, or the rocky cove on the other side if it's blowing from the southwest. Straddling the headland is *New Heaven* (℡01/981 2762; ❸), a laid-back, well-equipped place with a good kitchen; its pleasantly idiosyncratic en-suite bungalows enjoy plenty of elbow room and good views. The only other resort on Hat Sai Daeng is the less characterful, but adequate *Coral View* (℡01/ 970 0378 or 970 2280; ❸–❹), with a choice between concrete and wooden bun-galows on the slope behind the beach and a breezy, elevated restaurant.

The **south coast** is sheltered from the worst of both monsoons, and conse-quently **Ao Chaloke Ban Kao** has seen a fair amount of development, with several dive resorts taking advantage of the large, sheltered bay. *Buddha View Dive Resort* – which even has its own swimming pool for training divers – rents out one-person (B250/B400 per half-day/full day) and two-person (B400/B700) **kayaks**. Two accommodation options stand out from the crowd here. Run by a friendly, young bunch and home to Big Bubble Diving, *Viewpoint Bungalows* (℡ & ℻01/210 2207, ✉bigbubble@hotmail.com; ❶–❸) sprawl along the western side of the bay; the well-built, clean bungalows have shared or en-suite bathrooms, the best of them with verandas overlooking the sunset from the headland. *Ko Tao Cottage Resort* (℡ & ℻077/456133 or 456198, ✉divektc@samart.co.th; ❹–❻) is one of the island's few stabs at insti-tutionalized luxury and worth a splurge, especially if you're considering scuba diving with its diving school. The cottages, which have verandas, ceiling fans and plain, smart decor (some with sea views and mini-bars), are ranged around a shady garden and restaurant by the beach.

Nakhon Si Thammarat and around

NAKHON SI THAMMARAT, the south's second-largest town, occupies a blind spot in the eyes of most tourists, whose focus is fixed on Ko Samui, 100km to the north. Its neglect is unfortunate, for it's an absorbing place, though a bit short on accommodation and other facilities. The south's major pilgrimage site and home to a huge military base, Nakhon is relaxed, self-confident and sophisticated, well known for its excellent cuisine and tradition-al handicrafts. The stores on Thanon Thachang are especially good for local nielloware (*kruang tom*), household items and jewellery elegantly patterned in gold or silver on black, and *yan lipao*, sturdy basketware made from intricately woven fern stems of different colours. Nakhon is also the best place in the country to see how Thai shadow plays work, at Suchart Subsin's workshop.

The town is recorded under the name of Ligor (or Lakhon), the capital of the kingdom of Lankasuka, as early as the second century, and classical dance-drama, *lakhon*, is supposed to have been developed here. Well placed for trade with China and southern India, Nakhon was the point through which the Theravada form of Buddhism was imported from Sri Lanka and spread to Sukhothai, the capital of the new Thai state, in the thirteenth century.

Known as *muang phra*, the "city of monks", Nakhon is still the religious cap-ital of the south, and the main centre for **festivals**. The most important of these are the **Tamboon Deuan Sip**, held during the waning of the moon in the tenth lunar month (either September or October), and the **Hae Pha Khun That**, which is held twice a year, on Maha Puja (February full moon – see also p.65) and on Visakha Puja (May full moon – see p.66). The purpose of the for-mer is to pay homage to dead relatives and friends; it is believed that during this fifteen-day period all *pret* – ancestors who have been damned to hell – are allowed out to visit the world, and so their relatives perform a merit-making ceremony in the temples, presenting offerings from the first harvest to ease their suffering. A huge ten-day fair takes place at Sri Nakharin park (on the north side of town towards the airport) at this time, as well as processions, shadow plays and other theatrical performances. The Hae Pha Khun That also attracts people from all over the south, to pay homage to the relics of the Buddha at Wat Mahathat. The ceremonial centrepiece of this festival is the Pha Phra Bot, a strip of yellow cloth many hundreds of metres long, which is carried in a spectacular procession around the chedi.

The Town

The **town plan** is simple, but puzzling at first sight: it runs in a straight line for 7km from north to south and is rarely more than a few hundred metres wide, a layout originally dictated by the availability of fresh water. The modern centre for businesses and shops sits at the north end around the train station, with the main day market (to the east of the station on Thanon Pak Nakhon) in this food-conscious city displaying a particularly fascinating array of produce that's best around 8 or 9am. To the south, centred on the elegant, traditional mosque on Thanon Karom, lies the old Muslim quarter; south again is the start of the old city walls, of which few remains can be seen, and the historic centre, with the town's main places of interest now set in a leafy residential area.

Wat Mahathat

Missing out **Wat Mahathat** would be like going to Rome and not visiting St Peter's, for the Buddha relics in the vast chedi make this the south's most

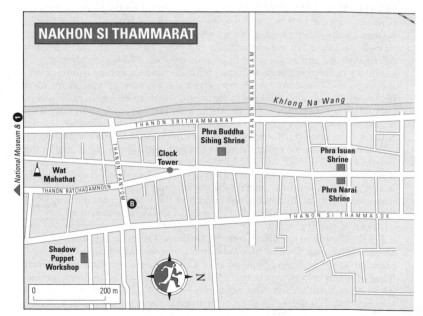

NAKHON SI THAMMARAT

important shrine. Inside the temple cloisters, which have their main entrance facing Thanon Ratchadamnoen about 2km south of the modern centre, the courtyard looks like a surreal ornamental garden, with row upon row of smaller chedis, spiked like bayonets, each surrounded by a box hedge and all in the shadow of the main chedi, the **Phra Boromathat**. This huge, stubby Sri Lankan bell supports a slender, ringed spire, which is in turn topped by a shiny pinnacle said to be covered in 600kg of gold leaf. According to the chronicles, relics of the Buddha were brought here from Sri Lanka two thousand years ago by an Indian prince and princess and enshrined in a chedi. It's undergone plenty of face-lifts since: an earlier Srivijayan version, a model of which stands at one corner, is encased in the present twelfth-century chedi. The most recent restoration work, funded by donations from all over Thailand, rescued it from collapse, although it still seems to be leaning dangerously to the southeast. Worshippers head for the north side's vast enclosed stairway, framed by lions and giants, which they liberally decorate with gold leaf to add to the shrine's radiance and gain some merit. In the left-hand shrine at the foot of the stairs here, look out for some fine stuccoes of the life of the Buddha.

The **Viharn Kien Museum** (hours irregular, but usually daily 8.30am–noon & 1–4pm), which extends north from the chedi, is an Aladdin's cave of bric-a-brac, said to house fifty thousand artefacts donated by worshippers, ranging from ships made out of seashells to gold and silver models of the Bodhi Tree. At the entrance to the museum, you'll pass the Phra Puay, an image of the Buddha giving a gesture of reassurance. Women pray to the image when they want to have children, and the lucky ones return to give thanks and to leave photos of their chubby progeny.

Outside the cloister to the south is the eighteenth-century **Viharn Luang**, raised on elegant slanting columns, a beautiful example of Ayutthayan

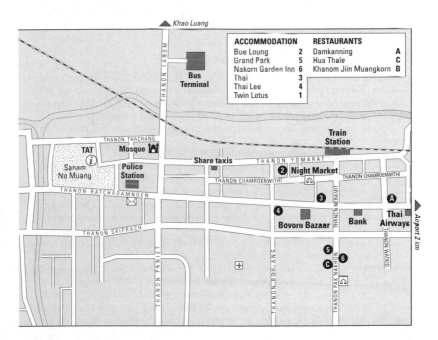

Khao Luang

ACCOMMODATION		RESTAURANTS	
Bue Loung	2	Damkanning	A
Grand Park	5	Hua Thale	C
Nakorn Garden Inn	6	Khanom Jiin Muangkorn	B
Thai	3		
Thai Lee	4		
Twin Lotus	1		

Bus Terminal

THANON KAROM

Train Station

THANON THACHANG

TAT

Mosque

Share taxis

THANON YOMARAT

Sanam Na Muang

Police Station

Night Market

THANON CHAMROENWITHI

THANON CHAMROENWITHI

THANON RATCHADAMNOEN

THANON SRIPRACH

Bovorn Bazaar

Bank

Thai Airways

THANON NERAMIT

THANON PANIET

THANON BOHLANG

THANON PAK NAKHON

THANON WATKID

Airport 2 km

architecture. The interior is austere at ground level, but the red coffered ceiling shines with carved and gilded stars and lotus blooms. Elsewhere in the spacious grounds, cheerful, inexpensive stalls peddle local handicrafts such as shadow puppets, bronze and basketware.

The National Museum

A few minutes' walk south again from Wat Mahathat, the **National Museum** (Wed–Sun 9am–noon & 1–4.30pm; B30) houses a small but diverse collection, mostly of artefacts from southern Thailand. In the prehistory room downstairs, look out for the two impressive ceremonial bronze kettledrums, dating from the fifth century BC and topped with chunky frogs (the local frogs are said to be the biggest in Thailand and a prized delicacy). Next door are some interesting Hindu finds and many characteristic Buddha images made in imitation of the Phra Buddha Sihing at the city hall, the most revered image in southern Thailand. Among the collections of ceramics and household articles upstairs, you can't miss the seat panel from Rama V's barge, a dazzling example of the nielloware for which Nakhon is famous – the delicate animals and landscapes have been etched onto a layer of gold which covers the silver base, and then picked out by inlaying a black alloy into the background.

The shadow puppet workshop

The best possible introduction to *nang thalung*, southern Thailand's **shadow puppet theatre**, is to head for 110/18 Soi 3, Thanon Si Thammasok, ten minutes' walk east of Wat Mahathat (☎075/346394): here Suchart Subsin, one of the south's leading exponents of *nang thalung*, and his son have opened up their workshop to the public, and, for a small fee (usually around B50), they'll show you a few scenes from a shadow play in the small open-air theatre. You can also see the intricate process of making the leather puppets and can buy the finished products as souvenirs: puppets sold here are of much better quality and design than those usually found on southern Thailand's souvenir stalls.

Other shrines and temples

In the chapel of the provincial office on Thanon Ratchadamnoen sits the **Phra Buddha Sihing**, which according to legend was magically created in Sri Lanka in the second century. In the thirteenth century it was sent by ship to the king of Sukhothai, but the vessel sank and the image miraculously floated on a plank to Nakhon. Two other images, one in the National Museum in Bangkok, one in Wat Phra Singh in Chiang Mai, claim to be the authentic Phra Buddha Sihing, but none of the three is in the Sri Lankan style, so they are all probably derived from a lost original. Although similar to the other two in size and shape, the image in Nakhon has a style unique to this area, distinguished by the heavily pleated flap of its robe over the left shoulder, a beaky nose and harsh features, which sit uneasily on the short, corpulent body. The image's plumpness has given the style the name *khanom tom* – "banana and rice pudding".

You're bound to pass the small, red-roofed Hindu shrines of **Phra Isuan** and **Phra Narai** on Thanon Ratchadamnoen, legacies of Nakhon's ancient commercial links with India (hours irregular, but usually Mon–Fri 8.30am–4pm, with a break for lunch). The former houses a lingam, a phallic representation of Shiva worshipped by women who want to conceive, and in its grounds there's a ritual swing, a smaller version of the Sao Ching Cha at Wat Suthat in Bangkok; the latter shelters a life-size image of Narai, an incarnation of Vishnu.

Shadow puppets

Found throughout southern Asia, shadow puppets are one of the oldest forms of theatre, featuring in Buddhist literature as early as 400 BC. The art form seems to have come from India, via Java, to Thailand, where it's called *nang*, meaning "hide": the puppets are made from the skins of water buffalo or cows, which are softened in water, then pounded until almost transparent, before being carved and coloured to represent the characters of the play. The puppets are then manipulated on sticks in front of a bright light, to project their image onto a large white screen, while the story is narrated to the audience.

The grander version of the art, nang yai – "big hide", so called because the figures are life-size – deals only with the *Ramayana* story (see box on p.75). It's known to have been part of the entertainment at official ceremonies in the Ayutthayan period, but has now almost died out. The more populist version, nang thalung – *thalung* is probably a shortening of the town name, Phatthalung (which is just down the road from Nakhon), where this version of the art form is said to have originated – is also in decline now: performances are generally limited to temple festivals, marriages and ordinations, lasting usually from 9pm to dawn. As well as working the sixty-centimetre-high *nang thalung* puppets, the puppet master narrates the story, impersonates the characters, chants and cracks jokes to the accompaniment of flutes, fiddles and percussion instruments. Not surprisingly, in view of this virtuoso semi-improvised display, puppet masters are esteemed as possessed geniuses by their public.

At big festivals, companies often perform the *Ramayana* sometimes in competition with each other; at smaller events they put on more down-to-earth stories, with stock characters such as the jokers Yor Thong, an angry man with a pot belly and a sword, and Kaew Kop, a man with a frog's head. Yogi, a wizard and teacher, is thought to protect the puppet master and his company from evil spirits with his magic, so he is always the first puppet on at the beginning of every performance.

In an attempt to halt their decline as a form of popular entertainment, the puppet companies are now incorporating modern instruments and characters in modern dress into their shows, and are boosting the love element in their stories. They're fighting a battle they can't win against television and cinemas, although at least the debt owed to shadow puppets has been acknowledged – *nang* has become the Thai word for "movie".

The Brahmin community based at these shrines supplies astrologers to the royal court and priests for the Ploughing Ceremony, held every May in Bangkok.

Practicalities

Nakhon's **bus terminal** and **train station** are both centrally placed, and even the **airport** is only 2km north of the centre, served by air-con minibus to and from the Thai Airways office at 1612 Thanon Ratchadamnoen (☎075/342491 or 343874). **Share-taxis** congregate towards the south end of Thanon Yomarat. For getting around Nakhon, small blue **share-songthaews** ply up and down Thanon Ratchadamnoen for B5 a ride.

TAT has an office in a restored 1920s government officers' club on Sanam Na Muang (daily 8.30am–4.30pm; ☎075/346515–6, ✉tatnakon@nrt.cscoms.com), which also covers the provinces of Trang and Phatthalung. The main **post office** (Mon–Fri 8.30am–4.30pm), nearby on Thanon Ratchadamnoen opposite the police station, has an **international phone office** upstairs which is open 24 hours a day.

Accommodation

Though most of Nakhon's **hotels** are dingy and soulless, there are enough exceptions to get by.

Bue Loung Hotel, 1487/19 Soi Luang Muang, Thanon Chamroenwithi ☎075/341518, ℗343418. Central but reasonably quiet; gets the thumbs-up from visiting businessmen, with a choice of fan or air-con in double or twin rooms. ❷–❸

Grand Park Hotel, 1204/79 Thanon Pak Nakhon ☎075/317666–73, ℗317674. If you're looking for something more upmarket in the centre of town, this newly established place is worth considering – it's large, stylish and bright, and staff are cheery and attentive. ❺

Nakorn Garden Inn, 1/4 Thanon Pak Nakhon ☎075/313333, ℗342926. A rustic but sophisticated haven in a three-storey red-brick building overlooking a tree-shaded yard. Large, smart rooms come with air-con, hot water, cable TV and mini-bars. The best moderately priced option in town. ❹

Thai Hotel, 1375 Thanon Ratchadamnoen ☎075/341509, ℗344858. Formerly top of the range in Nakhon, this large institutional high-rise can still offer clean, reliable, fan-cooled and air-con rooms, though staff can be surly, not to say rude. ❸–❹

Thai Lee Hotel, 1130 Thanon Ratchadamnoen ☎075/356948. For rock-bottom accommodation, the plain and basic rooms here aren't a bad deal (it's worth asking for a room at the back of the hotel to escape the noise of the main street). ❶

Twin Lotus, about 3km southeast of the centre at 97/8 Thanon Patanakarn Kukwang ☎075/323777, ℗323821. Gets pride of place in Nakhon – though not location; sports five restaurants, a swimming pool and a health club. ❻

Eating and drinking

Nakhon is a great place for inexpensive **food**. Most famous, and justifiably so, is the lunchtime-only *Khanom Jiin Muangkorn* on Thanon Panyom near Wat Mahathat: the rough-and-ready outdoor restaurant dishes up one of the local specialities, *khanom jiin*, noodles topped with hot, sweet or fishy sauce served with *pak ruam*, a platter of crispy raw vegetables. Also boasting rock-bottom prices for lunch is *Krua Nakhon* in the Bovorn Bazaar on Thanon Ratchadamnoen, a big, rustic pavilion with good *khanom jiin* and other local dishes: *kaeng som*, a mild yellow curry; *kaeng tai plaa*, fish stomach curry; and various *khanom wan*, coconut milk puddings.

Also in Bovorn Bazaar, *Hao Coffee* is a good spot for Thai or Western breakfast or lunch, with a wide selection of coffees, including Thai filter coffee, to wash it down. It's a busy, friendly place, modelled on an old Chinese-style coffee shop, packed full of ageing violins, clocks and other antiques. If you're not in the mood for nostalgic charm, head for the shiny, air-con *Ligor Bakery*, at the entrance to the Bovorn Bazaar, which offers plenty of cakes, decent Western-style breakfasts and good coffees.

The busy night market on Thanon Chamroenwithi near the *Bue Loung Hotel* is great for inexpensive food, such as *yam plaa meuk* and *yam kung*, and people-watching. In the old Muslim quarter, many stalls near the corner of Thanon Karom and Thanon Yomarat sell good Muslim food, such as *roti* (sweet pancake – also available at stalls in and around the night market) and chicken with curried rice.

The best of Nakhon's more conventional **restaurants** is *Hua Thale*, on Thanon Pak Nakhon opposite the *Nakorn Garden Inn* (daily 4–10pm), renowned among locals for its excellent, inexpensive seafood. Run by a friendly Thai who lived in Los Angeles for many years and who will take your order (no English menu), it's plain and very clean, with the day's catch displayed out front and relaxing patio tables out the back. Recommended dishes include whole baked fish and *hoy meng pho op mordin*, large green mussels in a delicious herb soup containing lemon grass, basil and mint. On the corner of Thanon Watkid and Thanon Ratchadamnoen, *Damkanning* is a decent fallback, one of many affordable, popular restaurants with pavement tables in the area.

If you're looking for somewhere to **drink**, head for *99% Rock*, a wooden open-air bar in the Bovorn Bazaar that's popular with Nakhon's sprinkling of expats, or to Thanon Watkid, where a group of congenial bars with names like *Lucky Light* and *Marine Pub* offer live music.

Khao Luang National Park

Rising to the west of Nakhon Si Thammarat and temptingly visible from all over town, is 1835-metre-high **Khao Luang**, southern Thailand's highest mountain. A huge national park encompasses Khao Luang's jagged green peaks, beautiful streams with numerous waterfalls, tropical rainforest and fruit orchards, as well as the source of the Tapi River, one of the peninsula's main waterways, which flows into the Gulf of Thailand at Surat Thani. **Fauna** here includes macaques, musk deer, civets, binturongs, as well as more difficult to see Malayan tapirs and serows, plus over two hundred bird species. There's an astonishing diversity of **flora** too, notably rhododendrons and begonias, dense mosses, ferns and lichens, plus more than three hundred species of both ground-growing and epiphytic orchids, some of which are unique to the park. The best time to visit is after the rainy season, from January onwards, when there should still be a decent flow in the waterfalls, but the trails will be dry and the leeches not so bad. However, the park's most distinguishing feature for visitors is probably its difficulty of access: main roads run around the 570-square-kilometre park with spurs into some of the waterfalls, but there are no roads across the park and very sparse public transport along the spur roads. Only **Krung Ching waterfall**, one of Thailand's most spectacular, which features on the back of one-thousand-baht notes, really justifies the hassle of getting there.

Before heading off to Khao Luang, be sure to drop into Nakhon's TAT office for a useful park **brochure**, with a sketch map and sketchy details of the walking routes to Krung Ching waterfall and to the peak itself (for the latter, which begins at Ban Khiriwong on the southeast side of the park and involves at least one night camping on the mountain, ask at TAT about the possibility of hiring local guides). Irregular **songthaews** on the main roads around the park and to Ban Khiriwong congregate on and around Thanon Chamroenwithi near the *Bue Loung Hotel* in Nakhon. The only **rental transport** available in town are pricey air-conditioned minibuses from Muang Korn Travel, 1242/67 Thanon Boh-Ang (☎075/356574; B1500 per day); otherwise you might try doing a deal with a share-taxi driver at the bottom of Thanon Yomarat to take you to the park

Park headquarters and Kharom waterfall
Park headquarters (B200 admission) lie 33km west of Nakhon, 3km off Highway 4015 to Chawang, on the south side of the mountain; songthaews will usually drop you at the turning off the highway, though you might find one that will leg it up the very steep access road to HQ. Around 300m beyond, **Kharom waterfall** is very popular with Thai picnickers at weekends but its extensive rocky cascades are a little disappointing – and not a patch on Krung Ching. If you need them, four-person bungalows are available at HQ (B300), and it's possible to camp with your own tent.

A trip to **Krung Ching**, a nine-tier waterfall on the north side of the park, makes for a highly satisfying day out, with a mostly paved nature trail taking you through dense, steamy jungle to the most beautiful, third tier. The easiest way to **get there** from Nakhon with your own transport is to head north on Highway 401 towards Surat Thani, turning west at Tha Sala onto Highway 4140, then north again at Ban Nopphitam onto Highway 4186, before heading south from Ban Huai Phan on Highway 4188, the spur road to Ban Phitham and the Krung Ching park office, a total journey of about 70km. Songthaews will get you from Nakhon to Ban Huai Phan in about an hour, but you'd then have to hitch the last 13km. Four-person bungalows are available at the park office (B300), as well as tents (B100); camping is free if you bring your own. There's a sporadically open canteen, and an informal shop selling snacks and drinks.

The shady four-kilometre **trail** to the dramatic main fall is very steep in parts, so you should allow four hours at least there and back. On the way you'll pass giant ferns, including a variety known as *maha sadam*, the largest fern in the world, gnarled banyan trees, forests of mangosteen and beautiful, thick stands of bamboo. You're bound to see beautifully coloured birds and insects, but you may well only hear macaques and other mammals. At the end, a long, stepped descent brings you down to a perfectly positioned wooden platform with fantastic views of the forty-metre fall; here you can see how, shrouded in thick spray, it earns its Thai name, Naan Fon Saen Ha, meaning "heavy rain".

Sichon

The coast north from Nakhon is dotted with small, Thai-orientated beach resorts, none of which can match the Ko Samui archipelago, lurking in the Gulf beyond, for looks or facilities. However, if you're searching for a quiet, low-key antidote to Samui's Western-style commercialism, the most interesting of these resorts, **SICHON**, might be just the place for you.

Buses and share taxis make the 65-kilometre journey north from Nakhon along the Surat Thani road to Talat Sichon, as the town's unpromising modern centre, with a few facilities such as banks and plenty of motorcycle taxis, is known. This half-hearted built-up area sprawls lazily eastwards for 3km to Pak Nam Sichon, a lively and scenic fishing port at the mouth of the eponymous river. Here, when they're not fishing in the bay, brightly coloured boats of all sizes draw up at the docks, backed by low-slung traditional wooden shophouses, the angular hills around Khanom beyond and, in the far distance, Ko Samui. About 1km south of the river mouth **Hat Sichon** (aka Hat Hin Ngarm) begins, a pretty crescent bay of shelving white sand, ending in a tree-tufted, rocky promontory. The beach is home to the best-value accommodation option in the area, *Prasarnsuk Villa* (☎075/335561–2, ℱ335562; ❸–❼), a neatly organized, welcoming place with a good, popular restaurant that stretches to a few tables and umbrellas on the beach. Amid spacious lawns, trees and flowers, bungalows range from decent, fan-cooled, en-suite affairs with verandas to "VIP" suites with air-con, hot water and TV. The next beach south, **Hat Piti**, is not quite so attractive, a long, straight, deserted stretch of white sand backed by palm trees. But if you want a few more facilities, this is where to come: *Piti Resort* (☎ or ℱ075/335301–4; ❼), 2km south of *Prasarnsuk*, can offer a small swimming pool, an entertainment club and a tastefully designed beachside restaurant, as well as hot water, air-con and cable TV in all bungalows.

Travel details

Trains

Cha-am to: Bangkok (12 daily; 3hr 10min–3hr 50min); Chumphon (10 daily; 4–5hr); Hua Hin (11 daily; 25min); Surat Thani (7 daily; 7hr 10min–8hr 25min).

Chumphon to: Bangkok (12 daily; 7hr–9hr 30min); Hua Hin (12 daily; 3hr 30min–5hr); Surat Thani (10 daily; 2hr 15min–4hr).

Nakhon Si Thammarat to: Bangkok (2 daily; 15hr).

Hua Hin to: Bangkok (12 daily; 15hr); Chumphon (10 daily; 3hr 30min–5hr 20min); Surat Thani (10 daily; 5hr 40min–8hr).

Phetchaburi to: Bangkok (8 daily; 2hr 45min–3hr 45min); Cha-am (12 daily; 35min); Chumphon (10 daily; 4hr 30min–6hr 30min); Hua Hin (12 daily; 1hr) Surat Thani (9 daily; 6hr 45min–9hr).

Surat Thani to: Bangkok (10 daily; 9–12hr); Butterworth (Malaysia; 1 daily; 11hr); Hat Yai (5 daily; 4–5hr); Nakhon Si Thammarat (2 daily; 3hr 30min), Phatthalung (5 daily; 3–4hr); Sungai Kolok (2 daily; 9hr); Trang (2 daily; 4hr); Yala (4 daily; 6–8hr).

Buses

Cha-am to: Bangkok (every 40min; 2hr 45min–3hr 15min); Chumphon (every 2hr; 4hr 10min–5hr 10min); Hua Hin (every 30min; 35min), Phetchaburi (every 30 min; 50min).

Chumphon to: Bangkok (12 daily; 6hr 30min–9hr); Hat Yai (4 daily; 7hr 30min); Hua Hin (every 40min; 3hr 30min–4hr 30min); Phuket (3 daily; 7hr); Ranong (hourly; 2hr); Surat Thani (every 30min; 2hr 45min).

Hua Hin to: Bangkok (every 40min; 3hr 30min); Cha-am (every 30min; 35min); Chumphon (every 40min; 3hr 30min–4hr 30min); Phetchaburi (every 30min; 1hr 30min); Pranburi (every 20min; 40min).

Ko Samui to: Bangkok (Southern Terminal; 3 daily; 15hr).

Nakhon Si Thammarat to: Bangkok (Southern Terminal; 10 daily; 12hr); Hat Yai (every 30min; 3hr); Ko Samui (1 daily; 5hr); Krabi (5 daily; 3hr); Phatthalung (every 30min; 3hr); Phuket (every 30min; 6–7hr); Songkhla (every 30min; 3hr); Surat Thani (every 20min; 3hr); Trang (1 daily; 3hr).

Phetchaburi to: Bangkok (every 30min; 2hr); Cha-am (every 30 min; 50min); Chumphon (about every 2hr; 5hr–6hr); Hua Hin (every 30 min; 1hr 30min).

Surat Thani to: Bangkok (Southern Terminal; 7 daily; 11hr); Chaiya (hourly; 1hr); Chumphon (every 30min; 2hr 45min); Hat Yai (9 daily; 5hr–6hr 15min); Krabi (hourly; 4hr); Nakhon Si Thammarat (every 20min; 3hr); Narathiwat (2 daily; 7hr); Phuket (20 daily; 4hr 30min–6hr); Phunphin (every 10min; 30min); Ranong (17 daily; 4hr); Trang (2 daily; 3hr).

Ferries

Chumphon to: Ko Tao (3 daily; 1hr 40min–6hr).

Don Sak to: Ko Samui (7 daily; 1hr 30min); Ko Pha Ngan (2 daily; 2hr 30min).

Khanom to: Ko Samui (4 daily; 1hr 30min).

Ko Pha Ngan to: Ko Samui (8 daily; 45min–1hr); Ko Tao (5 daily; 50min–3hr).

Surat Thani to: Ko Pha Ngan (1 nightly; 7hr); Ko Samui (1 nightly; 7hr).

Tha Thong to: Ko Pha Ngan (1 daily; 4hr); Ko Samui (1 daily; 2hr 30min).

Flights

Hua Hin to: Bangkok (1 daily; 30min); Ko Samui (1 daily; 1hr).

Ko Samui to: Bangkok (12–14 daily; 1hr 20min); Krabi (1 daily; 40min); Phuket (2 daily; 50min); Singapore (1 daily; 1hr 20min); U-Tapao, near Pattaya (1 daily; 1hr).

Nakhon Si Thammarat to: Bangkok (1–2 daily; 1hr 15min).

Surat Thani to: Bangkok (2 daily; 1hr 10min).

Southern Thailand:
the Andaman coast

CHAPTER 7

Highlights

* **Khao Sok National Park** – Sleep in a tree-house and wake to the sound of hooting gibbons. **p.625**

* **Ko Similan** – Remote chain of islands with some of the best diving in the world. **p.633**

* **Reefs and wrecks** – Dive Thailand's finest underwater sights from Phuket (**p.638**), Ao Nang (**p.681**) or Ko Phi Phi (**p.688**).

* **The Vegetarian Festival** – Awesome public acts of self-mortification on parade in Phuket. **p.643**

* **Northwest Phuket** – Quiet, affordable beaches at Hat Mai Khao (**p.645**), Hat Nai Thon (**p.649**) and Hat Kamala. **p.650**

* **Sea-canoeing along the Krabi coastline** – The perfect way to explore the region's myriad mangrove swamps and secret lagoons. **p.677**

* **Rock-climbing on Laem Phra Nang** – Get a bird's eye view of fabulous coastal scenery. **p.679**

* **Ao Phra-Ae** – Ko Lanta's loveliest white-sand beach. **p.702**

* **Ko Jum** – Tiny island where there's nothing to do but chill out. **p.705**

Southern Thailand: the Andaman coast

A s Highway 4 switches from the east flank of the Thailand peninsula to the **Andaman coast** it enters a markedly different country: nourished by rain nearly all the year round, the vegetation down here is lushly tropical, with forests reaching up to 80m in height, and massive rubber and coconut plantations replacing the rice and sugar-cane fields of central Thailand. In this region's heartland the drama of the landscape is enhanced by sheer limestone crags, topographical hallmarks that spike every horizon and make for stunning views from the road. Even more spectacular – and the main crowd-puller – is the Andaman Sea itself: translucent turquoise and so clear in some places that you can see to a depth of 30m, it harbours the country's largest **coral reefs** and is far and away the top diving area in Thailand.

Unlike the Gulf coast, the Andaman coast is hit by the **southwest monsoon** from May to October, when the rain and high seas render some of the outer islands inaccessible. However, conditions aren't generally severe enough to ruin a holiday on the other islands, while the occasional mainland cloudburst is offset by the advantages of notably less expensive and crowded accommodation.

Accommodation prices

Throughout this guide, guest houses, hotels and bungalows have been categorized according to the price codes given below. These categories represent the minimum you can expect to pay in the high season (roughly July, Aug & Nov–Feb) for a double room. If travelling on your own, expect to pay anything between sixty and one hundred percent of the rates quoted for a double room. Wherever a price range is indicated, this means that the establishment offers rooms with varying facilities – as explained in the write-up. Wherever an establishment also offers dormitory beds, the prices of these beds are given in the text, instead of being indicated by price code.

Remember that the top-whack hotels will add seven percent tax and a ten percent service charge to your bill – the price codes below are based on net rates after taxes have been added.

❶ under B150	❹ B400–600	❼ B1200–1800
❷ B150–250	❺ B600–900	❽ B1800–3000
❸ B250–400	❻ B900–1200	❾ B3000+

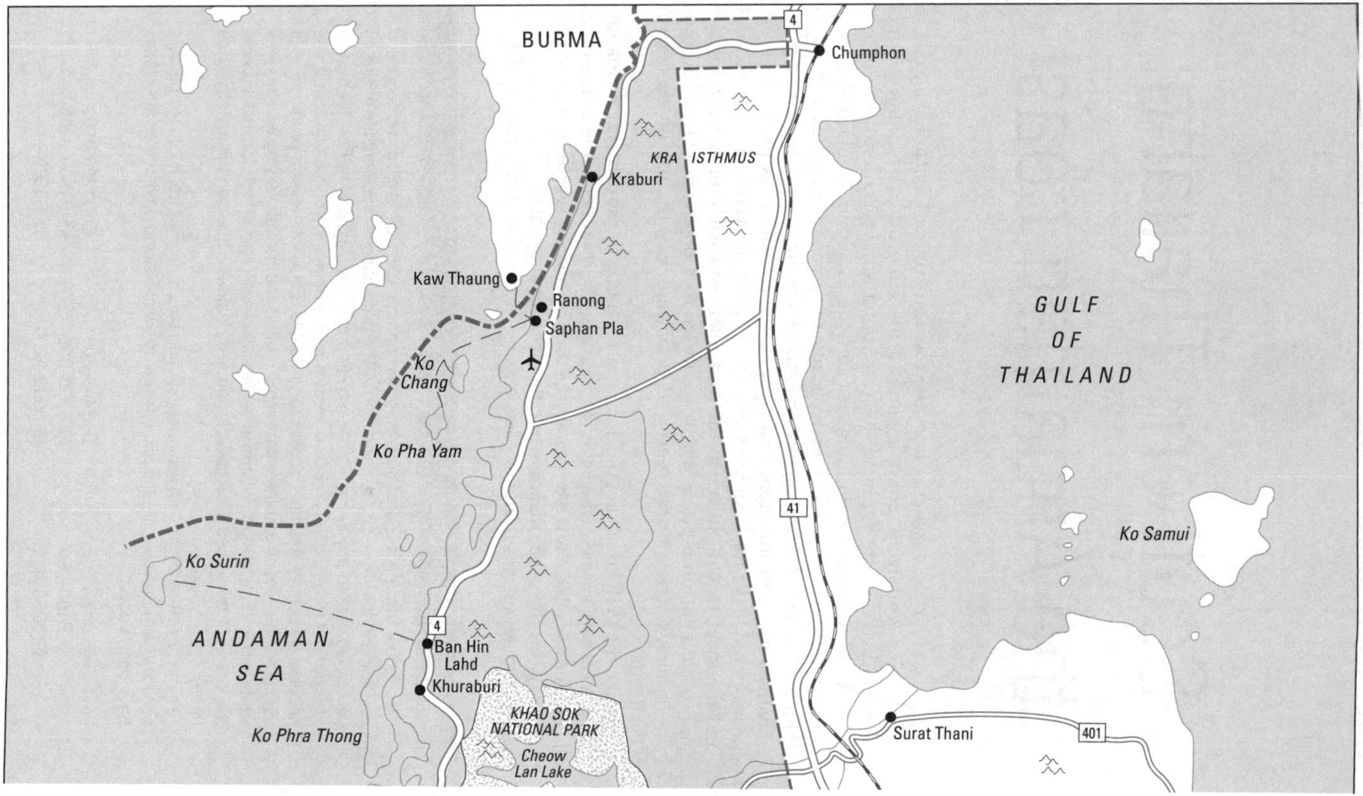
BURMA
Chumphon
4
KRA ISTHMUS
Kraburi
Kaw Thaung
Ranong
Saphan Pla
Ko Chang
Ko Pha Yam
GULF OF THAILAND
41
Ko Samui
Ko Surin
ANDAMAN SEA
4
Ban Hin Lahd
Khuraburi
KHAO SOK NATIONAL PARK
Cheow Lan Lake
Ko Phra Thong
Surat Thani
401

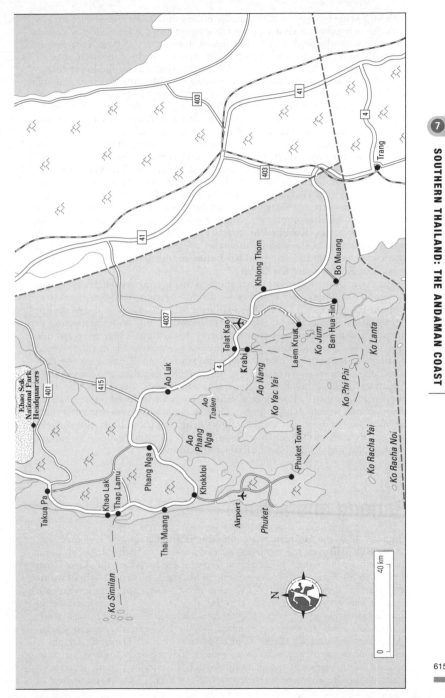

Although some bungalows at the smaller resorts shut down entirely during low season, nearly every beach detailed in this chapter keeps at least one place open.

Eager to hit the high-profile beaches of Phuket and Krabi, most people either fly over the first three-hundred-kilometre stretch of the west coast or pass through it on an overnight bus, thereby missing out on the lushly forested hills of **Ranong** province and bypassing several gems: the tiny and still idyllic island of **Ko Chang** (not to be confused with its larger, more famous namesake off the east coast); the **Ko Surin** and **Ko Similan** island chains, whose reefs rate alongside the Maldives and the Great Barrier Reef; the enjoyable **Khao Sok National Park**, where you can stay in a treehouse beneath the shadows of looming limestone outcrops; and the mid-market resort of **Khao Lak**, which hugs the rugged mainland coast on the edge of Khao Lak National Park. Tourism begins in earnest on **Phuket**, Thailand's largest island and the best place to learn to dive. The high-rises and consumerist gloss that characterize much of Phuket don't appeal to everyone, however, and many travellers opt instead for the slightly less mainstream but very popular beaches around the former fishing village of **Krabi**. Nearby the stunningly beautiful **Ko Phi Phi** attracts a lot of attention considering its size, and is beginning to crack under the strain, so many travellers have moved on again, searching out hideaways on **Ko Lanta** and bringing custom to the tiny retreats of **Ko Jum** and **Ko Bubu**.

Getting to Andaman coast destinations is made easy by Highway 4, also known as the Phetkasem Highway – and usually called Thanon Phetkasem when it passes through towns. The road runs from Bangkok to the Malaysian border, and frequent air-con and ordinary **buses** ply this route, connecting all major – and most minor – mainland tourist destinations. There is no rail line down the Andaman coast, but as the numerous cross-peninsula roads are served by frequent buses, many travellers take the **train** from Bangkok to the Gulf coast, enjoy the region's splendours for a while and then nip over to the Andaman coast by bus before proceeding southwards. **Ferries** to the most popular islands usually leave several times a day (with reduced services during the monsoon season), but for more remote destinations you may have to charter your own or wait for islanders' trading boats to pick you up. Alternatively, you can **fly** direct to the Andaman coast: there's a busy international airport on Phuket, plus useful local ones in Krabi and Ranong.

Ranong and around

Highway 4 hits the Andaman coast at **Kraburi**, where a signpost welcomes you to the **Kra Isthmus**, the narrowest part of peninsular Thailand. At this point just 22km separates the Gulf of Thailand from the inlet where the River Chan flows into the Andaman Sea, west of which lies the southernmost tip of mainland Burma, **Kaw Thaung** (aka Victoria Point). Ever since the seventeenth century, Thai governments and foreign investors have been keenly interested in this slender strip of land, envisaging the creation of an Asian Suez canal which would cut some 1500km off shipping routes between the Indian Ocean (Andaman Sea) and the South China Sea (the Gulf of Thailand). Despite a number of detailed proposals, no agreement has yet been reached, not least because of the political implications of such a waterway: quite apart from accentuating the divide between prosperous southern Thailand and the rest of the country, it would vastly reduce Singapore's role in the international shipping industry.

Seventy kilometres south of the isthmus, the channel widens out at the provincial capital of **Ranong**, which thrives on its proximity to Burma. Thai tourists have been coming here for years, to savour the health-giving properties of the local spring water, but foreign holidaymakers have only recently discovered that Ranong is a useful departure-point for the delightful nearby islands of **Ko Chang** and **Ko Pha Yam**. The other reason to stop off in Ranong is to make a day-trip to the Burmese town of Kaw Thaung and acquire a new thirty-day Thai tourist visa into the bargain – an option that's popular with Phuket expats.

Ranong is the capital of Thailand's wettest province, which soaks up over 5000mm of rain every year – a fact you'll undoubtedly experience first-hand if you linger in the region. The landscape to the south of Ranong town is particularly lush, and any journey along Highway 4 will whizz you between densely forested hills to the east and mangrove swamps, rubber plantations and casuarina groves to the west; much of this coastal strip is preserved as **Laem Son National Park**. The hillsides are streaked with waterfalls which are, of course, seen to their best advantage during the rainy season, though the effect is striking at almost any time of year.

The Town

Despite – or perhaps because – it's the wettest town in the whole country, **RANONG** has an enjoyable buzz and enthusiastic energy about it, fuelled in great part by the apparently amiable mix of Burmese, Thai, Chinese and Malay inhabitants. Many town-centre businesses promote their wares in curly Burmese script, and there's lots of pleasure to be had from simply enjoying the different faces and styles of dress. As with most border areas, however, there's also a flourishing illegal trade operating out of Ranong – in amphetamines, guns and labour apparently – though the closest you're likely to get to these activities is reading about them in the *Bangkok Post*.

The **geothermal springs** so favoured by Thai tourists are the focus of diminutive Raksawarin Park just off Thanon Phetkasem, ten minutes' walk north of the bus terminal or 1km southeast of the town centre – take songthaew #2 from the central Thanon Ruangrat or a motorbike taxi. You can't submerge yourself in the water here, but you can buy eggs to boil in the sulphurous 65°C water, or paddle in the cooler pools that have been siphoned off from the main springs. Picnickers throng here at weekends, but to properly appreciate the springs you need to soak in them: *Jansom Thara Hotel*, five minutes' walk away, channels the mineral waters into its public bath (B100 for non-guests).

If you haven't had already had enough of water features, you could make a trip out of town to the impressive **Nam Tok Ngao**, an enormous waterfall 12km south of Ranong, which cascades almost all the way down the eastern hillside in full view of Highway 4. Any south-bound bus will drop you there.

Practicalities

Bangkok Airways operates four weekly **flights** between Bangkok and Ranong, which arrive at the **airport** 20km south of Ranong on Highway 4; taxis meet the flights, or you can walk out of the airport on to Highway 4 and flag down any north-bound bus. Air tickets can be bought from the tours desk at the

Jansom Thara hotel (see below). All west-coast buses travelling between Bangkok or Chumphon and Takua Pa, Phuket or Krabi stop briefly at Ranong's **bus station** on Highway 4 (Thanon Phetkasem), 1500m southeast of the centre; coming from Surat Thani and Khao Sok, you'll probably need to change buses at Takua Pa. Several city **songthaews** serve Ranong bus station, including one that runs to the hotels, day market and nearby songthaew depot on Thanon Ruangrat, and another that shuttles between the bus station and the port area at Saphan Pla 5km to the southwest, where you pick up boats to Kaw Thaung in Burma and to Ko Chang and Ko Pha Yam; another songthaew runs direct from the market on Thanon Ruangrat to the Saphan Pla port area. Many songthaews have their destinations written in English on the side, and most charge B7–10 per ride. There is no official **tourist information** in town, but several hotels carry detailed advertisements for bungalows on Ko Chang and Ko Pha Yam, and you can book some island bungalows through the *Chaong Thong* restaurant (see opposite), whose English-speaking staff are very helpful.

Marking the town centre, Thanon Ruangrat is where you'll find the handful of budget hotels and traveller-oriented restaurants, as well as the day and night **markets**, a small **post office** (at the northern end), half a dozen places offering **internet access** (most of them north of the *Sin Tawee* hotel), and at the southern end, a Bangkok Bank with an ATM and an **exchange** counter. Thanon Ruangrat runs approximately northwest–southeast and at its southern end is crossed by Thanon Tha Muang, where the CAT **international phone office** (Mon–Fri 8am–8pm, Sat & Sun 8.30am–4.30pm), also with internet access, is located about 200m to the east of the Ruangrat junction. English-language books and newspapers are stocked at the **bookstore** diagonally across the road from the *Chaong Thong*. The Thonburi-Ranong **hospital** (℡077/834214) is at 41/142 Thanon Tha Muang. Ranong's **immigration office** is 5km out of town in Saphan Pla; for details on how to extend or renew your visa here see pp.619–620.

Accommodation

Most travellers linger in Ranong for just one night, and the town's budget Thai-Chinese **hotels** don't exactly encourage you to prolong your stay. The most popular is the decidedly average *Sin Tawee* at 81/1 Thanon Ruangrat (℡077/811213; ❷–❸), which offers cheap and simple en-suite fan and air-con rooms about 100m north of the day market and songthaew depot. Equally uninspired, but decent enough, the *Asia Hotel* (℡077/811113; ❷–❺) is at 39/9 Thanon Ruangrat, about 70m south of the market, and easily recognized by its pale blue colour scheme inside and out; staff speak English, the rooms are large, and you can choose between fan or air-con rooms. About 600m north up Thanon Ruangrat from the market, across from the branch post office, the *Boat Restaurant* rents out a few rooms at cheap prices (❷). With its mineral baths, jacuzzis and range of upmarket rooms, *Jansom Thara Hotel* (℡077/811510, ℻821821; ❻–❾), located about 1200m east of the town centre, near the hot springs and bus station at 2/10 Thanon Phetkasem, used to be the town's best accommodation; it's now been superseded by the more modern chain hotel the *Royal Princess*, slightly more centrally located off the west arm of Thanon Tha Muang (℡077/835240, ℻835238, Ⓦwww.royalprincess.com; ❽), which also has jacuzzis with spa water, and a swimming pool.

Eating and drinking

Ranong's ethnic diversity ensures an ample range of **eating** options, and a stroll up Thanon Ruangrat will take you past Muslim foodstalls and Chinese pastry shops as well as a small but typically Thai night market. Deservedly the most popular travellers' restaurant is *Chaong Thong*, 8–10 Thanon Ruangrat (Mon–Sat 6am–9.30pm), across from the *Asia Hotel* and south a bit, next to the Bangkok Bank; here you can choose from a long and varied selection of inexpensive dishes that includes Spanish omelette, shrimp curry and lemon-grass tea, as well as lots of veggie options and hearty breakfasts. About 100m north of the *Sin Tawee* hotel, the very cheap *Veetiang* boasts a long menu covering all manner of seafood cooked to myriad Thai and Chinese recipes, as well as standard over-rice dishes. Another 200m north up Thanon Ruangrat, across from the post office and next to the cinema, a small café serves vegetarian food every day until 6pm. A few metres north of the veggie place, at 301 Thanon Ruangrat, the *Sir Dol Pub* opens nightly at 7pm for pool, live music, beer and snacks.

Kaw Thaung (Ko Song)

The southernmost tip of Burma – known as Kaw Thaung in Burmese, Ko Song in Thai, and Victoria Point when it was a British colony – lies just a few kilometres west of Ranong across the River Chan estuary, and is easily reached from the Thai side of the border. So long as you follow the procedures detailed below, it's quite straightforward for foreign tourists to **enter Burma** at this point, and nipping across the border and back is a fairly popular way of getting a new thirty-day Thai tourist visa, but if you already have a sixty-day visa and are looking for another month, it's faster and a little cheaper (B500 plus two photos) to extend your existing visa at the Thai immigration office in Saphan Pla (see below) and avoid going into Burma at all – which also means you are not giving your money to the Burmese military regime.

Having said that, although there's nothing much to do in **KAW THAUNG** itself, it's an enjoyable focus for a trip out of Ranong, and sufficiently different from Thai towns to merit an hour or two's visit. Alighting at the quay, the market and tiny town centre lie before you, while over to your right, about twenty minutes' walk away, you can see an eye-catching hilltop pagoda, surmounted by a huge reclining Buddha and a ring of smaller ones. Once you've explored the covered market behind the quay and picked your way through the piles of tin trunks and sacks of rice that crowd the surrounding streets, it's fun to take a coffee break in one of the typically Burmese quayside pastry shops before negotiating a ride in a boat back to Saphan Pla; Thai money is perfectly acceptable in Kaw Thaung. There are also a couple of seafood restaurants on the quay, as well as the decent enough *Honey Bee Hotel* (**❺**) should you want to stay over.

Practicalities

Longtail boats to Kaw Thaung leave from **SAPHAN PLA**, Ranong's fishing port and harbour, which is about 5km southwest of the town centre and served by regular songthaews from Ranong's Thanon Ruangrat and bus station (20min; B7). All non-Thais must first get a Thai exit stamp before boarding a boat to Kaw Thaung, so get out of the songthaew at the Thai **immigration office** (daily 8.30am–4.30pm) on the outskirts of Saphan Pla: the office is clearly signed on the right, across the road from the Thai Farmers Bank. Boat boys usually hover outside the office to try and secure your custom, so once you've got your stamp you can either accompany them (in which case you'll probably end up chartering the boat) or just continue walking down the road for about fifteen minutes until you reach the PTT petrol station, where you should turn down to the right to find a quayside thick with longtails. There's another small quay a few hundred metres further up the quayside, but the PTT one is busier.

Longtails leave for Kaw Thaung when they have enough custom: the fare should be B50 per person in an already crowded boat, or B150 one-way to charter the whole boat. The crossing takes about thirty minutes, but the longtails have to stop en route at a tiny island containing the **Burmese immigration** office, where you buy your Burmese visa: US$5 (or B300) for a one-to three-day pass, or US$36 for thirty days. For stays of over a day you also need to change US dollars into Foreign Exchange Certificates (FECs): $50 for two to three days, or $300 for a month's stay. Legally, you are not allowed to travel beyond Kaw Thaung unless you have already bought a proper visa from a Burmese embassy (see p.22) to supplement the Kaw Thaung passes. If you do have a visa, you can fly to Rangoon from the airport 7km north of Kaw Thaung, but road travel from here to Rangoon is currently forbidden to foreigners.

If you're simply making the trip to get a new Thai visa you can take the boat straight back to Saphan Pla from the immigration island, though Kaw Thaung is just a few minutes' boat ride further on. If you do visit Kaw Thaung, when you return to Saphan Pla your boat will stop at the Burmese immigration island to collect your passport; once back on Thai soil you must return to the Thai immigration office to get your new Thai thirty-day tourist visa before catching a songthaew back to Ranong.

Ko Chang

Not to be confused with the much larger island of Ko Chang on Thailand's east coast (see p.439), Ranong's **KO CHANG** is a forested little island about 5km offshore, with less than perfect beaches but a charmingly low-key, friendly and laid-back atmosphere. The beaches are connected by tracks through the trees; there are no cars and only sporadic, self-generated supplies of electricity. With *Eden Bungalows* at one end and *Paradise Bungalows* at the other, you begin to get the picture, which for once doesn't stretch the imagination too far. The pace of life on Ko Chang is very slow, the emphasis strongly on kicking back and chilling out – bring your own hammock and you'll fit right in.

Many of the islanders live in the small **village** behind the long pier that juts out from the middle of Ao Yai, just north of the shallow khlong. Partially hidden amongst the trees beside the beach is the village wat and monks' quarters, with a sign that asks tourists to dress modestly when in the area and not to swim or sunbathe in front of it. The 800-metre-long stretch of **beach** that runs north from the pier is the most attractive on the island, with yellow and grey sand that swirls together in leopardskin-like patterns and has a texture so soft that it squeaks. This part of the beach is nice and wide even at high tide, and especially popular with kids. The beach that runs south of the pier and the khlong is less impressive: it's very narrow at high tide, but when the water goes out you have to walk a longish distance to find any depth. Southern Ao Yai, which begins just beyond the rocky divide occupied by *Ko Chang Resort*, has greyish sand but is fine for swimming.

Nearly all the bungalows on Ko Chang **close** down from June through October when the island is subjected to very heavy rain; many bungalow staff relocate to the mainland for this period, so you should phone ahead if you want to stay here then.

Practicalities

Longtail **boats** to Ko Chang leave from Ranong's port area, **Saphan Pla** (as do boats to Ko Pha Yam, see p.622), which is about 5km southwest of the town centre and served by regular **songthaews** from Thanon Ruangrat and the bus station (20min; B7). When the songthaew stops at the toll-booth entry to Saphan Pla you'll see a PTT petrol station to the right (which is the landmark for boats to Kaw Thaung in Burma) and a small soi on the left; turn down the left-hand soi (there are a couple of faded Ko Chang bungalow signs on the wall here) and follow it as it twists its way down to the water about 400m further on. At the waterfront you'll see a couple of small restaurants, including the Burmese-run *Quick Stop*, where you can find out when the next boat to the island is due to depart (the current timetable is also available at *Chaong Thong* restaurant in Ranong) and while away the time over a cup of Burmese tea.

At time of writing there was one scheduled daily boat **departure** at 10am, and usually another one in the early afternoon, but if there are more than six in your party, you can probably charter your own boat almost immediately; the journey takes about an hour and costs B100 per person. Tell the boatman which bungalow you want and he'll drop you as close as possible (though you'll probably have to wade in); if you haven't decided on one, you won't have to walk for long from wherever you get dropped. Very few boats travel to Ko Chang during the rainy months of June through October, and those that do drop passengers on Ko Chang's east coast, a three-kilometre walk from Ao Yai. During the tourist season, there's at least one boat a day from Ko Chang **back to Saphan Pla**, generally in the morning between about 7am and 9am – ask at your bungalows the day before. Any songthaew will take you back from Saphan Pla to Ranong, but if you want to go directly to the bus station be sure to catch a blue-coloured one.

To date there is no commercial activity at all on Ko Chang, save for one small beach **stall** at *Golden Bee* selling a few basic necessities, and a dive operator who runs his business from a hut just north of *Cashew Resort*. **Overseas phone calls** can be made at *Golden Bee* and *Cashew Resort*.

Accommodation

Most of the **bungalow** operations are simple bamboo affairs, comprising just a dozen huts and a small restaurant each. Though they nearly all have their own generators, it's a good idea to bring a torch as many bungalow managers bow to customers' preference to stick to candles and paraffin lamps.

Cashew Resort, north of the pier on central Ao Yai ⊕01/229 6667. The longest-running set of bungalows on the island, and also the largest, this place is located among the cashew trees and has simple wooden huts with shared bathrooms, as well as more solid en-suite versions with glass windows. Has more of a busy atmosphere than the other bungalows on Ao Yai. ❶–❷

Chang Tong, south of the pier on central Ao Yai ⊕077/833820. Simple, very clean wood and bamboo bungalows, well spaced in two rows. All have mosquito nets and some have bathrooms. ❶–❷

Eden Bungalows, north of the pier on central Ao Yai. Widely spaced and nicely secluded bungalows amongst the trees at the far north end of Ao Yai. ❶–❷

Full Moon, southern Ao Yai. Sturdy wooden bungalows along the beachfront, with or without private bathroom. ❶–❷

Golden Bee, south of the pier on central Ao Yai ⊕077/844485. Ultra-simple huts set among the palm trees near the pier. All huts have a mattress on the floor, and some have attached bathrooms. ❶–❷

Hornbill, north around two headlands from Ao Yai. Simple, unobtrusive bungalows built amongst the trees behind their own little gold-sand bay, just a few minutes' walk north of *Ko Chang Contex*, and within easy reach of Ao Yai. Lives up to its name, as majestic black and white hornbills are a common sight here. ❶–❷

Ko Chang Contex, north around the headland from Ao Yai. Located in its own peaceful little bay a short walk north of Ao Yai, the handful of huts here is scattered across the rocks above the beach, with just the resident black and white hornbills for company. ❶–❷

Ko Chang Resort, southern Ao Yai ⒺE sound_of_sea@lycos.com. Occupying a fabulous spot high on the rocks, the newer and sturdier en-suite wooden bungalows here have fine sea views from their balconies and are simply but thoughtfully designed inside. The older ones share bathrooms. There's a stylish restaurant with low tables, cushions and a similarly engaging panorama, and the swimmable beach is just a couple of minutes' scramble to the south. ❷

Lae Tawan, south around the headland from southern Ao Yai. Basic huts in their own small bay, with or without bathroom. Twenty minutes' walk from Ao Yai, with great sunset views. ❶–❷

Paradise, southern Ao Yai. Very popular, laid-back place, with some huts overlooking the rocks and others ranged up the bank at the back, looking down onto the beach. Some are en suite. ❶–❷

Sabay Jai, south of the pier on central Ao Yai. Friendly little place with a restaurant and just eight bungalows, some semi-detached, others freestanding and en-suite. ❶–❷

Sunset Bungalows, north of the pier on central Ao Yai. Set in a rather dark grove of cashew-nut trees on the edge of the beach, comprising decent huts with or without attached bathrooms. ❶–❷

Tadang Bay, southern Ao Yai. Set up on the headland at the far southern end of Ao Yai, the huts here enjoy nice long views of the whole bay. The price depends on the size of the hut; all share bathrooms. ❶

Ko Pha Yam

The tiny island of **KO PHA YAM** offers fine white-sand beaches and coral reefs and is home to around a hundred islanders, most of whom make a living by growing cashew nuts. It's a touch more developed than Ko Chang, having vehicle-worthy tracks and a few vehicles that use them, but it's still a peaceful place. Most islanders live in the fishing village on the northeast coast, where there's a pier and a temple as well as a couple of foodstalls and a phone office. From November through May there's at least one **boat** a day from Ranong's port area, Saphan Pla, to Ko Pha Yam, departing at 2pm and taking two hours to reach the east coast (B100) or about three hours for west-coast destinations (B150); see p.619 for details of how to get to the Saphan Pla pier from Ranong. The boat returns from the island's west coast at 7am, passing the east coast at about 8am. Boats are less regular during the rainy season, from June through October, and many bungalows close up, so call ahead during this period to check first and arrange transport.

The nicest beach on the island is the 2.5-kilometre-long **Ao Yai** on the southwest coast, where the sand is soft and blindingly white and there's snorkelling off the little rocky outcrop at the end of the bay. The sunsets are quite spectacular here too. Towards the southern end of the beach, *Ao Yai Bungalows* (☎077/821753; ❷) has a handful of nice wooden bungalows with attached bathrooms and offers discounts for stays of a week or more; it's open year-round. Nearby *Bamboo* (☎01/273 3437; ❷) has huts of a similar standard, also en suite. Further up on the northwest coast, on **Ko Kwai** beach, *Vijit* (☎077/834082; ❷) offers clean wooden en-suite bungalows set in a garden and surrounded by trees; you can walk from here to the village on the east coast in about 45 minutes. Across on the east coast, the dozen basic bungalows of *Ko Pha Yam Resort* (☎077/812297; ❸–❺) are scattered among a cashew plantation on the edge of the beach.

7

Ko Surin and around

The coastal town of **Khuraburi**, 110km south of Ranong on Highway 4, is the closest (though not necessarily the most convenient) departure point for the magnificent national park island chain of **Ko Surin**, a group of five small islands around 60km offshore, just inside Thai waters. Also accessible from Khuraburi is the island of **Ko Phra Thong**, said to be exceptionally rewarding for birdwatching and boasting a popular eco-resort.

Ko Surin

The spectacular shallow reefs around **KO SURIN** offer some of the best snorkelling and diving on the Andaman coast. The most beautiful and easily explored of the reefs are those surrounding the two main islands in the group, Ko Surin Nua (north) and Ko Surin Tai (south), which are separated only by a narrow channel. **SURIN NUA**, slightly the larger at about 5km across, holds the national park headquarters, visitor centre and park bungalows on its southwest coast. The water is so clear here, and the reefs so close to the surface, that you can make out a forest of sea anemones while sitting in a boat just 10m from the park headquarters' beach. Visibility off the east and west coasts of both islands stretches to a depth of 40m.

Across the channel, **SURIN TAI** is the long-established home of a community of *chao ley* (see p.624) who divide their time between boat-building and fishing. Every April, as part of the Songkhran New Year festivities, hundreds of *chao ley* from nearby islands (including those in Burmese waters) congregate here to celebrate with a ceremony involving, among other rites, the release into the sea of several hundred turtles, which are a symbol of longevity and especially precious to Thai and Chinese people.

Practicalities

Because the islands are so far out at sea, Ko Surin is effectively out of bounds during the monsoon season, when the sixty-kilometre trip becomes a potentially suicidal undertaking. During the rest of the year, getting to Ko Surin can be both time-consuming and expensive. The easiest way to reach the islands is to join an organized live-aboard **dive trip** with one of the dive operators in Khao Lak (see box on p.63) or Phuket (see box on p.638), which usually also feature other remote reefs such as Richelieu Rock or the Burma Banks, and cost from B16,000–20,000 for four days all inclusive with at least eight dives.

If you're determined to see the islands independently, you could try to catch one of the **national park boats** that sail at least once a week from November through April from the Khuraburi pier at Ban Hin Lad, about 8km north of Khuraburi town. To get to the pier, get off the bus at kilometre-stone 110 on Highway 4 (ask the driver for Ko Surin) and then take a motorcycle taxi down to the pier. The boats take from three to five hours and cost B1000 return; ask at the national park office near the pier-head (℡076/491378) for details. It's also possible to charter your own fishing boat from the pier for around B6000 a day (journey time 4–5hr): unless you speak fluent Thai the best way to arrange this is by calling the national park office. Once you're on the islands, you can **charter a longtail** to explore the coasts: a four-hour cruise is priced at around B500.

Sometimes called sea gypsies, the **chao ley** or *chao nam* ("people of the sea" or "water people") have been living off the seas around the west coast of the Malay peninsula for hundreds of years. Some still pursue a traditional nomadic existence, living in self-contained houseboats known as **kabang**, but many have now made permanent homes in Andaman coast settlements in Thailand and Malaysia.

Dark-skinned and sometimes with an auburn tinge to their hair, the sea gypsies are thought to be Austronesian or Malay in **origin**, and their migration probably first started west and then north from the Riau-Lingga archipelago, which lies between Singapore and Sumatra. It's estimated that around five thousand *chao ley* now live off the coasts of the Andaman Sea, divided into five groups, with distinct lifestyles and dialects.

Of the different groups, the **Urak Lawoy**, who have settled on Ko Lipe in Ko Tarutao National Park (see p.729) and in Phuket (see p.637), are the most integrated into Thai society. They are known as *Mai Thai*, or "New Thai", and many have found work on coconut plantations or as fishermen. Other groups continue in the more traditional *chao ley* **occupations** of hunting for pearls and sea shells on the ocean floor, attaching stones to their waists to dive to depths of 60m with only an air-hose connecting them to the surface; sometimes they fish in this way too, taking down enormous nets into which they herd the fish as they walk along the sea bed. Their agility and courage make them good birds'-nesters as well (see box on p.695), enabling them to harvest the tiny nests of sea swifts from nooks and crannies hundreds of metres high inside caves along the Andaman coast.

The **Moken** of Thailand's Ko Surin islands and Burma's Mergui archipelago are the most traditional of the *chao ley* communities and still lead remote, itinerant lives. They own no land or property, but are dependent on fresh water and beaches to collect shells and sea slugs to sell to Thai traders. They have extensive knowledge of the plants that grow in the remaining jungles on Thailand's west-coast islands, using eighty different species for food alone, and thirty for medicinal purposes.

The sea gypsies are **animists**, with a strong connection both to the natural spirits of island and sea and to their own ancestral spirits. On some beaches they set up totem poles as a contact point between the spirits, their ancestors and their shaman. The sea gypsies have a rich **musical heritage** too. The Moken do not use any instruments as such, making do with found objects for percussion; the Urak Lawoy on the other hand, due to their closer proximity to the Thai and Malay cultures, are excellent violin- and drum-players. During community entertainments, the male musicians form a semicircle around the old women, who dance and sing about the sea, the jungle and their families. See the discography on p.808 for details of *chao ley* music on CD.

Building a new boat is the ultimate expression of what it is to be a *chao ley*, and every newly married couple has a *kabang* built for them. But the complex art of constructing a seaworthy home from a single tree trunk, and the way of life it represents, is disappearing. In Thailand, where **assimilation** is actively promoted by the government, the truly nomadic flotillas have become increasingly marginalized, and the number of undeveloped islands they can visit unhindered gets smaller year by year. On Phuket, the Urak Lawoy villages have become sightseeing attractions, where busloads of tourists trade cute photo poses for coins and sweets, setting in motion a dangerous cycle of dependency. In Burma, the continued political instability and repression has further restricted their mobility, and there is a real danger of getting arrested and even forced into slave labour – nothing short of hell on earth especially for a people whose lives have always been determined by the waves and the wind.

Accommodation and eating

As boats to the islands tend to leave very early in the morning, you'll probably have to spend at least one night in a **Khuraburi hotel**. The fairly basic *Rungtawan* (❷) is next to the bus stop for the pier, at kilometre-stone 110 on Highway 4, or there are newer and more salubrious bungalows at *Thararin River Hut Resort* (❸–❹) a couple of kilometres out of town. Alternatively, try the attractively designed wooden chalets at *Khuraburi Greenview Resort* (ⓣ & ⓕ 076/421360; ❼–❽) which all have air-con, TV and use of the swimming pool and are located 12km south of Khuraburi, alongside Highway 4.

For accommodation on Ko Surin, you have the choice of renting one of the expensive six-person national park **bungalows** on Surin Nua (B1200, but deals for couples may be negotiable), settling for a dorm bed (B100) in the nearby longhouse or opting for a B100 two-person national park tent. Accommodation gets very booked up at weekends and on public holidays, so it's worth reserving a bed in advance by calling ⓣ 076/491378. Otherwise, you can camp in your own tent in the vicinity of the park buildings. Unless you take your own **food** to the islands, you'll be restricted to the three set meals a day served at the restaurant on Surin Nua for B300 (vegetarian and other special meals can be supplied if requested in advance).

Ko Phra Thong

One kilometre off the Khuraburi coast, **KO PHRA THONG** (Golden Buddha Island) is home to an eco-resort, the *Golden Buddha Beach Resort* (ⓣ 01/230 4744, ⓕ 02/863 1301, ⓔ sandler@mozart.inet.co.th) which, as well as renting out kayaks and running a turtle sanctuary, also hosts yoga retreats. Its bungalows have mosquito nets and open-air bathrooms, and are set among the trees beside the main beach, which is 7km long and blessed with fine white sand. The resort is run by a company called Lost Horizons (ⓦ www.losthorizonsasia.com), which charges B1200 per person per day to stay here, including all meals; they arrange transport from Ranong or Khuraburi if contacted in advance.

Khao Sok National Park

Forty kilometres south of Khuraburi, Highway 4 reaches the junction town of **Takua Pa**. Highway 401, which cuts east from here, is the route taken by most Surat Thani-bound buses from Phuket and Krabi, and it's a spectacular journey across the mountains that stretch the length of the peninsula, a landscape of limestone crags and jungle, scarred only by the road. Most of what you see belongs to **KHAO SOK NATIONAL PARK**, a tiny part of which – entered 40km east of Takua Pa – is set aside for overnight stays. Although the park is an increasingly popular destination for day-trippers from Khao Lak and Phuket, it definitely merits a good 48 hours: waking up to the sound of hooting gibbons and the sight of thick white mist curling around the karst formations is an experience not quickly forgotten, and there are plenty of opportunities for hikes and overnight treks into the jungle.

Access and accommodation

The park entrance is located at kilometre-stone 109, less than an hour by **bus** from Takua Pa, ninety minutes from Khao Lak, or two hours from Surat Thani.

Buses run at least every ninety minutes in both directions; ask to be let off at the park and you'll be met by a knot of competing guest-house staff waiting to give you a free lift to their accommodation, the furthest of which is 3km from the main road. Coming by bus from Bangkok, Hua Hin or Chumphon, take a Surat Thani-bound bus, but ask to be dropped off at the junction with the Takua Pa road, about 20km before Surat Thani, and then change onto a Takua Pa bus. Onward bus connections are frequent and guest-house staff will ferry you back to the main road. Most guest houses also offer a taxi service for a maximum of three people to Khao Lak (B1200), Surat Thani (B1400) and Phuket (B2000).

Accommodation

Despite the area being a national park, a cluster of appealing jungle **guest houses** has grown up along tracks to the south and east of the national park visitor centre and trail-heads: most are simple wood or bamboo huts set peacefully among the trees or beneath the limestone karsts. They all have restaurants and can arrange trekking guides as well. The longest-running and most peaceful guest houses are situated down a side track that branches off the north–south track from the main road to the visitor centre and runs alongside the river; the newer ones are located along the main north–south track. All guest houses serve food, and there are a couple of small restaurants along the main north-south track, as well two tiny minimarkets where you can buy essentials and change money.

Art's Riverview Jungle Lodge, about 800m east along the side track ℗076/421613. Efficiently run place comprising half a dozen wooden cabins (price depends on size and location) and three treehouses in a tropical garden located right next to a good swimming hole. It's popular with backpackers' tour groups, so advance booking is recommended. ❸–❺

Bamboo House, about 150m east along the side track. One of the first guest houses in the park and run by members of the park warden's family, this place offers simple bamboo huts with attached bathroom as well as sturdier but less atmospheric concrete ones. ❶–❺

Bamboo 2, beside the river, on the main track, about 1200m from the main road. Characterless concrete bungalows overlooking the river, though they might be worth the money if you're looking for an insect-proof option. ❸

Freedom House, on the main track, about 1km from the main road ℡ & ℗077/214974, ℡01/979 2765, ℅thaitour_surat@hotmail.com. Australian-managed place comprising a handful of big bamboo houses raised unusually high on stilts, with verandas that look straight into a patch of jungle. Standard simply furnished accommodation, with en-suite bathrooms. ❷

Garden Huts, on the main track, about 900m from the main road. Set well away from the main track

and prettily located beside a small pond surrounded by wild flowers, the half-dozen bungalows here are simple bamboo affairs with attached bathrooms, mosquito nets, fans and electricity, and nice views of the karsts. Run by a friendly, enthusiastic family. ❷

Khao Sok Jungle Huts, on the main track, about 1100m from the main road. Tall bamboo huts on stilts with long views out towards the karsts. Price depends on the size of the hut and on proximity to the track (some are pretty close); they all have attached bathrooms. ❶–❷

Nung House, about 200m east along the side track. Small, friendly place with just nine huts run by the park warden's son and his family. Choose between simple bamboo constructions with en-suite facilities, concrete bungalows, and treehouses. Their restaurant serves good food. ❶–❸

Our Jungle House, on a branch track off the side track ℗076/421706, ℅our_jungle_house@hotmail.com. The most romantically located of Khao Sok's guest houses is set in a secluded riverside spot beneath the limestone cliffs, about fifteen minutes' walk on from *Nung House*, along the left-hand fork in the track. Here you can choose between beautifully situated treehouses, private cabins by the river, and rooms in the main house. All accommodation has its own bathroom, but there's no electricity in the cabins and treehouses, so candles are provided. ❸–❺

Treetops River Huts, on the main track, about 1400m from the main road ☏077/299150, ℗285987. Located beside the river, very close to the visitor centre and trailheads, with a choice of accom- modation ranging from simple bamboo huts with bathrooms through to en-suite wood or stone ones. Comfortable but has a busier feel than many, partly because it's popular with small tour groups. ❷–❺

The park

The B200 national park **entrance fee** (B100 for kids) is payable at the check- point close to the visitor centre and is valid for three days – you'll need to pay this in addition to the fees for any guided treks or tours. Several trails radiate from the park headquarters and visitor centre, some of them more popular and easier to follow than others, but all quite feasible as day-trips. The **visitor cen- tre** (daily 8am–4pm) sells a small sketch map of the park and trails, as well as the recommended **guidebook** to the park, *Waterfalls and Gibbon Calls* by Thom Henley (B250), which includes lots of background information on the flora and fauna of Khao Sok as well as a full description of all the things to look out for on the interpretative trail (see below). If you don't buy the book, you might want to spend a few minutes looking at the exhibition inside the visi- tor centre, which also gives interesting details, in English and Thai, on Khao Sok's highlights.

When choosing your trail, consult the sketch map and the noticeboard at the trailheads, and then check with one of the rangers to make sure it's still acces- sible – rangers sometimes decommission trails if they get eroded or overgrown, or if animals and birds in the vicinity need to be shielded from too much human contact. Also, be prepared to remain alert to the course of your trail, as broken trail markers are now rarely replaced because of cuts to the park's budg- et. Take plenty of water as Khao Sok is notoriously sticky and humid.

Eight of the park's nine current **trails** follow the same route for the first 5km. This route heads directly west of the park headquarters and follows the course of the Sok river; it is clearly signed as leading to trails #1–8. The first 3.5km of the route is marked with numbered signposts which refer to the **interpreta- tive trail** described in *Waterfalls and Gibbon Calls*. The interpretative trail takes about ninety minutes one way and though not exciting in itself (a broad, road- like track most of the way) is made a lot more interesting if you refer to the descriptions in the book.

Most people carry on after the end of the interpretative trail, following signs for trail #1, which takes you to **Ton Gloy waterfall**. Nine kilometres from headquarters (allow 3hr each way), the falls flow year-round and tumble into a pool that's good for swimming. En route to Ton Gloy, you'll pass signs for other attractions including **Bang Leap Nam waterfall** (trail #4, 4.5km from head- quarters), which is a straightforward hike; and **Tan Sawan waterfall** (trail #3, 9km from headquarters), a more difficult route that includes a wade along the river bed for the final kilometre and should not be attempted during the rainy season.

The other very popular trail is #9 to **Sip-et Chan waterfall**, which shoots off north from the park headquarters and follows the course of the Bang Laen river. Though the falls are only 4km from headquarters, the trail can be difficult to follow and involves a fair bit of climbing plus half a dozen river crossings. You should allow three hours each way, and take plenty of water and some food. With eleven tiers, the falls are a quite spectacular sight; on the way you should hear the hooting calls of white-handed gibbons at the tops of the tallest trees, and may get to see a helmeted hornbill flying overhead.

Guided treks and tours

Longer **guided treks** into the jungle interior can be arranged through most of Khao Sok's guest houses, but if your accommodation doesn't come up with the goods try either *Freedom House, Nung House, Bamboo House* or *Treetops*. Note that all prices listed below are exclusive of the three-day national park pass, which costs B200 per person.

For B300–400 per person, you can join a trek along the main park trails (usually to Ton Gloy waterfall or Sip-et Chan falls) or to a nearby cave, but the most interesting treks start from **Cheow Lan lake**, which is studded with spectacular karst formations, with three impressive caves near the access trail; it's about an hour's drive from the accommodation area and is only open to guided treks. A typical day-trip to the lake (B1000–1200) includes a boat ride and swim, with a possible fishing option too, plus a trek to one of the nearby caves – one of which has a river running through it, so you may have to swim in parts. This is quite an adventurous outing: when not straining your neck to observe the gibbons in the treetops, you'll be wading through rivers and keeping an eye out for hungry leeches. Overnight trips to the lake generally cover the same ground and feature either camping in the jungle (B1800) or accommodation at the national park raft house on the lake (B2200); the more expensive version, run through *Freedom House*, adds on a trek to a waterfall, a night safari and night fishing (B2500).

Most guest houses also do **night safaris** along the main park trails, at around B300 for two hours or B500 for four hours, when you're fairly certain to see civets and might be lucky enough to see some of the park's rarer inhabitants, like elephants, tigers, clouded leopards and pony-sized black and white tapirs.

The **Sok river** that runs through the park and alongside many of the guest houses is fun for swimming in and inner-tubing down; tubes can be hired at *Bamboo House*. You can also go on a guided canoe trip down the river: a two-hour, ten-kilometre canoe ride costs B600–800 per person and can be arranged through *Bamboo House*. Many guest houses can also arrange **elephant rides** (2hr; B800) and trips to a rather uninteresting local cave temple (B300).

If you're in a hurry, consider organizing an overnight trekking expedition to Khao Sok through a **tour agent** in Khao Lak, Krabi or Phuket. A two-day trip including transport, raft-house accommodation, guided trekking and a night safari costs around B4800 per adult or B2800 per child; refer to the relevant town accounts for details. Santana in Phuket (℡076/294220, ℱ340360, ⓦwww.santanphuket.com) can also arrange overnight kayaking trips in Khao Sok.

Khao Lak and Bang Niang

Fringed by casuarina, palm and mangrove trees, the scenic strip of bronze-coloured beach at **KHAO LAK**, 30km south of Takua Pa, makes a reasonably appealing destination in its own right, though its main role is as a departure point for **diving trips** to Ko Similan (see p.633) and Ko Surin (see p.623). There's no real village to speak of at Khao Lak: most of the accommodation is down on the beach, about 500m west of Highway 4 on the other side of a rubber plantation, and the main road itself is lined with small restaurants, dive operators, several little shopping plazas and a few guest houses. During the monsoon, the crashing waves and squelchy mud can make Khao Lak seem

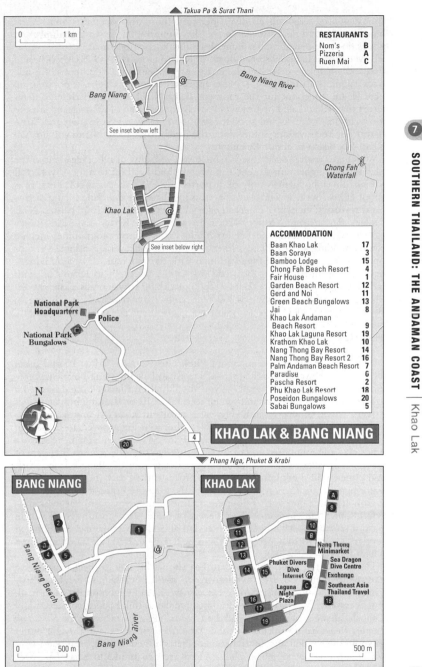

Takua Pa & Surat Thani

0 — 1 km

See inset below left

Bang Niang

Bang Niang River

Chong Fah
Waterfall

Khao Lak

See inset below right

RESTAURANTS

Nom's	**B**
Pizzeria	**A**
Ruen Mai	**C**

ACCOMMODATION

Baan Khao Lak	17
Baan Soraya	3
Bamboo Lodge	15
Chong Fah Beach Resort	4
Fair House	1
Garden Beach Resort	12
Gerd and Noi	11
Green Beach Bungalows	13
Jai	8
Khao Lak Andaman	
Beach Resort	9
Khao Lak Laguna Resort	19
Krathom Khao Lak	10
Nang Thong Bay Resort	14
Nang Thong Bay Resort 2	16
Palm Andaman Beach Resort	7
Paradise	6
Pascha Resort	2
Phu Khao Lak Resort	18
Poseidon Bungalows	20
Sabai Bungalows	5

National Park
Headquarters

Police

National Park
Bungalows

N

KHAO LAK & BANG NIANG

Phang Nga, Phuket & Krabi

BANG NIANG

Bang Niang Beach

Bang Niang River

0 — 500 m

KHAO LAK

Nang Thong
Minimarket

Phuket Divers
Dive
Internet

Sea Dragon
Dive Centre

Exchange

Laguna
Night
Plaza

Southeast Asia
Thailand Travel

0 — 500 m

almost wintry; although all dive operators, most tour operators and several bungalow operations close down for the duration, an increasing number of places do stay open and offer huge discounts as an enticement.

Development has now spread north of Khao Lak to **BANG NIANG** beach, two and a half kilometres up the coast and accessed by a kilometre-long side track running off Highway 4. New upmarket accommodation is popping up here all the time, but for the moment Bang Niang is still a smaller, quieter resort than Khao Lak. The beach is a lovely long stretch of golden sand, for the most part free of rocks and good for swimming between November and April. If you just keep walking south along the beach from Bang Niang you'll reach Khao Lak beach in about 45 minutes.

Whichever resort you're based at, once you've had your fill of trips out to the islands, you might want to rent a motorbike and head off to a local **waterfall** – Nam Tok Chongfah is only 5km north of Khao Lak, Nam Tok Lumphi is about 20km south. Several tour operators in Khao Lak and Bang Niang organize **day-tours**, including *Bamboo Lodge* and Jungle and Sea Tour, behind *Nang Thong Bay Resort* (076/420625), and Eco Khao Lak Adventure (076/420224), inside the Laguna Night Plaza. Typical programmes include elephant-riding and canoeing either just outside Khao Sok National Park, or on the coast in Si Phang Nga National Park (B2000 adults/B1000 children); sea-kayaking in Ao Phang Nga (B2150/1500); overnight in Khao Sok with trekking and a night safari (B4800/2800); trekking to waterfalls in nearby Sri Phang Nga National Park (B1200/600); and a day-trip to Kaw Thaung in Burma (B2000/1000).

Practicalities

All the regular **buses** running from Phuket to Ranong, Takua Pa and Surat Thani, and vice versa, pass the turn-offs to Khao Lak and Bang Niang; if you're coming from Krabi or Phang Nga you should take a Phuket-bound bus as far as **Khokkloi** bus terminal and switch to a Takua Pa or Ranong bus. Most bus drivers will be familiar with the big-name resorts in Khao Lak and Bang Niang and should drop you as near as possible; otherwise, for most Khao Lak beach hotels you should get off as soon as you see the Sea Dragon Dive Center, from where it's a five-hundred-metre walk west down the side road to the sea. For Bang Niang, alight when you see a cluster of signs for the Bang Niang resorts and either walk the kilometre down the road to the beach, following the relevant signs, or arrange a motorbike taxi at the roadside. When it comes to moving on, it's just a question of hopping on one of the frequent north- or southbound buses and changing where necessary (hotel staff can usually fill you in on bus schedules). Many guest houses and all tour operators can arrange taxi services for up to four people to Khao Sok (B900), Krabi (B1600) and Surat Thani ferry pier (B2100).

The **shops** and businesses in Khao Lak should be able to meet your everyday requirements, but for anything major you'll need to go to Takua Pa or Phuket. The Nang Thong minimart, across from Sea Dragon on the main road, stocks travellers' essentials like mosquito repellent, toilet paper, sunscreen and English-language newspapers, and the Laguna Night Plaza beside the *Khao Lak Laguna Resort* has a bookstore, clothes boutique, restaurant and souvenir outlet as well as car rental and several tour operators. Dotted along the main road you'll also find several tailors' shops. There are two **banks** in Khao Lak, with ATMs and exchange counters (daily 8.30am–6pm): one next to Sea Dragon and the other inside the Laguna Night Plaza. Several places on Highway 4 offer

Dive operators in Khao Lak

Though Khao Lak has charms enough of its own to keep you happy for a few days, most travellers are drawn here because of the **diving and snorkelling trips** to the Similan islands (see p.633) and beyond. These trips are extremely popular and don't leave every day so you should try to book them in advance. Normal live-aboard boats take around four or five hours to reach the Similans from Khao Lak, but some dive operators also use speedboats for day-trippers – these only take a couple of hours, but aren't recommended for anyone prone to seasickness. The diving season runs from November through April, though if you're in the area a couple of weeks either side of this period it may be worth enquiring about dive trips on the off-chance.

Kon-Tiki, inside the Laguna Night Plaza ☏076/420208, Ⓕ420120, ⓦwww.kontiki-khaolak.com. Swiss-run PADI Five-Star Instructor Development Centre, with another branch in Phuket. They use a speedboat for their one-day dive trips to the Similans (B3500), but also do two- and three-day live-aboards (around B9000 and B13,000), with accompanying snorkellers welcomed at about forty percent discount. Also run courses for kids aged 7–11 (B700), as well as one- and two-day Discover Scuba courses on the Similans (B4500/6500).

Phuket Divers, beside Highway 4 in central Khao Lak, and in front of *Gerd and Noi* on the beach ☏076/420628, ⓦwww.phuketdivers.com. Three-day trips on a comfortable live-aboard boat to the Similans for B14,000, or B16,500 for a four-day expedition to the Similans, Surin islands and Richelieu Rock. Snorkellers welcome on both for a reduced price. Four-day Openwater PADI dive courses can be done in Khao Lak for B8000 or added to above dive trips for B7000.

Poseidon, at *Poseidon Bungalows*, 7km south of central Khao Lak, near the village of Lam Kaen (see p.633) ☏076/443258, ⓦwww.similantour.nu. Highly recommended three-day live-aboard snorkelling trips to the Similans (B5500); can arrange dives for accompanying divers if requested. Current departures are twice weekly on Tuesdays and Fridays.

Sea Dragon Dive Center, beside Highway 4 in central Khao Lak, also bookable through *Paradise* in Bang Niang ☏076/420420, Ⓕ420418, ⓦwww.seadragondivecenter.com. The longest-running Khao Lak dive operator is managed by experienced and safety-conscious farangs, has a good reputation and is highly recommended. They have three live-aboard boats, and prices range from B9000 for a two-day trip to the Similans with six dives, to B16,000 for a four-day expedition with fourteen dives on the Similans, Surin islands, Ko Bon, Ko Tachai and Richlieu Rock. Snorkellers can accompany some trips at about one-third off the price. Aside from live-aboards you can also do one-day local dives for B1300–1800. All their PADI dive courses can be done in Khao Lak – one-day Discover Scuba around B1700, or four-day Openwater for B8000 – and some can be also be done while on one of the above dive trips.

internet access, as does *Bamboo Lodge* down by the beach. South-East Asia Thailand Travel (☏076/420611) sells international and domestic air tickets, arranges train tickets, organizes tours and can arrange accommodation if necessary; for day-trip operators, see opposite. *Green Beach* rents **mountain bikes**, Eco Khao Lak Adventure (☏076/420224) in the Laguna Night Plaza has **motorbikes** (B250/day) and mountain bikes (B150) for rent and is an outlet for Budget **car rental** (ⓦwww.budget.co.th). There's a **clinic** at *Krathom Thai* every evening from 4.30pm–9.30pm.

Bang Niang is less commercial, but has a small cluster of businesses beside Highway 4 at the turn-off to the beach, where you'll find a tour operator, internet access and an informal taxi service.

Accommodation and eating

The standard of **accommodation** in Khao Lak and Bang Niang is high, but rates are pricey (there's little under B550) and the trend is upmarket, with several places already building swimming pools; it's certainly not a budget travellers' resort. Unless otherwise stated, all accommodation occupies beachfront land, and generally you'll be staying in bungalows rather than rooms in a block. Accommodation in all categories is best reserved ahead as the resort is very popular with mid-market German and Swedish travellers as well as tourists on eco-packages. Those places that stay open during the rainy season, from May through October, usually offer discounts of up to fifty percent on the rates quoted below.

All the bungalow resorts in Khao Lak and Bang Niang have **restaurants**, and these are always popular: those at *Nang Thong Bay Resort* and *Jai* stand out. There are a few little dedicated restaurants along the roadside in Khao Lak, including the very inexpensive *Nom's*, which emphasizes home-style cooking and serves noodle and rice dishes as well as plenty of fresh seafood. At the other end of the spectrum, *Old Siam*, inside the Laguna Night Plaza, boasts a more refined, mid-priced menu featuring delicious fish cakes, *tom yam kung* and the like.

Khao Lak

Baan Khao Lak ☎ 076/420199, ⓕ 420198. Upmarket collection of 28 bungalows set in a garden around a shorefront swimming pool. ❽

Bamboo Lodge ☎ 076/420625. One of the cheaper options, with just half a dozen en-suite bungalows set back from the shore in a bamboo grove. ❹

Garden Beach Resort ☎ 076/420121, ⓕ 420129. Lots of rather uninspiring but reasonably priced whitewashed concrete bungalows, all with fan. Those on the beachfront cost more. Closed mid-May to mid-Oct. ❸–❺ .

Gerd and Noi, also known as *Khao Lak Bungalows* ☎ 076/420145, ⓕ 420144. Large, nicely furnished villas with huge glass windows that look out on to the tropical shorefront garden. All rooms have fans; price depends on the location. ❺–❻

Green Beach Bungalows ☎ 076/420043, ⓕ 420047. Forty fan and air-con bungalows set around a small khlong, each with a balcony, woven bamboo walls and mosquito screens. Rents mountain bikes. Open all year with forty percent discounts May–Oct. ❺–❻

Jai ☎ 076/420390. Friendly family-run place offering the cheapest accommodation in Khao Lak, comprising simple old-style bamboo bungalows furnished with mozzie nets and bathrooms, set close to the main road and some distance from the beach. There's a good restaurant here too. ❷

Khao Lak Andaman Beach Resort ☎ 076/420136, ⓕ 420134. Thirty huge bungalows,

all smartly outfitted and good value. There are a few fan-cooled ones but most have air-con; price depends on closeness to the sea. Recommended. ❺–❼

Khao Lak Laguna Resort ☎ 076/420200, ⓕ 076/431297, ⓔ khaolak2@png.a-net.net.th. The pick of the crop in Khao Lak, where guests stay in tasteful, traditional *sala*-style villas, equipped with fan or air-con, mini-bar and hot water. There's a swimming pool and a restaurant in the attractively landscaped beachfront grounds and a small shopping plaza beside the road. Very popular, so reserve ahead. Open all year; fifty percent discount May–Oct. ❾

Krathom Khao Lak ☎ 076/420149, ⓕ 431226, ⓔ krathom@hotmail.com. Nine comfortably furnished wood and thatch bungalows scattered among the trees some way back from the main road, with no beach access. Run by the local doctor's family and open all year. There's a restaurant and small bar here too. ❹

Nang Thong Bay Resort ☎ & ⓕ 01/229 2181. Efficiently run, popular place that offers a range of very clean, smartly maintained bungalows, all with fans and attached bathrooms; the most expensive ones are set in a garden that leads right down to the water, the cheaper ones are set in another garden on the other side of the track. The restaurant serves good but pricey food and has a book exchange. Open all year, with a fifty percent discount in low season. ❹–❻

Nang Thong Bay Resort 2 ☎ 076/420078, ⓕ 420080. Three dozen bungalows comfortably furnished to a similarly high standard as at its sister resort. The cheapest ones have fan and bathroom; the pricier accommodation has air-con and a fridge. Reserve ahead. Open all year. ④–⑦

Phu Khao Lak Resort ☎076/420141, ℱ420140. Diagonally across the main road from the *Laguna*, the spotlessly clean concrete bungalows at this family-run place sit prettily amid a coconut plantation. They're among the cheapest in the resort, though they're a bit of a walk from the beach. Price depends on the size of the bungalow. ③–④

Poseidon Bungalows ☎076/443258, ⓦwww.similantour.nu. Seven kilometres south of central Khao Lak, on a wild and rocky shore surrounded by jungle and rubber plantations, this Swedish-Thai-run guest house is a lovely place to hang out for a few days and it's also a long-established organizer of snorkelling expeditions to the Similan islands (see below). The smaller, cheaper bungalows share facilities, while the more expensive en-suite ones are larger and more comfortable; there's a good restaurant here too. To get here, ask to be dropped off the bus at the village of Lam Kaen (between kilometre-stone markers 53 and 54), from where it's a 1km walk or B40 motorbike-taxi ride to the bungalows. Motorbikes are available for rent. Closed May–October. ③–⑤

Bang Niang

Baan Soraya ☎076/420192, ⓔbaan_soraya@phang-nga.net. Just half a dozen very attractive bungalows, with stylish furnishings, hot water and some air-con; a mere hop and a skip from the sea, though only one bungalow actually enjoys a proper sea view. Run by a Dutch-Thai couple. Closed May–Oct. Recommended. ⑤–⑦

Chong Fah Beach Resort ☎076/420056, ℱ420055, ⓔchongfah@usa.net. The original hotel on Bang Niang beach, but poorly laid out, so that the small blocks of rooms overlook each other rather than the sea. Interiors are very comfortable though, some rooms have air-con, and the place is efficiently run. ⑤–⑧

Fair House, beside Highway 4, just north of the turn-off to the beach, ☎076/420394. A handful of concrete bungalows widely spaced in a garden set back from the main road, but a good kilometre's walk from the beach. ④

Palm Andaman Beach Resort ☎076/420185, ℱ420189, ⓔpalm_as1@hotmail.com. A rather stylish and relatively good-value outfit, whose very spacious air-con bungalows are attractively designed and have unusual open-air bathrooms. ⑧

Paradise ☎076/420184. One of the most popular places on Bang Niang, chiefly because it offers simple, old-style bamboo huts, rather than the concrete versions favoured by most resorts in this area. The huts all have fans, mosquito nets and bathrooms and are set in a palm grove that runs right down the shore; price depends on size and proximity to the beach. You can book Sea Dragon dive trips and courses here, rent motorbikes and organize local tours. From May through Oct you should phone ahead to check whether they're open. ③–⑤

Pascha Resort ☎076/420280, ℱ420282, ⓔpascha43@hotmail.com. Tastefully designed teak-wood bungalows, each one furnished in traditional Thai style and equipped with air-con, TV and mini-bar; a swimming pool is planned. Across a track from the beach. ⑦

Sabai Bungalows ☎076/420142. Run by the same people as *Gerd and Noi* on Khao Lak, *Sabai* offers the cheapest accommodation in Bang Niang, with ten bamboo bungalows set in a garden beside a track, less than 100m from the beach. Rooms have fans and good bathrooms. ③

Ko Similan

Rated by *Skin Diver* magazine as one of the world's top ten spots for both above-water and underwater beauty, the nine islands that make up the **KO SIMILAN** national park are among the most exciting **diving** destinations in Thailand. Massive granite boulders set magnificently against turquoise waters give the islands their distinctive character, but it's the thirty-metre visibility that draws the divers. The underwater scenery is nothing short of overwhelming here: the reefs teem with a host of coral fish, from the long-nosed butterfly fish to the black-, yellow- and white-striped angel fish, and the ubiquitous purple and turquoise parrot fish, which nibble so incessantly at the coral. A little further offshore, magnificent mauve and burgundy crown-of-thorns starfish stalk the sea bed, gobbling chunks of coral as they go – and out here you'll also see turtles, manta rays, moray eels, jacks, reef sharks, sea snakes, red grouper and quite possibly white-tip sharks, barracuda, giant lobster and enormous tuna.

The **islands** lie 64km off the mainland and are numbered from nine at the northern end of the chain to one at the southern end. In descending order, they are: Ko Bon (number nine), Ko Ba Ngu, Ko Similan, Ko Payoo, Ko Miang (actually two islands, numbers five and four, known collectively as Ko Miang), Ko Pahyan, Ko Pahyang and Ko Hu Yong. Only islands number eight (Ko Ba Ngu) and number four (Ko Miang) are inhabited, with the national park headquarters and accommodation located on the latter; some tour groups are also allowed to camp on island number eight. Ko Similan is the largest island in the chain, blessed with a beautiful, fine white-sand bay and impressive boulders; Ko Hu Yong has an exceptionally long white-sand bay and is used by **turtles** for egg-laying (see box on p.648) from November to February.

As well as suffering from indigenous predators and from the repercussions of El Niño in the 1990s, the Similan reefs have also been damaged in places by anchors and by the local practice of using dynamite in fishing. National parks authorities have recently responded by taking drastic action to protect this precious region, banning fishermen from the island chain (to vociferous and at times violent protest), enforcing strict regulations for tourist boats, and, at the time of writing, closing off islands one, two and three to all visitors. The whole Similan chain is closed to all visitors from May through October, when high seas make it almost impossible to reach anyway.

Practicalities

Ko Similan is not really a destination for the independent traveller, but if you have your own diving gear and want to do it on your own, you should head down to **Thap Lamu pier**, which is signed off Highway 4 about 8km south of central Khao Lak. A company called Met Sine Tourist, based at the Thap Lamu pier (T & F 076/443276), runs day-trips by speedboat from here to the Similans (B2100), which depart every day during the season at 8.30am, take two hours and can also be used by independent travellers wanting to stay on the island for a few days. It's also possible to buy one-way tickets to island number four on the daily Songserm speedboat which leaves Phuket every morning at 8.30am from December through April, takes approximately ninety minutes and cost B700 each way.

Limited **accommodation** is available on Ko Miang, in the shape of national-al park bungalows (B600 for four beds) and tents (B150), and there's an expensive restaurant here too. It's definitely worth booking your accommodation in advance with the national parks office on the Thap Lamu pier (T 076/411913–4), as the place can get crowded with tour groups, especially on weekends and holidays. There's no drinking water available outside Ko Miang, and campfires are prohibited on all the islands. Inter-island shuttles, the only way of getting from place to place, are expensive, at B250 per person per trip.

Organized snorkelling and diving tours

It's far simpler to do what most people do and join an organized **tour** (Nov–May only). Most travel agents in Phuket sell snorkelling **day-trips** to Ko Similan for B2300–3000, which either go by boat all the way from Phuket to the Similans or travel first to Thap Lamu by bus and then take a speedboat;

either way the whole journey takes around three hours. Kon-Tiki in Khao Lak (see box on p.631) also does one-day dive trips to the Similans (B3500).

The more rewarding option would be to do an **overnight** trip to the islands. Met Sine in Thap Lamu (T & F076/443276) runs two- and three-day Similan packages (B3200/4000), which include accommodation on Ko Miang and snorkelling equipment, while many dive companies sell two- to four-day all-inclusive live-aboard trips. Most live-aboard boats take four to five hours to reach Ko Similan from Khao Lak or Phuket. The cheapest, most informal tours are run out of Khao Lak, where prices average B9000 for a two-day live-aboard **diving** trip or B16,000 for four days, with about a forty percent discount for accompanying snorkellers; a three-day dedicated **snorkelling** trip costs B5300; for full details see box on p.631. Most of the Phuket-based dive operators (see p.638) only offer four-day live-aboards to the Similans (also featuring Richlieu Rock and a couple of other sites) for US$550–600; some trips are open to accompanying snorkellers at a slight discount.

Phuket

Thailand's largest island and a province in its own right, **Phuket** (pronounced "Poo-ket") has been a well-off region since the nineteenth century, when Chinese merchants got in on its tin-mining and sea-borne trade, before turning to the rubber industry. Phuket remains the wealthiest province in Thailand, with the highest per-capita income, but what mints the money nowadays is **tourism**: with an annual influx that tops one million, Phuket ranks second in popularity only to Pattaya, and the package-tour traffic has wrought its usual transformations. Thoughtless tourist developments have scarred much of the island, particularly along the west coast, and the trend on all the beaches is upmarket, with very few budget possibilities. As mainstream resorts go, however, those on Phuket are just about the best in Thailand, offering a huge range of **watersports** and magnificent **diving** facilities to make the most of the clear and sparkling sea. Remoter parts of the island are still attractive, too, particularly the interior: a fertile, hilly expanse dominated by rubber and pineapple plantations and interspersed with wild tropical vegetation.

Phuket's capital, Muang Phuket or **Phuket town**, lies on the southeast coast, 42km south of the Sarasin Bridge linking the island to the mainland. Most people pass straight through the town on their way to the beaches on the **west coast**, where three big resorts corner the bulk of the trade: high-rise **Ao Patong**, the most developed and expensive, with a nightlife verging on the seedy; the slightly nicer **Ao Karon**; and adjacent **Ao Kata**, the smallest and least spoilt of the trio. If you're really looking for peace and quiet you should turn instead to some of the beaches on the far northwest coast, such as the twelve-kilometre-long national park beach of **Hat Mai Khao**, its more developed neighbour **Hat Nai Yang** or the delightful little bays of **Hat Nai Thon** and **Hat Kamala**. Most of the other west-coast beaches have been taken over by one or two upmarket hotels, specifically **Hat Nai Harn**, **Hat Surin** and

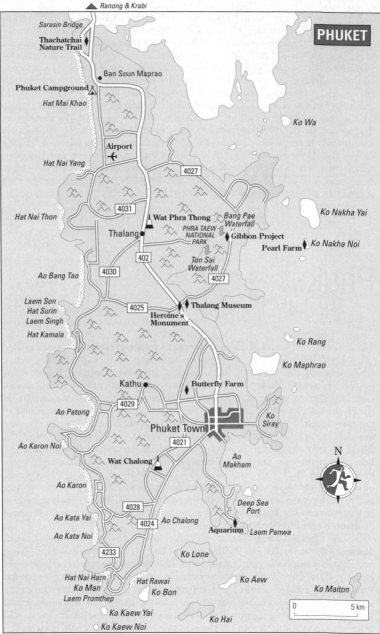

Ranong & Krabi

Sarasin Bridge

**Thachatchai
Nature Trail**

Ban Soun Maprao

Phuket Campground

Hat Mai Khao

Ko Wa

Airport

Hat Nai Yang

4027

Hat Nai Thon

4031

Ko Nakha Yai

Wat Phra Thong

Bang Pae
Waterfall

PHRA TAEW
NATIONAL
PARK

Gibbon Project

Thalang

Ton Sai
Waterfall

Pearl Farm

Ko Nakha Noi

402

4030

Ao Bang Tao

4025

4027

Thalang Museum

Laem Son
Hat Surin
Laem Singh
Hat Kamala

**Heroine's
Monument**

Ko Rang

Ko Maphrao

Kathu

Butterfly Farm

4029

Ao Patong

Ko
Siray

Phuket Town

Ao Karon Noi

4021

Ao
Makham

Wat Chalong

Ao Karon

Deep Sea
Port

4028

Aquarium

Laem Panwa

Ao Kata Yai

4024

Ao Chalong

Ko Lone

Ao Kata Noi

4233

Hat Nai Harn
Ko Man
Laem Promthep

Hat Rawai
Ko Bon

Ko Aew

Ko Maiton

Ko Kaew Yai

Ko Kaew Noi

Ko Hai

N

PHUKET

0   5 km

Ko Racha Yai

Ao Bang Tao. In complete contrast, the south and east coasts hold one of Thailand's largest seafaring *chao ley* communities (see p.624), but the beaches along these shores have nothing to offer tourists, having been polluted and generally disfigured by the island's tin-mining industry.

There's an excellent **website** about Phuket Ⓦ www.phuket.com, which has numerous links to Phuket tour operators and businesses and is particularly good for discounted accommodation on the island.

Getting to the island

Quite a few airlines operate direct **international flights** to Phuket, so if you're starting your Thailand trip in the south, it may be worth flying straight here or via another Asian city rather than having to make connections via Bangkok. Bangkok Airways also does a tempting thrice-daily shuttle between Phuket and Siem Reap in Cambodia.

Given that bus journeys from Bangkok are so long and tedious, you might want to consider taking a **domestic flight** from the capital – or elsewhere – to Phuket. Thai Airways runs seventeen flights a day between Phuket and Bangkok, and also links the island with Hat Yai daily; Bangkok Airways does two daily runs between Phuket and Ko Samui, and the Phuket-based airline Air Andaman flies daily to Krabi, Surat Thani and Nakhon Si Thammarat, and is intending to extend its service to include Chumphon and Ranong.

Phuket International Airport (☎076/327230) is located on the northwest coast of the island, 32km northwest of Phuket town. There is currently no reliable public transport system from the airport to the beaches, so you are more or less obliged to take a **taxi** to your chosen destination. These cost about B400–600 to the main west-coast beaches of Ao Patong, Ao Karon and Ao Kata, or about B300 to Phuket town. You can **rent cars** direct from the airport: both Avis (☎076/327358, Ⓦ www.avisthailand.com) and Budget (☎076/205396, Ⓦ www.budget.co.th) have desks in the arrivals area, and there's a **left-luggage** service at the airport too.

The cheapest way of **getting to the airport** is by Tour Royal Limousine, which charges B80 per person. Unfortunately their office and pick-up point is inconveniently located at 55/3 Thanon Vichitsongkhram (☎076/222062), 4km west of Phuket town centre. Limousine minivans depart from here at 6.30am and then hourly from 7am to 6pm and take about 45 minutes. Not surprisingly, most people take taxis instead, and nearly all hotels on Patong, Karon and Kata offer a taxi service to the airport for B400–600; the trip takes about an hour. The domestic **departure tax** of B30 is included in the price of the air ticket, but for international departures you will be charged B500 at check-in. Contact details for the Phuket offices of international and domestic airlines are given on p.644.

By bus

All direct **air-con buses** from Bangkok's Southern Bus Terminal make the journey overnight, leaving at approximately half-hourly intervals between 5.30pm and 7pm and arriving about fourteen hours later. Most air-con buses from Phuket to Bangkok also make the journey overnight, though there are a few departures during the morning. There is no train service to Phuket, but if you can't face taking the bus all the way from Bangkok, a more comfortable (and less nerve-wracking) alternative would be to book an overnight sleeper train to Surat Thani, about 290km east of Phuket, and take a bus from there to Phuket (about six hours). There are fourteen buses a day between **Surat Thani** and Phuket, all travelling via **Khao Sok**, **Takua Pa** and **Khao Lak**; and six

The reefs and islands within sailing distance of Phuket rate among the most spectacular in the world, and the desire to dive off the Andaman coast draws hordes of visitors to the resort. This is where you'll find Thailand's largest concentration of **dive centres**, offering some of the best-value certificated courses and trips in the country. All the dive centres listed below offer PADI- and/or NAUI-certificated diving courses and have qualified instructors and dive-masters; we have highlighted those centres that are accredited PADI Five-Star Centres (the Instructor Development Centres are one step higher than the Five-Star Centres); see p.75 for details. Nonetheless, you should still try to get recommendations from other divers before signing up with any dive centre, however highly starred. Always check the equipment and staff credentials carefully and try to get first-hand recommendations from other divers. You should also check that the dive centre is a member of Hyperbaric Services Thailand (HST), which runs Phuket's **recompression chamber**, located at 233 Thanon Song Roi Phi on Ao Patong (℡076/342518). The recompression chamber is available free to member organizations and their customers; non-members need to put down a deposit of B100,000 before they can get treated. All dive centres rent **equipment**, and many of them sell essential items too; for the full range, visit Dive Supply, at 189 Thanon Song Roi Phi on Ao Patong (daily 9.30am–7pm; ℡076/342511).

A half- or one-day introductory **diving course** averages B1500–2000, and a four-day Openwater course costs between B5000–9500, usually including equipment. The price of **day-trips** to local reefs depends on the distance to the dive site, and the operator, but generally falls between B2000–3500, including at least two dives, all equipment and food. Nearly all dive centres also offer **live-aboard** cruises: a typical four-day live-aboard trip to Ko Similan (see p.633) and Ko Surin (see p.623) costs US$500 including at least eight dives, all equipment and full board.

Snorkellers are usually welcome to join divers' day-trips (about B1000) and can sometimes go on live-aboard cruises at slightly reduced rates. In addition, all travel agents sell mass-market day-trips to Ko Phi Phi, which include snorkelling stops at Phi Phi Le and Phi Phi Don, an hour's snorkelling (mask, fins and snorkel provided) and a seafood lunch. Transport is on large boats belonging to the main local ferry companies, with prices averaging B1100, or B750 for children. Most of these companies also offer day-trips to Ko Similan, for B2300–3000, depending on the speed of the boat; some companies use boats from Phuket which take three hours, while other companies bus passengers to Thap Lamu and then use speedboats, which also takes around three hours in total.

Dive centres

All the centres listed below offer a variety of itineraries and cruises, with schedules depending on weather conditions and the number of divers. Check out the Phuket Island Access website (@www.phuketcom.co.th/diving/guide.htm) for links to Phuket dive operators and for some fine underwater pictures.

Ao Patong

Fantasea Divers, next to *Holiday Inn* at the southern end of Patong ℡076/340088, ℻340309, @www.fantasea.net.

Holiday Diving Club, at *Patong Beach Hotel*, south of Soi Bangla ℡076/341235, ℻340998, ℮seawalk@phuket-ksc.co.th.

Santana, 6 Thanon Sawatdirak ℡076/294220, ℻340360, @www.santanaphuket .com. Five-Star PADI Instructor Development Centre.

South East Asia Divers, 62 Thanon Thavee Wong ℡076/344022, ℻342530, @www.phuketdive.net. Five-Star PADI Instructor Development Centre.

Ao Karon/Ao Kata

Andaman Scuba, 114/24 Thanon Taina on the Kata/Karon headland ⓣ076/331006, ⓕ330591, ⓦwww.andamanscuba.com.

Dive Asia, 12/10 Thanon Patak, north Karon ⓣ076/396199; Kata/Karon headland ⓣ076/330598, ⓕ284033, ⓦwww.diveasia.com. Five-Star PADI Instructor Development Centre.

Kon-Tiki, c/o *Karon Villa*, central Karon ⓣ076/396312, ⓕ396313, ⓦwww.kon-tiki-diving.com. Five-Star PADI Dive Centre.

Marina Divers, next to *Marina Cottages* at 120/2 Thanon Patak ⓣ076/330272, ⓕ330998, ⓦwww.marinadivers.com. Five-Star PADI Instructor Development Centre.

Andaman coast dive sites

The major **dive sites** visited from Andaman coast resorts are listed below. In these waters you'll find a stunning variety of coral and a multitude of fish species, including sharks, oysters, puffer fish, stingrays, groupers, lion fish, moray eels and more. For more information on marine life see "Flora, Fauna and Environmental Issues" in Contexts, p.796; for detailed ratings and descriptions of Andaman coast dive sites, consult the **handbook** *Diving in Thailand*, by Collin Piprell and Ashley J. Boyd (Asia Books).

Anemone Reef, about 22km east of Phuket. Submerged reef of soft coral and masses of sea anemones that starts about 5m deep. Lots of fish, including reef sharks, tuna and barracuda. Usually combined with a dive at nearby Shark Point.

Burma Banks, about 250km northwest of Phuket. A series of submerged "banks", well away from any land mass and very close to the Burmese border. Visibility up to 25m.

Hin Daeng and Hin Muang, 26km southwest of Ko Rok Nok, near Ko Lanta (see box on p.698). Hin Daeng is a highly recommended reef wall, with visibility up to 30m. One hundred metres away, Hin Muang also drops to 50m and is a good place for encountering stingrays, manta rays, whale sharks and silvertip sharks. Visibility up to 50m.

King Cruiser, near Shark Point, between Phuket and Ko Phi Phi. Dubbed the Thai Tanic, this has become a wreck dive as of May 1997, when a tourist ferry sank on its way to Ko Phi Phi. Visibility up to 20m.

Ko Phi Phi, 48km east of Ao Chalong. Visibility up to 30m. Spectacular drop-offs; good chance of seeing whale sharks. See p.685.

Ko Racha Noi and **Ko Racha Yai,** about 33km and 28km south of Ao Chalong respectively. Visibility up to 40m. Racha Yai is good for beginners and for snorkellers; at the more challenging Racha Noi there's a good chance of seeing manta rays, eagle rays and whale sharks.

Ko Rok Nok and **Ko Rok Nai,** 100km southeast of Ao Chalong, south of Ko Lanta (see box on p.699). Visibility up to 18m.

Ko Similan, 96km northwest of Phuket. One of the world's top ten diving spots. Visibility up to 30m. Leopard sharks, whale sharks and manta rays, plus caves and gorges. See p.633.

Ko Surin, 174km northwest of Phuket. Shallow reefs particularly good for snorkelling; see p.623.

Richelieu Rock, just east of Ko Surin. A sunken pinnacle that's famous for its manta rays and whale sharks.

Shark Point (Hin Mu Sang), 24km east of Laem Panwa. Protected as a marine sanctuary. Visibility up to 10m. Notable for soft corals, sea fans and leopard sharks. Often combined with the King Cruiser dive and/or Anemone Reef.

private minibuses a day from Phuket to Surat Thani, which leave from opposite the *Montri Hotel* on Thanon Montri. Takua Pa is a useful interchange for local services to Khuraburi and Ranong, though there are four direct buses a day between **Ranong** and Phuket. As for points further south: seventeen buses a day run between **Krabi** and Phuket, via **Phang Nga**, and there are also frequent services to and from **Trang**, **Nakhon Si Thammarat** and **Hat Yai**.

Nearly all buses to and from Phuket use the **bus station** (T076/211977) at the eastern end of Thanon Phang Nga in Phuket town, from where it's a ten-minute walk or a short tuk-tuk ride to the town's central hotel area, and slightly further to the departure-point for the beaches in front of the fruit and vegetable market on Thanon Ranong.

By boat

If you're coming to Phuket **from Ko Phi Phi** or **Ko Lanta**, the quickest and most scenic option is to take the **boat**. During peak season, up to four ferries a day make the trip to and from Ko Phi Phi, taking between ninety minutes and two and a half hours and docking at the deep-sea port on Phuket's southeast coast; during low season, there's at least one ferry a day in both directions. Travellers from Ko Lanta have to change boats on Ko Phi Phi. Minibuses meet the ferries in Phuket and charge B100 per person for transfers to Phuket town and the major west-coast beaches, or B150 to the airport.

Island transport

Although the best west-coast beaches are connected by road, to get from one beach to another by **public transport** you nearly always have to go back into Phuket town; songthaews run regularly throughout the day from Thanon Ranong in the town centre and cost between B15 and B25 from town to the coast. **Tuk-tuks** do travel directly between major beaches, but charge at least B120 a ride. However, almost everyone on Phuket rides **motorbikes** (some of which would be more accurately described as mopeds), and you might consider saving time, money and aggravation by doing likewise. All the main resorts rent out motorbikes for B200–250 per day (be sure to ask for a helmet as well, as the compulsory helmet law is strictly enforced on Phuket); alternatively, rent a **jeep** for B800–1200. Be aware though that traffic accidents are legion on Phuket, especially for bikers: there were reportedly 179 motorcycle fatalities on Phuket in 1999 alone.

Phuket town

Though it has plentiful hotels and restaurants, **PHUKET TOWN** (Muang Phuket) stands distinct from the tailor-made tourist settlements along the beaches as a place geared primarily towards its residents. Most visitors hang about just long enough to jump on a beach-bound songthaew, but you may find yourself returning for a welcome dose of real life; Phuket town has an enjoyably authentic market and some of the best handicraft shops on the island. If you're on a tight budget, the town is worth considering as a base, as accommodation and food come a little less expensive, and you can get out to all the beaches with relative ease. Bear in mind, though, that the town offers little in

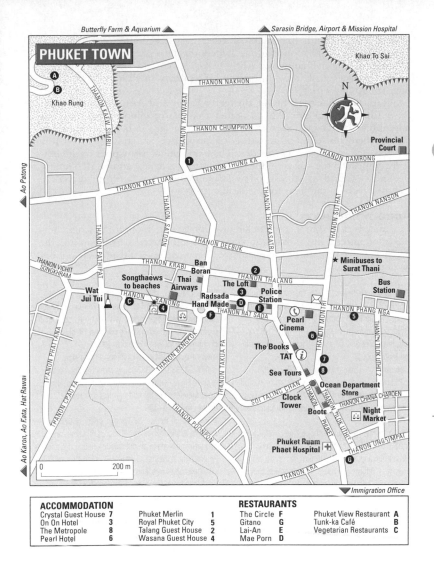

ACCOMMODATION				RESTAURANTS			
Crystal Guest House	7	Phuket Merlin	1	The Circle	F	Phuket View Restaurant	A
On On Hotel	3	Royal Phuket City	5	Gitano	G	Tunk-ka Café	B
The Metropole	8	Talang Guest House	2	Lai-An	E	Vegetarian Restaurants	C
Pearl Hotel	6	Wasana Guest House	4	Mae Porn	D		

the way of nightlife, and as public transport to and from the more lively beaches stops at dusk, you'll have to either rent your own wheels or spend a lot of money on tuk-tuks.

Aside from a manically bustling market on Thanon Ranong there's not a great deal to see, though a two-hour wander around the streets will take you past several faded **colonial-style residences** built by Chinese merchants at the turn of the century. Recognizable by their doors and shutters painted in pastel pinks, blues and greens, a string of these elegant old mansions lines Thanon Talang: the carved lintels and brightly painted shutters of the building next door to the Chinese temple are definitely worth an upward glance. You'll find relics of other historical buildings on Thanon Yaowarat, and on Thanon Ranong (where the Thai Airways office is a fine example), Thanon Phang Nga (the *On On Hotel*) and Thanon Damrong, where the town hall stood in for the US embassy in Phnom Penh in the film *The Killing Fields*.

Kids usually enjoy the **Phuket Butterfly Farm and Aquarium** (*Faam Phi Seua*; daily 9am–5.30pm; B200), located a couple of kilometres beyond the northern end of Thanon Yaowarat at 71/6 Soi Paneang in Ban Sam Kong, but though there are heaps of butterflies of various species, and a few reef fish, there's a lack of specific information. There's no public **transport** to the butterfly farm, but a tuk-tuk from the town centre should cost around B80 return. If you have your own vehicle, follow Thanon Yaowarat as far north as you can and then pick up the signs for the farm.

Accommodation

Few tourists choose to stay in Phuket town, preferring to opt for beach accommodation instead. But should you want to buck the trend – or if you find the beaches are packed out or too expensive – there are several reasonable options in all categories.

Crystal Guest House, 41/16 Thanon Montri ☎076/222774. One of several good, clean guest houses in the town centre; all rooms have attached bathroom, the more expensive have air-con, hot water and TV as well. internet access in the lobby. ❸–❹

Metropole, 1 Thanon Montri ☎076/215050, ℗215990. One of the largest hotels in town, and popular with package tourists and businesspeople. Rooms are comfortably equipped if not particularly stylish. ❸

On On Hotel, 19 Thanon Phang Nga ☎076/211154. This attractive, colonial-style 1920s building is a long-running favourite with travellers. Rooms are basic but adequate; they're all en suite and you can choose between fan and air-con. internet access in the lobby. ❷–❸

Pearl Hotel, 42 Thanon Montri ☎076/211044, ℗212911. Upper-mid-range hotel favoured by package tourists; facilities include a rooftop restaurant and swimming pool, which make it reasonable value for its class. ❼

Phuket Merlin, 158/1 Thanon Yaowarat ☎076/212866, ℗216429. Former top-class hotel that now aims mid-market, with decently equipped rooms, all furnished with air-con and TV, plus a swimming pool and nightclub. ❼

Royal Phuket City, 154 Thanon Phang Nga ☎076/233333, ℗233335, ⊛www.royalphuketcity.com. Huge chain hotel, with swimming pool, gym, business centre and comfortable rooms. The best in town. ❽–❾

Talang Guest House, 37 Thanon Talang ☎076/214225, ℮talanggh@phuket.ksc.co.th. Large fan and air-con rooms in an old wooden house in one of Phuket's most traditional streets. All rooms have attached bathrooms, and soap and towels are provided. A little faded but good value nonetheless. ❸–❹

Wasana Guest House, 159 Thanon Ranong ☎076/211754, ℗225424. Friendly, traveller-oriented guest house that's right next to the departure-point for Patong and Karon songthaews. The rooms, all en-suite and some with air-con, are good value for Phuket. ❷–❺

Eating and drinking

For authentically inexpensive and tasty Thai **food**, hit any one of the noodle shops along Rat Sada or Takua Pa roads, or check out the curries, soups and stews at the no-frills food centre on the top floor of the Thanon Montri Ocean department store (10am–10pm). Alternatively, there's always the night market which materializes around the square off Thanon Tilok Uthit 1 every evening at about 6pm. Foodstalls are also set up at night opposite the TAT office on Thanon Phuket, but the prices here are inflated because of the English-language menu.

The Circle, beside the roundabout on Thanon Rat Sada. Conveniently located a couple of blocks east of the songthaew stop, and open-fronted for maximum street-view, this place is ideal for a coffee and a snack, serving cappuccinos, real coffees (including hill-tribe blends from north Thailand), fabulous cakes, plus a few hot dishes.

Gitano, opposite *McDonalds* at 14 Thanon Ongsimpai. Lively, Columbian-managed music café that serves Californian and Thai dishes plus a range of cocktails. Stages regular special events including live music and comedy shows. Nightly 6pm–2am.

Lai-An, 58 Thanon Rat Sada. Large, busy, air-con Chinese restaurant offering a huge array of moderately priced dishes, including some Thai standards.

Mae Porn, 50–52 Thanon Phang Nga. Popular and very reasonably priced seafood restaurant serving typical Thai and Chinese dishes.

Phuket View Restaurant, on Thanon Kaew Simbu near the top of Khao Rung, the wooded hill on the northwestern outskirts of town. Middle-class Phuketians drive up to this slightly formal, mid-priced restaurant for outdoor seafood with a view. Bring mosquito repellent.

Tunk-ka Café, just above *Phuket View* on Thanon Kaew Simbu near the top of Khao Rung. Renowned for its (moderately priced) seafood, mixed grills, iced coffees and panoramic views.

Vegetarian Restaurants, Thanon Ranong. Two canteen-style restaurants side by side, staffed by volunteers from the nearby Wat Jui Tui Chinese temple. Most dishes are made with meat substitutes (usually soya), so the menu lists such delights as roast duck curry. It's a friendly place and very cheap. Opens for breakfast and lunch only.

Shopping

Phuket town has the best **bookshop** on the island: The Books (daily 11am–9.30pm), near the TAT office on Thanon Phuket, stocks a phenomenal range of English-language books about Thailand, plus a few shelves of coffee-table books and modern novels. Ban Boran, at 51 Thanon Yaowarat, specializes

Ngan Kin Jeh: the Vegetarian Festival

For nine days every October or November, at the start of the ninth lunar month, the streets of Phuket are enlivened by **Ngan Kin Jeh** – the Vegetarian Festival – which culminates in the unnerving spectacle of men and women parading about with steel rods through their cheeks and tongues. The festival marks the beginning of **Taoist Lent**, a month-long period of purification observed by devout Chinese all over the world, but celebrated most ostentatiously in Phuket, by devotees of the island's five Chinese temples. After six days' abstention from meat, alcohol and sex, the white-clad worshippers flock to their local temple, where drum rhythms help induce a trance state in which they become possessed by spirits. As proof of their new-found transcendance of the physical world they skewer themselves with any available sharp instrument – fishing rods and car wing-mirrors have done service in the past – before walking over red-hot coals or up ladders of swords as further testament to their otherworldliness. In the meantime there's much singing and dancing and almost continuous firework displays, with the grandest festivities held at Wat Jui Tui on Thanon Ranong in Phuket town.

The ceremony dates back to the mid-nineteenth century, when a travelling Chinese opera company turned up on the island to entertain emigrant Chinese working in the tin mines. They had been there almost a year when suddenly the whole troupe – together with a number of the miners – came down with a life-endangering fever. Realizing that they'd neglected their gods somewhat, the actors performed expiatory rites which soon effected a cure for most of the sufferers. The festival has been held ever since, though the self-mortification rites are a later modification, possibly of Hindu origin.

in **clothes** made from the handspun cotton of north and northeast Thailand; some of the fabric is exquisite, and they have some interesting designs too. Along the same road you'll find several **antiques** shops, displaying furniture and artefacts from the north and northeast, as well as pieces from Burma. Housed in a fine old colonial building at 36 Thanon Talang, The Loft (closed Sundays) also specializes in classy Asian **artefacts** and antiques, including Chinese, Korean and Japanese furniture, Vietnamese and Burmese antiques, Laotian textiles and Tibetan rugs. It's a fine place for a browse, and the temporary exhibitions of modern art displayed in the art gallery upstairs are generally worth a look too. For cheaper, good-quality Thai **handicrafts**, check out Radsada Hand Made, which sells textiles, carved wooden textile hangers, mango- and coconut-wood vases and bowls, silver jewellery and hill-tribe trinkets.

Listings

Airlines Air Andaman, at the airport ☏076/351374; Air Lanka c/o Phuket Centre Tour, 27 Thanon Rat Sada ☏076/212892; American Airlines, 156/13 Thanon Phang Nga ☏076/232511; Bangkok Airways, 158/2–3 Thanon Yaowarat ☏076/225033; China Airlines, at the airport ☏076/327099; Dragon Air, 37/52 Thanon Montri ☏076/215734; Emirates, as Air Lanka; EVA Air, as Air Lanka; Iberia, as American Airlines; Korean Airlines c/o Crown Family Tour, *Phuket Merlin Hotel*, Thanon Yaowarat ☏076/234775; Lauda Air c/o LTU Asia Tours ☏076/327432; Malaysia Airlines 1/8 Thanon Thungka ☏076/216675; Silk Air/Singapore Airlines, 183 Thanon Phang Nga ☏076/213895; Thai Airways, 78 Thanon Ranong (☏076/212499).

American Express, c/o Sea Tours, 95/4 Thanon Phuket (☏076/218417, ☏216979; Mon–Fri 8.30am–5pm, Sat 8.30am–noon). Refunds on lost traveller's cheques are usually available here within the hour, and staff keep poste restante letters and faxes for at least a month.

Banks and exchange All the main banks have branches on Thanon Phang Nga or Thanon Rat Sada, with adjacent exchange facilities open till at least 7pm and ATMs dispensing cash around the clock.

Hospitals The private Mission Hospital (aka Phuket Adventist Hospital), about 1km north of TAT on Thanon Thepkasatri (☏076/212386, emergencies 211173), has Phuket's best and most expensive facilities, including private rooms and an

emergency department; Phuket International Hospital (☏076/249400, emergencies 210935), on the airport bypass road just outside Phuket town, is a new hospital with good facilities, an emergency department and an ambulance service. Also in town are Bangkok Phuket Hospital at 2/1 Thanon Hongyok Utis ☏076/254425, and Wachira Phuket Hospital on Thanon Yaowarat ☏076/211114.

Immigration office At the southern end of Thanon Phuket, near Ao Makham ☏076/212108; Mon–Fri 8.30am–4.30pm.

Internet access At *Crystal Guest House*, 41/16 Thanon Montri; and *On On Hotel*, 19 Thanon Phang Nga; there's Catnet public internet access at the phone office on Thanon Phang Nga.

Mail The GPO is on Thanon Montri. Poste restante should be addressed c/o GPO Thanon Montri, Phuket 83000 and can be collected Mon–Fri 8.30am–4.30pm, Sat 8.30am–3.30pm.

Pharmacy There's a branch of Boots on Thanon Tilok Uthit 1.

TAT 73–75 Thanon Phuket (daily 8.30am–4.30pm ☏076/212213, ☏213582, ✉tathkt@phuket.ksc.co.th).

Telephones For international calls use the CAT phone office on Thanon Phang Nga (daily 8am–midnight).

Tourist Police 24hr help available on ☏1699, or contact the police station on the corner of Thanon Phang Nga and Thanon Thepkasatri ☏076/355015.

Around the island

This account of the island starts at the top of Phuket's most appealing coast and follows an anti-clockwise route around the perimeter, through the chief tourist centres. The west coast boasts a series of long sandy beaches punctuated by sheer rocky headlands, unprotected from the monsoons and consequently quite rough and windswept from May to October, but nevertheless heavily developed and packed with Phuket's best hotels and facilities. Shadowed by the mainland, the east coast is much more sheltered and thus makes a convenient docking point for ships, but is hopeless for swimming and sunbathing. The interior remains fairly untouched either by industry or by the tourist trade, and can make a refreshing break from the beaches.

Hat Mai Khao

Phuket's northwest coast kicks off with the island's longest and least-visited beach, the twelve-kilometre **HAT MAI KHAO**, which starts a couple of kilometres north of the airport and 34km northwest of Phuket town, and remains almost completely unsullied by any touristic enticements, with to date just a couple of discreet budget accommodations hidden behind a sandbank at the back of the shore. Together with Hat Nai Yang immediately to the south (see p.646), Hat Mai Khao constitutes **Sirinath National Park**, chiefly because giant marine turtles come ashore here between October and February to lay their eggs (see box on p.648). Mai Khao is also a prime habitat of a much-revered but non-protected species – the sea grasshopper or sea louse, a tiny crustacean that's considered a great delicacy. While you're at Mai Khao, you might want to make a trip to the Thachatchai Nature Trail, which also comes under the protection of the Sirinath National Park, but is actually on Phuket's northeast coast, very close to the Sarasin Bridge and about 8km north from the Hat Mai Khao accommodation; it's described on p.665.

If you're looking for peace, solitude and 12km of soft sand to yourself, then the Hat Mai Khao **accommodation** is for you. The two places to stay here, both run by members of the same family and both serving food, occupy adjacent plots at the back of the beach that are only accessible by a 1500-metre track. *Phuket Camp Ground* (T01/676 4318, Wwww.phuketdir/campground.com) rents out tents (B200) which you can either set up near their small restaurant or move down onto the beach a few metres away beyond the sandbank. On the other side of a small shrimp-breeding pond, *Mai Khao Beach Bungalows* (T01/895 1233, F076/206205, Ebmaikhao_beach@hotmail.com; ❷–❹) has just a few bungalows with fan and en-suite bathrooms as well as a handful of tiny, tent-like A-frame huts with mattresses, mosquito nets and shared bathrooms.

The easiest way to get to Hat Mai Khao is by long-distance **bus**. All buses travelling between Phuket town bus station and any mainland town (eg Krabi, Phang Nga, Khao Lak, Surat Thani) take Highway 402 to get on or off the island: just ask to be dropped in Ban Soun Maprao, a road junction just north of kilometre-stone 37. (If coming directly here from the mainland you'll waste a good couple of hours if you go into town and then come back out again.) Five songthaews a day also travel this far up Highway 402, but buses are faster and more frequent. From the bus drop, walk 1km down the minor road until you reach a signed track off to the west, which you should follow for 1500m to reach the accommodation and the beach; there's unlikely to be any

There are heaps of things to do on Phuket, from deep-sea fishing to rock climbing, cookery courses to mountain-bike tours. Tour agents on all the main beaches will be only too happy to fix you up with your activity of choice, or you can arrange it yourself by calling the relevant numbers. Transport from your hotel is usually included in the price of a day-trip. For details of dive operators in Phuket, see pp.638–9.

Activities

Bungy-jumping Catapult yourself off a 54-metre tower and look down over Ao Patong at Tarzan's Jungle Bungy Jump on Soi Sunset ℡01/464 1581.

Elephant trekking Too many treks to list, but every tour agent sells at least one. Treks last up to two hours, cost about B750 (kids B450) and follow a path through forest close to the beach. Some companies such as Siam Safari ℡076/280116 and the almost identical Island Safari ℡076/280858 offer combination programmes (around B1350/950 adults/children) featuring, for example, canoeing, a "jeep safari" and a monkey show as well as elephant riding.

Golf Phuket has four eighteen-hole courses open to the public: the Banyan Tree Club on Hat Bang Tao ℡076/324350, the Blue Canyon Country Club near Hat Nai Yang ℡076/327440; the Phuket Century Club in Kathu ℡076/321329, and the Phuket Golf and Country Club, also in Kathu ℡076/321038. Eighteen holes range from B2200 to 3500, with club rental B300–500 and caddies B200. You can arrange golf packages through Golf Phuket ℡076/280461, ⊛www.golfphuket.com or Phuket Golf Service ℡076/321278.

Horse riding Ride along jungle trails and sandy beaches with Laguna Riding Club ℡076/324199 on Hat Bang Tao, or Phuket Riding Club in Rawai ℡076/288213.

Paintball and shooting At Phuket Shooting Range, on the Kata/Karon road (daily 9am–6pm; ℡076/381667).

Rock climbing Practise your climbing skills on the fifteen-metre-high Quest Rock Climbing Tower on Hat Bang Tao ℡076/324062 before heading out to the real rock faces in Krabi (see p.679).

Thai cookery courses Half-day courses featuring a choice of half a dozen different menus, plus fruit-carving and lunch or dinner at the Supachai Thai Cookery School, 101/14 Moo Ban Irawadee (the bypass) just outside Phuket town (℡076/355291,

motorbike taxis to transport you, but you might get lucky. Travelling to Hat Mai Khao from the airport, is only a three-kilometre-ride in a metered taxi.

Hat Nai Yang

Despite also being part of the Sirinath National Park – and location of the national park headquarters – the long curved sweep of **HAT NAI YANG,** 5km south of Hat Mai Khao and 30km north of Phuket town, has become fairly developed, albeit in a relatively low-key way, with around thirty open-air restaurant-shacks and small bars set up along the beachfront road and the track that runs off it, and a small tourist village of tour operators, transport rental outlets, minimarkets, an internet centre and the inevitable tailors. For the moment though, the developments are fairly unobtrusive and the beach is a pleasant place to while away a few hours, ideally around lunch- or dinner-time when you can browse the restaurant menus at leisure – barbecued seafood and wood-fired pizzas are the local specialities. Eating out here in the shade of the feathery casuarina trees that run the length of the bay is a hugely popular

@www.phuketdir.com/supachai; B1500–2700 including transport); and every Saturday and Sunday at *The Boathouse* hotel on Kata beach (☎076/330015, @www.theboathousephuket.com; B2400).

Days out

Deep sea fishing Day-trips and overnight charters in custom-built boats from Andaman Hooker ☎076/282036, An Angling Experience ☎076/283270 and Phuket Sport Fishing Centre ☎076/214713; less strenuous freshwater line-casting at Phuket Fishing Park near the Heroine's Monument, off Highway 402 ☎076/239391.

Mountain-bike tours Graded routes around the island, through forests and to beaches; bike rental included in the price: Andaman Trails ☎076/235098, Asian Adventures ☎076/341799 and Phang Nga Discovery ☎076/340636.

Sea canoeing One and two-day self-paddling expeditions in sea kayaks around the limestone karsts of Phang Nga bay (see p.669) or through the jungles of Khao Sok (see p.625) for around B2700 per person per day: Santana ☎076/294220, @www.santanaphuket.com, Sea Canoe Thailand ☎076/212252, @www.seacanoe.com and Sea Cave Canoe ☎076/210434, @www.seacavecanoe.com

Nights out

Phuket Fantasea ☎076/271222. Enjoyable spectacular that's staged at the Fantasea entertainments complex just inland of Hat Kamala. The 75-minute show is a slick, hi-tech fusion of high-wire trapeze acts, acrobatics, pyrotechnics, illusionists, comedy and traditional dance – plus a depressing baby elephant circus. Transport is included in the steep ticket price (B1000/700 adults/children), with an optional pre-show dinner (B400). The show starts at 9pm every night except Tuesday; tickets can be bought through any tour operator.

Phuket Simon Cabaret ☎076/342011. Famous extravaganza in which a troupe of gorgeously feminine transvestites perform song-and-dance numbers, attired in outrageously flamboyant costumes. It's all very Hollywood – a little bit risqué but not at all sleazy, so the show is popular with tour groups and families. The cabarets are staged twice a night, and tickets can be bought from any tour agent for B500; agents should provide free transport to the theatre which is south of Patong, on the road to Karon.

Sunday pastime with local Thai families; to avoid the crowds, come during the week. Should you feel a little more energetic, the beach is fairly clean and fine for swimming, and there's a reasonable, shallow **reef** about 1km offshore (10min by longtail boat) from the national park headquarters, which are a fifteen-minute walk north of the tourist village. If you're staying here and have your own transport, you could make a trip to the Thachatchai Nature Trail (see p.665).

Practicalities

Accommodation is pleasingly limited on Hat Nai Yang. The cheapest and most peaceful place to stay is at the national park bungalows (☎076/327407; ❸–❺), prettily set out under the trees on a very quiet stretch of beach fifteen minutes' walk north from the tourist village. Two-person bungalows are basic but en-suite, their price depending on the size of the hut; they must be booked in advance. Tents are also available for B300 and can be pitched anywhere you like; if you bring your own you must first get permission from the park headquarters or visitor centre (both daily 8.30am–4.30pm). *Nai Yang Beach Resort*

Thailand is home to four species of **marine turtle**: the green, the leatherback, the Olive Ridley and the hawksbill; the loggerhead turtle also once swam in Thai waters, until the constant plundering of its eggs rendered it locally extinct. Of the remaining four species, the **green turtle** is the commonest, a mottled brown creature named not for its appearance but for the colour of the soup made from its flesh. Adults weigh up to 180kg and are herbivorous, subsisting on sea grass, mangrove leaves and algae. The **leatherback**, encased in a distinctive ridged shell, is the world's largest turtle, weighing in at between 250kg and 550kg; it eats nothing but jellyfish. The small **Olive Ridley** weighs up to 50kg and feeds mainly on shrimps and crabs. Named for its peculiar beak-like mouth, the **hawksbill** is prized for its spectacular carapace (the sale of which was banned by CITES in 1992); it weighs up to 75kg and lives off a type of sea sponge.

The survival of the remaining four species is by no means assured – prized for their meat, their shells and their eggs, and the frequent victims of trawler nets, all types of marine turtle are now **endangered species**. The worldwide population of female turtles is thought to be as small as 70,000 to 75,000, and only around fifty percent of hatchlings reach adulthood. As a result, several of the Thai beaches most favoured by egg-laying turtles have been protected as **marine parks**, and some equipped with special hatcheries. The breeding season usually starts in October or November and lasts until February, and the astonishing egg-laying ritual can be witnessed, under national park rangers' supervision, on Phuket's Hat Mai Khao (see p.645), Ko Surin Tai (p.623, and Ko Tarutao (p.728).

Broody female turtles of all species always return to the beach on which they were born to lay their **eggs**, often travelling hundreds of kilometres to get there – no mean feat, considering that females can wait anything from twenty to fifty years before reproducing. Once *in situ*, the turtles lurk in the water and wait for a cloudy night before wending their laborious way onto and up the beach: at 180kg, the green turtles have a hard enough time, but the 550kg leatherbacks endure an almost impossible uphill struggle. Choosing a spot well above the high-tide mark, each turtle digs a deep nest in the sand into which she lays ninety or more eggs; she then packs the hole with the displaced sand and returns to sea. Tears often stream down the turtle's face at this point, but they're a means of flushing out sand from the eyes and nostrils, not a manifestation of grief.

Many females come back to land three or four times during the nesting season, laying a new batch of ninety-plus at every sitting. Incubation of each batch takes from fifty to sixty days, and the temperature of the sand during this period determines the sex of the hatchling: warm sand results in females, cooler sand in males. When the **baby turtles** finally emerge from their eggshells, they immediately and instinctively head seawards, guided both by the moonlight on the water – which is why any artificial light, such as flashlight beams or camera flashes, can disorientate them – and by the downward gradient of the beach.

(℡076/328300, ℻328333, @nai-yang@phuket.ksc.co.th; ❺–❼) in the heart of the tourist village has a range of comfortable, mid-market bungalows set in a spacious garden on the inland side of the beachfront road, and offers a choice between fan and air-con. Just to the north is the less appealing *Crown Nai Yang Suite Hotel* (℡076/327420, ℻327322, Ⓦwww.phuket.com/crown-naiyang; ❽–❾) which has some strangely dark bedroom suites, including fully equipped kitchens, and pricier but nicer ones, all set around a swimming pool; it's used by airline crews. Best of the lot is the elegant and luxurious *Pearl Village*

(℡076/327006, ℻327338, ⓦwww.phuket.com/pearlvillage; ❾) where hotel rooms and pretty cottages are set in gorgeously landscaped tropical gardens that run down to the southern end of the beachfront road; facilities here include a swimming pool and tennis courts.

Hat Nai Yang is just 2km south of the **airport**, so a taxi ride down to the beach shouldn't cost much. An infrequent **songthaew** service (B30; 1hr 45min) runs between Phuket town and Hat Nai Yang via the airport, but a better public transport option might be to take any long-distance **bus** running to or from the mainland (they all use Highway 402) and get off at the turn-off to the airport. From here it should be easy to flag down a tuk-tuk, metered taxi or motorcycle taxi to Hat Nai Yang. A tuk-tuk from Phuket town to Hat Nai Yang costs around B300. There are plenty of transport touts in Nai Yang to help with return or onward journeys.

Hat Nai Thon

The next bay south down the coast from Hat Nai Yang is the small but perfectly formed **Hat Nai Thon**, one of the least commercialized beaches on the island. The 500-metre-long gold-sand bay is shaded by casuarinas and surrounded by fields and plantations of coconut, banana, pineapple and rubber trees, all set against a distant backdrop of hills. The access road off Highway 402 winds through this landscape, passing a few villages en route before reaching the shore, and to date there are just three formal places to stay at the beach, plus a couple of homes with rooms for rent, one dive operator, a few jeeps for hire and a restaurant attached to each hotel. There's good snorkelling at reefs that are easily reached by longtail, but otherwise you'll have to make your own entertainment. The best way to get to Nai Thon is to take one of the half-hourly **songthaews** (B20; 1hr 30min) from Phuket town to Ao Bang Tao, the next resort south down the coast, and then hire a taxi, which could cost as much as B150.

At the northern end of the shorefront road, across the road from the sea, *Phuket Naithon Resort* (℡076/205233, ℻205214; ❻- ❼) offers big, apartment-style **rooms** in terraced bungalows with the choice between (genuine) mountain views or (less interesting) sea views, and the option of air-con, balcony and TV. About 100m south down the road, *Naithon Beach Resort* (℡076/205379, ℻205381, ⓔnaithonbeachresort@hotmail.com; ❼–❽), set in a small garden across the road from the beach, has wooden fan and air-con bungalows with more character but lesser views. The nearby *Tien Sen* restaurant (℡076/205260; ❺) has rooms upstairs, at the cheapest rates in Nai Thon, though it's worth paying a bit more here to get the rooms with air-con and a sea view.

Ao Bang Tao

The eight-kilometre-long **AO BANG TAO** is effectively the private beach of the upmarket *Laguna Resort*, an "integrated resort" comprising five luxury hotels set in extensive landscaped grounds around a series of lagoons. There's free transport between the hotels, and for a small fee all *Laguna* guests can use facilities at any one of the five hotels – which include fifteen swimming pools, thirty restaurants, several children's clubs, a couple of spas and countless sporting facilities ranging from tennis courts to riding stables, windsurfers, and hobie-cats to badminton courts. There's also the eighteen-hole Banyan Tree golf course, the Quest Laguna outdoor sports centre and a kids' activity centre called Camp Laguna, with activities for 8- to 18-year-olds ranging from abseiling and rock climbing to team games and arts and crafts workshops. Not surprisingly the *Laguna* hotels are exceptionally popular with families, though beware of the undertow off the coast here, which confines many guests to the hotel pools. Half-hourly **songthaews** (B20; 1hr 15min) cover the 24km from Phuket town to Ao Bang Tao; taxis cost about B200 for the same journey. There are reputable **car-rental** desks at all the hotels, as well as small shopping arcades.

Accommodation

All *Laguna Phuket* **hotels** are in the top price bracket: the *Allamanda* has the cheapest rooms with high-season rates from US$150, and the *Banyan Tree Phuket* is the most exclusive option on the beach with rates starting at US$400; the cheapest rooms at the other three hotels average $285. The above quoted rates are generally discounted a little if you book via the *Laguna Phuket* website (Ⓦwww.lagunaphuket.com), and rates drop by up to fifty percent during the low season from May to October.

Allamanda Ⓣ076/324359, Ⓕ324360. Consciously family-oriented hotel comprising 235 apartment-style suites – all with a kitchenette – set round the edge of a lagoon and the fringes of the golf course. There are some special children's suites, three children's pools and a babysitting service. ❾

Banyan Tree Phuket Ⓣ076/324374, Ⓕ324375. The most sumptuous and exclusive of the *Laguna* hotels, with a select 108 villas, all gorgeously furnished and outfitted with private gardens and outdoor sunken baths. Also on site are the award-winning Banyan Tree spa and the eighteen-hole Banyan Tree golf course. ❾

Dusit Laguna Ⓣ076/324320, Ⓕ324174. Located between two lagoons, all rooms here have private balconies with good views. Facilities include a spa, a couple of swimming pools and a club for kids aged 4 to 12. ❾

Laguna Beach Resort Ⓣ076/324352, Ⓕ324353. Another family-oriented hotel, with a big water park, lots of sports facilities, Camp Laguna activities for children, plus luxury five-star rooms in the low-rise hotel wings. ❾

Sheraton Grande Laguna Ⓣ076/324101, Ⓕ324108. Built on its own island in the middle of one of the lagoons, with five-star rooms, nine bars and restaurants and conference facilities. ❾

Hat Surin (Ao Pansea)

The favourite haunt of royalty and Hollywood stars, dainty little **HAT SURIN** (also sometimes known as **Ao Pansea**) occupies the bay south of Ao Bang Tao, beyond Laem Son cape. Nearly always a peaceful spot, it boasts Phuket's most indulgent resort, the *Amanpuri* (Ⓣ076/324333, Ⓕ324100, Ⓦwww.phuket.com/amanpuri; ❾), part of the super-exclusive, Hong Kong-based Aman chain, where luxuries include a personal attendant, a private Thai-style pavilion and unlimited use of the black marble swimming pool; rates start at US$500. Also here are the delightful traditional-style thatched villas at *The Chedi* (formerly *The Pansea*; Ⓣ076/324017, Ⓕ324252, Ⓦwww.chedi-phuket.com; ❾) whose published prices start at a slightly more reasonable US$295. Songthaews travel the 24km between Phuket town and Hat Surin approximately every half-hour and cost B25.

Hat Kamala and Laem Singh

A small, characterful tourist development has grown up along the shorefront of **HAT KAMALA**, sandwiched between the beach and the inland Muslim village of Ban Kamala, about 200m west of the main Patong–Surin road and 26km northwest of Phuket town. With cheerfully painted houses, no high-rises or big hotels and an emphasis on garden compounds and rooms for rent, Hat Kamala has an almost Mediterranean ambience and is one of the most appealingly low-key resorts on Phuket. Aside from the accommodation, the little tourist village, which is clustered either side of Thanon Rim Had (also spelt Rim Hat), has several restaurants and bars, transport rental, internet access, a minimarket, a health centre, a post office and a tour operator. For anything else you'll need to head south around the headland to Ao Patong, just a few kilometres away. The Phuket Fantasea entertainments complex (see box on p.651) is about 1km northeast of Hat Kamala on the main Patong–Surin road. If you look closely you'll see that the shorefront land across the road from the Fantasea is actually a Muslim cemetery – the grass is dotted with small shards of rock indicating the burial plots. A few hundred metres north of the cemetery, a couple of steep paths lead west off the main road and down to **Laem Singh** cape, a pretty little sandy cove that's a picturesque combination of turquoise water and smooth granite boulders; it's nice for swimming and very secluded. The easiest way to get to Hat Kamala is by songthaew from Phuket town (every 30min, 1hr 15min; B25).

Accommodation and eating

Hat Kamala is popular with long-stay tourists, and many of the **hotels** offer rooms with kitchenettes; on the whole, prices here are reasonable for Phuket. A few of the hotels have **restaurants**, most notably the *Two Chefs* seafood restaurant at *Papa Crab Guest House*, and there are several independent restaurants along Thanon Rim Had as well, most of which, like *Roberta* and *Charoen Seafood*, emphasize seafood, the local speciality.

Benjamin Resort, 83 Thanon Rim Had, opposite the school at the southerly end of the beachfront road, ☎ & ℗076/325739. Set right on the beach, nearly all thirty rooms in this hotel have fine sea views from their balconies, as well as air-con, TV and a fridge. Lacks the character of some of the others but good value. ❺

Bird Beach Bungalow, central seafront road at 73/3 Thanon Rim Had ☎ & ℗076/279669. Popular, long-running place with well-furnished bungalows set around a courtyard. Rooms are a bit dark but comfortable and reasonable value, with a choice of fan or air-con. ❼

Kamala Beach Estate ☎076/270756, ℗324115, ⓦwww.phuket.com/kamala/beach. Stunningly located on Hat Kamala's far southern headland and set around a swimming pool in tropical gardens, this place offers luxury serviced apartments for rent and is favoured by long-term and repeat guests. ❾

Malinee House, 75/4 Thanon Rim Had ☎076/324094, ℗279465, ⓔmalineehouse@hotmail.com. Very friendly, traveller-oriented guest house with internet access and the Jackie Lee tour operator downstairs, and large, comfortably

furnished fan and air-con rooms upstairs, all of them with balconies. Good value and recommended. ❹–❺

Papa Crab Guest House, southerly end of the seafront road at 93/5 Thanon Rim Had ☎ & ℗076/324315. Exceptionally stylish decor in this three-storey block of rooms above the Swedish-managed *Two Chefs* restaurant. Striking mango-coloured paintwork, rattan furnishings and the option of fan or air-con rooms. Try to get a room on the top floor if possible. ❺

Phuket Kamala Resort, northern end of the seafront road at 74/8 Thanon Rim Had ☎076/324396, ℗324399, ⓔkamalaresort@hotmail.com. Efficiently run hotel with forty rooms in air-con bungalows set either round the swimming pool or in the garden to the rear. All rooms have TVs and some also have a kitchenette. There's a restaurant and tour desk here too. ❼

Seaside Inn, central seafront at 88/6 Thanon Rim Had ☎ & ℗076/270894. Two dozen nice bungalows ranged around a pretty garden across the road from the seafront. All rooms have air-con, TV and kitchenette. ❼

Ao Patong

The most popular and developed of all Phuket's beaches, **AO PATONG** – 5km south of Ao Kamala and 15km west of Phuket town – is where the action is: the broad, three-kilometre-long beach offers good sand and plenty of shade beneath the casuarinas and parasols, plus the densest concentration of top hotels, restaurants and bars and the island's biggest choice of watersports and diving centres. On the downside, a congestion of high-rise hotels, tour agents and souvenir shops disfigures the beachfront, and limpet-like touts are everywhere. Signs are that things can only get worse: "entertainment plazas" are mushrooming all over Patong, each one packed with hostess bars and strip joints that make this the most active scene between Bangkok and Hat Yai, attracting an increasing number of single Western men. Before long, this might be a second Pattaya.

Already close to saturation point, Patong just keeps on growing outwards and upwards, which can make it hard to orientate yourself. But essentially, the resort is strung out along the two main roads, **Thavee Wong** and **Raja Uthit/Song Roi Phi**, that run parallel to the beachfront, spilling over into a network of connecting sois which in turn have spawned numerous pedestrian-only "plazas". It's along the two major thoroughfares that you'll find most of the accommodation, while the two landmark sois connecting them have become established entertainment zones: **Soi Bangla** and its offshoots throb away at the heart of the nightlife district, while the more sedate **Soi Post Office** is dominated by tailors' shops and small cafés and restaurants.

Practicalities

Songthaews to Patong leave Phuket town's Thanon Ranong approximately every fifteen minutes between 6am and 6pm and take about twenty minutes. They approach the resort from the northeast, driving south along Thanon Thavee Wong as far as the *Patong Merlin*, where they usually wait for a while to pick up passengers for the return trip to Phuket town. A **tuk-tuk** from Patong to Ao Karon will probably set you back about B200. SMT/National **car rental** (℡076/340608) has a desk inside the *Holiday Inn*, or you can hire jeeps or motorbikes from the transport touts who hang out along Thanon Thavee Wong.

Most of the **tour agents** and **dive operators** have offices on the southern stretch of Thanon Thavee Wong: see the box on pp.646–7 for a roundup of available day-trips and activities, and the box on pp.638–9 for diving details. There are private **internet** centres every few hundred metres on all the main roads in the resort, which charge much less than the business centres in the top hotels. The **police station** is on Thanon Thavee Wong, across from the west end of Soi Bangla.

Accommodation

Moderately priced accommodation on Patong is poor value by usual Thai standards. Because demand is so great, rudimentary facilities cost twice as much here as they would even in Bangkok, and during high season it's almost impossible to find a vacant room for less than B600. Some of the best-value mid-range places are at the far northern end of Thanon Raja Uthit, beneath the hill road that brings everyone in from town; because this part of Patong is a 750-metre walk from the central shopping, eating and entertainment area (though only 100m from the sea itself), prices are noticeably lower, and rooms and bungalows larger into the bargain. In general, Patong's **upmarket** hotels are better value, and many occupy prime beachfront sites on Thavee Wong. Officially, the beach itself is a building-free zone, but a sizeable knot of developments has

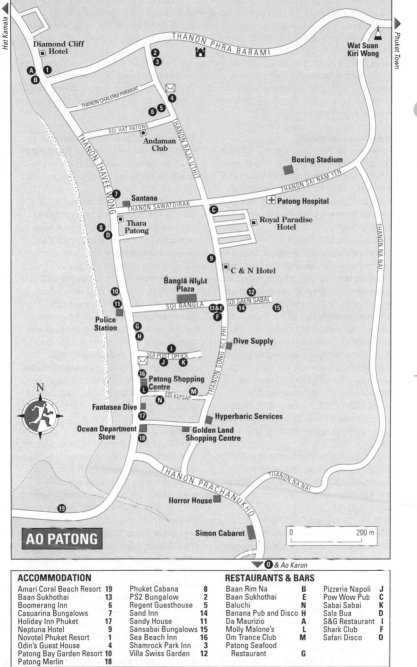

AO PATONG

& Ao Karon

ACCOMMODATION

Amari Coral Beach Resort	19
Baan Sukhothai	13
Boomerang Inn	6
Casuarina Bungalows	7
Holiday Inn Phuket	17
Neptuna Hotel	9
Novotel Phuket Resort	1
Odin's Guest House	4
Patong Bay Garden Resort	10
Patong Merlin	18
Phuket Cabana	8
PS2 Bungalow	2
Regent Guesthouse	5
Sand Inn	14
Sandy House	11
Sansabai Bungalows	15
Sea Beach Inn	16
Shamrock Park Inn	3
Villa Swiss Garden	12

RESTAURANTS & BARS

Baan Rim Na	B	Pizzeria Napoli	J
Baan Sukhothai	E	Pow Wow Pub	C
Baluchi	N	Sabai Sabai	K
Banana Pub and Disco	H	Sala Bua	D
Da Maurizio	A	S&G Restaurant	I
Molly Malone's	L	Shark Club	F
Om Trance Club	M	Safari Disco	O
Patong Seafood			
Restaurant	G		

somehow sprung up along the central stretch of sand between Soi Bangla and Thanon Sawatdirak. If you're travelling with **kids**, check out the facilities at the *Holiday Inn* which has some specially furnished children's bedrooms and a kids' club as well; *Novotel Phuket Resort* is another good option, with some of the most child-friendly facilities on the island.

High season here runs from November to April, but during the crazy fortnight over Christmas and New Year, when rooms should be reserved well in advance, most places add a supplementary charge of 25 percent. Every hotel drops its prices during the low season, when discounts of up to fifty percent on the rates listed are on offer.

Inexpensive and moderate

Boomerang Inn, Aroonsom Plaza, 5/3–4 Soi Hat Patong ☎076/342182, ℱ342868. Friendly small hotel that offers reasonably priced if rather faded rooms at the inland end of the soi, about 5min walk from the beach. Fan rooms have small windows, but the air-con versions are larger, lighter and have TV. ⑤

Neptuna Hotel, 82/49 Thanon Raja Uthit ☎076/340824, ℱ340627, ⓦwww.phuket-neptuna.com. Popular collection of air-con bungalows with all the trimmings in a pleasantly manicured if slightly congested garden. Excellent location, protected from the bustle, but only 200m walk from Soi Bangla. Recommended. ⑦

Odin's Guest House, 78/59 Thanon Raja Uthit ☎076/340732. The cheapest rooms in Patong, at the far northern end of the resort. Accommodation is in two-storey rows of very acceptable bungalows, all with fan and en-suite bathroom. ❸

PS2 Bungalow, 78/54 Thanon Raja Uthit ☎076/342207, ℱ290034. Close by *Odin's*, so also a fair walk from the main attractions. Large, good-value en-suite bungalows with fan or air-con. ❹–❻

Regent Guesthouse, 70 Aroonsom Plaza, Thanon Raja Uthit ☎076/341099, ℱ341664, ⓔregent@e-mail.in.th. Efficiently run small hotel with sizeable air-con rooms and internet access in the lobby. ❻–❼

Sand Inn, 171 Soi Saen Sabai ☎076/340275, ℱ341519, ⓔsand-inn@samart.co.th. Spotless, well-appointed air-con rooms, a little on the compact side, east off the bar-packed Soi Bangla. TV in all rooms and internet access downstairs. ❼

Sandy House, 87/14 Thanon Thavee Wong ☎076/340458, ⓔsandyhse@phuket.ksc.co.th. Right on the beach; two good but pricey rooms with beachfront view, plus several others with no view at all. All rooms have air-con. ❼–❽

Sansabai Bungalows, 17/21 Soi Saensabai ☎076/342948, ℱ344888, ⓦwww.phuket-sans-

abai.com. Plain but comfortable bungalows in a peaceful green oasis of a garden off the far end of the soi; the priciest options have air-con and TV. Close to the nightlife but secluded. Good value for Patong. ❻–❼

Sea Beach Inn, 90/1–2 Soi Permpong 2 ☎ & ℱ076/341616. Huge, slightly faded rooms with large balconies, a stone's throw from the beach and reached by following the signs through the warren of beachwear stalls. Fan and air-con available. Good value for Patong. ❺

Shamrock Park Inn, 17/2 Thanon Raja Uthit ☎076/342275, ℱ340990. Good value budget-oriented option that's near *Odin's* and *PS2*. Pleasant fan and air-con rooms in a two-storey complex, all with en-suite shower and many with balconies. There's a roof garden, too. ❹–❺

Villa Swiss Garden, 84/24 Soi Saen Sabai ☎076/341120, ℱ340726, ⓔvsgarden@phuket.ksc.co.th. East across Raja Uthit from Soi Bangla, this place has enormous air-con rooms, comfortably furnished with TV, fridge and ghetto-blaster. ❻

Expensive

Amari Coral Beach Resort, 104 Thanon Traitrang ☎076/340106–14, ℱ340115, ⓦwww.amari.com. Occupies a secluded spot on a cliff at the southernmost end of the beach; supremely luxurious with all facilities, including two swimming pools and a spa as well as tennis courts, a fitness centre and several restaurants. ❾

Baan Sukhothai, eastern end of Soi Bangla ☎076/340195, ℱ340197, ⓦwww.baan-sukhothai.com. A traditionally styled haven in a road packed with tacky modernity. Accommodation here is in lavishly done-out wooden bungalows, set in a landscaped garden with swimming pool and tennis courts. An excellent restaurant, too. ❾

Casuarina Bungalows, 92/2 Thanon Thavee Wong ☎076/341197, ℱ340123, ⓦwww.phuketdir.com/casuarina. Individual bungalows and rooms in a small block are set attractively in tree-covered grounds just across the road from the sea, in the least congested part of the resort. Swimming pool and sauna. ⑧–⑨

Holiday Inn Phuket, 86/11 Thanon Thavee Wong ☎076/340608, ⓕ340435, ⓦwww.phuket.com/holidayinn. Recommended upmarket option that offers very smart rooms while retaining a relaxed and informal atmosphere. Large pool and three restaurants, and an interesting programme of daily activities. Also has some kidsuites – bedrooms designed for children – and a kids' club. ⑨

Novotel Phuket Resort, Thanon Kalim Beach ☎076/342777, ⓕ342168. Smart, comfortable chain hotel set on the hillside at the quieter, northern end of the beach. Set in landscaped tropical gardens and offering fine views. Facilities include three restaurants and a multilevel swimming pool. Especially good for families as it offers heaps of sporting activities and runs a free kids' club with games, videos and craft-making. Free for under 16s sharing their parents' room. ⑨

Patong Bay Garden Resort, 33 Thanon Thavee Wong ☎076/340297, ⓕ340560, ⓔpatongbay@email.in.th. Small hotel set right on the beach, with many rooms having French windows that literally open out onto the (rather crowded) sand and others that give out onto the courtyard swimming pool. Rooms are comfortable and well equipped, with air-con and TV. ⑨

Patong Merlin, 99/2 Thanon Thavee Wong ☎076/340037, ⓕ340394, ⓦwww.merlinphuket.com. Huge hotel at the southern end of the road, with four hundred top-quality rooms and three swimming pools. Popular with tour groups. ⑨

Phuket Cabana, 94 Thanon Thavee Wong ☎076/340138, ⓕ340178, ⓦwww.impiana.com. Gorgeous collection of very tastefully designed bungalows, all equipped with air-con, TV and fridge, and set around a garden swimming pool. Right on the beach and definitely the choice option in its price bracket. ⑨

Eating

Western-orientated cafés squashed in among the high-rises and shops are popular for daytime snacks, with Italian food and seafood big favourites. Prices are fairly high however, and there's not always quality to match. One place where you can be sure of a cheap feed is at the **night market** that sets up after dark along Thanon Raja Uthit, between Soi Bangla and Soi Sai Nam Yen.

Baan Rim Na, far northern end of Thanon Thavee Wong ☎076/340789. Popular, elegant, traditional Thai restaurant, beautifully sited in a teak building overlooking the bay. Specializes in classic Thai dishes and unusual contemporary cuisines. Advance booking advised. Expensive.

Baan Sukhothai, hotel restaurant at the eastern end of Soi Bangla. Elegant upmarket restaurant, particularly recommended for its fine "Royal Thai" dishes. Expensive.

Baluchi, inside the *Horizon Beach Hotel* on Soi Kepsap. Perhaps the best Indian restaurant in the resort, specializing in North Indian cuisine and tandoori dishes. Moderate to expensive.

Da Maurizio, far northern end of Thanon Thavee Wong ☎076/344709. Superior Italian restaurant in a stunning location set on the rocks overlooking the sea. Authentic pasta and antipastos, and a good wine list. Reservations advisable. Expensive.

Patong Seafood Restaurant, on the central stretch of Thanon Thavee Wong. A deservedly popular, open-air restaurant which serves all manner of locally caught fish and seafood, particularly

Phuket lobster, cooked to Thai, Chinese and Western recipes. Moderate.

Pizzeria Napoli, Soi Post Office. Recommended Italian place, serving traditional wood-fired pizzas and home-made pasta. Moderate.

Roma de Mauro e Franco, 89/15 Soi Post Office. Fresh pasta served amid checked tablecloths, candles and an intimate ambience. Inexpensive to moderate.

Sabai Sabai, Soi Post Office. Family-run place serving the usual Thai and European dishes, as well as hearty American breakfasts and mixed grills. Inexpensive.

Sala Bua, Thanon Thavee Wong. Fabulously stylish, breezy, beach-view restaurant attached to the equally glamorous *Phuket Cabana* hotel. The innovative Pacific Rim menu includes ravioli stuffed with mud crabs and rock-lobster omelette. Expensive but worth it.

S&G Restaurant, Soi Post Office. The selection of real coffees and cappuccinos make this a good choice for breakfast. Inexpensive.

Much of Patong's **nightlife** is packed into the strip of neon-lit open-air "bar-beers" along Soi Bangla and the tiny sois that lead off it, where a burgeoning number of go-go bars (some of them advertising "couples welcome") add a seedier aspect to the zone. The bars and clubs listed below are the best of the more salubrious options. The **gay** entertainment district is mainly concentrated around the network of small sois and dozens of bar-beers in front of *Paradise Hotel* on Thanon Raja Uthit. If you're looking for something else to do with yourself or your kids in the evening, you could always try the **House of Horror** theme park on Thanon Prachanukho at the southern edge of Patong (daily 5pm–2am; B400), where an old hospital has been converted into sixteen horror chambers, each inspired by a different horror movie and populated by role-playing actors to get you spooked; you can also eat here at the *Graveyard Restaurant*, where kids get a free meal if accompanying adults. Alternatively, check out the nearby transvestite **Simon Cabaret**, or the spectacular show at **Phuket Fantasea**, both described in the box on p.647.

Banana Pub and Disco, 124 Thanon Thavee Wong. Very popular, very central upstairs disco and street-level bar attracting a mixed clientele of Thais, expats and tourists. Live music. Nightly 9pm–2am.

Molly Malone's, near *KFC* on the corner of the Patong Shopping Centre at 69 Thanon Thavee Wong. As you'd expect, the resort's original Irish pub serves draught Guinness and Kilkenny beer, dishes out bar food and entertains drinkers with an Irish band every night. Has a nice beer garden too. Daily 11am–2am.

Om Trance Club, Soi Kepsap. Psychedelic decor to go with the house and garage music. Nightly 9pm–2am.

Safari Disco, just beyond the southern edge of Patong, between Simon Cabaret and the *Le Meridien* beach at 28 Thanon Siriat. Decked out to look like a jungle theme park, complete with waterfalls, this is one of the most popular dance venues on Phuket, with two bands playing nightly from around 9pm; the music fuses disco beats from the 1980s with more recent techno sets. There's a restaurant here too. Shuts at 3am.

Shark Club, Thanon Song Roi Phi. Huge glitzy disco in the heart of the action, with laser-beam light shows and thumping sound systems. Nightly 9pm–2am.

Ao Karon

Twenty kilometres southwest of Phuket town, **AO KARON** is only about 5km south from Patong, but a lot less congested. With the help of a healthy scattering of café-bars, restaurants and relatively inexpensive guest houses, Ao Karon generally tempts the younger couples and mid-budget backpackers away from its increasingly manic neighbour. Although the central stretch of beachfront is dominated by large-capacity hotels, the beach itself is completely free of developments, and elsewhere you'll find mainly low-rise guest houses and bungalows, some of them set around gardens, interspersed with stretches of undeveloped grassland.

While long and sandy, the **beach** offers very little in the way of shade; south of the *Phuket Arcadia* it feels quite exposed because of the road that runs right alongside it, and it almost disappears at high tide. That said, it's a popular place to swim, and local entrepreneurs rent out parasols and deckchairs on some stretches. Be warned that the **undertow** off Ao Karon is treacherously strong during the monsoon season from May to October, so you should heed the warning signs and flags and ask for local advice – fatalities are not uncommon. For the rest of the year, there's plenty of scope for

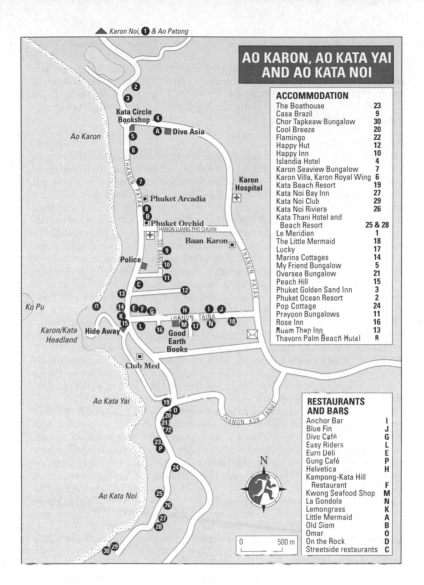

AO KARON, AO KATA YAI AND AO KATA NOI

ACCOMMODATION

The Boathouse	23
Casa Brazil	9
Chor Tapkeaw Bungalow	30
Cool Breeze	20
Flamingo	22
Happy Hut	12
Happy Inn	10
Islandia Hotel	4
Karon Seaview Bungalow	7
Karon Villa, Karon Royal Wing	6
Kata Beach Resort	19
Kata Noi Bay Inn	27
Kata Noi Club	29
Kata Noi Riviera	26
Kata Thani Hotel and Beach Resort	25 & 28
Le Meridien	1
The Little Mermaid	18
Lucky	17
Marina Cottages	14
My Friend Bungalow	5
Oversea Bungalow	21
Peach Hill	15
Phuket Golden Sand Inn	3
Phuket Ocean Resort	2
Pop Cottage	24
Prayoon Bungalows	11
Rose Inn	16
Ruam Thep Inn	13
Thavorn Palm Beach Hotel	8

RESTAURANTS AND BARS

Anchor Bar	I
Blue Fin	J
Dive Café	G
Easy Riders	L
Euro Deli	E
Gung Café	P
Helvetica	H
Kampong-Kata Hill Restaurant	F
Kwong Seafood Shop	M
La Gondola	N
Lemongrass	K
Little Mermaid	A
Old Siam	B
Omar	O
On the Rock	D
Streetside restaurants	C

Map labels: Karon Noi, Ao Patong, Kata Circle Bookshop, Dive Asia, Ao Karon, Karon Hospital, Phuket Arcadia, Phuket Orchid, THANON LUANG PHO CHUAN, Baan Karon, Police, SOI BANTIAO, THANON PATAK, Ko Pu, THANON TAINA, Karon/Kata Headland, Hide Away, Good Earth Books, Club Med, Ao Kata Yai, THANON KOK TANOT, N, Ao Kata Noi, 0 500 m

watersports here; windsurfing is good all year round, and the reefs around the tiny island of Ko Pu, just off the headland separating Karon from neighbouring Ao Kata Yai to the south, make for enjoyable snorkelling. The tiny bay just north of Ao Karon – known as Karon Noi or Relax Bay – is almost exclusively patronized by guests of the swanky *Le Meridien* hotel, but non-guests are quite welcome to swim and sunbathe here. For inland entertainment, you could do a round at Dino Park **mini-golf** (daily 10am–midnight; B200), next to *Marina Cottages* on the Kata/Karon headland, which is part of a pseudo-prehistoric theme park comprising a dino burger bar, a dino restaurant and an erupting "volcano"; or try the **House of Horror** theme park on Patong (see p.656).

Some of the posher hotels on Phuket's other beaches offer expensive **spa treatments** to their guests, but on Karon anyone is welcome to the Kata Hide Away Herbal Aromatic Spa, near *Peach Hill* at 116/9 Thanon Patak (℡076/330914), where local herbs are used in all their massage treatments which cost B400–950.

Practicalities

Songthaews for Ao Karon leave from the terminal on Thanon Ranong in Phuket town (every 20min; 30min; B20). They arrive in Karon via the outer stretch of Thanon Patak (the ring road encircling the resort), hitting the beach at the northern end of Ao Karon and then driving south along the beachfront length of Thanon Patak, continuing over the headland as far as *Kata Beach Resort* on Ao Kata Yai. To catch a songthaew back into town, just stand on the other side of the road and flag one down. If you're aiming for accommodation on Thanon Taina, you can save yourself at least ten minutes by getting off at the songthaew drop just north of the post office on the eastern, outer arm of Thanon Patak, where it intersects with the east end of Thanon Taina; the same is true in reverse when picking up a songthaew to travel back into Phuket town. For Soi Bangla accommodation, get off just after the *Baan Karon* hotel at the Thanon Luang Pho Chuan intersection.

Karon's main **shopping** areas are confined to four smallish knots: hotels, restaurants, dive shops and minimarts line the northern curve of Thanon Patak, location of the *Islandia Hotel*; there are banks, supermarkets and a post office on the central stretch of the beachfront, close to *Phuket Arcadia*, with similar businesses spilling eastwards along Thanon Luang Pho Chuan; and spread along Thanon Taina is a little tourist village – sometimes referred to as Kata Centre – full of tailors, beachwear outlets, craft shops, minimarts and café-bars.

There are several places offering **internet access** along Thanon Patak, and also around the *Islandia Hotel*; the more expensive hotels nearly all have business centres with (pricey) internet access. Karon's best secondhand **bookshop** (sometimes known as Karon Bookshop) is hidden away inside the Karon Circle supermarket at the roundabout on the northwest corner of Thanon Patak; it has thousands of paperbacks in all literary genres. The Good Earth Bookstore (closed Sun) on Thanon Taina has a smaller range. There's a **clinic** on Thanon Luang Pho Chuan and a **police station** on the central beachfront stretch of Thanon Patak. Avis **rental cars** has a counter at *Le Meridien* (℡076/340480), and National/SMT has a desk inside *Karon Villa* (℡076/396139, ⓦwww.avis.com); or try the cheaper vehicles hired out by transport touts throughout the resort.

Accommodation

Karon is less pricey than Patong, but during peak season you'd be lucky indeed to find any **accommodation** in the ❷ category, with most places only dropping their rates below ❸ on weekdays during the monsoon season. One of the best places to search for budget hotels is on the Karon/Kata headland, particularly along Thanon Taina, which bisects the road to Kata Yai. Not only are most guest houses here significantly less expensive than those on Karon proper, they're also convenient for bars, restaurants and shops, and yet less than ten minutes' walk from the beach. Soi Bangla, which runs south off Thanon Luang Pho Chuan, can also be a fruitful place to look.

High season here runs from November to April, but you'll almost certainly be charged an extra 25 percent over the Christmas and New Year fortnight when everything gets booked up weeks in advance. During the low season, expect to get discounts of up to fifty percent on the rates given below.

Inexpensive and moderate

Casa Brazil, 127/14 Soi Bangla, which runs south off Thanon Luang Pho Chuan ⓣ076/396317, ⓦwww.phukethomestay.com. Unusually stylish little hotel, designed in Santa Fe style, with adobe-look walls and funky decor and furnishings. The 21 rooms are comfortable and all have air-con. **❼**

Happy Hut, up a hill at the southern end of Karon ⓣ076/330230. One of the last remaining old-style bungalows on Phuket – and one of the cheapest. Pleasantly located in a grassy dip some 300m from the beach, with simple wooden huts all furnished with a bathroom and mosquito net; the price depends on the hut's size. Has a nice atmosphere. Recommended. **❷–❹**

Happy Inn, Soi Bangla ⓣ076/396260. Nice assortment of smart bungalows in a small garden that occupies a surprisingly peaceful spot. Price depends on the size of the bungalow and whether it has air con. Recommended. **❸–❺**

Karon Seaview Bungalow, 36/9 Thanon Patak ⓣ076/396798, ⓕ396799. Slightly grotty fan and air-con bungalows with attached bathroom, ranged either side of a tree-lined walkway just across the road from the beach in this central area. Reasonably priced considering the location. **❸–❹**

The Little Mermaid, 94/25 Thanon Taina ⓣ076/330730, ⓕ330733. Exceptionally good bungalow rooms, all with air-con, TV and comfortable furnishings, set round a swimming pool. Also some cheaper, city-style fan and air-con rooms in the central hotel block. Advance booking essential. **❸–❺**

Lucky, 110/44–45 Thanon Taina ⓣ076/330572. Inexpensive place offering good, bright en-suite rooms in a low-rise block (the best ones have balconies) and some rather plain semi-detached bungalows on land further back. **❸**

My Friend Bungalow, 36/6 Thanon Patak ⓣ076/396344, ⓕ396161, ⓔbaumlers@phuket-internet.co.th. Popular collection of fifty rather musty-smelling bungalows – the air-con versions are a bit more appealing – set back from the road in the northern central beach area. There's a streetside bar and restaurant. **❹–❺**

Peach Hill, 113 Thanon Patak ⓣ076/330603, ⓕ330895, ⓔpeachill@phuket.ksc.co.th. Popular and stylish mid-range place, perfectly located on a hill between the Thanon Taina bars and the beach. Some rooms are in the hotel wing and others are

in private bungalows set in the garden. All rooms have air-con and TV, and there are three pools. Recommended; booking ahead is essential. **❻**

Phuket Golden Sand Inn, northern end of Ao Karon ⓣ076/396493, ⓕ396117, ⓔgolsands@phuket.ksc.co.th. Medium-sized hotel, one of the least costly of its kind, with good-value fan or air-con bungalows, plus pricier rooms in the central block. Popular and friendly. **❻–❽**

Phuket Ocean Resort, behind the lagoon at the far northern end of Karon ⓣ076/396599, ⓕ396470, ⓦwww.phuket-ocean.com. Good, unpretentious hotel ranged up a slope and offering large rooms, all with air-con and balconies: price depends on whether you want a sea view or not. Three swimming pools and internet access in the lobby. **❽**

Prayoon Bungalows, up a gentle rise on Soi Bangla. Friendly, family-run place with just seven smart bungalows ranged across a grassy slope a little way off the beach. **❺**

Rose Inn, Thanon Taina ⓣ076/330582. Rooms here are a bit dark, but not bad for the price and area. Only 5min walk from Karon beach. All rooms with bathroom, some with air-con. **❹**

Ruam Thep Inn, far southern end of beachfront Thanon Patak ⓣ076/330281. Forty very good, fully equipped air-con bungalows, just 20m from the beach. Superbly situated restaurant terrace jutting out over the sea. **❽**

Expensive

Karon Villa, Karon Royal Wing, 36/4 Thanon Patak ⓣ076/396139, ⓕ396122, ⓦwww.karonvilla.com. The most attractive place on Ao Karon: a self-contained village in the central beach area. Bungalows built to several different designs stand in lovely gardens, with even more luxurious accommodation provided in the main "Royal Wing" building. Numerous restaurants and bars, plus a pool and fitness club. **❾**

Le Meridien, on Karon Noi (also known as Relax Bay), north Karon ⓣ076/340480, ⓕ340479, ⓔmeridien@phuket.ksc.co.th. Has the tiny bay all to itself; facilities include nine restaurants, a huge lake-style swimming pool (with islands), a spa, squash and tennis courts and private woods. A good place for kids, with special activities arranged every day for under-14s. Thai cookery classes also available. **❾**

Marina Cottages, 120 Thanon Patak, far southern end of Ao Karon, on the Karon/Kata headland ☎076/330625, ℱ330516, ⓦwww.marina-cottage.com. Full range of luxurious cottages in a gorgeous tropical garden that leads right down to the beach. Convenient for bars and restaurants. Advance booking recommended. ➒

Thavorn Palm Beach Hotel, 128/10 Thanon Patak, in the central beach area ☎076/381034, ℱ396090, ⓦwww.thavornpalmbeach.com. Top-quality high-rise accommodation in this large chain hotel, set in exuberantly landscaped gardens interlaced with five free-form pools and four children's pools. Also has tennis courts and several restaurants. Rates from $240. ➒

Eating

Many of Karon's more reasonably priced **restaurants** and bars are sprinkled along Thanon Taina on the Karon/Kata headland, though for the cheapest and most authentic Thai food you can't beat the hot-food carts that dish out noodle soup, satay and fried bananas on Thanon Taina throughout the day; there's also a very cheap local-food kitchen tucked away in a house next to the *Easy Riders* bar on Thanon Taina. Another very enjoyable place to eat is at the string of five open-fronted streetside restaurants just north of the *Ruam Thep Inn* on Thanon Patak. The food here is pretty inexpensive and ranges from king prawns to burgers and *matsaman* curries to spaghetti.

Dive Café, Thanon Taina. Popular, cheap and cheerful restaurant serving a good choice of authentic Thai curries – yellow, green and *matsaman* in various permutations – plus plenty of seafood. Inexpensive.

Euro Deli, across from *Marina Cottages* on Thanon Patak. Real coffee, fresh brioches, croissants and Danish pastries make this a good if pricey place to start the day.

Helvetica, Thanon Taina. Swiss-run restaurant that serves especially good breakfasts, including a basket of different home-made breads, muesli and *rösti*.

Kampong-Kata Hill Restaurant, Thanon Taina. Occupies a superb position on a steep slope just off the main road, its winding, flower-lined walkway lit up with fairylights after dark. As you'd expect, the food is fairly high-class, too, with quality Thai dishes a speciality. Moderate to expensive.

Kwong Seafood Shop, Thanon Taina. Very popular for its array of freshly caught fish and seafood which can be barbecued or cooked to order. Moderate.

La Gondola, Thanon Taina. Authentic Italian cuisine and exceptionally good pizzas. Expensive.

Lemongrass, Kata/Karon headland. Pleasant place with classy touches that specializes in good-quality Thai food (mainly curries, noodles and seafood) at reasonable prices; the shrimp curry is especially delicious. Moderate to expensive.

Little Mermaid, northern curve of Thanon Patak. Scandinavian joint that seems to be the most popular place in Karon for noon-time breakfasts. Their rye breads and foreign cheeses are tasty but expensive. Moderate.

Old Siam, in front of the *Thavorn Palm Beach Hotel*, Thanon Patak ☎076/396090. Large but fairly elegant teak-wood restaurant with indoor and outdoor dining areas; renowned for its traditional Royal Northern Thai cuisine. Stages classical Thai dance (Wed & Sat) and can feel overly touristy. Call for free transport here. Moderate to expensive.

On the Rock, in the grounds of *Marina Cottages*, Kata/Karon headland. Open-air seafood restaurant situated right on the rocks overlooking Ao Karon. Recommended. Moderate.

Drinking and nightlife

Most of the Thanon Taina **bars** are small, genial places, usually with just a handful of tables, a reasonable selection of beers and bar snacks, and a pool table; *Blue Fin* and *Anchor Bar* are both recommended, but there are plenty of others. Though there are as yet no go-go bars on Karon, the Patong bar scene has made inroads into the resort, and there are little clusters of bar-beers with hostess service around the *Islandia Hotel* on the northern curve of Thanon Patak and around the *Thavorn Palm Beach* in the central beachfront. For non-alcoholic entertainment, try the nearby transvestite **Simon Cabaret** or the spectacular show at **Phuket Fantasea** both of which are described in the box on p.647.

Ao Kata Yai and Ao Kata Noi

Tree-lined and peaceful, **AO KATA YAI** (Big Kata Bay) is only a few minutes' drive around the headland from Karon (17km from Phuket town), but both prettier and safer for swimming thanks to the protective rocky promontories at either end. The northern stretch of Kata Yai is completely given over to the unobtrusive buildings of the *Club Med* resort, and then it's a lengthy trek down to the rest of the accommodation at the southern end, where you'll also find the restaurants, bars, minimarkets, tour operators and transport rental outlets. A headland at the southernmost point divides Ao Kata Yai from the much smaller **AO KATA NOI** (Little Kata Bay), which is an attractive little gold-sand bay, very popular and so quite crowded with parasols and deckchairs. Kata Noi has its own small cluster of businesses including a minimarket, several restaurants and bars, transport rental and even a tailor's shop.

Most **songthaews** from Phuket go first to Karon, then drive south past *Club Med* and terminate at *Kata Beach Resort* on the headland between Kata Yai and Kata Noi. To get to Kata Noi, continue walking over the hill for about ten minutes, or take a tuk-tuk for about B100. A tuk-tuk from Kata Yai to Karon should cost you about the same. There are plenty of transport touts offering jeeps and motorbikes for rent.

Accommodation and eating

There is no budget **accommodation** on Kata Yai, and only a couple of places on Kata Noi with rooms for under B600. On Kata Yai, the **restaurant** of choice is *The Boathouse Wine and Grill,* which has a famously extensive wine list and an exquisite and extremely expensive menu of Thai and Western delicacies, and runs Thai cooking classes every Saturday and Sunday for B2400. Also managed by *The Boathouse* hotel is the less formal but still fairly pricey *Gung Café,* with beachfront seating and a menu that includes a range of Thai dishes as well as seafood and rock lobster ("*gung*"). For a nice change from the ubiquitous seafood, check out the Indian and Muslim dishes at *Omar* near *Cool Breeze* in Kata Yai, or the wood-fired pizzas at *Flamingo.*

Kata Yai

The Boathouse, 2/2 Thanon Patak ☎076/330015, ☏330561, ⑩www.theboathousephuket.com. Exclusive and very pricey beachfront boutique hotel with just 36 elegantly furnished rooms and a reputation for classy service. Room rates from B7400. ⑨

Cool Breeze, 5/5 Thanon Patak ☎076/330484, ☏330173. Sixteen appealing bungalows set up the hillside, above the streetside restaurant. The best ones have sea views; choose between fan and air-con. ⑤–⑦

Flamingo, 5/19 Thanon Patak ☎076/330776, ☏330814, ⑩www.flamingo-resort.com. Dozens of prettily positioned bungalows built among the trees on a steep incline above the pale pink restaurant and bar. Fan or air-con bungalows

available; most have verandas and some have sea views. ⑤–⑥

Kata Beach Resort, 5/2 Thanon Patak ☎076/330530, ☏330128, ⑩www.katagroup.com. Huge high-rise hotel with grounds that run down to the white-sand beach. Has a big swimming pool, a kids' pool and lots of watersports facilities, popular with families. ⑨

Oversea Bungalow 5/6 Thanon Patak ☎ & ☏076/284155. Nine large bungalows ranged up a hillside and accessed by a series of steep stairways. Some offer long-distance sea views; all have air-con. Fifty-percent discount May–Oct. ⑦

Pop Cottage, on the southern fringes of Kata Yai at 2/12 Thanon Patak ☎076/330181, ☏330794, ⑩www.phuket-popcottage.com. This mid-sized hotel on a hill a few minutes' walk from the beach has pleasant enough air-con rooms, some with long-range sea views. There's a large pool plus, for the kids, a separate games room and another pool. ⑦–⑨

Kata Noi

Chor Tapkeaw Bungalow, 4/13 Thanon Patak ☎076/330433, ℻330435. The best of Kata Noi's cheaper options, whose spacious and fairly comfortably furnished bungalows are ranged up the hillside at the far southern end of the road; the verandas give good sea views and the restaurant is right on the beach. Book ahead as there are only 24 rooms and it's very popular. ⑥

Kata Noi Bay Inn, 4/16 Thanon Patak ☎076/330570, ℻333308, ⓔkatanoi_bayinn@hotmail.com. Small, friendly little hotel attached to a seafood restaurant, offering good-value rooms with balconies and, in some cases, a distant sea view. Fan and air-con available. ④–⑥

Kata Noi Club, 3/25 Thanon Patak ☎076/284025, ℻330194, ⓔkatanoi_club@yahoo.com. Has some rather spartan bungalows at the far southern end of the beachfront road, as well as a few better, pricier air-con ones. ⑤–⑦

Kata Noi Riviera, 3/21 Thanon Patak ☎076/330726, ℻330294. Rooms here feel uninspired and rather box-like but they are the least expensive on this beach. The priciest ones have air-con. ④–⑦

Kata Thani Hotel and Beach Resort, 3/24 Thanon Patak ☎076/330124, ℻330426, ⓦwww.phuket.com/katathani. The biggest outfit on Kata Noi, occupying about half the beachfront and a good chunk of land 200m further down the road as well. Rooms here come in various degrees of luxury, but all feature air-con, use of the four swimming pools, tennis courts and kids' playground; there are restaurants, a dive shop and a shopping plaza on the premises too. Rates from B6300. ⑨

Hat Nai Harn and Laem Promthep

Around the next headland south from Kata Noi, **HAT NAI HARN** – 18km southwest of Phuket town – is generally considered to be one of the loveliest beaches on the island, given character by a sparkling saltwater lagoon and dominated by the luxurious hotel, the *Phuket Yacht Club*.

Follow the coastal road 2km south and you'll get to a small bay which has coral reefs very close to the shore, though the currents are strong and the sewage pipes uncomfortably close. A further 1km on, you reach the southernmost tip of Phuket at the sheer headland of **Laem Promthep**. Wild and rugged, jutting out into the deep blue of the Andaman Sea, the cape is one of the island's top beauty spots: at sunset, busloads of tour groups get shipped in to admire the scenery – and just to ensure you don't miss the spectacle, a list of year-round sunset times is posted at the viewpoint. Several reefs lie just off the cape, but it's safer to snorkel from a boat rather than negotiate the rocky shore.

Practicalities

Songthaews from Phuket (every 30min; B25) bypass Laem Promthep and follow the direct inland road between Nai Harn and Hat Rawai instead, so you may have to do the lengthy climb round the promontory on foot. It's a popular spot though, so it should be easy enough to hitch.

The internationally acclaimed *Le Royal Meridien Phuket Yacht Club* (☎076/381156, ℻381164, ⓦwww.phuket-yachtclub.com) is one of the most exclusive **hotels** on the whole island, offering superb rooms and exquisite service for a published price of $440 a night, but with huge discounts available online. For more moderately priced accommodation, head a little further round the headland to the minuscule Ao Sane, where *Jungle Beach Resort* (☎076/381108, ℻381542; ⑦–⑨) offers 44 comfortable air-con bungalows and a swimming pool.

Hat Rawai and its islands

The eastern side of Laem Promthep curves round into **HAT RAWAI**, Phuket's southernmost beach and the first to be exploited for tourist purposes. Twenty-five years on, the developers have moved to the softer sands of Kata and Karon and returned Rawai to its former inhabitants, the *chao ley*. A few bungalow outfits still operate here, but most visitors come either to eat seafood with Phuket's townspeople in one of the open-air seafood restaurants on the beachfront, or to hire a longtail out to the **islands** offshore. Of these, Ko Khai Nok, Ko Hai (aka Coral Island), Ko Racha Yai and Ko Racha Noi are good for snorkelling and diving – the visibility and variety of the reefs around **Ko Racha** in particular compare with those off Ko Similan further up the Andaman coast, and make a popular destination for Phuket's diving centres (see box on pp.638–9).

Hat Rawai boasts an idiosyncratic monument in the shape of the *Henry Wagner*, a very ordinary twelve-metre longtail boat set back from the road just west of the pier. In June 1987, five disabled men set off in this boat to pioneer a course across the Isthmus of Kra, and in just six weeks they navigated the rivers connecting the Andaman Sea to the Gulf of Thailand, without the aid of accurate charts. The captain and inspiration behind the enterprise was the late Tristan Jones, a Welsh-born 64-year-old amputee, veteran adventurer and campaigner for the disabled, who told the story of the trip in his book, *To Venture Further*.

Practicalities

Songthaews from Phuket town pass through Rawai (B20) on their way to and from Nai Harn. Longtail **boats** to the islands are easily chartered from Rawai; for a maximum of eight people, a boat to Ko Racha Yai (1hr) should cost around B2000 for a day-trip, including snorkelling time and return transport, or around B1000 for a simple transfer to Ko Racha Yai. Longtails to Ko Hai are cheaper at around B800 for a half-day snorkelling charter, or a bit less for a single journey to the island.

Unless you're keen on desolate beaches, Rawai makes a pretty dismal place to stay, but if you're just waiting for a boat out to one of the islands you could try the **bungalows** at *Porn Sri* (ⓣ076/381264, ⓕ288043; ❹–❻). Accommodation on nearby islands is much more appealing: on **Ko Racha Yai** you can stay at *Ban Raya Resort* (ⓣ076/354682, ⓕ224439, ⓦwww.phuket.com/banraya; ❼–❽) which has fan and air-con bungalows scattered through a palm grove on a headland, within a few minutes' walk of several lovely beaches. On **Ko Hai** there's *Coral Island Resort* (ⓣ076/281060, ⓕ381957, ⓦwww.phuket.com/coralisland; ❽–❾) with 64 bungalows and a pool set in lush tropical gardens and within easy reach of several beautiful white-sand beaches. Day-trippers are not allowed onto tiny little **Ko Maiton**, which is home to the very exclusive *Maiton Island Resort* (ⓣ076/214954, ⓕ214959, ⓦwww.phuket.com/maiton; ❾), whose luxurious traditional-style villas all have direct access to a blindingly white sand beach; rates start at B10,800.

The east coast

Tin mines and docks take up a lot of Phuket's east coast, which is thus neither scenic nor swimmable. East of Rawai, the sizeable offshore island of **Ko Lone** protects the broad sweep of **Ao Chalong**, where many a Chinese fortune was made from the huge quantities of tin mined in the bay. Ao Chalong tapers off eastwards into **Laem Panwa**, at the tip of which you'll find the **Phuket Aquarium** (daily 10am–4pm; B20), 10km south of Phuket town and accessible by frequent songthaews. Run by the island's Marine Research Centre, it makes a poor substitute for a day's snorkelling, but not a bad primer for what you might see on a reef. The research centre is also involved in the protection of marine turtles (see box on p.648); there's a hatchery on the premises, although it's out of bounds to casual visitors.

Around the other side of Laem Panwa, the island's main port of **Ao Makham** is dominated by a smelting and refining plant, bordered to the north by **Ko Siray** (aka Ko Sire), just about qualifying as an island because of the narrow canal that separates it from Phuket. Tour buses always stop off here to spy on Phuket's largest and longest-established *chao ley* community, an example of exploitative tourism at its worst. For more on the *chao ley* see p.624.

The interior

If you have your own transport, exploring the lush, verdant **interior** makes a good antidote to lying on scorched beaches. All the tiny backroads – some too small to figure on tourist maps – eventually link up with the arteries connecting Phuket town with the beaches, and the minor routes south of Hat Nai Yang are especially picturesque, passing through monsoon forest which once in a while opens out into spiky pineapple fields or regimentally ordered **rubber plantations**. Thailand's first rubber trees were planted in Trang in 1901, and Phuket's sandy soil proved to be especially well suited to the crop. All over the island you'll see cream-coloured sheets of latex hanging out to dry on bamboo racks in front of villagers' houses.

North of Karon, Phuket's minor roads eventually swing back to the central Highway 402, also known as Thanon Thepkasatri after the landmark monument that stands on a roundabout 12km north of Phuket town. This **Heroines' Monument** commemorates the repulse of the Burmese army by the widow of the governor of Phuket and her sister in 1785: the two women rallied the island's womenfolk who, legend has it, cut their hair short and rolled up banana leaves to look like musket barrels to frighten the Burmese away. All songthaews to Hat Surin and Hat Nai Yang pass the monument (as does all mainland-bound traffic), and this is where you should alight for **Thalang Museum** (Wed–Sun 8.30am–4pm; B20), five minutes' walk east of here on Route 4027. Phuket's only museum, it has a few interesting exhibits on the local tin and rubber industries, as well as some colourful folkloric history and photos of the masochistic feats of the Vegetarian Festival (see box on p.643). If you continue along Route 4207 you'll eventually reach the Gibbon Rehabilitation Project, described below.

Eight kilometres north of the Heroines' Monument, just beyond the crossroads in the small town of **Thalang**, stands **Wat Phra Thong**, one of Phuket's most revered temples on account of the power of the Buddha statue it enshrines. The solid gold image is half-buried and no one dares dig it up for fear of a curse that has struck down excavators in the past. After the wat was built around the statue, the image was encased in plaster to deter would-be robbers.

Phra Taew National Park

The road east of the Thalang intersection takes you to the visitor centre of **Phra Taew National Park**, 3km away. Several paths cross this small hilly enclave, leading you through the forest habitat of macaques and wild boar, but the most popular features of the park are the Gibbon Rehabilitation Project and the Ton Sai and Bang Pae waterfalls, which combine well as a day-trip. The

Gibbon Project is located about 10km northeast of the Heroines' Monument, off Route 4207. **Songthaews** from Phuket town, more frequent in the morning, will take you most of the way: ask to dropped off at Bang Pae (a 40min drive from town) and then follow the signed track for about 1km to get to the project centre. You can get drinks and snacks at the foodstall next to the Rehabilitation Centre, and the route to the waterfalls is signed from here.

The Gibbon Rehabilitation Project

Phuket's forests used once to resound with the whooping calls of indigenous white-handed lar gibbons, but because these primates make such cute and charismatic pets there is now not a single wild gibbon at large on the island. The situation has become so dire that the lar is now an endangered species, and in 1992 it became illegal in Thailand to keep them as pets, to sell them or to kill them. Despite this, you'll come across a good number of pet gibbons on Phuket, kept in chains by bar and hotel owners as entertainment for their customers or as sidewalk photo opportunities for gullible tourists. The **Gibbon Rehabilitation Centre** (daily 10am–4pm, last tour at 3.15pm; donation; ℡ 076/260491, ℻ 260492, ℮ gibbon@poboxes.com) aims to reverse this state of affairs, first by rescuing as many pet gibbons as they can, and then by resocializing and re-educating them for the wild before finally releasing them back into the forests. It is apparently not unusual for gibbons to be severely traumatized by their experience as pets. To begin with the young gibbons will have been taken forcibly from their mothers – who most likely would have been shot – and then they may have been taunted or even abused by their owners; in addition many "bar babies" never learn how to use their arms – a catastrophe for a wild lar who can swing through the trees at up to 30km per hour. Not surprisingly, the therapy takes a long time – to date only one gibbon has been reintroduced to the forests, and that's to an uninhabited island in Phang Nga bay.

Visitors are welcome at the project, which is centred in the forests of Phra Taew National Park, close to Bang Pae waterfall, but because the whole point of the rehab project is to minimize the gibbons' contact with humans, you can only admire the creatures from afar. There's a small exhibition here on the aims of the project, and the well-informed volunteer guides will fill you in on the details of each case and on the idiosyncratic habits of the lar gibbon (see Contexts on p.792 for more about Thailand's primates). Should you want to become a project volunteer yourself, you can fax or email the project centre.

Bang Pae and Ton Sai waterfalls

If you follow the track along the river from the Gibbon Project, you'll soon arrive at **Bang Pae waterfall**, a popular picnic and bathing spot, ten to fifteen minutes' walk away. Continue on the track for another 2.8km (about 1hr 30min on foot) and you should reach **Ton Sai waterfall**: though not a difficult climb, it is quite steep in places and can be rough underfoot, so take plenty of water and wear decent shoes. There are plenty of opportunities for cool dips in the river en route. Once at Ton Sai you can either walk back down to the Phra Taew National Park access road and try to hitch a ride back home, or return the way you came.

Thachatchai Nature Trail

Forty-one kilometres north of the Thalang intersection, just 700m south of the Sarasin Bridge exit to the mainland, a sign east off Highway 402 brings you to the **Thachatchai Nature Trail**, part of the Sirinath National Park (which also covers the west-coast beaches of Hat Mai Khao and Hat Nai Yang). Although probably not worth a special trip, the trail does combine nicely with a visit to Hat Mai Khao (see p.645) or Hat Nai Yang (see p.646) – and it's free. Any bus running between Phuket town and the mainland will drop you at the sign (it's across the road from the old headquarters of the Sirinath National Park, now moved to Hat Nai Yang), just be sure to get off before you cross the bridge. There's a visitor centre at the trailhead where you can pick up a leaflet, and a drinks stall next door.

The six-hundred-metre trail runs along a raised wooden walkway that loops through a patch of coastal mangrove swamp. Informative English-language interpretive boards are set at regular intervals to show you what **flora and fauna** to look and listen out for: you can't fail to spot the swarms of fiddler crabs scuttling about in the sand and mud around the roots of the mangrove trees, and with a little patience you might also notice a few of the crabs which you may already have encountered elsewhere, as they're the ones that give the distinctive taste to the green papaya salad, *som tam*. The "bok-bok" sound that you can hear above the roar of the distant highway is the sound the mangrove-dwelling shrimps make when they snap their pincers as they feed. For more on mangroves, see box on p.675.

Ko Phi Phi and the Krabi coast

East around the mainland coast from Phuket's Sarasin Bridge, the limestone pinnacles that so dominate the landscape of southern Thailand suddenly begin to pepper the sea as well, making **Ao Phang Nga** one of the most fascinating bays in the country. Most travellers, however, head straight for the hub of the region at **Krabi**, springboard for the spectacular mainland beaches of **Laem Phra Nang** and the even more stunning – and very popular – **Ko Phi Phi**. If it's tropical paradise minus the crowds that you're after, opt instead for the sizeable but more peaceful **Ko Lanta Yai** or the smaller **Ko Jum**.

All the major islands are served by frequent **ferries** from Krabi except during the rainy season (May–Oct), when convoluted routes via other mainland ports are sometimes possible. Buses and songthaews connect all mainland spots whatever the weather, and you can rent motorbikes in Krabi.

Ao Phang Nga

Protected from the ravages of the Andaman Sea by Phuket, **AO PHANG NGA** has a seascape both bizarre and beautiful. Covering some four hundred

the *Phang Nga Bay Resort* (☎ 076/412067, ℱ 412070; ❼–❽) boasts a swimming pool and good facilities, but has disappointing views considering the bayside location.

For **eating**, check out the *Phing Kan Restaurant* under the *Ratanapong Hotel*, where you can choose from a variety of noodle and rice standards detailed on the English-language menu. The well-established streetside restaurant nearby also has an English menu and a large selection of rice, noodle and fish dishes. Otherwise, plenty of noodle stalls line Thanon Phetkasem day and night.

Tours of the bay

The most popular budget tours are the **longtail-boat trips** operated by the long-established Sayan Tour (☎ 076/430348, ℮ sayuntour@hotmail.com), housed in an office inside the bus station (see opposite). Similar ones are organized from adjacent bus station offices by Mr Kaen Tour (☎ 076/430619) and James Bond Tour (☎ 076/413471), and by Mr Hassim at the *Muang Tong Hotel* across the road (☎ 076/412132). All offer half-day tours (daily at 8am & 2pm; 3–4hr) costing B200 per person (minimum four people), as well as full-day extensions which last until 4pm and cost B500 including lunch. (Take the 8am tour to avoid seeing the bay at its most crowded.) The tours leave from the tour operators' offices, but will pick up from the town's hotels if booked in advance; people staying at Tha Don, the departure-point for trips around Ao Phang Nga, can join the tours at the pier.

All tour operators also offer the chance to **stay** overnight on **Ko Panyi**. This can be tacked onto the half- or full-day tour for an extra B250; dinner, accommodation, and morning coffee are included in the price. Sayan Tour also offers overnight stays on the private Ko Yang Dang (aka Elephant Island), where you can swim and go canoeing; alternatively a couple of hours' canoeing can be added to the standard tour for B400.

If you have the money, the most rewarding way to see the bay is by **sea canoe**. Several companies in Phuket and Khao Lak now offer this activity, in which you paddle round the bay in two-person kayaks, exploring the hidden lagoons (*hongs*) inside the karst outcrops (see box on p.677), and observing the seabirds, kingfishers and crab-eating macaques that haunt the mangrove-fringed shores – without the constant roar of an engine to scare them away. Most outings also include snorkelling and swimming time, plus lunch on a deserted beach somewhere; some companies offer overnight trips with the chance to paddle into *hong*s after dark, and the longest-running operator, Sea Canoe, does expeditions lasting up to a fortnight. Everyone gets full paddling instruction and English-speaking guides should always be to hand; some companies have big support boats as well. Prices range from around B2200 (kids B1500) per person per day out of Khao Lak (see p.630) to B2700 (B1350) from Phuket (see box on p.647).

The bay

On tours, the standard itinerary follows a circular or figure-of-eight route around the bay, passing extraordinary karst silhouettes that change character with the shifting light – in the eerie glow of an early-morning mist it can be a breathtaking experience. Many of the formations have nicknames suggested by their weird outlines – like **Khao Machu**, which translates as "Pekinese Rock", and **Khao Tapu**, or Nail Rock. Others have titles derived from other attributes – **Tham Nak** (Naga Cave) gets its name from the serpentine stalagmites inside; and a close inspection of **Khao Kien** (Painting Rock) reveals a cliff wall decorated with paintings of elephants, monkeys, fish, crabs and hunting weapons, believed to be between three thousand and five thousand years old.

Ao Phang Nga's most celebrated feature, however, earned its tag from a movie: the cleft **Khao Ping Gan** (Leaning Rock) is better known as **James Bond Island**, after doubling as Scaramanga's hideaway in *The Man With the Golden Gun*. Every boat stops off here and the rock crawls with trinket vendors.

From Khao Ping Gan most of the boats return to the mainland via the eye-catching settlement of **Ko Panyi**, a Muslim village built almost entirely on stilts around the rock that supports the mosque. Nearly all boat tours stop here for lunch, so the island's become little more than a tourists' shopping and eating arcade. You're best off avoiding the expensive and noisy seafood restaurants out front, and heading towards the islanders' foodstalls around the mosque. The overnight tours, which include an evening meal and dormitory-style accommodation on the island, offer a more tranquil experience and a chance to watch the sun set and rise over the bay, though there's little to do in the intervening hours and you're confined to the village until a boat picks you up after breakfast.

At some point on your trip you should pass several small brick **kilns** on the edge of a mangrove swamp – once used for producing charcoal from mangrove wood – before being ferried beneath **Tham Lod**, a photogenic archway roofed with stalactites and opening onto spectacular limestone and mangrove vistas.

Krabi

The compact little fishing town of **KRABI** is both provincial capital and major hub for onward travel to some of the region's most popular islands, including Ko Phi Phi, Ko Lanta and the Laem Phra Nang beaches. So efficient are the transport links that you don't really need to stop here, but it's an attractive spot, strung out along the west bank of the Krabi estuary, with mangrove-lined shorelines to the east, a harbour filled with rickety old fishing vessels and looming limestone outcrops on every horizon. The main Thanon Utrakit runs north–south along the estuary, veering slightly inland just north of the Tha Reua Chao Fa (Chao Fa pier) and forming the eastern perimeter of the tiny town centre. There are plenty of guest houses, so it's possible to base yourself here and make day-trips to the Krabi beaches (see p.676), 45 minutes' ride away by boat or songthaew, though most people prefer to stay at the beaches. Krabi is at its busiest during high season from November through February, a period which officially begins with the annual Andaman Festival, a week of festivities featuring parades, outdoor concerts, fishing contests, a funfair and lots of street stalls that climaxes at Loy Krathong, the nationwide festival celebrated in late October or early November.

Arrival, transport and information

There are at least two daily Thai and/or Bangkok Airways **flights** between Bangkok and Krabi; Andaman Air shuttles between Phuket and Krabi three times a day. Diminutive Krabi **airport** (☏075/691940) is 18km east of town,

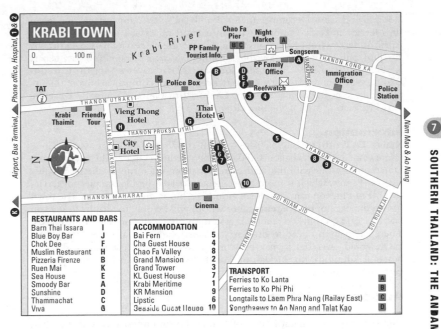

KRABI TOWN

0   100 m

Krabi River

Chao Fa Pier

Night Market · A

PP Family Tourist Info.

Songserm

THANON KONG KA

PP Family Office · A

Immigration Office

Reefwatch

Police Station

TAT

Police Box

Thai Hotel · G

THANON UTRAKIT

Krabi Thaimit · Friendly Tour

Vieng Thong Hotel

THANON PRUKSA UTHIT

City Hotel

THANON MAHARAT

Cinema

THANON ISARA

SOI RUAM JID

SOI RUAMJAI

Nam Mao & Ao Nang

Airport, Bus Terminal ◄ | Phone office, Hospital ◀ 1 & 2

RESTAURANTS AND BARS

Barn Thai Issara	I
Blue Boy Bar	J
Chok Dee	F
Muslim Restaurant	H
Pizzeria Firenze	B
Ruen Mai	K
Sea House	E
Smoody Bar	A
Sunshine	D
Thammachat	C
Viva	G

ACCOMMODATION

Bai Fern	5
Cha Guest House	4
Chao Fa Valley	8
Grand Mansion	2
Grand Tower	3
KL Guest House	7
Krabi Meritime	1
KR Mansion	9
Lipstic	6
Seaside Guest House	10

TRANSPORT

Ferries to Ko Lanta	A
Ferries to Ko Phi Phi	B
Longtails to Laem Phra Nang (Railay East)	C
Songthaews to Ao Nang and Talat Kao	D

just off Highway 4. Thai Airways minibuses transport passengers from the airport into town for B60, though these seem often to be commandeered by tour groups, so you may end up getting a taxi for B300 to Krabi or B500 to Ao Nang (maximum four passengers). Budget **car rental** have a desk in the airport arrivals area (℡075/620028, ⓦwww.budget.co.th), as do National/SMT (℡075/691939, Ⓔsmtcar@samart.co.th).

Direct air-con and VIP **buses** from Bangkok leave the Southern Bus Terminal at staggered intervals between 6.30pm and 8pm and take at least twelve hours. Air-con buses run hourly to and from Surat Thani, so if you're travelling from Bangkok, you could take an overnight **train** to Surat Thani and then pick up a Krabi bus. There are also hourly buses to and from Phuket via Phang Nga; if travelling to or from Khao Sok or Khao Lak you may have to change buses at Khokkloi. Only a few buses drop their passengers in central Krabi: most pull in at the **bus terminal** 5km north of town in the village of Talat Kao, which stands at the intersection of Thanon Utrakit and Highway 4. From here there's a frequent songthaew service to Krabi's Thanon Maharat.

When it comes to moving on from Krabi, you can buy combination bus and train tickets **to Bangkok** via Surat Thani (2 daily; 16hr; B600–850) from any travel agent; these firms also sell tickets on private buses, minibuses and boats to **Ko Samui** (2 daily; 6hr; B300–370), **Ko Pha Ngan** (2 daily; 6hr; B400), Bangkok's **Thanon Khao San** (daily; 14hr; B450–550), **Penang** (2 daily; 6hr; B400) and **Langkawi** (daily; 12hr; B550).

Two companies, Songserm and PP Family, run **ferries** from Krabi to Ko Phi Phi and to Ko Lanta; both companies use the two Chao Fa **piers**, and both have offices on nearby Thanon Kong Ka. There's nothing to choose between the two, whose prices and journey times are identical, but the timetables are different: PP Family runs year-round ferries **to Ko Phi Phi** at 10.30am and

2.30pm, and from December to April adds an extra 9am service; Songserm runs ferries at 11am and 3pm with an extra 9am service from December to April. All ferries from Krabi to Ko Phi Phi cost B200. Ferries **to Ko Lanta** via Ko Jum only run from November through May: PP Family's boats depart Krabi at 10.30am and 1.30pm, and Songserm's boat leaves at 8am; the trip costs B200. Every tour agent in town sells tickets for both companies or you can buy them on the boat. Longtail boats for **Laem Phra Nang** (45 min; B70) use the Chao Fa piers as well as the pier closer to TAT.

Information

Krabi's **TAT office** (daily 8.30am–4.30pm, ☎ 075/612740) is housed in a lone whitewashed hut on Thanon Utrakit at the northern edge of the town centre. Don't confuse this with the Tourist Information office run by the ferry operator PP Family, which is more conveniently located beside the pier for ferries to Ko Phi Phi; you can get information here, but it may be partisan. The town has no shortage of **tour agents**, all of whom will be only too happy to sell you bus, boat and train tickets and to fix you up with a room on one of the islands. There's actually no need to buy ferry tickets in advance as none of the boats has reserved seats, but it may be worth booking your first night's island or beach accommodation through one of these agents, as Ko Phi Phi especially gets packed out during peak season.

Accommodation

The least expensive guest houses offer rock-bottom **accommodation**, often cramped and windowless but perfectly adequate for one night: if all those listed are full, head for the pierside stretch of Thanon Kong Ka, where several tour operators advertise rooms for rent in the ❷ category.

Bai Fern, a 5min walk west from the pier along Thanon Chao Fa ☎ 075/630339. Sizeable, well-maintained rooms in a three-storey block that's away from the main fray; some rooms have private bathrooms and all have a balcony. ❷–❸
Cha Guest House, opposite the post office on Thanon Utrakit ☎ 075/621125, ⓦ www.thaisouth.com/cha. Long-standing traveller-oriented place with good rooms in bungalows set round a garden compound behind Krabi's most clued-up internet centre. Room rates depend on size and whether you want a private bathroom. Recommended. ❷–❸
Chao Fa Valley, a 7min walk west from the pier along Thanon Chao Fa ☎ 075/612499. Spacious en-suite bungalows arranged around a pretty flower garden with an appealingly calm atmosphere. Price depends on the size of the bungalow. ❷–❸
Grand Mansion, a 12min walk north up Thanon Utrakit from the pier ☎ 075/611371, ⓕ 611372. Though a little way from the town centre, this is the most convenient of Krabi's more comfortable hotels. The best rooms have air-con, hot water and TV. ❹–❺

Grand Tower Hotel, at the corner of Thanon Utrakit and Thanon Chao Fa ☎ 075/621456, ⓕ 611741. Central and deservedly popular, this is a very comfortable travellers' hotel with clean, nicely furnished and well-maintained rooms, all of them en suite and some with TV and air-con. internet access downstairs. Better than many pricier hotels in town. Recommended. ❸–❹
KL Guest House, Soi 2, Thanon Maharat ☎ 075/612511. No-frills, budget option; all rooms have a fan and shared bathroom, but the cheaper ones have no window. ❶–❷
KR Mansion, a 10min walk west from the pier along Thanon Chao Fa ☎ 075/612761, ⓕ 612545, ⓔ krmansion@hotmail.com. Popular travellers' haunt with clean and well-kept rooms, some with attached bathroom. Lots of traveller's information, a nice rooftop bar and a good restaurant. Also offer internet access, book exchange and bicycle rental. ❷–❺
Krabi Meritime, 2km north of town off Thanon Utrakit ☎ 075/620028, ⓕ 612992, ⓔ krabi@asianet.co.th. Beautifully located luxury hotel, set beside the limestone karsts and mangroves of the Krabi River. Rooms are attractive and

have fine views, there's a big pool, a spa, a kids' games room and babysitting service. Good value for its class; thirty percent discounts May–Oct. ❽
Lipstic, 20–22 Soi 2, Thanon Maharat ⌾075/612392, ✉kayanchalee@hotmail.com. Good budget choice tucked away off the street

with nice clean rooms, many with windows but none with private bathroom. ❷
Seaside Guesthouse, 8–10 Thanon Maharat ⌾075/630530, ⌾630529. Windowless cells with shared bathrooms; clean enough. internet access downstairs. ❷

Eating and drinking

Krabi has plenty of traveller-oriented restaurants, the best of which are detailed below, but for a truly inexpensive Thai meal, head for the riverside **night market**, which sets up around the pier-head every evening from about 6pm.

Barn Thai Issara, Soi 2, Thanon Maharat. Expensive home-made pizzas, fresh pasta dishes, Indian and Mexican food plus some unusual sourdough sandwiches.
Blue Boy Bar, Soi 4, Thanon Maharat. Downtown bar staging live music to help wash down the beer.
Chok Dee, Sea House and Sunshine, Thanon Kong Ka. Three independently run little restaurants next to each other on the road down to the pier, all deservedly popular, serving standard Thai and Western dishes, inexpensive set breakfasts, real coffee, curries and burgers. Service is friendly and relaxed.
Krabi Meritime, 2km north of the town centre off Thanon Utrakit. Fabulous views from the sky lounge on the eighth floor at Krabi's poshest hotel – a great place for a sundowner as you're admiring the riverine landscape of karsts and mangrove swamps.
Muslim Restaurant, Thanon Pruksa Uthit. Cheap and filling *rotis* (flat fried breads) served with a choice of curry sauces.
Pizzeria Firenze, Thanon Kong Ka. Authentic Italian dishes, including pizzas, pastas, sandwiches and ice creams. Tasty but pricey.

Ruen Mai, about 2km north of the town centre on Thanon Maharat. Popular with locals and well regarded, this typical garden restaurant is worth making the effort to get to, not least for the change from the more touristed options in the town centre. It serves a mid-priced menu of quality Thai dishes, including lots of seafood and *tom yam*.
Smoody Bar, Thanon Kong Ka. Nightly live music and reasonably priced beer on the waterfront at the edge of the night market.
Tamarind Tree, restaurant attached to *KR Mansion* on Thanon Chao Fa. Does a full range of slap-up organic and macrobiotic Thai and Western fare at reasonable prices. It's well worth coming here before sunset to soak up the distant mountain views from the separate rooftop bar (open 4pm–1am) and work your way through the cocktail menu.
Thammachat, Thanon Kong Ka. Boasts the best and most adventurous mid-priced menu in town, which is particularly strong on unusual Thai and vegetarian dishes. The veggie *hoh mok* (baked bean-curd omelette with basil and lemon grass) is highly recommended.

Listings

Airlines The Thai Airways office is just outside the *Krabi Meritime Hotel* on Thanon Utrakit ⌾075/622440; for flights with other carriers contact any Krabi tour operator.
Banks and exchange All major banks have branches on Thanon Utrakit with exchange counters and ATMs.
Car rental At Krabi airport (see p.671), and through some guest houses and tour companies, including Friendly Tour at 173 Thanon Utrakit

⌾075/612558, ✉krabifriendly@hotmail.com; and Krabi Thaimit at 177 Thanon Utrakit ⌾075/632054, ⌾www.asiatravel.com/thailand /krabicarrent; both rent jeeps for B1200 per 24hr and cars for B1500, including full insurance.
Cookery classes Available at the Krabi Thai Cookery School, just off the Krabi–Ao Nang road (10am–3pm; B1000 including transport; ⌾01/396 5237, ✉krabicookeryschool@hotmail.com), and bookable through any tour operator.

Dive centre Although there are dive centres at all the Krabi beaches, it's possible to organize trips and courses from Krabi town through the British-run Reefwatch Worldwide Dive Operator, 48 Thanon Utrakit ☎ 075/632650, ⊛ www.reefwatch-worldwide.com. They charge B7900 for the four-day Openwater course and run dive trips to local sites (see p.639) for B1400–2400, generally in a longtail boat.

Hospitals Krabi Hospital is about 1km north of the town centre at 325 Thanon Utrakit ☎ 075/611226.

Immigration office On Thanon Utrakit (Mon–Fri 8.30am–4.30pm; ☎ 075/611097).

Internet access At nearly every Krabi guest house; *Cha Guest House*, opposite the post office on Thanon

Utrakit has the most terminals. Catnet internet access at the phone office on Thanon Utrakit.

Mail The GPO is on Thanon Montri. Poste restante should be addressed c/o GPO and can be collected Mon–Fri 8.30am–4.30pm, Sat 8.30am–3.30pm.

Motorbike rental Through some guest houses and tour companies for about B250 per day.

Police 24hr help available on ☎ 1699, or contact the police station at the southern end of Thanon Utrakit ☎ 075/611222.

Telephones For international calls use the CAT phone office about 2km north of the town centre on Thanon Utrakit (Mon–Fri 8am–8pm, Sat & Sun 8.30am–4.30pm), which is easily reached on any songthaew heading up that road, or on foot.

Day-trips from Krabi

With time on your hands you'll soon exhaust the possibilities in Krabi, but there are a few trips to make out of town apart from the popular excursions to Laem Phra Nang (p.677), Hat Nopparat Thara (see p.684), Ao Phang Nga (see p.666) and Ko Phi Phi (see p.685). Alternatively, you could join one of the numerous **organized tours** sold by every Krabi travel agent, for example the tours of four or five islands which take in the reefs and beaches around Laem Phra Nang, or the hikes through the national park near Khlong Thom, home of the rare Gurney's pitta; because tour agencies sell the same basic itineraries, prices are kept competitive.

The mangroves

Longtail-boat tours of the **mangrove swamps** that infest the Krabi River estuary are an increasingly popular activity and can be organized directly with the boatmen who hang around Krabi's two piers (about B300 per hour for up to six people) or through most tour operators (average B500 per person for three hours). All mangrove tours give you a chance to get a close-up view of typical mangrove flora and fauna (see box opposite), and most will stop off at a couple of riverside caves on the way. The most famous features on the usual mangrove itinerary are the twin limestone outcrops known as **Khao Kanab Nam**, which rise a hundred metres above the water from opposite sides of the Krabi River near the *Krabi Meritime Hotel* and are so distinctive that they've become the symbol of Krabi. One of the twin karsts hides caves which can be easily explored – many skeletons have been found here over the centuries, thought to be those of immigrants who got stranded by a flood before reaching the mainland.

Even more fun than taking a longtail tour of the mangroves is a self-paddle **kayaking** tour of the mangroves and *hong*s, hidden lagoons found further north up the coast. Every tour operator in Krabi sells these outings; see the box on p.677 for itineraries and prices.

Wat Tham Seua

Beautifully set amid limestone cliffs 12km northeast of Krabi, the tropical for-est of **Wat Tham Seua** (Tiger Cave Temple) can be reached by taking a red songthaew from Thanon Utrakit (20min; B8), and then walking 2km down the

Life in a mangrove swamp

Mangrove swamps are at their creepiest at low tide, when their aerial roots are fully exposed to form gnarled and knotted archways above the muddy banks. Not only are these roots essential parts of the tree's breathing apparatus, they also reclaim land for future mangroves, trapping and accumulating water-borne debris into which the metre-long mangrove seedlings can fall. In this way, mangrove swamps also fulfil a vital ecological function: stabilizing shifting mud and protecting coastlines from erosion and the impact of tropical storms.

Mangrove swamp mud harbours some interesting creatures too, like the instantly recognizable **fiddler crab**, named after the male's single outsized reddish claw, which it brandishes for communication and defence purposes – the claw is so powerful it could open a can of baked beans. If you keep your eyes peeled you should be able to make out a few **mudskippers**; these specially adapted fish can absorb atmospheric oxygen through their skins as long as they keep their outsides damp, which is why they spend so much time slithering around in the sludge. As you'd imagine from the name, on land they move in tiny hops by flicking their tails, aided by their extra-strong pectoral fins. Of the bigger creatures who patrol the mangrove swamps in search of food, you might well come across **kingfishers** and white-bellied **sea eagles**, but you'd be very lucky indeed to encounter the rare crab-eating macaque. For more on mangrove ecosystems see Contexts, p.800.

To date, the Krabi mangroves have escaped the **environmentally damaging** attentions of the prawn-farming industry that has so damaged the swamps around Kanchanaburi (see "Environmental Issues" in Contexts, p.800, for more on this). But mangrove wood from this area has been used to make commercial charcoal, and on any boat trip around the Krabi coastline you'll almost certainly pass the remains of old tiny brick kilns near cleared patches of swamp.

signed track. As this is a working monastery, signs request that visitors wear respectable dress (no shorts or singlets for men or women), so bear this in mind before you leave town.

The temple's main **bot** – on your left under the cliff overhang – might come as a bit of a shock: alongside portraits of the abbot, a renowned teacher of Vipassana meditation, close-up photos of human entrails and internal organs are on display – reminders of the impermanence of the body. Any skulls and skeletons you might come across in the compound serve the same educational purpose. The most interesting part of Wat Tham Seua lies beyond the bot, reached by following the path past the nuns' quarters until you get to a couple of steep **staircases** up the 600-metre-high cliffside. The first staircase is long (1272 steps) and very steep, and takes about an hour to climb, but the vista from the summit is quite spectacular, affording fabulous karst views over the limestone outcrops and out to the islands beyond. There's a small shrine and a few monks' cells hidden among the trees at the top. The second staircase, next to the large statue of the Chinese fertility goddess Kuan Im, takes you on a less arduous route down into a deep dell encircled by high limestone walls. Here the monks have built themselves self-sufficient meditation cells, linked by paths through the lush ravine: if you continue along the main path you'll eventually find yourself back where you began, at the foot of the staircase. The valley is home to squirrels and monkeys as well as a pair of remarkable trees with overground **buttress roots** over 10m high. Triangular buttress roots are quite a common sight in tropical forests such as this, where the overhead canopy is so dense that it blocks out most of the sunlight, starving the soil of the nutrients necessary to sustain such enormous trees and rendering subterranean roots ineffective; these lateral extensions to the trunk both absorb foodstuff from the forest floor, in the form of fallen leaves and fungi, and act as the tree's anchor.

Susaan Hoi

Thais make a big deal out of **Susaan Hoi** (Shell Cemetery), 17km west around the coast from Krabi, but it's hard to get very excited about a shoreline of metre-long 40-centimetre-thick beige-coloured rocks that could easily be mistaken for concrete slabs. Nevertheless, the facts of their formation are impressive: these stones are 75 million years old and made entirely from compressed shell fossils. You get a distant view of them from any longtail boat travelling between Krabi and Ao Phra Nang; for a closer look take any of the frequent Ao Nang-bound songthaews from Thanon Utrakit.

Krabi beaches

Although the mainland beach areas west of Krabi can't compete with the local islands for underwater life, the stunning headland of **Laem Phra Nang** is accessible only by boat, so staying on one of its three beaches can feel like being on an island, albeit a crowded and potentially rather claustrophobic one. In contrast, a road runs right along the **Ao Nang** beachfront, which has enabled a burgeoning but likeable resort to thrive around its rather unexceptional beach. The next bay to the west, **Hat Nopparat Thara,** is long and unadulterated and has some appealingly solitary places to stay at its western end. Snorkelling conditions deteriorate at all Krabi beaches during the rainy season from May through October, so prices at all accommodation drops by up to fifty percent for this period, though a few places close down for the duration.

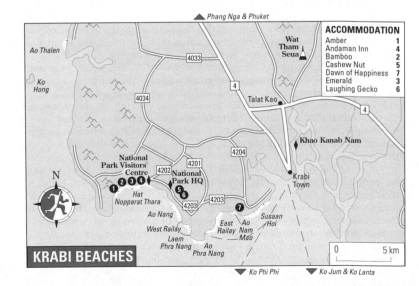

ACCOMMODATION

Amber	1
Andaman Inn	4
Bamboo	2
Cashew Nut	5
Dawn of Happiness	7
Emerald	3
Laughing Gecko	6

KRABI BEACHES

0   5 km

By far the most rewarding way of exploring the glories of the Krabi coastline is by **sea kayak**. Paddling silently and stealthily into the eerie mangrove swamps and secret lagoons, or *hongs*, hidden inside the limestone karsts is an awesome experience and gives you close-up views of birds, animals and plants that would be impossible in a roaring longtail.

Hongs are the *pièce de résistance* of south Thailand's coastline – invisible to any passing vessel, these secret tidal lagoons can only be accessed at certain tides in canoes and boats small enough to travel along the narrow tunnels that lead into the karst's central pool. Once inside a *hong* you are completely enclosed by a ring of cliff faces hung with strange plants which nourish a local population of flying foxes and monkeys and support an ecosystem that's remained unchanged for millennia. Like the karsts themselves, the *hong*s have taken millions of years to form, the softer limestone hollowed out from above by the wind and the rain, and from the side by the pounding waves. Eventually, when the two hollows met, the heart of the karst was able to fill with water via the wave-eroded passageway at sea level, creating a lagoon. At high water these tunnels are filled and so impassable to any human, but when the tide recedes – for about fifty minutes every six hours – some tunnels do become passable to kayaks, enabling people to navigate into the mysterious *hong* at the heart of the karst.

Many companies take tourists kayaking around the karsts and mangrove swamps along the Krabi coastline, to impressive spots such as **Ao Thalen** (aka Ao Talin or Talan), about 25km northwest of Krabi town, where you paddle out to the *hong*s and beaches of **Ko Hong** and **Ko Bileh**. Another 25km north up the Krabi coast, the **Ban Bor Tor** (aka Ban Bho Tho) area of **Ao Luk** bay is famous as much for its caves as for its mangroves and karst landscape, and is another popular destination for kayak trips. The most famous cave up here is **Tham Lod**, with a long tunnel hung with stalagmites and stalactites and an entrance that's obscured by vines. The walls of nearby **Tham Phi Hua Toe** display around a hundred prehistoric cave-paintings as well as some interestingly twisted stalactite formations. Most Ao Luk tours also feature a visit to the inland botanical gardens of **Than Bokkharani**, 1km south of Ao Luk. Called Than Bok for short, the tiny park is a glade of emerald pools, grottoes and waterfalls enclosed in a ring of lush forest; if you want to see them independently, catch an Ao Luk songthaew from Krabi (1hr) and then walk down to the gardens.

Kayaking **trips** to any of the above destinations usually cost about B1200–1700 for a full day or B700–900 for half a day. Timing is obviously crucial in the exploration of these *hong*s, so sea-kayaking tour operators have to arrange their itinerary day by day to coincide with the tide. They can be arranged through any tour operator in Krabi town, Laem Phra Nang or Ao Nang, or directly with reputable kayaking operators such as Sea Canoe (℡075/637170, ֍www.seacanoe.com) and Sea Kayak Krabi (℡075/630270). Sea Canoe also does longer trips of up to a fortnight, including the one-nighter based at their island camp (B7500 per person). All kayaking tours are priced for self-paddling, and tour leaders should give you full kayaking instruction; if asked, most tour operators can arrange for someone else to paddle you around for an extra B300.

Laem Phra Nang and Ao Nam Mao

Seen from the close quarters of a longtail boat, the combination of sheer limestone cliffs, pure white sand and emerald waters at **LAEM PHRA NANG** is spectacular – and would be even more so without the hundreds of other admirers gathered on its beaches. Almost every centimetre of buildable land on the cape has now been taken over by bungalows, but at least high-rises don't feature yet, and much of the construction is hidden among coconut palms or set amid prettily landscaped gardens. The headland has three beaches within ten minutes' walk of each other: **Ao Phra Nang** graces the southwestern edge, and is flanked by **east and west Railay**. The scene here is laid-back, but by no means comatose; it's as popular with backpackers as it is with couples on short breaks, and the accommodation and entertainment facilities reflect this. It's also a major rock-climbing centre, both for beginners and experienced climbers, many of whom hang out here for months at a time while ticking off the three hundred different routes. Even if you don't want to stay, it's worth coming for the day to gawp at the scenery and scramble down into the lushly vegetated area around the cape's enclosed lagoon. Just about visible from east Railay but only accessible from it by a ten-minute longtail ride, **Ao Nam Mao** feels secluded and is the site of just one mid-priced eco-resort.

The beaches

Set against a magnificent backdrop of cliffs and palms, diminutive **AO PHRA NANG** (aka Hat Tham Phra Nang) is the loveliest spot on the cape, attracting sunbathers to its luxuriously soft sand and snorkellers to the reefs some 200m offshore. Of the three beaches, it alone has no bungalows visible from the shore, just a couple of makeshift beachfront café-bars. Screened from the beach is just one luxury resort, with the sole means of direct access to Ao Phra Nang, but non-guests can walk there from east Railay in under ten minutes, following the resort's hedge until it gives onto a walkway which winds under the lip of the karst to the beach.

The beach and cape are named after a princess (*phra nang* means "revered lady"), whom the local fisherfolk believe lives here and controls the fertility of the sea. If you walk past the entrance to **Tham Phra Nang** (Princess Cave), hollowed out of the huge karst outcrop at the eastern edge of the bay, you'll see a host of red-tipped wooden phalluses stacked as offerings to her, by way of insurance for large catches. The numerous passageways and rocks around the cave are fun to clamber over, but getting down into **Sa Phra Nang** (Princess Lagoon) is more of a challenge. Buried deep inside the same rock, the lagoon is accessible only via a steep 45-minute descent that starts at the "resting spot" halfway along the walkway connecting the east edge of Ao Phra Nang with east Railay. After an initial ten-minute clamber, negotiated with the help of ropes, the path forks: go left for a panoramic view over the east and west bays of Hat Railay, or right for the lagoon. (For the strong-armed, there's the third option of hauling yourself up ropes to the top of the cliff for a bird's-eye view.) Taking the right-hand fork, you'll pass through the tropical dell dubbed "big tree valley" before eventually descending to the murky lagoon. The muddy banks have spawned a lagoonside gallery of clay models fashioned by visitors. The exterior face of Sa Phra Nang is popular with novice rock climbers, and courses are held here throughout the day during the dry season; see below for details.

Sometimes known as Sunset Beach, **WEST RAILAY** comes a close second to Ao Phra Nang, with similarly impressive karst scenery, crystal-clear water and a much longer stretch of good sand. There's some shade here too, and you only have to walk a few hundred metres to get beyond the longtails and the beachfront diners' line of vision. For more seclusion and an absence of longtails, wade or swim the few hundred metres to the lovely, uncrowded beach around the headland to the immediate north of west Railay (beyond the compound of the private time-share outfit, the *Railay Beach Club*).

The least attractive of the cape's beaches, **EAST RAILAY** (also sometimes known as Nam Mao, but not to be confused with the better known Ao Nam

Mao immediately to the east) is not suitable for swimming because of its fairly dense mangrove growth, a tide that goes out for miles and a bay that's busy with incoming longtails. Still, there's a greater concentration of inexpensive bungalows here, and none is more than ten minutes' walk from the much cleaner sands of west Railay and Ao Phra Nang. To get to east Railay from Ao Phra Nang, follow the walkway from the eastern edge; from west Railay walk through the *Railay Bay* or *Sand Sea* bungalow compounds.

AO NAM MAO is more suitable for swimming than east Railay though the tide here also runs out a long way and the sand is nothing like as deluxe as on west Railay. It's much less congested though, and you can walk to the Susaan Hoi shell cemetery in about twenty minutes.

Diving, climbing and kayaking

All bungalows on Laem Phra Nang organize **snorkelling trips** (B250–400 including equipment) to the nearby islands of Hua Kwan and Ko Poda, and some offer two-night trips to Bamboo Island (B2000). From October through May, Phra Nang Divers, located next to *Railay Village* on west Railay (T & F075/637064, W www.pndivers.com) runs one-day **diving trips** to nearby islands (B1800–2700), and two- and three-day live-aboards for B9000 and B15,500; they also offer a range of PADI-certificated diving courses (B9500 for the four-day Openwater). The most popular period for diving is January through March when it's worth reserving ahead if you're on a tight schedule. The nearest **recompression chamber** is on Ao Patong in Phuket (see p.638).

Given the topography, there's huge potential for **rock climbing**, abseiling and caving at Laem Phra Nang. There are some three hundred bolted sport-climbing routes on the cape, ranging in difficulty from 5a–8c, and no shortage of places where you can rent equipment and hire guides and instructors. Two of the longest-established climbing outfits are King Climbers (T075/637125, F612914, W www.railay.com/railay/climbing/climbing_intro.shtml), located at the back of the *Ya Ya* compound on east Railay, and Tex Climbing at the edge of *Railay Bay* (T075/631509, F621186, E texrock@loxinfo.co.th). It's a good idea to check with other tourists before choosing a climbing guide, as operators' safety standards vary. All the climbing centres rent out equipment (B1000 per day for two people) and offer a range of climbing **courses** and expeditions. A typical half-day introduction for novice climbers costs B800, a one-day climbing outing is B1500, and for B5000 you get a three-day course which should leave you experienced enough to strike out on your own. If you're already self-sufficient, you might want to get hold of the *Route Guide* to the Laem Phra Nang climbs, written by the guys at King Climbers and available from most of the climbing shops.

Limestone cliffs and mangrove swamps also make great landscapes for **kayaking**, and several places on east and west Railay rent them out for B100–150 per hour, with discounts for half- and full-day rental. Some places also offer kayaking tours of spectacular Ao Luk and Ko Hong (see p.677) for B850–900.

Practicalities

Laem Phra Nang is only accessible by **boat** from Krabi town, Ao Nang, Ao Nam Mao and Ko Phi Phi. Longtail boats to Laem Phra Nang depart from various spots along the **Krabi** riverfront and from Chao Fa pier (45min; B70), leaving throughout the day as soon as they fill up. There are usually several different boatmen touting for custom at the same time, but as they each need a minimum of six passengers (the maximum load is fourteen), it's often more efficient to make your own group of six before committing to one particular boatmen. Depending on the tide, all Krabi boats land on or off east Railay, so you'll probably have to wade; from east Railay it's easy to cut across to west Railay along any of the through-tracks. Krabi boats do run during the rainy season, but it's a nerve-wracking experience so you're advised to go via Ao Nang instead. **Ao Nang** is much closer to Laem Phra Nang, and longtails run from the beachfront here to west Railay (10min; B40) year-round. During high season there's one direct boat a day between Laem Phra Nang and **Ko Phi Phi**. The easiest way of getting to **Ao Nam Mao** is by songthaew: all Krabi–Ao Nang songthaews pass the resort's entrance (every 10min; B20). Demand for boats between Ao Nam Mao and Laem Phra Nang is small, but if you don't mind waiting an hour or so you should be able to get a longtail between the two for about B40 (10min).

The three big bungalow operations on west Railay all have tour agencies and shops selling beach gear and postcards. You can **change money** at nearly all the bungalow operations on the cape, but rates can be up to ten percent lower than at the Krabi banks. There is (slow and expensive) **internet access** at *Ya Ya* on east Railay, an **overseas phone** service at *SandSea* and *Railay Village*, a **clinic** in the *Railay Bay* compound, mid-way along the access track between east and west Railay, and a small **bookshop** stocked with new and secondhand books at *Railay Village*.

Accommodation and eating

Aside from the opulent *Rayavadee Premier* resort, **accommodation** on the headland is of a fairly uniform standard which tends to be more expensive and less good value than equivalent options on the mainland. The places on east Railay are more budget-orientated than those on west Railay, but most bungalows offer a range of choices, priced to reflect flimsiness of hut or nature of view, though bear in mind that no room on the cape is more than 200m from the sea. To get a decent room at a decent price during high season, it's essential to arrive on the beaches as early in the morning as possible and, if necessary, to hang around waiting for people to check out. Prices listed below are for high season, but rates can drop up to fifty percent from May to October.

All the bungalow operations have **restaurants** where food is generally pricey and unremarkable. Evening entertainment consists either of watching the restaurant videos – most places have twice-nightly screenings – or patronizing one of the relaxed beachfront **bars**, like *Rapala* and *Last Bar*, both near *Diamond 2* bungalows on east Railay. Rock-climbers tend to gravitate towards the *Sunset Bar* on west Railay, where there's fire-juggling most nights.

Ao Phra Nang

Rayavadee Premier, on Ao Phra Nang, right at the tip of the cape ☎ 075/620740, ℱ 620630, ⓦ www.rayavadee.com. Set in a beautifully landscaped compound bordering all three beaches, and the only place with direct access to Ao Phra Nang, this exclusive resort is an unobtrusively designed small village of supremely elegant two-storey pavilions costing a staggering B23,000 a night. The lack of beachfront accommodation is more than compensated for by a swimming pool with sea view. ⑨

West Railay

Railay Bay ☎ & ℱ 075/622330. A huge range of accommodation on land that runs down to both east and west Railay. The cheapest rooms are in small fan-cooled huts while the top-end bungalows are thoughtfully designed and have sea-view verandas and air-con. Some of the lower-priced huts are closer to east than west Railay. ④–⑧

Railay Village ☎ 075/622578, ℱ 622579. Attractive fan and air-con bungalows occupying landscaped grounds in between the two beaches, with nowhere more than 300m from the west Railay shore. Efficiently run and nicely maintained; recommended. ⑤–⑧

SandSea ⊕075/622167, ⊕622168. Comfortable bungalows with fan and bathroom, plus deluxe air-con versions with big windows and nice furniture. All accommodation is set around a lovely tropical garden, and the place feels peaceful and secluded from the fray. Recommended. ⑥–⑧

East Railay

Coco Bungalow, in the centre of the beach ⊕01/228 4258. The cheapest accommodation on the cape, comprising basic but pleasant enough en-suite bamboo huts in a small garden compound. Always fills up fast. ①

Diamond Cave Bungalows, at the far eastern end of the beach ⊕075/622589, ⊕622590. Huge range of rooms, mostly in detached bungalows, impressively located beside several karsts, including Diamond Cave itself. Rooms are plainly but comfortably furnished, some have air-con and TV, and the cheapest ones, which have shared bathrooms, are rented out to climbers at good monthly rates. ⑤–⑦

Diamond 2, at the far eastern end of the beach ⊕075/622591. Just a handful of ultra-basic, no-frills bamboo huts crammed into a small area at the far end of the beach. The cheaper rooms share facilities. ②

Sunrise Bay Bungalows, towards the western (Laem Phra Nang) end of the beach ⊕075/622591. Forty small concrete huts with private bathrooms; price depends on proximity to the beachfront. ④–⑤

Viewpoint, at the far eastern end of east Railay ⊕075/622587. Set up above the shore, which means that many of the bungalows enjoy good bay-views from the large picture windows; some rooms in a hotel block are also available. The terrace restaurant affords great vistas of the mangrove and karst-dotted seascape too, and is worth a visit from non-guests. ④–⑥

Ya Ya Bungalows in the centre of the beach ⊕075/622750. Dozens of huts and three-storey wooden towers jammed into a small area make this place seem a bit claustrophobic and leave the ground-floor rooms rather dark. All rooms have private facilities and some have air-con. ③–⑥

Ao Nam Mao

Dawn of Happiness, Ao Nam Mao ⊕01/895 2101, ⊕075/612914. A peaceful, self-styled eco-resort comprising just a handful of characterful rustic bungalows with bamboo walls, mosquito nets and cold-water showers. They run lots of soft-adventure tours to local spots, including snorkelling and kayaking, and overnight trips to Bamboo Island and to Khao Sok. Open all year, with forty percent discounts in low season. ⑤–⑥

Ao Nang

Now that Laem Phra Nang is full to bursting point, **AO NANG** (sometimes confusingly signed as Ao Phra Nang), a couple of bays further north up the coast, has blossomed into quite a lively resort. Though it lacks the cape's fine beaches, some people find it a friendlier and less claustrophobic place than Laem Phra Nang. A road runs right alongside a big chunk of Ao Nang's narrow shore, with the resort area stretching back over 1km along both arms of Highway 4203, but you only need to walk down the track that runs to the south of *Ao Nang Villa* to get to a much prettier and quieter part of the beach; better still, swim or wade around the small headland at the southernmost tip to find yourself on another long bay of fine gold sand. A half-hour walk in the other direction takes you to the unadulterated sands of Hat Nopparat Thara, or it's an impressive ten-minute boat ride from the Ao Nang shore to the beaches of Laem Phra Nang. In short, from wherever you stand, the expansive seaward view of crystal-clear water dotted with limestone monoliths remains pretty awesome.

Diving, snorkelling and kayaking

About ten **dive shops** operate out of Ao Nang, with offices on the beach road and up Route 4203, including Ao Nang Divers at *Krabi Seaview*

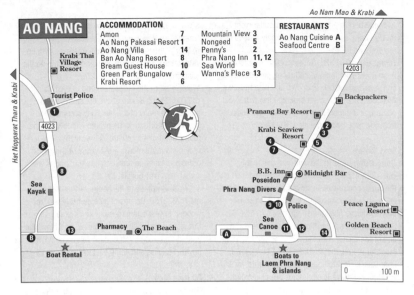

ACCOMMODATION

Amon	7	Mountain View	3
Ao Nang Pakasai Resort	1	Nongeed	5
Ao Nang Villa	14	Penny's	2
Ban Ao Nang Resort	8	Phra Nang Inn	11, 12
Bream Guest House	10	Sea World	9
Green Park Bungalow	4	Wanna's Place	13
Krabi Resort	6		

RESTAURANTS

Ao Nang Cuisine **A**
Seafood Centre **B**

(☎075/637242, ⓦwww.krabi-seaview.com), Calypso (☎075/637056), Coral Diving at *Krabi Resort* (☎075/637465), Phra Nang Divers (☎ & ⓕ075/637064, ⓦwww.pndivers.com), and Poseidon (☎075/637263). Most one-day **dive trips** head for the area round Ko Phi Phi (see p.685) and include dives at Shark Point and the "King Cruiser" wreck dive (see p.639 for descriptions) for B2000–2400 including two tanks, or B900 for snorkellers. Two dives in the Ao Nang area – at Ko Poda and Ko Yawasam – average B1800 (B500–700 for snorkellers) or B1400 if you opt to go in a longtail rather than a dive boat. PADI dive courses start at B1800 for the introductory day, or B9000 for the Openwater. The nearest **recompression chamber** is run by Hyperbaric Services Thailand and is located on Ao Patong in Phuket (see p.638); check to see that your dive operator is insured to use it.

It's quite common to arrange your own **snorkelling trips** with the longtail boatmen who congregate on the Ao Nang beachfront: a typical price would be B200 per person for a four- or five-hour snorkelling trip to Ko Poda and other nearby islets. Alternatively, all Ao Nang tour agents sell snorkelling and swimming day-trips such as those advertised as "four-island" tours. Most dive shops rent mask, snorkel and fins for about B150 the set.

Several tour agents in Ao Nang offer **kayaking** expeditions, including the longest-established and highly reputable SeaCanoe (☎075/637170, ⓦwww.seacanoe.com), which has an office on the beachfront road, and Seakayak Krabi (☎075/630270) which is based opposite the *Ban Ao Nang* hotel. For around B1700 they take you on self-paddle trips through the mangrove swamps and caves of Ao Luk or Ao Thalen, just south of Ao Phang Nga. See the box on p.677 for more on kayaking in the Krabi area. Some outlets also rent kayaks by the hour, at B100–150 per hour.

Practicalities

Access to Ao Nang is easy, as **songthaews** run from Krabi regularly throughout the day, taking about 45 minutes (every 10min from 6am–6.30pm, every

30min from 6.30pm–10.30pm; B20), and there are frequent longtail **boats** shuttling back and forth to west Railay on Laem Phra Nang (10min; B40). From November to May, a daily boat connects Ao Nang with Ko Phi Phi Don (1hr). There are plenty of facilities on Ao Nang, including official **money exchange** counters, lots of **internet** centres, several minimarkets, a proliferation of beachwear stalls, numerous tour operators and dive shops (see p.681), and the inevitable tailors' shops. The local **tourist police** are based next to the *Pakasai Resort* (☏075/637208). Most guest houses rent out **motorbikes** for B120–200 per 24 hours, and tour operators rent out jeeps for B1200/day. There's a *muay Thai* **boxing** stadium 1km west out of Ao Nang, near the *Laughing Gecko* guest house on Hat Nopparat Thara (see p.685), which stages regular bouts in high season; check local flyers for details.

Accommodation and eating

The tourist season at Ao Nang is short, so the high-season **hotel** prices listed below only apply from late November through February; if you're planning on coming here in January, the busiest month, you should definitely book your accommodation in advance. Outside high season, rates can drop by up to fifty percent, making early November and March the best-value time to stay here (being neither wet, nor crowded, nor expensive). Although **budget accommodation** may at first glance appear thin on the ground at Ao Nang, several budget and moderate places do exist, the best of them a few hundred metres north of the seafront, along Route 4203.

As for **eating**, *Ao Nang Cuisine*, on the beachfront road, has a good reputation for authentic, quality Thai seafood dishes, or try *Ao Nang Seafood*, in among the cluster of little bars and restaurants sometimes referred to as the Seafood Centre at the western end of the beachfront road, where you get very good fish dishes plus an uninterrupted view of the waves.

Inexpensive and moderate

Amon, on Route 4203 ☏075/637695. The en-suite concrete row-houses here have neither views nor atmosphere but come at a good price. ❸
Bream Guest House, on Route 4203 ☏075/637555, ✉bream-prapa@hotmail.com. Urban-style guest house offering some of the cheapest rooms in the resort, all with shared bathroom. ❸
Green Park Bungalow, on Route 4203 ☏075/637300. Friendly family-run place set in a shady grove of trees and offering bamboo huts with verandas and private bathrooms or more expensive concrete versions. Recommended budget option. ❷–❹
Mountain View, on Route 4203 ☏01/637294. Reasonably priced en-suite bungalows under a limestone cliff. ❹
Nongeed, on Route 4203 ☏075/637237. Range of rooms with the nicest and priciest on the upper floor, blessed with great karst views and air-con. The better downstairs rooms have TVs to compensate for the lack of outlook. Good value for Ao Nang. ❸–❺
Penny's, on Route 4203 ☏075/637295, ℻637468, ✉johneyre@loxinfo.co.th. Friendly,

family-run place offering very clean, comfortable rooms with or without bathroom and/or air-con. Located in a small block right under a limestone cliff, so there are magnificent views from the rooftop sun terrace. Discounts of up to fifty percent in low season. ❹–❼
Sea World, on Route 4203 ☏075/637388. Very good, well-priced rooms with bathroom, balcony and great views, with or without air-con; a few of the cheapest rooms share bathrooms. internet access downstairs. Very popular so try to reserve ahead. ❷–❺
Wanna's Place and Ao Nang Beach Bungalow, central beachfront road ☏075/637322, ☻www.wannasplace.com. This two-in-one operation is the most affordable of the few beachfront places and offers nice enough, if rather plain, fan and air-con bungalows around a garden with a swimming pool. It's very popular so worth reserving ahead. ❺–❻

Expensive

Ao Nang Pakasai Resort, on the road to Hat Nopparat Thara ☏075/637777, ℻637637,

@apakasai@loxinfo.co.th. Run by the same group as the *Krabi Meritime* in Krabi, this stylish resort is equally luxurious, with accommodation scattered up the hillside in landscaped grounds giving fine bay views. The rooms are beautifully furnished and there's a scenically located swimming pool, table tennis, games room and bicycle hire. Not suitable for guests with mobility difficulties. Rates from B5000. ❾

Ao Nang Villa, just off the beach ☏ & ℗075/637072, operation with attractive air-con bungalows and sea-view hotel rooms just off the beach. All rooms have air-con, TV and use of the pool. ❽

Ban Ao Nang Resort, opposite *Krabi Resort* on the road to Hat Nopparat Thara ☏075/637072,

℗637070, @baonan@loxinfo.co.th. A low-rise establishment just 2min walk from the sea; there's a pool here and the air-con rooms are comfortably furnished. ❽

Krabi Resort, just north of the main beachfront, on the road to Hat Nopparat Thara ☏075/637030, ℗637051. Set in a large tropical garden in a tiny bay; one of the poshest places on Ao Nang with both top-notch bungalows and rooms in a low-rise hotel. ❾

Phra Nang Inn, on the main beachfront ☏075/637130, ℗637134, @phranang@loxinfo.co.th. Elegant wooden hotel with spacious, well-equipped rooms and a small swimming pool. Big discounts May–Oct. ❽–❾

Hat Nopparat Thara

Follow the road northwest past *Krabi Resort* for about 1km and you come to the **eastern** end of two-kilometre-long **Hat Nopparat Thara**. Invariably almost deserted, this beach is part of the national marine park that encompasses Ko Phi Phi, with the park headquarters about two-thirds of the way along and the **visitor centre** another kilometre further on, beyond the T-junction. At low tide it's almost impossible to swim here, but the sands are enlivened by millions of starfish and thousands of hermit crabs, and you can walk out to the small offshore island if you tire of the supine life. There's some development on the inland side of the beachfront road here, with signs of more to come, so the distance between eastern beach accommodation and the restaurants and shops of Ao Nang is set to decrease.

The **western** stretch of Hat Nopparat Thara feels like a different beach as it's separated from the visitor centre and eastern Hat Nopparat Thara by a khlong, and can only be reached by the longtails which depart from the national park pier, Tha Hat Nopparat Thara (the 4WD track to the beach is private). Sometimes known as Hat Ton Son, western Hat Nopparat Thara currently has just four bungalow operations sharing the long swathe of peaceful casuarina- and palm-shaded shoreline, and is a great place to escape the crowds and commerce of other Krabi beaches. The views of the karst islands are magnificent – and you can walk to some of the nearer ones at low tide, though swimming here is just as tide-dependent as on eastern Hat Nopparat Thara. All the bungalow outfits here can arrange snorkelling trips to nearby islands, and *Andaman Inn* offers quite a range of day-trips inland.

Practicalities

All Krabi–Ao Nang **songthaews** go via the national park visitor centre (for the pier and boats to the western beach) and all travel the length of eastern Hat Nopparat Thara as well. The fare is B20 from Krabi (30min) or B10 from Ao Nang (10–15min). **Longtails** from Tha Hat Nopparat Thara leave for the western beach when full and will either drop you beside the closest set of bungalows, *Andaman Inn* (B10), from where you can walk to the accommodation of your choice, or at high tide they'll take you further up the beach if asked (B20–30).

As for **accommodation**, most of the western beach **bungalows** have electricity in the evenings only, and most close for the rainy season from May through October. You are quite free to camp anywhere on the beach, though on the eastern beach there's very little shelter, and the road is visible along most of it. All accommodation places on both beaches serve **food**, and there are a few hot-food and snack stalls near the national park bungalows.

Eastern Hat Nopparat Thara

Cashew Nut, 200m down a track from the main beachfront road. Fairly comfortable, sturdy concrete bungalows with fan and bathroom. ❹
Laughing Gecko, 200m down a track from the main beachfront road. En-suite, simply equipped bamboo huts managed by a friendly family. ❷
National Park Bungalows, beside the visitor centre and pier at the western end of the eastern beach ☏075/637159. Just a handful of spartan bungalows sleeping two, or four-person tents for hire at B200. ❸

Western Hat Nopparat Thara

Amber Bungalows, westernmost end of the beach, about 700m walk from the khlong ☏01/894 8761, amberandaman@hotmail.com. A very quiet spot, this welcoming Thai-French-run place has just nine spacious bamboo bungalows with mosquito nets and private bathrooms, each

enjoying a good sea view from the large verandas. In low season, call to check whether it's open. ❷–❸
Andaman Inn, 100m west of the khlong ☏01/956 1173. The most commercial and popular place on the western beach, with a huge range of huts, from very simple affairs with shared bathrooms to large en-suite versions. Does day-trips and snorkelling tours. ❶–❸
Bamboo, between *Emerald* and *Amber* ☏01/892 2532. The simplest and most *laissez faire* of the places on the beach, offering very basic bamboo huts, with or without private showers, and lamplight in the evenings. Closed April to mid–Nov. ❶–❷
Emerald Bungalows, next to *Andaman Inn* ☏01/956 2566, ☏075/631119. Offers the most comfortable accommodation on the beach, in big, brightly painted and nicely furnished wooden bungalows, all with sea views, private bathroom and fan. Runs boat trips to nearby islands at B1500 for up to eight people. Closed May–Aug. ❻

Ko Phi Phi

Now well established as one of southern Thailand's most popular destinations, the two islands known as **KO PHI PHI** lie 40km south of Krabi and 48km east of southern Phuket, encircled by water so clear that you can see almost to the sea bed from the surface, easily making out the splayed leaves of cabbage coral and the distinctively yellow-striped tiger fish from the boat as you approach the islands. The action is concentrated on the larger **Ko Phi Phi Don**, packed with bungalow operations and tourist enterprises serving the burgeoning ranks of divers, snorkellers and sybarites who just come to slump on the long white beaches. No less stunning is the uninhabited sister island of **Ko Phi Phi Leh**, whose sheer cliff-faces get national marine park protection on account of the lucrative bird's nest business (see box on p.695).

Inevitably, both islands have started to suffer the negative consequences of their outstanding beauty. Some of the beaches are now littered with plastic bottles and cigarette ends, and Phi Phi Don seems to be permanently under construction, with building rubble disfiguring the interior and piles of stinking rubbish left rotting behind the ranks of bungalows. This problem has worsened since Phi Phi Leh gained worldwide attention when it was used as the film location for the movie *The Beach*, with businesses on Phi Phi Don capitalizing

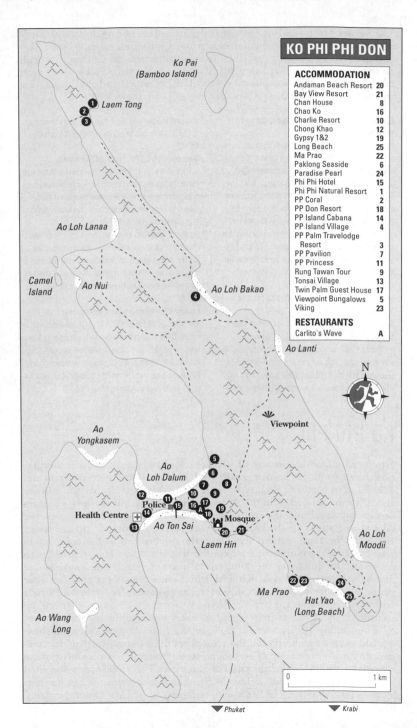

KO PHI PHI DON

ACCOMMODATION

Andaman Beach Resort	**20**
Bay View Resort	**21**
Chan House	**8**
Chao Ko	**16**
Charlie Resort	**10**
Chong Khao	**12**
Gypsy 1&2	**19**
Long Beach	**25**
Ma Prao	**22**
Paklong Seaside	**6**
Paradise Pearl	**24**
Phi Phi Hotel	**15**
Phi Phi Natural Resort	**1**
PP Coral	**2**
PP Don Resort	**18**
PP Island Cabana	**14**
PP Island Village	**4**
PP Palm Travelodge Resort	**3**
PP Pavilion	**7**
PP Princess	**11**
Rung Tawan Tour	**9**
Tonsai Village	**13**
Twin Palm Guest House	**17**
Viewpoint Bungalows	**5**
Viking	**23**

RESTAURANTS

Carlito's Wave	**A**

Ko Pai
(Bamboo Island)

Laem Tong

Ao Loh Lanaa

Camel
Island

Ao Nui

Ao Loh Bakao

Ao Lanti

N

Viewpoint

Ao
Yongkasem

Ao
Loh Dalum

Police

Health Centre

Ao Ton Sai

Mosque

Laem Hin

Ao Loh
Moodii

Ma Prao

Hat Yao
(Long Beach)

Ao Wang
Long

0   1 km

▼ Phuket   ▼ Krabi

mercilessly on the islands' increasing popularity, resulting in some of the worst-value accommodation in the whole of Thailand and a less than welcoming atmosphere. There are exceptions of course, but be warned that many tourists find Phi Phi a disappointment.

Getting to the islands

During peak season, **ferries** to Ko Phi Phi Don run at least four times daily **from Krabi** and up to six times a day from **Phuket**; ticket prices depend on the speed and comfort of the boat, though be warned that the glassed-in air-con ferries can be far stuffier and more fume-ridden than the open-sided ones. Buying a return ticket offers no advantages and can sometimes be limiting, as some ferries won't take tickets issued by other companies. In the rainy season the service from both Krabi and Phuket is reduced to once or twice daily. From November to May, there are also daily boats to Phi Phi Don from **Ao Nang** and **Ko Lanta Yai**. The only way you can get to Phi Phi Leh is by long-tail from Phi Phi Don or as part of a tour.

Because of the accommodation situation, you might prefer to see Phi Phi on a **day-trip**: tour agents in Phuket, Ao Nang, Krabi town and Ko Lanta all organize snorkelling excursions to Phi Phi Don and Phi Phi Leh, with prices starting from around B1100 including lunch and snorkelling equipment, or B750 for under-12s. Alternatively, you could organize your own outing to Phi Phi Don on the scheduled ferries: the return boat to Ko Lanta leaves Phi Phi Don at 2pm, while the last boats to Krabi and Phuket leave at around 3.30pm.

Onward transport from Phi Phi can be arranged through any of the numerous tour agents in Ton Sai village – they can fix pretty much anything from domestic flights to boat, bus and train tickets.

Ko Phi Phi Don

KO PHI PHI DON would itself be two islands were it not for the tenuous palm-fringed isthmus that connects the hilly expanses to east and west, separating the stunningly symmetrical double bays of Ao Ton Sai to the south and Ao Loh Dalum to the north. So steep is the smaller western half that the tiny population lives in isolated clusters across the slopes of the densely vegetated eastern stretch, while the tourist bungalows stick mainly to the intervening sandy flats, with a few developments on the beaches fringing the cliffs east and north of the isthmus.

All boats dock at **Ao Ton Sai**, the busiest bay on the island. From here you can catch a longtail to any of the other beaches or walk – there are a couple of short motorbike tracks but no roads on Phi Phi Don, just a series of paths across the steep and at times rugged interior, at points affording superb views over the bays. **Accommodation** on Phi Phi Don ranges from the exclusive to the ramshackle, but in the "budget" and mid-market categories you could end up paying as much as three times what you'd pay on the mainland. The prices listed below are for high season, which runs from October to April, but most bungalow operators slap on a thirty to fifty percent surcharge during the ridiculously hectic Christmas and New Year period; reservations are absolutely essential over this holiday fortnight, and are strongly recommended throughout high season. From May to September you should be able to negotiate up to fifty percent off the prices listed below. The commercial heart of the island is Ton Sai village, which has all sorts of tourist-oriented **facilities** including exchange counters, internet access, international telephone centres, postal services and lots of small shops.

More accessible than Ko Similan and Ko Surin, Ko Phi Phi and its neighbouring islands rate very high on the list of Andaman coast **diving and snorkelling** spots, offering depths of up to 35m, visibility touching 30m, and the possibility of seeing white-tip sharks, moray eels and stingrays. At uninhabited **Ko Pai** (or Bamboo Island), off the northeast coast of Phi Phi Don, much of the reef lies close to the surface, and gives you a chance of seeing the occasional turtle and possibly the odd silver- and black-striped banded sea snake – which is poisonous but rarely aggressive. At the adjacent **Ko Yung** (or Mosquito Island), the offshore reef plunges into a steep-sided and spectacular drop. Off the west coast of Phi Phi Don, **Ao Yongkasame** also has good reefs, as do the tranquil waters at **Ao Maya** on the west coast of Phi Phi Leh. For a description of the other local top sites, see p.639.

Dive centres on Phuket (see p.638), Ao Nang (p.681) and Laem Phra Nang (p.679) run daily excursions here, and there are also about twenty centres on Phi Phi itself. The biggest concentration is in Ton Sai village, where there are over a dozen competing outfits, so prices are cheap and some operators cut corners; because of this it's very important to check your operator's credentials and equipment and to try and talk to other divers about their experiences. Note that the cheaper dive trips are usually by longtail boat rather than the much more comfortable, better-equipped proper dive boats: ask to see a photo of your boat before booking. Many dive centres on Phi Phi sell American-made dive equipment, and they all rent equipment too. Recommended Ton Sai operators include the PADI Five-Star Instructor Development Centres Barrakuda (ⓣ & ⓕ 075/620698, ⓦ www.barakuda.com), Moskito (ⓣ 01/229 1361, ⓕ 076/217106, ⓦ www.moskitodiving.com) and Viking Divers (ⓣ 01/970 3644, ⓦ www.vikingdiversthailand.com). There are also small dive centres on Hat Yao, Ao Loh Bakao and Laem Tong. Average prices for **day-trips** including two tanks and lunch are: B1800 for local reefs off Phi Phi Leh; B2600 for the King Cruiser wreck; or B3600 for Hin Daeng and Hin Muang (by speedboat). Excalibur Liveaboards (ⓦ www.thailand-liveaboard.com), which currently runs out of Moskito, organizes liveaboard trips direct from Phi Phi to the Similans (about US$650 for four days) and Burma (US$1100, six days). **Dive courses** on Phi Phi cost B2500 for an introductory one-day session, B10,000 for the certificated four-day Openwater course, and

Ao Ton Sai

The constantly expanding village at **AO TON SAI** is now a full-blown low-rise holiday resort, and it's the liveliest – if not exactly the pleasantest – place to stay on the island. Backpacker-oriented shops, tour operators, restaurants and dive centres line the main track that parallels the beachfront and runs east as far as *Chao Ko* bungalows, while every available inch of land between the Ao Ton Sai shoreline and the resorts on Ao Loh Dalum is crammed with more makeshift stalls, tin-shack guest houses, beach bars, massage shops and cafés. If you can ignore the building debris at every turn, the constant hum of overworked generators and the pervasive whiff of sewage, it can be quite a fun place to hang out for a few hours; if not, head up the coast as fast as you can. All the main services are here, including two **exchange** counters run by national banks (daily 7am–10pm), a licensed post office, international telephone call centres and scores of little places offering **internet access**, where rates are higher than on the mainland but not outrageous. The island's **health centre** is at the western end of Ton Sai, in the compound of the *PP Island Cabana*, and there's a **police** box at the pier and another one next to the *Apache Bar* on the track to Laem Hin.

The **beach** itself is most attractive at the western end, under the limestone karsts, but even this stretch gets unbearably crowded in the middle of the day

B8000 for a two-day Advanced course. If you're short on time, email ahead to reserve a place on a dive course or live-aboard trip. The nearest **recompression chamber** is run by Hyperbaric Services Thailand and is located on Ao Patong in Phuket (see p.638); check to see that your dive operator is insured to use it.

Nearly all the tour operators and bungalow operations on Phi Phi Don organize day and half-day **snorkelling** trips. Prices range from B400–600 for a day-trip including lunch and snorkelling gear, with the price depending on the size of the boat and number of participants. In the case of snorkelling, the longtails that run from Ko Phi Phi are better than the larger fishing boats and the Phuket cruise ships, which are so popular you can rarely see the fish for the swimmers. Many dive operators will take accompanying snorkellers on their one-day dives for about B500.

The limestone cliffs and secluded bays of the Phi Phi islands make perfect **kayaking** territory, as the lagoons and palm-fringed coasts are much better appreciated in silence than over the roar of a longtail or cruise ship. If you rent a kayak for a whole day you can incorporate sunbathing and snorkelling breaks on small unpopulated bays nearby. Lots of tour operators in the village rent out kayaks at B150–300 per hour or B800–1000 per day, depending on size and quality, and there are also kayaks for rent on Hat Yao. Seafun Watersports at *PP Princess* on Ao Loh Dalum (℡01/897 2256, ℻075/612188, ✉sea_fun@hotmail.com) offers guided kayaking tours to Phi Phi Leh and Bamboo Island for B1000, including lunch, snorkelling gear and longtail transfer. They also teach **windsurfing** (B300 per hour or B700 half a day) and offer a variety of interesting **sailing trips** including a one-day tour of local islands (B1800), and trips around Ao Phang Nga ($75 per day) or to Langkawi in Malaysia (₵75 per day), lasting several days; the overnight trips need to be booked in advance.

Phi Phi's topography is also a gift for **rock-climbers** and several places in the village offer climbing instruction and equipment rental, including Hang Out Rock Climbing (✉suthida@hotmail.com), located close to *Carlito's Wave* on the track to Laem Hin. They charge B1000 for up to three climbs, with full instruction and equipment. The main climbing area is a small beach just to the west of Ao Ton Sai, and includes the Ton Sai Tower and the Drinking Wall, with heights of 15m and 30m.

when it plays host to hundreds of day-trippers who snorkel just off-shore and then eat lunch on the beach. The central part of the bay is far too busy with ferries and longtails to even consider swimming in, but the eastern stretch, in front of *Chao Ko*, is a little quieter.

Accommodation

Most of Ton Sai's **accommodation** is packed between the Ao Ton Sai and Ao Loh Dalum beaches, and at the foot of the hills to the east and west. The cheapest places are the ever-growing number of small guest houses stuffed cheek-by-jowl into extremely rickety shacks that look like a significant fire hazard and are very poor value for money.

Chan House, beside the path to the viewpoint on the northeast edge of the village. Welcoming staff but low-grade en-suite rooms in this small, simply designed block. ❹

Chao Ko, 10min walk east of the pier at the edge of the village ℡075/611313. Fills up fast because it's both close to the village action and more qui-

etly located on the less congested fringes. Standard concrete bungalows, all with private bathroom and some with air-con and partial sea view. ❹–❽

Chong Khao Bungalows, behind *Tonsai Village* and *PP Cabana*, at the western end of the village ℡01/894 8786. Set in a coconut grove, this place

feels peaceful, homely and spacious, and is just 200m from the beach at Ao Loh Dalum. There's a range of en-suite huts, from the ultra-basic to the fairly comfortable. ❸–❺

Phi Phi Hotel, 50m north (inland) from the pier ☎075/620599 ⓕ611233. Low-rise hotel with smart rooms, each equipped with air-con, TV, phone and mini-bar; some have sea view. ❽–❾

PP Island Cabana, just west (left) of the pier ☎075/620634, ⓕ612132, ⓦwww.phiphicabana-hotel.com. Cute mid-range bungalows set in a shorefront garden, plus more upmarket air-con rooms in the central hotel block. Swimming pool and restaurant on the premises. ❼–❾

Rung Tawan Tour, in the heart of the inland village ☎01/895 2395. Friendly place with very basic but bearable rooms in a rickety shack, all with bathrooms and most with a view of next door's wall. internet access downstairs. ❹

Tonsai Village, the far western end of the beach ☎ & ⓕ075/612434. Located under a cliff at the far end of the beach, these nicely appointed bungalows are kitted out with air-con, TV and comfortable furnishings, though they're a bit dark and close together. ❽

Twin Palm Guest House, north of *Mama's* restaurant in the thick of the inland scrum ☎01/958 8753, ⓔtwinpalm@phiphithailand.com. Scrapes by with a handful of dark Bangkok-style en-suite guest-house rooms, plus some slightly nicer bungalows. ❹–❼

Eating and drinking

Ton Sai is by far the best place to eat on the island – there are dozens of little **restaurants** in the village, ranging from bakeries to Muslim foodstalls, but the biggest crowd-puller is the seafood. At night almost every restaurant displays the day's catch, and huge barracuda, red snapper and sharks lie temptingly alongside crabs and lobsters. New restaurants spring up as old ones fold, but French-run *Mama's*, on the main track from the pier, is a long-standing favourite for seafood and good cakes; *Le Grand Bleu*, also on the main track, is another recommended French place, serving classy and expensive menus of the day. *Lemongrass*, next to the post office on one of the side tracks, serves only Thai food on its lengthy, mid-priced menu that includes mussels, red and green curries and some decent veggie options. Less expensive but just as tasty are the typically Thai curry-and-rice shops at the heart of the village, and there are always lots of hawkers flogging *rotis* and fried bananas from their hand-carts. The best places for breakfast are the two **bakeries** on opposite sides of the main track, where you're served real coffee to go with the huge selection of croissants, Danish pastries, home-made breads, cakes and cookies.

Small **bars** proliferate here too, adorned with hand-painted signboards and throbbing to the usual Bob Marley and Euro-pop standards. *Carlito's Wave*, next to *Chao Ko* on the eastern edge of the village, is a popular seafront joint with a big cocktails menu and laid-back atmosphere; further east along the track, *Apache Bar* is a huge multi-tiered bar and dance-floor which holds regular parties (check locally posted flyers) and has a long happy hour. In the heart of the village, *Reggae Bar* stages nightly bouts of Thai boxing for its customers.

Laem Hin

East along the coast from *Chao Ko*, about ten minutes' walk from the pier, is the promontory known as **Laem Hin**, beyond which is a small stretch of beach that's quieter than Ao Ton Sai and better for swimming. Bungalows cover the Laem Hin promontory and beach, and they're popular places to stay, being in easy reach of the restaurants and nightlife at Ao Ton Sai – a ten- to fifteen-minute walk that's feasible day or night – while feeling a little less claustrophobic and hectic.

Andaman Beach Resort, east of *PP Don Chukit* ☎075/621427. Large choice of fairly comfortable bungalows set on a grassy area running down to the sea. The sea-view ones in the front row have air-con and are the most expensive, but they're right beside the main track and subject to the roar of passing longtails; the cheapest places are poorly designed rooms in row-houses at the back of the compound. ⑤–⑧

Bay View Resort, far eastern end of Laem Hin beach ☎ & ☎075/621223. Nicely furnished air-con bungalows occupying a superb position high on the cliffside, their massive windows affording unbeatable views. Good value considering the competition. ⑧

Gypsy 1, inland, down the track between the mosque and *PP Don* ☎01/229 1674. Clean, pleasant, good-value concrete bungalows, all with attached bathroom; set round a lawn about 150m north of the water. Recommended. ④

Gypsy 2, 100m north along the track from *Gypsy 1*. Unadorned grey concrete huts run by relatives of the people at *Gypsy 1*. ④

PP Don Chukit Resort, just east of the promontory ☎01/894 2511. Uninspired collection of mid-range air-con bungalows, plus some overpriced fan rooms in single-storey blocks. ⑤–⑦

Ao Loh Dalum

Though less attractive than Hat Yao, **AO LOH DALUM** is a much quieter place for swimming and sunbathing than Ao Ton Sai, yet the bungalows here are only five or ten minutes' walk from Ton Sai's restaurants and nightlife. The bungalows' seafront bars on Loh Dalum are also popular and genial places to hang out. The main drawback here is that the tide goes out for miles, leaving you with a long trek over sodden sand before you can get a decent dip. Loh Dalum's mid-range and upmarket **bungalows**, are some of the most attractive on the island; they have good facilities too, including watersports equipment for hire at *PP Pavilion* and *PP Princess*.

The **viewpoint** which overlooks the far eastern edge of the beach affords a magnificent wraparound panorama of both Ao Loh Dalum and Ao Ton Sai: photographers slog up the steep half-hour climb for sunset shots of the two bays, but early morning is an equally good time to go, as the café at the summit serves simple breakfasts as well as cold drinks. To get there, follow the track inland (south) from beside *Paklong Seaside* and then branch off to your left (eastwards) near the water treatment plant. From the viewpoint you can descend the rocky and at times almost sheer path to **Ao Lanti**, a tiny bay on the east coast with choppy surf and a couple of resident *chao ley*. Theoretically, it should also be possible to reach the northeastern bay of Ao Loh Bakao (see p.694) by a path from near the viewpoint, but the two-kilometre route is unsignposted and overgrown.

Charlie Resort, in the middle of the beach ☎ & ☎075/620615. Mid-range place with relatively good-value fan-cooled bungalows, each one with its own tiny garden area out front; price depends on proximity to the seafront. Lively bar and restaurant on the beach. ④–⑥

Paklong Seaside, easternmost end of the beach ☎01/958 6371. Comfortable guest house right on the shore, with a handful of decent fan-cooled rooms in a small wooden building; price depends on the size of the room. ④–⑦

PP Pavilion, eastern end of the beach ☎075/620677, ☎620633, ☎pavilion@phiphithailand.com. Attractive upmarket wooden chalets, nicely spaced over the beachfront grounds. Fan and air-con available. ⑦–⑧

PP Princess, at the westernmost end of the beach, 300m north of the Ton Sai pier ☎075/622079, ☎612188, ☎www.ppprincess.com. Offers the plushest and most tastefully designed accommodation on the island: comfortably furnished wooden chalets with big windows, verandas, air-con, TV and mini-bar. They have an eco-friendly waste-disposal system too. Price depends on proximity to shorefront. ⑧–⑨

Viewpoint Bungalows, up the cliffside at the far eastern end of the beach ☎ & ☎ 075/622351. Strung out across the hillside, these attractive but pricey bungalows boast great views out over the bay. The most expensive have air-con and TV. ⑦–⑧

Hat Yao

With its deluxe sand and large reefs packed with polychromatic marine life just 20m offshore, **HAT YAO** (Long Beach) is the best of Phi Phi's main beaches. It's also the most crowded, with hundreds of sunbathers pitching up on the gorgeous sand every day and throngs of day-trippers making things even worse at lunchtime. Unperturbed by all the attention, shoals of golden butterfly fish, turquoise and purple parrot fish and hooped angel fish continue to scour Hat Yao's coral for food, escorted by brigades of small cleaner fish who live off the parasites trapped in the scales of larger species. For the best of the coral and the biggest reef in the vicinity, you should make for the submerged rock known as **Hin Pae** off the southern end of Hat Yao – novice divers get ferried out there by boat, but if you're a strong swimmer you can easily reach it from the beach. The Scuba Hut dive shop at *Long Beach* runs day-trips to local reefs and rents out diving and snorkelling equipment.

Longtail **boats** do the ten-minute shuttle between Hat Yao and Ao Ton Sai from about 8am to 8pm, but it's also possible to **walk** between the two in half an hour. At low tide you can get to Hat Yao along the shore, though this involves quite a bit of clambering over smooth wet rocks – not ideal when wearing a heavy rucksack, nor after a night spent trawling the bars of Ton Sai village (take a torch). The alternative route takes you over the hillside via the steps up from *Bay View Resort* on Laem Hin – with side tracks running off to the bays holding *Pirate*, *Ma Prao* and *Viking* – and then finally dropping down to Hat Yao. When returning, follow the path up into the trees from behind one of the last *Paradise Pearl* bungalows at the far western end of Hat Yao, and continue as far as you can along the track. You'll need to dip down to the shore briefly at *Ma Prao*, before finally coming down to sea level at *Bay View* on Laem Hin. Several other **paths** connect Hat Yao to the beaches of Ao Loh Dalum to the north and the tiny bay of Loh Moodii to the northeast: the trails start behind the last of the *Long Beach Bungalows*.

Accommodation

The most attractive of Hat Yao's **accommodation** is tucked away in a little cove west of Hat Yao itself, with easy access via a rocky path. The small, secluded and friendly Belgian-run *Ma Prao* (☎075/622486; ❷–❹) has a good selection of 32 simple wood and bamboo bungalows ranged across the hillside overlooking the sea, and a pleasant eating area out front. The cheapest huts share bathrooms, but some have a terrace; the more expensive options have private bathrooms, fans and decks. There's a small dive operation here, you can rent kayaks, and the kitchen produces a long and varied menu that includes eighty different cocktails and home-made yoghurt. Not surprisingly, it's a popular place, so call the day before to secure a room, or check in somewhere else and put yourself on the waiting list. Just around the rocks in the next tiny cove to the east sit the seven ultra-basic bamboo huts belonging to *Viking* (❶), Phi Phi's last remaining homage to the typical Asian beach experience: rudimentary facilities, laid-back staff and inexpensive rates.

Of the two bungalow operations on Hat Yao, most budget travellers head first for *Long Beach Bungalows* (☎075/612410; ❸–❹), which covers the eastern half of the beach. Some of the cheapest huts here are on the verge of collapse – and the proximity of rubbish dumps makes them no more enticing – but the newer, more expensive huts are better value, and most of these have private bathrooms. The larger, better-maintained bungalows at *Paradise Pearl* (☎ & ☞075/622100; ❹–❻) are decently spaced along the western half of the beach; all have attached bathrooms and some are very comfortably furnished. Prices mainly reflect proximity to the sea, though none is more than 20m from the water; front-row residents get the worst of the noise from incoming longtails.

Ao Loh Bakao and Laem Tong

Far removed from the hustle of Ao Ton Sai and its environs, a few exclusive resorts have effectively bought up the secluded northern beaches of Phi Phi Don. This is primarily package-holiday territory – you're unlikely to find a room free if you turn up unannounced – and it's difficult and expensive to get to the other parts of the island, so you should choose your hotel with care. There are no regular boats here from Ao Ton Sai, but longtail boats will take you for about B200; the trip takes around an hour to Ao Loh Bakao and a further half-hour north to Laem Tong. To charter a return boat at night, you're looking at B1000 for a round trip including waiting time.

Just over halfway up the coast, the eighty plush, fan-cooled and air-conditioned chalets on stilts at *Phi Phi Island Village* (T076/215014, F214918; ⑨) have the beach of **Ao Loh Bakao** all to themselves; the bungalows are designed in traditional Thai style and there's a pool in the gardens. At the northernmost tip, **Laem Tong** has three upmarket resorts on its shores and views across to nearby Bamboo Island and Mosquito Island. The beautifully designed *Phi Phi Palm Beach Travelodge Resort* (T01/676 7316, F076/215090, W www.phiphi-palmbeach.com; ⑨; room rates start at B6500) is a popular honeymoon spot, and a lovely location for anyone looking for a quiet, comfortable break: all bungalows are air-conditioned and there's a swimming pool, outdoor jacuzzi, dive centre and tennis courts here as well as batik and cookery courses and trips to local islands. The rustic wooden cabins at *PP Coral Resort* (T076/211348, F215455, W www.ppcoral.com; ⑧–⑨) are a little less deluxe – and a little more affordable – but the sense of seclusion is slightly marred by the daily arrival of lunching day-trippers. The furthest north is *Phi Phi Natural Resort* (T075/613010, F613000, W www.phiphinatural.com; ⑦–⑨), with stylish, reasonable-value chalets scattered around the tropical shorefront garden, plus a swimming pool and a terrace restaurant offering fine sea views; snorkelling, fishing and dive trips are all available here.

Ko Phi Phi Leh

More rugged than its twin Ko Phi Phi Don, and a quarter the size, **KO PHI PHI LEH** is home only to the **sea swift**, whose valuable nests are gathered by intrepid *chao ley* for export to specialist Chinese restaurants all over the world. Tourists descend on the island not only to see the nest-collecting caves but also to snorkel off its sheltered bays and to admire the very spot where *The Beach* was filmed; the anchoring of tourist and fishing boats has damaged much of the coral in the most beautiful reefs. Most snorkelling trips out of Phi Phi Don include Phi Phi Leh, which is only twenty minutes south of Ao Ton Sai, but you can also get there by hiring a longtail from Ao Ton Sai or Hat Yao (B500–700 per six-person boat). If you do charter your own boat, go either very early or very late in the day, to beat the tour-group rush. Alternatively, why not try paddling yourself in and out of the quiet bays in a kayak – see box on p.689 for details.

Most idyllic of all the bays in the area is **Ao Maya** on the southwest coast, where the water is still and very clear and the coral extremely varied – a perfect snorkelling spot and a feature of most day-trips. Unfortunately the discarded lunch boxes and water bottles of day-trippers now threaten the health of the marine life in **Ao Phi Leh**, an almost completely enclosed east-coast

Bird's nesting

Prized for its aphrodisiac and energizing qualities, **bird's-nest soup** is such a delicacy in Taiwan, Singapore and Hong Kong that ludicrous sums of money change hands for a dish whose basic ingredients are tiny twigs glued together with bird's spit. Collecting these nests is a lucrative but life-endangering business: sea swifts (known as edible nest swiftlets) build their nests in rock crevices hundreds of metres above sea level, often on sheer cliff-faces or in cavernous hollowed-out karst. **Nest-building** begins in January and the harvesting season usually lasts from February to May, during which time the female swiftlet builds three nests on the same spot, none of them more than 12cm across, by secreting an unbroken thread of saliva which she winds round as if making a coil pot. **Gatherers** will only steal the first two nests made by each bird, prising them off the cave walls with special metal forks. Gathering the nests demands faultless agility and balance, skills that seem to come naturally to the *chao ley*, whose six-man teams bring about four hundred nests down the perilous bamboo scaffolds each day, weighing about 4kg in total. At a market rate of B20,000–50,000 per kilo, so much money is at stake that a government franchise must be granted before any collecting commences, and armed guards often protect the sites at night. The *chao ley* themselves seek spiritual protection from the dangers of the job by making offerings to the spirits of the cliff or cave at the beginning of the season; in the Viking Cave, they place buffalo flesh, horns and tail at the foot of one of the stalagmites.

lagoon of breathtakingly turquoise water. Not far from the cove, the **Viking Cave** gets its misleading name from the scratchy wall-paintings of Chinese junks inside, but more interesting than these 400-year-old graffiti is the **bird's-nesting** that goes on here: rickety bamboo scaffolding extends hundreds of metres up to the roof of the cave, where the harvesters spend the day scraping the tiny sea-swift nests off the rockface.

Ko Lanta Yai

Although **KO LANTA YAI** can't compete with Phi Phi's stupendous scenery, the 25-kilometre-long island does offer plenty of fine sandy beaches and safe seas and is actually a much friendlier place to stay, not least because – despite a booming tourist industry – it still feels like it belongs to its twenty thousand residents (something which can't be said of Ko Phi Phi, Phuket or Ko Samui), the majority of whom are mixed-blood Muslim descendants of Malaysian and *chao ley* peoples. Aside from fishing, many of the islanders support themselves by cultivating the land between the beaches and the forested ridges that dominate the central and eastern parts of Lanta Yai; the others work mainly in the tourist industry, most of which is still run by local families. Traditional *chao ley* rituals are celebrated on Ko Lanta twice a year, when ceremonial boats are set afloat on the full moon nights in June and November (see p.624 for more on the *chao ley*).

The local *chao ley* name for the island is *Pulao Satak*, "Island of Long Beaches", an apt description of the string of silken **beaches** along the western coast, each separated by rocky points and strung out at quite wide intervals. The northernmost one, Hat Khlong Dao, is developed almost to full capacity,

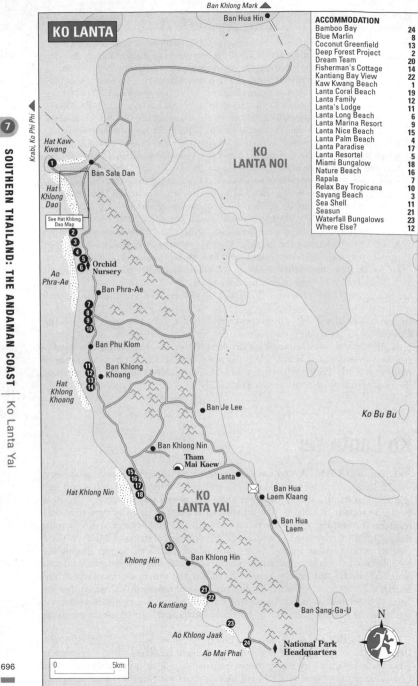

KO LANTA

Ban Khlong Mark ▲

Ban Hua Hin ●

KO
LANTA NOI

Krabi, Ko Phi Phi ▲

Hat Kaw
Kwang

①

Ban Sala Dan

Hat
Khlong
Dao

See Hat Khlong
Dao Map

②
③
④
⑤
⑥ Orchid
Nursery

Ao
Phra-Ae

Ban Phra-Ae

⑦
⑧
⑨
⑩

Ban Phu Klom

⑪
⑫ Ban Khlong
⑬ Khoang
⑭

Hat
Khlong
Khoang

● Ban Je Lee

Ko Bu Bu

● Ban Khlong Nin

**Tham
Mai Kaew**

⑮
⑯
⑰ Lanta ●
⑱

Hat Khlong Nin

✉ Ban Hua
Laem Klaang
●

KO
LANTA YAI

⑲

● Ban Hua
Laem

⑳

Khlong Hin

Ban Khlong Hin

㉑
㉒

Ao Kantiang

● Ban Sang-Ga-U

㉓

Ao Khlong Jaak

㉔

Ao Mai Phai

▲ **National Park
Headquarters**

N

0   5km

but deserted spots are not hard to find further south and they nearly all offer luxuriously soft sand and clear water. All the bungalow outfits advertise snorkelling trips to the reefs off Ko Lanta's myriad satellite islands, and diving is also a popular and rewarding activity; Ko Lanta's mangrove-fringed east coast is unsuitable for swimming but ideal for kayaking.

Ko Lanta is extremely popular during **high season** (Nov–Feb), when it's well worth either booking your first night's accommodation in advance or taking up the suggestions of the bungalow touts who ride the boats from the mainland. **Accommodation pricing** on Ko Lanta is extremely flexible and alters according to the number of tourists on the island: it's not uncommon, for example, for bungalow rates to triple in the thirty-day period from mid-November to mid-December, while between May and October rates are vastly discounted. The price range shown in our Ko Lanta accommodation listings are for the beginning and end of high season (generally Nov & March–April). All bungalows increase their rates for the peak months of December and January; most places double their prices for this period, the exceptions being many of the cheapest (❶–❸) places which can triple or even quadruple their prices, and the most expensive places (❼ and ❽) which usually "only" add around twenty percent. The island is much quieter during the **rainy season** (May–Oct), when the seas become too rough for boats to travel here from Krabi and the shores suffer from a fair bit of water-borne debris. A number of the more remote bungalow operations close down during this period, but most of the bungalows on the main beaches stay open, and many are willing to discount their rates too.

Getting to the island

From November to May two daily **ferries** run from Krabi to Ban Sala Dan on the northern tip of Ko Lanta Yai, and there's at least one ferry a day between Ko Phi Phi and Ban Sala Dan. Bungalow touts always meet the boats at Ban Sala Dan and transport you to the beach of your choice. During the rest of the year (the rainy season), you'll need to arrange **minivan** transport from Krabi with one of the tour agencies, which costs the same and takes about the same time if not a bit longer. The minivans take the **overland route**, going via Ban Hua Hin on the mainland, from where they drive onto a small ferry, get taken across to Ban Khlong Mark on Ko Lanta Noi, drive across to Lanta Noi's northwest tip, take another ferry over the channel to Ko Lanta Yai (every 20 min from 7am–9pm; 20min; B50 per car) and then drive down to whichever beach you've decided to stay on. This is also the route used year-round by transport operators from Trang and by anyone bringing their own vehicle on to the island: if you do come with your own wheels, be warned that Lanta's roads are far from perfect and in the south degenerate into extremely rough tracks.

When it comes to **moving on** from Ko Lanta, every tour operator in Ban Sala Dan and almost every bungalow outfit on the island can sell you onward transport to Krabi (three boats daily from November to May, two at 8am and the last at 1pm; B200) and Ko Phi Phi (daily from November to May at 8am; B200), as well as minibus tickets to Trang, onward bus from Trang or Krabi to Surat Thani or Hat Yai, and flights from Krabi or Trang airports.

Island practicalities

Though a road runs the entire length of Ko Lanta Yai's west coast, becoming quite rough just after Hat Khlong Nin and finally grinding to a bumpy halt at

Ko Lanta is a significant diving centre, with local reefs a lot quieter and more pristine than the ones round Phi Phi and Phuket, and an excellent place for seeing whale sharks. The diving season runs from November to April or mid-May, with all the dive centres running expeditions and diving courses during this period; outside these months the seas are too rough to travel on.

Some of Lanta's best dive sites are located between Ko Lanta and Ko Phi Phi, including the soft coral at Hin Bidah, where you get lots of leopard sharks, barracuda and tuna. West and south of Lanta, the Ko Ha island group offers four different dives on each of its five islands, including steep drop-offs and caves. Much further south, about four hours' boat ride, there's a fifty-metre wall at spectacular Hin Daeng and Hin Muang, plus a good chance of seeing tuna, jacks, silvertip sharks, manta rays and even whale sharks. See the descriptions of Andaman coast dive sites on p.639 for more on some of these reefs. A typical day-trip to some of these reefs costs B2200–3000 including equipment rental and two tanks (B600–800 for snorkellers), but all dive centres offer discounts if you do three consecutive one-day dives. For an overnight expedition to local islands with accommodation either on the boat or on one of the islands, and four tanks, you pay about B6000. Diving courses average out at B11,000 for the four-day Openwater course, or B7500–8000 for the two-day Advanced course.

Nearly all Ko Lanta dive centres have their headquarters in the village of Ban Sala Dan, and many also have branch offices on the beaches. Some of the best include the reputable and long-established Ko Lanta Diving Centre/Ko Lanta Tauchschule, on Ban Sala Dan's seafront road (T & F075/612969, Wwww.kohlantadivingcenter.com), run by prolific dive author and photographer Christian Mietz; British-run The Dive Zone (T075/684056, Wwww.thedivezone.com), which also has a branch at Golden Bay on Hat Khlong Dao; and the German-run Atlantis (T075/68 40 81, F612914, Wwww.top-com.com/atlantis), which also has a branch on Hat Khlong Dao. The nearest recompression chamber is located on Ao Patong in Phuket (see p.638); check to see that your dive operator is insured to use it.

Snorkelling

All tour operators and bungalow outfits also sell tickets for the large-scale outings in big boats that can hold around a hundred passengers: these go to three or four

the far southern tip, **transport** between the beaches is quite difficult as there's no regular songthaew service on the island. Once you're established on your beach you have either to hire a motorbike from your accommodation (about B40 per hour, B250 per day; B500 per day for a big trail bike), or cadge a lift with the bungalow operators when they go and meet the boats at Ban Sala Dan. Tour operators in Ban Sala Dan also rent jeeps (B1200 per day) as well as bikes. You can usually arrange a **motorbike taxi** in Ban Sala Dan to take you back to your bungalow (B20–30 from the village to Hat Khlong Dao, B30–40 to Ao Phra-ae), or you might be able to hitch a ride, though if you're staying on Hat Khlong Dao it's an easy half-hour walk to the village.

Most bungalows will **change money**, though you'll get the best rates at the bank in Ban Sala Dan. **Telephone** lines were laid on the island in 2001, so many businesses now have T075 numbers, though some are still using satellite phones with T01 codes; many bungalows offer international telephone services for guests. **internet** centres are popping up all over the place; there's a reliable one on the southern edge of Ban Sala Dan.

islands off the Trang coast (see pp.719–23 for island descriptions), usually including the enclosed emerald lagoon on the island of **Ko Mook** (aka Ko Muk), nearby **Ko Hai** (aka Ko Ngai) and **Ko Kradan**; they cost B650 per person including snorkelling gear and lunch. The twin islands of **Ko Rok Nok** and **Ko Rok Nai**, which are further south still at 47km from Ko Lanta, are another top destination but can only be reached by small speedboat, which takes just an hour to get there and costs B1200. Some bungalow operators offer private longtail-boat tours to the reefs off the **Ko Ha** island group (about two hours' boat ride from Lanta), with snorkelling or fishing as requested: Ko Lanta Tour at *Lanta Villa* on Hat Khlong Dao charges B3000 for a four-person boat including fishing and/or snorkelling gear.

Kayaking

The north coast of Ko Lanta Noi, around Ban Rapu, is rich in mangroves and caves which makes it fun to explore by **kayak**. Kayaking outings can be arranged from Ban Sala Dan tour operators for B1300 per person including transport, lunch and kayak.

Day-trips

Ko Lanta's biggest inland attraction is the **Tham Mai Kaew caves**, located in the heart of the island, and signposted from the west-coast road at Hat Khlong Nin. There are myriad chambers here, some of which you can only just crawl into, and they boast stalactites and interesting rock formations as well as a creepy cave pool and the inevitable bats. To properly explore the cave system you need to bring your own torch, and you need a guide: the Muslim family that live close to the caves act as caretakers and guides and give two-hour tours for B50 per person. The **waterfall** inland from Ao Khlong Jaak is another fairly popular spot, and can be reached from the bay by walking along the course of the stream for about two hours; alternatively join one of the numerous tours that combine visits to the caves and the waterfall in a half-day-trip for about B300, or B600 with a ninety-minute **elephant ride** thrown in. South Nature Travel tour operator in Ban Sala Dan also offers full-day tours of Ko Lanta for around B1300 (kids B950), which includes kayaking and snorkelling as well as a visit to a rubber plantation and to the **Lanta Orchid Nursery**. Located inland from Ao Phra-ae, near *Lanta Resortel*, the nursery includes an exhibition on orchid farming (open Nov to mid-April daily; B30, children B20).

Ban Sala Dan

During high season, direct boats from Krabi and Phi Phi arrive at Lanta's main settlement, the Muslim fishing port and village of **BAN SALA DAN**, located on the northernmost tip of Ko Lanta Yai. It's essentially a T-junction village, with about three dozen shops and businesses within easy walking distance of each other. Though many of these cater for tourists, the village has a low-key atmosphere, and fishing is still a significant income-earner. Several minimarkets sell essentials like mosquito repellent and sunscreen, as well as new and secondhand books, beachwear and postcards. There's a Siam City bank with currency **exchange** and a Visa cash advance service (Mon–Fri 8.30am–3.30pm), several places offering **internet** access, a **police** booth and a **health centre**, though for anything serious you'll need to go to Krabi or Phuket. Ban Sala Dan is the best place on the island to arrange a **diving** course or expedition and also has half-a-dozen tour operators offering all manner of **day-trips** (see box above for a guide to diving and day-tripping destinations), as well as bike and jeep rental and boat, bus, train and air tickets.

While you're in the village, it's well worth stopping for a breezy meal at one of the **restaurants** whose dining area juts out on a shaded jetty right over the water, giving enjoyable views of the fishing boats and Ko Lanta Noi. Both *Seaside* and the nearby *Sea View* have good, very inexpensive menus offering authentic Thai dishes from chicken and cashews to fish fried with chilli or garlic.

Hat Khlong Dao

Lanta Yai's longest and most popular beach is **HAT KHLONG DAO**, the northernmost of the west-coast beaches, about half an hour's walk from Ban Sala Dan, or 2–3km by road. The sand here is soft and golden, palms and casuarinas shade parts of the shore, the sunsets can be magnificent, and the whole is framed by a dramatic hilly backdrop. Not surprisingly, this is where you'll find the densest collection of bungalows on the island, but though most of the shorefront land has been developed, none encroaches on the sand itself and development is relatively discreet. The northern curve of Hat Khlong Dao juts out into a rocky promontory known as **Laem Kaw Kwang** (Deer Neck Cape), whose north-facing shore, **Hat Kaw Kwang**, is mainly characterized by mud flats and mangroves and is home to a *chao ley* settlement.

There's a tiny minimart next to *Lom Thaleh* at the southern end of Hat Khlong Dao, and dive shops at several of the bungalows; for anything else you'll need to go to Ban Sala Dan. The nicest way to walk to the village (about 30min from *Golden Bay*) is to head to the deer neck at the northern curve of the beach, and then take a right along the mostly shaded track which leads from *Kaw Kwang Bungalows* to the road into Ban Sala Dan.

All the bungalows have **restaurants** serving travellers' fare and standard Thai dishes, and at night they're lit up with fairy lights and low lanterns, which lends a nice mellow atmosphere to the evenings and makes a welcome change from the neon frenzy at other resorts. Most restaurants also offer fresh seafood at night, where you choose your specimen and the cooking method and are

HAT KHLONG DAO

N

0   200 m

Ban Sala Dan

RESTAURANTS

Danny's	**A**
Flower Power Bar	**C**
Otto	**B**

ACCOMMODATION

Andaman Lanta Resort	17
Diamond Sand Palace	7
Golden Bay Cottages	6
Hans	5
Kaw Kwang Bungalows	1
Khlong Dao Beach Bungalows	12
Laguna Beach Club	3
Lanta Bee Garden	16
Lanta Garden Home	14
Lanta Island Resort	10
Lanta Noble House	2
Lanta Sand	15
Lanta Sea House	11
Lanta Villa	9
Lom Taleh	13
Southern Lanta Resort	8
Sun, Fun & Sea	4

BAN KHLONG DAO

Ao Phra-ae

Relax Bay Tropicana ℡01/228 4213, ⓦwww.ko-lanta.com/hotels/relaxbay.htm. Set in its own tiny bay south around the next rocky point from *Lanta Marina*, this place has some fairly standard concrete bungalows as well as a few tastefully simple bamboo and rattan bungalows, most with big verandas and open-air bathrooms. ⑤

Sayang Beach Resort ℡075/612138, ⓦwww.lanta.de/sayang. Small and friendly place occupying expansive grounds with huts nicely spaced among the palm trees. All bungalows are built with natural materials and have decent bathrooms; price depends on location and size. ⑤–⑦

Hat Khlong Khoang

The lovely long beach at **HAT KHLONG KHOANG**, 2km south of *Relax Bay Tropicana*, is peppered with rocks and only really swimmable at high tide. That said, it's quite rewarding for snorkelling and has some very laid-back bungalow operations, mostly set in shorefront coconut groves and fostering an appealingly low-key atmosphere.

Accommodation

Coconut Greenfield ℡01/228/4602, ⓦwww.kolanta.net/coconutgreenfield. Memorably friendly place with good facilities, a laid-back atmosphere, twenty comfortable bungalow, and tents for rent at B80 a double. Also has a pool table, mini-golf, a small minimarket and a regular programme of traditional festivities, plus the beachfront *Robin Hood Bar*. Recommended. ②–⑤
Fisherman's Cottage ℡01/476 1529, ⓔfishermanscottage@hotmail.com. This quiet, low-key place at the southern end of the beach has just half-a-dozen bungalows, each with big glass windows, mosquito nets and decent bathrooms. ②

Lanta Family Ten large and well-kept bungalows ranged under the palm trees; mosquito nets supplied on request. ②–③
Lanta's Lodge ℡01/228 4378. Thirty sizeable, if a little spartan, wooden bungalows, some with aircon; the price depends on their proximity to the shorefront. Closed May–Oct. ②–④
Sea Shell Just three bungalows run by a Dutch-Thai couple; nicely furnished and with good bathrooms. ②–③
Where Else? As you might expect from the name, this has a relaxed, laid-back atmosphere and consists of just fifteen bamboo and coconut-wood bungalows, with attached coral-floored bathrooms. ②

Hat Khlong Nin to Khlong Hin

A further 5km on, the long, sandy stretch of **Hat Khlong Nin** is very good for swimming, though three of the four bungalow operations here are clustered together in a rather claustrophobic knot at the centre of the shore. You can walk the 3km to the Tham Mai Kaew caves from Khlong Nin in about an hour. *Miami Bungalow* rents **motorbikes** for B250 per day and has an international phone service.

All the **bungalows** on Hat Khlong Nin are open all year. Built on its own at the far northern end of the beach, *Lanta Nice Beach Resort* (℡075/629062; ①–③) does its name justice, being located on a broad swathe of sandy beach and offering twenty spacious concrete bungalows, many with sea views. The twenty sky-blue concrete bungalows at *Nature Beach Bungalow* (℡01/397 4184; ③–④) lack character inside, but are run by a friendly local family. Next door, at the long-running *Lanta Paradise* (℡01/607 5114; ①–③), you can choose between old bamboo huts and big, smart, concrete bungalows which are packed rather uncomfortably close together but feel spacious inside. The accommodation at neighbouring *Miami Bungalow* (℡01/228 4506; ①–④)

ranges from simple wooden huts with fans to larger concrete versions, some with air-con and sea view.

Just over a kilometre south of Hat Khlong Nin, the road passes diminutive **Khlong Nam Jun**, a tiny cove that's rocky in parts but enjoys a swimmable beach and just one set of bungalows, *Lanta Coral Beach* (T01/228 4326; ❹–❺; closed May–Oct). The seventeen good-sized concrete huts here are scattered among the palms (some of which are hung with hammocks) and have fans and well-appointed bathrooms. It's a quiet place, away from the crowds but not too remote.

The bungalows at *Dream Team* (T01/228 4184, Wwww.ko-lanta.com/hotels /dreamteam.htm; ❶–❺) have the next rocky headland known as **Khlong Hin** all to themselves and, though this beach is hopeless for swimming, there's a good sandy stretch just fifteen minutes' walk to the north. The bungalows are set in a pretty, cultivated flower garden and they range from ultra-basic to air-conditioned luxury; the mid-range ones are reasonably priced and quite comfortable. There's a good restaurant here too, with fine sea views.

Ao Kantiang, Ao Khlong Jaak and Ao Mai Pai

Three kilometres south of Khlong Hin, the secluded, almost remote fishing cove of **Ao Kantiang** boasts an impressively curved sweep of long, sandy bay backed by wild, jungle-clad hillsides whose resident monkeys occasionally pop down to seaside. The beach is good for swimming, and snorkelling and fishing trips are easily arranged from the bungalow outfits here. Right on the shore, *SeaSun* (❶–❷) offers inexpensive bamboo huts; the sixteen bamboo bungalows at neighbouring *Kantiang Bay View Resort* (T01/606 3546; ❷–❺) are set in two facing rows and furnished with fan and bathroom.

The road gets worse and worse as you head south from Ao Kantiang, eventually degenerating into a track that leads to the isolated little **Ao Khlong Jaak**, site of the exceptionally popular *Waterfall Bungalows* (T01/228 4014, F075/612084, Wwww.waterfallbaybeach.com; ❸–❺). The 23 huts here are simple but stylish, many with split-level accommodation in the roof and bathrooms downstairs; the huts nearer the sea are more expensive, as are those with air-con. It's a friendly, clued-in retreat and offers day-trips to the islands and the nearby national park, as well as pretty good food. Advance booking is essential and the place is open year-round.

An abysmal coastal track continues for 3km south of *Waterfall*, affording good sea views, passing a quiet sandy beach and then coming to a halt at the lighthouse. Few drivers will offer to bring you down here, however much you pay them, but if you like the quiet, solitary life it might be worth making the trip in order to stay at *Bamboo Bay* bungalows (❷–❹) at the pretty cove of **Ao Mai Pai**; the bamboo huts here are simple, but have large verandas and electricity in the evenings, and it's just an hour's boat ride to some nice snorkelling islands.

Ko Bubu and Ko Jum

Now that Ko Lanta is firmly registered on the beaten track, tourists in search of a more Robinson Crusoe-style haven have pushed on to a couple of other nearby islands. The minuscule **Ko Bubu**, only 7km off Lanta Yai's east coast, is the preserve of just one bungalow outfit, but in contrast to many one-resort islands, this is not an exclusive upmarket operation. The same is true of **Ko Jum**, which is slightly larger than Phi Phi Don but nevertheless offers only three accommodation options.

Ko Bubu

With a radius of not much more than 500m, wooded **KO BUBU** has room for just thirty bungalows at *Bubu Bungalows* (⊕01/228 4510; ❸–❺; closed May–Oct), plus a few tents for rent at B150 a double. The island is twenty minutes' chartered longtail ride (B100) from the small town of **Lanta** on Ko Lanta Yai's east coast and can also be reached direct **from Krabi** by following the rainy-season route for Ko Lanta Yai and taking a longtail from Bo Muang for B150. Most of Krabi's tour agents (see p.672) will book you in for the Ko Bubu bungalow resort and can organize through transport from Krabi.

Ko Jum (Ko Pu)

Situated halfway between Krabi and Ko Lanta Yai, **KO JUM** (also known as **Ko Pu**) is the sort of laid-back and simple spot that people come to for a couple of days, then can't bring themselves to leave. Its mangrove-fringed east coast holds two of the island's three fishing villages – Ban Ko Pu sits on the northeast tip and Ban Ko Jum, complete with it own beachfront school, is down on the southeast tip – while across on the sandy west coast there are a couple of small bungalow operations to the south of the third village, Ban Ting Lai. Much of the north is made inaccessible by the breastbone of forested hills, whose highest peak (395m) is Khao Ko Pu, and the ten-kilometre track that connects the north and south of the island runs around its northeastern flank. There's little to do here except hunt for shells, stroll the kilometre across the island to buy snacks in Ban Ko Jum or roast on the beach and then plunge into the sea. Sandflies can be quite a problem on Ko Jum, so bring plenty of insect repellent, and some bite-cream too in case it doesn't work.

The 35 smart wood and concrete **bungalows** of the long-running *Joy Bungalows* (⊕01/229 1502; ❷–❺) are comfortably equipped with balconies, beds and nets, and the bamboo huts are simple but fine enough. Close by *Joy, New Bungalow* (❶–❸) has just fifteen basic bamboo huts plus a couple of treehouses; their fish dinners are recommended. If you get sick of bungalow food, try the inexpensive and authentic Thai food at *Rimthang* on the track into Ban Ko Jum, or *Mama Cooking*, in Ban Ko Jum itself.

Both bungalows send **longtails** out to meet the Krabi–Ko Lanta ferries as they pass the west coast (1hr 30min from Krabi or about 45min from Ko Lanta). In the rainy season they sometimes organize a daily songthaew and longtail to cover the alternative mainland route, which runs from Krabi via the pier at **Laem Kruat**, 40km southeast, from where the boat takes you out to Ko Jum's east coast – ask any Krabi tour operator for songthaew departure times.

Travel details

Buses

Khao Lak to: Khao Sok (every 90min; 1hr 30min); Phuket (11 daily; 2hr 30min); Ranong (8 daily; 2hr 30min–3hr); Surat Thani (every 90min; 3hr 30min); Takua Pa (every 40min; 30min).

Khao Sok to: Khao Lak (every 90min; 1hr 30min); Surat Thani (every 90min; 2hr); Takua Pa (every 90min; 50min).

Krabi to: Bangkok (9 daily; 12–14hr); Hat Yai (13 daily; 4–5hr); Nakhon Si Thammarat (9 daily,

3–4hr); Penang (2 daily; 6hr); Phang Nga (17 daily;
1hr 30min–2hr); Phuket (17 daily; 3–5hr); Ranong
(3 daily; 4hr); Satun (2 daily; 5hr); Surat Thani
(hourly; 4hr); Takua Pa (4 daily; 3hr 30min–4hr
30min); Trang (14 daily; 3hr).

Phang Nga to: Bangkok (4 daily; 11hr–12hr 30min);
Krabi (hourly; 1hr 30min–2hr); Phuket (hourly; 1hr
30min–2hr 30min); Surat Thani (4 daily; 4hr).

Phuket to: Bangkok (at least 10 daily; 14–16hr);
Hat Yai (12 daily; 6–8hr); Khao Lak (14 daily; 2hr);
Khao Sok (14 daily; 3–4hr); Krabi (17 daily; 3–4hr);
Nakhon Si Thammarat (at least 7 daily; 7–8hr);
Phang Nga (17 daily; 2hr 30min); Phattalung (2
daily; 6–7hr); Ranong (4 daily; 5–6hr); Satun (2
daily; 7hr); Sungai Kolok (2 daily; 11hr); Surat
Thani (20 daily; 4hr 30min–6hr); Takua Pa (14
daily; 2hr 30min–3hr); Trang (22 daily; 5–6hr).

Ranong to: Bangkok (7 daily; 9–10hr); Chumphon
(every 90min; 2hr); Khuraburi (8 daily; 2hr); Phuket
(8 daily; 5–6hr); Takua Pa (8 daily; 2hr 30min–3hr).

Takua Pa to: Bangkok (10 daily; 12–13hr); Krabi
(4 daily; 3hr 30min–4hr 30min); Phuket (every
40min; 3hr); Ranong (8 daily; 2hr 30min–3hr);
Surat Thani (11 daily; 3hr).

Ferries

Ko Phi Phi Don to: Ao Nang (Nov–May 1 daily); Ko
Lanta Yai (Nov–May 2 daily; 1hr 30min); Krabi (4–6
daily; 1hr 30min–2hr); Phuket (Nov–May up to 4
daily; 1hr 30min–2hr 30min).

Krabi to: Ko Jum (1hr 30min); Ko Lanta Yai
(Nov–May 2 daily; 2hr 30min); Ko Phi Phi Don (4–6
daily; 1hr 30min–2hr).

Phuket to: Ko Phi Phi Don (2–6 daily; 1hr
30min–2hr 30min); Ko Similan (Dec–May daily;
1hr 30min).

Ranong to: Ko Chang (Nov–May 1–2 daily; 1hr);
Ko Pha Yam (Nov–May 1 daily; 1–2hr).

Thap Lamu (Khao Lak) to: Ko Similan (Nov–May
1 daily; 2hr).

Flights

Krabi to: Bangkok (2 daily; 65min); Phuket (3
daily; 30min).

Phuket to: Bangkok (17 daily; 1hr 25min); Hat Yai
(1–2 daily; 45min); Ko Samui (2 daily; 50min);
Krabi (3 daily; 30min); Nakhon Si Thammarat
(daily; 40min); Siem Reap (Cambodia; 3 daily; 2hr
20min); Surat Thani (daily; 40min).

Ranong to: Bangkok (4 weekly; 1hr 20min).

The deep south

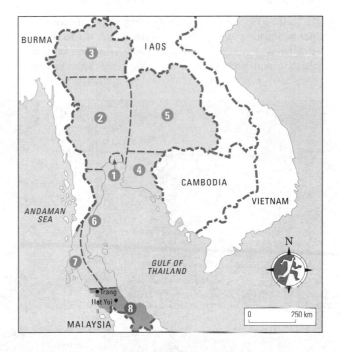

Highlights

* **Thale Noi Waterbird Park** – Boating on this fascinating inland lake isn't just for birdwatchers. **p.714**

* **Ko Mook** – best of the Trang islands, with laidback beach resorts and the stunning Emerald Cave. **p.720**

* **Ko Tarutao National Marine Park** – a largely undisturbed haven of beautiful land- and seascapes. **p.725**

* **Thale Ban National Park** – waterfalls, caves, noisy, sweaty jungle – and solitude. **p.724**

* **Songkhla** – sand-and-see all-rounder, with diverting sights, great accommodation and restaurants, and miles of beach. **p.735**

* **Southern Folklore Museum, Ko Yo** – stunning views and fascinating insights into southern Thai culture. **p.740**

The deep south

T he frontier between Thailand and Malaysia carves across the peninsula six degrees north of the equator, but the cultures of the two countries shade into each other much further north. According to official divisions, the southern Thais – the *thai pak tai* – begin around Chumphon, and as you move further down the peninsula you see ever more sarongs, yashmaks and towering mosques, and hear with increasing frequency a staccato dialect that baffles many Thais. In **Trang**, **Phatthalung** and **Songkhla** provinces, the Muslim population is generally accepted as being Thai, but the inhabitants of the four southernmost provinces – **Satun**, **Pattani**, **Yala** and **Narathiwat** – are ethnically more akin to the Malays: most of the 1,500,000 followers of Islam here speak Yawi, an old Malay dialect. To add to the ethnic confusion, the deep south has a large urban population of Chinese, whose comparative wealth makes them stand out sharply from the Muslim farmers and fishermen.

On a journey south, the first thing you might be tempted by is an atmospheric boat trip through the **Thale Noi Waterbird Park** near Phatthalung. The easiest route after that is to hop across to the great natural beauty of the **west coast**, with its sheer limestone outcrops, pristine sands and fish-laden coral stretching down to the Malaysian border. The spread of tourism outwards from Phuket is slowly inching its way south to the idyllic islands around

---

Accommodation prices

Throughout this guide, guest houses, hotels and bungalows have been categorized according to the **price codes** given below. These categories represent the minimum you can expect to pay in the high season (roughly July, Aug & Nov–Feb) for a **double room**. If travelling on your own, expect to pay anything between sixty and one hundred percent of the rates quoted for a double room. Wherever a **price range** is indicated, this means that the establishment offers rooms with varying facilities – as explained in the write-up. Wherever an establishment also offers **dormitory beds**, the prices of these beds are given in the text, instead of being indicated by price code.

Remember that the top-whack hotels will add seven percent tax and a ten percent service charge to your bill – the price codes below are based on net rates after taxes have been added.

❶ under B150
❷ B150–250
❸ B250–400
❹ B400–600
❺ B600–900
❻ B900–1200
❼ B1200–1800
❽ B1800–3000
❾ B3000+

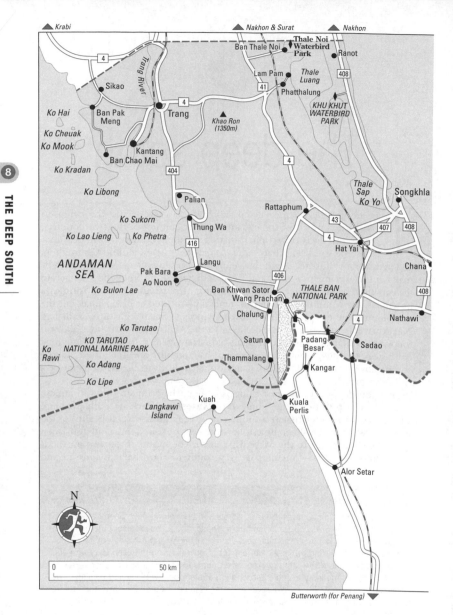

Trang, but for the time being at least these remain more or less unscathed, and further south in the spectacular **Ko Tarutao National Park**, you'll usually still have the beaches all to yourself.

On the less attractive **east** side of the peninsula, you'll probably pass through the ugly, modern city of **Hat Yai** at some stage, as it's the transport capital for the south and for connections to Malaysia, but a far more sympathetic place to stay is the old town of **Songkhla**, half an hour away on the seashore. The

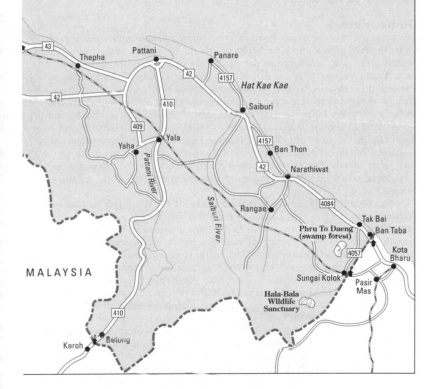

region southeast of here is where you'll experience Malay Muslim culture at its purest, though with the exception of **Narathiwat**, a pleasant stopover on the journey south to the border, it has little to offer the visitor.

As well as the usual bus services and the rail line, which forks at Hat Yai to Butterworth and Kuala Lumpur on the Malaysian west coast and Sungai Kolok on the eastern border, the deep south is the territory of **share-taxis** – sometimes grand old 1950s Mercs, which connect all the major towns for about twice the fare of ordinary buses. The cars leave when they're full, which usually means six passengers, with, quite possibly, babes-in-arms and livestock. They are a quick way of getting around and you should get dropped off at the door of your journey's end. A more recent phenomenon, run on almost exactly the same principles at similar prices, is **air-conditioned minibuses**; on these you'll be more comfortable, with a seat to yourself, and most of the various ranks publish a rough timetable – though the minibuses also tend to leave as soon as they're full.

There are eight **border crossings** to Malaysia – two by sea from Satun, the rest by land from Wang Prachan, Padang Besar, Sadao, Betong, Sungai Kolok, and Ban Taba – which are outlined in the relevant parts of this chapter. At any of them you can nip across and back to get a thirty-day Thai visa or to begin the second part of a double-entry visa; longer visas can be obtained at the Thai consulates at Penang on the west side of Malaysia and Kota Bharu on the east side (details on p.26 of Basics).

Some history

The central area of the Malay peninsula first entered Thai history when it came under the rule of Sukhothai, probably around the beginning of the fourteenth century. Islam was introduced to the area by the end of that century, by which time Ayutthaya was taking a firmer grip on the peninsula. **Songkhla** and **Pattani** then rose to be the major cities, prospering on the goods passed through the two ports across the peninsula to avoid the pirates in the Straits of Malacca between Malaysia and Sumatra. More closely tied to the Muslim Malay states to the south, Pattani began to **rebel** against the central power of Ayutthaya in the sixteenth century, but the fight for self-determination only weakened Pattani's strength. The town's last rebellious fling was in 1902, seven years after which Pattani was isolated from its allies, Kedah, Kelantan and Trengganu, when they were transferred into the suzerainty of the British in Malaysia.

During World War II the **Communist Party of Malaya** made its home in the jungle around the Thai border to fight the occupying Japanese. After the war they turned their guns against the British colonialists, but having been excluded from power after independence, descended into general banditry and racketeering around Betong. The Thai authorities eventually succeeded in breaking up the bandit gangs in 1989 through a combination of pardons and bribes, but the stability of the region then faced disruption from another source, a rise in **Islamic militancy**. The mid-1990s saw a concerted outburst of violence from the Pattani United Liberation Organization and other separatist groups, but the situation has since improved considerably, with closer co-operation between Thailand and Malaysia, and a string of progressive measures from the Thai government that have earned praise from other Islamic nations – among them lifting the ban on Islamic dress in state-run schools, observing Islamic holidays as official holidays in Muslim majority provinces and pumping money into development projects in the region.

Phatthalung and around

Halfway between Nakhon and Hat Yai, the hot, dusty town of **PHATTHALUNG** is worth a stop only if you're tempted by a boat trip through the nearby Thale Noi Waterbird Park, its beautiful watery landscape rich in exotic birds and vegetation. Although its setting among limestone outcrops is dramatic, the town itself is drab and unwelcoming: its only claims to fame are *nang thalung*, the Thai shadow puppet theatre to which it probably gave its name (see box on p.605), and bandits, though it has cleaned up its act in recent years.

If you've time to kill before or after a visit to the waterbird park, head for **Khao Hua Taek** or "Broken-Headed Mountain", the limestone outcrop with a dent in its peak which rises abruptly out of the west end of the centre. **Wat Kuha Sawan**, on the east side, has been built around a large, cool cave in the base of the outcrop, where a crude Buddha image is sheltered by a model of the bodhi tree hung with delicate brass leaves. Climb the concrete steps to the right of the cave, then follow the path to the left to reach the summit, where you'll get a good view over Phatthalung and the surrounding rice fields. To the east, you'll also be able to see **Khao Ok Taloo**, "Broken-Hearted Mountain", so called because of the natural tunnel through its peak: according to legend, Hua Taek and Ok Taloo were the wife and the mistress of a third mountain to the north, **Khao Muang**, over whom they had a fierce fight, leaving them with these wounds.

If a visit to Khao Hua Taek still leaves you with time on your hands, you could make a short trip out of town towards the resort of Lam Pam, half an hour away to the northeast: take one of the frequent songthaews from the rail crossing on Thanon Ramet. About 6km out on the right-hand side, stop off at the 200-year-old bot of **Wat Wang** to see a series of elegant and dynamic murals depicting the life of the Buddha – ask a monk for the key to the formidable cloisters which surround it. Two former **governor's palaces**, appealing examples of traditional southern Thai architecture, overlook a picturesque canal 200m beyond Wat Wang on the same side of the road. Nearer to the road, the "old" residence, Wang Khao, which dates from the middle of the nineteenth century, is built entirely of wood on inward-sloping stilts, a design whose tensile properties mean that it can be held together with tongue-and-groove joints rather than nails. In the so-called "new palace", Wang Mai, built in 1889 with a raised stone courtyard around a large tree, look out for the intricate traditional carvings on the main house, especially the "sunrise" gable, sometimes called the "crest of a monk's robe" because it resembles the edge of the robe gathered into pleats by a monk's hand. At **Lam Pam** itself there's nothing to do but eat and drink at minimal cost, while relaxing in a deckchair on the shady banks of the Thale Luang, the lagoon adjoining Thale Noi (see p.714).

Practicalities

Phatthalung is served by frequent **buses** from north and south and from Trang, 57km to the west, and is on the major rail line, which crosses the main street, Thanon Ramet, in the centre of town. Most buses stop near the **train station**, which is on the north side of Thanon Ramet; through buses only stop at the junction of highways 4 and 41, to the west, leaving a short songthaew hop into town.

Out of a poor selection of **hotels**, the best value is the friendly *Thai Hotel*, at 14 Thanon Disara Sakarin, behind the Bangkok Bank on Thanon Ramet (⊤074/611636; ❷–❸); rooms with attached bathrooms and a choice of fan or air-conditioning are clean and reasonably quiet. *Koo Hoo*, at 9 Thanon Prachabamrung (parallel to and south of Ramet), is an excellent, moderately priced **restaurant** – try the chicken with lemon sauce on a bed of fried seaweed, or the delicious giant tiger prawns.

Thale Noi Waterbird Park isn't just for bird-spotters – even the most recalcitrant city-dweller can appreciate boating through the bizarre fresh-water habitat formed at the head of the huge lagoon that spills into the sea at Songkhla. Here, in the "Little Sea" (*thale noi*), the distinction between land and water breaks down: the lake is dotted with low, marshy islands, and much of the intervening shallow water is so thickly covered with water vines, lotus pads and reeds that it looks like a field. But the real delight of this area is the hundreds of thousands of birds which breed here – brown teals, loping purple herons, white cattle egrets and nearly two hundred other species. Most are migratory, arriving here from January onwards from as far away as Siberia – March and April provide the widest variety of birds, whereas from October to December you'll spot just a small range of native species. Early morning and late afternoon are the best times to come, when the heat is less searing and when, in the absence of hunters and fishermen, more birds are visible.

To get from Phatthalung to **BAN THALE NOI**, the village on the western shore, take one of the frequent **songthaews** (1hr) from Thanon Nivas, which runs north off Thanon Ramet near the station. If you're coming from Nakhon or points further north by bus, you can save yourself a trip into Phatthalung by getting out at **Ban Chai Khlong**, 15km from Ban Thale Noi, and waiting for a songthaew there. **Longtail boats** can be hired at the pier in the village: for around B300 (depending on the number of people in your party), the boat-man will give you a two-hour trip around the lake. If you want to get a dawn start, stay in one of the few national park **bungalows** built over the lake (dona-tion required; book at least fifteen days in advance on ☏075/685230).

Trang province

Trang town, 60km west of Phatthalung, is fast developing as a popular jumping-off point for backpackers, drawn south from the crowded sands of Krabi to the pristine **beaches and islands** of the Trang coast. Its islands sport only a couple of bungalow outfits each, though some of these have moved upmarket in recent years and it won't be long before resorts multiply and prices rise. **Inland**, too, tourism is developing, and several outfits in Trang town now offer white-water rafting, kayaking and trekking excursions. So popular is the area becoming that it even has its own website: the excellent Ⓦwww.tran-gonline.com has plenty of well-presented information on attractions, tours and accommodation in the region, and allows online bookings.

Trang town

The town of **TRANG** (aka Taptieng), which prospers on rubber, oil palms, fish-eries and – increasingly – tourism, is a sociable place whose wide, clean streets are dotted with crumbling, wooden-shuttered houses. In the evening, restaurant tables sprawl onto the main Thanon Rama VI and Thanon Wisetkul, and dur-ing the day, many of the town's Chinese inhabitants hang out in the cafés, drink-ing the local filtered coffee. Trang's Chinese population makes the **Vegetarian Festival** at the beginning of October almost as frenetic as Phuket's (see box on p.643) – and for veggie travellers it's an opportunity to feast at the stalls set up

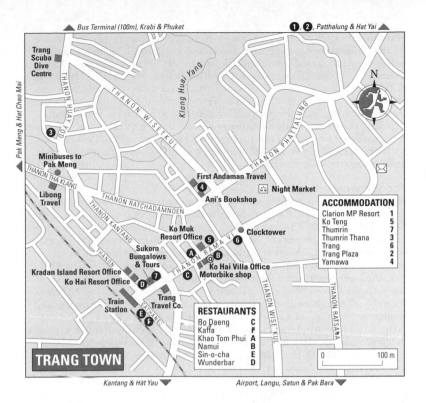

TRANG TOWN

Bus Terminal (100m), Krabi & Phuket

❶, ❷, Patthalung & Hat Yai

Trang Scuba Dive Centre

Pak Meng & Hat Chao Mai

THANON HUAY YOD

THANON WISETKUL

Klong Huai Yang

THANON PHATTALUNG

N

❸

Minibuses to Pak Meng

THANON THA KLANG

Libong Travel

THANON RATCHADAMNOEN

First Andaman Travel

❹

🎵 Night Market

Ani's Bookshop

THANON KANTANG

Ko Muk Resort Office ❺

Clocktower

❻

Sukorn Bungalows & Tours

THANON RAMA VI

Ⓐ

THANON

Kradan Island Resort Office

Ko Hai Resort Office

❼

Ⓐ@Ⓑ

Ko Hai Villa Office

Ⓒ

Motorbike shop

Ⓓ

Train Station

Trang Travel Co.

THANON SA THANG

Ⓔ

Ⓕ

THANON WISE KUL

THANON RATSADA

✉

ACCOMMODATION

Clarion MP Resort	1
Ko Teng	5
Thumrin	7
Thumrin Thana	3
Trang	6
Trang Plaza	2
Yamawa	4

RESTAURANTS

Bo Daeng	C
Kaffa	F
Khao Tom Phui	A
Namui	B
Sin-o-cha	E
Wunderbar	D

0   100 m

Kantang & Hat Yau ▼

Airport, Langu, Satun & Pak Bara ▼

---

around the temples. Getting there is easy, as Trang is ninety minutes from Phatthalung and well served by buses from all the surrounding provinces.

Practicalities

There are daily Thai Airways **flights** (around B2300 one way) between Bangkok and Trang **airport**, which is connected to Trang town by B30 air-conditioned minibuses, operated by Trang Travel Company (see p.716). Two overnight **trains** from the capital run down a branch of the southern line to Trang, stopping at the station at the western end of Thanon Rama VI. Most **buses** arrive at the terminal on Thanon Huay Yod, to the north of the centre; buses from Satun and Palian stop on Thanon Ratsada, which runs south from the eastern end of Thanon Rama VI. **Air-conditioned minibuses** for Hat Yai are based on Thanon Huay Yod near the main bus terminal; those for Nakhon Si Thammarat are found on Thanon Klong Huai Yang, off Thanon Wisetkul about 200m from the clocktower; and those for Ko Lanta leave from the offices of several travel agents around town who handle bookings for them, including Sukorn Beach Bungalows and Tours (see p.716). This agency also operate minibuses to Pak Bara in high season (roughly Nov–May); at other times of year you have to take a bus to Langu and then a songthaew.

There's an excellent **bookshop**, Ani's, round the corner from the *Yamawa Bed and Breakfast* at 285 Thanon Ratchadamnoen; it stocks a wide range of books in English and other languages, as well as souvenirs from Trang province. The owners are a good source of information on the area, and also have a couple of **motorbikes**, which they rent out for B150 per day. There's a greater choice available from the motorbike shop at 44 Thanon Rama VI (B200 per day), as well as air-conditioned vans, with driver, for B1700 per day. On Thanon Sathanee, both the Trang Travel Company at no. 99 (☎075/219598–9, 🖷211290, 📧trangtravel@hotmail.com) and Sukorn Beach Bungalows and Tours at no. 22 (☎ & 🖷075/211457, 🌐www.sukorn-island-trang.com) can arrange **car hire**, with driver, at similar rates. For self-drive car rental, contact Avis (☎075/691941, 📧tst@avisthailand.com), who have plans to open a branch at Trang airport. You can connect to the **internet** at 116 Thanon Rama VI (daily 8am–10.30pm; B1 per minute), and at the Trang Travel Company (daily 8am–8pm; B2 per minute).

Accommodation

Hotels in Trang are concentrated along Thanon Rama VI and Thanon Wisetkul. The town's outstanding **budget** choice is the *Yamawa Bed and Breakfast* at 94 Thanon Wisetkul (☎075/216617; ❷), a gem of a guest house whose six large rooms, with shared bathrooms, are spread over three floors, beautifully decorated throughout and festooned with plants; rates include breakfast. There's a restaurant on the ground floor, as well as a leafy roof terrace. The friendly Thai-Belgian family who run the guest house also organize treks in the Trang area. If you can't get a room here, a second best is the *Ko Teng Hotel* at 77–79 Thanon Rama VI (☎075/218622; ❷), a little rough around the edges, but friendly enough and with en-suite rooms that are large and clean.

The pick of the **moderate** range, *Trang Hotel*, 134/2–5 Thanon Wisetkul, at the junction with Thanon Rama VI overlooking the clocktower (☎075/218944, 🖷218451; ❹), has large, comfortable twin rooms with air-conditioning, hot water and television. *Thumrin Hotel*, on Rama VI near the station (☎075/211014, 🖷218057; ❹), used to be the town's only deluxe option, but is now looking down-at-heel, having been decisively usurped by no fewer than three **luxury** hotels: the *Trang Plaza*, 2km east of the centre at 132 Thanon Phattalung (☎075/226902–10, 🖷226901; ❻); the *Clarion MP Resort Hotel*, a little further out on the same road (☎075/214230–45, 🖷211177, 🌐www.mpresort.com; ❼); and the *Thumrin Thana*, 1km north of the train station at 69/8 Thanon Thana (☎075/211211, 🌐www.thumrin.co.th; ❽); note that hefty discounts are often available at all three hotels.

Eating and drinking

Trang's **food** comes into its own in the early evenings, when the excellent night market opens for business; it's around the back of the city hall, just off Thanon Rama VI, 100m north of the clocktower. Try the *khanom jiin*, soft noodles topped with hot, sweet or fishy sauces and eaten with crispy greens. *Khao Tom Phui*, 1/11 Thanon Rama VI (open from 5pm), is a very popular and reasonable pavement restaurant on the north side of the street. For something posher, head for *Namui* on the opposite side at no. 130, a large, clean institution specializing in good seafood; ignore the unprepossessing interior and head straight through the restaurant to the creeper-covered patio and outdoor seating at the back. An even nicer setting can be found at the *Riverside* restaurant, a boat permanently moored on the Trang River, 5km from the centre of town; you need to take a tuk-tuk there and back, but it's worth the extra effort for the breezy location and great Thai food.

There are several good places to sample Trang's **café** society. Diagonally opposite *Thumrin Hotel* on Thanon Rama VI, *Bo Daeng* serves the ubiquitous *kopii* (filtered coffee) with *patongkoh* (Chinese doughnuts) and *ahaan det diap*, plates of assorted tasty titbits such as spring rolls, baby corn and sausage. For a daytime coffee fix and Western-style cakes, head for *Sin-o-cha*, next to the station at 25/25–26 Thanon Sathanee, or the equally popular *Kaffa*, a few doors along at no. 25/47. Trang even boasts a farang **bar**, pandering to its small expat community and growing population of tourists: *Wunderbar*, at the bottom end of Rama VI near the station, offers a wide selection of drinks, Thai food, burgers, pizzas and other Western favourites.

Around Trang

From Ban Pak Meng, 40km due west of Trang town, to the mouth of the Trang River runs a thirty-kilometre stretch of lovely **beaches**, broken only by dramatic limestone outcrops which are pitted with explorable caves. Air-conditioned minibuses run from Trang to Pak Meng in the north, and via Hat Yao to Ban Chao Mai in the south, but if you want to explore the whole coastline, you'll need to rent or hire a motorbike, car or taxi in Trang.

Much nicer than the mainland beaches – and more geared towards foreign tourists – are the fantastic **islands** off the coast, most notable among them Hai, Mook and Kradan. Blessed with blinding white beaches, great coral and amazing marine life, these have managed, despite increasing popularity, to cling on to that illusory desert-island atmosphere which better-known places like Phuket and Samui lost long ago. The situation is changing fast, however: prices have risen in line with the number of tourists, accommodation is often fully booked at peak times and many resorts that were previously open in high season only (Nov–May) are now opening year round – though in practice many remain inaccessible out of season due to treacherous seas. We give details of opening seasons in the individual island accounts below, but it's sensible to phone ahead – either to the place you want to stay, or to its office in Trang town or Bangkok – to check on opening months, vacancies and transport. In addition to some public ferry services, there are boat services which many resorts run in the morning; at other times the resort you're interested in may well be willing to despatch a longtail to pick you up.

Besides the specific resort offices (detailed below in the island accounts), there are a couple of **travel agencies in Trang** which offer a wider range of services. The Trang Travel Company (see opposite) can provide information on, and make reservations at, any of the places on the islands, or if you just fancy a day exploring the islands, can organize a **boat trip** (mid-Oct to mid-May only) to Ko Mook, Ko Hai and Ko Cheuak ("Robe Island", so named after its limestone folds) for B600 per person including packed lunch; snorkelling gear can be rented (B30 per day) and the boat will drop you off at one of the islands if you wish. The well-organized Sukorn Beach Bungalows and Tours (see opposite) offer a similar range of services – accommodation booking, boat trips and car rental – in addition to running their own bungalow outfit on Ko Sukorn. The friendly Thai-Dutch owners are a great source of information on the area, and their office makes a good first stop in town. They can also book you onto any of the white-water rafting, canoeing and trekking trips run by Libong Travel (see p.718).

To do some **scuba-diving** off the Trang coast, contact Trang Scuba Dive Centre at 59/33–34 Thanon Huay Yod (☎075/222189, ℉222194, ℮trangscuba@thumrin.co.th); they offer day-trips to Ko Mook, Ko Hai and Ko Kradan for B2000–2500 per person, or can organize longer trips of up to a week (staying aboard or at one of the island resorts). Ko Hai also has its own dive shop, Rainbow Divers (see p.720).

Away from the beach, **inland** Trang Province has plenty to offer too. Outdoor pursuits have mushroomed in the last few years, and several operators now offer **trekking, white-water rafting** or **canoeing** excursions, most taking in some of the myriad caves and waterfalls which are scattered though the province. One of the longest established operators is Libong Travel, 59/1 Thanon Tha Klang (⊕075/222929 or 01/606 8530, ⓕ214676), opposite the minibus stand for Pak Meng; they offer a fairly typical spread of trips, including white-water rafting (B850 day-trip), canoeing through the mangroves near Ban Chao Mai and the caves along the Trang coast (B750 day-trip), and a three-day jungle trek up to the 1200-metre peak of nearby Mount Rutu (B1700). They also offer a day-trip to Thale Noi Waterbird Park near Phatthalung for B650 (see p.714), as well as island tours.

The coast: Pak Meng to Ban Chao Mai

Although it has a fine outlook to the headlands and islands to the west, the beach at **PAK MENG** is not the most attractive on the coast, a rather muddy strip of sand truncated at its northern end by a busy pier and to the south by a newly constructed promenade and sea wall. If it's just a day at the beach you're after, you're much better off continuing further south down the coast to Hat Yong Ling or Hat Yao. Getting to Pak Meng takes about an hour on one of the air-conditioned **minibuses** that leave when full (roughly hourly; B50) from Thanon Tha Klang, the northwesterly continuation of Thanon Ratchadamnoen in Trang. The nicest place **to stay** is the *Lay Trang Resort*, a stone's throw from the pier (⊕075/274027–8, ⓦwww.laytrang.com; ⑤); its smart brick air-conditioned bungalows, ranged around a large, peaceful garden, come with balconies and spacious hot-water bathrooms. The owners can organize longtail day-trips to Ko Mook, Ko Hai and Ko Kradan for B550 a head including lunch. There's a pleasant, reasonably priced **restaurant** attached – the seafood dishes are particularly good – and there are plenty of foodstalls and simple eateries lining the back of the beach.

A paved road heads south from Pak Meng, passing, after 7km, the turning for the headquarters of the **Hat Chao Mai National Park** (entry B200) at Hat Chang Lang. The park covers 230 square kilometres, including the islands of Mook and Kradan and the entire stretch of coastline from Pak Meng down to Ban Chai Mai. The headquarters have limited information available in English, but there are some eight-berth **bungalows** available to rent (B500 each), or for B200 a night, two-person tents can be pitched under the casuarina trees at the back of the sandy beach. You'll need to bring your own food unless you're prepared to retrace your steps a couple of kilometres north along the coast road to the *Chang Lang Resort* (⊕075/291008–9, ⓕ291008; ④), a decent bungalow outfit with attached restaurant, set back from the beach just off the main road – if you do eat here, try the oysters, for which Hat Chang Lang is famous. Primarily aimed at Thai weekenders, the pleasant resort has well-built concrete bungalows, some air-conditioned, and all with mosquito screens, en-suite bathrooms and their own verandas. The run-down concrete rooms at the nearby *Seasand Resort* (④) should be given a wide berth.

Four kilometres south of Hat Chang Lang is **Hat Yong Ling**, an attractive convex beach with a large cave which you can swim into at high tide or walk into at low tide. You'll need to pay the national park entrance fee and bring a picnic as there are no food or drink stalls, but the reward is a quiet, pristine strip of sand with crystal-clear waters, probably the nicest along this stretch of coast. Immediately beyond comes **Hat Yao** (Long Beach), also known as Hat Chao Mai, which runs in a broad five-kilometre white-sand strip, backed by casuarina trees and some simple restaurants. In a scenic spot at the southern end of the beach, *Sinchai's Chaomai Resort* (℡01/396 4838; ❶–❸) is very relaxed and friendly, and offers a choice between simple huts with mosquito nets, and rooms in sturdy wooden or concrete bungalows; two-person tents are also available for B50 per night. The laid-back owners can rustle up tasty Thai meals, there's a small English-language library, and fishing and snorkelling tours can be arranged on request.

A short walk away from *Sinchai's* is the Muslim village of **BAN CHAO MAI**, a straggle of simple thatched houses on stilts, which exists on fishing, especially for crabs. Hourly air-conditioned **minibuses** from Trang via Hat Yao reach Ban Chao Mai in about an hour (B100). By the harbour, the distinctive green tin-roofed *Had Yao Nature Resort* (℡01/894 6936, @natureresorts@thailand.com; ❷–❺) is an official YHA **hostel** – clean, friendly and efficiently run by a young Thai brother and sister, who are very clued up about eco-tourism in the area and recycle all their rubbish (they also own the *Libong Nature Beach Resort*, covered on p.722, and can arrange transport there). Dorm beds in the large house cost B100, and there are also some fan-cooled rooms with shared bath, as well as nicer self-contained bungalows with tables, chairs and their own balcony over the canal. The attached vegetarian restaurant serves up excellent grub. **Bikes** – an excellent means of transport for the nearby beaches – can be rented at the hostel for B100 per day, and there are also some **kayaks** available for exploring the mangrove swamps on the canal running behind the village (B200–300 per day). The owners organize kayak trips (B300 per person) to Tham Chao Mai, a nearby cave which is large enough to enter by boat; inside are impressively huge rock pillars and a natural theatre, its stage framed by rock curtains.

Ko Hai

Of all the Trang islands, **KO HAI** (aka Ko Ngai), 16km southwest of Pak Meng, is the most developed, though it's still pretty low-key. The island's action, such as it is, centres on the east coast: three resorts, and an unobtrusive *chao ley* (see p.624) hamlet, enjoy a dreamy panorama of jagged limestone outcrops, whose crags glow pink and blue against the setting sun, stretching across the sea to the mainland behind. A two-kilometre-long beach of fine, white sand has a gentle slope that's ideal for swimming, and there's some good snorkelling in the shallow water off the southeast tip – though be careful of sea urchins and the sharp stag coral. For the best snorkelling in the region you can rent a longtail on Ko Hai (half-day B600) to get to Ko Cheuak, Ko Maa and Ko Waen, just off Ko Hai to the east, where you can swim into caverns and explore a fantastic variety of multicoloured soft and hard coral. All three resorts on Ko Hai run excursions to Ko Mook's Emerald Cave.

Ko Hai's **resorts** are theoretically **open year round**, with prices dropping slightly in the low season, but bear in mind that out of season the sea is often too rough for boats to cross. When they're running, **boats** leave Pak Meng for the one-hour voyage at 10.30am, charging B150 one way; if you miss the boat, longtails can be chartered for B400. The cheapest of the island's resorts, *Ko Hai Villa* (℡01/677 0319; Trang office at 112 Thanon Rama VI, ℡075/210496; ❹–❺) has the beach much to itself. Simple, well-organized bamboo bungalows on a nice grassy plot boast verandas, small toilets and mosquito nets, or you could opt for a newer concrete bungalow or room in a concrete longhouse. The more upmarket *Ko Hai Resort* (℡075/211045; Trang office at 205 Thanon Sathanee, ℡075/210317, ℻227092; Bangkok reservations ℡02/316 3577, ℻316 7916; ❺–❽) occupies a sandy cove by the island's jetty; besides a good restaurant, it has a spread of rooms ranging from fan-cooled en-suite huts on the rocks to air-conditioned beachside bungalows with wooden verandas and spacious bathrooms. The resort also has a well-organized **dive shop**: the German-run Rainbow Divers (Ⓔrainbowtau@aol.com) offers day-trips around Ko Hai, Ko Rok and the nearby islands (two tanks and lunch US$50–60), as well as PADI certification (4–5 days; around US$300). Operated by the same company as *Ko Hai Resort*, the *Ko Hai Fantasy Resort* (Ⓣ075/216339, Ⓦwww.kohngai.com; Trang office details and Bangkok reservations as for *Ko Hai Resort*; ❽), 1km north of its sister resort on a secluded stretch of beach, is swankier still, with foot spas outside each bungalow to wash away the sand before you step inside. Its thirty pastel-coloured bungalows are set in a pretty garden under coconut palms, some right on the beach, and there's a good restaurant too.

Ko Mook

KO MOOK, about 8km southeast of Ko Hai, offers some of the best budget accommodation on the Trang islands, though at time of writing the resorts here were open in high season only. The island supports a comparatively busy fishing village on its east coast, but its main source of renown is **Tham Morakhot**, the stunning "Emerald Cave" on the west coast, which can only be visited by boat but shouldn't be missed. An eighty-metre swim through the cave – 10m or so of which is in pitch darkness – brings you to an inland beach of powdery sand open to the sky, at the base of a spectacular natural chimney whose walls are coated with dripping vegetation. Unless you're a nervous swimmer, avoid the organized tours on bigger boats offered by some of the resorts on nearby islands, and charter your own longtail instead: you won't get lifejackets and torches, but the boatman will swim through the cave with you and – if you're lucky – you'll avoid the tours and get the inland beach all to yourself, an experience not to be forgotten.

The peaceful **Hat Farang**, south of Tham Morakhot and a thirty-minute walk west from the island village, is by far the best beach on Ko Mook, with gently shelving white sand, crystal-clear water that's good for swimming and snorkelling, and beautiful sunsets. To get to Hat Farang from the mainland, either charter a longtail from Pak Meng direct to the beach (B400), or take the midday **ferry** from Kuantunku Pier (8km south from Pak Meng, connected by regular B40 minibus) to the island village, and then a motorbike taxi across (B30). The nicest of the three **bungalow** outfits here is *Charlie's* (Ⓣ01/476 0478; ❷), with simple bamboo huts and spacious well-ventilated two-man tents set right on the beach under the coconut palms. It has a spotlessly clean shower block, and a simple open-air restaurant serving Western snacks alongside the tasty Thai dishes. **Motorbikes** can be rented here to explore the island (B200 per day), and there's also some snorkelling gear available (B100 per day); a longtail charter to the Emerald Cave will set you back B300 per boat. If *Charlie's* is full, the simple bamboo huts and basic mattress-on-floor rooms at the *Hat Farang* (Ⓣ075/224475 in Trang after 7pm; ❷–❸) are a good second choice, set 50m or so back from the beach in a grassy plot and run by a friendly Thai woman. At the rocky, northern end of the beach, the *Sawatdee's* bamboo huts (book through *Wunderbar* in Trang – see p.717; ❸) are a little dilapidated, but compensate with uninterrupted sea views.

The beaches on the eastern side of the island are disappointing, often reduced to dirty mud flats when the tide goes out. On this coast just north of the village is the *Ko Mook Resort* (Ⓣ075/212613; Trang office at 45 Thanon Rama VI, Ⓣ & Ⓕ075/214441; ❸–❺); arrayed here on shady slopes around a decent restaurant are basic bungalows (with fans, mosquito screens and shared bathrooms) as well as big bamboo and wood versions with verandas and private bathrooms. Their office in Trang can arrange transport here by car and boat, departing from their office at 11.30am every day in season (B150 per person); otherwise longtails can be chartered at Pak Meng for around B300, or there's the midday ferry from Kuantunku. The resort runs free boat transport every day to nicer beaches around Ko Mook, and can also organize snorkelling trips to nearby islands.

Ko Kradan

About 6km to the southwest of Ko Mook, **KO KRADAN** is the remotest of the inhabited islands off Trang, and one of the most beautiful. An unimaginatively designed complex on the east coast, *Kradan Island Resort* (Trang office at 66/10 Thanon Sathanee, ⊤ & ℉075/211391; Bangkok reservations ⊤02/391 6091; ❺–❻) is Ko Kradan's only sign of life, offering reasonable **bungalows** with bathrooms, fans and mosquito-screened windows overlooking the beach, as well as cheaper accommodation in four-room wooden longhouses. The friendly staff speak good English and can arrange fishing trips and longtail tours of the surrounding islands and the Emerald Cave. You can swim at the long, narrow beach of steeply sloping, powdery sand in front of the resort – complete with its own coral reef – or at Sunset Beach, in a small bay ten minutes' walk away on the other side of the island. There's more good snorkelling among a great variety of hard coral in the clear waters off the island's north-eastern tip, while the waters off the southwest of the island are a popular spot for **windsurfing**; the resort rents out windsurfers if you want to give it a go. To get there, phone the resort's Trang office in advance to be picked up at Pak Meng for the ninety-minute voyage (B600 for the boat); the resort is officially **open all year**, but often inaccessible due to bad weather conditions.

Ko Libong

The largest of the Trang islands, **KO LIBONG**, lies 10km southeast of Ko Mook, opposite Ban Chao Mai on the mainland. Less visited than its northern neighbours, it's known mostly for its wildlife, although it has its fair share of golden beaches too. Libong is one of the most significant remaining refuges in Thailand of the **dugong** (also known as the manatee), a large marine mammal which feeds on sea grasses growing on the sea floor – the sea-grass meadow around Libong is reckoned to be the largest in Southeast Asia. Sadly, dugongs are now an endangered species, traditionally hunted for their blubber (used as fuel) and meat, and increasingly affected by fishing practices such as scooping, and by coastal pollution which destroys their source of food. The dugong has now been adopted as one of fifteen "reserved animals" of Thailand and is the official mascot of Trang province, but it remains to be seen how effective methods of conservation will be, especially with tourist interest in the dugong growing all the time – one Trang venture is proposing guaranteed-sighting money-back tours, tracking the normally elusive animals down by sonar.

Libong is also well known for its migratory **bird life**, which stops off here on its way south from Siberia, drawn by the island's food-rich mud flats (now protected by the Libong Archipelago Sanctuary, which covers the eastern third of the island). For those seriously interested in ornithology, the best time to come is during March and April, when you can expect to see crab plovers, great knots, Eurasian curlews, bar-tailed godwits, brown-winged kingfishers, masked finfoots and even the rare black-necked stork, not seen elsewhere on the Thai–Malay peninsula. Both of the island's resorts can arrange longtail charters with local fishermen (B800 per boat) out to the Juhol Cape, the prime viewing point on the island; late afternoon is best, when the bird life is more active.

Practicalities

Ferries depart daily year-round at 3pm from **Kantang** (reached by regular B40 minibus from Thanon Kantang near Trang's train station), arriving one hour later at Ban Hin Kao, Ko Libong's main settlement; from here motorbike taxis (B40) transport you across to Ban Lan Khao and the island's two resorts. Alternatively, the *Had Yao Nature Resort* in Ban Chao Mai offers a direct transfer to the *Libong Nature Beach Resort* for B100 per person.

Situated on the long, thin strip of golden sand which runs along the southwestern coast, both of Ko Libong's **resorts** are **open all year**. The beach is pretty enough, though at low tide the sea retreats for hundreds of metres, exposing rock pools that are great for splashing about in but not so good for a dip. The newly opened *Libong Nature Beach Resort* (T01/894 6936; Bangkok reservations T02/378 1428 or 378 1550; or book through *Had Yao Nature Resort* – see p.719; Enatureresorts@thailand.com; ❸–❺) is the nicer of the two, run by the same brother-and-sister team who operate the *Had Yao Nature Resort* on the mainland. Its simple bamboo huts and neat brick en-suite bungalows with cheerful green tin roofs are set slightly back from a secluded stretch of beach, a ten-minute walk south of the fishing village of Ban Lan Khao; there's a good restaurant attached too. Motorbikes are available to rent (B400 per day), and the helpful owners can also organize snorkelling, sea-kayaking, fishing and boat trips to nearby islands. Dugong-spotting excursions are also available; you're unlikely to see the animals themselves, but you can sometimes spot their feeding trails, 2–3m long, in the sea grass below. At *Libong Beach Resort* (T075/281160; Trang office at 18/2 Moo 6 Tambon Bankuan, T075/225205, Elibongbeach@hotmail.com; ❸–❹), on the opposite, northern, side of Ban Lan Khao, a little closer to the clutter of the village, simple wooden bungalows on stilts come with or without bathroom, and there's also a reasonable restaurant.

Ko Sukorn

A good way south of the other Trang islands, low-lying **KO SUKORN** lacks the white-sand beaches and beautiful coral of its neighbours but makes up for it with its friendly inhabitants, laid-back ambience and one excellent resort; for a glimpse of how island villagers – mainly fishermen and rubber farmers – live and work, this is the place to come.

The lush interior of the island is mainly given over to rubber plantations, interspersed with rice paddies, banana and coconut palms; there's a fringe of mangroves on the northern coast near the pier, while the island's main **beach** – 500m of gently shelving brown sand, backed by coconut palms – runs along the southwestern shore. It's here you'll find the excellent *Sukorn Beach Bungalows* (T01/228 3668; Trang office at 22 Thanon Sathanee, T075/211457, Wwww.sukorn-island-trang.com; ❸–❹), one of the few Trang resorts that's reliably open and accessible all year round (discounts of up to sixty percent are available in low season). The clued-up Thai-Dutch duo who run the place are keen to keep the resort low-key and work with the local islanders as much as possible, something that's reflected in the friendly welcome you get all over the island. Nicely decorated concrete and thatch bungalows and longhouses – all spotlessly clean and with en-suite bathrooms – are set around a lush garden dotted with deckchairs (prices vary with distance from the beach) and there's an excellent well-priced **restaurant**.

Boat excursions from the resort range from **fishing trips** (with baskets – for squid and crab – in the morning, with nets in the evening, and with rods all day) to **snorkelling trips** out to Ko Phetra, Ko Lao Lien and Ko Takieng (all part of the Ko Phetra National Marine Park; see p.730). The latter run in high season only, when the sea is calm enough; at other times of year you're restricted to the island itself, though there's plenty to occupy you. At thirty square kilometres, it's a good size for exploring, and the resort has both motorbikes (half-day B175) and mountain bikes (half-day B85) for rent, as well as a handy map which marks all the sights, including the crab market (daily at 11am), the village health centre (where you can get a massage) and a viewpoint – at 150m up, the island's highest point – which you can climb in the dry season.

A songthaew-and-boat **transfer to the island** (B70 per person) leaves the resort's office in Trang daily at 11.30am and takes a couple of hours. Leaving the island, there's no need to return to the mainland; *Sukorn Beach Bungalows* can organize **longtail-boat transfers** to any of the other Trang islands, as well as to Ko Bulon Lae (see p.730). The resort can also arrange to pick you up from these islands if you call ahead.

Satun province

Satun province, which lies south of Trang and flush against the Malaysian border, provides the first glimpse of Thailand for many travellers on their way up through the Thai-Malay peninsula. The sleepy provincial capital, **Satun**, offers few attractions for the visitor, but makes a good base for the nearby **Thale Ban National Park**, with its caves, waterfalls and luxuriant jungle. The province's main attraction, however, is the **Ko Tarutao National Marine Park**, one of the loveliest beach destinations in Thailand, with pristine stretches of sand and a fantastic array of marine life. North of the national park, the tiny islands of the **Ko Phetra National Marine Park** are much less visited, with the exception of **Ko Bulon Lae**, which has a good selection of privately run bungalows along its long and beautiful beach.

Satun

Nestling in the last wedge of Thailand's west coast, remote **SATUN** is served by just one road, Highway 406, which approaches the town through forbidding karst outcrops. Set in a green valley bordered by limestone hills, the town is leafy and relaxing but not especially interesting: the boat services to and from Malaysia are the main reason for farangs to come here, though some use the town as an approach to Thale Ban National Park (see p.724).

Frequent **buses** depart from Thanon Ratsada in Trang, and regular buses also come here from Hat Yai and from Phatthalung – if you don't get a direct bus from Phatthalung to Satun, you can easily change at **Rattaphum**, on the junction of highways 4 and 406. Buses arrive at the terminal on Thanon Satun Thani, the main road into town; share-taxis and air-con minibuses are based 400m southwest of the bus terminal around the junction of Thanon Saman Pradit (the main east–west thoroughfare) and Thanon Buriwanit, which runs parallel to Thanon Satun Thani. There's **internet access** at Satun CyberNet, 136 Thanon Satun Thani (daily 9am–10pm; B30 per hour).

Crossing into Malaysia from Satun

From Satun, it's possible to travel into Malaysia by songthaew or longtail boat. **Songthaews** leave every thirty minutes from opposite the *Rian Thong* hotel, heading to the Malaysian border via Wang Prachan in the Thale Ban National Park. The border checkpoint lies 2km beyond the park headquarters, and share-taxis wait at **Bukit Kayu Hitam** on the other side to ferry you south to Alor Setar or Penang.

From **Thammalang** pier, 10km south of Satun at the mouth of the river, **longtail boats** leave when full on regular trips (daily 8am–3pm; 30min; B100 per person) to **Kuala Perlis** on Malaysia's northwest tip, from where there are plentiful transport connections down the west coast. Four ferry boats a day are scheduled to cross to the Malaysian island of **Langkawi** from Thammalang (currently departing at 8.30am, 10am, 1.30pm & 4pm; 50min); buy tickets (B180) from the town's main travel agent, Satun Travel and Ferry Service, opposite the *Pinnacle Wangmai Hotel* at 45/16 Thanon Satun Thani (℡074/711453, ℱ721959), and check on departures, as they are sometimes cancelled if there are too few takers. Frequent songthaews (B20) and motorbike taxis (B100) run to Thammalang from the junction of Thanon Saman Pradit and Thanon Buriwanit, taking around thirty minutes. If you are **entering Thailand by sea** from Malaysia, be sure to report to the **immigration office** at Thammalang pier to have your passport stamped, otherwise you may have problems on your eventual departure from Thailand.

By the town pier, *Rian Thong*, 4 Thanon Saman Pradit (℡074/711036; ❷), is the best budget **hotel** in Satun; the owners are friendly, and some of the clean, well-furnished rooms overlook the canal. *Farm Gai* (℡074/730812; ❶), more or less in open country ten minutes' west of the centre (take a motorbike taxi; B20), is run by a Swiss who was once a pioneering bungalow-builder on Ko Samui. The comfortable, well-designed huts and rooms sit in a quiet, somewhat overgrown garden; the family prefers guests who will stay for a while to sample Thai country life, but don't insist on it. In complete contrast, *Pinnacle Wangmai Hotel*, out towards the bus depot at 43 Thanon Satun Thani (℡074/711607–8, ℱ722162, Ⓦwww.pinnaclehotels.com/satun.html; ❺), is a typical "deluxe" hotel with air-conditioned rooms in a modern concrete building; similar but more central is the newer *Sinkiat Thani*, 50 Thanon Buriwanit (℡074/721055–8, ℱ721059; ❺), where large bedrooms offer good views over the surrounding countryside. For **food**, try *Yim Yim* on Thanon Saman Pradit by the Chinese temple, a clean and popular restaurant which serves good, simple Chinese food from 6pm onwards. A good daytime option for ice creams and moderately priced Thai food is the air-conditioned *Time Restaurant*, next door to the *Pinnacle Wangmai Hotel* on Thanon Satun Thani.

If you're thinking of visiting the Ko Tarutao National Marine Park, it's worth checking whether Satun Travel and Ferry Service (see box above) have reinstated their weekend boat service to Ko Lipe; this was dropped due to lack of demand, but may well start up again as the park becomes more popular. With a journey time of just under two hours, it's a good, quick route to the island.

Thale Ban National Park

Spread over rainforested mountains along the Malaysian border, **THALE BAN NATIONAL PARK** is a pristine nature reserve which shelters a breathtaking variety of wildlife: from tapirs, Malayan sun bears and clouded leopards, to butterflies, which proliferate in March, and unusual birds such as bat hawks, booted eagles and flamboyant argus pheasants. Unfortunately for naturalists and casual visitors alike, few trails have been marked out through the jungle, but the lush, peaceful setting and the views and bathing pools of the Yaroy waterfall are enough to justify the trip.

From Satun, half-hourly songthaews leave from opposite *Rian Thong* hotel, passing through the village of **Wang Prachan** and reaching Thale Ban **headquarters** (℡074/797073), 2km further on, in an hour. **From Hat Yai**, share-taxis (B70) leave from opposite the post office north of the train station and take you straight through to the park headquarters.

Hemmed in by steep, verdant hills and spangled with red water lilies, the **lake** by the headquarters is central to the story that gives the park its name. Local legend tells how a villager once put his *ban* (headscarf) on a tree stump to have a rest; this caused a landslide, the lake appeared from nowhere, and he, the stump and the *ban* tumbled into it. The water is now surrounded by thirteen **bungalows** (B500–1000 per night depending on size), for which lower rates can be negotiated when business is slow. A **campsite** (B20 per person per night) with showers and toilets and a decent open-air **canteen** also overlook the lake.

One of the easiest trips from park headquarters brings you to **Tham Tondin**, a low, sweaty stalactite cave which gradually slopes down for 800m to deep water. It's about 2km north of headquarters back along the road to Khwan Sator – look out for the wooden sign in Thai, on the west side of the main road just north of kilometre-stone 18, then climb 30m up the slope to see the tiny entrance at your feet. If you time your visit so that you emerge just before dusk, you'll see hundreds of bats streaming out of the hole for the night. It's best to consult the detailed map at headquarters before you visit the cave, and you'll need a flashlight.

A more compelling jaunt, though, is to **Yaroy waterfall** – bring swimming gear for the pools above the main fall. Take the main road north from the head-quarters through the narrow, idyllic valley for 6km (beyond the village of Wang Prachan) and follow the sign to the right. After 700m, you'll find the main, lower fall set in screeching jungle. Climbing the path on the left side, you reach what seems like the top, with fine views of the steep, green peaks to the west. However, there's more: further up the stream are a series of gorgeous shady pools, where you can bathe and shower under the six-metre falls.

The most interesting **jungle walk** heads northeast from the headquarters, then west, approaching Yaroy waterfall from above after 16km. The trail, often steep and arduous, is marked with yellow distance markers on trees every 500m, with more frequent orange tape around trees, but these tapes are some-times pulled down by animals or people – someone at headquarters might be free to guide you for a small fee. If you set out early and at a decent pace, it's possible to complete the walk and get back from Yaroy waterfall to headquarters in a day (a minimum of about 8hr) or, if you're fully equipped, you could overnight at one of three marked **camping** areas by small streams near the trail. Along the way, you'll be rewarded with magnificent views that on a clear day stretch as far as the islands of Tarutao and Langkawi, you'll pass old ele-phant passages and mating playgrounds of argus pheasants, and you'll be unlucky not to spot at least boars, gibbons and bats.

Ko Tarutao National Marine Park

The unspoilt **KO TARUTAO NATIONAL MARINE PARK** is probably the most beautiful of all Thailand's accessible beach destinations. Occupying 1400 square kilometres of the Andaman Sea, the park covers 51 mostly unin-habited islands, of which three – Ko Tarutao, Ko Adang and Ko Lipe – are easy

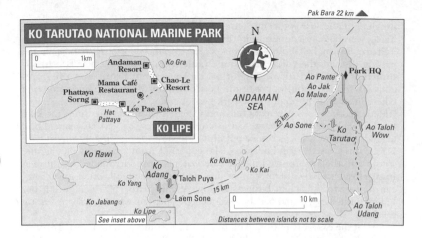

KO TARUTAO NATIONAL MARINE PARK

N

0   1km

Andaman   Ko Gra
Resort
              Chao-Le
Mama Café   Resort
Phattaya   Restaurant
Sorng
        Hat   Lee Pae Resort
     Pattaya

KO LIPE

Ko Rawi

Ko Adang

Ko Yang

Ko Jabang

Ko Lipe

See inset above

ANDAMAN
SEA

Ao Pante   Park HQ
Ao Jak
Ao Malae

25 km

Ao Sone   Ko   Ao Taloh
         Tarutao   Wow

Ko Klang

Ko Kai

Taloh Puya

15 km

Laem Sone

0   10 km

Ao Taloh
Udang

Distances between islands not to scale

to reach from the mainland port of **Pak Bara** and offer accommodation for visitors. The area's forests and seas support an incredible variety of **fauna**: langurs, crab-eating macaques and wild pigs are common on the islands, which also shelter several unique subspecies of squirrel, tree shrew and lesser mouse deer; among the hundred-plus bird species found here, reef egrets and hornbills are regularly seen, while white-bellied sea eagles, frigate birds and pied imperial pigeons are more rarely encountered; and the park is the habitat of about 25 percent of the world's fish species, as well as marine mammals such as the dugong, sperm whale and dolphins. The islands are also an important site for **turtle egg-laying** (see box on p.648): Olive Ridley, green, hawksbill and leatherback turtles lay their eggs on Ko Tarutao's sands between September and April, green turtles on Ko Adang from September to December; park rangers try to keep an eye on the nests and are generally happy to share the information with visitors. The park's delicate environment can bear the current level of tourism, but will be disastrously disturbed if proposals to set up regular boat connections with the highly developed Malaysian resort on Langkawi island, 8km from Ko Tarutao, are acted upon.

The park is officially **closed** to tourists from mid-May to mid-November (the exact dates vary from year to year), when storms can make the sea passage hazardous, and even in the open season, especially at its beginning or end, boats won't leave if conditions are bad or there aren't enough passengers to break even. On the other hand, private operators do still operate boat services to the islands out of season if there's enough demand, and while the park amenities on Tarutao and Adang islands remain closed outside the official months, the private bungalow concerns on Ko Lipe generally open their doors before the official season starts and remain open after it closes. Furthermore, as the Tarutao archipelago increases in popularity, it's possible that the entire park may begin to open year-round in the next few years – call the **Pak Bara visitor centre** (☏074/781285) for the latest.

You should have no problem finding somewhere to stay except at the three New Years (Thai, Chinese and Western), when it's best to book ahead in Bangkok (see p.48). Outside of Ko Lipe, the west coast of Ko Tarutao has the best facilities in the park. The *Traveler's Adventure Handbook* to Tarutao is a must-buy at B40, though sometimes out of print – try Pak Bara's visitor centre (they publish it) or the one at Ao Pante on Ko Tarutao. **Snorkelling gear** can be rented at either visitor centre or on Ko Adang for B50 per day, and is widely available from the private bungalow outfits on Ko Lipe. In recent years, several **diving** operations have started up in the Tarutao area; the best diving is to be found west of Ko Tarutao around Ko Klang, Ko Adang, Ko Rawi and Ko Dong, where encounters with whale and reef sharks, dolphins, stingrays and turtles are common. One of the longest-established operators is the Canadian-run Sabye Sports, 1080 Moo 3 Kampang, Satun (T&F074/734104 in Satun, T01/230 8195 on Ko Lipe, Wwww.sabye-sports.com); also very reliable is the American-run Starfish Scuba, 166 Thanon Phattalung, Songkhla (T074/321943 or 01/896 9319, Wwww.starfishscuba.com). For watery adventures above the surface, Paddle Asia, 93/6 Soi Samakit 2, Phuket (T076/254742, Wwww.paddleasia.com), organizes small-group **sea-kayaking** trips around the Tarutao islands, costing US$100–150 per person per day.

En route to Tarutao and Bulon Lae: Pak Bara

From Trang, Sukorn Beach Bungalows and Tours (see p.716) runs regular direct minibuses to **PAK BARA** in high season; at other times you'll need to take a Satun-bound bus (2hr 30min) or a share-taxi (1hr 30min) to the inland town of **Langu** and change there to a red songthaew for the ten-kilometre hop to the port. Frequent buses and taxis **from Satun** make the fifty-kilometre trip to Langu. Coming **from Hat Yai**, you're best off catching one of the air-conditioned minibuses (B60; 2hr) which leave every hour from an office on Thanon Prachathipat and take you all the way through to Pak Bara pier.

In season, **ferries** leave Pak Bara at 10.30am and 3pm daily for the ninety-minute voyage to Ao Pante on Ko Tarutao (B300 return); the 10.30am boat then continues on to Ko Adang (B800 return from Pak Bara), 40km west of Ko Tarutao, from where it's just a short longtail hop (B50) over to Ko Lipe. The Tarutao–Adang leg can take anything from two hours upwards, depending on the sea conditions. Coming back, boats leave Ko Adang at 9am, calling in at Ko Tarutao before returning to Pak Bara; there's also an additional 9am sailing from Ko Tarutao.

These ferries are supplemented by boats run by **private operators**, which set off regardless of the official season if there's enough demand and the sea conditions are safe; they charge the same as the ferries and leave when there's a full complement of passengers (generally in the early afternoon). If you're thinking of visiting the Tarutao islands out of season, it's best to call ahead to check if boats are running; Adang Sea Tours (T074/781268 or 01/609 2604) is one of the most reliable operators, or you could try Udom Tour (T01/963 6916 or 01/897 4755), Araya Travel (T074/781212 or 01/306 0213) or Andrew Tour (T074/781159 or 01/276 7866). All these operators have offices on the road leading up to Pak Bara pier; Araya Travel also offers **internet access**.

Simple **accommodation** is available in Pak Bara for people who miss the boats. The best choice is the friendly *Diamond Beach* (T074/783138; ❷–❸), 500m before the pier, which offers well-kept bamboo A-frames and simpler concrete huts in a shady compound by the beach, and serves good food. Slightly cheaper – and closer to the pier – is the *Bara Guesthouse* (T074/783068 or 01/478 6258; ❶–❷), which has some basic and rather dingy mattress-on-floor rooms as well as much nicer en-suite ones looking onto a small courtyard. At the time of writing, there were **no currency-exchange** facilities in Pak Bara or on the Tarutao islands, so you may well need to change money before you arrive.

Ko Tarutao

The largest of the national park's islands, **KO TARUTAO** offers the greatest natural variety: mountains covered in semi-evergreen rainforest rise steeply to a high point of 700m; limestone caves and mangrove swamps dot the shoreline; and the west coast is lined with perfect beaches for most of its 26-kilometre length. The last of these is also where you'll find the park's best facilities for visitors outside Ko Lipe.

Boats dock at **Ao Pante**, on the northwestern side of the island, where the admission fee (B200) is collected and where the **park headquarters** is situated. Here you'll find the only shop on the island, selling basic supplies, as well as a visitor centre, a well-stocked library and a simple restaurant. The **bungalows** (from B300 per bungalow sleeping six), which are spread over a large, quiet park behind the beach, are for the main part national park standard issue with cold-water bathrooms, but there are also a couple of newer two- or three-person bungalows with air-conditioning (B750–1500 per bungalow) as well as some basic mattress-on-floor four-person rooms in **bamboo longhouses**, sharing bathrooms (B400 per room, or B100 per person). No mosquito nets are provided here, so come with your own or bring plenty of mosquito repellent. Two-person **tents** can be rented for B200 a night; campers with their own gear are charged B20 per person per night.

Behind the settlement, the steep, half-hour climb to **To-Boo cliff** is a must, especially at sunset, for the view of the surrounding islands and the crocodile's-head cape at the north end of the bay. A fun one-hour boat trip (B40 per person; contact the visitor centre to book) can also be made near Ao Pante, up the canal which leads 2km inland from the pier, through the lush leaves and dense roots of a bird-filled mangrove swamp, to the entrance to **Crocodile Cave** – where you're unlikely to see any of the big snappers, reported sightings being highly dubious.

A half-hour walk south from Ao Pante brings you to the two quiet bays of **Ao Jak** and **Ao Malae**, fringed by coconut palms and filled with fine white sand. Behind the house at the south end of Ao Malae, a road leads over the headland to **Ao Sone** (a 2hr walk from Ao Pante), where a pretty freshwater stream runs past the ranger station at the north end of the bay, making this a good place for peaceful camping. A favourite egg-laying site for sea turtles, the main part of the bay is a three-kilometre sweep of flawless sand, with a ninety-minute trail leading up to a waterfall in the middle and a mangrove swamp at the far south end.

On the east side of the island, **Ao Taloh Wow** is a rocky bay with a ranger station, connected to Ao Pante by a twelve-kilometre road through old rubber plantations and evergreen forest. If you have a tent, you might want to set off along the overgrown, five-hour trail beyond Taloh Wow, which cuts through the forest to **Ao Taloh Udang**, a sandy bay on the south side where you can set up camp. Here the remnants of a penal colony for political prisoners are just visible: the plotters of two failed coup attempts were imprisoned here in the 1930s before returning to high government posts. The ordinary convicts, who used to be imprisoned at Ao Taloh Wow, had a much harsher time, and during World War II, when supplies from the mainland dried up, prisoners and guards ganged together to turn to piracy. Pirates and smugglers still occasionally hide out in the Tarutao archipelago, but the main problem now is illegal trawlers fishing in national park waters.

Ko Adang

At **KO ADANG**, a wild, rugged island covered in tropical rainforest, the boat pulls in at the **Laem Sone** park station on the southern shore, where the beach is steep and narrow and backed by a thick canopy of pines. As at Ao Pante, there are rooms in **bamboo longhouses** (B400 per room sleeping four, or B100 per person), sharing bathrooms; two-person **tents** can be rented (B200 a night), or campers can pitch their own tents for B20 per person per night. There's a **restaurant** here, though it's a bit pricey and only does a limited range of food.

The half-hour climb to **Sha-do** cliff on the steep slope above Laem Sone gives good views over the sand spit of the harbour and Ko Lipe to the south. About 2km west along the coast from the park station, the small beach is lined with coconut palms and an abandoned customs house, behind which a twenty-minute trail leads to the small **Pirate Waterfall**. For more ambitious explorations, the park handbook recommends "**snork-hiking**", an amphibious method of reaching distant attractions. Up the east coast, you can make such a day-trip to **Rattana waterfall**, 3km from the park station, and to the *chao ley* (see p.624) village of **Taloh Puya**, 1km further on, which has a fine coral reef directly offshore and a nice beach to the north.

Ko Lipe

KO LIPE, 2km south of Adang, makes a busy contrast to the other islands. A small, flat triangle, it's covered in coconut plantations and inhabited by *chao ley*, with shops, a school and a health centre in the village on the eastern side. By rights, such a settlement should not be allowed within the national park boundaries, but the *chao ley* on Lipe are well entrenched: Satun's governor forced the community to move here from Ko Lanta between the world wars, to reinforce the island's Thai character and prevent the British rulers of Malaya from laying claim to it. Relations with park rangers have been strained in the past, but the park authority is working on a scheme to demarcate village and national park areas, which will hopefully go some way towards both resolving the tensions and preserving some of the island's natural beauty.

There are several **bungalow** outfits on the island, mostly operated by enterprising newcomers from the mainland rather than the indigenous *chao ley*. None is outstanding, but the best choices can be found on **Hat Pattaya**, a crescent of white sand 1km from the village on the south side of the island; this is also the prettiest beach on Ko Lipe, and has a good offshore reef to explore too. At the western end of the beach, the Italian-run *Phattaya Song* (②–④) has a lovely location: basic but clean bamboo huts, all with attached cold-water bathrooms and mosquito nets, are strung out behind the beach or up on the steep hillside, with the nicest of all perched high up on the rocks and accessed by precarious bamboo ladders. There's an excellent cosy restaurant – the most popular on the island – and fishing and snorkelling trips can be arranged if you want to visit the coral reefs around Ko Jabang and Ko Yang, on the west side of Adang. For paddling about around Lipe, sea **canoes** can be rented for B600 per day. The beach's other resort, the *Lee Pae Resort* (☎074/712181 or 01/896 5491; ③–⑤), has more facilities but less charm: its 75 bungalows range from pleasant concrete cottages with fan, screens and en-suite bathroom, to basic bamboo huts with mosquito nets and a mattress on the floor.

Over on the other side of the island, there are a couple more options on the beach in front of the village: the *Chao-Le Resort* (☎074/729201; ②–⑤) offers neat concrete en-suite bungalows and cheaper wooden huts in a sandy, scrubby compound under the pine trees, while the *Andaman Resort* (☎074/729200;

❸–❹) has bungalows of a similar standard in a more secluded spot away from the clutter of the village. *Andaman Resort* also has some two-person tents to rent for B100 per night, or you can pitch your own for B30. The beach on this side of the island is nowhere near as nice as Hat Pattaya, though there's rewarding water and a beautiful coral reef around tiny **Ko Gra**, 200m out to sea from the village.

Midway along the path that connects the two beaches, the pretty garden of the *Mama Café Restaurant*, owned and run by a friendly *chao ley* family, is a nice place to stop for a simple lunch of fried fish and rice, or go there for breakfast and sample its "*chao ley* pastries", tiny pancakes that come in eighteen different flavours.

Ko Phetra National Marine Park

The thirty tiny islands of the **KO PHETRA NATIONAL MARINE PARK**, which sprinkle the sea between the Trang islands to the north and the Tarutao islands to the south, are for the most part inaccessible to tourists – with the notable exception of **Ko Bulon Lae** which, though it offically falls under the auspices of the park, has been allowed to develop much as it likes. A handful of the other islands can be visited on day-trips – there's fantastic snorkelling and diving, particularly around some of the more remote islands; Starfish Scuba (see p.727) organizes live-aboard **diving** excursions in the park.

The **park headquarters** (daily 8am–4.30pm; ☎074/783008) is on the mainland at Ao Noon, 4km south of Pak Bara (take a motorbike taxi); the staff here speak very little English, but they do have some leaflets on the park, and can advise on accommodation in **Ko Lidi**, one of the more accessible islands. Just 5km from the mainland (charter a longtail from Ao Noon for the 15min journey; B500), the quiet beaches of Ko Lidi are mainly popular with groups of Thai tourists; there are some simple eight-person tents (B300) available for visitors, but you'll need to bring your own mats, bedding and food. To the northwest, the steep limestone crags of **Ko Khao Yai** (charter a longtail) jut up from the water in fantastic gothic shapes; the lack of fresh water here means there's nowhere to stay, but there are some good coral reefs surrounding the island. The best snorkelling, however, is to be had at the more remote islands dotted around **Ko Phetra**, 40km or so from park headquarters just over the border in Trang province. These islands, with their small sandy coves and undisturbed reefs, are most easily and enjoyably reached through the excellent day-trips (Nov–May only) organized by *Sukorn Beach Bungalows* on nearby Ko Sukorn (see p.722). Ko Phetra itself, the main island of the group, is generally off-limits – there's big money in the birds' nests found here (see box on p.695) and concessions are jealously guarded – but trips take in the neighbouring islands of **Lao Lien** and **Takieng**, and it's even possible to camp overnight on the latter.

Ko Bulon Lae

The scenery at tiny **KO BULON LAE**, 20km west of Pak Bara, isn't as beautiful as that found elsewhere along Andaman coast, but it's not at all bad: a two-kilometre strip of fine white sand runs the length of the casuarina-lined east coast, while *chao ley* fishermen make their ramshackle homes in the tight coves of the western fringe. A reef of curiously shaped hard coral closely parallels the eastern beach, while **White Rock** to the south of the island has beautifully coloured soft coral and equally dazzling fish. **Snorkelling** gear, as well as boats for day-trips to White Rock and surrounding islands (B1000 per boat seating

up to eight people), can be rented at *Pansand*, the island's largest and best **resort**
(☎01/397 0802, ⓔpansand@cscoms.com; ❻–❼), where accommodation
ranges from neat little bamboo huts to swanky clapboard cottages with bathrooms, fans and mosquito screens on the windows. On the beach side of the
spacious, shady grounds, there's a sociable restaurant serving up good seafood
and other Thai dishes. To book a room here or find out about boats in the off-
season, contact the resort directly or First Andaman Travel at 82–84 Thanon
Wisetkul in Trang (☎075/218035, ⓕ211010). There are two other options on
the island, both of which have fans and mosquito nets in all bungalows: nearby *Moloney* (❷–❹), which offers a choice of en-suite or shared bathroom; and,
ten minutes' walk away in Ao Phangka Yai on the north coast, *Phangka Bay
Resort*, with well-designed, en-suite bungalows (❸–❹) and a good restaurant.

    Ferries for Ko Bulon Lae leave Pak Bara daily at 2pm (1hr 30min; B300
return), returning from the island at 9am the following day. They're scheduled
to run roughly from November to April, but sometimes set off in the low season. In addition, private operators will generally stop off at Ko Bulon Lae on
their way to Ko Tarutao if there is enough demand, or you can charter a longtail (B1500 for up to five people).

Hat Yai

HAT YAI, the transport axis of the region, was given a dose of instant
American-style modernization in the 1950s, since when it's commercially
usurped its own provincial capital, Songkhla. The resulting concrete mess, rem-
iniscent of Bangkok without the interesting bits, attracts over a million tourists
a year, nearly all of them Malaysians and Singaporeans who nip across the border to shop and get laid. If the concrete and the sleaze turn you off a protracted stay, remember that Songkhla (see p.735) is only 25km away.

    Hat Yai is one of the south's major centres for **bullfighting**, which in its Thai
version involves bull tussling with bull, the winner being the one which forces
the other to retreat. Fights can last anything from a few seconds to half an hour,
in which case the frantic betting of the audience becomes more interesting
than the deadlock in the ring. Every weekend, day-long competitions, beginning between 9 and 10am, are held at various points around the south.
Admission is usually B600–700 for the whole day, and it's best to get there in
the early afternoon as the big fights, involving betting of up to one million
baht, are lower down the card. It's worth checking with TAT for the latest
information but, at the time of writing, the most convenient events are at
Noen Khum Thong, 10km out of Hat Yai on the way to the airport, on the
first Saturday of the month (charter a songthaew to get there); and on the
fourth Saturday of the month at Ban Nam Krajai, 200m south of the Ko Yo
intersection on the Hat Yai–Songkhla road (catch a bus towards Songkhla).

Practicalities

On any extended tour of the south you are bound to end up in Hat Yai, and
you may as well take the opportunity to call in at the **TAT** office for Songkhla
and Satun provinces at 1/1 Soi 2, Thanon Niphat Uthit 3 (daily
8.30am–4.30pm; ☎074/243747, ⓕ245986, ⓔtatsgkhl@tat.or.th). The **tourist
police** have an office at Thanon Sripoovanart on the south side of town

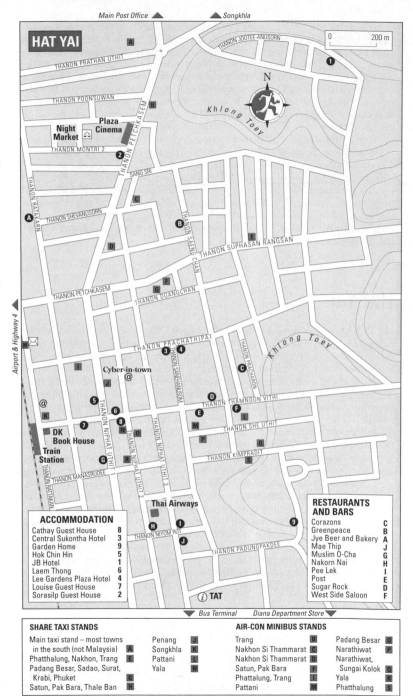

HAT YAI

Main Post Office ▲   ▲ Songkhla

THANON JOOTEE-ANUSORN

THANON PRATHAN UTHIT

THANON POONSUWAN

Night Market

Plaza Cinema

THANON MONTRI 2

THANON PETCHKASEM

SANG SRI

THANON SHEVANUSORN

THANON RATAKAN

Khlong Toey

N

THANON SAENG CHAN

THANON SUPHASAN RANGSAN

THANON PETCHKASEM

THANON DUANGCHAN

THANON PRACHATHIPAT

THANON PRACHARON

Cyber-in-town @

THANON SANGCHAN SOM

THANON THAMNOON VITHI

THANON SHE UTHIT

Khlong Toey

DK Book House

Train Station

THANON NIPHAT UTHIT 1

THANON NIPHAT UTHIT 2

THANON NIPHAT UTHIT 3

THANON KIMPRADIT

THANON MANASRUDEE

THANON RATAKAN

Airport & Highway 4 ◄

Thai Airways

THANON NIYOM ROT

THANON PADUNGPAKDEE

ⓘ TAT

0   200 m

ACCOMMODATION

Cathay Guest House	8
Central Sukontha Hotel	3
Garden Home	9
Hok Chin Hin	5
JB Hotel	1
Laem Thong	6
Lee Gardens Plaza Hotel	4
Louise Guest House	7
Sorasilp Guest House	2

RESTAURANTS AND BARS

Corazons	C
Greenpeace	B
Jye Beer and Bakery	A
Mae Thip	J
Muslim O-Cha	G
Nakorn Nai	H
Pee Lek	I
Post	E
Sugar Rock	D
West Side Saloon	F

▼ Bus Terminal   Diana Department Store ▼

SHARE TAXI STANDS

Main taxi stand – most towns
  in the south (not Malaysia) A
Phatthalung, Nakhon, Trang F
Padang Besar, Sadao, Surat,
  Krabi, Phuket G
Satun, Pak Bara, Thale Ban H

Penang J
Songkhla K
Pattani L
Yala N

AIR-CON MINIBUS STANDS

Trang B
Nakhon Si Thammarat C
Nakhon Si Thammarat D
Satun, Pak Bara F
Phatthalung, Trang I
Pattani M

Padang Besar O
Narathiwat P
Narathiwat,
  Sungai Kolok Q
Yala R
Phatthalung S

Crossing into Malaysia from Hat Yai

Hat Yai is only 50km from the border with Malaysia. The fastest way of getting across (5–6hr) is to take a **share-taxi** to Penang (where you can renew your visa at the Thai consulate); taxis depart every morning for about B250. Tickets for the more comfortable and slightly less expensive **air-conditioned minibuses** to Penang (B220) can be bought at Hat Yai travel agents, such as Cathy Tour at 93 Thanon Niphat Uthit 2 (T074/235044), or Golden Way, 132 Thanon Niphat Uthit 3 (T074/233917). Both these agents also handle minibuses to Sungai Kolok (3hr; B170), Alor Setar (3hr; B230) and Butterworth (5hr; B230), and VIP buses to Kuala Lumpur (12hr; B350) and Singapore (18hr; B550). The least expensive but most time-consuming method is to catch a bus to Padang Besar (every 15min; 1hr 40min), walk 800m across the border and take a share-taxi to Kuala Perlis (30min) or Alor Setar (1hr) – avoid the obvious route straight down Highway 4 to Sadao, because there's a long stretch between the opposing border posts which there's no inexpensive way of covering.

Most comfortable are the **trains**, though they're not very frequent: two a day run from Hat Yai to Sungai Kolok on the east-coast border, and one a day heads to Butterworth (for the ferry to Penang or trains on to Kuala Lumpur) via the frontier at Padang Besar.

(T074/246733), and the **immigration office** is on Thanon Petchkasem (T074/243019). The three central Niphat Uthit roads are known locally as *sai neung, sai sawng* and *sai saam*.

If you're leap-frogging into the deep south via Hat Yai **airport** you'll arrive 12km from town, then be shuttled into the centre by shared minibus (B50) or taxi (B240) straight to your destination; there are regular minibuses back to the airport from the Thai Airways office at 190/6 Thanon Niphat Uthit 2 (T074/234238) – the schedule is displayed outside. The smooth passage of Malaysian and Singaporean dirty-weekenders is facilitated by regular flights between Hat Yai and Johor Bahru, Kuala Lumpur, Kota Kinabalu, Kuching and Miri (all operated by Malaysia Airlines), and Singapore (Thai Airways).

The **train station** is on the west side of the centre at the end of Thanon Thammoon Vithi, and contains a useful left-luggage office (daily 6am–6pm; B10 per piece per day); the **bus terminal** is far to the southeast of town on Thanon Kanchanawanit, leaving you with a songthaew ride to the centre, but most buses make a stop at the Plaza Cinema on Thanon Petchkasem, on the north side of the centre. **Share-taxis** and **air-conditioned minibuses** should drop you off at your destination; for departure, they have a number of different ranks around town (marked on the map opposite) according to where you want to go. Both Avis (T074/352239, @hdy@avisthailand.com) and Budget (T074/239033 4, @brachy6@budget.co.th) have **car-rental** desks at the *Central Sukontha* hotel (see p.734), with daily rates starting from around B1400 for a jeep; Avis has another desk at the airport (T074/227259).

There's central **internet access** opposite the station at 4/4 Thanon Rattakan (daily 9.30am–8.30pm; B25 per hour), and at the swish Cyber-in-town, 56 Thanon Niphat Uthit 2 (Mon–Fri 10am–10pm, Sat 9am–10pm & Sun 9am–4pm; B40 per hour) – the latter has drinks and snacks available. DK Book House, just by the station at 2/4–5 Thanon Thammoon Vithi, is a good **book-shop** with a small but reasonably priced selection of English-language titles.

The helpful Cathy Tour (see box above) can **book flights** as well as bus tickets, and also runs private minibus services to many popular tourist destinations. C & P Tour, 129/1 Thanon Niphat Uthit 3 (T074/233388, F232243) offers an unusual minibus **tour** to **Khao Namkhang**, 80km south of Hat Yai near Sadao, to see the complex of tunnels here, an erstwhile hideout of the Communist Party of Malaya (see also p.712 & p.744).

Accommodation

Hat Yai has a huge range of **hotels**, none of them very good value and most worked by prostitutes, though a few in the budget range are geared to travellers.

Cathay Guest House, 93 Thanon Niphat Uthit 2 ☏074/243815, ☏354104. This friendly place is falling apart, but the fittings are reasonably clean; the café acts as a sociable meeting-place (and shows Western movies nightly), and the information board and guest comment books are guidebooks in themselves. Dorm beds B90. **❷**

Central Sukontha Hotel, 3 Thanon Sanehanusom ☏074/352222, ☏352223, ✉sukontha@hadyai.loxinfo.co.th. Luxury hotel in a handy central location next to the Central Department Store. Offers great views over the city from its two top-notch restaurants and coffee bar. **❽**

Garden Home, southeast of the centre at 51/2 Thanon Hoi Mook ☏074/236047, ☏234444. This pastiche of a grand mansion built around a plant-filled courtyard offers very good value; the large bedrooms show some sense of decor and boast a good range of facilities (air-con, hot water, TV and mini-bar). **❺**

Hok Chin Hin, 87 Thanon Niphat Uthit 1 ☏074/243258, ☏350131. The best of many cheap Chinese hotels around the three central Niphat Uthit roads. Offers rooms with en-suite bathrooms and ceiling fans or air-con above a café serving noodle soups and other simple fare. **❷–❸**

JB Hotel, 99 Thanon Jootee-Anusorn ☏074/234300–18, ☏234328, ⓦwww.jb-hotel.com. Hat Yai's best hotel furnishes quite enough luxury to justify the price – among the highlights are a large swimming pool, a top-class Chinese restaurant and the *Jazz Bistro*, a civilized place for Thai and Western fare or just a drink. **❽**

Laem Thong, 46 Thanon Thamnoon Vithi ☏074/352301, ☏237574, ✉laemthong99@hotmail.com. Large and efficient Chinese-run place, with a choice of fan-cooled or air-con rooms, most with hot water. **❷–❹**

Lee Gardens Plaza Hotel, 29 Thanon Prachatipat ☏074/261111, ☏353555. Upmarket option with great views of the city from its comfortable rooms. Facilities include a pool and jacuzzi. **❻**

Louise Guest House, by the train station at 21–23 Thanon Thamnoon Vithi ☏074/220966. Clean and very friendly Chinese-run place, with much the same facilities as the larger, more impersonal *Laem Thong*, though the fan-cooled rooms here are a little overpriced. **❸–❹**

Sorasilp Guest House, 251/7–8 Thanon Petchkasem ☏074/232635. On the upper floors of a modern building beside the Plaza Cinema. Friendly and clean, though a little noisy. **❷**

Eating, drinking and nightlife

Hat Yai's **restaurants**, a selection of which are listed below, offer a choice of Thai, Chinese, Muslim and Western food, while the sprawling **night market**, behind the Plaza Cinema on Thanon Montri 2, has something for everyone: seafood and beer, Thai curries, deep-fried chicken and the Muslim speciality *khao neua daeng*, tender cured beef in a sweet red sauce.

For a quiet **drink**, head for *Sugar Rock*, 114 Thanon Thamnoon Vithi, a pleasant café-bar with low-volume Western music. More lively are *West Side Saloon*, on the same road at no. 135/5, and *Corazons Latin Pub and Restaurant*, at 41 Thanon Pracharom – both are extremely popular nightspots, with excellent house bands that cover everything from Thai country music and "songs for life" (see p.804) to 1970s disco. To get away from it all, the five mini-theatres at Diana department store, on Thanon Sripoovanart on the south side of the centre, show Western **movies** with English soundtracks.

Greenpeace Restaurant, 50 Thanon Saeng Chan. Comes as a pleasant surprise in Hat Yai, with its leafy patio overlooking a quiet road; it's popular with local expats and offers a good menu of Thai and Western food. Open from 5pm.

Jye Beer and Bakery, Thanon Ratakarn. Good for a bit of a splurge – they do posh Thai and American food in a cosy, rustic atmosphere.

Mae Thip, 187/4 Niphat Uthit 3. Good reliable Thai place, popular with locals; also does a few Malay dishes, including satay.

Muslim O-Cha, 117 Niphat Uthit 1. A simple, clean restaurant which serves small portions of curried chicken and rice, and other inexpensive Muslim dishes. Daily until 8.30pm.

Nakorn Nai, 166/7 Niphat Uthit 2. Cool and comfortable, this is a reasonable place for all-day breakfasts, Western food and some interesting Thai dishes.

Pee Lek 59, 185/4 Niphat Uthit 3, at the junction with Thanon Niyom Rot. This welcoming place gets the thumbs-up for moderately priced Thai-style seafood – try *gataa rawn*, a sizzling dish of mixed marine life.

Post, Thanon Thamnoon Vithi. Popular with farangs, this comfy, spacious restaurant-bar has a large Western menu and shows nonstop music videos.

Songkhla and around

Known as the "big town of two seas" because it sits on a north-pointing peninsula between the Gulf of Thailand and the **Thale Sap** lagoon, **SONGKHLA** provides a sharp contrast to Hat Yai. A small, sophisticated provincial capital, it retains many historic buildings – such as the elegant Wat Matchimawat and the Chinese mansion that now houses the National Museum – and its broad, quiet streets are planted with soothing greenery. With some fine restaurants and excellent accommodation, and its proximity to the wonderful Southern Folklore Museum at Ko Yo, Songkhla makes a stimulating place in which to hole up for a few days.

The settlement was originally sited on the north side of the mouth of the Thale Sap, where a deepwater port has now been built, and flourished as a **trading port** from the eighth century onwards. The shift across the water came after 1769, when a Chinese merchant named Yieng Hao was granted permission by the Thai ruler, Taksin, to collect swallows' nests from Ko Si Ko Ha – now part of Khu Khut Waterbird Park. Having made a packet from selling them for their culinary and medicinal properties, he was made governor of Songkhla by Taksin and established the city on its present site. For seven generations the **Na Songkhla dynasty** he founded kept the governorship in the family, overseeing the construction of many of the buildings you see today. The town is now an unhurried administrative centre, which maintains a strong central Thai feel – most of the province's Muslim population live in the hinterland.

The Town

The town which the Na Songkhlas built has expanded to fill the headland, and makes a great place for strolling around. The western side, where the town first developed, shelters a fishing port which presents a vivid, smelly scene in the mornings. Two abrupt hills – **Khao Tung Kuan** and the smaller **Khao Noi** – border the north side of the centre, while in the heart of town lie the main tourist attractions, the **National Museum** and the extravagantly decorated **Wat Matchimawat**. Sitting on the fringe of town at the southern end of Hat Samila – the 8km of beach along the eastern shore – **Khao Saen** is an impoverished but vibrant fishing village, whose multicoloured boats provide

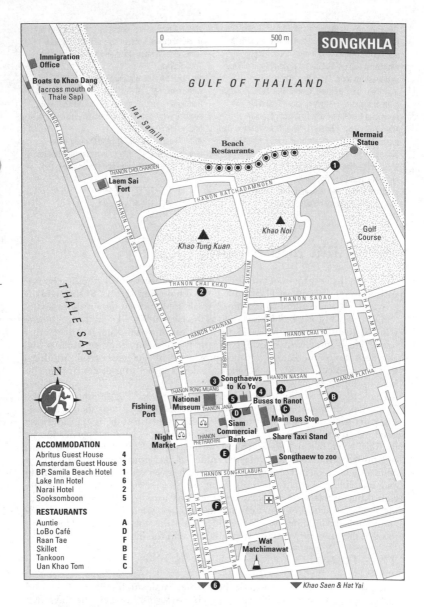

SONGKHLA

GULF OF THAILAND

Immigration Office

Boats to Khao Dang (across mouth of Thale Sap)

Hat Samila

THANON LANG PHRAM

THANON CHOLCHARDEN

Laem Sai Fort

THANON LAEM SAI

Beach Restaurants

Mermaid Statue

1

THANON RATCHADAMNOEN

THALE SAP

Khao Tung Kuan

Khao Noi

Golf Course

THANON RATCHADAMNOEN

THANON CHAI KHAO

2

THANON SADAO

THANON SUKHUM

THANON VICHANCHOM

THANON CHAINAM

THANON SAIBURI

THANON SISUDA

THANON CHAI YO

THANON PLATHA

THANON NASAN

N

3 Songthaews to Ko Yo

A

Buses to Ranot **B**

THANON RONG MUANG

National Museum

Fishing Port

THANON JANA

4

5

C

D

THANON RAMWITHI

THANON SAKE

THANON PHETHAXHIRI

Siam Commercial Bank

Main Bus Stop

Night Market

Share Taxi Stand

E

Songthaew to zoo

THANON SONGKHLABURI

F

THANON NAKHON NAI

THANON NANG NGAM

THANON NAKHON NAWK

Wat Matchimawat

6

Khao Saen & Hat Yai

ACCOMMODATION
Abritus Guest House	4
Amsterdam Guest House	3
BP Samila Beach Hotel	1
Lake Inn Hotel	6
Narai Hotel	2
Sooksomboon	5

RESTAURANTS
Auntie	A
LoBo Café	D
Raan Tae	F
Skillet	B
Tankoon	E
Uan Khao Tom	C

0   500 m

Songkhla's most hackneyed postcard image. If you're about on a Sunday, don't miss the hectic **morning market** – the largest in southeast Thailand – which fills the streets around Songkhla's main bus stop.

Khao Tung Kuan, Laem Sai Fort and Hat Samila

To get your bearings, climb up **Khao Tung Kuan** at the northwestern end of town; unfortunately the hill has become something of a hangout for local drug addicts, so it's safest to avoid it in the early morning and the evening, especially if you're on your own. From Thanon Laem Sai, on the western side of the hill, steps rise past simple monks' huts which surround what looks like a red-brick Wendy house – Rama V ordered the pavilion to be built at the height of his westernization programme, but the local artisans clearly couldn't get their heads round the monarch's conception. From the chedi at the top of the hill, you can look south over the town and the fishing port, and west over the Thale Sap to the island of Ko Yo. On the eastern side of the hill, down on the road that runs between Khao Tung Kuan and Khao Noi, you'll often see people turning up in the late afternoon to feed fruit to the macaque monkeys that live on the two hills.

Further up Thanon Laem Sai, you can visit **Laem Sai Fort**, with its low walls and cannon, which was built by the French in the seventeenth century, when they held favour with the kings of Ayutthaya. Just beyond lies palm-fringed **Hat Samila**; its famous **mermaid statue**, the symbol of the town, lies a few hundred metres east along the beach in front of the *BP Samila Beach Hotel*.

Songkhla National Museum

The **Songkhla National Museum** (Wed–Sun 9am–noon & 1–4pm; B30) on Thanon Jana, the main east–west street, is worth a visit for its architecture alone. Built in 1878 in south Chinese style and recently renovated to its original condition, this graceful mansion was first the residence of the governor of Songkhla and Nakhon, then the city hall, and later the local poorhouse before being converted into a museum in the 1970s. Its best side faces the garden at the back: from here you can see how the ornamental staircases and the roof were constructed in shapely curves to disorientate straight-flying evil spirits.

A jumble of folk exhibits, such as masks for the *manohra* (the southern Thai dance-drama) and agricultural implements, are strewn around the garden, while inside the wildly diverse collection includes well-preserved examples of Ban Chiang pottery, early Hindu statues and Mahayana Buddhist images from the Srivijaya period, and a selection of beautiful Chinese ceramics. Upstairs everything is upstaged by overblown Chinese and Thai furniture, all lacquer and mother-of-pearl and bas-relief carving.

Wat Matchimawat

From the museum, you can explore the atmospheric old streets of Nakhon Nai and Nakhon Nawk, which show European influence in their colonnaded pavements and crumbling stucco, on your way south to **Wat Matchimawat**, a grand, attention-grabbing affair set in ornamental grounds on Thanon Saiburi. What stands out most of all is the bot, a florid mixture of Chinese and Thai styles, which was apparently modelled on Wat Phra Kaeo in Bangkok. Fetching stone bas-reliefs decorate the low walls around the bot, depicting leafy scenes from the *Romance of the Three Kingdoms*, a Chinese historical novel which served as a handbook of manners and morals in the middle of the nineteenth century, when the temple was built. Every centimetre of the lofty interior is covered with colourful *Jataka* murals, telling of the previous lives of the Buddha, mixed in with vivacious tableaux of nineteenth-century Songkhla life. The bot is usually locked, but you can get the key from the adjacent informal museum (daily, irregular hours), which is filled with ceramics, votive tablets, stuffed animals and other clutter.

Khao Saen

To see the best of the Muslim shanty village of **Khao Saen**, set against a rocky headland on the southern edge of Songkhla's tide of development, visit in the

late afternoon, when the boisterous fish market is in full swing (except Fri). Songthaews from Thanon Platha make the trip in fifteen minutes. The crowded, rotting shacks of the village make a bleak contrast with the objects for which Khao Saen is most celebrated – its decorated prawn-fishing vessels. Drawn up in rows on the beach, these immaculate small boats have dragon prows wrapped in lucky garlands and hulls brightly painted with flags and intricate artwork. These pictures, which mostly depict mosques and idyllic landscapes, are the work of an artist at Saiburi, further down the coast (see p.746), and cost each fisherman a month's income.

Practicalities

Most **buses** arrive at the major junction of Thanon Ramwithi with Jana and Platha roads. People usually come here straight from Hat Yai, 25km southwest, but buses also run direct from Nakhon. **Taxis** for these towns and places further afield congregate on the south side of the main bus stop, just off Thanon Ramwithi. If the heat gets to you as you stroll around town, catch one of the **songthaews** (B5–10 per person) or motorbike taxis (B10–20) which cruise the streets. **Mountain bikes** can be rented at the *Amsterdam Guest House* for B100 per day, and they also have some motorbikes available (B200 per day), useful for getting to Songkhla zoo and Ko Yo. *LoBo Café* can also arrange motorbike and car rental (B200/B800 per day respectively).

There are several places for **internet access** around town, including Dot Com (Mon–Sat 8am–10pm, Sun 9am–10pm; B40 per hour), next door to the *Abritus Guest House*, and E-Milk, 72 Thanon Saiburi (daily 11am–9pm; same price); the latter also sells coffee, fruit shakes, pizza and waffles. Several **banks** with ATMs can be found in the centre, including Siam Commercial Bank on Thanon Saiburi. The **post office** is on Thanon Nakhon Nai. Songkhla's **immigration office** is at 1/65 Thanon Lang Praram (Mon–Fri 8.30am–4.30pm; ☎074/313480).

Accommodation

Budget travellers are spoilt for choice when it comes to **places to stay** in Songkhla, with a couple of excellent guest houses. For more luxury, the recently refurbished *BP Samila Beach* provides all the creature comforts.

Abritus Guest House, 28/16 Thanon Ramwithi ☎074/326047, ✉abritus_th@yahoo.com. Scores high on friendliness; the Bulgarian family who run the place are especially welcoming, and a mine of information on the town. Huge clean rooms with shared bathrooms are set above a popular café which dishes up great breakfasts – including German bread and filter coffee – as well as salads, omelettes and Bulgarian meatballs. ❷

Amsterdam Guest House, at 15/3 Thanon Rong Muang on the north side of the museum ☎074/314890. Of Songkhla's budget places to stay, this homely vine-covered place is best geared up to backpackers. The rooms, with shared bathrooms, are bright and clean; there's cable TV, lots of handy brochures, an English-language library and a relaxed downstairs seating area

that's well equipped with comfy sofas monopolized by dozing cats. Outside is a small shady patio, and next door an excellent little restaurant serves up beer and toasties alongside the delicious Thai dishes. ❷

BP Samila Beach Hotel, 8 Thanon Ratchadamnoen ☎074/440222, ☎440442. The best hotel in town, with outdoor swimming pools, a herb steamroom and the beach right on its doorstep; rooms come with sea or "mountain" view. ❻–❼

Lake Inn Hotel, 301 Thanon Nakhon Nawk ☎074/321411–2, ☎321044. Good hotel 500m south of the centre close by the Thale Sap lagoon; half of the tastefully furnished rooms face the lake and there's a good ground-floor restaurant, also with views of the water. ❺

Narai Hotel, 14 Thanon Chai Khao
⊕074/311078. Another friendly place situated in a quiet, rambling wooden house at the foot of Doi Tung Kuan. Good value; the cheapest of the budget options in Songkhla. ❷

Sooksomboon 2, 18 Thanon Saiburi
⊕074/323809–10, ⑨321406. Comfortable air-con rooms, all with hot-water bathrooms, at this good-value, centrally located hotel. ❹

Eating and drinking

A good spot for **breakfast** is the cosy *LoBo Café* at 10/1 Thanon Jana, which offers a huge list of pancakes alongside the usual Western breakfasts. For day-time eating, pull up a deckchair and relax at the shaded beach **restaurants** which congregate at the northern end of Thanon Sukhum and at the east end of Thanon Platha; or saunter down to the quiet and clean *Tankoon Restaurant*, 25/1 Thanon Saiburi (closes 8.30pm), where you can relax with a beer and some tasty Thai fodder in its peaceful leafy interior; the attached **coffee shop**, *Coffeebucks*, serves delicious iced coffee. Songkhla's most famous restaurant, *Raan Tae*, at 85 Thanon Nang Ngarm, is spotlessly clean and justly popular, serving especially good seafood – but it's closed between 2pm and 5pm, and after 8pm. Also specializing in seafood, as well as the rice porridge of its name, is *Uan Khao Tom*, Talat Rot Fai, where you can relax outdoors on a quiet street under fairy lights (opens 6pm). The **night market**, south of the post office on Thanon Nakhon Nai, is the place for budget-conscious travellers.

A ghetto of Westernized **bars** and restaurants on Saket, Sisuda and Sadao roads caters to the good ole boys who work on the offshore oil rigs: places such as the *Skillet* ("vittles and stuff"), on Thanon Saket near Platha, and *Auntie*, 62/1 Thanon Sisuda, are open until midnight and serve good American-style food and ice-cold beers, at a price.

Around Songkhla

The excellent **Southern Folklore Museum** on Ko Yo is the biggest draw outside Songkhla; a visit there is best combined with lunch at one of the island's renowned seafood restaurants. Slightly further afield, the **Khu Khut Waterbird Park** is similar to, though not as impressive as, Thale Noi (see p.714) near Phatthalung, but if you're not planning to visit Phatthalung, it's worth coming here on a day-trip.

Ko Yo

KO YO, the small island in the Thale Sap to the west of Songkhla, has long been a destination for day-trippers, and the road link with the land on both sides of the lagoon has accelerated the transformation of **Ban Nok** – the island's main settlement – into a souvenir market. Here you'll find durian cakes, an amazing variety of dried and treated seafood, and the high-quality fabrics – mostly cotton, but sometimes with small amounts of silk woven in – for which Ko Yo is famous; if you're around in the morning, you can fork left off the main road in the village to watch the weavers at work in their houses.

The best way of getting there **from Songkhla** is by songthaew (B10), which set off at regular intervals from Thanon Jana, opposite the *LoBo Café*. Alternatively, take one of the frequent Ranot-bound buses (every 30min; B5), which depart from the same street and take half an hour to get to Ko Yo, before continuing to Khu Khut Waterbird Park. If you're coming **from Hat Yai**, there's no need to go into Songkhla first: take a Songkhla-bound bus or minibus but get off on the edge of the suburbs at the junction with Highway 408, and catch a songthaew or bus across the bridge to Ko Yo.

The chief appeal of Ko Yo is the **Southern Folklore Museum** (daily 8.30am–5pm; B50), which sprawls over the hillside on the northern tip of Ko Yo just before the northern bridge. Affording stunning views over the water to Songkhla and of the fishing villages on the western side of the island, the park is strewn with all kinds of boats and wooden reproductions of traditional southern houses, in which the collections are neatly set out. The exhibits inside, such as the shadow-puppet paraphernalia and the *kris* – long knives with intricately carved handles and sheaths – show the strong influences of Malaysia and Indonesia on southern Thailand. Also on show are the elaborate dance costumes for the *manohra*, but probably the most fascinating objects are the *lek kood*, or coconut scrapers, which are set into seat-blocks carved into an offbeat variety of shapes – rabbits, elephants, phalluses, beauty queens. The museum's **shop** has the island's finest selection of fabrics, and there's a pleasant **café** with great views over the museum rooftops to the fishing villages below. Better still are the panoramas from the top of the **viewing tower** in the museum courtyard.

Ko Yo is renowned for its excellent seafood **restaurants**. One hundred metres south of the museum, a short slip road leads up to the popular *Suan Kaeo*, in a breezy spot overlooking the Thale Sap and Songkhla – try *hor mok thalay*, mixed fresh seafood in a chilli and coconut sauce. Alternatively, follow the access road to the museum west around the island for 200m to reach a couple of simpler places right on the water's edge – *Ko Kaeng* and *Ko Tong* – both with great seafood.

Khu Khut Waterbird Park

About 40km up Highway 408 from Songkhla, a left turn by the police station leads after 2km to the headquarters of **Khu Khut Waterbird Park**, a conservation area on the Thale Luang where over 140 species of mostly migratory birds are found. Ranot-bound buses only drop you off at the junction, from where you can take a motorbike taxi (B20) to reach the park. The best time of year to visit is from January to March, and the birds are at their most active in the early morning and late afternoon. A longtail trip to view the birds costs B200 for an hour, while for B400 you get a two-hour jaunt across the shallow lake, weaving between water reeds and crayfish traps, to **Ko Si Ko Ha**, the dramatic limestone islands where birds' nests (see box p.695) are gathered for Chinese gourmets. However, you won't be able to set foot on the islands as the concession-holders jealously guard their hugely profitable business from spies and thieves.

Songkhla Zoo

Songkhla's newest attraction, **Songkhla zoo** (daily 9am–6pm; B30), is situated some 15km south of the city on Highway 408, the Songkhla–Nathawi road. It's a huge place, spread over eleven square kilometres of hills, so making your way around it can be rather tiring – though the benefit of the elevation is the great view it gives back over Songhkla and Ko Yo. As yet the zoo is rather sparsely populated with animals, but it's growing fast, and plans in the future to become a breeding centre for tapirs. The easiest way to get here is to hire a motorbike from the *Amsterdam Guest House* or *LoBo Café* in Songkhla (see p.739); this gives the added benefit of a means of transport around the zoo itself (for an additional B10 entry fee). Alternatively, take a Chana-bound songthaew from Thanon Ramwithi (B10).

Pattani

PATTANI, the traditional centre of the Muslim south, is a rather forbidding town, but presents a fascinating cultural clash embodied by the discord between its polychrome Chinese temples and the remains of its sixteenth-century mosque. Founded around the beginning of the fifteenth century, not long after the introduction of Islam to the area, Pattani soon became an important port for trade in the Gulf of Thailand. The port eventually declined when the river silted up and became no longer easily navigable, but the industry and fisheries which in recent years have been established around the town have turned it into a busy, though rather ugly, commercial centre.

From the time of its founding, Pattani owed allegiance to the Thai kings at Ayutthaya, and after the capital was moved to Bangkok the city-state was fully integrated into Thailand. However, having close ties with fellow Islamic states to the south, it has always chafed against the central power – the separatist Pattani United Liberation Organization originated here – though in recent years a more positive relationship has developed. Pattani is also home to a sizeable Chinese community, whose rivalry with Islam is enshrined in the town's most famous legend. In the 1570s a certain Lim Toh Khiem, a notorious Chinese pirate, married a local woman and was converted to Islam. To show his conviction in his new faith, he began building a mosque – at which point, legend has it, his sister Lim Ko Niaw sailed from China to persuade him to renounce Islam and return to his homeland. When her mission failed she hanged herself from the nearest cashew-nut tree, which was later carved into a statue of her, preserved at the **San Jao Lim Ko Niaw**. The shrine, located on Thanon Arnoaru (a side street off the northern stretch of Thanon Yarang, the main north–south street), is gaudy and dimly lit, groaning with rich offerings and grimy with the soot of endless joss sticks; the doll-like image of Lim Ko Niaw is its centrepiece. During the annual Lim Ko Niaw festival, held in the mini-stadium opposite in the middle of the third lunar month (usually March), the image is carried through a raging bonfire by entranced devotees, who by this and other masochistic feats seek to prove their purity to their heroine goddess.

Lim Ko Niaw's suicide put a curse on her brother's mosque, the **Masjid Kreu Se**, which confounded his and his successors' attempts to finish it. Located 5km east of town towards Narathiwat, the roofless brick shell has an unofficial Muslim guard stationed near the entrance to prevent non-Muslims from walking onto the holy ruins. Next door to the mosque the Chinese have built an ostentatious shrine around the horseshoe burial mound of Lim Ko Niaw. The mosque can be visited by songthaew or bus from Thanon Ramkomud, the eastern continuation of Thanon Rudee, whose intersection with Thanon Yarang marks the centre of town.

Practicalities

Facilities for visitors are very limited, though at a pinch the town can be visited on a long day-trip from Hat Yai or as a break in the journey south; the **bus station** is towards the south end of Thanon Yarang, and share-taxis and minibuses are clustered a kilometre or so north on the same road. The pick of a pitiful choice of budget **hotels** in Pattani is the central *Palace*, on Thanon Preeda, between Thanon Pipit and Thanon Rudee (☎073/349711; ❷–❸), which has reasonably clean fan-cooled and air-conditioned rooms. Those who can afford it are much better off upgrading to the luxury *CS Pattani*, 299 Moo 4, Thanon Nongchik, on the western outskirts of town (☎073/335093–4; ❼). There's good, though pricey,

Chinese **food** at the *London Restaurant* at 89/5 Thanon Yarang; cheaper and just as tasty is the fare at the busy night market on the north side of Thanon Pipit.

South to Yala and the border

From Pattani, Highway 410 heads due south to **Yala**, a dull but efficient town 43km across the coastal plain, then on for 140km through the mountains to **Betong**, the most southerly point on the Thai–Malaysian border. This makes a quiet, scenic route into Malaysia but otherwise has little to offer.

Yala

YALA is the business and education centre of the Muslim border provinces, a town of tree-lined boulevards that's won awards as the cleanest town in Thailand. An uninspiring place, its liveliest time is during the **ASEAN Barred Ground Dove Festival**, usually in the first weekend of March, when hundreds of competitors flock here from all over Southeast Asia. The breeding of luck-bringing Java doves is an obsession among the Muslim population of the south, where most houses have a bird cage outside and many villages feature fields of metal poles six to eight metres tall on which to hang the cages during the competition season, which is normally March and April. The birds are judged on the pitch, melody and volume of their cooing and on their appearance; the most musical specimens change hands for as much as two million baht at the Yala jamboree.

Though staunchly Islamic (the town is home to the largest mosque in Thailand), Yala attracts busloads of Buddhist pilgrims, who come to revere the 25-metre-long reclining Buddha at **Wat Khuhaphimuk** (aka Wat Na Tham), 8km out of town on the road to Yaha and Hat Yai. The image's aura of holiness comes from its atmospheric setting in a broad, dank cave, and from its great age: it's said to have been constructed (and the temple founded) by a king of Palembang (Sumatra), some time around the end of the eighth century. To get there, take a bus from behind the *Thepvimarn* hotel, which will leave you with a five-hundred-metre walk south to the temple.

Practicalities

The **train station**, opposite which share-taxis and air-conditioned minibuses congregate, is on the northeast side of the centre. **Buses** from Pattani stop on Thanon Sirorot, north of the station and east of the tracks; those from Hat Yai stop 500m southwest on the same road. The best budget place to **stay** is *Thepvimarn* at 31 Thanon Sribumrung (☎073/212400 or 211655; **②–④**), which has large, clean fan-cooled and air-conditioned rooms; if you're coming from the train station, it's the first left off Thanon Pipitpakdee. The luxury *Yala Rama Hotel* is on the same road at no. 21 (☎073/212815; **④**). For an evening **meal** of simple, reasonable seafood, try the popular *Tara Seafood Restaurant* at the corner of Thanon Sribumrung and Thanon Pipitpakdee.

Betong

Perched on the tip of a narrow tongue of land reaching into Malaysia, the small town of **BETONG** is only worth considering if you're heading out of the country – it's notorious for its fog, and most of Betong's visitors come across the border for shopping and brothel-creeping. The mountains and thick jungle surrounding the town proved a perfect hiding ground for the headquarters of the **Communist Party of Malaya**, whose hidden underground camp of **Pitya Mit**, just 20km from Betong on the Yala road, survived undetected for almost twenty years under the noses of their enemies. Around 180 communists lived in the complex of **tunnels**, built over three months in 1976 – 10m deep and over 1km long – before peacefully giving themselves up in a 1989 settlement with the Thai government. Today the tunnels are open to the public, with several of the old communists acting as guides. The camp is open daily, but you'll need your own transport to get there. Several such tunnel complexes lie dotted around the south of Thailand; another, larger, one was recently opened to tourists at **Khao Namkhang** (see p.734 for details of a tour there from Hat Yai).

The mountainous route from Yala to Betong is largely the preserve of share-taxis and air-conditioned minibuses, which cover the ground in three hours, as the one sluggish bus a day takes around six hours. From here you can **cross the border** by taxi to Keroh in Malaysia, which gives access to Sungai Petani and the west coast.

Narathiwat and around

The coastal region between Pattani and the Malaysian border is one of the least developed areas of the deep south, although the main town of the region, **Narathiwat**, is slowly coming up in the world, with a brand-new regional tourist office and airport terminal both opening in the last few years. Increasingly popular with travellers stopping off on their way to or from the border, Narathiwat's an easy-going place in which to soak up the atmosphere for a couple of days, with a decent range of hotels and restaurants. It also offers the opportunity of a day at the beach (though if you're after a more protracted beach stay, you're better off on the other side of the Thai peninsula) and an excursion to the beautiful **Wat Chonthara Sing He**, 30km to the south in Tak Bai. Its most famous sight, however, the **Phra Buddha Taksin Mingmongkon**, touted near and far as the largest seated Buddha in Thailand, impresses only by virtue of its vital statistics (it's 24m high, 17m knee to knee).

Off the coast, tiny **Ko Losin**, 100km northeast of Narathiwat, is unremarkable but for the superb **diving** it offers on the coral-encrusted rock beneath the surface – some of the best in Thailand. Visibility is generally excellent, and much of the reef and its inhabitants – blacktip reef sharks, giant manta rays, whale sharks and turtles – can be viewed between 5m and 20m down. Divemaster, 100/63 Ladprao Soi 18, Thanon Ladprao, Bangkok (℡02/512 1664, ⓦwww.divemaster.net), and Songkhla's Starfish Scuba (see p.727) both run live-aboard charters to the island between June and September.

Narathiwat town

NARATHIWAT is set on the west bank of the slowly curving Bang Nara River, at the mouth of which, just five minutes' walk north of the centre, sits a shanty fishing village fronted by *korlae* boats (see p.747). It's worth getting up early on a Friday morning for the bustling, colourful **market** which sprawls over the north end of Thanon Puphapugdee (the main river-bank road). Local batiks are sold here, as well as all kinds of food, including the local fish sauce,

nam budu: all around the region you'll see hundreds of concrete and ceramic pots laid out along the roadside containing the fermenting fish that goes to make the sauce – it takes a year or so before the sauce can be bottled and sold.

Just beyond the fishing village, peaceful deckchair restaurants overlook Hat Narathat, a beach too dangerous for swimming. Fortunately, the best **beach** in the area, boulder-strewn **Ao Manao**, 3km south towards Tak Bai, then 3km left down a paved side road, is within easy reach by motorbike taxi. Known as Lemon Bay due to the long, gentle curve of its coastline, this beautiful stretch is lined with trees and dotted with seafood restaurants.

Narathiwat's annual **Khong Dee Muang Nara** festival takes place in September every year, coinciding with the royal family's one-month visit to the nearby Taksin Ratchaniwet palace (see p.748); the festival involves *korlae* boat racing along the river and a dove-cooing contest.

Practicalities

Narathiwat's two main streets run north–south: Thanon Puphapugdee and the inland Thanon Pichit Bamrung, where most **buses** make a stop to the south of the clocktower – though the bus terminal is on the southwest side of town. **Air-conditioned minibuses** for Pattani are based at the corner of Thanon Puphapugdee and Thanon Vejitchaiboon, those for Hat Yai at the corner of Thanon Pichit Bamrung and Thanon Jamroonara, and for Sungai Kolok and Ban Taba at 308/5 Thanon Pichit Bamrung; **share-taxis** for Hat Yai, Pattani and Yala hang around further north on the same road. The **airport**, served by minibuses (B50; B140 to Sungai Kolok), lies 12km north of town. **Trains** on the line to Sungai Kolok stop at **Tanyongmat**, a half-hour songthaew ride from the centre.

Narathiwat's **TAT** office (daily 8.30am–4.30pm; ☎073/516144, ℉522412, ⓔtatnara@tat.or.th), which has responsibility for Narathiwat, Yala and Pattani provinces, is inconveniently situated a couple of kilometres out of town on the Tak Bai road (take a motorbike taxi). The friendly office has a few English-

---

Crossing into Malaysia near Narathiwat

You can cross to Malaysia southeast of Narathiwat at either of two frontier posts, both of which are well connected to **Kota Bharu**, the nearest town on the other side. Frequent songthaews and buses from Narathiwat make the ninety-minute trip to the riverside frontier post of **Ban Taba**, a village 5km beyond Tak Bai with a couple of mediocre hotels in case you're really stuck. From here a ferry (B6) shuttles across to the Malaysian town of Pongalan Kubur, which has frequent taxis and buses to Kota Bharu.

If you're coming from points north of Narathiwat, transport connections are likely to draw you inland to **Sungai Kolok**, a seedy brothel town popular with Malaysian weekenders. The longer-established of the border posts, Sungai Kolok is the end of the rail line from Bangkok, its station in the northern part of town a mere 800m west of the frontier bridge; motorbike taxis and samlors cover the ground if you can't face the walk. Hat Yai and Narathiwat air-conditioned minibuses are based opposite the station, and most buses stop to set down or pick up there, too. From Rantau Panjang on the other side, frequent taxis and buses head for Kota Bharu. There should be no reason for you to stay in Kolok, but if you need a **hotel**, the best of the town's many budget places is the *Thanee*, at 4/1 Thanon Cheunmanka (☎073/611241; ❷–❸), five minutes' walk south from the train station down Thanon Charoenkhet (turn right at the *Merlin Hotel*); like most of Kolok's hotels, it doubles as a brothel, but the rooms, some with air-conditioning, are clean enough and the staff reasonably helpful.

language brochures, but a much better source of information on the town and its surroundings is the excellent *Baan Burong Riverside Guest House*; downstairs is a **travel agency** which can book plane, bus, minibus and train tickets, and arranges **visa runs** to the Thai consulate in Kota Bharu (transport costs B1500 per person). There's an **internet** shop (daily 9am–10pm; B30 per hour) next door to the *Royal Princess* hotel on Thanon Pichit Bamrung.

Accommodation and eating

One of the best places to **stay** in Narathiwat is the *Baan Burong Riverside Guest House* at 399 Thanon Puphapugdee (☏073/511027, ℻512001, ⓔnatini @chaiyo.com; ❸–❹). Situated in a 60-year-old Sino-Portuguese house in a central location overlooking the river, the guest house is nicely decorated and spotlessly clean, with just three air-conditioned rooms sharing hot-water bathrooms, and a living room with satellite TV, a small book collection and free tea and coffee. Guests have free use of bicycles and kayaks (for non-guests, bicycles are B50 per day, kayaks B50 per hour), and **motorbike rental** (B250 per day) and **car hire** with driver (B1800 per day) can also be arranged – useful for exploring the nearby coast. The helpful and friendly owner, Natini, can also organize a variety of activities, including Thai cooking courses (B200–400), batik-making (B350) and goat-milking (B150), as well as an exhaustive range of **tours**, everything from overnight fishing trips in nearby Saiburi (B1500 for boat), to morning hikes in Phru To Daeng, Thailand's last remaining swamp forest (B450), and two-day eco-tours of the Hala Bala tropical rainforest wildlife sanctuary, where ten of the world's twelve species of hornbill can be found.

Much cheaper than the *Baan Burong*, but nowhere near as nice, is the *Narathiwat Hotel*, which occupies a characterful wooden building on the same street at no. 341 (☏073/511063; ❶); the rooms on the upper level are reserved for foreign tourists and are clean enough, if rather basic. On a cross street towards the north end of town, the friendly and comfortable *Tanyong Hotel* at 16/1 Thanon Sopapisai (☏073/511477–9, ℻511834; ❹–❺) is highly recommended for a splurge, with some cheaper fan rooms available. Narathiwat's best hotel is the luxury *Royal Princess*, 228 Thanon Pichit Bamrung (☏073/515041–50, ℻515040, Ⓦwww.royalprincess.com; ❼), which offers a swimming pool and other smart international-standard amenities; it's generally booked solid in September when the royal family and their entourage decamp to Taksin Ratchaniwet.

The top **restaurant** in town is the swish *Mankornthong* at 433 Thanon Puphapugdee, with a floating platform at the back; the seafood is pricey but very good. Much simpler, and considerably cheaper, is the spotlessly clean Muslim restaurant *Chesenik* on Thanon Sopapisai, which specializes in *kai korlae* (chicken in a mild thick curry gravy). This dish can be found in its more traditional form – grilled on sticks – in the small **night market** opposite the *Royal Princess Hotel*, where you can also snack on excellent *roti*. Some distance out of town at 1/3 Thanon Rangae–Mukka, the idyllic *Baan Suan Gasoh Garden Restaurant* is worth the journey for its delicious, reasonably priced Thai food and lush garden setting; call ahead on ☏073/521700 or 511027 for a free pickup from your hotel.

The coast: Saiburi to Panare

From Narathiwat, a minor road (Route 4157) stretches all the way north up the coast to Panare – with a brief detour inland just before Saiburi – passing dozens of tiny Muslim fishing villages, protected from the winds that batter the coast during the monsoon by sturdy palm-frond windbreaks. It's a picturesque route, with goats and sheep straying onto the road and fish laid out to dry on racks by the roadside. The **beaches** that line much of this coastline are pretty enough, but cater mainly to Thai day-trippers; accommodation, where it exists at all, tends to be basic and rather seedy, while the beaches themselves can be blighted with litter from the omnipresent snack stalls. Note too that this is a fervently Muslim area, so women should cover up with a T-shirt on the beach. That said, a trip to one of the beaches listed below makes a pleasant day out, and during the week you'll have the added benefit of them all to yourself. The best way to reach them is to rent a **motorbike** or, if there's a small group of you, a chauffeured **car** from the *Baan Burong Riverside Guest House* in Narithiwat (see p.745); this will also give you freedom to take in a few other sights around the town. Alternatively, regular **songthaews** head all the way up the coast to Panare.

SAIBURI, 50km from Narathiwat on the bus route to Pattani, is a relaxing, leafy town sprinkled with evidence of its former importance as a trading port – ancient Chinese shophouses, dilapidated wooden mansions and the brick shell of a 400-year-old mosque, Masjid Khao, preserved in landscaped gardens. About 2km from the centre, across the Saiburi River and behind the fishing port, the quiet, tree-lined beach of **Hat Wasukri** is served by a handful of restaurants and the uninspiring *Muang Sai Resort* (☎073/411318; ❸), the town's only accommodation, whose dilapidated concrete bungalows are equipped with fans and bathrooms. The beach is the venue for the town's annual fishing competition, held every May.

The best of this area, however, lies further north towards **Panare**. The remote riverside village of **Dan Pasey Yawo** (Ban Bon), 2km up the road, is renowned as one of the best centres for the manufacture of **korlae** boats, the beautifully decorated smacks used by Muslim fishermen all along this coast, and visitors are welcome to watch the craftsmen at work in the shade of the village's coconut plantation. The intricacy and extent of their decoration is what makes these boats unique – floral motifs and pastoral scenes cover every centimetre, from the bird-of-paradise figurehead to the *singtoh* lion god at the stern, thought to protect the fishermen from the spirits of the sea. Each boat is entirely hand-made, takes four months to complete and sells for over B60,000, although B1000–3000 replicas are produced as a sideline.

About 15km further up towards Panare, you'll come to a turning (no English sign) for **Hat Kae Kae**, an idyllic seaside hamlet among shady palm trees, which gets its onomatopoeic name from the sound the sea makes when it hits the smooth boulders on the small, steeply sloping beach. If you're coming by songthaew, ask to be let off at Hat Kae Kae and you'll be left with a five-hundred-metre walk over a low rocky rise to reach the seashore, backed by some simple foodstalls.

Wat Chonthara Sing He and Taksin Ratchaniwet

South of Narathiwat, one of the finest bots in Thailand lies about 30km down the coast in TAK BAI. Standing in a sandy, tree-shaded compound by the river, the bot at **Wat Chonthara Sing He** (aka Wat Chon) was built in the middle of the last century, as an emblem of Thai sovereignty to prove that Narathiwat was an integral part of Thailand, at a time when the British were claiming the area as part of Malaya. The building's brightly coloured fifteen-tiered roof exemplifies the fashion for curvaceous Chinese styles, here mixed with typical southern Thai features, such as the spiky white nagas, to produce an elegant, dynamic structure. Ask a monk for the key and look at the liv well-preserved murals which completely cover the interior, portraying bawdy love scenes as well as typical details of southern life: bull- and goat-fighting, and men dressed in turbans and long sarongs.

The wat can be visited either as an easy day-trip from Narathiwat or on your way to the border – frequent buses bound for Sungai Kolok or buses and songthaews for Ban Taba pass through the small town. About 7km into the hour-long trip, you can't miss the **Taksin Ratchaniwet palace**, which stands on a wooded hill overlooking the sea. It is possible to visit the grounds when the king is not in residence (generally Oct–Aug daily 9am–4pm; free), but you'll need your own transport to get round the extensive grounds, and the excursion is only of real interest to devotees of the royal family. If you do make the trip, look out for the **gold-leaf vine** in the grounds; the velvety leaves of this highly prized plant, which is native only to the area around Narathiwat, turn an iridescent pink, then gold, then silver, each year from September to November. Other provinces have attempted to cash in on the vine's money-spinning appeal by planting it in other areas of Thailand – only to find that the leaves remain resolutely green all year round.

Travel details

Trains

Hat Yai to: Bangkok (5 daily; 16hr); Butterworth (Malaysia; 1 daily; 5hr 30min); Padang Besar (1 daily; 1hr 40min); Phatthalung (10 daily; 1–2hr); Sungai Kolok (2 daily; 3hr 30min); Surat Thani (8 daily; 4hr–6hr 30min); Yala (9 daily; 1hr 30min–3hr).
Phatthalung to: Bangkok (5 daily; 13hr 30min–16hr 30min); Hat Yai (10 daily; 1–2hr).
Sungai Kolok to: Bangkok (2 daily; 20hr); Hat Yai (2 daily; 3hr 30min–5hr); Nakhon Si Thammarat (1 daily; 9hr 40min); Phatthalung (5 daily; 5–7hr); Surat Thani (3 daily; 9–12hr); Yala (8 daily; 1hr 45min–2hr 30min).
Trang to: Bangkok (2 daily; around 16hr).
Yala to: Bangkok (4 daily; 18–20hr); Hat Yai (9 daily; 1hr 30min–3hr).

Buses

Hat Yai to: Bangkok (every 30min; 13hr); Chumphon (5 daily; 8hr 15min); Ko Samui (1 daily; 6hr 30min); Krabi (2 daily; 4–5hr); Nakhon (every 30min; 3–4hr); Narathiwat (5 daily; 3–4hr); Padang Besar (every 10min; 1hr 40min); Pak Bara (3 daily; 2hr 30min); Pattani (13 daily; 1hr 45min–2hr 40min); Phatthalung (16 daily; 1hr 50min); Phuket (13 daily; 7–9hr); Satun (every 15min; 1hr 30min); Songkhla (every 10min; 30min); Sungai Kolok (2 daily; 5hr); Surat Thani (9 daily; 5hr–6hr 15min); Trang (every 30min; 3–4hr); Yala (every 30min; 2–3hr).
Narathiwat to: Ban Taba (every 30min; 1hr 30min); Bangkok (3 daily; 17hr); Pattani (hourly;

1–2hr); Sungai Kolok (every 30min; 1–2hr); Tak Bai (every 30min; 1hr).
Pattani to: Bangkok (3 daily; 16hr).
Phattalung to: Bangkok (4 daily; 13hr).
Satun to: Bangkok (2 daily; 16hr); Trang (every 30min; 3hr).
Songkhla to: Chana (every 30min; 30min); Hat Yai (every 10min; 30min); Nakhon Si Thammarat (every 30min; 3hr); Ranot (every 30min; 1–2hr).
Sungai Kolok to: Bangkok (3 daily; 18–20hr); Hat Yai (5 daily; 4hr); Narathiwat (hourly; 1–2hr); Pattani (4 daily; 2–3hr); Surat Thani (3 daily; 9–10hr); Tak Bai (hourly; 30min); Yala (hourly; 3hr).
Trang to: Bangkok (8 daily; 14hr); Krabi (hourly; 2hr); Nakhon Si Thammarat (hourly; 2–3hr); Phatthalung (hourly; 1hr); Phuket (hourly; 4hr 30min); Satun (every 30min; 3hr).
Yala to: Bangkok (4 daily; 19hr); Betong (1 daily; 6hr); Hat Yai (every 30min; 2–3hr); Pattani (every 45min; 45min).

Flights

Hat Yai to: Bangkok (6 daily; 1hr 30min); Johor Bahru (Malaysia; 3 weekly via KL; 6hr); Kota Kinabalu (Malaysia; 3 weekly via KL; 7hr); Kuala Lumpur (Malaysia; 3 weekly; 1hr); Kuching (Malaysia; 3 weekly via KL; 7hr); Phuket (1–2 daily; 1hr); Singapore (1 daily; 1hr 35min).
Narathiwat to: Bangkok (1 daily; 3hr); Phuket (1 daily; 1hr).
Trang to: Bangkok (1 or 2 daily; 1hr 30min).

contexts

contexts

CONTEXTS

The historical framework

As long as forty thousand years ago, Thailand was inhabited by **hunter-gatherers** who lived in semi-permanent settlements and used tools made of wood, bamboo and stone. By the end of the last Ice Age, around ten thousand years ago, these groups had become **farmers**, keeping chickens, pigs and cattle, and – as evidenced by the seeds and plant husks which have been discovered in caves in northern Thailand – cultivating rice and beans. This drift into an agricultural society gave rise to further technological developments: the earliest **pottery** found in Thailand has been dated to 6800 BC, while the recent excavations at **Ban Chiang** in the northeast have shown that **bronze** was being worked at least as early as 2000 BC, putting Thailand on a par with Mesopotamia, which has traditionally been regarded as the earliest Bronze Age culture. By two thousand years ago, the peoples of Southeast Asia had settled in small villages among which there was regular communication and trade, but they had split into several broad families, differentiated by language and culture. At this time, the ancestors of the Thais, speaking proto-Thai languages, were still far away in southeastern China, whereas Thailand itself was inhabited by Austroasiatic speakers, among whom the Mon were to establish the region's first distinctive civilization, Dvaravati.

Dvaravati and Srivijaya

The history of **Dvaravati** is ill-defined to say the least, but the name is applied to a distinctive culture complex which shared the **Mon** language and **Theravada Buddhism**. This form of religion probably entered Thailand during the second or third centuries BC, when Indian missionaries were sent to Suvarnabhumi, "land of gold", which seems to correspond to the broad swath of fertile land stretching from southern Burma across the north end of the Gulf of Thailand.

From the discovery of monastery boundary stones (*sema*), clay votive tablets and Indian-influenced Buddhist sculpture, it's clear that Dvaravati was an extensive and prosperous Buddhist civilization which had its greatest flourishing between the sixth and ninth centuries AD. No strong evidence has turned up, however, for the existence of a single capital – rather than an empire, Dvaravati seems to have been a collection of city-states, which, at least in their early history, came under the lax suzerainty of **Funan**, a poorly documented kingdom centred in Cambodia. Nakhon Pathom, Lopburi, Si Thep and Muang Sema were among the most important Dvaravati sites, and their concentration around the Chao Phraya valley would seem to show that they gained much of their prosperity, and maintained religious and cultural contacts with India, via the **trade route** from the Indian Ocean over the Three Pagodas Pass.

Although they passed on aspects of their heavily Indianized art, religion and government to later rulers of Thailand, these Mon city-states were politically fragile and from the ninth century onwards succumbed to the domination of the invading Khmers from Cambodia. One northern outpost, the state of **Haripunjaya**, centred on Lamphun, which had been set up on the trade route with southern China, maintained its independence probably until the beginning of the eleventh century.

Meanwhile, to the south of Dvaravati, the shadowy Indianized state of Lankasuka had grown up in the second century, centred on Ligor (now

Nakhon Si Thammarat) and covering an area of the Malay peninsula which included the important trade crossings at Chaiya and Trang. In the eighth century, it came under the control of the **Srivijaya** empire, a Mahayana Buddhist state centred on Sumatra, which had strong ties with India and a complex but uneasy relationship with neighbouring Java. Thriving on seaborne trade between Persia and China, Srivijaya extended its influence as far north as Chaiya, its regional capital, where discoveries of temple remains and some of the finest stone and bronze statues ever produced in Thailand have borne witness to the cultural vitality of this crossroads empire. In the tenth century the northern part of Lankasuka, under the name **Tambralinga**, regained a measure of independence, although it seems still to have come under the influence of Srivijaya as well as owing some form of allegiance to Dvaravati. By the beginning of the eleventh century however, peninsular Thailand had come under the sway of the Khmer empire, with a Cambodian prince ruling over a community of Khmer settlers and soldiers at Tambralinga.

The Khmers

The history of central Southeast Asia comes into sharper focus with the emergence of the **Khmers**, vigorous empire-builders whose political history can be pieced together from the numerous stone inscriptions they left. Originally vassal subjects of Funan, the Khmers of **Chenla** – to the north of Cambodia – seized power in the latter half of the sixth century during a period of economic decline in the area. Chenla's rise to power was knocked back by a punitive expedition conducted by the Srivijaya empire in the eighth century, but was reconsolidated during the watershed reign of **Jayavarman II** (802–50), who succeeded in conquering the whole of Kambuja, an area which roughly corresponds to modern-day Cambodia. In order to establish the authority of his monarchy and of his country, Jayavarman II had himself initiated as a *chakravartin*, or universal ruler, the living embodiment of the **devaraja**, the divine essence of kingship – a concept which was adopted by later Thai rulers. Taking as the symbol of his authority the phallic lingam, the king was thus identified with the god Shiva, although the Khmer concept of kingship and thus the religious mix of the state as a whole was not confined to Hinduism: elements of ancestor worship were also included, and Mahayana Buddhism gradually increased its hold over the next four centuries.

It was Jayavarman II who moved the Khmer capital to **Angkor** in northern Cambodia, which he and later kings, especially after the eleventh century, embellished with a series of prodigiously beautiful temples. Jayavarman II also recognized the advantages of the lakes around Angkor for irrigating rice fields and providing fish, and thus for feeding a large population. His successors developed this idea and gave the state a sound economic core with a remarkably complex system of **reservoirs** (*baray*) and water channels, which were copied and adapted in later Thai cities.

In the ninth and tenth centuries, Jayavarman II and his imperialistic successors, especially **Yasovarman I** (889–900), confirmed Angkor as the major power in Southeast Asia. They pushed into Vietnam, Laos, southern China and into northeastern Thailand, where the Khmers left dozens of Angkor-style temple complexes, as seen today at Prasat Phanom Rung and Prasat Hin Phimai. To the west and northwest, Angkor took control over central Thailand, with its most important outpost at Lopburi, and even established a strong presence to the south on the Malay peninsula. As a result of this expansion, the Khmers were masters of the most important trade routes between India and

China, and indeed nearly every communications link in the region, from which they were able to derive huge income and strength.

The reign of **Jayavarman VII** (1181–1219), a Mahayana Buddhist who firmly believed in his royal destiny as a *bodhisattva*, sowed the seeds of Angkor's downfall. Nearly half of all the extant great religious monuments of the empire were erected under his supervision, but the ambitious scale of these building projects and the upkeep they demanded – some 300,000 priests and temple servants of 20,000 shrines consumed 38,000 tons of rice per year – along with a series of wars against Vietnam, terminally exhausted the economy.

In subsequent reigns, much of the life-giving irrigation system around Angkor turned into malarial swamp through neglect, and the rise of the more democratic creed of Theravada Buddhism undermined the divine authority which the Khmer kings had derived from the hierarchical Mahayana creed. As a result of all these factors, the Khmers were in no position to resist the onslaught between the thirteenth and fifteenth centuries of the vibrant new force in Southeast Asia, the Thais.

The earliest Thais

The earliest traceable history of the **Thai people** picks them up in southern China around the fifth century AD, when they were squeezed by Chinese and Vietnamese expansionism into sparsely inhabited northeastern Laos and neighbouring areas. The first entry of a significant number of Thais onto what is now Thailand's soil seems to have happened in the region of Chiang Saen, where it appears that some time after the seventh century the Thais formed a state in an area then known as **Yonok**. A development which can be more accurately dated and which had immense cultural significance was the spread of Theravada Buddhism to Yonok via Dvaravati around the end of the tenth century, which served not only to unify the Thais but also to link them to Mon civilization and give them a sense of belonging to the community of Buddhists.

The Thais' political development was also assisted by **Nan-chao**, a well-organized military state comprising a huge variety of ethnic groups, which established itself as a major player on the southern fringes of the Chinese empire from the beginning of the eighth century. As far as can be gathered, Nan-chao permitted the rise of Thai *muang* or small principalities on its periphery, especially in the area immediately to the south known as **Sipsong Panna**.

Thai infiltration continued until, by the end of the twelfth century, they seem to have formed the majority of the population in Thailand, then under the control of the Khmer empire. The Khmers' main outpost, at Lopburi, was by then regarded as the administrative capital of a land called "Syam" (possibly from the Sanskrit *syam*, meaning swarthy) – a mid-twelfth-century bas-relief at Angkor Wat, portraying the troops of Lopburi preceded by a large group of self-confident Syam Kuk mercenaries, shows that the Thais were becoming a force to be reckoned with.

Sukhothai

By the middle of the thirteenth century, the Thais, thanks largely to the decline of Angkor and the inspiring effect of Theravada Buddhism, were poised on the verge of autonomous power. The final catalyst was the invasion by Qubilai Khan's Mongol armies of China and Nan-chao, which began around 1215 and was completed in the 1250s. Demanding that the whole world should acknowledge the primacy of the Great Khan, the Mongols set their hearts on the "pacification" of the "barbarians" to the south of China, which obliged the Thais to form a broad power base to meet the threat.

The founding of the first Thai kingdom at **Sukhothai**, now popularly viewed as the cornerstone of the country's development, was in fact a small-scale piece of opportunism which almost fell at the first hurdle. At some time around 1238, the princes of two small Thai principalities in the upper Chao Phraya valley joined forces to capture the main Khmer outpost in the region at Sukhothai. One of the princes, **Intradit**, was crowned king, but for the first forty years Sukhothai remained merely a local power, whose existence was threatened by the ambitions of neighbouring princes. When attacked by the ruler of Mae Sot, Intradit's army was only saved by the grand entrance of Sukhothai's most dynamic leader: the king's nineteen-year-old son, Rama, held his ground and pushed forward to defeat the opposing commander, earning himself the name **Ramkhamhaeng**, "Rama the Bold".

When Ramkhamhaeng came to the throne around 1278, he saw the south as his most promising avenue for expansion and, copying the formidable military organization of the Mongols, seized control of much of the Chao Phraya valley. Over the next twenty years, largely by diplomacy rather than military action, Ramkhamhaeng gained the submission of most of the rulers of Thailand, who entered the **new empire**'s complex tributary system either through the pressure of the Sukhothai king's personal connections or out of recognition of his superior military strength and moral prestige. To the east, Ramkhamhaeng pushed as far as Vientiane in Laos; by marrying his daughter to a Mon ruler to the west, he obtained the allegiance of parts of southern Burma; and to the south his vassals stretched down the peninsula at least as far as Nakhon Si Thammarat. To the north, Sukhothai concluded an alliance with the parallel Thai states of Lanna and Phayao in 1287 for mutual protection against the Mongols – though it appears that Ramkhamhaeng managed to pinch several *muang* on their eastern periphery as tribute states.

Meanwhile **Lopburi**, which had wrested itself free from Angkor sometime in the middle of the thirteenth century, was able to keep its independence and its control of the eastern side of the Chao Phraya valley. Having been first a major cultural and religious centre for the Mon, then the Khmers' provincial capital, and now a state dominated by migrating Thais, Lopburi was a strong and vibrant place mixing the best of the three cultures, as evidenced by the numerous original works of art produced at this time.

Although the empire of Sukhothai extended Thai control over a vast area, its greatest contribution to the Thais' development was at home, in cultural and political matters. A famous **inscription** by Ramkhamhaeng, now housed in the Bangkok National Museum, describes a prosperous era of benevolent rule: "In the time of King Ramkhamhaeng this land of Sukhothai is thriving. There is fish in the water and rice in the fields . . . [The King] has hung a bell in the opening of the gate over there: if any commoner has a grievance which sickens his belly and gripes his heart . . . he goes and strikes the bell . . . [and King Ramkhamhaeng] questions the man, examines the case, and decides it justly for him." Although this plainly smacks of self-promotion, it seems to contain at least a kernel of truth: in deliberate contrast to the Khmer god-kings, Ramkhamhaeng styled himself as a **dhammaraja**, a king who ruled justly according to Theravada Buddhist doctrine and made himself accessible to his people. To honour the state religion, the city's temples were lavishly endowed: as original as Sukhothai's political systems were its religious **architecture and**

sculpture, which, though bound to borrow from existing Khmer and Sri Lankan styles, show the greatest leap of creativity at any stage in the history of art in Thailand. A further sign of the Thais' new self-confidence was the invention of a new **script** to make their tonal language understood by the non-Thai inhabitants of the land.

All this was achieved in a remarkably short period of time. After the death of Ramkhamhaeng around 1299, his successors took their Buddhism so seriously that they neglected affairs of state. The empire quickly fell apart, and by 1320 Sukhothai had regressed to being a kingdom of only local significance.

Lanna

Almost simultaneous with the birth of Sukhothai was the establishment of a less momentous but longer-lasting kingdom to the north, called **Lanna**. Its founding father was **Mengrai**, chief of Ngon Yang, a small principality on the banks of the Mekhong near modern-day Chiang Saen. Around 1259 he set out to unify the squabbling Thai principalities of the region, first building a strategically placed city at Chiang Rai in 1262, and then forging alliances with Ngam Muang, the Thai king of Phayao, and with Ramkhamhaeng of Sukhothai.

In 1281, after ten years of guileful preparations, Mengrai conquered the Mon kingdom of Haripunjaya based at Lamphun, and was now master of northern Thailand. Taking advice from Ngam Muang and Ramkhamhaeng, in 1292 he selected a site for an impressive new capital of Lanna at **Chiang Mai**, which remains the centre of the north to the present day. Mengrai concluded further alliances in Burma and Laos, making him strong enough to successfully resist further Mongol attacks, although he was eventually obliged to bow to the superiority of the Mongols by sending them small tributes from 1312 onwards. When Mengrai died after a sixty-year reign in 1317, supposedly struck by a bolt of lightning, he had built up an extensive and powerful kingdom. But although he began a tradition of humane, reasonable laws, probably borrowed from the Mons, he had found little time to set up sound political and administrative institutions. His death severely destabilized Lanna, which quickly shrank in size and influence.

It was only in the reign of **Ku Na** (1355–85) that Lanna's development regained momentum. A well-educated and effective ruler, Ku Na enticed the venerable monk Sumana from Sukhothai, to establish an ascetic Sri Lankan sect in Lanna in 1369. Sumana brought a number of Buddha images with him, inspiring a new school of art that flourished for over a century, but more importantly his sect became a cultural force that had a profound unifying effect on the kingdom. The influence of Buddhism was further strengthened under **King Tilok** (1441–87), who built many great monuments at Chiang Mai and cast huge numbers of bronze seated Buddhas in the style of the central image at Bodh Gaya in India, the scene of the Buddha's enlightenment. Tilok, however, is best remembered as a great warrior, who spent most of his reign resisting the advances of Ayutthaya, by now the strongest Thai kingdom.

Under continuing pressure both from Ayutthaya and from Burma, Lanna went into rapid decline in the second quarter of the sixteenth century. For a short period after 1546, Chiang Mai came under the control of Setthathirat, the king of Lan Sang (Laos), but, unable to cope with Lanna's warring factions, he then abdicated, purloining the talismanic Emerald Buddha for his own capital at Louang Phabang. In 1558, Burma decisively captured Chiang Mai, and the Mengrai dynasty came to an end. For most of the next two centuries, the

Burmese maintained control through a succession of puppet rulers, and Lanna again became much as it had been before Mengrai, little more than a chain of competing principalities.

Ayutthaya

While Lanna was fighting for its place as a marginalized kingdom, from the fourteenth century onwards the seeds of a full-blown Thai nation were being sown to the south at **Ayutthaya**. The city of Ayutthaya itself was founded on its present site in 1351 by U Thong, "Prince Golden Cradle", when his own town, Lopburi, was ravaged by smallpox. Taking the title **Ramathibodi**, he soon united the principalities of the lower Chao Phraya valley, which had formed the western provinces of the Khmer empire. When he recruited his bureaucracy from the urban elite of Lopburi, Ramathibodi set the **style of government** at Ayutthaya – the elaborate etiquette, language and rituals of Angkor were adopted, and, most importantly, the conception of the ruler as *devaraja*. The king became sacred and remote, an object of awe and dread, with none of the accessibility of the kings of Sukhothai: when he processed through the town, ordinary people were forbidden to look at him and had to be silent while he passed. This hierarchical system also provided the state with much-needed manpower, as all freemen were obliged to give up six months of each year to the crown either on public works or military service.

The site chosen by Ramathibodi turned out to be the best in the region for an international port, and so began Ayutthaya's rise to prosperity, based on its ability to exploit the upswing in **trade** in the middle of the fourteenth century along the routes between India and China. Flushed with economic success, Ramathibodi's successors were able to expand their control over the ailing states in the region. After a long period of subjugation, Sukhothai became a province of the kingdom of Ayutthaya in 1438, six years after Boromraja II had powerfully demonstrated Ayutthaya's pre-eminence by capturing the once-mighty Angkor, enslaving large numbers of its subjects and looting the Khmer royal regalia. (The Cambodian royal family were forced to abandon the palace forever and to found a new capital near Phnom Penh.)

Although a century of nearly continuous warfare against Lanna was less decisive, success generally bred success, and Ayutthaya's increasing wealth through trade brought ever greater power over its neighbouring states. To streamline the functioning of his unwieldy empire, **Trailok** (1448–88) found it necessary to make reforms of its administration. His **Law of Civil Hierarchy** formally entrenched the inequality of Ayutthayan society, defining the status of every individual by assigning him or her an imaginary number of rice fields – for example, 25 for an ordinary freeman and 10,000 for the highest ministers of state. Trailok's legacy is found in today's unofficial but fiendishly complex status system, by which everyone in Thailand knows their place.

Ramathibodi II (1491–1529), almost at a loss as to what to do with his enormous wealth, undertook an extensive programme of public works. In the 1490s he built several major religious monuments, and between 1500 and 1503 cast the largest standing metal image of the Buddha ever known, the Phra Si Sanphet, which gave its name to the temple of the royal palace. By 1540, the kingdom of Ayutthaya had grown to cover most of the area of modern-day Thailand.

Burmese wars and European trade

In the sixteenth century recurring tensions with Burma led **Chakkraphat** (1548–69) to improve his army and build brick ramparts around the capital.

This was to no avail however: in 1568 the Burmese besieged Ayutthaya with a huge army, said by later accounts to have consisted of 1,400,000 men. The Thais held out until August 8, 1569, when treachery within their own ranks helped the Burmese break through the defences. The Burmese looted the city, took thousands of prisoners and installed a vassal king to keep control.

The decisive character who broke the Burmese stranglehold twenty years later and re-established Ayutthaya's economic growth was **Naresuan** (1590–1605), who defied the Burmese by amassing a large army. The enemy sent a punitive expedition which was conclusively defeated at Nong Sarai near modern-day Suphanburi on January 18, 1593, Naresuan himself turning the battle by killing the Burmese crown prince. Historians have praised Naresuan for his personal bravery and his dynamic leadership, although the chronicles of the time record a strong streak of tyranny – in his fifteen years as king he had eighty thousand people killed, excluding the victims of war. A favoured means of punishment was to slice off pieces of the offender's flesh, which he was then made to eat in the king's presence.

The period following Naresuan's reign was characterized by a more sophisticated engagement in **foreign trade**. In 1511 the Portuguese had become the first Western power to trade with Ayutthaya, and Naresuan himself concluded a treaty with Spain in 1598; relations with Holland and England were initiated in 1608 and 1612 respectively. For most of the seventeenth century, European merchants flocked to Thailand, not only to buy Thai products, but also to gain access to Chinese and Japanese goods on sale there. The role of foreigners at Ayutthaya reached its peak under **Narai** (1656–88), but he overstepped the mark in cultivating close links with Louis XIV of France, who secretly harboured the notion of converting Ayutthaya to Christianity. On Narai's death, relations with Westerners were severely cut back.

Despite this reduction of trade and prolonged civil strife over the succession to the throne whenever a king died – then, as now, there wasn't a fixed principle of primogeniture – Ayutthaya continued to flourish for much of the eighteenth century. The reign of **Borommakot** (1733–58) was particularly prosperous, producing many works of drama and poetry. Furthermore, Thai Buddhism had by then achieved such prestige that Sri Lanka, from where the Thais had originally imported their form of religion in the thirteenth century, requested Thai aid in restoring their monastic orders in 1751.

However, immediately after the death of Borommakot the rumbling in the Burmese jungle to the north began to make itself heard again. Alaunghpaya of Burma, apparently a blindly aggressive country bumpkin, first recaptured the south of his country from the Mons, then turned his attentions on Ayutthaya. A siege in 1760 was unsuccessful, with Alaunghpaya dying of wounds sustained there, but the scene was set. In February 1766 the Burmese descended upon Ayutthaya for the last time. The Thais held out for over a year, during which they were afflicted by famine, epidemics and a terrible fire which destroyed ten thousand houses. Finally, in **April 1767**, the walls were breached and the city taken. The Burmese razed everything to the ground and tens of thousands of prisoners were led off to Burma, including most of the royal family. The king, Suriyamarin, is said to have escaped from the city in a boat and starved to death ten days later. As one observer has said, the Burmese laid waste to Ayutthaya "in such a savage manner that it is hard to imagine that they shared the same religion with the Siamese". The city was abandoned to the jungle, but with remarkable speed the Thais regrouped and established a new seat of power, further down the Chao Phraya River at Bangkok.

The early Bangkok empire

As the bulk of the Burmese army was obliged by war with China to withdraw almost immediately, Thailand was left to descend into banditry. Out of this lawless mess several centres of power arose, the most significant being at Chanthaburi, commanded by **Phraya Taksin**. A charismatic, brave and able general who had been unfairly blamed for a failed counter-attack against the Burmese at Ayutthaya, Taksin had anticipated the fall of the besieged city and quietly slipped away with a force of five hundred men. In June 1767 he took control of the east-coast strip around Chanthaburi and very rapidly expanded his power across central Thailand.

Blessed with the financial backing of the Chinese trading community, to whom he was connected through his father, Taksin was crowned king in December 1768 at his new capital of Thonburi, on the opposite bank of the river from modern-day Bangkok. One by one the new king defeated his rivals, and within two years he had restored all of Ayutthaya's territories. More remarkably, by the end of the next decade Taksin had outdone his Ayutthayan predecessors by bringing Lanna, Cambodia and much of Laos into a huge new empire. During this period of expansionism, Taksin left most of the fighting to Thong Duang, an ambitious soldier and descendant of an Ayutthayan noble family, who became the *chakri*, the military commander, and took the title **Chao Phraya Chakri**.

However, by 1779 all was not well with the king. Being an outsider, who had risen from an ordinary family on the fringes of society, Taksin became paranoid about plots against him, a delusion that drove him to imprison and torture even his wife and sons. At the same time he sank into religious excesses, demanding that the monkhood worship him as a god. By March 1782, public outrage at his sadism and dangerously irrational behaviour had reached such fervour that he was ousted in a coup.

Chao Phraya Chakri was invited to take power and had Taksin executed. In accordance with ancient etiquette, this had to be done without royal blood touching the earth: the mad king was duly wrapped in a black velvet sack and struck on the back of the neck with a sandalwood club. (Popular tradition has it that even this form of execution was too much: an unfortunate substitute got the velvet sack treatment, while Taksin was whisked away to a palace in the hills near Nakhon Si Thammarat, where he is said to have lived until 1825.)

Rama I

With the support of the Ayutthayan aristocracy, Chakri – reigning as **Rama I** (1782–1809) – set about consolidating the Thai kingdom. His first act was to move the capital across the river to Bangkok, a better defensive position against any Burmese attack from the west. Borrowing from the layout of Ayutthaya, he built a new royal palace and impressive monasteries, and enshrined in the palace wat the Emerald Buddha, which he had snatched back during his campaigns in Laos.

As all the state records had disappeared in the destruction of Ayutthaya, religious and legal texts had to be written afresh and historical chronicles reconstituted – with some very sketchy guesswork. The monkhood was in such a state of crisis that it was widely held that moral decay had been partly responsible for Ayutthaya's downfall. Within a month of becoming king, Rama I issued a series of religious laws and made appointments to the leadership of the monkhood, to restore discipline and confidence after the excesses of Taksin's reign. Many works of drama and poetry had also been lost in the sacking of

Ayutthaya, so Rama I set about rebuilding the Thais' literary heritage, at the same time attempting to make it more cosmopolitan and populist. His main contribution was the *Ramakien*, a dramatic version of the Indian epic *Ramayana*, which is said to have been set to verse by the king himself, with a little help from his courtiers, in 1797. Heavily adapted to its Thai setting, the *Ramakien* served as an affirmation of the new monarchy and its divine links, and has since become the national epic.

In the early part of Rama I's reign, the Burmese reopened hostilities on several occasions, the biggest attempted invasion coming in 1785, but the emphatic manner in which the Thais repulsed them only served to knit together the young kingdom. Trade with China revived, and the king addressed the besetting problem of manpower by ordering every man to be tattooed with the name of his master and his town, so that avoiding royal service became almost impossible. On a more general note, Rama I put the style of government in Thailand on a modern footing: while retaining many of the features of a *devaraja*, he shared more responsibility with his courtiers, as a first among equals.

Rama II and Rama III

The peaceful accession of his son as **Rama II** (1809–24) signalled the establishment of the **Chakri dynasty**, which is still in place today. This Second Reign was a quiet interlude, best remembered as a fertile period for Thai literature. The king, himself one of the great Thai poets, gathered round him a group of writers including the famous Sunthorn Phu, who produced scores of masterly love poems, travel accounts and narrative songs.

In contrast, **Rama III** (1824–51) actively discouraged literary development – probably in reaction against his father – and was a vigorous defender of conservative values. To this end, he embarked on an extraordinary redevelopment of Wat Po, the oldest temple in Bangkok. Hundreds of educational inscriptions and mural paintings, on all manner of secular and religious subjects, were put on show, apparently to preserve traditional culture against the rapid change which the king saw corroding the country. In foreign affairs, Rama III faced a serious threat from the vassal states of Laos, who in 1827 sent an invading army from Vientiane, which got as far as Saraburi, only three days' march from Bangkok. The king's response was savage: having repelled the initial invasion, he ordered his army to destroy everything in Vientiane apart from Buddhist temples and to forcibly resettle huge numbers of Lao in Isaan. Shortly after, the king was forced to go to war in Cambodia, to save Buddhism and its traditional institutions from the attentions of the newly powerful, non-Buddhist Vietnamese. A series of campaigns in the 1830s and 1840s culminated in the peace treaty of 1845–46, which again established Thailand as the dominant influence in Cambodia.

More significant in the long run was the danger posed by the increase in Western influence which began in the Third Reign. As early as 1825, the Thais were sufficiently alarmed at British colonialism to strengthen Bangkok's defences by stretching a great iron chain across the mouth of the Chao Phraya River, to which every blacksmith in the area had to donate a certain number of links. In 1826 Rama III was obliged to sign a limited trade agreement with the British, the **Burney Treaty**, by which the Thais won some political security in return for reducing their taxes on goods passing through Bangkok. British and American missions in 1850 unsuccessfully demanded more radical concessions, but by this time Rama III was seriously ill, and it was left to his far-sighted and progressive successors to reach a decisive accommodation with the Western powers.

Mongkut and Chulalongkorn

Rama IV, more commonly known as **Mongkut** (1851–68), had been a Buddhist monk for 27 years when he succeeded his brother. But far from leading a cloistered life, Mongkut had travelled widely throughout Thailand, had maintained scholarly contacts with French and American missionaries and, like most of the country's new generation of leaders, had taken an interest in Western learning, studying English, Latin and the sciences. He had also turned his mind to the condition of Buddhism in Thailand, which seemed to him to have descended into little more than popular superstition; indeed, after a study of the Buddhist scriptures in Pali, he was horrified to find that Thai ordinations were probably invalid. So in the late 1830s he set up a rigorously fundamentalist sect called *Thammayutika*, the "Order Adhering to the Teachings of the Buddha", and as abbot of the order he oversaw the training of a generation of scholarly leaders for Thai Buddhism from his base at Bangkok's Wat Bowonniwet, which became a major centre of Western learning.

When his kingship faced its first major test, in the form of a threatening British mission in 1855 led by **Sir John Bowring**, Mongkut dealt with it confidently. Realizing that Thailand was unable to resist the military might of the British, the king reduced import and export taxes, allowed British subjects to live and own land in Thailand and granted them freedom of trade. Of the **government monopolies**, which had long been the mainstay of the Thai economy, only that on opium was retained. After making up the loss in revenue through internal taxation, Mongkut quickly made it known that he would welcome diplomatic contacts from other Western countries: within a decade, agreements similar to the Bowring Treaty had been signed with France, the US and a score of other nations. Thus by skilful diplomacy the king avoided a close relationship with only one power, which could easily have led to Thailand's annexation.

While all around the colonial powers were carving up Southeast Asia amongst themselves, Thailand suffered nothing more than the weakening of its influence over Cambodia, which in 1863 the French brought under their protection. As a result of the open-door policy, foreign trade boomed, financing the redevelopment of Bangkok's waterfront and, for the first time, the building of paved roads. However, Mongkut ran out of time for instituting the far-reaching domestic reforms which he saw were needed to drag Thailand into the modern world.

The modernization of Thailand

Mongkut's son, **Chulalongkorn**, took the throne as Rama V (1868–1910) at the age of only 15, but he was well prepared by an excellent education which mixed traditional Thai and modern Western elements – provided by Mrs Anna Leonowens, subject of *The King and I*. When Chulalongkorn reached his majority after a five-year regency, he set to work on the reforms envisioned by his father. One of his first acts was to scrap the custom by which subjects were required to prostrate themselves in the presence of the king, which he followed up in 1874 with a series of decrees announcing the gradual abolition of slavery. The speed of his financial and administrative reforms, however, proved too much for the "**Ancients**" (*hua boran*), the old guard of ministers and officials inherited from his father. Their opposition culminated in the Front Palace Crisis of 1875, when a show of military strength almost plunged the country into civil war, and, although Chulalongkorn skilfully defused the crisis, many of his reforms had to be quietly shelved for the time being.

An important administrative reform which did go through, necessitated by the threat of colonial expansionism, concerned the former kingdom of Lanna. British exploitation of teak had recently spread into northern Thailand from neighbouring Burma, so in 1874 Chulalongkorn sent a commissioner to Chiang Mai to keep an eye on the prince of Chiang Mai and make sure that he avoided any collision with the British. The commissioner was gradually able to limit the power of the princes and integrate the region more fully into the kingdom.

In the 1880s prospects for reform brightened as many of the "Ancients" died or retired. This allowed Chulalongkorn to **restructure the government** to meet the country's needs: the Royal Audit Office made possible the proper control of revenue and finance; the Department of the Army became the nucleus of a modern armed services; and a host of other departments were set up, for justice, education, public health and the like. To fill these new positions, the king appointed many of his younger brothers, who had all received a modern education, while scores of foreign technicians and advisers were brought in to help with everything from foreign affairs to rail lines.

Throughout this period, however, the Western powers maintained their pressure on the region. The most serious threat to Thai sovereignty was the **Franco-Siamese Crisis** of 1893, which culminated in the French, based in Vietnam, sending gunboats up the Chao Phraya River to Bangkok. Flouting numerous international laws, France claimed control over Laos and made other outrageous demands, which Chulalongkorn had no option but to concede. In 1907 Thailand was also forced to relinquish Cambodia to the French, and in 1909 three Malay states fell to the British. In order to preserve its independence, the country ceded almost half of its territory and forewent huge sums of tax revenue. But from the end of the Fifth Reign, the frontiers were fixed as they are today.

By the time of the king's death in 1910, Thailand could not yet be called a modern nation-state – corruption and nepotism were still grave problems, for example. However, Chulalongkorn had made remarkable advances, and, almost from scratch, had established the political institutions to cope with twentieth-century development.

The end of absolute monarchy

Chulalongkorn was succeeded by a flamboyant, British-educated prince, **Vajiravudh** (1910–25), who was crowned Rama VI. The new king found it difficult to shake the dominance of his father's appointees in the government, who formed an extremely narrow elite, comprised almost entirely of members of Chulalongkorn's family. In an attempt to build up a personal following, Vajiravudh created, in May 1911, the **Wild Tigers**, a nationwide paramilitary corps recruited widely from the civil service. However, in 1912 a group of young army lieutenants, disillusioned by the absolute monarchy and upset at the downgrading of the regular army in favour of the Wild Tigers, plotted a **coup**. The conspirators were easily broken up before any trouble began, but this was something new in Thai history: the country was used to in-fighting among the royal family, but not to military intrigue from men from comparatively ordinary backgrounds.

Vajiravudh's response to the coup was a series of modernizing **reforms**, including the introduction of compulsory primary education and an attempt to better the status of women by supporting monogamy in place of the widespread practice of polygamy. His huge output of writings invariably encouraged people to live as modern Westerners, and he brought large numbers of commoners into high positions in government. Nonetheless, he would not relinquish his strong opposition to constitutional democracy.

When **World War I** broke out in 1914, the Thais were generally sympathetic to the Germans out of resentment over their loss of territory to the French and British. The king, however, was in favour of neutrality, until the US entered the war in 1917, when Thailand followed the expedient policy of joining the winning side and sent an expeditionary force of 1300 men to France in June 1918. The goodwill earned by this gesture enabled the Thais, between 1920 and 1926, to negotiate away the unequal treaties which had been imposed on them by the Western powers. Foreigners on Thai soil were no longer exempted from Thai laws, and the Thais were allowed to set reasonable rates of import and export taxes.

Yet Vajiravudh's extravagant lifestyle – during his reign, royal expenditure amounted to as much as ten percent of the state budget – left severe financial problems for his successor. Vajiravudh died without leaving a son, and as three better-placed contenders to the crown all died in the 1920s, **Prajadhipok** – the seventy-sixth child and last son of Chulalongkorn – was catapulted to the throne as Rama VII (1925–35). Young and inexperienced, he responded to the country's crisis by creating a Supreme Council of State, seen by many as a return to Chulalongkorn's absolutist "government by princes".

Prajadhipok himself seems to have been in favour of constitutional government, but the weakness of his personality and the opposition of the old guard in the Supreme Council prevented him from introducing it. Meanwhile a vigorous community of Western-educated intellectuals had emerged in the lower echelons of the bureaucracy, who were increasingly dissatisfied with the injustices of monarchical government. The final shock to the Thai system came with the Great Depression, which from 1930 onwards ravaged the economy. On June 24, 1932, a small group of middle-ranking officials, led by a lawyer, Pridi Phanomyong, and an army major, Luang Phibunsongkhram, staged a **coup** with only a handful of troops. Prajadhipok weakly submitted to the conspirators, or "Promoters", and 150 years of absolute monarchy in Bangkok came to a sudden end. The king was sidelined to a position of symbolic significance and in 1935 he abdicated in favour of his ten-year-old nephew, **Ananda**, then a schoolboy living in Switzerland.

To the 1957 coup

The success of the 1932 coup was in large measure attributable to the army officers who gave the conspirators credibility, and it was they who were to dominate the constitutional regimes that followed. The Promoters' first worry was that the French or British might attempt to restore the monarchy to full power. To deflect such intervention, they appointed a government under a provisional constitution and espoused a wide range of liberal Western-type reforms, including freedom of the press and social equality, few of which ever saw the light of day.

The regime's first crisis came early in 1933 when **Pridi Phanomyong**, by now leader of the government's civilian faction, put forward a socialist economic plan based on the nationalization of land and labour. The proposal was denounced as communistic by the military, Pridi was forced into temporary exile and an anticommunist law was passed. Then, in October, a royalist coup was mounted which brought the kingdom close to civil war. After intense fighting, the rebels were defeated by Lieutenant-Colonel **Luang Phibunsongkhram** (or Phibun), so strengthening the government and bringing Phibun to the fore as the leading light of the military faction.

Pridi was rehabilitated in 1934 and remained powerful and popular, especially among the intelligentsia, but it was Phibun who became prime minister after the decisive **elections of 1938**, presiding over a cabinet dominated by military men. Phibun encouraged a wave of nationalistic feeling with such measures as the official institution of the name Thailand in 1939 – Siam, it was argued, was a name bestowed by external forces, and the new title made it clear that the country belonged to the Thais rather than the economically dominant Chinese. This latter sentiment was reinforced with a series of harsh laws against the Chinese, who faced discriminatory taxes on income and commerce.

World War II

The outbreak of **World War II** gave the Thais the chance to avenge the humiliation of the 1893 Franco–Siamese Crisis. When France was occupied by Germany in June 1940, Phibun seized the opportunity to invade western Cambodia and the area of Laos lying to the west of the Mekhong River. In the following year, however, the threat of a Japanese attack on Thailand loomed. On December 8, 1941, almost at the same time as the assault on Pearl Harbour, the Japanese invaded the country at nine points, most of them along the east coast of the peninsula. The Thais at first resisted fiercely, but realizing that the position was hopeless, Phibun quickly ordered a ceasefire. Meanwhile the British sent a force from Malaysia to try to stop the Japanese at Songkhla, but were held up in a fight with Thai border police. The Japanese had time to establish themselves, before pushing down the peninsula to take Singapore.

The Thai government concluded a military alliance with Japan and declared war against the US and Great Britain in January 1942, probably in the belief that the Japanese would win the war. However, the Thai minister in Washington, Seni Pramoj, refused to deliver the declaration of war against the US and, in co-operation with the Americans, began organizing a resistance movement called **Seri Thai**. Pridi, now acting as regent to the young king, furtively co-ordinated the movement under the noses of the occupying Japanese, smuggling in American agents and housing them in a European prison camp in Bangkok.

By 1944 Japan's final defeat looked likely, and Phibun, who had been most closely associated with them, was forced to resign by the National Assembly in July. A civilian, Khuang Aphaiwong, was chosen as prime minister, while Seri Thai became well established in the government under the control of Pridi. At the end of the war, Thailand was forced to restore the annexed Cambodian and Lao provinces to French Indochina, but American support prevented the British from imposing heavy punishments for the alliance with Japan.

Postwar upheavals

With the fading of the military, the election of January 1946 was for the first time contested by organized political parties, resulting in Pridi becoming prime minister. A new constitution was drafted and the outlook for democratic, civilian government seemed bright.

Hopes were shattered, however, on June 9, 1946, when King Ananda was found dead in his bed, with a bullet wound in his forehead. Three palace servants were hurriedly tried and executed, but the murder has never been satisfactorily explained, and public opinion attached at least indirect responsibility for the killing to Pridi, who had in the past shown strong anti-royalist feeling. He resigned as prime minister, and in April 1948 the military made a decisive return: playing on the threat of communism, with Pridi pictured as a Red bogeyman, Phibun took over the premiership.

After the bloody suppression of two attempted coups in favour of Pridi, the main feature of Phibun's second regime was its heavy involvement with the US. As communism developed its hold in the region, with the takeover of China in 1949 and the French defeat in Indochina in 1954, the US increasingly viewed Thailand as a bulwark against the Red menace. Between 1951 and 1957, when its annual state budget was only about $200 million a year, Thailand received a total $149 million in American economic aid and $222 million in military aid. This strengthened Phibun's dictatorship, while enabling leading military figures to divert American money and other funds into their own pockets.

In 1955, his position threatened by two rival generals, Phibun experienced a sudden conversion to the cause of democracy. He narrowly won a general election in 1957, but only by blatant vote-rigging and coercion. Although there's a strong tradition of foul play in Thai elections, this is remembered as the dirtiest ever: after vehement public outcry, **General Sarit**, the commander-in-chief of the army, overthrew the new government in September 1957.

To the present day

Believing that Thailand would prosper best under a unifying authority – an ideology that still has its supporters – Sarit set about re-establishing the monarchy as the head of the social hierarchy and the source of legitimacy for the government. Ananda's successor, **King Bhumibol** (Rama IX), was pushed into an active role while Sarit ruthlessly silenced critics and pressed ahead with a plan for economic development. These policies achieved a large measure of stability and prosperity at home, although from 1960 onwards the international situation worsened. With the Marxist Pathet Lao making considerable advances in Laos, and Cambodia's ruler, Prince Sihanouk, drawing into closer relations with China, Sarit turned again to the US. The Americans obliged by sharply increasing military aid and by stationing troops in Thailand.

The Vietnam war

Sarit died in 1963, whereupon the military succession passed to **General Thanom**, closely aided by his deputy prime minister, **General Praphas**. Neither man had anything of Sarit's charisma and during a decade in power they followed his political philosophies largely unchanged. Their most pressing problem was the resumption of open hostilities between North and South Vietnam in the early 1960s – the **Vietnam War**. Both Laos and Cambodia became involved on the side of the communists by allowing the North Vietnamese to supply their troops in the south along the Ho Chi Minh Trail, which passed through southern Laos and northeastern Cambodia. The Thais, with the backing of the US, quietly began to conduct military operations in Laos, to which North Vietnam and China responded by supporting anti-government insurgency in Thailand.

The more the Thais felt threatened by the spread of communism, the more they looked to the Americans for help – by 1968 around 45,000 US military personnel were on Thai soil, which became the base for US bombing raids against North Vietnam and Laos, and for covert operations into Laos and beyond.

The effects of the **American presence in Thailand** were profound. The economy swelled with dollars, and hundreds of thousands of Thais became reliant on the Americans for a living, with a consequent proliferation of corruption and prostitution. What's more, the sudden exposure to Western culture led many to question the traditional Thai values and the political status quo.

The democracy movement and civil unrest

At the same time, poor farmers were becoming disillusioned with their lot and during the 1960s many turned against the Bangkok government. At the end of 1964, the **Communist Party of Thailand** and other groups formed a **broad left coalition** which soon had the support of several thousand insurgents in remote areas of the northeast. By 1967, the problem had spread to Chiang Rai and Nan provinces, and a separate threat had arisen in southern Thailand, involving **Muslim dissidents** and the Chinese-dominated **Communist Party of Malaya**, as well as local Thais.

Thanom was now facing a major security crisis, especially as the war in Vietnam was going badly. In 1969 he held elections which produced a majority for the government party but, still worried about national stability, the general got cold feet and in November 1971 he reimposed repressive military rule. However, the 1969 experiment with democracy had heightened expectations of power-sharing among the middle classes, especially in the universities. **Student demonstrations** began in June 1973, and in October as many as 500,000 people turned out at Thammasat University in Bangkok to demand a new constitution. Clashes with the police ensued but elements in the army, backed by King Bhumibol, prevented Thanom from crushing the protest with troops. On October 14, 1973, Thanom and Praphas were forced to resign and leave the country.

In a new climate of openness, **Kukrit Pramoj** managed to form a coalition of seventeen elected parties and secured a promise of US withdrawal from Thailand, but his government was riven with feuding. Meanwhile, the king and much of the middle class, alarmed at the unchecked radicalism of the students, began to support new, often violent, right-wing organizations. In October 1976, the students demonstrated again, protesting against the return of Thanom to Thailand to become a monk at Wat Bowonniwet. This time there was no restraint: supported by elements of the military and the government, the police and reactionary students launched a massive assault on Thammasat University. On October 6, hundreds of students were brutally beaten, scores were lynched and some even burnt alive; the military took control and suspended the constitution.

General Prem

Soon after, the military-appointed prime minister, **Thanin Kraivichien**, imposed rigid censorship and forced dissidents to undergo anti-communist indoctrination, but his measures seem to have been too repressive even for the military, who forced him to resign in October 1977. General Kriangsak Chomanand took over, and began to break up the insurgency with shrewd offers of amnesty. His power base was weak, however, and although Kriangsak won the elections of 1979, he was displaced in February 1980 by **General Prem Tinsulanonda**, who was backed by a broad parliamentary coalition.

Untainted by corruption, Prem achieved widespread support, including that of the monarchy, which was to prove crucial. In April 1981, a group of disaffected military officers seized government buildings in Bangkok, forcing Prem to flee the capital. However, the rebels' attempt to mobilize the army was hamstrung by a radio message from Queen Sirikit in support of Prem, who was easily able to retake Bangkok. Parliamentary elections in 1983 returned the military to power and legitimized Prem's rule.

Overseeing a period of strong foreign investment and rapid economic growth, Prem maintained the premiership until 1988, with a unique mixture

Under Prem and successive leaders, Thailand has taken a characteristically pragmatic attitude to the troubles of its neighbours, paying scant attention to world opinion. In 1979, the Vietnamese invaded **Cambodia** to oust the brutal Khmer Rouge, and continued to fight them in the 1980s, crossing into Thailand to attack their bases. In response to this perceived threat to national security, Prem supported and supplied the Khmer Rouge and a wide variety of other Cambodian guerrilla groups sheltering on Thai soil, while backing the United Nations and the Association of Southeast Asian Nations (ASEAN) in their attempts to persuade the Vietnamese to withdraw their troops. These attempts paid off with the 1991 Paris peace accords: Vietnamese forces withdrew, refugees on Thai soil were repatriated, and elections were held in Cambodia in May 1993 under UN auspices. The Khmer Rouge, however, obstructed the peace plan and continued to fight Phnom Penh's shaky coalition government, with Thailand effectively acting as the rebels' main financier and ally – Thai–Khmer Rouge trade in gems and timber, backed by Thai army commanders on the border, at one stage reached over US$1 million dollars a month. A ban on the export of logs from Cambodia, however, went into effect in May 1995, and Thai influence along its southeastern frontier has severely diminished with the break-up of the Khmer Rouge, culminating in the death of Pol Pot in 1998 and the surrender of the last remaining guerrillas in early 1999. Cambodia was allowed to join ASEAN in April 1999, but relations with Thailand remain frosty: Thai businesses continue to be involved in illegal logging and gemmining in Cambodia's border areas, and occasional disputes have flared because of uncertainty over the demarcation of the eight-hundred-kilometre border, which has not been properly surveyed for many years.

Thailand's policy towards **Burma** has been even more contentious. Despite brutal repression by the Burmese military dictatorship (SLORC) of pro-democracy demonstrations in 1988, despite its refusal to hand over power to Aung San Suu Kyi's elected opposition, and despite irrefutable evidence of its heinous human rights abuses, Bangkok has drawn its ASEAN partners into a policy of "constructive engagement" with the military regime in Rangoon, which culminated in Burma's admission to ASEAN in July 1997. This has allowed Thai businessmen and army officers to derive huge benefit from the devastation of Burmese teak forests and the exploitation of fishing grounds and mineral resources. Opposition to Bangkok's stance has come from the US and the European Union, who have imposed extensive sanctions against Burma. Thai ministers have become slightly more critical of the Burmese regime over the last few years, and have tentatively suggested moving away from ASEAN's policy of non-intervention in members' domestic affairs. However, Thailand's main concern has been with a danger to its own social fabric, accusing Burma of flooding it with narcotics: the Burmese military is involved with, or at least aids and abets, the traffickers who pour heroin and an estimated 600 million methamphetamine (*ya baa*) tablets a year over the border into Thailand; while the heroin mostly passes through to Western markets, the *yaa ba* is destined for young Thais. Relations between the two countries reached a low point in 2000, with the Burmese counter-claim that Thailand allowed "terrorists" and other anti-Rangoon elements to operate from its soil, following Thailand's perceived soft response to the seizure of the Burmese embassy in Bangkok (see p.770).

of dictatorship and democracy sometimes called Premocracy: although never standing for parliament himself, Prem was asked by the legislature after every election to become prime minister. He eventually stepped down because, he said, it was time for the country's leader to be chosen from among its elected representatives.

The 1992 demonstrations

Prem's wishes on his resignation in 1988 were respected, and the new prime minister was indeed an elected MP. **Chatichai Choonhavan**, a retired general with a long civilian career in public office, pursued a vigorous policy of economic development, filling his cabinet with businessmen and encouraging rampant foreign investment. The resultant economic boom, however, fostered widespread corruption, in which members of the government were often implicated. Following an economic downturn and Chatichai's attempts to downgrade the political role of the military, the armed forces staged a bloodless **coup** on February 23, 1991, led by Supreme Commander **Sunthorn** and General **Suchinda**, the army commander-in-chief.

Perhaps recognizing that coups were no longer a viable means of seizing power in Thailand, Sunthorn and Suchinda immediately installed a civilian caretaker government, led by a former diplomat, **Anand Panyarachun**, and promised elections within six months. A poll was eventually held on March 22, 1992, but the new constitution permitted the unelected Suchinda to barge his way to the premiership, at the head of a five-party pro-military coalition dubbed the "devils" by the Thai press. Democracy found its supporters in the shape of the four main opposition parties – the "angels" – and organized groups of academics, professionals and social activists; their campaign for the prime minister's resignation centred around **Chamlong Srimuang**, a popular former governor of Bangkok and head of the strongly Buddhist Palang Dharma party, who went on hunger strike. When Suchinda appeared to renege on earlier promises to make democratic amendments to the constitution, including a requirement that the prime minister be an elected MP, hundreds of thousands of ordinary Thais poured onto the streets in **mass demonstrations** between May 17 and 20. Hopelessly misjudging the mood of the country, Suchinda brutally crushed the protests, leaving hundreds dead or injured in the bloodiest chapter in Thai politics since 1976 – official figures proclaimed 52 deaths, but by the end of 1992 as many as two hundred others were still listed as missing. Having justified the massacre on the grounds that he was protecting the king from communist agitators, Suchinda was forced to resign when King Bhumibol expressed his disapproval in a ticking-off that was broadcast on world television. Anand was again invited to form an interim government, and quickly moved to restructure the armed forces.

Chuan's first premiership

Elections scheduled for September 13, 1992, were seen as the acid test – would Thais opt for a democratic form of government, or would they continue to sell their votes to the "traditional" politicians? In the event, vote-buying was still widespread, especially in rural areas, but the "angel" **Democrat Party**, led by **Chuan Leekpai**, a nine-time minister and noted upholder of democracy and the rule of law, gained the largest number of parliamentary seats. Chuan duly became prime minister, at the head of a coalition largely comprised of the parties who had opposed Suchinda's rise to power.

Against the background of a vague programme to spread wealth to rural areas, to provide "social justice for all" and to raise education standards, Chuan's popularity received two shots in the arm in 1994. In the middle of the year, the opposition was discredited when two of its MPs were refused visas to the US, on the grounds that they were suspected of drug trafficking – one of them a former deputy minister who was thought to have been involved in the heroin trade for over twenty years. Then Chuan took decisive action over the **Saudi gems case**, a saga dating back to 1989, when a Thai servant stole twenty million dollars' worth of jewellery from the Jeddah palace of Prince Faisal, son of Saudi Arabia's King Fahd. Back in Thailand, the servant went on a rather obvious spending spree, was arrested and sentenced to two years in prison. The story didn't end there, however: over half of the gems returned to Prince Faisal were found to be fake, and the Thai press enjoyed itself immensely, publishing photos of policemen's and politicians' wives and challenging readers to "spot the real Saudi jewellery". In 1990, three Saudi embassy officials were murdered in Bangkok in mysterious circumstances, almost certainly because of their links to the case. The Thai authorities, however, made no progress in getting to the bottom of the affair, thus souring relations with the Saudis, who put a freeze on visas for Thais wanting to work in their country and banned Saudi tourists from visiting Thailand. When, in July 1994, the wife and son of a Thai gems dealer thought to have handled some of the missing stones were found dead, Chuan stepped in over the heads of the dithering Interior Ministry: two police generals were arrested for ordering the murders, and investigations into three former police chiefs were instigated. Considering the rank of the police officers involved, it seems unlikely that the full facts of the case will ever emerge, but Chuan scored points by being seen to take firm action.

Chuan's reign as the longest-serving democratically elected prime minister in Thai history came to an abrupt end when, in May 1995, Chamlong Srimuang's Palang Dharma party withdrew from the ruling coalition, obliging Chuan to dissolve parliament and call a general election. Ironically, considering his squeaky-clean reputation, Chuan lost the support of Palang Dharma over alleged corruption in his **land reform scheme**. Almost 600,000 families, many of them landless peasants, had been given 4.4 million acres since 1993. However, ten people given free land in Phuket, among them relations of Democrat Party MPs, were not poor farmers but rich businessmen, who received land near the seafront suitable for hotel development.

Banharn and Chavalit

In the election on July 2, 1995, the largest party turned out to be Chart Thai (formerly led by the disgraced Chatichai Choonhavan), with 92 out of 391 seats. Its new leader, **Banharn Silpa-archa**, eventually formed a coalition, heading a seven-party bloc including Palang Dharma. Dubbed a "walking ATM" by the local press, a reference to his reputation for buying votes, Banharn was also known as a decisive go-getter and a wily political strategist.

However, Banharn immediately ran into opposition from the media and middle-class city-dwellers. With many Chart Thai MPs involved in construction businesses, and ministers thought to be more concerned with making money from their positions than running the country, his administration was criticized on the grounds of corruption. Criticism reached a crescendo with a no-confidence debate in parliament in September 1996. Just before the vote, **General Chavalit Yongchaiyudh**, leader of the 57-seat **New Aspiration Party** (NAP), struck a deal with Banharn: the NAP would vote for the prime minister in the no-confidence motion, as long as Banharn would then resign within a week. This Banharn agreed to do, and he duly won the vote, but then pulled the rug out from under Chavalit's feet by dissolving parliament, leaving Chavalit to fight a new election instead of being ushered in as prime minister after Banharn's resignation.

In November, Chavalit just won what was dubbed as the dirtiest election in Thai history, with an estimated 25 million baht spent on vote-buying in rural areas, especially the northeast. Chuan Leekpai's Democrats took 123 seats, among them nearly all of Bangkok, but were pipped by the NAP's 125 seats, which included the majority of the northeast.

Soon after entering office, Chavalit vowed to implement political reform, but when the time came for action, seemed reluctant to approve the proposed **new constitution**. Drawn up by an independent Constitution Drafting Assembly, its main points included: direct elections to the senate, rather than appointment of senators by the prime minister; acceptance of the right of assembly as the basis of a democratic society and guarantees of individual rights and freedoms; greater public accountability; and increased popular participation in local administration. The eventual aim of the new charter was to end the traditional system of patronage, vested interests and vote-buying, and so it did not naturally find favour with Chavalit's supporters – his interior minister, Snoh Thienthong, even went as far as claiming that communists were behind it. However, when the media, business groups and even military leaders came out in favour, Chavalit was obliged to give the new constitution the go-ahead in late 1997.

The economic crisis

At the same time as his post-election vow on political reform, Chavalit pledged to improve the country's financial situation, saying that Thais would "eat and live well". The economy was already on shaky ground, however, and in February 1997 foreign-exchange dealers, alarmed at the size of Thailand's private foreign debt – 250 billion baht owed by the unproductive domestic property sector alone – began to mount speculative **attacks on the baht**, which in turn affected the stock market. The government valiantly defended the pegged exchange rate, spending $23 billion of the country's formerly healthy foreign-exchange reserves, but at the beginning of July was forced to give up the ghost – the baht was floated and soon went into free-fall. Blaming its traditional allies the Americans for neglecting their obligations, Thailand sought help from Japan; Tokyo suggested the **IMF**, who in August put together a **rescue package** for Thailand worth US$17 billion. Among the conditions of the package, the Thai government was to slash the national budget, control inflation and open up financial institutions to foreign ownership.

By this stage, there were fears that the crisis could threaten the country's much-vaunted social stability, yet Chavalit's government was viewed as inept and more concerned with personal interests and political game-playing than managing the economy properly. For weeks Chavalit staunchly ignored demands from all sectors of society for his resignation, but on November 3 he caved in. After some undignified horse-trading, Chuan Leekpai was able to form a six-party coalition government, taking up what was widely seen as a poisoned chalice for his second term.

Chuan's second term

On his return to office, Chuan could at least call on the services of two respected technocrats, finance minister **Tarrin Nimmanhaeminda** and deputy prime minister **Supachai Panichpakdi**, to head his economic team, but the prospects looked bleak. Businesses unable to pay their debts were looking to lay off hundreds of thousands of employees (thousands of office workers, for example, were unemployed because of the suspension of 58 financial companies), and the IMF was keeping the squeeze on the government to implement its austerity measures. In response, Chuan took a hard line to try to restore confidence in the economy: he followed the IMF's advice, which among other things involved maintaining cripplingly high interest rates to protect the baht, and pledged to reform the financial system, including the gradual introduction of new banking regulations. Although this played well abroad, at home the government encountered increasing hostility. With interest rates peaking at twenty percent, the business community was starved of funds, and by the middle of 1998 activity was grinding to a halt. Meanwhile, unemployment, which had been as low as one million before the crisis, edged past two million by mid-1998. Huge numbers of jobless workers were returning to their villages and swelling the ranks of the country's six to eight million people living on the fringes of poverty. Inflation peaked at ten percent, and there were frequent public protests against the IMF.

Although Chuan's popularity was further dented by a series of minor corruption scandals among his coalition partners, by the end of the year his tough stance on the economy was paying off, with the baht stabilizing at just under 40 to the US dollar, and interest rates and inflation starting to fall. Foreign investors slowly began returning to Thailand, and by October 1999 Chuan was confident enough to announce that he was forgoing almost $4 billion of the IMF's planned $17 billion rescue package.

In foreign affairs, Thailand's involvement in **East Timor**, which descended into anarchy after voting for independence from Indonesia in August 1999, signalled a major new departure. Around 1500 Thai troops were sent to the region in support of a large Australian force, proving that the Thai military, so politically powerful and inward-looking up to the early 1990s, was now seeking a greater role in international affairs. It also demonstrated a new willingness by Thailand to become involved in the affairs of other Southeast Asian countries, and in a bizarre situation that arose later that year, Chuan showed he was not afraid to incur the displeasure of neighbouring Burma. On October 1, five student activists **captured the Burmese embassy** in Bangkok, holding forty staff and foreigners hostage. After hours of very public negotiations – during which Deputy Foreign Minister, Sukhumbhand Paribatra, became something of a hero by offering himself as a hostage – the five were taken by Thai helicopter to the Burmese border and dropped inside territory controlled by rebel Karens. Furious at what they saw as favourable treatment of the students, the Burmese military junta closed all land border crossings with Thailand for a while; however, the ensuing cross-border smuggling, if anything, benefited the Thais, while consumer goods in Burma rocketed in price.

The 2001 general election

The year 2000 was dominated by the build-up to the **general election** – Chuan was obliged to disband parliament by November at the latest, but held on for as long as he could, eventually setting the polls for January 6, 2001. It was to be the first such vote held under the 1997 constitution, which was intended, among other things, to take the traditionally crucial role of money, especially for vote-buying, out of politics. However, this election coincided with the emergence of a major new party, **Thai Rak Thai** (Thai Loves Thai), formed by one of Thailand's wealthiest men, telecoms tycoon **Thaksin Shinawatra**.

Although Thaksin denied the money attraction, over one hundred MPs from other parties, including the ruling Democrats, were drawn to Thai Rak Thai as the dissolution of parliament approached. However, in September, the **National Counter-Corruption Commission** announced an investigation into Thaksin's affairs, citing a failure to disclose fully his business interests in a declaration of assets when he joined Chavalit's 1997 government (under the new constitution, ministers can hold no more than a five percent stake in a business). The NCCC also wanted to know how members of Thaksin's household – including his maid, nanny, driver and security guard – came to hold over one billion baht's worth of stock in his businesses.

Campaigning proceeded largely regardless of the investigation, and for a change focused on policies rather than personalities, as had been the norm in Thai politics. While the Democrats reminded the country of their success in saving the country from the economic crisis, Thaksin touted some far more controversial policies: he promised to transfer one trillion baht in banks' non-performing loans into a state-owned asset-management company, and to issue a three-year loan moratorium for perennially indebted farmers; he also promised a one million baht development fund for each of the country's seventy thousand villages. Such proposals were obvious vote-winners, but at no stage did Thaksin reveal in detail where the money would come from.

Despite the prospect of stronger anti-corruption enforcement by the recently formed **Election Commission**, allegations of campaign irregularities had been made against around a hundred candidates even before election day. During the night before the vote, dogs were heard to howl even louder than ever – an election phenomenon Thais attribute to the commotion created by campaign bagmen on last-minute rounds. As expected, Thaksin achieved a sweeping victory, at one stage looking likely to win an unprecedented overall majority in parliament. However, after the Election Commission instigated new polls in 62 constituencies where there had been irregularities in the original vote, his final count came to 248 seats out of a possible 500. (Over a thousand other allegations of electoral fraud were not followed up by the commissioners, who appear to have reined themselves in to ensure their long-term survival.) Thaksin duly entered into a coalition with Chart Thai and New Aspiration, thereby controlling a healthy total of 325 seats.

Instead of a move towards greater democracy, as envisioned by the 1997 constitution, Thaksin's new government seemed to represent a full-blown merger between politics and big business, concentrating economic power in even fewer hands. His first cabinet was a motley crew of old-style vested interests, including former PM Chavalit, credited by many with having sparked Thailand's economic crisis, as deputy premier and defence minister. The regime got off to an inauspicious start: in February 2001, there was a fierce border skirmish near Chiang Rai between the Thai Third Army and the Burmese army, who were seeking to protect the drug trade from which they receive substantial kickbacks. Then in early March, an explosion ripped through a plane at Bangkok airport on which Thaksin was meant to be travelling, killing a member of the cabin crew. At the time of writing, it appears to have been a terrible accident involving an exploding fuel tank, rather than an assassination attempt. As this book went to press, it was announced that Thaksin had been cleared of a corruption charge by a narrow margin of 8–7 in the Constitutional Court.

Art and architecture

Aside from pockets of Hindu-inspired statuary and architecture, the vast majority of historical Thai culture takes its inspiration from Theravada Buddhism and, though the country does have some excellent museums, to understand fully the evolution of Thai art you have to visit its temples. For Thailand's architects and sculptors, the act of creation was an act of merit and a representation of unchanging truths, rather than an act of expression, and thus Thai art history is characterized by broad schools rather than individual names. This section is designed to help make sense of the most common aspects of Thai art and architecture at their various stages of development.

The basics

To appreciate the plethora of temples and religious images in Thailand, and the differences in the creations of different eras, you first need a grasp of the fundamental architectural forms and the iconography of Buddhism and Hinduism.

The wat

The **wat** or Buddhist temple complex has a great range of uses, as home to a monastic community, a place of public worship, a shrine for holy images and a shaded meeting-place for townspeople and villagers. Wat architecture has evolved in ways as various as its functions, but there remain several essential components which have stayed constant for some fifteen centuries.

The most important wat building is the **bot** (sometimes known as the *ubosot*), a term most accurately translated as the "ordination hall". It usually stands at the heart of the compound and is the preserve of the monks: lay people are rarely allowed inside, and it's generally kept locked when not in use. There's only one bot in any wat complex, and often the only way to distinguish it from other temple buildings is by the eight **sema** or boundary stones which always surround it. Positioned at the four corners of the bot and at the cardinal points of the compass, these stone *sema* define the consecrated ground and usually look something like upright gravestones, though they can take many forms. They are often carved all over with symbolic Buddhist scenes or ideograms, and sometimes are even protected within miniature shrines of their own. (One of the best *sema* collections is housed in the National Museum of Khon Kaen.)

Often almost identical to the bot, the **viharn** or assembly hall is for the lay congregation. This is the building tourists are most likely to enter, as it usually contains the wat's principal **Buddha image**, and sometimes two or three minor images as well. Large wats may have several viharns, while strict meditation wats, which don't deal with the laity, may not have one at all.

Thirdly, there's the **chedi** or stupa (known as a **that** in the north), a tower which was originally conceived as a monument to enshrine relics of the Buddha, but has since become a place to contain the ashes of royalty – and anyone else who can afford it. Of all Buddhist structures, the chedi has undergone the most changes and as such is often the most characteristic hallmark of each period (see box on p.205).

Less common wat buildings include the small square **mondop**, usually built to house either a Buddha statue or footprint or to contain holy texts, and the **ho trai**, or scripture library; there are good examples of traditional *ho trai* at

Wat Thung Si Muang in Ubon Ratchathani and at Wat Yai Suwannaram in Phetchaburi.

Buddhist iconography

In the early days of Buddhism, image-making was considered inadequate to convey the faith's abstract philosophies, so the only approved iconography comprised doctrinal **symbols** such as the *Dharmachakra* (Wheel of Law, also known as Wheel of Doctrine or Wheel of Life). Gradually these symbols were displaced by **images of the Buddha**, construed chiefly as physical embodiments of the Buddha's teachings rather than as portraits of the man (see p.784 for more on the life of the Buddha). Sculptors took their guidance from the Pali texts which ordained the Buddha's most common postures (*asanha*) and gestures (*mudra*).

Of the **four postures** – sitting, standing, walking and reclining – the **seated Buddha**, which represents him in meditation, is the most common in Thailand. A popular variation shows the Buddha seated on a coiled serpent, protected by the serpent's hood – a reference to the story about the Buddha meditating during the rainy season, when a serpent offered to raise him off the wet ground and shelter him from the storms. The **reclining** pose symbolizes the Buddha entering Nirvana at his death, while the **standing** and **walking** images both represent his descent from Tavatimsa heaven.

The most common **hand gestures** include: *Dhyana Mudra* (Meditation), in which the hands rest on the lap, palms upwards; *Bhumisparsa Mudra* (Calling the Earth to Witness, a reference to the Buddha resisting temptation), with the left hand upturned in the lap and the right-hand fingers resting on the right knee and pointing to the earth; *Vitarkha Mudra* (Teaching), with one or both hands held at chest height with the thumb and forefinger touching; and *Abhaya Mudra* (Dispelling Fear), showing the right hand (occasionally both hands) raised in a flat-palmed "stop" gesture.

All three-dimensional Buddha images are objects of reverence, but some are more esteemed than others. Some are alleged to have displayed human attributes or reacted in some way to unusual events, others have performed miracles, or are simply admired for their beauty, their phenomenal size or even their material value – if made of solid gold or of jade, for example. Most Thais are familiar with these exceptional images, all of which have been given special names, always prefixed by the honorific "Phra", and many of which have spawned thousands of miniaturized copies in the form of amulets. Pilgrimages are made to see the most famous originals.

It was in the Sukhothai era that the craze for producing **Buddha footprints** really took off. Harking back to the time when images were allusive rather than representative, these footprints were generally moulded from stucco to depict the 108 auspicious signs or *lakshanas* (which included references to the sixteen Buddhist heavens, the traditional four great continents and seven great rivers and lakes) and housed in a special mondop. Few of the Sukhothai prints remain, but Ayutthaya-Ratanakosin-era examples are found all over the country, the most famous being Phra Phutthabat near Lopburi, the object of pilgrimages throughout the year. The feet of the famous Reclining Buddha in Bangkok's Wat Po are also inscribed with the 108 *lakshanas*, beautifully depicted in mother-of-pearl inlay.

Hindu iconography

Hindu images tend to be a lot livelier than Buddhist ones, partly because there is a panoply of gods to choose from, and partly because these gods have

Once you've recognized the main characters of the Hindu pantheon, you'll want to know what they're up to in the murals and reliefs that ornament temple walls and ceilings. Of the hundreds of different episodes featured in as many interpretations by painters and sculptors – many taken from the *Ramayana* and *Mahabharata* – the following recur frequently.

The Churning of the Sea of Milk (in situ at Khao Phra Viharn and in reproduction at Ayutthaya's Historical Study Centre). A creation myth in which Vishnu appears in his second, tortoise, incarnation. The legend describes how the cosmic ocean (or "milk") was churned with a sacred inverted conical mountain to create the universes and all things in them ("the butter"). A *naga* was used as the churning rope, and the holy tortoise offered his shell to support the mountain – an image which gave rise to the notion of tortoise as the base and foundation stone of the world. The churning also produced a sacred nectar of immortality, which both the gods and the demons were keen to consume. Vishnu craftily encouraged the demons to hold the head-end of the *naga* rope while helping to make this nectar, giving the gods the tail-end, and encouraging the demons to drink the liquid at its early, alcoholic stage; the friction of the process caused the *naga* to heat up and breathe fire, burning the demons, who by this stage were so intoxicated that they promptly fell asleep, leaving the distilled nectar for the gods.

Reclining Vishnu Asleep on the Milky Sea of Eternity (the most accessible lintels at Phanom Rung, in the National Museum in Bangkok and at Wat Phra That Narai Cheng Weng near Sakhon Nakhon). Another common creation myth, this time featuring Vishnu as four-armed deity (sometimes referred to as Phra Narai), sleepily reclining on a *naga*, here representing the Milky Sea of Eternity. Vishnu is dreaming of creating a new universe, shown by the lotus blossoms which spring from his navel, and the four-faced god Brahma who perches atop them; as "Creator", Brahma will be responsible for putting this dream into practice.

Krishna Lifting Mount Govadhana (lintel at Phimai). A story of godly rivalry, in which a community of worshippers suddenly transferred allegiance from the god Indra to the interloping Krishna. Indra, the god of the elements, was so incensed that he attacked the turncoats with a raging storm; they called on Krishna for help, and he obliged by lifting up the mighty Mount Govadhana to provide an enormous umbrella.

The Dance of Shiva or Shiva's Dance of Destruction (at Phimai, Phanom Rung, Khao Phra Viharn and Wat Phra That Narai Cheng Weng near Sakhon Nakhon). A very powerful and highly symbolic image in which the multi-armed Shiva, as Nataraja, performs a wild, ecstatic dance that brings about the total destruction (through fire) of the extant world and replaces it with a new epoch (as represented by a double-sided drum). In the northeastern Khmer temples this dance is a fairly common subject of stone reliefs, nearly always set as a lintel above a major gateway into the sanctuary.

How Ganesh Came to Have an Elephant's Head. At the time of Ganesh's birth, his father, Shiva, happened to be away from home. On returning to his wife's apartments, Shiva was enraged to find a strange young man in Parvati's boudoir and rashly decapitated the youth. Of course, the boy turned out to be Ganesh, Shiva's own son; full of remorse, the god immediately despatched a servant to procure the head of the first living being he encountered so that his son could be restored to life. The servant returned with an elephant's head, which is why this endearing Hindu god has the pot-bellied body of a child and the head of a young elephant. An alternative version of the tale has Shiva overreacting after his baby son's cries woke him from a particularly pleasant daydream.

© CONTEXTS | Art and architecture

mischievous personalities and reappear in all sorts of bizarre incarnations. Central to the Hindu philosophy is the certainty that any object can be viewed as the temporal residence, embodiment or symbol of the deity; thus its iconography includes abstract representations (such as the phallic lingam for Shiva) as well as figurative images. Though pure Hinduism receded from Thailand with the collapse of the Khmers, the iconography has endured, as Buddhist Thais have incorporated some Hindu and Brahmin concepts into the national belief system and have continued to create statues of the three chief Hindu deities – Brahma, Vishnu and Shiva – as well as using lesser mythological beasts in modern designs.

Vishnu has always been especially popular: his role of "Preserver" has him embodying the status quo, representing both stability and the notion of altruistic love. He is most often depicted as the deity, but frequently crops up in other human and animal incarnations. There are ten of these manifestations in all, of which **Rama** (number seven) is by far the most popular in Thailand. The epitome of ideal manhood, Rama is the super-hero of the epic story the *Ramayana* (see box on p.125) and appears in storytelling reliefs and murals in every Hindu temple in Thailand; in painted portraits you can usually recognize him by his green face. Manifestation number eight is **Krishna**, more widely known than Rama in the West, but slightly less common in Thailand. Krishna is usually characterized as a flirtatious, flute-playing, blue-skinned cowherd whose most famous achievement is the lifting of Mount Govadhana (as depicted in relief at Phimai; see box on p.775), but he is also a crucial moral figure in the *Mahabharata*. Confusingly, Vishnu's ninth avatar is the **Buddha** – a manifestation adopted many centuries ago to minimize defection to the Buddhist faith. When represented as **the deity**, Vishnu is generally shown sporting a crown and four arms, his hands holding a conch shell (whose music wards off demons), a discus (used as a weapon), a club (symbolizing the power of nature and time), and a lotus (symbol of joyful flowering and renewal). The god is often depicted astride a **garuda**, a half-man, half-bird. Even without Vishnu on its back, the garuda is a very important beast – a symbol of strength, it's often shown "supporting" temple buildings.

Statues and representations of **Brahma** (the Creator) are very rare. Confusingly, he too has four arms, but you should recognize him by the fact that he holds no objects, has four faces (sometimes painted red), and is generally borne by a goose-like creature called a *hamsa*.

Shiva (the Destroyer) is the most volatile member of the pantheon. He stands for extreme behaviour, for beginnings and endings (as enacted in his frenzied Dance of Destruction, described in the box on p.775), and for fertility, and is a symbol of great energy and power. His godlike form typically has four, eight or ten arms, sometimes holding a trident (representing creation, protection and destruction) and a drum (to beat the rhythm of creation). In his most famous role, as **Nataraja**, or Lord of the Dance, he is usually shown in stylized standing position with legs bent into a balletic position, and the full complement of arms outstretched above his head. Three stripes on a figure's forehead also indicate Shiva, or one of his followers. In abstract form, he is represented by a **lingam** or phallic pillar (once found at the heart of every Khmer temple in the northeast). Primarily a symbol of energy and godly power, the lingam also embodies fertility, particularly when set upright in a vulva-shaped vessel known as a **yoni**. The yoni doubles as a receptacle for the holy water that worshippers pour over the lingam.

Close associates of Shiva include **Parvati**, his wife, and **Ganesh**, his elephant-headed son (the story of how Ganesh came to look as he does is explained in the box on p.775). Depictions of Ganesh abound, both as statues and, because he is the god of knowledge and overcomer of obstacles (in the path of learning), as the symbol of the Fine Arts Department – which crops up on all entrance tickets to museums and historical parks.

The royal, three-headed elephant, **Erawan**, usually only appears as the favourite mount of the god **Indra**, who is rather unremarkable without the beast but generally figures as the king of the gods, with specific power over the elements (particularly rain) – four statues of the god and his mount grace the base of the *prang* at Bangkok's Wat Arun.

Lesser mythological figures, which originated as Hindu symbols but feature frequently in wats and other Buddhist contexts, include the **yaksha** giants who ward off evil spirits (like the enormous freestanding ones guarding Bangkok's Wat Phra Kaeo); the graceful half-woman, half-bird **kinnari**; and finally, the ubiquitous **naga**, or serpent king of the underworld – often the proud owner of as many as seven heads, whose reptilian body most frequently appears as staircase balustrades in Hindu and Buddhist temples.

The schools

In the 1920s art historians and academics began compiling a classification system for Thai art and architecture which was modelled along the lines of the country's historical periods – these are the guidelines followed below. The following brief overview starts in the sixth century, when Buddhism began to take a hold on the country; few examples of art from before that time have survived, and there are no known earlier architectural relics.

Dvaravati (sixth–eleventh centuries)

Centred around Nakhon Pathom, U Thong and Lopburi in the Chao Phraya basin and in the smaller northern enclave of Haripunjaya (modern-day Lamphun), the **Dvaravati** state was populated by Theravada Buddhists who were strongly influenced by Indian culture.

Only one, fairly late, known example of a Dvaravati-era **building** remains standing: the pyramidal laterite chedi in the compound of Lamphun's Wat Kukut, which is divided into five tiers with niches for stucco Buddha images on each row. Dvaravati-era **artefacts** are much more common, and the national museums in Nakhon Pathom and Lamphun both house quite extensive collections of Buddha images from that period. In an effort to combat the defects inherent in the poor-quality limestone at their disposal, sculptors made their Buddhas quite stocky, cleverly dressing the figures in a sheet-like drape that dropped down to ankle level from each raised wrist, forming a U-shaped hemline – a style which they used when casting in bronze as well. Nonetheless many **statues** have cracked, leaving them headless or limbless. Where the faces have survived, Dvaravati statues display some of the most naturalistic features ever produced in Thailand, distinguished by their thick lips, flattened noses and wide cheekbones.

Nakhon Pathom, a target of Buddhist missionaries from India since before the first century AD, has also yielded a substantial hoard of **dharmachakra**, originating in the period when the Buddha could not be directly represented. These metre-high carved stone wheels symbolize the cycles of life and reincarnation, and in Dvaravati examples are often accompanied by a small statue of a deer, which refers to the Buddha preaching his first sermon in a deer park.

Srivijaya (eighth–thirteenth centuries)

While Dvaravati's Theravada Buddhists were influencing the central plains and, to a limited extent, areas further to the north, southern Thailand was paying allegiance to the Mahayana Buddhists of the **Srivijayan** empire. The key distinction between Theravada and Mahayana strands of thought is that Mahayanists believe that those who have achieved enlightenment should postpone their entry into Nirvana in order to help others along the way. These stay-behinds, revered like saints both during and after life, are called **bodhisattva**, and **statues** of them were the mainstay of Srivijayan art.

The finest Srivijayan *bodhisattva* statues were cast in bronze and show such grace and sinuosity that they rank among the finest sculpture ever produced in the country. Usually shown in the **tribunga**, or hipshot pose, with right hip thrust out and left knee bent, many are lavishly adorned, and some were even bedecked in real jewels when first made. By far the most popular *bodhisattva* subject was **Avalokitesvara**, worshipped as compassion incarnate. Generally shown with four or more arms and with an animal skin over the left shoulder or tied at the waist, Avalokitesvara is also sometimes depicted with his torso covered in tiny Buddha images. Bangkok's National Museum holds the most beautiful Avalokitesvara, found in Chaiya; most of the other best Srivijayan sculptures have been snapped up by Bangkok's curators as well.

As for Srivijayan **temples**, quite a number have been built over, and so are unviewable. The most typical intact example is the Javanese-style chedi at Chaiya's Wat Phra Boromathat, heavily restored but distinguished from contemporaneous Dvaravati structures by its highly ornamented stepped chedi, with mini chedis at each corner.

Khmer and Lopburi (tenth–fourteenth centuries)

By the end of the ninth century the **Khmers** of Cambodia were starting to expand from their capital at Angkor into the Dvaravati states, bringing with them the Hindu faith and the cult of the god-king (*devaraja*). As lasting testaments to the sacred power of their kings, the Khmers built hundreds of imposing stone **sanctuaries** across their newly acquired territory: the two top examples are both in southern Isaan, at Phimai and Phanom Rung, though there is also an interesting early one at Muang Singh near Kanchanaburi.

Each magnificent castle-temple – known in Khmer as a **prasat** – was constructed primarily as a shrine for a Shiva lingam, the phallic representation of the god Shiva. They followed a similar pattern, centred on at least one towering structure, or **prang**, which represented Mount Meru (the gods' heavenly abode), and surrounded by concentric rectangular enclosures, within and beyond which were dug artificial lakes and moats – miniature versions of the primordial ocean dividing heaven from earth.

The prasats' most fascinating and superbly crafted features, however, are the **carvings** that ornament almost every surface. Usually gouged from sandstone, but frequently moulded in stucco, these exuberant reliefs depict Hindu deities, incarnations and stories, especially episodes from the *Ramayana* (see box on p.125). Towards the end of the twelfth century, the Khmer leadership became Mahayana Buddhist, commissioning Buddhist carvings to be installed alongside the Hindu ones, and simultaneously replacing the Shiva lingam at the heart of each sanctuary with a Buddha or *bodhisattva* image. (See p.473 for more on the architectural details.)

The temples built in the former Theravada Buddhist principality of **Lopburi** during the Khmer period are much smaller affairs than those in Isaan, and are best represented by the triple-pranged temple of Phra Prang Sam Yot. The Lopburi classification is most usually applied to the Buddha statues that emerged at the tail end of the Khmer period, picking up the Dvaravati sculptural legacy. Broad-faced and muscular, the classic Lopburi Buddha wears a diadem or ornamental headband – a nod to the Khmers' ideological fusion of earthly and heavenly power – and the *ushnisha* (the sign of enlightenment) becomes distinctly conical rather than a mere bump on the head. Early Lopburi Buddhas come garlanded with necklaces and ornamental belts; later examples eschew the jewels. As you'd expect, Lopburi National Museum houses a good selection.

Sukhothai (thirteenth–fifteenth centuries)

Capitalizing on the Khmers' weakening hold over central Thailand, two Thai generals established the first real Thai kingdom in **Sukhothai** in 1238, and over the next two hundred years the artists of this realm produced some of Thailand's most refined art. Sukhothai's artistic reputation rests above all on its **sculpture**. More sinuous even than the Srivijayan images, Sukhothai Buddhas tend towards elegant androgyny, with slim oval faces that show little of the humanistic Dvaravati features or the strength of Lopburi statues, and slender curvaceous bodies usually clad in a plain, skintight robe that fastens with a tassel close to the navel (see box on p.265). The sculptors favoured the seated pose, with hands in the *Bhumisparsa Mudra*, most expertly executed in the Phra Buddha Chinnarat image, now housed in Phitsanulok's Wat Si Ratana Mahathat (replicated at Bangkok's Wat Benjamabophit) and in the enormous Phra Sri Sakyamuni, now enshrined in Bangkok's Wat Suthat. They were also the first to represent the **walking Buddha**, a supremely graceful figure with his right leg poised to move forwards and his left arm in the *Vitarkha Mudra*, as seen in the compounds of Sukhothai's Wat Sra Si.

The cities of Sukhothai and nearby Si Satchanalai were already stamped with sturdy relics of the Khmers' presence, but rather than pull down the sacred prangs of their predecessors, Sukhothai builders added bots, viharns and chedis to the existing structures, as well as conceiving quite separate **temple complexes**. Their viharns and bots are the earliest halls of worship still standing in Thailand (the Khmers didn't go in for large public assemblies), but in most cases only the stone pillars and their platforms remain, the wooden roofs having long since disintegrated. The best examples can be seen in the historical park at Sukhothai, with less grandiose structures at the parks in nearby Si Satchanalai and Kamphaeng Phet.

Most of the **chedis**, though, are in much better shape. Many were modelled on the Sri Lankan bell-shaped reliquary tower (symbolizing the Buddha's teachings ringing out far and wide), often set atop a one- or two-tiered square base surrounded by elephant buttresses – Si Satchanalai's Wat Chang Lom is a stylish example. The architects also devised a new type of chedi, as elegant in its way as the images their sculptor colleagues were producing. This was the **lotus-bud chedi**, a slender tower topped with a tapered finial that was to become a hallmark of the Sukhothai era. In Sukhothai both Wat Mahathat and Wat Trapang Ngoen display good examples.

Ancient Sukhothai is also renowned for the skill of its potters, who produced a **ceramic ware** known as Sawankhalok, after the name of one of the nearby kiln towns. Most museum ceramics collections are dominated by Sawankhalok ware, which is distinguished by its grey-green celadon glazes and by the fish and chrysanthemum motifs used to decorate bowls and plates.

Lanna (thirteenth–sixteenth centuries)

Meanwhile, to the north of Sukhothai, the independent Theravada Buddhist kingdom of Lanna was flourishing. Its art styles – known interchangeably as Chiang Saen and Lanna – evolved from an eclectic range of precursors, building on the Dvaravati heritage of Haripunjaya, copying direct from Indian sources and incorporating Sukhothai and Sri Lankan ideas from the south.

The earliest surviving Lanna **monument** is the Dvaravati-style Chedi Si Liem in Chiang Mai, built to the pyramidal form characteristic of Mon builders in fairly close imitation of the much earlier Wat Kukut in Lampang. Also in Chiang Mai, Wat Jet Yot replicates the temple built at Bodh Gaya in India to commemorate the seven sites where the Buddha meditated in the first seven weeks after attaining enlightenment – hence the symbolic seven pyramidal chedis, and hence also the name, which means "the temple of seven spires".

Lanna **sculpture** also drew some inspiration from Bodh Gaya: the early Lanna images tend to plumpness, with broad shoulders and prominent hair curls, which are all characteristics of the main Buddha at Bodh Gaya. The later works are slimmer, probably as a result of Sukhothai influence, and one of the most famous examples of this type is the Phra Singh Buddha, enshrined in Chiang Mai's Wat Phra Singh. Other good illustrations of both styles are housed in Chiang Mai's National Museum.

Ayutthaya (fourteenth–eighteenth centuries)

Although the Sukhothai era was artistically fertile, the kingdom had only a short political life and from 1351 Thailand's central plains came under the thrall of a new power centred on **Ayutthaya** and ruled by a former prince of Lopburi. Over the next four centuries, the Ayutthayan capital became one of the most prosperous and ostentatious cities in Asia, its rulers commissioning some four hundred grand wats as symbols of their wealth and power. Though essentially Theravada Buddhists, the kings also adopted some Hindu and Brahmin beliefs from the Khmers – most significantly the concept of *devaraja* or god-kingship, whereby the monarch became a mediator between the people and the Hindu gods. The religious buildings and sculptures of this era reflected this new composite ideology, both by fusing the architectural styles inherited from the Khmers and from Sukhothai and by dressing their Buddhas to look like regents.

Retaining the concentric layout of the typical Khmer **temple complex**, Ayutthayan builders played around with the component structures, most notably the prang, which they refined and elongated into a **corncob-shaped tower**, rounding it off at the top and introducing vertical incisions around its circumference. As a spire they often added a bronze thunderbolt, and into niches within the prang walls they placed Buddha images. In Ayutthaya itself, the ruined complexes of Wat Phra Mahathat and Wat Ratburana both include these corncob prangs, but the most famous example is Bangkok's Wat Arun, which though built during the subsequent Bangkok period is a classic Ayutthayan structure.

Ayutthaya's architects also adapted the Sri Lankan **chedi** so favoured by their Sukhothai predecessors, stretching the bell-shaped base and tapering it into a very graceful conical spire, as at Wat Sri Sanphet in Ayutthaya. The **viharns** of this era are characterized by walls pierced by slit-like windows, designed to foster a mysterious atmosphere by limiting the amount of light inside the building. As with all of Ayutthaya's buildings, few viharns survived the brutal 1767 sacking, with the notable exception of Wat Na Phra Mane. Phitsanulok's Wat Phra Ratana Si Mahathat was built to a similar plan – and in Phetchaburi, Wat Yai Suwannaram has no windows at all.

From Sukhothai's Buddha **sculptures** the Ayutthayans copied the soft oval face, adding an earthlier demeanour to the features and imbuing them with an hauteur in tune with the *devaraja* ideology. Like the Lopburi images, early

Ayutthayan statues wear crowns to associate kingship with Buddhahood; as the court became ever more lavish, so these figures became increasingly adorned, until – as in the monumental bronze at Wat Na Phra Mane – they appeared in earrings, armlets, anklets, bandoliers and coronets. The artists justified these luscious portraits of the Buddha – who was, after all, supposed to have given up worldly possessions – by pointing to an episode when the Buddha transformed himself into a well-dressed nobleman to gain the ear of a proud emperor, whereupon he scolded the man into entering the monkhood.

While a couple of wats in Sukhothai show hints of painted decoration, religious **painting** in Thailand really dates from the Ayutthayan era. Unfortunately most of Ayutthaya's own paintings were destroyed in 1767 and others have suffered badly from damp, but several temples in other parts of the country still have some well-preserved murals, in particular Wat Yai Suwannaram in Phetchaburi. By all accounts typical of late seventeenth-century painting, Phetchaburi's murals depict rows of *thep*, or divinities, paying homage to the Buddha, in scenes presented without shadow or perspective, and mainly executed in dark reds and cream.

Ratanakosin (eighteenth century to the 1930s)

When **Bangkok** emerged as Ayutthaya's successor in 1782, the new capital's founder was determined to revive the old city's grandeur, and the **Ratanakosin** (or Bangkok) period began by aping what the Ayutthayans had done. Since then neither wat architecture nor religious sculpture has evolved much further.

The first Ratanakosin **building** was the bot of Bangkok's Wat Phra Kaeo, built to enshrine the Emerald Buddha. Designed to a typical Ayutthayan plan, it's coated in glittering mirrors and gold leaf, with roofs ranged in multiple tiers and tiled in green and orange. To this day, most newly built bots and viharns follow a more economical version of this paradigm, whitewashing the outside walls but decorating the pediment in gilded ornaments and mosaics of coloured glass. Tiered temple roofs – an Ayutthayan innovation of which few examples remain in that city – still taper off into the slender bird-like finials called *chofa*, and naga staircases – a Khmer feature inherited by Ayutthaya – have become an almost obligatory feature of any major temple. The result is that modern wats are often almost indistinguishable from each other, though Bangkok does have a few exceptions, including Wat Benjamabophit, which uses marble cladding for its walls and incorporates Victorian-style stained-glass windows, and Wat Rajabophit, which is covered all over in Chinese ceramics. The most dramatic chedi of the Ratanokosin era – the tallest in the world – was constructed in the mid-nineteenth century in Nakhon Pathom to the original Sri Lankan style, but minus the elephant buttresses found in Sukhothai.

Early Ratanakosin sculptors produced adorned **Buddha images** very much in the Ayutthayan vein, sometimes adding real jewels to the figures, and more modern images are notable for their ugliness rather than for any radical departure from type. The obsession with size, first apparent in the Sukhothai period, has plumbed new depths, with graceless concrete statues up to 60m high becoming the norm (as in Roi Et's Wat Burapha), a monumentalism made worse by the routine application of browns and dull yellows. Most small images are cast from or patterned on older models, mostly Sukhothai or Ayutthayan in origin.

Painting has fared much better, with the *Ramayana* murals in Bangkok's Wat Phra Kaeo (see p.124) a shining example of how Ayutthayan techniques and traditional subject matters could be adapted into something fantastic, imaginative and beautiful.

Contemporary

Following the democratization of Thailand in the 1930s, artists increasingly became recognized as individuals, and took to signing their work for the first time. In 1933 the first school of fine art (now Bangkok's Silpakorn University) was established under the Italian sculptor Corrado Feroci, designer of the capital's Democracy Monument, and, as the new generation experimented with secular themes and styles adapted from the Western Impressionist, Post-impressionist and Cubist movements, later embracing Abstraction and Expressionism, Thai art began to look a lot more **"modern"**. Aside from a period during the 1970s, when massive political upheaval forced artists to address issues of social injustice and authoritarian rule, the leading artistic preoccupation of the past seventy years has been Thailand's spiritual heritage, with nearly every major figure on the contemporary art scene tackling religious issues at some point. For some artists this has meant a straightforward modernization of Buddhist legends or a reworking of particular symbols, while others have sought to dramatize the moral relevance of their religion in the light of political, social and philosophical trends.

Bangkok has a near-monopoly on Thailand's **art galleries**. While the permanent collections at the National Gallery are disappointing, regular exhibitions of more challenging contemporary work appear at both the Silpakorn University Art Gallery and the Queen Sirikit Convention Centre, as well as at a host of smaller gallery spaces dotted around the city. The listings magazine *Bangkok Metro* prints details of current exhibitions, and does features on prominent artists too. The headquarters of Bangkok's major banks and securities' companies also display works by modern Thai artists both established and lesser known, and in recent years have made a big show of backing substantial art prizes. For a preview of works by Thailand's best modern artists, visit the Rama IX Art Museum Foundation's Web site at ⊕www.rama9art.org.

One of the first modern artists to adapt traditional styles and themes was **Angkarn Kalayanapongsa**, whose most public work can be seen in temple murals such as those at Wat Sri Khom Kham in Phayao (see p.377). Characteristic of this aspect of Angkarn's work is the fusion of the elegant, two-dimensional styles of Ayutthayan mural painting (of which few original examples remain) with a surrealistic, dreamlike quality. Many of his paintings feature casts of *khon*-like figures and flying *thep* decked out with gilded crowns and ornamental armlets, anklets and necklaces in a setting studded with symbols from both Buddhism and contemporary culture.

Aiming for the more secular environments of the gallery and the private home, **Pichai Nirand** rejects the traditional mural style and makes more selective choices of Buddhist imagery, appropriating religious objects and icons and reinterpreting their significance. He's particularly well known for his fine-detail canvases of Buddha footprints, many of which can be seen in Bangkok galleries and public spaces.

Pratuang Emjaroen is probably most famous for his social commentary, as epitomized by his huge and powerful canvas *Dharma and Adharma; The Days of Disaster*, which he painted in response to the vicious clashes between the military and students in 1973. The 5m x 2m picture depicts images of severed limbs, screaming faces and bloody gun barrels amid shadowy images of the Buddha's face, a spiked *dharmachakra* and other religious symbols. Although it doesn't belong to any public collection, it is occasionally loaned to galleries around Thailand, as are many of Pratuang's other works, many of which discuss the theme of social injustice and display the artist's trademark use of strong shafts of light and bold colour.

The anti-democratic policies which climaxed in the violence of May 1992 (see p.767) have been addressed by **Vasan Sitthiket**, who exhibited a collection of expressionistic, childlike portraits of "sinners" in a show called "Inferno" in June of the same year, disingenuously claiming that his theme was the Buddhist Tosachat (the last ten lives of the Buddha). Currently one of Thailand's most outspoken and iconoclastic artists, he continues to highlight the tensions of modern Thai life, and to expose the hypocrisies of establishment figures such as monks, politicians and military leaders. His uncompromising pictures are shown at large and small galleries around the capital, though some still find him too hot to handle – like the curators at a Chulalongkorn University show in 2000 who asked him to withdraw some of his works at the last minute due to their politically inflammatory tone; Vasan responded by immediately filling the space with a provocative but accessible piece of performance art, a medium which has become his new and equally distinctive calling card.

Longer established, and only a little less controversial, **Thawan Duchanee** has tended to examine the spiritual tensions of modern life. His juxtaposition of religious icons with fantastical Bosch-like characters and explicitly sexual images prompted a group of fundamentalist students to slash ten of his early paintings in 1971 – an unprecedented reaction to a work of Thai art. Undaunted, Thawan has continued to produce challenging work, including interpretations of the *Ramayana*, the *Jataka* and the *Tri Phum*, in a bid to manifest the individual's struggles against the obstacles that dog the Middle Way, prominent among them lust and violence. In the last few years he has taken up a number of commissions from banks and car manufacturers, which has led to his being criticized by other artists for compromising his artistic integrity.

Jarassri Roopkamdee is renowned for her expressionist woodcut paintings, many of which deal with relationships and the everyday dramas of normal life; her work gets shown quite regularly in Bangkok galleries. She describes one of her most famous pieces, *Drunkards,* as being a depiction of the way men turn into monsters when they get drunk "causing car accidents, demanding sex". With its distorted, howling mouths, warped faces and sombre colours, *Remind of the Loving Time* is another yelp of pain, inspired by the artist's own family history. Jarassri divides her time between Thailand and Germany. Another of Thailand's top contemporary women artists, **Pinaree Santipak** also zooms in on gender roles, using paintings and multimedia pieces to re-examine traditional attitudes as in her 1999 show in Bangkok, Womanly Bodies.

Religion: Thai Buddhism

Over ninety percent of Thais consider themselves Theravada Buddhists, followers of the teachings of a holy man usually referred to as the Buddha (Enlightened One), though more precisely known as Gautama Buddha to distinguish him from three lesser-known Buddhas who preceded him, and from the fifth and final Buddha who is predicted to arrive in the year 4457 AD. Theravada Buddhism is one of the two main schools of Buddhism practised in Asia, and in Thailand it has absorbed an eclectic assortment of animist and Hindu elements into its beliefs as well. The other ten percent of Thailand's population comprises Mahayana Buddhists, Muslims, Hindus, Sikhs and Christians.

The Buddha: his life and beliefs

Buddhists believe that Gautama Buddha was the five-hundredth incarnation of a single being: the stories of these five hundred lives, collectively known as the **Jataka**, provide the inspiration for much Thai art. (Hindus also accept Gautama Buddha into their pantheon, perceiving him as the ninth manifestation of their god Vishnu.)

In his last incarnation he was born in Nepal as **Prince Gautama Siddhartha** in either the sixth or seventh century BC, the son of a king and his hitherto barren wife, who finally became pregnant only after having a dream that a white elephant had entered her womb. At the time of his birth astrologers predicted that Gautama was to become universally respected, either as a worldly king or as a spiritual saviour, depending on which way of life he pursued. Much preferring the former idea, the prince's father forbade anyone to let the boy out of the palace grounds, and took it upon himself to educate Gautama in all aspects of the high life. Most statues of the Buddha depict him with elongated earlobes, which is a reference to this early pampered existence, when he would have worn heavy precious stones in his ears.

The prince married and became a father, but at the age of 29 he flouted his father's authority and sneaked out into the world beyond the palace. On this fateful trip he encountered successively an old man, a sick man, a corpse and a hermit, and thus for the first time was made aware that pain and suffering were intrinsic to human life. Contemplation seemed the only means of discovering why this should be so – and therefore Gautama decided to leave the palace and become a **Hindu ascetic**.

For six or seven years he wandered the countryside leading a life of self-denial and self-mortification, but failed to come any closer to the answer. Eventually concluding that the best course of action must be to follow a "Middle Way" – neither indulgent nor over-ascetic – Gautama sat down beneath the famous riverside bodhi tree at **Bodh Gaya** in India, facing the rising sun, to meditate until he achieved enlightenment. For 49 days he sat cross-legged in the "lotus position", contemplating the causes of suffering and wrestling with temptations that materialized to distract him. Most of these were sent by **Mara**, the Evil One, who was finally subdued when Gautama summoned the earth goddess **Mae Toranee** by pointing the fingers of his right hand at the ground – the gesture known as *Bhumisparsa Mudra*, which has been immortalized by hundreds of Thai sculptors. Mae Toranee wrung torrents of water from her hair and engulfed Mara's demonic emissaries in a flood, an episode that also features in several sculptures and paintings, most famously in the statue in Bangkok's Sanam Luang.

Temptations dealt with, Gautama soon came to attain **enlightenment** and so become a Buddha. As the place of his enlightenment, the **bodhi tree** (or bo tree) has assumed special significance for Buddhists: not only does it appear in many Buddhist paintings and a few sculptures, but there's often a real bodhi tree (*ficus religiosa*) planted in temple compounds as well. Furthermore, the bot is nearly always built facing either a body of water or facing east (preferably both).

The Buddha preached his **first sermon** in a deer park in India, where he characterized his Dharma (doctrine) as a wheel. From this episode comes the early Buddhist symbol the **Dharmachakra**, known as the Wheel of Law, Wheel of Doctrine or Wheel of Life, which is often accompanied by a statue of a deer. Thais celebrate this first sermon with a public holiday in July known as Asanha Puja. On another occasion 1250 people spontaneously gathered to hear the Buddha speak, an event remembered in Thailand as Maha Puja and marked by a public holiday in February.

For the next forty-odd years the Buddha travelled the region converting non-believers and performing miracles. One rainy season he even ascended into the Tavatimsa heaven (Heaven of the thirty-three gods) to visit his mother and to preach the doctrine to her. His descent from this heaven is quite a common theme of paintings and sculptures, and the **Standing Buddha** pose of numerous Buddha statues comes from this story. He also went back to his father's palace where he was temporarily reunited with his wife and child: the Khon Kaen museum houses a particularly lovely carving of this event.

The Buddha "died" at the age of eighty on the banks of a river at Kusinarí in India – an event often dated to 543 BC, which is why the Thai calendar is 543 years out of synch with the Western one, so that the year 2004 AD becomes 2547 BE (Buddhist Era). Lying on his side, propping up his head on his hand, the Buddha passed into **Nirvana** (giving rise to another classic pose, the Reclining Buddha), the unimaginable state of nothingness which knows no suffering and from which there is no reincarnation. Buddhists believe that the day the Buddha entered Nirvana was the same date on which he was born and on which he achieved enlightenment, a triply significant day that Thais honour with the Visakha Puja festival in May.

Buddhist doctrine

After the Buddha entered Nirvana, his **doctrine** spread relatively quickly across India, and probably was first promulgated in Thailand in about the third century BC. His teachings, the *Tripitaka*, were written down in the Pali language – a derivative of Sanskrit – in a form that became known as Theravada, or "The Doctrine of the Elders".

As taught by the Buddha, **Theravada Buddhism** built on the Hindu theory of perpetual reincarnation in the pursuit of perfection, introducing the notion of life as a cycle of suffering which could only be transcended by enlightened beings able to free themselves from earthly ties and enter into the blissful state of Nirvana. For the well-behaved but unenlightened Buddhist, each reincarnation marks a move up a vague kind of ladder, with animals at the bottom, women figuring lower down than men, and monks coming at the top – a hierarchy complicated by the very pragmatic notion that the more comfortable your lifestyle the higher your spiritual status.

The Buddhist has no hope of enlightenment without acceptance of the **four noble truths**. In encapsulated form, these hold that desire is the root cause of all suffering and can be extinguished only by following the eightfold path or Middle Way. This **Middle Way** is essentially a highly moral mode of life that includes all the usual virtues like compassion, respect and moderation, and eschews vices such as self-indulgence and antisocial behaviour. But the key to it all is an acknowledgement that the physical world is impermanent and ever-changing, and that all things – including the self – are therefore not worth craving. Only by pursuing a condition of complete **detachment** can human beings transcend earthly suffering.

By the beginning of the first millennium, a new movement called **Mahayana** (Great Vehicle) had emerged within the Theravada school, attempting to make Buddhism more accessible by introducing a Hindu-style pantheon of *bodhisattva*, or Buddhist saints, who, although they had achieved enlightenment, nevertheless postponed entering Nirvana in order to inspire the populace. Mahayana Buddhism subsequently spread north into China, Korea, Vietnam and Japan, also entering southern Thailand via the Srivijayan empire around the eighth century and parts of Khmer Cambodia in about the eleventh century. Meanwhile Theravada Buddhism (which the Mahayanists disparagingly renamed "Hinayana" or "Lesser Vehicle") established itself most significantly in Sri Lanka, northern and central Thailand and Burma.

The monkhood

In Thailand it's the duty of the 200,000-strong **Sangha** (monkhood) to set an example to the Theravada Buddhist community by living a life as close to the Middle Way as possible and by preaching the Dharma to the people. A monk's life is governed by 227 strict rules that include celibacy and the rejection of all personal possessions except gifts.

Each day begins with an alms round in the neighbourhood so that the laity can donate food and thereby gain themselves merit (see opposite), and then is chiefly spent in meditation, chanting, teaching and study. The stricter of the Thai Sangha's two main sects, the **Thammayutika**, places strong emphasis on scholarship and meditation, but the much larger and longer-established **Mahanikai** sect encourages monks to pursue wider activities within the community. Always the most respected members of any community, monks act as teachers, counsellors and arbiters in local disputes and, in rural areas, they often become spokesmen for villagers' rights, particularly on environmental and land ownership issues. Although some Thai women do become nuns, they belong to no official order and aren't respected as much as the monks.

Monkhood doesn't have to be for life: a man may leave the Sangha three times without stigma and in fact every Thai male (including royalty) is expected to **enter the monkhood** for a short period at some point in his life, ideally between leaving school and marrying, as a rite of passage into adulthood. So ingrained into the social system is this practice that nearly all Thai companies grant their employees paid leave for their time as a monk. The most popular time for temporary ordination is the three-month Buddhist retreat period – **Pansa**, sometimes referred to as "Buddhist Lent" – which begins in July and lasts for the duration of the rainy season. (The monks' confinement is said to originate from the earliest years of Buddhist history, when farmers complained that perambulating monks were squashing their sprouting rice crops.) **Ordination ceremonies** take place in almost every wat at this time and make spectacular scenes, with the shaven-headed novice usually clad entirely in white and carried about on friends' or relatives' shoulders, or even on elephants as in Hat Siew near Si Satchanalai (see p.274) and Ban Ta Klang near Surin (see p.483). The boys' parents donate money, food and necessities such as washing powder and mosquito repellent, processing around the temple compound with their gifts, often joined by dancers or travelling players hired for the occasion.

Monks in contemporary society

In recent years, some monks have extended their role as village spokesmen to become influential activists: monks played a key role in the fierce campaign against the Pak Mun dam in Isaan (see p.497), for example, while the inhabitants of Wat Tham Krabok near Lopburi have successfully turned their temple into an international drug rehabilitation centre, and those of Wat Phai Lom near Bangkok have established the country's largest breeding colony of Asian open-billed storks. However, the increasing involvement of many monks in the secular world has not met with unanimous approval.

Less heroic, and far more disappointing to the laity, are those monks who **flout the precepts** of the Sangha by succumbing to the temptations of a consumer society, flaunting Raybans, Rolexes and Mercedes (in some cases actually bought with temple funds), chain-smoking and flirting, even making pocket money from predicting lottery results and practising faith-healing. With so much national pride and integrity riding on the sanctity of the Sangha, any whiff of a deeper scandal is bound to strike deep into the national psyche, and everyone was shocked when a young monk confessed to robbing and then murdering a British tourist in 1995. Since then Thai monks have been involved in an unprecedented litany of crimes, including several rapes and murders, and there's been an embarrassment of exposés of corrupt, high-ranking abbots caught carousing in disreputable bars, drug-dealing and even gun-running. This has prompted a stream of editorials on the state of the Sangha and the collapse of spiritual values at the heart of Thai society. The inclusivity of the monkhood – which is open to just about any male who wants to join – has been highlighted as a particularly vulnerable aspect, not least because donning saffron robes has always been an accepted way for criminals, reformed or otherwise, to repent of their past deeds. Interestingly, back in the late 1980s, the influential monk, Phra Bodhirak, was unceremoniously defrocked after criticizing what he saw as a tide of decadence infecting Thai Buddhism and advocating an all-round purification of the Sangha. He now preaches from his breakaway Santi Asoke sect headquarters on the outskirts of Bangkok, but his ascetic code of behaviour is not sanctioned by the more worldly figures of the Sangha Supreme Council.

Buddhist practice

In practice most Thai Buddhists aim only to be **reborn** higher up the incarnation scale rather than set their sights on the ultimate goal of Nirvana. The rank of the reincarnation is directly related to the good and bad actions performed in the previous life, which accumulate to determine one's **karma** or destiny – hence the Thai obsession with "making merit".

Merit-making (*tham bun*) can be done in all sorts of ways, from giving a monk his breakfast to attending a Buddhist service or donating money to the neighbourhood temple, and most festivals are essentially communal merit-making opportunities. For a Thai man, temporary ordination is a very important way of accruing merit not only for himself but also for his mother and sisters – wealthier citizens might take things a step further by commissioning the casting of a Buddha statue or even paying for the building of a wat. One of the more bizarre but common merit-making activities involves **releasing caged**

birds: worshippers buy one or more tiny finches from vendors at wat compounds and, by liberating them from their cage, prove their Buddhist compassion towards all living things. The fact that the birds were free until netted earlier that morning doesn't seem to detract from the ritual at all. In riverside and seaside wats, birds are sometimes replaced by fish or even baby turtles.

Spirits and non-Buddhist deities

The complicated history of the area now known as Thailand has, not surprisingly, made Thai Buddhism a strangely syncretic faith, as you'll realize when you enter a Buddhist temple compound to be confronted by a statue of a Hindu deity. While regular Buddhist merit-making insures a Thai for the next life, there are certain **Hindu gods and animist spirits** that most Thais also cultivate for help with more immediate problems. Sophisticated Bangkokians and illiterate farmers alike find no inconsistency in these apparently incompatible practices, and as often as not it's a Buddhist monk who is called in to exorcize a malevolent spirit. Even the Buddhist King Bhumibol employs Brahmin priests and astrologers to determine auspicious days and officiate at certain royal ceremonies and, like his royal predecessors of the Chakri dynasty, he also associates himself with the Hindu god Vishnu by assuming the title Rama IX – Rama, hero of the Hindu epic the *Ramayana*, having been Vishnu's seventh manifestation on earth.

If a Thai wants help in achieving a short-term goal, like passing an exam, becoming pregnant or winning the lottery, then he or she will quite likely turn to the **Hindu pantheon**, visiting an enshrined statue of either Brahma, Vishnu, Shiva, Indra or Ganesh, and making offerings of flowers, incense and maybe food. If the outcome is favourable, devotees will probably come back to show thanks, bringing more offerings and maybe even hiring a dance troupe to perform a celebratory *lakhon chatri* as well. Built in honour of Brahma, Bangkok's Erawan Shrine is the most famous place of Hindu-inspired worship in the country.

Whereas Hindu deities tend to be benevolent, **spirits** (or *phi*) are not nearly as reliable and need to be mollified more frequently. They come in hundreds of varieties, some more malign than others, and inhabit everything from trees, rivers and caves to public buildings and private homes – even taking over people if they feel like it. So that these *phi* don't pester human inhabitants, each building has a special **spirit house** (*phra phum*) in its vicinity, as a dwelling for spirits ousted by the building's construction. Usually raised on a short column to set it at or above eye-level, the spirit house must occupy an auspicious location – not, for example, in the shadow of the main building – so help from the local temple or village elder is usually required when deciding on the best position. Spirit houses are generally about the size of a dolls' house and designed to look like a wat or a traditional Thai house, but their ornamentation is supposed to reflect the status of the humans' building – thus if that building is enlarged or refurbished, the spirit house should be improved accordingly. Little figurines representing the relevant guardian spirit and his aides are sometimes put inside the little house, and daily offerings of incense, lighted candles and garlands of jasmine are placed alongside them to keep the *phi* happy – a disgruntled spirit is a dangerous spirit, liable to cause sickness, accidents and even death. As with any religious building or icon in Thailand, an unwanted or crumbling spirit house should never be dismantled or destroyed, which is why you'll often see damaged spirit houses placed around the base of a sacred banyan tree, where they are able to rest in peace.

Flora, fauna and environmental issues

Spanning some 1650km north to south, Thailand lies in the heart of Southeast Asia's tropical zone, its northernmost region just a few degrees south of the Tropic of Cancer, its southern border running less than seven degrees north of the Equator. As with other tropical regions across the world, Thailand's climate is characterized by high humidity and even higher temperatures, a very fertile combination which nourishes a huge diversity of flora and fauna in a vast range of habitats: mixed deciduous and dry dipterocarp forests in the mountainous north and arid northeast; semi-evergreen and hill evergreen forest at higher elevations throughout continental Thailand; wet tropical rainforests in the steamy south; flood plains in the central region; mangrove swamps along its coasts; and some of the world's most beautiful coral reefs off each coastline.

The country boasts some ten percent of the world's **bird** population (928 species) and at least six percent of its vascular plants (over 15,000 species so far recorded). These statistics, however, mask a situation that has deteriorated rapidly since World War II, as short-sighted economic development has taken a serious toll on Thailand's landscape.

Half of Thailand's forest is protected as **national park**, and it is in these reserves that the kingdom's natural heritage is best appreciated. The most rewarding of the country's national parks, including Khao Yai in the northeast, Doi Inthanon and Doi Suthep in the north, and Khao Sam Roi Yot and Khao Sok in the south, are described in detail in the guide; general practical information on national parks is given in Basics on p.75.

The geography of Thailand

Thailand has a **tropical monsoon climate**. Most rain is brought from the Indian Ocean by the southwest monsoon from May to October, the so-called rainy season. From November to February the northeast monsoon brings a much cooler and drier climate from China, the cold, dry season. However, this northeastern monsoon hits the peninsula, east coast after crossing the South China Sea, loading up with moist air and therefore extending this region's rainy season until January or later. The north–south divide is generally considered to lie just north of Ranong (10°N) – the capital of Thailand's wettest province – at the Kra Isthmus (see p.616).

Agriculture plays a significant role in Thailand's economy, and over fifty percent of Thais live off the land. Waterlogged rice paddies characterize the central plains; cassava, tapioca and eucalyptus are grown as cash crops on the scrubby plateau of the northeast; and rubber plantations dominate the commercial land-use of the south. Dotted along Thailand's coastline are mangrove swamps and palm forests; the country's coral reefs are discussed under "Wildlife" (see p.796).

Mixed deciduous and dry dipterocarp forests

An estimated 65 percent of Thailand's forests are of **deciduous** form (occasionally referred to as monsoon forest). These areas have to survive periods of up to six months with minimal rainfall, so the trees shed their leaves to conserve water. The family **Dipterocarpaceae** dominate these forests, a group of tropical hardwoods prized for their timber and, in places, their resin. The name comes from the Greek and means "two-winged fruit". Deciduous forests are often light and open, with canopies ranging from as low as 10m up to a maximum of about 40m. The undergrowth is usually fairly thick.

Teak was once a common species in northern deciduous forests, but following wholesale felling, only a few isolated teak forests now remain. Perhaps the most precious and sought-after monsoon-forest commodity, this solid timber is rich in silicic acid and oil, a combination which not only deters attacks by insects and fungi but also prevents the wood from warping, making it the ideal material for everything from houses to furniture. Often reaching 40m, teak trees are instantly recognizable, their large, elliptical leaves *in situ* from May to October or forming crunchy brown carpets beneath the trees for the rest of the year. Teak trees take around two hundred years to attain their full size, but artificial cultivation is becoming increasingly widespread in Thailand, and a teak tree's life-span on a plantation can be as short as fifteen years.

Bamboo thrives in a monsoon climate, shooting up at a remarkable rate during the wet season, but surviving undaunted at other times and often in soils too poor for other species; as a result bamboo often predominates in secondary forests (those where logging or clearing has previously taken place, and a new generation of plants has grown up – the majority of Thailand's forest). The smooth, woody, hollow stem characteristic of all varieties of bamboo is a fantastically adaptable material, used by the Thais for constructing everything from outside walls to chairs to water pipes (in hill-tribe villages) and musical instruments; and the bamboo shoot is an essential ingredient in Thai–Chinese cuisine.

Deciduous forest is relatively easy to fell, especially with the notorious slash-and-burn technique, and so a significant proportion of Thailand's deciduous forest has been cleared for both small and commercial cultivation purposes.

Tropical rainforests

Thailand's **tropical rainforests** occur in areas of high and prolonged rainfall in the southern peninsula, most accessibly in the national parks of Khao Sok, Thale Ban, Tarutao and Khao Luang. Some areas contain as many as two hundred species of tree within a single hectare, along with a host of other flora. Characteristic of a tropical rainforest is the multi-layered series of **canopies**. The uppermost storey of emergent trees sometimes reaches 60m, and these towering trees often have enormous buttressed roots for support; beneath this, the dense canopy of 25–35m is often festooned with climbers and epiphytes such as ferns, lianas, mosses and orchids; then comes an uneven layer 5–10m high consisting of palms, rattans, shrubs and small trees. The forest floor in tropical rainforests tends to be relatively open and free of dense undergrowth, owing to the intense filtering of light by the upper three layers.

Again, members of the *Dipterocarpaceae* family are dominant, and it is these trees, along with strangling figs, that form some of the most spectacular buttress roots. Though dipterocarps provide little food for fauna, they play an important role as nesting sites for hornbills, as lookout posts for gibbons – and as timber.

Semi-evergreen forests

Semi-evergreen forests are the halfway house between tropical rainforests and dry deciduous forests, showing characteristics of both habitats. It's a classification that includes all lowland and submontane evergreen forests from the

Epiphytes and strangling figs

Nearly all forest types play host to a plethora of **epiphytes**, of which there are over a thousand species in Thailand. These are plants that usually grow on other plants, though they do not feed from them. Instead they obtain nutrients from the atmosphere, the rain, and decaying plant and animal matter. Some of the commoner epiphytes in Thailand include the golden spiky-petalled *Bulbophyllum picturatum*, the bright yellow members of the genus *Dendrobium*, the ivory-coloured *Cymbidium siamensis*, the flame-red *Ascocentrum curvifolium* and the blue *Vanda coerulea*.

For the early years of its life, the **strangling fig** (*Ficus* sp) is also an epiphyte. The fig's peculiar life starts after the flower has been fertilized by a species-specific wasp host. The ripe fruit must then pass through the gut of a bird or animal and be dropped in a moist spot somewhere near the sunlit canopy of a support tree, often a dipterocarp. After germination, the fig lives a typical epiphytic lifestyle, but also spreads a lattice of roots down to the ground. Once tethered to the earth, the fig gives up its epiphytic role and feeds normally by extracting nutrients from the soil. After many years, the fig's roots completely enshroud the support tree, and eventually the crown spreads over and above its host, cutting off the support tree's light and therefore hastening its death. The support tree subsequently decomposes, leaving a hollow but structurally sound strangling fig. Strangling figs are excellent places to observe birds and mammals, particularly when in fruit, as they attract hornbills, green pigeons, barbets, gibbons, langurs and macaques.

plains to about 1000m. Semi-evergreen forests thrive in regions with distinctly seasonal rainfall where the humidity is relatively low; they share many similarities with the southern rainforests, though the canopies are lower and you'll find fewer palms and rattans. Fine examples can be found at Khao Yai and Kaeng Krachang national parks, and all along the Burmese border, all of which are potentially good places to observe large mammals, including elephants, gaurs, tigers and bears.

Hill evergreen (montane) forests

Above 1000m, the canopy of tall trees gives way to **hill evergreen forest** growth, consisting of oaks, chestnuts, laurels and other shorter temperate-zone tree families, many with twisted trunks and comparatively small leaves. Rainfall is frequent and often continuous at these elevations, so moss usually covers the forest floor and the undergrowth seems a lot denser, particularly with epiphytes, rhododendrons and various types of tree fern. These highland forests are exposed to the harshest winds and coolest temperatures, so only the hardiest, sturdiest tree and plant species survive.

Hill evergreen forest can occur within areas dominated by either monsoon forest or tropical rainforest. Good examples can be seen in Doi Inthanon and Phu Kradung national parks, and in parts of Doi Suthep and Khao Yai national parks. In the higher areas of the north not protected as national park, a lot of the primary hill evergreen forest has been cleared for cultivation, especially by local hill tribespeople who favour the slash-and-burn farming technique.

Mangrove swamps and coastal forests

Mangrove swamps are an important habitat for a wide variety of marine life (including 204 species of bird, 74 species of fish and 54 types of crab) but, like much of Thailand's natural heritage, they have fallen victim to destructive economic policies (see "Environmental Issues", p.800). Huge swathes of Thailand's coast used to be fringed with mangrove swamps, but now they are mainly found only along the west peninsular coast, between Ranong and Satun. On Phuket, the Thachatchai Nature Trail leads you on a guided tour through a patch of mangrove swamp, but an even better way of exploring the swamps is to paddle through them in a kayak; several tour operators in Phuket and in the Krabi area can arrange this. At high tide only the upper branches of the thirty or so species of mangrove are visible, thick with glossy, dark green leaves, but as the tide recedes, a tangled mass of aerial roots is exposed. These roots not only absorb oxygen, but also trap water-borne debris brought in by the tides, thus gradually extending the swamp area (reclaiming land from the sea) and simultaneously nurturing fertile conditions for the new mangrove seedlings.

Nipa palms share the mangrove's penchant for brackish water, and these stubby-stemmed palm trees grow in abundance in southern **coastal areas**, though commercial plantations are now replacing the natural colonies. Like most other species of palm indigenous to Thailand, the nipa is a versatile plant, its components exploited to the full – alcohol is distilled from its sugary sap, for instance, while roofs, sticky-rice baskets and chair-backs are constructed from its fronds.

Taller and more elegant, **coconut palms** grace some of Thailand's most beautiful beaches. On islands such as Ko Samui, they form the backbone of the local economy, with millions of coconuts harvested every month, most of them by specially trained pig-tailed macaques (see p.565), for their milk, their oil, their fibrous husks (used in matting and for brushes) and their wood.

Casuarinas also flourish in sandy soils and are common on the beaches of southern Thailand; because they are also fast-growing and attain heights of up to 20m, they are quite often used in afforestation programmes on beaches else-where. At first glance, the casuarina's feathery profile makes it look like a pine tree of some kind, but it's actually made up of tiny twigs, not needles.

The wildlife

Before World War II, Thailand's landscapes were virtually unspoiled and were apparently teeming with **wild animals** such as elephants, wild boars, rhinoc-eroses, bears and deer. So numerous were these species, in fact, that they were regarded as little more than an impediment to economic progress, an attitude which resulted in a calamitous reduction of Thailand's wildlife and its habitats.

Nonetheless, in zoogeographical terms, Thailand lies in an exceptionally rich "transition zone" of the Indo-Malayan realm, its forests, mountains and nation-al parks attracting creatures from both Indochina and Indonesia. In all, Thailand is home to 282 species of mammal (over forty of which are considered to be endangered) and 928 species of bird (190 of them endangered).

Mammals

In the main national parks of Khao Yai, Doi Inthanon, Khao Sok and the like, the animals you're most likely to encounter – with your ears if not your eyes – are **primates**, particularly macaques and gibbons. The latter spend much of their time foraging for food in the higher reaches of the forest canopy, while the former usually seek their sustenance lower down, often descending closer to the ground to rest and to socialize.

The gibbons are responsible for the unmistakable hooting that echoes through the forests of some of the national parks. Chief noise-maker is the **white-handed** or **lar gibbon**, an appealing beige- or black-bodied, white-faced animal whose appearance, intelligence and dexterity unfortunately make it a popular pet. The poaching and maltreating of lar gibbons has become so severe that a special Gibbon Rehabilitation Project has been set up in Phuket (see p.665).

Similarly chatty, macaques hang out in gangs of twenty or more. The **long-tailed** or **crab-eating macaque** lives in the lowlands, near the rivers, lakes and coasts of Krabi, Ko Tarutao, Ang Thong and Khao Sam Roi Yot, for example. It eats not only crabs, but mussels, other small animals and fruit, transporting and storing food in its big cheek pouch, when swimming and diving – activities at which it excels. The **pig-tailed macaque**, so called because of its short curly tail, excels at scaling the tall trees of Erawan, Khao Yai, Doi Inthanon and other national parks, a skill which has resulted in many of the males being captured and trained to pick coconuts – a practice that's very common in Surat Thani (see p.565).

You're almost certain to see deer in areas of protected forest, especially the **barking deer**, a medium-sized loner happy in pretty much any type of woodland (easily seen in Khao Yai, Phu Kradung and Erawan) and the large, dark-brown **sambar deer**, which prefers the deciduous forests of the same parks. The tiny **mouse deer** is less often seen, and at only 20cm from ground to shoulder it's Southeast Asia's smallest hoofed animal. Mouse deer live in the dense undergrowth of forests (Khao Yai, Erawan, Ko Surin) but their reputed tastiness could see them heading for the endangered species list.

Commonly sighted on night treks in Doi Inthanon, Doi Suthep, Khao Yai and Khao Sam Roi Yot national parks, the **civet** – species of which include the common palm and small Indian – is a small mongoose-type animal which hunts smaller mammals in trees and on the ground; it's known in the West for the powerful smell released from its anal glands, a scent used commercially as a perfume base. More elusive is the **Indochinese tiger**, which lives under constant threat from both poachers and the destruction of its habitat by logging interests, both of which have reduced the current population to somewhere between 150 and 250; for now Khao Yai and Khao Sok are the two likeliest places for sightings. The medium-sized arboreal **clouded leopard** is also on the endangered list, and is hard to spot anyway as it only comes out to feed on birds and monkeys under cover of darkness, rarely venturing out in moonlight let alone daylight.

The shy, nocturnal **tapir**, an ungulate with three-toed hind legs and four-toed front ones, lives deep in the forest of peninsular Thailand but is occasionally spotted in daylight. A relative of both the horse and the rhino, the tapir is the size of a pony and has a stubby trunk-like snout and distinctive colouring that serves to confuse predators: the front half of its body and all four legs are black, while the rear half is white. Another unusual ungulate is the **gaur**, recognizable by its brown coat, sharp horns, powerful off-white legs and sheer bulk – the largest member of the cattle family, it measures up to 2m at shoulder height and can weigh over a tonne. It feeds mainly at night, and is most frequently spotted at salt licks, for example in Khao Yai.

It's thought there are now as few as two thousand wild **elephants** left in Thailand: small-eared Asian elephants found mainly in Khao Yai and Khao Sok. The situation is so dire that an organization called the Elephant Help Project Phuket (ⓦwww.elephanthelp.org) has been established with the aim of buying captive elephants from Phuket tourist attractions and releasing them back into the wild via a protected reserve in Northern Thailand. For more on elephants in the wild and in captivity see the boxes on p.340 and p.151

Birds

Even if you don't see many mammals on a trek through a national park, you're certain to spot a satisfying range of **birds**. Because of its location at the zoogeographical crossroads of Southeast Asia, Thailand boasts a huge diversity of bird species. The forests of continental Thailand are home to many of the same birds that inhabit India, Burma and Indochina, while the mountains of the north share species with the Himalayas and Tibet, and the peninsular forests are home to birds found also in Malaysia and Indonesia. Khao Yai and Khao Nor Chuchi are prime year-round sites for bird-spotting, and, during the winter, Doi Inthanon is a good place for flycatchers and warblers, and Khao Sam Roi Yot a rewarding area to see migrant waders and waterfowl.

There are twelve species of **hornbill** in Thailand, all equally majestic with massive, powerful wings (the flapping of which can be heard for long distances) and huge beaks surmounted by bizarre horny casques. Khao Yai is the easiest place to spot at least two of the species, the plain black and white **oriental pied hornbill** and the flashier **great hornbill**, whose monochromic body and head are broken up with jaunty splashes of yellow; the little island of Ko Chang in Ranong province also has some resident oriental pied hornbills too.

The shyness of the gorgeous **pitta** makes a sighting all the more rewarding. Usually seen hopping around on the floor of evergreen forests, especially in Doi Inthanon, Doi Suthep and Khao Yai, these plump little birds – varieties of which include the **rusty-naped**, the **blue** and the **eared** – have dazzling markings in iridescent reds, yellows, blues and blacks. The one pitta you might see outside a rainforest is the **blue-winged** pitta, which occasionally migrates to drier bamboo forests. Thailand is also home to the extremely rare **Gurney's pitta**, found only in Khlong Thom National Park, inland from Ko Lanta.

Members of the pheasant family can be just as shy as the pittas, and are similarly striking. The black-and-white-chevron-marked **silver pheasant**, and the **green peafowl** are particularly fine birds, and the commonly seen **red jungle fowl** is the ancestor to all domestic chickens.

The striking orange-breasted and red-headed **trogons** live mainly in the middle layer of forests such as Khao Yai, as does the **barbet**, a little lime-green relative of the woodpecker. Less dramatic but more frequently sighted forest residents include the **abbot's babbler**, whose short tail and rounded, apparently ineffectual wings mean it spends most of its time on the forest floor; and the distinctive, deeply fork-tailed, glossy black **drongo**. The noisy, fruit-eating **bulbuls** are also commonly spotted; many bulbuls have confusingly similar green and brown colouring, but two easily recognized species are the yellow-chested olive-backed **black-crested bulbul**, and the black, brown and white **red-whiskered bulbul**. The **black-naped oriole**, small groups of which fly from tree to tree in gardens as well as forests, is also easy to single out, both by its loud chirping and by its yellow body, black head and wing markings and reddish beak.

Thailand's **rice fields** also attract a host of different birds, not only for the seeds and grasses but also for the insects, rodents and even fish that inhabit the paddies. Some of the most common rice-field visitors are the various species of **munia**, a chubby relative of the finch, whose chunky, conical beak is ideally suited to cracking the unripened seeds of the rice plant; the aptly named **scaly breasted** munia and the **white-headed** munia are the most recognizable members of the family, although all members are an assortment of browns and whites. **Egrets** and **herons** also frequent the fields, wading through the waterlogged furrows or perching on the backs of water buffaloes and pecking at cattle insects, while from November to April, thousands of **Asian open-billed storks** – so called because of the gap between the upper and lower mandibles – descend on agricultural land as well, building nests in sugar-palm trees and bamboos and feeding on pira snails – each baby stork polishing off at least half a kilo a day.

Coastal areas also attract storks, egrets and herons, and the mud flats of Khao Sam Roi Yot are a breeding ground for the large, long-necked **purple heron**. The magnificent **white-bellied sea eagle** haunts the Thai coast, nesting in the forbidding crags around Krabi, Phang Nga and Ko Tarutao and preying on fish and sea snakes. The tiny **edible nest swiftlet** makes its eponymous nest – the major ingredient of birds'-nest soup and a target for thieves – in the limestone crags, too, though it prefers the caves within these karsts; for more on these swiftlets and their nests see box on p.695.

Snakes

Thailand is home to around 175 different species and subspecies of **snake**, 56 of them dangerously venomous. Death by snakebite is not common, however, but all hospitals should keep a stock of serum, produced at the Snake Farm in Bangkok (see p.159).

Found everywhere and highly venomous, the two-metre, nocturnal, yellow-and-black-striped **banded krait** is one to avoid, as is the shorter but equally poisonous **Thai** or **monocled cobra**, which lurks in low-lying humid areas and close to human habitation. As its name implies, this particular snake sports a distinctive "eye" mark on its hood, the only detail on an otherwise plain brown body. The other most widespread poisonous snake is the sixty-centimetre **Malayan pit viper**, whose dangerousness is compounded by its unnerving ability to change the tone of its pinky-brown and black-marked body according to its surroundings.

The ubiquitous shiny black or brown **common blind snake**, also known as the flowerpot snake, grows to only 17cm, and is as harmless as its worm-like appearance suggests. Also non-venomous but considerably mightier, with an average measurement of 7.5m (maximum 10m) and a top weight of 140kg, the **reticulated python** is Thailand's largest snake, and the second largest in the world after the anaconda. Tan-coloured, with "reticulated" black lines containing whitish oval spots, like eyes, the reticulated python is found near human habitation all over Thailand, especially in the suburbs of Greater Bangkok. It feeds on rats, rabbits, small deer, pigs, cats and dogs which it kills by constriction; if provoked, it can kill humans in the same way.

Other common Thai snakes include the **iridescent earth** or **sunbeam snake**, named after the sheen of its scales which glisten and change from black to a dark brown in the sunlight. Non-venomous and burrowing, this snake reaches a length of 1.2m and is found all over Thailand. South of Chumphon, the **mangrove snake** lives in the humid swamps that fringe the river banks, estuaries and coastal plains. Arboreal, nocturnal and mildly venomous, it can grow to about 2.5m and is black with thin yellow bands set at fairly wide intervals. Finally, the **golden tree snake** is the most common of Thailand's flying snakes, so called because they can glide from tree to ground. Frequently sighted in Greater Bangkok, this mildly venomous tree snake is not golden but green with a dense pattern of black flecks, and grows to about 1.5m.

Quite a few of Thailand's snakes can swim if they have to, but the country is also home to 25 species of **sea snakes**, whose tails are flattened to act as an efficient paddle in water. Most sea snakes are venomous though not aggressive. Of the poisonous ones, the commonest and most easily recognized is the **banded sea snake**, which is silvery grey with thirty to fifty black bands and a slightly yellow underside at its front end. It grows to 1.5m and inhabits shallow coastal waters, coming onto land to lay its eggs.

Marine species

The Indian Ocean (Andaman Sea) and the South China Sea (Gulf of Thailand) together play host to over 850 species of open-water fish, more than one hundred species of reef fish and some two hundred species of hard coral.

As a result of the destruction of much of Thailand's **coral reef** due to tourism and dynamite fishing (see "Environmental Issues", p.800), the most rewarding places to observe underwater life are the stretches of water conserved as **national marine parks**. The best of these are detailed in the guide and include Ko Similan, Ko Surin, Ko Tarutao and Ang Thong; Thailand's major diving bases have their headquarters on Phuket, Ko Phi Phi and Ko Tao, and in Ao Nang, Khao Lak and Pattaya. (See also "Outdoor Activities" in Basics on p.75.)

Coral reefs are living organisms composed of a huge variety of marine life forms, but the foundation of every reef is its ostensibly inanimate **stony coral** – hard constructions such as boulder, mushroom, bushy staghorn and brain coral. Stony coral is composed of whole colonies of polyps – minuscule invertebrates which feed on plankton, depend on algae and direct sunlight for photosynthesis, and extract calcium carbonate (limestone) from sea water in order to reproduce. The polyps use this calcium carbonate to build new skeletons outside their bodies – an asexual reproductive process known as budding – and this is how a reef is formed. It's an extraordinarily slow process, with colony growth averaging somewhere between 5mm and 30mm a year.

The fleshy plant-like **soft coral**, such as dead man's fingers and elephant's ear, generally establishes itself on and around these banks of stony coral, swaying with the currents and using tentacles to trap all sorts of micro-organisms. Soft coral is also composed of polyps, but a variety with flaccid internal skeletons built from protein rather than calcium. **Horny coral**, like sea whips and intricate sea fans, looks like a cross between the stony and the soft varieties, while **sea anemones** have much the most obvious, and poisonous, tentacles of any member of the coral family, using them to trap fish and other large prey.

The algae and plankton that accumulate around coral colonies attract a whole catalogue of fish known collectively as **reef fish**. Most are small in stature, with vibrant colours which serve as camouflage against the coral, flattened bodies and broad tails for easy manoeuvring around the reef, and specially adapted features to help them poke about for food in the tiniest crannies.

Among the most typical and easily recognizable reef fish is the gorgeously coloured **emperor angel fish**, which boasts spectacular horizontal stripes in bright blue and orange, and an orange tail. The **moorish idol** is another fantastic sight, bizarrely shaped with a trailing streamer – or pennant fin – extending from its dorsal fin, a pronounced snout and dramatic black, yellow and white bands of colour. Similarly eye-catching, the ovoid **powder-blue surgeon fish** has a light blue body, a bright yellow dorsal fin and a white "chinstrap". The commonly spotted **long-nosed butterfly fish** is named for the butterfly-like movements of its yellow-banded silver body as it darts in and out of crevices looking for food. The bright orange **clown fish**, so called because the thick white stripes across its body resemble a clown's ruff, is more properly known as the anemone fish because of its mutually protective relationship with the sea anemone, near which it can usually be sighted. Equally predictable is the presence of **cleaner fish**, or cleaner wrasse, on the edges of every shoal of reef fish. Streamlined, with a long snout and jaws that act like tweezers, a cleaner fish spends its days picking parasites off the skins of other fish – a symbiotic relationship essential to both parties.

Some reef fish, among them the ubiquitous turquoise and purple **parrot fish**, eat coral. With the help of a bird-like beak, which is in fact several teeth fused together, the parrot fish scrapes away at the coral and then grinds the fragments down with another set of back teeth – a practice reputedly responsible for the erosion of a great deal of Thailand's reef. The magnificent mauve and burgundy **crown-of-thorns starfish** also feeds on coral, laying waste to as much as fifty square centimetres of stony coral in a 24-hour period. Its appearance is as formidable as its eating habits, with a body that measures up to 50cm in diameter protected by "arms" covered in highly venomous spines.

Larger, less frequent visitors to Thailand's offshore reefs include the **moray eel**, whose elongated jaws of viciously pointed teeth make it a deadly predator, and the similarly equipped **barracuda**, the world's fastest-swimming fish. **Sharks** are quite common off the Andaman coast reefs, where it's also sometimes possible to swim with a **manta ray**, whose extraordinary flatness, strange wing-like fins and massive size – up to 6m across and weighing some 1600kg – make it an astonishing presence. **Turtles** sometimes paddle around reef waters, too, but all four local species – leatherback, Olive Ridley, green and hawksbill – are fast becoming endangered in Thailand, so much so that the Royal Forestry Department has placed several of their egg-laying beaches under national park protection (see p.648), including those at Hat Mai Khao on Phuket, Thai Muang, Ko Surin Tai and Ko Tarutao.

Other commonly spotted creatures are the **sea urchin**, whose evil-looking spines grow up to 35cm in length, and the ugly but harmless **sea cucumber**, which looks like a large slug and lies half-buried on the sea bed. Deceptively slothful in appearance, sea cucumbers are constantly busy ingesting and excreting so much sand and mud that the combined force of those in a three-square-kilometre area can together redistribute one million kilogrammes of sea-bed material a year.

Environmental issues

Only in the 1970s did some sort of environmental awareness emerge in Thailand, when the politicization of the poor rural areas began to catch up with the power-brokers in Bangkok. For years farmers had been displaced from land on which they had long established a thriving ecological balance, to be resettled out of the way of the Bangkok-based logging interests. Discontent with this treatment finally led some of the farmers to join the student protests of 1973, and in the subsequent right-wing backlash many political ringleaders fled the capital to seek refuge in the north. Many have since returned under amnesty, and their experiences among the nation's dispossessed have ensured that the environment plays a major role in the mainstream politics of Thailand.

National parks

One significant outcome of the new environmental awareness was the creation in the 1970s of a National Parks Division and a Wildlife Conservation Division within the Royal Forestry Department (RFD). In 1972 Thailand had just four **national parks**, but there are now almost one hundred across the country, plus 37 wildlife sanctuaries, nearly fifty non-hunting grounds and several other protected zones. In all, they cover 66,000 square kilometres, or around thirteen percent of the country (a high proportion compared to other nations, such as Japan at 6.5 percent, and the US at 10.5 percent). More parks are scheduled but, as key parks planner Dr Surachet Chettamart warns, "Creating parks is not a numbers game, and when degraded areas are included, the whole parks system suffers. Some, such as Ko Phi Phi and Ko Samet, should be excised or reclassified since they have been transformed into holiday resorts."

The **touristification of national parks** such as Ko Phi Phi and Ko Samet is a hugely controversial issue, and was highlighted when the RFD allowed a film crew to "relandscape" part of Ko Phi Phi Leh in 1999 for the movie *The Beach* – to vociferous protest from environmental groups. There is no question that both Phi Phi and Samet have suffered huge environmental damage as a direct result of the number of overnight visitors they receive, and the contrast with national parks where the government has put its foot down – for example in Khao Yai, where all tourist businesses were unceremoniously kicked out in the early 1990s – is marked. More recently, the RFD began flexing its muscles in the Ko Similan National Marine Park, closing two of the nine islands to all visitors in 2000, imposing tight bureaucratic controls on the number and type of boats allowed to bring snorkellers and divers to the other seven and – most controversially – banning local fishermen from the area; the latter injunction caused intense outrage and resulted in two attempts on the life of the national park director involved. While most people understand that the role of the RFD is to conserve vulnerable and precious resources like the Similans, the dramatic hike in entrance fees payable by foreigners to national parks – from B20 up to B200 in 2000 – has been greeted with cynicism and anger, not least because there is little sign of anything tangible being done with the money; see Basics p.76 for more on this.

Deforestation

Undoubtedly the biggest crisis facing Thailand's environment is **deforestation**, the effects of which are felt all over the country. As well as providing shelter and sustenance for birds and animals (a single male tiger, for instance, needs about thirty square kilometres of forest to survive), forests act as an ecological sponge, binding soil and absorbing the impact of monsoon rains. When they are cut down, water and topsoil are both rapidly lost, as was demonstrated tragically in 1988, when villages in the south were devastated by mudslides that swept down deforested slopes, killing hundreds of people. A formal **ban** on most **commercial logging** was finally established in the following year, but much illegal activity has continued.

There was little likelihood that the ban would ever be fully observed, as nothing has been done to change the pattern of wood consumption and the government has instituted no supervisory body to ensure the cessation of illegal logging. To make matters worse, there's the endemic problem of "influence": when the big guns from Bangkok want to build a golf course on a forest reserve, it is virtually impossible for a lowly provincial civil servant to resist their money.

The timber firms and their financial backers and political protectors have various ways of circumventing the law. Much skulduggery goes on close to the Burmese border, where the lawbreakers can claim that the felled timber came from outside the country. Some of it does indeed come from Burma, where the vicious and greedy military regime has set up deals with some of the less scrupulous Thai timber merchants – a racket put in motion by a former chief of the Thai army.

Reforestation schemes

In many cases, commercial **reforestation** has actually worsened the situation. Backed by vested interests, the Royal Forestry Department has classified several areas as "degraded" forest, even though some of these are ancient virgin forest. Once thus designated, the hardwood forests are felled and cleared for commercial development. This usually takes the form of the plantation of fast-growing species such as **eucalyptus**, which are vital to the economically important – but grossly polluting – pulp and paper industries, but suck nutrients and water from the soil at a terrible rate, and are also impossible to mix with other crops. Moreover, some ten million people happen to live in these "degraded" forests.

Under the **khor jor kor** plan, part of Thailand's National Forest Policy of 1985, it's intended that some 25 percent of the country's land area is to remain covered with forest (including rubber plantations), with a further fifteen percent set aside for commercial plantation by the private sector and government agencies. The first phase of *khor jor kor* targeted some 250,000 Isaan families – labelled "encroachers" – for relocation from about 2500 villages, thereby reducing their living space by about one third. Some two thousand families have already been uprooted to make way for new plantations. Without warning, soldiers arrived at two villages in Khon Khaen province, ordered their inhabitants to leave and proceeded to demolish their dwellings. Each family was given temporary food rations and a nominal sum of money before being dumped in resettlement sites that had not been finished and had no attached farmland. Villagers were forced to kill their most valuable possessions – their buffalo – for food.

However, some important reforestation projects have been successfully carried out in national parks with pre-existing degraded areas, in particular at Nam Nao and Phu Hin Rongkla. And there seems to be a concerted effort to replant mountain slopes, roadsides and national park buffer zones with native species rather than commercial ones.

Infrastructure projects

Another major cause of deforestation is development of the country's **infrastructure**. The expanding road network, essential to Thailand's emergence as an industrialized nation, has inevitably damaged the ecology of the country, as have the quarries that supplied the construction boom of the 1980s. But nothing has stirred as much controversy as Thailand's hydro-electric schemes, which might be a lot cleaner than the production and burning of lignite – the low-grade coal that's Thailand's major source of energy – but destroys vast areas and, of course, displaces countless people.

The construction of the **Pak Mun dam** in southern Isaan was typical. It was completed in July 1994 despite vociferous and at times violent protest from local people and environmental pressure groups. Over three thousand local farming families ended up losing their homes, and scores of fishermen had their annual incomes severely depleted, with inadequate compensation being offered by the Electricity Generating Authority of Thailand. To add insult to injury, a study by the independent World Commission on Dams, released in November 2000, showed that the dam is a financial as well as an environmental disaster, see box on p.497 for the full story.

The one positive thing to come out of the Pak Mun debacle was the forming of the **Assembly of the Poor**. The women of the communities affected by the Pak Mun project started an anti-dam movement, and in 1995 joined forces with representatives from five other networks – consisting of people affected by other infrastructure projects, land and forest conflicts, slum issues and exploitation at work – to form the most powerful grassroots movement in Thailand. Uniting under the declaration that "the people must be the real beneficiaries of development, and the poor must participate in the decision-making on development projects that will affect them," the Assembly of the Poor has brought numerous development and poverty issues into the headlines, establishing protest villages at development sites and (their most successful campaign to date) organizing a 99-day sit-in in 1997, when twenty thousand villagers set up home for over three months outside Government House in Bangkok. As a result of the Assembly's efforts, some new consultative and compensation measures have been introduced and certain controversial infrastructure projects have been shelved. The United Nations Development Programme now points to the Assembly as a model for grassroots struggles for sustainable development.

No sooner is one controversial project completed than another one seems to rear its ugly head. At time of writing, the hot potato is the **Trans–Thai–Malaysia gas pipeline** and gas separation plant project, which the Petroleum Authority of Thailand (PTT) is planning to construct in Songkhla province, much to the consternation of many local residents, who see this as causing irreversible damage to both the physical environment and the social landscape. The separation plant would be constructed on the coast at Chana, south of Songkhla, from where gas would be piped down to Malaysia. The pipeline is the cornerstone of the proposed industrialization of the South, as it will supply the energy needed to power new factories and industries in the provinces on both sides of the Malaysian border.

Mangroves and coral reefs

In the past, **mangrove swamps** were used by rice farmers to raise **prawns**, using the tides to wash the larvae into prepared pools. Some rice farmers even converted their paddies into prawn farms, but generally the scale of this aquaculture was small and sustainable.

Then, in 1972, the Department of Fisheries began to promote modern technology, enticing many people to invest all they could afford – sometimes more – in this growth sector. It looked like good money, with farmers initially reporting profits of three hundred percent, which for people used to living on the breadline was a gift from the gods. However, big business swiftly moved in, so that today almost all prawn farming in Thailand is in the hands of a few companies.

This was bad for the local farmers, and disastrous for the ecology of the mangroves. Large-scale prawn farming uses vast amounts of sea water, which salinates the neighbouring land to the extent that rice farmers who used to produce two crops a year are now reduced to one small harvest. Furthermore, the chemicals used to feed the prawns and ward off disease are allowed to wash back into the swamps, damaging not only the mangroves themselves, but also the water used for irrigation, drinking and washing. Pollution also kills the very industry that produces it, forcing farmers to move their breeding pools along the coast, damaging yet more mangroves. This destruction of the mangrove forests to make way for new breeding pools is exemplified by the case of the Wen River National Forest Reserve in Kanchanaburi, where the RFD's own figures show that a mere ten percent of the fertile mangrove forest has survived intact. With Thailand now the world's leading producer of tiger prawns, some environmental action groups are calling for an international boycott until there's a proven supply of farmed tropical prawns.

Many of Thailand's **coral reefs** – some of which are thought to be around 450 million years old – are being destroyed by factors attributable to tourism. The main cause of tourism-related destruction is the pollution generated by the hotels and bungalows which have multiplied unchecked at many of the most beautiful sites on the coasts. The demand for coral souvenirs is exploited by unscrupulous divers and local traders, and many irresponsible dive leaders allow their customers to use harpoon guns, which cause terrible damage to reefs. Still, the destruction of coral by tourists is dwarfed by that wreaked by the practice of **dynamite fishing**, which goes on in areas away from the normal tourist haunts.

Endangered species and the wildlife trade

Having hunted many of its indigenous species to extinction (such as Schomburgk's deer, the Javan rhinoceros and the Sumatran rhinoceros), Thailand now acts as the "wildlife supermarket of the world", to quote the World Wide Fund for Nature, which in 1991 condemned Thailand as "probably the worst country in the world for the illegal trade in endangered wildlife". Thailand signed the Convention on the International Trade in Endangered Species – **CITES** – in 1973, but for years afterwards the Thais exploited the uncertainty as to whether CITES covered trade in species originating outside the trading country. Even now that it has been established that CITES applies to all commerce in all listed species, Thailand continues to make money out of imported animals and animal products.

Cambodia – not a signatory to CITES – is the major supplier of **live animals**. The main action is focused on border towns such as Aranyaprathet, where Thai middle-merchants can easily acquire monkeys, deer, wildcats, monitor lizards and various other reptiles, secure in the knowledge that official intervention will be minimal. The R.FD, which is charged with the suppression of wildlife trade, has a budget for only a handful of wildlife officers nationwide, and doesn't have the money to train them properly, so even if they do intercept a transaction in an endangered species, they probably won't know what they're looking at.

Several animal traders deal quite openly in Bangkok, chiefly at the Chatuchak Weekend Market (see p.161), but the capital's trade is weighted towards **animal products**. In a three-month WWF-sponsored survey of 111 hotels in 2000, 42 were found to be selling one or more of twenty different illegal wildlife products in their shops. Ninety percent of this trade involves ivory products, mostly imported from Burma and Laos, although some is native – despite the fact that the Asian elephant has long been protected by law in Thailand. The second-biggest share is of tiger body-parts, which end up on the black markets of China, Taiwan and Hong Kong, where bones, skin, teeth, whiskers and penis are prized for their "medicinal" properties; it's thought that much of Thailand's dwindling tiger population ends up in such lucrative pieces. Crocodile skins, many of which come from South America, are sold in huge numbers in Bangkok and other tourist areas, as are snake skins, corals and rare insects and butterflies.

Thailand's own legislation – the Wild Animals Reservation and Protection Act – is notoriously weak at protecting native Thai species not listed by CITES. For example, the WWF has accused Thailand of showing little interest in protecting its **orchid** species, which grow here in a profusion unmatched anywhere else. And although Thailand's politicians are sensitive to international disapproval when it comes to conservation issues, it seems that there is still a lack of real will to clamp down on the people who profit from the destruction of rare animals. Although there are occasional highly publicized raids on traders in endangered species, fines tend to be too small to act as a significant deterrent.

Contributions by Mark Read and Gavin Lewis

Music

Music is an important part of Thai culture, whether related to Buddhist activities in the local temple (still a focal point for many communities), animist rituals, Brahmanic ceremonies or the wide range of popular song styles. The most interesting types of Thai music, *luk thung* and *mor lam*, are incredibly popular and distinctively Thai in character. But they – and Thai popular music in general – are largely ignored by visitors to the country. The little that tourists do tend to hear is classical or court ensembles at restaurants or the National Theatre, or the discordant pipes and drums that accompany Thai boxing (*muay Thai*).

The classical tradition

Thai classical dance and music can be traced back to stone engravings during the Sukhothai period (thirteenth to fifteenth centuries), which show ensembles of musicians playing traditional instruments, called **phipat**. The *phipat* ensembles include a large array of percussion instruments, rather like the Indonesian gamelan – gong circles, xylophones and drums – plus a raucous oboe called the *phinai*. The music was developed to accompany classical dance-drama (*khon* or *lakhon*) or shadow-puppet theatre (*nang*) – an ensemble playing for a shadow-puppet show is depicted in the magnificent *Ramayana* murals in the Temple of the Emerald Buddha in Bangkok's Grand Palace complex.

Phipat music sounds strange to Western ears as the seven equal notes of the Thai scale fall between the cracks of the piano keyboard. But heard in the right environment – in a temple, at a dance performance or at a Thai boxing match – it can be entrancing. As there is no notation, everything is memorized. And, as in all Thai music, elements have been assimilated over the years from diverse sources, then synthesized into something new.

Despite the country's rapid Westernization, Thai classical music has been undergoing something of a revival in the past few years, partly as a result of royal patronage. There have been recent experiments, too, that attempt to blend Thai classical and Western styles – often jazz or rock – led by avant-garde groups like **Kangsadan** and **Fong Naam**. Recently **Boy Thai** have followed their lead, albeit with a more pop-oriented sound, and have had some mainstream success with two albums.

There are regular dance and classical music performances in Bangkok at the National Theatre and the Thai Culture Centre. Somewhat lacklustre **temple dancing** can usually be seen at the Erawan Shrine on Thanon Rama I and the *lak muang* shrine behind the Grand Palace; at these venues, people give thanks for their good fortune by paying for the temple musicians and dancers to go through a routine. A number of restaurants also mount music and dance shows for tourists, including regular shows by Fong Naam and **Duriyapraneet**, the latter being the country's longest-established classical band.

Folk music

Thailand's folk musics are often referred to as **pleng phua bahn**, which encompasses styles from the country's four distinct regions (central, north, northeast and south), with more than eighty languages and dialects. Despite the rapid social change of the past decade, numerous folk styles are still enthusiastically played, from the hill-tribe New Year dances in the far north to the all-night singing jousts of northeastern *mor lam glawn*, to the haunting Muslim vocals of *likay wolou* in the deep south.

Most Thais are familiar with the exciting central folk styles like *lam tad* and *pleng choi*, both of which feature raunchy verbal jousting between male and female singers. In 2000, the *lam-tad*-style folk song *ASEAN Samakee* was used to promote the thirty-third meeting of the Association of Southeast Asian Nations (ASEAN) in Bangkok. Styles like these and the ever-popular *mor lam* from the northeast (see p.807) are incorporated into modern popular styles like *luk thung* (see p.805).

One notable folk style to have grown in popularity in recent years is the uptempo and danceable northeastern instrumental style known as **bong lang** (the name comes from a wooden xylophone that is attached vertically to a tree). *Bong lang* is thought to predate Indian-Thai culture, and while it is clearly an ancient music, the style continues to be refined. As recently as the late 1970s, the *phin hai*, a jar with rubber stretched across the mouth, was introduced (though often only to put a cute young woman at the front of the band); its sound, made by plucking the rubber, is similar to that of a double bass.

The best place to see *bong lang* is upcountry, especially in Kalasin province in central Isaan between November and March. Folk music also features prominently at the major festivals held in the northeastern cities of Khon Kaen, Ubon Ratchathani and Udon Thani, particularly at Songkhran (April), the Bun Bang Fai rocket festival (May), and the Asanha Puja candle festival (July); check with TAT for specific dates and locations.

Popular styles

Despite the economic meltdown since the Asian economic crisis of 1997, the crippling problem of music piracy and a market dominated by a few major companies, the Thai **pop scene** remains vibrant and full of surprises. Thailand is the second biggest music market in Southeast Asia after Indonesia, and Bangkok is a major regional centre for pop music and popular culture.

Western orchestration for Thai melodies had been introduced in the 1930s and this led to the development of *dontree sakol*, or modern music, in the form of big band and swing, country and western, Hollywood film music, rock 'n' roll, and so on. In the early days, two distinctive Thai genres developed: *luk grung*, a schmaltzy romantic ballad form; and *luk thung* (Thai country). **Luk grung**, with its clearly enunciated singing style and romantic fantasies, was long associated with the rich strata of Bangkok society; it's the kind of music that is played by state organs like Radio Thailand. However, it was largely transformed during the 1960s by the popularity of Western stars like Cliff Richard; as musicians started to mimic the new Western music, a new term was coined, *wong shadow* (*wong* meaning group, *shadow* from the British group, The Shadows). This trend led to the development of *string*, Westernized Thai pop, in the 1980s. Currently the popular music market divides into forty percent *luk thung* (counting regional styles like *mor lam* and *kantrum* as well), thirty percent *string* and twenty percent *luk grung*, with *luk thung* particularly popular in the provinces.

String

The term **string** came into use as Thai-language pop music rapidly developed in the economic boom times of the 1980s. S*tring* encompasses ballads, rock and alternative, disco, techno/house, reggae, ska and rap; whatever trend is popular in the US, UK and increasingly Japan, gets picked up quickly and reassembled with Thai lyrics and a particular local flavour that often favours sweet melodies.

Megastars like veteran **Thongchai "Bird" Macintyre, Patiparn "Mos" Pattavikan** generally record on either of the two major labels, Grammy and RS Promotion, though another major star, **Tata Young**, is now signed to BEC-Tero. Grammy, which controls more than half the market, has an umbrella of labels that releases everything from best-selling soft rockers **LoSo** to **Mai Chareonpura** to the current top-selling *luk thung* act **Got Chakrapand**. Their most famous rock act, though, is the talented brothers **Asanee & Wasan**, now producing a new generation of rockers on their own label.

Since the mid-1990s, Bakery Music, originally an independent label but now linked with BMG, has led the two major pop trends to develop. Bakery broke the **alternative** scene with **Modern Dog**, probably the country's best rock act of the last decade, and helped develop the rap scene with the top-selling Thai language rapper **Joey Boy**. They also picked up on the popularity of Japanese culture and music with Thai youth and started a label, Dohjo, which specializes in **J-pop** (Japanese-influenced pop) and has produced top acts like the female duo **Triumph's Kingdom**. Bangkok is the best place to catch gigs – check the *Bangkok Metro* monthly listings magazine for dates.

Songs for life

Another big genre is **pleng phua chiwit**, or "songs for life", which started as a kind of progressive rock in the early 1970s, with bands like **Caravan** (no relation to the British songsters) blending *pleng phua bahn* (folk songs) with Western folk and rock. Caravan were at the forefront of the left-wing campaign for democracy with songs like *Khon Gap Kwai* (Human with Buffaloes):

> *Greed eats our labour and divides people into classes*
> *The rice farmers fall to the bottom*
> *Insulted as backward and ignorant brutes*
> *With one important and sure thing: death.*

Although an elected government survived from 1973 to 1976, the military returned soon after and Caravan, like many of the student activists, went into hiding in the jungle. There they performed to villagers and hill-tribe people and gave the occasional concert. When the government offered an amnesty in 1979, most of the students, and Caravan too, disillusioned with the Communist Party's support for the Khmer Rouge in Cambodia, returned to normal life.

In the 1980s a new group emerged to carry on Caravan's work, **Carabou**. The band split up but has had several reunions; their influence is still strong, with leader Ad Carabou and several others garnering awards at the annual Season Awards for popular music in 2001. However, despite the bloody street riots of 1992 (in protest at the then military-installed government) once again bringing "songs for life" artists out to support the pro-democracy protests, since the 1980s the strong social activism of Caravan's early years has generally been replaced by more individual and personal themes. The current top act is fresh-faced singer-songwriter **Pongsit Kamphee**, whose earnest approach and rise through the ranks (he was reportedly once a stagehand for Caravan) have garnered him a sizeable following.

Musically, the genre has changed little in 25 years, remaining strongly rooted in Western folk-rock styles. Songs for life fans should check out cassette stalls at Bangkok's Chatuchak Weekend Market (see p.161), several of which specialize in this genre.

Luk thung

Go to one of the huge **luk thung** shows held in a temple or local stadium on the outskirts of Bangkok, or to any temple fair in the countryside, and you'll hear one of the great undiscovered popular musics of Asia. The shows, amid the bright lights, foodstalls and fairground games, last several hours and involve dozens of dancers and costume changes. In contrast with *luk grung*, *luk thung* (literally, "child of the field") has always been associated with the rural and urban poor, and because of this has gained nationwide popularity over the past forty years.

According to *luk thung* DJ Jenpope Jobkrabunwan, the term was first coined by Jamnong Rangsitkuhn in 1962, but the first song in the style was *Oh Jow Sow Chao Rai* (Oh, the Vegetable Grower's Bride), recorded in 1937, and the genre's first big singer, **Kamrot Samboonanon**, emerged in the mid-1940s. Originally called *pleng talat* (market songs) or *pleng chiwit* (songs of life), the style blended together folk songs (*pleng pua bahn*), central Thai classical music and Thai folk dances (*ram wong*). Malay strings and fiddles were added in the 1950s, as were Latin brass and rhythms like the cha-cha-cha and mambo (Asian tours by Xavier Cugat influenced many Asian pop styles during the 1950s), as well as elements from Hollywood movie music and "yodelling" country and western vocal styles from the likes of Gene Autry and Hank Williams. In 1952, a new singer, **Suraphon Sombatjalern**, made his debut with a song entitled *Nam Da Sow Vienne* (Tears of the Vientiane Girl) and became the undisputed king of the style until his untimely murder (for serious womanizing, rumour has it) in 1967. Along with female singer **Pongsri Woranut**, Sombatjalern helped develop the music into a mature form.

Today, *luk thung* is a mix of Thai folk music and traditional entertainment forms like *likay* (travelling popular theatre), as well as a range of Western styles. There are certainly some strong musical affinities with other regional pop styles like Indonesian *dangdut* and Japanese *enka*, but what is distinctly Thai – quite apart from the spectacular live shows – are the singing styles and the content of the lyrics. Vocal styles are full of glissando, wavering grace notes and wailing ornamentation. A singer must have a wide vocal range, as the late *luk thung* megastar **Pompuang Duangjan** explained: "Making the *luk thung* sound is difficult, you must handle well the high and low notes. And because the emotional content is stronger than in *luk grung*, you must also be able to create a strongly charged atmosphere."

Pompuang had the kind of voice that turns the spine to jelly. She rose to prominence during the late 1970s, joining sweet-voiced **Sayan Sanya** as the biggest male and female names in the business. Like Sombatjalern, both came from the rural peasantry, making identification with themes and stories that related directly to the audience much easier. Songs narrate mini-novellas, based around typical characters like the lorry driver, peasant lad or girl, poor farmer, prostitute or maid; and the themes are those of going away to the big city, infidelity, grief, tragedy and sexual pleasure. Interestingly, it is not always the lyrics that carry the sexual charge of the song (and if lyrics are deemed too risqué by the authorities the song will be subject to strict censorship) but rather the vocal style and the stage presentation, which can be very bawdy indeed.

With the advent of TV and the rise in popularity of *string*, the number of large upcountry *luk thung* shows has declined. It's not easy, said Pompuang, to tour with over a hundred staff, including the dancers in the *hang kruang* (cho-

rus). "We play for over four hours," she says, "but *string* bands, with only a few staff members, play a paltry two hours!" Her response to the advent of *string* and the increasing importance of promotional videos was to develop a dance-floor-oriented sound – **electronic luk thung**. Few *luk thung* singers are capable of this, but Pompuang had the vocal range to tackle both ballad forms and the up-tempo dance numbers. Her musical diversification increased her popularity enormously, and when she died in 1992, aged only 31, up to 200,000 people, ranging from royalty to the rural poor, made their way to her funeral in her home town of Suphanburi.

Since Pompuang's death, the top *luk thung* slot has been occupied by **"Got" Chakrapand Arbkornburi**, whose switch from pop to full-time *luk thung* has brought many younger listeners to the style. Bangkok's first 24-hour *luk thung* radio station, Luk Thung FM (90MHz), was launched in August 1997, and it's even hip for the middle class to like *luk thung* these days. Listeners have been snapping up collections of *luk thung* classics, and several veteran singers have relaunched their careers, including **Sodsai Rungphothong**, who had a monster two-million seller with his *Rak Nong Porn* album. A new generation of singers has also emerged, with artists like **Monsit Kamsoi, Arpaporn Nakornsawan, Yingyong Yodbuangarm** and **Dao Mayuree**. There is some truth, however, in the criticism that some new *luk thung* stars are being artificially manufactured just like their pop and rock counterparts, and there's a tendency to rate a pretty face over vocal expertise.

For many years, *luk thung* was sung by performers from the Suphanburi area in the central plains, but more regional voices are being heard in the genre now, with northeasterners now outnumbering these singers. A slightly faster rhythm, *luk thung* Isaan, has developed, led initially by **Pimpa Pornsiri**, who called the style *luk thung prayuk*. The south, too, has its own *luk thung* star, in the enormously popular **Ekachai Srivichai**. But the most surprising development has been the emergence of not one but two blonde-haired, blue-eyed foreigners singing *luk thung* and *mor lam*. First up is Swede **Manat "Jonas" Andersson**, who rose to national prominence with his debut album, *Pom Cheu Jonas*; he's already a fixture on the *luk thung* circuits. Anglo-Dutch singer **Kristy Gibson** sings mainly *luk thung Isaan* and *mor lam*; her debut album, *Der Kha Der*, was also received rapturously by *luk thung* fans.

Mor lam

Mor lam is the folk style from the poor, dry northeastern region of Isaan, an area famed for droughts, hot spicy food, good boxers and great music. Over the last ten years, the modern pop form of this style has risen dramatically, at *luk thung*'s expense. Traditionally, a *mor lam* is a master of the *lam* singing style (sung in the Isaan dialect, which is actually Lao), and is accompanied by the *khaen* (bamboo mouth organ), the *phin* (two- to four-string guitar) and *ching* (small temple bells). Modern **mor lam** developed from *mor lam glawn*, a narrative form where all-night singing jousts are held between male and female singers, and from *mor lam soeng*, the group-dance form. Both still play an important part in many social events like weddings, births and deaths, festivals and temple fairs. A *mor lam* may sing intricate fixed-metre Lao epic poems or may relate current affairs in a spontaneous rap. In the large groups, Western instruments like guitar (replacing the *phin*) and synthesizer (for the *khaen*) are used.

The style came to national prominence some fifteen to twenty years ago, when a female *mor lam* singer, **Banyen Rakgan**, appeared on national TV. In the early 1980s the music was heard not only in Isaan but also in the growing

CDs produced in Thailand feature mainly *string* artists and a few *luk thung* bands. There are, however, a few excellent discs on Western labels. There is a lot more variety on Thai **cassettes**, the buying of which can be fun. In Bangkok, check out day and night markets, or the tape stores on Thanon Charoen Krung (New Road), and tell the sellers the name of an artist you'd like to hear. Most major *luk thung* or *mor lam* artists release a cassette every three months, which is often given an artist's series number. Old-style recordings of Suraphon Sombatjalern and the like can be found on the ground floor of the *Mah Boon Krong Centre* near Siam Square. All the releases listed here are CDs except where stated; the rest are Thai cassettes.

Classical

Fong Naam *The Hang Hong Suite* (Nimbus, UK). A good introduction to the vivacious and glittering sound of classical Thai music, from one of Thailand's best ensembles. The disc includes some very upbeat funeral music and a series of parodies of the musical languages of neighbouring cultures. *The Sleeping Angel* (Nimbus, UK) is also a splendid recording.

Musicians of the National Dance Company of Cambodia *Homrong* (Real World, UK). Some tracks on this disc are strikingly similar to Thai classical music; others are more folk-based and are clearly at the root of present-day *kantrum*. The story of the National Dance Company reviving the traditions of classical Cambodian music after the horrific destruction of the Pol Pot regime is inspiring.

The Prasit Thawon Ensemble *Thai Classical Music* (Nimbus, UK). The ensemble recorded this after a performance at the 5th International Conference of Thai Studies at London University in 1993. Brilliant playing (and outstanding recording quality) from some of Thailand's best performers, mainly of *piphat* style. Includes the overture *Homrong Sornthong* and, on *Cherd Chin*, some scintillating dialogues between different instruments.

Various *Thailande* (Auvidis/UNESCO, France). An atmospheric disc of three contrasting ensembles from Chiang Mai. Intricate textures that draw you in.

Hill-tribe music

Various *Thailand: Musiques et Chants des Peuples du Triangle d'Or* (Globe Music, France). Recordings of the traditional music of Thailand's main hill-tribe groups: Meo, Lisu, Shan, Lahu, Yao, Akha and Karen.

Chao ley (sea gypsy) music

Various *Sea Gypsies of the Andaman Sea* (Topic, UK). The traditional music of the nomadic fisherfolk in southern Thailand, mostly recorded in the Surin islands.

Luk thung

Pompuang Duangjan *Greatest Hits Vol 2* (BKP, Thailand). A representative selection of *luk thung* hits from the late star of popular country music with a full, rich voice unlike anyone else in the business. In Thailand, the best of many cassettes to go for is called *Pompuang Lai Por Sor* (Pompuang's Many Eras) (Topline, Thailand).

Monsit Khamsoi *Khai Kwai Chuay Mae* (Sell the Buffalo to Help Mum) and *Sang Nang* (While I'm Away) (both on Sure, Thailand). He came from nowhere and was considered too ugly to make it, but with his humility and that fabulously soft emotive voice, he captured the hearts of the entire nation and proved to be the best male *luk thung* singer to emerge for years. Lovely musical setting for his reinterpretations of the classics.

Pimpa Pornsiri *Tee Sud Khong Pimpa* (The Biggest of Pimpa) (Rota, Thailand). All the hits of *luk thung prayuk*'s biggest name.

Suranee Ratchasima *Jeep Dor* (Returning Courtship) (Sure, Thailand). Rising *luk thung* singer from Khorat shows off her pipes on this set of standards.

Sodsai Rungphothong *Rak Nong Porn* (I Love Young Porn) (Topline, Thailand). The killer comeback by veteran Sodsai, with the title track garnering two million in sales. Classic old-style *luk thung* – jangling temple bells and brass blaring, and Sodsai wailing over it all.

Sayan Sanya *Luk Thung Talap Thong* (*Luk Thung* from the Golden Tape) (Onpa, Thailand). Heir to Sombatjalern's throne, sweet-voiced Sanya has never sounded better than on this greatest hits collection.

Suraphon Sombatjalern *Luk Thung Talap Thong* (*Luk Thung* from the Golden Tape) (Onpa, Thailand). Greatest hits by the king of *luk thung*. Great voice, great songs, great backing – Siamese soul.

Ood Oh-pah Tossaporn *Pleng Wan* (Sweet Songs) (Onpa, Thailand). Rock singer Tossaporn made a stunning *luk thung* debut with this 1990 recording, with catchy Thai classical backing.

Mor lam/northeastern music

Jintara Poonlarp *Dam Jai Nam Da* (Depends on the Tears) (MGA, Thailand). Poonlarp has conquered *mor lam* over the past few years with her powerful voice and fast delivery.

Banyen Rakgan *Luk Thung, Mor Lam Sood Hit* (*Luk Thung, Mor Lam* Top Hits) (Rota, Thailand). Sixteen scorchers from the first national *mor lam* star. Rakgan's voice is a standout. Good example of the big-band *mor lam* sound.

Isan Slété *Songs and Music from North East Thailand* (Globestyle, UK). Excellent selection of traditional *mor lam*. Vocal and instrumental numbers, played by a band of master musicians.

Pornsak Songsaeng *Gaud Mawn Nawn Pur* (Holding the Pillow in my Delirium) (Onpa, Thailand). *Mor lam*'s top male act, a fine singer with a deep, distinctive voice.

Sarm Tone *Pong Pong Chung* (Sound of the Drum) (Kita, Thailand). An interesting group, founded in 1990, who mix *mor lam* and *luk thung* in a humorous urban pop style. Good fun live, too.

Various *Instrumental Music of Northeast Thailand* (King, Japan). Wonderful collection of *bong lang* and related instrumental northeastern styles. Lively and fun. Unmissable.

Various, featuring Chaweewan Damnoen *Mor lam Singing of Northeast Thailand* (King, Japan). The only female *mor lam* National Artist, Chaweewan Damnoen, headlines this fine collection of many *lam* (singing) styles. Most *mor lam glawn* narrative and dance styles, even spirit-possession rituals, are included on this, one of the best Thai CDs available.

String and songs for life

Carabou *Made in Thailand* and *Ameri-koi* (both Krabue, Thailand). Two classic albums from the songs-for-life giants. *Made in Thailand* was right in tune with the times and targeted social problems like consumerism, the sex trade and a failing education system. *Ameri-koi* (Greedy America) is even more nationalistic than the previous one but it also hits out at Thai migrant workers exploited by labour brokers.

Modern Dog *Modern Dog* (Bakery Music, Thailand). This album of alternative rock marked an important change of direction for the Thai rock scene.

Kantrum

Darkie *Darkie, Rock II: Buk Jah* (Movie Music, Thailand). The first-ever *kantrum* crossover album achieved nationwide stardom for the King of Kantrum. Darkie's booming voice moves from rap-like delivery to moans and wails, shadowed closely by the fiddle and some funky riddims. Unmissable.

Darkie *Kantrum Rock Vols I & II* (available on separate cassettes). Benchmark recordings by *kantrum*'s only major star: Darkie's fine wailing voice is featured in rock-*kantrum*, *kantrum* and *kantrum luk thung*.

slums of Bangkok, as rural migrants poured into the capital in search of work. By the end of the decade stars like **Jintara Poonlarp** (with her hit song "Isaan Woman Far From Home") and **Pornsak Songsaeng** could command the same sell-out concerts as their *luk thung* counterparts. The current bestseller is **Siriporn Ampaiporn**, whose strong vocals burst upon the scene with the monster-selling *Bor Rak Si Dam* album.

The format of a *mor lam* performance is similar to that of *luk thung* shows – lots of dancers in wild costumes, comedy skits and a large backing orchestra – as is the subject matter. The music is definitely hot, especially if you see it live, when bands will often play through the night, never missing the groove for a minute, driven on by the relentless *phin* and *khaen* playing. To some people, the fast plucking style of the *phin* gives a West African or Celtic tinge; the *khaen* has a rich sound – over a bass drone players improvise around the melody, while at the same time vamping the basic rhythm. Male and female singers rotate or duet humorous love songs, which often start with one of the *mor khaen* setting up the beat. They sing about topical issues, bits of news, crack lewd jokes or make fun of the audience – all very tongue-in-cheek.

Musically, however, *mor lam* and *luk thung* are very different; *mor lam* has a much faster, relentless rhythm and the vocal delivery is rapid-fire, rather like a rap. You'll immediately recognize a *mor lam* song with its introductory wailing moan "*Oh la naw*", meaning "fortune". *Mor lam* artists, brought up bilingually, can easily switch from *luk thung* to *mor lam*, but *luk thung* artists, who only speak the national central Thai dialect (Siamese), cannot branch out so easily.

In the 1990s, *mor lam* musicians headed off the challenge of increasingly popular *string* bands by creating **mor lam sing**, a turbo-charged modern version of *mor lam glawn* played by small electric combos. The number of large touring *luk thung* or *mor lam* shows has declined in recent years, owing to high overheads, TV entertainment and the popularity of *string* bands, so *mor lam sing* satisfies the need for local music with a modern edge.

Kantrum: Thai-Cambodian pop

"Isaan nua (north) has *mor lam*, Isaan dai (south) has *kantrum*," sings **Darkie**, the first – and so far only – star of **kantrum**, Thai-Cambodian pop, in his song, "Isaan Dai Sah Muk Kee" (Southern Isaan Unity). His music is a very specific offshoot, from the southern part of Isaan, where Thai-Cambodians mix with ethnic Lao and Thais. So far *kantrum* is only popular in Isaan, and that seems unlikely to change, as few people outside the region speak either Cambodian or the Thai-Cambodian dialect, Suay, in which the songs are sung.

Modern *kantrum* has developed from Cambodian folk and classical music, played in a small group consisting of fiddle, small hand drums and *krab* (pieces of hardwood bashed together rather like claves). This traditional style is now quite hard to find in Thailand; some ten or so years ago, musicians started to electrify the music, using both traditional and Western instruments. Shunning the synthesizer preferred by his competitors like Khong Khoi, Oh-Yot and Ai Num Muang Surin, Darkie puts the wailing fiddle centre-stage, cranks up the rhythms (*kantrum* has a harder beat than even *mor lam*) and sets off with his deep, distinctive voice. In 1997, he broke new ground with *Darkie Rock II: Buk Jah*, the first *kantrum* crossover album to have success in the mainstream pop market.

John Clewley
(Adapted from the *Rough Guide to World Music*)

The hill tribes

Originating in various parts of China and Southeast Asia, the hill tribes are often termed Fourth World people, in that they are migrants who continue to migrate without regard for established national boundaries. Most arrived in Thailand during the last century, and many of the hill peoples are still found in other parts of Southeast Asia – in Vietnam, for example, where the French used the *montagnards* ("mountain dwellers") in their fight against communism. Since 1975, a large percentage of the one million refugees that Thailand has accepted from Burma, Laos and Cambodia has been hill-tribe people. Some, however, have been around for much longer, like the Lawa, who are thought to have been the first settlers in northern Thailand, though these days they have largely been assimilated into mainstream Thai culture. Called **chao khao** (mountain people) by the Thais, the tribes are mostly preliterate societies, whose sophisticated systems of customs, laws and beliefs have developed to harmonize relationships between individuals and their environment. In recent years their ancient culture has come under threat, faced with the effects of rapid population growth and the ensuing competition for land, discrimination and exploitation by lowland Thais, and tourism. However, the integrity of their way of life is as yet largely undamaged, and what follows is the briefest of introductions to an immensely complex subject. If you want to learn more, visit the Tribal Museum in Chiang Mai (see p.316), or the Hill Tribe Museum and Handicrafts Shop in Chiang Rai (see p.381) before setting out on a trek.

Agriculture

Although the hill tribes keep some livestock, such as pigs, poultry and elephants, the base of their economy is **swidden agriculture**, a crude form of shifting cultivation also practised by many Thai lowland farmers. At the beginning of the season an area of jungle is cleared and burned, producing ash to fertilize rice, corn, chillies and other vegetables, which are replanted in succeeding years until the soil's nutrients are exhausted. This system is sustainable with a low population density, which allows the jungle time to recover before it is used again. However, with the increase in population over recent decades, ever greater areas are being exhausted, and the decreasing forest cover is leading to erosion and micro-climatic change.

As a result, many villages took up the large-scale production of **opium** to supplement the traditional subsistence crops, though the Thai government has now largely eradicated opium production in the north. However, the cash crops which have been introduced in its place have often led to further environmental damage, as these low-profit crops require larger areas of cultivation, and thus greater deforestation. Furthermore, the water supplies have become polluted with chemical pesticides, and, although more environmentally sensitive agricultural techniques are being introduced, they have yet to achieve widespread acceptance.

Religion and festivals

Although some tribes have taken up Buddhism and others – especially among the Karen, Mien and Lahu – have been converted by Christian missionaries bringing the incentives of education and modern medicine, the hill tribes are predominantly **animists**. In this belief system, all natural objects are inhabited by spirits which, along with the tribe's ancestor spirits and the supreme divine spirit, must be propitiated to prevent harm to the family or village. Most villages have one or more religious leaders, which may include a priest who looks after the ritual life of the community, and at least one shaman who has the power to mediate with the spirits and prescribe what has to be done to keep them happy. If a member of the community is sick, for example, the shaman will be consulted to determine what action has insulted which spirit, and will then carry out the correct sacrifice.

The most important festival, celebrated by all the tribes, is at **New Year**, when whole communities take part in dancing, music and rituals particular to each tribe: Hmong boys and girls, for instance, take part in a courting ritual at this time, while playing catch with a ball. The New Year festivals are not held on fixed dates, but at various times during the cool-season slack period in the agricultural cycle from January to March.

Costumes and handicrafts

The most conspicuous characteristics of the hill tribes are their exquisitely crafted **costumes** and adornments, the styles and colours of which are particular to each group. Although many men and children now adopt Western clothes for everyday wear, with boys in particular more often running around in long shorts and T-shirts with logos, most women and girls still wear the traditional attire at all times. It's the women who make the clothes too – some still spin their own cotton, though many Hmong, Lisu and Mien women are prosperous enough to buy materials from itinerant traders. Other distinctive hill-tribe artefacts – tools, jewellery, weapons and musical instruments – are the domain of the men, and specialist **blacksmiths** and **silversmiths** have such high status that some attract business from villages many kilometres away. Jewellery, the chief outward proof of a family's wealth, is displayed most obviously by Lisu women at the New Year festivals, and is commonly made from silver melted down from Indian and Burmese coins, though brass, copper and aluminium are also used.

Clothing and **handicrafts** were not regarded as marketable products until the early 1980s, when co-operatives were set up to manufacture and market these goods, which are now big business in the shops of Thailand. The hill tribes' deep-dyed coarse cloth, embroidered with simple geometric patterns in bright colours, has become popular among middle-class Thais as well as farang visitors. Mien material, dyed indigo or black with bright snowflake embroidery, is on sale in many shops, as is the simple but very distinctive Akha work – coarse black cotton, with triangular patterns of stitching and small fabric patches in rainbow colours, usually made up into bags and hats. The Hmong's much more sophisticated **embroidery** and **appliqué**, added to jacket lapels and cuffs and skirt hems, is also widely seen – Blue Hmong skirts, made on a base of indigo-dyed cotton with a white geometric batik design and embroidered in loud primary colours, are particularly attractive.

Besides clothing, the hill tribes' other handicrafts, such as knives and wooden or bamboo musical pipes, have found a market amongst farangs, the most saleable product being the intricate engraving work of their silversmiths, especially in the form of chunky bracelets. For a sizeable minority of villages, handicrafts now provide the security of a steady income to supplement what they make from farming.

The main tribes

Within the small geographical area of northern Thailand there are at least ten different hill tribes, many of them divided into distinct subgroups – the following are the main seven, listed in order of population and under their own names, rather than the sometimes derogatory names used by Thais. (The Thai Yai – or Shan – the dominant group in most of the west of the region, are not a hill tribe, but a subgroup of Thais.) Beyond the broad similarities outlined above, this section sketches their differences in terms of history, economy and religion, and describes elements of dress by which they can be distinguished.

Karen

The **Karen** (called Kaliang or Yang in Thai) form by far the largest hill-tribe group in Thailand with a population of about 500,000, and are the second oldest after the Lawa, having begun to arrive here from Burma and China in the seventeenth century. The Thai Karen, many of them refugees from Burma (see box on p.280), mostly live in a broad tract of land west of Chiang Mai, which stretches along the border from Mae Hong Son province all the way down to Kanchanaburi, with scattered pockets in Chiang Mai, Chiang Rai and Phayao provinces.

The Karen traditionally practise a system of **rotating cultivation** – ecologically far more sensitive than slash-and-burn – in the valleys of this region and on low hills. Their houses, very similar to those of lowland Thais, are small (they do not live in extended family groups), built on stilts and made of bamboo or teak; they're often surrounded by fruit gardens and neat fences. As well as farming their own land, the Karen often hire out their labour to Thais and other hill tribes, and keep a variety of livestock including elephants, which used to be employed in the teak trade but are now often found giving rides to trekking parties.

Unmarried Karen women wear loose white or undyed V-necked shift dresses, often decorated with grass seeds at the seams. Some subgroups decorate them more elaborately, Sgaw girls with a woven red or pink band above the waist, and Pwo girls with woven red patterns in the lower half of the shift. Married women wear blouses and skirts in bold colours, predominantly red or blue. Men generally wear blue, baggy trousers with red or blue shirts, a simplified version of the women's blouse.

Hmong

Called the Meo by the Thais (a term meaning "barbarian"), the **Hmong** (free people) originated in central China or Mongolia and are now found widely in northern Thailand; they are still the most widespread minority group in south China. There are two subgroups: the **Blue Hmong**, who live around and to the west of Chiang Mai; and the **White Hmong**, who are found to the east. A separate group of White Hmong (Gua'm-ba Meo) live in refugee camps along the border with Laos: they fled from Laos after the end of the Vietnam War, during which they had sided with the Americans. Their overall population in Thailand is about just over 111,000, making them the second-largest hill-tribe group.

Of all the hill tribes, the Hmong have been the quickest to move away from subsistence farming. In the past, Hmong people were more involved in opium production than most other tribes in Thailand, though now many have eagerly embraced the newer cash crops. Hmong clothing has become much in demand in Thailand, and Hmong women will often be seen at markets throughout the country selling their handicrafts. The women, in fact, are expected to do most of the work on the land and in the home.

Hmong **villages** are usually built at high altitudes, below the crest of a protecting hill. Although wealthier families sometimes build the more comfortable

Thai-style houses, most stick to the traditional house, with its dirt floor and a roof descending almost to ground level. They live together in extended families, with two or more bedrooms and a large guest platform.

The Blue Hmong dress in especially striking **clothes**. The women wear intricately embroidered pleated skirts decorated with parallel horizontal bands of red, pink, blue and white; their jackets are of black satin, with wide orange and yellow embroidered cuffs and lapels. White Hmong women wear black baggy trousers and simple jackets with blue cuffs. Men of both groups generally wear baggy black pants with colourful sashes round the waist, and embroidered jackets closing over the chest with a button at the left shoulder. All the Hmong are famous for their chunky **silver jewellery**, which the women wear every day, the men only on special occasions: they believe silver binds a person's spirits together, and wear a heavy neck ring to keep the spirits weighed down in the body.

Lahu

The **Lahu**, who originated in the Tibetan highlands, migrated to southern China, Burma and Laos centuries ago; only since the end of the nineteenth century did they begin to come into Thailand from northern Burma. They're called Muser – from the Burmese word for "hunter" – by the Thais, because many of the first Lahu to reach northern Thailand were professional hunters. With a population of about 82,000, they are the third-largest hill-tribe group: most of their settlements are concentrated close to the Burmese border, in Chiang Rai, northern Chiang Mai and Mae Hong Son provinces, but families and villages change locations frequently. The Lahu language has become the *lingua franca* of the hill tribes, since the Lahu often hire out their labour. About one-third of Lahu have been converted to Christianity (through exposure in colonial Burma), and many have abandoned their traditional way of life as a result. The remaining animist Lahu believe in a village guardian spirit, who is often worshipped at a central temple that is surrounded by banners and streamers of white and yellow flags. Village houses are built on high stilts with walls of bamboo or wooden planks, thatched with grass. While subsistence farming is still common, sustainable agriculture – plantations of orchards, tea or coffee – is becoming more prevalent, and cash crops such as corn and cotton have taken the place of opium.

Some Lahu women wear a distinctive black cloak with diagonal white stripes, decorated in bold red and yellow at the top of the sleeve, but traditional costume has been supplanted by the Thai shirt and sarong amongst many Lahu groups. The tribe is famous for its richly embroidered **yaam** (shoulder bags), which are widely available in Chiang Mai.

Akha

The poorest of the hill tribes, the **Akha** (Kaw or Eekaw in Thai) migrated from Tibet over two thousand years ago to Yunnan in China, where at some stage they had an organized state and kept written chronicles of their history – these chronicles, like the Akha written language, are now lost. From the 1910s the tribe began to settle in Thailand and is found in four provinces – Chiang Rai, Chiang Mai, Lampang and Phrae – with a population of nearly 50,000 in about 250 villages. The greatest concentration of Akha villages is in Chiang Rai province followed by northern Chiang Mai, near the Burmese border – recently many Akha have fled persecution in politically unstable Burma. A large Akha population still lives in Yunnan and there are communities in neighbouring Laos as well as in Burma.

The Akha are less open to change than the other hill tribes, and have maintained their old agricultural methods of **shifting cultivation**. The Akha's form of animism – *Akhazang*, "the way of life of the Akha" – has also survived in uncompromised form. As well as spirits in the natural world, *Akhazang* encompasses the worship of ancestor spirits: some Akha can recite the names of over sixty generations of forebears.

Every Akha village is entered through ceremonial **gates** decorated with carvings depicting human activities and attributes – even cars and aeroplanes – to indicate to the spirit world that beyond here only humans should pass. To touch any of these carvings, or to show any lack of respect to them, is punishable by fines or sacrifices. The gates are rebuilt every year, so many villages have a series of gates, the older ones in a state of disintegration. Another characteristic of an Akha villages is its giant **swing** (also replaced each year), and used every August in a swinging festival in which the whole population takes part.

Akha **houses** are recognizable by their low stilts and steeply pitched roofs, though some may use higher stilts to reflect higher status. Even more distinctive is the elaborate **headgear** which women wear all day; it frames the entire face and usually features white beads interspersed with silver coins, topped with plumes of red taffeta and framed by dangling hollow silver balls and other jewellery or strings of beads. The rest of their heavy costume is made up of decorated tube-shaped ankle-to-knee leggings, an above-the-knee black skirt with a white beaded centrepiece, and a loose-fitting black jacket with heavily embroidered cuffs and lapels.

Mien

The **Mien** (called Yao in Thai) consider themselves the aristocrats of the hill tribes. Originating in central China, they began migrating southward more than two thousand years ago to southern China, Vietnam, Laos and Thailand; in southern China they used to have such power that at one time a Mien princess was married to a Chinese emperor. In Thailand today the Mien are widely scattered throughout the north, with concentrations around Nan, Phayao and Chiang Rai, and a population of about 41,000. They are the only hill tribe to have a written language, and a codified religion based on medieval Chinese Taoism, although in recent years there have been many Mien converts to Christianity and Buddhism. In general, the Mien strike a balance between integration into Thai life and maintenance of their separate cultural base. Many earn extra cash by selling exquisite embroidery and religious scrolls, painted in bold Chinese style.

Mien villages are not especially distinctive: their houses are usually built of wooden planks on a dirt floor, with a guest platform of bamboo in the communal living area. The **clothes** of the women, however, are instantly recognizable: long black jackets with glamorous looking stole-like lapels of bright scarlet wool, heavily embroidered loose trousers in intricate designs which can take up to two years to complete, and a similarly embroidered black turban. The caps of babies are also very beautiful, richly embroidered with red or pink pom-poms. On special occasions, like weddings, women and children wear silver neck rings, with silver chains decorated with silver ornaments extending down the back, and even their turbans are crossed with lengths of silver. A Mien woman's wedding head-dress is quite extraordinary, a carefully constructed platform with arched supports which are covered with red fabric and heirlooms of embroidered cloth. Two burgundy-coloured fringes create side curtains obscuring her face, and the only concession to modernity is the black insulating tape that holds the structure to her head.

Lisu

The **Lisu** (Lisaw in Thai), who originated in eastern Tibet, first arrived in Thailand in 1921 and are found mostly in the west, particularly between Chiang Mai and Mae Hong Son, but also in western Chiang Rai, Chiang Mai and Phayao provinces, with a population of around 30,000. Whereas the other hill tribes are led by the village headman or shaman, the Lisu are organized into patriarchal clans which have authority over many villages, and their strong sense of clan rivalry often results in public violence.

The Lisu live in extended families at moderate to high altitudes, in houses built on the ground, with dirt floors and bamboo walls. Both men and women dress colourfully; the women wear a blue or green parti-coloured knee-length tunic, split up the sides to the waist, with a wide black belt and blue or green pants. At New Year, the women don dazzling outfits, including waistcoats and belts of intricately fashioned silver and turbans with multicoloured pom-poms and streamers; traditionally, the men wear green, pink or yellow baggy pants and a blue jacket.

Lawa

The history of the **Lawa** people (Lua in Thai) is poorly understood, but it seems very likely that they have inhabited Thailand since at least the eighth century; they were certainly here when the Thais arrived eight hundred years ago. The Lawa people are found only in Thailand; they believe that they migrated from Cambodia and linguistically they are certainly closely related to Mon-Khmer, but some archeologists think that their origins lie in Micronesia, which they left perhaps two thousand years back.

This lengthy cohabitation with the Thais has produced large-scale integration, so that most Lawa villages are indistinguishable from Thai settlements and most Lawa speak Thai as their first language. However, in an area of about 500 square kilometres between Hot, Mae Sariang and Mae Hong Son, the Lawa still live a largely traditional life, although even here the majority have adopted Buddhism and Thai-style houses. The basis of their economy is subsistence agriculture, with rice grown on terraces according to a sophisticated rotation system. Those identified as Lawa number just over ten thousand.

Unmarried Lawa women wear distinctive strings of orange and yellow beads, loose white blouses edged with pink, and tight skirts in parallel bands of blue, black, yellow and pink. After marriage, these brightly coloured clothes are replaced with a long fawn dress, but the beads are still worn. All the women wear their hair tied in a turban, and the men wear light-coloured baggy pants and tunics or, more commonly, Western clothes.

Books

The following books should be available in the UK, US or, more likely, Bangkok. Publishers' details for books published in the UK and US are given in the form "UK publisher; US publisher" where they differ; if books are published in one of these countries only, this follows the publisher's name; if books are published in Thailand, the city follows the publisher's name. The designation "o/p" means out of print – consult a library, specialist second-hand bookseller or online out-of-print-books service. Titles marked ⊠ are particularly recommended.

Travelogues

Carl Bock, *Temples and Elephants* (White Orchid Press, Bangkok). Nineteenth-century account of a rough journey from Bangkok to the far north, dotted with vivid descriptions of rural life and court ceremonial.

Ian Buruma, *God's Dust* (Phoenix Press). Modern portraits of various Southeast and East Asian countries, of which only forty pages are devoted to Thailand – worthwhile nevertheless for its sharp, unsentimental and stylish observations.

Donna Carrère, *Year of the Roasted Ear: Travels, Trials and Tribulations in Southeast Asia* (Summersdale, UK). Humorous and sharply observant warts-and-all account of the Carrère family's disaster-ridden holiday in Thailand and Malaysia.

⊠ **Karen Connelly**, *Touch the Dragon* (Silkworm Books, Chiang Mai). Evocative and humorous journal of an impressionable Canadian teenager, sent on an exchange programme to Den Chai in northern Thailand for a year.

Tristan Jones, *To Venture Further* (Adlard Coles Nautical, UK). Amazing tale of how the author, a veteran adventurer and an amputee, pioneered the crossing of the Kra isthmus in a longtail boat staffed by a disabled crew. Unusually forthright perspective on Thailand and its people.

Charles Nicholl, *Borderlines* (o/p in UK and US). Entertaining adventures and dangerous romance in the "Golden Triangle" form the core of this slightly hackneyed traveller's tale, interwoven with stimulating and well-informed cultural diversions.

⊠ **James O'Reilly and Larry Habegger** (eds), *Travelers' Tales: Thailand* (Travelers' Tales). Perfect background reading for any trip to Thailand: a collection of contemporary writings about the kingdom, some from established Thailand experts, social commentators and travel writers, others culled from enthusiastic visitors with unusual and often very funny stories to share. A great idea, thoughtfully and effectively executed.

⊠ **Alistair Shearer**, *Thailand: the Lotus Kingdom* (o/p in UK and US). Amusing, sensitive and well-researched contemporary travelogue: a cut above the competition.

Culture and society

Michael Carrithers, *The Buddha: A Very Short Introduction* (Oxford Paperbacks). Clear, accessible account of the life of the Buddha, and the development and significance of his thought.

Robert and Nanthapa Cooper, *Culture Shock! Thailand* (Kuperard; Graphic Art Center). Widely available but in every respect inferior to Denis Segaller's books on Thai culture (see opposite) – seems chiefly intended for prospective employers worried about how to deal with the Thai maid.

John R. Davies, *A Trekkers' Guide to the Hilltribes of Northern Thailand* (Footloose Books, o/p). Bite-sized but well-informed insight into hill-tribe cultures, including some practical information and a small dictionary of hill-tribe languages.

James Eckardt, *Bangkok People* (Asia Books, Bangkok). The collected articles of a renowned expat journalist, whose interviews and encounters with a gallery of different Bangkokians – from construction-site workers and street vendors to boxers and political candidates – add texture and context to the city.

Sanitsuda Ekachai, *Behind the Smile* (Thai Development Support Committee, Bangkok). Collected articles of a *Bangkok Post* journalist highlighting the effect of Thailand's sudden economic growth on the country's rural poor.

Jonathan Falla, *True Love and Bartholomew: Rebels on the Burmese Border* (Cambridge University Press). Well-written and sympathetic first-hand account of a year (1986-87) spent with the Karen inside their self-proclaimed independent state of

Kawtulay, about 15km west of the Thai/Burma border. An affectionate, informed and rare portrait of these persecuted people, their political demands and the minutiae of their daily lives. For more on the Karen, see box on p.280.

Marlane Guelden, *Thailand: Into the Spirit World* (Times Editions, Bangkok). In richly photographed coffee-table format, a wide-ranging, anecdotal account of the role of magic and spirits in Thai life, from tattoos and amulets to the ghosts of the violently dead.

★ **William J. Klausner,** *Reflections on Thai Culture* (Siam Society, Bangkok). Humorous accounts of an anthropologist living in Thailand since 1955. Entertaining mixture of the academic and the anecdotal; especially good on everyday life and festivals in Isaan villages.

★ **Elaine and Paul Lewis,** *Peoples of the Golden Triangle* (Thames and Hudson). Hefty, exhaustive work illustrated with excellent photographs, describing every aspect of hill-tribe life.

John McKinnon (ed.), *Highlanders of Thailand* (Oxford University Press, o/p). A rather dry but enlightening collection of essays on the hill tribes.

Trilok Chandra Majupuria, *Erawan Shrine and Brahma Worship in Thailand* (Tecpress, Bangkok). The most concise introduction to the complexities of Thai religion, with a much wider scope than the title implies.

★ **Cleo Odzer,** *Patpong Sisters* (Arcade Publishing). An American anthropologist's funny and touching account of her life with the prostitutes and bar girls of Bangkok's notorious red-light district. An enlightening and thought-provoking read, it's a surprisingly enjoyable page-turner too.

★ **Pasuk Phongpaichit and Sungsidh Piriyarangsan,** *Corruption and Democracy in Thailand* (Political Economy Centre, Faculty of Economics, Chulalongkorn University, Bangkok). Fascinating academic study, revealing the nuts and bolts of corruption in Thailand and its links with all levels of political life, and suggesting a route to a stronger society. Their sequel, a study of Thailand's illegal economy, *Guns, Girls, Gambling, Ganja*, co-written with Nualnoi Treerat (Silkworm Books, Chiang Mai) makes equally eye-opening and depressing reading.

Phya Anuman Rajadhon, *Some Traditions of the Thai* (DK Books, Bangkok). Meticulously researched essays written by one of Thailand's leading scholars, republished to commemorate the centenary of the author's birth.

Denis Segaller, *Thai Ways* and *More Thai Ways* (Asia Books, Bangkok). Fascinating collections of short pieces on Thai customs and traditions written for the former *Bangkok World* newspaper by a long-term English resident of Bangkok.

Pira Sudham, *People of Esarn* (Shire Books, Bangkok). Wry and touching potted life-stories of villagers who live in, leave and return to the poverty-stricken northeast, compiled by a northeastern village lad turned author.

Thanh-Dam Truong, *Sex, Money and Morality: Prostitution and Tourism in South-East Asia* (o/p in UK and US). Hard-hitting analysis of the marketing of Thailand as sex-tourism capital of Asia.

S. Tsow, *Thai Lite* (Asia Books, Bangkok). Humorous, occasionally insightful, collection of feature articles on a diverse range of subjects by a Bangkok-based journo.

William Warren, *Living in Thailand* (Thames and Hudson). Luscious coffee-table volume of traditional houses and furnishings, with an emphasis on the homes of Thailand's rich and famous; seductively photographed by Luca Invernizzi Tettoni.

Richard West, *Thailand: The Last Domino* (o/p in UK and US). Worthy attempt to get under the skin of "enigmatic Thailand", with a heady mix of political analysis, travelogue and anecdote. The author focuses on Thailand's relationships with neighbouring countries to show how it failed to become the "last domino" in the spread of communism.

History

Anna Leonowens, *The English Governess at the Siamese Court* (Tor Books, US). The mendacious memoirs of the nineteenth-century English governess that inspired the infamous Yul Brynner film *The King and I*; low on accuracy, high on inside-palace gossip.

Pasuk Phongpaichit and Chris Baker, *Thailand's Crisis* (Silkworm Books, Chiang Mai). Illuminating examination, sometimes heavy going, of the 1997 economic crisis and its political, social and cultural causes and effects, co-authored by a professor of economics at Bangkok's

Chulalongkorn University and a farang freelance writer.

Michael Smithies, *Old Bangkok* (Oxford University Press, o/p). Brief, anecdotal history of the capital's early development, emphasizing what remains to be seen of bygone Bangkok.

☐★ **William Stevenson**, *The Revolutionary King* (Constable, UK). Fascinating biography of the normally secretive King Bhumibol, by a British journalist who was given unprecedented access to the monarch and his family. The overall approach is fairly uncritical, but lots of revealing insights emerge along the way.

John Stewart, *To the River Kwai: Two Journeys – 1943, 1979* (Bloomsbury). A survivor of the horrific World War II POW camps along the River Kwai, the author returns to the region, interlacing his wartime reminiscences with observations on how he feels and what he sees 36 years later.

William Warren, *Jim Thompson: the Legendary American of Thailand* (Jim Thompson Thai Silk Co, Bangkok). The engrossing biography of the ex-intelligence agent, art collector and Thai silk magnate whose disappearance in Malaysia in 1967 has never been satisfactorily resolved.

Joseph J. Wright Jr, *The Balancing Act: A History of Modern Thailand* (Asia Books, Bangkok). Detailed analysis of the Thai political scene from the end of the absolute monarchy in 1932 until the February 1991 coup; plenty of anecdotes and wider cultural references make it a far from dry read.

☐★ **David K. Wyatt**, *Thailand: A Short History* (Yale University Press). An excellent treatment, scholarly but highly readable, with a good eye for witty, telling details. Good chapters on the story of the Thais before they reached what's now Thailand, and on recent (up to 1984) developments.

Art and architecture

☐★ **Steve van Beek**, *The Arts of Thailand* (Charles E. Tuttle). Lavishly produced and perfectly pitched introduction to the history of Thai architecture, sculpture and painting, with superb photographs by Luca Invernizzi Tettoni.

Jean Boisselier, *The Heritage of Thai Sculpture* (Asia Books, Bangkok). Weighty but accessible seminal tome by influential French art historian.

☐★ **Susan Conway**, *Thai Textiles* (University of Washington Press, US). A fascinating, richly illustrated work which draws on sculptures and temple murals to trace the evolution of Thai weaving techniques and cos-

tume styles, and to examine the functional and ceremonial uses of textiles.

Dorothy H. Fickle, *Images of the Buddha in Thailand* (Oxford University Press, o/p). Clear, concise, though rather arid examination of Thai Buddha images of all periods, and the historical and religious influences which have shaped their development. Well illustrated, with a short introduction on the life of the Buddha himself.

Betty Gosling, *Sukhothai: Its History, Culture and Art* (Oxford University Press). Overpriced but thoroughly researched dissection of the ruins of Sukhothai and the kings who commissioned the building.

★ **Sumet Jumsai**, *Naga: Cultural Origins in Siam and the West Pacific* (Oxford University Press, o/p). Wide-ranging discussion of water symbols in Thailand and other parts of Asia, offering a stimulating mix of art, architecture, mythology and cosmology.

★ **Apinan Poshyananda**, *Modern Art In Thailand* (Oxford University Press, Singapore). Excellent introduction – the only one of its kind – which extends up to the early 1990s, with very readable discussions on dozens of individual artists, and lots of colour plates.

★ **Smithi Siribhadra and Elizabeth Moore**, *Palaces of the Gods: Khmer Art and Architecture in Thailand* (River Books, Bangkok). Lavishly produced tome covering all known Khmer sites in the country, with detailed but accessible descriptions and artistic assessments, illustrated with stunning photographs by Michael Freeman.

William Warren and Luca Invernizzi Tettoni, *Arts and Crafts of Thailand* (Thames and Hudson). Good-value large-format paperback, setting the wealth of Thai arts and crafts in cultural context, with plenty of attractive illustrations and colour photos.

Natural history and ecology

Hans-Ulrich Bernard with Marcus Brooke, *Insight Guide to Southeast Asian Wildlife* (APA). Adequate introduction to the flora and fauna of the region, with a fairly detailed focus on several of Thailand's national parks. Full of gorgeous photos, but not very useful for identifying species in the field.

★ **Ashley J. Boyd and Collin Piprell**, *Diving in Thailand* (Times Editions; Hippocrene). A thorough guide to 84 dive sites, detailing access, weather conditions, visibility, scenery and marine life for each, slanted towards the underwater photographer; general introductory sections on Thailand's marine life, conservation and photography tips.

Denis Gray, Collin Piprell and Mark Graham, *National Parks of Thailand* (Industrial Finance Corporation of Thailand, Bangkok). Useful and readable handbook for naturalists, covering all the major national parks and detailing the wildlife and forest types you're likely to come across in each.

Margaret S. Gremli and Helen E. Newman, *Insight Guides Underwater: Marine Life in the South China Sea* (APA). Although not extending to the Andaman coast, Thailand's best snorkelling and diving area, this handy, at-a-glance reference guide to reef fish and coral formations covers pretty much everything you'll see there as well as on the Gulf coast. Packed with clear and informative colour photos, yet small enough for a day-pack.

★ **Thom Henley**, *Waterfalls and Gibbon Calls* (Limmark, Thailand). Though ostensibly a guide to the flora, fauna and trails of Khao Sok National Park, this book contains so much interesting and easily digestible stuff on the plants, animals and birds found all over Thailand that it's worth buying even if you're not going to the park.

Philip Hurst, *Rainforest Politics* (Zed Books). Case studies of alarming ecological destruction in six Southeast Asian countries, sponsored by Friends of the Earth, which clearly and powerfully assesses the causes and offers pragmatic solutions.

Eric Valli and Diane Summers, *The Shadow Hunters* (Suntree, Thailand). Beautifully photographed photo-essay on the birds'-nest collectors of southern Thailand, with whom the authors spent over a year, together scaling the phenomenal heights of the sheer limestone walls.

Literature

Kampoon Boontawee, *A Child of the Northeast* (DK Books, Bangkok). Over-sentimental prizewinning novel set in 1930s Isaan, but well worth reading for its wealth of local colour and insights into northeastern folklore and customs.

Alastair Dingwall (ed), *Traveller's Literary Companion: Southeast Asia* (Inprint Publishing; Passport, o/p). A useful though rather dry reference, with a large section on Thailand, including a book list, well-chosen extracts, biographical details of authors and other literary notes.

Khammaan Khonkhai, *The Teachers of Mad Dog Swamp* (Silkworm Books, Chiang Mai). The engaging story of a young teacher who encounters opposition to his progressive ideas when he is posted to a remote village school in the northeast. A typical example of the "novels for life" genre, which were fashionable in the 1970s and are known for their strong moral stance.

Chart Korpjitti, *The Judgement* (Thai Modern Classics). Sobering modern-day tragedy about a good-hearted Thai villager who is ostracized by his hypocritical neighbours. Contains lots of interesting details on village life and traditions and thought-provoking passages on

the stifling conservatism of rural communities. Winner of the S.E.A. Write award in 1982.

Nitaya Masavisut and Matthew Grose, *The S.E.A. Write Anthology of Thai Short Stories and Poems* (Silkworm Books, Chiang Mai). Interesting medley of short stories and poems by eleven Thai writers who have won Southeast Asian Writers' Awards, providing a good introduction to the contemporary literary scene.

Kukrit Pramoj, *Si Phaendin: Four Reigns* (2 vols; DK Books, Bangkok). A kind of historical romance spanning the four reigns of Ramas V to VIII (1892–1946) as experienced by a heroine called Ploi. Written by former prime minister Kukrit Pramoj, the story has become a modern classic in Thailand, made into films, plays and TV dramas, with Ploi as the archetypal feminine role model.

Rama I, *Thai Ramayana* (Chalermnit, Bangkok). Slightly stilted abridged prose translation of King Rama I's version of the epic Hindu narrative, full of gleeful descriptions of bizarre mythological characters and supernatural battles. Essential reading if you want anything like a full appreciation of Thai painting, carving and classical dance.

Nikom Rayawa, *High Banks, Heavy Logs* (Penguin, o/p). Gentle tale of a philosophizing woodcarver and his traditional elephant-logging community, which won the Southeast Asian Writers' Award.

J.C. Shaw, *The Ramayana through Western Eyes* (DK Books, Bangkok). The bare bones of the epic tale are retold between tenuously comparable excerpts from Western poets, including Shakespeare, Shelley and Walt Whitman. Much more helpfully, the text is interspersed with key scenes from the murals at Bangkok's Wat Phra Kaeo.

S.P. Somtow, *Jasmine Nights* (Hamish Hamilton, o/p). An engaging and humorous rites-of-passage tale, of an upper-class boy learning what it is to be Thai.

★ **Khamsing Srinawk**, *The Politician and Other Stories* (Oxford University Press, o/p). A collection of brilliantly satiric short stories, full of pithy moral observation and biting irony, which capture the vulnerability of peasant farmers in the north and northeast, as they try to come to grips with the modern world. Written by an insider from a peasant family, who was educated at Chulalongkorn University, became a hero of the left, and joined the communist insurgents after the 1976 clampdown.

Atsiri Thammachoat, *Of Time and Tide* (Thai Modern Classics). Set in a fishing village near Hua Hin, this poetically written novella looks at how Thailand's fishing industry is changing, charting the effects on its fisherfolk and their communities.

Thailand in foreign literature

★ **Dean Barrett**, *Kingdom of Make-Believe* (Village East Books, US). Despite the clichéd ingredients – the Patpong go-go bar scene, opium smuggling in the Golden Triangle, Vietnam veterans – this novel about a return to Thailand following a twenty-year absence turns out to be a rewarding read, with engaging characters and a multi-dimensional take on the farang experience.

Botan, *Letters from Thailand* (DK Books, Bangkok). Probably the best introduction to the Chinese community in Bangkok, presented in the form of letters written over a twenty-year period by a Chinese emigrant to his mother. Branded as both anti-Chinese and anti-Thai, this 1969 prizewinning book is now mandatory reading in school social studies' classes.

Pierre Boulle, *The Bridge Over the River Kwai* (Random House). The World War II novel which inspired the David Lean movie and kicked off the Kanchanaburi tourist industry.

★ **Alex Garland**, *The Beach* (Penguin; Riverhead). Gripping and hugely enjoyable cult thriller about a young Brit who gets involved with a group of travellers living a utopian existence on an uninhabited Thai island. Tensions rise as people start to reveal their true personalities, and when the idyll begins to sour the book turns into a mesmerizing page-turner.

★ **Spalding Gray**, *Swimming to Cambodia* (Theatre Communications Group, US). Hugely entertaining and politically acute account of the actor and monologist's time in Thailand on location for the filming of *The Killing Fields*.

Christopher G Moore, *God Of Darkness* (Asia Books, Bangkok). Thailand's best-selling and most prolific expat novelist specializes in intricately woven thrillers packed with incisive detail of contemporary Thai life; this one is set during the economic crisis of 1997, which makes it an especially good read, with plenty of meat on endemic corruption and the desperate struggle for power within family and society.

Collin Piprell, *Yawn: A Thriller* (Asia Books, Bangkok). Enjoyable page-turner that spins a good yarn from the apparently disparate worlds of scuba diving and Buddhist retreats.

Set mainly in Pattaya and a thinly disguised Ko Pha Ngan, it stars a Canadian couple and a predictable cast of big-hearted hookers, degenerate ex-pats and an evil godfather figure.

Darin Strauss, *Chang & Eng* (Allison & Busby, UK). The imagined autobiography of the famous nineteenth-century Siamese twins, following their journey from houseboat on the Mekhong River via the freak shows of New York and London to married life in smalltown North Carolina.

Food and cookery

★ **Vatcharin Bhumichitr**, *The Taste of Thailand* (Pavilion; Collier, o/p). Another glossy introduction to this eminently photogenic country, this time through its food. The author runs a Thai restaurant in London and provides background colour as well as about 150 recipes adapted for Western kitchens.

Jacqueline M. Piper, *Fruits of South-East Asia* (Oxford University Press, o/p). An exploration of the bounteous fruits of the region, tracing their role in cooking, medicine, handicrafts and rituals. Well illustrated with photos, watercolours and early botanical drawings.

Travel guides

John R. Davies, *Touring Northern Thailand* (Footloose Books, o/p). Comprehensive listings of places of interest in the north, essentially for travellers with their own transport, with very useful odometer distances given throughout. Stretches as far south as Sukhothai and Mae Sot, though little attention paid to the area around Nan; published in 1991, so some information, especially on accommodation, out of date.

Oliver Hargreave, *Exploring Chiang Mai: City, Valley and Mountains*

(Within Books, Chiang Mai). Thorough guide to the city and out-of-town trips, with plenty of useful small-scale maps, written by a long-time resident.

William Warren, *Bangkok's Waterways: An Explorer's Handbook* (Asia Books, Bangkok). A cross between a useful guide and an indulgent coffee-table book: attractively produced survey of the capital's riverine sights, spiced with cultural and historical snippets.

Language

Thai belongs to one of the oldest families of languages in the world, Austro-Thai, and is radically different from most of the other tongues of Southeast Asia. Being tonal, Thai is extremely difficult for Westerners to master, but by building up from a small core of set phrases, you'll soon get the hang of enough to get by. Most Thais who deal with tourists speak some English, but once you stray off the beaten track you'll probably need at least a few words in Thai. Anywhere you go, you'll impress and get better treatment if you at least make an effort to speak a few words.

Distinct dialects are spoken in the north, the northeast and the south, which can increase the difficulty of comprehending what's said to you. **Thai script** is even more of a problem to Westerners, with 44 consonants to represent 21 consonant sounds and 32 vowels to deal with 48 different vowel sounds. However, street signs in touristed areas are nearly always written in Roman script as well as Thai, and in other circumstances you're better off asking than trying to unscramble the swirling mess of symbols, signs and accents. Transliteration into Roman script leads to many problems – see the box in the Introduction.

For the basics, the most useful **language book** on the market is *Thai: A Rough Guide Phrasebook* (Rough Guides), which covers the essential phrases and expressions in both Thai script and phonetic equivalents, as well as dipping into grammar and providing a menu reader and fuller vocabulary in dictionary format (English–Thai and Thai–English). Among pocket dictionaries available in Thailand, G.H. Allison's *Mini English–Thai and Thai–English Dictionary* (Chalermnit) has the edge over *Robertson's Practical English–Thai Dictionary* (Asia Books), although it's more difficult to find.

The best **teach–yourself course** is the expensive *Linguaphone Thai*, which includes six cassettes; *Colloquial Thai* (Routledge) covers some of the same ground less thoroughly. For a more traditional text book, try *The Fundamentals of the Thai Language* (Marketing Media Associates Co, UK), which is comprehensive, though hard going; G.H. Allison's *Easy Thai* (Tuttle) is best for those who feel the urge to learn the alphabet.

Pronunciation

Mastering **tones** is probably the most difficult part of learning Thai. Five different tones are used – low, middle, high, falling, and rising – by which the meaning of a single syllable can be altered in five different ways. Thus, using four of the five tones, you can make a sentence just from just one syllable: *mái mài mâi mãi* – "New wood burns, doesn't it?" As well as the natural difficulty in becoming attuned to speaking and listening to these different tones, Western efforts are complicated by our tendency to denote the overall meaning of a sentence by modulating our tones – for example, turning a statement into a question through a shift of stress and tone. Listen to native Thai speakers and you'll soon begin to pick up the different approach to tone.

The pitch of each tone is gauged in relation to your vocal range when speaking, but they should all lie within a narrow band, separated by gaps just big enough to differentiate them. The **low tones** (syllables marked `), **middle tones** (unmarked syllables), and **high tones** (syllables marked ´) should each

Greetings and basic phrases

Whenever you speak to a stranger in Thailand, you should end your sentence in *khráp* if you're a man, *khâ* if you're a woman – these untranslatable politening syllables will gain good will, and should always be used after *sawàt dii* (hello/goodbye) and *khàwp khun* (thank you). *Khráp* and *khâ* are also often used to answer "yes" to a question, though the most common way is to repeat the verb of the question (precede it with *mâi* for "no"). *Châi* (yes) and *mâi châi* (no) are less frequently used than their English equivalents.

Hello	*sawàt dii*
Where are you going? (not always meant literally, but used as a general greeting)	*pai nãi?*
I'm out having fun/ I'm travelling (answer to *pai nãi*, almost indefinable pleasantry)	*pai thîaw*
Goodbye	*sawàt dii/ la kàwn*
Good luck/cheers	*chôk dii*
Excuse me	*khãw thâwt*
Thank you	*khàwp khun*
It's nothing/it doesn't matter/ no problem	*mâi pen rai*
How are you?	*sabai dii rẽu?*
I'm fine	*sabai dii*
What's your name?	*khun chêu arai?*
My name is...	*phõm (men)/ diichãn (women) chêu...*
I come from...	*phõm/ diichãn maa jàak...*
I don't understand	*mâi khâo jai*
Do you speak English?	*khun phûut phasãa angkrìt dâi mãi?*

Do you have...?	*mii...mãi?*
Is there...?	*...mii mãi?*
Is...possible?	*...dâi mãi?*
Can you help me?	*chûay phõm/ diichãn dâi mãi?*
(I) want...	*ao...*
(I) would like to...	*yàak jà...*
(I) like...	*châwp...*
What is this called in Thai?	*nîi phasãa thai rîak wâa arai?*

Getting around

Where is the...?	*...yùu thîi nãi?*
How far?	*klai thâo rai?*
I would like to go to...	*yàak jà pai...*
Where have you been?	*pai nãi maa?*
Where is this bus going?	*rót nîi pai nãi?*
When will the bus leave?	*rót jà àwk mêua rai?*
What time does the bus arrive in...?	*rót theũng... kìi mohng?*
Stop here	*jàwt thîi nîi*
here	*thîi nîi*
over there	*thîi nâan/thîi nôhn*
right	*khwãa*
left	*sái*
straight	*trong*
north	*neũa*
south	*tâi*
east	*tawan àwk*
west	*tawan tòk*
near/far	*klâi/klai*
street	*thanõn*
train station	*sathàanii rót fai*
bus station	*sathàanii rót meh*
airport	*sanãam bin*
ticket	*tũa*
hotel	*rohng raem*
post office	*praisanii*
restaurant	*raan ahãan*
shop	*raan*
market	*talàat*

hospital	*rohng pha-yaabaan*
motorbike	*rót mohtoesai*
taxi	*rót táksîi*
boat	*reua*

Accommodation and shopping

How much is...?	*...thâo rai/kìi bàat?*
How much is a room here per night?	*hâwng thîi nîi kheun lá thâo rai?*
Do you have a cheaper room?	*mii hâwng thùuk kwàa mãi?*
Can I/we look at the room?	*duu hâwng dâi mãi?*
I/We'll stay two nights	*jà yùu sãwng kheun*
Can you reduce the price?	*lót raakhaa dâi mãi?*
Can I store my bag here?	*fàak krapão wái thîi nîi dâi mãi?*
cheap/expensive	*thùuk/ phaeng*
air-con room	*hãwng ae*
ordinary room	*hãwng thammadaa*
telephone	*thohrásàp*
laundry	*sák phâa*
blanket	*phâa hòm*
fan	*phát lom*

General adjectives

alone	*khon diaw*
another	*ìik...nèung*
bad	*mâi dii*
big	*yài*
clean	*sa-àat*
closed	*pìt*
cold (object)	*yen*
cold (person or weather)	*não*
delicious	*aròi*
difficult	*yâak*
dirty	*sokaprok*
easy	*ngâi*
fun	*sanùk*
hot (temperature)	*ráwn*

hot (spicy)	*pèt*
hungry	*hiũ khâo*
ill	*mâi sabai*
open	*pòet*
pretty	*sũay*
small	*lek*
thirsty	*hĩu nám*
tired	*nèu-ai*
very	*mâak*

General nouns

Nouns have no plurals or genders, and don't require an article.

bathroom/toilet	*hãwng nám*
boyfriend or girlfriend	*faen*
food	*ahãan*
foreigner	*fàràng*
friend	*phêuan*
money	*ngoen*
water	*nám*

General verbs

Thai verbs do not conjugate at all, and also often double up as nouns and adjectives, which means that foreigners' most unidiomatic attempts to construct sentences are often readily understood.

come	*maa*
do	*tham*
eat	*kin/thaan khâo*
give	*hâi*
go	*pai*
sit	*nâng*
sleep	*nawn làp*
take	*ao*
walk	*doen pai*

Numbers

zero	*sũun*
one	*nèung*
two	*sãwng*
three	*sãam*
four	*sìi*
five	*hâa*
six	*hòk*
seven	*jèt*
eight	*pàet*
nine	*kâo*
ten	*sìp*
eleven	*sìp èt*

continued overleaf

continued from previous page

twelve, thirteen, etc	*sìp sǎwng, sìp sǎam...*	1pm	*bài mohng*
		2–4pm	*bài sǎwng mohng– bài sìi mohng*
twenty	*yîi sìp/yíip*	5–6pm	*hâa mohng yen–hòk mohng yen*
twenty-one	*yîi sìp èt*		
twenty-two, twenty-three, etc	*yîi sìp sǎwng, yîi sìp sǎam...*	7–11pm	*nèung thûm–hâa thûm*
thirty, forty, etc	*sǎam sìp, sìi sìp...*	midnight	*thîang kheun*
one hundred, two hundred, etc	*nèung rói, sǎwng rói...*	What time is it?	*kìi mohng láew?*
one thousand	*nèung phan*	How many hours?	*kìi chûa mohng?*
ten thousand	*nèung mèun*	How long?	*naan thâo rai?*

Time

The commonest system for telling the time, as outlined below, is actually a confusing mix of several different systems. The State Railway and government officials use the 24-hour clock (9am is *kâo naalikaa*, 10am *sìp naalikaa*, and so on), which is always worth trying if you get stuck.

		minute	*naathii*
		hour	*chûa mohng*
		day	*waan*
		week	*aathít*
		month	*deuan*
		year	*pii*
		today	*wan níi*
1–5am	*tii nèung–tii hâa*	tomorrow	*phrûng níi*
6–11am	*hòk mohng cháo–sìp èt mohng cháo*	yesterday	*mêua wan*
		now	*dǐaw níi*
		next week	*aathít nâa*
		last week	*aathít kàwn*
		morning	*cháo*
		afternoon	*bài*
		evening	*yen*
noon	*thîang*	night	*kheun*

be pronounced evenly and with no inflection. The **falling tone** (syllables marked ^) is spoken with an obvious drop in pitch, as if you were sharply emphasizing a word in English. The **rising tone** (marked ~) is pronounced as if you were asking an exaggerated question in English.

As well as the unfamiliar tones, you'll find that, despite the best efforts of the transliterators, there is no precise English equivalent to many **vowel and consonant sounds** in the Thai language. The lists below give a rough idea of pronunciation.

Vowels

a as in dad.

aa has no precise equivalent, but is pronounced as it looks, with the vowel elongated.

ae as in there.

ai as in buy.

ao as in now.

aw as in awe.

e as in pen.

eu as in sir, but heavily nasalized.

i as in tip.

ii as in feet.

o as in knock.

oe as in hurt, but more closed.

oh as in toe.
u as in loot.

uay: "u" plus "ay" as in pay.
uu as in pool.

Consonants

r as in rip, but with the tongue flapped quickly against the palate – in everyday speech, it's often pronounced like "l".
kh as in keep.
ph as in put.
th as in time.

k is unaspirated and unvoiced, and closer to "g".
p is also unaspirated and unvoiced, and closer to "b".
t is also unaspirated and unvoiced, and closer to "d".

Glossary

Amphoe District.

Amphoe muang Provincial capital.

Ao Bay.

Aspara Female deity.

Avalokitesvara Bodhisattva representing compassion.

Avatar Earthly manifestation of a deity.

Ban Village or house.

Bencharong Polychromatic ceramics made in China for the Thai market.

Bhumisparsa mudra Most common gesture of Buddha images; symbolizes the Buddha's victory over temptation.

Bodhisattva In Mahayana Buddhism, an enlightened being who postpones his or her entry into Nirvana.

Bot Main sanctuary of a Buddhist temple.

Brahma One of the Hindu trinity – "The Creator". Usually depicted with four faces and four arms.

Celadon Porcelain with distinctive grey-green glaze.

Changwat Province.

Chao ley/ Chao nam "Sea gypsies" – nomadic fisherfolk of southern Thailand.

Chedi Reliquary tower in Buddhist temple.

Chofa Finial on temple roof.

Deva Mythical deity.

Devaraja God-king.

Dharma The teachings or doctrine of the Buddha.

Dharmachakra Buddhist Wheel of Law (also known as Wheel of Doctrine or Wheel of Life).

Doi Mountain.

Erawan Mythical three-headed elephant; Indra's vehicle.

Farang A foreigner; a corruption of the word *français*.

Ganesh Hindu elephant-headed deity, remover of obstacles and god of knowledge.

Garuda Mythical Hindu creature – half-man half-bird; Vishnu's vehicle.

Gopura Entrance pavilion to temple precinct (especially Khmer).

Hamsa Sacred mythical goose; Brahma's vehicle.

Hang yao Longtail boat.

Hanuman Monkey god and chief of the monkey army in the *Ramayana*; ally of Rama.

Hat Beach.

Hin Stone.

Hinayana Pejorative term for Theravada school of Buddhism, literally "Lesser Vehicle".

Ho trai A scripture library.

Indra Hindu king of the gods and, in Buddhism, devotee of the Buddha; usually carries a thunderbolt.

Isaan Northeast Thailand.

Jataka Stories of the five hundred lives of the Buddha.

Khaen Reed and wood pipe; the characteristic musical instrument of Isaan.

Khao Hill, mountain.

Khlong Canal.

Khon Classical dance-drama.

Kinnari Mythical creature – half-woman, half-bird.

Kirtimukha Very powerful deity depicted as a lion-head.

Ko Island.

Ku The Lao word for *prang*; a tower in a temple complex.

Laem Headland or cape.

Lakhon Classical dance-drama.

Lak muang City pillar; revered home for the city's guardian spirit.

Lakshaman/Phra Lak Rama's younger brother.

Lakshana Auspicious signs or "marks of greatness" displayed by the Buddha.

Lanna Northern Thai kingdom that lasted from the thirteenth to the sixteenth century.

Likay Popular folk theatre.

Longyi Burmese sarong.

Maenam River.

Mahathat Chedi containing relics of the Buddha.

Mahayana School of Buddhism now practised mainly in China, Japan and Korea; literally "the Great Vehicle".

Mara The Evil One; tempter of the Buddha.

Mawn khwaan Traditional triangular or "axe-head" pillow.

Meru/Sineru Mythical mountain at the centre of Hindu and Buddhist cosmologies.

Mondop Small, square temple building to house minor images or religious texts.

Moo/muu Neighbourhood within an *amphoe*.

Muang City or town.

Muay Thai Thai boxing.

Mudra Symbolic gesture of the Buddha.

Mut mee Tie-dyed cotton or silk.

Naga Mythical dragon-headed serpent in Buddhism and Hinduism.

Nakhon Honorific title for a city.

Nam Water.

Nam tok Waterfall.

Nang thalung Shadow-puppet entertainment, found in southern Thailand.

Nielloware Engraved metalwork.

Nirvana Final liberation from the cycle of rebirths; state of non-being to which Buddhists aspire.

Pak Tai Southern Thailand.

Pali Language of ancient India; the script of the original Buddhist scriptures.

Pha sin Woman's sarong.

Phi Animist spirit.

Phra Honorific term – literally "excellent".

Phu Mountain.

Prang Central tower in a Khmer temple.

Prasat Khmer temple complex or central shrine.

Rama Human manifestation of Hindu deity Vishnu; hero of the *Ramayana*.

Ramakien Thai version of the *Ramayana*.

Ramayana Hindu epic of good versus evil: chief characters include Rama, Sita, Ravana, Hanuman.

Ravana Rama's adversary in the *Ramayana;* represents evil. Also known as Totsagan.

Reua Boat.

Reua hang yao Longtail boat.

Rishi Ascetic hermit.

Rot ae/rot tua Air-conditioned bus.

Rot thammadaa Ordinary bus.

Sala Meeting hall or open-sided pavilion.

Samlor Passenger tricycle; literally "three-wheeled".

Sanskrit Sacred language of Hinduism; also used in Buddhism.

Sanuk Fun.

Sema Boundary stone to mark consecrated ground within temple complex.

Shiva One of the Hindu trinity – "The Destroyer".

Shiva lingam Phallic representation of Shiva.

Soi Alley or side road.

Songkhran Thai New Year.

Songthaew Pickup used as public transport; literally "two rows", after the vehicle's two facing benches.

Takraw Game played with a rattan ball.

Talat Market.

Talat nam Floating market.

Talat yen Night market.

Tavatimsa Buddhist heaven.

Tha Pier.

Thale Sea or lake.

Tham Cave.

Thanon Road.

That Chedi.

Thep A divinity.

Theravada Main school of Buddhist thought in Thailand; also known as Hinayana.

Totsagan Rama's evil rival in the *Ramayana*; also known as Ravana.

Tripitaka Buddhist scriptures.

Tuk-tuk Motorized three-wheeled taxi.

Uma Shiva's consort.

Ushnisha Cranial protuberance on Buddha images, signifying an enlightened being.

Viharn Temple assembly hall for the laity; usually contains the principal Buddha image.

Vipassana Buddhist meditation technique; literally "insight".

Vishnu One of the Hindu trinity – "The Preserver". Usually shown with four arms, holding a disc, a conch, a lotus and a club.

Wai Thai greeting expressed by a prayer-like gesture with the hands.

Wang Palace.

Wat Temple.

Wiang Fortified town.

Yaksha Mythical giant.

Yantra Magical combination of numbers and letters, used to ward off danger.

index

and small print

Index

map entries are in colour

INDEX

INDEX

Ⓘ

Twenty Years of Rough Guides

In the summer of 1981, Mark Ellingham, Rough Guides' founder, knocked out the first guide on a typewriter, with a group of friends. Mark had been travelling in Greece after university, and couldn't find a guidebook that really answered his needs. There were heavyweight cultural guides on the one hand – good on museums and classical sites but not on beaches and tavernas – and on the other hand student manuals that were so caught up with how to save money that they lost sight of the country's significance beyond its role as a place for a cool vacation. None of the guides began to address Greece as a country, with its natural and human environment, its politics and its contemporary life.

Having no urgent reason to return home, Mark decided to write his own guide. It was a guide to Greece that tried to combine some erudition and insight with a thoroughly practical approach to travellers' needs. Scrupulously researched listings of places to stay, eat and drink were matched by careful attention to detail on everything from Homer to Greek music, from classical sites to national parks and from nude beaches to monasteries. Back in London, Mark and his friends got their Rough Guide accepted by a far-sighted commissioning editor at the publisher Routledge and it came out in 1982.

The Rough Guide to Greece was a student scheme that became a publishing phenomenon. The immediate success of the book – shortlisted for the Thomas Cook award – spawned a series that rapidly covered dozens of countries. The Rough Guides found a ready market among backpackers and budget travellers, but soon acquired a much broader readership that included older and less impecunious visitors. Readers relished the guides' wit and inquisitiveness as much as the enthusiastic, critical approach that acknowledges everyone wants value for money – but not at any price.

Rough Guides soon began supplementing the "rougher" information – the hostel and low-budget listings – with the kind of detail that independent-minded travellers on any budget might expect. These days, the guides – distributed worldwide by the Penguin group – include recommendations spanning the range from shoestring to luxury, and cover more than 200 destinations around the globe. Our growing team of authors, who mostly come to Rough Guides initially as outstandingly good letter-writers telling us about their travels, are spread all over the world, particularly in Europe, the USA and Australia. As well as the travel guides, Rough Guides publishes a series of dictionary phrasebooks covering two dozen major languages, an acclaimed series of music guides running the gamut from Classical to World Music, a series of music CDs in association with World Music Network, and a range of reference books on topics as diverse as the internet, pregnancy and unexplained phenomena. Visit www.roughguides.com to see what's cooking.

Help us update

We've gone to a lot of effort to ensure that the fourth edition of **The Rough Guide to Thailand** is accurate and up to date. However, things change – places get "discovered", opening hours are notoriously fickle, restaurants and rooms raise prices or lower standards. If you feel we've got it wrong or left something out, we'd like to know, and if you can remember the address, the price, the time, the phone number, so much the better.

We'll credit all contributions, and send a copy of the next edition (or any other Rough Guide if you prefer) for the best letters. Everyone who writes to us and isn't already a subscriber will receive a copy of our full-colour twice-yearly newsletter. Please mark letters: **"Rough Guide Thailand Update"** and send to: Rough Guides, 62–70 Shorts Gardens, London WC2H 9AH, or Rough Guides, 4th Floor, 345 Hudson St, New York, NY 10014. Or send an email to: **mail@roughguides.co.uk**

Rough Guide Credits

Text editor: Richard Lim
Series editor: Mark Ellingham
Editorial: Martin Dunford, Jonathan Buckley,
Jo Mead, Kate Berens, Ann-Marie Shaw,
Paul Gray, Helena Smith, Judith Bamber, Orla
Duane, Olivia Eccleshall, Ruth Blackmore,
Geoff Howard, Claire Saunders, Alexander
Mark Rogers, Polly Thomas, Joe Staines,
Gavin Thomas, Duncan Clark, Peter Buckley,
Lucy Ratcliffe, Clifton Wilkinson, Alison
Murchie, Matthew Teller (UK); Andrew
Rosenberg, Stephen Timblin, Yuki Takagaki,
Richard Koss (US)
Production: Susanne Hillen, Andy Hilliard,
Link Hall, Helen Prior, Julia Bovis, Michelle
Draycott, Katie Pringle, Mike Hancock, Zoë
Nobes, Rachel Holmes, Andy Turner

Cartography: Melissa Baker, Maxine Repath,
Ed Wright, Katie Lloyd-Jones
Picture research: Louise Boulton, Sharon
Martins
Online: Kelly Cross, Anja Mutic-Blessing,
Jennifer Gold, Audra Epstein, Suzanne
Welles (US)
Finance: John Fisher, Gary Singh, Edward
Downey, Mark Hall, Tim Bill
Marketing & Publicity: Richard Trillo, Niki
Smith, David Wearn, Chloë Roberts, Claire
Southern, Demelza Dallow (UK); Simon
Carloss, David Wechsler, Kathleen Rushforth
(US)
Administration: Tania Hummel, Julie
Sanderson

Publishing Information

This fourth edition published October 2001
by **Rough Guides Ltd,**
62–70 Shorts Gardens, London WC2H 9AH.
Penguin Putnam, Inc. 375 Hudson Street,
NY 10014, USA. Reprinted August 2002.
Distributed by the Penguin Group
Penguin Books Ltd,
80 Strand, London WC2R 0RL
Penguin Putnam, Inc.
375 Hudson Street, NY 10014, USA
Penguin Books Australia Ltd,
487 Maroondah Highway, PO Box 257,
Ringwood, Victoria 3134, Australia
Penguin Books Canada Ltd,
10 Alcorn Avenue, Toronto, Ontario,
Canada M4V 1E4
Penguin Books (NZ) Ltd,
182–190 Wairau Road, Auckland 10,
New Zealand
Typeset in Bembo and Helvetica to an
original design by Henry Iles

Printed in Italy by LegoPrint S.p.A

864pp includes index
A catalogue record for this book is available
from the British Library

ISBN 1-85828-719-7

The publishers and authors have done their
best to ensure the accuracy and currency of
all the information in **The Rough Guide to
Thailand,** however, they can accept no
responsibility for any loss, injury, or
inconvenience sustained by any traveller as a
result of information or advice contained in
the guide.

SMALL PRINT

Acknowledgements

The **authors** jointly would like to thank: Ron Emmons and Claire Saunders for their tireless researching and thoughtful updating; Julia Kelly, Nicky Agate and Narrell Leffman for additional Basics research; our editor, Richard Lim, for his insightful editing and resourceful enthusiasm; staff at the Bangkok Tourist Bureau and TAT offices all over the country, especially in Khorat and Ko Samui; Tom Vater for the piece on the *chao ley*; John Clewley for updating the music article; Phil Cornwel-Smith; Randy Campbell; Andrew Spooner; Iain Stewart; Bangkok Airways. Thanks also to Jennifer Speake for vigilant proofreading; Mike Hancock, Katie Pringle, Rachel Holmes and Andy Hilliard for typesetting; and Melissa Flack and Maxine Repath for maps.

From **Lucy**, thanks to: Chris Lee and Abi Batalla at London TAT; Mawn in Trat; Tan and Michel in Sukhothai; Mark Read in Khao Yai; Pornprasong and A-No-Thai in Mae Sot; Terry McBroom in Pattaya.

Thanks from **Claire** to: Pongsan Pitakmahaket at Nakhon Phanom TAT and Navaporn Chuachomket at Narathiwat TAT; Khun Niyana in That Phanom; Khun Vincent on Ko Libong; Arnat Buathong in Hat Yai; Khun Kannika in Narathiwat; Ravat Krailadsiri in Mukdahan; Sylvie Lecompte at Avis; and – especially – to Dick te Brake and Worrawut Wadee in Trang, Khun Natini in Narathiwat, Gareth and Christina in Bangkok, and Ian for selflessly helping research all those beaches.

Ron thanks Annette and Pon Kunigagon in Chiang Mai, Shane Beary in Tha Ton, Ung Fhu in Nan and Anirut Ngerncome in Chiang Khong.

Readers' letters

John Aliband, Lisa Anderson, Mr & Mrs K. Ansell, Kiersten Aschauer, Sue Barber, Caroline Bennett, Mitchell Berger, Leonard Billen, Rupert Blum, Luke Boag, Alan Booth, Vanessa Breakwell, Hillary Brill, Dr Adrian R. Brown, Rona Brown, Carolyn Bullock & Liz Donkin, Wendy Byrne, George and Fiona Carmichael, Simon Chapman & Becky Edser, Stephen Constant, Neville Cornwell, Peter Cunningham, Nick Davison, Alex Dawson, Emma Daykin, Richard Dion, B.H. & A. Dobson, Joe Dodson, Iain Dunlop, Jacquelyn M Dunn, Michael Edwards, Carsten Engel, Maura Fearon, Madeline Feeney, Lynne Fender, Isabella Forrest, Lawrence Forrester, Vesa Frantsila, M. Froetscher, John Garratt, Emma Gervasio, D.C. Godfrey, Dan Goodacre, Julie & Barry Green, Helen Griffith, Madeline Grove, Martin Gunther & Simone von der Forst, Richard Harvey, Garvin Heath, Andrew Hedger & Clare Spallini, Lisa Herbert, Scott Herbstman, Alan Hickey, Bryony Inge, Roger & Maureen Jonstone, Kaoriy, Suzanne Kay, Keesin, Michael Kelly, Malousch Köhler, Paul Lawlor, Jonty Levin, Henry Lew, Janet Lock, Roger Loxley, Marc Lyall, Padraig F. MacDonnchadha, Monica Mackaness and John Garratt, Jamie MacSween, John Maley, Eric Manes & E. Gail Richardson, Bob & Ann Marshall, Ann Matthews, Kirsteen McFadzean, Keith McGhie, Lorenzo Menghini, Marc Mills, Robin Mitchell, Muriel Mora, Lisa Naylor, Ellie Norris, P. John O'Neill, Selena Oldham, Martin Platt, Joost van Praag Sigaar, Emily Prince, Polly Rashbrooke & Nic Macdonald, Peter C. Ray, Emma Reilly, John Richardson, Rebecca Ridgway, Robert Rushmer, Lance Saunders, Elizabeth Savur, Steve Scott, Susan Shaw, Sheryl & Mike, Rachel N. Smith, Hilary Sneller, Ruud Spek, Andrew Spooner, Kerry Start & Tony Shilling, Iain Stewart, Graham Tate, Ben & Rhian Taylor, Steve Taylor, Les Thompson, Roy Turner, Nicki W., Nicole Wainwright & Jacob Loomisu, Nic & Kim Walker, Kylie Weeks, David Whalley, Donal Wickham, Ross Williamson, M.T. Willis, Peter Yarranton, Jennifer Yoe, Ytene, Jo Yuen, Rona Yuthasasrakosol, R.A. Zambardino.

Photo Credits

Music

Acoustic Guitar
Blues: 100 Essential
 CDs
Cello
Clarinet
Classical Music
Classical Music:
 100 Essential CDs
Country Music
Country: 100
 Essential CDs
Cuban Music
Drum'n'bass
Drums
Electric Guitar
 & Bass Guitar
Flute
Hip-Hop
House
Irish Music
Jazz
Jazz: 100 Essential
 CDs
Keyboards & Digital
 Piano
Latin: 100 Essential
 CDs
Music USA: a Coast-
 To-Coast Tour
Opera
Opera: 100 Essential
 CDs
Piano
Reading Music
Reggae
Reggae: 100
 Essential CDs
Rock
Rock: 100 Essential
 CDs
Saxophone
Soul: 100 Essential
 CDs
Techno
Trumpet & Trombone
Violin & Viola
World Music: 100
 Essential CDs

World Music Vol1
World Music Vol2

Reference

Children's Books,
 0–5
Children's Books,
 5–11
China Chronicle
Cult Movies
Cult TV
Elvis
England Chronicle
France Chronicle
India Chronicle
The Internet
Internet Radio
James Bond
Liverpool FC
Man Utd
Money Online
Personal Computers
Pregnancy & Birth
Shopping Online
Travel Health
Travel Online
Unexplained
 Phenomena
Videogaming
Weather
Website Directory
Women Travel
World Cup

Music CDs

Africa
Afrocuba
Afro-Peru
Ali Hussan Kuban
The Alps
Americana
The Andes
The Appalachians
Arabesque
Asian Underground
Australian Aboriginal
 Music
Bellydance
Bhangra

Bluegrass
Bollywood
Boogaloo
Brazil
Cajun
Cajun and Zydeco
Calypso and Soca
Cape Verde
Central America
Classic Jazz
Congolese Soukous
Cuba
Cuban Music Story
Cuban Son
Cumbia
Delta Blues
Eastern Europe
English Roots Music
Flamenco
Franco
Gospel
Global Dance
Greece
The Gypsies
Haiti
Hawaii
The Himalayas
Hip Hop
Hungary
India
India and Pakistan
Indian Ocean
Indonesia
Irish Folk
Irish Music
Italy
Jamaica
Japan
Kenya and Tanzania
Klezmer
Louisiana
Lucky Dube
Mali and Guinea
Marrabenta
 Mozambique
Merengue & Bachata
Mexico
Native American
 Music
Nigeria and Ghana
North Africa

Nusrat Fateh Ali
 Khan
Okinawa
Paris Café Music
Portugal
Rai
Reggae
Salsa
Salsa Dance
Samba
Scandinavia
Scottish Folk
Scottish Music
Senegal
 & The Gambia
Ska
Soul Brothers
South Africa
South African Gospel
South African Jazz
Spain
Sufi Music
Tango
Thailand
Tex-Mex
Wales
West African Music
World Music Vol 1:
 Africa, Europe and
 the Middle East
World Music Vol 2:
 Latin & North
 America,
 Caribbean, India,
 Asia and Pacific
World Roots
Youssou N'Dour
 & Etoile de Dakar
Zimbabwe

Rough Guides music, reference & CDs

NOTES

NOTES